# BEHAVIORAL ASSESSMENT OF CHILDHOOD DISORDERS

**THE GUILFORD
BEHAVIORAL ASSESSMENT SERIES**
*John D. Cone and Rosemery O. Nelson, Editors*

BEHAVIORAL ASSESSMENT OF ADULT DISORDERS
*David H. Barlow, Editor*
BEHAVIORAL ASSESSMENT OF CHILDHOOD DISORDERS
*Eric J. Mash and Leif G. Terdal, Editors*

# BEHAVIORAL ASSESSMENT OF CHILDHOOD DISORDERS

EDITED BY

## ERIC J. MASH

*University of Calgary*

*and*

## LEIF G. TERDAL

*University of Oregon Health Sciences Center*

*Foreword by Gerald R. Patterson*

THE GUILFORD PRESS

NEW YORK    LONDON

## TO HEATHER AND MARGE

© 1981 The Guilford Press, New York
A Division of Guilford Publications, Inc.
200 Park Avenue South, New York, N.Y. 10003

Printed in the United States of America

Library of Congress Cataloging in Publication Data

Main entry under title:

Behavioral assessment of childhood disorders.

    (The Guilford behavioral assessment series)
    Includes bibliographies and indexes.
    1. Child psychopathology—Diagnosis. 2. Psychodiagnostics. I. Mash, Eric J. II. Terdal, Leif G., 1937—    [DNLM: 1. Child behavior. 2. Psychopathology—In infancy and childhood. 3. Mental disorders—In infancy and childhood. 4. Mental disorders—Diagnosis. 5. Behavior therapy—In infancy and childhood. WS350 B4182]
RJ503.5.B43     618.92′89075     80-22914
ISBN 0-89862-141-0

# CONTRIBUTORS

BEVERLY M. ATKESON, PhD, Department of Psychology, University of Georgia, Athens, Georgia

BARBARA A. BALASCHAK, PhD, Seizure Unit, Department of Neurology, Children's Hospital Medical Center of Boston, Boston, Massachusetts

RUSSELL A. BARKLEY, PhD, Departments of Neurology and Psychiatry, The Medical College of Wisconsin and Milwaukee Children's Hospital, Milwaukee, Wisconsin

BILLY A. BARRIOS, PhD, Department of Psychology, University of Virginia, Charlottesville, Virginia

ANTHONY R. CIMINERO, PhD, Veterans Administration Medical Center, Miami, Florida

THOMAS J. COATES, PhD, Division of Pediatric Cardiology, The John Hopkins University School of Medicine, Baltimore, Maryland

CHARLES G. COSTELLO, PhD, Department of Psychology, University of Calgary, Calgary, Alberta, Canada

DANIEL M. DOLEYS, PhD, Center for Developmental and Learning Disorders, Medical Center, The University of Alabama in Birmingham, Birmingham, Alabama. Current address: Brookwood Medical Center, Birmingham, Alabama

REX FOREHAND, PhD, Department of Psychology, University of Georgia, Athens, Georgia

JOHN P. FOREYT, PhD, Diet Modification Clinic, National Heart and Blood Vessel Research and Demonstration Center, Baylor College of Medicine and The Methodist Hospital, Houston, Texas

ROBERT M. FRIEDMAN, PhD, Adolescent Project, Child, Adolescent, and Community Program, Florida Mental Health Institute, Tampa, Florida

G. KEN GOODRICK, PhD, Department of Psychology, University of Houston, Houston, Texas

CHARLES R. GREENWOOD, PhD, Juniper Gardens Children's Project, Bureau of Child Research, University of Kansas, Kansas City, Kansas

DONALD P. HARTMANN, PhD, Department of Psychology, University of Utah, Salt Lake City, Utah

MARIO HERNANDEZ, MS, Department of Psychology, University of South Florida and Florida Mental Health Institute, Tampa, Florida

HYMAN HOPS, PhD, Oregon Research Institute, Eugene, Oregon

SUZANNE BENNETT JOHNSON, PhD, Department of Psychiatry, J. Hillis Miller Health Center, University of Florida, Gainesville, Florida

PAUL KAROLY, PhD, Department of Psychology, University of Cincinnati, Cincinnati, Ohio

ERIC J. MASH, PhD, Department of Psychology, University of Calgary, Calgary, Alberta, Canada

BARBARA G. MELAMED, PhD, Department of Clinical Psychology, J. Hillis Miller Health Center, University of Florida, Gainesville, Florida

DAVID I. MOSTOFSKY, PhD, Department of Psychology, Boston University, and Seizure Unit, Department of Neurology, Children's Hospital Medical Center of Boston, Boston, Massachusetts

CRIGHTON NEWSOM, PhD, Suffolk Child Development Center, Smithtown, New York, and Department of Psychology and Special Education, State University of New York at Stony Brook, Stony Brook, New York

GEORGE A. REKERS, PhD, Department of Family and Child Development, Kansas State University, and Logos Research Institute, Inc., Manhattan, Kansas

ARNOLD RINCOVER, PhD, Department of Psychology, University of North Carolina at Greensboro, Greensboro, North Carolina

JACK SANDLER, PhD, Department of Psychology, University of South Florida, Tampa, Florida

MARK S. SCHWARTZ, PhD, Section of Psychology, Mayo Clinic, Rochester, Minnesota

CAROL SHIGETOMI, PhD, Department of Psychology, University of Utah, Salt Lake City, Utah

LEIF G. TERDAL, PhD, Department of Medical Psychology, University of Oregon Health Sciences Center, Portland, Oregon

CARL E. THORESEN, PhD, School of Education, Stanford University, Stanford, California

DAVID A. WOLFE, PhD, Department of Psychology, University of South Florida, Tampa, Florida

# FOREWORD

It was only a generation ago that all aspiring child clinical students spent hundreds of hours in the intimate embrace of the Rorschach and its entourage. Given such a history, a volume such as this gives one a tremendous sense of relief. This volume draws upon some of the best investigators who represent a whole new generation of psychologists. Here the emphasis is upon behavior rather than upon signs and symbols. The inferences that are made lend themselves to empirical testing. This is the kind of child clinical enterprise which can grow and change. The attention to methodology and psychometric critique builds the feedback loop which guards against an assessment technology that has aura and mystique but no content.

In the mid 1960s, there was a pressing need for better means of measuring changes brought about by treatment of spouses, families, and problem children in the classroom. The research suggested that parent reports were biased to report change when none had occurred. Parent reports of child rearing had little relation to what parents actually did in the home. These were earth-shaking complications, for the edifice of socialization theory rested upon such data!

At that time, the fire-and-brimstone operant iconoclasts from Washington, Kansas, Harvard, and Illinois were going out into the real world and taking frequency counts on such things as "number of towels hoarded," "number of times out of chair," and so on. Those drawn into the behavior-change movement became observers because observation was an integral part of the new operant approach to treatment. Within a short time, we found ourselves engaged with the traditional psychometric problems of interobserver agreement, validity, stability of behavior over time, bias, the effects of observer presence, and normative data. The old questions are still with us. If anything, they were more demanding and more difficult to answer. At that time, Steve Johnson and his group at Oregon, Dan O'Leary at Stony Brook, Eric Mash at Calgary, and John Reid at Wisconsin were working on their classic studies of these and related questions.

As work went on, it became apparent that the scope of what was being assessed needed to be enlarged. Observation data per se had built-in limitations: such data could not, for example, assess the frequency of such low-base-rate events as fire setting or stealing; tell us about the family's support system as it functioned in the community; or tell us about how the mother felt about herself or about the child. Complete behavioral assessment required that these variables be included. Familial crises and insularity co-vary with what the observers see the family doing. These variables also co-vary with mood changes. If one is to understand *interaction* in any setting, it will be necessary to invent assessment devices that measure both molecular and molar variables.

It seems, then, that the wheel has come full turn. The present volume attests to the fact that behavioral assessment now includes self-report measures; families are being interviewed and subjects are asked to rate themselves and others. What, then, has been added? I think that the full impact of the mid-1960s' breakaway is still to be realized. The genesis for the forthcoming change lies in the format by which some of the new data were being collected. Several of the observation code systems collected the data in sequential form. Interactional events were arranged along a time line. The data itself generate questions about what goes with what. Data relating to these kinds of functional relations mean that a psychology of interaction is being built. The people who are building it come from diverse fields, but they have two things in common: they construct observation tools and the data are cast in sequential form (Cairns, 1979; Lamb, Suomi, & Stephensen, 1979). Given repeated samples of data over extended intervals, then, the study of structure and interaction will lead, in turn, to the study of process, that is, changes in structure over time.

A new generation of assessment devices that measure interactional structure? An evaluation of treatment outcomes by delineation of process changes? Perhaps. But whether or not this comes to pass, the clinical enterprise is building a solid new empirical base. The contributors to this volume are not just telling us how to diagnose hyperactivity, social withdrawal, or problem behaviors in general. Rather, they are also telling us about determinants for these behaviors. The techniques and data presented in this volume are solid contributions. Reading these chapters gives one a sense of excitement about seeing things at their beginning. Taken in their aggregate, the chapters in this volume speak to the fact that the field of assessment is growing up.

GERALD R. PATTERSON
*Social Learning Center*

Eugene, Oregon

## References

Cairns, R. B. (Ed.). *The analysis of social interactions: Methods, issues and illustrations.* Hillsdale, N.J.: Lawrence Erlbaum Associates, 1979.

Lamb, M. E., Suomi, S. J., & Stephensen, G. R. *Social interaction analysis: Methodological issues.* Madison: University of Wisconsin Press, 1979.

# PREFACE

This is a book about assessment and diagnosis, child and family development, child psychopathology, psychological measurement, clinical psychology, psychometrics, social values, ethics, behavior therapy—and other things. Although this statement may appear ridiculously ambitious, and more descriptive of an institute than a book, it is intended only to sensitize the reader to our view that all assessments of children with problems are characteristically embedded in a complex network of overlapping disciplines and bodies of knowledge. These complexities of developing children and their social systems are a fact that renders any narrow approach to child assessment inadequate.

This volume considers the assessment of children with problems from a behavioral perspective. In its simplest formulation, such a perspective emphasizes that assessment should proceed as an empirically based enterprise. The approach to the behavioral assessment of childhood disorders taken in this volume, consistent with current practices, is that of a general problem-solving strategy for understanding children and their behavior. These strategies are, for the most part, atheoretical and make few a priori assumptions regarding etiology.

Recent discussions of behavioral assessment have provided an extensive description of the underlying conceptual framework and characteristic procedures. Although there is currently no singular definition for behavioral assessment, commonly occurring concepts have included a focus on the importance of situational determinants and a methodological emphasis on the direct observation of behavior in context. A major theme has been the need to formulate assessment information in a way that is meaningful for clinical decision making about individual children and their families.

In spite of a rapid growth in the number of articles, books, and journals dealing with the topic of behavioral assessment, there is some evidence to suggest that the actual use by students and practitioners of behavioral assessment procedures with children has not paralleled this growth. It is our belief that this state of affairs is related to a lack of behavioral assessment developments for *specific* populations of children. A major impetus for undertaking the preparation of this volume was to address this need for greater specificity. The current presentation formulates assessment questions and procedures in relation to particular classes of problems characteristic of disturbed children. As such, it presents not only assessment information but also information concerning the determinants of the disorders under consideration. The underlying premise of this entire volume is that adequate behavioral assessment requires an understanding both of assessment principles and methodology and of the specific parameters associated with particular childhood problems.

The problem-oriented focus of this volume makes it not only a book about assessment but also a book about child psychopathology. In most chapters, authors provide an extensive functional analysis of the problem being considered. The levels of analysis characterizing the different chapters reflect gradations in the current state of the art. A blend of empirical data, theory, and technique is evident for all chapters, however, with differing degrees of emphasis. In some chapters, the presentation of technique is extensive. In others, information is presented that serves to provide a foundation on which adequate technique might be developed. This variability is a reflection of the differential attention given to the various childhood disorders by behavioral assessors. For example, more work has been done with acting-out types of childhood problems than with other disorders, such as social withdrawal or childhood depression. We view this variability as a healthy sign of a developing and self-evaluating discipline. The number of chapters in this volume dealing with the assessment of health-related disorders recognizes the increasingly greater attention being given to these problems by behavioral researchers and practitioners.

We have attempted to include chapters covering the widest possible range of childhood disorders and problems. It was with some discomfort that we decided to loosely organize chapters in this volume according to what may appear to be traditional diagnostic categories, since eschewal of such nomenclature has been part of the behavioral assessment tradition. However, in defense of our heterodoxy, we believe that children present themselves to professionals with characteristic classes of problems and that organizing information for assessment according to such commonalities in behavior and determinants serves an important heuristic function. Consequently, the chapter headings were selected to reflect commonly occurring classes of problems, but not static diagnostic entites. As with any venture of this kind, there were chapters that we would have liked to include but for various reasons were unable to do so. Among these were chapters relating to the assessment of language difficulties, mental retardation, and adolescent delinquency and substance abuse. In any case, we hope that this book will be appropriate for use in assessment, child psychopathology, and behavior therapy courses at both the advanced undergraduate and graduate levels in areas such as psychology, education, counseling, social work, and medicine, and, in addition, that it will satisfy a need in applied settings and training programs for those practitioners who wish to introduce new child assessment procedures into their work.

The chapters in this volume include the most up-to-date information on behavioral assessment with children. In this regard, they represent the culmination of approximately 25 years of effort on the part of behaviorally oriented researchers and practitioners. At the same time, they also represent a starting point. They provide an integration and organization which we hope will stimulate the development and use of more standardized, more sophisticated, and more empirically based assessment procedures with children. We trust that the eventual outcome of these developments will be to generate assessments that provide greater benefit to those children and families who are being assessed.

We would like to extend our thanks to the contributors to this volume for their receptiveness to editorial feedback and their efforts in working within sometimes unrealistic time schedules. We are also indebted to a number of students who provided insightful comments on earlier drafts of the chapters in this volume, including Sherry Pitcher, Jeff Sosne, and especially Charlotte Johnston. A number of our colleagues and friends also gave invaluable feedback, including Russell Barkley, Bonnie Kaplan, and Charles Costello. The editorial support of Seymour Weingarten throughout the conception and birth of this volume was also of great help. During the preparation of this book, Eric Mash was supported by a Canada Council Leave Fellowship and by research grants from the Alberta Mental Health Advisory Council and Health and Welfare Canada. This support greatly facilitated work on this volume and is gratefully acknowledged. Finally, we would like to thank our families, Heather, Marge, Erik, and Paul.

ERIC J. MASH
LEIF G. TERDAL

Calgary, Alberta
Portland, Oregon

# CONTENTS

# INTRODUCTION

# BEHAVIORAL ASSESSMENT OF CHILDHOOD DISTURBANCE

**Eric J. Mash**          **Leif G. Terdal**

*University of Calgary     University of Oregon Health Sciences Center*

## INTRODUCTION

The assessment, evaluation, and labeling of children in our society is both fact and promise. Within formal and informal contexts, the assessment of children is pervasive in any society that values its young (Kessen, 1979; Lomax, Kagan, & Rosenkrantz, 1978). Almost from conception the child is evaluated as to progress in such areas as physical growth and maturation, cognitive development, educational status and achievement, social relationships, emotional maturity, and psychological functioning. Parents, teachers, physicians, and the social community in general all serve in the role of evaluators. As part of this ongoing assessment, some children are identified as deviating from a normal course of development, in terms of either their behavior or some violation of the norms and/or expectations of their social milieu. If a negative value is assigned to this deviation, the child is especially likely to be labeled as belonging to a category of children who differ in this way. It is these children and their families who then come to the attention of society's professional assessors, who utilize special strategies to build upon the assessments that have already been conducted informally. This book is concerned with the special strategies for the assessment of childhood disorders encompassed under the label "behavioral assessment."

Recent discussions of behavioral assessment (Cone, 1978; Hartmann, Roper, & Bradford, 1979; Mash, 1979) and childhood disorder (Achenbach, 1978; Achenbach & Edelbrock, 1978a; Clarizio & McCoy, 1976; Erickson, 1978; Knopf, 1979; Quay & Werry, 1979; Ross, 1974) have pointed up the continuing lack of conceptual and methodological clarity characterizing both of these areas. Although there is much agreement regarding the need for systematic assessment of children, particularly children with problems, there is much disagreement regarding how childhood disorders should be conceptualized, what child characteristics should be assessed, by whom and in what situations they should be assessed, and how the outcomes of such assessments should be interpreted.

In spite of these disagreements, there is a consensus regarding the need for viewing the development of effective assessment strategies not as an endpoint but rather as a necessary prerequisite for improving and evaluating services for children. As noted by Achenbach and Edelbrock (Note 1), "unless more precise assessment of children is accompanied by efforts to determine differential outcomes under various conditions, it will not benefit the children who are assessed" (p. 40). This "functional–utilitarian" view for the behavioral assessment of children is perhaps the major theme underlying all of the chapters in this book, a theme that transcends many of the conceptual and methodological problems, differences, and preferences that will emerge in this discussion.

Although there is currently no single definition of child behavior assessment (O'Leary, 1979), we believe that there are characteristically occurring concepts (e.g., importance of situational influence as a behavioral determinant), methods (e.g., direct observation of naturally occurring events), and purposes (e.g., treatment evaluation) that serve to define the field. There is no single element that characterizes a particular assessment as behavioral; rather, it is a series or pattern of overlapping emphases that serves to identify an assessment as such (Mash, 1979). The purpose of this initial chapter will be to outline some of the current concepts and practices (Nelson & Hayes, 1979; O'Leary, 1979) associated with the behavioral assessment of disturbed children and to discuss some of the issues and concerns surrounding the development of these concepts and practices. Recognizing the likelihood of ongoing and future changes in assessment strategies related to new empirical findings, emergent ideas, practical concerns, and shifts in the broader sociocultural milieu in which assessments are carried out, this chapter—indeed, this book—should be viewed as a working framework for understanding current behavioral approaches to the assessment of children.

## Some General Observations on Behavioral Assessment

The rate at which behavioral assessment has emerged as a distinct area of study is remarkable. Equally remarkable is the rate at which excellent descriptions of this emergence have themselves emerged (e.g., Hartmann *et al.*, 1979; Nelson & Hayes, 1979). Indicative of the recent and rapid growth in behavioral assessment has been the appearance of numerous conference papers and symposia (e.g., Terdal, Note 2), books (e.g., Barlow, 1981; Ciminero, Calhoun, & Adams, 1977; Cone & Hawkins, 1977; Haynes, 1978; Hersen & Bellack, 1976; Mash & Terdal, 1976; Nay, 1979), book chapters (e.g., Ciminero & Drabman, 1977; Evans & Nelson, 1977; Marholin & Bijou, 1978), new journals (*Behavioral Assessment*, 1979; *Journal of Behavioral Assessment*, 1979), and journal articles. These developments do not reflect the additional attention given to behavioral assessment issues in discussions that do not focus exclusively on the topic. Although it was noted earlier by several writers (e.g., Cone & Hawkins, 1977; Mash & Terdal, 1974) that serious attention to assessment procedures and issues in behavior therapy lagged behind the development of treatment techniques, this no longer seems to be the case.

In considering current developments in behavioral assessment, three general observations are germane to this discussion:

1. In spite of the burgeoning literature in behavioral assessment, the proportion of this literature that deals specifically with the assessment of children is small. Many of the more comprehensive texts on behavioral assessment give minimal attention to the assessment of children (e.g., Ciminero, Calhoun, & Adams, 1977; Hersen & Bellack, 1976). Few book chapters dealing exclusively with the assessment of children (e.g., Ciminero & Drabman, 1977; Evans & Nelson, 1977) have appeared. The disproportionate emphasis given to assessment of adults in the literature is characteristic of psychological assessment generally and likely reflects some of the difficulties that are inherent in child assessment, such as rapid developmental change and restricted language abilities.

2. With few exceptions (e.g., Johnson & Melamed, 1979), discussions of behavioral assessment have focused on the general principles and issues of such assessment and are not specific as to the characteristics of the population being assessed. Consequently, although a general framework for the development of specific strategies is available, particular conceptual issues and methodological parameters associated with the assessment of differing populations of children have not been explicated to any great extent. The need for considering such population-specific assessment strategies was a major consideration in the development of this book.

3. There appears to be a disparity between the quantity of literature recommending how behavioral assessments should be carried out and the extent to which these recommendations are realized in practice. Several recent surveys (e.g., Swan & MacDonald, 1978; Wade, Baker, & Hartmann, 1979) have reported that behavioral assessors continue to use traditional assessment strategies, including projective techniques, and may not utilize to any great extent those procedures (e.g., direct observation) frequently viewed as an integral part of behavioral assessment. Why is there such infrequent and nonexclusive use of behavioral assessment by behavioral practitioners?

Several answers immediately come to mind, including institutional demands for traditional diagnoses and tests, excessive time and personnel costs associated with direct observation in natural contexts, and the absence of readily available and psychometrically sound behavioral instruments for specific populations. There is, however, another possible reason.

Historically, assessment techniques have received favor because they have provided information about children that was not otherwise readily apparent. Such assessment have typically involved much inference, and, from horoscopes to Rorschach tests, interpretations of behavior are clearly not readily apparent to untrained observers (McReynolds, 1975). Behavioral assessment has intentionally maintained a low level of inference; in doing so, it provides information that may in fact be readily apparent to consumers of assessment information, although not in as accurate or as reliable a form. Consequently, some behavioral assessments may not be perceived as skilled acts and therefore may be viewed as less relevant. For example, informing a mother that her child shows five deviant responses per hour after an hour of observation may not have the appeal of assessments that forecast the child's masculinity or femininity based on response to inkblots or to the distressed looks of puppies who have yet to be toilet trained. Regardless of the validity of the latter interpretations, there may be an obvious difference in appeal to both users and consumers, and greater acceptance of behavioral methods may occur only after behavioral assessors begin to make more data-based interpretations and predictions than has been the case. Such data-based interpretations should attempt to look at broader patterns of behavior over time and to focus on procedures and controlling variables that are specific to certain populations of children. Many of the chapters in this volume address these types of assessment issues and interpretations, and, it is hoped, will promote the increased use of behavioral assessment by practitioners.

## Definition of Behavioral Assessment

The development of behavioral approaches for the assessment of disturbed children has been inextricably related to the emergence of behavior therapy/behavior modification as a therapeutic strategy (Kanfer & Saslow, 1969; Kazdin, 1978). Although the practice of behavioral assessment is by no means restricted to these situations in which behavioral treatments are being considered or used (Adams & Turner, 1979), it is believed that current views of behavioral assessment can best be understood within the context of behavioral intervention. In fact, many of the recent changes in behavioral assessment have directly mirrored changes in the concepts and practices of behavior therapy.

For example, the increasing use of cognitive change procedures (e.g., Kendall & Hollon, 1979; Meichenbaum, 1977) and social skills training (e.g., Combs & Slaby, 1977) and the growth of behavioral medicine and behavioral pediatrics (e.g., Christopherson & Rapoff, 1979; Coates & Perry, 1979; Pomerleau, 1979; Pomerleau & Brady, 1979; Schwartz & Weiss, 1977, 1978) as areas of speciality have served to stimulate parallel developments concerned with the assessment of parent and child cognitions (e.g., Kendall & Hollon, 1980) and affect (e.g., Meichenbaum & Butler, 1979; Prinz, Rosenblum, & O'Leary, 1978), social skills (e.g., Deluty, 1979; Reardon, Hersen, Bellack, & Foley, 1979; VanHasselt, Hersen, Whitehill, & Bellack, 1979), and a variety of health-related difficulties (*Professional Psychology*, 1979) in areas such as physical medicine (e.g., Rosenbaum & Drabman, 1979a), dentistry (Levy, Knight-Lertora, Olson, & Charney, Note 3), and neuropsychology (e.g., Goldstein, 1979).

Early behavioral approaches to the treatment of childhood disorders (Ullmann & Krasner, 1965) involved the specification of the target behaviors in need of change and their alteration through the arrangement or rearrangement of environmental contingencies in a manner loosely conforming to operant learning principles as described by Skinner (1953). Approval was given to retarded youngsters for good eye contact and smiling (Hopkins, 1968), tantrums were ignored (Williams, 1959), and all over the world (particularly in places like Washington, Kansas, and Kalamazoo) the echo of "That's a good child!" was heard following appropriate behavior. This was the heyday of M & M's and Sugar Pops, a time when dental associations and Feingold parent groups did not attempt to muddy the sugar-laden waters. Behavioral assessment consisted primarily of obtaining frequency, rate, and duration measures of the behaviors of interest by observing and counting. "Pinpoint, record, and consequate" provided a straightforward and oftentimes extremely effective method of remediating problem behavior. Following the operant tradition, applied behavior analysis (Baer, Wolf, & Risley, 1968) fueled a behavior assessment approach and further emphasized the need to examine not only the behaviors of interest but also the events that immediately preceded and followed these behaviors (Bijou & Peterson, 1971). As described by O'Leary (1979), the cardinal feature of early behavioral assessments was an emphasis on observable events, current behavior, and situational determinants of problematic behavior.

The importance of systematic assessment of target behavior at this point in the development of behavior therapy cannot be underestimated; accurate observations and objective recording are still the foundations upon which the behavioral assessment of children is built (Cooper, 1974; Gelfand & Hartmann, 1975; Sulzer-Azaroff & Mayer, 1977). The early work stimulated what might be described as a broadly empirical approach to child clinical problems, pointed up the need for evaluating treatment outcomes through the utilization of objective measures, and led to the development of methods having high face validity (Kanfer, 1979; O'Leary, 1979).

As behavior therapy with children evolved, greater emphasis was placed on viewing the child as part of a larger network of interacting social systems (Patterson, 1976; Wahler, 1976) and on the important role of cognition and affect in mediating child behavior change (Bandura, 1969, 1977; Kanfer & Phillips, 1970; Karoly, Chapter 2, this volume; Meichenbaum, 1977; Mischel, 1973, 1979). These developments have changed the quality of behavioral assessment from target behavior measurement to a more general problem-solving strategy based upon ongoing functional analysis and encompassing a greater range of independent and dependent variables. Current views of behavioral assessment of children are reflected in the following statement taken from a sensitive and scholarly chapter on the topic by Evans and Nelson (1977):

> Behavior assessment of children can best be considered an exploratory strategy rather than a routine application of specific procedures. The elements of the strategy are complex, but they include an emphasis on the psychology of child development and an extension of the experimental method, although in practice the latter is often more

reminiscent of Piaget's *méthode clinique* than a controlled experiment in the formal sense. (p. 610)

In this volume, the term *behavioral assessment* will be used to describe a range of deliberate problem-solving strategies for understanding children and childhood disorders. As shall be discussed in this chapter, these strategies (1) are usually carried out in relation to a set of circumscribed purposes; (2) are based on a particular point of view about children's functioning and its determinants; (3) have as their focus certain behaviors, signs, and cues, which, it is believed, are important to assess; and (4) possess a unique methodology for gathering, integrating, and interpreting information. The outcome of these problem-solving strategies should be to afford us a picture of the child that possesses more detail, accuracy, and utility than would be the case without their use (McReynolds, 1975). As noted by Nelson and Hayes (1979), "the goal of behavioral assessment is to identify meaningful response units and their controlling variables for the purposes of understanding and of altering behavior" (p. 1).

In summary, the behavioral assessment of children involves a process of hypothesis testing regarding the nature of the problem, its causes, and the likely effects of various treatments. Such hypothesis testing proceeds from a particular assumptive base and is carried out in relation to existing data, with specific methodologies and purposes. The nature of the assumptive base, methodologies, and purposes will be elaborated on in this and subsequent chapters. It is believed that the generation of better hypotheses to test can best proceed from an understanding of child development, knowledge regarding specific child psychopathologies, and the general principles of psychological assessment. This viewpoint is reflected throughout this volume.

## A Comparison of Behavioral and Traditional Assessment

Most discussions and definitions of behavioral assessment have included a comparison with more traditional assessment approaches (e.g., Cone & Hawkins, 1977; Goldfried & Kent, 1972; Hartmann *et al.*, 1979; Mash & Terdal, 1976; Mischel, 1968). Such contrasts have served to identify some of the major defining characteristics of behavioral assessment, although they have also resulted in definitions based more on what behavioral assessment is not, than on what it is (Mash, 1979). It is clear that the categories "behavioral" and "traditional" encompass a heterogeneous range of assessment approaches and that broad comparisons obscure many of the subtle and important distinctions that exist within each. This differentiation is apparent when one compares behavioral assessments that focus on the overt responses of children to those that attempt to assess the rules and problem-solving strategies that children utilize in organizing their behavior (Karoly, Chapter 2, this volume; Meichenbaum & Butler, 1979; Mischel, 1979). It would be possible, in this instance, to compare traditional assessment with both traditional behavioral assessment and current behavioral assessment approaches. Having identified that global comparisons inevitably result in oversimplification, it is still useful to highlight some of the major differences that have been cited in contrasting the two approaches.

### Conceptions of Personality and Abnormal Behavior

Behavioral approaches have generally avoided the use of underlying and inferred personality constructs, focusing, instead, on what the child does in specific circumstances. In contrast, traditional assessment approaches view personality as a reflection of underlying and stable traits. Within behavioral approaches, the maintaining conditions for both normal and deviant behavior are presumed to be present in the current environment, whereas in traditional approaches, the focus has been on universal and temporally remote events (e.g., early toilet training practices) and/or on inferential constructs regarding internal states (e.g., intrapsychic conflicts) as primary causes of disturbance (Kessler, 1966).

The most frequently cited writings in support of the behavioral viewpoint of personality have been those of Mischel (1968, 1973). However, the following statement by Mischel (1979) suggests that the great "behavioral denial" of personality traits may have been, and continues to be, a straw man. In referring to his now classic volume, *Personality and Assessment* (1968), Mischel states:

> My intentions in writing that book were not to undo personality but to defend individuality and the uniqueness of each person against what I saw as the then prevalent form of clinical hostility: the tendency to use a few behavioral signs to categorize people enduringly into fixed slots on the assessor's favorite nomothetic trait dimensions and to assume that these slot positions were sufficiently informative to predict specific behavior and to make extensive decisions about a person's whole life. (p. 740)

Mischel is also explicit in pointing out that his 1968 analysis of the status of traits was related to the goals of clinicians involved in assessing the problems of individuals. With the goals of individually oriented clinical assessment and treatment as a focus, there was a need to emphasize situational specificity of behavior because traditional trait approaches to personality had persistently neglected the discriminativeness and situational sensitivity in behavior. Finally, as Mischel (1979) goes on to state, "the original excitement of the behavioral approach for me lay in its promise to focus on the client-defined problematic behavior in its context rather than on the clinician's inferences about the symptomatic meaning of that behavior as a sign of generalized dispositions or psychodynamics" (p. 743).

It is evident from preceding statements that the behavioral view of personality is a pragmatic one that reflects not a denial of trait dimensions or constructs but rather a reemphasis of the importance of assessing the child's individuality and uniqueness for the purpose of designing effective treatments. Similarly, the behavioral view that the maintaining conditions for behavior resided in the child's current external environment represented an emphasis based upon the relative neglect of such factors by traditional approaches. Such a view serves as a focus of convenience for the goal of clinical intervention with children, not as a denial of the importance of internal events as determinants of behavior. Although the nature of the internal events inferred within a behavioral paradigm has differed greatly from that typically inferred within traditional psychodynamic formulations of childhood disorder (Mahoney, 1974), behavioral assessors have consistently and increasingly shown a greater recognition of the importance of intraorganismic variables in child assessment. Whether traits or internal events influence behavior—obviously they do—is not an important issue at present. Rather, the important issues in behavioral assessment involve the identification and reliable measurement of those traits and intrapersonal events that are meaningful in relation to the purposes for which behavioral assessments are typically carried out.

### Situational Consistency of Behavior

Related to the traditional view of personality as consisting of stable and enduring traits is the notion that child behavior will be relatively stable across situations. In terms of a nomothetic trait position, the view is not that the absolute level of child behavior will remain untouched by situational variation but rather that the rank ordering of children on a particular trait dimension should maintain itself across situations (Guilford, 1959; Goldberg, Note 4). The behavioral view, which follows from an emphasis on situational determinants, has been one of situational specificity, that is, that the patterning and organization of an individual's behavior across situations may be highly idiographic (Mischel, 1968, 1973). The theoretical debates surrounding this issue have been extensive (Bem & Funder, 1978; Endler & Magnusson, 1976; Mischel, 1973) and will not be discussed here. However, the pragmatic outcomes of the emphasis on situational specificity in behavioral assessment were a greater sensitivity to the need for measurement of situational characteristics and an increase in the range of environments sampled, so that home, school, and playground observations, for example, were added to those samples of the child's behavior obtained under highly controlled testing conditions in the clinic.

A current child assessment issue related to the situational consistency of behavior is the identification of meaningful dimensions by which situations can be classified. Without such information, it is impossible to investigate the question. The types of cross-situational studies that have been carried out with children have involved comparisons across global situations defined as different with respect to broad physical characteristics or spatial separation, such as home versus classroom (Bernal, Delfini, North, & Kreutzer, 1976; Johnson, Bolstad, & Lobitz, 1976), classroom versus school playground (A. Harris, 1979), and laboratory versus home (Martin, Johnson, Johansson, & Wahl, 1976; Yuzwak, Note 5). The findings from these studies have tended to yield mixed results, in part, because of the uncertainties associated with identifying functional properties within situations and the variability in the types of behaviors that were assessed. Other possibilities for classifying situations, in addition to physical properties, could include similarities in the nature of contingency systems (Mash, 1976) and subjectively perceived equivalencies on the part of both child and adult participants (Mischel, 1979).

A second issue related to cross-situational consistency involves the possible interactions between specific child characteristics and the degree of behavioral stability. This issue reflects the more general concern for defining the conditions under which cross-situational consistency might or might not be expected. Particularly relevant to this topic are those discussions (e.g., Mischel, 1973) and findings that suggest greater cross-situational stability of behavior for deviant than for nondeviant children (e.g., Mash & Mercer, 1979). Such a prediction follows from the assumption that certain types of disturbed children (e.g., hyperactive) may have difficulty regulating their behavior in relation to situational demands and therefore may continue to behave in similar ways even when the situation requires a different response. Other types of problem children (e.g., withdrawn) may continue to behave similarly across situations as a function of having a restricted response repertoire upon which to draw. Additional findings that are relevant to child behavior–situation interactions as a potential determinant of cross-situational stability come from studies demonstrating differences between problem and nonproblem children in some situations but not in others, for example, those with high versus low task demands (e.g., Campbell, 1973, 1975). More attention must be paid to the identification of both intrasituational and intersituational response relationships, and it is hoped that the continuing debate regarding global questions about the existence of cross-situational stability will diminish.

### Temporal Consistency of Behavior

Traditional personality approaches tend to view behavior as consistent over time, concomitant with the stable and enduring nature of underlying causes. Conceptually, at least, behavioral views would predict either consistency or variability in child behavior over time, as a function of stability or of variation in behavioral context. Because externally and internally induced situational variation appears to be the norm rather than the exception throughout childhood, the rational behavioral view should be one that predicts the relative absence of consistency in behavior over time. This view, however, fails to capture the complexity of the question in a number of ways. First, consistency can be assessed in relation to many levels of behavior, and, depending on the specificity of the behavior under consideration, different results may obtain (Mash, 1976). If a child's behavior is described in terms of a highly idiographic response topography (e.g., whining), then we may find little consistency over time, whereas behavioral definitions based on broader response classes (e.g., aggression) that encompass a wide range of behaviors, both within and across age levels, may have more enduring qualities.

Mischel (1979) has recently stated that "no one seriously questions that lives have continuity and that we perceive ourselves and others as relatively stable individuals who have substantial identity and stability over time, even when our specific actions change across situations (Mischel, 1968, 1973, 1979)" (p. 742). This statement suggests that at least one behavioral viewpoint of temporal consistency, in this case a cognitive social learning perspective, may not be dramatically different from a traditional view because temporal stability is predicated on the assumption of the enduring quality of a number of inferred constructs (e.g., construction competencies, encoding strategies, expectancies, subjective values, and goal plans), albeit these constructs may differ from those inferred in traditional theories of personality. Pressing concerns in assessing temporal stability are the length of time to be considered in identifying patterns of behavior and the unit of response and stimulus–response chains to be used in defining a pattern. Thus far, behavioral assessors have examined the question of temporal consistency over very short periods and, because of sampling problems, with relatively short stimulus–response chains (e.g., dyadic interaction).

The type of child characteristic being assessed also has implications for the question of temporal stability. For example, cognitive styles, intellect, problem-solving strategies (Mischel, 1973), aggression (Olweus, 1979), and general temperament (Thomas, Chess, & Birch, 1968) may be especially consistent over time, whereas specific social behaviors may be less so. Some early characteristics have been suggested as showing persistence over time, such as introversion–extroversion or sociability, especially in boys (Kagan & Moss, 1962; Schaeffer & Bayley, 1963); general activity levels (Halverson & Waldrop, 1976); and individual preferences for types and amounts of stimulation. Early temperament difficulties have also been suggested as persistent, including biological irregularities in feeding, sleeping, and elimination; inflexibility; slow adaptation to novel situations; avoidance of new situations; fussiness; and crying (Thomas, Chess, Birch, Hertzig, & Korn, 1963). That many of these characteristics are present in early infancy suggests a possible genetic basis, and clearly their presence channels the nature of early parental reactions to the child and subsequent socialization experiences (Bates, Freeland, & Lounsbury, 1979).

The question of temporal consistency in behavioral assessment is especially important from the standpoint of the types of childhood disorders and problems that are likely to persist over time and that are predictive of adult disturbance. Although the data in this regard are scarce, because of the methodological difficulties and ethical concerns associated with longitudinal study, available data would suggest that aggressive, conduct-disorder, hyperactive, and peer relationship difficulties are the most predictive of later adult problems (Robins, 1966, 1979). Specific neurotic-type symptoms, such as early fears, seem less predictive of negative outcomes; however, it is possible that the long-term negative outcomes of these types of early disturbance may be present, although not as obvious or as severe as those associated with acting-out problems.

### Other Differences

Several other differences between behavioral and traditional assessment approaches have been specified, many of which follow from the distinctions outlined previously. These differences, which are discussed in other chapters of this volume, are, briefly, as follows:

1. Behavioral approaches have emphasized contemporaneous controlling variables, whereas traditional approaches have focused more on historical causes.
2. Behavioral positions are more often concerned with a response as a direct sample of the behaviors of interest, whereas traditional approaches view

responses as important only to the extent that they reflect underlying causes.

3. Behavioral approaches focus on obtaining assessment information that is directly relevant to treatment or treatment evaluation in contrast to traditional assessments, which have emphasized diagnosis and prognosis.

4. Behavioral approaches have tended to utilize more direct assessment methods, such as naturalistic observation, in contrast to indirect methods such as interview or verbal self-report.

5. Behavioral approaches have attempted to maintain a low level of inference in interpreting observations (Goldfried & Kent, 1972).

6. In contrast to traditional assessments of child disturbance, which often occur on one or two occasions and prior to treatment, behavioral assessments are ongoing and self-evaluating. In part, the need for further assessment is dictated by the efficacy of treatment; however, the relationship between assessment and treatment with behavioral approaches is generally a very close one.

It will become apparent to the reader that many of these contrasts are not nearly as distinct as one might suppose, especially when one considers the range of concepts and procedures characterizing contemporary behavioral assessment as described in this volume. These contrasts, however, have served to stimulate attention to assessment questions and procedures that had been relatively neglected in clinical child assessment.

## COMMON ASSESSMENT PURPOSES

Assessments of children are carried out for varying purposes. Whether explicit or implicit, these purposes will influence what behaviors and settings are attended to in assessment, the types of methods used, and even the working assumptions and conceptualizations about child behavior that underlie the assessment. Most questions surrounding the assessment of childhood disturbance can be considered only within the context of the intended assessment purpose; therefore, decisions regarding the appropriateness or usefulness of particular methods and procedures are usually relative ones. For example, a multiple-category observation code system may be appropriate for assessments designed to identify potential controlling variables to be altered with treatment but inappropriate for evaluating the outcome of a highly focused intervention.

Several writers (Cone & Hawkins, 1977; Mash & Terdal, 1976, 1980; Hawkins, Note 6) have outlined some of the common purposes of child behavior assessment, including *diagnosis*, or determinations of the nature of the child's problem; *design*, or the gathering of information that will be relevant for treatment; and *evaluation*, or assessments intended to evaluate the effectiveness of treatment. Although these purposes are characteristic of behavioral assessments of children, they are not specific to any one theoretical, methodological, or therapeutic orientation. Because these purposes have been discussed previously and will be dealt with in relation to specific disorders in the chapters following, we shall comment on them only briefly here.

## Diagnosis

The three purposes of assessment mentioned often occur in phases for individual cases. Early diagnostic assessments are concerned with questions relating to general screening and administrative decision making (e.g., is the child appropriate for this particular agency or educational program?), whether or not there is a problem (e.g., does the child's behavior deviate from an appropriate norm?), and the nature and extent of the problem (e.g., what is it that the child is doing or not doing that results in a distressed family or school situation?). Some of the pivotal distinctions between behavioral and traditional approaches have centered on how the diagnostic phase of assessment is viewed. Diagnoses within traditional child assessments have been described as involving a clinical determination of individual disease pictures, employing categories drawn from a system of classification of diseases, often with etiological and prognostic implications (Prugh, Engel, & Morse, 1975). This view of diagnosis is somewhat discrepant with the behavioral stereotyping of traditional assessments as often terminating with assignment of the child to some diagnostic category. However, regardless of whether traditional clinical diagnoses should in principle do more than assign children to categories, they typically have not generated much information that is directly relevant to the design of treatments.

The diagnostic phase within behavioral assessment is conducted with the expectation that assessment will lead directly into treatment recommendations and evaluations. Children are typically not assigned to categories; when they are, the implicit classification systems used in behavioral assessment have involved a highly descriptive nomenclature (e.g., behavioral excesses, deficits, and assets) in contrast to the inferential nomenclature characteristic of the more traditional diagnostic approaches (e.g., hyperactive, conduct disorder, etc.). Diagnostic information within traditional assessment is often used to answer questions such as Is the child hyperactive? Is he learning disabled? Is he autistic? or Is the child retarded? The questions more often asked in the diagnostic phase of behavioral assessment are, What is the child doing, either overtly or covertly, that brings him or her into conflict with the environment? and What are the potential controlling variables for these behaviors? Behavioral assessment does not reject etiologic diagnosis, as some nonbehavioral writers have suggested (e.g., Kessler, 1971). However, instead of using traditional diagnostic categories, which often assume a common etiology, a behavioral diagnosis should be highly individualized and based on direct empirical support. Both behavioral and traditional diagnoses should be tentative and provisional until substantiated; in practice, however, it is behavioral diagnosis that more often reflects the use of working hypotheses that are accepted or rejected based upon the ongoing gathering of assessment information. The methods employed in the early diagnostic phases of behavioral assessment tend to be global and extensive—they have been described as showing "broad bandwidth but low fidelity"—and the use of unstructured interviews, global checklists, observational narratives, and multicategory code systems is common.

## Design

The design phase of behavioral assessment of children focuses on obtaining information that is directly relevant to the formulation of effective treatment strategies. This gathering of information includes further specification and measurement of potential controlling variables (e.g., patterns of social reward and punishment), determination of the child's own resources for change (e.g., behavioral assets and/or self-controlling behaviors), assessment of potential social and physical environmental resources that can be utilized in carrying out treatment, assessment of the motivation for treatment for both the child and significant others, indication of potential reinforcers, specification of realistic and specific treatment objectives, and recommendation of the types of treatment that are most likely to be effective.

Hypothesis testing during this phase is the norm, and the effectiveness of, or the need for further, assessment is based on whether specified goals are achieved. The assessment procedures characterizing this phase are more focused than during the diagnostic phase, and specific types of problem checklists (e.g., fears, activity level, self-control), observational situations (e.g., command–compliance observation analogues), and behavior codes (e.g., on-task, self-stimulation, aggression) are used. Although relevance for treatment is the major criterion associated with assessment information at this time, the decision rules involved in the selection of target behaviors and treatments have often not been made explicit. This issue will be discussed subsequently in the chapter.

## Evaluation

The evaluation phase of behavioral assessment commonly involves the use of procedures designed to determine whether treatment objectives are being met, whether changes that have occurred are attributable to the interventions, whether the changes are long lasting, the economic viability of the treatment, and whether treatments and treatment outcomes are subjectively acceptable to the participants. The assessments for determining whether treatment goals are being met require the measurement of target behavior(s) over time. Such measurement will indicate the presence or absence of changes, which may be adequate in many instances. However, to determine whether these changes were a function of the treatments introduced, it is necessary to collect observations within the constraints of a single-subject experimental design (see Hersen & Barlow, 1976, for an extensive discussion of the use of single-case designs in behavioral assessment). Evaluations relative to the acceptability of treatments and treatment changes have been discussed recently under the heading of social validity (Kazdin, 1977; Wolf, 1978), and behavioral assessors have become increasingly sensitive to some of the measurement issues surrounding long-term follow-up (Mash & Terdal, 1980). The questions raised during the evaluation phase are typically those included under the term "accountability," and the methods used tend to be highly focused and specific relative to earlier assessment phases. One of the major contributions of behavioral approaches has been the greater emphasis given to evaluating treatment outcomes, in contrast to the evaluation efforts associated with other treatment approaches.

In practice, the assessment phases outlined are rarely sequential or distinct from one another. However, they reflect the more common general purposes associated with the behavioral assessment of children and highlight the need to consider such purposes in determining the appropriateness of particular assessment strategies. The purposes described thus far relate to clinical decision making for individual children, since this is characteristically the focus of most behavioral assessments. There is also a need, however, to recognize that broader societal and institutional purposes often underly assessment practices with children. These include classification for administrative record keeping, program development and evaluation, policy planning, and the advancement of scientific knowledge (Hawkins, Note 6). The types of assessment methods needed to carry out these purposes may differ substantially from those required for the assessment of individual children.

# CHILDREN'S FUNCTIONING AND ITS DETERMINANTS

## Childhood Disorders versus Target Behaviors

Behavioral approaches to disordered states in children have been explicit in their rejection of traditional models of child psychopathology (e.g., Kessler, 1966), from the standpoints of both etiological constructs and classificatory systems for diagnosis (Ullmann & Krasner, 1965). It may therefore be surprising to the reader who has examined the organization of this volume to note that many of the chapter headings follow what might be described as traditional child diagnostic labels, as opposed to descriptive headings such as "behavioral excesses" or "behavioral deficits." A comment by Phillips, Draguns, and Bartlett (1975), made with respect to other behaviorally oriented texts, seems pertinent here. They state:

> Behavior modification has not quite succeeded, however, in eschewing classificatory entities; in at least two prominent texts written from the point of view of behavior modification (Ullmann and Krasner, 1969; Yates, 1970), the subject matter is divided into chapters corresponding to traditional diagnostic units. (p. 34)

A similar criticism might be made of this volume. However, the decision to present assessment methodology within the context of categories of childhood disorder is by no means an endorsement of more traditional views of childhood disturbance. Rather, it reflects the view that children often present themselves for assessment showing characteristic behavior–situation patterns or clusters, rather than specific target symptoms, and that assessment can best proceed from an understanding of such characteristic patterns. There is evidence to suggest that broad patterns of child disturbance labeled "undercontrolled" (e.g., aggressive, delinquent, and hyperactive) and "overcontrolled" (e.g., schizoid, anxious, depressed, having somatic complaints, and withdrawn) are relatively stable over time and across raters (Achenbach & Edelbrock, 1978a). We concur with Kanfer's (1979) position that "different problem areas require development of separate methods and conceptualizations that take into account the particular parameters of that area," and that "it may turn out that in some domains progress in behavioral assessment will be blocked until conceptual models or data are available to permit a functional analysis on which target selection for assessment and rules for generalization of observations can be based" (p. 39). Each chapter in this volume provides a conceptual model and data for the problem being considered, and the assessment strategies presented follow from this framework.

The designation of particular categories of childhood disorder as a basis for discussing assessment strategies is suggestive of the syndrome and trait views that behavioral assessors have characteristically avoided. However, as described by Achenbach and Edelbrock (1978a, p. 1294), there are different ways of viewing the role of syndromes in classifying children:

1. The syndrome may be viewed as representing a personality or character type that endures beyond the immediate precipitating events requiring professional attention.
2. The syndrome may be viewed as a reaction type, whose form is as much a function of specific precipitating stresses as of individual characteristics.
3. The syndrome may be viewed as a collection of behaviors that happen to be statistically associated because the environmental contingencies supporting them are statistically associated.
4. The syndrome may be viewed as reflecting dimensions or traits, so that children are best described individually in terms of their scores on all syndromes rather than by categorization according to their resemblance to a particular syndrome.

The view of syndromes as representing either reaction types or classes of correlated behaviors would appear consistent with the assumptions underlying behavioral assessment. In fact, some of the recent work in behavioral assessment focusing on response covariations in deviant child behavior (e.g., Wahler, 1975) suggests the utility of this view, especially when correlated, but dissimilar, child behaviors are related to the occurrence of common controlling variables. An interesting demonstration of response class membership based on similarity of stimulus control function was reported by Patterson and Bechtel (1977). Initial correlational analysis suggested natural covariations of responses, such as making noise, hitting, pinching and pushing, and talking to neighbor, in a 7-year-old hyperactive boy. The behaviors in this response class covaried as a function of changes in setting variables (e.g., group vs. individual work). However, behaviors that were not members of this response class, such as movement around the room, varied in different ways with similar setting changes. Although this work is of a preliminary nature, it does suggest the utility of considering childhood disorders in terms of empirically derived stylistic consistencies in behavior and situational reactions rather than exclusively in terms of specific target problems.

It should also be recognized that commonalities are found not only in terms of the reactions of children to precipitating stimuli but also in environmental reactions to specific types of child behavior as a precipitating event. There may be stylistic consistencies in the manner in which parents react to their hyperactive children (Cunningham & Barkley, 1979; Campbell, 1973), as indicated by attempts to direct or control the child's behavior. However, this style may reflect a predictable child-behavior-induced reaction in that normalization of the child's behavior through the use of stimulant medication results in a reduction in the parent's controlling behavior (Barkley & Cunningham, 1979).

The view of categories of childhood disorder suggested here is based on commonalities in patterns of behavior and behavior–context disturbance rather than on target symptoms. Many previous presentations of behavioral assessment have focused on assessment techniques, such as the interview, the self-report, and direct observation (Haynes, 1978; Mash & Terdal, 1976; Nay, 1979). However, this volume considers these techniques only in relation to the specific problem context in which they are to be used. Ross (1978) notes that "the emphasis in behavior therapy should be on the conceptualization of problems and not on specific techniques" (p. 592). This statement is equally applicable to behavioral assessment. Although there are some general principles associated with the development and use of particular behavioral assessment techniques, the nature of an interview with the parent of a depressed child should be different from that conducted with the parent of a socially aggressive child. It is believed that an understanding of the parameters associated with childhood depression or social aggression, in addition to the general principles of behavioral interviewing, will serve to generate more specialized and ultimately more useful assessments in each of those areas respectively.

## Classification and Diagnosis

Probably the most controversial area in the assessment and treatment of disturbed children has been the use of diagnostic labels based upon global classification systems. In commenting on the high proportion (estimates of 40%) of clinic-referred children who are labeled in global and nondescript terms such as "adjustment reaction" (e.g., Cerreto & Tuma, 1977), Dreger, Lewis, Rich, Miller, Reid, Overlade, Taffel, and Flemming (1964) state, "looked at realistically, what this means in that after the elaborate procedures used in most clinics are completed, the child is placed in a category, which says exactly what we knew about him in the first place, that he has a problem" (p. 1). In some studies, as many as 30% of parents surveyed who had been in contact with professionals indicated that their children had been described with three or more labels (Gorham, Des Jardins, Page, Pettis, & Scheiber, 1975), and unsubstantiated diagnoses and client labels have been consistently cited as being among the most common errors in child and family treatment research (O'Leary & Turkewitz, 1978). Criticisms of existent systems for the classification and labeling of children have been directed at the etiological assumptions upon which they are based, their unreliability with respect to both test–retest and interrater agreement, lack of demonstrated validity, lack of utility with respect to prognosis and treatment, and general abuses and misuses related to the potentially iatrogenic effects associated with the assignment of labels (Hobbs, 1975a, 1975b).

Several writers have recently described and commented upon the types of classification systems that have been developed for disordered child behavior (Achenbach & Edelbrock, 1978a; Harris, 1979; Kessler, 1971; Quay, 1979), and it is likely that such discussions will increase with the appearance of the most recent edition of the American Psychiatric Association's (1979) *Diagnostic and Statistical Manual* (DSM-III), with its increased number of categories for describing children's disorders and its more detailed specifications for diagnosis and clinical decision making. There is, in the literature, some consensus regarding the general neglect of meaningful taxonomic frameworks for describing children and the need for the development of classification schemes for guiding theory, research, and practice. For example, Achenbach and Edelbrock (1978a) state, "the study of psychopathology in children has long lacked a coherent taxonomic framework within which training, treatment, epidemiology, and research could be integrated" (p. 1275). However, these same authors also note that the "lack of entrenched categories for child psychopathology may ultimately prove a blessing if it promotes efforts to develop a more clinically useful, reliable, and empirically based foundation for the study of child disorders" (p. 1276). These two statements reflect a commonly expressed attitude about child classification, which includes a dissatisfaction with things as they are and a hope for something better, but also a noted lack of significant progress in identifying mutually acceptable categories or in overcoming recurrent reliability and validity problems.

Behavioral assessments of children have been characterized as rejecting child classification and diagnosis (Kessler, 1971; Prugh *et al.*, 1975). This view is not accurate, for, as noted by Prugh *et al.* (1975), "to argue against *any system of classification* because of attendant difficulties, as has often been done recently, is to abandon the scientific and the clinical approach" (p. 264). It is the attendant difficulties of existing classification systems that behavioral assessors find objectionable, not the act of classification itself. Such difficulties include empirical inadequacy (e.g., lack of reliability), implicit etiological assumptions based on highly inferential psychodynamic constructs that underlie many of the categories, the static nature of categories as applied to a developing child, the lack of demonstrated relevance to treatment, the undesirable consequences of labeling, and the failure of previous classification systems to attend adequately to situational influences.

It is also the case, however, that behavioral assessors have failed to develop an alternative to existing classification systems in spite of the longstanding recognition of this need (Adams, Doster, & Calhoun, 1977; Arkowitz, 1979; Ferster, 1965). In part, the lack of behavioral assessment development in this area likely reflects a priority related to idiographic and treatment-oriented assessment goals. It is not clear that the development of global classification systems for child disorders will do much to facilitate these goals, albeit they have potential usefulness for improving communication, combining data obtained from diverse sources, epidemiologic study, comparison of treatments, and understanding of causes (Kessler, 1971).

Classification efforts for childhood disorders have followed two traditions. The first has involved the development of clinically derived categories for classification based upon subjective consensus, as characterized by those systems developed by the Group for the Advancement of Psychiatry (Note 7), the American Psychiatric Association (DSM-I, 1952; DSM-II, 1968; DSM-III, 1979), and the World Health Organization (multiaxial classification—Rutter, Lebovici, Eisenberg, Sneznevskij, Sadoun, Brooke, & Lin, 1969; Rutter, Shaffer, & Shepherd, 1975). Although it is beyond the scope of this chapter to review these systems in any detail, commonly occurring major categories are exemplified by those provided in DSM-III. These include attention deficit disorders, or hyperkinesis; conduct disorders of a socialized and unsocialized nature; and anxiety–withdrawal disorders. Other categories include mental retardation, developmental disorders of a pervasive and specific nature, and more specific problems related to eating, speech, and stereotyped movements. Problems related to the use of these systems involve their coverage, reliability and validity, utility, and the fact that they are based on disease models of behavior (McLemore & Benjamin, 1979; McReynolds, 1979; Schacht & Nathan, 1977). The interested reader is referred to reviews by Achenbach & Edelbrock (1978a), Harris (1979), Hobbs (1975a, 1975b), Kessler (1971), and Quay (1979) for a detailed discussion of these classification systems. Given the differing assumptions upon which these systems are based, it is doubtful that they will be of much direct use to behavioral assessors for purposes other than administrative requirement.

The second major effort toward classifying childhood disorders is an empirical one, involving the utilization of multivariate statistical methods such as factor analysis and cluster analysis. Such approaches assume that there are a number of independent dimensions for behavior and that all children possess these sets of behavior to varying degrees. In contrast to the previously described typological approaches characterized by the use of clinically derived categories emphasizing qualitatively different types of childhood disorder, the dimensional approach, which focuses on empirically derived categories of behavioral covariation, seems more consistent with the assumptions of behavioral assessment, if not with the practice. Although empirically derived classifications are more objective and potentially more reliable, they also possess associated problems, including how to determine the constituent behaviors that go into the analysis, interactions between the methods of data collection (e.g., ratings, direct observations, questionnaires) or the informant (e.g., parent vs. teacher) and the dimensions that emerge, and the sensitivity of the global dimensions to situational influences.

The multivariate studies (see Achenbach & Edelbrock, 1978a) are consistent in identifying two broad dimensions of child behavior: the first, labeled undercontrolled (aggressive, externalizing, acting out, conduct disorder), and the second, labeled overcontrolled (inhibited, internalizing, shy–anxious, personality disorder). More specific dimensions that have been identified in studies have included academic disability, aggressiveness, anxiousness, delinquency, depression, hyperactivity, immaturity, obsessive–compulsive behavior, schizoid behavior, sexual problems, sleep problems, social withdrawal, somatic complaints, and uncommunicativeness (Achenbach & Edelbrock, 1978a). The reliability of many of these dimensions, however, is questionable, and their generality depends on both the informant and the method used to obtain data. Although the multivariate approach continues to hold promise for the development of taxonomies to be used in research designed to enhance our understanding of childhood disorder and to evaluate treatment outcomes, its utility for the individualized assessment and treatment of childhood disturbance is less apparent. This state of affairs was summarized by Peterson (1968):

> The unitary traits we have so far defined seem to be determined more by the perceptual tendencies of observers than by the behavioral tendencies of the people under observation. And even if situation and method generality could be attained it is not immediately clear what the descriptions have to do with treatment. This is what we are up to, after all. No dimensional system available today is very useful in providing the kinds of information needed to help the people we labor so hard to describe. (p. 7)

In spite of the fact that many multivariate studies have been carried out since this statement was made, it is still believed to be accurate. The potential utility of multivariate procedures in clinical practice is yet to be demonstrated.

### Outcomes of Labeling Children

Much has been written about the positive and negative aspects of assigning diagnostic labels to children. On the positive side, it is argued that labels help to summarize and order observations, to facilitate communication among professionals with different backgrounds, to guide treatment strategies in a global fashion, to put therapists in touch with a preexisting relevant body of more detailed experimental and clinical data, and, consistent with scientific goals, to facilitate etiological, epidemiological, and treatment outcome studies (Rains, Kitsuse, Duster, & Friedson, 1975). On the negative side are criticisms regarding how effectively currently existing child diagnostic labels achieve any of the aforementioned purposes and a concern about the negative outcomes associated with assigning labels to children, including how others tend to perceive and react to the children and how the label influences the children's perceptions of themselves (Guskin, Bartel, & Macmillan, 1975) and their behavior.

The use of existing labels has also been noted to bias professionals toward seeing psychopathology in children, although there is some evidence that behavior therapists may be less easily biased by labels (Langer & Abelson, 1974). Several studies have demonstrated that a particular behavior, when believed to be exhibited by a "disturbed" child, may produce different reactions than when believed to be exhibited by a "nondisturbed" child (e.g., Stevens-Long, 1973). Labeling children as behaviorally disturbed or as normal has also been shown to result in distortions in recall, on the part of trained observers, for negative (Yates, Klein, & Haven, 1978) and, under some circumstances, positive behaviors (Yates & Hoage, Note 8). Yates et al. (1978) found an observer tendency to overestimate the occurrence of negative behavior in a group labeled behaviorally disturbed and to underestimate the occurrence of negative behavior in a group labeled normal. Similarly, the effects of labeling on recall were demonstrated in a study by Cantor and Mischel (1977), which found that the induction of the trait concepts "extrovert" and "introvert" biased the recognition of associated personality characteristics. Other studies have demonstrated the role that labels play in producing negatively stereotypical expectancies on the part of teachers (e.g., Foster, Ysseldyke, & Reese, 1975). These illustrative studies, as well as many others, provide indirect support for some of the potentially negative effects of diagnostic labeling by professionals.

On the positive side, some investigators have suggested that labels may serve as a convenient reference point for tolerance toward and acceptability of particular sets of child behaviors (Algozzine, Mercer, & Countermine, 1977) or may provide parents with closure and understanding regarding what might be wrong with their child (e.g., Fernald & Gettys, Note 9). If parents were to believe that the label explained why their child is the way he or she is, then attention may be directed at coping with the problem rather than at searching for the "real cause" through successive contacts with agencies and professionals. Whether such suggested "benefits" outweigh the negative effects of labeling is yet to be demonstrated.

It is believed that the important outcomes associated with the labeling of disturbed children may not be those involving the assignment of labels by professionals. Rather, it is the informal labeling processes and interpretations of formal labels by parents, teachers, and children themselves that are likely to have the greatest impact. Further study of how parents and teachers use labels to organize their experiences with both normal and disturbed children, and how such labeling influences their responses to and feelings about children, is likely to increase our understanding of childhood disorder. Although behavioral assessors have rejected the use of existing diagnostic labels, especially with individual children, labeling is a prepotent human response for organizing experiences and cannot be legislated out of existence by fiat. There is a need to assess some of the natural and common ways in which child behavior is ordered by those in contact with the child. The issue is not whether the use of labels should be supported or rejected, but rather the identification of the types of labels that are used, the conditions under which they are used, and the effects associated with their use.

## Etiological Assumptions Regarding Childhood Disorders

The most prevalent misconception associated with behavioral views of childhood disorder is that deviant behaviors are acquired exclusively as a function of interaction with the external physical and social environment. Implicit in this view is that child deviancy represents faulty learning and, therefore, that in assessing the problem one should look for causes in the external environment, giving minimal attention to organismic events or internal cognitions and affects.

To be sure, behavioral views of childhood disorder have emphasized the significant role of environmental events as relevant controlling conditions, but certainly not to the exclusion of other important variables. If anything, behavioral and social learning viewpoints that emerged in the 1960s (e.g., Bandura, 1969; Kanfer & Phillips, 1970; Ullmann & Krasner, 1965) provided a more balanced approach to the study of childhood psychopathology, which historically had emphasized physical causes, such as brain dysfunction, or internal events, such as unconscious impulses and drives. It was unfortunate that the attempt to give greater attention to important and observable environmental influences was inaccurately perceived by many as a rejection of all intraorganismic controlling variables. In any event, behavioral assessment of childhood disorders does not assume that problematic behavior must be learned, although in many instances it may well be. Methodologically, behavioral assessment tends toward being atheoretical. It does assume that socioenvironmental controlling variables play an important causal and maintaining role in all forms of childhood disorders, as do organismic variables. The relative importance of organismic and environmental variables and their interaction is not to be assumed for any class of problems but rather should follow from a careful and empirically based functional analysis of the problem. A number of general points that are related to a behavioral assessment view of childhood disorder are as follows:

1. The first point concerns multiple causality. Given that the child is embedded in a complex physical–social system, it is likely that many potentially relevant controlling variables contribute to the problem, including physical and social environmental events, as well as organismic variables of both a physical and cognitive nature.

2. No a priori assumptions are made regarding the primacy of controlling variables in contributing to childhood disorders. Such a view rejects particular sets of controlling variables as necessarily more important than others (e.g., physical vs. social causes) either contemporaneously or historically and is intended to counteract the popular belief in many child assessment and treatment settings that identification of malfunctioning physical systems through neuropsychological testing, medical examination, or historical information somehow provides a complete

or more fundamental explanation of why the child is exhibiting problems. Such an analysis is both incomplete and inaccurate because it gives greater weight to physical causes in explaining child behavior and ignores potential environment factors of equal importance.

3. Although there are no assumptions in behavioral assessment regarding the primacy of controlling conditions with respect to etiology, primacy may be given to classes of variables for the sake of methodological and practical expediency. Variables that are observable, measurable, and readily modifiable may become the focus for assessment when such an approach facilitates remediation of the problem.

4. It is assumed that there is an ongoing and reciprocal interaction between relevant controlling variables, so that attempts to identify original causes in assessment are not likely to be fruitful. "Causes" that occur earlier in development (e.g., birth injury or early social deprivation) cannot be assumed to be more significant contributors to the child's difficulties than current physical conditions and social interactions.

5. The processes by which the relevant controlling variables for deviant child behavior exert their influence are assumed to be similar to those underlying non-deviant child behavior, and general principles related to both physiology and learning apply equally for both populations. However, in some circumstances it may be demonstrated that children exhibiting particular deficits may respond differently to environmental and physical input than children who do not. For example, hyperactive children may respond differently to rewards and punishments than non-hyperactive children (Cunningham & Knights, 1979; Firestone & Douglas, 1975), although it is not clear whether this difference is related to an inherent child deficit or is acquired as a function of ongoing interactions. A popular view has been that hyperactive children respond "paradoxically" to stimulant medications relative to normal children (see Barkley, 1977, for review); recent findings, however, do not support this view (Rapoport, Buchsbaum, Zahn, Weingartner, Ludlow, & Mikkelson, 1978). In any event, qualitative differences between deviant and normal children should be empirically demonstrated and not based exclusively on theoretical prediction.

6. Although controlling variables that are contemporaneous and situationally present are frequently emphasized as "causes" in behavioral views of childhood disorder, there is also a need to consider both extrasituational and temporally more remote causes. For example, external stressors such as marital discord (Oltmanns, Broderick, & O'Leary, 1977) may have direct effects on a mother's immediate reaction to her child's behavior. Passman and Mulhern (1977) have shown that a mother's punitiveness toward her child may increase with the amount of external stress to which she is exposed, and Wahler (1980) has reported an inverse relationship between extrafamily contacts and child behavior problems. There is increasing evidence to suggest that situationally present child behaviors are only one contributor to parental reactions to their children, which may be influenced by external factors of the type just mentioned, as well as by general rules and strategies that parents may follow in interacting with their children (Lytton, 1979; Chapman, Note 10). It is not surprising, therefore, that treatment-induced behavioral altera-

tions in the child may not necessarily lead to subsequent changes in parental behavior or perceptions toward the child.

## DIMENSIONS OF CHILD BEHAVIOR ASSESSMENT

The most important characteristic of developing children is the active dialogue that takes place between themselves and their biological makeup, physical and social environments, and the cultural context into which they are born. Pushed along by genetic endowment and neuromuscular maturation, groping and grasping to understand physical realities and the expectations of those around them, children are nurtured, shaped, and socialized. Rather than being passive partners in this dialogue, children, in return, shape and socialize the world around them, setting their own expectations and demands (Bell & Harper, 1977). This developmental engagement is characterized by cognitive–social conflict and equilibrium and almost always by movement and change. It begins at the time of conception and continues thereafter. Any consideration of the assessment of children must begin with a recognition of the ebb and flow of this developmental dialogue, because it has important implications for conceptualizing, measuring, classifying, diagnosing, changing, and evaluating changes in child behavior. This recognition that childhood behavior is embedded within normal developmental sequences and occurs within a context of social and situational influence, perceptions, and expectations on the part of significant adults as well as within the broader context of societal and cultural norms (Bronfenbrenner, 1977; Cochran & Brassard, 1979), necessitates a view of child behavior assessment as both unique and multidimensional, requiring consideration of the totality of the child's current life situation as well as significant developmental history (Ross, 1978). The multidimensionality that is characteristic of child behavior in context leads to several generalizations regarding assessment:

1. Developing children represent a unique population for which there are special assessment considerations of both a conceptual and a practical nature.
2. The assessment of childhood disorders necessarily involves normative comparisons encompassing social judgments, developmental deviation, and variation with respect to an appropriate reference group.
3. Assessments of children invariably involve multiple targets, including somatic and physiological states, overt behavior, cognitions, and affect.
4. Given the large number and wide range of behaviors that are necessarily implicated in most types of childhood disorders, guidelines are needed for the selection of meaningful target behaviors for cost-efficient and effective assessments and treatments.
5. The range of situations within which children interact is necessarily various and includes the family, school, and formal and informal peer groups. Therefore, multisituational analysis is the rule.

6. The pervasiveness of developmental change and situational variation in children suggests the need to assess patterns of behavior over time as well as more global situational consistencies.

Each of these generalizations will be discussed in the sections to follow.

## Special Considerations

Although assessments with adults and children have much in common, there are several characteristic conditions and constraints associated with the assessment of children that are not ordinarily encountered when assessing adults. The uniqueness of child assessment follows from generalizations about children as a group, characteristics of children at different ages that interact with the type of assessment being conducted, and commonalities within the types of situations in which children ordinarily function and in which they are assessed.

### *Rapid and Uneven Developmental Change*

With respect to generalizations about children as a group, the most noteworthy characteristic is rapid and uneven developmental change (Ciminero & Drabman, 1977; Evans & Nelson, 1977). Such change has implications both for judgments concerning childhood deviancy and for the selection of appropriate methods for assessment. Some studies have described both the age trends characterizing many child behaviors (Kagan & Moss, 1962; MacFarlane, Allen, & Honzik, 1954; Achenbach & Edelbrock, Note 1) and how the social significance and meaning of a problem may vary with the age of the child (Prugh et al., 1975). Developmental deviation has been defined empirically in relation to a deviation from some observed behavioral norm (Achenbach & Edelbrock, Note 1) and/or theoretically in terms of a deviation from some expected behavioral patterns characteristic of particular stages of cognitive or psychosexual development (Santostefano, 1971). A behavioral assessment approach would place greater emphasis on developmental norms based upon observed behavior than on norms derived from inferred theoretical constructs. Unfortunately, there are few data of a cross-sectional or longitudinal nature describing age trends for child behavior, and the data that are available typically constitute global parental reports regarding the frequency of occurrence for problem child behaviors at different ages (MacFarlane et al., 1954; Achenbach & Edelbrock, Note 1). Although such parental reports of problem child behavior at different ages are extremely important in establishing age trends, it is also important to supplement these descriptions with direct observations of behavior over time and to establish norms for prosocial behaviors. Additionally, although there is some information regarding the proportion of children at given ages exhibiting various problems, there is less information regarding some of the more qualitative shifts in behavior that may occur. Although such qualitative changes over time are more difficult to assess, it would appear that many child behaviors, such as fears (Graziano, DeGiovanni, & Garcia, 1979; Johnson & Melamed, 1979) and hyperactivity (Ross & Ross, 1976), change both qualitatively and quantitatively with age. Judgments regarding deviancy must be made in relation to both types of change.

Rapid and uneven developmental change also carries implications for the stability of assessment information over time. Assessment of behavior at one age may not be predictive of behavior at a later time, especially when assessments are obtained with very young children. For example, in examining aggressive behavior in males, Olweus (1979) reported that the degree of stability tended to decrease linearly as the interval between the two times of measurement increased and that stability in aggressive behavior could be broadly described as a positive linear function of the interval covered and the subject's age at the time of first measurement, expressed in the age ratio $T_1:T_2$. As the child ages, there does seem to be greater behavioral stability between successive assessments. However, it is not always easy to determine whether this reflects consistency in child behavior or consistency in the methods being used in assessment. For example, the homogeneity of test items is likely to be greater for assessments with 7-year-old and 10-year-old children than for assessments with 2-year-old and 5-year-old children. This would likely be the case for assessments of both social behavior and cognitive abilities.

### Plasticity and Modifiability

A second characteristic of children as a group that has implications for assessment and treatment relates to the plasticity and modifiability of the young in relation to environmental influence. That child behavior is under the strong and immediate social control of parents and other children suggests that the need for assessment of these environmental influences is relatively greater than would be the case for assessments with adults.

### Age and Sex Characteristics

A third characteristic of children as a group is that they are various, both within and across ages. Age-related characteristics have implications not only for judgments regarding deviancy but also for the assessment methods that are appropriate. One obvious difference relates to the constraints placed on the use of child self-report as a function of age-related verbal and cognitive abilities. The quality of the child's reaction to being observed may also vary with age. Assessment of young children may be affected by the child's wariness of strangers, whereas adolescents may be wary of assessments by adults, but for different reasons, and they could therefore react in different ways.

Sex of the child also seems to play an important role in judgments of deviancy, with concomitant implications for the interpretation of assessment information. Numerous studies have shown that both the norms that are used in making judgments about child behavior and the overt behavioral reactions of parents and teachers will vary as a function of whether the child is male or female. Other studies have shown sex differences for different types of childhood disorder (see Eme, 1979, for review), and the factors emerging from multivariate studies of child behavior problems differ for boys and girls (Achenbach & Edelbrock, Note 1).

### Commonalities in Assessment Situations

There are several commonalities in the types of situations in which children are evaluated that also have implications for assessment (Ciminero & Drabman, 1977; Evans & Nelson, 1977). That children are typically referred by adults means that they may not be experiencing subjective distress and may not understand the reasons for assessment. It also suggests the need to consider those factors that have been shown to influence referral, including social class (Harris, 1974) and type of problem (Lorion, Cowen, & Caldwell, 1974). Additionally, assessments designed to develop effective treatments must be conducted with the realization that there have likely been prior attempts to modify the child's behavior and that assessment and treatment are highly interrelated.

There is also a strong relationship between learning and behavior problems during childhood, and behavioral assessments are often carried out in the context of cognitive or intellectual evaluations. This interrelationship between learning and behavior problems reflects the more general observation that problematic child behavior rarely occurs in isolation. This typically means that child assessment is multidisciplinary, involving a range of professionals, including educators, psychologists, and a variety of medical personnel. The multidisciplinary nature of child assessment frequently results in fragmented assessments and poor communication. Consequently, the need for assessments that can be readily understood and used by a range of professionals is especially important with children.

It is also the norm that children who are referred for assessment will undergo repeated evaluations. This is especially the case for children with chronic conditions, for which repeated evaluation and planning may be dictated by legislative requirements. Repeated evaluation also applies to children with less severe problems, reflecting both the fragmentation that is characteristic of mental health delivery systems for children and, more positively, the reevaluation of children following remedial behavioral or educational programming. Repeated evaluations require the development of assessment methods that are robust across ages and relatively insensitive to the effects of practice.

### Normative Comparisons

Behavioral assessors, with their emphasis on the functioning of individual children, have given little attention to the development of normative information that attempts to establish the individual child's position on some dimension relative to the performance of other members of a suitable reference group. In recognizing the role of assessment in monitoring changes associated with treatment, the focus has been on the establishment of intraindividual as opposed to group norms. For example, such intraindividual normative comparisons are implicit in any assessment that examines the performance of a child relative to the same child's behavior under baseline conditions. Although intraindividual comparisons of this type will identify the child as improving, not improving, or getting worse, they give little guidance as to whether the child's level of performance is meaningful with respect to some generally accepted performance criterion.

In this regard, assessment approaches that emphasize the child's performance not in relation to some reference group average but, rather, to specific performance criteria would appear to be consistent with the treatment emphasis in behavioral assessment (Hartmann et al., 1979). Such edumetric or criterion-referenced testing approaches (Carver, 1974) seem especially applicable in areas such as academic performance, athletic skill, or job completion, where easily identifiable and sometimes absolute performance goals are available. On the other hand, in areas related to social behavior and adjustment, the current lack of availability of accepted standards of performance makes a criterion-referenced approach more difficult to apply. However, recent efforts to identify the types of child social behaviors that may lead to popularity with peers or that are reinforced by peers (see Hops & Greenwood, Chapter 8, this volume) or the types of responses that are likely to be approved of or viewed as disturbing by adults (e.g., Mooney & Algozzine, 1978) may one day provide a basis for generally acceptable criterion standards in some of the more relativistic areas of social performance.

In considering the applicability of group norms in behavioral assessment, two issues are important. The first involves the utility of normative comparison, and the second, what kind of normative information is likely to be most useful. Hartmann et al. (1979) have recently outlined some potentially useful purposes of normative comparisons in behavioral assessment. Included among these are the following:

1. Normative comparisons would be useful in the identification of deficient, excessive, or otherwise problematic performance, as would be the case if the child engaged in excessively high rates of aggressive behavior. Under such circumstances, normative information about the rates of aggression in comparable situations by comparable children would serve as a basis for identifying the child as potentially problematic, depending on social judgments and environmental reactions to the behavior.

2. Where presenting complaints about children reflect parental expectations that differ markedly from existing norms, the target for, and type of, treatment may be different than would be the case in the absence of such normative information.

3. Where norms exist that suggest certain types of childhood problems to be both common and transient (e.g., early reactions to separation) at particular ages, such information may lead to decisions regarding whether or not to treat the problem.

4. Where norms exist for skilled versus inept performances, such information may be used for establishing both intermediate treatment targets and final

treatment goals. Such use exemplifies the criterion-referenced approach described previously.

5. Norms may be useful for grouping children into relatively homogeneous treatment groups, which subsequently could produce greater precision with respect to the types of treatment most appropriate for children with particular kinds of difficulties.

6. Normative information permits the direct comparison of studies using differing samples of children.

7. Normative information for specific assessment measures may facilitate the comparability of findings obtained through different data sources. For example, measures of parental report and direct observation may yield equivalent information should the scores on each reflect a particular amount of deviation, as in the case of a child who was one standard deviation above the mean on the two different measures.

8. Normative information may be used to evaluate the clinical significance or social validity of treatment outcomes (Kazdin, 1977).

In addition to the preceding uses described by Hartmann *et al.* (1979), normative information regarding important situational determinants may also help to identify some situations as being high risk for the development of particular problems. For example, normative information regarding the quality of the child's school environment—for example, high expectations, good group management, effective feedback with ample use of praise, setting of good models of behavior by teachers, pleasant working conditions, and giving pupils positions of trust and responsibility—may serve as a basis for early detection of potential problems where such conditions do not exist, with a subsequent focus on the design of preventative programs (Rutter, 1979). Similarly, norms regarding the presence or absence of certain family background variables for particular childhood disorders—for example, those related to social class and to parental history of alcoholism or child abuse—may also serve as a basis for identifying some children as high risk.

Normative information within the context of child assessment has typically been conceptualized in one of two ways. The first approach is reflected in the average child's performance under ''usual'' conditions. Such an approach has given primacy to age-related characteristics, and implicit in such developmental norms is the assumption that similar underlying processes, conceptualized in terms of either maturation or age-related developmental tasks, are applicable to most, if not all, children. This assumption has resulted in little attention to situational information in describing normative performances, with the exception of such marker variables as the child's age and sex.

The second approach to normative information has looked at the average child's performance under ''highly specific'' and controlled conditions, as would be the case with standardized tests of intelligence, language ability, or academic achievement. In contrast to the use of developmental norms, this approach creates a circumscribed and often narrow set of conditions under which to assess children's performance.

Both of these approaches, reflecting either homogeneity or standardization of situations, assume or create a consistent set of stimulus conditions against which differences among children will emerge. They focus on the child's performance typically in a limited number of areas and give little attention to either situational differences or similarities. A behavioral assessment view toward the establishment of norms requires a somewhat different emphasis.

To begin, the important role given to relevant contextual variables in children's functioning requires the establishment not only of average levels of child performance but also of norms for physical and social environments. Normative information for specific populations of children, regarding such things as the frequency and quality of parental commands (Cunningham & Barkley, 1979), natural rates of teacher approval and disapproval in the classroom (Van Houten, 1978; White, 1975), the amount of time spent interacting with siblings (Leitenberg, Burchard, Burchard, Fuller, & Lysaght, 1977) or in different physical environments, and the kinds of situations that most typically lead to conflict, is as essential as norms for child behavior. The general need in behavioral assessment is for norms that establish the child's performance under a representative range of conditions, for example, not just the norm that children may be more compliant as they get older but also the rates of compliance for different types of commands. Although this view of behavior–situation norms is not entirely different in concept from norms obtained in a standard test situation, it differs in that the range and representativeness of situations and behaviors sampled should be more extensive and more representative of the child's natural environments.

With few exceptions, behavior–situation norms for children are not currently available. In part, this reflects the lack of standardized methods and situations that have been employed in the behavioral assessment of children. However, this situation is changing, and several chapters in this volume provide normative information in such areas as parent–child interaction, sex-role behaviors, and social skills, under a standard range of conditions.

It should also be noted that even where norms for children have not included situational information, they have tended to focus more on physical and cognitive development than on commonly occurring child behaviors. Where norms have been provided for behavior, they have tended to be extremely global and overinclusive, as reflected in such terms as "out of control," "inwardized," or "balanced" (e.g., Ilg & Ames, 1955). Additionally, such norms have been based on reports by others rather than direct observation. There is a need for normative information regarding specific child behavior obtained through direct observation as well as through the reports of significant others (Achenbach & Edelbrock, Note 1).

## Multiple Targets

Behavioral assessments of children have typically been directed at behavior and at potential controlling variables. Early approaches tended to focus on behavior as reflected in the overt motor reactions of the child, whereas recent views have accepted a broader view of child behavior, which encompasses all organismic activity, including physiological reactions and subjective covert cognitions and affect. Controlling variables for behavior are those antecedent and consequent events in the social and physical environments that serve to influence the occurrence of the behavior. The heuristic *S-O-R-K-C*, originally presented by Lindsley (1964) and elaborated on by Kanfer & Phillips (1970) and others (e.g., Goldfried & Sprafkin, 1976), serves as a convenient way of organizing relevant classes of assessment information into broad categories of antecedent and consequent events, any of which may be designated as targets for treatment.

*S* refers to prior stimulation, or to the external and internal environments that have some functional relationship to the behavior. Given that the functional properties of environments for many child behaviors have not been empirically established, assessment often involves the designation of *S* variables that may be hypothesized as potentially important.

*O* refers to the biological state of the child, including the wide range of genetic, physiological, neurological, biochemical, and mechanical variables that influence the form and function of behavior. The numerous studies supporting the interaction between biological and social variables in child functioning require that medical information regarding the child's biological condition be brought to bear in any assessment, if only at times to be eliminated as a possible relevant determinant for specific types of behavior. Such information is especially important with children, given the frequent and rapid physical changes that are occurring throughout childhood and adolescence. The blending of assessment information related to biological and social variables is especially evident in the section of this volume dealing with health-related disorders.

*R* refers to the response, which has been taken in behavioral assessment as encompassing motor behavior, cognitive–verbal behavior, and physiological–emotional behavior (Lang, 1968). Developments in behavioral assessment, because of both theory and practicality, have occurred largely with respect to the measurement of motor behavior, and to a lesser extent, with physiological responses. However, there is an increasing emphasis on the definition and measurement of more covert cognitive events. Mischel's (1973) discussion of person variables, including construction competencies, encoding strategies, expectancies, values, and plans, and some of Meichenbaum's (e.g., Butler & Meichenbaum, 1980; Meichenbaum, Burland, Gruson, & Cameron, Note 11) recent writings on self-statements and metacognitive assessment provide useful frameworks for the examination of covert processes. Some of the problems involved in multiple-response-mode assessment, including that of reaching adequate consensus regarding the definitions of cognitive, motor, and physiological systems and the lack of correlation between the three systems, have been recently discussed by Cone (1979).

*K* refers to the contingency relationships between behavior and its consequences, including such things as the frequency and timing of response outcomes. Schedules of reinforcement (Ferster & Skinner, 1953) clearly influence the form and topography of child behavior and constitute an important category of assessment information. It has been suggested, for example, that under continuous reward conditions, the performance of hyperactive and normal children may not differ, whereas under conditions of partial reward, hyperactive children may exhibit response decrements (Firestone & Douglas, 1975).

*C* refers to the consequences of behavior and includes a wide variety of pleasant and unpleasant events. As was the case with prior stimulation, it is important to distinguish between events following behavior that are functionally related in altering future probabilities and consequent events that are contiguous but that have not been demonstrated to have response-controlling properties (Mash & Terdal, 1976).

It should be evident from this brief overview that the preceding designations, although useful in organizing assessment information, are arbitrary and reflect a somewhat static view of the relationship between child behavior and context. The categories are foci of convenience, and responses may serve as antecedents or consequences, depending upon one's perspective. With the view that child-behavior environment relationships are continuous, ongoing, and interactive, it is apparent that behavior may be a controlling variable for environmental events and for itself, as emphasized in much of the work on behavioral self-regulation (Kanfer & Karoly, 1972). Many studies have shown that a child's behavior may alter the contingency systems to which he or she is exposed. For example, children's reactions immediately prior to adult-administered consequences such as punishment have been shown to influence the amount of punishment they receive (Parke & Sawin, Note 12). Children who seek to make reparation for misdeeds receive less punishment from adults than those who act defiantly. The reader who is interested in a more detailed discussion of some of the complexities of *S-O-R-K-C* definitions and interactions is referred to Kanfer and Phillips (1970).

## Selection of Target Behaviors

The identification of problem behaviors that, in turn, are targeted for change within a behavioral intervention program has been a hallmark of behavioral assessments with children. However, several writers (Hawkins, 1975; Mash & Terdal, 1976) have called attention to the fact that many studies begin with a designation of problems to be treated, with little information as to the decision processes utilized in their selection.

### Interassessor Agreement

The need for interassessor agreement on problem identification is an empirical question. However, limited data are currently available (Hartmann *et al.*, 1979). An exception is a recent study by Hay, Hay, Angle, and Nelson (1979), who assessed the reliability of problem identification using a behavioral interview with adult clients exhibiting drug abuse problems. In an exemplary design, four interviewers interviewed the same four clients, and it was found that although it was possible to generalize across interviewers with respect to the overall number of areas identified as problematic, there was little agreement among interviewers on specific problem areas. In addition, interview rather than client variability in behavior seemed to be the major factor contributing to low reliability, suggesting the need for standardized interview procedures. The findings of this study suggest the need for further examination of interassessor reliability in target behavior selection. Additionally, although such investigations should be method-specific—multiple methods of assessment are typically the norm with children—interactive effects must also be considered. For example, is reliability enhanced or attenuated by the use of multiple methods in problem identification? The assumption has been that multimethod assessment may enhance reliability, but this has not been tested directly.

Additionally, there is little information to support the view that given essentially equivalent assessment information, different behavioral assessors will reliably pinpoint the same problem as the primary intervention target. However, it is also not clear that such reliability of target behavior selection is a necessary condition for successful treatment because, hypothetically, similar outcomes could be achieved through different means. This view would largely reflect the model of behavior change that underlies assessment and treatment. Models that view behavior change as being mediated via unifying intrapersonal constructs such as self-efficacy, as proposed by Bandura (1977), would likely acknowledge that different treatment targets could produce equivalent outcomes to the extent that a change in any target behavior altered the child's belief that he or she could perform successfully. For example, similar outcomes for a child with learning difficulties might be achieved by increasing either the rate at which the child gave correct answers in the classroom or the rate of successful completion of homework assignments.

That children typically exhibit a multiplicity of presenting problems (Wittlieb, Eifert, Wilson, & Evans, 1979), many of which may be both common and transient, and that it is typically an adult report that defines child behavior as problematic make target behavior selection especially complex. Regardless of the outcomes of future studies designed to assess the importance of interassessor agreement about problem identification, there is a pressing need for assessors to be more explicit about what factors influence the specification of target behaviors. A recent report by Wittlieb et al. (1979) provides some information in this regard. These authors reviewed 36 single-case studies of children under 17 years of age, all of which appeared in *Behavior Therapy*. Although 67% of the studies reported the child as exhibiting more than one problem behavior, only one-third reported the treatment of all mentioned problems. In a few instances, the target behavior was completely different from the problems mentioned in the case description. Slightly more than half the studies provided reasons for the selection of the particular target behavior, and these were divided into five categories by Wittlieb et al. (1979):

1. The behavior was dangerous to the life or health of the child.
2. The behavior was considered detrimental to the child's school performance and/or adjustment.
3. The behavior was judged socially repugnant.

4. The behavior was viewed as having influence on some other deviant behavior.
5. The behavior was selected to prove that a particular treatment procedure could be successfully applied to that type of behavior.

Wittlieb *et al.* (1979) noted that target behavior selection involves three processes: the identification of all problems, the prioritizing of problems, and the choice of targets for treatment. It was not possible to determine whether the reasons given previously were the basis for problem identification or prioritization. Additionally, the possibility that other reasons could have been involved cannot be excluded. For example, such factors as therapist treatment preferences and the convenience of behaviors with respect to available resources could also be determining factors.

### Conceptual Guidelines

Some general attempts have been made to provide conceptual guidelines for assisting clinicians in their attempts to identify treatment targets and treatment techniques. For example, Kanfer and Grimm (1977) present a detailed framework for organizing information obtained in interviews. The categories were generated pragmatically by attempting to integrate frequently encountered presenting complaints with commonly used interventions. This framework does not provide guidelines specific to target behavior selection in children, although the categories are clearly applicable across a wide age range.

Despite the absence of data supporting the utilization of specific decision rules for the selection of treatment targets with children, some consistent guidelines emerge from the literature (Nelson & Hayes, 1979). These guidelines have typically been formulated in terms of either conceptual or empirical criteria. It should be noted that in most instances with children, a general issue is whether the choice of target behavior reflects a concern for the child or for significant others. What must be considered is whether the behavior selected for change will provide real benefit to the child (e.g., improved academic performance) or whether it only serves to make the situation more "manageable" for adults, as would be the case with classroom programs that emphasized compliance to authority while ignoring educational objectives (Winett & Winkler, 1972).

Some of the most commonly cited conceptual criteria for selecting particular child behaviors for treatment are as follows:

1. The behavior is considered to be physically dangerous to the child and/or to others in the child's environment.
2. The behavior should provide an entry point into the natural reinforcement community of the child. The term "behavior trap" (Baer & Wolf, 1967) has been used in reference to positive behaviors that are likely to be supported and maintained by significant others.
3. The target behaviors selected should be positive, in order to avoid a problem focus in treatment. Targets that specify what is desirable for the

child to do, rather than what the child should not be doing, provide the child with appropriate resources for action.

4. Behaviors that are viewed as essentials for development are frequently given high priority. For example, language, cognitive development and school performance, motor skills, rule-governed behavior (see Karoly, Chapter 2, this volume), and, more recently, peer relationships (Hartup, 1979; see Hops & Greenwood, Chapter 8, this volume) are frequently targeted behaviors. Implicit in this emphasis is the notion that many of these behaviors are embedded in normal developmental sequences such that the failure to take corrective action early will result in cumulative deficits, with the child falling even further behind.

5. Behaviors that are viewed as essential early elements for more complex response chains have also been given priority. Classes of general imitative behavior and particular cognitive styles have been viewed as requisite behaviors that permit the occurrence of a range of other responses.

6. Behaviors that maximize the flexibility of the child in adapting to changing new environments are viewed as important treatment targets. Recent emphasis on coping skills strategies and self-control (e.g., O'Leary & Dubey, 1979; Rosenbaum & Drabman, 1979b) would fall into this category.

7. Behaviors that dramatically alter the existing contingency system for the child, such that maladaptive environmental reactions to the child are altered, are viewed as likely to contribute to long-term benefit (Stokes, Fowler, & Baer, 1978). Giving the child social skills that "turn on" parents and teachers who are "turned off," such as ways of being reinforcing to adults, has the potential for increasing positive exchanges.

## Empirical Guidelines

Some of the more commonly cited empirical criteria for selecting particular child behaviors for treatment are as follows:

1. Behaviors that are consistent with some developmental or local norms for performance.

2. Behaviors that have been shown, as a result of careful task analysis, to be critical components for successful performance. Teaching classroom survival skills (e.g., attending, peer discussions about classwork) as described by Hops and Cobb (1973) is an example of this approach.

3. Behaviors that are subjectively rated as positive by recognized community standards (Wolf, 1978).

4. Behaviors that effectively discriminate between "skilled" and "non-skilled" performers.

5. Behaviors whose natural history is known to have a poor long-term prognosis. For example, conduct disorders (Robins, 1966), hyperactivity (Ross & Ross, 1976), and peer acceptance/rejection have all been associated with poor long-term outcomes.

The preceding guidelines represent tentative decision-making rules in the selection of treatment targets. Clearly, further empirical specification is needed before such recommendations can be adopted. A question related to the identification of target behavior is, having identified many potentially desirable behavioral goals, in what order should problems be treated? In addition to practical considerations, such as client and therapist resources, recommendations have included guidelines such as altering the behavior that is most irritating to the child's social environment, changing behavior that is easiest to change (e.g., to be sure that early success is achieved), and changing behavior that is most difficult to change (e.g., to show just how effective the therapist is). The few data that are available suggest that the order in which problems are treated may not be a significant factor in treatment outcome (Eyberg & Johnson, 1974).

## Physical and Social Contexts

Thus far, we have been discussing target behavior selection in terms of child behavior. This emphasis is inconsistent with the behavioral assessment view of child behavior as being embedded in a social context. It is important to recognize that many of the preceding guidelines are equally as applicable to the selection of treatment targets involving the child's physical and social environments. It is clear that in many instances the parent's view of the child's problem may be a primary treatment target (e.g., Lobitz & Johnson, 1975a), especially when the parent exaggerates or applies faulty norms in assessing the child's performance (e.g., complaints regarding limited expressive vocabulary on the part of a 1-year-old child). Additionally, parents' communication style and the linguistic complexity in issuing commands (Roberts, McMahon, Forehand, & Humphreys, 1978) may be more salient treatment targets than child noncompliance.

Physical environments or situational structures (e.g., classroom) may also, at times, be more appropriate targets than child behavior. For example, the rate at which learning materials are presented (Dalby, Kinsbourne, Swanson, & Sobol, 1977) and the amount of structure in the classroom (Jacob, O'Leary, & Rosenblad, 1978) have both been shown to affect the performance of hyperactive children significantly. It may be more efficient to alter the environmental situation in which the child is functioning than to target child behavior for change. These examples suggest that an interactional position complicates the task of identifying meaningful target behavior, because it is necessary to consider not only what child behaviors are relevant targets but also what features of the child's environment both alone and in combination with child behavior constitute appropriate intervention targets.

In keeping with the problem-specific focus of this volume, it is recommended that common treatment targets for specific populations be indicated. Initial empirical analyses of existing literature might prove useful in this regard. For example, Emery and Marholin (1977) examined the treatment targets in studies of applied behavior analysis conducted from 1968–1976. These studies dealt with legal deviance in children aged 8½ to 16 years. The target behaviors serving as the focus of the investigations, in order of frequency, were: social interpersonal behavior (35.6%); program behaviors (21.4%); school behaviors (17.2%); compliance with authorities (11.2%); ecological behavior, such as not littering (7.4%); delinquent behaviors (3.7%); and vocational behaviors (3.5%). It was also reported that only 29.6% of the studies showed a clear relationship between referral problem (e.g., truancy) and target behavior. These types of findings, although not indicative of what behavior should be targeted for treatment, indicate those behaviors that commonly are and thus may provide further insight into factors influencing problem behavior selection with specific populations of children.

## Multisituational Analysis

Information regarding the context in which child behavior occurs is an essential ingredient for any child behavioral assessment concerned with the identification of relevant controlling variables to be utilized in the design of effective treatments (McReynolds, 1979). This is especially important, because the range of situations in which children function is diverse. Identification of the functional properties of specific setting events permits behavioral alteration based on the utilization of stimulus control procedures. Situational analysis, especially with respect to physical environments or structure, has been referred to as "ecological assessment" (Willems, 1973, 1974) and, in spite of its acknowledged importance in child behavior assessment, has been an area of relative neglect. Frequently, situational analysis is carried out in a global fashion, as would be the case in comparisons of the child's behavior in the home versus the school setting. It is believed that greater within-situation differentiation, which recognizes both the differences and the potential similarities in dissimilar environments, is necessary (Moos, 1975) if the potential of situational analysis in developing effective treatments is to be realized.

One type of molecular situational analysis has examined differential child responses to varying antecedent social stimuli, as would be the case with studies examining the effects of parents' utilizing different types of commands (Forehand, 1977) or language constructions in directing the child's behavior. Other studies have attempted to identify differing types of home, classroom, or institutional situations or task structures that might be predictive of particular child responses. For example, certain home situations involving the mother being occupied, or those possessing time constraints (e.g., dinnertime—Jewett & Clark, 1979; bedtime; getting dressed; and going to school) or elements of social evaluation, such as shopping trips (Clark, Greene, Macrae, McNees, Davis, & Risley, 1977) and visits to others' homes and to restaurants, seem to be high risk for the occurrence of problematic behavior in both normal and disturbed children (Barkley, Chapter 3, this volume; Risley, Clark, & Cataldo, 1976).

Other studies have examined classroom activity structures that are predictive of different types of child behavior, involving such things as group versus individual activities (Patterson & Bechtel, 1977), quiet versus noisy conditions (Whalen, Henker, Collins, Finck, & Dotemoto, 1979), self-paced versus other-paced activities (Whalen *et al.*, 1979), room size, seating arrangements, groupings of children based on different levels of ability, and formal versus informal task requirements (Jacob *et al.*, 1978). Similar variables have been examined in institutional and daycare environments (e.g., Risley *et al.*, 1976). In addition, general environmental conditions related to space, noise, and temperature provide other variables of potential importance. For example, Russell and Bernal (1977) reported systematic variations in the rates of desirable and undesirable child behavior in the home, associated with temporal and climatic variables such as time of day, day of the week, precipitation, and temperature. That children characteristically come into contact with multiple settings suggests the importance of further specification of situational variables and their functional relationship with behavior.

## Expanded Temporal and Contextual Base

A core assumption of early approaches to the behavioral assessment of children was the focus on contemporaneous behavior and controlling conditions (Ullmann & Krasner, 1965). Current influences were viewed as being proximal not only in time to the behavior being assessed but also with respect to the situation. For example, an observational assessment of parent–child interaction looked for "causes" of child behavior as reflected in the responses (e.g., cues and reinforcers) provided to the child by the parent in that situation. Developmental–historical information was not given a particularly important role, so that maternal response to the child was viewed as being a direct reaction to the child's ongoing behavior in the situation rather than as a function of the cumulative effect of many prior negative interactions with the child. That parents of aggressive, in contrast to normal, children may punish the child more, even when he or she is behaving appropriately (Patterson, 1976), suggests that the parents may be responding to more than the immediate behaviors of the child.

Similarly, behavioral assessment of children has tended to ignore some of the broader contextual variables that might be related to ongoing child behaviors. Such factors as parental personality, family climate, marital relationships, and community support systems may be equally potent sources of control for child behavior as the reactions of significant others to the child's behavior at the time of its occurrence. Some studies have shown the warmth and permissiveness of the home to be a significant factor in the effectiveness of social reinforcement by parents (Patterson, Littman, & Hinsey, 1964); as mentioned, others have demonstrated that maternal punitiveness to the child can be influenced by the degree of external stress placed on the mother in the situation (Passman & Mulhern, 1977). Friedrich (1979) reported that marital satisfaction was the best overall predictor of the coping behaviors of mothers of handicapped children, and Wahler (1980) has reported a positive relationship between problem child behavior and the degree of "insularity" of the family.

Given the likelihood that these situationally and temporally more remote variables represent important determinants of both child behavior and treatment outcomes, the exclusive reliance on contemporaneous information in behavioral assessment is no longer tenable. Although still a core condition for behavioral assessment, contemporaneous information should be buttressed and interpreted within a broader temporal and social context. As noted by Skinner (1953), "although it is necessary that science confine itself to selected segments in a continuous series of events, it is to the whole series that any interpretation must eventually apply" (p. 151).

# METHODS OF ASSESSMENT

The methods employed by child behavior assessors cannot in and of themselves be considered unique. The use of verbal reports obtained through structured and nonstructured interviews, behavioral checklists and questionnaires (Humphreys & Ciminero, 1979), and direct observation of behavior (Kent & Foster, 1977) obviously predates the recent emergence of behavioral assessment as a distinct approach. What is unique about behavioral assessment methods has been (1) the relative emphasis given to certain methods as opposed to others, for example, to direct observation versus verbal report; (2) the content of the instruments used, which usually represents a sample of the behaviors and situations of interest rather than an indirect sign of some underlying trait; and (3) the way in which the information obtained is utilized and interpreted. In spite of these differing emphases, it should be noted that the methods of behavioral assessment have in common with traditional methods the usual psychometric concerns related to adequate reliability, validity, and utility (Hartmann et al., 1979; Hay et al., 1979; O'Leary & Johnson, 1979).

We do not intend to review here the voluminous number of behavioral assessment methods that have been utilized with children or to identify all of the issues associated with their use. There are now many excellent reviews (e.g., see Ciminero & Drabman, 1977; Evans & Nelson, 1977), detailed book chapters (e.g., see Ciminero, Calhoun, & Adams, 1977; Haynes, 1978; Nay, 1979), and journal articles dealing with each method. Rather, we will attempt to highlight some of the more prevalent current concerns and issues associated with the use of particular methods. The major contribution of this volume to the assessment methods will be the elaboration and evaluation of previously described general methods in relation to specific child problems.

It should be noted that method preference in behavioral assessment is directly related to the relative importance ascribed to specific behaviors and controlling variables in behavioral theory and practice. For example, there has been a re-emergence of the use of self-report measures relative to direct observation, concomitant with the increasing attention to cognitive controlling variables and treatments. Method preference has also shifted with the collection of data that have bearing on the reliability, validity, or utility of particular procedures. For example, although naturalistic observation in the child's home or classroom environment was once viewed as the sine qua non of behavioral assessment (Johnson & Bolstad,

1973), problems associated with representativeness, reactivity, and economy have led to the conclusion that such observational assessments may not always be the preferred procedure. Such data-based alterations in methodological preference are viewed as a healthy development that is entirely consistent with the empirical emphasis characteristic of behavioral assessment.

Precise information regarding the types of assessment methods utilized most frequently by behavior therapists is not readily available. A survey of behavior therapists by Swan and MacDonald (1978) provides some information regarding the types of methods used most often with clients. The percentage of clients with which each of the following are used suggests that a multimethod approach is the norm: interviews (89.4%), self-monitoring (51.5%), interviews with significant others (49.2%), direct observations *in situ* (39.6%), information from consulting professionals (36.6%), role playing (34.3%), written self-report (31.7%), demographic questionnaires (20.1%), personality inventories (20.2%), and projective tests (10.1%). It should be noted that method use as described in this study was for adult and child practice combined; thus, one would predict that the reported percentages would be somewhat different for child assessments exclusively.

## Selection of Methods

Traditional approaches to the assessment of childhood problems have frequently adhered to a "test battery" model. Children presenting themselves to professionals for assessment received a standardized evaluation that included an interview with the parent, IQ test, projective personality test, and a test for organicity or perceptual dysfunction. Criticisms of these procedures as being insufficient for diagnosis and treatment have come from both behaviorally and nonbehaviorally oriented clinicians (e.g., Santostefano, 1978).

One criticism of this test battery approach has been the conceptual adequacy, utility, and cost efficiency of giving all children all assessments. Behavioral assessors, although espousing a view of individualized assessment, have probably perpetuated the test battery model under a different label, that of "multimethod assessment." Although the behavioral test battery may differ in the methods used (e.g., observation vs. projective tests), the assumption characterizing any situation where multiple assessments are routinely carried out with all children is that the more information there is available, the better we are able to understand and treat children. An additional, and very old, assumption is that the more convergent assessment information we have, the greater the degree of confidence in our inferences and conclusions about the child (McReynolds, 1975).

It should be recognized that the foregoing statements are assumptions. Although there is a good deal of empirical support for the notion that different methods may and often do yield different information about the child, the hypothesis that using as many different methods as possible will result in a truer or more useful description of the child has not been tested. It is important that behavioral assessors give some attention to the incremental validity associated with using multiple methods, in order to avoid the perpetuation of potentially unnecessary and costly procedures. Presumably, such incremental validity could be assessed by examining the relationship between amount and type of assessment information obtained and positive treatment outcomes (Mash, 1979).

The multiple purposes for which assessments with children are carried out suggest that all children should not be assessed in all possible ways and, therefore, that there is a need for identifying those factors that go into determining which method of assessment should be used. Although it is not possible to discuss these factors in detail, included would be such things as the nature of the target behavior (e.g., overt versus covert, chronic versus acute), characteristics of the child (e.g., age, cognitive and language skills) and of significant others (e.g., social class and education), the assessment setting (e.g., classroom, home, or institution), characteristics of the assessor (e.g., level of training and available time), characteristics of the method (e.g., complexity and amount of technical resources or training required, sensitivity to treatment), and assessment purpose. Some of the more common considerations in the selection of particular methods for specific populations of children are discussed in each of the chapters in this volume.

## Standardization, Reliability, and Validity

The need for standardized measures in child psychopathology (Achenbach, 1978) and child development generally (Bell & Hertz, 1976), and in child behavior assessment in particular, has been pointed out by many writers (Cone & Hawkins, 1977; Kanfer, 1972; Mash & Terdal, 1977; Nelson & Bowles, 1975) over the past decade. In spite of this recognition, there has been a proliferation of methods for assessing children that are idiosyncratic to the situation in which they are used, unstandardized, and of unknown reliability and validity. The rejection of many traditionally used psychological tests by behavioral assessors, concomitant with an emphasis on individual-focused assessment, served to produce a void that was filled by instruments that have face validity but that are of unknown psychometric characteristics. Standardized assessments are critical when the concern with assessment is in the relative standing of individual children with respect to some reference group. However, when assessments focus on identifying relevant behavior and controlling variables for the individual child, in order to design effective treatments, the need for standardization seems less evident. If a particular child's behavior does not fit a code definition within a behavior observation system, then one can alter the definition of the code so that it will encompass the behavior of this child. Such situation-specific procedural alteration has been common practice and has tended to retard the development of a common pool of standardized procedures.

That the same instruments have not been used repeatedly by different assessors has limited the accumulation of meaningful reliability and validity information. This state of affairs is especially prevalent with children. Although there are several adult measures (e.g., Fear Survey Schedule, Reinforcer Survey Schedule, Assertiveness Questionnaire) that have received extensive use (Kanfer, 1972), with the exception of a few comprehensive observational systems that were originally developed for specific research purposes (e.g., Mash, Terdal, & Anderson, 1973; Wahler, House, & Stambaugh, 1976; O'Leary, Romanczyk, Kass, Dietz, & Santagrossi, Note 13; Patterson, Ray, Shaw, & Cobb, Note 14), there are few standardized behavioral assessment methods for children.

The lack of standardization in behavioral assessment also seemed to create a gap between developers and users of behavioral instruments. Although many potentially useful behavioral measures were developed, they either did not appear in the literature because of unestablished reliability and validity, or they appeared in an abbreviated form that tended to make them unusable. In the latter circumstance, a footnote to the effect that "a manual for this observation code is available on request" usually appeared. However, by the time the article appeared in print, readers wrote to the author, received a copy, and began to use the procedure, the original user had often revised, altered, or abandoned the reported assessment procedure. These changes were often in response to inadequacies of the measure that had been identified through repeated use. However, this did not change the fact that the old form of the assessment was now being used and passed on to others, often with further revision. It is likely that most of the behavioral assessment measures developed for children in the past ten years are buried in the stacks of conference paper presentations and unpublished papers that typically accumulate in file cabinets and inconspicuous office corners.

It is evident that if behavioral assessment with children is to have any scientific and clinical merit, the proliferation of idiosyncratic assessment methods must be replaced by the development and use of more standardized and population-specific behavioral assessments. There are several recommendations as to how this might be achieved. To begin, it is felt that the lack of a population-specific assessment focus tended to necessitate revision of existing measures to make them applicable to the population of children under consideration. Assessments developed specifically for children with certain classes of problems, such as those presented and suggested in the chapters of this volume, are less likely to need revision. For example, a structured command situation for looking at parent–child interaction is more likely to be used in its exact form if the nature of the structure (e.g., type of commands to be given by the mother) and the specific parent–child behaviors coded reflect some of the more common deficits and excesses characteristic of particular childhood disorders.

In addition to population-specific assessment procedures as a way of increasing the likelihood that standardized measures be utilized, other writers have suggested the need for a clearinghouse for behavioral assessment instruments (Mash, 1979) or the use of journals' manuscript acceptance policies requiring submission of assessment manuals that could then be placed in an archival storage and retrieval system (Hartmann et al., 1979). Editorial policies that encouraged the use of one of the few best instruments available for particular child problems could also promote greater standardization.

The relevance of traditional psychometric concepts of reliability and validity for behavioral assessment methods was originally considered by Johnson and Bolstad (1973) in a now classic paper. This issue has since received extensive discussion and will not be dealt with in any detail here (see Cone, 1977, 1978; Goldfried, 1977; Goldfried & Linehan, 1977; Hartmann *et al.*, 1979; Hartmann, Note 15, for discussion). A major issue has been whether conceptualizations that view behavior as situation-specific and variable over time are incompatible with classical test theory concepts of reliability and validity. For example, if one does not adopt the view that stable traits manifest themselves in similar ways over time, then viewing variability of scores over time as reflecting an unreliable measuring instrument rather than inherent behavioral inconsistency would be inappropriate (Kazdin, 1979). Similarly, concurrent validity has little meaning if one accepts cross-situational variability as the norm, because a lack of situational consistency reflects things as they are, rather than being an invalid measurement procedure. Several writers have discussed these concerns and have noted ways in which psychometric procedures and generalizability theory might be applied to behavioral assessment, even with the differing assumptions (Cone, 1977; Jones, 1977; Hartmann, Note 15).

## Nonstructured Interviews

Regardless of therapeutic orientation, the interview continues to be the most universally used clinical assessment procedure (Swan & MacDonald, 1978). However, as noted by O'Leary and Turkewitz (1978), the information obtained in the interview, the meaning assigned to that information, and the extent of standardization will vary with one's theoretical orientation. Consequently, although interviews have been used extensively in behavioral assessments of children, these interviews have often been quite different in purpose and style than those conducted by individuals with nonbehavioral orientations. Given that a social learning conceptualization of childhood disorder involves other individuals in an ongoing network of reciprocal causality, and because children are typically referred by adults, it is almost always necessary to obtain descriptions from adults about the nature of the child's difficulties, social circumstances, physical status, and development (Evans & Nelson, 1977). Most typically the child's parent(s), usually the mother, will be the primary informant. However, other adults—for example, teachers (Spivack & Swift, 1973), relatives, and neighbors—and other children—for example, siblings and peers—although less frequently called upon, can provide potentially useful assessment information as well.

Interviews with the parents will provide information about the child, about the parent, and about the parent–child relationship. The amount of focus given to each of these areas will vary with the purpose for which the interview is carried out, although behavioral assessors have characteristically given less attention to information about the parent than to information about the child and the parent–child relationship. This is especially so when contrasted with traditional analytic approaches, in which parental personality disturbance is viewed as a major and often direct determinant of child psychopathology.

Several writers have recently outlined the varying purposes for which behavioral interviews are conducted (Haynes, 1978; Linehan, 1977; Morganstern, 1976; Nay, 1979). These functions have been summarized generally by Haynes and Jensen (1979) and, adapting their points to interviews with parents, would include the following:

1. Gathering information about parental concerns and goals.
2. Assessing parental perceptions as to the nature of the child's problems, concerns, and goals.
3. Identifying factors maintaining or eliciting problem behaviors.
4. Obtaining historical information about problem and nonproblem behaviors and about prior treatment efforts.
5. Identifying potentially reinforcing events for both child and parent.
6. Educating the parent with respect to the nature of the childhood problem in terms of prevalence, prognosis, and possible etiologies.
7. Providing the parent with an adequate rationale for proposed interventions.
8. Assessing the parents' motivation for changing the situation and their resources for taking an active role in helping to mediate behavior change.
9. Obtaining informed consent.
10. Providing data for the assessment of treatment outcomes.
11. Communicating with parents about the procedures and setting realistic goals for assessment and intervention.

The multiplicity of purposes described means that the degree of structure, the content, and the style of parental interviews will vary greatly, and a general lack of uniformity is the rule rather than the exception. There are several general points related to behavioral interviews with parents that should be discussed.

### Generality and Flexibility

The first concern involves the level of generality and flexibility. Typically, interviews with parents have been used either as diagnostic or screening instruments to determine treatment eligibility or as methods of gaining information that will facilitate the design of effective treatments. These purposes necessarily define the interview as being general and also require the interviewer to be flexibly tolerant in adapting to the various concerns being raised by parents. The degree of structure and standardization within parental interviews is usually low but could be increased for other interview purposes, for example, when interview information is to be used as an outcome measure. Alternatively, if pretreatment questionnaires included life history information and/or reinforcement surveys, then initial interviews could be more structured and focused. The advantage of such increased standardization would likely be greater reliability and validity.

A number of guidelines and standardized formats have been suggested for behavioral interviews with parents (e.g., Bersoff & Grieger, 1971; Holland, 1970; Kanfer & Saslow, 1969; Wahler & Cormier, 1970). Although these formats are useful, they are also quite general and make no a priori assumptions regarding the specific interview content that is likely to be most meaningful. In effect, these nonspecific interview formats ignore the information available from informal assessments that have already taken place and the existing empirical literature related to the class of problems the child and parent are experiencing. Typically, existent information and empirical findings are brought to bear under the ambiguous label of "clinical skills." Clinical experience and training are presumed to lead the interviewer into asking the "right" questions within some of the general areas suggested by the formats that have been presented. Consistent with the theme of this book, it is believed that problem-specific interview formats are necessary. Interviews with parents of autistic children should systematically probe for information regarding commonly identified problems and controlling variables (e.g., self-stimulation, language, possible negative reinforcers). Rather than assuming that interviewers will have the necessary specific information to guide interview content and process, it is believed that interview schedules that include disorder-specific information will lead to more systematic, standardized, efficient, and useful interviews possessing greater reliability and validity.

### Reliability and Validity

Another concern involves the reliability and validity of parental interview information. With respect to reliability, the concern relates to (1) whether information obtained on one occasion is comparable to information that was obtained or that would have been obtained on other occasions from the same parent (e.g., test–retest reliability); (2) whether information obtained from the parent is comparable to information obtained from another informant, for example, mother versus father (e.g., interobserver agreement); (3) whether the information given by the parent is consistent with other information given by the parent in the same interview (e.g., internal consistency); and (4) whether the information obtained by one interviewer is comparable to that obtained by another interviewer with the same parent (e.g., method error). All of these concerns, with the possible exception of the third, are attenuated somewhat by behavioral conceptualizations about the situational variability of behavior.

The first reliability concern mentioned is especially relevant in relation to interviews that require parents to report retrospectively on the child's developmental/social history, one of the more common elements of most child assessments (Yarrow, Campbell, & Burton, 1970). In reviewing the reliability of such recall by parents, Evans and Nelson (1977) conclude that these retrospective reports are likely to be unreliable and frequently distorted in the direction of socially desirable responses and dominant cultural themes. Interestingly, the degree of reliability appears related to the nature of the events that parents are reporting (e.g., pleasantness vs. unpleasantness) and the level of specificity of behavior being described (e.g., Lapouse & Monk, 1958). It should be recognized, however, that although parental reports may conform to the demand characteristics of the interview situation, such characteristics may not always predict socially desirable responses. For example, there may be a parental bias toward reporting more negative behaviors and greater distress if eligibility for treatment is an issue, whereas posttreatment interviews may be discriminative for reports of positive child behavior and the absence of distress. This latter point is especially important when interview information is to be used as an outcome measure for treatment. Interobserver agreement in relation to mother–father and teacher report is difficult to evaluate, because disagreement may reflect differences in the situation in which each of these informants observe the child. In general, mothers may be more reliable informants than fathers.

Validity of the behavioral interview with parents may be considered from the standpoint of (1) the extent to which interview information corresponds to that obtained through other methods (concurrent validity) and (2) the degree to which interview information predicts either treatment plan or treatment outcome (predictive validity). Research would suggest that there is a general lack of correspondence between different data sources indicating the need to use multiple methods of assessment. There are virtually no data that have examined the validity of interview information from parents in predicting either treatment or treatment outcome.

Situation-specific views within behavioral assessment suggest that different interview informants may be appropriate for information related to different child settings. Consequently, assessments of school behavior and functioning typically involve interviews with the child's teacher. Most of the general concerns expressed previously in relation to the parental interview are applicable to the teacher interview. However, because the latter interview is likely to be more focused (e.g., school behavior and performance), some of these concerns may be lessened.

Interviews with other significant adults or with the child's friends or peers may be potentially useful but have received little attention in assessment because of ethical concerns associated with obtaining such information. For example, interviews with peers may further stigmatize the child as being a problem, with subsequent alterations in the manner in which others were to interact with the child. At the same time, data suggest that peer evaluation may be particularly sensitive in identifying children with problems (Cowen, Pederson, Babigian, Izzo, & Trost, 1973), although it is not known whether peer judgments regarding the specific nature of these problems are likely to be accurate. The general problems associated with verbal report in children, particularly with younger children, suggest that structured tasks or game-like assessment procedures involving child and peer interaction may be more sensitive measures than unstructured interviews with peers. Information obtained from siblings could also be important in that many problem child situations are characterized by high rates of sibling conflict (Leitenberg *et al.*, 1977). Some studies have suggested that children's views of their siblings are frequently negative, especially when contrasted with parental views as to how their children view one another.

## Structured Parental Reports about Child Behavior

### Global Checklists

In addition to unstructured pretreatment interviews with parents, reports concerning child behavior and adjustment have been obtained from parents utilizing other, more structured methods (Humphreys & Ciminero, 1979). The first of the two most prevalent strategies has been the use of behavior checklists requiring either binary judgments concerning the presence or absence of particular child behaviors (e.g., Miller, Hampe, Barrett, & Noble, 1971—*Louisville Behavior Check List*; Sines, Pauker, Sines, & Owen, 1969—*Missouri Children's Behavior Checklist*) or Likert-type scale ratings concerning the degree to which the behavior is present or a problem (e.g., Achenbach & Edelbrock, 1978b; Achenbach & Edelbrock, 1979—*Child Behavior Checklist*; Conners, 1970—*Conner's Parent's Questionnaire*; Cowen, Huser, Beach, & Rappaport, 1970—*Parent Attitudes Test*; Peterson, 1961; Quay & Peterson, 1967, Note 16—*Behavior Problem Checklist*; Wimberger & Gregory, 1968—*Washington Symptom Checklist*). The second strategy has involved the use of structured interviews requiring the presentation of a standard set of questions to parents by trained interviewers (e.g., Graham & Rutter, 1968; Lapouse & Monk, 1958, 1959; Richman & Graham, 1971; Shepherd, Oppenheim, & Mitchell, 1966).

Behavior checklists have received extensive use for a number of reasons, not the least of which is their ease and practicality of administration. Checklists have served as a comprehensive, but rough, screening instrument, most typically during the diagnostic phase of assessment, for the identification of the range of problems being exhibited by the child. As such, they provide a reasonable estimate of parental perceptions of the child's behavior and adjustment in the home. Several studies (e.g., Eyberg & Johnson, 1974) have reported a lack of correspondence between parental checklist scores and observed child behavior. This is not surprising, given that checklists may reflect global appraisals and attitudes about child behavior rather than reported frequencies of behavioral occurrence. However, it should also be noted that most checklist scores encompass responses to a range of items, some referring to global child characteristics (e.g., happy or sad) and others to specific behaviors (e.g., wets the bed). In contrast, direct observations tend to be highly specific with respect to the behavior codes employed and to their definition. Consequently, lack of correspondence between checklist scores and observations may well reflect the fact that checklist measures are a polyglot rather than reflecting presumed inaccuracies or biases of parent report.

Checklists have also been used as a relatively simple measure of behavior and/or attitude changes associated with treatment. With such use, corroborative information is necessary, because a lack of correspondence between parent report and observed behavior following treatment (e.g., Schnelle, 1974) may be predictive of later problems. The other major use of parent checklists has been as a basis for the empirical classification of syndromes of child psychopathology, as characterized by the multivariate approach described previously. Two recent reviews (Achenbach & Edelbrock, 1978a; Humphreys & Ciminero, 1979) have discussed some of the psychometric properties and considerations associated with the uses of parental report measures.

In spite of the purported biases associated with parental reports about child behavior (Evans & Nelson, 1977), parents are of necessity the primary informants in child behavior assessment, because it is parental perception that determines what, if anything, will be done about their children (Achenbach, 1978). Furthermore, there is some suggestion that professionals' judgments regarding childhood disorder may be influenced more by what parents say about their children than by observed child behavior. Because parent-completed checklists can provide more information more quickly than could be obtained through interviews and are also more economical with respect to cost, effort, and therapists' time, they are likely to receive continued use in child behavior assessments. It is believed that the utility of such checklists for the assessment and treatment of individual children could be enhanced through the use of more situational content in their construction.

## Behavior-Specific Parent Ratings

In addition to global checklists and structured interviews, several parent-completed measures concerned with more specific areas or problems have also been developed. These include parental ratings of the child's hyperactivity (e.g., Werry & Sprague, 1970), general development (Ireton & Thwing, 1972), self-control (Kendall & Wilcox, 1979), and preferred reinforcers (Clement & Richard, 1976). In general, these types of measures are more focused than the global checklists and include more contextual information. Ratings that deal with child behavior, because of their specificity with regard to the problem, are frequently utilized as outcome measures.

Another type of parent report, often used to monitor changes during treatment, has been parent recordings of targeted child behavior. Typically, parents will collect baseline data on one or two general (e.g., compliance) or specific (e.g., swearing) behaviors that may subsequently be designated for modification. Less frequently, parents may also collect systematic data about antecedent and consequent events in order to identify potentially important controlling variables to be utilized in treatment. Many different forms have been presented to assist parents in recording their child's behavior (e.g., Madsen & Madsen, 1972). Such forms are common fare in almost all manuals that have been used in behaviorally oriented parent training programs (see Bernal & North, 1978, for a review of 26 commonly used parent training manuals).

Records kept by parents have the advantage of providing ongoing *in situ* information about behaviors of interest that might not otherwise be accessible to observation and may also provide secondary benefits that are not directly related to assessment. These include teaching parents better observation and tracking skills, assessing parental motivation, and providing parents with more realistic estimates of their child's rate of responding and with feedback regarding the effects of treatment. On the negative side, there are practical problems in getting parents to keep accurate records, and parental recordings of behavior may be reactive in the home situation, producing unrepresentative data. Additionally, although parent recordings have been used extensively, there is little reliability or validity information available concerning their use.

## Parent Self-Ratings

Writings about behavioral assessment with children have not been explicit concerning the importance of information reported by parents about themselves. With traditional assessments of children, information about the parents' personality functioning obtained through interview and through objective and projective personality tests were viewed as essential for understanding, and often as a precursor of, the child's disordered behavior. Where behavioral assessments have utilized parental reports about themselves, they typically have been in areas related directly to problems the child is experiencing (e.g., How does it make you feel when he does not listen to you?). Information concerning parents' feelings, attitudes, and cognitions is often considered only as a moderator variable in relation to the way in which it influences how parents will respond to the child or as a predictor of how likely the parents are to fulfill their responsibilities as mediators in treatment.

To some extent, parent checklists and ratings about the child's behavior represent a measure of the parents' own perceptions of the severity and scope of the child's problem. That the same objectively presented behavior may be perceived as more or less severe by different parents indicates that these ratings are measures of both child and parent characteristics, reflecting such things as the parents' tolerance for certain types of child behavior, the degree to which they perceive the child as sick or disturbed, and how much they like or dislike the child. The extent to which these variables are functionally related to how parents treat the child is a question in need of further empirical elaboration; several investigators, however, have suggested that positive changes with treatment may be related to whether or not parents continue to view the child as sick or disturbed (e.g., Lovaas, Koegel, Simmonds, & Long, 1973; Patterson, Reid, Jones, & Conger, 1975).

Other measures have provided parents with standard situations involving children, presented via written materials (e.g., Gordon, Jones, & Nowicki, 1979), audiotape (e.g., Martin et al., 1976), or videotape (e.g., Miller & Clarke, 1978). The parents are then requested to give their reactions to the child, indicating how they might reward or punish the behavior. Such analogue measures are a reflection of how parents think they would respond, and the degree of correspondence between expressed intent and actual parent behavior in these situations has received little empirical investigation. Such measures have the potential for providing information economically. However, it seems likely that such reports would be biased toward social desirability, consistent with currently accepted child-rearing practices.

Several measures of parental attitude have also been utilized in child behavior assessment. These measures describe parental attitudes about children and child-rearing in general (e.g., Schaefer & Bell, 1958), about the degree of comfort and/or stress associated with being a parent (e.g., Abidin & Burke, Note 17), and about the degree to which specific types of child behavior are perceived as "disturbing" (e.g., Mooney & Algozzine, 1978). Although relationships between such attitudinal measures and child behavior have been demonstrated, the directionality of such effects is not known. Parents of hyperactive children may feel less competent as parents, but clearly such views can develop as a function of repeated encounters with a "difficult" child rather than serving as a basis for child behavior problems.

Recent work has included parent report measures of their own mood states, such as depression (e.g., Griest, Wells, & Forehand, 1979), marital satisfaction and adjustment (Oltmanns et al., 1977), and the availability of community support systems (Wahler, Leske, & Rogers, 1978). It would appear that these measures reflect factors that may contribute to how parents react to their disturbed children and to treatment programs. However, the use of these types of measures in child behavior assessment is recent, reflecting an increasing interest in cognitive and affective variables, and therefore their usefulness in individual assessments has yet to be demonstrated. Whether the parental characteristics being assessed by these measures reflect reactions to child disturbance, precursors of child disturbance, or both, as is likely, they will need to be systematically assessed and dealt with in treatment if effective long-term outcomes are to be achieved.

## Child Self-Report

Child self-report has played a relatively minor role in behavioral assessments with children, presumably because of concerns about reliablity, validity, and methodological difficulty in obtaining such information, especially from younger children. However, children's position as unique observers of their own behavior and the behavior of those around them suggests that the self-reported perceptions and behaviors of children are necessary, but often neglected, types of assessment information. Child self-reports that have been utilized include interviews with the child, child-completed checklists and questionnaires, and child self-monitoring of behavior.

The purposes of interviews with children are varied (e.g., Yarrow, 1960), but typically include attempts to elicit information regarding children's perceptions of themselves and their problem and to obtain a sample of how children can handle themselves in a social situation with an adult (Evans & Nelson, 1977). Children's views of the circumstances that brought them to the clinic, their expectations for improvement, and their comprehension of the assessment situation are all important. Additionally, children's perceptions of their parents, siblings, teachers, and peers will likely determine their reactions to them and are therefore especially important when one is considering the use of such individuals as potential mediators in behavioral intervention programs. Interviews may also focus on obtaining specific types of information that children are in a unique position to report, such as their preferred reinforcers (Nay, 1974) or preferences for immediate versus delayed rewards (Weiss & Gallimore, 1973). Also, with the increasing recognition of cognitive variables in behavioral assessment, the interview situation provides a method for assessing such things as the child's use of strategies for planning and self-regulation (see Karoly, Chapter 2, this volume). Using a structured interview format, Mischel (1979) reported that children as young as 8 years of age seemed able to discuss and give examples of how they use plans, and by age 10, some children interviewed showed well-developed ideas about the nature, organization, and function of plans in their own lives.

A variety of child-completed checklists and questionnaires have been used in behavioral assessment, especially with older children. Many areas of functioning have been assessed with these questionnaires, including general personality dimensions such as introversion/extroversion (Eysenck & Rachman, 1965) and perceived locus of control (Bugental, Whalen, & Henker, 1977; Switzky & Haywood, 1974). Although such personality measures have been traditionally viewed by behavioral assessors as not especially useful for the design of treatments, there is some emerging evidence to suggest the utility of such measures in predicting the differential efficacy of particular interventions. For example, Bugental *et al.* (1977) reported that hyperactive children with an internal locus of control benefited more from a self-control program in contrast to children with an external locus of personal causality, who appeared more responsive to externally administered rewards. Such trait–treatment interactions suggest the potential relevance and utility of child-completed personality inventories.

Other child-completed checklists have focused on the child's assertiveness (Reardon *et al.*, 1979), self-esteem (e.g., Coopersmith, 1967; Piers & Harris, Note 18), self-concept regarding classroom activities (e.g., Williams & Workman, 1978), peer relationships and popularity (see Hops & Greenwood, Chapter 8, this volume), or reinforcement preferences (e.g., Clement & Richard, 1976; Tharp & Wetzel, 1969). Specific examples of these checklists are given in many of the chapters that follow. For the most part, these checklists have not been as sensitive to situational dimensions as a behavioral approach would demand, tending to be concerned with general behavioral traits. An exception to this is the *Children's Action Tendency Scale* (Deluty, 1979), a self-report measure of aggressiveness, assertiveness, and submissiveness in third- to sixth-grade children, which was developed following the behavioral analytic method described by Goldfried and D'Zurilla (1969). Responses to this scale are to specific conflict situations (e.g., another child shoves you out of line), and although the relationship between self-report and behavioral ratings of assertiveness in children may be questionable (Reardon *et al.*, 1979), it is believed that more questionnaires reflecting situational content are needed in both child and parent report measures.

In general, the use of child-completed questionnaires appears to have some promise in behavioral assessment, provided that greater attention is given to standardization, reliability, and validity (Herjanic, Herjanic, Brown, & Wheatt, 1975). Reliability and validity in relation to differences in children's language ability are important areas to consider (Gorsuch, Henighan, & Barnard, 1972). Child self-reports are often necessary when covert processes or constructs such as self-concept or mood are to be assessed and can be used to supplement or confirm more direct behavioral measures. It is likely that the increasing recognition of covert processes by behavioral assessors will result in the further development of child report measures.

A third type of child self-report measure has involved the use of self-monitoring procedures. A number of reviews of the type of self-monitoring procedures that have been used in assessment, as well as related methodological issues, are available (e.g., Ciminero, Nelson, & Lipinski, 1977). Children have used self-monitoring for such behaviors as classroom attending (Broden, Hall, & Mitts, 1971), academic responses (Lovitt, 1973; Sagotsky, Patterson, & Lepper, 1978), class attendance (McKenzie & Rushall, 1974), talking out in class (Broden *et al.*, 1971), aggression (Lovitt, 1973), room-cleaning (Layne, Rickard, Jones, & Lyman, 1976), and appropriate verbalizations (Nelson, Lipinski, & Boykin, 1978). However, in most instances, the use of self-monitoring with children has been employed as part of a larger set of procedures of self-assessment, including recording and evaluation, which are intended to modify the behavior being monitored. There are few descriptions of children self-monitoring their own behavior and life situations in order to obtain diagnostic information in developing treatment or to use as a treatment outcome measure. Consequently, the assessment functions of self-monitoring with children have not received much elaboration.

## Direct Observations of Behavior

We have previously defined a direct observational procedure as "a method for obtaining samples of behaviors and settings determined to be clinically important (in relation to diagnosis, design, and evaluation), in a naturalistic situation or in an analogue situation that is structured in such a way as to provide information about behaviors and settings comparable to what would have been obtained *in situ*" (Mash & Terdal, 1976, p. 261). As noted by Jones, Reid, and Patterson (1974, p. 4), direct observational methods involve recording behavior when it occurs, the use of trained and impartial observers following clearly specified rules and procedures for recording, and behavioral descriptions that require a minimal degree of inference.

The role given to direct observations of ongoing child behavior in context as the sine qua non of behavioral assessment (Johnson & Bolstad, 1973) has been so great that the use of observational procedures has in some instances been viewed as synonymous with the practice of behavioral assessment. Many reports, for example, present only direct observation of target behavior as a measure of change. The strong and sometimes overzealous emphasis on direct observations of child behavior as the primary data source in behavioral assessment was likely related to an increased recognition of the need for greater objectivity in clinical child assessment and the compatability of direct and less inferential behavioral data sources with the nonmediational focus characterizing earlier behavior therapy approaches.

There has been a lessening emphasis on direct observation as an exclusive assessment procedure, concomitant with the increasing admissability of cognitive variables in both behavior therapy and assessment. Implicit in some of the earlier writings in support of direct observations of children was the notion that behavior samples should be especially veridical statements about children, in light of children's restricted cognitive–mediational processes for regulating their behavior in general and their reactions to being observed (e.g., Kent & Foster, 1977). Consistent with this assumption is the view that direct observation may be more appropriate with younger than older children (Lytton, 1971). There is, however, no explicit support for the notion that direct observation is a truer estimate of functioning for children than for adults, because, with the possible exception of young infants, active cognitive processes and reactivity to being observed are likely characteristic of individuals at any age (Mash & Hedley, 1975). Even if it were the case that children were less reactive than adults to observation, that children are typically observed during interactions with parents or teachers substantially lessens the importance of this rationale for using observations with children. A positive and important outcome of the preceding assumption, however, has been a significant emphasis on the development of useful observation procedures for children, along with a concern for, and systematic investigation of, related reliability and validity questions.

The behavioral assessment emphasis on direct observational procedures was also part of the general reaction against the indirect and often highly inferential assessments characterizing traditional child assessments (Goldfried & Kent, 1972). Parent ratings, personality inventories, and children's self-report and responses to projective test stimuli or doll play situations as they have traditionally been used to generate inferences regarding emotional conflict and intrapsychic processes often seemed far removed from the major presenting problems of the child and his or her family.

It has also been argued that direct observation is less subject to bias and distortion than verbal reports from either children or parents and teachers. Support for this argument, however, comes more from studies demonstrating poor reliability and validity associated with verbal report (Evans & Nelson, 1977) than from studies directly demonstrating observational data to be accurate and unbiased. In fact, many studies have shown that observed behavior can be readily distorted by biases on the part of both observers and those being observed (see Kent & Foster, 1977, for review). For example, Johnson and Lobtiz (1974) demonstrated that normal parents could make their children look either "good" or "bad" when instructed to do so (see also Lobitz & Johnson, 1975b). As noted by Kent and Foster (1977), such data do not prove that potential biases are the norm, only that they can occur. Although recognizing the need for further empirical investigation of this question, it seems unlikely, given the demand characteristics of most observation situations, that parents would not attempt to systematically influence that which is observed. Decisions relating to problem diagnosis, eligibility for treatment, educational placement, legel adjudications, and evaluations of treatment change represent only a few of the demand characteristics that provide a framework for parents in presenting specific self- and child behaviors. To believe that parents would not do so reflects an overly simplistic and inaccurate underestimation of some very basic problem-solving and hypothesis-testing human attributes.

The issue, then, is not that parents and children bias what is observed, but rather that there is a need to identify the types of observational situations by individual interactions that are likely to generate particular rules and/or cognitions for organizing and presenting a particular pattern of behavior to outside observers who are there for a reason. Such rules and strategies are no different from other types of controlling variables, for example, physical and social environment parameters, that will influence observations. It is unfortunate that child and parent behavior that attempts to conform to the demand characteristics of being observed has been labeled "bias," because such a term carries extraneous negative valence. In this regard, a parent who failed to regulate his or her behavior in response to an external observer should not be viewed as any less biased than one who did. Both are responding deliberately to the presence of observers, only in different ways.

The central issue has been formulated in terms of whether the behavior of children or parents in the presence of an observer is typical of what occurs when the observer is not present. The thorny methodological and ethical issues surrounding this question have resulted in only a few direct (White, 1977) and indirect (Patterson & Harris, Note 19) empirical studies with parents, the findings of which have been equivocal. However, several studies have suggested that students and teachers may be minimally reactive to classroom observation (Dubey, Kent, O'Leary, Broderick, & O'Leary, 1977; Mercatoris & Craighead, 1974; Nelson, Kapust, & Dorsey, 1978; Weinrott, Garrett, & Todd, 1978). Even without substantiating data, it is often assumed that an observer-present versus observer-absent difference in behavior indicates that observer-present data lack validity. This assumption, however, is only partially true. A lack of correspondence between unobserved and observed behavior would cast doubt on the validity of observations that were intended to establish existing rates and patterns of behavior (e.g., in accordance with "nature"), as would be the case in assessments that had as their purpose the evaluation of treatment outcomes. It would, for example, be important to show that a child was compliant to maternal requests not only in the presence of an observer but at other times as well. However, when observational assessments are intended to generate hypotheses concerning treatment plans and targets, variations in base rates of behavior may be less of a threat to the validity of the assessment than would variations in patterning of behavior. Thus, a mother might exhibit a lower rate of negative behavior when observed but still be negative in a representative stylistic way.

Frequently, direct observation is pitted against verbal report, and it is not uncommon that they do not agree (Lytton, 1973). This lack of agreement is often taken as evidence for the unreliability of verbal report, with the view that direct observation is a less biased measure. This is a fallacious argument in support of the accuracy of direct observation, because in the absence of agreement between the two measures it is equally plausible that either may represent the more valid indicator, or that both may be equally invalid. Clearly, a lack of agreement suggests not that one measure is accurate and the other is not, but rather that each may be tapping a different dimension; it is therefore important to obtain both types of information.

The preceding general comments are not intended to cast aspersion on the importance of direct observational procedures for behavioral assessments of child disturbance. Rather, they are intended to caution against the steadfast adherence to observational methods as the best type of assessment under all circumstances in the face of an increasing conceptual emphasis on cognitive variables, contradictory empirical findings related to bias and reactivity, the relativity of assessment purposes, and practical concerns associated with their use.

## Observational Procedures with Children

A wide range of observational procedures have been utilized in assessing children, ranging from simple single-behavior recordings that can be conducted with a minimal amount of observer training to fairly complex and exhaustive multibehavior/multicontext interaction code systems (e.g., Mash et al., 1973; Wahler et al., 1976; Patterson et al., Note 14) requiring substantial initial and ongoing observer training. The factors involved in selecting an appropriate observational procedure are numerous and include such things as the stage of the assessment process, the characteristics of the behaviors of interest, the situation in which observation is to occur, observer characteristics, and technical resources (Mash & Terdal, 1976).

Currently, there are several detailed discussions of direct observational procedures and of some of the methodological issues surrounding their use (e.g., Haynes, 1978; Kent & Foster, 1977; Mash & Terdal, 1976; Nay, 1979; Wildman & Erickson, 1977). These issues are concerned with factors influencing the objectivity and reliability of observations, such as code system characteristics (e.g., number of categories); characteristics of the behaviors being observed (rate and complexity); methods of assessing reliability (e.g., awareness of reliability checks); observer characteristics (e.g., age, sex); methods of calculating interobserver agreement; sources of observer and observee bias under a range of conditions; and reactivity to being observed (Mash & Hedley, 1975). Extensive discussion of these issues is beyond the scope of this chapter, but a sensitivity to methodological concerns of this kind is a necessary part of any observational assessment of children, because they have a direct bearing on the validity of the findings. A minimally acceptable set of criteria for any observational code would be that it is objective (e.g., two observers would classify behavior in the same way), that it has mutually exclusive subcategories, and that it provides data that are amenable to objective analysis. Given these minimal requirements, further validation as to a wide range of goals and purposes is possible.

### Selecting Code Categories

The use of observational codes with children requires decisions relating to both the content (e.g., what categories to include) and the structure (e.g., number of categories, temporal base, and mechanics for observing and recording) of the code system. With regard to content, the selection of particular categories of child behavior to observe, either in the construction of one's own code system or in the selection of an already existing code system, presupposes an existing set of hypotheses. In effect, the behavioral assessor is controlling his or her experiences through choice of an observational scheme; consequently, the choice of what to observe takes on great importance. As noted by Butler, Rice, and Wagstaff (1963), "his classification scheme may simply be an objectified set of prejudices having much to do with the misguided imagination of the observer but containing no insight about the kind of organisms observed" (p. 8).

There are many such prejudices that are implicit within available observational codes for children. For example, the greater prevalence and range of codes for categorizing child compliance and parental directiveness, relative to codes for children's and parents' affectional responses, have followed from and contributed to the development of hypotheses of disturbed child behavior centering around command–compliance sequences (e.g., Patterson, 1976). This is not to say that such hypotheses lack validity and/or utility, but rather that the nature of an existing code system may favor some assessment outcomes over others. That most observational codes for children have examined family interactions to a greater extent than interactions with peers has likely limited the identification of many potentially important controlling variables.

For the most part, code selections and observational system construction for the behavioral assessment of children have been conducted on a rational basis. Consistent with the view of maintaining low levels of inference, the child and parent behaviors observed are often those directly reported as problematic by parent and teachers or that fit with the theories or experiences of the assessor. Also, established code systems, because of their procedural development, availability, and ease of application, often may be utilized inappropriately with particular populations or in situations that differ from those established in the initial rationale for construction. It is believed that category and code system selection could be improved with greater attention to the parameters associated with the specific populations of children being observed and the settings in which they function. Specialized codes of this nature are provided in the chapters of this volume related to aggression, fears and anxieties, and autism. The categories included reflect behaviors and setting variables that have been empirically shown to be relevant to the population under study. As one example, such empirically constructed code systems might result in an emphasis in classroom codes related to task performance rather than to task attention when school achievement is a source of difficulty (Ayllon & Rosenbaum, 1977).

It would also be useful to examine existing code systems used with children in order to identify base rates with which particular categories are used in assessment and the reasons given for their inclusion or exclusion. Such data are available in the literature but have not, to date, been summarized. Additionally, the ways in which similar categories have been defined need further specification. Reflecting the lack of standardization mentioned previously, it is not uncommon for similarly labeled behavior categories to be defined in quite different ways (Mash & Dalby, 1979). Such idiosyncratic code construction seems unnecessary and can only contribute to poor communication between assessors. Perhaps a behavior and setting code dictionary that provided standardized classifications and definitions relevant to specific child populations and settings would stimulate greater consistency in the use of observational categories.

## Settings for Observation

Following from a situation-specific view of behavior, observational assessments with children have been carried out in a wide range of settings, the most common being the clinic, the home, and the classroom. Other examples of observational settings include institutional environments, such as group homes for delinquent adolescents; living environments for retarded or autistic children; playgrounds; supermarkets; and children's groups. More specific situations within each of these global settings have also provided structure for observation, for example, free play versus command–compliance instructions in the clinic or observation at mealtime or bedtime in the home.

A major concern associated with the choice of observational settings has been the degree of control that is imposed on the situation by the assessor. Behavioral assessors have emphasized the importance of observing in the child's natural environment, imposing the least amount of structure as is possible, in order to see things "as they typically occur." This emphasis has reflected a reaction against the nonrepresentative and exclusive clinic observation conditions characteristic of most traditional clinical child assessments. Although *in situ* assessment is still recognized as an important part of behavioral assessment with children, there has also been an increased recognition that nonstructured observations, in the home, for example, may not always be the most efficient or practical method for obtaining samples of the behaviors of interest. Observation in the home—in fact, observation in general—may be unrevealing with behaviors that occur at a low rate or that are especially reactive to observation. In addition, the assumptions that home observations are "natural" and that observations in the clinic are "artificial" are oversimplifications. Home observations may, at times, provide us with artificial reactions to natural conditions, whereas clinic observations may provide us with natural reactions to artificial conditions. Which information is more meaningful depends much on the purpose of the assessment. Cross-setting comparisons of behavior—for example, home versus clinic—when they do not agree cannot be assumed to be a function of the unrepresentativeness of behavior in the clinic unless there is some independent verification of the representativeness of the home observation. In most instances there is not, and it is therefore inaccurate to equate representativeness with the naturalness of physical settings, as is often done.

When home or classroom observations have been neither feasible nor appropriate, behavioral assessors have utilized a wide range of structured laboratory or clinic observation settings for sampling the behaviors of interest (see Hughes & Haynes, 1978, and Lytton, 1971, for reviews). Such so-called analogue situations are assumed to provide more efficient access to the behaviors of interest than observation in the natural environment. Analogue situations have provided a wide range of structures for assessing parent–child behaviors, including free play interactions between mother and child (e.g., Forehand, King, Peed, & Yoder, 1975; Mash & Terdal, 1973); a variety of command–compliance situations, such as the mother having the child clean up or put away play materials (e.g., Mash, Lazere, Terdal, & Garner, 1973); occupying himself or herself while the mother is busy reading or talking on the telephone (e.g., Hatfield, Ferguson, & Alpert, 1967); academic task situations (Herbert, Pinkston, Hayden, Loeman, Sajwaj, Pinkston, Cordua, & Jackson, 1973); problem-solving situations, such as figuring out how to play a game together (Parsons & Alexander, 1973); and highly structured observations of the social reinforcement properties (e.g., Patterson, Littman, & Hinsey, 1964) or punishment styles (e.g., Passmann & Mulhern, 1977) of parents. The range of potentially relevant analogue situations to be used in behavioral assessment is restricted only by the ingenuity and physical resources of the assessor. The challenge, however, is for systematic reliability and validity assessment that would permit the use of more standardized and psychometrically well-developed analogues than has been the case thus far.

## Using and Interpreting Observational Data

Direct observational data have been utilized for a number of purposes, including serving as treatment outcome measures, providing a data base for the construction of theories about childhood disorder (Patterson, 1976), and serving as a basis for making recommendations for treatment. In practice, the latter use is perhaps the most frequent but the least understood, because the processes by which direct observations have been translated into clinical recommendations are often poorly defined, unspecified, or oversimplified. For example, the observation of a positive adult response to a negative child behavior (e.g., teacher attention for misbehavior) or of a negative adult response to a positive child behavior (e.g., parental scoldings following a child's use of age-appropriate grammatical constructions) may lead to treatment recommendations centering around better contingency management. Alternatively, adult presentations of ambiguous antecedent cues for behavior (e.g., overly complex parental commands) may result in treatments centering around the alteration of stimulus control functions. However, in practice, these types of observation–treatment recommendations represent informal hypothesis testing rather than systematically or empirically derived outcomes. It is also not clear whether such recommendations represent a fitting of observations to preferred and to common hypotheses regarding contingencies or the derivation of hypotheses that are based upon what has been observed.

Interpretations of observational data have typically followed from summarizations of child behavior–adult response over relatively short time intervals. It is often the pattern of behavior based upon interactional responses in immediately adjacent time intervals about which interpretations are made with the assumption that immediate cues and reactions serve as major controlling events. A mother's reaction to her child's behavior is assumed to follow from the child's response that preceded it. However, the causes for both child and adult behavior may emanate from more remote points in observational sequences than those immediately adjacent in time, and there is a need for empirical and conceptual criteria that can be utilized to formulate interpretations of observational data based on stylistic patterns of responding.

## Formal Testing with Children

Regardless of whether behavioral assessment represents a break from traditional psychometric test approaches or a logical extension of such approaches, as some have suggested (e.g., Evans & Nelson, 1977), the fact remains that the use of developmental scales (e.g., Bayley, 1969; Boyd, 1974), intelligence tests, achievement tests, perceptual–motor tests, tests for organicity, and comprehensive neuropsychological assessments with children is common practice among both behavioral and nonbehavioral clinicians. Intelligence estimates, such as the Wechsler Intelligence Scale for Children and the Stanford–Binet Intelligence Scale, which are the tests reported to be the most frequently used by practitioners (Brown & McGuire, 1976; Lubin, Wallis, & Paine, 1971), are ranked by clinicians as having the highest psychometric quality among frequently used tests and are rated by practicing professionals as important in the training of clinical psychology students (Wade & Baker, 1977). Additionally, the use of formal tests is frequently dictated by institutional or legislative requirements, situational expectancies, ease of administration, habit, and perceived usefulness.

It is beyond the scope of this chapter to review the extensive literature dealing with the uses and misuses of traditional tests with children. The reader is referred to chapters by Evans and Nelson (1977) and Ciminero and Drabman (1977) for discussions about the role of formal tests within child behavior assessment generally and to individual chapters in this volume for discussions of the utility of specific tests within the context of behavioral assessment with specific populations of disturbed children.

## Informal Uses of Formal Test Situations

Both behaviorally (e.g., Evans & Nelson, 1977) and nonbehaviorally oriented writers (e.g., Brooks, 1979) have suggested the utility of formal test situations for obtaining information other than test scores, although perhaps for different reasons. Process variables in formal assessment related to cognitive, educational, and intellectual functioning (Aliotti, 1977; Kratochwill, 1977) and to emotional functioning have been discussed (Brooks, 1979). With respect to psychoeducational evaluations, a number of writers (see Brooks, 1979) have suggested using the formal test situation not only to obtain grade level or ability test scores but also for the following:

1. The assessment of learning styles or underlying cognitive structures rather than specific skills.

2. Teaching a child learning strategies during an evaluation in order to assess how well he or she can learn and benefit from these strategies.
3. Using limit testing or a modified format (e.g., reinforcing test performance) following the administration of standardized test procedures in order to obtain additional information about learning capacity.
4. Using test teaching when test tasks closely approximate the skill to be learned. With such a view, the distinction between traditionally used "formal tests" and "behavioral tests" becomes blurred.

Brooks (1979) also describes a number of additional process variables that may be assessed within the context of psychoeducational assessment. These include an assessment of what testing means to children (e.g., to prove they are stupid, a form of punishment, to help them learn); an assessment of children's perceived self-competence or self-efficacy (Bandura, 1977) in the test situation, as well as their coping style; and an assessment of children's ability to form relationships with the examiner, as an estimate of a more general ability to form alliances with adults.

All of the preceding suggestions seem consistent with behavioral assessment views in that they use the test situation to obtain samples of behavior that are to be utilized in individualizing child treatment rather than for the purpose of normative comparisons.

## Integrating and Presenting Assessment Information

The diversity of assessment information collected across multiple situations and with multiple informants suggests the need for guidelines for integrating and communicating such information to others. In spite of this need, there have been few presentations in the literature of illustrative comprehensive behavioral assessments with children. Kanfer and Saslow (1969) have provided a general framework for assessing and summarizing assessment information; however, their heuristic organizational scheme does not deal with some of the specific problems that are involved in summarizing assessment information. General textbooks on psychological report writing (e.g., Tallent, 1976) provide little specific information relevant to summarizing behavioral assessments with disturbed children.

Exceptions to the general neglect of integrating and communicating behavioral assessment information come from a relatively detailed description of the assessment of a 5-year-old boy showing discipline and school problems reported by Ciminero and Drabman (1977) and several case illustrations described by Haynes (1978). Ciminero and Drabman's (1977) illustrative case report includes sections dealing with (1) test results and a description of behavioral deficits and abilities; (2) behavioral assessment data gathered from child, parent, and teacher interviews and the results of problem checklists and behavioral observations of the child at home and at school; (3) recommendations for setting placements and characteristics that would be most beneficial to the child; (4) recommendations for specific educational prescriptions, to be used by teachers and/or parents, designed to improve academic performance and discipline problems; and (5) other therapeutic recommendations based upon all assessment results. Noteworthy in this report is the degree of specificity associated with treatment recommendations, in contrast to many psychological evaluations with children that offer little in the way of direct suggestions as to what can be done about the problem.

The following characteristics of behavioral assessment with children present special difficulties in presenting and communicating assessment results:

1. The highly specific information characteristic of behavioral assessment may be cumbersome to present without utilizing summary interpretive statements. However, such statements may obscure much of the behavioral and situational detail needed for the design of effective treatments. Guidelines for translating descriptive and low-level-of-inference information into more interpretive analytic statements are needed.

2. The amount of quantitative and technical information (e.g., base rates, conditional probabilities) generated by behavioral assessments of disturbed children may also be difficult to summarize. Graphic presentation may help to simplify, although with multiple behaviors and situations, graphic display may be time consuming and difficult to follow.

3. That behavioral assessment is ongoing creates the need for a flexible system for updating and modifying reports based on new information. Although a large proportion of behavior therapists report that it takes them two or fewer sessions to conceptualize their client's problem (Swan & MacDonald, 1978), behavior assessment should, in theory, progress over extended time periods. Ongoing assessment presents a practical challenge in relation to how new information can be communicated to consumers.

4. If behavioral assessments and reports are to include routinely specific recommendations for treatment, ethical concerns may arise in those situations in which the assessor is not likely to be involved as the primary agent of treatment. Assessment summaries that include highly specific treatment recommendations in the absence of resources for continuing assessor involvement may produce potentially negative outcomes.

More attention to these and other issues is needed if behavioral assessment is to receive greater use than it has thus far. Further illustrations and case presentations of behavioral assessments with disturbed children are needed, and the development of standardized formats for summarizing and communicating assessment information about particular childhood disorders would be useful.

# SUMMARY

In this introductory chapter, we have described some of the more general issues characterizing the behavioral assessment of disturbed children. In doing so, we have tried to set the stage for the detailed discussions concerning the assessment of specific types of childhood disturbance in the chapters that follow. We have presented the view that behavioral assessment with children represents a general problem-solving strategy for understanding children's behavior and its determinants. It is a highly empirical approach to clinical child assessment, which is based on an understanding of child development, child psychopathology, and psychological testing. This problem-solving strategy typically is carried out in relation to recurrent purposes, follows from a particular set of assumptions about children's behavior and its causes, designates particular behaviors and controlling variables as important, and emphasizes particular methods.

The purposes, assumptions, and methods outlined are those that we believe characterize contemporary approaches to the behavioral assessment of children. A general theme that has been emphasized is that behavioral assessments of childhood disturbance will be most meaningful if they follow from functional analyses and procedural developments for specific types of childhood disorder. It is this theme that underlies most of the chapters that follow.

## Acknowledgments

Sincere appreciation is expressed to Charlotte Johnston and Charles Costello for their helpful comments on an earlier draft of this chapter. Thanks also to Dorothy Cowell for her typing of the chapter. During the preparation of this chapter, the first author was supported by a Canada Council Leave Fellowship and by research grants from the Alberta Mental Health Advisory Council. This support is gratefully acknowledged.

## Reference Notes

1. Achenbach, T. M., & Edelbrock, C. S. *Behavior problems and competencies reported by parents of normal and disturbed children aged 4 through 16.* Unpublished manuscript, National Institute of Mental Health, Washington, D.C., 1979.
2. Terdal, L. G. (Chair). *Behavioral assessment of childhood disorders.* Symposium presented at the annual meeting of the American Psychological Association, New York City, September 1979.
3. Levy, R. L., Knight-Lertora, A., Olson, D. G., & Charney, C. *Evaluation of a behavioral training program for senior dental students.* Paper presented at the annual meeting of the Society of Behavioral Medicine, San Francisco, December 1979.
4. Goldberg, L. R. *Some recent trends in personality assessment.* Paper presented at the annual meeting of the American Psychological Association, Washington, D.C., September 1971.
5. Yuzwak, W. J. *The effect of setting and mother's education on mother–child interaction.* Unpublished master's thesis, University of Calgary, 1979.
6. Hawkins, R. P. *The functions of assessment: Implications for selection and development of devices for assessing repertoires in clinical, educational, and other settings.* Unpublished manuscript, University of West Virginia, 1979.
7. Group for the Advancement of Psychiatry. *Psychopathological disorders in childhood: Theoretical considerations and a proposed classification* (Report No. 62). New York: Author, 1966.
8. Yates, B. T., & Hoage, C. M. *Mnemonic stigma in behavior observation: An interaction of diagnostic label, relative frequency of positive versus negative behavior, and type of behavior recalled.* Paper presented at the meeting of the Association for the Advancement of Behavior Therapy, San Francisco, December 1979.
9. Fernald, C. D., & Gettys, L. *Effects of diagnostic labels on perceptions of children's behavior*

*disorders*. Paper presented at the annual meeting of the American Psychological Association, Toronto, Canada, August 1978.

10. Chapman, M. *Isolation of effects in experimentally produced changes in parent–child interaction*. Paper presented at the annual meeting of the American Psychological Association, New York City, September 1979.

11. Meichenbaum, D., Burland, S., Gruson, L., & Cameron, R. *Metacognitive assessment*. Paper presented at the Conference on the Growth of Insight, Wisconsin Research and Development Center, October 1979.

12. Parke, R. D., & Sawin, D. B. *The child's role in sparing the rod*. Unpublished manuscript, University of Illinois, 1977.

13. O'Leary, K. D., Romanczyk, R. G., Kass, R. E., Dietz, A., & Santogrossi, D. *Procedures for classroom observations of teachers and children*. Unpublished manuscript, State University of New York at Stony Brook, 1971.

14. Patterson, G. R., Ray, R. S., Shaw, D. A., & Cobb, J. A. *Manual for coding family interactions* (6th rev.), 1969. (Available from ASIS National Auxiliary Publications Service, CCM Information Services, Inc., 909 Third Avenue, New York, N.Y. 10022. Document No. 01234.)

15. Hartmann, D. P. *Must the baby follow the bathwater? Psychometric principles—behavioral data*. Paper presented at the annual meeting of the American Psychological Association, Washington, D.C., September 1976.

16. Quay, H. C., & Peterson, D. R. *Manual for the Behavior Problem Checklist*. Unpublished manuscript, 1975.

17. Abidin, R. R., & Burke, W. T. *Parenting stress index*. Unpublished manuscript, University of Virginia, 1978.

18. Piers, E. V., & Harris, D. B. *The Piers–Harris Self-Concept Scale*. Unpublished manuscript, Pennsylvania State University, 1963.

19. Patterson, G. R., & Harris, A. *Some methodological considerations for observation procedures*. Paper presented at the annual meeting of the American Psychological Association, San Francisco, 1968.

# References

Achenbach, T. M. Psychopathology of childhood: Research problems and issues. *Journal of Consulting and Clinical Psychology*, 1978, *46*, 759–776.

Achenbach, T. M., & Edelbrock, C. S. The classification of child psychopathology: A review and analysis of empirical efforts. *Psychological Bulletin*, 1978, *85*, 1275–1301. (a)

Achenbach, T. M., & Edelbrock, C. S. The child behavior profile: II. Boys aged 12–16 and girls aged 6–11 and 12–16. *Journal of Consulting and Clinical Psychology*, 1978, *47*, 223–233. (b)

Adams, H. E., Doster, J. A., & Calhoun, K. S. A psychologically based system of response classification. In A. R. Ciminero, K. S. Calhoun, & H. E. Adams (Eds.), *Handbook of behavioral assessment*. New York: Wiley, 1977.

Adams, H. E., & Turner, S. M. Editorial. *Journal of Behavioral Assessment*. 1979, *1*, 1–2.

Algozzine, B., Mercer, C. D., & Countermine, T. The effects of labels and behavior on teacher expectations. *Exceptional Children*, 1977, *44*, 131–132.

Aliotti, N. C. Covert assessment in psychoeducational testing. *Psychology in the Schools*, 1977, *14*, 438–443.

American Psychiatric Association. *Diagnostic and statistical manual of mental disorders* (1st ed.). Washington, D.C.: Author, 1952.

American Psychiatric Association. *Diagnostic and statistical manual of mental disorders* (2nd ed.). Washington, D.C.: Author, 1968.

American Psychiatric Association. *Diagnostic and statistical manual of mental disorders* (3rd ed.). Washington, D.C.: Author, 1979.

Arkowitz, H. Behavioral assessment comes of age. *Contemporary Psychology*, 1979, *24*, 296–297.

Ayllon, T., & Rosenbaum, M. S. The behavioral treatment of disruption and hyperactivity in school settings. In B. B. Lahey & A. E. Kazdin (Eds.), *Advances in clinical child psychology* (Vol. 1). New York: Plenum, 1977.

Baer, D. M., Wolf, M. M., & Risley, T. R. Some current dimensions of applied behavior analysis. *Journal of Applied Behavior Analysis*, 1968, *1*, 91–97.

Bandura, A. *Principles of behavior modification.* New York: Holt, Rinehart & Winston, 1969.

Bandura, A. Self-efficacy: Toward a unifying theory of behavioral change. *Psychological Review*, 1977, *84*, 191–215.

Barkley, R. A. A review of stimulant drug research with hyperactive children. *Journal of Child Psychology and Psychiatry*, 1977, *18*, 137–165.

Barkley, R. A., & Cunningham, C. E. The effects of Ritalin on the mother–child interactions of hyperactive children. *Archives of General Psychiatry*, 1979, *36*, 201–208.

Barlow, D. H. (Ed.). *Behavioral assessment of adult disorders.* New York: The Guilford Press, 1981.

Bates, J. E., Freeland, C. A., & Lounsbury, M. L. Measurement of infant difficultness. *Child Development*, 1979, *50*, 794–803.

Bayley, N. *The Bayley scales of infant development.* New York: Psychological Corporation, 1969.

*Behavioral Assessment.* New York: Pergamon, 1979.

Bell, R. Q., & Harper, L. V. *Child effects on adults.* Hillsdale, N.J.: Lawrence Erlbaum, 1977.

Bell, R. Q., & Hertz, T. W. Toward more comparability and generalizability of developmental research. *Child Development*, 1976, *47*, 6–13.

Bem, D. M., & Funder, D. C. Predicting more of the people more of the time: Assessing the personality of situations. *Psychological Review*, 1978, *85*, 485–501.

Bernal, M. E., Delfini, L. F., North, J. A., & Kreutzer, S. L. Comparison of boys' behaviors in homes and classrooms. In E. J. Mash, L. A. Hamerlynck, & L. C. Handy (Eds.), *Behavior modification and families.* New York: Brunner/Mazel, 1976.

Bernal, M. E., & North, J. A. A survey of parent training manuals. *Journal of Applied Behavior Analysis*, 1978, *11*, 533–544.

Bersoff, D. N., & Grieger, R. M. An interview model for the psychosituational assessment of children's behavior. *American Journal of Orthopsychiatry*, 1971, *41*, 483–493.

Bijou, S. W., & Peterson, R. F. Functional analysis in the assessment of children. In P. McReynolds (Ed.), *Advances in psychological assessment* (Vol. 2). Palo Alto, Calif.: Science and Behavior Books, Inc., 1971.

Boyd, R. D. *The Boyd developmental progress scale.* San Bernadino, Calif.: Inland Counties Regional Center, Inc., 1974.

Broden, M., Hall, R. V., & Mitts, B. The effect of self-recording on the classroom behavior of two eighth grade students. *Journal of Applied Behavior Analysis*, 1971, *4*, 191–199.

Bronfenbrenner, U. Toward an experimental ecology of human development. *American Psychologist*, 1977, *32*, 513–531.

Brooks, R. Psychoeducational assessment: A broader perspective. *Professional Psychology*, 1979, *10*, 708–722.

Brown, W. R., & McGuire, J. M. Current psychological assessment practices. *Professional Psychology*, 1976, *7*, 445–484.

Bugental, D. B., Whalen, C. K., & Henker, B. Causal attributions of hyperactive children and motivational assumptions of two behavior-change approaches: Evidence for an interactionist position. *Child Development*, 1977, *48*, 874–884.

Butler, L., & Meichenbaum, D. The assessment of interpersonal problem-solving skills. In P. C. Kendall & S. D. Hollon (Eds.), *Cognitive–behavioral interventions: Assessment methods.* New York: Academic Press, 1980.

Butler, J. M., Rice, L. N., & Wagstaff, A. K. *Quantitative naturalistic research.* Englewood Cliffs, N.J.: Prentice-Hall, 1963.

Campbell, S. B. Mother–child interaction in reflective, impulsive, and hyperactive children. *Developmental Psychology*, 1973, *8*, 341–349.

Campbell, S. B. Mother–child interaction: A comparison of hyperactive, learning disabled, and normal boys. *American Journal of Orthopsychiatry*, 1975, *45*, 51–57.

Cantor, N., & Mischel, W. Traits as prototypes: Effects on recognition memory. *Journal of Personality and Social Psychology*, 1977, *35*, 38–48.

Carver, R. P. Two dimensions of tests: Psychometric and edumetric. *American Psychologist*, 1974, *29*, 512–518.

Cerreto, M. C., & Tuma, J. M. Distribution of DSM-II diagnoses in a child psychiatric setting. *Journal of Abnormal Child Psychology*, 1977, *5*, 147–153.

Christopherson, E. R., & Rapoff, M. A. Behavioral pediatrics. In O. F. Pomerleau & J. P. Brady (Eds.), *Behavioral medicine: Theory and practice*. Baltimore: Williams & Wilkins, 1979.

Ciminero, A. R., Calhoun, K. S., & Adams, H. E. (Eds.). *Handbook of behavioral assessment*. New York: Wiley, 1977.

Ciminero, A. R., & Drabman, R. S. Current developments in the behavioral assessment of children. In B. B. Lahey & A. E. Kazdin (Eds.), *Advances in clinical child psychology* (Vol. 1). New York: Plenum, 1977.

Ciminero, A. R., Nelson, R. O., & Lipinski, D. P. Self-monitoring procedures. In A. R. Ciminero, K. S. Calhoun, & H. E. Adams (Eds.), *Handbook of behavioral assessment*. New York: Wiley, 1977.

Clarizio, H. F., & McCoy, G. F. *Behavior disorders in children* (2nd ed.). New York: T. Y. Crowell, 1976.

Clark, H. B., Greene, B. F., Macrae, J. W., McNees, M. P., Davis, J. L., & Risley, T. R. A parent advice package for family shopping trips: Development and evaluation. *Journal of Applied Behavior Analysis*, 1977, *10*, 605–624.

Clement, P. W., & Richard, R. C. Identifying reinforcers for children: A children's reinforcement survey. In E. J. Mash & L. G. Terdal (Eds.), *Behavior therapy assessment: Diagnosis, design, and evaluation*. New York: Springer, 1976.

Coates, T. J., & Perry, C. Multifactor risk reduction with children and adolescents: Taking care of the heart in behavior group therapy. In D. Upper & S. Ross (Eds.), *Behavior group therapy: An annual review*. Champaign, Ill.: Research Press, 1979.

Cochran, M. M., & Brassard, J. A. Child development and personal social networks. *Child Development*, 1979, *50*, 601–616.

Combs, M. L., & Slaby, D. A. Social-skills training with children. In B.. B. Lahey & A. E. Kazdin (Eds.), *Advances in clinical child psychology* (Vol. 1). New York: Plenum, 1977.

Cone, J. D. The relevance of reliability and validity for behavioral assessment. *Behavior Therapy*, 1977, *8*, 411–426.

Cone, J. D. The behavioral assessment grid (BAG): A conceptual framework and a taxonomy. *Behavior Therapy*, 1978, *9*, 882–888.

Cone, J. D. Confounded comparisons in triple response mode assessment research. *Behavioral Assessment*, 1979, *1*, 85–95.

Cone, J. D., & Hawkins, R. P. (Eds.). *Behavioral assessment: New directions in clinical psychology*. New York: Brunner/Mazel, 1977.

Conners, C. K. Symptom patterns in hyperkinetic, neurotic, and normal children. *Child Development*, 1970, *4*, 667–682.

Cooper, J. O. *Measurement and analysis of behavioral techniques*. Columbus, Ohio: Charles E. Merrill, 1974.

Coopersmith, S. *The antecedents of self-esteem*. San Francisco: W. H. Freeman, 1967.

Cowen, E. L., Huser, J., Beach, D. R., & Rappaport, J. Parental perceptions of young children and their relation to indexes of adjustment. *Journal of Consulting and Clinical Psychology*, 1970, *34*, 97–103.

Cowen, E. L., Pederson, A., Babigian, H., Izzo, L. D., & Trost, M. A. Long-term follow-up of early detected vulnerable children. *Journal of Consulting and Clinical Psychology*, 1973, *41*, 438–445.

Cunningham, C. E., & Barkley, R. A. The interactions of normal and hyperactive children with their mothers in free play and structured tasks. *Child Development*, 1979, *50*, 217–224.

Cunningham, S. J., & Knights, R. M. The performance of hyperactive and normal boys under differing reward and punishment schedules. *Journal of Pediatric Psychology*, 1978, *3*, 195–201.

Dalby, J. T., Kinsbourne, M., Swanson, J. M., & Sobol, M. P. Hyperactive children's underuse of learning time: Correction by stimulant treatment. *Child Development*, 1977, *48*, 1448–1453.

Deluty, R. H. Children's Action Tendency Scale: A self-report measure of aggressiveness, assertiveness, and submissiveness in children. *Journal of Consulting and Clinical Psychology*, 1979, *47*, 1061–1071.

Dreger, R. M., Lewis, P. M., Rich, T. A., Miller, K. S., Reid, M. P., Overlade, D. C., Taffel, C., & Flemming, E. L. Behavioral classification project. *Journal of Consulting Psychology*, 1964, *28*, 1–13.

Dubey, D. R., Kent, R. N., O'Leary, S. G., Broderick, J. E., & O'Leary, K. D. Reactions of children and teachers to classroom observers: A series of controlled investigations. *Behavior Therapy*, 1977, *8*, 887–897.

Eme, R. F. Sex differences in child psychopathology: A review. *Psychological Bulletin*, 1979, *86*, 574–595.

Emery, R. E., & Marholin, D. An applied behavior analysis of delinquency: The irrelevancy of relevant behavior. *American Psychologist*, 1977, *32*, 860–873.

Endler, N. S., & Magnusson, D. (Eds.). *Interactional psychology and personality*. Washington, D.C.: Hemisphere, 1976.

Erickson, M. T. *Child psychopathology: Assessment, etiology, and treatment*. Englewood Cliffs, N.J.: Prentice-Hall, 1978.

Evans, I. M., & Nelson, R. O. Assessment of child behavior problems. In A. R. Ciminero, K. S. Calhoun, & H. E. Adams (Eds.), *Handbook of behavioral assessment*. New York: Wiley, 1977.

Eyberg, S. M., & Johnson, S. M. Multiple assessment of behavior modification with families: Effects of contingency contracting and order of treated problems. *Journal of Consulting and Clinical Psychology*, 1974, *42*, 594–606.

Eysenck, H. J., & Rachman, S. *The causes and cures of neurosis*. London: Routledge & Kegan Paul, 1965.

Ferster, C. B. Classification of behavioral pathology. In L. Krasner & L. P. Ullmann (Eds.), *Research in behavior modification: New developments and implications*. New York: Holt, Rinehart & Winston, 1965.

Ferster, C. B., & Skinner, B. F. *Schedules of reinforcement*. New York: Appleton-Century-Crofts, 1953.

Firestone, P., & Douglas, V. I. The effects of verbal and material rewards and punishers on the performance of impulsive and reflective children. *Child Study Journal*, 1975, *7*, 71–78.

Forehand, R. Child noncompliance to parent commands: Behavioral analysis and treatment. In M. Hersen, R. M. Eisler, & P. M. Miller (Eds.), *Progress in behavior modification* (Vol. 5). New York: Academic Press, 1977.

Forehand, R., King, H. E., Peed, S., & Yoder, P. Mother–child interactions: Comparison of a noncompliant clinic group and a nonclinic group. *Behaviour Research and Therapy*, 1975, *13*, 79–84.

Foster, G. G., Ysseldyke, J. E., & Reese, J. H. I wouldn't have seen it, if I hadn't believed it. *Exceptional Children*, 1975, *41*, 469–473.

Friedrich, W. N. Predictors of the coping behavior of mothers of handicapped children. *Journal of Consulting and Clinical Psychology*, 1979, *57*, 1140–1141.

Gelfand, D. M., & Hartmann, D. P. *Child behavior analysis and therapy*. New York: Pergamon, 1975.

Goldfried, M. R. Behavioral assessment in perspective. In J. D. Cone & R. P. Hawkins (Eds.), *Behavioral assessment: New directions in clinical psychology*. New York: Brunner/Mazel, 1977.

Goldfried, M. R., & D'Zurilla, T. J. A behavioral-analytic model for assessing competence. In C. D. Spielberger (Ed.), *Current topics in clinical and community psychology* (Vol. 1). New York: Academic Press, 1969.

Goldfried, M. R., & Kent, R. N. Traditional versus behavioral assessment: A comparison of methodological and theoretical assumptions. *Psychological Bulletin*, 1972, *77*, 409–420.

Goldfried, M. R., & Linehan, M. N. Basic issues in behavioral assessment. In A. R. Ciminero, K. S. Calhoun, & H. E. Adams (Eds.), *Handbook of behavioral assessment*. New York: Wiley, 1977.

Goldfried, M. R., & Sprafkin, J. N. Behavioral personality assessment. In J. T. Spence, R. C. Carson, & J. W. Thibaut (Eds.), *Behavioral approaches to therapy*. Morristown, N.J.: General Learning Press, 1976.

Goldstein, G. Methodological and theoretical issues in neuropsychological assessment. *Journal of Be-

*havioral Assessment*, 1979, *1*, 23–41.

Gordon, D. A., Jones, R. H., & Nowicki, S. A measure of intensity of parental punishment. *Journal of Personality Assessment*, 1979, *43*, 485–496.

Gorham, K. A., Des Jardins, C., Page, R., Pettis, E., & Scheiber, B. Effect on parents. In N. Hobbs (Ed.), *Issues in the classification of children*. San Francisco: Jossey-Bass, 1975.

Gorsuch, R. L., Henighan, R. P., & Barnard, C. Locus of control: An example of dangers in using children's scales with children. *Child Development*, 1972, *43*, 579–590.

Graham, P., & Rutter, M. The reliability and validity of the psychiatric assessment of the child: II. Interview with the parent. *British Journal of Psychiatry*, 1968, *114*, 581–592.

Graziano, A. M., DeGiovanni, I. S., & Garcia, K. A. Behavioral treatment of children's fears: A review. *Psychological Bulletin*, 1979, *86*, 804–830.

Griest, D., Wells, K. C., & Forehand, R. An examination of predictors of maternal perceptions of maladjustment on clinic-referred children. *Journal of Abnormal Psychology*, 1979, *88*, 277–281.

Guilford, J. P. *Personality*. New York: McGraw-Hill, 1959.

Guskin, S. L., Bartel, N. R., & MacMillan, D. L. Perspective of the labeled child. In N. Hobbs (Ed.), *Issues in the classification of children*. San Francisco: Jossey-Bass, 1975.

Halverson, C. F., & Waldrop, M. F. Relations between preschool activity and aspects of intellectual and social behavior at age 7½. *Developmental Psychology*, 1976, *12*, 107–112.

Harris, A. An empirical test of the situation specificity/consistency of aggressive behavior. *Child Behavior Therapy*, 1979, *1*, 257–270.

Harris, S. L. The relationship between family income and number of parent-perceived problems. *International Journal of Social Psychiatry*, 1974, *20*, 109–112.

Harris, S. L. DSM-III—Its implications for children. *Child Behavior Therapy*, 1979, *1*, 37–46.

Hartmann, D. P., Roper, B. L., & Bradford, D. C. Some relationships between behavioral and traditional assessment. *Journal of Behavioral Assessment*, 1979, *1*, 3–21.

Hartup, W. W. Peer relations and the growth of social competence. In M. W. Kent & J. E. Rolf (Eds.), *Primary prevention of psychopathology. Volume III: Social competence in children*. Hanover, N.H.: University Press of New England, 1979.

Hatfield, J. S., Ferguson, L. R., & Alpert, R. Mother–child interaction and the socialization process. *Child Development*, 1967, *38*, 356–414.

Hawkins, R. P. Who decided *that* was the problem? Two stages of responsibility for applied behavior analysis. In W. S. Wood (Ed.), *Issues in evaluating behavior modification*. Champaign, Ill.: Research Press, 1975.

Hay, W. M., Hay, L. R., Angle, H. V., & Nelson, R. O. The reliability of problem identification in the behavioral interview. *Behavioral Assessment*, 1979, *1*, 107–118.

Haynes, S. N. *Principles of behavioral assessment*. New York: Gardner Press, 1978.

Haynes, S. N., & Jensen, B. J. The interview as a behavioral assessment instrument. *Behavioral Assessment*, 1979, *1*, 97–106.

Herbert, E. W., Pinkston, E. M., Hayden, E. M., Loeman, M., Sajwaj, T. E., Pinkston, S., Cordua, G., & Jackson, C. Adverse effects of differential parental attention. *Journal of Applied Behavior Analysis*, 1973, *6*, 15–30.

Herjanic, B., Herjanic, M., Brown, F., & Wheatt, T. Are children reliable reporters? *Journal of Abnormal Child Psychology*, 1975, *3*, 41–48.

Hersen, M., & Barlow, D. H. *Single-case experimental designs: Strategies for studying behavior change*. New York: Pergamon, 1976.

Hersen, M., & Bellack, A. S. (Eds.). *Behavioral assessment: A practical handbook*. New York: Pergamon, 1976.

Hobbs, N. *Issues in the classification of children*. San Francisco: Jossey-Bass, 1975. (a)

Hobbs, N. *The futures of children*. San Francisco: Jossey-Bass, 1975. (b)

Holland, C. J. An interview guide for behavioral counseling with parents. *Behavior Therapy*, 1970, *1*, 70–79.

Hopkins, B. L. Effects of candy and social reinforcement, instructions and reinforcement schedule leaning on the modification and maintenance of smiling. *Journal of Applied Behavior Analysis*, 1968, *1*, 121–129.

Hops, H., & Cobb, J. A. Survival behaviors in the educational setting: Their implications for research and intervention. In L. A. Hamerlynck, L. C. Handy, & E. J. Mash (Eds.), *Behavior change: Methodology, concepts, and practice*. Champaign, Ill.: Research Press, 1973.

Hughes, H. M., & Haynes, S. N. Structured laboratory observation in the behavioral assessment of parent–child interactions: A methodological critique. *Behavior Therapy*, 1978, *9*, 428–447.

Humphreys, L. E., & Ciminero, A. R. Parent report measures of child behavior: A review. *Journal of Clinical Child Psychology*, 1979, *5*, 56–63.

Ilg, F. L., & Ames, L. B. *Child behavior*. New York: Harper & Row, 1955.

Ireton, H., & Thwing, E. *The Minnesota Child Development Inventory*. Minneapolis: Interpretive Scoring Systems, 1972.

Jacob, R. G., O'Leary, K. D., & Rosenblad, C. Formal and informal classroom settings: Effects on hyperactivity. *Journal of Abnormal Child Psychology*, 1978, *6*, 47–59.

Jewett, J. F., & Clark, H. B. Teaching preschoolers to use appropriate dinnertime conversation: An analysis of generalization from school to home. *Behavior Therapy*, 1979, *10*, 589–605.

Johnson, S. B., & Melamed, B. G. The assessment and treatment of children's fears. In B. B. Lahey & A. E. Kazdin (Eds.), *Advances in clinical child psychology* (Vol. 2). New York: Plenum, 1979.

Johnson, S. M., & Bolstad, O. D. Methodological issues in naturalistic observation: Some problems and solutions for field research. In L. A. Hamerlynck, L. C. Handy, & E. J. Mash (Eds.), *Behavior change: Methodology, concepts, and practice*. Champaign, Ill.: Research Press, 1973.

Johnson, S. M., Bolstad, O. D., & Lobitz, G. K. Generalization and contrast phenomena in behavior modification with children. In E. J. Mash, L. A. Hamerlynck, & L. C. Handy (Eds.), *Behavior modification and families*. New York: Brunner/Mazel, 1976.

Johnson, S. M., & Lobitz, G. K. Parental manipulation of child behavior in home observations. *Journal of Applied Behavior Analysis*, 1974, *7*, 23–32.

Jones, R. R. Conceptual vs. analytic uses of generalizability theory in behavioral assessment. In J. D. Cone & R. P. Hawkins (Eds.), *Behavioral assessment: New directions in clinical psychology*. New York: Brunner/Mazel, 1977.

Jones, R. R., Reid, J. B., & Patterson, G. R. Naturalistic observation in clinical assessment. In P. McReynolds (Ed.), *Advances in psychological assessment* (Vol. 3). San Francisco: Jossey-Bass, 1974.

*Journal of Behavioral Assessment*. New York: Plenum, 1979.

Kagan, J., & Moss, H. *Birth to maturity*. New York: Wiley, 1962.

Kanfer, F. H. Assessment for behavior modification. *Journal of Personality Assessment*, 1972, *36*, 418–423.

Kanfer, F. H. A few comments on the current status of behavioral assessment. *Behavioral Assessment*, 1979, *1*, 37–39.

Kanfer, F. H., & Grimm, L. G. Behavioral analysis: Selecting target behaviors in the interview. *Behavior Modification*, 1977, *1*, 7–28.

Kanfer, F. H., & Karoly, P. Self-control: A behavioristic excursion into the lion's den. *Behavior Therapy*, 1972, *3*, 398–416.

Kanfer, F. H., & Phillips, J. S. *Learning foundations of behavior therapy*. New York: Wiley, 1970.

Kanfer, F. H., & Saslow, G. Behavioral diagnosis. In C. M. Franks (Ed.), *Behavior therapy: Appraisal and status*. New York: McGraw-Hill, 1969.

Kazdin, A. E. Assessing the clinical or applied importance of behavior change through social validation. *Behavior Modification*, 1977, *1*, 427–452.

Kazdin, A. E. *History of behavior modification: Experimental foundations of contemporary research*. Baltimore: University Park Press, 1978.

Kendall, P. C., & Hollon, S. D. (Eds.). *Cognitive–behavioral interventions: Theory, research, and procedures*. New York: Academic Press, 1979.

Kendall, P. C., & Hollon, S. D. (Eds.). *Cognitive–behavioral interventions: Assessment methods*. New York: Academic Press, 1980.

Kendall, P. C., & Wilcox, L. E. Self-control in children: Development of a rating scale. *Journal of Consulting and Clinical Psychology*, 1979, *47*, 1020–1029.

Kent, R. N., & Foster, S. L. Direct observational procedures: Methodological issues in naturalistic settings. In A. R. Ciminero, K. S. Calhoun, & H. E. Adams (Eds.), *Handbook of behavioral assessment*. New York: Wiley, 1977.

Kessen, W. The American child and other cultural inventions. *American Psychologist*, 1979, *34*, 815–820.

Kessler, J. W. *Psychopathology of childhood*. Englewood Cliffs, N.J.: Prentice-Hall, 1966.

Kessler, J. W. Nosology in child psychopathology. In H. E. Rie (Ed.), *Perspectives in child psychopathology*. Chicago: Aldine-Atherton, 1971.

Knopf, I. J. *Childhood psychopathology: A developmental approach*. Englewood Cliffs, N.J.: Prentice-Hall, 1979.

Kratochwill, T. R. The movement of psychological extras into ability assessment. *Journal of Special Education*, 1977, *11*, 299–311.

Lang, P. J. Fear reduction and fear behavior: Problems in treating a construct. In J. M. Shlien (Ed.), *Research in Psychotherapy* (Vol. 3). Washington, D.C.: American Psychological Association, 1968.

Langer, E. J., & Abelson, R. P. A patient by any other name . . . : Clinician group difference in labeling bias. *Journal of Consulting and Clinical Psychology*, 1974, *42*, 4–9.

Lapouse, R., & Monk, M. A. A epidemiologic study of behavior characteristics in children. *American Journal of Public Health*, 1958, *48*, 1134–1144.

Lapouse, R., & Monk, M. A. Fears and worries in a representative sample of children. *American Journal of Orthopsychiatry*, 1959, *29*, 803–818.

Layne, C. C., Rickard, H. C., Jones, M. T., & Lyman, R. D. Accuracy of self-monitoring on a variable ratio schedule of observer verification. *Behavior Therapy*, 1976, *7*, 481–488.

Leitenberg, H., Burchard, J. D., Burchard, S. N., Fuller, E. J., & Lysaght, T. V. Using positive reinforcement to suppress behavior: Some experimental comparisons with conflict. *Behavior Therapy*, 1977, *8*, 168–182.

Lindsley, O. R. Direct measurement and prosthesis of retarded behavior. *Journal of Education*, 1964, *147*, 62–81.

Linehan, M. Issues in behavioral interviewing. In J. D. Cone & R. P. Hawkins (Eds.), *Behavioral assessment: New directions in clinical psychology*. New York: Brunner/Mazel, 1977.

Lobitz, G. K., & Johnson, S. M. Normal versus deviant children: A multimethod comparison. *Journal of Abnormal Child Psychology*, 1975, *3*, 353–373. (a)

Lobitz, G. K., & Johnson, S. M. Parental manipulation of the behavior of normal and deviant children. *Child Development*, 1975, *46*, 719–726. (b)

Lomax, E. M. R., Kagan, J., & Rosenkrantz, B. G. *Science and patterns of child care*. San Francisco: W. N. Freeman and Company, 1978.

Lorion, R. P., Cowen, E. L., & Caldwell, R. A. Problem types of children referred to a school-based mental health program. *Journal of Consulting and Clinical Psychology*, 1974, *42*, 491–496.

Lovaas, O. I., Koegel, R., Simmons, J. Q., & Long, J. S. Some generalization and follow-up measures on autistic children in behavior therapy. *Journal of Applied Behavior Analysis*, 1973, *6*, 131–166.

Lovitt, T. C. Self-management projects with children with learning disabilities. *Journal of Learning Disabilities*, 1973, *6*, 15–28.

Lubin, B., Wallis, R. R., & Paine, C. Patterns of psychological test usage in the United States: 1955–1969. *Professional Psychology*, 1971, *2*, 70–74.

Lytton, H. Observational studies of parent–child interaction: A methodological review. *Child Development*, 1971, *42*, 651–684.

Lytton, H. Three approaches to the study of parent–child interaction: Ethological, interview, and experimental. *Journal of Child Psychology and Psychiatry*, 1973, *14*, 1–17.

Lytton, H. Disciplinary encounters between young boys and their mothers and fathers: Is there a contingency system? *Developmental Psychology*, 1979, *15*, 256–268.

MacFarlane, J. W., Allen, L., & Honzik, M. P. *A developmental study of the behavior problems of normal children between twenty-one months and fourteen years*. Berkeley, Calif.: University of California Press, 1954.

Madsen, C. K., & Madsen, C. H. *Parents, children, discipline: A positive approach*. Boston: Allyn & Bacon, 1972.

Mahoney, M. J. *Cognition and behavior modification*. Cambridge, Mass.: Ballinger, 1974.

Marholin II, D., & Bijou, S. W. Behavioral assessment: Listen when the data speak. In D. Marholin II (Ed.), *Child behavior therapy*. New York: Gardner Press, 1978.

Martin, S., Johnson, S. M., Johansson, S., & Wahl, G. The comparability of behavioral data in laboratory and natural settings. In E. J. Mash, L. A. Hamerlynck, & L. C. Handy (Eds.), *Behavior modification and families*. New York: Brunner/Mazel, 1976.

Mash, E. J. Behavior modification and methodology: A developmental perspective. *Journal of Educational Thought*, 1976, *10*, 5–21.

Mash, E. J. What is behavioral assessment? *Behavioral Assessment, 1979, 1*, 23–29.

Mash, E. J., & Dalby, J. T. Behavioral interventions for hyperactivity. In R. L. Trites (Ed.), *Hyperactivity in children: Etiology, measurement, and treatment implications*. Baltimore: University Park Press, 1979.

Mash, E. J., & Hedley, J. Effect of observer as a function of prior history of social interaction. *Perceptual and Motor Skills*, 1975, 40, 659–669.

Mash, E. J., Lazere, R., Terdal, L., & Garner, A. Modification of mother–child interactions: A modeling approach for groups. *Child Study Journal*, 1973, *3*, 131–143.

Mash, E. J., & Mercer, B. J. A comparison of the behavior of deviant and non-deviant boys while playing alone and interacting with a sibling. *Journal of Child Psychology and Psychiatry*, 1979, *20*, 197–207.

Mash, E. J., & Terdal, L. G. Modification of mother–child interactions: Playing with children. *Mental Retardation*, 1973, *11*, 44–49.

Mash, E. J., & Terdal, L. G. Behavior therapy assessment: Diagnosis, design, and evaluation. *Psychological Reports*, 1974, *35*, 587–601.

Mash, E. J., & Terdal, L. G. *Behavior therapy assessment: Diagnosis, design, and evaluation*. New York: Springer, 1976.

Mash, E. J., & Terdal, L. G. After the dance is over: Some issues and suggestions for follow-up assessment in behavior therapy. *Psychological Reports*, 1977, *41*, 1287–1308.

Mash, E. J., & Terdal, L. G. Follow-up assessments in behavior therapy. In P. Karoly & J. J. Steffen (Eds.), *The long-range effects of psychotherapy: Models of durable outcome*. New York: Gardner Press, 1980.

Mash, E. J., Terdal, L. G., & Anderson, K. The response-class matrix: A procedure for recording parent–child interactions. *Journal of Consulting and Clinical Psychology*, 1973, *40*, 163–164.

McKenzie, T. L., & Rushall, B. S. Effects of self-recording on attendance and performance in a competitive swimming training environment. *Journal of Applied Behavior Analysis*, 1974, 7, 199–206.

McLemore, C. W., & Benjamin, L. Whatever happened to interpersonal diagnosis?: A psychosocial alternative to DSM-III. *American Psychologist*, 1979, *34*, 17–34.

McReynolds, P. Historical antecedents of personality assessment. In P. McReynolds (Ed.), *Advances in psychological assessment* (Vol. 3). San Francisco: Jossey-Bass, 1975.

McReynolds, P. The case for interactional assessment. *Behavioral Assessment*, 1979, *1*, 237 247.

McReynolds, W. T. DSM-III and the future of applied social science. *Professional Psychology*, 1979, *10*, 123–132.

Meichenbaum, D. A cognitive-behavior modification approach to assessment. In M. Hersen & A. S. Bellack (Eds.), *Behavioral assessment: A practical handbook*. New York: Pergamon, 1976.

Meichenbaum, D. *Cognitive-behavior modification: An integrative approach*. New York: Plenum, 1977.

Meichenbaum, D., & Butler, L. Cognitive ethology: Assessing the streams of cognition and emotion. In K. Blankstein, P. Pliner, & J. Polivy (Eds.), *Advances in the study of communication and affect: Assessment and modification of emotional behavior* (Vol. 6). New York: Plenum, 1979.

Mercatoris, M., & Craighead, W. E. Effect of nonparticipant observation on teacher and pupil classroom behavior. *Journal of Educational Psychology*, 1974, *66*, 512–519.

Miller, H., & Clarke, D. *Effective parental attention* (videotape), 1978. (For information contact authors at Parent Training Clinic, Department of Psychiatry, University of California, Los Angeles, California.)

Miller, L. C., Hampe, E., Barrett, C., & Noble, H. Children's deviant behavior within the general population. *Journal of Consulting and Clinical Psychology*, 1971, *37*, 16–22.

Mischel, W. *Personality and assessment*. New York: Wiley, 1968.

Mischel, W. Toward a cognitive social learning reconceptualization of personality. *Psychological Review*, 1973, *80*, 252–283.

Mischel, W. On the interface of cognition and personality: Beyond the person–situation debate. *American Psychologist*, 1979, *34*, 740–754.

Mooney, C., & Algozzine, B. A comparison of the disturbingness of behaviors related to learning disability and emotional disturbance. *Journal of Abnormal Child Psychology*, 1978, *6*, 401–406.

Moos, R. H. Assessment and impact of social culture. In P. McReynolds (Ed.), *Advances in psychological assessment* (Vol. 3). San Francisco: Jossey-Bass, 1975.

Morganstern, K. P. Behavioral interviewing: The initial stages of assessment. In M. Hersen & A. S. Bellack (Eds.), *Behavioral assessment: A practical handbook*. New York: Pergamon, 1976.

Nay, W. R. Comprehensive behavioral treatment in a training school for delinquents. In K. S. Calhoun, H. E. Adams, & K. M. Mitchell (Eds.), *Innovative treatment methods in psychopathology*. New York: Wiley, 1974.

Nay, W. R. *Multimethod clinical assessment*. New York: Gardner Press, 1979.

Nelson, R. O., & Bowles, T. E. The best of two worlds—Observation with norms. *Journal of School Psychology*, 1975, *13*, 3–9.

Nelson, R. O., & Hayes, S. C. Some current dimensions of behavioral assessment. *Behavioral Assessment*, 1979, *1*, 1–16.

Nelson, R. O., Kapust, J. A., & Dorsey, B. L. Minimal reactivity of overt classroom observations on school and teacher behaviors. *Behavior Therapy*, 1978, *8*, 695–702.

Nelson, R. O., Lipinski, D. P., & Boykin, R. A. The effects of self-recorders' training and the obtrusiveness of the self-recording device on the accuracy and reactivity of self-monitoring. *Behavior Therapy*, 1978, *9*, 200–208.

O'Leary, K. D. Behavioral assessment. *Behavioral Assessment*, 1979, *1*, 31–36.

O'Leary, K. D., & Johnson, S. B. Psychological assessment. In H. C. Quay & J. S. Werry (Eds.), *Psychopathological disorders of childhood* (2nd ed.). New York: Wiley, 1979.

O'Leary, K. D., & Turkewitz, H. Methodological errors in marital and child treatment. *Journal of Consulting and Clinical Psychology*, 1978, *46*, 747–758.

O'Leary, S. G., & Dubey, D. R. Applications of self-control procedures with children: A review. *Journal of Applied Behavior Analysis*, 1979, *12*, 449–465.

Oltmanns, T. F., Broderick, J. E., & O'Leary, K. D. Marital adjustment and the efficacy of behavior therapy with children. *Journal of Consulting and Clinical Psychology*, 1977, *45*, 724–729.

Olweus, D. Stability of aggressive reaction patterns in males: A review. *Psychological Bulletin*, 1979, *86*, 852–875.

Parsons, B. V., & Alexander, J. F. Short-term family intervention: A therapy outcome study. *Journal of Consulting and Clinical Psychology*, 1973, *41*, 195–201.

Passman, R. H., & Mulhern, R. K. Maternal punitiveness as affected by situational stress: An experimental analogue of child abuse. *Journal of Abnormal Psychology*, 1977, *86*, 565–569.

Patterson, G. R. The aggressive child: Victim and architect of a coercive system. In E. J. Mash, L. A. Hamerlynck, & L. C. Handy (Eds.), *Behavior modification and families*. New York: Brunner/Mazel, 1976.

Patterson, G. R., & Bechtel, G. G. Formulating the situational environment in relation to states and traits. In R. B. Cattell & R. M. Greger (Eds.), *Handbook of modern personality theory*. Washington, D.C.: Halstead, 1977.

Patterson, G. R., Littman, R. A., & Hinsey, W. C. Parental effectiveness as reinforcer in the laboratory and its relation to child-rearing practices and child adjustment in the classroom. *Journal of Personality*, 1964, *32*, 180–199.

Patterson, G. R., Reid, J. B., Jones, R. R., & Conger, R. E. *A social learning approach to family intervention: Families with aggressive children* (Vol. 1). Eugene, Ore.: Castalia Publishing Company, 1975.

Peterson, D. R. Behavior problems of middle childhood. *Journal of Consulting Psychology*, 1961, *25*, 205–209.

Peterson, D. R. *The clinical study of social behavior*. New York: Appleton-Century-Crofts, 1968.

Phillips, L., Draguns, J. G., & Bartlett, D. P. Classification of behavior disorders. In N. Hobbs (Ed.), *Issues in the classification of children*. San Francisco: Jossey-Bass, 1975.

Pomerleau, O. F. Behavioral medicine: The contribution of the experimental analysis of behavior to medical care. *American Psychologist*, 1979, *34*, 654–663.

Pomerleau, O. F., & Brady, J. P. Introduction: The scope and promise of behavioral medicine. In O. F. Pomerleau & J. P. Brady (Eds.), *Behavioral medicine: Theory and practice*. Baltimore: Williams & Wilkins, 1979.

Prinz, R. J., Rosenblum, R. S., & O'Leary, K. D. Affective communication differences between distressed and non-distressed mother–adolescent dyads. *Journal of Abnormal Child Psychology*, 1978, *6*, 373–378.

*Professional Psychology*. Special issue: Psychologists in health care settings, 1979, *10*, Whole No. 4.

Prugh, D. G., Engel, M., & Morse, W. C. Emotional disturbance in children. In N. Hobbs (Ed.), *Issues in the classification of children*. San Francisco: Jossey-Bass, 1975.

Quay, H. C. Classification. In H. C. Quay & J. S. Werry (Eds.), *Psychopathological disorders of childhood* (2nd ed.). New York: Wiley, 1979.

Quay, H. C., & Peterson, D. R. *Manual for the Behavior Problem Checklist*. Champaign, Ill.: University of Illinois, Child Research Center, 1967.

Quay, H. C., & Werry, J. S. (Eds.). *Psychopathological disorders of childhood* (2nd ed.). New York: Wiley, 1979.

Rains, P. M., Kitsuse, J. I., Duster, T., & Friedson, E. The labeling approach to deviance. In N. Hobbs (Ed.), *Issues in the classification of children*. San Francisco: Jossey-Bass, 1975.

Rapoport, J. L., Buchsbaum, M. S., Zahn, T. P., Weingartner, H., Ludlow, C., & Mikkelson, E. J. Dextroamphetamine: Cognitive and behavioral effects in prepubertal boys. *Science*, 1978, *199*, 560–563.

Reardon, R. C., Hersen, M., Bellack, A. S., & Foley, J. M. Measuring social skill in grade school boys. *Journal of Behavioral Assessment*, 1979, *1*, 87–105.

Richman, N., & Graham, P. J. A behavioral screening questionnaire for use with three-year-old children: Preliminary findings. *Journal of Child Psychology and Psychiatry*, 1971, *12*, 5–33.

Risley, T. R., Clark, H. B., & Cataldo, M. F. Behavioral technology for the normal middle-class family. In E. J. Mash, L. A. Hamerlynck, & L. C. Handy (Eds.), *Behavior modification and families*. New York: Brunner/Mazel, 1976.

Roberts, M. W., McMahon, R. J., Forehand, R., & Humphreys, L. The effect of parental instruction-giving on child compliance. *Behavior Therapy*, 1978, *9*, 793–798.

Robins, L. N. *Deviant children grow up*. Baltimore: Williams & Wilkins, 1966.

Robins, L. N. Follow-up studies. In H. C. Quay & J. S. Werry (Eds.), *Psychopathological disorders of childhood* (2nd ed.). New York: Wiley, 1979.

Rosenbaum, M. S., & Drabman, R. S. Goniometry in behavior modification: A useful assessment technique. *Journal of Applied Behavior Analysis*, 1979, *12*, 354. (a)

Rosenbaum, M. S., & Drabman, R. S. Self-control training in the classroom. *Journal of Applied Behavior Analysis*, 1979, *12*, 457–485. (b)

Ross, A. O. *Psychological disorders of children: A behavioral approach to theory, research, and therapy*. New York: McGraw-Hill, 1974.

Ross, A. O. Behavior therapy with children. In S. L. Garfield & A. E. Bergin (Eds.), *Handbook of psychotherapy and behavior change: An empirical analysis*. New York: Wiley, 1978.

Ross, D. M., & Ross, S. A. *Hyperactivity: Research, theory, and action*. New York: Wiley, 1976.

Russell, M. B., & Bernal, M. E. Temporal and climatic variables in naturalistic observation. *Journal of Applied Behavior Analysis*, 1977, *10*, 399–405.

Rutter, M. Maternal deprivation, 1972–1978: New findings, new concepts, new approaches. *Child Development*, 1979, *50*, 283–305.

Rutter, M., Lebovici, S., Eisenberg, L., Sneznevskij, A. V., Sadoun, R., Brooke, E., & Lin, T. A tri-axial classification of mental disorders in childhood. *Journal of Child Psychology and Psychiatry*, 1969, *10*, 41–61.

Rutter, M., Shaffer, D., & Shepherd, M. *A multi-axial classification of child psychiatric disorders: An evaluation of a proposal.* Geneva, Switzerland: World Health Organization, 1975.

Santostefano, S. Beyond nosology: Diagnosis from the viewpoint of development. In H. E. Rie (Ed.), *Perspectives in child psychopathology.* Chicago: Aldine-Atherton, 1971.

Santostefano, S. *A biodevelopmental approach to clinical child psychology: Cognitive controls and cognitive control therapy.* New York: Wiley, 1978.

Schacht, T., & Nathan, P. E. But is it good for psychologists? Appraisal and status of DSM-III. *American Psychologist,* 1977, *32,* 1017–1025.

Schaefer, E. S., & Bell, R. Q. Development of a parent attitude research instrument. *Child Development,* 1958, *29,* 339–361.

Schaeffer, W. W., & Bayley, N. Maternal behavior, child behavior, and their intercorrelations from infancy through adolescence. *Monographs of the Society for Research in Child Development,* 1963, *28,* 1–127.

Schnelle, J. F. A brief report on the invalidity of parent evaluations of behavior change. *Journal of Applied Behavior Analysis,* 1974, *7,* 341–343.

Schwartz, G., & Weiss, S. What is behavioral medicine? *Psychosomatic Medicine,* 1977, *36,* 377–381.

Schwartz, G. E., & Weiss, S. Behavioral medicine revisited: An amended definition. *Journal of Behavioral Medicine,* 1978, *1,* 249–251.

Shepherd, M., Oppenheim, A. N., & Mitchell, S. Childhood behavior disorders and the child-guidance clinic: An epidemiological study. *Journal of Child Psychology and Psychiatry,* 1966, *7,* 55–89.

Sines, J., Pauker, J. D., Sines, L. K., & Owen, D. R. Identification of clinically relevant dimensions of children's behavior. *Journal of Consulting and Clinical Psychology,* 1969, *33,* 728–734.

Skinner, B. F. *Science and human behavior.* New York: Macmillan, 1953.

Spivack, G., & Swift, M. The classroom behavior of children: A critical review of teacher administered rating scales. *Journal of Special Education,* 1973, *7,* 55–89.

Stevens-Long, J. The effect of behavioral context on some aspects of adult disciplinary practice and affect. *Child Development,* 1973, *44,* 476–484.

Stokes, T. F., Fowler, S. A., & Baer, D. M. Training preschool children to recruit natural communities of reinforcement. *Journal of Applied Behavior Analysis,* 1978, *11,* 285–303.

Sulzer-Azaroff, B., & Mayer, G. R. *Applying behavior-analysis procedures with children and youth.* New York: Holt, Rinehart & Winston, 1977.

Swan, G. E., & MacDonald, M. L. Behavior therapy in practice: A national survey of behavior therapists. *Behavior Therapy,* 1978, *9,* 799–807.

Switzky, H. N., & Haywood, H. C. Motivational orientation and the relative efficacy of self-monitored and externally imposed reinforcement systems in children. *Journal of Personality and Social Psychology,* 1974, *30,* 360–366.

Tallent, N. *Psychological report writing.* Englewood Cliffs, N.J.: Prentice-Hall, 1976.

Tharp, R. G., & Wetzel, R. J. *Behavior modification in the natural environment.* New York: Academic Press, 1969.

Thomas, A., Chess, S., & Birch, H. G. *Temperament and behavior disorders in children.* New York: New York University Press, 1968.

Thomas, A., Chess, S., Birch, H., Hertzig, M., & Korn, S. *Behavioral individuality in early childhood.* New York: New York University Press, 1963.

Ullmann, L. P., & Krasner, L. (Eds.). *Case studies in behavior modification.* New York: Holt, Rinehart & Winston, 1965.

Ullmann, L. P., & Krasner, L. *A psychological approach to abnormal behavior.* Englewood Cliffs, N.J.: Prentice-Hall, 1969.

VanHasselt, V. B., Hersen, M., Whitehill, M. B., & Bellack, A. S. Social skill assessment and training for children: An evaluative review. *Behaviour Research and Therapy,* 1979, *17,* 413–437.

Van Houten, R. Normative data: A comment. *Journal of Applied Behavior Analysis,* 1978, *11,* 110.

Wade, T. C., & Baker, T. B. Opinions and use of psychological tests: A survey of clinical psychologists. *American Psychologist,* 1977, *32,* 874–882.

Wade, T. C., Baker, T. B., & Hartmann, D. P. Behavior therapists' self-reported views and practices. *The Behavior Therapist,* 1979, *2,* 3–6.

Wahler, R. G. Some structural aspects of deviant child behavior. *Journal of Applied Behavior Analysis*, 1975, *8*, 27–42.

Wahler, R. G. Deviant child behavior in the family: Developmental speculations and behavior change strategies. In H. Leitenberg (Ed.), *Handbook of behavior modification and behavior therapy*. Englewood Cliffs, N.J.: Prentice-Hall, 1976.

Wahler, R. G. The insular mother: Her problems in parent–child treatment. *Journal of Applied Behavior Analysis*, 1980, *13*, 207–219.

Wahler, R. G., & Cormier, W. H. The ecological interview: A first step in out-patient child behavior therapy. *Journal of Behavior Therapy and Experimental Psychiatry*, 1970, *1*, 279–289.

Wahler, R. G., House, A. E., & Stambaugh, E. E. *Ecological assessment of child problem behavior: A clinical package for home, school, and institutional settings*. New York: Pergamon, 1976.

Wahler, R. G., Leske, G., & Rogers, E. S. The insular family: A deviance support system for oppositional children. In L. A. Hamerlynck (Ed.), *Behavioral systems for the developmentally disabled: I. School and family environments*. New York: Brunner/Mazel, 1978.

Weinrott, M. R., Garrett, B., & Todd, N. The influence of observer presence on classroom behavior. *Behavior Therapy*, 1978, *9*, 900–911.

Weiss, L. B., & Gallimore, R. Some problems of behavioral classification in cross-cultural research. In S. MacDonald & G. Tanabe (Eds.), *Focus on classroom behavior: Theory and research*. Springfield, Ill.: Charles C. Thomas, 1973.

Werry, J. S., & Sprague, R. L. Hyperactivity. In C. G. Costello (Ed.), *Symptoms of psychopathology: A handbook*. New York: Wiley, 1970.

Whalen, C. K., Henker, B., Collins, B. E., Finck, D., & Dotemoto, S. A social ecology of hyperactive boys: Medication effects in structured classroom environments. *Journal of Applied Behavior Analysis*, 1979, *12*, 65–81.

White, G. D. Effects of observer presence on family interaction. *Journal of Applied Behavior Analysis*, 1977, *10*, 734.

White, M. A. Natural rates of teacher approval and disapproval in the classroom. *Journal of Applied Behavior Analysis*, 1975, *8*, 367–372.

Wildman, B. G., & Erickson, M. T. Methodological problems in behavioral observation. In J. D. Cone & R. P. Hawkins (Eds.), *Behavioral assessment: New directions in clinical psychology*. New York: Brunner/Mazel, 1977.

Willems, E. P. Go ye into all the world and modify behavior: An ecologist's view. *Representative Research in Social Psychology*, 1973, *4*, 93–105.

Willems, E. P. Behavioral technology and behavioral ecology. *Journal of Applied Behavior Analysis*, 1974, *7*, 151–165.

Williams, C. D. The elimination of tantrum behavior by extinction procedures. *Journal of Abnormal and Social Psychology*, 1959, *59*, 269.

Williams, R. L., & Workman, E. A. The development of a behavioral self-concept scale. *Behavior Therapy*, 1978, *9*, 680–681.

Wimberger, H. C., & Gregory, R. J. A behavior checklist for use in child psychiatry clinics. *Journal of the American Academy of Child Psychiatry*, 1968, *7*, 677–688.

Winett, R. A., & Winkler, R. C. Current behavior modification in the classroom: Be still, be quiet, be docile. *Journal of Applied Behavior Analysis*, 1972, *5*, 499–504.

Wittlieb, E., Eifert, G., Wilson, F. E., & Evans, I. M. Target behavior selection in recent child case reports in behavior therapy. *The Behavior Therapist*, 1979, *1*, 15–16.

Wolf, M. M. Social validity: The case for subjective measurement or how applied behavior analysis is finding its heart. *Journal of Applied Behavior Analysis*, 1978, *11*, 203–214.

Yarrow, L. J. Interviewing children. In P. Mussen (Ed.), *Handbook of research methods in child development*. New York: Wiley, 1960.

Yarrow, M. R., Campbell, J. D., & Burton, R. V. Recollections of childhood: A study of the retrospective method. *Monographs of the Society for Research in Child Development*, 1970, *35*, Serial No. 138.

Yates, A. J. *Behavior therapy*. New York: Wiley, 1970.

Yates, B. T., Klein, S. B., & Haven, W. G. Psychological nosology and mnemonic reconstruction: Effects of diagnostic labels on observers' recall of positive and negative behavior frequencies. *Cognitive Therapy and Research*, 1978, 2, 377–387.

# EXTERNALIZING DISORDERS

# SELF-MANAGEMENT PROBLEMS IN CHILDREN

**Paul Karoly**

*University of Cincinnati*

A central issue in contemporary child assessment is how best to conceptualize disorders of self-guidance. As with some deficits in cognitive or interpersonal skills, self-management problems are often described in negative terms (as things children won't or can't do) while being linked to interiorized "causes" (e.g., ego weakness, inadequate socialization, nervous system hyperreactivity). "Can you teach my 14-year-old daughter self-respect?" asks a distraught parent. "She just can't say no to boys."

Sharing many of the inadequacies inherent in the general domain of child assessment (e.g., the lack of standardization in measurement operations, limited developmental relevance), the study of self-management also encounters a set of unusual obstacles—philosophical and theoretical, rather than purely technical, in nature. First, self-management appears to be a superordinate, rather than a primary, adjustment construct. However, we cannot, for any practical purpose, speak of self-management in general, but only as reflected in more familiar categories of action, thought, or feeling. As clinicians, teachers, or parents, we might be interested, for example, in children's capacity for controlling their desire to overeat, for regulating their classroom study habits, or for independently solving an interpersonal dilemma. Rarely do adults concern themselves with psychological abstractions ("As long as we're here, doctor, could you check Johnny's ego strength?").

A related difficulty is the inferential nature of hypothesized self-management processes, such as self-knowledge, self-observation, intentionality, planning, and the like. Indeed, in some mediational systems, the basic components not only are inaccessible via direct observation but are endowed with additional characteristics that appear to violate the canons of parsimony and operationalization (e.g., the linking of ego functions to sexual motives, or the assumption of a hierarchical arrangement of cognitive control mechanisms). Also, in what is assuredly a mixed blessing, self-management psychology does not possess strong ties to traditional clinical-interventive or diagnostic practices. Short of the presumption that children and adults differ in their readiness (capacity and motivation) to employ various self-management maneuvers, the empirical literature contains scant reference to descriptive accounts of self-management disorders in children or to extended naturalistic observations of children's self-management in the general context of (1) other behaviors, (2) the child's situational perceptions and interpretations, or (3) the preceding and consequential behavior of significant others. The traditional separation in child psychology between laboratory-based, purely theoretical or analogue approaches and clinic-based, practical concerns (cf. Santostefano, 1978) is nowhere better illustrated than in the domain of self-management.

Laboratory studies of self-regulation and self-control (primarily of a behavioral nature), which have the best chance of proving predictively useful (valid) and descriptively reliable, are nonetheless tied to a model that has been aptly criticized for its representation of children as passive, stimulus-bound reactors to the world rather than as creative, interpretive actors upon it. Can a model of children's self-management possess both clinical and experimental vitality? I am committed to the view that it is possible to speak with both precision and sensitivity about children's successes and failures at self-direction. In the absence of such a dual approach, the field is destined to see further caricaturistic efforts to "cure" children's reaction times on laboratory tests or to locate and strengthen the "observing ego" in knife-wielding adolescents.

## FUNDAMENTAL ASSUMPTIONS AND DEFINITIONS: METATHEORY

It is extremely difficult to separate a psychological process from its explanatory network. Our view of the nature of "intelligence" colors our measurement procedures and our educational–remedial designs. And so it is with self-management. One group of students of human behavior may adopt the natural science ethic and seek to account for self-direction (as any set of actions) using the principles of learning or conditioning. Still another large contingent assumes that self-guidance is an innate given (in a neurologically healthy child or adult). Freedom versus determinism, willpower versus Big Brother, an internal (personality) perspective versus environmentalism—these are the provocative alternatives offered us. However, when operant advocates claim that they can unravel the processes of self-management by "objective" functional analyses, or when psychodynamic theorists make similar unraveling claims but instead employ psychoanalysis, the discovery process is, in reality, a synthetic putting together, or a creative endeavor. Of course, self-management is a fiction. But so, too, are all psychological constructs. The truly important question is, "Is it a useful fiction?"

The recognition of such a question is important in many respects. The assumption that self-management is a point of view obviates the debate between those who would seek to prove that external, rather than internal, happenings are the "first causes" and those who hold the truth of self-directiveness to be self-evident. The utility of self-management concepts is an empirical question, to be settled by experimentation and not by philosophical debate (cf. Coates & Thoresen, 1979; Goldiamond, 1976; Mahoney, 1976).

Being free to create as they please, psychologists may next inquire into the most productive means of building a workable psychology of self-management, taking care to avoid the traps of either-or and ultimate-cause reasoning, which only serve to limit creative solutions. Elsewhere I have suggested (Karoly, 1977, in preparation) that one route to the development of a viable theory of self-management would involve a thorough examination of extant conceptions with an eye toward identifying the commonalities. The search for common elements is seen as a way of preserving the insights of the many thoughtful individuals who have labored to understand self-directiveness. It may also provide the raw materials (e.g., the metatheory) for a more complete, internally consistent, and clinically useful approximation to a genuine theory of self-management than has hitherto been provided by hard-line true believers or "no-line" eclectics. Three essential tenets are identifiable: personal mediation, temporal and contextual relativity, and reciprocal determinism.

## Personal Mediation

Over the years, human self-management has evolved from a supernatural or biological prerequisite, assuring the survival of organized society, to a personal quality that presumedly interacts with current and historical contextual features to determine whether an individual's behavioral efforts will either successfully sustain goal-directedness (self-regulation) or successfully alter goal-directedness (self-control) in the face of a neutral or nonfacilitative environment (Kanfer & Karoly, 1972). Whether viewed as an intrapsychic agency (in psychoanalytic terms), a temperament, a trait (or dispositional) construct, a moral orientation, an aspect of intelligence, a motivational orientation, or a learned set of behaviors, the concept of self-management nonetheless includes a person at the center.

The self-management construct requires a focus upon private, relatively infrequent, self-assessed behaviors, which the actor is in the best position to evaluate and revise in accordance with changing internal and external conditions. The *self* in self-management implies not an independent or ultimate source of control, not a homunculus, not a formless entity existing in hyperspace, but the point of origin of an extended series of actions and reactions and the source of continuity that ties contemporary actions to distant goals and outcomes.

To suggest that self-management is a personally mediated process is to suggest that it is subjective. Unfortunately, a belief in subjective mediation (or the phenomenological perspective) is often likened to a belief in God in the context of an essentially atheistic discipline (cf. Mahoney, 1974). Is there any room for "theism" within a science groping for objectivity? Is there any room for a position based on personalistic, subjective criteria in a book on *behavioral* assessment? I think that such room not only exists but is vital to the continued success of a learning-theory model of behavior change and behavior persistence (Karoly, 1980). The arguments against subjectivity are simply outdated.

For example, subjectivity is said to describe a stance, with respect to the extraction and the use of knowledge, that emphasizes the special position of the actor. The subjectivist believes that one can know more than one can tell and that the individual knows differently and uniquely about the world (and his or her own role in it). I stand in a unique position vis-à-vis my perception of things because no one else has direct access to "my experience." If this is so, then by definition, a scientific assault on the psychology of my experience, or anybody's experience, is impossible because one of the basic tenets of scientific method, observer interchangeability, is ruled out. Radical behaviorism, physicalism, and logical positivism have provided psychology with an alternative—if you want to study subjective experience, do not.

What is wrong with the surgical solution to the mind–body problem? Other than the obvious incompleteness that it forces upon psychological theory, there are the factual or logical errors in the preceding arguments. Psychologists who adhere to "mindlessness" as a metatheory have been misled about both the nature of subjective experience and the proper use of the scientific method. Consider the following assertions:

1. If subjective experience is purely metaphysical, a science of subjective experience is ruled out.
2. If science rests solely upon the manipulation of observable events, then a science of subjective experience is ruled out.

Both of these assertions are undoubtedly logical, but their premises are invalid. Hence, they are inapplicable. Until recently, American psychologists have not questioned the validity of these premises, probably because the relative success of behavioral technology and the ease of laboratory experimentation made it unnecessary to do so. The contemporary interest in generalizability, naturalistic research, theory-building, cognition, and the long-term effectiveness of psychological treatments has caused us to reexamine our premises.

If subjective experience is not metaphysical, then it should be studied. If science is not synonymous with control and direct measurement, subjectivity can be studied. With regard to the first "if," Natsoulas (1978) has reviewed the philosophical arguments against assuming that because "I" know the physical and the psychological "me" differently than any observer can, this knowledge must, by definition, exist on a plane higher than the physical. Natsoulas (1978) points out that "there is no subject of experience distinct from the organism to which the experiences occur" (p. 270). The person is capable of being aware of himself or herself as an object of environmental action ("I am in pain"; "I am being manipulated by others"), which is called "objective self-awareness," or as an actor on the environment, as the origin of behavior ("I can do it"; "I am in charge"), which is called "subjective self-awareness" (Duval & Wicklund, 1972). The corporeal "I" gains such awareness by interacting with an environment that is really out there (naive realism). Nothing supernatural is required. And if the "self" is not a metaphysical entity, its perspective can at least be appreciated, although not totally understood. Personal experiences are not fantasies and may therefore be approached as "shared," to the degree that the observer uses his or her own similar experiences as an anchor. Such understanding, however, will always be partial.

With regard to the second "if," although it is indeed true that subjectivity as a subject matter implies a loss of what philosophers of science call "analytical tractability" (i.e., directness of assessment, control over one's observations, admissibility of quantification and manipulation), it is also true that science proceeds by "instrumental congruence," which is simply the attempt to bring the appropriate analytical tools to bear on the problem at hand (cf. Sutherland, 1973). Whereas positivism fits as an analytical mode to phenomena that are readily accessible, stable over time, and least prone to observer interference, an inferential or deductivist mode is appropriate when the phenomenon under investigation (i.e., the self-managing child) is changing over time and in relation to specific settings and setting demands (cf. also Sampson, 1978). The self-management psychologist, at this stage of our knowledge, must be a deductivist. Such a fate is not altogether shameful, for as Sutherland (1973) notes:

> The deductivist, then, is something of a scavenger, building what often amounts to a work of art out of components which had heretofore never been integrated, leaving some connections unvalidated and often introducing some innovations. . . . [In] his scavenging and logical machinations lies the future of a truly integrated science and the most sound platform for treating those problems which simply cannot effectively be reduced to isolated, mechanical units of analysis. (p. 177)

Therefore, if it is asserted that self-management involves internal processes (conscious problem recognition, decision making, planning, and the like), and if it is acknowledged that total objectivity in our approach to these processes is an impossibility, one should not be misled into thinking that our perspective is inherently nonpsychological or nonempirical. On the contrary, it is deeply psychological and altogether in keeping with the principles of scientific validation.

If a set of fundamental beliefs was to be articulated about self-management based upon the apparently universal acknowledgment of personal mediation (and the appropriateness of inference as a necessary means of investigation), it would involve assumptions about the existence of the following capacities:

- The child's capacity for active awareness of distal and proximal stimulation
- The child's capacity for building an internal representation of self and the environment
- The child's capacity to act in accordance with internalized codes and preferences

### Temporal and Contextual Relativity

The eight relatively distinct approaches to self-management previously mentioned (the dynamic, motivational, moral, etc.) also appear to converge in their acknowledgment (though sometimes tacit) that children are ever-changing and discriminating. Children cannot, therefore, be studied in a temporal vacuum or apart from the context in which their self-guiding activities occur. Self-management problems (e.g., study skills deficiencies, impulse control, pain tolerance) may be specific to one's subculture, age, gender, and setting, as well as being tied to a particular historical period. Certainly a middle-class child in contemporary America does not face the demands for delay of gratification that might have confronted the denizen of Oliver Twist's England. Contemporary "trait" theorists and "ego" psychologists seem to recognize the role of the environment, as social learning theorists acknowledge the role of "person variables" (cf. Buss & Plomin, 1975; Loevinger, 1976; Mischel, 1973). Self-management can no more be defined as a global capacity that one has and will invariably use than it can be defined as a simple set of actions that one displays on cue. Self-management is neither an enduring personal attribute nor an automatic, momentary happening.

An extremely important characteristic of self-management (self-control and self-regulation) is that we cannot rely on information about specific instances in order to define or identify its occurrence. We cannot simply calculate a behavior rate, note a response type, measure an intensity level, or collect isolated behavior ratings and de facto label an action as self-controlling or self-regulating. Although Mahoney and Arnkoff (1978) correctly point out that "the context and history of a given behavior are the primary factors which determine whether it is labeled 'self-control' " (p. 693), we should keep in mind that we are rarely interested in a "given behavior" but are, instead, concerned with labeling extended patterns and time-bound outcomes. No meaningful answer is possible to the often-asked question, "Is that [action, choice] an example of self-control (or self-regulation)?" Such a question might be likened to asking a painter "Is that brush stroke an example of art?"

Certainly one can find authors who defend the theoretical superiority of trait theory or of environmentalism. Yet no piece of research or clinical case study has ever been published in which an "impulsive" child, for example, has been shown to be impulsive in all settings or at all times (or even in a reasonably broad sampling of contexts and occasions).

A simplified schematic depicting the relationships between the person $(P)$, the setting $(S)$, the emitted response $(R)$, and time $(T_1 \ldots T_n)$ is presented in Figure 1 to help concretize the present line of reasoning.

While examining the figure, consider the following vignette. Suppose an obese child finds himself in the situation, at Time 1, of being faced with a jar full of tasty jelly beans. Likewise, assume that he has not eaten for a few hours (the physiological state of the child at $T_1$ is one of hunger). The child has a history of eating candy between meals and of being reprimanded (mildly) when caught in the act. At this time, the child is alone and is quite sure of not being detected (he knows his parents will not be home for an hour). He makes the response $(R_1)$ of reaching for a piece of candy.

If we freeze the action at the point at which the child reaches for a jelly bean, what can we say about his self-control? The unqualified or absolute trait view might

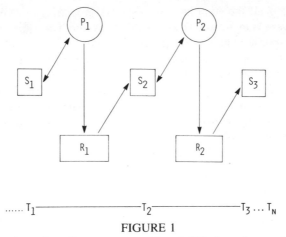

FIGURE 1

The flow of behavior, where $P_1$ = person at Time 1 ($T_1$); $S_1$ = the psychological situation at Time 1; and $R_1$ = the response emitted at Time 1 (be it an instrumental, cognitive, affective, or physiological response).

lead us to administer a test of self-control that essentially requires the child to sum all of his recollections of his preferences, attitudes, expectancies, and actions toward between-meal snacking (and other forms of transgression) in order to tell us whether he is the "type" to go ahead and consume the tempting morsel he will soon have within his grasp. The assumption is that what the child does is a function of the drawing power of the candy and his inner capacity, but with the inner capacity playing a more central role in the predictive equation. This assumption of centrality is precisely why the "consistency of personality" view fails to accommodate to the ebb and flow of the behavior–environment stream and why it generally lacks genuine predictive power (cf. Fiske, 1978). If the child does not eat the candy, the "personologist" will hindsightfully attribute control to the "self," but if the child consumes it, then the environment will be awarded the prize. It is bad enough to approach behavior control in either-or terms, but to do so with only the potential for retrospective attribution suggests an even shakier conceptual foundation.

Lest the dyed-in-the-wool behaviorist be forgotten, note that the requirements for predicting how the child will respond in a specified setting are no less complicated procedurally than the task that devout trait theorists set for themselves. The behaviorist must conduct a fine-grain analysis of contingency relationships between self-management responses and environmental cues and consequences. Among the questions a behavioral assessor would seek to answer are the following: What aspects of the environment serve to elicit the undesirable behaviors (reaching for the candy)? Is the presence of the candy alone responsible for the child's response, or is the effective cue some combination of setting properties and events? Can the individual discriminate between cues that signal consumption and cues for response suppression? What is the role of emotional factors in the problematic response? And, if all the stimulus and response properties of overeating for the specific child were known, would we be able to predict with certainty whether the consumption response would be made? In all likelihood, we would not.

The point of this discussion is that neither a mechanistic *S-R* model nor a static trait (dispositional, cognitive, or temperament) model is capable of addressing children's potential for change, conditional discrimination, and/or flexibility. Most contemporary writers on the subject would agree. The old debates between the willpower and learning perspectives were both oversimplified and misdirected (Coates & Thoresen, 1979).

Specific assumptions based upon a relativity view include the following:

- That the appropriateness of specific episodes of self-control or self-regulation is a function of fluctuating internal and external requirements (time, place, culture, etc.).
- That children's behaviors in pursuit of self-control or self-regulation are only the means to an end. Knowing whether children are capable of and/or motivated to emit specific component behaviors is not sufficient. We must also understand the circumstances under which children actually perceive the need to self-manage and the factors influencing their successful co-ordination of efforts over an extended period.
- That data about self-management skills should be collected in natural environments, as well as in artificial or constrained conditions, because laboratory studies cannot reveal what the child's environment expects and demands as criterial performance or how the expectations and demands shift as a function of where, when, and with whom the child behaves.

### Reciprocal Determinism

It is but a short step from acknowledging that the person and the environment are equally real and important to the view that they are mutually interactive. The simple and sovereign determinisms of the past (e.g., the biological, sociological, intra-psychic, emotional, rational) have given way, in modern personality theory, to an appreciation for interactionism (cf. Ekehammar, 1974; Endler & Magnusson, 1976; Pervin, 1978).

It is my contention that the majority of contemporary theorists in the domain of self-management generally agree with the view that successful self-directive efforts require the interdependent functioning of personal, environmental, and overt behavioral components. Whereas investigators associated with the social-learning framework have perhaps been the most outspoken advocates of interactionism in self-management (e.g., Bandura, 1977, 1978; Kanfer, 1977; Mahoney, 1974; Mischel, 1973; Staats, 1975), a close look at the other popular personality perspectives will reveal a similar turn of mind.

For example, current versions of ego psychology consider specific and measurable "cognitive styles" to be important in the child's display of affect and behavior control (Klein, 1976; Santostefano, 1978) and assume that environments both activate and facilitate their effectiveness. Temperament theorists (e.g., Buss & Plomin, 1975) discuss interactions between genetic proclivities toward impulsivity and predictable, socially mediated developmental "crises" (cf. also Chess, Thomas, & Birch, 1967). Those who view self-control as an emergent moral process nonetheless respect individual differences in children's rule following as a function of the home and school environment (e.g., Kohlberg, 1976). Contemporary models of achievement motivation (a presumed determinant of self-mastery and task persistence) are clear derivatives of Murray's (1938) essentially interactional personality system.

A notable implication of the interactional view is the need to exercise caution when using the term *self-management* (or *self-control* or *self-regulation*). The individual is not the only, or necessarily the most important, source of influence in adaptation. Keeping personal, environmental, temporal, and behavioral elements consistently in mind means greater theoretical richness, multicomponent assessment, and enlarged interventive opportunities (Coates & Thoresen, 1979; Staats, 1975). Among the key assumptions generated by an interactional, or an interdependent systems, approach are the following:

- That the only potentially unbiased indicator of successful self-management is a tangible product or outcome. Given a real-world accomplishment (such as weight loss or improvements in grades), the assessor can then work backward to ascertain the relative contribution of internal and/or external factors.
- That the confluence of different factors suggests that at any time there exists a dynamic balance, or what systems theorists call a *steady state*. Whereas certain skills, attitudes, or goals may be relatively long-lived, the display of self-management is dependent upon the joint influence of historical and currently acting determinants.
- That task-relevant thoughts and feelings are as legitimate to study as the concrete, instrumental behaviors underlying self-management. The best avenue for clinical intervention is always an empirical question.

## A CONCEPTUAL FRAMEWORK: FOUR-FACTOR THEORY

The interrelated doctrines of personal mediation, relativism, and reciprocal determinism represent metatheoretical beliefs, the usually implicit groundwork upon which theories and technologies are constructed. Prior to formulating hypotheses about specific variables (including how best to measure them), scientists must possess rudimentary definitions (a focus for their work) and criteria for evaluating the value or meaningfulness of their efforts. It is not possible, therefore, to debate or disprove the theories of those who believe in either unconscious determinism or direct environmental control of behavior. We can only doubt the utility of such metatheoretical foundations and proceed in our own direction. Having asserted that a good psychology of self-management rests upon three fundamental beliefs (and a set of corollaries), we can now begin to formulate a conceptual model consistent with this metatheory. The working model must be clinically encompassing, internally coherent, empirically testable, and adaptable as a guide to therapeutic intervention and assessment. The discussion that follows will emphasize the assessment implications.

However, before stating *how*, we should clarify the *what*. The following definitions of self-control and self-regulation are in keeping with the cognitive social learning perspective and the aforementioned metatheoretical notions.

*Self-control* refers to a set of aroused processes (cognitive and instrumental) through which an individual consciously and consistently contributes to changing the likelihood of engaging in a behavior with conflicting temporal contingencies. The behavior in question either may result in immediate reward but have eventual aversive consequences (as in various addictive disorders) or may involve immediately unpleasant, but long-range positive, outcomes. The aroused processes help to facilitate either avoidance (of the short-range positive payoff) or approach (to the short-run negative outcome). Typically, the individual must be motivated to counteract the cues in the immediate environment, which are arranged so as to facilitate the more probable, but maladaptive, patterns of responding (approach to the short-range positive outcomes or avoidance of short-range discomfort or loss).

*Self-regulation* refers to a set of aroused processes through which an individual consciously and consistently contributes to maintaining the course of goal-directed behavior in the relative absence of external supports or when external supports are of limited utility.

## Hypothetical Components

### Rules Discrimination

Historically, the concept of self-management has been associated with the question of how best to instill in the developing child an understanding and mastery of various standards of conduct. Much human socialization is concerned with making voluntary that which was originally evoked by external pressures—an outcome variously named *internalization, identification*, or *self-discipline*.

Theorists and researchers with varied conceptual commitments have tended to converge in identifying the central problems of self-management psychology as those involving the dual processes of curbing, or of keeping, commitments to action (cf. Kanfer, 1977; Kanfer & Karoly, 1972). Further, whether they are termed "moral" or merely "adaptive," and whether they are assumed to be innate or acquired, the standards of behavior by which children are expected to live must be activated and sustained over relatively long periods. In the absence of constant external reminders, the only efficient mode of behavior control is to teach children to be rule carriers, rule detectors, rule formers, and rule users. There is not a single theoretical position on self-management that does not concern itself with children's conformity to rules. However, the manner in which rules have been conceived has not been as empirically or clinically productive as it might be. For example:

- Children's rule following has generally been approached unilaterally rather than interactionally, either as developmentally determined (Piaget, Freud) or as acquired (learning theories).
- Self-management is often reduced to nothing but rule conformity, rendering children "inert" as contributors to the process.
- Conformity to rules is usually operationalized as conformity to inhibitory rules (or "stop commands"). Curbing of impulses is more often discussed than the redirection of energies or their continued mobilization (self-regulation).
- What is known about children's rule following has come from experimentation in which adults have engaged in direct and explicit rule giving. The focus on experimenter-imposition of rules severely limits our knowledge of how and when children learn to recognize (or detect) situational requirements for self-control or self-regulation in their natural environments. Because youngsters can be rule users when the task requirements and motivational options are clearly laid out (as they have been in 99% of the empirical research on children's self-control), it cannot be assumed that children have accepted the rule, that they will preserve it for future use, that they could recognize its applicability in other (noncontrived) contexts, or that they would modify or revise it when circumstances so warranted.

As Parke (1974) has noted:

> The model of the child as a possive recipient of adult-controlled input is no longer adequate. . . . As our findings illustrate, children as well as adults function as rule transmitters and rule enforcers. (p. 141)

Therefore, there is a need to understand an individual's orientation toward rules calling either for the alteration of a highly probable approach or avoidance response (self-control) or for sustaining efforts toward a goal in the absence of, or in opposition to, present external demands (self-regulation). Dysfunctions in self-control or self-regulation imply that some relevant rules are not being followed. To clarify the problem, it will be necessary to assess children's (1) sensitivity to self-management rules, (2) acceptance of the content and logic of rules, (3) memory for rules, and (4) ability to recognize the generalized utility of certain codes of conduct. The reader will note the multidimensionality of these formulations as compared with the view that children's rule-related behavior is simply the result of appropriate conditioning or the consequence of having reached the requisite stage of moral development.

### Perceptual–Cognitive Tuning: The Selective Awareness of Short- and Long-Run Consequences

The knowledge that self-management is the rule, norm, or requirement in a particular situation is necessary, but not sufficient, to guarantee a child's involvement in a series of behaviors requiring effort expenditure. In addition to recognizing standards, then, the child must see the personal relevance (or value) of his or her engaging in behavior X to obtain reward Y, at the possible cost of Z (a tangible or intangible outcome). In other words, the child must perceive that adhering to this rule represents a problem in need of solution. As previously stated elsewhere (Karoly, 1977):

> Recognition of the possibility of system change and personal responsibility is an invariant initial component of self-management. Although occasionally addressed, the recognition stage has remained largely implicit—neglected by researchers, theorists, and child clinicians. (p. 216)

A fundamental blow to the external validity of the majority of laboratory-based studies of children's self-management (in addition to the experimental imposition of rule structuring) is the experimental structuring and/or control of short- and long-run incentives. A child who will readily indicate a preference for two bags of peanuts in an hour over one bag to be delivered immediately (a choice used in the assessment of delay-of-gratification propensities among young children) might not be able, on his or her own, to discern the real-life temporal conflict associated with a particular set of actions. What I have summarized under the heading of "perceptual tuning" includes the following components, which require careful assessment in all instances of self-management dysfunction: (1) the accuracy of the child's awareness of the short-term nature and effects of his or her behavior, (2) the accuracy of the child's awareness of the long-term nature and effects of present behaviors, (3) the child's recognition of the behavioral links that connect short- and long-range outcomes, (4) the child's recognition of the problematic aspects of the short-run behavioral patterns, and (5) the child's awareness of the potential impact (both short- and long-term) of his or her behavior on significant others.

The emphasis on the component processes of rule discrimination and perceptual–cognitive tuning derives largely from the tenets of personal mediation and of contextual relativity outlined previously in this chapter. It is my contention that these two components of the hypothesized self-management construct have been either neglected or oversimplified in most theoretical accounts (cf. also Karoly, 1977, in preparation, Note 1). Surely, in almost every experimental study of children's self-control (e.g., delay of gratification) or self-regulation (e.g., self-reinforced academic performance) the experimenter has obviated what would be a major part of the child's job in the natural environment, that is, identifying the rules, recognizing the temporal conflict, and specifying the value and relevance of the available response options. The assessment of these processes cannot be omitted in the clinical appraisal of maladjusted children, at least not insofar as the present conceptual model is concerned.

### Motivation—Effort and Commitment

Over the years, self-management has been taken to represent a motivational subsystem unique to *Homo sapiens*. With the exception of those concepts of self-control or self-regulation built upon animal models of learning or upon biological predeterminism, theoretical accounts have tended to focus on how children come to "tame" their impellent emotions via higher order mental processes. In place of such nebulous constructs as *will, self,* and *ego,* contemporary psychological descriptions of self-management include such operations as imagery, expectancy, and self-directed language (Staats, 1971). Indeed, the current use of the term *freedom* in psychology refers not so much to a philosophical tenet opposed to determinism, but to the view that both instrumental and emotional behavior can be mediated by thought as well as by environmental cues and contingencies (Weiner, 1976).

Cognitive processes in self-management are typically not invoked to influence activities about which the individual is neutral. Children who must resist the urge to spend all their money on candy and save it for lunch, or who must serve as their own monitors of academic output while the teacher is out of the room, are usually being required to engage in low probability behavior (at least insofar as they are concerned). Thus, in addition to the discrimination of rules or response requirements and the awareness of the long- and short-range implications of behavior, the self-managing child must also be affectively aroused to the degree that he or she is willing to work for self-change or self-directed maintenance of behavior. Effort and commitment must be expended against whatever factors are operating to prevent change or the continuation of ongoing activity. The child for whom saving money or working on mathematical problems is unequivocally enjoyable (and of high probability) does not need to engage in self-management.

A specific episode of self-control or self-regulation, therefore, must be set in motion (i.e., motivated), not only by internal or external events signaling a need for self-directed activity (the perceptual–cognitive tuning factor) but also by cognitions supportive of the individual's conscious decision to expend the necessary energy to succeed. Somehow the child must find the power to "get new behavior patterns up over a very steep hill" (Thoresen, Kirmil-Gray, & Crosbie, 1977). The statement "I know I ought to, but I just don't want to" is ubiquitous among youngsters with behavior problems. A big part of the task of the self-management psychologist is to understand why children and adolescents cannot mobilize the commitment to exercise self-control or self-regulation.

The view of self-management psychologists is that commitment (or intentionality) is influenced by immediate situational factors, physical states of the organism, and generalized expectancies and problem-solving habits (cf. Bellack & Schwartz, 1976; Kanfer & Karoly, 1972; Karoly, 1977, 1980). Among the motivational factors that will require careful assessment in preparation for self-management training are the following:

1. The child's perception of the value of the self-managed response as compared with the perceived alternatives (e.g., dieting vs. remaining obese; obtaining an "A" in English vs. obtaining a "C"; practicing the piano vs. playing basketball)
2. The nature of potentially active physiological factors (e.g., calmness vs. arousal) either facilitating or inhibiting the desire to self-manage

3. The child's willingness to "make promises," and his or her history of fulfilling them
4. The stringency or leniency of the child's self-evaluative standards
5. The child's expectancy of future goal attainment compared with the perceived costs of engaging in self-management (costs that include personal losses or interpersonal ones)
6. The child's belief in his or her ability to engage successfully in self-management (cf. Bandura's "self-efficacy" concept, 1977)
7. The child's habitual mode of attributing responsibility for the accomplishment of tasks relevant to self-management (e.g., "Obesity is inherited"; "I've got my father's temper")

### Skills for Extended Self-Management

The specific skills for execution of self-managed responses have been the subject of intense empirical investigation since the mid-1960s, during which time Bandura, Kanfer, Mischel, Aronfreed, Rotter, Walters, Staats, and other social-learning advocates began speculating on the means for extending learning theories to accommodate human self-directiveness. Working from an implicit metatheoretical commitment to personal mediation, scores of investigators have demonstrated the potential utility of such self-mediated operations as (1) self-observation, (2) self-recording, (3) self-evaluation and standard setting, (4) the self-administration of rewards and punishments, (5) verbal self-instructional control of attention and motor repertoires, (6) information-processing style (e.g., different modes of encoding, storage, retrieval, and organization of experience in memory), (7) planning and problem-solving style, (8) imaginal control of thought and affect, (9) self-perception and causal attribution, and (10) the deliberate manipulation of stimulus–response, response–outcome, and self-efficacy expectancies.

The active research, both laboratory-based and applied, dealing with so-called mechanisms or skill components has tended to obscure a number of fundamental conceptual issues within self-management psychology.

Certainly the "knowing how" component is essential to the success of any endeavor. In self-management, the awareness components ("knowing why") and the motivational component ("wanting to") cannot be expected to yield successful self-control or self-regulation if the requisite instrumental and/or cognitive competencies are lacking. Yet an exclusive focus upon the mechanisms of self-change or self-directed maintenance of behavior is not likely to clarify questions of value (e.g., When is individualism counterproductive for the person or the society?) or to impose order upon a field that relies upon ad hoc, usually unvalidated procedures for measuring isolated skills for brief periods under contrived conditions.

The relativistic (contextual or holistic) metatheory has often been overlooked in the pursuit of a universally applicable self-management technology. The clinician cannot afford to lose sight of the facts (1) that component skills must be empirically related to effective self-management in the natural environment before their relevance to self-control or self-regulation can be acknowledged, (2) that prior to systematic assessments, there is no reason for interpreting certain clinical disorders (such as hyperactivity, antisocial or criminal behavior, depression, or academic failure) as being self-management disorders by definition, (3) that component skills probably do not function in isolation from each other, (4) that a higher order integrative ability must also be assumed, (5) that efficient use of component skills may be as important as the frequency of their use, and (6) that environmental contingencies are central to the support of cognitive and behavioral competencies.

Armed, now, with some fundamental beliefs and a conceptual roadmap that emphasizes four basic dimensions of self-management (see Figure 2), we can begin to collect interpretable data about children's performance problems. The assessment model employed must be sufficiently broad so as to include children's judgments, cognitions, and complex instrumental skills.

# FUNCTIONAL – COMPONENT – CRITERION ANALYSIS: AN ASSESSMENT MODEL

Such a hybrid term as *functional–component–criterion* should make it clear that the familiar functional analytic view of how best to describe clinical assessment is seen to be in need of supplementation. This is so because, as Meichenbaum (1976) has noted, in a strict behavioral account, cognitive processes are reduced to the status of behaviors embedded in a response chain (and thereby subject to the same laws, or principles, of learning as are overt motor acts) or are simply dismissed as epiphenomena. The interactional philosophy underlying the current model does not allow any dimension (the internal or the external) to be ruled secondary by fiat. In fact, mediational processes are typically a central concern of those interested in children's self-management.

## Functional Aspects

In almost every case a child's behavior problem will be considered within the scope of self-management psychology if the assessor suspects (1) that the client will be required either to change or to maintain goal-directed behavior largely free of external guidance or monitoring, (2) that cognitive mediation is either lacking or ineffective, and/or (3) that a cognitively oriented intervention could yield an efficient and durable solution to the problem. But, whereas these are the initial considerations that make self-management relevant as a clinical model, the ultimate utility of the viewpoint is an empirical question. The outcomes or products of personal mediation (effective and/or ineffective) are observable actions upon the environment (e.g., refusing fattening foods, cooperative play, and putting in the study time prior to a test, or overindulgence in between-meal snacks, stealing from other children, and refusal to complete homework assignments). In many instances, the efficient causes

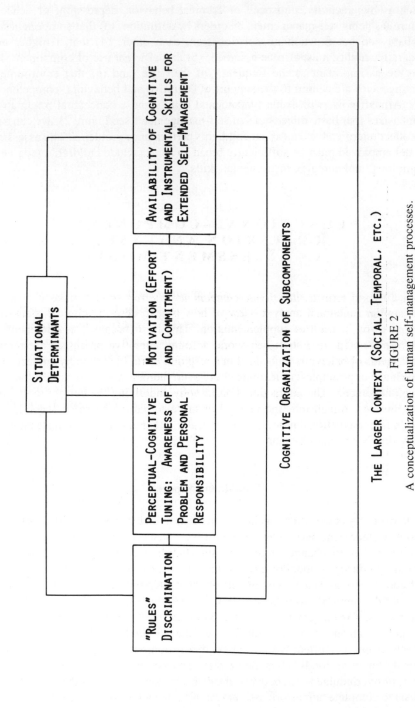

THE LARGER CONTEXT (SOCIAL, TEMPORAL, ETC.)

FIGURE 2

A conceptualization of human self-management processes.

of dysfunctional behavior are more readily identified in the immediate situation. It is incumbent upon the clinician to find the path of least resistance. Therefore, consider that, as a general rule, no problem is a self-management problem by definition.

The following fictionalized case might illustrate the issue best.

> Scott is 10 years old. He was referred to an outpatient clinic by a school psychologist. He is described as intelligent and resourceful. During the past three months he has been on temporary suspension from school because of two incidents, one, in which he broke into the school at night and vandalized some property, and another, in which he provoked a classmate into helping him set a fire in a broom closet. Reports from both teachers and parents suggest a history of minor rule infractions and some physical aggressiveness. Warnings and physical reprimands have had the effect of increasing disruptive behavior. Scott seems to react positively to being "challenged"—that is, "I'll bet you couldn't stop lighting matches even if you wanted to!" School authorities believe that he is too "disturbed" to be treated in school and have urged Scott's parents to consider sending the boy to a military academy, "where the discipline is tighter."

A number of characteristics of Scott's case would suggest interventions aimed at altering his style of managing himself in social settings. Particularly noteworthy are the apparent failures of externally managed remedial efforts and the relatively low frequency of the child's engagement in serious (attention-getting) episodes of misbehavior. The inculcation of problem-solving skills or prosocial values might well produce longer lasting results than punitive restrictions or harsh discipline. But before trumpeting "This looks like a job for self-control training!" and leaping to tall conclusions at a single bound, the active situational components must be considered more fully.

*Is the low-rate behavior a correlate of an identifiable high-rate behavior?* If Scott's serious delinquent acts (vandalism, fire setting) are occasionally coincidental to his more frequent tendency to become embroiled in verbal battles with his teachers, and if Scott could acknowledge that his acting out is an attempt to "get even," then an externally managed program designed to decrease arguments in class might, if successful, lead to a cessation of the infrequent but extreme delinquent behavior.

*Is the child acting in response to peer pressure or deviant models?* If so, then Scott may not be deficient in managing his behavior. Rather, he may be managing it in accordance with antisocial "demands" that are not readily apparent in the classroom context. Scott may likewise be more responsive to peer-controlled contingencies (both rewarding and punishing) than to adult-mediated outcomes.

*Is the deviant behavior a response to emotional disruption?* Scott may well be able to recognize the situational requirements as well as his own role in facilitating the unwanted behavior. He may also be capable of motivating himself to self-manage and may possess the requisite skills. However, his disruptive behavior may occur at times when sudden and extreme environmental or physiological changes act to momentarily interfere with rational problem solving. Identifying the stimuli or events that induce emotionality and eliminating them might be more efficient and effective than, say, a program of self-instructional training.

The reader is cautioned to keep in mind the larger environmental setting when dealing with problems that appear ill-suited to behavioral engineering approaches (cf. Karoly, 1975). Consider also the following statement (Bijou & Baer, 1978):

> If any of the critical responses or response-produced stimuli are not observable, application of the concept of self-management is *totally unprofitable and dangerous* in the sense of producing false knowledge. (p. 114, emphasis added)

Although such an assertion is inconsistent with every one of our metatheoretical commitments, it nonetheless warns of a very real possibility that clinicians face when approaching a child's problematic behavior from the mediational perspective, that is, the possibility of the dangers of weak inference, mentalistic thinking, and excursions down clinical blind alleys.

Ruling out some of the subtler environmental ingredients, the assessor may decide to consider employing a self-management model. However, a number of preliminary questions may yet be raised. Figure 3 provides a self-explanatory flowchart that should be of further assistance in the initial phases of self-management assessment.

## Component Analysis

If self-management theory is inadequate, then any measurement technology will likewise suffer. An adequate conceptualization can only assist the clinician by providing clues as to what to look for and why. Included among the specific components targeted for assessment in self-management programs have been such now familiar elements as the client's ability to detect and manipulate controlling stimuli in the environment, self-monitoring skills and habits, self-evaluative and standard-setting styles, self-reward and self-punishment propensities, attributional styles, problem-solving skills, the effectiveness of verbal self-instructions, information-processing and attentional abilities, and general intelligence (cf. Coates & Thoresen, 1979; Bellack & Schwartz, 1976; Kanfer, 1975; Karoly, 1977). The conceptual framework presented in the preceding section of this chapter (see Figure 2) may be most useful in organizing the assessment of the various mediational elements and in suggesting some untapped dimensions for careful analysis.

An appreciation for individual and developmental differences in component processes is essential to a complete clinical assessment. That the literature contains many examples of uniform, prescriptive intervention or measurement "packages" should not be taken too seriously by the clinician. Researchers tend to be more concerned with time constraints and publication pressures than is the average practitioner. Group treatment plans and statistical confidence limits are luxuries that most therapists can ill afford when confronted with a child in trouble with the law, school authorities, peers, or parents. The business of component analysis is slow and tedious, requiring clinical artistry as well as theoretical sophistication.

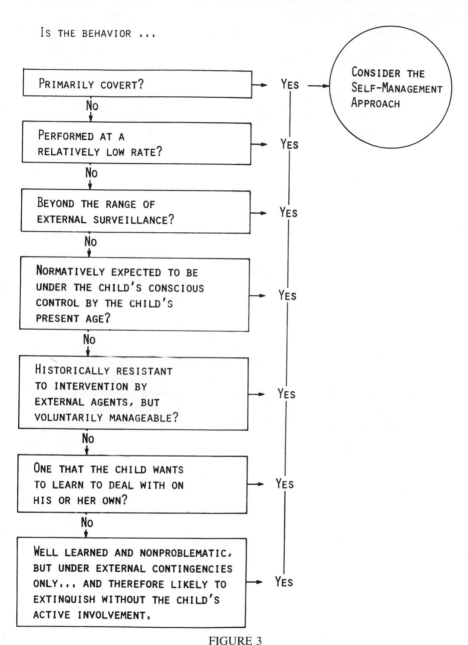

FIGURE 3

Questions guiding the decision to employ a self-management model.

The multicomponent model may, however, provide a rough guide as to the order in which self-management components should be assessed. Just as a tailor would not measure a person for a suit he did not want, the clinician should not embark upon a costly and time-consuming skills assessment (e.g., of self-monitoring, self-evaluative, or self-rewarding capacities) before determining whether the child perceives the relevance of self-management to his or her life. A telling criticism of the published work to date in self-control and self-regulation training is the possibility that investigators may have provided children with clothes they will not likely wear outside the treatment context (Tirrell & Scott, Note 2).

Thus, clinicians are advised to begin by gauging children's metamanagement,[1] which includes not only their knowledge about the situation-specific rules and their awareness of the short- and long-term consequences of their current behavior patterns but their understanding of what motivates them and how they can set about putting their various self-mastery skills into operation (see section on four-factor theory). Metamanagement deficiencies, once identified, can be addressed through didactic means, probably using less time and resources than would be necessary to motivate children effectively or to build a cognitive and/or instrumental skill repertoire. Indeed, self-management training efforts should always be guided by the principles of least intervention and program simplicity (cf. Hall, 1980). Of course, if deficits are not found in the cognitive–perceptual arena, the assessor would move on to a multifaceted examination of incentives and behavioral competencies (see section on methods and assessment targets, later in this chapter).

## Criterion Analysis

The objective, or functional, approach to behavior assessment is insufficiently dynamic. By this I do not mean that it is open to criticism because it fails to acknowledge the contribution of unconscious determinants. Rather, the S-R model does not easily accommodate the tenets of reciprocal determinism or temporal–contextual relativity. The functional view is not dynamic in the sense that Cattell's (1977; 1980) structured learning analysis is dynamic. That is, Cattell acknowledges that an adjustment problem does not exist in a situational or behavioral vacuum. Goals change (triggered by physiologic and cognitive changes), as do environmental demands. Problems of adjustment (including self-management) occur when environmental outlets and fluctuating human needs (wants, drives, values) come into conflict. The standard or criterion for "healthy" or "desirable" behavior is not static, absolute, or tied to a universal or recurring set of antecedent stimuli. Whenever a behavior is labeled "excessive" or "deficient" as regards

---

[1]This term is patterned after Flavell's (1977) concept of *metamemory*, which refers to children's knowledge about memory. Similar derivations are Litrownik & Steinfeld's (in press) use of the term *metacontrol*, Walter Mischel's studies in the development of children's knowledge about self-control (Mischel, Mischel, & Hood, Note 3; Mischel, Mischel, & Hood, Note 4), and Meichenbaum and Asarnow's (1979) discussion of metacognitive development and its implications for cognitive–behavioral interventions in classroom settings.

self-management, it is important to remember that judgments of appropriateness are often subjective, always relative (i.e., meaningful only in context), and should be outcome, as opposed to process, oriented.

One of the most blatant examples of inadequate criterion analysis involves the diagnosis of cognitive and/or behavioral impulsivity in children. Fast reaction times and a tendency toward immediate consumption of rewards are often automatically judged to be maladaptive. But can we not always ask "How fast is too fast?" or "Is slower always better?"

Data exist suggesting that in certain settings involving different ethnic groups, fast responders and nondelayers may be the more successful children (Mischel, 1974; Price-Williams & Ramirez, 1974). It seems that the widespread focus among parents, educators, physicians, and clinicians upon the form of children's behavior, instead of upon their relative achievements, reflects premature standard setting rather than fair, pragmatic, and product-oriented appraisals of changing situational requirements (cf. Gilbert, 1978).

Basically, then, the criterion, or task analysis, approach supplements the functional analysis of the immediate causes of maladaptive behavior and the component analysis of potential mediational links by focussing on what the child should be doing and/or thinking in order to succeed at a particular self-management task. Determining that a child is an inaccurate self-monitor, that the child sets high minimal goal levels, or that he or she is sometimes deficient at "means–ends thinking" does not provide sufficient information for the design of a clinical intervention. Note (following Belmont & Butterfield, 1977) (1) that mediational strategies do not operate equivalently across tasks or problem areas, (2) that different means can often bring about the same desired ends, and (3) that there are variations within children as to the methods selected to cope with changing situational demands.

Models for criterion analyses come from several sources, including education, industrial psychology, personnel selection, human factors engineering, and the clinical-personality area (cf. Belmont & Butterfield, 1977; Gilbert, 1978; Goldfried & D'Zurilla, 1969; Gottman & Markman, 1978; Livingston, 1977; Stern, Stein, & Bloom, 1956; White, 1977). Most investigators agree that a performance standard should not derive exclusively from theory or armchair speculation. As White (1977) notes, "a criterion-referenced assessment is one in which the child's performance is compared against the level of performance required to be 'successful' in a task" (p. 351).

The key question is, of course, how to identify success (or to derive the criterion of optimal performance). The metatheoretical commitments dictate that assessors must examine the transaction of person and environment, consider the shared expectancies of the child and significant adults (parents and teachers), and observe performance over meaningful periods. Procedurally, assessors may apply the analytic method (Stern, Stein, & Bloom, 1956), or what is currently called the behavioral–analytic model (Goldfried & D'Zurilla, 1969). The steps or stages in such an assessment generally include (1) situational analysis—determining the critical self-control or self-regulation problems for the child (from the perspective of the child and significant others), (2) response enumeration—determining the potential behavior sequences and mediational strategies in each of the problem contexts, and (3) response evaluation—determining the actual (not the theoretical) effective responses in each situation. Proficiency and motivation are expected to change over time and across settings. Thus, there is no need to seek to establish absolute cut-off points for dichotomizing children into self-managers versus non-self-managers (although such a division might be useful for some research purposes).

## COMMON ASSESSMENT PURPOSES

To a large extent, clinical assessment in self-management has taken a back seat to research-oriented measurement (Karoly, 1977). That is, there have been relatively fewer applied studies of self-control and self-regulation as compared with laboratory-based investigations, whereas many of the published clinical studies have "raided" the analogue domain for treatment foci and outcome indexes. Thorough, integrated, multidimensional preintervention assessments are unfortunately the exception. The rule seems to be the use of convenient measures to tap the investigator's pet facet of self-management (e.g., self-reinforcement rate, delay preference, transgression latency) with little apparent concern for the relationship of that facet to criterial performance.

Among the potentially important general questions with which the clinical self-management assessor might be concerned are the following:

1. Would a self-management treatment model be applicable in this case (see section on functional aspects)?
2. Has the child's overt behavioral disturbance ever been conceptualized within a self-management framework? Is there an attendant literature on measurement techniques and/or treatment effects?
3. Would a set of interventions that are self-management oriented contribute to the maintenance of adaptive learning or to the prevention of future dysfunction?
4. Is a self-mediated form of treatment particularly warranted on ethical grounds?
5. How much of an investment does the child have in changing a high probability response pattern?
6. Does the assessor have access to data on the child's day-to-day transactions with significant others in important settings (school, home) over extended periods (for purposes of diagnosis, treatment, and outcome evaluation)?
7. Is it possible to identify the primary cause(s) of the child's failure to achieve criterial performance by systematically ruling out the role of (a) knowledge deficiencies, (b) developmental or biologic incapacities, (c) motivational insufficiencies, (d) skills deficits, or (e) nonfacilitative environments?

# METHODS AND TARGETS OF ASSESSMENT

Considered thus far have been why a self-management approach might be useful, what broad aspects of thought and behavior to assess, and, generally, how a systematic assault on the clinical problems of children might be orchestrated. The next step is to consider the techniques for accomplishing varied assessment purposes and the specific psychological processes an assessor might seek to elucidate. The remaining remarks will be confined to the component and criterion forms of assessment, as the functional approach is aptly illustrated elsewhere in this volume.

### Situation-Specific Self-Report via Clinical Interview

Often maligned and generally ignored, the behavioral interview is still an indispensable avenue for discovering and pinpointing treatment objectives and for gauging the feasibility of various modes of intervention (Ciminero & Drabman, 1977; Linehan, 1977; Morganstern, 1976). It is particularly important in self-management assessment to gather information about the child's level of problem awareness and metacognitions; his or her beliefs, goals, and intentions; and the degree of match or mismatch between the child and important adults with regard to the problem formulation.

Typically, when one is interviewing a youngster for the first time, a referral problem has already been identified—by an adult. The child may be too boisterous in class, a fire setter, 50 pounds overweight with "no self-control whatever", or unable to keep up in school despite an IQ of 134. Adult reports are vital in providing a picture of the expected behaviors of, or the environmental demands upon, the child. In deriving a criterion for a particular child in a specific context, the assessor should try to determine how realistic the adult expectations are:

1. Is the expected behavior readily observable in the majority of the child's peers?
2. How many informants agree on the problematic nature of the child's behavior?
3. Does the target child have a "reputation"? If so, are adults reporting what they have actually seen or only what they have heard?
4. Are there contexts in which the child's "problem" behavior(s) may be considered appropriate or actually or potentially rewarding (positively or negatively)?

In the examination of the self-reports of young children, a popular concern centers on their accuracy. Inaccuracy is typically defined as "discrepant from adult reports," and such discrepancy is equated with dishonesty or an absence of insight. The tendency to dismiss, indeed, to avoid obtaining, children's reports is an unfortunate consequence, which our personal mediation metatheory should help to guard against. As noted previously, it may be more clinically efficacious to seek to bring children's perceptions in line with situational requirements than to assume a skill deficiency and then to engage in an ill-fitting treatment program.

### Recounting an Episode of Misbehavior

An excellent data-gathering procedure is to recount with a puzzled attitude the vague details of an episode of misbehavior and to seek clarification from the child. For example:

> T: Your teacher tells me that yesterday a bunch of kids in your class "went wild" with paints, throwing them around the room and at other kids.
> C: Yeah.
> T: That really happened?
> C: Yeah. So?
> T: I guess the teacher just doesn't know how to handle kids.
> C: She's okay.
> T: Then what happened?
> C: The kids were bored.
> T: Were you bored?
> C: Yeah, I guess.
> T: Did you enjoy throwing the paints?
> C: What do you mean?
> T: Was it a way to be less bored?
> C: Sure . . . for awhile.
> T: Then what happened?
> C: We had to clean the place up. It took all afternoon.
> T: Did you think you would have to clean up?
> C: I don't know.
> T: Was it unfair for her to make you clean up?
> C: The janitor should do it.
> T: But the kids made the mess.
> C: Mrs. Masters [the teacher] is supposed to give us stuff to do.

From this fragment of an interview, information can be obtained that an observer in the classroom probably would not have garnered, that an informed adult might not have been able to supply, and that a standardized children's self-report inventory would surely overlook. For example, it may be concluded (in the context of other corroborative evidence, it is hoped) that the child's understanding of classroom convention includes the view that the teacher is responsible for keeping the pupils occupied at all times. It seems that the child's previous teacher did just that, and the child merely presumed that these rules still applied. The teacher, for her part, was of the opinion that her pupils should be able to busy themselves at their desks for periods of up to an hour without her supervision. Although it may be possible to show that the child tends to overestimate the passage of time and tends not to think too far into the future, the clinical resolution of the self-management problem in this case could be instituted (1) by explaining to the child that he or she should be able to work without teacher structuring and approval for brief periods and (2) by suggesting to the teacher that her pupils might be allowed to leave their desks and go to a play area after their work is completed. (Recall that the self-management problem is not in the child but in the time-limited transaction between the child and the environment.)

### Use of Fictitious Stories

Recently, Mischel and his colleagues have been exploring some of the determinants of young children's understanding of effective strategies for delay of gratification (Mischel *et al.*, Notes 3 and 4). Children, presented with a brief story about a child of the same sex having to wait for a preferred, but delayed, reward, are required to choose between alternative strategies (of which some have been empirically shown to be more effective in laboratory-based delay situations). The use of fictitious stories to assess children's general problem solving, analytic, imaginal, self-evaluational, information storage and retrieval, or rule-following skills has also been suggested by a number of cognitively oriented investigators (Coates & Thoresen, 1979; Meichenbaum, 1976, 1977; Spivack, Platt, & Shure, 1976).

For purposes of clinical assessment, it would be advisable to construct stories about problem situations similar to those in which the referred child has been involved. The assessor should ask questions about what the child might be feeling as well as thinking. Interviews with children (peers) who have not evidenced adjustment difficulties in the situations depicted might also be conducted to provide a rough comparison, or "norm." Children's narratives might be tape-recorded so that not only the content, but the sequence, of thoughts and images can be examined (as recommended by Meichenbaum, 1976, 1977, 1979). Finally, the inquiry should not be confined to questions about children's preferences for self-control or self-regulatory tactics or strategies. Note that the use of skills for extended self-management is the last of the components suggested by the model presented previously.

Consider a child of 8 years who has been referred because of his "raging temper," his tendency toward physical aggression, and his general lack of cooperation with teachers. A note on his report card reads "Out of control most of the day. Extremely immature." The assessor might draft and read to the child a story such as this one:

> This is a story about 8-year-old Johnny. He goes to public school. Johnny wants Billy's skateboard, so he decides to push Billy off the board and take it. He pushes Billy off. The other kids in the schoolyard laugh. Billy gets up and says "Gimme my skateboard." Johnny punches Billy in the eye and keeps the skateboard.

Although the assessor would certainly wish to determine if the client could spontaneously produce or identify a strategy for avoiding a fight, he or she should first ascertain the child's perceptions regarding the desirability of so doing (e.g., What is Johnny supposed to do if he wants Billy's skateboard? What do you think is the best thing to do? Does Johnny have a problem? If so, what is it?). Similarly, the child's perception of the possibly conflicting short- and long-term consequences of impulsive actions can be ascertained (e.g., What does Johnny feel like after he takes the skateboard? What will Johnny feel like tomorrow when he sees Billy again?).

Finally, the assessor would need to investigate the child's understanding of the motives for exercising self-restraint (e.g., Can you think of any reason(s) why Johnny might *not* want to push Billy and take his skateboard, even though he really really wants a skateboard?). It would be worth knowing whether a child's sole motivation centered on avoiding punishment or was based upon a recognition of standards of social conduct. I would predict limited extratherapy use of a specific self-control strategy (such as inhibitory self-verbalizations) by a child who is motivated to comply out of fear of external punishment, especially if that child were convinced that transgression could go undetected. A thorough assessment of children's multiple cognitions about self-management, on the other hand, might lead to a sequential treatment, where alterations in self-evaluative habits could be targeted prior to whatever behavioral skills training were required.

### Dialoguing

The distinction between treatment and assessment may often become blurred, as the adult's inquiries tend to stimulate children to think in newer and perhaps more productive ways. The methods here suggested for assessing children's metacognitions about self-management closely resemble the technique of problem-solving training that Shure and Spivack (1978) term *dialoguing*. Dialoguing refers to the process of drawing out the child's thoughts about a particular problem. Shure and Spivack (1978) offer eight basic dialoguing principles, which include nonaccusatory questioning, the use of a matter-of-fact tone, and the process of guiding a child to evaluate the quality of his or her point of view or proposed solution to a problem.

### Interviews with Relevant Adults

Real and hypothetical child problem situations might also be presented to relevant adults (parents and teachers usually) in order to obtain information about their role in formulating, clarifying, and enforcing rules, in providing modeling cues for standard setting and for the sequential enactment of complex self-managing behaviors, and in generally providing a facilitative/nonfacilitative environment for the child's display of self-management. Adults will also play a prominent role in treatment programs; it is essential that assessors probe, in the interview, the possible reinforcing consequences for the adult involved in the child's behavior problem. It is not uncommon for parents with socially inept, fearful, or dependent children who seek self-regulatory training (e.g., "To make my child more self-sufficient") to be deriving some personal source of fulfillment from "being needed." For example:

T: How would your life change if Anne could be taught to dress herself, get herself ready for school, and work on her models without your constant supervision?

M: Oh, I'd have more time for myself. I've got a life too.

T: Of course. Can you tell me how you'll be spending your free time?

M: I haven't thought about it really. (*Pause*) I don't think Anne can get along without me.

As arbitrary as the process may be, the fact remains that adults are frequently the "creators" of children's self-management dilemmas by virtue of their establishing the task demands and by withdrawing (to varying degrees) their explicit guidance. Therefore, from both a theoretical and practical standpoint, it behooves the clinical investigator to assess the processes by which parents and teachers categorize and label the tasks of childhood (cf. also Meichenbaum, 1979).

### Performance Tests and Simulations

Determining the proficiency level of self-management skills potentially in need of upgrading is best accomplished by means of performance tests—naturalistic and/or simulated. However, do not be misled by the term *performance* into assuming that only countable motor acts are relevant here. When assessing the effectiveness of instrumental skills under changing environmental circumstances, the assessor should focus with equal vigor upon the mediational underpinnings of self-management. The important point to bear in mind is that assessors need to know not only the way children conceptualize their problems—what they think about self-management (their attitudes and perceptions)—but also how they think and feel about self-management *in vivo* and how their "executive functions" link to specific behavioral outcomes. A discussion of the cognitive mechanisms hypothesized to underlie competent self-management is beyond the scope of a single chapter. Similarly, a range of determinants has been suggested that extends and blurs the boundaries of the four-factor model herein presented. At this stage in our knowledge, we welcome the fact that no single test battery is yet available that supposedly taps the components of children's self-management. However, to familiarize the reader with the potential mediational links in children's self-control and self-regulatory performances, Table 1 is presented, containing a summary of the components suggested by investigators in the cognitive social learning domain.

It should not be surprising that no single investigation has (or is likely to) include all of the elements listed in Table 1 as part of its assessment package. At this time, few hints can be offered with respect to narrowing the dysfunctional components to specific clinical disorders. Over the years, the popularity of various components has been affected primarily by the availability of measuring instruments and the salesmanship of conceptual advocates. Starting out with a self-instructional, problem-solving, or conceptual-tempo view of hyperactivity, aggression, retardation, and so forth, researchers have had no trouble in showing that each of these disorders is characterized (to some degree) by deficiencies in self-instructional control, problem solving, and/or performance on Kagan's (1966) *Matching Familiar*

TABLE 1

Hypothesized Components of Self-Management According to Contemporary Social-Learning Models

---

*Awareness (content-specific) and metacognitive factors[a]*
Knowledge of general role requirements
Knowledge of situation-specific rules and sanctions
Awareness of one's own motives and goals
Awareness of the conflictful nature of the short- and long-term consequences of one's behavior and the need for change (a self-control metacognition)
Awareness of the need for self-determination of standards and self-administration of incentives (a self-regulatory metacognition)
Awareness of the need to employ specific self-management strategies and knowledge of their content

*Motivational factors[b]*
Task-specific success/failure expectancies
Performance and self-efficacy attributions
Task perception units (e.g., goals and intentions viewed as temporally extended or as short-term operants)
Nature of self-evaluative dimensions
Leniency/stringency of self-evaluative standards
Consistency of self-application of consequences
Type of self-administered reward/punishment (e.g., symbolic–tangible, contingent– noncontingent)
Social comparison (reference or "norm" group against which performance is compared)
Affective arousal as a function of performance feedback

*Attentional skills[c]*
Efficiency of scanning/listening
Sustained focal attention versus distractibility
Selective attention to external and/or internal cues
Generalized alertness

*Information-processing skills[c]*
Storage and retrieval of task-relevant and background information
Labeling
Accuracy of time estimation
Accuracy of event sequencing
Information organization

*Problem-solving skills[c]*
Problem identification (also a metacognitive factor)
Alternative solution generation
Knowledge of effective self-management strategies
Means–ends thinking
Foresight
Decision making
Sequential planning
Role-taking and role-playing ability
Hypothesis testing and appraisal

*Verbal skills[c]*
Self-instructional control over attention, listening, and motor responding
Overt and covert verbal control over response latency and decision time
Verbal self-distraction

TABLE 1 *(continued)*

Verbal control over emotional reactivity (e.g., inhibition of anger, aggression, or anxiety)
Adequacy of self-expression (interpersonal communication)

*Cognitive–imaginal competencies[c]*
Symbolic representation
Concept formation/abstraction/inference
Memory (storage capacity)
Comprehension
Categorization
Discriminated self-observation (self-monitoring)
Organization and rehearsal of complex thought/behavior sequences
Formation and control of imagery

*Instrumental competencies[c]*
Physical coordination (gross and fine)
Sensorimotor capacities
Visual–motor abilities
Endurance and discomfort tolerance
Observational skills
Vocational skills

[a]Components related to the first two factors of the four-factor model.
[b]Components related to the third factor of the model.
[c]Components related to the fourth factor of the model.

*Figures Test* (MFFT). It is possible that the clinical disorders of children may be more aptly differentiated on the basis of how the various components coordinate (or miscoordinate) rather than on the basis of a specific component dysfunction.

The term *undifferentiated performance measures* of self-control and self-regulation (Karoly, 1977) refers to extended tests that require the child to achieve a discernible goal, such as altering the probability of approaching a tempting goal in order to avoid a long-range loss of reward (delay of gratification). During the repeated performance of such a task, children's motor behaviors can be observed while their strategic responses can be ascertained observationally, by requiring them to think out loud, and through a posttest interview. The assessor is also advised to alter systematically the demands of the task and the instructions and to note children's adaptive reactions.

Meichenbaum (1976) suggests three types of deliberate manipulation that may be useful in what he calls a "cognitive–functional" assessment. The first involves altering the psychological task demands, such as by instituting a speed (or slowness) requirement or a time boundary, by changing the stimulus display (its nature, rate of presentation, etc.), by increasing the external pressure to deviate (from a self-control course) via adult or peer pressure, or by preventing certain cognitive strategies from operating (having the child count backward aloud to prevent rehearsal or covert self-instruction). As Meichenbaum (1976) has stated:

> Through this approach one can assess both the client's capabilities as well as his deficits, under which task parameters the client is able to demonstrate competence, and under which conditions the client's performance begins to deteriorate. (p. 164)

Changing environmental features not directly linked to the self-management task—such as the sex of the assessor (the instruction giver), the nature of distracting stimuli in the environment, or the quality of the adult–child interaction prior to task presentation—can also facilitate the determination of skill dysfunctions.

Third, the cognitive–functional approach would suggest the use of specific task and instructional aides to gauge the child's ability to profit from structuring and to pinpoint areas of strength and/or weakness. The assessor can insert aides to attention, information processing, memory, problem analysis and solution, verbal self-direction, and so forth (see Table 1), and measure their effects on task performance.

A particularly apt performance test approach to the assessment of children's orientation toward self-management-relevant rules is to examine (via observation and interview) the manner in which children instruct other children and how they enforce the rules in control or regulation-type tasks (cf. Parke, 1974). Similarly, a mixed interview–performance test approach to the analysis of children's meta-cognitions, attitudes, expectancies, and so forth, is possible by videotaping the behaviors of one child in a self-managment setting and displaying the tape to another child who is asked to explain and interpret what is seen and to predict the outcome(s).

A more economical approach to assessment, one that is important in the design of clinical intervention, if not in diagnosis, and one that is useful when information exists to suggest a specific form of dysfunction, is the examination of component skills via interview and performance tests. Because assessment is directed not only at pinpointing targets for training but also at determining what aspects of a preexisting training program stand the best chance of being consistently self-applied, it will often be necessary to arrange practice periods wherein specific self-management skills are scrutinized.

Can the child accurately self-observe or keep records of his or her own performance? What is the nature of self-observational distortions? The assessor must have detailed information about self-monitoring abilities and habits not just for treatment design and planning, but for evaluating therapeutic outcome (cf. Bellack & Schwartz, 1976; Ciminero, Nelson, & Lipinski, 1977). It is during the preintervention assessment phase that clinicians will determine whether to have children use simple mechanical counting devices to gather data or to trust that children can keep more detailed records (diaries, data cards).

Habits of self-evaluation and self-administered praise and/or criticism (reward/punishment) are considered by social learning theorists to be central components of self-management (Bandura, 1969; Kanfer, 1970; Thoresen & Mahoney, 1974). Yet these aspects may go undetected in interview or performance test assessments unless the assessor is expressly looking for them. Because knowledge of these procedures comes primarily from clinical work and laboratory studies of adults and from narrow-band experimental studies of children (cf. Masters & Mokros, 1974), their explicit assessment with individual children should be rather detailed and open-ended. Assessors might ask children to tell them, subsequent to a self-management task, whether they succeeded or failed, how they know when they succeed or fail, how they feel inside, what they think about after a success or failure experience, whether there are certain times when they like themselves better than at other times, and whether they can point to specific actions or personal characteristics as being central to their feeling of success or failure (see also the listing of motivational factors in Table 1).

Certainly, during the conducting of an interview, in combination with performance tests, the assessor can delve into the hypothetical components of self-management, such as are listed in Table 1. However, it is very easy to get into the bad habit of asking leading questions and then presuming that data have been produced about children's representative modes of mediating self-management. For example, an assessor might ask a child, "Did you like what you did?" After an affirmative reply, the question could be followed up with "Do you think you deserve a prize or a reward?" Obtaining two affirmative answers, the assessor might be prompted to infer that the particular child will spontaneously engage in self-reward following task performance. There are many times, however, when children do not do what they are capable of doing. One obtains a healthy respect for individual and developmental differences in skills and motives when conducting mini-experiments focusing on children's component abilities.

### Self-Evaluation

Among the most critical and least understood of components, and one deserving of special mention, is the self-evaluation dimension. Suppose a clinician who has discovered no peculiarity in a child's self-reinforcement propensities decides to "train" the child in self-reinforcement because it is felt that self-reward will help maintain the other self-management skills newly acquired in treatment. The child, who was capable of self-administering tangible rewards in a laboratory game, may be less than adequate as a supplier of contingent self-congratulation during real-life performances. Why?

One avenue of explanation is that the child's natural mode of self-evaluation may be tied to personal characteristics unlike those simulated during the assessment period. There are also some data to suggest that, with age, individuals employ more differentiated categories for self-appraisal (Mullener & Laird, 1971). Similarly, it might be hypothesized that tasks themselves differ on the complexity of self-impressions required to yield masterful performance. Consider whether you could master tennis if all you evaluated was how hard you hit the ball, or how well you looked in your tennis shorts? If assessments of children's self-evaluations are limited to the good–bad or fast–slow dimensions (as has been the case in much of the published research), we could be collecting reliable information about irrelevant mediators. The assessor is advised to perform all tasks required of the child and to examine his or her own processes of problem appraisal and self-evaluation as one means of determining the evaluative dimensions of the task.

### Linguistic or Verbal Self-Instructional Control

A second theoretically compelling component of self-management also deserving special attention is the dimension of language and the verbal self-instructional control of behavior. What makes this aspect of self-guidance noteworthy is the widespread belief that language development influences not only the communication competencies of children but also their conceptual and problem-solving competencies. Thus, language is more than a component skill; it is a potential mediator of each of the hypothesized components of self-direction listed in Table 1.

Over the years, research has been conducted linking linguistic or verbal mediators to the tasks of attention (Douglas, 1972; Pick, Christy, & Frankel, 1972), time perception (Blank, 1974), concept learning (McKaughan, 1974), memory (Asarnow, Note 5), the control of motor responding (Luria, 1961; Meichenbaum, 1977; Wozniak, 1972), the control of aggression (Camp, Blom, Hebert, & Van Doorninck, 1977; Parke, Ewall, & Slaby, 1972), and the various processes involved in effective problem solving (Gagne & Briggs, 1974; Meichenbaum & Asarnow, 1979). Thus, the assessor is advised to pay particular attention not only to the content of children's verbalizations (as they think out loud in the course of a self-management behavior test) but also to the relationship between children's speech and the various ingredients of competent performance. That is, can the child effectively use self-presented, overt speech cues to guide his or her visual search of the environment, the initiation and cessation of action, the inhibition of initial and continued approach to a tempting stimulus, the appraisal of relevant and irrelevant task information, and the formulation of self-management plans or strategies and/or to self-administer meaningful incentives (i.e., self-reward and self-punishment)?

By virtue of its ease of administration and the hypothesized relationship between children's performances and various forms of adjustment difficulty, Kagan's *Matching Familiar Figures Test* (MFFT) (Kagan, Rosman, Day, Albert, & Phillips, 1964) may be employed as an analogue verbal control device that simulates the demands of a problem-solving situation. The instrument is a 12-item, matching-to-sample test, wherein the child's latency in selecting a pictorial match and the correctness of the choice can be viewed as reflecting "typical" styles of information search (search-and-scan behavior) and decision making under conditions of uncertainty (the general style being called "conceptual tempo"). Although the MFFT is often used to support a questionable typological differentiation between children (such as "reflective" vs. "impulsive"), children's test performance (in group studies, of course) seems to correlate with a number of self-management-relevant dimensions, such as classroom adjustment (Glenwick, Barocas, & Burka, 1976; Kendall & Wilcox, Note 6) and response inhibition and discrimination learning (Stein & Prindaville, 1976). Scores also relate to the clinical syndromes of hyperactivity and learning disability (Messer, 1976), as well as to various non-conceptual-tempo measures of self-control such as delay choice and resistance to temptation (Toner, Holstein, & Hetherington, 1977).

Children's performance on the MFFT appears to be influenced to varying degrees by factors such as age, sex, IQ, the nature of the task instructions, and other person and setting dimensions. In some instances the error score is predictive of real-life measures; in some cases, the latency score is more useful as a correlate. Thus, there is little reason to view the test as a measure of a cross-situational, unitary trait. Rather, where performance on the test can be shown (not assumed) to vary with performance on some criterial self-management performance dimension (a real-life self-control or self-regulation situation), then the assessor may find the test an economical tool for efficiently assessing the child's ability to use verbal cues to mediate conceptual tempo and for evaluating the effects of a clinical intervention (cf. Kendall & Finch, 1979), particularly one involving verbal self-instructional elements.

The Porteus Mazes may also serve as a handy procedure for exploring children's verbal control over motor behavior—before, during, and after treatment. Other devices (more complex and expensive than the Porteus or Kagan tests) that have been used to gauge verbal self-management competencies are described by Schubert (Note 7) and Litrownik (Note 8).

## Self-Monitoring—Children's Recordkeeping

Mischel (1978) has suggested that one of the key tasks of the psychologist working with troubled persons is to help them discover ways of ordering their lives based upon their own unique experiences. Such a *person-centered functional analysis* is offered in opposition to the more familiar tactic of convincing clients (subtly to be sure) to adopt the clinician's view of the world. If children are typically more malleable than adults, then a person-centered assessment–treatment model is even more vital in clinical work with youngsters. Self-monitoring, or child-centered recordkeeping, represents one means of collecting information about a child that is founded neither upon theory-derived measurement operations nor upon unrealistic normative standards, but upon the day-to-day interactions of the youngster and his or her changing external environments.

Skillful self-monitoring cannot be assumed, and deficiencies in the child's attentional repertoire (ability to discriminate internal responses and stimulus–behavior–outcome sequences) may well be a determinant of self-management failure (cf. Kanfer & Grimm, 1977). Where performance test data reflect inaccuracies in self-observation or self-recording, explicit feedback and training should be instituted. For example, Mahoney and Thoresen (1974) have suggested a period of external surveillance of a relatively discrete behavior, along with requiring the child to self-monitor. Feedback, prompting, modeling, and contingent reward for accuracy (or punishment for inaccuracy) can enhance the correspondence of the child's report with that of an objective observer (cf. Lyman, Rickard, & Elder, 1975; Risley & Hart, 1968).

Of course, reliable self-monitoring of an overt behavior may not predict similar accuracy with regard to a covert response, particularly if the internal reaction is socially undesirable and a source of displeasure or embarrassment to the child. Children may need to be taught to monitor first the neutral covert events with which an observable product is associated. (For example, the correct solution of a mathematical problem without the use of paper and pencil is a product that can reasonably be associated with certain monitorable mental operations.)

Among the important considerations to bear in mind when seeking accurate self-monitored records from children is (1) whether the children want to provide such information to the adult assessor and (2) whether the form of data collection is appropriate to the task. Clues to motivational concomitants of inaccurate self-observation may derive from the semistructured interview. The child may display uncharacteristic naïveté, forgetfulness, silliness, or distractibility when asked to recall instances of "misbehavior." On performance tests requiring self-monitoring, the child may display variability in instruction following, dependent upon the presence or absence of adult observers. Also, children may give evidence of conformity to self-monitoring instructions only when an instance of a positive (desirable) behavior is the proposed target. Motivational barriers may be overcome by discussion with the child aimed at minimizing the potential for punitive use of the self-collected information ("No, I won't show the numbers to anyone else. They might not understand anyway."). In addition, the assessor may wish to phrase his or her request for records of target behaviors (like urges to light a match) in the form of requests for records of an associated (dependent), but neutral, response (e.g., ask the child to record each time he or she thinks "Where can I find some matches?").

Second, the inappropriateness of the method of self-monitoring may reduce accuracy even when children are willing and able (under better conditions) to self-observe and self-record. Mahoney (1977) has suggested that the choice of a self-monitoring instrument be guided by considerations of simplicity of operation, reliability, and compatibility with the nature of the response to be assessed. For example, with a high-frequency "negative" behavior (e.g., self-critical thoughts in a teenager maintaining a low social profile in his or her high school), the use of frequency-counting devices (like wrist counters or hand-held tallying machines) may be embarrassing, intrusive, and reactive. A spot-check method, whereby data are recorded in an all-or-none fashion at a convenient time and place, might yield more useful and accurate information in such instances (Nelson, 1977). Diaries may be most effective with complex monitoring tasks, whereas simple, easy-to-carry cumulative counters might be best for young children monitoring relatively discrete activities of moderate frequency.

The assessor should not lose sight of the need for clinical importance in the behavior (overt or covert) to be monitored. As pointed out earlier, the preintervention interviews and performance tests should produce sufficient information to help the assessor pinpoint excesses or deficiencies in the components of self-management. Whereas the accuracy and reactivity aspects of the self-monitoring process have been given appropriately wide attention, comparatively less stress has fallen on the systematic determination of the most meaningful or representative target for self-observation.

Once again, the analogue studies have been minimally helpful. Frequently the *what* of self-monitoring is of secondary concern and is chosen primarily as a function of convenience. Despite the general commitment to reciprocal determinism and the importance of the adult–child interaction, few clinicians have asked children to record the "parental antedecent–internal reaction–parental response" sequence across various settings. Yet, in many cases, it is this sort of key information that the assessor will be unable to obtain through indirect, and even through direct, observational means. Mahoney (1977), in discussing the *what* of self-monitoring, likewise cautions against premature closure in deciding on the target(s) of self-observation:

> If [assessors] find *one* variable which seems to correlate with the target behavior, they eagerly conclude that they have found *the* culprit variable. . . . [Therefore] don't handicap your own effectiveness by refusing to attend to supplementary input. . . . In most of the self-monitoring forms I employ, there is an open-ended column for client comments. (p. 251)

Mahoney's recommendations would appear as valid when applied to the process of children's recordkeeping as they are in the case of adult self-assessment.

### Ratings by Peers, Parents, Teachers, and Other Observers

A danger in conducting a largely cognitively oriented assessment program is the tendency to become absorbed in the measurement of mediational processes, sometimes to the exclusion of the behavioral manifestations they are presumed to influence. The contemporaneous assessment of the overt behavioral evidence for self-management deficiencies or excesses (along with the analysis of hypothesized components) should keep assessors attuned to the ultimate products and objectives of their inquiry and, it is hoped, prevent them from getting lost in the kinds of conjecture that have hampered traditional (nonbehavioral) forms of assessment. Both the starting point and finishing line for any clinical measurement operation must be represented by the collection of overt behavior samples (recall the second assumption made on page 87).

From a reality standpoint, assessors usually begin their work with observers' reports of the occurrence of "misbehavior." The difference between the present cognitively based system of assessment and strict *S-R* conceptions is the belief that assessors cannot end their analysis with exclusively overt measurements (recall the discussion of personal mediation previously in this chapter). The "truth" of self-management disorders is, however, not dictated by theory, but rather by observations of children acting upon the real world, who thereby signal us as to what behaviors to be concerned about, when, where, and in relation to what other behaviors in their repertoire (cf. Cone, 1978, Note 9).

Also from a practical standpoint, the assessment of clinical success/failure and the determination of therapeutic maintenance, generalization, and transfer require multiple measurements over multiple settings by members of the child's natural community. The use of behavior ratings by significant members of the target child's extratherapy world is largely a practice that has been ignored in both research and clinical intervention.

For example, in one of the best experimental studies to date on the effects of a cognitively oriented treatment program on hyperactivity (a common self-regulatory problem), the research team (Douglas, Parry, Marton, & Garson, 1976) included only one observational rating of naturalistic (in this case, classroom) behavior—the Conners (1969) short-form (10-item) rating scale for parent and teacher reports of behaviors associated with hyperactivity. In general, the observational data that are collected in clinic or classroom-based self-management studies focus on the target responses but do not bear directly on the children's actual use of the "trained" self-management skills (Rosenbaum & Drabman, 1979).

Recently, Kendall and Wilcox (Note 6) developed a self-control rating scale (SCRS) for use by classroom teachers. The scale contains 10 items descriptive of what I would label self-management skills (reflecting both self-regulatory and self-control behaviors), 13 items indicative of impulsivity, and 10 items allowing the rater to choose between an impulsive or a self-managing alternative. Kendall and Wilcox administered their rating scale to teachers of 110 third- through sixth-grade children. In addition, children were tested or observed in order to assess intelligence, delay-of-gratification choice, impulsivity as indexed by MFFT and Porteus Maze performance, and self-control dysfunction behaviors emitted during the testing session (i.e., out of seat, interruptions, off-task physical and verbal behavior, and not paying attention to the examiner). The SCRS evidenced significant relationships with other indexes of self-control (on the order of .20 to .35), with the exception of the delay-choice measure. Scores on the SCRS also did not correlate with intelligence test scores, providing some discriminant validation for the Kendall–Wilcox instrument. The SCRS has been used to discriminate successfully between a group of classroom behavior problem children and a group of nonreferred children (Kendall & Wilcox, Study 2, Note 6) and as one mode of assessing the effects of a brief cognitive–behavioral treatment program for classroom-based impulsivity problems in children aged 8 through 10 (Kendall & Wilcox, Note 10).

Ratings are best obtained from multiple sources (not only teachers or parents, but peers and the target children themselves) and across the behavior settings in the child's lifespace that occupy central importance as far as self-management is concerned. The lack of cross-situational consistencies in ratings would represent a problem only to those who adhere to a unitary or trait view of children's self-management. Low intersetting consensus would be grounds for the cognitive–behavioral assessor to delve further into children's differential perceptions and metacognitions and into the nature of the settings themselves (the home, classroom, church, playground, etc.) insofar as demands for self-managed performance can be shown to vary in strength and clarity.

Rating methods also permit the study of the interrelationships among self-management skills and attitudes and between self-management responses and other behaviors in the child's repertoire. The use of multibehavior–multiobserver matrices (cf. Cone, Note 11), patterned after the classic multitrait–multimethod matrix approach to construct validation (Campbell & Fiske, 1959), can be of use to both the clinician and the researcher. The task of component analysis is not only to determine the level of children's cognitive and behavioral competencies but also to point to interdependencies and causal connections. Rating procedures represent perhaps the most economical means of measuring the repeated occurrence and covariation of different responses across settings. For the process researcher, the multibehavior–multimethod approach permits the determination of the variance due to ratings versus self-assessments and/or direct observations. The charting of response generalization and transfer, not to mention pretreatment–posttreatment changes, is available to the investigator of self-management training efforts via multibehavior–multiobserver-type (setting) analyses. For an example of the use of a multibehavior–multiobserver instrument for classroom assessment (with relevance to self-management), the reader is referred to the work of Barclay and his associates (e.g., Barclay, 1974).

## Direct, Naturalistic Observation Methods

The difference between ratings and direct behavioral observations revolves around the retrospective or reconstituted nature of the former as compared to the latter, wherein records are made of "clinically relevant behavior at the time and place of its occurrence" (Cone, 1978, p. 884). The *in vivo* assessment of children's naturally occurring self-control or self-regulatory sequences or dysfunctions for purposes of research or treatment is relatively rare, despite the fact that all assessment measures (data derived from self-reports, interviews, role plays, simulations, rating scales, etc.) are most appropriately validated by virtue of their relationship to real-life experiences and behaviors. Although the rationale for the use of direct observations is the same as that for behavior ratings in natural settings, the costs of real-time behavior sampling are much higher.

Among the major obstacles associated with direct observation methods are the time and the expense involved in training judges (observers) to apply behavior codes and sampling procedures reliably so as to capture for later analysis the flow of ongoing activity. Filming or audiotaping children's behaviors transforms fleeting information into more or less permanent recordings, but, eventually, trained observers must carefully code these data also. To engage in such assessments, one usually needs a cadre of highly motivated assistants and an equipment budget that only a government grant can underwrite. Finally, the types of target behaviors in which the self-management assessor might be interested may not readily be assessed via naturalistic observation. As Haynes (1978) states:

> The efficiency (information gained/assessment time) of naturalistic observation procedures is particularly low when low-frequency or highly reactive behaviors are the targets of assessment. For example, an unacceptably large amount of observation time might be necessary to observe target behaviors such as stealing, lying, marital fights, tantrums, etc. (p. 201)

To the list of troublesome targets for the observational method the following might be added: self-critical thoughts, daydreaming, between-meal snacking, attention-deployment, planning, cigarette smoking, and covert self-instruction, among others (see Table 1).

Although the use of direct observational methods may not be easy, the clinician should devote some thought to innovative ways of collecting information about children's real-world action tendencies. To the extent that self-management researchers have validated their rating scales, questionnaires, self-recording methods, and simulations against naturalistic criteria, the clinician may simply use the alternative techniques in place of direct behavior sampling in the natural environment. However, the theoretical outlook set forth here (including all three metaconceptions, particularly relativism) would lead to the assertion that indirect methods could never adequately replace naturalistic observation as a source of reliable data (cf. also Jeffrey, 1974).

One approach that is growing in popularity is the training of parents to observe their children's ongoing behavioral excesses or deficits, prior to parent-applied intervention (e.g., Graziano, 1977; O'Dell, 1974). One of the major problems with the use of parents as data collectors is that their intimate, reciprocal relationship with their children may preclude the reliable gathering and coding of usable information about the stimulus–response–outcome sequences that constitute their children's problems. Second, individual clinicians may not be equipped to engage in the intensive training of parents that would be necessary to ensure "objective" home observations or in the recruitment and training of non-family-member observers.

In my clinical work with parents and children I have relied upon relatively inexpensive and minimally intrusive methods, such as having one of the parents switch on a tape recorder during an episode of problem behavior (an aggressive interaction between siblings, a child's vain efforts to work on a model car kit without becoming angry and frustrated, etc.). Where predictable crisis points are identifiable (e.g., bedtime, going off to school in the morning, turning off the television to encourage homework completion), the parent can arrange for a tape recorder to be routinely ready (on a variable schedule) to record the action. Strategically placed tape recorders can provide important information to clinicians about children's extratherapy employment of specific self-management techniques that may have been the subject of training (particularly verbal methods, such as overt self-instructions, coping statements, and the like). A mother who was instructed in how to help her son use coping self-statements to overcome his fear of the dark (patterned after the experimental work of Kanfer, Karoly, & Newman, 1975) was also asked to turn on a tape recorder in the child's room before turning off the child's room light. Listening to a series of 60-minute tapes, I was able to determine the content and timing of the child's use, misuse, and disuse of the "therapeutic" self-instructions. Certainly much more work is needed in the development of simple, inexpensive, nonreactive measurements of children's (and parents') behaviors, motor as well as verbal, in the natural environment.

## Structured Measures of Fundamental Social and Intellectual Achievements

In research studies of children's self-management, investigators take great pains (1) to select participants who are likely to respond to the task instructions and (2) to equate groups of children on the basis of intelligence, age, and relevant experience with the experimental materials and arrangements. Prior to training children in various self-management tactics, careful investigators also seek to ascertain the level of development of prerequisite skills (e.g., object naming, counting, or simple instruction following). The purpose of this section is simply to remind practitioners of the fact that self-management assessment for diagnostic and training purposes must include measures of the cognitive, linguistic, emotional, and motoric prerequisites to effective self-direction.

Staats (1971) discusses such "basic repertoires" as inner speech control over behavior, attentional skills, memory span, expressive vocabulary, labeling (of self and the external world), logical reasoning, and social awareness as underlying effective and efficient self-guidance in children. Staats' notion of *cumulative hierarchical learning* provides an important conceptual bridge from theory-derived measurement and a concern for specific and isolated skills to the realities of the child's biology, physiology, and development. According to Staats (1971):

> A child who more quickly has developed a good attentional repertoire, has learned how to follow directions, and so on can be given training in other skills sooner than a child who has not learned these basic repertoires. Then, having acquired the additional skills, he can again be trained to the next type of skill. The general statement here is that acceleration in the acquisition of one repertoire accelerates the acquisition of the next. (pp. 288–289)

It therefore behooves the clinician to assess such building blocks as children's receptive and expressive language, motor control, habits of visual scanning and attention deployment, memory capacity and styles of encoding, storage, retrieval and rehearsal, interpersonal sensitivity, verbal mediation and habits of labeling, auditory perception, and general neurological development. Clues to possible dysfunctions are often derived from an intellectual assessment (e.g., Stanford–Binet, WISC, Slosson). Detailed analyses of specific learning disabilities may also be indicated. Whereas the clinician should not presume inherent limitations of self-management capacities in children with sensory impairments or developmental delays, neither should uniform training efforts be initiated in the belief that all children of a given mental and chronological age (and native speakers of the assessor's language) are equally prepared for training.

### Integrating Diverse Sources of Information

Among the greatest needs in the general assessment area is systemization. Because most targets of measurement are studied in isolation, the process of integrating observations and making generalizations is quite arbitrary. The key question is simply this: After collecting data from multiple vantages about thoughts, feelings, actions, and interbehavioral transactions, how should the assessor put it all together? Metatheoretical commitments would prompt assessors to assume (1) that no process of information integration or synthesis would be applicable across all settings and/or times, (2) that no data source is superior to any other, insofar as its "truth value" is concerned (cf. also Golding, 1978), and (3) that discordance between the child's view of his or her self-management problem(s) and the view of external observers is likely to be a common occurrence. Perhaps the best rule of thumb to offer now is to suggest that clinicians approach the child's problem behavior as it naturally unfolds and as free from etiological preconceptions as possible. In the last analysis, the child might integrate the clinical data for you—if you pay sufficiently careful attention.

## ASSESSMENT–TREATMENT RELATIONSHIPS

Efforts at self-management training are perhaps too new, too specialized, and too analogue-like for clearcut linkages to have been established between preintervention assessment procedures and prescriptive interventions. As is the case for a close developmental cousin, social skills training (see Chapter 8), clinical self-management methods are typically instituted on the basis of their apparent relationship to children's adjustment problems rather than in response to a demonstrated need (e.g., Hops, in press). Researchers studying therapy outcome have generally been motivated by a desire to test the clinical utility of a specific operant, observational learning, or cognitive–behavioral treatment package rather than by a concern for clarifying the varieties of pathology in children's self-directiveness. Once again, research models do not necessarily make good clinical (applied) models.

If the model of children's self-management presented previously in this chapter has any heuristic value, it may be revealed eventually by the extent to which the long-range success of therapeutic outcomes varies with the completeness of preintervention assessment (i.e., inclusive of all the hypothesized components; see Figure 2). A second major requirement is realism (or pragmatism) in the assessment–treatment relationship. That is, cognitive–behavioral clinicians must devote time not only to the careful, integrated analysis of performance deficits but also to the consideration of whether therapeutic goals (or criteria) are worthy, with worth defined as the ratio of value to cost (cf. Gilbert, 1978).

Because so many of the published treatment studies have been primarily feasibility studies involving what I consider partial assessments and a focus upon disconnected outcomes, there are few examples of systematic assessment leading to systematic intervention. Instead, as has been noted previously, individuals are making etiological assumptions (e.g., that depressed children do not self-regulate effectively because they set their self-evaluative standards too high), failing to test their fundamental assumptions (e.g., that depressed children are, indeed, less able than normal children to self-regulate), selecting a narrow range of subjects (e.g., children who score at the extremes of an unvalidated Depression Inventory), assessing an isolated "causal" component (standard setting on a laboratory task, of questionable meaning to the child), and, finally, training their subjects to perform differently (presumably as "normal" children would) on the selected component of self-management, usually without relating task performance to real-life, criterial behaviors. Although analogue experiments are vitally important (when questions of internal and external validity are thoughtfully addressed), clinicians can hardly be asked to rely upon them as a guide to the design of comprehensive interventions.

## Recommendations

The following is a set of recommendations for consolidating the assessment–treatment relationship in clinical settings:

1. Remember that the decision to label a child's problem as self-management-related should be dictated by a belief in the unique contribution of a cognitive–behavioral intervention, beyond those therapeutic effects possible with familiar external control methods. The assessor should be able to articulate clearly his or her rationale.

2. The boundaries of self-management assessment and training are set by the level of cooperativeness of the child, of significant others, and of the child's natural environment. Always try to ascertain early the degree to which the system is capable of sharing information and responding to feedback. Do not presume that clinical expertise can overcome a system that strongly rewards children's misbehaviors.

3. Guard against the prevalent tendency to assume that children's disorders are attributable to skill or motivational deficiencies. Start the assessment with a thorough examination of the higher-order metacognitive, informational, and rule-learning components. Determine also the child's level of social knowledge and functional intellectual capacities.

4. A surefire recipe for clinical failure is "Assess in a vacuum, train in a vacuum."

5. Respect the child's individuality by not evaluating the success of training against uniform learning criteria. What the child says or does (form) is less important than the actual accomplishment of tangible results.

6. Diagnostic and process assessment should not be considered separable. Measure, both during and after training, the extent to which the child actively uses the strategies, overt maneuvers, and/or linguistic controls taught in the context of the cognitive–behavioral intervention. The more components taught, the more the treatment will need to be carefully monitored.

7. Where assessment reveals multiple dysfunctions (across several of the components of self-management), training should be conducted in such a way as to assist the child to integrate the separately enacted skills. Model extended response sequences and generalizable rationales rather than isolated instances of, and reasons for, desirable behavior.

8. There will always be alternative clinical routes to the institution of the desirable, self-managing pattern, and the method(s) employed should be chosen on the basis of efficiency—cost in clinician, child, parent, and/or teacher time divided into the expected change in task-relevant behavior. The clinician who attempts to mirror, in an individual case, the comprehensiveness of a major, multimodal treatment study may be guilty of overkill. In treating an obese adolescent, instruction in stimulus control and contingent self-reward may be sufficient to assist the youngster in gaining control over eating patterns. The addition of clinical components beyond those necessary to alter the maladaptive pattern (e.g., teaching complex self-instructions, reattribution, self-labeling, or problem solving to the obese client) is justified only if the interview and case history suggest that maintenance of treatment gains is likely to be a problem.

9. Whereas group outcome researchers are often content with statistical indications of treatment success, the assessor–clinician relies upon the value of normative outcome criteria. Unfortunately, the "normal" limits of many self-managed response systems will be difficult to determine. Although physicians, legal authorities, and classroom teachers may be able to provide predictively valid estimates of pathological overweight, deviation from lawful pursuits, or classroom disruptiveness, there may be considerably more ambiguity associated with determining appropriate or inappropriate levels of self-managed affect, social approach–avoidance, interpersonal dominance–submission, altruism, obedience to vague cultural "regulations," and other complex patterns to which our contextual relativity metatheory most clearly applies. Local, rather than absolute, standards may therefore be the assessor's only basis for measurement.

10. Assessors should also be cognizant of the need for economical measures of treatment maintenance, generalization, and transfer to be taken at periodic intervals after treatment. Determination of the appropriate follow-up period has been a neglected concern in psychotherapy research in general (Mash & Terdal, 1980) and is particularly troublesome in clinical work with children, because of the supposedly confounding effects of maturation (physical and psychological), changing environments, developmental crises, and an expanding knowledge–experience base. However, Mash and Terdal (1980) have distinguished between types of follow-up assessments, especially those that do and those that do not provide useful information regarding treatment reformulation.

I suggest that clinicians will rarely be concerned with conducting follow-ups to support a particular theory or the comparative potency of a particular intervention. Rather, they will want to employ diagnostic follow-ups, in order to detect adverse effects, deterioration of effects, changing perceptions (metacognitions), and alterations in the performance demands placed upon the child (across time and settings). Although such follow-ups may be scheduled at regular, or at preplanned but irregular, intervals, the assessor may also wish to allow the school or the family to call for periodic assessments. In general, to the extent that interventions with children have focussed on complex skills, relatively long follow-up intervals are needed to give the training time to take hold and generalize and to give the school or family system time to adapt.

# SUMMARY

The movement in this chapter has been from the general to the specific. Interpreting in the broadest way the needs of the assessor confronted with children's problems of self-guidance, I have sought to provide a philosophical, as well as a conceptual, roadmap.

The stream of child behavior does not label itself, but minding its own business (as George Kelly used to say), awaits clinical translation. If assessors are to speak the language of children's self-management, they must recognize its extralinguistic characteristics: reciprocal determinism, personal mediation, and temporal/contextual relativity. Acknowledging metatheory, cognitive–behavioral assessors can avoid the incongruous blending of viewpoints, such as (1) the repudiation of cross-situational trait concepts and the assessment of impulsivity versus reflectiveness, (2) the rejection of subjectivity and the measurement of imagery and self-talk, or (3) the endorsement of response specificity and the recommended use of standardized instruments and prepackaged treatments.

Following the discussion of metatheory, a working model of children's self-management was proposed, highlighting four semi-independent, necessary constituents: (1) discrimination of the rules or situational response requirements, (2) awareness that one's non-self-managing behavior has become dissonant with the environmental demands and problematic insofar as the pursuit of rewarding outcomes is concerned, (3) the motivation to work for self-directed change and/or self-directed maintenance of behavior, and (4) the availability of the instrumental and cognitive skills prerequisite to effective self-guidance.

A general assessment model—the functional–component–criterion analysis—and a set of specific measurement guidelines were also offered. Six approaches to the clinical calibration of children's self-management-related perceptions, motives, and skills were recommended: the interview, performance tests and simulations (contrived and naturalistic), self-monitoring, multisource rating systems, direct observational methods, and the structured assessment of prerequisite social and intellectual achievements.

Finally, suggestions were offered on how the clinician might productively translate systematic assessment data into systematic intervention. In a very real sense, the recommendations for self-management assessment and treatment were presented despite, not because of, the currently available research literature. The measurement of children's self-guidance is a field that has yet to catch up with its conceptual potential or to earn its popular appeal. The author would be most gratified if the present offering were to facilitate in some modest fashion the eventual arrival of a mature clinical science of children's self-management.

## Reference Notes

1. Karoly, P. *Toward a synthesis in the psychology of self-control: The interactive effects of cognition and affect*. Paper presented at the fifth biennial meeting of the Southeastern Conference on Human Development, Atlanta, Georgia, 1978.
2. Tirrell, F. J., & Scott, N. A. *Behavioral self-control: The inadequacy of current laboratory analogue designs*. Paper presented at the first annual meeting of the Midwestern Association of Behavior Analysis, Chicago, 1975.
3. Mischel, H. N., Mischel, W., & Hood, S. W. *The development of knowledge about self-control*. Unpublished manuscript, Stanford University, 1978.
4. Mischel, W., Mischel, H. N., & Hood, S. W. *The development of knowledge of effective ideation to delay gratification*. Unpublished manuscript, Stanford University, 1978.
5. Asarnow, J. R. *Verbal rehearsal and serial recall: The mediational training of kindergarten children*. Unpublished master's thesis, University of Waterloo, 1977.
6. Kendall, P. C., & Wilcox, L. E. *Self-control in children: The development of a rating scale*. Unpublished manuscript, University of Minnesota, 1979.

7. Schubert, J. *The VRB apparatus.* Unpublished manuscript, University of Saskatchewan, Regina, 1973.
8. Litrownik, A. J. *Self-control and self-regulatory processes in TMRs* (Final report, Grant No. G00-75-06670). U.S. Department of Health, Education and Welfare, USOE, Bureau of Education for the Handicapped.
9. Cone, J. D. *Truth and sensitivity in behavioral assessment.* Paper presented at the meeting of the Association for the Advancement of Behavior Therapy, Chicago, 1978.
10. Kendall, P. C., & Wilcox, L. E. *A cognitive–behavioral treatment for impulsivity: Concrete versus conceptual labeling with nonself-controlled problem children.* Unpublished manuscript, University of Minnesota, 1979.
11. Cone, J. D. *Multitrait–multimethod matrices in behavioral assessment.* Paper presented at the meeting of the American Psychological Association, Washington, D.C., 1976.

# References

Bandura, A. *Principles of behavior modification.* New York: Holt, Rinehart & Winston, 1969.
Bandura, A. *Social learning theory.* Englewood Cliffs, N.J.: Prentice-Hall, 1977.
Bandura, A. The self-system in reciprocal determinism. *American Psychologist,* 1978, *33,* 344–358.
Barclay, J. R. System-wide analysis of social interaction and affective problems in schools. In P. O. Davidson, F. W. Clark, & L. A. Hamerlynck (Eds.), *Evaluation of behavioral programs in community, residential and school settings.* Champaign, Ill.: Research Press, 1974.
Bellack, A. S., & Schwartz, J. S. Assessment for self-control programs. In M. Hersen & A. S. Bellack (Eds.), *Behavioral assessment: A practical handbook.* New York: Pergamon, 1976.
Belmont, J. M., & Butterfield, E. C. The instructional approach to developmental cognitive research. In R. V. Kail & J. W. Hagen (Eds.), *Perspectives on the development of memory and cognition.* Hillsdale, N.J.: Lawrence Erlbaum, 1977.
Bijou, S. W., & Baer, D. M. *Behavior analysis of child development.* Englewood Cliffs, N.J.: Prentice-Hall, 1978.
Blank, M. Cognitive functions of language in the preschool years. *Developmental Psychology,* 1974, *10,* 229–245.
Buss, A. H., & Plomin, R. *A temperament theory of personality development.* New York: Wiley, 1975.
Camp, B., Blom, G., Hebert, F., & Van Doorninck, W. Think aloud: A program for developing self-control in young aggressive boys. *Journal of Abnormal Child Psychology,* 1977, *8,* 157–169.
Campbell, D. T., & Fiske, D. W. Convergent and discriminant validation by the multitrait–multimethod matrix. *Psychological Bulletin,* 1959, *56,* 81–105.
Cattell, R. B. Structured learning theory, applied to personality change. In R. B. Cattell & R. M. Dreger (Eds.), *Handbook of modern personality theory.* Washington, D.C.: Hemisphere, 1977.
Cattell, R. B. The structured learning analysis of therapeutic change and maintenance. In P. Karoly & J. J. Steffen (Eds.), *The long-range effects of psychotherapy: Models of durable outcome.* New York: Gardner Press, 1980.
Chess, S., Thomas, A., & Birch, H. G. Behavior problems revisited: Findings of an anterospective study. *Journal of the American Academy of Child Psychiatry,* 1967, *6,* 321–331.
Ciminero, A. R., & Drabman, R. S. Current developments in the behavioral assessment of children. In B. B. Lahey & A. E. Kazdin (Eds.), *Advances in clinical child psychology* (Vol. 1). New York: Plenum, 1977.
Ciminero, A. R., Nelson, R. O., & Lipinski, D. P. Self-monitoring procedures. In A. R. Ciminero, K. S. Calhoun, & H. E. Adams (Eds.), *Handbook of behavioral assessment.* New York: Wiley-Interscience, 1977.
Coates, T. J., & Thoresen, C. E. Self-control and educational practice, or Do we really need self-control? In D. Berlinger (Ed.), *Review of research in education.* Itasca, Ill.: Praeger, 1979.
Cone, J. D. The behavioral assessment grid (BAG): A conceptual framework and taxonomy. *Behavior Therapy,* 1978, *9,* 882–883.

Conners, C. K. A teacher rating scale for use in drug studies with children. *American Journal of Psychiatry,* 1969, *126,* 884–888.

Douglas, V. Stop, look, and listen: The problem of sustained attention and impulse control in hyperactive and normal children. *Canadian Journal of Behavioral Science,* 1972, *4,* 259–276.

Douglas, V., Parry, P., Marton, P., & Garson, C. Assessment of a cognitive training program for hyperactive children. *Journal of Abnormal Child Psychology,* 1976, *4,* 389–410.

Duval, S., & Wicklund, R. A. *A theory of objective self-awareness.* New York: Academic Press, 1972.

Ekehammar, B. Interactionism in personality from a historical perspective. *Psychological Bulletin,* 1974, *81,* 1026–1048.

Endler, N. S., & Magnusson, D. Toward an interactional psychology of personality. *Psychological Bulletin,* 1976, *83,* 956–974.

Fiske, D. W. *Strategies for personality research.* San Francisco: Jossey-Bass, 1978.

Flavell, J. H. *Cognitive development.* Englewood Cliffs, N.J.: Prentice-Hall, 1977.

Gagne, R., & Briggs, L. *Principles of instructional design.* New York: Holt, Rinehart & Winston, 1974.

Gilbert, T. F. *Human competence: Engineering worthy performance.* New York: McGraw-Hill, 1978.

Glenwick, D. S., Barocas, R., & Burka, A. A. Some interpersonal correlates of cognitive impulsivity in fourth-graders. *Journal of School Psychology,* 1976, *14,* 212–221.

Goldfried, M. R., & D'Zurilla, T. J. A behavioral–analytic model for assessing competence. In C. D. Spielberger (Ed.), *Current topics in clinical and community psychology* (Vol. 1). New York: Academic Press, 1969.

Goldiamond, I. Self-reinforcement. *Journal of Applied Behavior Analysis,* 1976, *9,* 509–514.

Golding, S. L. Toward a more adequate theory of personality: Psychological organizing principles. In H. London (Ed.), *Personality: A new look at metatheories.* Washington, D.C.: Hemisphere, 1978.

Gottman, J., & Markman, H. J. Experimental designs in psychotherapy research. In S. L. Garfield & A. E. Bergin (Eds.), *Handbook of psychotherapy and behavior change* (2nd ed.). New York: Wiley, 1978.

Graziano, A. M. Parents as behavior therapists. In M. Hersen, R. M. Eisler, & P. M. Miller (Eds.), *Progress in behavior modification* (Vol. 4). New York: Academic Press, 1977.

Hall, S. M. Self-management and therapeutic maintenance. In P. Karoly & J. J. Steffen (Eds.), *The long-range effects of psychotherapy: Models of durable outcome.* New York: Gardner Press, 1980.

Haynes, S. N. *Principles of behavioral assessment.* New York: Gardner Press, 1978.

Hops, H. Social skills training for socially isolated children. In P. Karoly & J. J. Steffen (Eds.), *Advances in child behavior analysis and therapy.* New York: Gardner Press, in press.

Jeffrey, D. B. Self-control: Methodological issues and research trends. In M. J. Mahoney & C. E. Thoresen (Eds.), *Self-control: Power to the person.* Monterey, Calif.: Brooks/Cole, 1974.

Kagan, J. Reflection–impulsivity: The generality and dynamics of conceptual tempo. *Journal of Abnormal Psychology,* 1966, *71,* 17–24.

Kagan, J., Rosman, B. L., Day, D., Albert, J., & Phillips, W. Information-processing in the child: Significance of analytic and reflective attitudes. *Psychology Monographs,* 1964, *78* (1, Whole No. 578).

Kanfer, F. H. Self-regulation: Research, issues, and speculations. In C. Neuringer & J. L. Michael (Eds.), *Behavior modification in clinical psychology.* New York: Appleton-Century-Crofts, 1970.

Kanfer, F. H. Self-management methods. In F. H. Kanfer & A. P. Goldstein (Eds.), *Helping people change.* New York: Pergamon, 1975.

Kanfer, F. H. The many faces of self-control, or behavior modification changes its focus. In R. B. Stuart (Ed.), *Behavioral self-management: Strategies, techniques, and outcome.* New York: Brunner/Mazel, 1977.

Kanfer, F. H., & Grimm, L. G. Behavioral analysis: Selecting target behaviors in the interview. *Behavior Modification,* 1977, *1,* 7–28.

Kanfer, F. H., & Karoly, P. Self-control: A behavioristic excursion into the lion's den. *Behavior Therapy,* 1972, *3,* 398–416.

Kanfer, F. H., Karoly, P., & Newman, A. Reduction of children's fear of the dark by competence-related and situational threat-related verbal cues. *Journal of Consulting and Clinical Psychology,*

1975, *43*, 251–258.

Karoly, P. Operant methods. In F. H. Kanfer & A. P. Goldstein (Eds.), *Helping people change*. New York: Pergamon, 1975.

Karoly, P. Behavioral self-management in children: Concepts, methods, issues, and directions. In M. Hersen, R. M. Eisler, & P. M. Miller (Eds.), *Progress in behavior modification* (Vol. 5). New York: Academic Press, 1977.

Karoly, P. Person variables in therapeutic change and development. In P. Karoly & J. J. Steffen (Eds.), *The long-range effects of psychotherapy: Models of durable outcome*. New York: Gardner Press, 1980.

Karoly, P. *Self-management in children: Principles and practices*. New York: Gardner Press, in preparation.

Kendall, P. C., & Finch, A. Developing non-impulsive behavior in children: Cognitive–behavioral strategies for self-control. In P. C. Kendall & S. D. Hollon (Eds.), *Cognitive–behavioral interventions: Theory, research, and procedures*. New York: Academic Press, 1979.

Klein, G. S. *Psychoanalytic theory: An exploration of essentials*. New York: International Universities Press, 1976.

Kohlberg, L. Moral stages and moralization: The cognitive–developmental approach. In T. Lickona (Ed.), *Moral development and behavior*. New York: Holt, Rinehart & Winston, 1976.

Linehan, M. K. Issues in behavioral interviewing. In J. D. Cone & R. P. Hawkins (Eds.), *Behavioral assessment: New directions in clinical psychology*. New York: Brunner/Mazel, 1977.

Litrownik, A. J., & Steinfeld, B. I. Developing self-regulation in retarded children. In P. Karoly & J. J. Steffen (Eds.), *Advances in child behavior analysis and therapy*. New York: Gardner Press, in press.

Livingston, S. A. Psychometric techniques for criterion-referenced testing and behavioral assessment. In J. D. Cone & R. P. Hawkins (Eds.), *Behavioral assessment: New directions in clinical psychology*. New York: Brunner/Mazel, 1977.

Loevinger, J. *Ego development: Conceptions and theories*. San Francisco: Jossey-Bass, 1976.

Luria, A. *The role of speech in the regulation of normal and abnormal behaviors*. New York: Liveright, 1961.

Lyman, R. D., Rickard, H. C., & Elder, I. R. Contingency management of self-report and cleaning behavior. *Journal of Abnormal Child Psychology*, 1975, *3*, 155–162.

Mahoney, M. J. *Cognition and behavior modification*. Cambridge, Mass.: Ballinger, 1974.

Mahoney, M. J. Terminal terminology: A self-regulated response to Goldiamond. *Journal of Applied Behavioral Analysis*, 1976, *9*, 515–517.

Mahoney, M. J. Some applied issues in self-monitoring. In J. D. Cone & R. P. Hawkins (Eds.), *Behavioral assessment: New directions in clinical psychology*. New York: Brunner/Mazel, 1977.

Mahoney, M. J., & Arnkoff, D. B. Cognitive and self-control therapies. In S. L. Garfield & A. E. Bergin (Eds.), *Handbook of psychotherapy and behavior change* (2nd ed.). New York: Wiley, 1978.

Mahoney, M. J., & Thoresen, C. E. (Eds.). *Self-control: Power to the person*. Monterey, Calif.: Brooks/Cole, 1974.

Mash, E. J., & Terdal, L. G. Follow-up assessments in behavior therapy. In P. Karoly & J. J. Steffen (Eds.), *The long-range effects of psychotherapy: Models of durable outcome*. New York: Gardner Press, 1980.

Masters, J. C., & Mokros, J. R. Self-reinforcement processes in children. In H. Reese (Ed.), *Advances in child development and behavior* (Vol. 9). New York: Academic Press, 1974.

McKaughan, L. Propositional self-control in children. *Journal of Experimental Child Psychology*, 1974, *17*, 519–538.

Meichenbaum, D. A cognitive-behavior modification approach to assessment. In M. Hersen & A. S. Bellack (Eds.), *Behavioral assessment: A practical handbook*. New York: Pergamon, 1976.

Meichenbaum, D. *Cognitive-behavior modification: An integrative approach*. New York: Plenum, 1977.

Meichenbaum, D. Teaching children self-control. In B. Lahey & A. E. Kazdin (Eds.), *Advances in clinical child psychology* (Vol. 2). New York: Plenum, 1979.

Meichenbaum, D., & Asarnow, J. Cognitive-behavior modification and metacognitive development:

Implications for the classroom. In P. C. Kendall & S. D. Hollon (Eds.), *Cognitive–behavioral interventions: Theory, research, and procedures*. New York: Academic Press, 1979.

Messer, S. B. Reflection–impulsivity: A review. *Psychological Bulletin*, 1976, *83*, 1026–1052.

Mischel, W. Toward a cognitive social learning reconceptualization of personality. *Psychological Review*, 1973, *80*, 252–283.

Mischel, W. Processes in delay of gratification. In L. Berkowitz (Ed.), *Advances in experimental social psychology* (Vol. 7). New York: Academic Press, 1974.

Mischel, W. Personality research: A look at the future. In H. London (Ed.), *Personality: A new look at metatheories*. Washington, D.C.: Hemisphere, 1978.

Morganstern, K. P. Behavioral interviewing: The initial stages of assessment. In M. Hersen & A. S. Bellack (Eds.), *Behavioral assessment: A practical handbook*. New York: Pergamon, 1976.

Mullener, N., & Laird, J. D. Some developmental changes in the organization of self-evaluations. *Developmental Psychology*, 1971, *5*, 233–236.

Murray, H. A. *Explorations in personality*. New York: Oxford University Press, 1938.

Natsoulas, T. Residual subjectivity. *American Psychologist*, 1978, *33*, 269–283.

Nelson, R. O. Methodological issues in assessment via self-monitoring. In J. D. Cone & R. P. Hawkins (Eds.), *Behavioral assessment: New directions in clinical psychology*. New York: Brunner/Mazel, 1977.

O'Dell, S. Training parents in behavior modification: A review. *Psychological Bulletin*, 1974, *81*, 418–433.

Parke, R. D. Rules, roles, and resistance to deviation: Recent advances in punishment, discipline, and self-control. In A. Pick (Ed.), *Minnesota symposia of child psychology* (Vol. 8). Minneapolis: University of Minnesota Press, 1974.

Parke, R. D., Ewall, W., & Slaby, R. G. Hostile and helpful verbalizations as regulators of nonverbal aggression. *Journal of Personality and Social Psychology*, 1972, *23*, 243–248.

Pervin, L. A. *Current controversies and issues in personality*. New York: Wiley, 1978.

Pick, A. D., Christy, M. D., & Frankel, G. W. A developmental study of visual selective attention. *Journal of Experimental Child Psychology*, 1972, *14*, 165–175.

Price-Williams, R. D., & Ramirez, M. Ethnic differences in delay of gratification. *Journal of Social Psychology*, 1974, *93*, 23–30.

Risley, T. R., & Hart, B. Developing correspondence between the nonverbal and verbal behavior of preschool children. *Journal of Applied Behavior Analysis*, 1968, *1*, 267–281.

Rosenbaum, M. S., & Drabman, R. S. Self-control training in the classroom. *Journal of Applied Behavior Analysis*, 1979, *12*, 467–485.

Sampson, E. E. Personality and the location of identity. *Journal of Personality*, 1978, *46*, 552–568.

Santostefano, S. *A biodevelopmental approach to clinical child psychology*. New York: Wiley, 1978.

Shure, M. B., & Spivack, G. *Problem-solving techniques in childrearing*. San Francisco: Jossey-Bass, 1978.

Spivack, G., Platt, J. J., & Shure, M. B. *The problem-solving approach to adjustment*. San Francisco: Jossey-Bass, 1976.

Staats, A. W. *Child learning, intelligence, and personality*. New York: Harper & Row, 1971.

Staats, A. W. *Social behaviorism*. Homewood, Ill.: Dorsey, 1975.

Stein, N., & Prindaville, P. S. Discrimination learning and stimulus generalization by impulsive and reflective children. *Journal of Experimental Child Psychology*, 1976, *21*, 25–39.

Stern, G. G., Stein, M. I., & Bloom, B. S. *Methods in personality assessment*. Glencoe, Ill.: Free Press, 1956.

Sutherland, J. W. *A general systems philosophy for the social and behavioral sciences*. New York: George Braziller, 1973.

Thoresen, C., Kirmil-Gray, K., & Crosbie, P. Processes and procedures of self-control: A working model. *Canadian Counselor*, 1977.

Thoresen, C., & Mahoney, M. J. *Behavioral self-control*. New York: Holt, Rinehart & Winston, 1974.

Toner, I. J., Holstein, R. B., & Hetherington, E. M. Reflection–impulsivity and self-control in preschool children. *Child Development*, 1977, *48*, 239–245.

Weiner, B. Motivation from the cognitive perspective. In W. K. Estes (Ed.), *Handbook of learning and cognitive processes* (Vol. 3). Hillsdale, N.J.: Lawrence Erlbaum, 1976.

White, O. R. Data-based instruction: Evaluating educational progress. In J. D. Cone & R. P. Hawkins (Eds.), *Behavioral assessment: New directions in clinical psychology*. New York: Brunner/Mazel, 1977.

Wozniak, R. H. Verbal regulation of motor behavior—Soviet research and non-Soviet replications: A review and explication. *Human Development*, 1972, *15*, 13–57.

# HYPERACTIVITY

## Russell A. Barkley

*Medical College of Wisconsin and Milwaukee Children's Hospital*

The behavior disorder known as hyperactivity is the most frequently referred problem to child guidance clinics in this country (Safer & Allen, 1976; Stewart, Pitts, Craig, & Dieruf, 1966). It is therefore necessary that professionals working with such children in a clinical or research setting have some knowledge of the nature of this disorder and of its development, prognosis, assessment, and treatment. It is the aim of this chapter to provide a conceptual framework within which to approach the tasks of assessment and treatment and to make specific suggestions for their accomplishment.

## DESCRIPTION AND DEFINITION

Hyperactive children are often described as overactive, inattentive, impulsive, difficult to discipline, and unable to inhibit their activity to situational demands (Cantwell, 1975; Ross & Ross, 1976; Routh, 1978; Safer & Allen, 1976). Frequently, they have great difficulties in interacting with peers, accomplishing academic assignments, and following directions given by parents and teachers (Stewart *et al.*, 1966). Problems with depression, alcohol abuse, obeying the law, and truancy often develop as they mature (Cantwell, 1978; Minde, Lewin, Weiss, Lavigeur, Douglas, & Sykes, 1971; Ross & Ross, 1976; Weiss, Minde, Werry, Douglas, & Nemeth, 1971). The outcome for these children in adulthood is often described as dismal (Barcai & Rabkin, 1974; Heussy & Cohen, 1976; Menkes, Rowe, & Menkes, 1967; Routh & Mesibov, 1980), and their long-term response to treatment as poor (Barkley, 1977a; Mash & Dalby, 1979; Routh, 1978; Weiss *et al.*, 1971). In short, they constitute a group of children plagued with conduct and reactive emotional problems throughout most of their lives.

Hyperactivity is believed to comprise anywhere from 2% to 20% of the U.S. school-age population (Safer & Allen, 1976; Sroufe and Stewart, 1973; Stewart *et al.*, 1966; Wender, 1971). A realistic estimate of prevalance used by most investigators is 4–5% of school-age children, or about one child in every classroom. Although, initially, hyperactivity was believed to be primarily an American problem because of the extremely low incidence rates reported in other countries (Rutter, Graham, & Yule, 1970; Stewart, 1970), more recent studies suggest that from 4% to 10% of the childhood population of most countries suffer from this disorder (Trites, Dugas, Lynch, & Ferguson, 1979; Sprague, Cohen, & Eichlseder, Note 1) but that it is classified under a different diagnosis, such as conduct disorder (Sandberg, Rutter, & Taylor, 1978). That the disorder occurs more in boys than in girls is readily accepted by most investigators, with ratios ranging from 3:1 to 9:1 (Safer & Allen, 1976; Trites *et al.*, 1979).

Early efforts at defining the disorder focused heavily on motor activity levels; hence the diagnosis of "hyperactivity" (Werry, 1968a). As noted by Ross and Ross (1976), these quantitative descriptions were flawed by the lack of normative data for children and failed to provide information on the qualitative aspects of the activity level, such as duration, intensity, relevance to a task, and goal directedness. Other problems with the quantitative approach pertained to a lack of common measurement systems, the multidimensional nature of activity level, the daily and often situational fluctuation of such levels, and its failure to correspond to the complaints of the adults referring the child for treatment (Barkley, 1977b; Barkley & Cunningham, 1979a; Barkley & Ullman, 1975; Kenny, Clemmens, Hudson, Lentz, Cicci, & Nair, 1971; Ross & Ross, 1976; Kasper, Note 2).

Later, definitions began to focus more heavily on deficits of attention and impulse control (Douglas, 1972, 1974, 1976), with the American Psychiatric Association changing the label to attention deficit disorder in its recent revision of the DSM-II. More recently, Routh (1978) and Safer and Allen (1976) have emphasized as being of major importance to the diagnosis, the inability of these children to restrict their activity level in an age-appropriate fashion as a situation demands. In addition, the difficulties these children have with social conduct and adjustment are receiving greater attention (Barkley, 1979; Routh & Mesibov, 1980; Sandberg *et al.*, 1978; Shaffer, McNamara, & Pincus, 1974; Kasper, Note 2), with some researchers questioning whether hyperactivity is truly different from the larger category of conduct disorders of childhood (Sandberg *et al.*, 1978).

From a review of these previous efforts to define the disorder, one finds several common themes. First, most investigators have stressed the excessive nature of the child's behavior, whether in activity level or attention span, as a hallmark of hyperactivity. Second, emphasis has been placed on the child's difficulty with self-control (failure to inhibit or restrict behavior as a situation demands). Third, each, in some way, has noted the qualitative or socially inappropriate aspect of the child's behavior. Finally, all have attempted to exclude from their definitions of hyperactivity other disorders such as mental retardation, gross brain damage, psychosis, or sensory or motor impairment (see Safer & Allen, 1976). Although the disorder may fit into the larger category of conduct disorders, it is distinguished from them by its early onset and cross-situational nature. However, this does not preclude the possibility that other conduct disturbances might develop concomitantly.

# REVIEW OF RESEARCH

Many studies have investigated the nature of hyper-
ship to secondary prob

on the assessment of hyperactive children.

## Primary Behavior Problems

As noted previously, there is a consensus that hyperactive children are overactive, inattentive, and impulsive. Despite this concordance, efforts to measure these discriminating behaviors objectively have proven surprisingly difficult.

This conclusion is especially true with regard to activity level, which is often assumed to be global and unidimensional in nature. However, this construct has presented both definitional and measurement problems. As Cromwell, Baumeister, and Hawkins (1963) discuss, activity level can refer to the frequency or intensity of a given behavior, its situational appropriateness, or its goal directedness. In addition, it can encompass qualitatively different types of motor behavior, from locomotion to discrete movements of an appendage, or even respiration rate. Not surprisingly, the construct of activity level is now viewed as a multidimensional one (Barkley, 1977b; Barkley & Ullman, 1975; Cromwell et al., 1963)

Attempts to assess differences in activity level between hyperactive children and other populations of children have produced inconsistent results. Some studies find hyperactive children to be more active than normal children across many settings (Barkley, 1977b; Pope, 1970), whereas others do not (Barkley & Ullman, 1975; Kenny et al., 1971; Shaffer et al., 1974). The nature of the setting and the type of measure utilized appear to account for the differences in findings, with measures of locomotion or seat activity in more structured (task-oriented) situations being the most sensitive to differences between hyperactive and normal children. However, efforts to discriminate hyperactive children from other deviant populations on these same measures have not proven successful (Sandberg et al., 1978; Shaffer et al., 1974; Firestone & Martin, Note 3). Thus, excessive rates of activity appear to be characteristic of many psychopathological populations of children, not simply of hyperactive children.

The second problem characterizing hyperactive children is difficulty with attention. Although the research findings in this area are more consistent in finding hyperactive children to be generally more inattentive than normal children, the notion that attention is unidimensional in nature has also been discarded (Douglas, 1972, 1974; Douglas & Peters, 1979). More specific definitions of the types of attention affected and of the manner in which they are measured are preferred. Hyperactive children seem to have shorter attention spans, greater distractibility, smaller focus of attention, and difficulties with selective attention (discrimination) compared to normal children (Barkley, 1977b; Bremer & Stern, 1976; Douglas & Peters, 1979; Ross & Ross, 1976; Routh & Schroeder, 1976). Measures of attention also appear to discriminate between hyperactive children and other deviant groups (Sandberg *et al.*, 1978; Shaffer *et al.*, 1974; Firestone & Martin, Note 3). Thus, a great deal of support exists for the notion that problems with attention are a major difficulty of hyperactive children.

Differences between hyperactive and normal children in impulsivity have been frequently demonstrated (Douglas, 1972, 1976; Meichenbaum, 1976, 1978; Ross & Ross, 1976; Schleifer, Weiss, Cohen, Elman, Cvejic, & Kruger, 1975). The most often-used measures have been the Matching Familiar Figures Test and the Porteus Mazes. Rapid responding with frequent errors on these tests is construed as impulsivity and reflects an inability to delay responding, to evaluate the nature of the problem, and to emit a correct response. Hyperactive children are therefore seen as deficient in one or more of these areas.

## The Concept of a Syndrome

The belief that hyperactivity is a syndrome rests on the notion that the primary problems of hyperactivity tend to co-vary to a significant degree. However, enumerable studies have not found a significant interrelationship among these problems behaviors for either hyperactive or normal children (Barkley, 1977b; Barkley & Ullman, 1975; Langhorne, Loney, Paternite, & Bechtholdt, 1976; Routh & Roberts, 1972; Shaffer *et al.*, 1974; Ullman, Barkley, & Brown, 1978; Werry, Weiss, & Douglas, 1964). Thus, the term *hyperactivity* as it is currently used refers to a heterogeneous group of children, some overactive, some inattentive, some impulsive, and others having all of these problems.

## Associated Behavior Problems

In addition to the problems with impulse control, attention, and activity level, hyperactive children have been found to show difficulties in other areas as well. Safer and Allen (1976) estimate that 70–80% of hyperactive children have at least one specific learning disability, although this is not always demonstrated (Cantwell & Satterfield, 1978). Often, they are found to be clumsy and awkward and to have fine and gross motor incoordination (Ross & Ross, 1976). Problems with academic achievement are common (Cantwell & Satterfield, 1978; Dykman, Peters, & Ackerman, 1973; Weiss, Kruger, Danielson, & Elman, 1975), and the likelihood that these children will have failed at least one grade in school before the high school level is high (Menkes *et al.*, 1967; Minde, Weiss, & Mendelson, 1972; Weiss *et al.*, 1975).

As noted previously, many develop poor peer relationships at an early age (Ross & Ross, 1976), which are a continuing concern to the child and his family (Safer & Allen, 1976). Problems with aggression (Patterson, 1976), poor social skills (Pelham, Note 4), and immature emotional control (Weiss et al., 1971) probably contribute to these peer relationship problems. Another problem of considerable importance to parents and teachers, which will receive more detailed discussion later, is that of noncompliance (Barkley & Cunningham, 1979a; Barkley & Ullman, 1975; Battle & Lacey, 1972, Campbell, 1973; Cunningham & Barkley 1979), Ullman, 1975; Battle & Lacey, 1972, Campbell, 1973; Cunningham & Barkley 1966; Ullman, Barkley, & Brown, 1978). In fact, some of these studies suggest that it is noncompliance, rather than overactivity or inattentiveness, that greatly frustrates parents and teachers and results in referral for treatment (Barkley & Cunningham, 1979a).

## Associated Physical Problems

A number of studies have attempted to determine whether hyperactive children are brain damaged or have dysfunction or immaturity of the central nervous system relative to normal children. These studies have not supported the notion that hyperactivity is related to brain damage (Rutter, 1977). Nevertheless, many studies find hyperactive children to have significantly more minor physical anomalies, histories of birth complications, soft neurologic signs, motor coordination problems, and minor EEG abnormalities than normal children, although not all hyperactive children have all or even a few of these difficulties (Hastings & Barkley, 1978; Hertzig, Bortner, & Birch, 1969; Paine, Werry, & Quay, 1968; Waldrop & Goering, 1971; Werry, 1968b). A recent review of the literature on psychophysiological studies (Hastings & Barkley, 1978) indicates that where differences in psychophysiological functioning are found between hyperactive and normal children, they consistently find hyperactive children to be underreactive to stimulation. That is, when stimulated, many of these children show lower amplitudes, shorter latencies, and faster habituation of various psychophysiological responses. It is by no means established that this underreactivity is even related to their behavior problems, symptomatic of underlying central nervous system deficiencies, or related to treatment responsiveness.

Although hyperactive children seem to show more signs of physical or central nervous system disturbances than normal children, it is not known whether such disturbances are specific to hyperactive populations or are characteristic of other psychiatric conditions as well. Some research on minor physical anomalies (Firestone & Martin, Note 3) and soft neurologic signs (Sandberg et al., 1978) indicates that these signs relate only to the presence or the absence of psychiatric disorders, not specifically to hyperactivity (Rutter, 1977).

## Developmental Course

Early literature on hyperactivity optimistically held that such children tended to outgrow their behavior problems by adolescence (Wender, 1971). However, follow-up studies of hyperactive children in their teenage and early adulthood years have not supported this belief.

Despite the observation that hyperactive children are most likely to be referred for professional help between the ages of 5 and 12 years (Kenny et al., 1971; Routh, 1978), most have manifested their hyperactive behaviors since ages 2 and 3 years (Stewart et al., 1966). It seems that the referrals occur later in development because of the social pressures brought to bear on the families of these children once they enter school.

Ross and Ross (1976) have provided an excellent description of the developmental course for hyperactive children. As infants, they are often described as temperamental, colicky, restless, difficult to feed, hyperreactive to stimulation, and having short sleep patterns (Campbell, Schleifer, & Weiss, 1978; Carey & McDevitt, 1978; Chamberlin, 1977; McInerny & Chamberlin, 1978). By ages 2 or 3 years, they are described as being more active, noncompliant, talkative, restless, and prone to accidents or poisonings than normal children (Minde et al., 1971; Ross & Ross, 1976; Stewart et al., 1966; Stewart, Thach, & Freidin, 1970).

Upon entry into preschool or kindergarten, hyperactive children are found to be more active, aggressive, and inattentive in the classroom and to have irregularity of mood, often throwing temper tantrums or reacting with rage following slight frustrations (Campbell et al., 1978; Ross & Ross, 1976; Schleifer et al., 1975). Their speech may be somewhat immature (Creager & Van Riper, 1967; Nichamin, 1972), although this is not well established (Barkley, Cunningham, & Karlsson, Note 5), and their interactions with peers are generally poor compared to normal children. It has been my observation that these children are more often likely to be retained in kindergarten because of their social immaturity and lack of readiness for beginning first grade.

In middle childhood, greater peer problems seem to emerge, and aggression may become a salient problem (Ross & Ross, 1976; Safer & Allen, 1976). Over time, there are delays in academic achievement despite normal intelligence (Cantwell & Satterfield, 1978; Safer & Allen, 1976), and the child may fail at least one or more grades before junior high school (Weiss et al., 1975). Emotional problems such as low self-esteem, depression, and threats of suicide become apparent, probably as a reaction to a history of social and academic failure. Disruptive classroom behavior and problems with compliance at home continue through this age range (Campbell et al., 1978).

Emergence into adolescence brings with it a continuation of problems of restlessness and inattentiveness, although gross motor activity levels have declined (Shaffer et al., 1974; Weiss et al., 1975). Social interaction problems and conduct disorders seem to reach their peak at this time, with delinquency, stealing, lying, and trouble with the law being more frequent compared to normal adolescents (Cantwell, 1978; Minde et al., 1972; Ross & Ross, 1976). In addition, hyperactive adolescents seem more likely to abuse alcohol than nonhyperactive, learning disabled adolescents (Blouin, Bornstein, & Trites, 1978). Rebelliousness and antiauthoritarian attitudes are common (Mendelson, Johnson, & Stewart, 1971; Minde et al., 1972), and hyperactive boys continue to be described by parents and teachers as immature, acting out, and disruptive. Academically, many have repeated at least one grade and are still below classmates in achievement skills and classroom conduct (Ackerman, Dykman, & Peters, 1977; Dykman *et al.*, 1973). Truancy from school and quitting school are also more frequent than in normal adolescents (Ross & Ross, 1976).

In adulthood, some of the difficulties have lessened, partly because these individuals are now out of school and able to seek out environments that are more tolerant of their behavior. Although activity level and attention are improved over that observed in childhood, these individuals remain more restless and have trouble concentrating compared to normal adults. Nonetheless, they are not rated by their employers as significantly different from others (Weiss, Hechtman, Perlman, Hopkins, & Wener, 1978), and their rate of unemployment is not unusual. Yet, differences from normal still persist, with alcohol abuse, psychopathy, depression, lower-than-expected economic status, smoking, and problems with the law (Borland & Heckman, 1976; Menkes *et al.*, 1967; Weiss *et al.*, 1978).

In summary, hyperactivity appears to be a chronic problem throughout life, with difficulties in concentration, impulse control, and social conduct persisting into adulthood. Although the core behavior problems show some decline with age, as they do in normal children, for many hyperactive children they remain troublesome. It also seems that with increasing emergence into larger social contexts, problems in social adjustment become more evident. Hyperactive children are therefore more likely to be referred during the following peak crisis periods: (1) at symptom onset (ages 2–4 years); (2) upon entry into the school setting; and (3) upon emergence into the broader context of society during adolescence.

## The Families of Hyperactive Children

Several studies have attempted to evaluate globally the family environments of hyperactive children. These studies suggest that hyperactive children more often come from lower socioeconomic groups (Safer & Allen, 1976) and have poorer relationships with their families (Battle & Lacey, 1972; Stewart *et al.*, 1966; Weiss *et al.*, 1971). Studies also suggest that alcoholism, psychopathy, and hysteria are frequent problems in these families (Cantwell, 1972, 1978; Morrison & Stewart, 1971). A significant number of the parents (between 10% and 20%) report that they were also probably hyperactive as children, and these tend to be the parents with the greatest difficulties with alcoholism and conduct problems (Morrison & Stewart, 1971, 1973a). It seems that the very problems many of these children have as adults were experienced by their parents, leading some to speculate that the disorder may be familial (Cantwell, 1972; Routh, 1978), if not specifically genetic (Cantwell, 1975; Morrison & Stewart, 1973a). Studies of the siblings of hyperactive children find significantly more of them to be hyperactive, anxious, or depressed compared to a control group (Welner, Welner, Stewart, Palkes, & Wish, 1977).

Recently, studies of the social interactions between hyperactive children and their parents (typically mothers) suggest that mothers of such children are more

commanding, directive, negative, and controlling of their children and less responsive to their interactions than mothers of normal children (Battle & Lacey,
1972; Campbell, 1973, 1975; Cunningham & Barkley, 1979; Humphries Kins.
bourne, & Swanson, 1970). In these interactions, hyperactive children (typically
boys) are less compliant, more negative, and less interactive with their mothers
and engage in more independent, inappropriate play compared to normal children
(Campbell, 1973, 1975; Cunningham & Barkley, 1979). Caution is required in
determining the direction of effects in these interactions as the child may be equally
as influential as the adult in determining the nature of the interaction (Bell, 1971;
Bell & Harper, 1977). Several recent studies of drug effects on the interactions of
hyperactive children with their mothers suggest that the directive, controlling behaviors of mothers might be a reaction to, rather than an initial cause of, the child's
hyperactive behavior (Barkley & Cunningham, 1979b; Cunningham & Barkley,
1978; Humphries et al., 1978). Nevertheless, this directive parental style may serve
to exacerbate the existent aversive behaviors of the child (Patterson, 1976).

## Early Predictors of Hyperactivity

The early onset of hyperactive behavior in children has led many investigators to
search for possible predictors of children at risk for developing this disorder. The
results suggest several promising predictors. One may be a history of hyperactivity
in the childhood of one or both parents, or another, alcoholism and sociopathy in
the parents (Cantwell, 1972), although these require more thorough study. Minor
physical anomalies in the newborn have been repeatedly shown to predict later
learning and behavior problems. However, they are also found in higher frequencies
in psychotic and autistic children (Halverson & Victor, 1976; Waldrop, Bell,
McLaughlin, & Halverson, 1978; Waldrop, Pedersen, & Bell, 1968). Certainly,
one of the strongest predictors appears to be infant temperament. Temperament
comprises habit regularity (sleeping and eating patterns), reactivity to stimulation,
activity level, irritability, withdrawal, or negative mood. Infants with high ratings
in these areas have reliably been found to be diagnosed as behavior problems in
early childhood (Cameron, 1978; Campbell et al., 1978; Carey & McDevitt, 1978;
Graham, Rutter, & George, 1973; Kalverboer, Touwen, & Prechtl, 1973; McInerny
& Chamberlin, 1978). Activity level alone has also shown some predictive utility
in that preschool children who showed vigorous and intense activity levels were
more likely to have lower intelligence estimates, poorer cognitive skills, and poorer
interactions at age 7½ years (Halverson & Waldrop, 1976). Although not specifically predictive of hyperactivity, poor peer judgements of a child appear to be
predictive of later conduct problems (Halverson & Waldrop, 1976; Roff, 1961;
Ross & Ross, 1976).

Although each of these predictors shows some promise in terms of identifying
young children at risk for later hyperactivity, some caution in their interpretation
seems warranted. No factor by itself seems to offer any clinical utility in predicting
which children will or will not become hyperactive, despite statistically significant

correlations with later behavior problems. A multifactor regression equation is probably more helpful in that a child with several such factors may be at greater risk than a child with only one. Nevertheless, the usefulness of even a multifactor approach is limited for decisions on individual cases.

## Etiology

One of the earliest and most frequently proposed etiologies of hyperactivity was brain damage or injury, usually postulated to have occurred around the time of birth. The use of the term brain damage requires that one be able to demonstrate through autopsy, neurologic evaluation, or hard neurologic signs that the child's brain has suffered structural injury or alteration. Brain damage has been found to be associated with hyperactivity in only a very small proportion of children, although it does predict the child to be at risk for general psychiatric problems (Rutter, 1977; Sandberg et al., 1978; Werry, 1968b).

Although the brain injury hypothesis has not been supported, the etiologic concept of neurologic dysfunction still receives wide endorsement (Hertzig et al., 1969; Wender, 1971). The evidence for this concept is inconsistent and often inferential, based primarily on the findings of a greater number of "soft" neurologic signs (increased slow-wave activity on EEG, fine motor incoordination, etc.) and developmental histories with prenatal, perinatal, or postnatal complications in hyperactive as compared to normal children (see Millichap, 1977; Wender, 1971). The nature of the proposed dysfunction varies with the investigator and may involve disturbances of neurotransmitters (Wender, 1971), diencephalic dysfunction (Laufer, Denhoff, & Solomons, 1957) or brain stem arousal problems (Rosenthal, 1973). Support for these notions was often derived from the belief that the response of hyperactive children to stimulant drugs was different from that of normal children and indicative of the underlying central nervous system disturbance—a belief that has recently been questioned by stimulant drug studies with normal children (Rapoport, Buchsbaum, Zahn, Weingartner, Ludlow, & Mikkelsen, 1978). The most that one can conclude at this point is that neurologic dysfunction of some sort may eventually be shown to play a role in the hyperactivity of some children, although the nature of this dysfunction awaits specification and empirical support.

Neurologic immaturity has also been advanced as a possible cause of hyperactivity (Kinsbourne, 1977). The general thesis behind this argument is that those areas of cortex underlying the functions of attention and motor inhibition are experiencing a lag in development, perhaps related to the myelination of those areas. Support for this theory is found in the often-reported observation that many hyperactive children (30–50%) show patterns of underarousal on EEG suggestive of cortical immaturity (Hastings & Barkley, 1978). The reports of these children being socially and emotionally immature (Safer & Allen, 1976) are also consistent with this etiology. However, as with neurologic dysfunction, the concept requires greater clarification and research support.

A genetic basis for hyperactivity is receiving increasing attention and rests on reports that children born into families with alcoholism, psychopathy, and hyperactivity are more likely to be hyperactive, even when raised by adoptive parents (Morrison & Stewart, 1973a, 1973b). Despite the numerous confounding variables in such research, Cantwell (1975) has reviewed the evidence for this position and finds it promising, although in need of much research. The safest conclusion at this time is that there seems to be a familial component in the hyperactivity of some children that may prove to be hereditary in nature, although the actual model of inheritance awaits elucidation.

Various chemical toxins have been proposed as a basis for hyperactivity. The strongest support has been shown for lead poisoning or increased lead absorption (David, 1974). Research comparing children with elevated blood lead levels to those without such levels generally finds 25–35% of the lead-exposed group to be hyperactive, significantly more than in the control group (Baloh, Sturm, Green, & Gleser, 1975; de al Burde & Choate, 1972, 1974). These results do not address whether lead poisoning actually causes hyperactivity or whether hyperactive children are simply more likely to ingest lead, as they are found to do with other toxins (Stewart et al., 1970).

Another chemical cause of hyperactivity may be seen in the response of some children to tranquilizers and anticonvulsants. One recent study (Wolf & Forsythe, 1978) found that 42% of children placed on these drugs became hyperactive, with the hyperactivity diminishing upon discontinuance of the drug. Allergic reactions to food additives have also been proposed as a possible cause of hyperactivity (Feingold, 1975). Research, however, provides only weak support for this position, with most studies finding that food additives have minimal or no effect on objectively measured behavior (see Millichap, 1977, for a discussion; also Conners, Goyette, Southwick, Lees, & Andrulonis, 1976; Harley, Matthews, & Eichman, 1978; Wender, 1977). Yet, one recent study (Rose, 1978) noted a functional relationship between the ingestion of artificial food colors and increased behaviors typically observed in hyperactive children. The subjects, however, were two girls selected for their prior history of diet responsiveness. Hence, the study fails to address what percentage of hyperactive children are actually diet-responsive or the extent to which artificial colors in diet contribute to the etiology of hyperactivity.

Efforts to establish environmental or social causes of hyperactivity have been few, and therefore the influence of environmental variables cannot be judged at this time (Routh, 1978). Certainly, hyperactive behavior varies across situations (Barkley, 1977b; Campbell et al., 1978, Rapoport & Benoit, 1975) and can be readily influenced by its consequences, whether they be changes in parental or teacher attention (Ayllon, Layman, & Kandel, 1975; Mash & Dalby, 1979; Willis & Lovaas, 1977) or punishment (Cunningham & Knights, 1978). Both hyperactive and normal children can be influenced by hyperactive or hypoactive models (Barkley & Routh, 1974; Kasper, Note 2), as well as by the degree of environmental stimulation (Zentall & Zentall, 1976). Nonetheless, a well-explicated environmental theory of hyperactivity that can adequately account for previous research findings remains to be developed.

# BEHAVIORAL CONCEPTUALIZATION OF HYPERACTIVITY

The previous discussion does not include an examination of those stimuli or response consequences that exert a considerable influence over the occurrence of hyperactive behaviors. However, to specify guidelines for assessment and treatment of these behaviors, their controlling variables require specification and elucidation. What follows, then, is a behavioral analysis of hyperactivity that in some instances is speculative but in most remains closely tied to what is commonly accepted about hyperactivity.

## Analysis of Hyperactive Behavior

Among the many deficits observed in hyperactive children, those of poor attention span and poor self-control have been repeatedly emphasized. Skinner (1953) has provided a behavioral conceptualization of attention that may serve as a framework for understanding the problems of hyperactive children. Skinner (1953) describes attention as involving a functional relationship between a controlling stimulus and a response. Deficits in attention are viewed as disturbances in one or more aspects of the relation between a discriminative stimulus and the behavior typically evoked by that stimulus. The problem is in the relationship between these events, not necessarily with the behavior itself.

Although there are numerous facets in this relation between stimulus and response, several important ones seem to be especially problematic for hyperactive children. One of these appears to be the duration of responding to a stimulus, or attention span. Hyperactive children are often reported to have great difficulty staying "on-task," or completing activities. Second, the time interval between the unpredictable occurrence of a stimulus and the occurrence of the appropriate response is often significantly longer in hyperactive than in normal children. This is most often witnessed in simple reaction-time tasks, where hyperactive children are consistently observed to be slower to react to the experimental stimulus than are normal children (Douglas, 1972; Douglas & Peters, 1979). Interestingly, a third, but related, problem occurs when the stimulus is not an uncertain one. In this case, hyperactive children appear to respond significantly faster to the stimulus and often to an incorrect, but more obvious, dimension of the stimulus. These three difficulties appear to be similar to the often-cited symptoms of poor attention span, poor concentration or distractibility, and poor impulse control in hyperactive children.

A second area of difficulty for the hyperactive child that is of greater social significance is self-control (see Karoly, Chapter 2, this volume). Skinner (1953) defines *self-control* as the emission of a response by an individual that alters the probability of a subsequent response by that individual. For instance, setting an alarm clock at bedtime is viewed as self-control because it increases the probability of awakening at a particular time the next morning. Skinner also points out that self-control does not remove the individual from control by his environment—it is merely a shift of control from social stimuli, such as other people, to nonsocial stimuli, such as inanimate objects or internal stimuli (those within the body that are otherwise referred to as private events). Hyperactive children appear to have difficulty with this shift of control from external to internal stimuli. In fact, this seems to be precisely what many parents of hyperactive children complain of in describing their children—their greater need for supervision and control by others (Barkley & Cunningham, 1979a).

### Contingency-Shaped versus Rule-Governed Behavior

Skinner (1953, 1967) goes on to point out that the absence or presence of self-control can be thought of as contingency-shaped versus rule-governed behavior. *Contingency-shaped behavior* refers to behavior that is shaped or consequated by the immediately occurring natural consequences in a given situation. For instance, a child who touches a hot stove and quickly withdraws his hand when burned is said to show contingency-shaped behavior when, in a similar subsequent situation, the child avoids the hot stove. This is contrasted with *rule-governed behavior*, where the behavior emitted is in response to a verbal stimulus providing information about that response, the response is in general accord with that information, and the response is consequated by socially (unnaturally) arranged contingencies. Following the preceding example, the child, in this case, is told by his mother not to touch the hot stove and is praised for not doing so or is punished by his mother for going too near the stove or reaching out to touch it. The avoidance of the hot stove in subsequent situations when the mother says to avoid it is referred to as rule-governed behavior by the child. In future situations, should the child avoid the hot stove in the absence of his mother, he is said to show self-control. Actually, in this situation, the child is likely responding to "internalized," or private, stimuli representing the initially overt rule, such as repeating the rule to oneself subvocally (self-speech).

Although such instances of rule-governed behavior may produce results similar to contingency-shaped behavior (avoidance of the stove), they do not produce identical behaviors, as the contingencies and consequating events in these two situations are quite different. In one instance, the child is actually burned and learns to avoid the stove, whereas in the other, he is never exposed to the natural consequences. Rule-governed behavior appears to be of critical importance to the socialization of children as (1) it permits the community to train the child to respond to the long-term consequences of an event, (2) it prevents the child's behavior from being shaped by the possibly spurious or inconsistent natural consequences of an immediate event, and (3) it prevents exposure of the child to harmful or life-threatening consequences (i.e., touching a hot stove or running into a busy street). It therefore appears to be the use of language or symbolic stimuli (typically verbal) that permits the verbal community to train the child to respond to rules of the community and eventually to bring the child's behavior under the control of non-social stimuli (such as objects or private events)—that is, to develop self-control.

Hence, deficiencies in self-control, as seen in hyperactive children, are probably deficiencies in some aspect of rule-governed behavior.

### Processes Leading to Rule-Governed Behavior

The major processes leading to rule-governed behavior and hence to many forms of self-control appear briefly to be as follows: (1) the possession of a language by the social community; (2) the presence of the neurological substrate needed to perceive and reproduce the language; (3) the training of the child in the language of the community; (4) the presence of an intact neurologic substrate permitting the translation of linguistic stimuli into motor responses or behavior; (5) the training of the child to comply with (respond to) rules provided by others in that language; (6) the training of the child to respond to his memory of those rules (internalized rules or self-speech); and (7) the training of the child in problem solving, or second-order, rule-governed behavior. Problems occurring in any of these steps or processes would lead to deficiencies in some or all aspects of later steps. The earlier in the sequence the deficiency occurs, the more widespread or severe the deficiency in self-control. However, self-control would be less likely to be disturbed in the older child or adult should these prerequisite steps later become defective. Obviously, according to this model, some problems in self-control in children can be environmentally caused (i.e., poor training), whereas others may be neurologically based (i.e., damage or dysfunction of critical neurologic substrates)

With respect to hyperactive children, it is assumed that processes 1 through 3 have occurred or exist without difficulty. The problems with self-control must therefore lie somewhere in processes 4 through 7. Following this line of reasoning, some hyperactive children may have damage or dysfunction in the neurologic substrate permitting the translation of linguistic symbols into the appropriate motor responses, which they dictate or represent. The likely location of this substrate is the frontal cortex, especially the left anterior frontal region in most people (Hecaen & Albert, 1977; Luria, 1966). The frontal cortex has also been shown to play a key role in sustained attention and in motor planning, regulation, and execution, areas in which some hyperactive children have problems (poor attention and motor incoordination). Certainly, the inadequate training of the child to comply with the rules provided by others, or poor parental management, may also lead to problems in self-control despite adequate neurologic development. Again, one of the major difficulties of hyperactive children is in compliance to parental commands (Barkley & Cunningham, 1979a; Cunningham & Barkley, 1979b). Inadequacies in training may also occur in teaching the child compliance with self-speech (internalized rules) and in problem solving, though problems in compliance to adult commands would probably not be as severe if these were the only defective steps in self-control. Thus, the major difficulties for most hyperactive children probably reside in process 4 or 5—defective neurologic substrates or inadequate training in compliance to social rules—or in both.

Although this may be the case, some discussion is needed of compliance to internal language or self-speech as well as problem solving by the child. Once a child has been adequately conditioned to comply with the rules provided by the verbal community, the community (i.e., parents) begins to limit its repeated provision of the same rules, instead consequating the child's behavior for compliance or noncompliance in the absence of the overt or external rule. This apparently conditions children to comply with their own memory of that rule instead of the external rule, or to rely on self-speech, or children's covertly repeating the rule to themselves. Once compliance to internal speech is adequately developed, the final phase of problem solving can begin, although it probably overlaps to some extent with earlier steps. Skinner (1953) refers to problem solving as second-order rule-governed behavior, in that it involves the individuals' asking questions of themselves or others (second-order rules) aimed at eliciting first-order rules or relevant descriptions of the contingencies operating in the problem situation. This leads to the generation of a rule (solution) that the person uses in subsequent similar situations. Assuming that a major problem with hyperactive children rests in their acquiring compliance to external rules provided by others, one would expect them also to show difficulties in developing and responding to self-speech and in problem solving as described here. The studies of Meichenbaum (1976) and others (Douglas, 1976) lend some support to this argument, although much more research is required to test these hypotheses.

Nonetheless, it will be the proposition of this chapter that the essence of hyperactivity in children is not simply a deficit in attention but also a deficit in the acquisition of age-appropriate rule-governed behavior and self-control. From these difficulties can easily arise those impressions of poor concentration, impulsivity, lack of inhibition, poor social relationships, and poor academic achievement often noted in hyperactive children.

## Behavioral Definition of Hyperactivity

From the previous discussion and review of the literature comes the following definition of hyperactivity: *Hyperactivity is the developmental deficiency of age-appropriate attention and rule-governed behavior (self-control) that is present in the child since at least ages 2–4 years, that is pervasive in nature (cross-situational), and that cannot be attributed to mental retardation, psychosis, or gross neurologic, sensory, or motor impairments.* As such, it is certainly a type of conduct disorder, but one that is distinguished from others of childhood by its early onset, poor attention span, and pervasive nature of problems in rule-governed behavior. In addition, it can occur as the result either of early poor socialization or training experiences or of as yet unrecognized minor injury, dysfunction, or immaturity of prerequisite neurologic substrates.

## Behavioral Analysis of Hyperactive Behavior within the Family

If hyperactivity is a deficiency of attention, rule-governed behavior, and self-control, it is worth examining how such behavior affects the parents and family members who must interact with the hyperactive child and whether their responses to the child exacerbate his or her problems or, indeed, create and maintain them.

An excellent model for conceptualizing the effects of child behaviors on adults has been set forth by Bell (see Bell & Harper, 1977). Since Bell's (1968) classic review of the literature in this area, many studies have been amassed that indicate that the characteristics and behaviors of a child serve as a source of controlling stimuli over the responding of parents to that child. As such, the child has a great deal of influence over the manner in which he or she is treated. In addition, the children's health, appearance, temperament, muscle tone, emotional reactivity, activity level, language development, intellectual level, and prior experience with adults all affect the nature of children's behavior toward parents and thus the parents' responding to them (Bell, 1968, 1971; Bell & Harper, 1977; Harper, 1971; Lamb, 1978, Passman & Mulhern, 1977).

In this theory, Bell (1977) assumes that parents possess upper and lower limits, or thresholds, relative to the frequency, intensity, duration, and situational or age appropriateness of their child's behavior. In the case where behavior by the child exceeds these limits in either direction, certain repertoires of parental behavior will be elicited as a result of their history of affecting these child behaviors. These may reduce excessive responding in the child or may serve to elicit higher levels of behavior where they are inappropriately infrequent.

Where the child's behavior is inappropriately excessive, as it often is in the hyperactive child, it will typically elicit a repertoire of responses that Bell (1977) calls *upper limit controls*. These generally consist of ignoring the child, perhaps providing reasons to him for restricting his behavior, or giving him restrictive commands, threats, or social or physical punishment. Following the principle of negative reinforcement, such parental behaviors are probably elicited and maintained because of their prior history of success in reducing excessive child behaviors.

The behavior of the parent may be hierarchically or sequentially organized such that in the initial stages, the parent may respond to excessive behavior by ignoring it and then by reasoning. Where these are unsuccessful, subsequent responses may consist of restrictive commands or threats, social punishment, and, ultimately, physical disciplining of the child. It is not necessary for the parent to proceed through this hierarchy of controls on each new occasion of excessive behavior. In fact, what is likely to occur is that earlier unsuccessful parental behaviors are extinguished with this particular child, and the parent responds immediately with more severe upper limit controls and, in some cases, physical punishment or abuse. In addition, events unrelated to the child that place further stress on the parent are likely to result in an increase in the use of punishment in response to excessive or hyperactive behaviors (Passman & Mulhern, 1977).

I have found in work on parent–child interactions with hyperactive children (Barkley & Cunningham, 1979a) that mothers of these children complain greatly of their inability to control the child's behavior. Many say that their final solution to coping with the child's chronic noncompliance is acquiescence rather than aggression, although they often vacillate between these alternatives. Hence, after a series of repeated commands to a chronically noncompliant child in a given situation, these parents report that they no longer escalate their reactions in a negative direction but simply give up enforcing the command and, in some instances, complete their own commands (i.e., pick up toys or dress the child). In conjunction with this acquiescence in enforcing commands, these mothers often report withdrawing from interactions with the child in an effort to avoid future command–noncompliance confrontations. Thus, the end stage of adjustment of some parents to chronically noncompliant children may not be high levels of upper limit controls or disciplining (because this, too, may prove ineffective), but acquiescence to the child or reduction in enforcing commands. Such a response by the parent, however, may only serve to strengthen the already noncompliant behavior of the child.

Where the child displays appropriate behavior that falls between the upper and lower limit controls of the parent, the typical reaction of the parent is likely to be the use of *equilibrium controls*. These response repertoires serve to maintain or reinforce the ongoing child behaviors and are probably maintained by the child's continuation of appropriate behavior. Such parental behaviors as observing, describing or narrating the child's behavior, positive social interactions, praise, physical contact, and affection may all serve to reinforce appropriate child behaviors.

However, in parents of hyperactive children, the likelihood of the parent's responding to appropriate child behaviors with equilibrium controls may be reduced, as in parents of aggressive children (Patterson, 1976). Because of the history of aversive interactions with the child, the parents, as noted previously, may withdraw from the child in an effort to prevent recurrences of confrontations. In my experience, many of the parents of these children say that when the child is playing quietly or behaving appropriately, they actively avoid interactions with him or her so as to sustain the child's behavior. They report that apparently when they have previously paid attention to the child's good behavior, it has provoked episodes of disruptive behavior from the child.

Parental behaviors called *lower limit controls* are elicited when a child's behavior is inappropriately infrequent or unresponsive. Low activity level, delayed language development, and mental retardation may create low-rate behaviors in children to which the parent responds with lower limit controls. These typically consist of drawing the child's attention to stimuli, coaxing, questioning, prompting, encouraging, and praising, as well as giving provocative (activity eliciting) commands and physical guidance. As with upper limit controls, equilibrium and lower limit response sets by the parent are probably hierarchically organized and show a sequential pattern over time in interactions with the child (Bell, 1977).

These effects of child behaviors on parents were well documented in a recent study by Cunningham and Barkley (1978). Two severely hyperactive twin boys were observed individually interacting with their mother in a clinic playroom for a 30-minute period. Half of this time was spent in free play and half accomplishing several tasks, such as having the child pick up the toys in the room. Observations were made once each week over a four-week period for both boys. The first session served as a baseline, while in the remaining weeks the boys experienced a double-blind, drug–placebo reversal design using 15 mg of Ritalin or of placebo prior to each observation session. The parent–child interactions were recorded using the

Response Class Matrix (Mash, Terdal, & Anderson, 1973), and activity level was measured by actometers (Johnson, 1971). This interaction coding system permits the recording of reciprocal interactions between parent and child by using two observers; one records the parent's response to the child's behavior, and the other records the child's response to the parent's behavior.

When the boys were off medication, actometer measures found them to be extremely active during both play and task sessions. When the children were on Ritalin, the activity level was reduced substantially. The more salient results for the interaction measures appears in Figure 1. As the figure shows, the boys were extremely noncompliant while off medication or on placebo. While taking medication, their levels of compliance were significantly improved. In response, their mother became significantly less commanding, more rewarding of compliance, and more positively responsive to the children's interactions and play. By rendering the children's behavior more appropriate, the Ritalin resulted in substantial changes in maternal behavior toward the children, with decreases in upper limit controls and increases in equilibrium controls.

As this study shows, parent and child behaviors can be viewed as a reciprocal feedback system where the behavior of each serves as both controlling stimuli and consequating events for the behavior of the other. Wahler (1976) has discussed this manner of viewing family interactions with deviant children. As he notes, the child's behavior, although identified as deviant by the family, is probably very adaptive within the family's contingencies of reinforcement. Similarly, so are the responses of the family members to the deviant child. In the case of hyperactive children, the frequently high levels of commands and negative behavior of the parents toward the children are at least in part a response to the hyperactive behaviors of the children and are probably maintained by the response of the children to the control (Barkley & Cunningham, 1979b; Cunningham & Barkley, Note 5).

Both Wahler (1976) and Patterson (1976) believe that the excessive oppositional behaviors of deviant children are developed or maintained by the operation of negative reinforcement. This explanation states that when a child initially emits an aversive behavior, such as screaming or a temper tantrum, the parent is likely to respond in an effort to reduce the ongoing aversiveness. Typically, this consists of reacting with upper limit controls such as commands or disciplining. The subsequent reduction in aversive behavior by the child negatively reinforces the commanding and negative behavior of the parent toward the child under future situations. However, under other circumstances, the child's aversive behavior may have met initially with parental negative behavior, which, with continued aversive behavior by the child, capitulated to acquiescence by the parent, as noted previously. Obviously, this parental response negatively reinforces the child's repertoire of sustaining his or her aversive behavior, even though it initially meets with negative parental behaviors.

Both of these instances probably operate to some degree in interactions between hyperactive children and their parents, producing what Patterson (1976) calls *coercive interaction patterns*. Patterson (1976) suggests that whether the parent's initially negative reaction to the child's aversive behavior is successful at reducing the

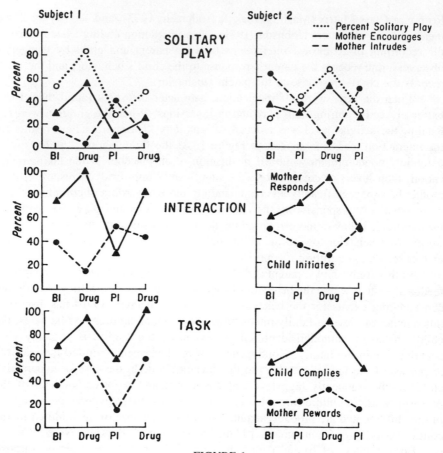

FIGURE 1

Selected behavioral measures from the Response Class Matrix (Mash, Terdal, & Anderson, 1973) for two hyperactive twin boys and their mother during baseline (Bl), drug, and placebo (Pl) sessions. Solitary play and interaction measures were derived from a 15-minute free play session, and task measures were taken from a 15-minute task session. From "The Effects of Ritalin on the Mother–Child Interactions of Hyperkinetic Twin Boys" by C. Cunningham and R. Barkley, *Developmental Medicine and Child Neurology*, 1978, *20*, 634–642. Copyright 1978 by Spastics International Medical Publications. Reprinted by permission.

behavior or whether the parent will acquiesce depends on the rate of escalation of negative behavior by the parent or child. If the parent's initial reaction escalates quickly to intensely negative behavior to the child, it may succeed in reducing the child's behavior. Yet, if the child's aversive behavior escalates faster than the parent's behavior to an intense and high rate of aversiveness, the parent acquiesces. In either case, negative interactions or coercion (Patterson, 1976) may come to be developed and sustained in both parent and child by negative reinforcement. The general effect is to increase coercive negative interactions in the family system, which may come to be adopted by other family members as the common mode of interaction.

In summary, regardless of the initial cause of the hyperactive child's difficulties with attention, rule-governed behavior (compliance), and self-control, the eventual impact can be quite disruptive and destructive to the overall functioning of the family. Initial parental reactions to the child's problems may consist of typical upper limit controls but, without success, may escalate to more negative, intense reactions to the child. Again, where ineffective, these reactions are also extinguished, with the parent ultimately either using aggression against the child or adopting a strategy of acquiescence, neither of which is an effective long-term solution to the problems of the hyperactive child. That greater marital or psychiatric problems in the parents of these children would develop or become exacerbated by such interaction patterns is obvious, especially where one parent (the mother) may be experiencing the greater difficulties with the child.

# IMPLICATIONS FOR ASSESSMENT

Several broad implications can be drawn from the previous review and discussion for the assessment of hyperactive children. These implications are as follows:

1. The primary behavior problems of hyperactive children appear to have an early onset and are chronic, making several demands on assessment procedures. First, the methods used should be reliable over time and valid across age levels, permitting comparability of findings obtained from repeated assessments. Second, the changing nature of the disorder over time, especially with respect to increasing social and academic problems, necessitates the use of measures that assess social interactions and social skills, as well as cognitive and academic deficits. The reader is referred to the chapters in this book dealing with conduct disorders, learning disabilities, self-control, and social skills for the most promising of the assessment methods for these behavior disorders. Third, the use of measures that have developmental norms is imperative if one is to assess and reassess the age-appropriateness of the hyperactive child's behavior and to draw conclusions as to whether it is or remains problematic or statistically atypical.

2. Hyperactivity is often cross-situational in nature, which suggests that more than one informant should be used in assessing the child's problems. Most often, parents, teachers, social workers, relatives, or other clinicians serve in this capacity, representing the different major situations in which most children participate, that is, home, school, clinic, and so forth. I have often found that mothers and fathers frequently disagree on the existence, nature, and severity of a child's problems. Such disagreement should not be construed as inaccuracy on either parent's part, because hyperactive children may behave differently for one parent than for the other. The opinions of each parent should be recorded and judged as credible for that parent's interactions with the child until proven otherwise.

3. Given the likelihood of the parents' or other family members' having

psychological difficulties, the evaluation must be broadened to assess these factors. Parent conduct problems, poor impulse control, alcoholism, and hysteria have a great impact on parent–child interactions and will confound the clinician's efforts at intervention if not assessed and treated where necessary. In my experience, these parental problems, when present, often interfere with the acquisition and utilization of behavior management skills.

4. The behavioral perspective of hyperactivity taken here—a deficiency in attention, rule-governed behavior, and self-control—leads to the inescapable conclusion that the assessment of the hyperactive child cannot simply focus on a single response class such as motor activity levels. Instead, one must assess the child's ability to sustain attention to activities as well as to follow commands, directives, and rules across a variety of situations at home, at school, or in public. Pertinent questions requiring attention during assessment involve whether or not the child has trouble following rules (noncompliance), and if so, under what situations, with what types of commands, and with what individuals. As was noted previously, where problems in compliance and rule-governed behavior exist, difficulties with self-control and problem solving might also require assessment (see Chapter 2, this volume, for specific methods of evaluation). Because social conduct with others draws upon one's knowledge of and ability to follow rules of conduct or etiquette, hyperactive children are also likely to manifest deficits in social skills (Pelham, Note 4). These, too, require assessment (see Chapter 8, this volume).

5. The problems with rule-governed behavior in hyperactive children obviously occur in some social context. The child's hyperactive behaviors have been seen to have a great deal of influence on others and on the manner in which they respond to the child. Because the response of others (typically parents, siblings, and teachers) can exacerbate the child's initial problems, the behavior of these individuals toward the child must also be assessed. The examiner should be especially sensitive to the development or existence of coercive social interaction patterns within the families of hyperactive children.

6. Given the reciprocal influences involved in parent–child interactions, the assignment of blame or fault is arbitrary and can no longer be unilaterally ascribed to either member of the interaction. Even where the initial problem with the child may be neurological, its existence within a social interaction system determines its expression and severity, and thus the parent shares responsibility for the problem. It is the interaction, not the parent or child, that is "at fault" and it is that interaction that should be the focus of assessment and treatment.

These general implications should provide a basis for selecting various assessment methods with which to evaluate the hyperactive child.


## ASSESSMENT


The assessment of hyperactive children typically involves both a parental and child interview, the use of rating scales, and the objective assessment of the child's social interactions.

## Parental Interview

*Purposes*

Despite its possible unreliability, the parental interview is an indispensable part of the assessment of behavior problem children. Such an interview serves many purposes. First, it establishes rapport among the parents, child, and examiner, which will prove invaluable in gaining the parents' cooperation. Second, it provides descriptive information regarding the parents' view of the child's problems, which aids in narrowing the focus for later, more direct observations. Third, provided it is acceptable to the parents, the child can be permitted to remain in the office or clinic playroom during the interview. In our clinic, a playroom is available with observation facilities where later direct assessment of the parent–child interactions will occur. The interview is usually conducted in this playroom, with the hyperactive child present. This permits the child to become accustomed to the room for more than an hour before the observation and testing takes place. I believe that such a habituation period is necessary for hyperactive children, as their behavior is usually not disruptive during the initial visit to a clinic (Kenny *et al.*, 1971) but worsens as they become familiar with the situation (Barkley, 1977b). Allowing the child in the room during the interview also permits some initial observations of parent–child interactions, especially while the parent is trying to talk to the examiner. Many hyperactive children present problems for their parents when visitors are in the home; structuring the interview in this way allows the examiner to see if similar problems develop. Fourth, the interview serves as an initial introduction for parents to those factors considered important in behavioral assessment (Wahler, 1976). As Wahler (1976) reports, many parents tend to emphasize developmental–historical causes for childhood problems. The process of the behavioral interview serves to focus parental attention on stimulus–response–consequation factors, thereby preparing them for initial training in observing problem behaviors. Some would add that a fifth purpose of the inverview is to assist in diagnosis of the child's disorder. This, however, is a much less important goal with hyperactive children compared to the elucidation of specific problem interactions and behaviors and their controlling events and consequences. Viable treatment recommendations flow from the latter and generally not from a diagnosis, because the treatments will hinge on the individual problems of the child and family.

After obtaining the typical demographic data related to the child—his or her school placement and age, family size, parental occupations, and so forth—the interview proceeds to a consideration of the specific concerns of the family and their nature and history. It is important that general statements or descriptors of problem behaviors be elaborated upon, as reports of "overactivity" or "stubbornness" are rarely helpful by themselves (Wahler, 1976). Parents of hyperactive children frequently respond to the opening broad question about current concerns with general descriptors such as "the child cannot sit still or pay attention," "he fights with everyone," or "she has got us at our wits' end." Their hasty launch into other problems usually requires redirection to the initially expressed problems for clarification. As in any behavioral interview, the focus is on clarifying current controlling stimuli and consequences for specific problem behaviors. Once this information is obtained, questioning about the history of the problem behaviors can proceed and, as noted previously, often reveals difficulties since early childhood. If so, parents should be queried as to what factors prompted referral at the present time. This question usually suggests that other community agencies (school, health care clinic) or individuals (neighbors, relatives) were integral to defining the child's behavior as deviant and urging the family to seek help. Less frequently, the parents have sought help on their own, perhaps in response to the intolerable pitch of negative family interactions or even as a result of reading popular articles on hyperactivity. The specific factor prompting referral often reveals much regarding parental motivation for treatment.

## *Format*

At this point, the interview should shift to a review of common home and public situations in which the parents and child interact. I have found it extremely useful to follow an interview format adapted from that used by Hanf (see Table 1). A standard set of questions (right column of Table 1) is used to obtain information on parent–child interactions in at least 14 different situations (left column). For each setting, the examiner should determine the general nature of the child's behavior, whether the parent feels a problem exists, and if so, what specific kind. In addition, one should ask what events in that setting trigger the problem behavior, how the parent usually responds initially, and what subsequent responses are likely

TABLE 1
Parental Interview Format

| Situations to be discussed with parents | Follow-up questions for each problematic situation |
|---|---|
| General—overall interactions<br>Playing alone<br>Playing with other children<br>Mealtimes<br>Getting dressed in morning<br>During washing and bathing<br>While parent is on telephone<br>While watching television<br>While visitors are at home<br>While visiting others' homes<br>In public places (supermarkets, shopping centers, etc.)<br>While mother is occupied with chores or activities<br>When father is at home<br>When child is asked to do a chore<br>At bedtime<br>Other situations (in car, in church, etc.) | 1. Is this a problem area? If so, then proceed with questions 2 through 9<br>2. What does the child do in this situation that bothers you?<br>3. What is your response?<br>4. What will the child do next?<br>5. If the problem continues, what will you do next?<br>6. What is usually the outcome of this interaction?<br>7. How often do these problems occur in this situation?<br>8. How do you feel about these problems?<br>9. On a scale of 0 to 10 (0 = no problem; 10 = severe problem), how severe is this problem to you? |

*Note.* Adapted from C. Hanf, University of Oregon Health Sciences Center, 1976.

to be made by the child. If problem behaviors continue in this interaction, it is helpful to learn what the parent's subsequent responses will be, and how effective they are. The frequency of these problem interactions in this setting over time is then determined. Finally, the parent is asked how he or she feels about the problem interactions and what effect they have had on him or her or the family. The parent is asked to rate the problems in the particular situation on a scale of zero (no problem) to ten (severe problem), to permit the collection of numerical data from the interview. Each problem situation is followed up with this series of questions.

The value of this interview format is illustrated by the following example:

EXAMINER: How does your child generally behave when there are visitors at your home?

MOTHER: Terrible! He embarrasses me tremendously.

E: Can you give me some idea of what he does specifically that is bothersome in this situation?

M: Well, he won't let me talk with the visitors without interrupting our conversation, tugging on me for attention, or annoying the guests by running back and forth in front of us as we talk.

E: Yes? And what else is he likely to do?

M: Many times, he will fight with his sister or get into something he shouldn't in the kitchen.

E: How will you usually respond to him when these things happen?

M: At first I usually try to ignore him. When this doesn't work, I try to reason with him, promise I'll spend time with him after the visitors leave, or try to distract him with something he usually likes to do just to calm him down so I can talk to my guests.

E: How successfully does that work for you?

M: Not very well. He may slow down for a few moments, but then he's right back pestering us or his sister, or getting into mischief in the kitchen. I get so frustrated with him by this time. I know what my visitors must be thinking of me not being able to handle my own child.

E: Yes, I can imagine it's quite distressing. What will you do at this point to handle the situation?

M: I usually find myself telling him over and over again to stop what he is doing, until I get very angry with him and threaten him with punishment. By now, my visitors are making excuses to leave and I'm trying to talk with them while yelling at my son.

E: And then what happens?

M: Well, I know I shouldn't, but I'll usually grab him and hold him just to slow him down. More often, though, I may threaten to spank him or send him to his room. He usually doesn't listen to me though until I make a move to grab him.

E: How often does this usually happen when visitors are at your home?

M: Practically every time; it's frustrating.

E: I see. How do you feel about your child creating such problems in front of visitors?

M: I find myself really hating him at times (*cries*); I know I'm his mother and I shouldn't feel that way, but I'm so angry with him, and nothing seems to work for me. Many of our friends have stopped coming to visit us, and we can't find a babysitter who will stay with him so we can go out. I resent having to sacrifice what little social life we have. I'm likely to be angry with him the rest of the day.

This case illustrates the valuable data on parent–child interactions that can be obtained using this format and how it fits in nicely with the earlier conceptualization by Bell (1977) of child effects on parents. Note the hierarchical arrangement of parental responses that sequentially come into play when prior responses prove useless. The escalation to upper limit controls by the mother is evident, as is the coercive interaction pattern of the child discussed by Patterson (1976) and Wahler (1976). Also, the mother's initial positive responses to ongoing aversive child behaviors probably reinforces them, making subsequent aversive behaviors more likely. The treatment recommendations derived from such an interview will be discussed in a succeeding section of this chapter.

The noncompliance of the hyperactive child permeates many, though not all, of the situations covered in this behavioral interview, and the general nature of the parent–child problem interactions remains quite similar across them. Frequently, the parent initially responds by ignoring the child or by reasoning with him or her. This changes to repetition of the initial command three or four times with increasing negative emotion. At this point, the parent usually escalates to using a threat with the repeated command. This may be repeated twice before the interaction, now highly emotionally charged for the parent, terminates with the parent using aggression against the child, acquiescing to the child and forgetting the command, or carrying out the command (i.e., eventually picking up the toys the child refused to clean up). The additional presence of external stress for the parent when entering such an interaction often results in near abuse of the child, self-imposed confinement by the parent to avoid abuse of the child, or temporary desertion of the household by the parent. Treatment, therefore, should be aimed at disrupting this escalating chain of aversive interaction early in the sequence.

The situations in the interview that are likely to prove most problematic for the hyperactive child are presented in Table 2. This table summarizes the parent's ratings of severity of the compliance problems in each situation for 27 hyperactive children and 13 normal children recently screened as part of a research project. The percentage of each group having problems in that setting is also provided. As these data show, the hyperactive child is likely to have problems across a wide variety of settings, with the most salient ones in situations involving play with other children, dressing in the morning, when the parent is on the phone, while visitors are in the house, in public places such as shopping centers, and during chore performance. Most of these children present fewer compliance problems for their fathers. In addition, problems during solitary play rarely develop, as the parents often report that the child rarely plays alone. The data in Table 2 underscore the utility of this interview format in distinguishing hyperactive from normal children in their parent–child interactions and in suggesting which situations will later prove most fruitful for observing and recording problematic interactions.

TABLE 2

Percentage and Parent-Rated Severity of Problems for Hyperactive and Normal Children, as Derived from the Parental Interview

| Situation from interview | Hyperactives (n = 27) | | Normals (n = 13) | |
|---|---|---|---|---|
| | % | Rating[a] | % | Rating[a] |
| Overall interactions | 74 | 5.0 | 0 | 0.0 |
| Play alone | 22 | 1.3 | 7 | 0.3 |
| Play with others | 81 | 6.1 | 7 | 0.1 |
| Mealtimes | 63 | 4.2 | 7 | 0.2 |
| Dressing in morning | 67 | 3.9 | 0 | 0.0 |
| Washing and bathing | 33 | 1.6 | 15 | 0.5 |
| Parent on telephone | 82 | 5.0 | 31 | 1.4 |
| During television | 48 | 2.8 | 7 | 0.6 |
| Visitors at home | 82 | 5.4 | 0 | 0.0 |
| Visiting others' homes | 67 | 4.5 | 0 | 0.0 |
| In public places | 89 | 5.9 | 7 | 0.4 |
| While mother is occupied | 48 | 2.6 | 0 | 0.0 |
| Father at home | 33 | 2.1 | 7 | 0.4 |
| Chores | 59 | 3.6 | 7 | 0.2 |
| Bedtime | 67 | 5.7 | 38 | 2.0 |
| Other situations | 70 | 5.3 | 15 | 0.7 |

[a]The severity of each problem was rated by the parent on a scale of 0 (no problem) to 10 (severe problem); these ratings are the mean ratings for each group.

In assessing the child's noncompliance through interview and direct observation, attention needs to be paid to the nature of the noncompliance, because treatment recommendations will vary as a function of this information. This is substantiated by a review of Table 3, where the different types of disturbance in compliance are briefly presented along with treatment suggestions for each type. Any child may show one or all of these stimulus control problems, and thus any or all treatment suggestions may apply. If later direct observations of the child are not feasible, it is imperative that greater time be given to these issues in the interview.

As noted previously, hyperactive children are likely to have learning disabilities and/or behavioral problems in school (see Chapter 10, this volume, for a discussion of the assessment of learning disabilities). With respect to school behavior problems, an approach similar to the parental interview can be followed. The history, nature, frequency, and controlling variables of the hyperactive behavior as discussed with the parents are later discussed with the teacher.

The parents should then be queried as to the child's developmental and medical history in order to determine the potential contribution of these factors to the presenting problems. Parents should be questioned specifically about early exposure to lead or lead poisoning and about whether the child is currently on anticonvulsants or tranquilizers, as these etiologic possibilities have specific medical treatments (chelation therapy, removal from or change in drugs, etc.). Where medical or neurologic problems are suspected from the history, referral to a physician is essential. Without any suggestions of treatable medical problems, however, referral

TABLE 3
Problems Leading to Noncompliance

| Problem | Corrective action |
| --- | --- |
| Vague, ambiguous, or distorted commands presented by parents | Instruct parents on presenting clear and concise direct commands. |
| Parental command given as a question | Train parent in use of direct commands without voice inflection implying a question or without direct questions. |
| Refusal by child to initiate compliance to parental command | Train parents to provide positive attention contingent on episodes where compliance is initiated within 5 seconds and to use brief time-out periods contingent upon noncompliance after 5 seconds. |
| Inability of child to sustain compliance to a command | Train parents to provide positive attention for very brief periods of compliance. Then train them to shape or increase gradually the intervals of compliance for which they will give positive attention. When child terminates compliance before task completion, train parents to give one warning for child to return to the task and then apply brief time out. |
| Excessive duration of child's compliance | Use a kitchen timer with child by setting timer to interval somewhat greater than that eventually desired for the task. Make attention and praise contingent on compliance within the interval, and time out contingent on failure to do so within interval. Gradually reduce the time interval on timer until desired compliance time is achieved; gradually remove use of timer. |
| Poor quality of compliance | Ensure that parents have concisely specified the desired behaviors for the task and desired outcome and that the child has the requisite skills. Parent then models desired behavior, consequates child's behavior for (non)imitation, and specifies in writing on a chore card (for children who can read) the desired outcome. Parents then consequate task performance on basis of adherence to modeled or written standards. Reduce use of written standards as needed. |
| Frequent parental intrusions while child correctly complies with commands | This problem often results from the child's poor quality of compliance, excessive duration of compliance, or parent's provision of vague command to the child. If so, then treat as above. Otherwise, the problem may be that the child, for his or her age, complies correctly but that the parent intrudes on compliance because of excessively high/strict parental expectations for compliance. When |

TABLE 3 *(continued)*

| Problem | Corrective action |
|---|---|
| | this is detected, focus treatment on altering parental expectations to more appropriate levels. |
| Developmental language or intellectual delay of child | This can lead to any or all of the previous problems. When suspected, the child should receive thorough developmental testing. Parents can then be trained in all preceding methods, but especially in reducing the number and complexity of commands to the child. |
| Inadequate consequation of child's (non)compliance by parents | This may be observed in conjunction with any or all of the preceding problems. The parent may ignore the child's appropriate compliance when it does occur, may fail to punish noncompliance, or may fail to consequate (non)compliance within a short time after its occurrence. Parents can be trained to provide only one command and to consequate (non)compliance within 5 seconds after command. |
| Presence of stimuli that elicit child behavior that competes with compliance (i.e., having TV on while doing homework) | Reduce or remove competing stimuli. |

to a physician for examination may not serve to expedite behavioral change (Kenny *et al.,* 1971; Safer & Allen, 1976; Werry & Sprague, 1968).

The interview should then progress to an examination of family-related variables, such as marital adjustment, parental psychiatric disorder, parental use of medication, problems with employment or health, and problems with siblings. Problems in these areas are more likely to occur in families of hyperactive children and, where present, will have some influence on treatment and follow-up. Special emphasis should also be given to how these problems must contribute to the troublesome parent–child interactions revealed earlier in the interview.

Finally, as with other behavioral disorders of childhood, some time should be spent in asking the parents about salient reinforcers for the child that can be utilized in treatment. In addition, some determination of the parents' motivation and expectations for treatment is required, as difficulties or misconceptions in these areas may become the first priority in designing a program of intervention.

## Child Interview

Depending on the child's age and intellectual level, some time in the initial assessment should be devoted to interviewing the child. If the child was present during the parental interview, some observations about his or her language, behavior, and social skills may already have been collected. The interview should focus on the child's perceptions of the reasons for the evaluation, as well as his or her descriptions of parent–child interaction in the situations that were already discussed with the parents. This may reveal some variation from the parents' description as to how the child views the triggering events and outcome of the interaction. Some discussion of peer interactions is also desirable, to determine the child's awareness of problems in this domain and any feelings he or she may have about them. Where social skills problems are revealed, the examiner should assess them thoroughly (see Chapter 8, this volume). Querying the child as to desired rewards and activities should generate useful possibilities for reinforcers in later intervention programs. Research by Whalen (Whalen & Henker, 1976) suggests that children's perception of what factors are responsible for their misbehavior may influence their response to drug and behavioral interventions. Children who viewed their behavior as outside their means of control responded better to drug treatment than those who viewed themselves as having some control in the matter. The latter group responded better to behavioral treatments. Should these results be replicated, they suggest another area in which the child might be questioned.

In my experience, interviews with the child may not prove particularly productive for treatment planning, except in establishing a necessary rapport and in elaborating on some of his or her physical, cognitive, and behavioral characteristics. Interviews usually reveal the children to have little perception of their difficulties, because their self-reflection is generally poor, and to have little insight into the reactions of others toward them. Lying or distorting information in a more socially acceptable or pleasing direction is more frequent, as are impulsive responses to questions. Nonetheless, the beneficial aspects of the interview outweigh its problems, especially with older hyperactive children (over 8 or 9 years of age).

## Parent/Teacher Behavior Rating Scales

There are a number of rating scales available for use with hyperactive children (Loney, 1978; Ross & Ross, 1976). Many of these scales have the advantage of providing numerical data on a variety of childhood behaviors, which can be used to determine whether the problem behaviors are statistically deviant from normal and to monitor a child's improvements during and after intervention. Most of these rating scales lack adequate reliability and validity data and have few norms, especially those related to the age and sex of the child. In addition, most of them provide no information about the stimulus events that control the behavior and the consequences that follow the response. Thus, rating scales may be helpful in diagnosis but are not especially useful in generating suggestions for treatment.

Four rating scales are available that have generally adequate standardization data for use with hyperactive children. The Werry–Weiss–Peters Activity Rating Scale (Werry, 1968b) is a 31-item questionnaire completed by the parents regarding the child's behavior across seven general settings: mealtime, television, homework, play, sleep, public places, and school. The parents indicate whether the child shows none, some, or much of the behavior listed for an item. Scores of 0, 1, or 2 points are credited for these answers, respectively, with the sum across all items yielding a total score of "hyperactivity." Routh, Schroeder, and O'Tuama (1974) modified the scale by deleting the school-related items and standardizing it for children aged 3 through 9 years. This modified form appears in Table 4, and the means and standard deviations from the Routh *et al.* (1974) study are given in Table 5. The scale has been shown to discriminate hyperactive from normal children (Sprague *et al.*, 1970) and to be sensitive to stimulant drug effects (Barkley, 1977a). However, it may have little prescriptive utility in clinic practice.

Conners has constructed (Conners, 1969, 1970, 1973) and standardized (Goyette, Conners, & Ulrich, 1978) two widely used rating scales for hyperactive children. One scale is completed by the parents and consists of 93 items relating to various behaviors. The scale was recently shortened somewhat and slightly reworded (Goyette *et al.*, 1978), with new norms being provided. The scale was also factor analyzed by Goyette *et al.* (1978) and was found to yield factor groupings identical to those of previous studies with the older scale, the groupings being conduct problems, learning problems (attention), psychosomatic problems, impulsive–hyperactive, and anxiety. Separate factor scores are derived from the questionnaire for comparison with the norms and have been shown to be highly related to the age and sex of the child, as well as to the sex of the parent rating the child. Mothers reported significantly more problems with their children than fathers (Goyette *et al.*, 1978).

The second rating scale was developed for use by teachers (Conners, 1969). It is a 39-item scale that has also recently been reworded, standardized, and factor analyzed (Goyette *et al.*, 1978). The factor structures are similar to those from the parent scale. Both scales appear to discriminate hyperactive and normal children (Conners, 1970), to be drug sensitive (Barkley, 1977a; Conners, 1972), and to correlate highly with the Werry–Weiss–Peters parent scale (Barkley & Cunningham, 1979a). The scales are often used for subject selection in research studies and are helpful where a diagnosis is important. Specific treatment recommendations, however, rarely follow from their use, with one exception. Previous research suggests that children who are anxious and display nervous tics will probably respond poorly to stimulant drug treatment (Barkley, 1976, 1977a; Fish, 1971). Hence, a high score on the anxiety factor of these scales may possibly rule against stimulant drug treatment.

The fourth rating scale to be considered here is the Child Behavior Checklist recently developed by Achenbach (1978) for use with boys and girls aged 4–16 years. It is a 114-item scale of a variety of problem behaviors, and it yields scores for several factored subscales, depending on the age and sex of the child. One factor has been labeled for hyperactivity. Although the scale discriminates between disturbed and normal children (Achenbach, 1978), no research currently exists demonstrating its discriminative validity for hyperactive children. In addition, it is subject to all of the criticisms of the other scales with regard to treatment planning. Its one advantage over other scales, however, is that it assesses strengths or competencies of the child as well as deviant behavior.

TABLE 4
Werry–Weiss–Peters Activity Rating Scale

---

1. During meals, is the child up and down at the table?
   No    Some    Much    NA (not applicable)
2. During meals, does the child interrupt others without regard for what they are trying to say?
   No    Some    Much    NA
3. During meals, does the child fiddle with things?
   No    Some    Much    NA
4. During meals, does the child wriggle?
   No    Some    Much    NA
5. During meals, does the child talk too much?
   No    Some    Much    NA
6. When watching television, does the child get up and down during the program?
   No    Some    Much    NA
7. When watching television, does the child wriggle?
   No    Some    Much    NA
8. When watching television, does the child play with objects or his or her body?
   No    Some    Much    NA
9. When watching television, does the child talk too much?
   No    Some    Much    NA
10. When watching television, does the child do things that interrupt others?
    No    Some    Much    NA
11. Is the child unable to play quietly?
    No    Some    Much    NA
12. When at play, does the child keep going from one toy to another?
    No    Some    Much    NA
13. When at play, does the child seek the attention of an adult?
    No    Some    Much    NA
14. When at play, does the child talk too much?
    No    Some    Much    NA
15. When at play, does the child disrupt the play of other children?
    No    Some    Much    NA
16. Does the child have difficulty settling down to sleep?
    No    Some    Much    NA
17. Does the child get too little sleep?
    No    Some    Much    NA
18. Is the child restless during sleep?
    No    Some    Much    NA
19. Is the child restless during travel?
    No    Some    Much    NA
20. Is the child restless during shopping (including touching everything)?
    No    Some    Much    NA
21. Is the child restless during church or at the movies?
    No    Some    Much    NA
22. Is the child restless while visiting relatives?
    No    Some    Much    NA

---

*Note.* Scale adapted from Werry (1968b) as modified by Routh, Schroeder, and O'Tuama (1974). Parents complete the scale, and 1 point is credited for every answer of "Some," 2 points for every answer of "Much." The total score is derived by summing across all answers. See norms in Table 5.

TABLE 5

Means and Standard Deviations, by Age, for the Werry–Weiss–Peters Activity Rating Scale

| Age (years) | Mean score | 1 $SD^a$ | 2 $SD$ |
|---|---|---|---|
| 3 | 15.20 | 20.96 | 26.72 |
| 4 | 12.35 | 20.25 | 28.15 |
| 5 | 11.13 | 16.25 | 21.37 |
| 6 | 12.40 | 21.32 | 30.24 |
| 7 | 9.95 | 14.50 | 19.05 |
| 8 | 9.30 | 13.84 | 18.38 |
| 9 | 8.08 | 12.12 | 16.16 |

*Note.* Means and standard deviations are derived from the study by Routh, Schroeder, and O'Tuama (1974) and are collapsed across sex of child and sex of parent completing the questionnaire. Scores apply only to the modified version of the scale as used in Routh *et al.* (1974).

[a]*SD* = standard deviation above the mean.

Where possible, I prefer direct observation and behavioral interview data to the use of these scales. Where such data cannot be obtained, use of a parent- and teacher-completed questionnaire may be helpful. When viewed from the standpoint of the present conceptualization of hyperactivity (poor attention and rule-governed behavior), these rating scales are seen as shedding little, if any, light on the nature of a child's problems.

## Teacher Interview

The hyperactive child is likely to have problems with classroom behavior and/or academic achievement. Should these prove to be concerns of the parents in the initial evaluation, then contact with the child's teacher(s) is imperative, preferably via a school visit and direct observation of the child's behavior. Where this is not feasible, telephone contact with the teacher is absolutely essential. In addition, one might also utilize the Conners Teacher Rating Scale.

Whether in person or by telephone, the interview with the teacher, as with the parents, should stress the specific nature of the child's behavior problems, the situations in which they are most likely to develop (individual work, group work, recess, lunchroom, hallways, etc.), and the current responses of others toward the child. Like many parents, teachers also tend to use global descriptions of the child's behavior ("aggressive," "won't listen," "restless") without regard to situational antecedents or consequating events. Most often with hyperactive children these descriptions center on the child's short attention span, restlessness, impulsivity, and poor peer relationships. As noted previously, these complaints are best understood as problems in attention and rule-governed behavior and should be assessed accordingly. Care should be taken to obtain highly specific descriptions of the teacher's interactions with the child and of the child's interactions with other children in the problem situations. The follow-up questions used in the parental interview to assess such interactions will also prove helpful here. One also needs to determine what the child's expectations or demands are in each situation and what time constraints are placed on him or her for satisfactory work accomplishment.

From this interview, the examiner is likely to find that the hyperactive child's greatest difficulties are in sustained attention and following the rules of appropriate conduct in the school. During individual work periods, the child is likely to be described as moving frequently (squirming in the chair), distracting other children by talking to them or otherwise intruding on their work, wandering about the classroom engaging in play with other objects, and initiating frequent interactions with the teacher, usually on the premise of seeking help or just being sociable, for example, "Teacher, do you know what I did last week?" It is the inappropriateness of these activities for the situation (noncompliance), and usually not their content or nature, that is distressing to others. In some cases, however, such as with aggression, the nature of the child's interaction is inappropriate regardless of the situation and relates to the child's failure to follow more general rules of social conduct. During group work periods, the child is likely to be reported as talking out of turn, initiating interactions with peers instead of attending to the teacher, and playing with inappropriate objects. Again, the essence of the problem is noncompliance to situational rules. At recess periods, the descriptions of problem behaviors of hyperactive children will be quite similar to those noted during play with peers at home. As with the parental interview, the teacher should be questioned as to the nature of the child's interactions with peers.

## Objective Assessment Methods

At this point in the evaluation, the examiner should have some idea as to the nature of the child's difficulties in following rules, the settings in which they are likely to occur, and the reactions of others toward the child. This information serves to narrow the focus of subsequent direct observations and permits the selection of particular observational methods that will derive the most useful information for treatment decisions. If one follows the traditional view of hyperactivity, then one is likely, at this point, to begin to measure objectively the child's rates of various types of activity levels in various situations to see if he or she is truly overactive. Objective measures of attention span and impulsivity may also be invoked. Various measures are available for use in the clinic or in a natural setting, but they are too numerous to review here. The important issue is whether such measures provide useful data for treatment planning. I do not believe that they do, and a brief survey of some of these measures should illustrate this point.

Innumerable measures of activity level in children are available, seemingly limited only by technology and one's creative genius (see for reviews Cromwell, Baumeister, & Hawkins, 1963; Ross & Ross, 1976; Werry & Sprague, 1968).

Modified self-winding wristwatches called "actometers" are available for measuring wrist and ankle movements (Johnson, 1971), as are pedometers for attaching to belt, wrist, or ankle (Barkley, 1977b). Other measures consist of pneumatic floor pads to count footsteps (Montagu & Swarbrick, 1975), sound-wave generators for assessing movement in a room (McFarland, Peacock, & Watson, 1966), motion-sensitive chairs for evaluating "seat restlessness" (Barkley, 1977b; Christensen & Sprague, 1973), and grid-marked playrooms in which machines or observers record the number of lines a child traverses in the room (Barkley, 1977b; Routh & Schroeder, 1976; Touwen & Kalverboer, 1973) as measures of locomotor activity. All of these and others have been used in research and, in some cases, in clinic practice to assess hyperactive children.

From the standpoint of behavioral assessment, these measures have serious limitations as to their clinical utility despite their ability to discriminate hyperactive from normal children (Barkley & Ullman, 1975; Ullman et al., 1978). First, the quantitative scores they yield generally show poor reliability over time. Second, normative data are not readily available on most measures, making their interpretation suspect. Third, the measures have been shown to be highly influenced by situational variables (Barkley & Ullman, 1975; Ullman et al., 1978) and to demonstrate only low-order correlations across situations (Barkley & Ullman, 1975; Rapoport & Benoit, 1975) or with other measures of activity level. Fourth, the scores so obtained give no information on the controlling variables affecting the activity level or its consequating events. And fifth, the results of these measures are not likely to correlate with those aspects of the child's behavior that the parent or teacher actually finds objectionable. For instance, measures of activity level have repeatedly failed to correlate with various measures of parent or teacher opinion of hyperactivity, such as the rating scales described previously (Barkley & Ullman, 1975; Routh & Schroeder, 1976; Shaffer et al., 1974; Ullman et al., 1978). Instead, these rating scales are most highly correlated with measures of compliance and interaction problems in parent–child interactions (Barkley & Cunningham, 1979a; Rapoport & Benoit, 1975; Routh & Schroeder, 1976; Shaffer et al., 1974). If one accepts the position set forth here that hyperactivity is a problem in compliance to rules (stimulus control), then these setting and social interaction aspects are critical to its understanding and treatment.

Similar criticisms can be leveled at the objective tests or laboratory measures of attention span (see Barkley, 1977b) and impulsivity, where quantitative scores are all that the measures provide. Hence, such measures are not recommended for use in clinical evaluations of hyperactive children unless information is derived on the stimulus and consequating variables affecting the score, as well as on the social context in which it was taken. More critical, it seems, to the assessment of hyperactive children are those methods of recording social interactions of the child with others, because it is these other people who establish the rules that the child has difficulty following and who provide the most salient consequating events for their noncompliance. Measures of parent–child, teacher–child, and peer–child interactions involving the hyperactive child are therefore viewed as the best available assessment devices for obtaining useful data for treatment planning and follow-up.

The remainder of this section is given to a review of the most useful social interaction measures for evaluating the hyperactive child.

## Clinical Analogue Observations

Where time, finances, or resources do not permit direct home or school observations of hyperactive children, then observation in analogue settings within the clinic prove essential. Where circumstances preclude even this form of assessment, parents and teachers should be requested to keep diaries of the child's interactions in select problem situations for 1 to 2 weeks before intervention is undertaken. An obvious difficulty with clinic playroom observations is their potential unrepresentativeness of parent–child interactions within the home or other public places (Martin, Johnson, Johanssen, & Wahl, 1976). This difficulty is one of stimulus similarity or generality between home and clinic playroom. Theoretically, one would expect that the more similarity between the two settings, the greater the likelihood that playroom observations are representative of home behavior by parent and child. This is especially true with respect to the nature of the rules to be followed in the clinic playroom or of the commands given by the parent.

### *The Setting*

Circumstances in our clinic do not easily permit direct home observation of the hyperactive children evaluated. Hence, we have had to develop a clinic analogue setting that enhances the likelihood of eliciting the problem parent–child interactions that are of concern to the parents. This has been accomplished with good success by following several procedures. First, furnishings were selected for the playroom that are similar to those found in a home (sofa, coffee table, plants, bookshelves, rocking chair, a sink, wall pictures, etc.). Second, the data from the parental interviews were examined for the types of situations at home that are likely to be problematic for the child. The rules or commands likely to be used in these settings were then selected for use in the playroom by the parent. Third, as noted previously, the child is often permitted to play in this room during the parental interview to allow for habituation to the room. Fourth, the parent is informed of the need for the interactions in this setting to parallel as closely as possible those occurring at home. Fifth, the mother is always the parent observed with the child because she is almost always the one who has greater difficulty gaining compliance from the child. Finally, the parents are queried after the playroom observation to determine their opinion of how close the playroom behavior problems were to those usually noted at home. In many cases, the parents believe that the problems seen are sufficiently close to those at home to permit an adequate understanding of the child's problems. Where the parent does not feel that we have observed the problem behaviors, then greater discussion of the difference between our observations and the behaviors at home will occur, and, if necessary, home observations will be scheduled.

A more thorough description of the playroom setting and measures is found elsewhere (Barkley & Cunningham, 1979b; Terdal, Jackson, & Garner, 1976). Briefly, the mother and child are placed in a clinic playroom with toys available (standard across children) and are asked to play together as they might do at home for about 15 minutes. At the end of this time, the examiner enters the playroom and gives the mother a list of three commands to give the child. These were derived from a review of problem interactions characteristic of many hyperactive children. The commands are to have the child (1) pick up all the toys and place them on a table at the back of the playroom; (2) sit beside the mother at the small table and copy a series of geometric designs on a piece of paper (geared to child's age level); and (3) select only one toy to play with, go to a marked-off section of the playroom (indicated with black tape on the floor), and play only in this area, while the mother reads magazines at the other side of the room. In this last task, the child is told by the mother not to leave that area and not to talk to her or to bother her. The last task has, to date, proven to be highly effective at eliciting behavior problems from hyperactive children. These three tasks were selected because they appeared to represent general types of commands that hyperactive children have trouble with, these being: (1) interrupting an ongoing desirable activity (free play) to do an undesirable one requested by the parent (pick up the toys); (2) accomplishing sustained paper-and-pencil tasks (copying designs) with the mother where activity is restricted to a small area (table and chair); and (3) avoiding the interruption of activities of the parent (reading a magazine) while restricting one's own activities.

### The Measurement System

During the free play and task 15-minute periods, the observations are recorded by two coders behind the one-way mirror, using the Response Class Matrix (Mash *et al.*, 1973). One coder scores the mother's behavior and the child's responses to her, while the other scores the child's behavior and the mother's responses to him or her. This permits the recording of the reciprocal influences between mother and child. The coder using the mother antecedent–child consequent matrix records the mother's behavior in seven well-defined categories (command, command–question, question, praise, negative, interaction, and no response) and the child's responses to her in six categories (compliance, independent play, question, negative, interaction, and no response). The coder recording the child antecedent–mother response matrix uses identical scoring categories but with the child's behavior now viewed as the stimulus to maternal responses. In addition, this coder uses a seventh child behavior category for "competing," or noncompliant, behavior as an antecedent event to subsequent maternal behaviors. The coders utilize 15-second time intervals, in which the interaction is observed for 10 seconds, with 5 seconds used to record the last scorable interaction in the previous 10 seconds. A tape recorder is used to cue the coders for these time intervals. Sixty coded interactions are therefore recorded for free play and sixty for the task period. Intercoder reliability is quite satisfactory (.80 to .98), depending on the behavioral category (Barkley & Cunningham, 1979b; Mash *et al.*, 1973; Terdal *et al.*, 1976).

This coding system and analogue setting have proven highly sensitive to differences in interactions between hyperactive and normal children (Cunningham & Barkley, 1978), language-delayed versus normal children (Cunningham, Siegel, & Van Der Spuy, Note 6), and retarded versus normal children (Terdal *et al.*, 1976), with the interaction patterns differing for the deviant populations as a function of the characteristics of that population. The task period especially has proven highly sensitive to the problems of hyperactive children. The interaction measures correlate with parent rating scales of hyperactive behavior, especially the command and compliance categories (Barkley & Cunningham, 1979a), and are sensitive to drug treatment of the hyperactive child (Barkley & Cunningham, 1979b; Cunningham & Barkley, 1978).

Most important, the system, in conjunction with the parental interview and notes on the quality of the playroom interaction, lead to highly useful treatment recommendations. Additionally, the sensitivity of the system to treatment effects makes it ideal for periodic assessment both during and after treatment. Normative data are being collected at this time (Barkley & Murphy, Note 7) for six age levels of children, which will supplant the data published for a small group ($n = 20$) of normal children of varying ages (Cunningham & Barkley, 1978). Even in the absence of thorough norms at present, the system shows great utility for generating hypotheses as to child behavior problems and for monitoring over time within-subject changes due to intervention.

The task period can be easily modified to assess the commands that the child has difficulty obeying according to the mother simply by introducing that situation as part of the task. For instance, hyperactive children who show problem interactions while their mother is on the telephone can have a telephone call placed to their mother in the playroom from elsewhere in the clinic to see if this elicits problem behaviors. Or, if getting the child to accomplish school homework related to reading or math is a problem, it can be assessed in the clinic by providing these materials as part of the task.

Some of the more salient data obtained from an evaluation of a 4-year-old hyperactive boy and his mother are illustrated in Table 6. (The complete set of measures generated from this system is available in the report by Barkley & Cunningham, 1979b.) Also in Table 6 are the means for the measures on 20 normal children, which were obtained for comparative purposes (see Cunningham & Barkley, 1979).

The data indicate that in free play, the 4-year-old hyperactive child responded significantly less (only 42% of the time) to his mother's interactions, was much less compliant to her commands, and was much more questioning of her than normal children in a similar situation. The boy's mother proved to be significantly less interactive and questioning with this boy and more commanding and directive. In addition, she was much less responsive to his interactions when they did occur. This pattern of free play interaction suggests that the bulk of the interactions

TABLE 6

Observation Measures for the Mother–Child Interactions of a 4-Year-Old Hyperactive Boy as Compared to Means and Standard Deviations for Normal Children

| Interaction measure | Percentage of interactions for 4-year-old child | Mean (*SD*) for 20 normal children |
|---|---|---|
| During free play | | |
| Mother initiates interaction | 32 | 54 (13) |
|   Child responds | 42 | 84 (16) |
| Child initiates interaction | 52 | 68 (18) |
|   Mother responds | 65 | 92 (8) |
| Child plays independently | 20 | 30 (19) |
|   Mother controls play | 17 | 6 (8) |
|   Mother encourages play | 58 | 53 (11) |
| Mother commands | 45 | 10 (12) |
|   Child complies | 48 | 90 (16) |
| During task period | | |
| Mother commands | 53 | 21 (11) |
|   Child complies | 44 | 95 (9) |
| Child compliance duration[a] | 1.3 | 9.0 (4.0) |
| Mother encourages compliance | 18 | 30 (14) |

*Note.* Measures are derived from the Response Class Matrix (Mash, Terdal, & Anderson, 1973) as defined in Barkley and Cunningham (1978). Means and standard deviations for normal children are derived from Cunningham and Barkley (1978b).

[a]All measures are expressed as percentages except for this measure, which is the total number of intervals of compliance divided by the number of commands given by the parent, giving the mean duration of compliance per command.

centered around command–compliance problems, whereas with normal children, free play generally consists of positive interactions and play. Equally significant was the generally low level of each person's responsiveness to the other when interactions were initiated.

In the task period, greater problems with the child's compliance are evident, with the child complying with only 44% of his mother's commands compared to 95% for normal children. Probably as a result, this mother was significantly more directive toward the child compared to mothers of normal children. More than half of the mother's interactions during this time were commands, as compared to a 21% command level for mothers of normal children. Overall, these data suggest a serious problem of noncompliance with this child and excessive directiveness by the mother, with both individuals being less responsive to each other's interactions than is seen in normal parent–child dyads. Treatment, therefore, should focus on changing these parameters if the overall quality of the interaction is to improve.

Other measurement systems besides the Response Class Matrix can be employed in clinic analogue settings, and some of them are reviewed under the next section on home observations. The reader is referred to Chapter 4, this volume, for a detailed discussion of the coding system by Patterson (1976) and his colleagues (see Reid, 1978) and by Hanf (see Forehand, Sturgis, McMahon, Aguar, Green, Wells, & Breiner, 1979; Hanf, Note 8). All of these systems capture reciprocity effects in dyadic interactions and are therefore of value in generating useful treatment planning for the hyperactive child. Where interactions with siblings are problematic and one desires to assess such three-way interactions (parent, child, sibling) in a clinic playroom, the systems of Patterson (1976) or Wahler (1975; Wahler, House, & Stambaugh, 1976) can be used. Reviews of the literature on analogue settings (Hughes & Haynes, 1978) and parent–child interaction measures (Roberts & Forehand, 1978) should be consulted by anyone wishing to utilize these assessment strategies.

## Home Observations

Where time and resources permit, home observations may prove very useful for assessing hyperactive behavior and parent–child problem interactions. The time of day and the type of home setting used for observation can be geared to those salient problem situations noted in the parental interview. Nonetheless, direct home observations are prone to the same problems as clinic analogue observations, such as reactivity to being observed, observer bias, coder drift, demand characteristics, response sets, and instrument decay (Johnson & Bolstad, 1973). Indeed, the structure imposed on the home situation to accomplish the observations may transform it to a "standard" situation. Furthermore, as Terdal et al. (1976) point out, although home observations may yield information not readily obtained in the clinic playroom, there is no evidence that such information is essential to making treatment recommendations or a necessary condition for behavior change.

Where home observations are undertaken, the interaction coding systems of Patterson (1976) or Wahler et al. (1976) are recommended, although the Response Class Matrix (Mash et al., 1973) can also be utilized, provided that only dyadic interactions are of interest. In the systems designed by Wahler, 18 behavior categories are used to assess the behavior of the child and his or her interactions with peers and adults. It can be employed across a wide variety of settings involving any number of individuals interacting with the child. Unfortunately, it does not capture the sequence (antecedent–consequent) of interaction effects and therefore provides less information on the reciprocal influence involved in social interactions.

In any case, whatever the system employed, the emphasis in home observations is on capturing data about the hyperactive child's social interactions, his or her ability to comply with rules and commands, and the stimulus–consequent factors affecting his or her compliance. As with clinic analogue observations, one is likely to find the hyperactive child to have higher levels of noncompliance, aggression, negative interactions, and independent, inappropriate play compared to normal children. In addition, the parents are likely to give more punishment and less praise and to respond significantly less to the child's interactions than parents of normal children (Delfini, Bernal, & Rosen, 1976; Wahler, 1976).

## School Observations

Many, though by no means all, hyperactive children present problems in the classroom similar to compliance problems presented in the home. Difficulty in completing classwork is often observed, as the child spends much of the time talking excessively with others, disrupting them, wandering about the classroom, or playing with objects (Barkley, Copeland, & Sivage, 1980; Jacob, O'Leary, & Rosenblad, 1978). As a result, some assessment of classroom behavior is generally required.

Where resources do not permit direct classroom observations, the Conners Teacher Rating Scale should be used in conjunction with a thorough behavioral interview with the teacher, similar to the parental interview, and daily teacher written records or diaries describing the child's behavior. If possible, however, school observations should be undertaken, as parents will not generally prove to be reliable reporters of their child's behavior in the classroom and teacher reports are not likely to reveal antecedent–consequent events as well as direct observation. More important, the social interactions of peers and the teacher with this child should be observed, as they provide the most salient stimuli and consequating events for the child. Again, the social interaction coding systems by Patterson (1976) and Wahler et al. (1976) are the best available for assessing classroom interactions and for generating data useful for treatment programs.

Other systems for recording classroom behaviors of hyperactive children are available; these generally employ time sampling or interval recording procedures for hyperactive behaviors such as "out of seat," disruption, attending, aggression, noncompliance, and vocalizing. Their disadvantages stem from their failure to capture antecedent and consequent events related to the behavior. An example of one such system is that used by Jacob et al. (1978). An interval sampling system is used to record such behaviors as solicitaton, aggression, refusal, change of position, daydreaming, and making "weird" sounds, which are specifically defined and show intercoder agreement ranging from .60 to 1.00, depending on the behavioral category. The measures clearly differentiate hyperactive from normal children, particularly in formal or highly structured classroom settings (Jacob et al., 1978). Another such system is that of Abikoff, Gittelman-Klein, and Klein (Note 9), which is specifically designed for observing the classroom behavior of hyperactive children. The system contains 14 behavioral categories scored on an interval sampling basis, with intercoder agreement averaging .76 but being highly related to the category being scored. Twelve of the 14 categories discriminated hyperactive from normal children, with the categories for motor activity being significantly and inversely related to age.

Although other coding systems have been used with hyperactive children, most have neglected attention and rule-governed behavior, except where categories of noncompliance are coded. In addition, their emphasis has not been on assessing reciprocal social interactions. Hence, I am inclined to use systems assessing teacher–child or peer–child interactions, as noted previously, or to design such a system for use with a particular child. Whatever system one adopts, observations are most likely to prove useful when conducted in highly structured situations, such as individual work periods, and during peer interactions at recess.

## Summary

The assessment of the hyperactive child should at least involve parent and teacher interviews, parent–teacher behavior rating scales, and daily record keeping of specified behavioral events. Whenever possible, these may be supplemented by direct observations in a clinic analogue setting or in the home and classroom, as resources dictate. In any case, emphasis in evaluating hyperactivity in children is best focused on their difficulties in attention and in following rules, as well as on the nature of the child's noncompliance. Social interactions with the child are critically important to understanding fully the hyperactive behaviors and their antecedent–consequent events. Treatments derived from these data are likely to focus on the child's deficits in compliance, self-control, problem solving, and social skills. From the current perspective, efforts at assessing motor activity or impulsivity by traditional laboratory methods are outdated and result in only short-term treatment recommendations without tackling the essence of the disorder.

# TREATMENT IMPLICATIONS

Two assumptions are generally made in the evaluation and treatment of hyperactive children. First, the distinction between assessment and intervention from a behavioral perspective is arbitrary. The first session for evaluation can actually be viewed as treatment, because its goal and that of subsequent treatment sessions is the specification of problem behaviors and their controlling variables as well as the implementation or adjustment of treatment programs. Hence, assessment and treatment are intertwined throughout the course of involvement with the parents and the child.

Second, the approach of Tharp and Wetzel (1969) is seen as essential to implementing treatment. That is, the parents are viewed as the direct therapists working with the child, while the clinician serves as trainer/consultant to the parents or other adult mediators, such as teachers. Because the problems with the child's compliance occur in social interactions with these adults, treatment is most logically carried out with them rather than in direct therapist–child encounters. By altering the stimulus and consequating events that parents or teachers provide for the child, it is believed that the problematic social interactions with the child will be improved.

It is felt that by doing so, treatment generalization will be enhanced over that achieved by direct therapist intervention with the child.

Viewed as a disorder of attention and rule-governed behavior, hyperactivity is most effectively treated by interventions that affect the processes involved in them. Generally, the control of behavior by rules is treated or developed by providing clearly stated rules to the child, which are geared to his or her level of language development and which, when followed, are consequated by positive reinforcement, and, when not followed, by punishment. Obviously, the consequating events must closely follow the child's responses to rules and must be consistent between both parents, as well as over time with each parent, if rule-governed behavior in the child is to be developed.

More specifically, treatments for hyperactivity should encompass the following aspects, which are derived from the present conceptualization of the disorder: (1) training of parents in methods of conditioning compliance and rule-governed behavior; (2) training parents to teach or develop problem-solving skills (higher order rule-governed behavior); (3) training of the parents in rule-governed and problem-solving behaviors during child-rearing or caregiver interactions with the child; and (4) the regular scheduling of periodic "booster," or re-intervention, sessions with the family. Where classroom problems occur, teachers can be trained in points 1 and 2 for direct application to classroom interactions with the child. Further, the possible use of stimulant medications is not ruled out as an adjunct to these other intervention programs. Each of these aspects of intervention will be briefly discussed.

## Parent Training

An initial aspect of any program with parents should be to provide them with information on the nature of the disorder, such as that provided in the introduction to this chapter. This often alleviates many of the misconceptions parents have about the disorder and usually makes them much better consumers of information (often overdramatized) that they are likely to encounter in lay publications or to receive from friends and relatives. In addition, they develop the attitude of coping with, rather than curing, hyperactive behaviors and are much more realistic in their expectations of therapy and of its likely need in the future. This aspect of treatment necessitates that the therapist be well informed as to the literature on the subject. The books of Ross and Ross (1976) and Safer and Allen (1976) are two excellent starting points.

A second step in parent training requires that the parent come to be a salient dispenser of social attention and rewards to the child. This requirement stems from the research of Patterson (1976) and Wahler (1976) indicating that the social attention and praise frequently dispensed by parents of oppositional children have less reinforcement value to the child than that given by other people. This probably stems from the long history of coercive, mutually aversive parent–child interactions within these families. Often, the parent's negative feelings toward the child are equally shared by the child toward the parent. The free play observations of parent–child interactions in the clinic or at home will frequently permit some judgment as to the degree to which the problem interferes with parent–child interactions. The frequency, duration, and quality of the attention and praise delivered by the parent often serve as excellent indicators of this problem, as does the response of the child to these social interactions.

Where such a problem exists, as it so often does in older hyperactive children, programs for parents by Patterson (1976), Forehand *et al.* (1979), and Hanf (Note 8) would seem useful. Such programs stress the initial use of frequent, high-rate, high-quality positive social attention and praise to the child, contingent simply on any behaviors that are *not* inappropriate. Like Hanf and Forehand, I require that the parents spend at least 20 minutes each day with the child in free play, where the parent observes, describes, narrates, and praises ongoing appropriate play by the child. Such a procedure not only increases the parents' tracking of the child's behavior, which some believe is deficient in such parents (Mash & Dalby, 1979; Patterson, Note 10), but also alters the ratio of approving to disapproving remarks by parents toward greater relative approval. Hence, parents are likely to become more effective dispensers of social praise and attention.

The third step in parent training involves having parents utilize their positive attention contingently for compliance to commands. At this point, if problems in the manner in which a parent delivers commands or establishes household rules were observed during the assessment, efforts would be made to teach the parent to provide clearcut, unambiguous rules geared to the child's level of language development. For instance, I have frequently noted that mothers of hyperactive children often turn direct commands into command-questions, which are probably less effective in eliciting or controlling child compliance (Forehand *et al.*, 1979). This is illustrated by such statements by the mother as "Pick up the toys, OK?" or "Would you like to get ready for school now?" which clearly give the child the option of not complying. It is as if the mothers were asking a favor of these children as a hedge against the strong possibility that the child will not comply. If he or she does not, the need for disciplining the child for noncompliance is greatly reduced because of its optional nature.

Whatever the reason, training parents to reduce command frequency, complexity, and ambiguity go far in reducing confrontations with the child over noncompliance. Once accomplished, the parents can then be taught, as noted previously, to utilize social attention contingent on compliance to rules and commands. This suggests that another aspect of parent training should *not* be the design and implementation of various behavior modification procedures for use in each problem situation with the child. It will be recalled from Table 2 that the problem behaviors are frequently seen across many situations; hence at least five or more separate programs would be required. Instead, the problems in most situations are best conceptualized as noncompliance, with one program being developed around this core difficulty—the control of child behavior by rules. This also permits dispensing with much of the behavioral jargon of more traditional parent-training programs, which have been found both difficult for teaching to poorly educated parents and unnecessary for successful behavior change.

Subsequently, parents can be taught how to use various forms of acceptable punishment, such as time out, removal of social attention, loss of privileges, and, in some cases, mild spanking contingent upon noncompliance (Hanf, Note 8). If rule-governed behavior is to be conditioned rapidly and effectively in this step of the program, several guidelines must be followed:

1. Punishment must be delivered swiftly, with as little emotional upset by the parent as possible.
2. Punishment must be rendered immediately upon noncompliance to the first statement of the command so as to enhance its effectiveness as well as to disrupt the chain of aversive–coercive interactions, which escalate when commands are repeated frequently (Patterson, 1976).
3. No other activities by the child are permitted during punishment, such as getting a drink of water or playing with a toy while in time out.
4. Once the punishment is terminated, the child should correctly comply with the initial command where possible (i.e., pick up the toys).
5. Once the compliance is completed, the parent positively attends to the child for the next occurrence of appropriate behavior of any sort. This last process serves to prevent the parent from becoming a discriminative stimulus exclusively for punishment and ensures that the ratio of approval to punishment across interactions remains reasonably balanced.

### Considerations in Training

Programs that encompass the aforementioned steps for parent training already exist (Forehand et al., 1979; Patterson, 1978; Hanf, Note 8) and are effective in increasing compliance in oppositional children. With hyperactive children, however, several other steps appear to be needed, as indicated by the results of assessment. One of these is that the last step (punishment for noncompliance) be implemented gradually by parents, beginning with only one or two types of commands. Given the pervasive nature of the child's noncompliance, initial introduction of punishment across all command situations would result in a high rate of time out or other punishment for these children. By applying this procedure to one or two new commands per week, it permits the occurrence of stimulus generalization to other commands subsequently given by the parent such that punishment would not be necessary. Within 2 weeks or so, the procedure can be generalized to all parental commands without resulting in high levels of discipline for the child.

A second additional consideration is that some form of punishment is often required in addition to the emphasis on positive reinforcement in parent training. Several studies (Cunningham & Knights, 1978; Worland, 1976) suggest that hyperactive children show greater improvements in learning on laboratory tasks in response to punishment compared to normal children or compared to conditions involving only positive social attention. This result, plus the high rate of oppositional behaviors, often dictates the use of some punishment procedure in addition to reinforcement techniques.

A third consideration is that, depending on which aspects of compliance are problematic (see Table 3), suggestions can be made to the parents for improving these problems. For example, many hyperactive children are seen to initiate immediate compliance to a command but to dawdle and stretch out the duration of complying to an inappropriately long time. Parents usually respond with repeated commands, coaxing, or encouragement to hurry the child up—approaches that only encourage greater malingering. Use of a kitchen timer in such cases provides the child with an external, concrete stimulus for monitoring the passage of time. Parents can consequate the child's compliance on the basis of its adherence to the timed interval. Successive shortening of the intervals and less reliance on the timer may assist the child in relying upon more "internal" cues of time to hasten his compliance. To enhance the internalization of rules by the child, parents are taught to diminish gradually their reminders to the child regarding commonly accepted situational rules. In the absence of adult commands, (non)compliance to these rules is now consequated in an effort to teach the child to rely on his memory of the rule.

At this point, a further consideration in treatment of hyperactive children involves their probable deficits in self-speech and problem-solving skills (second-order rule-governed behavior), as discussed in the recent literature (Douglas, 1976; Douglas & Peters, 1979; Meichenbaum & Goodman, 1977). The conceptualization presented here of deficient rule-governed behavior is consistent with these observations in that problem-solving skills have as a prerequisite the ability of speech, and especially self-speech, to govern behavior. Viewed as such, hyperactive children are also deficient in the series of questions with which one typically queries oneself when faced with a potentially problematic situation (second-order rules). These questions are likely to result in the most effective analysis of the contingencies of the problem situation and enhance the likelihood of their accurate description (rule generation). Once specified or solved, the rule guides subsequent responses in the situation. Thus, although somewhat speculative at this time, teaching problem-solving skills to hyperactive children would seem imperative from this behavioral analysis. Such training probably should not occur (or would likely be less successful) until the hyperactive child is trained in compliance to external commands by others.

The techniques advocated by Meichenbaum and Goodman (1977) for teaching hyperactive children self-instruction, combined with the problem-solving training advocated by D'Zurilla and Goldfried (1971) would seem most suited to this aspect of intervention. Rather than the therapist directly training the hyperactive child, the parents should be taught the methods necessary to train the child. In our program, parents are trained to select one problem situation (such as the supermarket) and to train the child to (1) delay responding upon entering the situation; (2) ask himself or herself what behavior is expected there or what is appropriate; (3) have him or her describe the appropriate behavior; (4) provide the appropriate rules should the child's statements be inaccurate and then have him or her repeat them aloud; (5) have the child implement the correct responses; (6) provide positive social attention during steps 1 through 5; and (7) have the child evaluate his or her own behavior aloud upon leaving the problem situation. Subsequent trials in the problem situation can involve increasingly less external self-speech, with greater emphasis on "internal" self-speech to guide behavior (Meichenbaum, 1978). Barkley, Copeland, and Sivage (1980) and others (Douglas, 1976; Meichenbaum, 1978) have found this method easily taught to hyperactive children and highly effective in those settings where it is trained or with those persons conducting the training (see also Mash & Dalby, 1979). Again, the use of parents as therapists has at least some intuitive rationale in this regard. Once the method has been trained in one situation, others can be used such that the child is being required to show "self-control" or rule-governed behavior across more and more situations.

The next logical consideration in training parents of hyperactive children consists of training the parents themselves in rule-governed and problem-solving behavior during caretaker interactions with the child when problem behaviors arise. If the present analysis is correct, many parents of hyperactive children may show as many problems with rule-governed behavior as their children, especially in coercive parent–child interactions, where they are likely to respond impulsively to the child. Hence, training in problem-solving skills (second-order rules or questions) is likely to prove useful. To some degree, this is precisely what the therapist has at least implicitly been training parents to do throughout this entire process. That is, they have been trained to follow the "rules" provided by the therapist during parent–child interactions and have been rewarded accordingly by the therapist's praise and attention. Now, however, the process should be made more explicit, and the parents should be trained in self-instruction or problem solving when faced with child-rearing problems. I have only now begun to use this step in parent training programs and thus no data on its utility are available. Nonetheless, from an intuitive standpoint, it would seem worthy of clinical use and, more important, of future research in the treatment of hyperactive children and their families.

## Classroom Intervention

The same features of parent training apply to the training of teachers of hyperactive children. In addition, numerous behavioral techniques are available for use with such children in the classroom (see Ayllon & Rosenbaum, 1977; O'Leary & O'Leary, 1976). Again, the emphasis in the treatment of hyperactivity is on the training of rule-governed behavior and compliance rather than on sitting still and paying attention. To the extent that behavioral methods can be devised to facilitate the former, the latter results are also likely to occur. Again, the use of a timing device such as a timer or a tape-recorded signal (Barkley *et al.*, 1980; Glynn & Thomas, 1974) may assist the teacher in bringing the hyperactive child's classroom productivity and performance under the control of time, where necessary. Where learning disabilities are involved, the reader is referred to Chapter 10, this volume, for treatment recommendations.

## Drug Treatment

Currently, stimulant drugs constitute the most common treatment for hyperactive children. Consequently, some discussion of this form of treatment is necessary (for more detailed discussion see reviews by Barkley, 1976, 1977a; Cantwell & Carlson, 1978; Sroufe, 1975). The reviews cited suggest that the primary effects of the stimulant drugs (mainly Ritalin, Dexedrine, and Cylert) are improved concentration, reduced impulsivity, and, in some settings, reduced activity level. Other changes in behavior, such as improved compliance to commands (Barkley & Cunningham, 1979a) and occasionally reported improvements in intellectual and academic tests (see Barkley, 1977a), are related to the improvements in attention. Academic achievement, intelligence, or other higher cognitive skills are generally not improved by these drugs (Barkley & Cunningham, 1978). In addition, the long-term psychosocial outcome of the hyperactive child has not been shown to change as a result of stimulant medication given for as long as 3–5 years in childhood (Barkley, 1977a; Weiss et al., 1971). However, no studies have been done to determine *if the families* of the hyperactive children on medication have a better outcome as far as stability, marital problems, or other psychiatric difficulties. In short, the stimulant drugs are useful as far as short-term behavior management is concerned. They are unlikely, however, to change the long-term academic or conduct problems that these children are prone to experience.

### *Guidelines for Drug Use*

What role, then, should these drugs play in behavioral treatments of hyperactivity? There do not seem to be any hard and fast rules that answer this question. Certainly the drugs are useful, but not as the sole treatment of hyperactivity if one's aim is to alter long-term outcome. The following guidelines are often used in our clinics for making this determination:

1. Are the problems with hyperactive behavior of long-standing duration? If so, drugs may prove useful in quickly reversing chronic oppositional behavior and poor compliance to commands (Barkley & Cunningham, 1979a). If not, the behavior problems may be situational or reactive in nature, and the key to their resolution rests in a functional analysis of that situation, not in prescribing a drug.

2. Does the family have any other psychiatric problems that might create or maintain chronic oppositional behavior? If so, drugs may still be employed, but a simultaneous referral for psychological assistance for the other difficulties is imperative. Drugs alone will reduce the irritant value of the child's behavior and hence reduce the family's likelihood of seeking help for other problems. The drugs may be used in addition to parent training in child management as discussed previously. Although no research currently exists on the matter, it may be that the stimulant drugs enhance the ability of the parents to acquire new behavior management methods by reducing oppositional behavior that may create trouble for the parent who is newly applying such skills and by making compliant behaviors more likely so that the opportunity for parent reinforcement of behavior is greater. My

clinical experience with these combined treatments suggests that they are promising and deserving of future research.

3. Have other, nonmedical approaches to management been tried first? If so, then we are more inclined to use medication. In doing so, it has often been found that lower doses and less frequent uses of medication may be necessary once parent training has been completed. In other cases, no medication is necessary, as the parents report after training that, although the child is still fairly active, his or her compliance has improved and the parents now know how to handle those instances of oppositional behavior that do arise. If no other treatments have been used, parent training is recommended first instead of drugs.

4. Does the child show nervous tics, high rates of anxious behavior, or evidence of a thought disorder (i.e., loose, fragmented speech)? If so, medication is contraindicated, as such children appear to be among the small percentage of children who respond adversely to stimulant drugs.

5. Even where the answers to the preceding questions appear to rule against the use of drugs, they may be used effectively in cases where some form of immediate "crisis" intervention is necessary. We have often used these drugs to preclude possible abuse of the child by a highly frustrated parent who calls for help after a long series of coercive–aversive interactions with the child. In such cases, no type of behavioral treatment can act so swiftly as can the stimulant drugs to improve child behavior until the family can come in for evaluation and treatment. Once the family is enrolled in treatment, the drugs can be withdrawn gradually as the parents acquire new skills to prevent the recurrence of such crises.

When it is determined that drugs may prove helpful, referral to a physician for collaboration in the treatment of the child is necessary. By monitoring the changes in the parent–child interaction measures (which should be repeated periodically throughout treatment), information of great value can be provided to the physician for use in titrating medication. The drugs are usually discontinued after parent training is completed or once each year at the beginning of school to see if they are still required for use with behavior management. Studies suggest that such medications can be withdrawn once behavior modification programs are under way, with little exacerbation of the behavior problems (O'Leary & Pelham, 1978). The current practice of prescribing stimulants for use only on school days, and their short-lived effects (about 3–5 hours), suggest that it is the teacher, not the parents, who directly profits from the child's use of medication. The training of parents in behavior management is therefore almost always required with these children, as well as some training of the teacher(s), because the drugs rarely are enough to resolve all of the child's difficulties.

## Other Treatments

Although other treatments of hyperactivity have appeared in the literature, most of them are inconsistent with the present conceptualization and on this basis alone would be expected to be ineffective in the long run. Such treatments as diets free of food additives (Feingold, 1975), removal of certain aspects of fluorescent lighting (Mayron, Ott, Nations, & Mayron, 1974; O'Leary, Rosenbaum, & Hughes, 1978), and biofeedback for relaxation or arousal enhancement (see Mash & Dalby, 1979, for a critique) do not address the central deficits of these children with respect to rule-governed behavior. Their likelihood of offering a truly useful form of intervention therefore seems remote.

One form of intervention deserving comment as well as research attention is that of environmental restructuring to reduce or preclude hyperactive behaviors. Although in essence this is what is involved in parent or teacher training, the method described here is the alteration of the nonsocial environment. Such programs as reducing bright colors, shapes, or other stimulating objects in a room, or sequestering the hyperactive child in a cubicle to cut down distractions, are examples of this. Others more typically suggested involve locking up all household substances that might endanger the child, placing gates in various doorways to curtail nighttime wanderings, and so forth. Although they have some intuitive support, their actual utility awaits demonstration (Routh, 1978).

## Interplay of Assessment and Treatment

As noted in the introduction to this book, the repeated assessment of behavior problems throughout treatment and periodically at follow-up is essential to a behavioral approach to these problems. This is especially true of hyperactive children. Reassessment of parent–child interactions and/or classroom interactions suggests what effects intervention is having at each point in the course of treatment, as well as what skills or methods the parent or teacher still require in order to alter child behaviors further. For instance, reassessment may reveal that the parents still continue to pay positive attention to oppositional behaviors or to coercive child interactions despite instructions and practice during training not to do so. Such data can be used not only to confront parents about these continued problem interactions but also to show them how many successful changes are occurring in the parent–child interactions when progress is being made.

Once parent or teacher interventions are formally terminated, arrangements can be made for periodic regular contact by the examiner to monitor the maintenance of treatment gains and to apply "booster" sessions where necessary. The time intervals involved here cannot be determined from an a priori basis, nor can the length of follow-up itself necessarily be specified (Mash & Terdal, 1977), although several contacts per year over the subsequent year or two seem desirable.

During such reassessments, the instruments or methods to be utilized should consist at least of the behavioral interview format discussed previously and of parent and teacher rating scales. Where feasible, clinic analogue or home/classroom observations would greatly enhance the evaluation of treatment outcome. Should problems in learning disabilities or social skills also be involved, as they are likely to be, periodic re-evaluation using the methods described in Chapter 10 and Chapter 8 of this book, respectively, would be useful.

# ETHICAL CONSIDERATIONS

Although the psychological evaluation of any child brings with it a host of ethical issues, there are some that have more applicability to the evaluation and treatment of hyperactivity. One is the process of labeling the child as hyperactive. Many persons legitimately argue that such labels bring more harm than good. With hyperactive children, the label itself, among lay people, is likely to connote brain damage or dysfunction, which to some suggests that the child's behavior may be immutable—hence, why try to change him or her? To others it suggests the automatic use of prescription drugs, which would not usually be considered for the child with social skills problems or learning disabilities alone. Somehow, the addition of the label "hyperactivity" gives license to drug treatment, which, as shown previously, requires careful consideration. Another issue of labeling is the degree to which it obviates parental or social responsibility for attempting to alter the child's behavior. The phrase "He can't help it, he's hyperactive" employs a circularity of reasoning while explaining nothing. Both the child and parent may come to adopt this attitude, which precludes any motivation for behavioral interventions. Further difficulties with labeling may arise when the parent desires a label for the child that is not appropriate. A few parents I have seen wish extra help for the child at school, extra financial benefits for care of the child, or relief from the social responsibility that the label may bring despite the child's not being hyperactive. In such cases, the parents may bias their information in this desired direction. On the other hand, the label "hyperactivity" not only serves as a convenient short-hand term among professionals to suggest a common cluster of problems but also permits some general impression of prognosis when placed in the context of follow-up studies with this population. The best approach to labeling, then, is one of discretion.

The use of punishment with hyperactive children raises a second area of possible ethical problems. Where these methods are taught, parents may tend to use them more readily than positive reinforcement methods (Patterson, 1976). One therefore needs to insist on the training of parents in the use of positive reinforcement methods *before* that involving punishment and to emphasize repeatedly the need for positive attention and praise throughout the entire course of treatment. Despite initial coverage of positive reinforcement skills in parent training, toward the end of training parents have often slipped into almost exclusive use of the punishment methods, perhaps because of their perceived greater effectiveness in quelling oppositional behavior. For whatever reason, such a shift in parental behavior across the course of treatment requires close monitoring by the therapist and intervention to reverse the trend when indicated.

The use of drugs with children invites ethical concerns that are too numerous to detail here. These are discussed in other sources (Barkley & Cunningham, 1978; Sprague, 1978; Sroufe, 1975) and are mentioned here only to draw attention to their existence. Although they apply more to the physician prescribing the drug, therapists involved must realize that their information is weighed heavily in decisions to medicate a child and thus that they are indirectly responsible for such ethical matters as well.

# SUMMARY

Hyperactive children present problems of poor attention, impulse control, and restriction of activity from an early age, which, in many children, persist into adulthood. The possibility of the development of secondary conduct disorders and reactive emotional problems with these children is quite high in later childhood and adolescence. Learning disabilities may also co-exist with the behavioral problems. The causes of the disorder, although multiple, possibly involve familial or even hereditary mechanisms, with brain damage, chemical toxicity, or poor early training probably playing only minor roles in its genesis. The disorder is distinguished from more general conduct problems by its very early onset (ages 2 to 4 years or earlier), its greater involvement of attentional problems, the possibly greater involvement of underreactivity to stimulation of the nervous system, and the chronic and pervasive nature of the core behavior problems.

A behavioral analysis of the disorder results in its conceptualization as a developmental deficiency in age-appropriate attention and rule-governed behavior, which is of early onset in development and which leads to problems in second-order rule-governed behavior (problem solving) and self-control by the child. Emphasis in behavioral assessment is therefore placed on the evaluation of the types of problems with noncompliance (rule-governed behavior) that the child displays, their social context in interactions with others (parents and teachers especially), their cross-situational nature, and the larger family and social systems in which they occur. Greatest focus is placed on an assessment of parent–child interactions and their sequential progression over time. Treatments for hyperactivity stem directly from this assessment and conceptualization and are aimed (through parent training) at developing the child's rule-governed and problem-solving behavior. Interventions also emphasize the possibility of training parents in greater rule-governed and problem-solving behavior during caretaker interactions with the child. The attitude of teaching parents to cope with, not cure, the hyperactivity of the child is viewed as central to these treatments, with the need for periodic re-intervention highly likely over the course of the disorder. Stimulant drugs may serve as a useful adjunct to these other treatments, but they have little long-term utility when used alone.

## Acknowledgments

The author acknowledges his sincere appreciation to Jennifer Karlsson, Eve Strzelecki, Susan Wisth, and Deanna Andre for their assistance and to Eric Mash, Leif Terdal, Donald Routh, and Ronald Trites for comments on an earlier draft of this chapter.

# Reference Notes

1. Sprague, R. L., Cohen, M. N., & Eichlseder, W. *Are there hyperactive children in Europe and the South Pacific?* Paper presented at the meeting of the American Psychological Association, San Francisco, September 1977.
2. Kasper, J. C. *Research in distractibility and activity level: A review.* Paper presented at the meeting of the American Psychological Association, New Orleans, September 1974.
3. Firestone, P., & Martin, J. E. *An analysis of the hyperactive syndrome: A comparison of hyperactive, behavior problem, asthmatic and normal children.* Unpublished manuscript, Carleton University, 1978.
4. Pelham, W. E. *Social skills training with hyperactive children.* Paper presented at the meeting of the Association for the Advancement of Behavior Therapy, Chicago, November 1978.
5. Barkley, R. A., Cunningham, C. E., & Karlsson, J. A. *The speech of hyperactive children and their mothers: Comparisons with normal children and stimulant drug effects.* Unpublished manuscript, The Medical College of Wisconsin, 1978.
6. Cunningham, C., Siegel, L., & Van Der Spuy, H. *The mother–child interactions of retarded, language-delayed, and normal children.* Paper presented at the meeting of the American Psychological Association, Toronto, Ontario, August 1978.
7. Barkley, R. A., & Murphy, J. V. *Drugs and the social behavior of hyperactive children.* National Institute of Health Grant, 1979.
8. Hanf, C. *A two-stage program for modifying maternal controlling during mother–child (m–c) interaction.* Paper presented at the meeting of the Western Psychological Association, Vancouver, British Columbia, April 1969.
9. Abikoff, H., Gittleman-Klein, R., & Klein, D. *Validation of a classroom observation code for hyperactive children.* Unpublished manuscript, Long Island Jewish–Hillside Medical Center, 1978.
10. Patterson, G. R. *Programmatic research for families of aggressive children.* Symposium presented at the meeting of the Association for the Advancement of Behavior Therapy, Chicago, November 1978.

# References

Achenbach, T. The child behavior profile: Boys aged 6–11. *Journal of Consulting and Clinical Psychology*, 1978, *46*, 478–488.

Ackerman, P., Dykman, R., & Peters, J. Teenage status of hyperactive and nonhyperactive learning disabled boys. *American Journal of Orthopsychiatry*, 1977, *47*, 577–596.

Ayllon, T., & Rosenbaum, M. S. The behavioral treatment of disruption and hyperactivity in school settings. In B. Lahey & A. Kazdin (Eds.), *Advances in clinical child psychology* (Vol. 1). New York: Plenum, 1977.

Ayllon, T., Layman, D., & Kandel, H. A behavioral–educational alternative to drug control of hyperactive children. *Journal of Applied Behavior Analysis*, 1975, *8*, 137–146.

Baloh, R., Sturm, R., Green, B., & Gleser, G. Neuropsychological effects of chronic asymptomatic increased lead absorption. *Archives of Neurology*, 1975, *32*, 326–330.

Barcai, A., & Rabkin, L. Y. A precursor of delinquency: The hyperkinetic disorder of childhood. *Psychiatric Quarterly*, 1974, *48*, 387–399.

Barkley, R. Predicting the response of hyperactive children to stimulant drugs. *Journal of Abnormal Child Psychology*, 1976, *4*, 327–348.

Barkley, R. A. A review of stimulant drug research with hyperactive children. *Journal of Child Psychology and Psychiatry*, 1977, *18*, 137–165. (a)

Barkley, R. A. The effects of methylphenidate on various measures of activity level and attention in hyperkinetic children. *Journal of Abnormal Child Psychology*, 1977, *5*, 351–369. (b)

Barkley, R. A. Recent developments in research on hyperactive children. *Journal of Pediatric Psy-

*chology*, 1979, *3*, 158–163.

Barkley, R. A., Copeland, A. P., & Sivage, C. A self-control classroom for hyperactive children. *Journal of Autism and Developmental Disorders*, 1980, *10*, 75–89.

Barkley, R. A., & Cunningham, C. E. Do stimulant drugs improve the academic performance of hyperactive children? A review of outcome research. *Clinical Pediatrics*, 1978, *17*, 85–92.

Barkley, R. A., & Cunningham, C. E. The parent–child interactions of hyperactive children and their modification by stimulant drugs. In R. Knights & D. Bakker (Eds.), *Rehabilitation, treatment, and management of learning disabilities*. Baltimore: University Park Press, 1979. (a)

Barkley, R. A., & Cunningham, C. E. The effects of Ritalin on the mother–child interactions of hyperactive children. *Archives of General Psychiatry*, 1979, *36*, 201–208. (b)

Barkley, R. A., & Routh, D. K. Reduction of children's locomotor activity by modeling and the promise of contingent reward. *Journal of Abnormal Child Psychology*, 1974, *2*, 117–131.

Barkley, R. A., & Ullman, D. G. A comparison.of objective measures of activity and distractibility in hyperactive and nonhyperactive children. *Journal of Abnormal Child Psychology*, 1975, *3*, 213–244.

Battle, E. S., & Lacey, B. A context for hyperactivity in children, over time. *Child Development*, 1972, *43*, 757–773.

Bell, R. Q. A reinterpretation of the direction of effects in studies of socialization. *Psychological Review*, 1968, *75*, 81–95.

Bell, R. Q. Stimulus control of parent or caretaker behavior by offspring. *Developmental Psychology*, 1971, *4*, 63–72.

Bell, R. Q. Socialization findings reexamined. In R. Bell & L. Harper (Eds.), *Child effects on adults*. New York: Wiley, 1977.

Bell, R. Q., & Harper, L. (Eds.). *Child effects on adults*. New York: Wiley, 1977.

Blouin, A. G., Bornstein, M. A., & Trites, R. L. Teenage alcohol abuse among hyperactive children: A five year follow-up study. *Journal of Pediatric Psychology*, 1978, *3*, 188–194.

Borland, B., & Heckman, H. K. Hyperactive boys and their brothers. *Archives of General Psychiatry*, 1976, *33*, 669–675.

Bremer, D. A., & Stern, J. A. Attention and distractibility during reading in hyperactive boys. *Journal of Abnormal Child Psychology*, 1976, *4*, 381–387.

Cameron, J. R. Parental treatment, children's temperament, and the risk of childhood behavioral problems: 2. Initial temperament, parental attitudes, and the incidence and form of behavioral problems. *American Journal of Orthopsychiatry*, 1978, *48*, 140–147.

Campbell, S. Mother–child interaction in reflective, impulsive, and hyperactive children. *Developmental Psychology*, 1973, *8*, 341–347.

Campbell, S. Mother–child interaction: A comparison of hyperactive, learning disabled, and normal boys. *American Journal of Orthopsychiatry*, 1975, *45*, 51–57.

Campbell, S. B., Schleifer, M., & Weiss, G. Continuities in maternal reports and child behaviors over time in hyperactive and comparison groups. *Journal of Abnormal Child Psychology*, 1978, *6*, 33–45.

Cantwell, D. P. Psychiatric illness in the families of hyperactive children. *Archives of General Psychiatry*, 1972, *27*, 414–427.

Cantwell, D. P. (Ed.) *The hyperactive child*. New York: Spectrum, 1975.

Cantwell, D. P. Hyperactivity and antisocial behavior. *Journal of the American Academy of Child Psychiatry*, 1978, *252–262*.

Cantwell, D. P., & Carlson, G. A. Stimulants. In J. Werry (Ed.), *Pediatric psychopharmacology*. New York: Brunner/Mazel, 1978.

Cantwell, D. P., & Satterfield, J. The prevalance of academic underachievement in hyperactive children. *Journal of Pediatric Psychology*, 1978, *3*, 168–171.

Carey, W. B., & McDevitt, S. C. Stability and change in individual temperament diagnoses from infancy to early childhood. *Journal of the American Academy of Child Psychiatry*, 1978, 331–337.

Chamberlin, R. W. Can we identify a group of children at age two who are at risk for the development of behavioral or emotional problems in kindergarten or first grade? *Pediatrics* (Supplement), 1977, *59*, 971–981.

Christensen, D., & Sprague, R. Reduction of hyperactive behavior by conditioning procedures alone and combined with methylphenidate. *Behaviour Research and Therapy*, 1973, *11*, 331–343.

Conners, C. K. A teacher rating scale for use with drug studies with children. *American Journal of Psychiatry*, 1969, *127*, 884–888.

Conners, C. K. Symptom patterns in hyperkinetic, neurotic and normal children. *Child Development*, 1970, *41*, 667–682.

Conners, C. K. Pharmacotherapy for psychopathology in children. In H. Quay & J. Werry (Eds.), *Psychopathological disorders of childhood*. New York: Wiley, 1972.

Conners, C. K. Rating scales for use in drug studies with children. *Psychopharmacology Bulletin* (Special issue, pharmacotherapy in children), 1973, 24–29.

Conners, C. K., Goyette, C. H., Southwick, D. A., Lees, J. M., & Andrulonis, P. A. Food additives and hyperkinesis: A controlled double-blind experiment. *Pediatrics*, 1976, *58*, 154–166.

Creager, R. O., & Van Riper, C. The effect of methylphenidate on the verbal productivity of children with cerebral dysfunction. *Journal of Speech and Hearing Research*, 1967, *10*, 623–628.

Cromwell, R. L., Baumeister, A., and Hawkins, W. F. Research in activity level. In N. R. Ellis (Ed.), *Handbook of mental deficiency*. New York: McGraw-Hill, 1963.

Cunningham, C. E., & Barkley, R. A. The effects of Ritalin on the mother–child interactions of hyperkinetic twin boys. *Developmental Medicine and Child Neurology*, 1978, *20*, 634–642.

Cunningham, C. E., & Barkley, R. A. A comparison of the interactions of hyperactive and normal children with their mothers in free play and structured task. *Child Development*, 1979, *50*, 217–224.

Cunningham, S., & Knights, R. The performance of hyperactive and normal boys under differing reward and punishment schedules. *Journal of Pediatric Psychology*, 1978, *3*, 195–201.

David, O. J. Association between lower level lead concentrations and hyperactivity. *Environmental Health Perspective*, 1974, 17–25.

de la Burde, B., & Choate, M. Does asymptomatic lead exposure in children have latent sequelae? *Journal of Pediatrics*, 1972, *81*, 1088–1091.

de la Burde, B., & Choate, M. Early asymptomatic lead exposure and development at school age. *Journal of Pediatrics*, 1974, *87*, 638–642.

Delfini, L. F., Bernal, M. E., & Rosen, P. M. Comparison of deviant and normal boys in home settings. In E. J. Mash, L. A. Hamerlynck, & L. C. Handy (Eds.), *Behavior modification and families*. New York: Brunner/Mazel, 1976.

Douglas, V. I. Stop, look and listen: The problem of sustained attention and impulse control in hyperactive and normal children. *Canadian Journal of Behavioural Science*, 1972, *4*, 159–282.

Douglas, V. I. Sustained attention and impulse control: Implications for the handicapped child. In J. A. Swets & L. L. Elliott (Eds.), *Psychology and the handicapped child*. Washington, D.C.: U.S. Office of Education, 1974.

Douglas, V. I. Perceptual and cognitive factors as determinants of learning disabilities: A review chapter with special emphasis on attentional factors. In R. Knights & D. Bakker (Eds.), *The neuropsychology of learning disorders: Theoretical considerations*. Baltimore: University Park Press, 1976.

Douglas, V. I., & Peters, K. G. Toward a clearer definition of the attentional deficit of hyperactive children. In G. A. Hale & M. Lewis (Eds.), *Attention and the development of cognitive skills*. New York: Plenum, 1979.

Dykman, R. A., Peters, J. E., & Ackerman, P. T. Experimental approaches to the study of minimal brain dysfunction: A follow-up study. *Annals of the New York Academy of Sciences*, 1973, *205*, 93–108.

D'Zurilla, T. J., & Goldfried, M. R. Problem solving and behavior modification. *Journal of Abnormal Psychology*, 1971, *78*, 107–126.

Feingold, B. *Why your child is hyperactive*. New York: Random House, 1975.

Firestone, P., & Douglas, V. The effects of verbal and material rewards and punishers on the performance of impulsive and reflective children. *Child Study Journal*, 1977, *7*, 71–77.

Fish, B. The "one child, one drug" myth of stimulants and hyperkinesis. *Archives of General Psychiatry*, 1971, *25*, 193–203.

Forehand, R., Sturgis, E., McMahon, R., Aguar, D., Green, K., Wells, K., & Breiner, J. Parent behavioral training to modify child noncompliance: Treatment generalization across time and from home to school. *Behavior Modification*, 1979, *3*, 3–25.

Glynn, E., & Thomas, J. Effect of cueing on self-control of classroom behavior. *Journal of Applied Behavior Analysis*, 1974, *7*, 299–306.

Goyette, C. H., Conners, C. K., & Ulrich, R. F. Normative data on revised Conners parent and teacher rating scales. *Journal of Abnormal Child Psychology*, 1978, *6*, 221–236.

Graham, P., Rutter, M., & George, S. Temperamental characteristics as predictors of behavior disorders in children. *American Journal of Orthopsychiatry*, 1973, *43*, 328–339.

Halverson, C. F., Jr., & Victor, J. B. Minor physical anomalies and problem behavior in elementary school children. *Child Development*, 1976, *47*, 281–285.

Halverson, C. F., Jr., & Waldrop, M. F. Relations between preschool activity and aspects of intellectual and social behavior at age 7½. *Developmental Psychology*, 1976, *12*, 107–112.

Harley, J., Matthews, C. G., & Eichman, P. Synthetic food colors and hyperactivity in children: A double-blind challenge experiment. *Pediatrics*, 1978, *62*, 975–983.

Harper, L. V. The young as a source of stimuli controlling caretaker behavior. *Developmental Psychology*, 1971, *4*, 73–88.

Hastings, J. E., & Barkley, R. A. A review of psychophysiological research with hyperactive children. *Journal of Abnormal Child Psychology*, 1978, *7*, 413–447.

Hecaen, H., & Albert, M. *Human neuropsychology*. New York: Wiley, 1977.

Hersen, M., & Bellack, A. S. *Behavioral assessment: A practical handbook*. New York: Pergamon, 1976.

Hertzig, M. E., Bortner, M., & Birch, H. G. Neurologic findings in children educationally designated as "brain damaged." *American Journal of Orthopsychiatry*, 1969, *39*, 437–446.

Heussy, H. R., & Cohen, A. H. Hyperkinetic behaviors and learning disabilities followed over seven years. *Pediatrics*, 1976, *57*, 4–10.

Hughes, H. M., & Haynes, S. N. Structured laboratory observation in the behavioral assessment of parent–child interactions: A methodological critique. *Behavior Therapy*, 1978, *9*, 428–447.

Humphries, T., Kinsbourne, M., & Swanson, J. Stimulant effects on cooperation and social interaction between hyperactive children and their mothers. *Journal of Child Psychology and Psychiatry*, 1978, *19*, 13–22.

Jacob, R. G., O'Leary, K. D., & Rosenblad, C. Formal and informal classroom settings: Effects on hyperactivity. *Journal of Abnormal Child Psychology*, 1978, *6*, 47–59.

Johnson, C. F. Hyperactivity and the machine: The actometer. *Child Development*, 1971, *42*, 2105–2110.

Johnson, S. M., & Bolstad, O. D. Methodological issues in naturalistic observations: Some problems and solutions for field research. In L. A. Hamerlynck, L. C. Handy, & E. J. Mash (Eds.), *Behavior change: Methodology, concepts and practice*. Champaign, Ill.: Research Press, 1973.

Kalverboer, A. F., Touwen, B. C. L., & Prechtl, H. F. R. Follow-up of infants at risk of minor brain dysfunction. *Annals of the New York Academy of Sciences*, 1973, *205*, 173–187.

Kenny, T. J., Clemmens, R. L., Hudson, B. W., Lentz, G. A., Jr., Cicci, R., & Nair, P. Characteristics of children referred because of hyperactivity. *Journal of Pediatrics*, 1971, *79*, 618–622.

Kinsbourne, M. The mechanism of hyperactivity. In M. Blaw, I. Rapin, & M. Kinsbourne (Eds.), *Topics in child neurology*. New York: Spectrum, 1977.

Lamb, M. E. Influence of the child on marital quality and family interaction during the prenatal, perinatal, and infancy periods. In R. M. Lerner & G. B. Spanier (Eds.), *Child influences on marital and family interaction: A life-span perspective*. New York: Academic Press, 1978.

Langhorne, J., Jr., Loney, J., Paternite, C., & Bechtholdt, H. Childhood hyperkinesis: A return to the source. *Journal of Consulting and Clinical Psychology*, 1976, *85*, 201–209.

Laufer, M. W., Denhoff, E., & Solomons, G. Hyperkinetic impulse disorder in children's behavior problems. *Psychosomatic Medicine*, 1957, *19*, 38–49.

Loney, J. Childhood hyperactivity. In R. H. Woody (Ed.), *Encyclopedia of clinical assessment*. New York: Jossey-Bass, in press.

Luria, A. R. *Higher cortical functions in man*. New York: Basic Books, 1966.

Martin, S., Johnson, S. M., Johansson, S., & Wahl, G. The comparability of behavioral data in laboratory and natural settings. In E. J. Mash, L. A. Hamerlynck, & L. C. Handy (Eds.), *Behavior modification and families*. New York: Bruner/Mazel, 1976.

Mash, E. J., & Dalby, J. T. Behavioral interventions for hyperactivity. In R. Trites (Ed.), *Hyperactivity in children: Etiology, measurement and treatment implications*. Baltimore: University Park Press, 1979.

Mash, E. J., & Terdal, L. G. After the dance is over: Some issues and suggestions for follow-up assessment in behavior therapy. *Psychological Reports*, 1977, *41*, 1287–1308.

Mash, E. J., Terdal, L. G., & Anderson, K. The response class matrix: A procedure for recording parent–child interactions. *Journal of Consulting and Clinical Psychology*, 1973, *40*, 163–164.

Mayron, L. M., Ott, J. N., Nations, R., & Mayron, E. L. Light, radiation, and academic behavior: Initial studies on the effects of full spectrum lighting and radiation shielding on behavior and academic performance of school children. *Academic Therapy*, 1974, *10*, 33–47.

McFarland, J. N., Peacock, L. J., & Watson, J. A. Mental retardation and activity level in rats and children. *American Journal of Mental Deficiency*, 1966, *71*, 376–380.

McInerny, T., & Chamberlin, R. W. Is it feasible to identify infants who are at risk for later behavioral problems? *Clinical Pediatrics*, 1978, *17*, 233–238.

Meichenbaum, D. Cognitive–functional approach to cognitive factors as determiners of learning disabilities. In R. Knights & D. Bakker (Eds.), *Neuropsychology of learning disorders*. Baltimore: University Park Press, 1976.

Meichenbaum, D. Teaching children self-control. In B. Lahey & A. Kazdin (Eds.), *Advances in clinical child psychology* (Vol. 2). New York: Plenum, 1978.

Meichenbaum, D., & Goodman, S. The nature and modification of impulsivity. In M. Blaw, I. Rapin, & M. Kinsbourne (Eds.), *Topics in child neurology*. New York: Spectrum, 1977.

Mendelson, W., Johnson, N., & Stewart, M. Hyperactive children as teenagers: A follow-up study. *Journal of Nervous and Mental Disease*, 1971, *153*, 273–279.

Menkes, M. M., Rowe, J. S., & Menkes, J. H. A twenty-five year follow-up study on the hyperkinetic child with minimal brain dysfunction. *Pediatrics*, 1967, *39*, 393–399.

Millichap, J. G. *Learning disabilities and related disorders*. New York: Year Book Medical Publishers, 1977.

Minde, K., Lewin, D., Weiss, G., Laviguer, H., Douglas, V., & Sykes, E. The hyperactive child in elementary school: A 5-year, controlled, follow-up. *Exceptional Children*, 1971, *38*, 215–221.

Minde, K., Weiss, G., & Mendelson, B. A 5-year follow-up study of 91 hyperactive school children. *Journal of the American Academy of Child Psychiatry*, 1972, *11*, 595–610.

Montagu, J. D., & Swarbrick, L. Effect of amphetamines in hyperkinetic children: Stimulant or sedative? A pilot study. *Developmental Medicine and Child Neurology*, 1975, *15*, 293–298.

Morrison, J. R., & Stewart, M. A. A family study of the hyperactive child syndrome. *Biological Psychiatry*, 1971, *3*, 189–195.

Morrison, J. R., & Stewart, M. A. The psychiatric status of the legal families of adopted hyperactive children. *Archives of General Psychiatry*, 1973, *28*, 888–891. (a)

Morrison, J. R., & Stewart, M. A. Evidence of polygenetic inheritance in the hyperactive child syndrome. *American Journal of Psychiatry*, 1973, *130*, 791–792. (b)

Nichamin, S. J. Recognizing minimal cerebral dysfunction in the infant and toddler. *Clinical Pediatrics*, 1972, *11*, 255–257.

O'Leary, S. G., & O'Leary, K. D. Behavior modification in the school. In H. Leitenberg (Ed.), *Handbook of behavior modification and behavior therapy*. Englewood Cliffs, N.J.: Prentice-Hall, 1976.

O'Leary, S. G., & Pelham, W. E. Behavior therapy and withdrawal of stimulant medication in hyperactive children. *Pediatrics*, 1978, *61*, 211–216.

O'Leary, K. D., Rosenbaum, A., & Hughes, P. C. Fluorescent lighting: A purported source of hyperactive behavior. *Journal of Abnormal Child Psychology*, 1978, *6*, 285–289.

Paine, R. S., Werry, J. S., & Quay, H. C. A study of minimal cerebral dysfunction. *Developmental Medicine and Child Neurology*, 1968, *10*, 505–517.

Passman, R. H., & Mulhern, R. K. Stress affects maternal punitiveness: A model for investigating child-abuse. *Journal of Abnormal Psychology*, 1977, *86*, 565–569.

Patterson, G. R. The aggressive child: Victim and architect of a coercive system. In E. J. Mash, L. A. Hamerlynck, & L. C. Handy (Eds.), *Behavior modification and families*. New York: Brunner/Mazel,

1976.

Pope, L. Motor activity in brain injured children. *American Journal of Orthopsychiatry*, 1970, *40*, 783.

Rapoport, J. L., & Benoit, M. The relation of direct home observations to the child evaluation of hyperactive school age boys. *Journal of Child Psychology and Psychiatry*, 1975, *16*, 141–147.

Rapoport, J. L., Buchsbaum, M., Zahn, T., Weingartner, H., Ludlow, C., & Mikkelsen, E. Dextroamphetamine: Cognitive and behavior effects in normal prepubertal boys. *Science*, 1978, *199*, 511–514.

Reid, J. B. (Ed.). *A social learning approach to family intervention* (Vol. 2): *Observation in home settings*. Eugene, Ore.: Castalia, 1978.

Roberts, M. W., & Forehand, R. The assessment of maladaptive parent–child interaction by direct observation: An analysis of methods. *Journal of Abnormal Child Psychology*, 1978, *6*, 257–270.

Roff, M. Childhood social interactions and young adult bad conduct. *Journal of Abnormal and Social Psychology*, 1961, *63*, 333–337.

Rose, T. L. The functional relationship between artificial food colors and hyperactivity. *Journal of Applied Behavior Analysis*, 1978, *11*, 439–449.

Rosenthal, J. H. Neurophysiology of minimal cerebral dysfunctions. *Academic Therapy*, 1973, *8*, 291–294.

Ross, D. M., & Ross, S. A. *Hyperactivity*. New York: Wiley, 1976.

Routh, D. K. Hyperactivity. In P. Magrab (Ed.), *Psychological management of pediatric problems* (Vol. 2). Baltimore: University Park Press, 1978.

Routh, D. K., & Mesibov, G. Psychological and environmental intervention: Toward social competence. In H. Rie & E. Rie (Eds.), *Handbook of minimal brain dysfunctions*. New York: Wiley, 1980.

Routh, D. K., & Roberts, R. D. Minimal brain dysfunction in children: Failure to find evidence for a behavioral syndrome. *Psychological Reports*, 1972, *31*, 307–314.

Routh, D. K., & Schroeder, C. S. Standardized playroom measures as indices of hyperactivity. *Journal of Abnormal Child Psychology*, 1976, *4*, 199–207.

Routh, D. K., Schroeder, C. S., & O'Tuama, L. Development of activity level in children. *Developmental Psychology*, 1974, *10*, 163–168.

Rutter, M. Brain damage syndromes in childhood: Concepts and findings. *Journal of Child Psychology and Psychiatry*, 1977, *18*, 1–21.

Rutter, J., Graham, P., & Yule, B. A neuropsychiatric study in childhood. *Clinics in Developmental Medicine*, Nos. 35/36. London: Spastics International Medical Publications, 1970.

Safer, R., & Allen, D. *Hyperactive children: Diagnosis and management*. Baltimore: University Park Press, 1976.

Sandberg, S. T., Rutter, M., & Taylor, E. Hyperkinetic disorder in psychiatric clinic attenders. *Developmental Medicine and Child Neurology*, 1978, *20*, 279–299.

Schleifer, M., Weiss, G., Cohen, N., Elman, M., Cvejic, H., & Kruger, E. Hyperactivity in preschoolers and the effect of methylphenidate. *American Journal of Orthopsychiatry*, 1975, *45*, 38–50.

Shaffer, D., McNamara, N., & Pincus, J. H. Controlled observations on patterns of activity, attention, and impulsivity in brain-damaged and psychiatrically disturbed boys. *Psychological Medicine*, 1974, *4*, 4–18.

Skinner, B. F. *Science and human behavior*. New York: Macmillan, 1953.

Skinner, B. F. *Cumulative record: A selection of papers*. New York: Appleton-Century-Crofts, 1967.

Sprague, R. L. Principles of clinical trials and social, ethical and legal issues of drug use in children. In J. S. Werry (Ed.), *Pediatric psychopharmacology*. New York: Brunner/Mazel, 1978.

Sprague, R. L., Barnes, K., & Werry, J. Methylphenidate and thioridizine: Learning, reaction time, activity, and classroom behavior in disturbed children. *American Journal of Orthopsychiatry*, 1970, *40*, 615–628.

Sroufe, A. Drug treatment of children with behavior problems. In F. Horowitz (Ed.), *Review of child development research* (Vol. 4). Chicago: University of Chicago Press, 1975.

Sroufe, A., & Stewart, M. Treating problem children with stimulant drugs. *New England Journal of Medicine*, 1973, *289*, 407–413.

Stewart, M. A. Hyperactive children. *Scientific American*, 1970, *222*, 94–98.

Stewart, M. A., Pitts, F. N., Craig, A. G., & Dieruf, W. The hyperactive child syndrome. *American Journal of Orthopsychiatry*, 1966, *26*, 861–867.

Stewart, M. A., Thach, B. T., & Freidin, M. R. Accidental poisoning and the hyperactive child syndrome. *Diseases of the Nervous System*, 1970, *31*, 403–407.

Terdal, L. G., Jackson, R. H., & Garner, A. M. Mother–child interactions: A comparison between normal and developmentally delayed groups. In E. J. Mash, L. A. Hamerlynck, & L. C. Handy (Eds.), *Behavior modification and families*. New York: Brunner/Mazel, 1976.

Tharp, R. G., & Wetzel, R. J. *Behavior modification in the natural environment*. New York: Academic Press, 1969.

Touwen, B. C., & Kalverboer, A. F. Neurologic and behavioral assessment of children with minimal brain dysfunction. *Seminars in Psychiatry*, 1973, *5*, 79–94.

Trites, R. L., Dugas, F., Lynch, G., & Ferguson, B. Incidence of hyperactivity. *Journal of Pediatric Psychology*, 1979, *4*, 179–188.

Ullman, D. G., Barkley, R. A., & Brown, H. W. The behavioral symptoms of hyperactive children who successfully responded to methylphenidate treatment. *American Journal of Orthopsychiatry*, 1978, *48*, 425–437.

Wahler, R. G. Some structural aspects of deviant child behavior. *Journal of Applied Behavior Analysis*, 1975, *8*, 27–42.

Wahler, R. G. Deviant child behavior within the family: Developmental speculations and behavior change strategies. In H. Leitenberg (Ed.), *Handbook of behavior modification and behavior therapy*. Englewood Cliffs, N.J.: Prentice-Hall, 1976.

Wahler, R. G., House, A. E., & Stambaugh, E. G. *Ecological assessment of child problem behavior*. New York: Pergamon, 1976.

Waldrop, M. F., Bell, R. Q., McLaughlin, B., & Halverson, C. F., Jr. Newborn minor physical anomalies predict short attention span, peer aggression, and impulsivity at age 3. *Science*, 1978, *199*, 563–564.

Waldrop, M. F., & Goering, J. D. Hyperactivity and minor physical anomalies in elementary school children. *American Journal of Orthopsychiatry*, 1971, *41*, 602–607.

Waldrop, M. F., Pedersen, F. A., & Bell, R. Q. Minor physical anomalies and behavior in preschool children. *Child Development*, 1968, *39*, 391–400.

Weiss, G., Hechtman, L., Perlman, T., Hopkins, J., & Wener, A. Hyperactive children as young adults: A controlled prospective 10-year follow-up of the psychiatric status of 75 hyperactive children. *Archives of General Psychiatry*, 1979, *36*, 675–681.

Weiss, G., Kruger, E., Danielson, U., & Elman, M. Effect of long-term treatment of hyperactive children with methylphenidate. *Canadian Medical Association Journal*, 1975, *112*, 159–165.

Weiss, G., Minde, K., Werry, J., Douglas, V., & Nemeth, E. Studies of the hyperactive child: VII. Five-year follow up. *Archives of General Psychiatry*, 1971, *24*, 409–414.

Welner, Z., Welner, A., Stewart, M., Palkes, H., & Wish, E. A controlled study of siblings of hyperactive children. *Journal of Nervous and Mental Disease*, 1977, *165*, 110–117.

Wender, E. Food additives and hyperkinesis. *American Journal of Diseases of Children*, 1977, *131*, 1204–1206.

Wender, P. H. *Minimal brain dysfunction in children*. New York: Wiley, 1971.

Werry, J. S. Developmental hyperactivity. *Pediatric Clinics of North America*, 1968, *15*, 581–599. (a)

Werry, J. S. Studies of the hyperactive child: IV. An empirical analysis of the minimal brain dysfunction syndrome. *Archives of General Psychiatry*, 1968, *19*, 9–16. (b)

Werry, J. S., & Sprague, R. L. Hyperactivity. In C. G. Costello (Ed.), *Symptoms of psychopathology*. New York: Wiley, 1968.

Werry, J. S., Weiss, G., & Douglas, V. I. Studies of the hyperactive child: I. Some preliminary findings. *Canadian Psychiatric Association Journal*, 1964, *9*, 120–130.

Whalen, C., & Henker, B. Psychostimulants and children; a review and analysis. *Psychological Bulletin*, 1976, *83*, 1113–1130.

Willis, T. J., & Lovaas, O. I. A behavioral approach to treating hyperactive children: The parent's role. In J. G. Millichap (Ed.), *Learning disabilities and related disorders*. New York: Year Book Medical Publications, 1977.

Wolf, S. M., & Forsythe, A. Behavior disturbance, phenobarbital, and febrile seizures. *Pediatrics*,

1978, *61*, 728–731.

Worland, J. Effects of positive and negative feedback on behavior control in hyperactive and normal boys. *Journal of Abnormal Child Psychology*, 1976, *4*, 315–326.

Zentall, S. S., & Zentall, T. R. Activity and task performance of hyperactive children as a function of environmental stimulation. *Journal of Consulting and Clinical Psychology*, 1976, *44*, 693–697.

C H A P T E R   4

# CONDUCT DISORDERS[1]

**Beverly M. Atkeson**     **Rex Forehand**
*University of Georgia*     *University of Georgia*

In surveying the presenting problems of children described in the behavioral literature, it is clear that the vast majority of studies deal with children whose behavior can generally be described as "out of control" of the parents and/or community. Chief complaints of these children's parents include aggressiveness toward others (hitting, kicking, fighting); physical destructiveness; disobedience to adult authorities; temper tantrums; high-rate annoying behaviors (e.g., yelling, whining, high activity level, and threatening others); and, to a lesser extent, community rule violations such as stealing or fire setting (Bernal, Duryee, Pruett, & Burns, 1968; Hawkins, Peterson, Schweid, & Bijou 1966; O'Leary, O'Leary, & Becker, 1967; Patterson, 1974; Peed, Roberts, & Forehand, 1977; Wahler, 1969). Typically, these behaviors do not occur in isolation but as a complex or "class," and children displaying such behaviors have been labeled "disruptive," "oppositional," "socially aggressive," and "conduct-disordered" by various authors (e.g., Patterson, 1974; Wahler, 1969). Furthermore, factor analytic studies of children's behavior problems have repeatedly isolated a primary factor that is often labeled "conduct disorders," adding validity to the clinical descriptions of this behavioral "syndrome" (Conners, 1970; Jenkins, 1966; Patterson, 1964; Quay, Morse, & Cutler, 1966; Sines, Pauker, Sines, & Owen, 1969).

The need for developing and evaluating effective assessment approaches for the conduct-disordered child is evidenced by the fact that these children are the most common referrals to mental health centers. Surveys indicate that from one-third to one-half of all child referrals from parents and teachers concern these kinds of problems (Patterson, Reid, Jones, & Conger, 1975; Roach, 1958; Wolff, 1961). Other referral problems, such as hyperactivity and learning disabilities, may also display conduct disorders and are probably frequently included in surveys as conduct-disordered children. Developmental studies of nonclinic children indicate that

---

[1]Portions of this chapter also appear in a chapter entitled "Childhood Behavior Problems in the Home" by K. Wells and R. Forehand, which will appear in S. M. Turner, K. S. Calhoun, and H. E. Adams (Eds.), *Handbook of clinical behavior therapy.* New York: Wiley, in press.

even these children may exhibit conduct-disordered behaviors at some point in their childhood and adolescence (MacFarlane, Allen, & Honzik, 1954). For both clinic and nonclinic children the number of problem behaviors declines with age (e.g., MacFarlane *et al.*, 1954; Lapouse & Monk, 1959). However, children with severe conduct disorders are likely to exhibit similar patterns of behavior into adulthood if left untreated (Morris, 1956; Robins, 1966). Given the frequency with which these families present themselves to mental health facilities for help, the gloomy statistics on outcome of traditional psychotherapy, and the consequences of doing nothing, it is not surprising that much of the research on behavioral approaches with children has been focused on this target population.

The primary purpose of this chapter will be to present and evaluate critically the procedures currently used to assess conduct disorders in children. A secondary purpose is to familiarize the reader with the behavioral characteristics of conduct-disordered children and their families and to present a conceptual framework for the development and maintenance of conduct disorders in children.

## CHARACTERISTICS OF CONDUCT-DISORDERED CHILDREN AND THEIR FAMILIES

Before reviewing the various assessment approaches used with conduct-disordered children, it may be useful to describe in more detail the clinical picture presented by these families. Several behavior-analytic studies have been conducted describing the behavioral characteristics of conduct-disordered children and their families, as well as comparing these families to matched normal control groups. In one study conducted by Patterson (1976), 14 behaviors were identified that field observations indicated occurred with a high frequency for boys labeled "aggressive." Multiple observations were conducted in the homes of 27 aggressive and 27 nonproblem boys using a complex behavioral coding system and revealed that boys labeled "aggressive" displayed significantly higher rates of "coercive behavior," such as negative commands, disapproval, humiliation, noncompliance, negativism, teasing, physically negative acts, and yelling. Validity studies have indicated that all of these behaviors are considered deviant by parents (Adkins & Johnson, Note 1). A comparative study by Lobitz and Johnson (1975) employed a coding system similar to that used by Patterson and indicated that conduct-disordered children displayed a significantly higher proportion of deviant behavior (a summary score consisting of the combined rates of 15 behaviors similar to those listed previously), high-intensity deviant behavior (low-rate, highly objectionable behavior such as destructiveness), and a significantly lower proportion of positively valanced behavior (such as approval expressed to others, positive attention, independent activity, laughing, and talking). Studies by other investigators have essentially replicated these findings (Delfini, Bernal, & Rosen, 1976; Forehand, King, Peed, & Yoder, 1975; Green, Forehand, & McMahon, 1979; Moore, Note 2).

In addition to the differences in child behavior obtained in studies comparing normal and deviant families, many studies also report significant differences in the behavior of parents toward their children. Forehand *et al.* (1975) found that mothers who referred their children to a clinic for treatment of conduct disorders emitted a significantly higher rate of commands and criticisms to their children than did a group of nonclinic mothers. Delfini *et al.* (1976) replicated these findings and showed that a significantly greater proportion of commands emitted by parents of conduct-disordered children were posed in a threatening, angry, or nagging way. Finally, in addition to replicating the data on commands, Lobitz and Johnson (1975) found that parents of referred children responded with a greater proportion of negative behavior in general and supplied more negative consequences to deviant as well as nondeviant child behavior than parents of nonreferred children.

These studies indicate that the families of conduct-disordered children are characterized by a high rate of what Patterson (1976) has called "coercive" interactions among family members. Children engage in excessive rates of behaviors aversive to parents (e.g., noncompliance, physically aggressive behavior, and temper tantrums), and parents retaliate with equally excessive rates of aversive responses (e.g., threatening commands and criticisms), designed to "turn off" their children's negative behavior. The validity of these conclusions is evident as similar results have been obtained from four different laboratories using different coding systems, subjects, and operational definitions (Delfini *et al.*, 1976; Forehand *et al.*, 1975; Lobitz & Johnson, 1975; Patterson, 1976).

However, the results of these behavior-analytic studies must not be interpreted too rigidly. Each study demonstrated that *statistically* significant differences existed between referred and nonreferred families on the child and parent behavioral variables. In the Delfini *et al.* (1976) and Lobitz and Johnson (1975) studies considerable overlap existed between the distributions of scores for each group on behavioral variables. That is, a considerable number of children in the referred groups could not be differentiated on behavioral measures from children in the normal groups and vice versa. In contrast, the overlap between groups of referred and nonreferred children using questionnaires assessing parental *perception* of child deviance was much smaller (i.e., clearcut differences between the groups were obtained).

Thus, it appears that some children's parents perceive them as deviant, even though behaviorally they cannot be differentiated from normal children. Methodological problems could account for this apparent lack of convergence between behavioral and parental report measures (e.g., parental manipulation of child behavior during observations). Nevertheless, as Lobitz and Johnson (1975) have suggested, it is also possible that in some cases factors other than actual child deviance may be contributing to negative parent attitudes and the subsequent referral of the child for treatment. With respect to this issue, recent research has demonstrated relationships between personal and marital adjustment of parents and observed child deviance (Johnson & Lobitz, 1974; Oltmanns, Broderick, & O'Leary, 1977), suggesting that such variables may be an integral component of the clinical picture in many disturbed families. Our clinical experience suggests that excessively high parental standards for child behavior may be another variable to consider in the assessment of these families. Failure to assess and treat each of the salient variables contributing to the presenting clinical picture of conduct-disordered children and their families could lead to inappropriate or incomplete treatment, resulting in treatment failure or relapse.

## BEHAVIORAL FORMULATION OF CONDUCT DISORDERS IN CHILDREN

Behavioral formulations on the development of conduct disorders in children have been offered by Patterson (1976), Wahler (1976), and others. As mentioned previously, Patterson emphasizes the coercive, or controlling, nature of conduct disorders and has developed a "coercion hypothesis" to account for their development and maintenance. According to this hypothesis, rudimentary aversive behaviors, such as crying, may be instinctual in the newborn infant. Such behaviors could be considered highly adaptive in the evolutionary sense in that they quickly shape the mother in the skills necessary for the infant's survival (e.g., feeding and temperature control). Presumably, as most infants grow older, they substitute more appropriate verbal and social skills for the rudimentary coercive behaviors. However, according to Patterson (1976), a number of conditions might ensure that some children continue to employ aversive control strategies. For example, parents might fail to model or reinforce more appropriate prosocial skills and/or may continue to respond to the child's coercive behavior. As far as this latter point is concerned, Patterson and Reid (1973) have emphasized the role of negative reinforcement in the escalation and maintenance of coercive behaviors. In the negative reinforcement model, coercive behavior on the part of one family member is reinforced when it results in the removal of an aversive event being applied to another family member. The following examples illustrate how parent and child are negatively reinforced for engaging in coercive behavior.

*Application of aversive* ◄———*Coercive child*————►*Removal of aversive event.*
*event*                         *response*
Mother gives command.     Child whines,              Mother gives up (with-
                          screams, noncomplies.     draws the command) rather
                                                    than listen to whining
                                                    and screaming child.

In this example, the child's coercive behaviors are negatively reinforced when mother withdraws the aversive stimulus (command). In the following example, coercion escalates.

*Application of aversive* ◄———*Coercive child*————►*Application of aversive*
*event 1*                       *response*             *event 2*
Mother gives command.     Child whines,             Mother raises her voice;
                          noncomplies.              repeats command.

*Child response 2* ◄─────────── *Aversive stimulus 3* ─────────► *Removal of aversive child response*

Child yells louder, noncomplies.

Mother begins to yell; repeats command again.

Child complies.

In this example the mother's escalating coercive behavior is reinforced by the child's eventual compliance.

It is apparent in the preceding examples that negative reinforcement can function to increase the probability of the occurrence of aggressive control techniques by both child and parent. In addition, as this "training" continues over long periods, significant increases in rate and intensity of these coercive behaviors occur as both family members are reinforced by engaging in aggressive behaviors. Furthermore, the child also observes his or her parents engaging in coercive responses, which provides the opportunity for modeling of aggression to occur (Patterson, 1976; Patterson & Reid, 1973).

Although the "negative reinforcement trap" that has been delineated is probably the most powerful process contributing to conduct-disordered child behavior, Wahler (1976) has also emphasized the role of positive reinforcement in shaping these behaviors. In this model the parent applies positive reinforcers, such as verbal or physical attention, to the child's disruptive behaviors. In a common scenario, the child might throw a tantrum at bedtime. A typical parental response to this coercive behavior might be to approach the child and spend several minutes talking, trying to "understand" his or her anger or to reason with him or her. Assuming that parental verbal attention is a reinforcing event for the child, the parent has, in effect, spent several minutes rewarding the very behavior he or she is trying to eliminate.

Both Patterson's and Wahler's models focus on the role of parent–child interactions in developing and maintaining conduct-disordered child behaviors in the home setting. Little has been written concerning the development and maintenance of conduct-disordered child behaviors in the classroom setting. Obviously the same mechanisms, both positive and negative reinforcement, can operate in teacher–child interactions.

# ASSESSMENT OF CONDUCT DISORDERS IN CHILDREN

Behavioral approaches to the assessment of conduct disorders in children have typically included one or more of the following three procedures: behavioral interviews, behavioral questionnaires, and behavioral observations. The use of each of these procedures will be presented and evaluated. Although the emphasis will be on preintervention assessment and a functional analysis of conduct disorders in children, each of these procedures can also be used to evaluate treatment as it progresses and treatment outcome at termination and follow-up.

Before presenting the three assessment procedures, it is necessary to point out two problem areas that frequently accompany conduct disorders and for which additional assessment procedures are necessary. If the presenting problem concerns classroom behavior, a functional analysis of the problem behaviors should also include an assessment of the child's academic behavior. Although the three sets of procedures to be presented can provide information concerning the child's academic behavior, additional evaluation in the form of intelligence and achievement tests is necessary to determine if the child has learning difficulties in addition to his or her conduct-disorder problems. Chapter 10 of this volume provides a complete review of assessment strategies with which to evaluate learning problems. Frequently, conduct-disordered children also have problems with appropriate peer interactions. If the information from the behavioral interviews, questionnaires, and observations indicates that this is a problem area for a particular child, additional assessment of the child's social skills is necessary. Traditionally, assessment of social skills has involved behavioral observations, sociometric measures, and questionnaires. Chapter 8 of this volume provides strategies for the assessment of social skills.

## The Behavioral Interview

The interview is usually the first contact the therapist has with the identified client (i.e., the child) and the significant adults in the child's life (i.e., parents, teachers). The primary function of the interview is to identify verbally the behaviors to be targeted for treatment and the stimulus conditions, both antecedent and consequent, currently maintaining the problem behaviors. Because the etiology of child conduct disorders is conceptualized in terms of parent–child interactions and/or teacher–child interactions, the interview focuses on both adult and child behaviors and, more specifically, on the pattern of interaction between the child and the adult. As a consequence, the responses identified for treatment during the interview include parent and child behaviors and/or teacher and child behaviors.

Although the major purpose of an interview from a behavioral viewpoint is to determine factors currently operating to maintain the problem interactions, the initial contact with significant adults in the child's life can have other important uses (Ciminero & Drabman, 1977; Evans & Nelson, 1977; Haynes, 1978). A second function of the initial interview is to obtain a developmental history of the conduct-disordered child and the problem interactions. Although rarely useful in designing a treatment program, a developmental history of the problem parent–child and/or teacher–child interactions may be useful in the following ways: (1) it may suggest conditions under which the problem behavior may reappear after successful modification; (2) it may provide information concerning controlling variables; (3) it may promote understanding for the client of how behavior problems begin; and (4) the historical information may be relevant to the development of preventive programs (Haynes, 1978). In addition, a developmental history of the interactional problems provides the behavior therapist with a better understanding of the strength of the learned behaviors and the extent and severity of the conduct-disordered behaviors. Finally, a general developmental history of the child is useful in confirming the diagnosis of conduct disorder and in eliminating other diagnoses, such as hyperactivity (see Chapter 3, this volume).

A third function of the initial interview is to assess both the motivation of the parents and/or teacher for working in therapy and their ability to understand and execute behavioral programs. Closely related to this is the fourth function: clear communication to the parents and/or teacher of the conceptual framework of behavior therapy and the nature of the intervention process. Unless parents and/or teachers are highly motivated, can understand and execute programs, and are receptive to a behavioral approach, the implementation of programs to modify conduct disorders will be futile. Haynes (1978) provides a more complete discussion concerning these and other functions of the behavioral interview.

### Interview with Parents

If the receptionist has not already done so, the therapist first obtains demographic information concerning the child and his or her family. Included are such data as the child's date of birth, grade in school, number of siblings, siblings' sex and grades in school, and parents' age, education, and occupation. Having obtained this information, the therapist is ready to pursue the major purpose of the initial interview: determining the nature of the typical parent–child interactions that are problems, the antecedent stimulus conditions under which problem behaviors occur, and the consequences that accompany such behaviors.

This portion of the interview typically begins with a general question such as "Tell me what types of problems you have been having with your child" or "What brings you to the clinic?" In our experience, most parents, not surprisingly, respond globally to such a global question. To structure the way in which information is obtained from parents concerning current problem parent–child interactions, the interview format used by Hanf (Note 3) is extremely useful. Following this format, the therapist presents situations that may or may not be problem areas for the particular family. Parents are asked if their child is disruptive in the following situations: getting dressed in the morning, mealtime, playing alone, playing with other children, visiting in a friend's home, riding in the car, shopping, adult–adult conversations, telephone conversations, homework, cleaning up, naptime, bathtime, and bedtime. If the parents respond "no," the therapist moves to the next situation. If the parents report that a particular situation is a problem area for them, then the therapist examines the antecedent conditions of the situation (What happens just before the problem interaction?), the child's behavior (What does the child do?), the parents' response (What do you do?), and the child's reaction to the parents' intervention (What does the child do then?).

The analysis of both the parents' and child's behavior in the problem situation should be continued until the therapist has a clear understanding of the nature and extent of the parent–child interaction. Other relevant information, such as the frequency (How often . . .) and duration (How long . . .) of the problem behavior, should also be obtained. At this point, it is also appropriate to ask historical-developmental questions specific to the problem interaction. Following is a portion of an initial interview that will exemplify the analysis of a problem situation:

THERAPIST: Do you have any problems with Mark at bedtime?

PARENT: Oh my gosh, yes. It takes forever for him to go to sleep. He gets out of bed again and again.

T: Tell me about your family's routine during the half-hour before Mark's bedtime.

P: At 7:30 I help Mark with his bath. After he brushes his teeth and goes to the bathroom, I read him a story. Then Bob and I kiss him goodnight.

T: OK, then what happens?

P: Well, things are quiet for about 10–15 minutes. Then Mark is up. He gets out of bed and comes into the den where Bob and I are watching TV.

T: What does Mark do when he gets up?

P: He usually comes in and climbs in either Bob's or my lap and complains that he can't sleep.

T: What do you do then?

P: Sometimes we let him sit with us for a while, but usually I take him back to bed and tell him goodnight again.

T: What happens then?

P: Mark stays there for a while, but he's soon out again.

T: And then what do you do?

P: I may tell him he's being a bad boy. Then I take him back to bed. Usually I read him another story—hoping he'll get sleepy this time.

T: Does that work?

P: No, he's up again before I have time to get settled in my chair.

T: What happens then?

P: The whole thing repeats itself. I put him in bed, read him another story, and he gets up again.

T: How long does this go on?

P: For about 2 or 3 hours—until Bob and I go to bed.

T: What happens when you and your husband go to bed?

P: Mark still gets up, but we let him get in bed with us and he goes to sleep then.

T: How many nights a week does this happen?

P: Every night! I can't think of a night's peace in the last few months.

T: How long has Mark been doing this?

P: Oh, I would guess for about a year.

T: Have you or your husband tried any other ways of handling Mark at bedtime?

P: Sometimes I get angry and yell at him. Sometimes Bob tries spanking him, but then Mark just ends up crying all evening. At least my way, we have a little peace and quiet.

In this sample interview, the therapist obtained a description of the events preceding the problem situation fairly quickly. The therapist had to repeat "What happens then?" or some variation thereof several times until a clear description was obtained of the consequent events currently maintaining the problem behavior. Based on this assessment, the problem behavior—"getting out of bed"—is occurring at a high rate and has been for some time.

The next sample interview centers around the same problem situation— bedtime—but in this clinical case the antecedent events emerged as the factors maintaining the problem interaction.

T: Do you have a problem with Timmy at bedtime?

P: Certainly! He's impossible. He starts to scream and cry the minute we put him to bed.

T: Tell me about your family's routine the half-hour before Timmy's bedtime.

P: Well, Timmy takes his bath and puts on his pajamas right after supper. Then we usually watch television together. He knows his bedtime is 8:30, so when the program ends his father says "bedtime." Then the problems begin. Timmy tries to stall, begging to see the next show. We ignore this. His father usually ends up carrying Timmy—screaming all the way—to bed.

T: What happens then?

P: He used to get up again and again. Each time we would spank him and put him back to bed. Now when we put him to bed the first time, we just lock his door. He crys for a while and then drops off to sleep.

T: How many nights a week does this happen?

P: Let me see. Nearly all the time.

T: Thinking back over the past week, how many nights out of the last seven have you had problems with Timmy at bedtime?

P: Hmmm. Four.

T: How long has Timmy been difficult at bedtime?

P: For the last six months.

Based on this interview assessment, the therapist concluded that the antecedent events (the abrupt announcement of bedtime and removal of the child to bed) were maintaining the child's whine–cry–scream behavior at bedtime. Instructing the parents to institute a pre-bedtime ritual, similar to that used by the parents in the first interview, quickly eliminated the problem interactions at bedtime. The second interview sample was included to emphasize the importance of assessing the antecedent conditions in any problem parent–child interaction.

Patterson (Patterson et al., 1975) structures the initial interview with parents somewhat differently from Hanf (Note 3). Instead of focusing on situations, the therapist and parents together fill out a Symptom Checklist containing 31 child behavior problems. The 31 problems are: aggression, arguing, bedwetting, competitiveness, complaining, crying, defiance, destructiveness, fearfulness, fighting with siblings, fire setting, hitting others, hyperactiveness, irritability, lying, negativism, noisiness, noncomplying, not eating, pants wetting, pouting, running around, running away (wandering), sadness/unhappiness, soiling, stealing, talking back to mother, teasing, temper tantrums, whining, and yelling. As each behavior is read to the parents, a behavioral definition is also given, to ensure that the parent understands the descriptive term used. The parents are asked to indicate whether they think that the behavior occurs often enough to be a real problem now and whether the behavior is something they wish to change. If the parents' answer is "yes," then they are asked about the setting in which the problem behavior occurs, how they have tried to handle the problem, and what they think causes the problem.

After the therapist has determined the situations (or the behaviors in the case of Patterson's interview format) that are currently problems for the parents and the child, as well as the antecedent and consequent factors maintaining the problem parent–child interactions, a developmental history of the child is obtained. This should cover any difficulties during pregnancy, birth, and early childhood; the ages for developmental milestones such as sitting, standing, walking, and talking; and childhood illnesses and accidents.

At the end of the initial interview, the therapist briefly summarizes the problem interactions that have been selected as appropriate for treatment. In addition, he or she makes clear the behavior therapist's conceptualization of the problem behavior and the intervention approach to be adopted.

The interview as an assessment tool does not end with the first contact but continues throughout treatment formulation and implementation. The interview is used to obtain information (e.g., potential rewards and punishers) necessary for the development of treatment programs, to assess the programs as they are implemented, and to alter these programs if necessary. Portions of Holland's (1970) interview guide provide questions appropriate for the specification of problem behaviors, determination of reinforcers and punishers, and the development of treatment strategies (see Table 1).

### Interview with Teacher

If the presenting problem concerns classroom behavior, an interview with the child's teacher(s) is necessary. There are two prerequisites that must be fulfilled prior to the interview: parental permission to contact the school and, subsequently, approval from the school principal to contact the teacher(s). Once these prerequisites are accomplished, the teacher(s) can be contacted and an interview arranged. The interview with the teacher is structured similarly to Hanf's (Note 3) interview format used with parents, in that the therapist questions whether various classroom situations are problem areas. Situations to be covered include working alone, working in groups, structured activities, unstructured activities, recess, lunch, free time, and particular academic topics (e.g., mathematics, social studies). If the teacher indicates that a particular situation is a problem, then the therapist obtains a description of the situation (What is the class doing?), the child's behavior in that situation (What does the child do?), the teacher's responses to the child (What do you do?), and the child's responses to the teacher's interventions (What does the child do then?). Other information relevant to the problem situation includes the frequency and duration of the problem and the role of other children in escalating or inhibiting the problem.

reinforcement survey (Cautela, 1977) for use later in the development of treatment programs. In addition to content information, the interview with the child provides the therapist with a subjective evaluation of the child's cognitive and behavioral characteristics (e.g., verbal skills, social skills).

## Limitations

For the behavior therapist, the interview is a necessary, but not a sufficient, assessment procedure. Despite its extensive use, the behavioral interview—its structure, reliability, and validity—has been researched very little. Several studies (e.g., Yarrow, Campbell, & Burton, 1970) have investigated maternal retrospective reports of child behavior and have found that developmental information is generally biased in the desired direction. Studies examining the validity or reliability of parents' descriptions of current child behavior have yet to be done. However, in reviewing the research on parental interviews, Ciminero and Drabman (1977) conclude that there is some evidence to suggest that the more specific the interview questions, the more accurate the information obtained.

With respect to child interviews, Herjanic, Herjanic, Brown, and Wheatt (1975) compared the responses of children, aged 6 to 16 years, with the responses of their mothers in a structured interview and concluded that children are reliable reporters. The average agreement between children and their mothers was 80%. The agreement was highest (84%) for questions concerning factual information (e.g., age, address) and was lowest (69%) for questions dealing with mental status. Of more interest to the behavior therapist, children's responses to questions concerning behavior at home, with peers, and at school were in agreement with parents' responses 75% of the time. Data concerning the validity of either the mothers' or children's responses were not presented.

Research on the reliability and validity of teacher interviews is also lacking. Bolstad and Johnson (1977) compared the global labels (e.g., "best behaved," "average behaved," and "least well-behaved") teachers used to describe children in their classrooms with teacher ratings on questionnaires, teacher estimates of child classroom behaviors, and behavioral observations in the classrooms. Their results suggest that teachers' verbal reports are valid, at least with respect to global labels. Studies on the reliability and validity of more specific teacher verbal descriptions of child classroom behavior are not available.

In summary, the behavioral interview is, and will certainly continue to be, an indispensible part of behavioral assessment. Because of its limited empirical basis, however, it must be used in conjunction with other assessment procedures in developing a valid functional analysis of the referral problem.

## Behavioral Questionnaires

With conduct disorders, behavioral questionnaires are used primarily as an extension of the behavioral interview and might be described more accurately as a structured paper and pencil interview. Compared with interviews, they have several advantages: (1) they are self-administered; (2) they require relatively little time to administer, score, and interpret; and (3) they yield quantitative data (Haynes, 1978). In addition, because they may include a more extensive list of problem behaviors, use of questionnaires may identify problem behaviors for treatment that were missed in the behavioral interview (Ciminero & Drabman, 1977).

Although there are numerous questionnaires for use with parents and teachers (for reviews, see Humphreys & Ciminero, 1979; Spivack & Swift, 1973), currently there are none exclusively designed for assessment of conduct disorders in children. Instead, available questionnaires include aggressive, acting-out behaviors along with other child behavior problems. For practical purposes, four questionnaires will be presented here. Three are frequently used in the research literature to assess conduct disorders in children at home and at school (Atkeson & Forehand, 1978). The fourth questionnaire is included because it is the most extensively researched (Ciminero & Drabman, 1977).

### The Becker Bipolar Adjective Checklist

The Becker Bipolar Adjective Checklist, as originally developed by Becker (1960), consisted of 72 bipolar adjective pairs (e.g., excitable–calm, obedient–disobedient). Patterson and Fagot (1967) reduced the scale to 48 bipolar adjectives by sampling the six factors derived with Becker's (1960) original scale. In the questionnaire, each adjective pair functions as the end points of a seven-point Likert scale. The following example shows the presentation of one adjective pair in the questionnaire:

|  | ( ) | ( ) | ( ) | ( ) | ( ) | ( ) | ( ) |  |
|---|---|---|---|---|---|---|---|---|
| Excitable | 3 | 2 | 1 | 0 | 1 | 2 | 3 | Calm |

The instructions are to "place a check mark within the set of parentheses at the point on each scale which most accurately describes your evaluation of your child" (Patterson et al., 1975, p. 151).

Becker's (1960) factor analysis of the protocols from 64 nonclinic parents and 11 clinic parents yielded six factors: (1) Hostile–Withdrawn versus Warm–Extroversion, (2) Relaxed Disposition versus Nervous Disposition, (3) Lack of Aggression, (4) Schoolroom Efficiency, (5) Submission versus Dominance, and (6) Conduct Problems. A subsequent factor analysis by Patterson and Fagot (1967) of the responses of 40 parents replicated five of Becker's six factors. Becker's Submission-versus-Dominance factor loaded on the Conduct Problems factor and was therefore dropped by Patterson and Fagot (1967).

Although the questionnaire is scored so that the child being assessed receives a separate score for each factor, there are no standard scores or cut-off scores to indicate deviance either within or across scales. In addition, normative data for the questionnaire are inadequate because of the small samples used in the Becker and Patterson and Fagot studies. Interrater reliabilities reported range from .34 to .76 (Becker, 1960) and from .13 to .51 (Patterson & Fagot, 1967). Bolstad and Johnson (1977) reported test–retest reliabilities for teachers ranging from .63 to .84. Concerning validity, Lobitz and Johnson (1975) found significant differences on all five factors between 28 clinic children and 28 matched control children.

Most of the items on the questionnaire are subjective (e.g., "trusting," "tough," "responsible"). As a result, examination of the parent/teacher responses to the adjective pairs will not reveal any previously missed problem child behaviors. Reviewing the extremely negative responses with the parents and/or the teacher might provide the therapist with additional information, but the effort to get them from a subjective label (e.g., "irresponsible") to a specific problem behavior may be quite time consuming. In general, the use of this questionnaire is not recommended as an extension of the behavioral interview.

Despite its problems with reliability and normative data, the Becker Bipolar Adjective Checklist has been used frequently in research to evaluate treatment effectiveness with conduct-disordered children (e.g., Eyberg & Johnson, 1974; Johnson, Bolstad, & Lobitz, 1976; Patterson, 1974; Patterson, Cobb, & Ray, 1973; Peed et al., 1977). Most studies report significant pretreatment-to-posttreatment changes in the parents' ratings of their children on at least four of the five factors (e.g., Eyberg & Johnson, 1974; Patterson, 1974). Unfortunately, Peed et al. (1977) found that a waiting list control group demonstrated changes similar to those displayed by a treatment group for all factors except Conduct Problems. These results bring into question the validity of this instrument for assessing the effectiveness of behavior therapy treatment programs.

### The Parent Attitude Test

The Parent Attitude Test (PAT), developed by Cowen, Huser, Beach, and Rappaport (1970), includes four separate scales to measure parent attitudes and perceptions of child behavior: (1) the Home Attitude Scale, (2) the School Attitude Scale, (3) the Behavior Rating Scale, and (4) the Adjective Checklist Scale. The Home and School Attitude Scales consist of seven and four items, respectively. Each item is rated on a five-point scale to reflect the parents' perception of the child's adjustment at home and school. For example, a statement on the Home Attitude Scale is "As far as my child's behavior at home is concerned, he is doing . . . ," with five response options ranging from "very well" to "very poorly." An example from the School Attitude Scale is "When my child talks about school, it seems as if he . . . ," with five response choices ranging from "likes it very much" to "dislikes it very much." The Behavior Rating Scale consists of 25 items, each of which refers to an overt deviant behavior problem. Most of the items on this scale would be considered conduct-disordered behaviors (e.g., temper tantrums, crying); however, a few of the items refer to other types of child behavior problems (e.g., has trouble eating). Each item is rated on a five-point scale, ranging from "does not apply" to "shows very strongly." The Adjective Checklist Scale consists of 34 adjectives, each describing a child behavior or personality characteristic (e.g., alert, careless, defiant, shy, tense, helpless). Each adjective is rated on a three-point scale, ranging from "does not show at all" to "shows very strongly," to indicate the degree to which the adjective describes the child. Each scale is scored separately by summing the scores of the items within the scale. Neither normative data nor cut-off scores are available to interpret individual scores with respect to the general population.

Cowen *et al.* (1970) report test–retest reliabilities ranging from .57 (School Attitudes) to .72 (Adjective Checklist). No interrater reliabilities are reported. With respect to validity, Cowen *et al.* (1970) compared teacher ratings of children's adjustment, using other instruments, with the parent ratings on the PAT. Based on the teacher ratings of adjustment, the children were divided into two groups (the top two-thirds and the bottom one-third). Subsequent analysis indicated significant differences in the PAT scores of the two groups. Additionally, Liem, Yellot, Cowen, Trost, and Izzo (1969) found significant correlations between parent ratings on the PAT and clinicians' ratings for the early detection of emotional disorder in children. Forehand *et al.* (1975) also reported significant differences between clinic and nonclinic children on parent-completed PATs.

The Behavior Rating Scale of the PAT can be used as an extension of the behavioral interview with the parents. Because it contains fairly specific overt problem behaviors, examination of parent responses to the Behavior Rating Scale may reveal problem behaviors omitted during the interview. If this does occur, the specific behaviors are discussed with the parents. To obtain a functional analysis of each problem behavior, the format used by Patterson (Patterson *et al.*, 1975) is recommended (see section on interview with parent). Another use of the PAT is the comparison of parent attitudes to actual child behavior collected by independent observers and parents. Discrepancies in these measures may suggest that parent perceptions and attitudes rather than, or in addition to, child problem behavior should be modified. Forehand (Forehand, Griest, & Wells, 1979; Griest, Wells, & Forehand, 1979) recently has reported data suggesting that scores yielded by the PAT are not always congruent with observer-collected data.

The PAT has been used to evaluate treatment effectiveness with conduct-disordered children (Forehand & King, 1977; Forehand, Sturgis, McMahon, Aguar, Green, Wells, & Breiner, 1979; Peed *et al.*, 1977). Forehand and King (1977) report significant pretreatment-to-posttreatment changes in parent ratings on the Home Attitude, Behavior Rating, and Adjective Checklist Scales. The School Attitude Scale was not used. The changes were maintained at a 3-month follow-up. Forehand *et al.* (1979) reported similar findings, as well as maintenance of change at a 12-month follow-up. Peed *et al.* (1977) found that a treatment group changed significantly more than a waiting list control group on the Home Attitude and Behavior Rating Scales, but not on the Adjective Checklist Scale.

### The Walker Problem Behavior Identification Checklist

The Walker Problem Behavior Identification Checklist (Walker, 1970) contains 50 items that constitute overt problem behaviors. Although this questionnaire was developed for use by teachers (Walker, 1967), it has also been used by parents to indicate conduct-disordered child behaviors (e.g., Christophersen, Barnard, Ford, & Wolf, 1976). The items on the checklist are overt, requiring little inference by the rater (e.g., steals things from other children; disturbs other children—teasing, provoking fights, interrupting others; argues and must have last word in verbal exchanges). In completing the checklist, the teacher and/or parent indicates only if each behavioral item has been observed in the child in the last two months.

A factor analysis by Walker (cited in Spivack & Swift, 1973) yielded five factors: (1) Acting out, (2) Withdrawal, (3) Distractibility, (4) Disturbed Peer Relations,[2] and (5) Immaturity. Responses to the checklist are tallied so that the child being assessed receives a score on each factor. T-score norms are presented for each of the factors by sex but not by age. Walker (1967) reports a split-half reliability of .98; Bolstad and Johnson (1977) reported a test–retest reliability of .86 for teachers. With respect to validity, Walker (Spivack & Swift, 1973) compared the total scores of 38 children identified as behavior problems by an independent criterion with the total scores of a matched group of 38 children and found significant differences in the two groups. Similarly, Bolstad and Johnson (1977) found that children scoring high and low on teacher-completed Walker Checklists differed significantly in appropriate classroom behavior. Green, Forehand, and McMahon (1979) found that nonclinic and conduct-disordered clinic-referred children were rated differentially by their parents on the Acting-Out and Distractibility factors.

The acting-out scale is composed of items describing disruptive and aggressive behaviors (e.g., does not obey until threatened with punishment, reacts with defiance to instructions or commands, has temper tantrums). As such, teacher/parent responses to items on this scale can be used to reveal problem behaviors omitted previously in the interview. Because the list of behaviors on this scale is selective (14 items), the therapist cannot conclude that through its use he or she has a thorough understanding of the specific problem behaviors exhibited by a particular child.

Johnson, Bolstad, and Lobitz (1976) have reported data for four subjects that indicated significant changes in teacher-completed Walker scores with implementation of a classroom behavioral program. Changes in the checklist scores were congruent with changes in observer-collected classroom data for three of the four children. Christophersen et al. (1976) have reported significant changes in parent-completed Walker scores following treatment of parent–child pairs in their family training program. Similar changes were not demonstrated by a child guidance treatment group, which served as a comparison treatment approach for the behavioral parent training program utilized by Christophersen et al. (1976).

## The Behavior Problem Checklist

The Behavior Problem Checklist, developed by Peterson (1961), is a rating scale that lists 55 frequently occurring problem behaviors in children and adolescents.

---

[2]As was mentioned previously, conduct-disordered children may also have disturbed peer relations as part of their aggressive, disruptive behavior pattern. The Walker Checklist provides measures of both the child's acting-out behaviors and his or her peer relations and, as such, can serve as a screening instrument for further evaluation of social skills.

The problem behaviors included were selected from 427 child guidance clinic case Some of the items refer to overt behaviors (e.g., fighting), whereas others refe to personality characteristics (e.g., feelings of inferiority) (Spivack & Swift, 1973). Each problem behavior is rated on a three-point scale to indicate the severity of the problem.

Factor-analytic studies of this instrument have been conducted with several child populations: public school children, institutionalized juvenile delinquents, students in classes for the emotionally disturbed, and children seen at a child guidance clinic (Quay & Peterson, 1967). Based on these studies, four factors have emerged: (1) Conduct Disorder (psychopathy, unsocialized aggression), (2) Personality Disorder (neuroticism, anxious–withdrawn), (3) Inadequacy–Immaturity, and (4) Subcultural (socialized) Delinquency.

Quay and Peterson (1967) present means and standard deviations for both normal and clinical groups on each of the four factors. The norms are derived from ratings by teachers in a school setting. Norms are not available for ratings by parents in the home setting (Humphreys & Ciminero, 1979; Speer, 1971). Studies examining interrater reliability report correlations ranging from .23 to .77 (Quay & Peterson, 1967). The correlations are higher for mother–father ratings and teacher–teacher ratings; interrater reliability declines when comparisons are made across settings (e.g., mother–teacher, father–teacher). Test–retest reliabilities are also low, with correlations ranging from .21 to .52 (Quay & Peterson, 1967). With respect to validity, Speer (1971) found significant differences on the Conduct Disorder, Personality Disorder, and Inadequacy–Immaturity factors when parent ratings of clinic-referred children were compared with parent ratings of nonclinic children.

Although the Behavior Problem Checklist is by far the most extensively researched questionnaire, it has not been adopted by behavior therapists for use in evaluating treatment effectiveness with conduct-disordered children. Therefore, data are not available to indicate how sensitive the instrument is to behavioral interventions.

In summary, questionnaires can be used to assess parent and/or teacher perceptions of conduct-disordered children and to specify target behaviors omitted in the parent or teacher interviews. As such, they provide the therapist with an efficient method of obtaining quantitative data. Questionnaires are limited, however, in that they do not indicate antecedent and consequent events currently maintaining the problem behaviors. Because of their problems with test–retest reliabilities, questionnaires are also limited as an outcome measure of treatment effectiveness.

## Behavioral Observation

Because of problems inherent in other assessment strategies (e.g., interviews, questionnaires), direct behavioral observation is the most accepted procedure for obtaining a reliable and valid description of current child–parent interactions and/or child–teacher interactions. Through the appropriate use of behavioral observation, the therapist is able to obtain measures on the frequency and duration of child problem behavior and on the relations between child and parent and/or teacher behaviors and thus is able to quantify the problem interactions targeted for treatment. However, direct behavioral observation is not without problems. Difficulties include (1) loss of information with the use of a coding system, (2) assessment and calculation of reliability, (3) stability of data, (4) observer error, (5) subject reactivity to being observed, and (6) the effect of setting instructions. Others (Hersen & Barlow, 1976; Kent & Foster, 1977; Lipinski & Nelson, 1974) have addressed these difficulties in detail.

### Observation in the Clinic

Although extremely valuable to assessment and treatment, behavioral observations by independent observers in the natural environment are very expensive and time consuming—that is, they lack efficiency. An assessment procedure that reduces the time and cost associated with observation in the natural setting and that, unfortunately, may also reduce the validity of the information gained is the observation of parent–child interactions in a structured setting in the clinic. Use of a structured clinic observation is advantageous for two reasons. One, it efficiently elicits the problem parent–child interactions, and, two, the standard situation allows the therapist to make within- and between-client comparisons (Hughes & Haynes, 1978).

Typically, the structured setting is a playroom in a clinic, equipped with age-appropriate toys and games. Observation occurs unobtrusively through one-way mirrors. Instructions to the parents may vary from "play with your child" to highly specific guidelines for emitting a list of commands to the child. Similarly, behavior observation systems vary in complexity. For an excellent review and critique of behavior observations in the clinic, the reader is referred to Hughes and Haynes (1978).

Although several structured observation procedures are available for use in assessing parent–child interactions in the clinic (e.g., Eyberg & Johnson, 1974; Glogower & Sloop, 1976; Tavormina, 1975), only one will be presented. Forehand (e.g., Forehand & Peed, 1979) has modified the assessment procedure developed by Hanf (Note 3) for the observation of parent–child interactions in the clinic. Each parent–child pair is observed in a clinic playroom equipped with a one-way mirror and wired for sound. The playroom contains various age-appropriate toys, such as building blocks, toy trucks and cars, dolls, puzzles, crayons, and paper. An observer codes the parent–child interaction from an adjoining observation room. Prior to the clinic observation, each parent is instructed to interact with his or her child in two different contexts, referred to as the "child's game" and the "parent's game." In the child's game, the parent is instructed to engage in any activity that the child chooses and to allow the child to determine the nature and rules of the interaction. Thus, the child's game is essentially a free play situation. In the parent's game, the parent is instructed to engage the child in activities whose rules and nature are determined by the parent. Thus, the parent's game is essentially a command situation.

The clinic observation consists of coding the parent–child interaction from behind a one-way observation window for 5 or 10 minutes in both the child's and parent's games. Three child behaviors and six parent behaviors are recorded during the observation. The parent behaviors are as follows:

1. *Rewards*: praise, approval, or positive physical attention that refers to the child or to the child's activity; verbal rewards include both specific (labeled) and nonspecific (unlabeled) reference to "praiseworthy" behavior.
2. *Attends*: descriptive phrases that follow and refer to (a) the child's ongoing behavior, (b) objects directly related to the child's play, (c) his or her spatial position (e.g., "you're standing in the middle of the room"), or (d) his or her appearance.
3. *Questions*: interrogatives to which the only appropriate response is verbal.
4. *Commands*
   a. Alpha commands: an order, rule, suggestion, or question to which a motoric response is appropriate and feasible.
   b. Beta commands: commands to which the child has no opportunity to demonstrate compliance. Beta commands include parental commands that are (1) so vague that proper action for compliance cannot be determined, (2) interrupted by further parental talking before enough time (5 seconds) has elapsed for the child to comply, or (3) carried out by the parent before the child has an opportunity to comply.
5. *Warnings*: statements that describe aversive consequences to be delivered by the parent if the child fails to comply to a parental command.
6. *Time out*: A procedure used by the parent that clearly is intended to remove the child from positive reinforcement because of the child's inappropriate behaviors (e.g., placing the child in a chair in the corner of the room).

The child behaviors are as follows:

1. *Child compliance*: an appropriate motoric response initiated within 5 seconds following a parental alpha command.
2. *Child noncompliance*: failure to initiate a motoric response within 5 seconds following a parental alpha command.
3. *Child inappropriate behavior:* behavior that includes (a) whine–cry–yell–tantrum, (b) aggression (e.g., biting, kicking, hitting, slapping, and grabbing an object from someone), and (c) deviant talk (e.g., repetitive requests for attention, stated refusals to comply, disrespectful statements, and commands to parents that threaten aversive consequences).

Forehand, Peed, Roberts, McMahon, Griest, and Humphreys (Note 4) have developed a coding manual for training observers to score these behaviors.

Following the clinic observation, the data are summarized for both the child's game and the parent's game. Parent behaviors are expressed as rate per minute of attends, rewards, questions, alpha commands, beta commands, warnings, time outs, and total commands. Child behaviors are expressed in percentages: percentage of child compliance to alpha commands, percentage of child compliance to total commands, and percentage of child inappropriate behavior. In addition, the percentage of parental attention contingent upon child compliance (i.e., rewards plus attends emitted within 5 seconds following child compliance) is computed. Because the time spent in assessing the parent–child interactions is relatively short (10 minutes), this clinic observation procedure can be repeated at each clinic visit, thus providing the therapist with a continuous assessment of treatment effects. This same coding system can also be used for home observations of parent–child interactions (e.g., Peed *et al.*, 1977).

Figure 1 shows a sample score sheet for the observation of parent–child interactions during the parent's game in the clinic. Data are recorded in 30-second intervals. With one exception, the frequency of occurrence of each behavior is scored in each interval. Inappropriate behavior is recorded on an occurrence/nonoccurrence basis for each 30-second interval. The data from the sample observation are summarized at the bottom of the figure. As can be seen, the child engaged in inappropriate behavior (e.g., whining, crying, hitting) in 40% of the ten 30-second observation intervals. His compliance to the total number of commands given by the parent was 19%. However, his compliance to clear, direct commands (alpha commands) was much higher (75%). The parent provided positive consequences to only 17% of the child's compliances. Differentiating child compliance to alpha and to beta commands provides the therapist with information concerning the antecedent events maintaining child noncompliance. In this example, the large difference between the percentage compliance to alpha commands and that to total commands indicates that modification of the parents' command behavior is essential to treatment success. Based on this observation, the treatment goals would be (1) to teach the parent to give alpha commands, (2) to decrease the number of beta commands, (3) to increase the parent's positive consequation of child compliance, and (4) to decrease the child's inappropriate behavior by teaching the parent a time-out procedure.

Using this coding system, Forehand (Forehand & Peed, 1979) reports an average interobserver reliability of 75%. Data from repeated observations of non-intervention parent–child interactions are stable and consistent with this coding system (Peed *et al.*, 1977), yet the observation procedure is also sensitive enough to measure significant treatment effects in the clinic and home (Forehand, Griest, & Wells, 1979; Forehand, Sturgis, McMahon, Aguar, Green, Wells, & Breiner, 1979; Humphreys, Forehand, McMahon, & Roberts, 1978; Peed *et al.*, 1977).

Given that the coding system and structured situation produce a reliable and sensitive assessment instrument, the next question concerns the validity of the instrument. Forehand (Forehand *et al.*, 1975) found significant differences with respect to rate of parental commands and percentage of child compliance between clinic and nonclinic parent–child interactions observed in a clinic. In other studies, Forehand (e.g., Peed *et al.*, 1977) has shown that parent–child interactions in the clinic are similar to those observed in the home. More specifically, treatment effects observed in the clinic coincide with treatment effects observed in the home.

Child's Name  Begood, Jack            Page _____
              Last      First

Date _____          Time _____

Coder's Name _____

Session _____    Place  Clinic

1  C C A C C
       N C                            ⟨0⟩

2  A A C C Q C
           C                          ⟨0⟩

3  C C Q Q C C
           C                          ⟨1⟩

4  R C C C Q
         N                            ⟨1⟩

5  C C Q A C C
           C                          ⟨0⟩

6  C C Q C C C                        ⟨1⟩

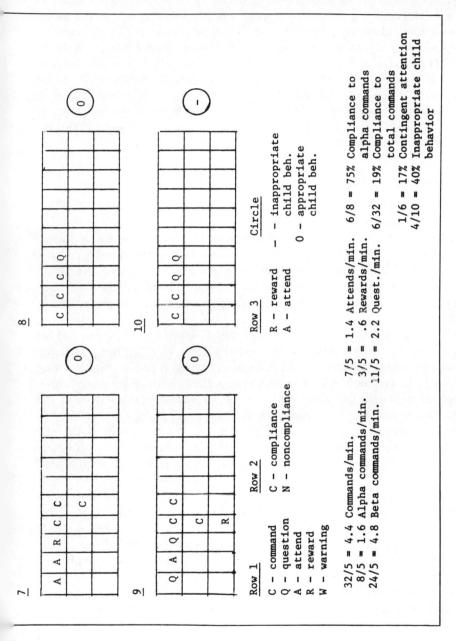

FIGURE 1

Sample score sheet for the observation of parent–child interactions during the parent's game in the clinic.

In their review of structured observation procedures, Hughes and Haynes (1978) report similar data with respect to reliability, sensitivity, and validity of clinic observations by a number of investigators. However, conflicting evidence does exist concerning the generality of parent–child interactions in the clinic to parent–child interactions in the home. Several studies report findings similar to those of Forehand (e.g., Mash, Lazere, Terdal, & Garner, 1973). However, Johnson (Eyberg & Johnson, 1974; Martin, Johnson, Johansson, & Wahl, 1976), among others, failed to find a correspondence between home and clinic observations. If home observations of parent–child interactions are not feasible, it is necessary to question both the parents and the child carefully concerning the similarity of behavior observed in the clinic to that displayed at home.

### Observation in the Home

Several behavioral coding systems have been developed to measure conduct-disordered child behavior in the home (e.g., Patterson, Ray, Shaw, & Cobb, 1969; Wahler, House, & Stambaugh, 1976; Forehand et al., Note 4; Bernal, Kreutzer, North, & Pelc, Note 5). Two of the systems that have been reported in the research literature as the most frequently used for home observations will be presented in this section. A third system, designed for use in both the home and the clinic, was presented in the preceding section on clinic observations (i.e., Forehand et al., Note 4).

The Behavioral Coding System (BCS) was developed by Patterson and his colleagues at the Oregon Research Institute (Patterson et al., 1969). Although designed to record social interactions among family members in their natural setting (the home), the system is not completely unstructured. Prior to the observation, members of the family are given the following instructions: (1) everyone in the family must be present; (2) no guests should be present during observations; (3) the family is limited to two rooms (4) no telephone calls are to be made, and incoming calls must be answered briefly; (5) no television viewing is permitted; and (6) no conversations may be held with observers while they are coding (Patterson et al., 1975).

Preintervention assessment usually consists of 6 to 10 hours of observation collected in approximately 1-hour segments. During an observation period, the subject's behavior and the responses by other family members to the subject's behavior are coded in order to provide a sequential account of the subject's interactions with other family members. Each member of the family is randomly designated the subject for 5-minute segments of the observation period. When each member has been observed for 5 minutes, the series is repeated once. Twenty-nine behavioral categories are used to describe the subject–family interactions. These behavioral categories are divided into two groups—responses and consequences. The behavioral categories labeled "responses" are: command, command negative, cry, humiliate, laugh, negativism, whine, yell, touch, self-stimulation, destructiveness, high rate, talk, physical negative, dependency, proximity, normative, receive things, play, tease, and work. The behavioral categories labeled "consequences" are: ignore, approve, physical positive, compliance, disapproval, non-compliance, attention, and no response (Patterson *et al.*, 1973). Patterson and Cobb (1971) provide complete definitions, with examples, for each of the 29 categories.

Following 6 to 10 hours of preintervention observation, the conduct-disordered child's behavior is summarized by computing the frequency of each deviant behavior and the frequency of total deviant behavior (Patterson *et al.*, 1973). In addition, the relationship of particular antecedent and consequent behaviors can be examined (Patterson, 1975, 1977a). As treatment progresses, observation data can also be used to determine changes in targeted and nontargeted deviant behavior (Patterson *et al.*, 1973) and in parent consequation of conduct-disordered behaviors (Taplin & Reid, 1977).

The observation procedure developed by Wahler and his associates at the Child Behavior Institute in Tennessee (Wahler *et al.*, 1976) is similar to Patterson's BCS in that it is designed to record a child's interactions with other persons in his or her environment. As with the BCS, certain rules are imposed on the family during the observation period. All family members must remain in the house, and all television sets, radios, and record players must be turned off. Observation periods are 30 minutes in length. The number of observation periods varies, depending on the length of time required to obtain a valid preintervention assessment. During the observation period, 19 behavioral response categories are used to record the child's behavior, and 6 behavioral stimulus categories are used to record the behaviors of other persons in the child's environment. The 19 categories for child behaviors are: compliance, opposition, aversive opposition, complaint, self-stimulation, object play, self-talk, sustained noninteraction, sustained schoolwork, sustained toy play, sustained work, sustained attending, mand adult, mand child, social approach adult, social approach child, social interaction adult, and social interaction child. The 6 stimulus categories are: instruction adult—nonaversive, instruction adult—aversive, social attention adult—nonaversive, social attention adult—aversive, social attention child—nonaversive, and social attention child—aversive. Wahler *et al.* (1976) provide definitions and behavioral examples for each of these categories.

Following the preintervention observations, the percentage of occurrence of selected child and parent behaviors is computed (e.g., Wahler, Note 6). These frequencies are compared with information obtained in the initial interview with the child's parents and discrepancies are explored. Repeated observations during treatment can be used to document changes in specific behavior categories. Posttreatment observations provide quantitative information on treatment effect, both immediate and long term.

The reliability and validity of Patterson's and Wahler's coding systems are similar to that reported by Forehand (see section on observations in the clinic). Patterson (1977b; Patterson *et al.*, 1973) reports interobserver agreement ranging from 73% to 80%, with the average agreement approximating 75%. Wahler (Wahler *et al.*, 1976) has found that interobserver agreement with his coding system usually reaches 80% or better. With respect to validity, Patterson's coding system has been shown to discriminate between the total deviant behavior of aggressive boys and that of normal boys matched on relevant demographic variables (Reid & Hendricks, 1973). Correlations between observations using the BCS and those using other measures (e.g., parent reports, parent-collected data) are also significant (Patterson, 1974, 1977b).

The validity data on Wahler's coding system are not as extensive. Using Wahler's system, Moore (Note 2) found that teacher-identified problem children displayed less appropriate behavior in both home and school than did teacher-identified nonproblem children. Adequate validity has also been reported, based on an assessment via a congruence evaluation of a child's behavior profile as expected on the basis of the interview data and the data from the behavioral categories of the coding system (Wahler *et al.*, 1976).

Each of the three coding systems (i.e., Forehand's, Patterson's, and Wahler's) was developed for use in clinical research to provide a rigorous assessment of treatment effectiveness with conduct-disordered children and their parents. The use of these systems in general clinical practice is desirable but rare. To obtain data on conduct-disordered behavior and antecedent and consequent events, the coding systems are, by necessity, complex. Partially as a result of their complexity, the time to train and maintain adequate levels of reliability by independent observers is lengthy. For example, Forehand (Forehand, Griest, & Wells, 1979) reports that observers receive at least 50 hours of training prior to the start of observations and weekly one-hour training sessions during the collection of observations. In addition to training time, the observations themselves require a certain amount of time and flexibility. With Patterson's coding system, there are 6 to 10 one-hour preintervention observations, 2 one-hour observations during treatment, and 18 one-hour observations spread over the year following termination (Patterson *et al.*, 1973). All of Patterson's home observations take place in the evening, just before dinner, so that the presence of the entire family is maximized. Forehand (Wells, Forehand, & Griest, Note 7), however, plans observations to coincide with the times when the problem child behaviors are more likely to occur and thus requires more flexibility in his independent observers' schedules.

As is evident from the preceding discussion, few clinical settings have the resources to provide such extensive assessment. In general, we recommend the use of structured clinical observations to assess parent–child interactions. If there is a discrepancy between the clinic observations and the parent reports of interactions at home, home observations are necessary.

### Observation in the School

Direct observations in the classroom have the same practical problems as those previously mentioned for home observations. Training of reliable observers and observation time are similar. Unfortunately, unlike home observation, the therapist does not have the option of observing teacher–child interactions in the clinic. Therefore, if the presenting problem concerns classroom behavior, observation in the school is usually necessary.

As with teacher interviews, the therapist must first obtain the permission of the parents, the principal, and the teacher(s) before scheduling the observations. As with home observations, behavior observations in the classroom should be timed so as to occur when the problem interactions are most frequent. For example, if the teacher reports that the child is particularly disruptive during seat work in the morning, the observation should take place during that period, not during reading class in the afternoon.

Patterson's BCS, originally developed for use in the home, has been extended to use in the school (Patterson *et al.*, 1973). Wahler's coding system was originally developed for use in both the home and the school. Adoption of either of these coding systems has the advantage of making cross-situational (home–school) comparisons during assessment and treatment (Ciminero & Drabman, 1977).

A third coding system, developed by Cobb and Hops (Note 8), was designed specifically for the acting-out child in the classroom. With this coding system, the behaviors of teachers and peers that precede and follow the conduct-disordered child's behavior are recorded, thus providing a sequential pattern identifying the antecedent and consequent events of the conduct-disordered child's behavior. There are 37 different behavioral categories, which can be grouped under eight headings: approvals and disapprovals, attention and looking at, management questions, talk academic, commands, disruption and inappropriate locale, physical negative and punishment, and miscellaneous. The coding manual by Cobb and Hops (Note 8) provides definitions and examples for each of the 37 categories. Using a modified form of the coding system, which included 19 categories, Walker and Hops (1976) reported reliabilities above 95%. Furthermore, the system discriminated between teacher-referred behavior problem children and their classroom peers in terms of appropriate behavior.

## Observation by Significant Adults

Another alternative to observations by independent observers in the natural setting is to train significant adults in the child's environment to observe and record certain types of child behavior. Wahler (Wahler *et al.*, 1976), Patterson (Patterson *et al.*, 1975), and Forehand (Forehand, Griest, & Wells, 1979) report the use of parents and/or teachers as observers in addition to the use of independent observers in the natural setting.

Patterson *et al.* (1975) employ a simplified observation procedure for parents. The conduct-disordered behaviors that the parents identified in the initial interview as of greatest concern to them are placed on a checklist. When the independent observers come to the child's home, the parents are asked to record the occurrence/nonoccurrence of each problem behavior for that particular day. Other researchers have used a similar format with success (e.g., Walter & Gilmore, 1973). Patterson (1975) reports a correlation of .69 between the independent observer's total deviant scores and the mean frequency of problem behaviors recorded by parents. Thus, parents are able to provide daily reports of the occurrence/nonoccurrence of specific child behaviors.

The observation procedure used by Wahler (Wahler *et al.*, 1976) is more complex than Patterson's, but it provides the behavior therapist with more information. With Patterson's procedure, data concerning antecedent and consequent events are lost because the parent is recording only specific child behaviors. With Wahler's procedure, the adult (parent or teacher) records, at most, 2 of the 19 child behavior categories, but he or she also records the instructional and attention categories for the adult's own behavior. Wahler (Wahler *et al.*, 1976) reports data to indicate that teachers can accurately record a child's conduct-disordered behavior in the classroom. No data are reported concerning the reliability of the teacher's recording of his or her own behavior.

With Forehand's procedure (Forehand, Griest, & Wells, 1979), parents select 3 problem behaviors from a list of 11 at the initial interview. These behaviors are: whine, physically negative, humiliate, destructive, tease, smart talk, noncompliance, ignore or fails to answer, yell, demand attention, and temper tantrum. These behaviors were identified by Adkins and Johnson (Note 1) as aversive child behaviors, as determined by parental ratings and parental consequences applied to the behaviors. Parents are required to record the frequency of each of the three selected problem behaviors during the 24 hours preceding four home observations both before and after treatment. The independent observers collect the parent-recorded data at the end of each 24-hour period when they visit the home for observations. No reliability data have been reported. Furthermore, Forehand, Griest, and Wells (1979) reported that the parent-recorded data during the 24-hour period did not correlate with observer measures of child compliance and child deviant behavior during a subsequent 40-minute observation, suggesting that the two methods of data collection may yield different conclusions.

With certain low-rate behaviors, such as stealing, fire setting, and truancy, parent- and/or teacher-collected data may be the only sources of information on the occurrence of these behaviors. Patterson and his colleagues (e.g., Patterson *et al.*, 1975) have developed specific techniques for the assessment and treatment of children who steal. Because behaviors such as stealing are rarely observed, the target behavior is redefined as "the child's taking, or being in possession of, anything that does not clearly belong to him" or the parent's "receiving a report or complaint by a reliable informant" (Patterson *et al.*, 1975, p. 137). A short, daily telephone interview for collecting data on the occurrence/nonoccurrence of stealing behavior and information related to the stealing event (e.g., What was stolen? Where did theft take place? How did you learn about theft? What did you do?) from parents has also been developed (Jones, Note 9).

In summary, behavioral observation is, to date, the most reliable and valid assessment procedure for obtaining a functional analysis of conduct disorders in children. It is also the most costly in terms of therapist's time. As a result, efforts are being made to develop alternative assessment procedures that are more efficient but that maintain the quality of the information obtained. Bernal, Gibson, Williams, and Pesses (1971) and Johnson and Bolstad (1975) have initiated research in this area by using audio recording equipment to collect home observation data. Comparisons of these data to observer-collected data yield similar results. Subsequent studies (Johnson, Christensen, & Bellamy, 1976; Christensen, Johnson, Phillips,

Rosen, & Glasgow, Note 10) have also used audiotaped data to evaluate treatment effectivenesses. More research of this type is needed in order to develop efficient behavioral observation procedures so that they become practical assessment instruments for general clinical use.

# ADDITIONAL ASSESSMENT STRATEGIES: SOCIAL VALIDATION

Data from behavioral observations before and after intervention can be used to assess whether therapeutic changes have occurred in the target parent–child and/or teacher–child interactions. But is this enough? Wolf (1978) has suggested that assessment procedures be expanded to include social validation of behavioral interventions. More specifically, he recommends that social validation occur at three stages in the intervention process. First, the social significance of the treatment goals should be assessed—that is, are the behaviors selected for treatment important to the child and to individuals in the child's environment? Second, the social appropriateness of the particular treatment procedure should be assessed. Although several treatment procedures are available that can reduce problem behaviors in children, which of these is most acceptable to the child, parents, teachers, and others? Third, the social importance of the treatment effects should be assessed—that is, are the child and the individuals in his or her environment satisfied with the results of treatment?

Kazdin (1977) has addressed the third type of social validation and has suggested two ways in which treatment effects can be assessed with respect to social importance. These two methods are *social comparison* and *subjective evaluation*. With the social comparison method, the behavior of the conduct-disordered child is compared to the behavior of nonproblem peers before and after treatment in order to assess whether the former child's behavior after treatment is similar to that of his or her peers. With the subjective evaluation method, individuals in the child's environment (e.g., parents, teachers) are asked to evaluate the child's problem behaviors in order to determine whether the intervention has resulted in qualitative differences in the way in which the child is perceived by others. Questionnaires and interviews are two procedures that attempt to assess changes in parent and/or teacher perceptions of the child.

Social comparison and subjective evaluation can also be used to address Wolf's first type of social validation, the social importance of treatment goals. Comparison of the conduct-disordered child's behavior with that of his or her peers can delineate behavioral differences and specific behaviors that are important to target for treatment. Interviews and questionnaires provide procedures by which significant adults in the child's environment can communicate the behaviors that they consider inappropriate and thus important to change.

The second type of social validation delineated by Wolf, that of social acceptability of treatment procedures, has received little attention. Most therapists consider the alternative treatment strategies available but present only one to the child's parents and/or teacher(s), thus not involving the child, the parents, or the teacher in this decision process. Involvement of the consumers in the choice of treatment strategy would be one way for them to provide input into the acceptability of various treatment procedures. Use of a questionnaire to assess consumer satisfaction with intervention strategies at the end of treatment is another alternative.

## CONCLUSIONS

Each of the procedures presented has its own strengths and weaknesses with respect to assessment of conduct-disordered child behavior. Yet, by carefully selecting a combination of procedures, the therapist can determine the target parent–child and/or teacher–child interactions for treatment intervention. Behavioral interviews provide the therapist with a verbal description of the problem behaviors and the antecedent and consequent events currently maintaining the behaviors. Equally important, the interview allows the therapist the opportunity to assess the motivation and abilities of the significant adults who will be responsible for executing the treatment programs. Questionnaires are an extension of the interview process and, as such, yield quantifiable data on child problem behaviors. In addition, they provide a measure of the parents' and/or teacher's perception of the conduct-disordered child. Although not without its own limitations, behavioral observation is the most accepted procedure for obtaining valid and reliable data pertaining to the child's problem behaviors and to the child's relevant interactions with others in his or her environment. Thus, through the use of interviews, questionnaires, and observation, the therapist can obtain a functional analysis of the child's problem behaviors and information concerning the significant adults' (e.g., parents, teacher) perceptions of the child's behavior. Furthermore, these same assessment procedures can be used to evaluate the outcome of treatment with conduct-disordered children, although different procedures may yield different conclusions (Atkeson & Forehand, 1978; Forehand, Griest, & Wells, 1979).

Behavioral assessment procedures for conduct-disordered children have been developed, expanded, and refined over the past ten years. The importance of systematic assessment prior to implementing treatment is now recognized. Use of multiple assessment measures is accepted as common practice. In short, significant advances have been made in the methods and procedures for behavior assessment of conduct-disordered children.

Attention now needs to be focused on the refinement of the assessment process such that it specifies the most effective strategy for treatment (Ciminero & Drabman, 1977). This determination is still a matter for clinical judgment. For example, the assessment procedures presented can specify the problem behaviors and their antecedent and consequent events for a particular child in a classroom, but these same procedures do not provide information concerning the most effective intervention for this child and his or her teacher. Criteria are not yet available to the therapist for determining whether he or she should select a home-based reinforcement program (Atkeson & Forehand, 1979), a self-control procedure (Drabman, Spitalnik, & O'Leary, 1973), or a classroom token system (Kazdin & Bootzin, 1972) to effectively decrease the child's problem behavior. Until the link between assessment and the specification of treatment is determined by empirical investigation, it is critical to employ social validation assessment strategies that allow the therapist to select a treatment strategy that is most acceptable to this type of problem child and his or her parents and teacher(s).

## Acknowledgment

Preparation of this chapter was supported in part by NIMH grant MH-28859-01.

## Reference Notes

1. Adkins, D. A., & Johnson, S. M. *What behaviors may be called deviant for children? A comparison of two approaches to behavior classification.* Paper presented at the Western Psychological Association Convention, Portland, Oregon, April 1972.
2. Moore, D. R. *Determinants of deviancy: A behavioral comparison of normal and deviant children in multiple settings.* Unpublished manuscript, University of Tennessee, 1975.
3. Hanf, C. *Shaping mothers to shape their children's behavior.* Unpublished manuscript, University of Oregon Medical School, 1970.
4. Forehand, R., Peed, S., Roberts, M., McMahon, R., Griest, D., & Humphreys, L. *Coding manual for scoring mother–child interaction* (3rd ed.). Unpublished manuscript, University of Georgia, 1978.
5. Bernal, M. E., Kreutzer, S. L., North, J. A., & Pelc, R. E. *Scoring system for home and school: Rationale, use, reliability, and validity.* Paper presented at the annual meeting of the American Psychological Association, Montreal, 1973.
6. Wahler, R. G. *The insular mother: Her problems in parent–child treatment.* Unpublished manuscript, University of Tennessee, 1979.
7. Wells, K. C., Forehand, R., & Griest, D. *The use of self-control procedures to enhance temporal generality of parent-training program.* Paper presented at the meeting of the Association for the Advancement of Behavior Therapy, Chicago, November 1978.
8. Cobb, J. A., & Hops, H. *Coding manual for continuous observation of interactions by single subjects in an academic setting* (Report No. 9). Center at Oregon for Research in the Behavioral Education of the Handicapped, University of Oregon, 1972.
9. Jones, R. R. *"Observation" by telephone: An economical behavior sampling technique* (Vol. 14, No. 1). Oregon Research Institute Technical Report, 1974.
10. Christensen, A., Johnson, S. M., Phillips, S., Rosen, G. M., & Glasgow, R. E. *Cost effectiveness in behavioral family therapy.* Unpublished manuscript, University of Oregon, 1978.

## References

Atkeson, B. M., & Forehand, R. Parent behavioral training for problem children: An examination of studies using multiple outcome measures. *Journal of Abnormal Child Psychology*, 1978, *6*, 449–460.

Atkeson, B. M., & Forehand, R. Home-based reinforcement programs to modify classroom behavior: A review and methodological evaluation. *Psychological Bulletin*, 1979, *86*, 1298–1308.

Becker, W. C. The relationship of factors in parental ratings of self and each other to the behavior of kindergarten children as rated by mothers, fathers, and teachers. *Journal of Consulting Psychology*, 1960, *24*, 507–527.

Bernal, M. E., Duryee, J. S., Pruett, H. L., & Burns, B. J. Behavior modification and the brat syndrome. *Journal of Consulting and Clinical Psychology*, 1968, *32*, 447–455.

Bernal, M. E., Gibson, D. M., Williams, D. E., & Pesses, D. I. A device for automatic audio tape recording. *Journal of Applied Behavior Analysis*, 1971, *4*, 151–156.

Bolstad, O. D., & Johnson, S. M. The relationship between teachers' assessment of students and the students' actual behavior in the classroom. *Child Development*, 1977, *48*, 570–578.

Cautela, J. R. *Behavior analysis forms for clinical intervention*. Champaign, Ill.: Research Press, 1977.

Christophersen, E. R., Barnard, J. D., Ford, D., & Wolf, M. M. The family training program: Improving parent–child interaction patterns. In E. J. Mash, L. C. Handy, & L. A. Hamerlynck (Eds.), *Behavior modification approaches to parenting*. New York: Brunner/Mazel, 1976.

Ciminero, A. R., & Drabman, R. S. Current developments in the behavioral assessment of children. In B. B. Lahey & A. E. Kazdin (Eds.), *Advances in clinical child psychology* (Vol. 1). New York: Plenum, 1977.

Conners, C. K. Symptom patterns in hyperkinetic, neurotic, and normal children. *Child Development*, 1970, *41*, 667–682.

Cowen, E. L., Huser, J., Beach, D. R., & Rappaport, J. Parental perceptions of young children and their relation to indexes of adjustment. *Journal of Consulting and Clinical Psychology*, 1970, *34*, 97–103.

Delfini, L. F., Bernal, M. E., & Rosen, P. M. Comparison of deviant and normal boys in home settings. In E. J. Mash, L. A. Hamerlynck, & L. C. Handy (Eds.), *Behavior modification and families*. New York: Brunner/Mazel, 1976.

Drabman, R. S., Spitalnik, R., & O'Leary, K. D. Teaching self-control to disruptive children. *Journal of Abnormal Psychology*, 1973, *82*, 110–116.

Evans, I. M., & Nelson, R. O. Assessment of child behavior problems. In A. R. Ciminero, K. S. Calhoun, & H. E. Adams (Eds.), *Handbook of behavioral assessment*. New York: Wiley, 1977.

Eyberg, S. M., & Johnson, S. M. Multiple assessment of behavior modification with families: Effects of contingency contracting and order of treated problems. *Journal of Consulting and Clinical Psychology*, 1974, *42*, 594–606.

Forehand, R., Griest, D., & Wells, K. C. Parent behavioral training: An analysis of the relationship among multiple outcome measures. *Journal of Abnormal Child Psychology*, 1979, *7*, 229–242.

Forehand, R., & King, H. E. Noncompliant children: Effects of parent training on behavior and attitude change. *Behavior Modification*, 1977, *1*, 93–108.

Forehand, R., King, H. E., Peed, S., & Yoder, P. Mother–child interations: Comparison of a noncompliant clinic group and a nonclinic group. *Behaviour Research and Therapy*, 1975, *13*, 79–84.

Forehand, R., & Peed, S. Training parents to modify noncompliant behavior of their children. In A. J. Finch, Jr., & P. C. Kendall (Eds.), *Treatment and research in child psychopathology*. New York: Spectrum, 1979.

Forehand, R., Sturgis, E. T., McMahon, R., Aguar, D., Green, K., Wells, K. C., & Breiner, J. Parent behavioral training to modify child noncompliance: Treatment generalization across time and from home to school. *Behavior Modification*, 1979, *3*, 3–25.

Glogower, F., & Sloop, E. W. Two strategies of group training parents as effective behavior modifiers. *Behavior Therapy*, 1976, *7*, 177–184.

Green, K. D., Forehand, R., & McMahon, R. J. Parental manipulation of compliance and noncompliance in normal and deviant children. *Behavior Modification*, 1979, *3*, 245–266.

Griest, D. L., Wells, K. C., & Forehand, R. An examination of predictors of maternal perceptions of maladjustment in clinic-referred children. *Journal of Abnormal Psychology*, 1979, *88*, 277–281.

Hawkins, R. P., Peterson, R. F., Schweid, E., & Bijou, S. W. Behavior therapy in the home: Amelioration of problem parent–child relations with the parent in a therapeutic role. *Journal of Experimental Child Psychology*, 1966, *4*, 99–107.

Haynes, S. N. *Principles of behavioral assessment.* New York: Gardner Press, 1978.

Herjanic, B., Herjanic, M., Brown, F., & Wheatt, T. Are children reliable reporters? *Journal of Abnormal Child Psychology,* 1975, *3,* 41–48.

Hersen, M., & Barlow, D. H. *Single-case experimental designs: Strategies for studying behavior change.* New York: Pergamon, 1976.

Holland, C. J. An interview guide for behavioural counseling with parents. *Behavior Therapy,* 1970, *1,* 70–79.

Hughes, H. M., & Haynes, S. N. Structured laboratory observation in the behavioral assessment of parent–child interactions: A methodological critique. *Behavior Therapy,* 1978, *9,* 428–447.

Humphreys, L. E., & Ciminero, A. R. Parent report measures of child behavior: A review. *Journal of Clinical Child Psychology,* 1979, *8,* 56–63.

Humphreys, L., Forehand, R., McMahon, R., & Roberts, M. Parent behavioral training to modify child noncompliance: Effects on untreated siblings. *Journal of Behavior Therapy and Experimental Psychiatry,* 1978, *9,* 235–238.

Jenkins, R. Psychiatric syndromes in children and their relation to family background. *American Journal of Orthopsychiatry,* 1966, *36,* 450–457.

Johnson, S. M., & Bolstad, O. D. Reactivity to home observations: A comparison of audio recorded behaviors with observers present or absent. *Journal of Applied Behavior Analysis,* 1975, *8,* 181–185.

Johnson, S. M., Bolstad, O. D., & Lobitz, G. K. Generalization and contrast phenomena in behavior modification with children. In E. J. Mash, L. A. Hamerlynck, & L. C. Handy (Eds.), *Behavior modification and families.* New York: Brunner/Mazel, 1976.

Johnson, S. M., Christensen, A., & Bellamy, G. T. Evaluation of family intervention through unobtrusive audio recordings: Experiences in "bugging" children. *Journal of Applied Behavior Analysis,* 1976, *9,* 213–219.

Johnson, S. M., & Lobitz, G. K. The personal and marital adjustment of parents as related to observed child deviance and parenting behaviors. *Journal of Abnormal Child Psychology,* 1974, *2,* 193–207.

Kazdin, A. E. Assessing the clinical or applied importance of behavior change through social validation. *Behavior Modification,* 1977, *1,* 427–452.

Kazdin, A. E., & Bootzin, R. R. The token economy: An evaluative review. *Journal of Applied Behavior Analysis,* 1972, *5,* 343–372.

Kent, R. N., & Foster, S. L. Direct observation procedures: Methodological issues in naturalistic settings. In A. R. Ciminero, K. S. Calhoun, & H. E. Adams (Eds.), *Handbook of behavioral assessment.* New York: Wiley, 1977.

Lapouse, R., & Monk, M. Fears and worries in a representative sample of children. *American Journal of Orthopsychiatry,* 1959, *29,* 803–818.

Liem, G. R., Yellot, A. W., Cowen, E. L., Trost, M. A., & Izzo, L. D. Some correlates of early-detected emotional dysfunction in the schools. *American Journal of Orthopsychiatry,* 1969, *39,* 619–626.

Lipinski, D., & Nelson, R. Problems in the use of naturalistic observation as a means of behavioral assessment. *Behavior Therapy,* 1974, *5,* 341–351.

Lobitz, G. K., & Johnson, S. M. Normal versus deviant children: A multimethod comparison. *Journal of Abnormal Child Psychology,* 1975, *3,* 353–374.

MacFarlane, J., Allen, L., & Honzik, M. *A developmental study of the behavior problems of normal children between twenty-one months and fourteen years.* Berkeley: University of California Press, 1954.

Martin, S., Johnson, S. M., Johansson, S., & Wahl, G. The comparability of behavioral data in laboratory and natural settings. In E. J. Mash, L. A. Hamerlynck, & L. C. Handy (Eds.), *Behavior modification and families.* New York: Brunner/Mazel, 1976.

Mash, E. J., Lazere, R., Terdal, L., & Garner, A. Modification of mother–child interactions: A modeling approach for groups. *Child Study Journal,* 1973, *3,* 131–143.

Morris, H. H. Aggressive behavior disorders in children: A follow-up study. *American Journal of Psychiatry,* 1956, *112,* 991–997.

O'Leary, K. D., O'Leary, S., & Becker, W. C. Modification of a deviant sibling interaction in the home. *Behaviour Research and Therapy,* 1967, *5,* 113–120.

Oltmanns, T. F., Broderick, J. E., & O'Leary, K. D. Marital adjustment and the efficacy of behavior therapy with children. *Journal of Consulting and Clinical Psychology*, 1977, *45*, 724–729.

Patterson, G. R. An empirical approach to the classification of disturbed children. *Journal of Clinical Psychology*, 1964, *20*, 326–337.

Patterson, G. R. Interventions for boys with conduct problems: Multiple settings, treatments, and criteria. *Journal of Consulting and Clinical Psychology*, 1974, *42*, 471–481.

Patterson, G. R. A three-stage functional analysis for children's coercive behaviors: A tactic for developing a performance theory. In B. C. Etzel, J. M. LeBlanc, & D. M. Baer (Eds.), *New developments in behavioral research: Theory, methods, and applications. In honor of Sidney W. Bijou.* Hillsdale, N.J.: Lawrence Erlbaum Associates, 1975.

Patterson, G. R. The aggressive child: Victim and architect of a coercive system. In E. J. Mash, L. A. Hamerlynck, & L. C. Handy (Eds.), *Behavior modification and families.* New York: Brunner/Mazel, 1976.

Patterson, G. R. Accelerating stimuli for two classes of coercive behaviors. *Journal of Abnormal Child Psychology*, 1977, *5*, 335–350. (a)

Patterson, G. R. Naturalistic observation in clinical assessment. *Journal of Abnormal Child Psychology*, 1977, *5*, 309–322. (b)

Patterson, G. R., & Cobb, J. A. A dyadic analysis of "aggressive" behaviors. In J. P. Hill (Ed.), *Minnesota symposia on child psychology* (Vol. 5). Minneapolis: University of Minnesota Press, 1971.

Patterson, G. R., Cobb, J. A., & Ray, R. S. A social engineering technology for retraining the families of aggressive boys. In H. Adams & L. Unikel (Eds.), *Issues and trends in behavior therapy.* Springfield, Ill.: Charles C. Thomas, 1973.

Patterson, G. R., & Fagot, B. I. Selective responses to social reinforcers and deviant behavior in children. *Psychological Record*, 1967, *17*, 369–378.

Patterson, G. R., Ray, R. S., Shaw, D. A., & Cobb, J. A. *Manual for coding of interactions* (1969 rev.). New York: Microfiche, 1969.

Patterson, G. R., & Reid, J. B. Intervention for families of aggressive boys: A replication study. *Behaviour Research and Therapy*, 1973, *11*, 383–394.

Patterson, G. R., Reid, J. B., Jones, R. R., & Conger, R. E. *A social learning approach to family intervention: Families with aggressive children* (Vol. I). Eugene, Ore.: Castalia Publishing Company, 1975.

Peed, S., Roberts, M., & Forehand, R. Evaluation of the effectiveness of a standardized parent training program in altering the interaction of mothers and their noncompliant children. *Behavior Modification*, 1977, *1*, 323–350.

Peterson, D. R. Behavior problems of middle childhood. *Journal of Consulting Psychology*, 1961, *25*, 205–209.

Quay, H. C., Morse, W. C., & Cutler, R. T. Personality patterns of pupils in special classes for the emotionally disturbed. *Exceptional Children*, 1966, *35*, 297–301.

Quay, H. C., & Peterson, D. R. *Manual for the Behavior Problem Checklist.* Champaign, Ill.: Children's Research Center, University of Illinois, 1967.

Reid, J. B., & Hendricks, A. F. C. J. A preliminary analysis of the effectiveness of direct home intervention for treatment of pre-delinquent boys who steal. In L. A. Hamerlynck, L. C. Handy, & E. J. Mash (Eds.), *Behavior change: Methodology, concepts, and practice.* Champaign, Ill.: Research Press, 1973.

Roach, J. L. Some social–psychological characteristics of child guidance clinic caseloads. *Journal of Consulting Psychology*, 1958, *22*, 183–186.

Robins, L. N. *Deviant children grown up: A sociological and psychiatric study of sociopathic personality.* Baltimore: Williams & Wilkins, 1966.

Sines, J., Pauker, J. D., Sines, L. K., & Owen, K. D. R. Identification of clinically relevant dimensions of children's behavior. *Journal of Consulting and Clinical Psychology*, 1969, *33*, 728–734.

Speer, D. C. Behavior Problem Checklist (Peterson–Quay): Baseline data from parents of child guidance and nonclinic children. *Journal of Consulting and Clinical Psychology*, 1971, *36*, 221–228.

Spivack, G., & Swift, M. The classroom behavior of children: A critical review of teacher-administered rating scales. *Journal of Special Education*, 1973, *7*, 55–89.

Taplin, P. S., & Reid, J. B. Changes in parent consequation as a function of family intervention. *Journal of Consulting and Clinical Psychology*, 1977, *45*, 973–981.

Tavormina, J. B. Relative effectiveness of behavioral and reflective group counseling with parents of mentally retarded children. *Journal of Consulting and Clinical Psychology*, 1975, *43*, 22–31.

Wahler, R. G. Oppositional children: A quest for parental reinforcement control. *Journal of Applied Behavior Analysis*, 1969, *2*, 159–170.

Wahler, R. G. Deviant child behavior within the family: Developmental speculations and behavior change strategies. In H. Leitenberg (Ed.), *Handbook of behavior modification and behavior therapy*. Englewood Cliffs, N.J.: Prentice-Hall, 1976.

Wahler, R. G., House, A. E., & Stambaugh, E. E. *Ecological assessment of child problem behavior*. New York: Pergamon, 1976.

Walker, H. M. Construction and validation of a behavior checklist for identification of children with behavior problems. *Dissertation Abstracts*, 1967, *28*, 978–979.

Walker, H. M. *The Walker Problem Behavior Identification Checklist*. Los Angeles: Psychological Services, 1970.

Walker, H. M., & Hops, H. Use of normative peer data as a standard for evaluating classroom treatment effects. *Journal of Applied Behavior Analysis*, 1976, *9*, 159–168.

Walter, H., & Gilmore, S. K. Placebo versus social learning effects in parent training procedures designed to alter the behaviors of aggressive boys. *Behavior Therapy*, 1973, *4*, 361–377.

Wolf, M. M. Social validity: The case for subjective measurement or how applied behavior analysis is finding its heart. *Journal of Applied Behavior Analysis*, 1978, *11*, 203–214.

Wolff, S. Symptomatology and outcome of preschool children with behaviour disorders attending a child guidance clinic. *Journal of Child Psychology and Psychiatry*. 1961, *2*, 269–276.

Yarrow, M. R., Campbell, J. D., & Burton, R. V. Recollections of childhood: A study of the retrospective method. *Monographs of the Society for Research in Child Development*, 1970, *35*, No. 5.

C H A P T E R   5

# CHILD ABUSE

### Robert M. Friedman
*Florida Mental Health Institute*

### Jack Sandler
*University of South Florida*

### Mario Hernandez
*University of South Florida and Florida Mental Health Institute*

### David A. Wolfe
*University of South Florida*

The abuse of children has a lengthy and well-documented history. However, the "discovery" of child abuse as a significant social and clinical problem by human service professionals is of more recent origin, dating back only to the 1950s and 1960s. During the four-year period beginning in 1962, legislatures of all 50 states passed statutes against the abuse of children by their caretakers (Pfohl, 1977).

Interest in the problem of child abuse by behavioral scientists has been even slower in developing. For example, a review of *Psychological Abstracts* for the five years from January 1971 to December 1975 shows a total of 64 child abuse listings, of which only seven were in psychological journals (Friedman & Friedman, Note 1). Five of these seven listings were from a special issue of the *Journal of Clinical Child Psychology*, "Violence against Children" (1973). During this same five-year period, *Psychological Abstracts* contained 1463 listings on the topic of aggression or aggressive behavior, more than 20 times as many as for child abuse.

A major reason for this relative lack of interest in child abuse by behavioral scientists is that the professionals most frequently called upon to deal with actual cases of abuse come from service- rather than research-oriented disciplines. These include social work, law, law enforcement, and the medical specialities of pediatrics, psychiatry, and radiology. The inclusion in this volume of a chapter on child abuse is an important indication of the growing concern for child abuse among behavioral scientists and practitioners.

## DEFINITIONS OF CHILD ABUSE

There have been three primary approaches to the definition of child abuse. The first one focuses solely on the outcomes of acts; in this case, *abuse* is defined in

221

terms of injuries inflicted upon children. Although this approach has the advantage of emphasizing observable, measurable, and even quantifiable conditions, it has the shortcoming of grouping together accidental and nonaccidental injuries. Also, it excludes those incidents where a parent strikes out at a child but fails to injure the child. For these reasons, most researchers in child abuse have rejected a definition expressed solely in terms of the outcome of the act.

The second approach requires that injuries be "intentionally" inflicted upon the child. The major problem with this definition is that intentionality cannot be directly observed, and so its presence can only be determined inferentially. The major means for determining intentionality in child abuse are: (1) admission of the act by a parent or parent substitute; (2) a statement by the child or a responsible witness; (3) evidence of previous severe injuries that were probably inflicted, or an explanation for the injuries that is incompatible with medical findings; and (4) an evaluation of the circumstances under which the incident took place.

The third approach to defining child abuse is to view it not as a set of behaviors, but rather as a "culturally determined label which is applied to behavior and injury patterns as an outcome of a social judgment on the part of the observer" (Parke & Collmer, 1975). This approach emphasizes that the use of the label is a function of the values, background, and experiences of the labeler, as well as of the norms of the community in general. Aggressive behavior toward children under certain circumstances and in particular communities may be normative and considered appropriate.

The variety of approaches to defining the problem raises the question of the degree of interjudge agreement on the presence or absence of child abuse. This is obviously an important question from both a legal and a research perspective, and one that has received relatively little attention. For the practitioner, however, this problem may pose fewer difficulties. Acts of abuse are rarely observed directly, and the approach to assessment and treatment typically focuses on other behaviors that are presumed to be related to abuse rather than directly on the abusive act.

# INCIDENCE OF CHILD ABUSE

The actual incidence of child abuse has eluded clear determination, with reports differing considerably, probably reflecting differences in definition. The primary means of determining incidence has been through the examination of official reports of abuse. However, this approach probably produces serious underestimates, because an undetermined number of instances are never reported. Using a procedure of examining reporting rates in Florida, where a well-publicized toll-free telephone number was established for statewide reporting of child abuse, and extrapolating from the reported rates there to the rest of the country, Nagi (1975) arrived at an estimate of 167,000 reported cases of abuse annually and of an additional 91,000 unreported cases.

Recently, Gelles (1978) presented the results of a self-report interview study of family violence. The study sample consisted of 1146 parents in two-parent homes, with at least one child between the ages of 3 and 17 years living at home. The interviewers in this study used a "conflict tactics technique," which required the interviewees to indicate the types of behaviors they had used to resolve a conflict with the referent child in the course of their interactions in the past year. Gelles found that 58.2% of the parents reported having slapped or spanked their child in the past year; 40.5% reported having pushed, grabbed, or shoved; 13.4% hit with something; 3.2% kicked, bit, or hit with fist; and 1.3% "beat up" their child (defined as "more than a single punch"). Extrapolating from these data, Gelles concluded that between 3.1 and 4.0 million children have been kicked, bitten, or punched by parents at some time in their lives, and that between 1.0 and 1.9 million experienced such treatment in the target year (1975). Further, between 1.4 and 2.3 million children were beat up while growing up.

Gelles' estimates are considerably higher than what has typically been found, even where other self-report procedures have been used (Gil, 1970). Gelles points out that this may be attributable partly to the fact that this study did not look at outcomes or actual injuries of children, but rather at acts of parents; presumably, many physical acts of parents toward children do not result in physical injuries. Gelles also indicates that, given the self-report nature of the study, the fact that only households with two parents were included in the sample, and the age restriction of 3 to 17 years, it is likely that his figures are still underestimates of the incidence of such physical acts by parents toward children. Gelles does report data by age of child, which show a progressive reduction in most acts as children get older. For example, whereas 84.1% of children aged 3–4 years were slapped or spanked during 1975, only 23% of children aged 15–17 years had been exposed to such treatment.

Another important component of the magnitude of child abuse is the seriousness of the acts of abuse. Estimates of the number of children killed each year by parents or guardians are around 700 (Fontana, 1973; Gil, 1970).

The research on incidence of child abuse is probably the most controversial area of study in the field. Criticisms of the recently completed study by Gelles are already surfacing (Pelton, 1979), and it is unlikely that this issue will be clearly resolved in the near future. Although such disagreements make it difficult to evaluate trends and to do large-scale preventive planning in this problem area, all estimates clearly indicate an incidence rate high enough to justify the increased attention that the problem has received in the 1970s.

# SPECIAL ISSUES IN CHILD ABUSE

## Protection versus Treatment

Because of the very serious and irreversible consequences that may result from child abuse, practitioners must give precedence to considerations of child protection before issues of treatment strategy can be addressed. A determination must be made of whether the child, if left in the home and in the custody of his or her parent(s), is likely to be seriously harmed. This critical question is much more essential in dealing with abuse than with almost all of the other target problems covered in this volume, because the immediate risk to the child is not as great in other problem areas.

The responsibility for taking action in cases of potential risk to a child is one of the most serious and demanding issues in human services work, and the decision to take action must frequently be made in the face of limited information and shaky empirical findings. The problems involved in predicting violent behavior, and the lack of success in doing so, have been attested to by several reviewers (Ennis & Litwack, 1974; Megargee, 1970; Stone, 1975). This chapter will include recommendations for assessment procedures geared to predicting the likelihood of further acts of abuse, although the main focus will be on assessment for the purpose of developing interventions.

## Parent Behavior versus Child Behavior

This chapter differs from all others in this volume in that the target problem under examination is in fact a *parental* action, and not a behavior of the child. In the field of child development, there has been considerable debate over the role of the child in shaping parental behavior (Bell, 1968, 1971; Hoffman, 1975), and this debate has carried over into the study of child abuse. Numerous investigators have attempted to identify special characteristics of child abuse victims (Elmer & Gregg, 1967; Gaines, Sandgrund, Green, & Power, 1978; Stern, 1973). However, no matter how "effective" the child may be in shaping parental behavior, the act of abuse is still a parental act. Therefore, most of the assessment of an abusive family must focus clearly upon the caretakers, although the influence of the child should not be overlooked.

## Relationship between Child Abuse and Child Neglect

There has been a tendency in the professional literature to link the study of child abuse and child neglect. This is a natural association, because both problems are typically placed under the jurisdiction of the protective services component of child welfare agencies as a result of the potentially injurious effects upon the victim. In several important ways, however, the two problems differ, and combining them may hinder research efforts. Acts of abuse are typically low-frequency events, which can often be traced to a sequence of antecedent events. Furthermore, abusive parents are typically not neglectful in the sense of failing to provide for the basic needs of their children; indeed, some studies (Gil, 1970) suggest that a majority of parents have at one time or another felt capable of abusing their children. Neglect, however, is more a "chronic" pattern of behavior than a low-frequency pattern.

Neglect may be characterized by parents' having very little interaction with a child or by their failing to provide a clean house with adequate clothes, food, and medical care, circumstances that are not characteristic of child abuse. The study of neglect, then, is a large and significant one in and of itself. For these reasons, the focus of this chapter will be on acts of commission (abuse) rather than on acts of omission, or those that characterize neglect (Polansky, Hally, & Polansky, 1975).

## Relationship of Child Abuse to Physical Punishment

As an outgrowth of the general interest in child abuse, some authorities have begun to focus their attention on the relationship between physical punishment and abuse. The distinction between these two acts is not always a clear one. Some investigators have hypothesized that condoning physical punishment as a means of discipline in our Western society creates an environment that facilitates child abuse (Gil, 1970, 1973). Others are opposed to the use of physical punishment with children (Feshbach, 1973; Feshbach & Feshbach, 1973), whatever the form, partly because of the presumed risk of injury, but also because of its hypothesized relationship to abuse.

The more general issue of the use of physical punishment is beyond the scope of this chapter. However, the increasing concern about physical punishment does stem, in part, from the problem of child abuse and should be of great interest to behavioral practitioners and researchers.

## Investigation of Low-Frequency, Private Behaviors

The investigator interested in studying problems such as noncompliance, hyperactivity, or aggression in children can typically observe the behaviors of concern directly, using any of a variety of observational procedures. Such direct observational procedures are at the very core of behavioral assessment. Child abuse, however, does not lend itself to direct observation, partly because of the relatively low frequency of its occurrence, but also because it is illegal and is socially discouraged and thus typically occurs in the privacy of the family setting. Further, should an observer be in a position to view threatening or abusive behavior, considerations for the child's safety would likely result in action to prevent the abuse rather than uninvolved observation.

The assessment of any problem that cannot be observed directly is complex. A common strategy is to observe other behaviors that occur more frequently and that are presumed to be related to the problem behavior. One might observe, for example, parents' negative verbal behavior toward a child, under the assumption that negative verbal and negative physical behaviors are part of the same response class. By modifying the frequency of one member of that class, one may change the frequency of other members of that class. As another example, assuming that abusive behavior is a result of general parental ineffectiveness, general child management procedures can be examined and be modified by increasing parental effectiveness. Ultimately, these inferences must withstand empirical tests of their validity. The low frequency of occurrence of abuse and the after-the-fact difficulty of identifying the precise sequence of actions that led to the abuse make it difficult to conduct such empirical tests. The present state of knowledge in child abuse is such that inferences about the relationship between abusive acts and other behaviors, such as inadequate general parenting skills or negative verbal behaviors, have not been adequately tested. Nevertheless, the recommendations to be made in this chapter for behavioral assessment of abuse will include observation of other behaviors presumed, on a conceptual basis, to be related to abuse.

## FUNCTIONAL ANALYSIS OF CHILD ABUSE

Causal analyses within the field of child abuse have primarily emphasized one of two different models. The first model examines sociocultural variables that operate to produce differential rates of abuse among subgroups in the United States or between the United States and other countries. The second model is a "psychological" one, in which the intent has been to identify the particular characteristics of individuals, families, or situations that lead to abuse. These two models will be examined briefly.

One of the major sociocultural variables studied has been the cultural attitude toward the general use of physical punishment. Gil (1970, 1973) has stressed the view that the high rate of child abuse in the United States is a reflection of a general societal attitude toward the use of force. Others have supported this view by pointing to the lower rates of abuse in such countries as Japan (Goode, 1971) and China (Parke & Collmer, 1975), where physical punishment is used less than it is in the United States.

Another sociocultural variable that has been extensively discussed is poverty, along with the related aspects of unemployment and crowded and inadequate housing. The investigation of the relationship between economic variables and abuse has been impaired by potential reporting biases, in which abuse among families of a lower socioeconomic class is more likely to be reported than is abuse among middle- and upper-class families. Over and above this potential bias, the preponderance of data supports the position that abuse is a higher frequency occurrence in lower socioeconomic groups (Gelles, 1979; Pelton, 1978).

Gil (1975) has also discussed as a sociocultural factor contributing to abuse the "social construction of childhood and social definition of children's rights," with its emphasis on children as possessions of parents. Garbarino (1977) has similarly emphasized that the privacy given to families in our society facilitates the occurrence of abuse. These variables will not be considered in depth in this chapter, because the primary focus is on a practical behavioral assessment. However, such factors clearly need to be considered in taking a comprehensive look at the problem, particularly from a prevention standpoint.

The primary focus of investigators pursuing a psychological model of abuse has been to identify specific personality traits, or forms of psychopathology, that have caused abuse. The findings of these studies have been reviewed several times (Friedman, 1975; Gelles, 1973; Parke & Collmer, 1975), and the consistent conclusion has been that the practical usefulness of this approach is limited. Only within the past four years have there been many attempts to conceptualize child abuse from a behavioral perspective.

### Components of Functional Analysis

The functional analysis to be presented here will utilize the *S-O-R-K-C* model, which focuses on the stimulus situation (*S*), the individuals involved (*O*), the responses (*R*), and the contingency (*K*) and consequences (*C*). In identifying the major factors within each of the components of the functional analysis, a combination of data sources will be used. These will include the self-reports of individuals involved in abuse, the official reports of acts of abuse, and data gathered on nonabusive behavior that is believed to be related to abuse. The research and conceptual literature on aggression will also be utilized, because child abuse can be viewed as a special instance of aggression.

### *Stimulus (S)*

Most of the data on antecedent stimulus events in child abuse have been reports of broad descriptions of occurrences. For example, Gil (1970) studied a sample of 1380 cases of abuse and found that in about 63% of the cases, the situation was described as one of "immediate or delayed response to specific act of child." Johnson (1974) and Thomson, Paget, Bates, Mesch, and Putnam (1971) also found high frequencies of reports that the act of abuse was a response to some specific aversive behavior of the youngster.

More specific descriptions of the antecedent behaviors emerge from studies of fatal abuse. Weston (1968) listed "crying" as the single most frequent stimulus where abuse had occurred just once. In instances where the child had previously been abused, soiling, wetting of pants, and excessive crying were the most common events. In a similar study of fatal cases of abuse, Scott (1973) found that the precipitating stimulus often was refusal of food, vomiting, crying, screaming (especially at night when the television was on), or swearing. Many of these instances, as Scott points out, are essentially inseparable from infancy. These findings are in contrast to the findings of several authors who studied filicide (Adelson, 1961; Myers, 1970; Resnick, 1969). In filicide, the act appears to have been premeditated, whereas in fatal instances of abuse, the acts appear to be more spontaneous.

Conflict between parents was found to precede acts of child abuse in 22–30% of two small, retrospective samples (Smith, Hanson, & Noble, 1974; Terr, 1970).

The frequency with which marital conflict immediately precedes abuse as well as other parent–child interactions may be underestimated by behaviorists. Typically, behavioral observation procedures have been limited to dyads, usually parent and child. As a result, potentially important interactions between husband and wife, or between parent and another child, are not included in the observational protocol. In order to get data on the full range of potentially important antecedent stimulus events, it would be necessary to observe simultaneously multiple dyads or triads (Schrader, Panzer, Long, Gillet, & Kornblath, Note 2).

Research in other areas of aggression would suggest that severe acts of physical violence are typically the result of an escalating sequence of negative interactions in which the probability and intensity of aggressive behavior increases with each successive component in the sequence (Goldstein, Davis, & Herman, 1975; Patterson & Cobb, 1973; Toch, 1969). There are ample clinical and anecdotal reports in the child abuse literature to suggest that such is often the case with parent–child aggression as well.

In developing a general model of aggression, Bandura (1973) distinguishes between aggressive behavior as a response to an aversive stimulus and as a response to anticipated positive consequences. Although such a distinction has rarely been made in the field of child abuse, most of the identified circumstances seem to involve responses to antecedent aversive events. There has been very little suggestion in the child abuse literature that acts of abuse are in response to the anticipation of positive reinforcement.

The current perspective that emerges from these considerations, then, suggests that child abuse may be understood as a special case of aggression, in which the child's aversive behavior provokes an aggressive reaction that escalates in intensity over a period of time until tissue damage results. Although many authorities accept such an explanation, perhaps on the basis of face validity, this model of child abuse may not encompass all of the possible circumstances. The results of one recent study, for example, (Wolfe & Sandler, Note 3) involve high rates of aversive parental behavior that were unrelated to "provocation" or deviant behavior on the part of target children.

In summary, whereas there has been very little systematic and detailed research on the antecedent stimulus events for abuse, the data seem to indicate the occurrence of some aversive event, typically on the part of the abused child, but sometimes on the part of a spouse. The precise sequence of events that leads from that aversive stimulus to an aggressive act of such intensity so as to be called abusive has not been directly examined.

### Individuals (O)

In discussing this component of the functional analysis, we shall consider first the perpetrator and then the abused child. When attention was first being directed to the causes of child abuse in the 1960s, the explanations offered were likely to focus on specific characteristics of the abuser. In particular, it was felt that abusers were seriously emotionally disturbed, if not psychotic. Most data to date, however, suggest that the percentage of abusers who might be considered psychotic is approximately 5% (Boisvert, 1972; Delsordo, 1963; Kempe, 1973; Schmitt & Kempe, 1975).

An important characteristic of the abuser that has been discussed is knowledge of children and child development. In particular, abusive parents have been reported to have unrealistic expectations for their children (Steele & Pollock, 1968) and to respond inappropriately to events that are normal for infants and young children. Although there is an absence of systematic data on this issue, an important dimension to be included in a behavioral assessment of an abusive family is the knowledge and expectations of child and infant behavior (Sandler, VanDercar, & Milhoan, 1978).

Much attention has also been paid to the perpetrator's experiences as a child and to his or her general personality characteristics. Although it is generally accepted that the abusive parent was exposed, as a child, to abusive models by his or her parents (Fontana, 1971), there are only a few data on this issue. Investigation of this issue as part of a behavioral assessment may be limited to an examination of intergenerational relationships within the family; for example, does the grandparent of the abused child create for the parent the expectation that severe discipline should be used in raising a child, and is the approval of that grandparent a significant reinforcer for punitive parental behavior?

Attempts to identify the "distinctive personality attributes" (Melnick & Hurley, 1969) of abusers have produced inconsistent results that are of little practical value in conducting assessments. Nor have there been any strong findings regarding the presence of alcohol or drug abuse problems in the abuser.

In contrast, there have been consistent findings regarding the social and community relationships of abusers. Helfer (1973) has indicated that an important factor in abuse is the social isolation of the perpetrator—specifically, an inability to use other people to assist in times of distress. This position has been supported by several other researchers (Bryant, Billingsley, Kerry, Leefman, Merrill, Senecal, & Walsh, 1963; Elmer, 1967; Holter & Friedman, 1968; Nurse, 1964; Smith, Hanson, & Noble, 1974). The finding requires that the traditional scope of behavioral assessment be expanded to include an analysis of existing social and community supports.

Analysis of the characteristics of the abused child has been more limited and of more recent concern than the focus on the abuser. The research data have consistently shown that premature and/or low-birth-weight children are especially at risk for abuse (Elmer & Gregg, 1967; Klein & Stern, 1971; Silver, Dublin, & Lourie, 1971; Skinner & Castle, 1969; Stern, 1973; Brown & Bakeman, Note 4). Also, the rate of physical and general developmental deviations in abused children is greater than in normal comparison groups (Ebbin, Golub, Stein, & Wilson, 1969; Elmer & Gregg, 1967; Gil, 1968, 1970; Johnson & Morse, 1968; Wight, 1969). However, specific causal linkages between these conditions and abuse, as well as specific descriptions of behavioral deficits of abused children, have not been presented. This is one area in which behavioral technology, with its heavy emphasis on careful observation and measurement of behaviors, can make a substantial contribution to the study of child abuse.

## Response (R)

The abusive response has been found to vary considerably. It may include such behaviors as striking with an open hand or closed fist; hitting with an object; burning with a cigarette, stove, or hot water; pushing; or kicking. The significance of the response topography has not yet been determined in terms of either its treatment implications or its predictive value regarding the likelihood of repeated acts of abuse. Nor has there been much recognition of the fact that abusive behavior really represents a continuum of behavior in terms of severity. Largely because the legal issues involved in abuse often require a dichotomous judgment between abusive and nonabusive acts, the question of degree, which may have implications for the protection of the child, has not received much attention.

There also have not been many investigations of the behavioral skills in the repertoire of the abuser. Burgess and Conger (1978) have examined this most closely in a well-controlled descriptive study. They found that abusive parents show a lower rate of positive reinforcement than control parents matched on socioeconomic variables. Burgess and Conger gathered their data through direct observation in the home while families were performing a structured set of tasks.

Assessment of typical patterns of family interaction in abusive families has been done using very unstructured situations (Panyan & Friedman, Note 5), loosely structured situations (Sandler, VanDercar, & Milhoan, 1978; Wolfe & Sandler, Note 3; Reid & Taplin, Note 6), and highly structured tasks (Burgess & Conger, 1978). The methodologies of these varying studies can be utilized for assessment of individual abusive families. In order to derive a total picture of the family, it is important to obtain adequate samples of parental behavior in response to aversive actions, as well as to positive actions, by their children. Additionally, it becomes important to assess behavioral skills as distinguished from the patterns of behavior typically shown in the family. The data collection involved in sampling a wide enough variety of situations in order to get a comprehensive look at the behavioral practices and skills in abusive families is quite time consuming but may be extremely important in leading to decisions about the specific focus of treatment.

## Contingency (K) and Consequences (C)

The most neglected area of consideration in the child abuse literature has been the contingencies and consequences operating upon the behavior. Instead, the main focus has been on identifying antecedent stimulus events and the characteristics of the individuals involved. With low-frequency events, it is not unusual to neglect the potential consequences and instead to focus exclusively on "psychopathology" and personality traits. This section will therefore draw heavily upon case findings and research in related areas.

The most obvious of the possible positive consequences of abusive behavior is the cessation of an aversive stimulus, such as crying or yelling (process of negative reinforcement). Reliance upon punitive techniques to bring about a termination of aversive events would clearly seem to be related to a lack of parental effectiveness. As children get older, however, and physical control procedures are used more and more, the child begins to habituate or counteraggress to the punishing response. This may require a short-term increase in the intensity of the punitive response, with the increased risk of injurious behavior.

Other potentially reinforcing events may be praise, approval, or some similar response from the spouse or significant other. The role of the nonabusive spouse in child abuse has typically been described as "passive" (Paulson, Afifi, Thomason, & Chaleff, 1974; Terr, 1970; Young, 1964). The response of the spouse, however, may not be simply passive but actually approving in some instances. It has also been suggested that parents of the abuser or other adults may reinforce what they perceive to be firm and strong disciplinary procedures.

In general, very little attention has been directed at assessing the impact of significant others in child abuse. It seems reasonable to assume, for example, that the other parent is a potential source of influence in such events and that this influence may range from placing restraint on the abusing partner to facilitating or provoking child abuse. It may be the case, for example, that normal families can be distinguished from abusive families on the basis of such an analysis; thus, the normal family would be represented by those situations in which one parent serves as a restraint against extreme acts by the other parent. Conversely, the most potentially dangerous situation would involve the other end of the continuum. The difficulties involved in such an assessment are considerable, of course, and might require a reconceptualization of conventional points of view. For example, given the norms that exist in our society, that is, that parents moderate extreme acts for one another, the *omission* of negative reaction on the part of the nonabuser may actually have the same effect as implicit reinforcement for such behavior.

Another potential source of social reinforcement that has been overlooked is a nonabused child. In studying patterns of interaction in abusive families, for example, Panyan and Friedman (Note 5) found that the rate of parental reinforcement applied to a child varied with the presence or absence of a second child. The second child responded negatively toward mother when she was positive to the first child. This observation, which emerged because the families were observed over repeated sessions with different family members present, illustrates how positive behavior toward one child may be punished by a second child.

Abuse has also been shown to be preceded by marital arguments. One potential response by a spouse to provocation by the other spouse may be to punish the partner by hurting that spouse's preferred child. Such a process, commonly called "displacement," permits a spouse to aggress against a target that is "safer" than the other spouse. Again, to get a complete picture of these types of interactions it would be necessary to conduct extended observations and to observe not just dyads, but entire family groupings. It is important to determine not only general rates of behaviors but also conditional probabilities given particular complex antecedent stimuli.

The performance of abusive behavior is also a function of the absence of negative consequences for the behavior. The passivity of spouses of abusers has already been mentioned. This suggests that even if the spouses do not explicitly reinforce the abusive behavior by giving approval, they are unlikely to respond negatively to the act. Paulson *et al.* (1974), have used the term *passive abusers* to describe those spouses "who either were aware of the risk of potential abuse and made no intervention, or in an indirect manner participated passively in the maltreatment" (p. 388).

Garbarino (1977) has stressed that the privacy of family life is an important and cherished part of our cultural tradition. Yet, as he points out, such privacy makes it more likely that acts such as abuse will go undetected and therefore not be negatively consequated. This is clearly consistent with the fact that very little abuse is observed to occur in public settings or with outsiders in the home. The absence of constraints upon abuse seems even more critical than the potential gain of positive reinforcement in contributing to abuse.

The schedules of reinforcement for abusive behavior are even more difficult to determine than the potential reinforcers. Of possible special significance is the well-understood principle that extinction of a response will produce temporary increases in the frequency and magnitude of that response. The parent whose physically punishing response is suddenly not as effective as it had previously been might very well be expected to increase the intensity of the punishment in an attempt to produce the desired reinforcement.

### Summary

This discussion has revealed that there is much overlap among the components of functional analysis. In addition to identifying the key dimensions to be included in a behavioral assessment, we touched on some factors that may have generated much discussion within the field of abuse but seem of potentially limited value in contributing to a behavioral assessment. The next section will look at assessment procedures that can be used with abusive families.

## TECHNIQUES FOR BEHAVIORAL ASSESSMENT OF CHILD ABUSE

The task of assessing all of the problems and needs of abusive families is a large and potentially overwhelming one. It involves the collection of data on several individuals from multiple sources, using a variety of assessment procedures and instruments. As a whole, the procedures to be presented here would be beyond the resources of most practitioners and researchers. It is hoped, however, that the assortment of procedures presented will permit the individual assessor to select those techniques that will yield the most useful data in the most efficient way for particular families.

Although this section will be organized into three major areas—assessment of the abusive parent, assessment of the abused child, and general assessment of the abusive situation—there will be considerable overlap among the areas. The major emphasis is on interaction effects between situational and individual variables. This interactionist perspective is receiving increased recognition as the soundest strategy for predicting behavior (Bem & Funder, 1978; Averill, 1973; Endler, 1975; Mischel, 1968, 1973).

Unlike many adult clients seen by behavioral practitioners, child abusers typically have been referred for service rather than being self-referred. This observation has implications in terms of both the referral information received as a starting point for the assessment and the early client–practitioner interactions. The practitioner can develop a structured questionnaire to be completed by the referral source, which can be very helpful in providing introductory information on the family history, background, circumstances surrounding the abusive incident, and current state of family functioning. This will enable the assessor to make preliminary judgments about the priority areas for assessment.

Because most abusive parents are not strictly "voluntary" participants and have been referred because of serious aggressive behavior, they are understandably resistant toward their involvement. At the earliest opportunity, the family should be interviewed by a member of the assessment team to clarify the reasons for referral, determine what the family's expectations regarding the assessment procedures are, and resolve any misconceptions. The initial interview should function as a source of encouragement and support for the family, as well as an opportunity for clarification and information gathering. The interviewer may wish to proceed from discussion of general issues that are not highly threatening to more direct discussion of significant personal concerns. The interviewer should look for opportunities to provide positive reinforcement to the family and, particularly, to encourage them to be willing to look at their characteristic style of family interaction. By avoiding criticism and by being supportive to the parents, the interviewer can elicit useful data concerning the family situation and can enhance the family's cooperation for continued assessment and treatment.

Although it is important for the interviewer to reinforce parental behaviors frequently, the interviewer also needs to be cautious about overdoing this. Some families, involved in delicate legal and child care negotiations, may misinterpret positive comments as support for their past actions or may distort the interviewer's comments and use them to manipulate other professionals involved in the situation. Other families, feeling ashamed of their past actions, may view excessive positive comments by the interviewer as insincere, and may view him or her as untrustworthy. The relationship developed at this initial interview is very important to further assessment and ultimately to treatment and must be handled carefully.

## Assessment of Parent

The assessment of the abusive parent will be broken down into the following five components: child management skills, knowledge of child development, anxiety and anger management, psychopathology, and community supports.

*Child Management Skills*

There is a great deal of formal and informal evidence that highlights the ineffective child management skills used by abusive parents (Burgess, 1979; Dubanoski, Evans, & Higuchi, 1978; Spinetta & Rigler, 1972). Because these parents have often been raised in punitive environments themselves, they may never have had appropriate child management skills modeled for them. Their intention may not be to injure the child, but to control his or her behavior. An assessment of the parents' current methods of controlling and teaching their child is an essential precursor to treatment.

These methods can be assessed through direct, systematic observation. There are several ways to approach this task, but unfortunately there are not enough data to determine the relative efficacy of one approach over another. Observation sessions can be held in a clinic, where it is possible to observe through one-way mirrors and even to videotape sessions; alternatively, the observer could gather these data by scheduling several home visits. Videotaping has advantages in that it may capture the interactions of more than just dyads and may permit those interactions to be tallied systematically through re-viewing of the tape several times. Both videotaping and office interviewing do increase the reactivity of the observational procedure, however.

Burgess and Conger (1978) structure their observation sessions, which are conducted in the home, by instructing the parents to interact with their child in a certain fashion (i.e., teaching a task, command–compliance situations, and free interactions). This procedure of presenting structured tasks appears to yield more relevant data in a more efficient manner than could be obtained in unstructured situations. For example, Panyan and Friedman (Note 5) observed families in their own homes with minimal structure such that individual family members could leave the scene of the observation if they chose. This procedure yielded significant data on what may be the most representative patterns of interaction in the family, but it requires considerable time to gather enough data to develop prescriptive intervention programs. This unstructured procedure is of greater use for obtaining general descriptions of abusive families.

An important part of the assessment procedure should be to observe family interactions with different constellations, or subgroupings, of people present. This permits a more precise determination of the significant antecedent and consequent controlling variables. Such observation may be done, for example, by requiring each parent separately to teach a task to a child and then bringing the parents together to teach the task. Such an approach also permits important data to be collected on how each spouse consequates the other spouse's behavior with the children. The importance of looking at these different groupings of family members has been recognized within family systems approaches (Haley, 1971, 1977; Minuchin, 1974). Although such an approach to families is entirely consistent with a behavioral approach and in fact represents a logical extension of attempts to identify controlling stimuli, it has typically not been used within behavioral assessment of family interactions.

The particular groupings of family members to be studied in depth will depend on the circumstances surrounding the abusive acts. If abuse was found to occur when the mother was alone with the child, for example, then that may be a grouping to be closely observed. Similarly, if the father reports having greater difficulty managing the behavior of a particular child when the mother is present, then the triad of mother, father, and child and the dyad of father and child will merit close examination.

Precise quantitative assessment of the family interactions requires the use of a structured procedure for scoring the behaviors. Existing systems, such as the Family Interaction Coding System (Reid & Taplin, Note 6) or the Behavioral Observation Scoring System (Burgess and Conger, 1978), have been used with abusive families and would typically be preferable to the development of a new system.

An additional method of assessing parental competency in child management is to use a criterion-based performance measure (e.g., Sweitzer & Boyd, Note 7). Such a checklist would be used to assess a specific skill dimension. Parents can be scored following an observation session or during a series of role-play situations. The checklist might include items such as the manner in which praise is used, type of instructions given, and descriptions of behavior provided to children when consequences are being given. Such a checklist can be an invaluable aid to the development and implementation of a competency-based parent training program.

The assessment of child management skills should be broadly focused. It should include separate assessments of parental skills and patterns for dealing with positive as well as negative behavior, instruction giving, problem-solving strategies, teaching, and general household organization, because parents may be competent in some areas but lacking in skills in others. Such an assessment will essentially yield a profile of parental skills in various areas and also a description of the stimulus circumstances under which particular behaviors are more likely to occur. The procedure of calculating conditional probabilities (Patterson, 1973, 1974) as a means of identifying antecedent stimulus control is strongly recommended because of its utility in identifying precise situations to which responses need to be changed.

### Knowledge of Child Development

Abusive behavior often occurs in response to child behaviors that are quite normal and common for children at a particular developmental level (e.g., Scott, 1973; Weston, 1968). It therefore becomes important to determine how accurate and realistic parents' expectations are concerning their child's behavior.

Through brief interviewing or a short questionnaire, the practitioner can assess the parents' knowledge of the capabilities of an infant or child at different ages (e.g., when they expect a child to walk, to be toilet trained, to cry, to talk, to grow out of certain behaviors). In addition, the Michigan Screening Profile of Parenting (MSPP) (Helfer, Hoffmeister, & Schneider, 1978), an instrument developed specifically to identify parents at risk for abuse, contains a subscale called "expectations of children," which may be used for the purpose of assessing parental expectations of their children. Also of use in assessing this area is the Infant Temperament Scale (Carey, 1972), which was developed for the purpose of assessing parental attitudes toward small children.

This assessment of parental expectations may yield different results for two spouses or may indicate that one or both parents are unrealistic in one or more areas of expectation. Either of these findings lends itself quite clearly to some informational training about the behavior of children.

### Anxiety and Anger Management

Interacting with deficiencies in child management skills and in knowledge about children is the parent's propensity to become easily anxious or angry. Therefore, it is important to assess the circumstances that frequently lead to anxious and angry responses on the part of the parents.

Some of this information can be gathered during the interview, or it may be described by the parent using a tool such as a Problem Behavior Workbook (Wolfe & Sandler, Note 3). Such a workbook asks the parents to identify problem situations with their children and to describe how often the problem occurs and how they respond to the problem. The situations identified may generate the greatest anxiety or anger. The MSPP (Helfer, Hoffmeister, & Schneider, 1978) also contains a subscale that measures the individual's coping abilities when under stressful circumstances.

To determine further the situations that are likely to produce high levels of anxiety and anger, the establishment of a hierarchy of frustrating and stressful situations is helpful. The Novaco Anger Scale (Novaco, 1978), consisting of 80 items for which the respondent rates his or her degree of anger on a five-point scale, may be helpful in identifying key situations. Although this instrument has not been used specifically with abusive parents and may need some modification for this population, the approach and format are applicable.

The types of situations that may produce high anxiety and anger can be wide ranging. Situations involving significant others outside of the nuclear family should be looked at closely. Members of the extended family may be significant reinforcers for the parents, for example, and situations in which they will be "judging" the parents' effectiveness in child management may be especially stressful. Similarly, abusive parents frequently are extremely sensitive to the reactions of others, be they school personnel, neighbors, merchants, or friends, and therefore it becomes important to assess reactions to these people.

The findings from this type of assessment lend themselves directly to the development of interventions. These interventions may involve skill training to deal with particularly stressful situations, desensitization to certain situations, and/or general training in anxiety and anger management.

### Psychopathology

Although the percentage of abusive parents who have been found to be psychotic or seriously emotionally disturbed is low, a thorough assessment should include screening for psychopathology. This is of considerable importance, because the parent whose perceptions are grossly distorted may be likely not only to repeat incidents of abuse but also to inflict serious harm. Therefore, considerations of child protection make it imperative that some screening be done for severe psychopathology.

Much of this screening can be done in an interview. Parents' perceptions of the child's behaviors and motives and their reports concerning the circumstances of abuse or potential abuse can serve as good indications of severe perceptual disturbance. Some parents, for example, may report that their 3-month-old infant is "out to get them" and that the baby's crying is an indication of that, or they may claim that the child must be cleansed of "bad blood" that was inherited from the father. In such extreme cases, consideration of the child's safety must take first priority.

Standardized psychological tests, such as the Minnesota Multiphasic Personality Inventory (MMPI), are also useful as a general screening procedure for severe psychopathology. Although not designed specifically for that purpose, the MSPP can also be helpful in identifying parents whose reactions are extreme.

Information concerning the parents' alcohol and drug intake is also very helpful. This can sometimes be gathered from the referral source or from significant informants. Although a strong link between child abuse and either alcoholism or drug abuse has not been demonstrated in studies with large samples, the significance of their presence in individual families can be great. In addition to finding out about parental alcohol and drug habits, it also is important to determine the types of response patterns the parents typically show when under the influence. An essential component of a treatment program for an abusive family may need to include modifying drinking or drug-taking behavior.

### Community Supports

The relative social isolation of abusive parents has been identified as a contributor to abuse by several authors (Bryant et al., 1963; Helfer, 1973; Smith et al., 1974). This is consistent with the general view that a person's social networks are an important part of his or her personal resources (Garbarino, Burston, Raber, Russell, & Crouter, 1978). The view of networks as resources has been apparent in the increased attention being given in recent years to the whole area of social and community support systems (Collins & Pancoast, 1976; Gottlieb, Note 8). The likelihood of severely deviant behavior, according to this view, increases with the size of the discrepancy between the demands of a situation and the resources available to meet those demands (French, Rogers, & Cobb, 1974). To the extent that a parent, when faced with great physical and emotional demands in child-rearing, is without sources of social support, the likelihood of events such as abuse increases.

Unfortunately, the measurement of social isolation and social support has not kept pace with the increasing interest in this topic. Tolsdorf (1976, Note 9), however, has presented a set of questions that can be used to determine the number of contacts that a person has outside of the immediate nuclear family and the nature and function of those contacts. These contacts can constitute tangible support, such as financial support or the sharing of tools or equipment, or emotional and behavioral support, such as assistance in dealing with a problem. Although Tolsdorf has not used his instrument directly with abusive families, he has used it to demonstrate differences between adults who function well and those who do not, and it seems that it would be applicable to abusive families.

Less formal procedures can also be used to tap the area of social isolation. Parents can be asked to report the number and the nature of the contacts they have had outside of the nuclear family within the past week. They can be asked to keep diaries of their activities. They can also be asked about the people who seem most helpful to them and how often they see them. These can be friends, family, employers, fellow employees, clergy, merchants, neighbors, and so forth. Parents can further be asked to reconstruct difficult situations that they have experienced with their children for purposes of looking at their use (or lack of use) of other people for assistance in these situations.

Important sources of support who are identified in this manner can be involved in the treatment program. They can be included in the sessions with the parents' permission, so that they may reinforce the efforts the parents are making to deal with their deficiencies. They can also be requested to call the parents regularly to prompt compliance with the treatment program and to reinforce such compliance. Parents can be taught skills to interact with potentially supportive individuals in the community, so that they can develop a network that will serve as a protection against further acts of abuse. This component of treatment has not typically played a major role in behavioral interventions; yet, the focus on social supports fits in very strongly with behavioral approaches.

First, such an effort helps create a number of well-functioning models and reinforcing agents in the community, thus not only facilitating new learning but also increasing the likelihood that positive changes will come under the control of reinforcers in the natural environment. Second, it can serve as a useful mechanism for getting parents to follow through on assignments given in treatment. This is a notorious problem in behavioral parent training programs, but with significant people in the individual's social network prompting good follow-through and reinforcing it, the likelihood of the parents' completing their assignments will increase. Third, support people can provide a parent with an alternate response to abuse when the negative interactions in the family begin to escalate. The parent can call the support individual, thereby possibly receiving assistance in dealing with the situation or just providing an opportunity for de-escalation of the situation. Support individuals can also provide much-needed occasional relief from child care for the parents. This is especially important for families of lower socioeconomic class who cannot afford to pay for child care.

## Assessment of Child

As described previously in this chapter, one general theoretical model of aggression suggests that aggressive behavior frequently occurs as a reaction to aversive events on the part of other individuals (Bandura, 1973). In the case of child abuse, this principle is frequently formulated in the context of the child's "contribution" to the abusive situation (Gelles, 1973; Helfer, 1973; Milowe & Lourie, 1964).

Several authorities and investigators have proposed a variety of predetermining conditions that are considered to increase the likelihood of abuse. It is important to bear in mind, however, the cautions expressed previously regarding the difficulties involved in analyzing child abuse; that is, the abusive act is typically private in nature and of low-occurring frequency. Therefore, most investigators have relied upon indirect measures, such as impaired parenting styles, poor child management skills, and negative parental perceptions. Given the limitations of such procedures for explaining child abuse and the relatively sparse evidence of a more direct nature regarding the causes of child abuse, many of the assertions relative to the child's contribution to abuse must be relegated to the realm of conventional wisdom rather than being considered demonstrated facts, at least for the present.

This section will review the state of knowledge and present assessment procedures relating to early infantile "risk" circumstances, temperamental contributors, serious childhood disorders, general child behavior, and general child characteristics.

### Early Infantile Risk Circumstances

A popular position in the child abuse literature is that abuse is more likely to occur if there have been early infantile "risk" conditions, such as prematurity and low birth weight. Stern (1973), for example, in a retrospective study found that 23% of a sample of 51 abused children were of low birth weight and that two of the three children in this study who required more than two months' separation from their mothers eventually died from abusive behavior.

Support for this position may also be inferred from those studies showing that low-birth-weight and premature infants are overrepresented in the population of abused children. Friedrich and Boriskin (1976) cite a number of studies reporting a much higher percentage of low-birth-weight and premature children in the abused population (from 12% to 44%), compared to the percentage of low-birth-weight and premature children in the general population (from 6% to 8%). In addition to these findings, several investigators have reported case studies that bear on this issue (Kaplan & Mason, 1960; Owens, 1964; Solnit and Stack, 1961). The major thrust of these reports is that negative parental reactions are high-probability responses to prematurity and other atypical infant conditions, because such conditions require extended hospitalization of the infant, which may interfere with the bonding of the parent and the child and the development of attachment. In addition, the behavioral repertoire of such atypical infants may be limited, therefore making the parenting task more demanding.

The inadequate methodologies employed in most of the studies, as cited by Friedrich and Boriskin (1976), suggest that the status of this argument, particularly the types of causal linkages that are hypothesized, is still ambiguous. Nevertheless, most authorities consider prematurity, low birth weight, and other conditions requiring intensive care shortly after birth as important contributors to child abuse, even when their own results are contradictory (Smith, Schwartz, Mandell, Silberstein, Dalack, & Sacks, 1969).

For these reasons, it is important to determine, in assessing individual families, the extent to which unusual conditions were present at birth or shortly thereafter. This information can typically be obtained at little response cost through direct inquiry, as well as through access to medical records. In particular, those conditions requiring special care and involving relatively long periods of separation (two weeks or more) would be considered high-risk circumstances by many authorities. Information about the type of parent–child relationship maintained during the period of prolonged separation and about the manner in which the parents and significant others responded to this separation may be useful in identifying the development of patterns of interaction. This information would obviously be of most value in cases where the abused child is still quite young.

## Temperamental Contributors to Child Abuse

A second hypothesis argues that the presence of any of a variety of "irritability" characteristics also increases the possibility of child abuse (Friedrich & Boriskin, 1976). Children obviously differ from one another in such temperamental dimensions as sleep–wake cycles, responsiveness to adults, sensitivity to stimuli, restlessness, and activity rates. These individual differences lend themselves to the logical argument that children who are more difficult in one or more of these dimensions are at greater risk for abuse than children who are "easier." In a study that supports this general position, though it does not deal directly with child abuse, Pederson (Note 10) has demonstrated different degrees of positive parental behavior to 6-week-old infants with differing levels of "irritability." There are, however, virtually no well-controlled studies in the child abuse literature that directly support this position.

During the interview, however, inquiries can be made about such factors as child responsiveness, sleep–wake cycle, periods of crying, and other related dimensions. Again, these are factors that are of greatest significance with younger children. Although most behavioral observation has focused on children beyond infancy, even informal observation of infant behavior and parent–infant interaction can help in assessing the family situation.

## Serious Childhood Disorders

Perhaps the strongest arguments regarding the child's contribution to abuse have concerned the manner in which serious childhood disorders impair parent–child relationships in general. Ferster and DeMyer (1962) and Rimland (1964) represent this position. In analyzing parent reactions to autism, Rimland, for example, suggests that the lack of responsiveness to normal social stimuli on the part of the autistic child is largely responsible for the lack of warmth and affection frequently observed in the parents of such children. The resulting parental styles can clearly be explained in terms of extinction and punishment; that is, parental attempts at providing affection are not reciprocated or perhaps are even rebuffed by the child, thereby resulting in a reduction in the frequency of such gestures. Such severe atypical conditions may clearly produce a host of impaired parent–child relationships, including those that contribute to child abuse.

Again, the evidence in support of a causal relationship between abuse and developmental dsorders is far from convincing, although numerous authors have presented data on the existence of physical and general developmental deviations in abused children (Ebbin, et al., 1969; Elmer & Gregg, 1967; Gil, 1968, 1970; Johnson & Morse, 1968; Wight, 1969). It may very well be that both the abuse and the developmental problems are a result of deficient parenting rather than the one being the cause of the other.

Nonetheless, such observations suggest that the risk of abuse is greater where serious disorders are present that result in excessive behavioral demands on the parents or in lack of responsiveness of the children. A careful assessment of the nature and severity of such disorders is therefore warranted. A number of formal and informal assessment procedures are available for such purposes. For example, suspected intellectual and/or learning deficits should be thoroughly evaluated by means of standardized diagnostic procedures. Behavioral disturbances should be further evaluated by means of observational procedures and problem behavior scales (see the section on general child behavior) that provide information about the child's behavior and the parent's perception of the problem. In many cases, it may be best to have the child evaluated by a qualified professional specializing in such problems, in order to determine the best program of remediation for the deficiency.

## General Child Behavior

Part of the assessment of the child should be observation of him or her and administration of problem behavior scales. The observational procedures described in the parent assessment section provide information about the child as well and are perfectly applicable for child assessment. Such procedures as the Family Interaction Coding System (Reid & Taplin, Note 6) and the Behavioral Observation Scoring System (Burgess & Conger, 1978) have been used with abusive families and yield information on a variety of child behaviors.

These instruments have typically been used to assess child behavior during interaction with parents or other family members. A thorough assessment should include observations of the child outside of the family context. With a child who is in nursery or elementary school, the school setting is an important place for observation. This provides an opportunity to determine if the child shows a generalized pattern of aversive behaviors, for example, or if his or her behavior is rather well differentiated according to the stimulus situation. Contrived situations, in which the child is interacting with peers and other adults, may also be helpful for this purpose. The reports of significant others, such as teachers and counselors, who see the child outside of the family are also very useful. Though these reports often deviate from accurate behavioral descriptions, they provide an important indication of how the child is perceived by others.

The Eyberg Child Behavior Inventory (Eyberg & Ross, 1978) of child conduct problems is a well-developed instrument that assesses parental perceptions of a child's behavior. The instrument is easy to administer and score and provides normative data for children aged 2 to 7 years. The inventory yields both an intensity and a problem score, which reflect the degree to which the parent sees a given behavior as undesirable. An instrument such as this is useful not only for assessment purposes but also as an outcome measure of change in parental perception following intervention. Changes in parental perception of behavior are at least as important in predicting enduring improvements in the family as actual behavior changes by the child in the absence of changes in parental perceptions. In addition to the Eyberg Child Behavior Inventory, the Patterson version of the Becker Adjective Checklist (Patterson, Reid, Jones, & Conger, 1975) is another useful measure of parental attitudes toward their children, although it does not describe problem behaviors exhibited by children as specifically as the Eyberg Inventory.

### General Child Characteristics

In addition to the areas of child behavior just covered, there are several other areas identified in the child abuse literature that can be assessed quickly, generally through interview questions. Green et al. (1974) describe "accidental" traits of a child that might place him or her at special risk. These include looking like a hated person, being an unwanted child, or having been "fathered" or "mothered" by someone who is now strongly disliked. Thomson et al. (1971) make the same point in a slightly different way, reporting that in a small portion of their sample of abused children, the child's perceived similarity, either physical or behavioral, to a spouse was a risk factor.

Steele and Pollock (1968) talk of the infant who may be premaritally conceived or who is born sooner after marriage than desired as sometimes being "unwelcome" by the parents. Although this situation and the others discussed are not high-frequency contributors to abuse, they can be easily assessed during an interview and, in individual cases, can be important factors.

One issue that bears on the role of the child is the extent to which abuse tends to be restricted to one child in a multichild family. If there is a high percentage of multichild families in which only one child is abused, then the potential importance of the child in contributing to this is underscored. However, the results of several studies question whether this is the case. For example, Silver, Dublin, and Lourie (1971) found that siblings also were abused in 19 of 34 cases; Lauer Ten Broeck, and Grossman (1974) found abuse of siblings in 53% of cases; and Skinner and Castle (1969) found abuse of more than one child in 20 of 41 cases. In fact, the results of research on this issue suggest that a particular high-risk factor may be having several children, particularly of preschool age, close together in age. In such a situation, the overall demand of parenting, combined with the parental deficiencies, appears to be the greatest contributor to abuse, and the role of the individual child seems smaller.

## Assessment of the Situation

This section will focus on assessment of the situational context for abuse and how this factor interacts with the parent and child characteristics already discussed to result in abusive behavior. Although early studies in the field of abuse looked almost exclusively at characteristics of the perpetrator to explain the abusive behavior, the importance of considering the interaction between situational and individual difference variables is now receiving greater recognition. For example, it is increasingly acknowledged that the likelihood that a parent with poor parenting skills will commit abuse varies as a function of the social and marital supports he or she may have. Conversely, a parent with weak support, but strong parenting skills, may have a low likelihood of abuse. A more complete and accurate understanding of abuse, therefore, comes when individual differences and situational variables and their interactions are examined.

Situational assessment can be conducted from two perspectives. The first of these involves assessing the situation on the basis of how it is perceived by those involved, whereas the second involves the more objective definition and description of the situation. This difference in perspective is based on the question of whether to define the stimulus (situation) independent of the observer. The assessment procedures included in this section will feature both perspectives. For example, procedures for objectively examining marital interactions will be discussed and so will be instruments that provide data on how each marital partner perceives the relationship. The actual rate of positive behavior from spouse to spouse can therefore be considered as one important measure, and each spouse's perception of that rate as another important measure.

A broad range of situational variables will be covered, including those closest to the abusive behavior temporally and some general socioeconomic dimensions. The following topics will be discussed: the immediate precipitating stimulus, the marital relationship, and the overall family environment.

### Immediate Precipitating Stimulus

The functional analysis of abuse included data on the types of stimulus events that have most often and immediately preceded acts of abuse. Most frequently reported were child behaviors that were sudden and aversive to the perpetrator. In conducting the types of behavioral observations discussed in the preceding assessment sections, using both structured and unstructured tasks, the practitioner will have an opportunity to observe parental responses to negative child behavior. A close analysis of parental behavior in these situations is an important part of the overall assessment. In looking at stimulus control in naturalistic situations, the research and conceptual model of Patterson (1973, 1974) is potentially extremely useful in analyzing the stimulus situation. Patterson quantitatively identifies particular responses based on antecedent stimuli that facilitate or inhibit the occurrence of particular responses and on an examination of the conditional probability of the target behavior in the presence and absence of that antecedent stimulus. In examining dyadic behavior, Patterson also looks at the manner in which particular behaviors serve to accelerate or decelerate the likelihood of positive or negative counterresponses. In extending this sequential analysis of behavior through several behaviors by each of the members of the dyad, Patterson erects a probability tree that illustrates how negative behavior may escalate and presumably culminate in high-magnitude, intense responses.

The type of detailed analysis that Patterson has conducted is clearly beyond the capability of most practitioners. Furthermore, the number of opportunities to observe this escalation process is typically restricted to a limited percentage of the overall behaviors observed. Still, the concept of a probability tree in which one can view extended sequences of behavior and identify facilitating and inhibiting stimuli and accelerating and decelerating responses can be most helpful to the assessor. It provides an important framework for guiding both formal and informal observational procedures.

Other more contrived procedures should be used to determine the types of responses parents typically make, not just to negative behavior on the part of their children, but to a chain of such behaviors. This can include simulations using role-playing procedures, in which parents are confronted with negative actions that continue despite the parents' initial attempts to stop them. Such role playing has the potential of generating considerable anxiety in the parents and should be approached gradually, with easy-to-handle situations being presented first. Yet, to find out the types of skills that parents call upon to handle a situation—for example, where one child is crying and another one is yelling and neither stops despite initial parental attempts—a simulation can be very helpful. An alternative way of getting some of the same information is to generate some sample situations and to have the parents write their responses to them. This is a more contrived technique and produces varied responses, partly because of differences in parental writing skill and in parental styles of dealing with very difficult situations.

The use of desensitization procedures to help parents manage particularly hard-to-handle situations has already been discussed. As a part of that procedure, it is essential to identify the specific situations that are most likely to result in the parent's losing control and acting too aggressively. These situations can be identified partly from a study of the circumstances surrounding the incident of abuse, partly from the report of the family members during an interview, and partly from the observations of the family. The use of a questionnaire such as the Novaco Anger Scale (Novaco, 1978) has also been discussed. In addition, parents can be asked to keep a diary of situations that generate strong tendencies to act aggressively, and these can then be used both for studying available responses in order to deal with them and for building a hierarchy for purposes of desensitization. These procedures can help increase parental awareness of high-anxiety- or anger-producing situations.

In analyzing the types of precipitating stimulus situations that may lead to abusive behavior in particular families, it is again important not to oversimplify the antecedent stimulus. If there were more than two people present, for example, the actions of each of the individuals, in addition to the actions of the abused child, constitute an important part of that stimulus. Further, although behavior can be best explained in terms of the stimuli that are closest to it temporally, it is also helpful to backtrack over other possible significant events of the hour and even of the day. The response to the immediately controlling antecedent stimulus may have been affected by an accumulation of negative events during the day. Where that is the case, treatment strategies can be developed to help parents to identify when such circumstances are increasing and then to learn methods for dealing with this escalation, such as requesting special assistance from family and/or friends, before the aggressive behavior occurs.

## Marital Relationship

The marital relationship is important to include in the overall situational assessment for several reasons. As described in the functional analysis, marital relationships in abusive families are typically quite weak, and marital conflict frequently precedes the abusive act. Further, even the ordinary demands of parenting require a marital relationship in which the spouses regularly support and assist each other. Finally, the role of the nonabusive spouse in possibly reinforcing the aggressive behavior, or at least in not preventing it from happening, is also important to an understanding of abuse.

Again, part of the evaluation of these dimensions of the marital relationship will come from the direct observational procedures already discussed. However, as suggested previously, it is important to extend the assessment to include the whole range of family relationships, not just the parent–child dyads.

Marital relationships can also be assessed directly through the use of structured tasks presented to the couple. For example, Olson and Ryder (1970) developed the Inventory of Marital Conflicts, which consists of 18 vignettes portraying common marital problems. Of these, 12 are written so that each spouse separately receives information portraying the other spouse as responsible for the conflict. The spouses then discuss the issue. This procedure, in slightly modified form, has been used in combination with the Marital Interaction Coding System, a 29-category behavioral coding system (Vincent, Weiss, & Birchler, 1975; Weiss, Hops, & Patterson, 1973). Other investigators have developed useful tasks for stimulating interaction between husband and wife (e.g., Watzlawick, 1966).

Marital relationships can also be assessed through questionnaires. The most frequently used instrument has been the Locke–Wallace Marital Adjustment Scale (Locke & Wallace, 1959), which requires just a brief time for administration and provides useful general information about the marital relationship. Similarly, the newer Dyadic Adjustment Scale (Spanier, 1976) provides general information about the relationship through a series of six-point rating items. Azrin, Naster, and Jones (1973), as part of their reciprocity marital counseling procedure, employ a marital rating procedure that has ten dimensions. Such questionnaires and rating procedures provide information about the perceptions of the marriage by each party, whereas observation procedures yield more objective data on actual behavior between the spouses.

## Overall Family Environment

Most of the attempts to assess the overall family environment have developed outside of traditional behavioral circles. For example, the journal *Family Process* probably contains the largest number of studies using rather well-operationalized measures to assess family behavior. Typically, these assessments have been conducted from a family systems theoretical base; because these assessments have tended to focus on observable behaviors and analyzed patterns of interaction between family members, they not only are consistent with behavioral approaches but have the potential of enriching and strengthening such approaches (Friedman, Note 11). Reviews of the findings of these studies are available (Doane, 1978; Jacob, 1975; Riskin & Faunce, 1972) that illustrate the methodologies used in family assessment.

One psychometric instrument that is specifically designed to assess overall family environment is the Moos Family Environment Scale (Moos, 1975). This scale requires that each family member complete a brief questionnaire of family activities as he or she perceives them, resulting in a family profile along ten dimensions. The Moos instrument is directed at families with children above the age of 5 years and has been found to discriminate between groups of families in terms of psychiatric status of family members, drinking patterns, and family size. Another overall family assessment procedure that provides a multidimensional description of families was developed by Deykin (1972). Although originally designed for use with adolescents, this procedure is applicable for families with younger children, because the primary data source is family-member responses to interview questions. This procedure yields family scores along the dimensions of decision making, marital interaction, child-rearing, emotional gratification, perception of and response to crisis, and perception of and response to community.

Situational stresses within a family have been examined in relationship to child abuse by Justice and Duncan (1976). These investigators administered, to abusive parents and control parents, the Social Readjustment Rating Scale (Holmes & Rahe, Note 12), which analyzes major stresses, such as change of job, new apartment or house, major illnesses, and sizeable changes in financial status of family. They found that the abusive parents had undergone a greater number of recent changes than had the control parents and concluded that an overall "life crisis" occurred during the 12 months preceding the abusive act. The end result of such a crisis state is exhaustion, decreased ability to adjust, and increased risk of losing control. The assessment of these types of life stresses is a useful part of the evaluation of abusive families. Those families for whom abuse followed several of these critical changes may benefit from training in how to adjust to general life pressures and how to organize their lives to avoid, as much as possible, the concentration of such events in a relatively short period.

One such life stress can be the addition of a new child to a family. If the adjustment to a new child is made more difficult by financial pressures and overcrowded living conditions, the likelihood of abuse may increase. As part of the overall assessment of the family, it therefore is important to examine the economic condition of the family and the physical surroundings in which family members live. Certainly, poverty has been considered a major factor in abuse. Giovannoni (1971), after finding that parents who had mistreated their children were frequently themselves "victimized by the stresses of poverty," raised the question of whether the conception of parental mistreatment of children should be changed, because the context for mistreatment is frequently "societal violence" toward families. Some of these factors may not lend themselves to direct intervention in treatment. However, a knowledge of the physical surroundings of the family may provide information about how to rearrange the environment in order to prevent conflict from developing. This may include anything from providing individuals who are frequently aggressive with as much private space as possible, to removing safety hazards, to removing items that present temptations for children to act against their parents' wishes. The issue of space becomes even more critical when there are several young children in the family. In crowded circumstances, the yelling or crying of one child may disrupt or wake up a second child, thereby creating a more difficult situation for the parents to handle as well as providing a greater instigation for aggression by the parents. Although the economic components of the problem are not amenable to direct intervention, parts of the physical arrangement may lend themselves very well to an environmental design approach, and families can be further assisted by their getting as much help as possible with their financial problems from other sources..

One instrument that was specifically developed to look at the area of child neglect is the Childhood Level of Living Scale (Polansky, DeSaix, & Sharlin, 1972). This scale looks at the general adequacy of child care in the family. As was pointed out previously, many abusive families are not neglectful and provide adequate care in most regards. On the other hand, where there is a question of parents' failing to fulfill their responsibilities in a variety of areas, this scale can be a very useful instrument. Completed by the assessor, it looks at such specific areas as the safety of the home, the hygiene practices, sleeping arrangements, clothing, and parental relationships with the children. In families who are found to show a strong and clear pattern of inadequate child care, the development of skills to deal with anger-provoking situations, for example, may become a lower priority.

## LEGAL AND ETHICAL CONSIDERATIONS

An analysis of child abuse would be incomplete without an acknowledgment of the legal and ethical ramifications involved in such circumstances. Because these issues are complex, are still in the emerging stages, and differ from state to state, only a brief survey of the most salient features will be described here.

Essentially, there are two legal codes to be considered in dealing with child abuse: (1) the adult offender statutes and (2) the child welfare statutes. With regard to the former, any given case of child abuse may be adjudicated as a criminal assault in criminal court. For example, under the relevant circumstances, a given parent may be charged with assault and battery (from a misdemeanor to a felony) and be subject to the usual course of events that prevails in such criminal cases.

Concurrently, and more or less independent of these actions, the state may take action in family or civil court to protect the welfare of the child. The state may act to remove the child from parental custody or to place the family under protective service supervision, with such decisions based on actions ranging from physical, sexual, or emotional abuse to neglect and abandonment. The state may take such actions even though no criminal charges are filed or pursued against the parents. Indeed, until recent years, few cases of purported abuse were being handled in the criminal court because of the difficulty in presenting adequate evidence for a trial. More and more, however, abusive parents are being tried in criminal court.

In addition to cases of abuse being tried in criminal court, the child advocacy movement had recently become more vigorously concerned with protecting the rights and safety of children. Initially restricted to blatant instances of abuse and neglect, the child advocacy effort has effected dramatic changes in limiting historically sanctioned parental prerogatives in child care. The trend is clearly toward protecting the child's rights, even though such action may conflict with parental rights.

For the practitioner involved in child abuse and neglect cases, the ethical concerns are exceedingly complex. In any given case, for example, a practitioner, in deciding whether to transfer custody and remove a child from his or her parents, must consider the possible short-range and long-range effects on the child, on other siblings, and on other family members. The impact of the various placement options, such as foster care, must also be considered. The current thrust is to permit a child to remain in his or her own home so long as it is not grossly dangerous or harmful. This position results more from the lack of positive alternatives than from concern with parents' prerogatives. More often than not, therefore, there is no entirely satisfactory option, and such decisions are made on the basis of the "least-of-the-evils" principle, despite the limited information that is available regarding the impact of that decision. This is a difficult situation to handle, particularly for the practitioner who has a strong empirical background; however, decisions concerning the safety of children cannot be postponed and need to be made using the best available information, however imperfect that may be.

A second ethical dilemma relates to those statutes that require practitioners to report acts of abuse that they become aware of to either child welfare or police authorities. Practitioners who are accustomed to invoking the "confidentiality" of their relationships with their clients must recognize that with regard to child abuse and neglect, the professional can be held liable for failure to report properly suspected abuse or neglect. This requirement means that the contract between the helping person and the client needs to be clearly described in terms of this issue. Professionals must inform their clients from the beginning of their relationship of what actions they must and will take if they learn of incidents of abuse or neglect. Although this may occasionally result in parents' withholding information from the therapist, there is very little margin of flexibility in this area.

Another special issue that will frequently arise in dealing with abusive families is their voluntary participation in treatment. Although most professionals working with families are accustomed to voluntary participation by the family, in many abusive families the parents may be ordered by the court into treatment. Accompanying such an order are expectations by the referral agency of particular types of information that will be provided about attendance at sessions, follow-through on treatment plans, and progress in treatment. It is very important, therefore, that practitioners have a clear understanding of the court's or agency's expectations, that the parents have a similarly clear understanding, and that all parties feel comfortable about working within that set of expectations. One of these expectations, which is often left implicit when it should be made explicit, is that the professional provide a recommendation about whether the child should be removed from the home if the situation does not improve and that he or she be available as an expert witness in court.

When an agency or the court makes a referral or issues a court order for treatment, the consequences for failure to attend sessions or to follow through with treatment plans are often left unclear. If the referral is a voluntary one, then the agency typically imposes no consequences. In the absence of having control in such a case, however, the agency worker, eager to have the parents continue treatment, may resort to bluffs or threats that the child will be removed from the home. The therapist then becomes associated with such contingencies, even though he or she may not approve, and this can serve as a barrier (or in some cases, as an aid) to treatment. Similar types of consequences, but usually those with more potential for follow-through, can be presented by agency staff to parents who have been ordered by the court to obtain treatment. In view of the potentially severe consequences of failing to cooperate with treatment, it is important for the practitioner to have a clear understanding of how the agency plans to operate from the beginning. If the professional feels comfortable with the mode of operation, he or she can then discuss it openly with the clients at the beginning of the assessment/treatment and not have the issue emerge at a later time as an obstacle to treatment. The court-ordered treatment can definitely be helpful with particular families who might otherwise prematurely cease to continue with treatment. However, before deciding whether to offer professional services, the practitioner must weigh the advantages of the arrangement against the position in which he or she may be placed should the clients not cooperate.

# SUMMARY

This chapter has provided an overview of the special issues related to child abuse, a functional analysis of the problem, a description of assessment procedures that can be used, and a brief look at special legal and ethical considerations. Low-frequency private behaviors present special problems and challenges for behaviorists, who have been accustomed to being able to observe target behaviors. In order to assess abusive families effectively and to develop treatment programs in view of the special problems that are presented, it is necessary to integrate traditional behavioral assessment procedures with other approaches that yield complementary information. Therefore, a variety of assessment procedures have been presented, including direct observation in naturalistic settings, observation with structured tasks, questionnaires, tests, interviews, and diaries. Using the total set of assessment procedures presented, however, is beyond the capability of most clinical practitioners. A comprehensive set of procedures was provided in order to enable practitioners to select those that appear to have the most value for particular types of abusive families.

The consistent emphasis within this chapter has been on examining abuse in terms of the context in which it occurs, including the immediate family, the situational context, and the larger community. Characteristics of individual parents and children were examined primarily in terms of how they interact with contextual variables to affect the likelihood of abusive behavior. The environment was conceptualized as a multidimensional one, in which behavioral, economic, physical, and community variables are all important. The family was viewed as a system in which the behavior of any one person is a function of the behaviors of all other members. The procedure of looking at dyads alone was therefore found to be a useful, but frequently oversimplified, way of examining family interactions.

The variety of assessment focuses and procedures discussed here highlights the complexity of the problem of child abuse. Behaviorists have been late in attending to the problem but can now contribute maximally, to the extent that they can work jointly with other experienced professionals in the area, adding their own special contributions. It is the professionals in such fields as social work, law enforcement, and pediatrics who deal with the problem of abuse at its most pressing, acute stage and who are confronted with the need to make immediate major decisions. Cooperative efforts among the mental health professionals who typically are involved at a later stage, after initial medical treatment for abuse has been given, and the on-the-line child welfare, medical, and law enforcement professionals stand to improve our capability for dealing with this troubling and perplexing problem.

## Reference Notes

1. Friedman, R. M., & Friedman, F. A. *The relationship between basic research in aggression and practice in child abuse: Implications for education.* Paper presented at the annual meeting of the Council on Social Work Education, Philadelphia, March 1976.
2. Schrader, C., Panzer, C., Long, J., Gillet, P., & Kornblath, R. *Modifying maladaptive communication patterns in adolescent–parent triads.* Unpublished manuscript, Long Island Jewish–Hillside Medical Center, Glen Oaks, N.Y., 1977.
3. Wolfe, D. A., & Sandler, J. *Parent training and contingency contracting with child abuse parents.* Unpublished manuscript, University of South Florida, Tampa, 1978.

4. Brown, J. V., & Bakeman, R. Untitled unpublished manuscript, Georgia State University, Atlanta, 1974.
5. Panyan, M., & Friedman, R. M. *Naturalistic observations of abusive families.* Paper presented at the annual meeting of the Association for the Advancement of Behavior Therapy, New York, December 1976.
6. Reid, J. B., & Taplin, P. S. *A social interactional approach to the treatment of abusive families.* Paper presented at the annual meeting of the Association for the Advancement of Behavior Therapy, New York, December 1976.
7. Sweitzer, M., & Boyd, A. *Parent Performance Checklist: A behavioral assessment of parent skills.* Unpublished manuscript, Florida Mental Health Institute, Tampa, 1979.
8. Gottlieb, B. *Primary groups as supportive milieu: Applications to community psychology.* Paper presented at the annual conference of the American Psychological Association, San Francisco, August 1977.
9. Tolsdorf, C. C. *The multiproblem family: Stress, support, and coping in the social network.* Paper presented at the annual meeting of the American Psychological Association, Toronto, Ontario, August 1978.
10. Pederson, F. A. *Relationships between parental behavior and mother–infant interaction.* Paper presented at the annual meeting of the American Psychological Association, Chicago, September 1975.
11. Friedman, R. M. *Enriching a behavioral approach to families with family systems concepts.* Unpublished manuscript, Florida Mental Health Institute, Tampa, 1978.
12. Holmes, T. H., & Rahe, R. *Schedule of Recent Experience (SRE).* Unpublished manuscript, University of Washington School of Medicine, Seattle, 1967.

# References

Adelson, L. Slaughter of the innocents: A study of forty-six homicides in which the victims were children. *New England Journal of Medicine*, 1961, *264*, 1345–1349.

Averill, J. R. The dis-position of psychological dispositions. *Journal of Experimental Research in Personality*, 1973, *6*, 275–282.

Azrin, N. H., Naster, B. J., & Jones, R. Reciprocity counseling: A rapid learning-based procedure for marital counseling. *Behaviour Research and Therapy*, 1973, *11*, 365–382.

Bandura, A. *Aggression: A social learning analysis.* Englewood Cliffs, N.J.: Prentice-Hall, 1973.

Bell, R. Q. A reinterpretation of the direction of effects in studies of socialization. *Psychological Review*, 1968, *75*, 81–95.

Bell, R. Q. Stimulus control of parent or caretaker behavior of offspring. *Developmental Psychology*, 1971, *4*, 63–72.

Bem, D. J., & Funder, D. C. Predicting more of the people more of the time: Assessing the personality of situations. *Psychological Review*, 1978, *85*, 485–506.

Boisvert, M. J. The battered-child syndrome. *Social Casework*, 1972, *53*, 475–480.

Bryant, H. D., Billingsley, A., Kerry, G. A., Leefman, W. V., Merrill, E. J., Senecal, G. R., & Walsh, B. Physical abuse of children—An agency study. *Child Welfare*, 1963, *52*, 125–130.

Burgess, R. L. Child abuse: A behavioral analysis. In B. B. Lahey & A. E. Kazdin (Eds.), *Advances in clinical child psychology* (Vol. 2). New York: Plenum, 1979.

Burgess, R. L., & Conger, R. D. Differentiating abusing and neglecting parents by direct observation of parent–child interaction. In M. L. Lauderdale, R. N. Anderson, & S. E. Cramer, (Eds.), *Child abuse and neglect: Issues on innovation and implementation—Proceedings of the second annual national conference on child abuse and neglect.* Washington, D.C.: National Center on Child Abuse and Neglect, 1978.

Carey, W. B. Measuring infant temperament. *Journal of Pediatrics*, 1972, *81*, 414.

Collins, A., & Pancoast, D. *Natural helping networks.* Washington, D.C.: National Association of Social Workers, 1976.

Delsordo, J. D. Protective casework for abused children. *Children*, 1963, *10*, 213–218.

Deykin, E. Life functioning in families of delinquent boys: An assessment model. *Social Service Review*, 1972, *46*, 90–102.

Doane, J. A. Family interaction and communication deviance in disturbed and normal families: A review of research. *Family Process*, 1978, *17*, 357–376.

Dubanoski, R. A., Evans, J. M., & Higuchi, A. A. Analysis and treatment of child abuse: A set of behavioral propositions. *Child Abuse and Neglect*, 1978, *2*, 153–172.

Ebbin, A. J., Golub, M. H., Stein, A. M., & Wilson, M. G. Battered child syndrome at the Los Angeles County General Hospital. *American Journal of Diseases of Children*, 1969, *118*, 660–667.

Elmer, E. *Children in jeopardy*. Pittsburgh: University of Pittsburgh Press, 1967.

Elmer, E., & Gregg, G. Developmental characteristics of abused children. *Pediatrics*, 1967, *40*, 596–602.

Endler, N. S. The case for person–situation interactions. *Canadian Psychological Review*, 1975, *16*, 12–21.

Ennis, B. J., & Litwack, T. R. Psychiatry and the presumption of expertise: Flipping coins in the courtroom. *California Law Review*, 1974, *62*, 693–752.

Eyberg, S., & Ross, A. W. Assessment of child behavior problems: The validation of a new inventory. *Journal of Clinical Child Psychology*, 1978, *7*, 113–116.

Ferster, C. B., & DeMyer, M. K. A method for the experimental analysis of the behavior of autistic children. *American Journal of Orthopsychiatry*, 1962, *32*, 89–98.

Feshbach, N. D. The effects of violence in childhood. *Journal of Clinical Child Psychology*, 1973, *2*, 28–31.

Feshbach, S., & Feshbach, N. D. Alternatives to corporal punishment: Implications for training and controls. *Journal of Clinical Child Psychology*, 1973, *2*, 46–49.

Fontana, V. J. Which parents abuse children? *Medical Insight*, 1971, *3*, 195–199.

Fontana, V. J. *Somewhere a child is crying: Maltreatment—Causes and prevention*. New York: Macmillan, 1973.

Friedrich, W. N., & Boriskin, J. A. The role of the child in abuse: A review of the literature. *American Journal of Orthopsychiatry*, 1976, *46*, 580–590.

Friedman, R. M. Child abuse: A review of the psychosocial research. In Herner Co. (Eds.), *Four perspectives on the status of child abuse and neglect research*. Springfield, Va.: National Technical Information Service, 1975. (NTIS No. PB-250-852/AS)

Gaines, R., Sandgrund, A., Green, A. H., & Power, E. Etiological factors in child maltreatment: A multivariate study of abusing, neglecting, & normal mothers. *Journal of Abnormal Psychology*, 1978, *87*, 531–540.

Garbarino, J. A preliminary study of some ecological correlates of child abuse: The impact of socioeconomic stress on mothers. *Child Development*, 1976, *47*, 178–185.

Garbarino, J. The price of privacy in the social dynamics of child abuse. *Child Welfare*, 1977, *56*, 565–575.

Garbarino, J., Burston, N., Raber, S., Russell, R., & Crouter, A. The social maps of children approaching adolescence: Studying the ecology of youth development. *Journal of Youth and Adolescence*, 1978, *7*, 417–428.

Gelles, R. J. Child abuse as psychopathology: A sociological critique and reformulation. *American Journal of Orthopsychiatry*, 1973, *43*, 611–621.

Gelles, R. J. Violence toward children in the United States. *American Journal of Orthopsychiatry*, 1978, *48*, 580–592.

Gelles, R. J. Interpreting family violence data: The author replies. *American Journal of Orthopsychiatry*, 1979, *47*, 372–374.

Gil, D. G. Incidence of child abuse and demographic characteristics of persons involved. In R. E. Helfer & C. H. Kempe (Eds.), *The battered child*. Chicago: University of Chicago Press, 1968.

Gil, D. G. *Violence against children: Physical child abuse in the United States*. Cambridge, Mass.: Harvard University Press, 1970.

Gil, D. G. (Statement in) U.S. Congress, Senate Committee on Labor and Public Welfare, *Child abuse prevention act, 1973*. Hearings before the Subcommittee on Children and Youth on S. 1191, 93rd

Congress, 1st Session. Washington, D.C.: U.S. Government Printing Office, 1973.

Gil, D. G. Unraveling child abuse. *American Journal of Orthopsychiatry*, 1975, *45*, 346–356.

Giovannoni, J. M. Parental mistreatment: Perpetrators and victims. *Journal of Marriage and the Family*, 1971, *33*, 649–657.

Goldstein, J. H., Davis, R. W., & Herman, D. Escalation of aggression: Experimental studies. *Journal of Personality and Social Psychology*, 1975, *31*, 162–170.

Goode, W. J. Force and violence in the family. *Journal of Marriage and the Family*, 1971, *33*, 624–636.

Green, A. H., Gaines, R. W., & Sandgrund, A. Child abuse: Pathological syndrome of family interaction. *American Journal of Psychiatry*, 1974, *131*, 882–886.

Haley, J. (Ed.). *Changing families*. New York: Grune & Stratton, 1971.

Haley, J. *Problem solving therapy*. San Francisco: Jossey-Bass, 1977.

Helfer, R. E. The etiology of child abuse. *Pediatrics*, 1973, *51*, 777–779.

Helfer, R. E., Hoffmeister, J. K., & Schneider, C. *A manual for use of the Michigan Screening Profile of Parenting*. Boulder, Colo.: Test Analysis & Development Corp., 1978.

Hoffman, M. L. Moral internalization, parental power, and the nature of parent–child interaction. *Developmental Psychology*, 1975, *11*, 228–239.

Holter, J. C., & Friedman, S. B. Child abuse: Case findings in the emergency department. *Pediatrics*, 1968, *42*, 128–138.

Jacob, T. Family interaction in disturbed and normal families: A methodological and substantive review. *Psychological Bulletin*, 1975, *82*, 33–65.

Johnson, B., & Morse, H. A. Injured children and their parents. *Children*, 1968, *15*, 147–152.

Johnson, C. L. *Child abuse in the Southeast: Analysis of 1172 reported cases*. Athens, Ga.: Regional Institute of Social Welfare Research, 1974.

*Journal of Clinical Child Psychology*. Violence against children, 1973, *2*.

Justice, B., & Duncan, D. F. Life crisis as a precursor to child abuse. *Public Health Reports*, 1976, *91*, 110–115.

Kaplan, D. M., & Mason, E. A. Maternal reactions to premature birth viewed as an acute emotional disorder. *American Journal of Orthopsychiatry*, 1960, *30*, 539–546.

Kempe, C. H. A practical approach to the protection of the abused child and the rehabilitation of the abusing parent. *Pediatrics*, 1973, *51*, 804–812.

Klein, M., & Stern, L. Low birth weight and the battered child syndrome. *American Journal of Diseases of Childhood*, 1971, *122*, 15–18.

Lauer, B., Ten Broeck, E., & Grossman, M. Battered child syndrome: Review of 130 patients with controls. *Pediatrics*, 1974, *54*, 67–70.

Locke, H. J., & Wallace, K. M. Short-term marital adjustment and prediction tests: Their reliability and validity. *Journal of Marriage and the Family*, 1959, *21*, 251–255.

Megargee, E. I. The prediction of violence with psychological tests. In C. D. Spielberger (Ed.), *Current topics in clinical and community psychology* (Vol. 1). New York: Academic Press, 1970.

Melnick, B., & Hurley, J. R. Distinctive personality attributes of child-abusing mothers. *Journal of Consulting and Clinical Psychology*, 1969, *33*, 746–749.

Milowe, I., & Lourie, R. The child's role in the battered child syndrome. *Society for Pediatric Research*, 1964, *65*, 1079–1031.

Minuchin, S. *Families and family therapy*. Cambridge, Mass.: Harvard University Press, 1974.

Mischel, W. *Personality and assessment*. New York: Wiley, 1968.

Mischel, W. Toward a cognitive social learning reconceptualization of personality. *Psychological Review*, 1973, *80*, 252–283.

Moos, R. *Family environment scale*. Palo Alto, Calif.: Consulting Psychologists Press, 1975.

Myers, S. A. Maternal filicide. *American Journal of Diseases of Children*, 1970, *120*, 534–536.

Nagi, R. Child abuse and neglect programs: A national overview. *Children Today*, 1975, *4*, 13–17.

Novaco, R. W. Anger and coping with stress. In J. Foreyt & D. Rathjen (Eds.), *Cognitive behavior therapy: Research and applications*. New York: Plenum, 1978.

Nurse, S. M. Familial patterns of parents who abuse their children. *Smith College Studies of Social Work*, 1964, *34*, 11–25.

Olson, D. H., & Ryder, R. G. Inventory of Marital Conflicts (IMC): An experimental interaction procedure. *Journal of Marriage and the Family*, 1970, *32*, 443–448.

Owens, C. Parents' reactions to defective babies. *American Journal of Nursing*, 1964, *64*, 83–86.

Parke, R. D., & Collmer, C. W. Child abuse: An interdisciplinary analysis. In E. M. Hetherington (Ed.), *Review of child development research* (Vol. 5). Chicago: University of Chicago Press, 1975.

Patterson, G. R. Changes in status of family members as controlling stimuli: A basis for describing treatment process. In L. A. Hamerlynck, L. C. Handy, & E. J. Mash (Eds.), *Behavior change: Methodology, concepts, and practice*. Champaign, Ill.: Research Press, 1973.

Patterson, G. R. A basis for identifying stimuli which control behaviors in natural settings. *Child Development*, 1974, *45*, 900–911.

Patterson, G. R., & Cobb, J. A. Stimulus control for classes of noxious behaviors. In J. Knutson (Ed.), *The control of aggression: Implications from basic research*. Chicago: Aldine, 1973.

Patterson, G. R., Reid, J. B., Jones, R. R., & Conger, R. E. *A social learning approach to family intervention* (Vol. 1). Eugene, Ore.: Castalia Publishing Co., 1975.

Paulson, M. J., Afifi, A. A., Thomason, M. L., & Chaleff, A. A descriptive measure of psychopathology in abusive parents. *Journal of Clinical Psychology*, 1974, *30*, 387–390.

Pelton, L. H. Child abuse and neglect: The myth of classlessness. *American Journal of Orthopsychiatry*, 1978, *48*, 608–617.

Pelton, L. H. Interpreting family violence data. *American Journal of Orthopsychiatry*, 1979, *49*, 194; 392.

Pfohl, S. J. The "discovery" of child abuse. *Social Problems*, 1977, *24*, 310–323.

Polansky, N. A., DeSaix, C., & Sharlin, S. *Child neglect: Understanding and reaching the parent*. New York: Child Welfare League of America, 1972.

Polansky, N. A., Hally, C., & Polansky, N. F. *Profile of neglect*. Washington, D.C.: Social & Rehabilitation Service, 1975.

Resnick, P. J. Child murder by parents: A psychiatric review of filicide. *American Journal of Psychiatry*, 1969, *126*, 325–334.

Rimland, B. *Infantile autism: The syndrome and its implications for a neural theory of behavior*. New York: Appleton-Century-Crofts, 1964.

Riskin, J., & Faunce, E. An evaluative review of family interaction research. *Family Process*, 1972, *11*, 365–456.

Sandler, J., VanDercar, C., & Milhoan, M. Training child abusers in the use of positive reinforcement practices. *Behaviour Research and Therapy*, 1978, *16*, 169–175.

Schmitt, B. D., & Kempe, C. H. The pediatrician's role in child abuse and neglect. *Current Problems in Pediatrics*, 1975, *5*, 3–47.

Scott, P. D. Fatal battered baby cases. *Medicine, Science, and the Law*, 1973, *13*, 197–206.

Silver, L. B., Dublin, C. C., & Lourie, R. S. Agency action and interaction in cases of child abuse. *Social Casework*, 1971, *52*, 164–171.

Skinner, A. E., & Castle, R. L. Seventy-eight battered children: A retrospective study. Hoddeston, Herts., England: Thomas Knight, 1969.

Smith, S. M., Hanson, R., & Noble, S. Social aspects of the battered baby syndrome. *British Journal of Psychiatry*, 1974, *125*, 568–582.

Smith, N., Schwartz, J., Mandall, W., Silberstein, R., Dalack, G., & Sacks, S. Mothers' psychological reactions to premature and full-size newborns. *Archives of General Psychiatry*, 1969, *21*, 177–181.

Solnit, A. J., & Stack, M. H. Mourning the birth of a defective child. *Psychoanalytic Study of the Child*, 1961, *16*, 523–537.

Spanier, G. B. Measuring dyadic adjustment: New scales for assessing the quality of marriage and similar dyads. *Journal of Marriage and the Family*, 1976, *38*, 15–28.

Spinetta, J. J., & Rigler, D. The child-abusing parent: A psychological review. *Psychological Bulletin*, 1972, *77*, 296–304.

Steele, B. F., & Pollock, C. B. A psychiatric study of parents who abuse infants and small children. In R. E. Helfer & C. H. Kempe (Eds.), *The battered child*. Chicago: University of Chicago Press, 1968.

Stern, L. Prematurity as a factor in child abuse. *Hospital Practice*, 1973, *8*, 117–123.

Stone, A. A. *Mental health and law: A system in transition*. Rockville, Md.: National Institute of Mental

Health, 1975.

Terr, L. A family study of child abuse. *American Journal of Psychiatry*, 1970, *127*, 665–671.

Thomson, E. M., Paget, N. W., Bates, D. W., Mesch, M., & Putnam, T. I. *Child abuse: A community challenge*. New York: Henry Stewart, 1971.

Toch, H. *Violent men*. Chicago: Aldine, 1969.

Tolsdorf, C. C. Social networks, support, and coping: An exploratory study. *Family Process*, 1976, *15*, 407–417.

Vincent, J. P., Weiss, R. L., & Birchler, G. R. A behavioral analysis of problem-solving in distressed and nondistressed married and stranger dyads. *Behavior Therapy*, 1975, *6*, 475–487.

Watzlawick, P. A structured family interview. *Family Process*, 1966, *5*, 256–271.

Weiss, R. L., Hops, H., & Patterson, G. R. A framework for conceptualizing marital conflict, a technology for altering it, some data for evaluating it. In L. A. Hamerlynck, L. C. Handy, & E. J. Mash (Eds.), *Behavior change: Methodology, concepts, and practice*. Champaign, Ill.: Research Press, 1973.

Weston, J. T. The pathology of child abuse. In R. E. Helfer & C. H. Kempe (Eds.), *The battered child*. Chicago: University of Chicago Press, 1968.

Wight, B. W. The control of child–environment interaction: A conceptual approach to accident occurrence. *Pediatrics*, 1969, *44*, 799–805.

Young, L. *Wednesday's children*. New York: McGraw-Hill, 1964.

# INTERNALIZING DISORDERS

CHAPTER 6

# FEARS AND ANXIETIES IN CHILDREN

**Billy A. Barrios**      **Donald P. Hartmann**
*University of Virginia*        *University of Utah*
**Carol Shigetomi**
*University of Utah*

## INTRODUCTION

Investigations of children's fears have played a surprisingly major role in the development of modern theories of behavior. Early in the 20th century, three case reports of children's animal phobias sparked dramatic changes in the conceptualization of human behavior. In 1909 Freud (1962) published his analysis of a fear of horses in a 5-year-old boy, Little Hans, which marked the beginning of child psychoanalysis (Jones, 1955) and which appeared to provide critical support for psychoanalytic theory. According to Glover (1956), the case of Little Hans "greatly reinforced and amplified . . . [the] concepts of phobia formation, of the positive Oedipus complex, of ambivalence, [and of] castration anxiety and repression, to name but a few" (p. 73).[1]

Shortly thereafter, the new theory called *behaviorism* gained support from a case of a childhood fear reported by the theory's founder, Watson, and his associate, Rayner (Watson & Rayner, 1920). This report described the conditioning of a small-animal (rat) phobia in a year-old infant, Albert. The often-cited study of Albert has been widely interpreted by Watson and others as providing a successful empirical test of a conditioning theory of behavior and of emotional development.[2]

A few years later, Watson's student, Jones (1924), published the first systematic application of behavioral techniques in the treatment of a child. Her classic study of Peter, an otherwise healthy 3-year-old who was afraid of rabbits as well

---

[1]See Wolpe and Rachman (1960) for an incisive, and sometimes amusing, critical analysis of the case of Little Hans.

[2]Harris (1979), in his review of exaggerations and other incorrect citations of the case of Albert, described the study as "interesting but uninterpretable" (p. 158).

as of a white rat, a fur coat, a feather, and cotton wool, successfully employed counterconditioning and social imitation. Jones's description of the treatment of Peter also foreshadowed the use of a passive form of behavioral avoidance test (BAT), a technique now commonly reported in the assessment of children's fears.

With such an auspicious beginning to the study of children's fears, one might expect that the entire field, including the assessment of fearful and anxious behavior, would be highly developed. As will be seen in the pages that follow, such a description of the assessment technology would be substantially in error. In fact, reliable information in the entire area of children's fears is so scarce that Miller, Barrett, and Hampe (1974) entitled a chapter "Phobias of Childhood in a Pre-scientific Era." Graziano and DeGiovanni's (1979) review of the behavior treatment literature of childhood phobias further highlights the undeveloped nature of this area. Although their review spans some 60 years, it includes only 28 controlled experiments and 40 uncontrolled case studies. In contrast, the four major behavioral journals (*Behavior Therapy, Behavior Therapy and Experimental Psychiatry, Behaviour Research and Therapy*, and the *Journal of Applied Behavior Analysis*) published that number of reports on *adult* fears and anxieties in the 5-year span extending from 1972 to 1976 (Ciminero, Doleys, & Williams, 1978).

The remainder of this introductory section includes a working definition of fears and anxieties; an examination of developmental, prognostic, and other factors related to the decision to treat or not to treat a fearful or anxious child; a brief description of behavioral techniques for treating children's fears and anxieties; and a discussion of issues involved in selecting from among these techniques. In the following two sections, we describe and evaluate the instruments available for assessing children's fearful and anxious behavior and provide a brief discussion of the areas in need of additional research and development.

## Fears, Anxieties, and Related Phenomena

Children's fears and anxieties have been considered part of a superordinate class of problems, the anxiety–withdrawal disorder identified through factor analyses (Quay, 1979). Research efforts to identify environmental and social variables associated with the disorder have not been very productive. Thus it seems that such a broad category is of limited utility in revealing etiology or in directing treatment.

The next level of classification has been to distinguish between fears and anxieties. Children's fears are typically described as reactions to perceived threats, involving avoidance of the threatening stimuli, subjective feelings of discomfort, and physiological changes such as sweating and palpitations. Anxieties are distinguished from fears largely on the basis of the specificity of the eliciting stimuli and of the accompanying response (Jersild, 1954). Fear reactions typically are highly differentiated and made in response to a specific stimulus, such as a natural event (lightning or the dark) or an abstract concept (war or rejection). Anxiety reactions are more diffuse—what Johnson and Melamed (1979) refer to as "apprehension without apparent cause" (p. 107). Although the behavioral literature does not clearly distinguish between fears and anxieties, one might expect that the latter would pose a more difficult assessment problem because of the ambiguity of both response and eliciting stimuli.

Clinical fears (phobias) or anxiety reactions are distinguished from their normal counterparts on the basis of their persistence, maladaptiveness, and magnitude (e.g., Marks, 1969; Miller, *et al.*, 1974; also see Berecz, 1968, and Crider, 1949, for reviews of writings that deal with definitions of phobias). In the case of clinically serious fears, the disturbed child may describe feelings of panic, of tension, or even of imminent death. Physiological changes may include rapid respiration, palpitation, breathlessness, nausea, and the like. Rachman (1968) describes a 7-year-old child, who, when confronted by a bee, would become "white, sweaty, cold and trembly, and his legs were like jelly" (p. 4). Behavioral responses may include screams, cries, and pleas for assistance, as well as gross motor responses ranging from exaggerated flight responses to complete immobility.

These traditional definitions of fears, anxiety reactions, and phobias have a number of problems that detract from their utility. First, the distinctions between fears and anxieties and between normal fears and clinical phobias may be difficult to operationalize. Second, labeling a child "fearful" or "anxious" provides limited information concerning how that child will behave. Relationships between physiological, cognitive, and behavioral–motoric responses may be highly variable (Lang & Lazovik, 1963; Rachman & Hodgson, 1974), and a distressed child might display a unique pattern of responding. For example, a dog-fearful child may imagine that dogs are life threatening, but may nonetheless approach them reluctantly and display no unusual physiological responses. Third, at least some of the classic fear responses can be developed and maintained independently of a threatening stimulus. For example, school avoidance can be maintained, at least in part, by parent-mediated consequences rather than by fear-eliciting qualities of the school. Although we will employ traditional definitions of fear and anxiety in the material that follows, one should not lose sight of their imperfections.

Children's phobic reactions vary in terms of the nature and complexity of the threatening stimulus, the nature and extent of the response modalities affected, and whether the phobia is self-contained or associated with other problem behavior. In view of the multidimensional character of phobias, it is perhaps not surprising that they have been subjected to a variety of classification schemes. At one time it was fashionable to provide long lists of exotic-sounding phobias, such as paraliphobia (fear of precipitating disaster by having omitted or forgotten something), pantophobia (fear of practically everything), and phobophobia (fear of phobias).[3] More recently, phobias have been divided into broader categories on the basis of either analytical or empirical methods. Hebb (1946) grouped phobias into etiological classes such as those produced by conflicts or sensory deficit or those arising from constitutional disturbances or maturation. Miller, Barrett, Hampe, and Noble (1972) based their classification on the results of a factor analysis and grouped phobic reactions into fears of physical injury, of natural events, and of psychic stress.

---

[3]For extended lists of phobias, see Masserman (1946) and Kanner (1957).

With the limited data currently available, it is not clear that these or other proposed classification schemes have "carved nature at its joints"; nor is it clear that any of the proposed schemes would be of particular use to behavior assessors. Indeed, the safest procedure from a behavioral point of view would be to consider each child's phobic behavior as a unique class defined by the stimulus that elicits the fearful and avoidance responses, the nature and degree of these responses, and other information required for a functional analysis of the individual case. School-phobic children may be an exception to this completely idiographic approach. Some writers (e.g., Miller, *et al.*, 1974; Yates, 1970) have suggested that classification of school phobics into two or three broad classes may have some diagnostic utility.

## Developmental Considerations

The incidence and the course of children's fearful and anxious behavior have been explored in a number of epidemiological and related investigations (see reviews by Berecz, 1968; Graziano, DeGiovanni, & Garcia, 1979; Jersild, 1954; Marks, 1969; and Miller *et al.*, 1974). Differing procedures and methodological problems make these studies difficult to compare, but a few generalizations can be made with reasonable confidence.[4]

### Incidence

Normal children have a surprisingly large number of fears. Jersild and Holmes (1935) noted that mothers reported that their 2- through 6-year-old children averaged between four and five fears and displayed a fearful reaction once every 4½ days. MacFarlane, Allen, and Honzik (1954), in their classic longitudinal study of normal children from ages 2 through 14 years, found that specific fears were reported at least once for 90% of their sample. Investigating a large sample of 6- through 12-year-old children, Lapouse and Monk (1959) indicated that 43% of their mothers reported having children with seven or more fears, and 15% reported having children with three or more anxious behaviors such as nail biting, teeth grinding, and thumb sucking. The results of a smaller ($n = 193$) validation sample further indicated that maternal reports may underestimate the prevalence of these behaviors. In contrast to the children's own reports, mothers reported 41% fewer fears and anxieties.

### Age Trends

The frequency of fearful and anxious behavior in children appears to decline with increasing age (see reviews by Miller *et al.*, 1974, and by Rachman, 1968). Holmes (1935), for example, observed common childhood fears (e.g., fear of strangers, of being left alone, and of the dark) in 2- through 5-year-olds and found that age

---

[4]See Graziano *et al.* (1979) for a discussion of the shortcomings of these studies.

was inversely related to the number of fears displayed. Lapouse and Monk (1959) reported similar age trends for 6- through 12-year-olds, Bauer (1976) for 4- through 12-year-olds, and MacFarlane *et al.* (1954) for 2- through 14-year-olds. Other studies, however, have not reported significant age trends (e.g., Croake & Knox, 1973; Dunlop, Note 1).

In addition to an apparent overall decline in children's fears with increasing age, the predominant fears at each age vary. Young infants are frightened by the loss of support, by height, and by sudden, intense, and unexpected stimuli such as loud noises (e.g., Jersild, 1954). As children mature and face new developmental challenges, their fears also change. One- and 2-year-old children are afraid of strangers, of toileting activities, and of being injured (e.g., Miller *et al.*, 1974), but are as yet unafraid of snakes (Jones & Jones, 1928). Imaginary creatures are common sources of fear for preschool children, as are animals and the dark (e.g., Jersild & Holmes, 1935). Young elementary school children continue to be frightened by animals, are also concerned for their safety, and are fearful of natural events such as lightning and thunder (e.g., Croake & Knox, 1973). School- and health-related fears also become prominent at this time. For example, Kennedy (1965) estimated the incidence of serious phobic reactions to school at 17 per 1000, whereas Stricker and Howitt (1965) indicate that as many as 16% of school-aged children exhibit serious fear and avoidance reactions to dental treatment. Older school children become increasingly fearful of injury and of economic and political catastrophes such as war (e.g., Angelino, Dollins, & Mech, 1956).

### Seriousness

Although common, most childhood fears are not serious. For example, Rutter, Tizard, and Whitmore (1970) screened the total population of 10- and 11-year-olds on the Isle of Wight and found a prevalence rate for serious fears of only 7 per 1000, with animal, darkness, school, and disease phobias the most common. Prevalence data of this kind prompted Miller *et al.* (1974) to suggest that the intensity of children's fears is best described by a J-shaped distribution curve, with numerous reports of mild fears and infrequent reports of severe fear reactions. The data reported by some investigators (e.g., MacFarlane *et al.*, 1954) provide a good fit with this description, whereas the data presented by other investigators (e.g., Croake & Knox, 1973) apparently do not.

Reports based on referrals to treatment agencies tend to support the notion that most fears are not sufficiently indisposing to children or irritating to their parents or teachers to require professional care. Johnson and Melamed's (1979) review indicates that phobic disorders account for only 3–4% of all child cases referred for treatment. Graham (Note 2), for example, reports only 10 specific phobias in 239 consecutive cases referred to the Maudsley Children's Department. Although behavior therapists spend more of their time treating fearful and anxious clients than any other type (Wade, Baker, & Hartmann, 1979; Swan & MacDonald, 1978), it would appear that these clients are typically not children. Based on a small and perhaps unrepresentative survey of child behavior therapists, Graziano and DeGiovanni (1979) found relatively few children (7–8%) referred for specific fear-related behavior. When children are referred for treatment, school phobia accounts for the majority of cases (69% according to Miller *et al.*, 1974), although it is by no means the most common phobia.

## Prognosis

The bulk of research evidence suggests that most childhood fears are short-lived (e.g., MacFarlane *et al.*, 1954; Marks, 1969). Slater (1939), for example, reported that the frequent displays of fearful and anxious behavior (e.g., tics, requests for mothers, and postural tensions) in 2- and 3-year-old nursery school children had almost completely abated after 4 weeks. Cummings (1944, 1946) reported that fears, though not generalized anxiety reactions, were quite transitory in 2- through 7-year-olds. Hagman (1932) similarly reported that most childhood fears were short-lived: 54% had disappeared after 3 months, and the more recalcitrant fears were gone after 3 years.

Serious childhood phobic reactions also generally seem to disappear within relatively brief periods. In a 5-year follow-up of an earlier epidemiological study, Agras, Chapin, and Oliveau (1972) found that, of the 10 children initially identified as phobics, all were improved or had recovered.

Other studies also present an encouraging view of the prognosis for fearful and avoidance behaviors in children. Hampe, Noble, Miller, and Barrett (1973), reporting a 2-year follow-up of treated phobic children, found that only 7% of the children continued to have serious fear reactions, whereas 80% were "symptom free." Similarly, Robins's (1966) analysis of the adult status of 525 child guidance clinic patients indicated that adults who displayed neurotic behavior such as nervousness, fears, tics, and shyness as children had a lower rate of neurotic disturbances when they reached adulthood than did members of a control group. Retrospective studies of adult phobics provide results generally consistent with the results of prospective studies. Although adult phobics report having more childhood fears than control group members (Solyom, Beck, Solyom, & Hugel, 1974), the fears of adult phobics typically do not begin during childhood (Agras, Sylvester, & Oliveau, 1969), with the possible exception of specific animal phobias (Marks & Gelder, 1966).

The bulk of epidemilogical and related evidence suggests that behavior assessors would do well to maintain a developmental perspective when evaluating children's fears and anxieties. According to this perspective, the seriousness of a fear response would be based partly on the extent to which that response was common to children of a similar age. Thus, a fear of ghosts-under-the-bed might be of minor concern if displayed by a 5-year-old, but might be a more serious matter if reported by a 13-year-old. A developmental perspective might also help restrain assessors inclined to overinterpret children's fearful reactions. Kanner (1960) provides an amusing example of the salutary effects of developmental norms relevant to this point. In the early years of child psychopathology, the seemingly innocent response of nail biting was variously viewed as "a stigma of degeneration," as "an exquisite psychopathic symptom," and as "a sign of an unresolved Oedipus complex." A survey disclosing that 66% of school children had been nail biters at one time or another prompted Kanner to remark that it was "hardly realistic to assume that two-thirds of our youth are degenerate, exquisitely psychopathic, or walking around with an unresolved Oedipus complex" (p. 18).

An additional implication for behavior assessors can be drawn from the various sources of data relating to the outcome of children's fears. Treated fears, with the exception of some cases of school phobia, have a favorable outcome. Even many untreated fears can be expected to improve with the passage of time. Although this latter fact may be of little immediate consolation to distressed parents, behavior assessors should consider cost-effectiveness before recommending treatment. Favorable cost-effective outcomes may be limited to inexpensive treatments that produce rapid and significant improvements (Gelfand, 1978) or that also serve preventive functions.

## To Treat or Not to Treat: Other Considerations

Although developmental and prognostic factors are important in deciding whether or not to accept a fearful or anxious child for treatment, many other factors will also contribute to that decision. Assessors may want to consider the child's and the adults' views of the problem, the relationship of the fear or anxiety to other problem behaviors, the anticipated costs and benefits associated with available treatments, and other practical and ethical factors. The following questions highlight these issues.

*Who is complaining?* Children are rarely self-referred for treatment; instead, they are referred by parents, teachers, or physicians (Evans & Nelson, 1977). The perceptions of these adults, not the child's fearful or anxious behavior, may be more important in determining whether the child is brought to the attention of a behavior therapist (Lobitz & Johnson, 1975). Thus, even though the child is fearful or anxious, he or she may be unmotivated or otherwise unwilling to participate in treatment. In other cases, the child's behavior may be appropriate, but the adult's demands or expectations for fearless behavior are unreasonable. When this occurs, the adult rather than the child may be the appropriate recipient of treatment.

*How is the behavior a problem?* According to Karoly (1975), a problem exists when a behavior reliably disrupts one's pursuit of personal goals, one's ability to adjust to the environment, or one's sense of comfort, satisfaction, and freedom. With a child client, the behavior assessor would want to examine the fear's or the anxiety's impact on individual, family, and classroom functioning; its interference with normal development and learning experiences; and the resulting curtailment of behavior choices and creation of subjective discomfort.

*How are fears related to other areas of the child's behavior?* The fearful or anxious behavior identified by an adult may not be the problem that needs modifying. Enuresis, tantrums, and sleep disturbances may occur in conjunction with anxiety reactions (Kanner, 1957). Anxiety may also be a reaction to other problems, such as learning difficulties, faulty parenting techniques, or physical illnesses, and an acute anxiety attack or phobia may precede or accompany a psychotic reaction (Chess & Hassibi, 1978). The child's fear may be linked to problems of a parent or indicative of maladaptive family functioning (Eisenberg, 1958; Gambrill, 1977; Singer, 1965). The presence of associated difficulties may mean that a problem other than the child's fear or anxiety should be treated or that both the fear or anxiety and another problem should be treated.

*What are the costs of treatment, assuming that there are effective interventions for the problem?* A child might be embarrassed or resentful of treatment, despite the promise of improved behavior and increased attractiveness to others. For parents and other adults, treatment involves expending time, money, and effort and disrupting regular activities in return for a fearless child.

*What would be different for the child and others in his or her natural environment without the problem?* The therapist must examine alternatives to the current situation and determine whether changes would be a positive event for all the persons involved. What are the implications of not treating a child's fear or anxiety? Although epidemiological data suggest that most childhood fears are transient, a therapist's refusal to provide the best available intervention might result in ethical or legal problems. The therapist must also consider the short- and long-term consequences for the child that are associated with a failure to treat. For example, children's fears of dentists, injections, and other medical procedures may be short-lived; the fears' interference with adequate care, however, may contribute to permanent physical damage, serious disease, and general poor health.

Answers to questions such as these will assist in deciding whether treatment is warranted. If the decision is to treat the child, then other issues must be considered by the behavioral assessor in order to select effective treatment procedures. Before turning to these issues, we will briefly describe the treatment options available to behavior therapists.

## Treatment Techniques

Most behavior therapists are familiar with the techniques commonly used in the treatment of children's fears and anxieties. Recommended for those who desire a more thorough discussion and examples of applications are Gelfand (1978); Graziano, DeGiovanni, and Garcia (1979); Hatzenbuehler and Schroeder (1978); and Richards and Siegel (1978).

### Counterconditioning Techniques

Counterconditioning involves pairing a positive emotional response with a graded sequence of exposures to the feared stimulus, arranged so that the child continues to experience a positive emotion while exposure is increased. Positive emotional states, supposedly incompatible with anxiety, may be relaxation, pleasure, pride, or the like. Perhaps the most famous example of this technique is Jones's (1924) classic treatment of little Peter's fear of rabbits. The most common form of counterconditioning is systematic desensitization, in which deep muscle relaxation is paired with gradual imaginal presentations of increasingly more anxiety-provoking stimuli. Mann and Rosenthal (1969), for example, used this technique to treat test anxiety. Emotive imagery was developed as an alternative to systematic desensitization for children who may not be able to master the relaxation induction procedures. In this technique, the child imagines himself or herself in a pleasant or exciting scene, into which are introduced images of progressively more fear-provoking stimuli. Lazarus and Abramovitz (1962), who developed the method, treated children's dog, school, and darkness fears.

Implosion is a technique sometimes grouped with counterconditioning procedures. With implosion, the child is subjected to presentation of the most extreme version of the feared stimulus through imagery, without suffering adverse consequences. Smith and Sharpe (1970) used implosion in the treatment of school phobia. Therapists must exercise caution in using implosion with children. Graziano (1975) has questioned its use on ethical grounds, and Gelfand (1978) and Ullmann and Krasner (1975) have pointed out practical difficulties in using the technique.

### Modeling Techniques

In modeling treatments, the child observes a model engage in progressively more intimate encounters with a feared stimulus, without adverse consequences to the model. In participant modeling, the child watches a model and then performs the demonstrated behavior, receiving encouragement, praise, or other rewards for his or her efforts. The therapist may provide physical guidance for the child's performance (guided participant modeling or contact desensitization). Melamed and Siegel (1975) used a filmed model in their work with children facing surgery.

Because modeling techniques involve demonstrations of appropriate behaviors and active practice, they are employed with children who are skill deficient, as well as with those who have adequate, but inhibited, skill repertoires. For successful modeling treatments, therapists must select procedures that will facilitate the component processes of modeling (Rosenthal & Bandura, 1978). For example, if the modeled performance is too threatening to children, they may avert their gaze and not even attend to the model. Model characteristics, such as age, must also be considered. Coping models, or those experiencing anxiety and dealing with it, are usually more effective than mastery models, those who show no fear or anxiety (Kazdin, 1973, 1974; Meichenbaum, 1971). Bandura (1969), Rimm and Masters (1974), and Rosenthal and Bandura (1978) provide extensive discussions of imitation-based treatments.

### Operant Techniques

Several treatments have used contingency management procedures. Positive reinforcement approaches often incorporate prompting, shaping, stimulus fading, and extinction. Leitenberg and Callahan (1973) treated a child's fear of the dark by having the child repeatedly practice a desirable response and giving reinforcement for success. Neisworth, Madle, and Goeke (1975) used stimulus fading procedures to treat separation anxiety.

Punishment must be used cautiously, as it can exacerbate the anxiety and avoidance behavior it was intended to treat. Time out, in which the child is removed from a reinforcing situation contingent on undesirable behavior, was used by Van Der Kooy and Webster (1975) in their treatment of elective mutism.

### Self-Control Strategies

Self-control procedures provide a strategy whereby the child manages his or her own anxiety responses by performing certain behaviors such as relaxation and task-facilitating self-talk (see Chapter 2, this volume). This coping skills approach to intervention comprises a variety of specific techniques, including self-monitoring, self-reinforcement, self-instruction, thought stopping, applied relaxation, problem solving, and stress inoculation training (Mahoney & Thoresen, 1974; Kanfer & Goldstein, 1975; Stuart, 1977). Although individual techniques may be based on operant or counterconditioning principles, they are referred to as self-control procedures because of their emphasis on the execution of active coping efforts and their potential for anxiety and fear prevention. Applications of this approach have consisted of teaching children relaxation and self-instructional skills in order to prevent anxiety associated with surgery (Peterson & Shigetomi, Note 3) and to reduce fear of darkness (Kanfer, Karoly, & Newman, 1975).

### Considerations in Selecting a Treatment

In selecting individualized treatment for a fearful or anxious child, the behavior assessor will want to perform a careful functional analysis similar to that suggested by Kanfer and Saslow (1969). The following questions will highlight some issues of particular concern in performing a functional analysis of fearful or anxious behavior.

*What is the target response?* To elaborate on the anxiety or fear response's topography, the behavior assessor should examine physiological, cognitive, and motor responses. Physiological responses such as heart rate, skin conductance, and respiration rate might be increased or otherwise disrupted by exposure to a feared stimulus. To change physiological responses, the therapist will consider using treatments that deal with physiological arousal, such as systematic desensitization or coping skills training techniques.[5]

Cognitive fear and anxiety responses are images and self-statements, including catastrophic thoughts. A child may be labeling a situation as dangerous regardless

---

[5]Although we suggest that treatments may be optimum under different circumstances, the effectiveness of the various techniques, with the exception of modeling, has not been demonstrated (Graziano *et al.*, 1979).

of physiological and behavioral responses. Counterconditioning therapies or those emphasizing self-instructions may be useful in altering images, self-statements, attributions, and interpretations of situations.

Problematic motor responses include behaviors that are inadequate or inappropriate for the situation or that provide escape or avoidance of the situation. In view of a child's limited repertoire, the anxious behaviors may be an appropriate reaction to a harmful, dangerous, or punishing situation (Borkovec, Weerts, & Bernstein, 1977). For example, social skill deficits may play a prominent role in anxiety and withdrawal problems because a socially inexperienced young child is less likely than an adult to have learned the necessary behaviors (Gelfand, 1978). If the anxiety response is attributable to a skill deficit, techniques that build alternative behaviors, such as participant modeling or shaping, are in order. Examining the antecedents of the anxiety or fear reactions can yield information on skill deficits. If the problem behavior occurs fairly uniformly across situations, then the child may have a skill deficit, but if the response is discriminated by the situation so that the appropriate behavior occurs under certain conditions, then the child has a situation-specific fear. In the latter case, in which skills are present but are inhibited by anxiety, techniques such as systematic desensitization may be sufficient (Gelfand, 1978; Rimm & Masters, 1974).

If the avoidance behavior is severe, Hatzenbuehler and Schroeder (1978) suggest that treatment should first emphasize passive association techniques that pair the feared stimulus with an antagonistic response as in counterconditioning, because active participation procedures such as participant modeling might be too frightening. For the moderately avoidant child, active participation might be more effective than passive techniques, and a combination of the two would be superfluous.

*Under what conditions does the problem response occur?* We have already suggested that careful analysis of the problem setting can aid in distinguishing between skill deficits and other causes of inadequate approach behavior. Careful analysis of situational variables may also indicate whether it is likely that consequences control the fear or anxiety response. For example, a child may display fear of traffic or of rodents only when in the presence of one or both parents. Treatment in such a case would attempt to alter the parents' consequences for inappropriate responding. In some cases fear- or anxiety-provoking stimuli may not be readily identifiable, and hence traditional counterconditioning efforts may be inapplicable. If the child can be taught to identify the onset of fearful or anxious behaviors, coping skills training involving relaxation training may be useful (e.g., Gambrill, 1977).

*What child characteristics must be considered in treatment selection?* The child's skills in language and imagery and his or her ability to follow directions or to relax muscles on command may determine the range of possible treatments for the fear or anxiety. Perceived locus of control might determine the effectiveness of contingency management programs, especially positive reinforcement (Switzky & Haywood, 1974). The child's potential for self-management, ability or willingness to engage in role play, and biological functioning with vision, hearing, and mobility will also affect treatment selection. If the treatment program involves the manipulation of reinforcers, then the child's reinforcers must be identified (e.g., Gelfand & Hartmann, 1975).

*What information about the child's environment is useful in treatment selection?* With children's problems, it is especially important to assess relevant adults' behaviors, skills, and motivations to see how they may be contributing to the problem behavior (Ciminero & Drabman, 1977). The parents' fears and anxieties, expectations for the child, general parenting skills, emotional response to the child's anxiety, and general relationship with the child are important (Stedman, 1976). If treatment will involve a mediator, such as a parent, teacher, peer, or sibling, the therapist must assess the potential mediator's ability to implement the program (Evans & Nelson, 1977). For example, if a school phobia involves a child's unwillingness to leave his or her mother, the therapist must assess the mother's willingness and ability to separate from the child and the teacher's ability to cooperate in the treatment (Gelfand, 1978). For contingency management programs, the therapist must assess the potential mediator's possession of the child's highranked reinforcers and ability to dispense the reinforcers contingently (Tharp & Wetzel, 1969).

In order to assist the behavior assessor in selecting effective intervention, the issues raised in this section, as well as related issues, are summarized in Table 1. It should be noted that our recommendations regarding treatment selection are speculative. Very little systematic research that attempts to identify the relationships among optimal outcome, response topography, antecedent conditions, and interventions has been conducted (e.g., Berecz, 1968; Hersen, 1971). A notable exception is the study by Trower, Yardley, Bryant, and Shaw (1978). The suggestions that have been made regarding treatment selection emanate largely from the theoretical models of the various interventions. The role of models in the assessment procedures is discussed in greater detail in the final section of this chapter.

Many of the assessment issues raised are common to a wide range of child behavior problems. Information relevant to these issues might be obtained from general assessment devices, such as interviews, checklists, and direct observation. Other questions are unique to children's fearful and anxious behavior, and necessary information is more efficiently acquired from specialized measurement procedures, which will be discussed in the next section.

# METHODS OF ASSESSING FEAR AND ANXIETY

This section will focus on the instruments utilized to gather information concerning motor, cognitive, and physiological aspects of common childhood fears and anxiety reactions and on novel methods that appear to hold promise for the assessment of children's anxieties.

Before describing the measurement techniques, it is important to distinguish

TABLE 1
Recommendations for Treatment Selection Based on Assessment Information

| Assessment information | Treatment technique[a] | | | | | | | |
|---|---|---|---|---|---|---|---|---|
| | CC | | | | CM | | | |
| | SD | ID | EI | M | PR | P | SP | SS |
| Fear–anxiety response topography | | | | | | | | |
| Physiological | + | + | + | + | | | | |
| Cognitive | | | | + | | | + | + |
| Motoric | + | + | + | + | + | | | |
| Functional analysis | | | | | | | | |
| Stimuli discriminating target responses | | | | | + | | | |
| Stimuli eliciting target responses | + | + | + | + | | | + | + |
| Cognitive mediators of target responses | | | | | | | | + |
| Consequences of target responses | | | | | + | | + | + |
| Child characteristics | | | | | | | | |
| Skill deficit | − | − | − | + | + | | | |
| Inability to relax | − | − | − | | | | | |
| Poor control over images | − | − | − | | | | | |
| Poor control of self-statements | | | | | | | − | |
| Low verbal skills | − | | | | | | − | |
| Failure to identify consequent stimuli | | | | | − | − | | |
| Poor potential for self-management | | | | | | | − | − |
| Other | | | | | | | | |
| Identification of effective mediator | | | | | + | + | | |

Note. This table is intended to serve as a framework for treatment selection. It is not meant to be a definitive source, because there are few data on procedures for selecting optimal treatment. A plus (+) indicates that the technique should be considered. A minus (−) indicates that the technique is counterindicated. An open cell indicates that the intervention is not clearly relevant.

[a]Abbreviations: CC, counterconditioning; SD, systematic desensitization; ID, *in vivo* desensitization; EI, emotive imagery; M, modeling (including participant modeling and contact desensitization); CM, contingency management; PR, positive reinforement; P, punishment; SP, self-control procedures; SS, self-statements.

between the mode of the instrument and the component that it is designed to assess (Cone, 1978). Each of the three components—motor, cognitive, and physiological—can be measured by an instrument whose mode may be behavioral, self-report, or physiological. For example, information concerning the motor response component of anxiety may be obtained by having the child complete a fear survey, which asks to what degree he or she avoids confronting various objects and situations. These ratings measure motor responding, even though they are obtained via the self-report mode. This important distinction between the mode of an instrument and the response that it is designed to assess has not been made in a number of previous discussions of the behavioral assessment of anxiety (Lick & Katkin, 1976). It is apparent that unless these distinctions are made, considerable confusion can arise.

## Motor Components of Fear and Anxiety

Motoric aspects of fear and anxiety have been the most extensively examined of the three response components. This should not come as a surprise because it is consistent with behavior therapy's theoretical and methodological foundations and also with the common immediate need to reduce the child's escape or avoidance behavior. Although the clinical goal is to modify all relevant response systems, behavior therapists have tended to focus on maladaptive motor components because they may maintain subjective discomfort (Bandura, 1978) and restrict activities, which may limit opportunities to acquire or strengthen beneficial behaviors. Direct observation of relevant behavior by trained observers is by far the most frequently employed assessment method, yet a number of instruments rely upon self-reports.

### *Behavioral Measures*

BEHAVIORAL AVOIDANCE TESTS. The typical behavioral measure of motor performance has been some form of the Behavioral Avoidance Test (BAT). Although BATs have been used since the early 1900s (Jersild & Holmes, 1935), the Lang and Lazovik (1963) procedure stands as the prototype of behavioral fear measures. This procedure involves asking the client/subject to enter a room containing a feared object and then to approach, touch, and handle the object. Performance on the BAT provides a number of behavioral measures of avoidance, such as distance moved toward the feared object, number of approach tasks completed and their latency, and time spent in the presence of the fear-eliciting stimulus (Kazdin, 1973).

Some form of BAT has been used to assess children's reactions to small animals, high buildings, water, medical procedures, darkness, solid foods, and separation. Procedurally, the BATs are quite simple and can be administered without difficulty by nonprofessionals. In instances where the child cannot perform the active approach responses because of physical limitations, a passive BAT, such as that designed by Murphy and Bootzin (1973), can be used. Active and passive BAT performances correlate highly in children (Murphy & Bootzin, 1973), as they do in adults (Borkovec & Craighead, 1971). Table 2 describes some of the major characteristics of commonly employed BATs.

Although the BAT remains the primary device for assessing children's fear and anxiety, the technique has problems that may limit its utility. First, BAT procedures are not standardized. Each investigator designs a unique version of the measure, with a different number of tasks and type and mode of instructions. For example, our review of children's BATs revealed that the number of steps or tasks involved ranged from 4 (Kuroda, 1969) to 29 (Ritter, 1968). Segmentation of the BAT into smaller, less difficult tasks may result in greater approach behavior (Nawas, 1971). Such variability in the assessment of the motoric component makes comparisons across studies and across target objects risky at best.

The tests also differ widely in their instructions. Some BATs provide factual information concerning the characteristics of the feared object, whereas others

TABLE 2

Characteristics of Behavioral Avoidance Tests for Assessing Children's Fears and Anxieties

| Reference | Fear | Number of steps | Comments |
|---|---|---|---|
| Bandura, Grusec, and Menlove (1967) | Dogs | 17 | Employed with children ranging in age from 3 to 5 years. In addition to measure of avoidance, scores also obtained for degree of fearfulness, vacillation, and reluctance that preceded and accompanied each approach response. No specific estimates of test–retest reliabilities reported, but children in a control condition exhibited a mean increase of six approach steps after a 4-day period. |
| Freeman, Roy, and Hemmick (1976) | Physical examination | 11 | Steps correspond to those in physical examination procedure. Employed in case study. No data available on reliability and relationship to other measures. |
| Hill, Liebert, and Mott (1968) | Dogs | 3? | Procedure involved requesting child to approach a dog 18 feet away. No information provided on temporal stability of performance or relationship to other measures. |
| Kanfer, Karoly, and Newman (1975) | Darkness | Passive | Procedure measured time child will tolerate the dark. Variations of this method required the child |

*(continued)*

TABLE 2 (continued)

| Reference | Fear | Number of steps | Comments |
|---|---|---|---|
| | | | to operate rheostat dial to darken room and remain in it. Control subjects exhibited very little change, suggesting adequate temporal stability over brief periods. High negative relationship between duration and intensity measures, with the greater the exposure to darkness the less self-reported fear. |
| Kelley (1976) | Darkness | 5 | No estimates of temporal stability reported. Two posttest BATs that differed in demand for approach. High demand instructions resulted in greater approach behavior. Relationship between BAT scores and Fear Thermometer ratings was nonsignificant but in the expected direction. |
| Kornhaber and Schroeder (1975) | Snakes | 14 | Control subjects exhibited very little change in performance from pretesting to posttesting, suggesting some test–retest reliability. BAT scores related significantly to a self-report measure of snake avoidance. |
| Kuroda (1969) | Frogs; earthworms; cats | 3 | Reliability and relationship to other measures not reported. |
| Leitenberg and Callahan (1973) | Darkness | Passive | Measured duration child could tolerate total darkness and dimly |

| | | | |
|---|---|---|---|
| | | | lit room. Control children exhibited little change during 4-week interval. |
| Lewis (1974) | Water | 16 | Measures skill and approach. Interrater reliabilities of skill ratings quite high. Control children exhibited little change in performance over a 5-day period. BAT scores correlated with instructor's ratings of skill, fear, and avoidance. |
| Murphy and Bootzin (1973) | Snakes | 8–18 | Both active and passive procedures used. Passive test was more fear eliciting. Control subjects' performance related to level of fear. No significant improvement in most fearful control subjects as a result of repeated testing; least fearful controls improved almost as much as treated subjects. |
| Ritter (1968) | Dogs | 29 | No specific estimates of temporal stability provided, but control subjects exhibited mean increase of 2.14. No strong relationship found between performance and self-report ratings. |

simply instruct the child to perform the tasks. Providing factual information may facilitate the performance of children who are avoidant because of ignorance and not because of fear (Bernstein & Paul, 1971). The BATs also differ in the information they provide concerning the degree of realistic threat posed by the target stimulus. Reducing the uncertainty associated with the BAT target results in greater approach behavior and less physiological arousal (Lick, Unger, & Condiotte, 1978). The precise instructions for terminating the BAT may also contribute to performance differences. Most BATs instruct children to say "No" or "I don't want to" when they wish to stop. Merely requesting children to "try as hard as you can" results in significantly greater approach behavior (Kelley, 1976). Considerable variability also exists in the method of delivering BAT instructions. In some instances, a live experimenter presents sequential instructions in the testing room, whereas in others, a single exposure to taped instructions is given prior to the child's entering the testing room. Research with adults indicates that exposure to a live experimenter presenting sequential instructions facilitates approach behavior (Bernstein & Nietzel, 1973).

Second, research on the influence of demand characteristics and procedural variations on BAT performance has been conducted with adults rather than children (see Kelley, 1976, for an exception). Consequently, it is unclear to what degree these methodological factors affect children's BAT performance. Kelley's (1976) work suggests that children, who often must comply with adult demands, may be particularly sensitive to these variations. She found that the simple instruction to "try as hard as you can" significantly increased approach behavior. Because such a subtle demand for approach behavior elicited performance changes, it seems probable that more obvious procedures would also.

Third, investigators have been lax in presenting reliability and validity data on children's BAT performance. Although the BAT performance of untreated adults is stable over time (Borkovec & Craighead, 1971; Lang & Lazovik, 1963), estimates of temporal stability have not been reported for children. Data are also lacking on the external validity or generalizability of BAT performance. BATs provide a restricted range of fear-eliciting stimuli in a safe environment. Exhibiting appropriate behavior in the laboratory does not ensure similar performance in naturalistic settings (Lick & Unger, 1975, 1977). Research is needed to establish the level of setting and temporal generalizability in children's BAT performance.

OBSERVATIONAL RATING SCALES. Several observational rating scales have been developed for assessing fears that do not lend themselves to BAT assessment. Generally, use of these scales involves observing children in either contrived laboratory or natural settings and scoring their performance in terms of explicitly defined response categories, such as visual contact, physical proximity, posture, and facial expressions. An observational rating system frequently employed with adults is Paul's (1966) Timed Behavior Checklist. Based on an earlier factor-analytic study of anxiety signs in speech research (Clevanger & King, 1961), the checklist was constructed to measure overt anxiety in a public-speaking situation and includes 20 behaviors such as stammering, hand tremors, and foot shuffling.

Use of the Timed Behavior Checklist method with children's public-speaking anxiety has yielded promising results (Cradock, Cotler, & Jason, 1978).

Another observational scale used to assess the motor component of children's anxiety is the Teacher's Rating Scale (Sarason, Davidson, Lighthall, Waite, & Ruebush, 1960). This measure of test anxiety contains 17 items (e.g., "Does the child's voice tremble when s/he is asked to recite?"), which are rated by the teacher on a five-point Likert scale. Observational rating scales have also been used to assess children's social withdrawal or avoidance of social interaction with peers. The methods described by O'Connor (1969) and Ross, Ross, and Evans (1971) involve observing children in their usual school environments and scoring their social interactions in terms of specified behavioral patterns. The resulting observational data are used to assist in identifying socially isolated children and in evaluating the clinical significance or social validity of treatment outcomes (Kazdin, 1977).

Recently, behavior therapists have begun to apply behavioral principles in the treatment of medically related problems (Gentry & Williams, 1977) and to collaborate with medical personnel in order to facilitate efficient health care and to minimize distress associated with certain medical procedures. Children's fears and anxiety concerning various medical treatments have received considerable attention. Observational rating systems have been developed for measuring children's responses to hospitalization (Vernon, Foley, & Schulman, 1967), anesthesia induction (Vernon, 1973), surgery (Melamed & Siegel, 1975), and dental treatment (Melamed, Hawes, Heiby, & Glick, 1975; Melamed, Weinstein, Hawes, & Katin-Borland, 1975; Melamed, Yurcheson, Fleece, Hutcherson, & Hawes, 1978). Instruments such as the Post-hospital Behavior Questionnaire (Vernon, Schulman, & Foley, 1966) have parents compare various child behaviors (e.g., fears of leaving the house and of the dark and excessive demands for physical proximity) upon discharge with their behaviors prior to hospitalization.[6] Individual ratings are summed to generate a total score. Summed-score measures of this kind generally lack the specificity required for tracking individual responses targeted for intervention. However, they might have some utility for assessing either generalized positive effects of treatment or undesirable side effects of treatment.

Melamed and Siegel (1975) developed the Observer Rating Scale of Anxiety to measure the motor component of anxiety related to surgery. A time sampling procedure is used, in which an observer indicates the presence or absence of each of 29 responses, such as stuttering, crying, trembling hands, and talk about hospital fears, separation from mother, and going home. Specific response categories may be singled out for study of individual children, a procedure that we highly recommend in light of the response stereotypy associated with anxiety reactions (Borkovec et al., 1977). Patterson, Ray, and Shaw (1968) also suggest that specific component scores provide a more sensitive index of change than do total scores,

---

[6]Psychometric considerations suggest that separate ratings of pretreatment and posttreatment performance are superior to retrospective ratings of change (e.g., see Hartmann, Roper, & Gelfand, 1977).

based upon their research on children's inappropriate acting-out behavior.

Another technique developed by Melamed and her colleagues, the Behavior Profile Rating Scale (Melamed, Hawes, Heiby, & Glick, 1975; Melamed, Weinstein, Hawes, & Katin-Borland, 1975), was designed to provide an objective measure of child behaviors that lead to disruption of dental treatment. The scale includes 27 categories, such as crying, refusal to open mouth, white knuckles, rigid posture, verbal complaints, kicking, eyes closed, choking, cries at injections, clings to mother, and leaves or stands up in chair. Each category is weighted by a factor that indicates the degree of disruption as determined by dentists' ratings. The total score is obtained by multiplying the frequency of behaviors in each category by its weight and summing the category scores. The weighting of behaviors according to their level of disruption may assist in the identification of treatment outcome. The procedure might be applied advantageously to other fears.

Separation anxiety has been the subject of considerable attention because of the current interest in attachment behavior (Ainsworth, 1973; Bowlby, 1973; Gewirtz, 1969). Separation anxiety, or the child's unwillingness to leave the presence of his or her parents, has been assessed by several behavioral methods. For example, Glennon and Weisz's (1978) Preschool Observation Scale of Anxiety rates the occurrence of 30 behavioral indicators (e.g., physical complaint, cry, whisper, nail biting, lip licking, sucking or chewing objects, and touching genitals) while children perform various tasks in the presence or absence of their mothers.

Procedures used to assess the motor component of children's fear and anxiety reactions by means of observations and ratings made by others share a number of problems. These problems include expectation biases, reactivity, reliability, observer drift, and expenses incurred in training observers and in purchasing equipment. Some of these issues are touched upon in Table 3, which summarizes reliability and validity data and other relevant applied concerns for some of the currently available observational rating systems. Other issues are discussed in the summary portion of the section on the behavioral components of fearful and anxious behavior. The interested reader may want to consult a number of sources that discuss these issues in some detail (e.g., Kazdin, 1977; Kent & Foster, 1977; Wildman & Erickson, 1977).

### Self-Report Measures

Information on fearful and anxious motor responses may also be gathered by means of children's evaluations of their own behavior. Children's self-reports of these responses are generally obtained through ratings of responses to a variety of potentially anxiety- and fear-eliciting stimuli or of descriptions of overt behavior exhibited when exposed to a specific stimulus. These ratings commonly require children to evaluate their fear or anxiety rather than their degree or probability of avoidance behavior. Fear and anxiety are rarely operationalized, and descriptive anchors are infrequently applied to the levels of the rating scales.

The self-report instruments discussed in this section have been placed here

TABLE 3

Characteristics of Observational Rating Systems for Assessing Children's Fears and Anxieties

| Reference | Fear | Reliability/validity | Comments |
|-----------|------|----------------------|----------|
| Glennon and Weisz (1978) | Separation | Interrater reliability is high. Scores relate to teacher and parent reports. | Items selected on basis of a literature search of behavioral indications of anxiety in children, recommendations by child clinical psychologists, and pilot testing indicating potential for accurate and reliable observation. System's usefulness may be limited by large number of response categories (30) and extensive training procedures required of observers. Response categories include physical complaint, cry, whisper, nail biting, lip licking, chewing or sucking objects, and touching genitals. |
| Melamed and Siegel (1975) | Surgery | Average interrater reliability is excellent. Relationships with other measures not reported. | 29 categories of verbal and skeletal-motor behavior thought to represent behavioral manifestations of anxiety in children. Categories include crying, trembling hands, stutters, and talks about going home. Complexity of the scale and the necessity of possibly extensive observer training may make it impractical for clinical use. |

*(continued)*

TABLE 3 (continued)

| Reference | Fear | Reliability/validity | Comments |
|---|---|---|---|
| Melamed, Yurcheson, Fleece, Hutcherson, and Hawes (1978); Melamed, Weinstein, Hawes, and Katin-Borland (1975); Melamed, Hawes, Heiby, and Glick (1975) | Dental treatment | Excellent interrater reliability. Substantial correlations between scores and dentists' ratings and children's self-report. | 27 response categories (e.g., crying, refusal to open mouth, white knuckles, rigid posture, verbal complaints, kicking, leaves or stands up in chair, eyes closed, choking, cries at injection, clings to parent and faints) that lead to disruption of the dental treatment procedure. Categories weighted by a factor that indicates the degree of a disruption as determined by dentists' ratings. |
| Neisworth, Madle, and Goeke (1975) | Separation | Interrater agreement quite high. Scores obtained in experimental setting related to mother's reports of similar behavior exhibited in different settings. | Duration recording of crying, screaming, and sobbing. Small number of response categories makes system feasible for clinical practice. Idiosyncratic responding on part of child may render system inappropriate for assessment. |
| O'Connor (1969) | Social interaction | Interobserver reliability is extremely high. | Five response categories include physical proximity, verbal interaction, looking at, and interacting with. May be used in naturalistic or laboratory settings. Certain categories emphasize the reciprocal quality of social interaction, which may make scoring difficult for nonprofessionals or minimally trained observers. |
| Paul (1966) | Public | Excellent interrater reliabilities. Scores correlate significantly with self-report and physiological measures. | 20 response categories, such as speech blocking, pacing, swaying, foot shuffling, hand tremors, perspiration, and quivering voice. Training of observers usually involves practice with both live and videotaped speech presentation; thus may not be feasible for typical clinical use. Only one inves- |

| | | | |
|---|---|---|---|
| | | | tigation (Cradock, Cotler, & Jason, 1978) has employed the rating system for assessment of speech-anxious children. |
| Ross, Ross, and Evans (1971) | Social interaction | High interrater agreement. | 11 response categories denoting social interaction and avoidance behavior (e.g., physical contact, verbal interaction, nonverbal motor interaction). Interval recording procedure may present problems for the nonprofessional, but should be relatively straightforward for professionals and experienced therapists. |
| Sarason, Davidson, Lighthall, Waite, and Ruebush (1960) | Test | No reliability estimates reported. Significant correlations found between scores and children's self-report. Fairly high negative correlations found between scores and achievement. | Using five-point Likert scale, teacher rates the child on 17 items (e.g., voice trembling when asked to recite, physical complaints on test days, upset when corrected). Infrequently employed by behavior therapists, the instrument generally lacks precision and situational specificity. May have some utility as relatively quick and simple screening measure. |
| Vernon (1973) | Anesthesia induction | Interrater agreement adequate. Significant relationships between scores and physiological measures and doctors' ratings. | Ratings of the global mood of the child according to a seven-interval scale at various time periods. Scale intervals are anchored with ambiguous behavior descriptions. Simplicity of system makes it attractive, but amount of information generated is limited. |
| Vernon, Schulman, and Foley (1966) | General | Some evidence of test–retest reliability and validity. Scores related to data obtained from interviews | 27 items describing a specific behavior, such as refusal to leave home, enter the dark, or leave presence of parents. Parents compare children's behavior at various times. |

somewhat arbitrarily. Questionnaires that did not include items with specific references to images, self-statements, or physiological processes were included for description and review in this section.

FEAR SURVEY SCHEDULES. These schedules have served as the prototypic self-report instrument for gathering information on responses to a wide range of objects and situations. Although several adult fear inventories have been developed (Tasto, 1977), only two instruments are available for use with children. The Fear Survey Schedule for Children, developed by Scherer and Nakamura (1968), comprises 80 items drawn from the Wolpe–Lang (Wolpe & Lang, 1964) Fear Survey Schedule and suggestions from graduate students and school personnel. The items are grouped into the following categories: school, home, social, physical, animal, travel, classical phobia, and miscellaneous. The child is instructed to rate his or her level of fear on each item according to a five-point scale. A related technique, the Louisville Fear Survey Schedule (Miller, Barrett, Hampe, & Noble, 1972), consists of 81 items covering a broad range of situations and objects. The items are rated on a three-point scale by either the child or an adult familiar with the child's behavior. Unfortunately, parent and child ratings are not interchangeable and may show substantial inconsistency (Miller, Barrett, Hampe, & Noble, 1971). Until reliability and validity issues with these instruments are further clarified (e.g., Graziano *et al.*, 1979), they should probably be restricted to rough screening functions.

FEAR THERMOMETER. Walk's (1956) fear thermometer, originally developed for use with adults, has been adapted for assessing children's fear of specific situations or objects. Kelley's (1976) version of the fear thermometer consists of an apparatus that can be manipulated by the child to indicate one of five levels of fear differentiated by color. Some instruments patterned after the fear thermometer have used pictures of faces representing various levels of fear. The child is asked to choose a face that best corresponds to how he or she felt during a specific situation. This method has generally lacked adequate reliability and validity (Glennon & Weisz, 1978; Peterson & Shigetomi, Note 3). Despite the questionable utility of the "faces test," techniques based on the fear thermometer seem potentially useful in that they simplify the rating task for children and remove some of the variability attributable to language skills that occurs when young children respond to questionnaires.

OTHER INSTRUMENTS. Few self-report instruments focus exclusively on assessment of a specific object or event or a set of thematically similar objects or events. Instruments designed to provide detailed and specific information include the Hospital Fears Rating Scale (Melamed & Siegel, 1975), the Snake Attitude Measure (Kornhaber & Schroeder, 1975), and the Personal Report of Confidence as a Speaker (Paul, 1966). The latter questionnaire has been employed primarily with adults and is discussed in detail elsewhere (Klorman, Weerts, Hastings, Melamed, & Lang, 1974; Paul, 1966). The Hospital Fears Rating Scale comprises eight items from the medical fears subscale of the Fear Survey Schedule for Children, eight items with face validity for assessing hospital fears, and nine filler items. The Snake Attitude Measure is a self-report device for assessing children's fear or avoidance using pictures rather than complex auditory or written materials. The measure comprises 16 sets of three pictures. Most sets of pictures include a snake and two other reptiles, amphibians, mammals, insects, or birds. For each picture set, children are asked to indicate which animal they like most and which animal they dislike most. A child's score is the number of snake pictures liked minus the number of snake pictures disliked.

## Discussion

The procedures used for assessing the motor components of fear and anxiety can all be implemented and interpreted by professionals or paraprofessionals with a moderate degree of training. However, assessors should be aware of several issues related to the use of these instruments. As previously indicated, performance on the BAT and related techniques may be influenced by demand characteristics and procedural variation; furthermore, the external validity of these laboratory procedures is open to question. Assessment procedures that rely upon the ratings of observers must also contend with the issues of observer bias and drift and of reactivity (Kent & Foster, 1977). Behavior assessors need to examine the influence of these factors on the data obtained from observational procedures discussed in this section. In addition, the behavioral categories used should be critically examined for traces of theoretical bias (Evans & Nelson, 1977). For example, in the modification of separation anxiety, it may be useful to assess noncompliance, enuresis, encopresis, pouting, refusal to go to bed at scheduled times, and the like. Our conceptual bias against the possibility of "symptom substitution" would preclude the examination of these maladaptive substitute behaviors.

A number of instruments require parents, teachers, or some other adult familiar with the child to rate the child's behavior. These checklists and rating scales may yield inaccurate behavioral estimates. Schnelle (1974), for example, obtained data on children's school attendance from school records and from parent reports. The two sources not only failed to agree ($r = -.20$), but parents overestimated their children's attendance. As suggested by their data, child behavior assessors should exercise caution in employing checklists that have not been adequately validated.

The majority of self-report instruments reviewed here have serious defects. Most are deficient in data on norms, reliability, and validity. Normative data on children's fears and anxieties are particularly critical in view of the developmental nature of these problems. Many of the items included in fear survey schedules and checklists also lack descriptive detail. For example, available procedures use single-stimulus words such as "dog" rather than more detailed phrases such as "small caged spaniel you are asked to approach slowly and then to pick up." As a result, these items tend to correlate more poorly with overt performance measures than do more specific and detailed self-report items (Lick, Sushinsky, & Malow, 1977). Another concern with the self-report techniques is that the correspondence among the various measures is unknown. This is a matter of some importance, inasmuch as investigators have tended to generate new self-report techniques for each study rather than employ already available instruments. As a result, there is a wealth of outcome data, but differences with respect to instrumentation make cross-study comparisons difficult.

The problems discussed suggest a number of lines of potentially fruitful study. First, investigators should perform systematic research on the reliability and validity of individual instruments and on the influence exerted by demand characteristics. Second, evaluations of the social significance of the behavior exhibited during assessment are warranted. Too often, issues of external validity and clinical significance are overlooked for the sake of experimental precision. Behavioral assessors need to establish the social validity of the behaviors measured (Kazdin, 1977) by their assessment procedures. Third, the potential value of fear survey schedules and behavior checklists for providing information about appropriate and inappropriate collateral effects of treatment deserves examination. Fourth, assessment procedures traditionally employed with adults should be examined for their utility with children. Anxiety associated with test taking, public speaking, social interactions, and mathematics is quite prevalent among both children and adults. Assessment instruments such as the Timed Behavior Checklist (Paul, 1966), Personal Report of Confidence as a Speaker (Paul, 1966), Phobic Test Apparatus (Levis, 1969), Behavioral Assertiveness Test (Eisler, Miller, & Hersen, 1973), Anagrams Task (Brown, Note 4), and the Situation Test (Rehm & Marston, 1968) may, with some modifications, be used with children. The potential of role-playing tests with children warrants systematic study. Role-playing procedures are capable of exposing the child to a wide range of fear-eliciting situations, are inexpensive and generally simple to administer, and may facilitate the identification of skill deficits. As is true with other laboratory methods, it is important to determine the degree of correspondence between role-playing measures and performance exhibited during *in vivo* tests.

## Cognitive Components of Fear and Anxiety

Generally, one of the major sources of discomfort for the anxious and fearful child is cognitive distress. Unless distressful and unpleasant cognitions are markedly reduced, children are unlikely to be satisfied with the outcome of treatment, regardless of the magnitude of behavioral or physiological change. In recent years, behavior therapists have devoted greater attention to the role that cognitions (e.g., self-statements and images) play in anxiety and fear reactions. Unfortunately, relatively little research has been directed toward assessing children's cognitions (Kendall & Korgeski, 1979). In fact, only a handful of instruments exist for the assessment of children's cognitions associated with anxiety and fear, and none of these instruments was developed by behavior therapists. Perhaps because these instruments come from a nonbehavioral orientation, they lack the situational specificity ideally characteristic of behavioral assessment procedures.

Reviewed in this section are the devices currently available for assessing the cognitive component of children's anxiety and fear. All instruments employ self-report procedures.[7] Also included is a review of procedures for assessing imagery abilities of children, because a number of interventions presumably require clear and vivid imagery in order for the interventions to be successful.

### Self-Report Measures

One of the most widely employed self-report instruments is the Children's Manifest Anxiety Scale (Castaneda, McCandless, & Palermo, 1956), a children's version of the Manifest Anxiety Scale (Taylor, 1951). Other frequently employed scales include the General Anxiety Scale for Children (Sarason et al., 1960), the State–Trait Inventory for Children (Spielberger, 1973), and the revised version of the Children's Manifest Anxiety Scale (Reynolds & Richmond, 1978). Most of these instruments conceive of the cognitive component of anxiety as a cross-situational characteristic.

Two instruments are available for examining the cognitive component of specific anxiety reactions. These are the Test Anxiety Scale for Children (Sarason et al., 1960) and Horner's (1968) measurement of the fear of success. In a few investigations, behavior therapists have used projective tests to measure the cognitive aspect of anxiety. Melamed and Siegel (1975) included the Human Figure Drawing Test (Koppitz, 1968), and Vernon (1973) employed a modified version of a projective test developed by Amen (Dorkey & Amen, 1947).

The major characteristics of these general, specific, and projective instruments are presented in Table 4.

Several behavior therapy techniques, such as systematic desensitization, implosion, and covert modeling, employ imagined representations of feared stimuli. Effective use of these techniques assumes that the child can generate appropriate images. Although a number of instruments exist for assessing imagery in adults (Hiscock, 1978; Richardson, 1969; Wade, Note 5), relatively few are available for use with children, and those that have been developed are rarely used by child therapists. Johnson and Bommarito (1971) review three instruments designed to assess children's imagery. Descriptions of the measures and their utility are presented in Table 4.

### Discussion

The most obvious feature of the majority of the instruments reviewed here is that they were developed by nonbehavioral investigators. Because the techniques were spawned by trait or dynamic orientations, they lack the situational specificity required of behavioral assessment instruments. Inventories that attempt to index cross-situational cognitive components of fears or anxiety often fail to describe individual

---

[7]Although these instruments typically contain items dealing with the motor and physiological components of anxiety and fear as well as the cognitive components, they are included for discussion in this section because the majority of the items are concerned with cognitions.

TABLE 4

Characteristics of Self-Report Instruments for Assessing Children's Fears and Anxieties

| Title | Reference | Fear | Channel | Reliability/validity | Comments |
|---|---|---|---|---|---|
| Amen's Projective Test | Vernon (1973) | Hospitalization | Cognitive | No data on reliability, but some data on validity. Scores correlated with nurses' ratings of children's general level of fear and nervousness during hospitalization. | Instrument lacks specificity. The faces format has been found to be insensitive and unstable in assessing children's fears. |
| Children's Manifest Anxiety Scale | Castaneda, McCandless, and Palermo (1956) | General | Cognitive | Good test–retest reliability for up to a month. Scores relate to learning task errors and to behavior problems. No relationship with teachers' ratings and IQ measures. | Normative data available for a variety of child groups. Items lack situational specificity. Could be used as a rough screening device for generalized treatment effect and cross-situational cognitive strategies. |
| Children's Manifest Anxiety Scale—Revised | Reynolds and Richmond (1978) | General | Cognitive | Internal consistency adequate. Temporal stability and validity data lacking. | Revised scale lessens administration time, increases clarity of items, and lowers the reading level. Suitable for primary-grade children. Limitations and potential utility same as for Children's Manifest Anxiety Scale |
| Fear Survey Schedule for Children | Scherer and Nakamura (1968) | General | Motor | Good internal consistency and temporal stability. Correlates with Children's Manifest Anxiety Scale and physiological measures. | Utility as a screening measure and for assessing generalization effects. By combining items and expanding certain fear categories, instrument can be used to assess specific fear. |

More detailed descriptions might increase predictive validity.

| Measure | Reference | Fear situation | Response system | Reliability/validity | Comments |
|---|---|---|---|---|---|
| Fear Thermometer | Kelley (1976) | Darkness | Motor | No data on temporal stability. Low negative relationship with BAT. | Simple to administer; may need to be increased beyond five scoring categories in order to achieve adequate sensitivity for detection of change. |
| | Melamed, Yurcheson, Fleece, Hutcherson, and Hawes (1978) | Dental treatment | Motor | High temporal stability and significant correlations with Fear Survey Schedule for Children and observational ratings. | Administration simple; interpretation of scores straightforward. Research on its utility with other target behaviors needed. |
| General Anxiety Scale for Children | Sarason, Davidson, Lighthall, Waite, and Ruebush (1960) | General | Cognitive | No reliability data available. Positive correlations with Test Anxiety Scale for Children. Low negative correlations with IQ and achievement measures. | Items lack detail and specificity. Potentially useful as a screening procedure and for assessing cross-situational cognitive style. |
| Global Self-Ratings | Glennon and Weisz (1978) | Separation | Motor | No adequate reliability and validity data. No relationship with other self-report, observational, and performance measures. | Not recommended. |
| Hospital Fears Rating Scale | Melamed and Siegel (1975) | Hospitalization/surgery | Motor | No within-group changes across measurement periods. Not related to physiological measures and behavioral observation scores. | Not recommended at this time. |

(continued)

TABLE 4 (continued)

| Title | Reference | Fear | Channel | Reliability/validity | Comments |
|---|---|---|---|---|---|
| Human Figure Drawing | Melamed and Siegel (1975) | Surgery | Cognitive | Interrater agreements excellent. No relationship with measures of motor and physiological channels and other estimates of the cognitive channel. Not sensitive to treatment. | Not recommended. |
| Louisville Fear Survey Schedule | Miller, Barrett, Hampe, and Noble (1972) | General | Motor | Internal consistency high. Data lacking on temporal stability and validity. Little congruence between child's ratings and parents' observations of level of fear. | Potentially useful for screening and assessment of generalization effects. Possibly useful for assessment of specific fears by combining related items and describing items in greater detail. |
| Memory for Objects | Radaker (1961) | None (imagery) | Cognitive | Test–retest reliability adequate. Scores related to Memory for Word Forms and to Memory for Designs. | Employed exclusively with retarded children. |
| Personal Report of Confidence as a Speaker | Paul (1966); Cradock, Cotler, and Jason (1978); Johnson, Tyler, Thompson, and Jones (1971) | Public speaking | Motor | Acceptable reliability and relationship to other measures. | Employed primarily with adults. Norms not available. Easy to administer and interpret. Provides detailed information on fear of public speaking. |

| Measure | Author (year) | Stimulus | Type | Reliability/Validity | Comments |
|---|---|---|---|---|---|
| Snake Attitude Measure | Kornhaber and Schroeder (1975) | Snakes | Motor | No data on temporal stability, but children in a no-treatment control condition exhibited small mean change scores for an unknown time interval. Scores correlate highly with BAT. | Administration and scoring of responses relatively simple. Employed only with second- and third-grade girls. Norms not available. More data needed on sensitivity. |
| State–Trait Anxiety Inventory for Children | Spielberger (1973) | General | Cognitive | Good reliability. Negative correlations with verbal IQ, aptitude, and achievement; positive correlations with school grades and Children's Manifest Anxiety Scale. Scores change as a function of stress and other anxiety producing stimuli. | Possibly useful as preliminary screening device or for assessment of generalization effect and cross-situational cognitive styles. |
| Test Anxiety Scale for Children | Sarason, Davidson, Lighthall, Waite, and Ruebush (1960) | Test | Cognitive | Good reliability. Some data on construct validity. | Not widely employed by behavior therapists because of lack of specificity. Slight modifications may make the scale useful. |
| Tri-Modal Imagery Scale | Bergan and Macchiavello (Note 8) | None (imagery) | Cognitive | Internal consistency high. Correlates with reaching achievement. | Used only with fourth-grade children. |
| Visual Imagery Index | Radaker (1961) | None (imagery) | Cognitive | Good test–retest reliability over 2-week period. No data on relationship with other instruments. | Used exclusively with mentally retarded children. |

situations adequately. For example, an item on the Children's Manifest Anxiety Scale states "I often worry about something bad happening to me." Identifying situations, such as school, going to the zoo, being alone, and interacting with peers, would yield information as to the generality and antecedents of the child's concerns. A related shortcoming associated with the instruments is their failure to identify the specific nature of the cognitive concerns. Terms such as "worry" and "think a lot about" do not pinpoint the cognitive stimuli, such as catastrophizing self-verbalizations or images, which may occur.

It appears that behavior therapists will continue to employ these instruments despite the aforementioned limitations (Wade, Baker, & Hartmann, 1979), primarily because they are economical of cost, effort, and time and provide data that are easily quantified. Modified versions of the instruments may provide information that is of some utility to child behavior assessors. However, a more profitable approach would seem to lie in abandoning these traditional measures and developing cognitive assessment devices that more nearly meet our needs.

Meichenbaum (1976) has suggested some procedures for assessing cognitions that child behavior assessors might find useful. Among these are self-monitoring, "talking out loud" when engaging in performance tests such as the BAT, viewing videotapes of performance and recalling cognitions present at that time, role playing, and imagery methods. Slight modifications in performance tests can generate valuable information concerning cognitions (Barrios, Note 6). For example, having the child "think out loud" during role-play tasks or vocalizing self-statements while imagining an approach to some feared stimulus may aid in identifying performance-debilitating cognitions (Smith & Sharpe, 1970). In their review of methods for assessing cognitions, Kendall and Korgeski (1979) examine seven approaches. Most of the measures that they review have been designed for use with adults, although they may be adapted for use with children. One promising approach is the *in vivo* thought-sampling technique operationalized by Klinger (1978). A subject carries a portable beeper; at varying intervals the device beeps, and the subject records his or her cognitions. The utility of the *in vivo* thought-sampling technique and of others proposed for use with children warrants investigation.

The ability to summon clear mental images of anxiety-arousing stimuli is a major skill requirement for the application of systematic desensitization and some cognitive-behavior modification techniques. The three instruments described in this section and several of those employed with adults seem promising for the assessment of children's imagery. Perhaps the major reason for the paucity of data on imagery assessment procedures is the infrequent application of imagery-based interventions with children. The reluctance on the part of child therapists to utilize imaginal techniques may be attributable, in part, to Tasto's (1969) report of a 4-year-old boy's failure to comprehend imagery instructions. However, the child literature does include a number of cases of successful use of imagery with children (Lazarus & Abramovitz, 1962; Rose, 1972; Smith & Sharpe, 1970).

Behavior assessors might also direct their attention to other cognitive issues that relate to the acquisition, maintenance, and modification of anxious behavior. These issues include children's expectations of treatment, their comprehension of assessment, and their perceptions of their competency and skill levels of the contingencies operating in the environment, as well as of the consequences associated with various behaviors (Bandura, 1977, 1980). To obtain accurate and reliable measures of these cognitive variables, the verbal demands of the assessment procedure should be congruent with the language abilities of the children.

As Kendall and Korgeski (1979) point out, the assessment of cognitions serves two functions. First, it enables assessors to examine the role that cognitions play in the acquisition and maintenance of fear and anxiety. Second, assessment of cognitions permits us to test the validity of techniques designed to alter cognitions. If these functions are to be served adequately, the assessment procedures must provide accurate data. Because of the inherent difficulties involved in studying covert phenomena, progress in this area may be gradual. Nevertheless, continued efforts are likely to prove fruitful for the understanding and development of effective interventions for the treatment of children's fears and anxieties.

## Physiological Components of Fear and Anxiety

Assessment of the physiological components of anxiety and fear involves substantial time, energy, and resources. Considerable expertise in the design of physiological assessment and in the selection and use of appropriate electrodes, transducers, and recording equipment is required. Unless the behavior assessor is well versed in the complexities of psychophysiology, misleading or erroneous conclusions may be reached.

Early behavioral research employing physiological measures adhered to a unidimensional theory of arousal. Physiological anxiety assessment assumed that peripheral physiological measures provided a straightforward index of a massive and diffuse sympathetic arousal that serves to energize the overt responses of anxiety and to determine the cognitive experience of fearfulness. Conceptions of arousal as a unidimensional continuum (Cannon, 1915; Duffy, 1962) are being modified to accommodate an increasing number of studies that fail to find reliable monolithic indicants of arousal. Johnson and Lubin (1972) point out that no single measure or combination of measures has been found that reliably relates to arousal across subjects or situations. The Laceys (Lacey, 1959; Lacey & Lacey, 1967) have provided evidence critical of the unidimensional conception of arousal, demonstrating repeatedly that complex and specific patterns of autonomic responses are elicited by specific stress stimuli. This accumulation of information strongly suggests that anxiety assessment should use more than one physiological measure.

Several psychophysiological principles and issues limit the utility of a simple stimulus–response arousal model of physiological responding. Among these are the Law of Initial Values (Wilder, 1950), adaptation (Lang, 1971), the orienting response (Sokolov, 1963), and the duration of response measurement (Averill & Opton, 1968). Extensive discussion of these and other aspects of physiological measurement are beyond the scope of this chapter. Those seeking such information should consult one of the several psychophysiological texts or handbooks (Brown,

1967; Greenfield & Sternbach, 1972; Prokasy & Raskin, 1973; Venables & Martin, 1967).

### Physiological Measures

Although there are many measures of physiological arousal, this section will be confined to a review of heart rate and electrodermal responses, which are the most frequently monitored physiological responses for fear and anxiety assessment.

Heart rate can be continuously monitored preceding and during presentations of feared stimuli. Anxiety-provoking stimuli can be presented *in vivo*, in fantasy, by means of imagery, and pictorially or auditorially through slide projections, videotapes, or audio recordings. The various presentation media influence heart rate through the cognitive and motor demands of the setting. Thus, comparison conditions involving low-fear stimuli should be included to control for these effects.

Although few investigations have assessed the physiological response component of children's fears and anxiety reactions, there is a handful of studies that illustrate the feasibility and importance of measuring these responses. In an investigation of children's responses to injections, Shapiro (1975) monitored anticipatory heart rate in addition to measuring behavioral and self-reported fear. Shapiro (1975) found that self-report and behavioral ratings interacted with heart rate changes. An increase in self-reported needle avoidance on the day children were to receive their injections coincided with heart rate increases; the lower the preinjection heart rate, the less avoidance behavior (e.g., crying, screaming) emitted during needle penetration.

Melamed *et al.* (1978) monitored children's heart rate during the viewing of various modeling films designed to reduce their anxiety associated with dental treatment. Unfortunately, Melamed and her colleagues did not report correlations between heart rate during film viewing and additional behavioral and self-report measures that were collected.

Electrodermal responses are highly active and complex and are influenced by a host of environmental and psychological variables. For example, electrodermal responses are extremely sensitive to novel and interesting stimuli (Raskin, 1973; Sokolov, 1963), thus large responses will occur with almost any stimulus when it is first presented. The intricacies of this response are far too great to cover adequately in this chapter. Readers who are interested in acquiring expertise in the measurement of electrodermal responses should consult the excellent reviews of this literature (Edelberg, 1972; Prokasy & Raskin, 1973; Venables & Martin, 1967).

As with heart rate, very few investigations have measured electrodermal responses of children to feared stimuli. The investigations by Shapiro (1975) and Melamed (Melamed *et al.*, 1978; Melamed & Siegel, 1975) are notable exceptions. In the Shapiro (1975) investigation already discussed, tape bands were applied to the child's left-hand index finger for 3 minutes, and the darkness of the fingerprint was judged on a ten-point scale by two independent raters. Although the procedure has excellent interrater reliability, its validity must be questioned in view of its exceptional sensitivity to nonemotional sources of sweat production. Shapiro (1975) discovered that finger sweat and ambient temperature were highly related, and a sizable proportion of the variance in finger sweat scores could be accounted for by temperature. This finding illustrates one hazard of collecting physiological measures in the natural environment and the need to be sensitive to the variables that influence responding.

Melamed and her colleagues (Melamed *et al.*, 1975, 1978; Melamed & Siegel, 1975) have employed the Palmar Sweat Index (e.g., Johnson & Dabbs, 1967). This index involves use of a plastic impression method that permits quantification of sweat gland activity of the hand. Interrater reliabilities are very satisfactory (*r* values in the middle .90s), and electrodermal responses correlated significantly with children's general fears and specific dental fears as reported on the Children's Fear Survey Schedule (Melamed *et al.*, 1978).

### Discussion

Assessment of the physiological component of fear and anxiety requires careful selection and interpretation of measures. Assessors must be alert to stimulus and situation demands, response stereotypy, and stimulus complexity, novelty, and cognitive difficulty. Physiological assessment of children poses additional difficulties. For example, many children may find it difficult to remain stationary during recording of physiological responses. The movement artifacts produced can be reduced by conducting several habituation sessions prior to actual data-gathering sessions. Alternatively, the artifacts can be measured and their effects removed from the data (Fehr, 1970).

Because very few investigations of children's fears have employed physiological measures, relatively little is known of the effects that such features as the laboratory setting, ambient noise, and instructional set have upon physiological responding. In a study of the effects of instructional set on physiological response to stressful imagery, Beiman (1976) found that the expectancies of fearful female college students influenced their physiological responses to aversive stimuli. In light of the results of the Kelley (1976) study, which found children's performance on behavioral tests to be easily manipulated by instructions, it appears likely that children's physiological responses also would be influenced by expectancy effects.

Assessment of the physiological response component of children's fears presents a challenge to behavior therapists. Availability of equipment and access to the child may dictate which method is to be employed. Self-report instruments can be used in cases in which equipment is not conveniently available. Inventories such as the Autonomic Perception Questionnaire (Mandler, Mandler, & Uviller, 1958) may be modified for use with children. Self-monitoring of certain physiological responses may also have some value. For example, children could be taught to take their own pulse and thus provide heart rate data for a variety of situations such as test taking and public speaking. Telemetry devices (Evans & Nelson, 1977; Wolffe, 1967) have been cited as offering the greatest assessment possibilities because they permit unobtrusive measurement in a wide range of situations and avoid the difficulties associated with laboratory measures. The use of telemetric devices in research efforts appears promising; its clinical utility has yet to be examined. The sweat bottle method (Strahan, Todd, & Inglis, 1974), a simple measure of palmar sweating applicable for naturalistic research, represents an additional instrument that may be well suited for assessment of children's fears.

Some readers may question the inclusion of physiological measures in the assessment of children's fears and anxiety. Because most of the current interventions focus on either the motor or cognitive components, assessment of physiological responses might seem superfluous. There are, however, instances in which appropriate motor behavior and self-statements are emitted but in which the child experiences distressful levels of autonomic arousal (Lang, 1978). In cases such as those, physiological assessment becomes critical.

## SUMMARY AND RECOMMENDATIONS

A prominent emphasis in behavior therapy is the intimate relationship between assessment and intervention (e.g., Bandura, 1969; Kanfer & Phillips, 1970). The treatment-related aspects of behavior assessment include selection of the target behavior, elaboration of the problem and its context in order to select a treatment technique, and evaluation of treatment effects, both during and after treatment. Presumably, information about the child, the problem behavior, the circumstances under which the problem occurs, and other variables, such as age norms and likely prognosis, would enable one to determine whether treatment is warranted, and if so, to select the specific target, the optimal treatment technique, and the primary and collateral dependent variables. Unfortunately, reality falls short of this ideal. There is no generally accepted model for selecting target and treatment, so decisions are often based on clinical impression or availability of technique (Ciminero & Drabman, 1977; Mash & Terdal, 1976). Only in developing a technology for measuring dependent variables and evaluating effectiveness have behavior assessors achieved reasonable success (Hartmann, Roper, & Bradford, 1979).

### Need for a Target and Treatment Selection Model

Several conditions contribute to this problem. First, assessors do not have a functional or generally accepted classification system for children's fears, although a number of frameworks have been proposed (e.g., Miller et al., 1974). Classification is no doubt made difficult by idiosyncrasies in the topography and interrelationship of children's fearful and anxious behaviors. Although motor, cognitive, and physiological responses apparently are not independent (Hodgson & Rachman, 1974; Rachman & Hodgson, 1974; Sartory, Rachman, & Grey, 1977), substantial disagreement exists over the specific form of their organization (Bandura, 1969, 1977, 1978; Lang, 1971).

Second, according to Marks (1977) and Graziano et al. (1979), none of the theoretical models proposed to explain the acquisition and maintenance of fear and anxiety is sufficiently comprehensive to provide a complete understanding of the cultural, interpersonal, and constitutional factors that may be relevant to these behavior disorders. Marks discusses seven aspects of naturally occurring fearful and anxious behaviors that are not well explained by current models. These include (1) selection of the phobic stimulus, (2) individual differences in susceptibility, (3) maturational changes, (4) physiological controlling variables, (5) social influences, (6) the role of trauma, and (7) the association of fears with other psychological disturbances. Although more work is required in this area, consideration of currently prominent models may nonetheless aid in the assessment process.

The utility of some conceptual models may derive largely from the insight they provide regarding the onset or origin of fearful or anxious behavior. One such model is the prepotency or preparedness model recently described by Marks (1969) and Seligman (1971). According to this theory, some stimuli (e.g., snakes, spiders, dogs, and heights) may "act as a magnet for phobias" (Marks, 1977, p. 194), whereas other stimuli (e.g., wooden ducks, macaroni, and shoelaces) apparently are less likely to acquire the capacity to elicit fears. The recent work of Öhman and his colleagues (Fredrikson & Öhman, 1979; Hugdahl, Fredrikson, & Öhman, 1977; Öhman, Fredrikson, & Hugdahl, 1978) has demonstrated the accuracy of preparedness theory in predicting differential rates in resistance to conditioning and in extinguishing emotional responses to various stimuli.

Other models may sensitize assessors to critical information that otherwise may be overlooked. The imitation learning model, for example, may direct attention to the fearful behavior of the parents and siblings of phobic children. Research has supported some of these theoretically derived expectations. For example, May (1950) found substantial correlations between self-reported fears in siblings, and Hagman (1932) described a high positive relationship between self-reported fears in children and their mothers. The cognitive–mediational model may alert us to images and self-statements involved in the acquisition and maintenance of avoidance behavior (Wade, Malloy, & Proctor, 1977). The frequently overlooked role of autonomic nervous system activity may receive greater attention as a result of physiological-based models (Costello, 1971; Lader & Mathews, 1968). A chronic state of overarousal is associated with certain phobic disorders. Explorations of the physiological processes of arousal and habituation in children may provide assessors with valuable information regarding the prevention of fears.

The most important function of conceptual models for treatment-oriented behavior assessors is the role of these models in treatment planning. Lick and Katkin (1976), for example, proposed three models that have treatment-related implications: the S-R, or classical conditioning, model; the cognitive–mediational model; and the response–reinforcement model. Of course, in any particular case of anxiety or fear, a combination of models may be applicable. For example, a child's fear of dogs might have started with a traumatic encounter with a large and snarling beast, but it may be maintained by reassurance, comfort, and other forms of attention from the parents or by self-generated images and self-statements. Furthermore, the theoretical basis for originally developing a technique may not be valid and thus not aid in selecting the treatment. For example, systematic desensitization, originally interpreted as counterconditioning, has been given other conceptual interpretations (Gambrill, 1977; Rimm & Masters, 1974). Despite the inadequacies of existing models, we believe that their use can facilitate assessment conducted with fearful and anxious children.

Third, a target and treatment selection model would require more reliable and valid assessment data than are currently available. Most devices for assessing children's fears or anxiety, whether in the motor, cognitive, or physiological domains, are unstandardized, lack norms, and have inadequately evaluated reliability and validity. Relatively little is known about the consistency of children's performance across repeated assessment or across settings (e.g., between performance in laboratory settings and in the child's usual life settings) or about the degree of correspondence between measures within or across domains.

In addition to these common problems, each type of measurement has its unique difficulties. For example, most self-report procedures are based on trait assumptions and hence lack the level of specificity required for most behavior assessment purposes. Both the cognitive and physiological domains have gone largely unexplored by behavior assessors. The former requires extensive test construction efforts, whereas the latter necessitates adaptation of adult procedures to children. Behavioral assessors might also profit from other work performed on fearful and anxious adults. Investigations of adults suggest that cognitive variables play an important role in the etiology and treatment of fears and anxieties (Arkowitz, 1977; Mahoney, 1977; Twentyman, Boland, & McFall, Note 7). As a result, greater attention is being devoted to the assessment of cognitions (Kendall & Korgeski, 1979). It is not the assessment variables alone that are changing; assessment techniques also have a new look. Behavioral assessors are abandoning their longstanding practice of being guided by common sense and clinical judgment in determining questionnaire items, role-playing situations, and response scoring methods. Increasing numbers of assessment instruments (Glass, Gottman, & Shmurak, 1976; Goldsmith & McFall, 1975; Perri, Richards, & Goodrich, 1978) are being constructed according to the behavior-analytic strategy outlined by Goldfried and D'Zurilla (1969).

Fourth, research that would enable us to predict a child's response to treatment on the basis of problem, setting, and child variables is lacking (Ciminero & Drabman, 1977; Evans & Nelson, 1977; Hersen, 1971). Continued reliance on single-subject investigations in which treatment failures tend not to be reported and information may not be systematically accumulated over several cases may very well delay the discovery of person by treatment interactions. The adoption of group factorial designs may be necessary to answer these questions.

At this time, the utility of assessment is not easy to evaluate (Evans & Nelson, 1977). Nevertheless, our working assumption is that the assessment of children's fearful and anxious behavior is valuable—that a thorough and objective formulation of these problems substantially facilitates resolving them.

## Reference Notes

1. Dunlop, G. *Certain aspects of children's fears.* Unpublished master's thesis, University of North Carolina, Raleigh, 1952.
2. Graham, P. *Controlled trial of behavior therapy vs. conventional therapy: A pilot study.* Unpublished D.P.M. dissertation, University of London, 1964.
3. Peterson, L., & Shigetomi, C. *The use of a self-control procedure to minimize pain and anxiety in hospitalized children.* Unpublished manuscript, University of Utah, 1978.
4. Brown, M. *A set of eight parallel forms of the digit symbol test.* Unpublished set of tests, University of Waterloo, 1969.
5. Wade, T. C. *Multitrait, multimethod analysis of imagery assessment.* Unpublished manuscript, University of Utah, 1976.
6. Barrios, B. A. *The cognitive revolution: Implications for behavioral assessment and intervention.* Unpublished manuscript, University of Utah, 1978.
7. Twentyman, C. T., Boland, T., & McFall, R. M. *Five studies exploring the problem of heterosocial avoidance in college males.* Unpublished manuscript, State University of New York at Binghamton, 1978.
8. Bergan, J. R., & Macchiavello, A. *Visual imagery and reading achievement.* Paper presented at American Education Research Association, Chicago, 1966.

## References

Agras, S., Sylvester, D., & Oliveau, D. The epidemiology of common fears and phobias. *Comprehensive Psychiatry*, 1969, *10*, 151–156.

Agras, W. S., Chapin, H. N., & Oliveau, D. C. The natural history of phobia. *Archives of General Psychiatry*, 1972, *26*, 315–317.

Ainsworth, M. D. The development of infant–mother attachment. In A. Caldwell & H. Ricciuti (Eds.), *Review of child development research* (Vol. 3). Chicago: University of Chicago Press, 1973.

Angelino, H., Dollins, J., & Mech, E. V. Trends in the "fears and worries" of school children as related to socio-economic status and age. *The Journal of Genetic Psychology*, 1956, *89*, 263–276.

Arkowitz, H. Measurement and modification of minimal dating behavior. In M. Hersen, R. M. Eisler, & P. M. Miller (Eds.), *Progress in behavior modification* (Vol. 5). New York: Academic Press, 1977.

Averill, J. R., & Opton, E. M. Psychophysiological assessment: Rationale and problems. In P. R. McReynolds (Ed.), *Advances in psychological assessment* (Vol. 1). Palo Alto, Calif.: Science and Behavior Books, 1968.

Bandura, A. *Principles of behavior modification.* New York: Holt, Rinehart & Winston, 1969.

Bandura, A. *Social learning theory.* Englewood Cliffs, N.J.: Prentice-Hall, 1977.

Bandura, A. Reflections on self-efficacy. *Advances in Behaviour Research and Therapy*, 1978, *1*, 237–269.

Bandura, A. Self-referent thought: The development of self-efficacy. In J. H. Flavell & L. D. Ross (Eds.), *Development of social cognition.* New York: Prentice-Hall, 1980.

Bandura, A., Grusec, E., & Menlove, F. L. Vicarious extinction of avoidance behavior. *Journal of Personality and Social Psychology*, 1967, *5*, 16–23.

Bauer, D. An exploratory study of developmental changes in children's fears. *Journal of Child Psychology and Psychiatry*, 1976, *17*, 69–74.

Beiman, I. The effects of instructional set on physiological response to stressful imagery. *Behaviour Research and Therapy*, 1976, *14*, 175–179.

Berecz, J. M. Phobias of childhood: Etiology and treatment. *Psychological Bulletin*, 1968, *70*, 694–720.

Bernstein, D. A., & Nietzel, M. T. Procedural variation in behavioral avoidance tests. *Journal of Consulting and Clinical Psychology*, 1973, *41*, 165–174.

Bernstein, D. A., & Paul, G. L. Some comments on therapy analogue research with small animal "phobias." *Journal of Behavior Therapy and Experimental Psychiatry*, 1971, *2*, 225–237.

Borkovec, T. D., & Craighead, W. E. The comparison of two methods of assessing fear and avoidance behavior. *Behaviour Research and Therapy*, 1971, *9*, 285–291.

Borkovec, T. D., Weerts, T. C., & Bernstein, D. A. Assessment of anxiety. In A. R. Ciminero, K. S. Calhoun, & H. E. Adams (Eds.), *Handbook of behavioral assessment*. New York: Wiley, 1977.

Bowlby, J. *Separation and loss*. New York: Basic Books, 1973.

Brown, C. C. (Ed.). *Methods in psychophysiology*. Baltimore: Williams & Wilkins, 1967.

Cannon, W. B. *Bodily changes in pain, hunger, fear and rage*. New York: Appleton-Century-Crofts, 1915.

Castaneda, A., McCandless, B. R., & Palermo, D. S. The children's form of the manifest anxiety scale. *Child Development*, 1956, *27*, 317–326.

Chess, S., & Hassibi, M. *Principles and practice of child psychiatry*. New York: Plenum, 1978.

Ciminero, A. R., Doleys, D. M., & Williams, C. L. Journal literature on behavior therapy 1970–1976: Analysis of the subject characteristics, target behaviors, and treatment techniques. *Journal of Behavior Therapy and Experimental Psychiatry*, 1978, *9*, 301–307.

Ciminero, A. R., & Drabman, R. S. Current developments in the behavioral assessment of children. In B. B. Lahey & A. E. Kazdin (Eds.), *Advances in clinical child psychology* (Vol. 1). New York: Plenum, 1977.

Clevanger, T., & King, T. R. A factor analysis of the visible symptoms of stage fright. *Speech Monographs*, 1961, *28*, 296–298.

Cone, J. D. The behavioral assessment grid (BAG): A conceptual framework and taxonomy. *Behavior Therapy*, 1978, *9*, 882–888.

Costello, C. G. Anxiety and the persisting novelty of input from the autonomic nervous system. *Behavior Therapy*, 1971, *2*, 321–333.

Cradock, C., Cotler, S., & Jason, L. A. Primary prevention: Immunization of children for speech anxiety. *Cognitive Therapy and Research*, 1978, *2*, 389–396.

Crider, B. Phobias: Their nature and treatment. *Journal of Psychology*, 1949, *27*, 217–229.

Croake, J. W., & Knox, F. H. The changing nature of children's fears. *Child Study Journal*, 1973, *3*, 91–105.

Cummings, J. D. The incidence of emotional symptoms in school children. *British Journal of Educational Psychology*, 1944, *14*, 151–161.

Cummings, J. D. A follow-up study of emotional symptoms in school children. *British Journal of Educational Psychology*, 1946, *16*, 163–177.

Dorkey, M., & Amen, E. W. A continuation study of anxiety reactions in young children by means of a projective technique. *Genetic Psychology Monographs*, 1947, *35*, 139–183.

Duffy, E. *Activation and behavior*. New York: Wiley, 1962.

Edelberg, R. Electrical activity of the skin: Its measurement and uses in psychophysiology. In N. S. Greenfield & R. A. Sternbach (Eds.), *Handbook of psychophysiology*. New York: Holt, Rinehart & Winston, 1972.

Eisenberg, L. School phobia: A study in the communication of anxiety. *American Journal of Psychiatry*, 1958, *114*, 712–718.

Eisler, R. M., Miller, P. M., & Hersen, M. Components of assertive behavior. *Journal of Clinical Psychology*, 1973, *29*, 295–299.

Evans, I. M., & Nelson, R. O. Assessment of child behavior problems. In A. R. Ciminero, K. S. Calhoun, & H. E. Adams (Eds.), *Handbook of behavioral assessment*. New York: Wiley, 1977.

Fehr, F. S. A simple method for assessing body movement and potential artifacts in the physiological recording of young children. *Psychophysiology*, 1970, *7*, 787–789.

Fredrikson, M., & Öhman, A. Cardiovascular and electrodermal responses conditioned to fear-relevant stimuli. *Psychophysiology*, 1979, *16*, 1–7.

Freeman, B. J., Roy, R. R., & Hemmick, S. Extinction of a phobia of physical examination in a seven-year-old mentally retarded boy—A case study. *Behaviour Research and Therapy*, 1976, *14*, 63–64.

Freud, S. Analysis of a phobia in a five-year-old boy. *Complete psychological works* (Vol. 10). London: Hogarth Press, 1962.

Gambrill, E. D. *Behavior modification: Handbook of assessment, intervention, and evaluation*. San

Francisco: Jossey-Bass, 1977.

Gelfand, D. M. Behavioral treatment of avoidance, social withdrawal and negative emotional states. In B. B. Wolman, J Egan, & A. O. Ross (Eds.), *Handbook of treatment of mental disorders in childhood and adolescence*. Englewood Cliffs, N.J.: Prentice-Hall, 1978.

Gelfand, D. M., & Hartmann, D. P. *Child behavior: Analysis and therapy*. New York: Pergamon, 1975.

Gentry, W. D., & Williams, R. B. (Eds.). *Behavioral approaches to medical practice*. Cambridge, Mass.: Ballinger, 1977.

Gewirtz, J. L. Mechanisms of social learning: Some roles of stimulation and behavior in early human development. In D. A. Goslin (Ed.), *Handbook of socialization theory and research*. Chicago: Rand McNally, 1969.

Glass, C. R., Gottman, J. M., & Shmurak, S. H. Response acquisition and cognitive self-statement modification approaches to dating skills training. *Journal of Counseling Psychology*, 1976, *23*, 520–526.

Glennon, B., & Weisz, J. R. An observational approach to the assessment of anxiety in young children. *Journal of Consulting and Clinical Psychology*, 1978, *46*, 1246–1257.

Glover, E. *On the early development of mind*. New York: International Universities Press, 1956.

Goldfried, M. R., & D'Zurilla, T. J. A behavior-analytic model for assessing competence. In C. D. Spielberger (Ed.), *Current topics in clinical and community psychology* (Vol. 1). New York: Academic Press, 1969.

Goldsmith, J. B., & McFall, R. M. Development and evaluation of an interpersonal skill-training program for psychiatric inpatients. *Journal of Abnormal Psychology*, 1975, *84*, 51–58.

Graziano, A. M. Reduction of children's fear. In A. M. Graziano (Ed.), *Behavior therapy with children* (Vol. 2). Chicago: Aldine, 1975.

Graziano, A. M., & DeGiovanni, I. S. The clinical significance of childhood phobias: A note on the proportion of child-clinical referrals for the treatment of children's fears. *Behaviour Research and Therapy*, 1979, *17*, 161–162.

Graziano, A. M., DeGiovanni, I. S., & Garcia, K. A. Behavioral treatment of children's fears: A review. *Psychological Bulletin*, 1979, *86*, 804–830.

Greenfield, N. S., & Sternbach, R. A. (Eds.). *Handbook of psychophysiology*. New York: Holt, Rinehart & Winston, 1972.

Hagman, E. R. A study of fears of children of pre-school age. *Journal of Experimental Education*, 1932, *1*, 110–130.

Hampe, E., Noble, H., Miller, L. C., & Barrett, C. L. Phobic children one and two years posttreatment. *Journal of Abnormal Psychology*, 1973, *82*, 446–453.

Harris, B. Whatever happened to Little Albert? *American Psychologist*, 1979, *34*, 151–160.

Hartmann, D. P., Roper, B. L., & Bradford, D. C. Some relationships between behavioral and traditional assessment. *Journal of Behavioral Assessment*, 1979, *1*, 3–21.

Hatzenbuehler, L. C., & Schroeder, H. E. Desensitization procedures in the treatment of childhood disorders. *Psychological Bulletin*, 1978, *85*, 831–844.

Hebb, D. O. On the nature of fear. *Psychological Review*, 1946, *53*, 259–276.

Hersen, M. The behavioral treatment of school phobia. *Journal of Nervous and Mental Disease*, 1971, *153*, 99–107.

Hill, J. H., Liebert, R. M., & Mott, D. E. W. Vicarious extinction of avoidance behavior through films: An initial test. *Psychological Reports*, 1968, *22*, 192.

Hiscock, M. Imagery assessment through self-report: What do imagery questionnaires measure? *Journal of Consulting and Clinical Psychology*, 1978, *46*, 223–230.

Hodgson, R., & Rachman, S. II. Desynchrony in measures of fear. *Behaviour Research and Therapy*, 1974, *12*, 319–326.

Holmes, F. B. An experimental study of the fears of young children. In A. T. Jersild & F. B. Holmes (Eds.), *Child Development Monograph* No. 20. Chicago: University of Chicago Press, 1935.

Horner, M. S. Sex differences in achievement motivation and performance in competitive and non-competitive situations (Doctoral dissertation, University of Michigan, 1968). *Dissertation Abstracts International*, 1969, *30*, 407 8. (University Microfilms No. 60-12, 135)

Hugdahl, K., Fredrikson, M., & Öhman, A. "Preparedness" and "arousability" as determinants of electrodermal conditioning. *Behaviour Research and Therapy*, 1977, *15*, 345–353.

Jersild, A. T. Emotional development. In L. Carmichael (Ed.), *Manual of child psychology* (2nd ed.). New York: Wiley, 1954.

Jersild, A. T., & Holmes, F. B. Children's fears. *Child Development Monograph*, 1935, No. 20.

Johnson, L. C., & Lubin, A. On planning psychophysical experiments: Design, measurement, and analysis. In N. S. Greenfield & R. A. Sternbach (Eds.), *Handbook of psychophysiology*. New York: Holt, Rinehart & Winston, 1972.

Johnson, O. G., & Bommarito, J. W. *Tests and measurements in child development: A handbook*. San Francisco: Jossey-Bass, 1971.

Johnson, R., & Dabbs, J. M. Enumeration of active sweat glands: A simple physiological indicator of psychological changes. *Nursing Research*, 1967, *16*, 273–276.

Johnson, S. B., & Melamed, B. G. The assessment and treatment of children's fears. In B. B. Lahey & A. E. Kazdin (Eds.), *Advances in clinical child psychology* (Vol. 2). New York: Plenum, 1979.

Johnson, T., Tyler, V., Thompson, R., & Jones, E. Systematic desensitization and assertive training in the treatment of speech anxiety in middle-school students. *Psychology in the Schools*, 1971, *8*, 263–267.

Jones, E. *Sigmund Freud: Life and work* (Vol. 2). London: Hogarth Press, 1955.

Jones, H. E., & Jones, M. C. Fear. *Childhood Education*, 1928, *5*, 136–143.

Jones, M. C. A laboratory study of fear: The case of Peter. *Pedagogical Seminary*, 1924, *31*, 308–315.

Kanfer, F. H., & Goldstein, A. P. Introduction. In F. H. Kanfer & A. P. Goldstein (Eds.), *Helping people change*. New York: Pergamon, 1975.

Kanfer, F. H., Karoly, P., & Newman, A. Reduction of children's fear of the dark by competence-related and situational threat-related verbal cues. *Journal of Consulting and Clinical Psychology*, 1975, *43*, 251–258.

Kanfer, F. H., & Phillips, J. S. *Learning foundations of behavior therapy*. New York: Wiley, 1970.

Kanfer, F. H., & Saslow, G. Behavioral diagnosis. In C. M. Franks (Ed.), *Behavior therapy: Appraisal and status*. New York: McGraw-Hill, 1969.

Kanner, L. *Child psychiatry*. Springfield, Ill.: Charles C. Thomas, 1957.

Kanner, L. Do behavior symptoms always indicate psychopathology? *Journal of Child Psychology and Psychiatry*, 1960, *1*, 17–25.

Karoly, P. Operant methods. In F. H. Kanfer & A. P. Goldstein (Eds.), *Helping people change*. New York: Pergamon, 1975.

Kazdin, A. E. The effect of suggestion and pretesting on avoidance reduction in fearful subjects. *Journal of Behavior Therapy and Experimental Psychiatry*, 1973, *4*, 213–222.

Kazdin, A. E. The effect of model identity and fear-relevant similarity on covert modeling. *Behavior Therapy*, 1974, *5*, 624–635.

Kazdin, A. E. Assessing the clinical or applied importance of behavior change through social validation. *Behavior Modification*, 1977, *1*, 427–452.

Kelley, C. K. Play desensitization of fear of darkness in preschool children. *Behaviour Research and Therapy*, 1976, *14*, 79–81.

Kendall, P. C., & Korgeski, G. P. Assessment and cognitive–behavioral interventions. *Cognitive Therapy and Research*, 1979, *3*, 1–22.

Kennedy, W. A. School phobia: Rapid treatment of fifty cases. *Journal of Abnormal Psychology*, 1965, *70*, 285–289.

Kent, R. N., & Foster, S. L. Direct observational procedures: Methodological issues in naturalistic settings. In A. R. Ciminero, K. S. Calhoun, & H. E. Adams (Eds.), *Handbook of behavioral assessment*. New York: Wiley, 1977.

Klinger, E. Modes of normal conscious flow. In K. S. Pope & J. L. Singer (Eds.), *The stream of consciousness: Scientific investigations into the flow of human experience*. New York: Plenum, 1978.

Klorman, R., Weerts, T. C., Hastings, J. E., Melamed, B. G., & Lang, P. J. Psychometric description of some specific-fear questionnaires. *Behavior Therapy*, 1974, *5*, 401–409.

Koppitz, E. M. *Psychological evaluation of children's human figure drawings*. New York: Grune &

Stratton, 1968.

Kornhaber, R. C., & Schroeder, H. E. Importance of model similarity on extinction of avoidance behavior in children. *Journal of Consulting and Clinical Psychology*, 1975, *43*, 601–607.

Kuroda, J. Elimination of children's fears of animals by the method of experimental desensitization: An application of learning theory to child psychology. *Psychologia: An International Journal of Psychology in the Orient*, 1969, *12*, 161–165.

Lacey, J. I. Psychophysiological approaches to the evaluation of psychotherapeutic process and outcome. In E. A. Rubinstein & M. B. Parloff (Eds.), *Research in psychotherapy.* Washington, D.C.: American Psychological Association, 1959.

Lacey, J. I., & Lacey, B. C. The law of initial value in the longitudinal study of autonomic constitution: Reproducibility of autonomic responses and response patterns over a four year interval. *Annals of the New York Academy of Sciences*, 1967, *38*, 1257–1290.

Lader, M. H., & Mathews, A. M. A physiological model of phobic anxiety and desensitization. *Behaviour Research and Therapy*, 1968, *6*, 411–421.

Lang, P. J. The application of psychophysiological methods to the study of psychotherapy and behavior modification. In A. E. Bergin & S. L. Garfield (Eds.), *Handbook of psychotherapy and behavior change: An empirical analysis.* New York: Wiley, 1971.

Lang, P. J. Self-efficacy theory: Thoughts on cognition and unification. *Advances in Behaviour Research and Therapy*, 1978, *1*, 187–192.

Lang, P. J., & Lazovik, A. D. Experimental desensitization of a phobia. *Journal of Abnormal and Social Psychology*, 1963, *66*, 519–525.

Lapouse, R., & Monk, M. A. Fears and worries in a representative sample of children. *American Journal of Orthopsychiatry*, 1959, *29*, 223–248.

Lazarus, A., & Abramovitz, A. The use of "emotive imagery" in the treatment of children's phobias. *Journal of Mental Science*, 1962, *108*, 191–195.

Leitenberg, H., & Callahan, E. J. Reinforced practice and reduction of different kinds of fears in adults and children. *Behaviour Research and Therapy*, 1973, *11*, 19–30.

Levis, D. J. The phobic test apparatus: An objective measure of human avoidance behavior to small objects. *Behaviour Research and Therapy*, 1969, *7*, 309–315.

Lewis, S. A comparison of behavior therapy techniques in the reduction of fearful avoidance behavior. *Behavior Therapy*, 1974, *5*, 648–655.

Lick, J. R., & Katkin, E. S. Assessment of anxiety and fear. In M. Hersen & A. S. Bellack (Eds.), *Behavioral assessment.* New York: Pergamon, 1976.

Lick, J. R. Sushinsky, L. W., & Malow, R. Specificity of fear survey schedule items and the prediction of avoidance behavior. *Behavior Modification*, 1977, *1*, 195–203.

Lick, J. R., & Unger, T. External validity of laboratory fear assessment: Implications from two case studies. *Journal of Consulting and Clinical Psychology*, 1975, *43*, 864–866.

Lick, J. R., & Unger, T. E. The external validity of behavioral fear assessment. *Behavior Modification*, 1977, *1*, 283–306.

Lick, J. R., Unger, T., & Condiotte, M. Effects of uncertainty about the behavior of a phobic stimulus on subjects' fear reactions. *Journal of Consulting and Clinical Psychology*, 1978, *46*, 1559–1560.

Lobitz, G. K., & Johnson, S. M. Normal versus deviant children: A multimethod comparison. *Journal of Abnormal Child Psychology*, 1975, *3*, 353–374.

MacFarlane, J., Allen, L., & Honzik, M. *A developmental study of the behavior problems of normal children.* Berkeley: University of California Press, 1954.

Mahoney, M. J. Reflections on the cognitive-learning trend in psychotherapy. *American Psychologist*, 1977, *32*, 5–13.

Mahoney, M. J., & Thoresen, C. E. *Self-control: Power to the person.* Monterey, Calif.: Brooks/Cole, 1974.

Mandler, G., Mandler, J. M., & Uviller, E. T. Autonomic feedback: The perception of autonomic activity. *Journal of Abnormal and Social Psychology*, 1958, *56*, 367–373.

Mann, J., & Rosenthal, T. Vicarious and direct counter-conditioning of test anxiety through individual and group desensitization. *Behaviour Research and Therapy*, 1969, *7*, 359–367.

Marks, I. *Fears and phobias.* New York: American Press, 1969.

Marks, I. Phobias and obsessions: Clinical phenomena in search of laboratory models. In J. D. Maser & M. E. P. Seligman (Eds.), *Psychopathology: Experimental methods.* San Francisco: W. H. Freeman, 1977.

Marks, I. M., & Gelder, M. G. Different onset ages in varieties of phobia. *American Journal of Psychiatry*, 1966, *123*, 218–221.

Masserman, T. *Principles of dynamic psychiatry.* Philadelphia: Saunders, 1946.

Mash, E. J., & Terdal, L. G. Behavior therapy assessment: Diagnosis, design and evaluation. In E. J. Mash, & L. G. Terdal (Eds.), *Behavior therapy assessment.* New York: Springer, 1976.

May, R. *The meaning of anxiety.* New York: Ronald, 1950.

Meichenbaum, D. Examination of model characteristics in reducing avoidance behavior. *Journal of Personality and Social Psychology*, 1971, *17*, 298–307.

Meichenbaum, D. A cognitive-behavior modification approach to assessment. In M. Hersen & A. S. Bellack (Eds.), *Behavioral assessment: A practical handbook.* New York: Pergamon, 1976.

Melamed, B. G., Hawes, R., Heiby, E., & Glick, J. The use of filmed modeling to reduce uncooperative behavior of children during dental treatment. *Journal of Dental Research*, 1975, *54*, 797–801.

Melamed, B. G., & Siegel, L. J. Reduction of anxiety in children facing hospitalization and surgery by use of filmed modeling. *Journal of Consulting and Clinical Psychology*, 1975, *43*, 511–521.

Melamed, B. G., Weinstein, D., Hawes, R., & Katin-Borland, M. Reduction of fear-related dental management using filmed modeling. *Journal of the American Dental Association*, 1975, *90*, 822–826.

Melamed, B. G., Yurcheson, R., Fleece, E. L., Hutcherson, S., & Hawes, R. Effects of filmed modeling on the reduction of anxiety-related behaviors in individuals varying in level of previous experience in the stress situation. *Journal of Consulting and Clinical Psychology*, 1978, *46*, 1357–1367.

Miller, L. C., Barrett, C. L., & Hampe, E. Phobias of childhood in a prescientific era. In S. Davids (Ed.), *Child personality and psychopathology.* New York: Wiley, 1974.

Miller, L. C., Barrett, C. L., Hampe, E., & Noble, H. Revised anxiety scales for the Louisville Behavior Check List. *Psychological Reports*, 1971, *29*, 503–511.

Miller, L. C., Barrett, C. L., Hampe, E., & Noble, H. Factor structure of childhood fears. *Journal of Consulting and Clinical Psychology*, 1972, *39*, 264–268.

Murphy, C. M., & Bootzin, R. R. Active and passive participation in the contact desensitization of snake fear in children. *Behavior Therapy*, 1973, *4*, 203–211.

Nawas, M. M. Standardized scheduled desensitization: Some unstable results and an improved program. *Behaviour Research and Therapy*, 1971, *9*, 35–38.

Neisworth, J. T., Madle, R. A., & Goeke, K. E. "Errorless" elimination of separation anxiety: A case study. *Journal of Behavior Therapy and Experimental Psychiatry*, 1975, *6*, 79–82.

O'Connor, R. D. Modification of social withdrawal through symbolic modeling. *Journal of Applied Behavior Analysis*, 1969, *2*, 15–22.

Öhman, A., Fredrikson, J., & Hugdahl, K. Orienting and defensive responding in the electrodermal system: Palmardorsal differences and recovery rate during conditioning to potentially phobic stimuli. *Psychophysiology*, 1978, *15*, 93–101.

Patterson, G. R., Ray, R. S., & Shaw, D. A. Direct intervention in families of deviant children. *Oregon Research Institute Research Bulletin*, 1968, *8*, No. 9.

Paul, G. L. *Insight vs. desensitization in psychotherapy.* Stanford, Calif.: Stanford University Press, 1966.

Perri, M. G., Richards, C. S., & Goodrich, J. D. Heterosocial adequacy test (HAT): A behavioral role-playing test for the assessment of heterosical skills in male college students. *JSAS Catalog of Selected Documents in Psychology*, 1978, *8*(1), 16.

Prokasy, W. F., & Raskin, D. C. (Eds.). *Electrodermal activity in psychological research.* New York: Academic Press, 1973.

Quay, H. C. Classification. In H. C. Quay & J. S. Werry (Eds.), *Psychopathological disorders of childhood* (2nd ed.). New York: Wiley, 1979.

Rachman, S. *Phobias: Their nature and control.* Springfield, Ill.: Charles C. Thomas, 1968.

Rachman, S., & Hodgson, R. Synchrony and desynchrony in fear and avoidance. *Behaviour Research and Therapy*, 1974, *12*, 311–318.

Radaker, L. D. The visual imagery of retarded children and the relationship to memory for word forms. *Exceptional Children*, 1961, *27*, 524–530.

Raskin, D. C. Attention and arousal. In W. F. Prokasy & D. C. Raskin (Eds.), *Electrodermal activity in psychological research*. New York: Academic Press, 1973.

Rehm, L. P., & Marston, A. R. Reduction of social anxiety through modification of self-reinforcement: An instigation therapy technique. *Journal of Consulting and Clinical Psychology*, 1968, *32*, 565–574.

Reynolds, C. R., & Richmond, B. O. What I think and feel: A revised measure of children's manifest anxiety. *Journal of Abnormal Child Psychology*, 1978, *6*, 271–280.

Richards, C. S., & Siegel, L. J. Behavioral treatment of anxiety states and avoidance behaviors in children. In D. Marholin II (Ed.), *Child behavior therapy*. New York: Wiley, 1978.

Richardson, A. *Mental imagery*. New York: Springer, 1969.

Rimm, D. C., & Masters, J. C. *Behavior therapy: Techniques and empirical findings*. New York: Academic Press, 1974.

Ritter, B. The group treatment of children's snake phobias using vicarious and contact desensitization procedures. *Behaviour Research and Therapy*, 1968, *6*, 1–6.

Robins, L. N. *Deviant children grown up*. Baltimore: Williams & Wilkins, 1966.

Rose, S. D. *Treating children in groups*. San Francisco: Jossey-Bass, 1972.

Rosenthal, T., & Bandura, A. Psychological modeling: Theory and practice. In S. L. Garfield & A. E. Bergin (Eds.), *Handbook of psychotherapy and behavior change: An empirical analysis* (Vol. 2). New York: Wiley, 1978.

Ross, D. M., Ross, S. A., & Evans, T. A. The modification of extreme social withdrawal by modeling with guilded participation. *Journal of Behavior Therapy and Experimental Psychiatry*, 1971, *2*, 273–279.

Rutter, M., Tizard, J., & Whitmore, K. *Education, health and behavior*. New York: Wiley, 1970.

Sarason, S. B., Davidson, K. S., Lighthall, F. F., Waite, R. R., & Ruebush, B. K. *Anxiety in elementary school children*. New York: Wiley, 1960.

Sartory, G., Rachman, S., & Grey, S. An investigation of the relation between reported fear and heart rate. *Behaviour Research and Therapy*, 1977, *15*, 435–438.

Scherer, M. W., & Nakamura, C. Y. A fear survey schedule for children (FSS-FC): A factor analytic comparison with manifest anxiety (CMAS). *Behaviour Research and Therapy*, 1968, *6*, 173–182.

Schnelle, J. F. A brief report on invalidity of parent evaluations of behavior change. *Journal of Applied Behavior Analysis*, 1974, *1*, 341–343.

Seligman, M. E. P. Phobias and preparedness. *Behavior Therapy*, 1971, *2*, 307–320.

Shapiro, A. H. Behavior of kibbutz and urban children receiving an injection. *Psychophysiology*, 1975, *12*, 79–82.

Singer, E. *Key concepts in psychotherapy*. New York: Random House, 1965.

Slater, E. Responses to a nursery school situation of 40 children. *Society for Research in Child Development Monograph*, 1939, *11*, No. 4.

Smith, R. E., & Sharpe, T. M. Treatment of a school phobia with implosive therapy. *Journal of Consulting and Clinical Psychology*, 1970, *35*, 239–243.

Sokolov, V. N. *Perception and the conditioned reflex*. New York: Macmillan, 1963.

Solyom, I., Beck, P., Solyom, C., & Hugel, R. Some etiological factors in phobic neurosis. *Canadian Psychiatry Association Journal*, 1974, *19*, 69–78.

Spielberger, C. D. *Manual for the state–trait anxiety inventory for children*. Palo Alto, Calif.: Consulting Psychologists Press, 1973.

Stedman, J. M. Family counseling with a school-phobic child. In J. D. Krumboltz & C. E. Thoresen (Eds.), *Counseling methods*. New York: Holt, Rinehart & Winston, 1976.

Strahan, R. F., Todd, J. B., & Inglis, G. B. A palmar sweat measure particularly suited for naturalistic research. *Psychophysiology*, 1974, *11*, 715–720.

Stricker, G., & Howitt, J. W. Physiological recording during simulated dental appointments. *New York State Dental Journal*, 1965, *31*, 204–213.

Stuart, R. B. (Ed.). *Behavior self-management: Strategies, techniques, and outcome*. New York: Brunner/Mazel, 1977.

Swan, G. E., & MacDonald, M. L. Behavior therapy in practice: A national survey of behavior therapists. *Behavior Therapy*, 1978, *9*, 799–807.

Switzky, N. N., & Haywood, H. C. Motivational orientation and the relative efficacy of self-monitored and externally imposed reinforcement symptoms in children. *Journal of Personality and Social Psychology*, 1974, *30*, 360–366.

Tasto, D. L. Systematic desensitization, muscle relaxation and visual imagery in the counterconditioning of a four-year-old phobic child. *Behaviour Research and Therapy*, 1969, *1*, 409–411.

Tasto, D. L. Self-report schedules and inventories. In A. R. Ciminero, K. S. Calhoun, & H. E. Adams (Eds.), *Handbook of behavioral assessment*. New York: Wiley, 1977.

Taylor, J. A. The relationship of anxiety to the conditioned eyelid response. *Journal of Experimental Psychology*, 1951, *42*, 183–188.

Tharp, R. G., & Wetzel, R. J. *Behavior modification in the natural environment*. New York: Academic Press, 1969.

Trower, P., Yardley, K., Bryant, B. M., & Shaw, P. The treatment of social failure: A comparison of anxiety-reduction and skills-acquisition procedures on two social problems. *Behavior Modification*, 1978, *2*, 41–60.

Ullmann, L. P., & Krasner, L. *A psychological approach to abnormal behavior* (2nd ed.). Englewood Cliffs, N.J.: Prentice-Hall, 1975.

Van Der Kooy, D., & Webster, C. D. A rapidly effective behavior modification program for an electively mute child. *Journal of Behavior Therapy and Experimental Psychiatry*, 1975, *6*, 149–152.

Venables, P., & Martin, I. (Eds.). *A manual of psychophysiological methods*. New York: Wiley, 1967.

Vernon, D. Use of modeling to modify children's responses to a natural, potentially stressful situation. *Journal of Applied Psychology*, 1973, *58*, 351–356.

Vernon, D. T. A., Foley, J. M., & Schulman, J. L. Effect of mother–child separation and birth order on young children's responses to two potentially stressful experiences. *Journal of Personality and Social Psychology*, 1967, *5*, 162–174.

Vernon, D. T. A., Schulman, J. L., & Foley, J. M. Changes in children's behavior after hospitalization. *American Journal of the Diseases of Children*, 1966, *3*, 581–593.

Wade, T. C., Baker, T. B., & Hartmann, D. P. Behavior therapist's self-reported views and practices. *The Behavior Therapist*, 1979, *2*, 3–6.

Wade, T. C., Malloy, T. E., & Proctor, S. Imaginal correlates of self-reported fear and avoidance behavior. *Behaviour Research and Therapy*, 1977, *15*, 17–22.

Walk, R. D. Self-ratings of fear in a fear-invoking situation. *Journal of Abnormal and Social Psychology*, 1956, *52*, 171–178.

Watson, J. B., & Rayner, P. Conditioned emotional reactions. *Journal of Experimental Psychology*, 1920, *3*, 1–14.

Wilder, J. The law of initial values. *Psychosomatic Medicine*, 1950, *12*, 392–401.

Wildman, B. G., & Erickson, M. T. Methodological problems in behavioral observation. In J. D. Cone & R. P. Hawkins (Eds.), *Behavioral assessment*. New York: Brunner/Mazel, 1977.

Wolffe, H. S. Radio telemetry. In P. Venables & I. Martin (Eds.), *A manual of psychophysiological methods*. New York: Wiley, 1967.

Wolpe, J., & Lang, P. J. A fear survey schedule for use in behavior therapy. *Behaviour Research and Therapy*, 1964, *2*, 27–30.

Wolpe, J., & Rachman, S. Psychoanalytic "evidence": A critique based on Freud's case of Little Hans. *Journal of Nervous and Mental Disease*, 1960, *130*, 135–148.

Yates, A. J. *Behavior therapy*. New York: Wiley, 1970.

# CHILDHOOD DEPRESSION

### Charles G. Costello
*University of Calgary*

## THE CONCEPT OF CHILDHOOD DEPRESSION

Although clinicians have reported the existence of depression in children from the early 1920s (e.g., Bleuler, 1934), it is only recently that an appreciable number have done so. A review of the literature by Coll and Bland (1979) indicates that in 1921 Kraepelin reported that, in his sample of 900 manic–depressive patients, .4% had their first manic–depressive episode before the age of 10. Nevertheless, the concept of childhood depression is only now in the process of receiving official recognition. Childhood depression was not included in the World Health Organization's 1974 *Glossary of Mental Disorders* or in the second version of the *Diagnostic and Statistical Manual of Mental Disorders* (DSM-II) of the American Psychiatric Association. In the third version of the manual (DSM-III), childhood depression has been included, but one has a sense of the uncertainty regarding the status of the concept. It is not listed under the heading "Disorders first evident in infancy, childhood or adolescence." However, in the discussion of age-specific associated features of depressive episodes, the following comments are made:

> Although the essential features of a major depressive episode are similar in infants, children, adolescents and adults, there are differences in the associated features.
>
> In prepubertal children separation anxiety may develop and cause the child to cling, to refuse to go to school, and to fear that he or she or the parents will die. A previous history of separation anxiety may result in more intense anxiety symptoms with the onset of a episode of major depressive episode.
>
> In adolescent boys negativistic or frankly antisocial behavior may appear. Feelings of wanting to leave home or of not being understood or approved of, restlessness, grouchiness, and aggression are common. Sulkiness, a reluctance to cooperate in family ventures, and withdrawal from social activities, with retreat to one's room, are frequent. School difficulties are likely. There may be inattention to personal appearance and increased emotionality, with particular sensitivity to rejection in love relationships. Substance Abuse may develop. (pp. 211–212)

These comments do not indicate very clearly how one would go about differentiating depression from other childhood disorders.

At another point in DSM-III, the following comment is made: "Major Depression may begin at any age, including infancy" (p. 215).

The first edition of the *American Handbook of Psychiatry* (Arieti, 1959) does not include childhood depression in its list of contents or in its index. However, a whole chapter is devoted to the topic in the second edition (Toolan, 1974).

Although there is some uncertainty in the official recognition of childhood depression, since the early 1950s there has been a large number of reports of childhood depression in the literature[1] and three books on the topic have appeared (Schulterbrandt & Raskin, 1977; Annell, 1972; Leese, 1974). A good review of some of the clinical literature, with the transcript of a debate that followed its presentation, can be found in Conners (1976). Unfortunately, these clinical reports do not put the concept on a very firm basis. Even a recent and more detailed analysis on a large sample (Pearce, 1978) does not help very much. Pearce investigated 784 children aged 3 to 17 years who attended a hospital department of child psychiatry over a period of 2 years. Each child was rated on an item sheet, which recorded demographic data and the symptoms present during the past year. Pearce does not note who the informant was in his study. A total of 42 symptoms could be rated as "absent," "doubtful," or "present." The item marked "morbid depression, sadness, unhappiness, tearfulness" was selected for further study. All children who had an organic or schizophrenic psychosis, who had an IQ below 50, or who were rated as having a doubtful symptom of depression were excluded from the study. Of the remaining 547 children, 126 (23%) were rated as having the symptom of depression, and this group was compared with the group of children who were not rated as depressed. The symptoms shown in Table 1 were found to occur significantly more frequently in children with symptoms of depression. With the exception of school refusal and phobias, the symptoms showed remarkable resemblance to those that are associated with depression in adults. Table 2 presents the symptoms that are negatively associated with depression in children.

The two clusters of symptoms presented in Tables 1 and 2 remind one of the second-order factors that are found in many investigations with children and that are sometimes labeled "internalizing" and "externalizing" (Achenbach & Edelbrock, 1978). One suspects that Pearce would have got similar results had he

---

[1] Reviews of the clinical literature on childhood depression have tended to select a few often-quoted reports. It seemed worthwhile, therefore, to bring a more complete list together here: Anthony and Scott (1960); Brumback and Weinberg (1977); Campbell (1952, 1955); Connell (1972); Cytryn and McKnew (1972, 1974); Feinstein and Wolpert (1973); Frommer (1967, 1968); Glaser (1967); Harrington and Hassan (1958); Hollon (1970); Kasanin (1952); Krakowski (1970); Leese (1974); Ling, Oftedal, and Weinberg (1970); McConville, Boag, and Purohit (1973); McKnew and Cytryn (1973); Malmquist (1971); Ossofsky (1974); Poznanski, Krahenbuhl, and Zrull (1976); Poznanski and Zrull (1970); Renshaw (1974); Rie (1966); Sandler and Joffe (1965); Sperling (1959); Toolan (1962); Varsamis and MacDonald (1972); Warneke (1975); Weinberg, Rutman, Sullivan, Penick, and Deitz (1973); Welner, Welner, McCrary, and Leonard (1977); White and O'Shanick (1977); Zrull, McDermott, and Poznanski (1970).

TABLE 1
Symptoms Significantly Associated with Depression in Children

| Symptom | Not depressed | Depressed | Significance |
|---|---|---|---|
| Morbid anxiety | 15% | 54% | $p < 0.001$ |
| Sleep disturbance | 23% | 46% | $p < 0.001$ |
| Irritability | 22% | 36% | $p < 0.001$ |
| Suicidal | 2% | 31% | $p < 0.001$ |
| Eating disturbance | 15% | 30% | $p < 0.001$ |
| School refusal | 18% | 28% | $p < 0.025$ |
| Phobias | 13% | 24% | $p < 0.01$ |
| Alimentary disorder/ abdominal pain | 11% | 23% | $p < 0.001$ |
| Ruminations/obsessions | 4% | 15% | $p < 0.001$ |
| Hypochondriasis | 3% | 13% | $p < 0.001$ |
| Altered perception | — | 12% | $p < 0.001$ |

Note. From "The Recognition of Depressive Disorder in Children" by J. B. Pearce, *Journal of the Royal Society of Medicine*, 1978, *71*, 496. Copyright 1978 by *Journal of the Royal Society of Medicine*. Reprinted by permission.

selected the "morbid anxiety" item to divide his children into those who had the symptom of anxiety and those who did not.

## Criticisms of the Concept

Though the concept of childhood depression appears to be gaining increased acceptance, criticisms of it have appeared. Some of the critics hold theoretical views that will not permit them to accept the concept. Rochlin (1959) noted that since clinical depression is a superego phenomenon, it does not occur in childhood, and Mahler (1961) argued that the immature personality structure of the infant or older

TABLE 2
Symptoms Negatively Associated with Depression in Children

| Symptom | Not depressed | Depressed | Significance |
|---|---|---|---|
| Disobedience | 55% | 43% | $p < 0.025$ |
| Fighting/aggression | 28% | 17% | $p < 0.025$ |
| Truancy | 26% | 14% | $p < 0.01$ |
| Enuresis | 21% | 10% | $p < 0.01$ |
| Encopresis | 10% | 3% | $p < 0.025$ |

Note. From "The Recognition of Depressive Disorder in Children" by J. B. Pearce, *Journal of the Royal Society of Medicine*, 1978, *71*, 496. Copyright 1978 by *Journal of the Royal Society of Medicine*. Reprinted by permission.

child is not capable of producing a state of depression such as that seen in the adult. Rie (1966) discussed at length these and other theoretical blocks to the acceptance of childhood depression and revealed his own theoretical block in stating that "there may be reason to believe that the fully differentiated and generalized primary affect characterising depression, namely, despair or hopelessness, is one of which children—perhaps prior to the end of the latency years—are incapable" (p. 682).

Some critics, though accepting the possibility that childhood depression exists, reject the concept of "masked depression" (Kovacs & Beck, 1977; Welner, 1978). The argument has been made by some clinicians (Cytryn & McKnew, 1974; Glaser, 1967; Leese, 1974; Renshaw, 1974; Toolan, 1962) that depression in children may be masked by other symptoms, such as aggressiveness, or that, expressing the same idea, the child may develop "symptom equivalents." As might be expected, this notion has caused a lot of confusion because almost every behavior or symptom possible has been nominated as an indicator of depression in the child. It would be advisable, therefore, for the concept of masked depression to be abandoned. Doing so is not to deny that the constellation of behaviors in depressed children may differ from those found in adults, but is to affirm that one should still look for some key symptoms such as depressed mood or loss of interest.

Some authors, such as Frommer (1968), have argued that evidence that a child's disorder is depression in disguise can be obtained by determining the response to antidepressant drugs. If the child responds, then he or she is depressed, whatever the symptoms being manifested. As Rutter (1972) has pointed out, however, this strategy is of doubtful validity. The circumstances under which antidepressant drugs may relieve adult depressive disorders have by no means been established, and, in particular, there are considerable individual differences in response to the drugs, which may or may not be related to differences in types of depression (Blackwell & Shepherd, 1968; Costello & Belton, 1970; Melia, 1970). Furthermore, antidepressant drugs may have therapeutic effects even in the absence of depression. For instance, there is some evidence that antidepressant drugs reduce enuresis (Shaffer, Costello, & Hill, 1968).

Graham (1974) based his criticism of the concept of childhood depression on some empirical data. He noted that in the Rutter Isle of Wight study (Rutter, Tizard, & Whitmore, 1970), teachers' and parents' ratings of a child's sadness and misery were not significantly related. Graham commented that this suggests that children behave differently at school from the way they do at home and that this, in turn, militates against the idea of an all-pervading clinical depressive condition that is manifest in all situations. Graham's (1974) general conclusion is as follows:

> There is lack of evidence to suggest that sadness and misery, when they occur in relation to the common emotional and conduct disorders of middle childhood, have any genetic or special psychopathological link with adult depression. In children such disorders are usually best viewed as a reaction rather than illness. (p. 347)

There would probably be little debate that sadness and misery may occur in children whose primary complaint is other than depression. For instance, Agras (1959) presented data on seven phobic children, indicating that in six cases there were frequent outbursts of weeping coming on for no apparent reason in a previously happy child, together with a great deal of unhappy, miserable, whining behavior. Three children manifested both fear of dying and the wish to die, and one made several suicidal gestures. However, most of the proponents of the concept of childhood depression consider it to be the *primary* problem in some children. On the other hand, they would not necessarily view the disorder as an illness and would not see any need to make assumptions about the genetic contributions to the disorder.

The most thorough criticism of the concept of childhood depression is provided by Lefkowitz and Burton (1978). One cannot but agree with their conclusion, arrived at on the basis of a close examination of the literature, that no reliable and valid method for assessing the putative condition of childhood depression exists and that, without supporting normative data, the notion of a syndrome of childhood depression rests largely on surmise. Nevertheless, there are some basic, but questionable, assumptions in the Lefkowitz and Burton (1978) paper, which have been examined at length elsewhere (Costello, 1980). These assumptions are:

1. If the behaviors thought to constitute the syndrome of depression are prevalent in normal children, they cannot be considered pathological and therefore the syndrome does not exist.
2. If the behaviors thought to constitute the syndrome of depression are found to disappear as a function of time, they cannot be considered pathological.
3. Problems that remit spontaneously do not need clinical intervention.

Briefly, the first assumption is questioned because it relies too heavily on a statistical deviation definition of pathology. Furthermore, it is the prevalence of *constellations* of behavior that is relevant to the question of the existence of a *syndrome* of depression in children. The second assumption is questioned on the grounds that the transitoriness of behavior seen in an individual and viewed developmentally gives one no more a priori justification for considering it to be normal than would the transitoriness of behavior seen in a society and viewed historically. The third assumption is questioned because it overlooks the way in which problem behavior in childhood may, in interaction with other factors, increase the likelihood of adult disorders.

There is evidence for childhood depression in the more systematic investigations (Rutter, Tizard, & Whitmore, 1970; Rutter, Graham, Chadwick, & Yule, 1976), but this evidence suggests that the syndrome, if it exists, is very rare. It seems likely, therefore, that, insofar as professionals are concerned with the syndrome of depression rather than the individual behaviors commonly associated with depression, they are going to be involved, in the initial stages of their work, in general survey or epidemiological investigations.

For this reason, I shall first review those assessment procedures and instruments that have been designed to assess what have been variously called constellations, factors, clusters, and syndromes of depressive behaviors. The purpose of this review will be (1) to comment on the psychometric properties and possible uses of the various instruments and (2) to list the items of the constellations found by the different investigators in order to give the reader an opportunity to consider the similarities and dissimilarities among the constellations.

The review will be restricted to those assessment procedures that have been developed specifically for prepubescent children and early adolescents. The assessment of depression in late adolescents will not be discussed because, for the most part, the procedures developed for adults are suitable for these adolescents. There are already many good reviews of the self-report and rating scales designed for assessing the syndrome of depression in adults (e.g., Becker, 1974; Rehm, 1976). There is some evidence that the Beck Depression Inventory (BDI) is suitable for adolescents (Albert & Beck, 1975). The data from the BDI, when it was administered to 36 boys and 27 girls ranging in age from 11 to 15 years, indicated that 33.3% of the sample fell into the "range of moderate to severe depressive symptomatology" and 2.2%, into the "severe range." Albert and Beck also note that "analysis of teacher evaluation of academic performance and individual depression scores showed that all students rated 'excellent' by the teachers had low depression scores, while all students rated 'poor' by teachers had high depression scores" (Albert & Beck, 1975, p. 304). The authors commented as follows:

> Teacher evaluation, paralleling the depression scores, raises questions concerning the grading system and adult feedback which possibly derogates the student's self concept. It appears plausible that the interpersonal relationships between students and teachers have direct bearing on the student's self concept and subsequent emotional health. It seems likely that the low-achieving student gets caught up in a vicious cycle in which substandard performance and depression reinforce each other. (p. 305)

Albert and Beck's (1975) paper is noteworthy because of the very high prevalence of depression that it reports and because it indicates how Beck's cognitive theory of depression is being utilized to account for childhood depression. At the very least, this paper should stimulate similar investigations with large samples of children and with more direct and systematic testing of hypotheses about the causes of depression in such young people.

## MEASURES OF CONSTELLATIONS OF DEPRESSIVE BEHAVIORS

The epidemiological investigations that have been done so far have depended on general screening instruments or interviews designed to identify children with any behavioral or emotional disorder, including depression. For instance, Rutter's (1967) Teachers' Questionnaire consists of 26 descriptions of behavior, only one of which, on the face of it, assesses depression: "Often appears miserable, unhappy, tearful or distressed." Rutter (1967) presented the reliability and validity data on total adjustment scores but did not present data specifically in relation to the assessment of depression. Rutter's Parental Questionnaire (Rutter, Tizard, & Whitmore, 1970) consists of 31 items, including the aforementioned item and two items that concern problems traditionally associated with depression, that is, eating problems and sleeping problems. Rutter, Tizard, and Whitmore (1970) present reliability and validity data on total adjustment scores, but not on individual items.

## Psychiatric Interview

Rutter and Graham (1968) developed a semistructured half-hour psychiatric interview for children aged 7 to 12 years, which includes the questions "Do you get fed up sometimes? Or feel miserable? Or do you cry sometimes? Do you ever feel really unhappy?" Positive responses to such questions are followed by probes regarding the severity, frequency, and setting of the emotions ("Do you ever feel so miserable that you want to go away and hide? Or that you want to run away? How often do you feel like that? What sort of things seem to make you feel fed up? Do you feel like that at home, at school, etc.?"). Included in the rating schedule to be completed on the basis of the child's report during the interview are the following scales: loneliness, misery, depression, self-depreciation, suicidal ideas. Scales included in the rating schedule to be completed on the basis of observation of the child's behavior during the interview are: sad–miserable, tearful, gross activity level, smiling, spontaneous talk.

Using this format, two psychiatrists separately interviewed 25 children attending a psychiatric clinic and found that there was only 40% agreement for the overall rating of depression. Ratings for individual behaviors usually associated with depression were higher: gross activity level (84% agreement), spontaneous talk (72%), smiling (72%), preoccupation with depressive topics (72%), sad–miserable expression (72%), and tearfulness (92%). Between the two interviews of each child, there was an interval of between 1 and 4 weeks; as Rutter and Graham (1968) noted, the ratings of items such as depression were probably affected by changes in clinical states between the two interviews. It is not possible, therefore, to determine the sources of any disagreements in the ratings.

To assess the validity of the psychiatric interview with the child, a random control group of 159 children and an "abnormal" group of 108 children were compared in Rutter's Isle of Wight epidemiological study. Rutter and Graham (1968) made a few interesting observations in relation to depression. They noted that "depressive items . . . differentiated quite well between the psychiatric group and the control group, but it was striking that in this age group depression was as frequent among children with anti-social disorders as among those with neurotic disorders" (p. 574). Also, most of the symptoms and behaviors in the rating schedules, apart from the depressive items, differentiated between the psychiatric and the control group. Furthermore, Rutter and Graham (1968) stated:

> Although in the present study an overall rating of psychiatric abnormality proved to be a satisfactory measure, not all of the individual ratings on specific aspects of behavior were equally reliable or equally useful. In particular, it was striking that some of the most global and inferential items were at least as reliable (as well as being more useful) as some of the specific and apparently objective pieces of behavior.

> For example, the overall rating of psychiatric abnormality and the rating on "emotional responsiveness" were both more reliable than "startle" or "muscular tension" or "friendliness." This difference was most striking in the "across interview" comparison and it may be that the more molecular and objective items were relatively situation-specific and therefore did not reflect enduring aspects of psychopathology, which were better measured by the global and inferential measures. (p. 575)

One may question to what extent "muscular tension" could be considered an objective piece of behavior, at least as measured by simple observation. One may also wonder on what grounds Rutter and Graham state that the global and inferential items are more useful than the measures of specific behaviors. That global and inferential items may be as reliable as the observations of more specific behaviors, however, is worth noting; in developing assessment procedures for childhood depression, it might be advisable to determine the reliability and validity of such global and inferential procedures.

Another observation made by Rutter and Graham (1968) is well worth noting:

> Depression proved to be a more difficult item than anxiety to rate reliably. Sadness or misery were often difficult to differentiate from emotional inhibition for other reasons, and all psychiatrists in the study found the quiet, shy, dull, uncommunicative children the most difficult to assess. (p. 575)

The Rutter and Graham (1968) paper provides a useful format for the conducting of interviews with children in order to assess behavior disorders. The rating schedules to be used in connection with the interviews cover, apart from emotional and behavioral disorders, an extensive set of ratings in relation to life and activities outside the school and to attitudes toward parents and school. Of course, no matter how skillfully the interview is conducted, it can only be considered the first step in the assessment of the child's problem. The various empirically determined sources of unreliability and invalidity in interviews with children or about children have been reviewed in Evans and Nelson (1977).

## Questionnaires and Checklists

Most of the investigators whose work is of relevance to the assessments of constellations of depressive behaviors have developed questionnaires or item checklists to be completed by parents. For instance, Arnold and Smeltzer (1974) have presented a child behavior checklist for use by parents. Factor analysis of data obtained from the parents of 185 children (130 boys and 55 girls) aged 12 years or younger and attending a child psychiatry clinic resulted in six factors, including one labeled "withdrawal–depression." The following items loaded (> .40) on this factor: sullen–sulky, says people don't like him, would rather be alone, gets confused in his thinking, is hard to know what he's trying to tell you, does the same thing over and over, sad, listless–uninterested. A similar factor was obtained from data from the parents of 166 children (86 boys and 80 girls) aged 13 to 18 years. Four of the aforementioned items—sullen–sulky, would rather be alone, sad, and listless–uninterested—loaded on the factor for older children. In addition, the items "can be cold and indifferent" and "things must be done the same way every time" loaded on the factor for older children. Because neither reliability nor validity data are presented for the total checklist scores or for the individual factor scores, one cannot comment on the clinical or investigative usefulness of this analysis.

## Personality Inventory for Children

Wirt, Lachar, Klinedinst, and Seat (1977) developed a 600-item Personality Inventory for Children (PIC), which contains clinical scales, including one for depression. The PIC is to be completed by an observer of the child, preferably the mother. It can be used with children from 3 to 16 years of age. The Depression Scale is composed of those items judged by practicing clinical psychologists to reflect childhood depression. In view of the controversy over the existence of childhood depression, at least at the syndrome level, one would have thought the development of such a scale to be a difficult task. Nevertheless, the designers of the instrument seemed to have had no difficulty; all items nominated by at least four of the seven judges involved in the designing are included in the final 46-item scale.

The scale items and their factor groupings are presented in Table 3. The test–retest reliability of the Depression Scale, based on 34 children attending an outpatient psychiatric clinic (the test interval was 4–72 days; $\bar{x} = 15.2$ days), was .94. For 46 normal children (the test interval was 13–102 days; $\bar{x} = 50.96$ days) it was .80. For 45 normal children over a shorter interval (2 weeks) it was .93.

Although no validity data were available for the Depression Scale, apart from data indicating that the scale's scores are high for various clinical samples, it would seem to be an instrument worth considering for use in screening. However, the Depression Scale is only one of many scales in the PIC, others of which may be of interest to those working in the area of childhood depression (e.g., Withdrawal Scale and Social Skills Scale).

## Child Behavior Checklist

Another system for classifying children with behavior and emotional disorders is the Child Behavior Checklist developed by Achenbach and his colleagues (Achenbach, 1978; Achenbach & Edelbrock, 1978). The checklist comprises 113 behavior problem items to which a parent responds by circling 0, 1, or 2, "with 0 indicating that the item is *not true* of the child, 1 indicating that the item is *somewhat or sometimes true* of the child, and 2 indicating that it is *very true or often true* of the child" (Achenbach & Edelbrock, 1979, p. 224).

The Child Behavior Checklist also comprises scales of involvement and attainment in the following three areas:

1. *Activities.* This scale consists of scores for the amount and quality of the child's participation in (a) sports; (b) nonsports hobbies, activities, and games; and (c) jobs and chores.

TABLE 3
Depression Scale (D) Items Grouped in Relation to Factors

I.  Brooding, Moodiness (40.28%)[a]
    My child seems unhappy about our home life. (T)[b]
    My child broods some. (T)
    My child often complains that others don't understand him (her). (T)
    Others often remark how moody my child is. (T)

II. Social Isolation (15.52%)
    My child usually plays alone. (T)
    My child often plays with a group of children. (F)
    My child doesn't seem to care to be with others. (T)
    My child seldom talks. (T)
    My child really has no real friend. (T)
    I often wonder if my child is lonely. (T)
    It is not too unlikely that my child will stay in the house for days at a time. (T)

III. Crying Spells (8.99%)
    My child often will cry for no apparent reason. (T)
    My child often has crying spells. (T)
    My child whines a lot. (T)
    My child cries when scolded. (T)

IV. Lack of Energy (8.43%)
    My child has as much pep and energy as most children. (F)
    My child seems tired most of the time. (T)

V.  Pessimism, Anhedonia (5.55%)
    My child usually looks at the bright side of things. (F)
    My child is almost always smiling. (F)
    My child is usually in good spirits. (F)
    My child has a good sense of humor. (F)
    Usually my child takes things in stride. (F)
    My child is as happy as ever. (F)

VI. Concern with Death and Separation (5.43%)
    My child often talks about death. (T)
    My child is afraid of dying. (T)
    My child is worried about sin. (T)
    My child worries about things that usually only adults worry about. (T)
    My child often asks if I love him (her). (T)

VII. Serious Attitude (4.26%)
    Everything has to be perfect or my child isn't satisfied. (T)
    My child seems too serious minded. (T)
    My child hardly ever smiles. (T)

VIII. Sensitivity to Criticism (3.57%)
    Little things upset my child. (T)
    My child's feelings are hurt easily. (T)
    My child takes criticism easily. (F)
    My child tends to pity him (her) self. (T)

IX. Indecisiveness, Poor Self-Concept (3.05%)
    My child has little self-confidence. (T)
    My child has trouble making decisions. (T)
    My child speaks of him (her) self as stupid or dumb. (T)
    My child will worry a lot about starting something new. (T)

TABLE 3 *(continued)*

---

X.   Uncommunicativeness (2.65%)
     My child has usually been a quiet child. (T)
     My child keeps thoughts to him (her) self. (T)
     Other
     Eating is no problem for my child. (F)
     My child doesn't seem to care for fun. (T)
     My child often stays in his (her) room for hours. (T)
     Several times my child has threatened to kill him (her) self. (T)
     My child is easily embarrassed. (T)

---

*Note.* Adapted from *Multidimensional Description of Child Personality: A Manual for the Personality Inventory for Children* by R. D. Wirt, D. Lachar, J. K. Klinedinst, and P. Seat, pp. 23–24. Copyright 1977 by Western Psychological Services. Reprinted by permission.
   [a]Indicates percentage of common variance.
   [b]T, true; F, false.

2. *Social.* This scale consists of scores for (a) the child's membership and participation in organizations; (b) number of friends and the child's contacts with them; and (c) behavior with others and when alone.
3. *School Scale.* This scale consists of scores for (a) the average of the child's performance in academic subjects; (b) placement in a regular or special class; (c) being promoted regularly or held back; and (d) the presence or absence of school problems.

Achenbach (1978, Note 1) and Achenbach and Edelbrock (1979) have reported the results of a series of factor-analytic studies for boys aged 4 and 5 years, 6 to 11 years, and 12 to 16 years and for girls aged 6 to 11 years and 12 to 16 years. A factor of Depression was found for boys aged 4 and 5 years and 6 to 11 years and for girls aged 6 to 11 years. A factor of Depressed Withdrawal was found for girls aged 12 to 16 years. The items loading on these factors are presented in Table 4.

Further psychometric data on specific scales is not available at present; and what is available refers mostly to all the scales in general. Achenbach (1978) reported data obtained with the checklist for 12 normal boys between 6 and 11 years old whose mothers were interviewed on two occasions (the interval range was 7–12 days; $\bar{x} = 8$ days). Pearson correlation coefficients between the scale scores on the two occasions ranged from .72 to .97, with a mean of .89. In the same paper, Achenbach reported that the intercorrelations between the checklist data of the mothers and of the fathers of 38 boys attending a clinic ranged from .58 to .87, with a mean of .74.

Attempts to obtain stable factors of depression in adults using simple checklists of the Achenbach sort have not been very successful (Costello, 1970). It will not be too surprising to find in the future the same lack of consistency across studies in the factors of childhood depression. Solutions to factor analysis are notoriously

TABLE 4

Items Loading on the Factor of Depression, Extracted from Data Obtained for Boys Aged 4 and 5 Years and 6 to 11 Years and for Girls Aged 6 to 11 Years, and on the Factor Depressed Withdrawal for Girls Aged 12 to 16 Years

| | Depression | | | Depressed Withdrawal |
| Item | Boys 4 and 5 years[a] | Boys 6 to 11 years[b] | Girls 6 to 11 years[c] | Girls 12 to 16 years[d] |
|---|---|---|---|---|
| Feels worthless | × | .68 | .66 | |
| Feels guilty | × | .67 | .55 | |
| Needs to be perfect | × | .58 | .41 | |
| Feels unloved | × | .55 | .47 | |
| Worrying | × | .52 | .67 | |
| Sad | × | .51 | .49 | .57 |
| Fears own impulses | × | .48 | .49 | |
| Lonely | × | .40 | .46 | |
| Anxious | × | .39 | .57 | |
| Self-conscious | × | .39 | .41 | .38 |
| Feels persecuted | × | .34 | .46 | |
| Sulks | × | .32 | .30 | .45 |
| Nervous | | .31 | .35 | |
| Suicidal talk | | .46 | | |
| Cries much | × | .39 | | |
| Suspicious | × | .30 | | |
| Harms self | | .30 | | |
| Fears school | | | .44 | |
| Clings to adults | | | .34 | |
| Withdrawn | × | | .32 | .63 |
| Is teased | | | .31 | |
| Shy, timid | × | | .31 | .55 |
| Secretive | × | | | .56 |
| Likes to be alone | | | | .55 |
| Slow moving | × | | | .53 |
| Won't talk | | | | .53 |
| Stubborn | | | | .38 |
| Sleeps much | | | | .38 |
| Stares blankly | | | | .37 |
| Overtired | | | | .33 |
| Obsessions | × | | | |
| Jealous | × | | | |
| Fears | × | | | |
| Nightmares | × | | | |
| Hoarding | × | | | |
| Moody | × | | | |
| Sex preoccupation | × | | | |

[a]From Achenbach (Note 1). The factor loadings for boys aged 4 and 5 years are not available in Achenbach (Note 1).    [b]From Achenbach (1978). Copyright 1978 by the American Psychological Association. Reprinted by permission.    [c]From Achenbach and Edelbrock (1978). Copyright 1978 by the American Psychological Association. Reprinted by permission.    [d]From Achenbach and Edelbrock (1979). Copyright 1979 by the American Psychological Association. Reprinted by permission.

vulnerable to slight changes in sample and item characteristics and to different factoring procedures (Comrey, 1978). Furthermore, some of the items in Achenbach's Child Behavior Checklist (e.g., "feels worthless," "feels guilty," and "needs to be perfect"), although providing some useful preliminary information, may be too general for adequate behavioral assessment.

### Peer Nomination Inventory

An interesting alternative way of assessing the adjustment of children was developed by Wiggins and Winder (1961). The instrument is called the Peer Nomination Inventory (PNI). The work that has been done with the PNI seems to have been confined to boys, and the currently available data suggest that, though depression may be among the dimensions measured by the inventory, it may be an elusive dimension. In the following discussion of the PNI, "Depression Scale" refers to the items grouped to form the scale on an a priori basis, not to a factor of depression.

The PNI does not seem to have been widely adopted despite its potential usefulness. In this respect, Wiggins and Winder (1961) noted that the social stimulus value of a child to his peers is a source of observational data that has not been fully exploited as a criterion measure of adjustment. The researchers note two good reasons for using peer ratings: (1) judgments as to the appropriateness of any given social behavior might do well to include the opinions of members of the social group in question; and (2) peers have opportunities for continuous observation over extended periods, both inside and outside the classroom.

The PNI is a 62-item inventory, the format of which is indicated in Figure 1. The instructions to the children are as follows:

> We have been having boys describe things they do. Now we want to know how many boys here do the same sort of things. So we have written down lots of things that kids do. You can check which boys in your class do these things. You just guess the best you can.
>
> Now turn to the first page. See the number 1. After the number 1, it says "He is absent from school a lot." Now look across the names. Who is absent from school a lot? Put a check mark under his name. Put a check mark under the name of every boy who is absent from school a lot. Now look at number 2. After number 2 it says, "He's pretty short." Put a check mark under every boy who is pretty short. If a boy is pretty short put a check mark under his name.

The basic score is the number of raters who nominated a given child on an item. Wiggins and Winder (1961) reported data from a factor-analytic study. The depression items and their loadings on the factors obtained are presented in Table 5. Wiggins and Winder noted that the depression items do not measure a behavior dimension that can clearly be distinguished from social isolation.

In investigating the psychometric properties of the final form of the PNI, data were obtained from 710 boys ranging in age from 8 to 12 years. The internal consistency coefficient for the Depression Scale was .78, indicating that this scale is a relatively homogeneous one. When teacher ratings were used to assess the

| | JERRY ASH | BOB BAKER | JOE GRANT | JOHN HALL | TOM JONES | CARL LOVE | SAM SMITH | BILL WEST |
|---|---|---|---|---|---|---|---|---|
| 1. He's absent from school a lot | | | | | | | | |
| 2. He's pretty short | | | | | | | | |
| 3. He's always losing things | | | | | | | | |
| 4. He's a fast runner | | | | | | | | |

FIGURE 1

Test format of the Peer Nomination Inventory. From "The Peer Nomination Inventory: An Empirically Derived Sociometric Measure of Adjustment in Preadolescent Boys" by J. S. Wiggins and C. L. Winder, *Psychological Reports*, 1961, *9*, 653, Figure 1. Reprinted by permission.

concurrent validity of the peer ratings, the mean (and the median) ρ between the teacher and the peer ratings was .42. This is not a high correlation, but then the observational base of teachers and peers differs to some degree—indeed, that was one of the reasons for the development of the PNI. Therefore, this was not a particularly good way of assessing concurrent validity. The product moment correlation coefficient between the scores obtained at two sessions, one year apart, for 339 boys was .37 for the Depression Scale. The stability coefficients of the individual depression items, however, ranged from .30 to .50, with a mean tetrachoric $r$ of $+.42$. Wiggins and Winder note that the individual items demonstrate greater temporal stability that does the total depression score and suggest, on this basis, that the scale may not be unidimensional. However, the internal consistency coefficient they reported (.78) does suggest that the scale is a relatively homogeneous one. The time between testings was probably far too long to be able to say very much about the stability of the scores, the contribution to real variance in the scores, and the differences between total and item scores as it relates to the problem of homogeneity.

Winder and Wiggins (1964) reported validity data on the Aggression and Dependency Scales of the PNI, and Siegelman (1966a) reported validity data on the Withdrawal Scale, but there seem to be no data on the validity of the Depression Scale. Siegelman (1966b) obtained a factor he labeled "Withdrawal–Depression" from the PNI data of 113 fourth-, fifth-, and sixth-grade boys. The loadings of the depression items on this factor are listed in the right-hand column of Table 5. It can be seen that Siegelman's Withdrawal–Depression factor is similar to Wiggins and Winder's Social Isolation factor.

TABLE 5

Factor Loadings of Depression Items of the Peer Nomination Inventory

| Depression item | Wiggins and Winder's factors[a] | | | | | | Siegelman's factor[b] |
|---|---|---|---|---|---|---|---|
| | I Social Isolation | II Hostility | III Crying | V Attention Getting | VII Minor | VIII Factors (unlabeled) | Withdrawal–Depression |
| 37. Someone makes fun of him and he starts crying. | .45 | | .70 | | | | .08 |
| 38. He cries if you hurt his feelings. | .34 | | .76 | | | | −.01 |
| 39. He cries when he doesn't do something right. | | | .81 | | | | .02 |
| 40. No matter what he does, it's wrong. | .57 | | | | | | .40 |
| 41. He's a little too sensitive to everybody. | .38 | | | .40 | | −.66 | .22 |
| 42. He feels left out. | .78 | | | | | | .86 |
| 43. He's not sure of himself in anything. | .62 | | | | | | .61 |
| 44. He says he can't do things. | .52 | | | | | | .69 |
| 45. He cries when he doesn't know how to play. | .41 | | .62 | | | | .22 |
| 46. He just can't stand anybody laughing at him. | | −.58 | | | −.42 | | .13 |
| 47. He's sort of unhappy. | .72 | | | | | | .72 |
| 48. He seems to think that he's nobody. | .70 | | | | | | .87 |

[a]From Wiggins and Winder (1961). Copyright 1961 by *Psychological Reports*. Reprinted by permission.
[b]From Siegelman (1966). Copyright 1966 by *Journal of Psychology*. Reprinted by permission.

## The Lefkowitz and Tesiny Inventory

A new peer nomination inventory (PNID) designed specifically for assessing depression has been presented by Lefkowitz and Tesiny (1980). In the group administration of the inventory, 20 items of the form "Who often plays alone?" are read aloud twice, and the children are instructed to draw a line through all the names on their class roster that "best fit the question." Other examples of the items are: Who doesn't try again when they lose? Who often sleeps in class? Who often cries? Who worries a lot? Who doesn't play? Who often looks sad? Of the 20 items, 14 are concerned with depression, 4 are concerned with happiness, and 2 are concerned with popularity.

The Lefkowitz and Tesiny inventory contains a greater variety of depression items than the Wiggins and Winder inventory, without any loss of internal consistency—$\alpha$ for the 13 depression items ("Who thinks they are sad?" was removed from the inventory) was .85, compared with an $\alpha$ of .78 for the Wiggins and Winder inventory.

Lefkowitz and Tesiny (1980) reported an extensive and thorough study of the psychometric properties of their inventory using data from 452 boys and 492 girls in 61 classrooms (the average age was 10.24 years; the standard deviation was .78). The total sample of 944 subjects was divided into a standardization (S) sample ($n = 472$) and a cross-validation (C) sample ($n = 472$). The most important findings were the following:

1. There were no sex differences on the inventory.

2. The test–retest coefficient for a sample of 177 children drawn at random from the first 506 children was .79 for the total depression score when retesting was done after approximately 2 months.

3. Factor analyses conducted separately for the S-sample and the C-sample resulted in three "depression" factors—Loneliness, Inadequacy, and Dejection—and a "happiness" factor. The depression factors accounted for 37.8% and 38.4% of the total variance in the S-sample and the C-sample, respectively. The authors noted that "the factor structures for the S- and the C-sample proved to be isomorphic, indicating successful cross-validation" (p. 46).

3. Treating raters (nominators) as items in a test and calculating the coefficient $\alpha$ for each of the 61 classes resulted in a mean $\alpha$ of .75, indicating an acceptable level of interrater agreement.

4. Scores on the inventory correlated significantly with a modified form of the Zung Self-Rating Depression Scale (Zung, 1965) (.14); with a modified form of the Children's Depression Inventory (CDI) (Kovacs & Beck, 1977) (.23), which is discussed subsequently in this chapter; and with teacher-rated depression (.41).

5. In order to determine the construct validity of the PNID, a number of relationships between PNID scores and "a set of variables related to the construct of childhood depression were predicted" (p. 46). Some of these predictions were tested by examining correlations between PNID item scores and PNID total scores, which does not seem to be a very appropriate method. Looking at the predicted relationships that were not tested in that manner, it was found that high PNID

scores predicted the following: (a) low intelligence scores ($r$ values for a number of measures of intelligence ranged from $-.10$ to $-.27$); (b) poor social behavior as rated by teachers ($r = +.22$); (c) low self-esteem as determined by Coopersmith's Self-Esteem Inventory (Coopersmith, 1967) ($r = -.12$); (d) external locus of control as determined by the Nowicki–Strickland Locus of Control Scale for Children (Nowicki & Strickland, 1973) ($r = +.19$); (e) absences from and lateness at school ($r$ values of $+.14$ and $+.09$, respectively); and (f) membership in lower socioeconomic categories ($r = -.19$).

In a factor analysis using the data from the PNID, as well as the measures used in establishing concurrent and construct validity, four factors were obtained: (1) Achievement–Socioeconomic, (2) Self-Rated Depression, (3) Other-Rated Depression, and (4) School Attendance.

In step-wise multiple regression analyses, the significant predictors of PNID scores were teacher-rated depression, social achievement (measured from peer nominations of happiness and popularity and therefore somewhat suspect), and self-rated depression on the modified CDI.

The Lefkowitz and Tesiny (1980) study has been presented in some detail because it is a model of the kind of thorough analysis that must be made of assessment instruments. It would be valuable if further study of the construct validity of this inventory included behavioral observation. Perhaps the data presented by Lefkowitz and Tesiny on construct validity are the least convincing. It is quite likely that the variables predicted by the PNID could be just as well or better predicted by other general or specific measures of disturbance. Construct validity for a measure can be convincingly demonstrated only if, at the same time, discriminant validity can be demonstrated. Lefkowitz and Tesiny (1980) did note the following:

> Some evidence for discriminant validity was obtained by a demonstration that hyperactive children in the sample were not nominated by their peers as significantly more depressed. Children categorized by their mothers (in a personal, precoded interview) "to be overly active compared to other children his/her age" had mean PNID scores that were not significantly different from children categorized to be not overly active. (p.48)

One wonders, though, if the measures of hyperactivity might not have had a predictive relationship to the same set of variables predicted by the PNID scores.

One also wonders what the effects of completing a PNID might be on the behaviors of the nominators and the nominated. This is a matter that should be investigated, because there could very well be iatrogenic effects of such an assessment procedure.

### Childhood Depression Inventory

The Childhood Depression Inventory (Kovacs & Beck, 1977) is a 27-item questionnaire designed specifically for assessing childhood depression. The CDI is a research instrument designed to be administered to children between the ages of

8 and 13 years. The child marks his or her answers directly on the inventory, but an interviewer reads the items aloud. Feelings and ideas for the 2 weeks preceding the interview are covered. Data currently available (Kovacs, Note 2) indicate that (1) for a sample of 875 normal children, $\alpha$ was .86, indicating acceptable internal consistency; (2) factor analysis resulted in only one factor; and (3) total scores did not correlate significantly with sex of age.[2]

Raskin (1977) has criticized the CDI on the grounds that it does not include behaviors generally cited under the rubric of "masked depression," such as temper tantrums, disobedience, running away from home, delinquency, and truancy. But, as proposed previously in this chapter, it is probably just as well at this stage not to work on the assumption that depression in children is masked. On the other hand, multiscale approaches to cover a variety of behavioral constellations are probably advisable. Raskin (1977) has also suggested that one should not rely solely on the child for the completion of the CDI. He argues that the child may be the best source for rating his or her inner feeling states but may not be especially reliable in rating such things as sleep disturbances and expressions of hostility. This is a more serious criticism, and it probably would be necessary to obtain information from sources other than the child.

In general, in screening children even for the sole purpose of detecting those who are depressed, it is advisable to cover a wide variety of behaviors and behavioral constellations. In this connection, a noteworthy comment has been made by Achenbach and Edelbrock (1979), referring to the relationship between age and the presence or absence of constellations of depressive behaviors:

> The depressed syndrome that was so clear-cut for young children of both sexes did not occur at all for adolescent boys and was combined with the Withdrawal syndrome for adolescent girls. The failure of depressive items to form a distinct factor for adolescents—especially the boys—does not imply that a diagnosis of depression would necessarily be inconsistent with the picture provided by the Profile, since clinical diagnoses should take account of overall Profile patterns and other data about the child and family, rather than being based exclusively on individual scale scores. In fact, the items that loaded highest on the Depressed factor for the younger boys were spread over several factors in the adolescent boys' sample, with three or more of them loading $\geq$ .30 on the Schizoid, Uncommunicative, and Hostile Withdrawal factors. The other items loading on these factors are consistent with the picture of an unhappy child, but there was no distinctive clustering of depressive items on any factor in the various rotations. (p. 321)

Short screening interviews, questionnaires, and checklists cannot be recommended as methods of assessing childhood depression in individual children. They could, perhaps, be adopted as research tools, but even their usefulness in this respect remains to be demonstrated.

---

[2]Further information on the CDI can be obtained from Maria Kovacs, Ph.D., Assistant Professor of Psychiatry, Western Psychiatric Institute and Clinic, 3811 O'Hara Street, Pittsburgh, Pa. 15261; telephone (412) 624-2043.

# BEHAVIORAL ASSESSMENT OF BEHAVIORS COMMONLY ASSOCIATED WITH DEPRESSION

Little attention has been paid by behavioral investigators to depression in children, and there is virtually no literature on the behavioral assessment of depression in children. There is a need, therefore, to apply the principles of behavioral analysis to the problem. These general principles have been presented in several articles and books, including this volume. This chapter will be concerned with the potential, in work with children, of behavioral procedures that have been used in assessing depression in adults.

Rehm (1976) noted that depression does not show quite the same situationality as anxiety. Consequently, she argued, the specific eliciting stimuli for depression are not readily identifiable, so that severity of depression is not measurable in terms of the numbers of situations in which it occurs. Furthermore, one is not able to assess overt motor or physiological responsivity to some set of depression-eliciting stimuli. Rehm's assumption here is that anxiety is situation-specific and depression is not, being, rather, a pervasive mood or condition. In actuality, situationally produced anxiety is only one form of anxiety. Another serious, if not more serious, form of anxiety is generalized anxiety. Generalized anxiety does, of course, affect many kinds of responses in all situations and presents some problems for both behavioral analysis and behavioral intervention. But Rehm's (1976) argument about the pervasiveness of depression has not been empirically demonstrated, and the data from Rutter and Graham (1968), presented previously, go against the argument.

## Depression and Response-Contingent Reinforcement

The best-known behavioral conceptualizations of depression are those involving, in some way or another, the concept of reinforcement. For some (Ferster, 1966, 1973; Lewinsohn, 1974), the important antecedent to depression is a loss of response-contingent reinforcement. For others, the important antecedent is the belief that there is no systematic relationship between one's behaviors and a probability of reinforcement (Seligman, 1975). I have proposed (Costello, 1972) that whatever reinforcers have to do with the causes of depression, depression itself is characterized by a loss of reinforcer effectiveness.

### *Pleasant Events Schedule*

Lewinsohn has, by far, done the greatest amount of work on the hypothesis relating the lack of, or the loss of, response-contingent reinforcement to depression. In his work, he has used one form or another of the Pleasant Events Schedule (PES). The schedule has a list of up to 320 positive events, such as "taking a bath" and "eating good meals." The schedule has been subjected to a considerable amount of psychometric investigation. Although all of Lewinsohn's work has been done with adults, a brief account of his procedure may serve to indicate the kind of approach to childhood depression that could be taken with a suitably modified PES. Data obtained with the PES could not, of course, be used to decide whether or not the child is or had been depressed. For this diagnostic purpose, one would have to have normative data on the PES, and, indeed, one would want to have the relationship between reinforcement and depression established on a firmer scientific basis than it is at present.

In Lewinsohn's retrospective use of the PES, subjects are first asked to indicate the frequency with which each event occurred within the past 30 days on a three-point scale: 1—not happened, 2—a few (1–6) times, and 3—often (7 or more times). Subjects then go through the list a second time, indicating how pleasant and enjoyable each event was, again on a three-point scale (1—not pleasant, 2—somewhat pleasant, and 3—very pleasant). Three scores can be derived from these ratings: (1) activity level, that is, the sum of the frequency ratings; (2) reinforcement potential, the sum of the pleasantness ratings; and (3) obtained reinforcement, the sum of the product of the frequency and pleasantness ratings for each item. In Lewinsohn's prospective studies including the monitoring of therapy, subjects have selected their 160 most pleasant items on the PES; this list is used as a daily activity checklist. Daily pleasantness ratings for events engaged in are also obtained. In one study (Lewinsohn & Graf, 1973), schedules of 160 items, selected as described previously, were kept for 30 days by ten depressed patients. The ten items whose scores for each subject most highly correlated with variations in daily mood as measured by the Depression Adjective Checklist (DACL) (Lubin, 1967) were selected as targets to be increased with behavior modification procedures.

Users of an instrument such as the PES must keep in mind the following problems:

1. Any retrospective use of the PES must deal with the problem that depressed people tend to underestimate the frequency of past pleasant or successful experiences (Wener & Rehm, 1975; Kuiper, 1978; Buchwald, 1977). These studies have been done with adults, but it is very likely that the same tendency would be found in depressed children. This may be a problem not only in retrospective studies but also in prospective studies, if the PES is filled out at the end of each day. If the child is depressed when the ratings are done, one might expect a cognitive distortion of past events. This may be of interest in itself but can be investigated only if data are also collected from second-party recorders, such as parents, or through direct observation by trained observers.

2. As Rehm (1976) has pointed out, self-monitoring may influence the behaviors being observed. This may be especially true for an instrument such as the PES, since, by definition, it taps only pleasant activities. Mood may improve as a result of the redirection of attention to pleasant events. In the assessment of an intervention, therefore, baseline data would be absolutely essential.

3. It may be found that, when children do self-monitoring with the PES, the data are unreliable and that more reliable data can be obtained from parents and teachers.

Lewinsohn has also designed a 160-item unpleasant events schedule (Lewinsohn, 1975), which includes items such as "being alone" and "being in a fight." Scoring procedures are similar to those applied to PES data. Though less work has been done with the unpleasant events schedule than with the PES, the currently available data suggest that it is a promising instrument for work with depressed adults and that the development of a form for use with children might very well be worthwhile.

## Reinforcement Survey Schedule

Another instrument designed for use with adults that might be modified for use with children is the Reinforcement Survey Schedule designed by Cautela and Kastenbaum (1967). The schedule is divided into four main sections. In the first three sections, the respondent is asked to rate items on a five-point scale representing the degree to which the stimuli give joy or other pleasurable feelings. Section 1 consists of items that could be presented to a client in most settings (e.g., item one, "eating," consists of six specific kinds of food). Section 2 consists of 54 items that could be presented only through facsimile or imagination, including activities such as watching sports (with nine specific sports listed), playing sports, watching television, and sleeping. Section 3 presents six brief "situations I would like to be in." For example:

> #4. You are walking alone a mountain pathway with your dog by your side. You notice attractive lakes, streams, flowers and trees. You think to yourself "It's great to be alive on a day like this, and to have the opportunity to wander alone out in the countryside." (Cautela & Kastenbaum, 1967, p. 1122)

The client is to indicate on a five-point scale how much he or she would like to be in the situation, from "not at all" to "very much."

In Section 4, clients are asked to list things they do or think about more than 5, 10, 15, and 20 times a day. This section was designed to provide data that would enable a therapist to apply the Premack principle in interventions. This well-known principle states that, for any set of responses, the most probable response in a free-choice situation will serve to reinforce less probable behaviors when presented at a subsequent time in a contingency relationship. The principle has been extended to state that less probable responses, if presented contingently, will serve to punish more probable responses. One important caveat here is that there is little empirical support for the assumption that a preferred activity assessed through verbal measres as in Section 4 of the Cautela and Kastenbaum schedule is equivalent in its empirical properties to a preferred activity assessed by observing the duration of an activity in a free-choice situation. Data relevant to this point will be noted at the end of this section, after other similar assessment procedures have been reviewed.

## Other Instruments

Some instruments have been developed specifically for use with children, and they are extremely simple. For very young children, Homme (1970) has suggested that

1. My favorite grown-up (adult) is _____
   What do you like to do with him? _____
2. The best reward anybody can give me is _____
3. My favorite school subject is _____
4. If I had ten dollars I'd _____
5. My favorite relative in Tucson is _____
6. When I grow up I want to be _____
7. The person who punishes me most is _____
   How? _____
   Effectiveness? _____
   Other punishments used? _____
   Which works best with you? _____
8. Two things I like to do best are _____
9. My favorite adult at school is _____
10. When I do something well, what my mother does is _____
    _____
11. I feel terrific when _____
12. The way I get money is _____
13. When I have money I like to _____
14. When I'm in trouble my father _____
15. Something I really want is _____
16. If I please my father, what he does is _____
17. If I had a chance, I sure would like to _____

FIGURE 2

potentially reinforcing events be written or drawn on a poster or in a booklet, to make up what he calls a "reinforcement menu." Homme (1970) and Daley (1976) present illustrations of such procedures.

Clement and Richard (1976) have presented an open-ended Children's Reinforcement Survey that is similar to the Cautela and Kastenbaum (1967) survey. It can be used either by the child or by a second-party informant. The survey covers people, places, things, and activities.

Tharp and Wetzel (1969) presented a procedure to aid in the determination of reinforcers and mediators of reinforcement. The Mediator–Reinforcer Incomplete Blank (MRB) is a 34-item, incomplete-sentence blank (see Figure 2). In their work, Tharp and Wetzel have read aloud to the child the items of the MRB. Throughout

18. The person I like most to reward me is _____

    How? _____

19. I will do almost anything to avoid _____

20. The thing I like to do best with my mother is _____

21. The thing I do that bothers my teacher the most is ._____

22. The weekend activity or entertainment I enjoy most is _____

23. If I did better at school I wish my teacher would _____

24. The kind of punishment I hate most is _____

25. I will do almost anything to get _____

26. It sure makes me mad when I can't _____

27. When I am in trouble, my mother _____

28. My favorite brother or sister in Tucson is _____

29. The thing I like to do most is _____

30. The only person I will take advice from is _____

31. Not counting my parents, a person I will do almost anything for is

    _____

32. I hate for my teacher to _____

33. My two favorite TV programs are _____

34. The thing I like to do best with my father is _____

Subject's Ranking of Reinforcers

_____

_____

_____

_____

Mediator–Reinforcer Incomplete Blank. From *Behavior Modification in the Natural Environment* by R. G. Tharp and R. J. Wetzel, pp. 225–226. Copyright 1969 by Academic Press, Inc. Reprinted by permission.

the interview, the subject is asked to describe the reinforcers clearly and to specify referent behaviors of the mediators when a positive or negative statement is made about them. Tharp and Wetzel give, as an example, a subject who says that the best reward he or she can receive is "love" and who then is asked what he or she would like people to do to show their love. The number of times that a subject mentions a particular reinforcer or potential mediator and the tone of voice used (such as enthusiasm or lack of enthusiasm) are used by the interviewer in assessing the relative strength and importance to the subjects of the reinforcers and mediators. At the end of the interview, the interviewer lists all the stated reinforcers and asks the subject to rank them. Tharp and Wetzel (1969, p. 77) also suggest that the reinforcers can be rated 1 through 9 according to the following scale:

9—Highly reinforcing; rarely fails to be effective

8

7—Quite reinforcing; will work hard for it (or avoid it)

6

5—Reinforces fairly well; moderately effective

4

3—Weak reinforcer; only works sometimes

2

1—Has reinforcing property of a very low or indeterminate power

Tharp and Wetzel present a good discussion of the way in which their instruments can be used clinically, as well as some case material. However, they do not present any data that would enable one to discuss the reliability or validity of the procedure. This is true, also, of the other procedures designed specifically for children that have been discussed so far.

Bersoff and Moyer (1976) have presented a Positive Reinforcement Observation Schedule (PROS), which they suggest can be used as a mediator reinforcement preference scale and as an observation schedule. The scale, presented in Table 6, consists of ten categories of positively reinforcing behaviors that may be emitted by adults interacting with a child. The categories described are more appropriate to the activities of classroom teachers, psychometricians, and behavior modifiers, but they could be easily reworded for use by parents. Bersoff and Moyer (1976) presented data indicating that

1. In a study of consensual validation, 147 judges perceived the ten categories to describe positive reinforcements.
2. When 38 of the original 147 judges repeated the judgment task 15 days after their first judgments, the mean percentage agreement between the two sessions was 82%, and the mean rank order correlation between the two administrations was .88.
3. When, in a series of studies, different observers made observations of the frequency of the PROS events emitted by teachers in elementary classrooms, the average interobserver correlation was .94.
4. Manipulation of positive reinforcements emitted by the teacher using the PROS significantly increased the arithmetic achievement of students in a third-grade classroom.

The instrument looks as though it might be of considerable value. Bersoff and Moyer (1976) suggest some potential uses of the PROS apart from its use as an observation schedule. These uses are:

1. The measurement of the disparity of reinforcement preferences between behavioral consultants and mediators such as teachers and parents. Bersoff and Moyer suggest that the reinforcement preferences of the mediator be assessed before an intervention approach is recommended, so that the consultants do not suggest reinforcers that are devalued by the consultee, with a resultant refusal or resistance to participate in the modification procedure.

TABLE 6

Definitions and Symbols of Categories of the Positive Reinforcement Observation Schedule

*Administration of Concrete Rewards (Direct) (CRD)*
Giving of direct concrete rewards, such as candy, money, or free time. This category also consists of those instances when the teacher/tester gives concrete but symbolic rewards (such as giving flashcards to a child contingent upon correct answer to that card) that have no backup or other value.

*Administration of Concrete Rewards (Token) (CRT)*
Giving of symbolic rewards that will be redeemed for direct concrete rewards at some future time. Common examples are poker chips, tallies, colored sticks, stars, and stickers.

*Affirmation of Appropriate Behavior (AAB)*
Verbal contact indicating approval, commendation to a child that his or her responses are correct or acceptable, or that his or her behavior is appropriate. Verbal affirmation may be either loud or soft and consists of such examples as "That's good," "Fine," "You're studying well."

*Rapport–Praise (RP)*
Evaluative reactions that go beyond the teacher's/tester's level of simple affirmation or positive feedback by verbally complimenting the child. RP communicates a positive evaluation or a warm personal reaction to the child and not merely an impersonal communication. Teacher/tester responses are considered RP if the verbal content (Yes, Unhuman, Fine, Good) or nonverbal content (head nod) is accompanied by nonverbal communication of warmth, joy, or excitement.

*Positive Facial Attention (FA + )*
Looking at a child when teacher/tester is smiling or attending to what the child is doing or what the child is saying. Teacher/tester might nod head, wink, or give other indication of approval while smiling. Concerted looking or attending to a child also belongs in this category, but a 5-second interval must elapse between one attend episode and another for this category to be scored again.

*Positive Physical Contact (PC + )*
Actual physical contact, such as patting, embracing, holding arm, or taking hand, as a sign of approval.

*Accepts Feelings (AF)*
Teacher/tester accepts and clarifies the feeling tone of the child in a nonthreatening manner. Feelings or student emotions may be positive or negative. Predicting or recalling feelings is included. Teachers/testers accept feelings when they say they understand how the child feels, that he or she has a right to these feelings, and that they will not punish the child for his or her feelings.

*Accepts Ideas (AI)*
Clarifying, building, or developing ideas suggested by the child. Teacher/tester may paraphrase the student's statement, restate the idea more simply, or summarize what the student has said. The key teacher/tester behaviors are clarifying and developing ideas. Simple restatement without building, such as when teacher/tester verbalizes student answer during recording on chalkboard or test booklet, is not scored.

*Adjuvant Mastery (AM)*
Urging, prompting, fostering, promoting confidence and success, providing encouragement for response production. When the child refuses to answer, the teacher/tester may suggest guessing, give encouragement ("You just got the last one"), or systematically employ a graded series of suggestions.

*Aiding by Example (AE)*
Demonstration of appropriate behavior by teacher/tester when the child is either nonresponsive or incorrect in exhibiting expected response.

*Note.* From "Positive Reinforcement Observation Schedule (PROS): Development and Use" by D. N. Bersoff and D. Moyer, in E. J. Mash and L. G. Terdal (Eds.), *Behavior Therapy Assessment.* Copyright 1976 by Springer Publishing Company, Inc. Reprinted by permission.

2. The assessment of mediators' change in attitude toward the events of the PROS during training and intervention.
3. With modification of difficulty levels of the category descriptions, the PROS could be used as a child reinforcer preference schedule.

The preceding methods of assessing potential reinforcers cannot simply be taken at their face value. Mash and Terdal (1976) have noted the problems involved in attempts to assess potential reinforcers for children through interviews or by obtaining reports on survey schedules from second-party informants such as the child's parents or teachers. The two primary problems are:

1. The informant is likely to think more in terms of absolute than of functional reinforcement properties. Though the event reported may have positive features, they may not necessarily be exercising positive (response-strengthening) control over the child's behavior.
2. The informant may have had limited opportunity to observe the child in situations that may be important for the identification of reinforcers. Mash and Terdal give as an example reinforcers provided by peers during play-ground interaction that has not been observed by the informant.

Despite the problems, interviews and second-party reports may be of value, as Mash and Terdal noted, if one is careful to determine things such as (1) the consistency or discrepancy between the parents' reports and the teacher's reports, (2) the consistency or discrepancy between second-party reports and the reports and behavior of the child, and (3) the actual reinforcing capacity of the events identified by the informant.

It is the third point that is particularly important. One cannot assume that verbal statements of preferences will always predict the actual reinforcing strength of the stimuli when the stimuli are made contingent on behavior (Schutz & Naumoff, 1964; Whitehurst & Domash, 1974). It will probably be some time before the relationships among intrinsic reinforcement, extrinsic reinforcement, pleasantness ratings, and response-strengthening properties have been teased out. Until then, assessment of reinforcers cannot be done in any routine clinical manner, but, then, the notion of routine methods is incompatible with the spirit of behavioral analysis. It is primarily through an experimental approach to assessment that some of the solutions to the complexities surrounding the concept of reinforcements will be found.

## Social Skills and Depression

Several writers have discussed the relationship between poor social skills and depression in adults. Although assessing social skills in children is reviewed in Chapter 8 of this volume, it may be useful to note the procedures used for investigating social skills in depressed adults so that one may consider their potential utility for investigating social skills in depressed children.

Assessing social skills in children would seem to be of particular importance. Rutter, Tizard, and Whitmore (1970), in their Isle of Wight general population survey of 10-year-olds, found that the description "not much liked by other children" was one of the best indicators of the presence of psychiatric disturbance. Hartup (1976), Roff (1970), and Rutter (1978) have reviewed the evidence that poor peer relationships are not only a good indicator of current problems but also a good predictor of later difficulties. More generally, adequate assessment of any childhood problems requires assessment of the child's relations with the social environment, because, as Evans and Nelson (1977) have pointed out, the young child is typically under much stronger sources of social control than the adult client.

In Lewinsohn's theory of depression, *social skill*, defined as the emission of behaviors that are positively reinforced by others, is seen as an area of deficit especially important in the development of depressive behaviors. One of the causes of depression, according to Lewinsohn, is the person's lack of ability to emit those behaviors that could, in turn, elicit positive reinforcement from others. Home observations have been used, as reported, for instance, in Lewinsohn and Shaffer (1971), in order to assess and modify a depressed person's interaction with other members of the family. Home visits, lasting about an hour each, are scheduled around mealtimes (usually the evening meal), when all members of the family are present. The observations arc usually done for 2 or 3 days in succession. Two observers station themselves at the edge of the dining room area in such a way that they can see all family members. Interactions are coded in 30-second intervals, using a system for coding interactions, which is shown schematically in Figure 3.

The system enables one to record the content of the action (c.g., "self"), the general category of the action (e.g., "criticism"), the "source" (the individual who emits an "action"), the "object" of the action (the person toward whom the action is directed), the "reactor," and the general category, the "reaction." Two forms of recording the interactions have been presented. One of them (Lewinsohn & Shaffer, 1971) involves an interaction matrix, as presented in Figure 4. The other form of recording is presented in Figure 5.

One of the disadvantages of the Lewinsohn and Shaffer matrix presented in Figure 3 is that it does not enable one to sec the relationship between any particular action and reaction. The Response Class Matrix, such as that designed by Mash, Terdal, and Anderson (1976) and illustrated in Figure 6, does permit one to record information about the antecedents or consequents for a given behavior.

Haynes (1978) has suggested that the disadvantage of either form of matrix is that one may be restricted to a portion of a long response chain. This can be overcome by numbering the entries into the matrix in relation to their occurrence in a sequence. However, the data provided by such matrices, like the data from the recording form designed by Lewinsohn (1976) and presented in Figure 4, may require complex methods of statistical analyses.

A set of category codes similar to that developed by Lewinsohn but specifically designed for the observation of the social interactions with other children and adults has been devised by Wahler and his colleagues (Wahler, 1975; Wahler, Breland,

## "ACTION"

**Interactional Categories**

| | | | | "REACTION" | | |
|---|---|---|---|---|---|---|
| | | | | **Positive** | | **Negative** |
| Psychol. Complaint | (PC) | Psy C | Affection | (AF) | Aff | Criticism ...... (CF) Crit |
| Somatic Complaint | (SC) | Som C | Approval | (AP) | App | Disapproval ...... (CP) Disapp |
| Criticism | (CI, CO) | Crit — I, — O | Agree | (AG) | Agr | Disagree ...... (OG) Disagree |
| | | | Laughter | (LP) | L + | Ignore ...... (IG) Ign |
| Praise | (PR) | Pr | Interest | (IN) | Int | Change Topic ...... (CG) Ch T |
| Information Request | (IM) | I — | Continues talking about | (CT) | Con T | Interrupts ...... (IR) Inter |
| Personal Problem | (PP, PM) | PP + — , — + topic | | | | Physical Punishment ...... (PU) Pun |
| Instrument Problem | (IL) | IP | Physical Affection | (PA) | Phys | |
| Other People's Problems | (OI, OE) | OP — I, — O | | | Aff | |
| Talking about abstract, impersonal, general, etc. | (TA) | Ta | | | | |

|  |  |
|---|---|
| | Object _____ Reactor |
| Source _____ | |
| Action _____ | Reaction |

**Content-Topics**

| | |
|---|---|
| School | Sch |
| Self | X,Y,Z |
| Other People (group, family) | X,Y,Z |
| Treatment | Rx |
| Sex | Sx |
| Therapist | T |

FIGURE 3

Behavior rating schedule. From "Manual of Instructions for the Behavior Ratings Used for the Observation of Interpersonal Behavior" by P. M. Lewinsohn, in E. J. Mash and L. G. Terdal (Eds.). *Behavior Therapy Assessement*, p. 337. Copyright 1976 by Springer Publishing Company, Inc. Reprinted by permission.

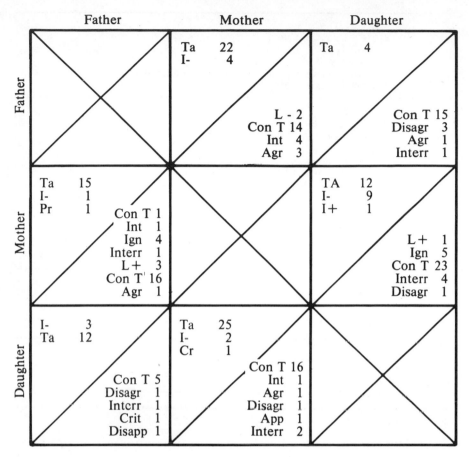

FIGURE 4

Sample matrix of coded observations. (Items above the diagonal are "actions," and those below the diagonal in each cell are "reactions." Thus, the first cell under "Mother" reads: Mother emits 26 actions, talking 22 times to Father and asking him 4 questions (I−). She emits 23 reactions, laughing twice, continuing the topic 14 times, showing interest 4 times, and agreeing 3 times.) From Lewinsohn and Shaffer (1971, p. 89).

Coe, & Leske, 1977). Brief descriptions of these categories are presented in Table 7. The complete coding system is presented in Wahler, House, and Stambaugh (1976).

One of the problems, of course, with procedures such as those of Lewinsohn and Wahler is that they are time-consuming and expensive. Because of these problems, McClean, Ogston, and Grauer (1973) devised a useful procedure that required patients to make half-hour tape recordings of problem discussion with their spouses at home. The recordings were divided into 30-second intervals and coded for positive and negative initiations and reactions using Lewinsohn's (1976)

1.

$$\text{A: } I\text{-} \frac{T}{R_X} \text{ B Con T}$$

A: What are we supposed to do here? Addressed to T.
B responds: I guess anybody knows.

2.

$$\text{A:I-} \frac{B}{\text{his work}} \text{ B-Int}$$

A: What did you do at the office today?
B: Oh, you should have been there, etc.

3.

$$\text{S: Crit} \underline{\quad\quad} \text{ M Ch T}$$
$$\text{"people"}$$

Sam: "People are so phony these days."
Martha: "I was late for class today."

4.

5.

6.

7.

FIGURE 5

Observation data sheet. From "Manual of Instructions for the Behavior Ratings Used for the Observation of Interpersonal Behavior" by P. M. Lewinsohn, in E. J. Mash and L. G. Terdal (Eds.), *Behavior Therapy Assessment*, p. 343. Copyright 1976 by Springer Publishing Company, Inc. Reprinted by permission.

manual. Interrater agreement ranged from 73% to 97%, with an average agreement of 88%. A similar method could possibly be used at least with older children. It would probably also be worthwhile, at this point, to investigate the possible relationships between (1) behaviors assessed in interviews; (2) laboratory observation of behaviors; and (3) social skills in the natural environment. For instance, several

| Child's Antecedent | MOTHER'S CONSEQUENT | | | | | | |
|---|---|---|---|---|---|---|---|
| | Command | Command question | Question | Praise | Negative | Inter-action | No response |
| Compliance | | | | | | | |
| Play | | | | | | | |
| Competing | | | | | | | |
| Negative | | | | | | | |
| Interaction | | | | | | | |
| No response | | | | | | | |

FIGURE 6
Response Class Matrix. From Mash, Terdal, and Anderson (1973).

investigators (Hinchliffe, Lancashire, & Roberts, 1971b; Rutter & Stephenson, 1972; Waxer, 1974) have found that depressed adults maintain significantly less eye contact than nondepressed adults. Similarly, slow speech, which has been found to be characteristic of depressed adults (Hinchliffe, Lancashire, & Roberts, 1971a), may occur in some children and contribute to difficulties in social situations.

## Retardation and Agitation

Both retardation and agitation have been found to be associated with adult depression. On the other hand, for the factors of depression found in the Achenbach studies reviewed previously, the only relevant item that showed a significant loading was "slow moving," which loaded on the Depressed Withdrawal factor found in 12- to 16-year-old girls. This lack of representation of retardation and agitation on the depression factors found with younger children may be attributable, in part, to their inadequate representation on the Child Behavior Checklist. There is only one item that appears to be directly related to agitation: "Can't sit still, restless or hyperactive."

From a behavioral point of view, impoverishment of behavior has been considered one of the defining characteristics of depression. This impoverishment can be manifested in terms of reduced probability of behavior, reduced frequency, reduced duration, reduced amplitude, and increased latency of responding. Activity schedules of the sort that have been reviewed in the section on reinforcers may give an indication of reduced probabilities, reduced frequencies, and reduced du-

TABLE 7

Brief Descriptions of Category Codes Used to Record Direct Observations of Subjects and Their Interaction Associates at School and at Home[a]

Target child behaviors

1. *Compliance* (C).[b] Any instance of compliance with an adult instruction (except those instructions forbidding some activity).

2. *Rule violation* (RV). Any instance of noncompliance with a permanent rule or temporary rule (see Nonaversive adult instruction, IA+).

3. *Opposition* (O). Any full 10-second interval of noncompliance with an instruction.

4. *Aversive opposition* (O−). Valence quality of a Rule violation or Opposition that is also scored if an occurrence of either of these has an aversive quality (see Aversive adult instruction).

5. *Complaint* (CP). Any instance of whining, crying, or any verbal or nonverbal act of protest.

6. *Self-stimulation* (S). Any rubbing of any body part against the body or some other surface at least three times during an interval (e.g., foot-tapping, finger-drumming, scratching).

7. *Object play* (OP). Idle or nonpurposive manipulation of an object—three of the same movements within an interval (e.g., rocking a chair, pencil tapping).

8. *Self-talk* (T). Any instance of recognizable language spoken by the child to himself or herself.

9. *Sustained noninteraction* (NI). A full interval of no meaningful interaction with person or object.

10. *Sustained school work* (SS). A full 10-second interval of any school-related work.

11. *Sustained toy play* (ST). A full interval of appropriate play with some object, with or without other children—for example, (1) running a car around on the rug, (2) pushing a stick in the dirt, (3) riding a bicycle, (4) reading a comic book, (5) playing with a doll, (6) pushing a pencil around on the table.

12. *Sustained work* (SW). A full 10-second interval of adult-approved work (e.g., cleaning his or her room, washing dishes, taking out the garbage).

13. *Sustained attending* (SA). A full 10-second interval of directing visual or auditory attention toward a single person or event.

14. *Approach child* (AC). Any initiation of an interaction with another child during the interval by the target child. May be verbal or nonverbal.

15. *Approach adult* (AA). Same as Approach child, only to an adult.

16. *Social interaction child* (SIC). Social behavior by the target child (toward another child) that is either part of an interaction in progress when the interval began or in response to initiation by another child. May be verbal or nonverbal.

17. *Social interaction adult* (SIA). The same as Social interaction child, only toward an adult.

18. *Mand child* (MC). Any instance of the target child commanding or giving an instruction to another child.

19. *Mand adult* (MA). Same as Mand child, only toward an adult.

20. *Slash* (SL). Any target child behavior that is not covered by any of the other categories.

Behaviors by other people toward the target child

21. *Nonaversive adult instruction* (IA+ or IAP). Instructions to the target child by an adult. May command the child to engage in some activity or may forbid the child from engaging in some activity. In the latter case, it is scored like a rule until the setting changes and is called a "temporary rule."

TABLE 7 *(continued)*

22. *Aversive adult instruction* (IA − or IAM). Same as Nonaversive adult instruction, only judged aversive in delivery because of (1) content (threat, ridicule), (2) tone (loud, angry), or (3) assertiveness (e.g., gesture, posture).

23. *Nonaversive adult social attention* (SA + or SAP). Any noninstructional contact by an adult with the target child. May be verbal or nonverbal.

24. *Aversive adult social attention* (SA − or SAM). Same as Nonaversive adult social attention, only aversive (see Aversive adult instruction).

25. *Nonaversive child social attention* (SC + or SCP). Any contact by another child with the target child. May be instructional or not, and verbal or nonverbal.

26. *Aversive child social attention* (SC − or SCM). Same as Nonaversive child attention, only aversive (see Aversive adult instruction).

27. *Visually present* (FP, MP). These categories are scored, respectively, for the visual presence to the target child for any instance of the father (FP) or the mother (MP). "Visually present" means that the child could look up from his or her current position (swiveling 360°, if necessary) and see the other person. If the child would have to get up to look over or around an obstacle, the other person is not considered visually present.

*Note.* From Wahler, Breland, Coe, and Leske (1977, p. 223).
[a]See Wahler, House, and Stambaugh (1976) for complete definitions, with examples.
[b]Note that these categories are not mutually exclusive. One behavior may be scored as several categories at the same time.

rations of behaviors. Increased latency of responding may be measured in terms of either discrete responses, as in measurement of simple or complex reaction times, for instance, or a chain of responses, as in the measurement of tapping speed and speed of writing. There are two problems to be faced, however. First, though there are studies demonstrating that depressed adults are slower in responding than nondepressed adults, no norms are available on speed of responding for either adults or children. Second, the work of Weckowicz and his colleagues (Weckowicz, Nutter, Cruise, & Yonge, 1972; Weckowicz, Nutter, Cruise, Yonge, & Cairns, 1978) suggests that the retardation of depressives is not attributable to some simple physiological process but is a result of complex motivational and situational variables.

Nevertheless, despite the absence of normative data, a clinician may adopt the hypothesis that a child is slow in responding on the basis of teachers' and parents' reports. The approach would then be to make speed of responding the target behavior and to determine the variables affecting the child's speed of responding. In the laboratory, measurements could be taken of standard reaction time and speed of tapping equipment and simple writing and drawing tasks. In the natural environment speed of responding in conversations, for instance, could be measured. In view of the findings of Weckowicz and his colleagues noted previously, it would also be advisable, in both the laboratory and the natural environment situations, to manipulate social and monetary incentives to determine how readily the speed of responding could be improved. Two other variables that have been related to speed of responding and that should be considered in any assessment procedure are level of anxiety and distraction by depressive thoughts (Payne, 1970).

A more elaborate procedure to determine activity levels in depressed adults has been described by Kupfer, Detre, Foster, Tucker, and Delgado (1972). The procedure would be used for children who were inpatients. The apparatus enables one to obtain 24-hour telemetric recording of activity. The transmitter, including battery, weighs 50 g, and the range is approximately 33.33 m. Kupfer, Weiss, Foster, Detre, Delgado, and McPartland (1974) found that unipolar depressives had significantly higher levels of activity than bipolar depressives prior to drug treatment. They also found, however, that whereas there was not a significant correlation between activity level and self-reported depression, there was a significant correlation (.85) between self-reported anxiety and activity levels. It would seem, therefore, that activity levels, as recorded by this device, may be more related to anxiety than to depression. But since anxiety appears to often co-exist with depression in adults, the instrument may be of value to the clinician interested in taking measurements related to anxiety, even though the primary problem of the child is suspected to be depression. Many rating scales and instruments have been disigned to assess activity levels in hyperactive children (see Chapter 3, this volume), some of which might be adopted for the assessment of retardation and agitation in the depressed child.

## The Measurement of Mood

The behavioral assessment of moods is not an easy task. For older children, Aitken's extremely simple Visual Analogue Scale might be worth considering (Aitken, 1969; Aitken & Zealley, 1970). This is a 100-mm graphic scale, anchored only at the ends by "normal mood" and "most depressed." As Aitken and Zealley (1970) have noted, "as moods vary in a continuous fashion it seems logical to present the patient with a kind of symbol which will avoid the need for him to rate in categories" (p. 222). One of the advantages of such an approach is that measurement to the nearest millimeter provides a sufficiently large number of categories to allow considering it as a continuum, and therefore the scores meet the assumptions necessary for parametric analysis.

## Behaviors and Constellations of Behaviors

In our behavioral assessments of disorders, constellations of behaviors have probably not received as much attention as they might have. Other researchers, however, have not neglected the issue. For instance, Wahler (1975) has written:

> The importance of pursuing response-class phenomena is evident from both practical and theoretical perspectives. *If a child's behavior repertoire is indeed organized into functional "clusters," it is conceivable that his or her deviant actions might be*

*modified indirectly*. Thus, behavior difficult to deal with directly, such as stealing, might be modified by the contingent management of behaviors more easily dealt with. In contrast, it is possible that contingent management o deviant behavior might produce undesirable changes in the child's behavioral repertoire. Both of these possibilities are of enormous practical importance. (p. 28)

In the case of childhood depression, negative self-concepts and sleep disturbances (see Chapter 15, this volume) may, for instance, be difficult to modify directly. They may, however, be modified indirectly if they co-vary with behaviors such as level of activity and social skills, which can be more directly modified.

Because assessing a number of behaviors across situations and over time is usually done in behavioral assessment, one would have the data with which to determine whether the behaviors measured do co-vary. Let us look briefly at how this might be done following the procedure described by Wahler (1975). Assume that the occurrence and nonoccurrence of each category of a set of behaviors have been recorded in each scoring period within a series of sessions. One can then obtain the percentage occurrence of each category for each session. These percentages for each category can be arranged as a distribution of scores across sessions. The category–score distributions can then be subjected to correlational analysis. The intercorrelation can be determined within sessions (baseline, treatment 1, etc.), within settings (e.g., home, school), and across settings (e.g., home and school data combined). The matrices of intercorrelations can then be subjected to one or another clustering technique to extract groupings of correlated behavior categories.

Before examining the environmental determinants of the clusters obtained, one would want to determine if a cluster identified within a setting was stable across sessions within that setting. If any cluster were found to be stable, the following type of analysis could be done. To determine if the categories of behavior within a cluster are under the control of the same environmental stimuli, one would conduct within-session analyses of the behavior clusters. One would assess the temporal relationship between the behaviors in each cluster and the environmental categories measured. To do this, one would compute three sets of conditional probabilities for each behavior category in each cluster. These computations involve determining stimulus occurrence probabilities (1) in the *same* time interval as that containing a relevant behavior, (2) in the interval *before* the behavior, and (3) in the interval *after* the behavior.

The procedures for determining the co-variation of behaviors in the cluster are not complicated, but the interpretation of the data obtained is likely to be difficult. For instance, in some cases, contingency management procedures that change one behavior in a cluster may result in systematic changes in environmental stimuli for other behaviors in the cluster. To the extent that the behaviors in which a clinician is interested do co-vary, problems are presented in using multiple baseline procedures for testing the specificity of the effects of interventions. For instance, if one attempted to modify a child's crying and found that there was a significant change during treatment in other behaviors, such as levels of activity, sleep, and social skills, one could not assume that the intervention was not specific in effect.

That would be one alternative hypothesis. The other, of course, is that the behaviors are functionally related and that, therefore, of necessity, when one intervenes with one behavior in the cluster, the others will change also.

That clinicians dealing with the problem of depression in children might have to face difficulties of this sort is indicated in a report by Zeiss, Lewinsohn, and Muñoz (1979). They found that in treating depressed adults, treatment focusing on either interpersonal skills, cognitions, or pleasant events significantly alleviated depression as measured by the Minnesota Multiphasic Personality Inventory (MMPI) Depression Scale. However, no treatment modality had specific impact on the target behavior alone. Instead, all patients improved on most dependent variables, regardless of whether or not they were directly addressed in treatment. The authors suggested that these results could best be interpreted in terms of Bandura's (1977) self-efficacy model.

# CONCLUSION

It would be unethical to assume that a child manifesting no clear signs of depression is nevertheless depressed, particularly if this resulted in the administration of antidepressant drugs. It would be unwise and unscientific, however, to assume that depression, as a primary problem, does not occur in children. The functional analysis of depressive behaviors in children and the investigation of their co-variation during and in the absence of interventions should be a high-priority endeavor. Behavioral checklists will probably play only a very preliminary role in such work. To know that a child cries is not likely to be of much help without a functional analysis of the crying. Such functional analyses of depressive behaviors in children have not been discussed because no such studies have been done and the general principles of such analyses are readily avilable in other portions of this book and elsewhere.

My object has been simply to present the observations on childhood depression and the possibly relevant procedures used with adult depressives, which may serve as a base from which the behavioral analyst can start work. Such work will benefit from attention being paid to the possible existence of constellations of depressive behaviors and by the effort to formulate theories of behavior that will account for the co-variations in such constellations. Indeed, for a thorough understanding of the depressed child's behavior, assessors may have to adopt methods of social systems analysis such as those proposed by Patterson (1976) and Wahler *et al.* (1977). Then we shall be concerned not only with the constellations of a child's behavior but also with the constellations of behaviors of the child's family and how these family behaviors, in turn, co-vary with the behaviors of people in other social units, such as other families, schools, and public agencies. The work of Coyne (1976) with depressed adults has shown how the depressed person's behavior may affect and be affected by the behaviors of other members of the family, and it would not be too surprising to find the same kind of interactions between depressed children and their families. On the other hand, we might find that the families of depressed children are insulated from the community in a manner described by Wahler *et al.* (1977). They found that the behaviors of the members of insulated families were not affected by the behaviors of those outside the family. In an investigation of women in the Outer Hebrides (Brown, Davidson, Harris, Maclean, Pollock, & Prudo, 1977), it was found that higher rates of depression occurred in women who were the least integrated into the community.

## Acknowledgment

Preparation of this chapter was supported by an Alberta Mental Health grant.

## Reference Notes

1. Achenbach, T. M. *The Child Behavior Profile: Edition for boys aged 4 and 5 years.* Unpublished manuscript, Laboratory of Developmental Psychology, National Institute of Mental Health, 1978.
2. Kovacs, M. Personal communication, February 14, 1979.

## References

Achenbach, T. M. The child behavior profile: I. Boys aged 6–11. *Journal of Consulting and Clinical Psychology,* 1978, *46,* 478–488.
Achenbach, T. M., & Edelbrock, C. S. The classification of child psychopathology: A review and analysis of empirical efforts. *Psychological Bulletin,* 1978, *85,* 1275–1301.
Achenbach, T. M., & Edelbrock, C. S. The child behavior profile: II. Boys aged 12 through 16 and girls aged 6–11 and 12–16. *Journal of Consulting and Clinical Psychology,* 1979, *47,* 223–233.
Agras, A. The relationship of school phobia to childhood depression. *American Journal of Psychiatry,* 1959, *116,* 533–539.
Aitken, A. C. B. Measures of feeling using analogue scales. *Proceedings of the Royal Society of Medicine,* 1969, *62,* 989–993.
Aitken, A. C. B., & Zealley, A. R. Measurement of moods. *British Journal of Hospital Medicine,* 1970, *4,* 215–224.
Albert, N., & Beck, A. T. Incidence of depression in early adolescence: A preliminary study. *Journal of Youth and Adolescence,* 1975, *4,* 301–307.
Annell, A. L. (Ed.). *Depressive states in childhood and adolescence.* Stockholm: Almquist & Wiksell, 1972.
Anthony, J., & Scott, P. Manic–depressive psychosis in childhood. *Journal of Child Psychology and Psychiatry,* 1960, *1,* 53–72.
Arieti, S. *American handbook of psychiatry.* New York: Basic Books, 1959.
Arnold, L. E., & Smeltzer, D. J. Behavior checklist factor analysis for children and adolescents. *Archives of General Psychiatry,* 1974, *30,* 799–804.
Bandura, A. Self-efficacy: Toward a unifying theory of behavioral change. *Psychological Review,* 1977, *84,* 191–215.
Bersoff, D. N., & Moyer, D. Positive reinforcement observation schedule (PROS): Development and use. In E. J. Mash & L. G. Terdal (Eds.), *Behavior therapy assessment: Diagnosis, design and evaluation.* New York: Springer, 1976.
Blackwell, B., & Shepherd, M. Prophylactic lithium: Another therapeutic myth? *Lancet,* 1968, *1,* 968–971.

Bleuler, E. *Textbook of psychiatry*. New York: Macmillan, 1934.

Brown, G. W., Davidson, S., Harris, T., Maclean, U., Pollock, S., & Prudo, R. Psychiatric disorder in London and North Uist. *Social Science and Medicine*, 1977, *11*, 367–377.

Brumback, R. A., & Weinberg, W. A. Childhood depression: An explanation of a behavior disorder in children. *Perceptual and Motor Skills*, 1977, *44*, 911–916.

Buchwald, A. M. Depressive mood and estimates of reinforcement frequency. *Journal of Abnormal Psychology*, 1977, *86*, 433–446.

Campbell, J. D. Manic–depressive psychosis in children. *Journal of Nervous and Mental Diseases*, 1952, *116*, 424–439.

Campbell, J. D. Manic–depressive disease in children. *Journal of the American Medical Association*, 1955, *158*, 154–157.

Cautela, J. R., & Kastenbaum, R. A reinforcement survey schedule for use in therapy, training and research. *Psychological Reports*, 1967, *20*, 1115–1130.

Clement, P. W., & Richard, R. C. Identifying reinforcers for children: A children's reinforcement survey. In E. J. Mash & L. G. Terdal (Eds.), *Behavior therapy assessment: Diagnosis, design and evaluation*. New York: Springer, 1976.

Coll, P. G., & Bland, R. Manic–depressive illness in adolescence and childhood. *Canadian Psychiatric Association Journal*, 1979, *24*, 255–263.

Comrey, A. L. Common methodological problems in factor analytic studies. *Journal of Consulting and Clinical Psychology*, 1978, *46*, 648–659.

Connell, H. M. Depression in childhood. *Child Psychiatry and Human Development*, 1972, *4*, 71–85.

Conners, C. K. Classification and treatment of childhood depression and depressive equivalents. In D. M. Gallant & G. M. Simpson (Eds.), *Depression: Behavioral, biochemical, diagnostic and treatment concepts*. New York: Spectrum, 1976.

Coopersmith, S. *The antecedents of self-esteem*. San Francisco: W. H. Freeman, 1967.

Costello, C. G. Classification and psychopathology. In C. G. Costello (Ed.), *Symptoms of psychopathology: A handbook*. New York: Wiley, 1970.

Costello, C. G. Depression: Loss of reinforcers or loss of reinforcer effectiveness. *Behavior Therapy*, 1972, *3*, 240–247.

Costello, C. G. Childhood depression: Three basic but questionable assumptions in the Lefkowitz and Burton critique. *Psychological Bulletin*, 1980, *87*, 185–190.

Costello, C. G., & Belton, G. P. Depression: Treatment. In C. G. Costello (Ed.), *Symptoms of psychopathology: A handbook*. New York: Wiley, 1970.

Coyne, J. C. Depression and the responses of others. *Journal of Abnormal Psychology*, 1976, *85*, 186–193.

Cytryn, L., & McKnew, D. H. Factors influencing the changing clinical expression of the depressive process in children. *American Journal of Psychiatry*, 1974, *131*, 879–881.

Cytryn, L., McKnew, D. H., & Levy, E. Z. Proposed classification of childhood depression. *American Journal of Psychiatry*, 1972, *129*, 149–155.

Daley, M. F. The "reinforcement menu": Finding effective reinforcers. In E. J. Mash & L. G. Terdal (Eds.), *Behavior therapy assessment: Diagnosis, design and evaluation*. New York: Springer, 1976.

Evans, I. M., & Nelson, R. O. Assessment of child behavior problems. In A. R. Ciminero, K. S. Calhoun, & H. E. Adams (Eds.), *Handbook of behavioral assessment*. New York: Wiley, 1977.

Feinstein, S. C., & Wolpert, E. A. Juvenile manic–depressive illness: Clinical and therapeutic considerations. *Journal of the American Academy of Child Psychiatry*, 1973, *12*, 123–126.

Ferster, C. B. Animal behavior and mental illness. *Psychological Record*, 1966, *16*, 345–356.

Ferster, C. B. A functional analysis of depression. *American Psychologist*, 1973, *28*, 857–870.

Frommer, E. A. Treatment of childhood depression with antidepressant drugs. *British Medical Journal*, 1967, *1*, 729–732.

Frommer, E. A. Depressive illness in childhood. In A. Coppen & A. Walk (Eds.), *Recent developments in affective disorder*. London: British Journal of Psychiatry Special Publication No. 2, 1968.

Glaser, K. Masked depression in children and adolescents. *American Journal of Psychotherapy*, 1967, *21*, 565–575.

Graham, P. Depression in pre-pubertal children. *Developmental Medicine and Child Neurology*, 1974, *16*, 340–349.

Graham, P., & Rutter, M. The reliability and validity of the psychiatric assessment of the child: II. Interview with the parent. *British Journal of Psychiatry*, 1968, *114*, 581–592.

Harrington, M., & Hassan, J. Depression in girls during latency. *British Journal of Medical Psychology*, 1958, *31*, 43–50.

Hartup, W. W. Peer interaction and the behavioral development of the individual child. In E. Schopler & R. S. Reichler (Eds.), *Psychopathology and child development*. New York: Plenum, 1976.

Hinchliffe, M. K., Lancashire, M., & Roberts, F. J. Depression: Defence mechanisms in speech. *British Journal of Psychiatry*, 1971, *118*, 471–472. (a)

Hinchliffe, M. K., Lancashire, M., & Roberts, F. J. Study of eye contact in depressed and recovered patients. *British Journal of Psychiatry*, 1971, *119*, 213–215. (b)

Hollon, T. H. Poor school performance as a symptom of masked depression in children and adolescents. *American Journal of Psychotherapy*, 1970, *24*, 258–263.

Homme, L. E. *How to use contingency contracting in the classroom*. Champaign, Ill.: Research Press, 1970.

Kasanin, J. The affective psychoses in children. *Journal of Nervous and Mental Diseases*, 1952, *116*, 424–429.

Kovacs, M., & Beck, A. T. An empirical–clinical approach toward a definition of childhood depression. In J. G. Schulterbrandt & A. Raskin (Eds.), *Depression in childhood: Diagnosis, treatment and conceptual models*. New York: Raven Press, 1977.

Krakowski, A. J. Depressive reactions of childhood and adolescence. *Psychosomatics*, 1970, *11*, 429–433.

Kuiper, N. A. Depression and causal attributions for success and failure. *Journal of Personality and Social Psychology*, 1978, *3*, 236–246.

Kupfer, D. J., Detre, T. P., Foster, F. G., Tucker, G. J., & Delgado, J. The application of Delgado's telemetric mobility recorder for human studies. *Behavioral Biology*, 1972, *7*, 585–590.

Kupfer, D. J., Weiss, B. L., Foster, F. G., Detre, T. P., Delgado, J., & McPartland, R. Psychomotor activity in affective states. *Archives of General Psychiatry*, 1974, *30*, 765–768.

Leese, S. Depression masked by acting-out behavior patterns. *American Journal of Psychotherapy*, 1974, *28*, 352–361. (a)

Leese, S. *Masked depression*. New York: Jason Aronson, 1974. (b)

Lefkowitz, M. M., & Burton, N. Childhood depression: A critique of the concept. *Psychological Bulletin*, 1978, *85*, 716–726.

Lefkowitz, M. M., & Tesiny, E. P. Assessment of childhood depression. *Journal of Consulting and Clinical Psychology*, 1980, *48*, 43–50.

Lewinsohn, P. M. Clinical and theoretical aspects of depression. In K. S. Calhoun, H. E. Adams, & K. M. Mitchell (Eds.), *Innovative treatment methods in psychopathology*. New York: Wiley, 1974.

Lewinsohn, P. M. Behavioral study and treatment of depression. In M. Hersen, R. M. Eisler, & P. M. Miller (Eds.), *Progress in behavior modification*. New York: Academic Press, 1975.

Lewinsohn, P. M. Manual of instructions for the behavior ratings used for the observation of interpersonal behavior. In E. J. Mash & L. G. Terdal (Eds.), *Behavior therapy assessment: Diagnosis, design and evaluation*. New York: Springer, 1976.

Lewinsohn, P. M., & Graf, M. Pleasant activities and depression. *Journal of Consulting and Clinical Psychology*, 1973, *41*, 261–268.

Lewinsohn, P. M., & Shaffer, M. Use of home observations as an integral part of the treatment of depression: Preliminary report and case studies. *Journal of Consulting and Clinical Psychology*, 1971, *37*, 87–94.

Ling, W., Oftedal, G., & Weinberg, W. Depressive illness in childhood presenting as a severe headache. *American Journal of Disabled Children*, 1970, *120*, 122–124.

Lubin, B. *Manual for the depression adjective checklist*. San Diego: Educational and Instructional Testing Service, 1967.

McClean, P. D., Ogston, R., & Grauer, L. A behavioral approach to the treatment of depression. *Journal of Behavior Therapy and Experimental Psychiatry*, 1973, *4*, 323–330.

McConville, B. J., Boag, L. C., & Purohit, A. P. Three types of childhood depression. *Canadian Psychiatric Association Journal*, 1973, *18*, 133–138.

McKnew, D. H., & Cytryn, L. Historical background in children with affective disorders. *American Journal of Psychiatry*, 1973, *130*, 1278–1280.

Mahler, M. S. Sadness and grief in infancy and childhood. *Psychoanalytic Study of the Child*, 1961, *16*, 332–351.

Malmquist, C. P. Depression in childhood and adolescence. *New England Journal of Medicine*, 1971, *284*, 887–893; 955–961.

Mash, E. J., & Terdal, L. G. (Eds.). *Behavior therapy assessment: Diagnosis, design and evaluation*. New York: Springer, 1976.

Mash, E. J., Terdal, L. G., & Anderson, K. The response class matrix: A procedure for recording parent–child interactions. In E. J. Mash & L. G. Terdal (Eds.), *Behavior therapy assessment: Diagnosis, design and evaluation*. New York: Springer, 1976.

Melia, P. I. Prophylactic lithium: A double blind trial in recurrent affective disorders. *British Journal of Psychiatry*, 1970, *116*, 621–624.

Nowicki, S. Jr., & Strickland, B. R. A locus of control scale for children. *Journal of Consulting and Clinical Psychology*, 1973, *40*, 148–154.

Ossofsky, H. J. Endogenous depression in infancy and childhood. *Comprehensive Psychiatry*, 1974, *15*, 19–25.

Patterson, G. R. The aggressive child: Victim and architect of a coercive system. In E. J. Mash, L. A. Hamerlynck, & L. C. Handy (Eds.), *Behavior modification and families*. New York: Brunner/Mazel, 1976.

Payne, R. W. Disorders of thinking. In C. G. Costello (Ed.), *Symptoms of psychopathology: A handbook*. New York: Wiley, 1970.

Pearce, J. B. The recognition of depressive disorder in children. *Journal of the Royal Society of Medicine*, 1978, *71*, 494–500.

Poznanski, E., Krahenbuhl, V., & Zrull, J. P. Childhood depression: A longitudinal perspective. *Journal of the American Academy of child Psychiatry*, 1976, *15*, 491–501.

Poznanski, E., & Zrull, J. P. Childhood depression: Clinical characteristics of overtly depressed children. *Archives of General Psychiatry*, 1970, *23*, 8–15.

Raskin, A. Depression in children: Fact or fallacy? In J. G. Schulterbrandt & A. Raskin (Eds.), *Depression in childhood: Diagnosis, treatment and conceptual models*. New York: Raven Press, 1977.

Rehm, L. P. Assessment of depression. In M. Hersen & A. S. Bellack (Eds.), *Behavioral assessment: A practical handbook*. New York: Pergamon, 1976.

Renshaw, D. C. Suicide and depression in children. *Journal of School Health*, 1974, *44*, 487–489.

Rie, H. E. Depression in childhood: A survey of some pertinent contributions. *Journal of American Academy of Child Psychiatry*, 1966, *5*, 653–685.

Rochlin, G. The loss complex. *Journal of the American Psychoanalytic Association*, 1959, *7*, 299–316.

Roff, M. Some life history factors in relation to various types of adult maladjustment. In M. Roff & D. F. Ricks (Eds.), *Life history research in psychopathology* (Vol. 1). Minneapolis: University of Minnesota Press, 1970.

Rush, A. J., Khatami, M., & Beck, A. T. Cognitive and behavior therapy in chronic depression. *Behavior Therapy*, 1975, *6*, 398–404.

Rutter, M. A children's behavior questionnaire for completion by teachers: Preliminary findings. *Journal of Child Psychology and Psychiatry*, 1967, *8*, 1–11.

Rutter, M. Early sources of security and competence. In J. S. Bruner & A. Gaston (Eds.), *Human growth and development*. Oxford: Clarendon Press, 1978.

Rutter, M., & Graham, P. The reliability and validity of the psychiatric assessment of the child: I. Interview with the child. *British Journal of Psychiatry*, 1968, *114*, 563–579.

Rutter, D. R., & Stephenson, G. M. Visual interaction in a group of schizophrenic and depressed patients. *British Journal of Social and Clinical Psychology*, 1972, *11*, 57–65.

Rutter, M., Tizard, J., & Whitmore, K. *Education, health and behavior*. London: Longman, 1970.

Sandler, J., & Joffe, W. G. Notes on childhood depression. *International Journal of Psychoanalysis*, 1965, *46*, 88–96.

Schulterbrandt, J. G., & Raskin, A. *Depression in childhood: Diagnosis, treatment and conceptual models*. New York: Raven Press, 1977.

Schutz, R. E., & Naumoff, H. The relationship between paired comparison scale values of stimuli and their function as reinforcers of a free operant response with young children. *Psychological Record*, 1964, *14*, 89–93.

Seligman, M. E. P. *Helplessness*. San Francisco: W. H. Freeman, 1975.

Shaffer, D., Costello, A. J. C., & Hill, D. Control of enuresis with imipramine. *Archives of Disorders of Childhood*, 1968, *43*, 665–671.

Siegelman, M. Psychometric properties of the Wiggins and Winder Peer Nomination Inventory. *Journal of Psychology*, 1966, *64*, 143–149. (a)

Siegelman, M. Loving and punishing parental behavior and intraversion tendencies in sons. *Child Development*, 1966, *37*, 985–992. (b)

Sperling, M. Equivalents of depression in children. *Journal of the Hillside Hospital*, 1959, *8*, 138–148.

Tharp, R. G., & Wetzel, R. J. *Behavior modification in the natural environment*. New York: Academic Press, 1969.

Toolan, J. M. Depression in children and adolescents. *American Journal of Orthopsychiatry*, 1962, *32*, 404–414.

Toolan, J. M. Depression and suicide. In S. Arieti (Ed.), *American handbook of psychiatry* (2nd ed.). New York: Basic Books, 1974.

Varsamis, J., & MacDonald, S. M. Manic–depressive disease in childhood. *Canadian Psychiatric Association Journal*, 1972, *17*, 279–281.

Wahler, R. G. Some structural aspects of deviant child behavior. *Journal of Applied Behavior Analysis*, 1975, *8*, 27–42.

Wahler, R. G., Breland, R. M., Coe, T. D., & Leske, G. Social systems analysis: Implementing an alternative behavioral model. In A. Rogers-Warren & S. F. Warren (Eds.), *Ecological perspectives in behavior analysis*. Baltimore: University Park Press, 1977.

Wahler, R. G., House, A. E., & Stambaugh, E. E. *Ecological assessment of child problem behavior*. New York: Pergamon Press, 1976.

Warneke, L. A case of manic–depressive illness in childhood. *Canadian Psychiatric Association Journal*, 1975, *20*, 195–200.

Waxer, P. Nonverbal cues for depression. *Journal of Abnormal Psychology*, 1974, *83*, 319–322.

Weckowicz, T. E., Nutter, R. W., Cruise, D. G., & Yonge, K. A. Speed in test performance in relation to depressive illness and age. *Canadian Psychiatric Association Journal*, 1972, *17*, 241–250.

Weckowicz, T. E., Nutter, R. W., Cruise, D. G., Yonge, K. A., & Cairns, M. Speed in test performance in relation to depressive illness and age (an appendix). *Canadian Psychiatric Association Journal*, 1978, *23*, 107–109.

Weinberg, W., Rutman, J., Sullivan, L., Penick, E. C., & Dietz, S. G. Depression in children referred to an educational diagnostic center: Diagnosis and treatment. *Journal of Pediatrics*, 1973, *83*, 1065–1072.

Welner, Z. Childhood depression: An overview. *Journal of Nervous and Mental Diseases*, 1978, *166*, 588–593.

Welner, Z., Welner, A., McCrary, M. D., & Leonard, M. A. Psychopathology in children of in-patients with depression: A controlled study. *Journal of Nervous and Mental Diseases*, 1977, *164*, 408–413.

Wener, A., & Rehm, L. P. Depressive affect: A test of behavioral hypotheses. *Journal of Abnormal Psychology*, 1975, *84*, 211–227.

White, J. H., & O'Shanick, G. Juvenile manic–depressive illness. *American Journal of Psychiatry*, 1977, *134*, 1035–1036.

Whitehurst, C., & Domash, M. Preference assessment for application of the Premack Principle. *Psychological Reports*, 1974, *35*, 919–924.

Wiggins, J. S., & Winder, C. L. The peer nomination inventory: An empirically derived sociometric measure of adjustment in preadolescent boys. *Psychological Reports*, 1961, *9*, 643–677.

Winder, C. L., & Wiggins, J. S. Social reputation and social behavior: A further validation of the peer nomination inventory. *Journal of Abnormal and Social Psychology*, 1964, *68*, 681–684.

Wirt, R. D., Lachar, D., Klinedinst, J. K., & Seat, P. D. *Multidimensional description of child personality: A manual for the personality inventory for children.* Los Angeles: Western Psychological Services, 1977.

World Health Organization. *Glossary of mental disorders and guide to their classification.* Geneva: Author, 1974.

Zeiss, A. M., Lewinsohn, P. M., & Muñoz, R. F. Nonspecific improvement effects in depression using interpersonal skills training, pleasant activity schedules or cognitive training. *Journal of Consulting and Clinical Psychology*, 1979, *47*, 427–439.

Zrull, J. P., McDermott, J. F., & Poznanski, E. Hyperkinetic syndrome: The role of depression. *Child Psychiatry and Human Development*, 1970, *1*, 33–40.

Zung, W. W. A self-rating depression scale. *Archives of General Psychiatry*, 1965, *12*, 63–70.

# SOCIAL SKILLS DEFICITS

**Hyman Hops**          **Charles R. Greenwood**

*Oregon Research Institute*          *University of Kansas*

The past decade has witnessed a geometric increase in studies examining the influence of peer social interaction on growth and development of social competencies from infancy through adolescence (Hartup, 1970; Kent & Rolf, 1979). The evidence clearly shows that peer social interaction begins during infancy and provides unique learning experiences for the developing child (Lewis & Rosenblum, 1975). Concurrently, interest has grown in methods to increase the amount and improve the quality of social relationships for children identified as deficient in social interaction skills or in peer group status (Combs & Slaby, 1977; Furman, 1980; Hops, in press). This chapter will examine these trends, with specific reference to their implications for the accurate, reliable, and valid assessment of social skills as a critical ingredient of programs designed to improve children's social adjustment.

## RECENT INTEREST IN PEER RELATIONSHIPS

The sudden growth in studies of peer influence and treatment of social deficits is in direct contrast to the virtual neglect of child–child social research over the past 25 years. Strain, Cooke, and Apolloni (1976) have cited American educators' failure to attend to children's social–emotional growth. Achenbach (1978) has also noted the limited development of meaningful classification systems for childhood in contrast to adult behavior disorders. Lewis and Rosenblum (1975) have persuasively argued that much of this inattention has been a direct function of the Piagetian and psychoanalytical theorizing that has dominated the area for so long, overemphasizing the saliency of adult–child relationships for adequate development of social, emotional, and cognitive competencies in children. Peer influences traditionally have been seen as secondary and only important in later childhood and early adolescence as children increasingly spend less time within the family structure.

However, the recent developmental literature uniformly shows that peer interaction provides unique opportunities for learning specific skills not attainable otherwise (Hartup, 1979). An ethological study of infants up to 12 months of age in a free play setting found that they touched each other several hundred times each day, the number increasing with age. Half the touches were mediated by toys (Meighan & Birr, Note 1). Interaction becomes more frequent and complex in toddlers (Mueller & Brenner, 1977), leading to more mature forms of toy play (Rubenstein & Howes, 1976). Social play requires the development of abstract concepts, such as reciprocity and general rules of game playing (Garvey, 1976), and social fantasy play among children facilitates divergent thinking (Johnson, 1976). Play may also act to mitigate social aggression and provide practice for appropriate adult functioning (Suomi & Harlow, 1976).

Peer acceptance/rejection, as measured by a variety of sociometric instruments, has been shown to be predictive of school dropouts (Ullmann, 1952), delinquency (Roff, Sells, & Golden, 1972), and psychiatric referrals up to 13 years later (Cowen, Pederson, Babigian, Izzo, & Trost, 1973). Although these studies are not homogeneous with respect to methodology, taken together, the evidence is strongly indicative of the importance of social interaction among children for optimum social, emotional, and cognitive development. A low level of social interaction is one of the variables considered a significant indicator of vulnerability and risk in children (Rolf & Hasazi, 1977).

## Spectrum of Current Applications

Most current studies of children's social behavior occur within five broad, but overlapping, areas: (1) normal development of interactive behavior, (2) deficit responding in social withdrawal, (3) excessive responding in social aggression, (4) assertion training to reduce passivity in social interaction, and (5) peer selection of preferred or nonpreferred partners for social activities. Although the objective of this chapter is not a comprehensive review of these areas, a brief overview of their activities, focus, and methodologies will be attempted here.

The work of Mueller and colleagues (Mueller, 1972; Mueller & Brenner, 1977; Mueller & Vandell, 1979) is an example of a current study of the normal acquisition of children's social behavior. Assessment here is primarily observational, descriptive, and conducted within laboratory preschool settings. Children are studied in groups over months to obtain longitudinal descriptions of interactive topographies and processes. Much of the data is derived from videotaped records, later coded by observers using complex coding systems (Mueller & Vandell, Note 2). A product of this research has been the establishment of reciprocity as a key ingredient in social interaction at toddler ages. Their data have described the emergence of new topographical forms of social behavior as a function of time and events within a controlled preschool peer group. This research, however, is devoid of attempts at structured intervention.

Increasingly, socially withdrawn children are coming to the attention of behavior change agents in mental health and special education settings (Hops, in press). Such children do not initiate peer interactions or respond to peer initiations, tend to be less verbal in their interactions when they do occur, and spend more time in solitary activities (Greenwood, Walker, Todd, & Hops, Note 3). Such behavior appears to be predictive of later lower school achievement (Kohn & Rosman, 1972; Victor & Halverson, 1976). Current studies of social withdrawal have focused on interventions designed to increase the frequency and range of specific social skills and social contacts (Hops, in press). Assessment procedures have included teacher and parent rankings, ratings, and behavioral checklists in addition to observations, the latter conducted primarily in the natural setting (e.g., preschool, playground). Assessment is targeted at identifying specific problematic behaviors and monitoring planned interventions.

The study of socially aggressive behavior has occurred primarily in family (Patterson, 1974a, 1976, 1979, 1980) and extraeducational peer group settings, for example, the playground or lunchroom (Walker, Hops, & Greenwood, in press). As described by Patterson, Reid, Jones, and Conger (1975) and Walker et al. (in press), socially negative/aggressive children appear to have acquired a behavior pattern based primarily on the aversive control of others. As such, aggressive behavior is highly instrumental in producing submission in others and also control of activities, situations, and so forth. It is not surprising that aggressive children are more frequently referred to mental health agencies and for special education services than the socially withdrawn. Our research has shown them to be near normal levels of appropriate responding but with excessively high levels of such aggressive behaviors as destruction of property, name calling, physical pestering, threatening, or abusive gestures (Walker et al., in press). Short- and long-range effects have been negatively related to lowered school achievement (Cobb, 1972) and later life adjustment (Zax, Cowen, Rappoport, Beach, & Laird, 1968) and have been positively associated with delinquency (Roff et al., 1972).

The types of assessment methods, and their purposes, that are used for studying aggressive children are similar to those used with the socially withdrawn (i.e., observations, rankings, ratings, and checklists for both description and treatment evaluation). Interventions have focused concomitantly on (1) the reduction of aggressive, coercive social behaviors and (2) their replacement with positive prosocial behaviors that elicit reciprocal responding by the social environment.

A newly developing area of interest in children's peer relations is seen in extensions of adult-oriented assertion training to children. To date, studies of assertiveness in children have been few and have been conducted primarily in clinical/analogue settings (Bornstein, Bellack, & Hersen, 1977). Assessment methodologies are designed to measure specific social topographies that countermand submissive responding, for example, clarifying intentions and negotiating change in peer behavior. Primary interest has focused on the processes by which assertive, aggressive, and passive social styles develop and can be modified.

Assessing the acceptance and/or rejection of peers as partners for various social and academic activities is the fifth global area to be described here. Wide use has been made of sociometric interview and rating methods for measuring children's reports of positive and negative partner selection. A major focus has been the mental-health-related aspects of social isolation, for example, the effects of low acceptance and/or rejection by peers on children's later life adjustment. Other important spinoffs of the study of natural peer groups have been concerned with interrace and intrarace relations (Singleton, Asher, & Alston, Note 4). Gottlieb, Agard, Kaufman, and Semmel (1976) have also applied sociometric methodology in attempts to integrate mentally retarded students into regular academic classroom settings. Observational procedures have also been used to study the effects on social interaction of integrating handicapped and normal children, using observational indexes of peer preferences and social contacts (Allen, Benning, & Drummond, 1972; Apolloni & Cooke, 1977; Guralnick, 1976).

In combination, these five general areas of children's social behavior provide a wealth of interesting and important problems for research and clinical and educational practice. The methods of assessment appropriate to each area continue to develop as increasing demands are placed upon behavior change agents to understand and manage these problems. These developments have also been enhanced by distinctive views of intervention possibilities and interaction processes.

## Behavioral Conceptualization of Social Interaction

Social interaction has been overwhelmingly described as interdependent and reciprocal in nature (Mueller, 1972; Patterson & Reid, 1970; Strain & Shores, 1977; Greenwood, Walker, Todd, & Hops, Note 5). Moreover, a behavioral view of interaction necessarily focuses upon the controlling nature of antecedent stimuli and the reinforcing functions of consequences as causal factors in the development and maintenance of social interaction. Yet, to date, only in select instances has applied research been carried out within this framework with children (e.g., Hops, Walker, & Greenwood, 1979; Strain, Shores, & Timm, 1977; Walker, Greenwood, Hops, & Todd, 1979). As described by Strain and Timm (1974) and Strain and Shores (1977), many of the early behavior change studies dealing with social behavior assessed the treated monadic social responses of the target subject—for example, cooperative play and smiling—independent of stimulus events provided by peers involved in the interactions as they occurred. Through the application of reinforcing consequences of adults in the setting, these monadic behaviors were systematically modified. However, without information on the *exchange* of peers interacting, on the quality of interactive responses, and on the duration of the interaction, changes in the peer interaction process cannot be completely understood (Strain & Shores, 1977).

## A Reciprocal Model Controlling Moment-to-Moment Interaction

As in a tennis match, social interaction (play) can occur only following (1) an initiation (serve) by one member of the dyad and (2) a response to that initiation (return) by the other. Mueller (1972) defines a *successful social initiation* as one that is responded to by a peer. Without reciprocity in interaction, the aims of the subject's initiations would not be achieved and consequently reinforced.

Following the return of the serve, interactions continue as a volley of alternative responses between individuals. During this time, the topography of the responses can vary (e.g., positive, negative, verbal, nonverbal, and physical). Interactions terminate with cessation of exchange in responding. For example, Walker *et al.* (1979) arbitrarily defined *termination* as 5 seconds without an observable exchange.[1]

Within this framework, it is possible to study individual children's topographies, with respect to peer initiations of various types, throughout a complete interaction sequence over time. Similarly, subjects' initiations can be studied in terms of the number and diversity of children with whom they initiate interactions, the topography and quality of initiations made, and the degree to which they are responded to and/or positively reinforced by peers. Greenwood *et al.* (Note 3) found that selected socially unresponsive children tended not to respond to children's initiations at normal levels and that when they did respond, a greater proportion of their responses was nonverbal (i.e., gestural and physical). The excessive reliance on nonverbal behavior suggests that withdrawn children do not effectively reinforce peers' initiations with them. Fortunately, the probability of peers' responding to initiations by withdrawn or nonwithdrawn peers is very high (.90 + ), in spite of the withdrawn peers' lower initiation rates. These data support the notions that withdrawn children (1) are not under good stimulus control (i.e., that they fail to respond to peers' initiations), (2) may lack age-appropriate language and play skills, and (3) do not reinforce peers for initiating interactions with them in terms of the actual probability of responding to initiations and in the quality of the responses made.

Research is currently under way within this framework in an attempt to identify the precise social skills of normal children that ensure the highest probabilities of peer reciprocity occurring. Tremblay, Strain, Hendrickson, and Shores (in press) found that, for 3- to 5-year-old preschoolers, (1) rough and tumble play, (2) share, (3) play organizer, and (4) assistance were the social initiations that were most effective in producing positive peer responses. Vocal attention, attention seeking, vocal initiation, and statement were the least effective. Rough and tumble play, for example, produced positive responses in 92% of its occurrences. Vocal attention, in contrast, was effective in only 31% of its occurrences, producing no response 69% of the time.

Mueller (1972) found that some behaviors mediate the success of particular initiations. For example, the best predictor of successful initiations was listener attention prior to or during the initiation. Unclear sentences and/or utterances were most predictive of failure of reciprocated initiations.

### Ecological Determinants

Although reciprocity appears to control ongoing interaction once under way, the

---

[1]The decision-making rules governing the end of interactions can be arbitrary and can vary with the situation. More precise determination will require further empirical study.

larger environmental context also greatly affects peer social-responding opportunities. Interaction can be occasioned by setting variables such as the structure of the physical environment (desks, work centers, play centers), adults present, teaching and instructional formats used, objects in the environment (e.g., games, toys—Quilitch & Risley, 1973), and the number and availability of peers (Campbell, 1977; Greenwood, Todd, Walker, & Hops, Note 6).

These variables function to control peers' social interaction. Research has demonstrated that games and toys and their joint behavior requirements can affect peer social interactions (Risley, 1977). Games require structured peer interchanges (e.g., flashcards) or solitary or independent involvement (e.g., monkey bars). Greenwood et al. (Note 3) demonstrated that the levels of reciprocal interactions in free play settings with limited teacher-imposed structure allowed significantly higher rates of interaction than an assigned task structure that required the children to be at desks or tables engaged in a teacher-directed task. Hops, Fleischman, Guild, Paine, Street, Walker, and Greenwood (Note 7) use games requiring increasingly unstructured joint play requirements in their treatment program for withdrawn children. The availability of peers and the number of peers within specific environments can also affect the levels of interaction. Greenwood et al., (Note 5) found a significant negative correlation between the number of peers in a classroom and the rate of interaction. These data suggest that social interaction of specific subjects may not require many peers to optimize its occurrence. Other researchers have found that increasing space and reducing peer density adversely affect joint play and interaction (Alevizos, Labrecque, & Gregersen, Note 8; White, Labrecque, & Gregersen, Note 9).

Individual characteristics also affect interaction, the most notable of which is sex. The documented preference for same-sex interaction occurs across all levels of childhood and early adolescence (Hartup, 1970; Singleton et al., Note 4). Females prefer more sedentary interaction, with fewer peers; in contrast, males are more active, with wider ranging contacts (Mueller, 1972; Raph, Thomas, Chess, & Korn, 1968; Rubin, Maioni, & Hornung, 1976; Waldrop & Halverson, 1975). Games and toy preferences also appear to be mediated by sex-related factors, even in young children (Fagot & Patterson, 1969).

Age has also been shown to be a factor in both the frequency and quality of interaction (Mueller, 1972; O'Connor, 1975; Raph et al., 1968; Reuter & Yunik, 1973; Rubin et al., 1976; Greenwood et al., Note 5), as have race (Singleton et al., Note 4), physical appearance (Waldrop, Bell, & Goering, 1976), and physical competencies (Broekhoff, 1976, 1977).

The search for effective social behavior interventions and assessment procedures lies at three levels within this discussion: (1) the peer–peer level of exchange and reciprocity, (2) the level of environment ecology, and (3) the interaction between 1 and 2. Teachers wishing to increase interaction can structure classroom ecology, including their lessons, instructions, and use of reinforcing consequences, with peer interaction in mind. For specific children, the assessment of ecology and interaction can generate data on the environments and settings in which peer–peer social interventions are or are not required. In this fashion, normative data on children's interaction rates in environments can be developed, in addition to the specific age- and sex-appropriate competencies.

## Social Skills Training and Treatments

Within a behavioral framework, social skills intervention assumes that there are individuals with conceptual and/or behavioral excesses or deficits that preclude their successful functioning in interpersonal situations (Hersen & Bellack, 1977). Consequently, the goals of training should result in more effective social responding and improved interpersonal relationships.

A classic study by Chittenden (1942) provided a promising empirical model for designing children's social skills training. Using direct observation, Chittenden identified two forms of assertive behavior, dominant and cooperative. Her data analysis suggested that dominant noncooperative children appeared unable to evaluate social situations properly and to behave accordingly.

Chittenden developed a comprehensive program to train children to discriminate between dominant and cooperative behavior and to provide them with a greater number of alternative responses in interpersonal problem situations. The results were only moderately successful. However, conceptually and methodologically, the study was a significant attempt to demonstrate how specific social skills deficits could be empirically determined in the natural setting and how training programs could be established to teach these behaviors to children with excessively dominant behaviors. As it turned out, there was a 20-year hiatus before such thinking re-emerged in developmental psychology.

Interest in treating social behavior disorders in children revived in the middle 1960s. Treatment procedures varied in their specificity from vague instructions to teachers to provide "socializing experiences" for low-status children (Bonney, 1971) to adult social reinforcement for specific responses such as, smiling and sharing (Cooke & Apolloni, 1976). The complexity of treatment also varied from contingent reinforcement for general social behavior (Allen, Hart, Buell, Harris, & Wolf, 1964) to the use of multiple antecedent/consequent components (Hops *et al.*, Note 7). Early intervention studies used primarily adult social change agents (Hart, Reynolds, Baer, Brawley, & Harris, 1968); more recently the involvement of peer confederates as treatment agents has assumed increasing roles (Furman, Rahe, & Hartup, 1979; Hops *et al.*, 1979; Peck, Apolloni, Cooke, & Raver, 1975; Strain *et al.*, 1977). Children targeted for interventions have included the developmentally delayed (Ballard, Corman, Gottlieb, & Kaufman, 1977), the retarded (Apolloni & Cooke, 1977), preschool-aged children (Todd, Note 10), children in kindergarten programs (Hops *et al.*, Note 7), and children in elementary school programs (Weinrott, Corson, & Wilchesky, 1979).

To date, social skills training procedures have only demonstrated moderate success (Hops, in press). Short-term powerful effects have been noted across a wide spectrum of treatment modalities (Combs & Slaby, 1977; Furman, 1980; Hops, in press). Long-term follow-up effects have been more elusive. In a review of the literature on social skills training of withdrawn/isolate children, it was found that maintenance of increased social ability was likely to occur following lengthy, more complex, intensive interventions regardless of the procedures used (Hops, in press). Those showing greater persistence of gains from 2 months to 1 year or more following termination of treatment generally involved interventions lasting at least one-half hour daily for a period of 8 weeks or more (Baer & Wolf, 1970; Ballard *et al.*, 1977; Weinrott *et al.*, 1979; Johnson, Goetz, Baer, & Green, Note 11; Street, Walker, Greenwood, Todd, & Hops, Note 12). Consequently, research must still look for precise variables that may be accounting for long-term success of programs, if they be other than time and the duration of intervention procedures. Isolation of more effective components may lead to shorter duration, cost-effective interventions that produce greater long-term effects.

# ASSESSMENT OF SOCIAL SKILLS

Assessors have yet to agree upon a precise definition of social competence. Consequently, we lack specific external criteria required to validate many of our procedures (Anderson & Messick, 1974; Zigler & Trickett, 1978). This lack of consensus is reflected in the heterogeneity of treatment designs and assessment instruments, and especially in the multitudinous definitions of social ''skills'' and/or ''deficits.''

As a result, treatment and assessment of social behavior are somewhat confounded because investigators propounding one type of treatment very likely rely on one form of assessment. For example, two distinct literatures appear to be developing with respect to the treatment of socially withdrawn/isolate behavior (Gottman, 1977b). For the most part, sociometric instruments have been used to assess the outcome of coaching or tutoring of isolate children (Gottman, Gonso, & Schuler, 1976; Oden & Asher, 1977; Hymel & Asher, Note 13). The effect of contingent reinforcement procedures, on the other hand, has been assessed with direct observation of the children in the natural setting (Allen *et al.*, 1964; Walker & Hops, 1973; Weinrott *et al.*, 1979). Similarly, assertiveness training is dependent upon observation of behavior within specific test situations outside the natural setting to demonstrate its effect (Bornstein, *et al.*, 1977). Few studies have been carried out using a multimethod and/or a multipurpose approach.

Even among investigators using a relatively homogeneous treatment procedure there exists considerable variability in specifying dependent measures and criteria for selection. Ten studies that have employed symbolic modeling procedures with withdrawn/isolate children can serve as a useful illustration. Table 1 summarizes the major assessment measures used in each of these studies in order to point out their similarities and differences.

In almost every case, children were identified in a two-step process: teacher nomination or rating, followed by direct observation of social behavior in the natural setting. In the preschool studies, the settings were generally less structured

TABLE 1

Symbolic Modeling Studies and Related Selection Criteria

| Authors | Grade | Setting | Number of minutes per child | Number of days | Selection criteria | Final sample | Percentage of total population | Percentage female |
|---|---|---|---|---|---|---|---|---|
| O'Connor (1969) | Preschool | Random | 8 | 8 | ≤ 15% social | 13 | 5 | 61 |
| O'Connor (1972) | Preschool | Random | 16 | | ≤ 15% social | 31 | 10 | 60 |
| Evers and Schwarz (1973) | Preschool | Free play | 20 | 2 | ≤ 20% social | 13 | 18 | 38 |
| Keller and Carlson (1974) | Preschool | Free play | 6 | 14 | ≤ 50% social[a] | 24 | [b] | 63 |
| Evers-Pasquale and Sherman (1975) | Preschool | Free play | 10 | 2 | ≤ 20% social | 19 | 25 | 44 |
| Jakibchuk and Smeriglio (1976) | Preschool | Free play | 14 | 2 | ≤ 40% social[c] | 22 | [b] | 50 |
| Gottman (1977a) | Headstart | | 8 | 1 | ≤ 15% social | 32 | 28 | 47 |
| Walker and Hops (1973) | Grade 1 | Unstructured | 710 | 16–30 | $\bar{x}_s = .14$ $\bar{x}_p = .38$[d] | 3 | 1 | 100 |
| Walker, Hops, Greenwood, and Todd (Note 30) | Primary | Regular class | 300 | 5 | $\bar{x}_s = .05$ $\bar{x}_p = .29$[d] | 6 | 3 | 80 |

*Note.* Teacher selection served as a first step in the screening process. In preschools, teachers nominated or rank-ordered children; in the primary grades, they completed the Walker Problem Behavior Identification Checklist (Walker, 1970).

[a] In addition to the interaction criterion, each subject could give or receive behaviors coded as reinforcing in no more than 50% of the coded intervals.

[b] Insufficient data in study precluded calculation.

[c] In addition to the interaction criterion, each subject could give or receive behaviors coded as reinforcing in no more than 50% of the intervals.

[d] Consistent discrepancy between subject and peer interaction rates.

and more likely to be free play. In the primary grade studies, children were observed in more structured settings within the regular classroom. At this point, the similarities among studies and procedures become less clear. The criterion for selection based on observational data varied greatly. In some classes, social "isolates" spent 15% or less of their time interacting with their peers (Gottman, 1977a; O'Connor, 1969, 1972; in others, they spent up to 50% of the time engaged in social behavior (Keller & Carlson, 1974). The varying criteria result in different proportions of the available population being identified as isolate, ranging from 5% (O'Connor, 1969) to 28% (Gottman, 1977a), and averaging 25% across the seven preschool studies. In the Walker, Greenwood, and Hops studies at the primary grade level (Hops *et al.*, 1979; Walker *et al.*, 1979), socially withdrawn children were selected on the basis of normative peer discrepancy in interaction. Target subjects had interaction rates (based upon 5 or more days of data) consistently below those of their peers. Such children were found to occur in about one of every two classrooms, in this case accounting for 1–3% of the population.[2] It is interesting that such selection variabilities exist even when the assessment procedures and the target children were selected using direct observation in each study.

These data are illuminating. They echo the recent interest in social skills training and assessment and the current state of infancy in developing procedures. Further, they suggest the need to reconsider the goals of selection and treatment in more functional terms. Social behavior assessment must be examined within a purposeful framework in relation to intervention objectives and/or criteria. Few studies have targeted behaviors for intervention that were empirically selected. As in the adult social skills training literature (Hersen & Bellack, 1977), investigators have been more concerned with developing treatments rather than appropriate, accurate, valid, and reliable assessment techniques. Arguing for the necessity of specifying objectives in effective teaching, Mager (1962) concluded that if we do not know where we are going, we may end up somewhere else. This argument is valid with respect to social skills training.

It is clear that we will require a methodological system within a purposeful and empirical framework in order to determine functionally what constitutes social competence and what procedures are most effective in assessing and establishing social skills in children.

## A Multipurpose–Multimethod Structure for Social Skills Assessment

Several authors have presented useful models for conceptualizing assessment functions in behavioral research and practice (Cone & Hawkins, 1977; Mash & Terdal, 1974, 1976). Generally, such models are complex and reflect a multipurpose–

---

[2]In related studies, Weinrott *et al.* (1979) found the incidence of withdrawn children meeting their criteria to be approximately 2–3 per 100. Greenwood *et al.* (Note 5), in a study of 29 preschool classrooms, estimated that one child meeting their criteria would be found in every two classrooms.

multimethod approach to behavioral assessment. In this section, we will attempt to show that utilizing multiple methods may be best for diverse goals such as screening, identifying problematic deficit–excess target behaviors, evaluating intervention process/outcome over the short run and the long run (Greenwood, Walker, & Hops, 1977), and determining the social validity of procedures (Kazdin, 1977). Examples extracted from the literature and from our experience will be used to illustrate useful strategies.

A major consideration in this chapter will be methods of practical utility for change agents in applied settings, for example, teachers and school psychologists. Although a measurement device may have demonstrated reliability and validity, it may remain impractical because its implementation requires highly trained specialists and/or it provides more data than are necessary for making decisions about the treatment or placement of children. A useful instrument must provide meaningful data for decision making at the level of staff expertise in the natural setting. In our experience, practitioners too often assume they must use the same assessment measures as researchers. More attention must be paid to the development of practical assessment devices that have good psychometric and functional properties but that also are of practical value to the less-skilled applied behavior analyst.

The discussion will now turn to the purposes and methods of assessing children's social behavior. The categories used to organize the discussion of assessment are necessarily arbitrary and based on models provided by Cone and Hawkins (1977) and Mash and Terdal (1976). As will be seen, there is considerable overlap among these categories. Frequently, it will be evident that the same assessment methodology can be used for different purposes. However, we will try to identify the most practical and functional method(s) for achieving specific goals.

## Diagnosis

The first basic question to be asked is whether or not a problem exists. This question may be approached at two levels: (1) screening at a gross level of measurement to determine whether a problem exists in a general sense and (2) more precise measurement to determine the nature of the difficulty and perhaps to generate hypotheses about potential interventions/or treatment settings.

### Screening

The primary purpose of screening in behavioral assessment is to identify children who may be either currently problematic or at risk for later, more severe behavioral disturbances (Garmezy, 1973). Referral of problematic social behavior by parents and teachers is probably the most frequent method by which target children are brought into contact with potential treatment sources. Although increases have been noted in early detection screening as part of large-scale preventative programs (Cowen, Dorr, Izzo, Madonia, & Trost, 1971; Rolf & Hasazi, 1977; Spivack & Shure, 1974), regular screening is practiced primarily in medical and educational settings, but not usually for socially related problems. Two systematic forms of screening methods will be reviewed here: (1) rankings by familiar adults and (2) peer ratings or preferences as measured by sociometrics.

RANKINGS. In the studies reviewed in Table 1, targeted children were initially screened using two of the most common procedures found in large settings: nominations and/or rankings. Yet surprisingly, none of the studies commented on the reliability, validity, or degree of teacher accuracy as confirmed by the subsequent observations. In contrast, Greenwood et al. (1977) and Greenwood, Walker, Todd, and Hops (1979) studied teacher screening accuracy in detail. They found that rank ordering children on the frequency of peer verbal interaction was a surprisingly reliable and valid procedure for identifying the least socially responsive child in the classroom. Of 26 preschool teachers, 20 (77%) identified the lowest interacting child (based on independent observations) within the first five ranks. This finding was replicated in a similar study conducted one year later (Greenwood, Walker, Todd, & Hops, Note 14).

Rank ordering of children is the first step in a screening/identification process developed for socially withdrawn school children (Greenwood et al., Note 6). Taking no more than 15 minutes, the rankings are completed in three steps, which systematize the procedure and ease the administration. As seen in the example provided in Figure 1, the teacher (1) lists all of the children in the class, (2) divides them into the most and least talkative groups, and (3) rank orders them according to the criterion. Preschoolers have been shown to be highly verbal and to use grammatically correct language forms frequently (Mueller, 1972; Mueller & Brenner, 1977; Greenwood et al., Note 6). Low rankings could indicate failure to develop both language and/or peer social skills.

Although rankings and nominations are highly cost effective in screening many children in a short time, they have at least two major limitations. First, the nominal type of identification provides little information that is useful in determining the goals of treatment or the specific nature of the problem. Screening simply identifies children who *may* require some form of intervention. Second, without specific item content, nominations rely extensively on the judgment of adults in the child's social environment. Consequently, some children (e.g., withdrawn) are less likely to be referred simply because adults may not consider certain social behaviors as problematic or they may place lower priorities on remediating specific deficits as opposed to others (Evans & Nelson, 1977; Hops et al., 1979; Westbrook, 1970).

Teachers have been characteristically eager to refer aggressive, acting-out children whose management demands inordinate amounts of teacher attention and energy. On occasion, we have had to prepare teachers to identify withdrawal behaviors in the classroom as the first step in the screening process. In the PEERS program for socially withdrawn children (Hops et al., Note 7), the initial teacher referral form contains brief descriptions of different forms of isolate behavior to help teachers discriminate withdrawal from other types (see Figure 2). In our experience, children who are highly aggressive and thus rejected by their peers are often incorrectly referred to as withdrawn. Children who are described as "seems to have fewer friends than most due to negative, bossy, or annoying behaviors

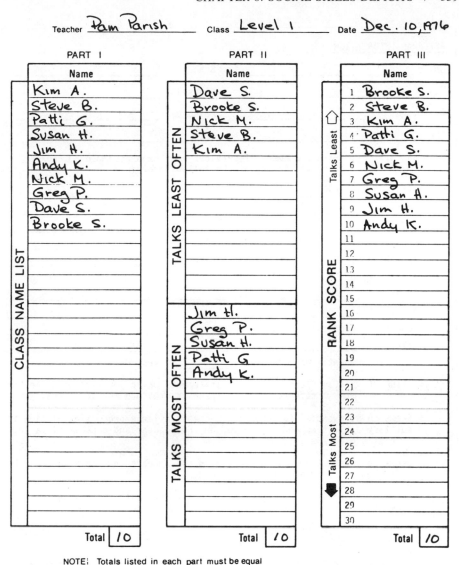

Teacher _Pam Parish_     Class _Level 1_     Date _Dec. 10, 1976_

| PART I | PART II | PART III |
|---|---|---|
| **Name** | **Name** | **Name** |

PART I — CLASS NAME LIST:
Kim A.
Steve B.
Patti G.
Susan H.
Jim H.
Andy K.
Nick M.
Greg P.
Dave S.
Brooke S.

Total | 10

PART II — TALKS LEAST OFTEN:
Dave S.
Brooke S.
Nick M.
Steve B.
Kim A.

TALKS MOST OFTEN:
Jim H.
Greg P.
Susan H.
Patti G
Andy K.

Total | 10

PART III — RANK SCORE (Talks Least → Talks Most):
1 Brooke S.
2 Steve B.
3 Kim A.
4 Patti G.
5 Dave S.
6 Nick M.
7 Greg P.
8 Susan H.
9 Jim H.
10 Andy K.
11
12
13
14
15
16
17
18
19
20
21
22
23
24
25
26
27
28
29
30

Total | 10

NOTE: Totals listed in each part must be equal

FIGURE 1

The SAMPLE ranking form for student verbal frequency interaction.

which turn others off'' may, in fact, warrant assessment and treatment of aggressive interaction styles. In such cases, interventions designed for withdrawal may be considered inappropriate. Walker, Street, Garrett, Crosson, Hops, and Greenwood (Note 15) present data showing that children referred to as negative/aggressive have rates of such aversive behaviors that are nearly seven times greater than those of a group of normal classroom peers, although both groups do not differ on rates of positive social interaction. For such children, programs that emphasize the control

REFERRAL INFORMATION:

Child_____     School_____

Teacher_____     Counselor_____

Consultant_____     Principal_____

Grade _____     Date_____

REFERRAL HISTORY: Please comment if services have been recommended and/or
received in any of the following areas.

Psychological Testing_____

Hearing Test_____

Vision Test_____

Speech Test_____

Tutoring, Remedial Help or Special Class Placement_____

Medical History of:

    Asthma_____

    Neurological_____

    Congenital Condition_____

    Other_____

    Is child presently on medication?_____ If yes, why?_____

DESCRIPTION OF CHILD: Please check any statements which you feel describe the
referred child. Space is provided for additional comments.

_____ Seems to be a social isolate (i.e., spends a large proportion of time in
solitary activities and may be judged independent and capable of taking
care of himself/herself.

_____ Seems to interact less with classmates and appears shy and timid; may be
described as somewhat anxious with others.

_____ Seems to spend less time involved in activities with others due to a
lack of social skills and/or appropriate social judgment.

_____ Seems to have fewer friends than most due to negative, bossy or annoying
behaviors which "turn off" others.

_____ Seems to spend less time with classmates than most due to awkward or
bizarre behaviors.

ADDITIONAL COMMENTS: _____

_____

_____

CORBEH © 1978

FIGURE 2
The PEERS program referral form.

of aversive responding seem more appropriate (cf. RECESS program for socially negative/aggressive children—Walker et al., Note 15).

SOCIOMETRICS. Although more costly in a number of ways, sociometrics can be used for screening. Sociometric procedures can locate children with low peer status for further study. Sociometric measures have been shown to correlate moderately with various measures of social competency (Asher, Oden, & Gottman, 1976; Gottman, Gonso, & Rasmussen, 1975) and to predict school dropout (Ullmann, 1952), delinquency (Roff et al., 1972), and adult psychiatric referrals (Cowen et al., 1973).

The most common sociometric procedure used is that of partial ranking or peer nomination. Children are asked to choose a predetermined number of classmates for specific referent situations, such as a playmate, a best friend, a workmate, or someone to go home with. Scores derived from such measures indicate levels of acceptance and rejection (i.e., percentage of positive and negative nominations) by the peer group. A number of studies have shown only moderate to low correlations between acceptance and rejection scores (Asher, Singleton, Tinsley, & Hymel, 1979), indicating that they may be measuring independent dimensions. Positive and negative nominations have also been shown to be distinct functionally (Ballard et al., 1977). Consequently, it may be necessary to obtain both measures in order to identify more precisely distinct groups of children. For example, true social isolates may be those children who are referred to as neglected, that is, those receiving few, if any, positive or negative choices. Several studies have discriminated between scores measuring the degree of popularity—the number of positive nominations—and an index of friendship—the number of reciprocal choices (Busk, Ford, & Schulman, 1973; Schulman, Ford, Busk, & Kaspar, 1973). They also found that the reciprocal measure was more stable over time.

A second method for determining peer status uses a rating scale rather than a nomination procedure (Asher et al., 1979). Each child is rated by every other child on a three- to seven-point Likert-type scale with reference to the specific situation presented (e.g., best friends). The rating scale provides better distributed scores across the entire peer group. It also ensures that every individual in the group is given equal consideration, which is a problem in the nomination procedure (Greenwood et al., 1977). For these reasons, the rating scale sociometric procedure may be best suited as a screening procedure for identifying children with few friends in the classroom. It also does not require children to consider the ethical question of rejecting specific classmates as potential playmates or workmates.

Cohen and Van Tassel (1978) have used a third type of sociometric procedure with preschoolers, the paired comparison technique. In this case, the child is presented with all possible pairs of pictures of his or her classmates and is asked to make a choice in each case dependent upon the referent situation. High test–retest reliabilities have been reported with this method for preschoolers (Cohen & Van Tassel, 1977). Its major drawback is the lengthy administration procedure. Cohen (Note 16) reports that no more than 30 minutes is required for a complete administration, but for a 3-year-old child, this may require two sessions.

As a screening instrument, sociometric procedures have certain strengths and limitations. For older children (fourth grade and higher) in classroom settings, it has been shown to be reliable and easily administered to entire classrooms in relatively brief periods (Busk *et al.*, 1973; Hymel & Asher, Note 13). It can provide an estimate of the child's popularity in the classroom, an index of his or her friendship status, and even work status. As such, it can be useful in identifying children with low peer status, who should be considered for more intensive assessment.

Limitations of sociometrics include the following:

1. As a screening device for younger children it is more expensive than a teacher ranking nomination system. It requires pictures of each child and from 15 to 30 minutes or more of individual administration time.
2. Administration of sociometrics with preschool-aged children (3–6 years) is likely to be less reliable (Greenwood *et al.*, 1979) unless more time consuming procedures (e.g., ratings—Asher *et al.*, 1979; or paired comparisons—Cohen & Van Tassel, 1978) are used.
3. Elementary schools are becoming more flexible in offering curriculum options. Consequently, the "homeroom" is becoming less and less the appropriate reference group for sociometric administration (Allen, Chinsky, Larsen, Lockman, & Selinger, 1976).
4. Greenwood *et al.* (1979) and Gottman (1977b) have reported difficulties in relating sociometric acceptance measures to observational indexes of social interaction in preschoolers. The validity of sociometrics with respect to socially unresponsive, withdrawn behavior has not been shown to be as functional as, for example, teacher rankings.
5. As previously mentioned in reference to teacher rankings, sociometrics do not provide *specific* information that can be used for designing interventions or determining the precise nature of the problem.

### Problem Definition

The second function of assessment is to verify screening/referral results in relation to actual behavior and in terms of relationships to outside criteria. Does more intensive measurement confirm or reject suspected behavioral deficits? If deficits are confirmed, what are the individual's specific strengths and weaknesses, in what settings, and what considerations should be made of intervention programs or of special program placement? In many instances, this type of assessment device has been used concurrently with screening or referral.

BEHAVIOR RATINGS AND CHECKLISTS. Behavior ratings and checklists filled out by parents and teachers have been commonly used to describe behavior deficits. The Walker Problem Behavior Identification Checklist is a 50-item teacher checklist, factor analyzed into five subscales: (1) Acting-Out, (2) Distractability, (3) Disturbed Peer Relations, (4) Withdrawal, and (5) Immaturity (Walker, 1970). The scale's norms were originally obtained from a sample of 534 intermediate-grade students. A total adjustment score on the checklist was shown to discriminate between students referred for behavior problems and nonreferred students. The scale has been widely used in educational and research settings (Greenwood, Hops, Walker, Guild, Stokes, Young, Keleman, & Willardson, 1979; Weinrott *et al.*, 1979; Greenwood *et al.* Note 3).

Several teacher rating scales were developed in our work with socially withdrawn and aggressive children as a second step in the referral process. Using seven-point Likert-type scales, descriptive behavior items were selected that discriminated between observational indexes of appropriate referrals and normal peers. In the PEERS program for withdrawn children (Hops *et al.*, Note 7), a score of 28 or less on an eight-item rating scale (see Figure 3) discriminated between referred children and their normal nonreferred classmates at better than 90%. Each item correlated significantly with observed time engaged in social behavior during recess.

Similar procedures were used to develop the Social Behavior Rating Positive Scale (SBR +) (see Figure 4) used in the SAMPLE identification kit for preschoolers (Greenwood *et al.*, Note 6). Both the individual items and the average scale composite score were significantly related to both social interaction rate and sociometric

FIGURE 3

The PEERS program Social Interaction Rating Scale (SIRS) for teachers.

| Child's Name _____ | Teacher _____ |
| School _____ | Grade _____ |
| Date _____ | Consultant _____ |

|  | not descriptive or true | moderately descriptive or true | very descriptive or true |
|---|---|---|---|
| 1. Verbally responds to a child's initiation. | | 1.....2.....3.....4.....5.....6.....7 | |
| 2. Engages in long conversations (more than 30 seconds). | | 1.....2.....3.....4.....5.....6.....7 | |
| 3. Shares laughter with class-mates. | | 1.....2.....3.....4.....5.....6.....7 | |
| 4. Spontaneously contributes during a group discussion. | | 1.....2.....3.....4.....5.....6.....7 | |
| 5. Volunteers for "show and tell." | | 1.....2.....3.....4.....5.....6.....7 | |
| 6. Freely takes a leadership role. | | 1.....2.....3.....4.....5.....6.....7 | |
| 7. Spontaneously works with a peer(s) on projects in class. | | 1.....2.....3.....4.....5.....6.....7 | |
| 8. Verbally initiates to a peer(s). | | 1.....2.....3.....4.....5.....6.....7 | |

CORBEH © 1978          TOTAL SCORE: ☐

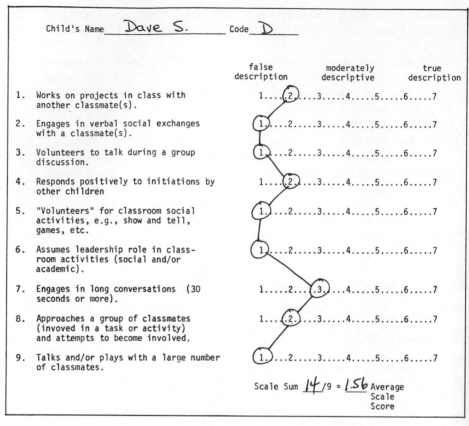

Child's Name __Dave S.__      Code _D___

| | false description | moderately descriptive | true description |
|---|---|---|---|

1. Works on projects in class with another classmate(s).      1...(2)...3.....4.....5.....6.....7

2. Engages in verbal social exchanges with a classmate(s).      (1)...2.....3.....4.....5.....6.....7

3. Volunteers to talk during a group discussion.      (1)...2.....3.....4.....5.....6.....7

4. Responds positively to initiations by other children      1...(2)...3.....4.....5.....6.....7

5. "Volunteers" for classroom social activities, e.g., show and tell, games, etc.      (1)...2.....3.....4.....5.....6.....7

6. Assumes leadership role in class-room activities (social and/or academic).      (1)...2.....3.....4.....5.....6.....7

7. Engages in long conversations (30 seconds or more).      1.....2...(3)...4.....5.....6.....7

8. Approaches a group of classmates (invoved in a task or activity) and attempts to become involved.      1...(2)...3.....4.....5.....6.....7

9. Talks and/or plays with a large number of classmates.      (1)...2.....3.....4.....5.....6.....7

Scale Sum _14_/9 = _1.56_ Average Scale Score

FIGURE 4

A "withdrawn profile" on the SAMPLE Social Behavior Rating Positive Scale (SBR+) for teachers.

acceptance. The RECESS program for socially negative/aggressive children (Walker *et al.*, Note 15) also contains a 33-item rating scale for teachers. The seven items found to discriminate best between normal peers and aggressive children selected on the basis of observation data are presented in Table 2 (Walker *et al.*, Note 15).

DIRECT OBSERVATION. Direct observation in natural or analogue settings has provided the major dependent variables in behavior analysis and behavioral assessment. Its use as a baseline assessment often has an implied dual purpose: as a diagnostic procedure to identify problematic behaviors in children and as a preintervention measure against which it is possible to evaluate treatment effects. The second use will be covered later in the chapter. In most cases, these are the same data.

Behavioral observation systems will vary according to recording technique (e.g., checklist vs. stopwatch), sampling strategy (e.g., real time vs. time sampling), and content (single vs. multiple code categories) (Sackett, 1978). Each will vary depending upon the objectives of the observations and the settings in which

TABLE 2

RECESS Normative Rating Scores on Negative Social Behavior Items for a Sample of Socially Negative/Aggressive Children and a Sample of Normal Children

| | Negative social behavior | | | |
| | Negative/aggressive (n = 19) | | Normal (n = 21) | |
| Negative social behavior item | $\bar{x}$ | SD | $\bar{x}$ | SD |
|---|---|---|---|---|
| Disturbs other children: teases, provokes fights, interrupts others. | 5.42 | .75 | 1.19 | 1.43 |
| Openly strikes back with angry behavior to teasing of other children. | 5.21 | 1.20 | 1.19 | 1.40 |
| Argues and must have the last word in verbal exchanges. | 4.68 | 1.56 | .86 | 1.28 |
| Displays physical aggression toward objects or persons. | 5.32 | 1.13 | .90 | 1.34 |
| Uses coercive tactics to force the submission of peers: manipulates, threatens. | 3.89 | 1.83 | .52 | 1.14 |
| Speaks to others in an impatient or cranky tone of voice. | 5.60 | .66 | .94 | 1.18 |
| Says uncomplimentary or unpleasant things to other children; for example, engages in name calling, ridicule, verbal derogation. | 4.50 | 1.63 | .72 | 1.04 |

they occur. Research requirements may involve the sequential recording of complex social interactions specifying both the social antecedents and the social consequents of a subject's behavioral stream. Although social behavior is essentially dyadic and interactive, an additional concern is the relative sophistication of the observer, the amount of training required for reliable recording, and the practical utility in clinical or educational settings. Consequently, the goals of clinical observations may be satisfied with simple frequency counts of one or two social behaviors (e.g., prosocial vs. socially aggressive) by relatively untrained professional school or mental health personnel. This chapter will focus on and present samples of observation systems for social behaviors that can be used in clinical settings.

The direct and systematic observation of children's social behavior has been practiced, off and on, for more than half a century (Goodenough, 1928). Parten's (1932) data on the social behavior of 34 preschoolers, collected in 1927, provided the basic norms for preschool populations for some 40 years (Barnes, 1971). However, these and other popular observation codes (Hartup, Glazer, & Charlesworth, 1967) were not designed for use by practitioners (e.g., mental health workers, teachers), nor did they contain dyadic interactive information that might provide useful targets for intervention. Although social behavior is naturally dyadic and complex (Mueller, 1972; Strain & Shores, 1977), applied behavior analysts require simpler coding systems that make available to them useful information about the social behavior of problematic children.

We and our colleagues have developed several observation coding systems for applied personnel as part of social behavior identification and intervention packages. They were designed specifically for school counselors, psychologists, and teachers and can be effectively used with minimal training. They serve to identify socially withdrawn children in the preschool (Greenwood et al., Note 6) and primary grades (Hops et al., Note 7) and socially negative/aggressive children in the primary grades (Walker et al., Note 15). All of these have been developed empirically, report reliability and validity indexes, and are supported by extensive normative data bases that provide the final criterion for selection as intervention targets.

A relatively simple method of counting reciprocal interactions is seen in the SAMPLE Observation System (SOS) developed for preschool children. An *interaction* is defined as a verbal, nonverbal, or physical exchange of signals between the target child and a peer. To use the code, an observer must be able to discriminate between (1) an initiation (the first social response in a chain), (2) a response to the initiation, (3) continuing responses in the chain, and (4) termination of the interaction (a 5-second delay by both members of the dyad). The observer records only initiations and their responses, but must be able to identify continuing responses in the chain and must note when an interaction has terminated.

Figure 5 provides a sample of the observation coding form used in the SOS. Within each box, reading from left to right, initiations are recorded on the left and peer responses on the right. Thus, "A-Sue" reads "Amy initiated to Sue and Sue responded." When a 5-second delay separates interactive responses, the interaction is considered terminated, and any subsequent responding is coded as a new interaction.

The SOS offers several advantages. This system yields information about the (1) frequency and rate of subject initiation, (2) the frequency and probability of a subject's initiation being responded to, (3) the number and range of peers with whom the subject interacted. Further, the system is simple enough so that teachers can learn to use it reliably. Its disadvantages include lack of differentiation between various types of topographic responding and limited sampling of the first two responses in a chain, with no data on the duration of the interaction.

The Consultant Social Interaction Code (CSIC, pronounced "seasick") is designed for recording social behavior on playground settings. This system is part of a complete social behavior intervention program for primary-grade withdrawn children (Hops et al., Note 7). It was developed as a screening and evaluation tool to be used by a teacher–consultant responding to a teacher referral. Using a 5-second interval recording procedure, the CSIC provides data on (1) percentage of positive social behavior, (2) percentage of talk, (3) rate of starts (initiations by target child), (4) rate of answers (target responses to peer initiations), (5) rate of interaction, and (6) ratio of starts to answers (a sociability ratio devised by Green-

Part I

Session No. **1**   Date **3/12/76**  Class **M**   Teacher **Jm**

Total
Obs. Time **8 min.**

| IDENTIFICATION | |
| --- | --- |
| Name | Code |
| AMY | A |

| CALCULATIONS | | SCORES |
| --- | --- | --- |
| # Interactions ÷ Minutes = | | Rate |
| 14 ÷ 8 = | | 1.75 |

Part II

| TIME Start Stop | FREEPLAY INTERACTIONS | | | | |
| --- | --- | --- | --- | --- | --- |
| 9:00 | A-Sue | A-Tina | Sue-A | Sue-A | Tina-A |
|  | A-Bill | A-Dave | Dave-A | Bill-A | Tina-A |
|  | Sue-A | A-Bill | Bill-A | Sue-A |  |
| 9:08 STOP |  |  |  |  |  |
|  |  |  |  |  |  |
|  |  |  |  |  |  |
|  |  |  |  |  |  |
|  |  |  |  |  |  |
|  |  |  |  |  |  |
|  |  |  |  |  |  |
|  |  |  |  |  |  |
|  |  |  |  |  |  |
|  |  |  |  |  |  |
|  |  |  |  |  |  |
|  |  |  |  |  |  |

FIGURE 5

A coding record illustrating the SAMPLE Observation System (SOS).

wood *et al.*, Note 17). The primary codes are Positive Social Behavior (PS) and Negative/Alone (NA). The former includes all forms of positive social behavior; the latter codes instances of nonsocial or inappropriate social behavior. The simple dichotomy allows consultants to learn the system in a short period with minimal training and is sufficient to identify socially withdrawn primary-grade children on the playground. A sample of coded interaction is provided in Figure 6.

The CSIC yields both initiation and interaction rate measures and indicates the duration of overall positive social behavior, as well as specific behavioral targets for intervention, such as talk, start, answer,[3] providing qualitative as well as quantitative information on a child's social responding.

---

[3]Normative data are not yet available on these specific targets.

Name **Sam L.** School **Westend** Date **2/9/78**

Grade **3** Teacher **Bronson** Consultant **Witherspoon** Page **1**

Recess: AM [X] Lunch [ ] PM [ ] In-Class [ ]

Phase: Screen [X] Baseline [ ] Intervention [ ] Fadeout [ ] Followup [ ]

SAT Rules: Slash ALL Unstructured SAT's — Circle ALL Praised SAT's

| Tally |
|---|
| NA 23 |
| PS 37 |
| S 2 |
| A 5 |
| T 11 |
| P 5 |
| TB 60 |
| M 5 |

| To Find | Compute | Results |
|---|---|---|
| Total Boxes | 37 [PS] + 23 [NA] | 60 *TB |
| Total Minutes | 60 [TB] ÷ 12 | 5 *M |
| Percent Positive Social | 37 [PS] ÷ 60 [TB] x 100 | 62 %PS |
| Percent Talk | 11 [T] ÷ 60 [TB] x 100 | 18 %T |
| Start Rate | 2 [S] ÷ 5 [M] | 0.4 S/minute |
| Answer Rate | 5 [A] ÷ 5 [M] | 1.0 A/minute |
| Interaction Rate | ( 2 [S] + 5 [A] ) ÷ 5 [M] | 1.4 I/minute |
| Start:Answer Ratio | 2 [S] ÷ 5 [A] | 0.4 S:A |
| Praise Rate | 5 [P] ÷ 5 [M] | 1.0 P/minute |

*Enter in Tally column also

CORBEH © 1978

FIGURE 6

A coding record illustrating the PEERS Consultant Social Interaction Code (CSIC).

Both the SOS and the CSIC have been shown to be useful and reliable when used by school personnel for both the diagnosis and the evaluation of social behavior programming. For research purposes, however, more complex coding systems are still required. Other codes developed in our laboratory provide data on more than 28 social interaction variables for children in a free play setting (e.g., Peer Interaction Recording System II—Garrett, Hops, & Stevens, Note 18; Preschool Interaction Code—Todd, Hudsen, & Greenwood, Note 19). These systems have been developed empirically, report validity and reliability indexes, and are supported by normative data bases. However, they require approximately 2 weeks of training to achieve acceptable agreement between observers and are not recommended for most clinical settings.

NORMATIVE DATA FOR DECISION MAKING. The availability of normative data can be helpful in making treatment decisions about referred children regarding the presence or absence of deficits or the suitability of the current level of social behavior(s) (Kazdin, 1977; Walker & Hops, 1976). For example, the identification of withdrawn children and the specific behaviors viewed as problematic in the majority of recent studies have been based largely on arbitrary criteria.

Two different behavioral strategies have been used for establishing norm-referent data bases. One specifies the use of normative data based on peer behavior collected within the same setting as the target child (Patterson, 1974a; Walker & Hops, 1976). The assumption is made that "similar" stimulus conditions are affecting interaction of all students in that setting. Observations are conducted on randomly selected individuals (Hops et al., 1979) or on the entire peer group (Walker & Hops, 1973) within the child's own classroom at the same time that the target child's behavior is observed. The peer group's data control for normally changing stimulus conditions as well as the potentially dramatic effects of random stimuli introduced into a social environment. For example, we found tenfold increases in social behavior of withdrawn children on separate days during baseline because a teacher had set up a "new" game during recess and had directly involved the child. Without the peer group data, which showed concomitant increases during those same periods, we might have mistakenly concluded that the child's social behavior was higher, more variable, and/or less problematic than it actually was under less structured conditions.

A second strategy for establishing normative criteria for social behavior involves the collection of peer group observation data on a larger scale and within similar settings (e.g., playground), but across a variety of schools. Representative normative data bases can greatly improve decision making, especially for practitioners whose schedules preclude the collection of local norms.

Large-scale normative data should also reflect differences that may occur as a function of developmental level, age, and setting effects. Differences in social behavior levels were noted for preschoolers (Greenwood et al., Note 5) and primary-grade children (Hops et al., Note 7). Greenwood et al. (Note 5) also found interaction rates varying by sex and by classroom structure. Preschool norms for social interaction rates during free play, presented in Figure 7, are based on a sample of 463 children ages 3–7 years. The dark band represents 1.5 standard deviations

TABLE 3

PEERS Program Normative Data Base ($n$ = 109) for Social Behavior Levels in the Primary Grades

| Grade | Mean percentage social behavior | Normal range | |
|-------|--------------------------------|--------------|--------------|
| | | −1 *SD* | +1 *SD* |
| K–1 | 46.40 | 30.89 | 61.91 |
| 2 | 60.81 | 48.62 | 73.00 |
| 3 | 70.61 | 58.74 | 82.48 |

below the mean, indicating that 90% of the norm group had higher interaction rates. In Table 3, norms are presented for social behavior levels in the primary grades based on a sample of 109 classmates of children referred for socially withdrawn behavior. No significant differences were found between the levels for kindergarten and first grade and between males and females.

To illustrate the use of these norms for problem identification, let us consider the PEERS program procedures. Teacher referral and rating scale completion is the first step in the diagnostic process. If the teacher's ratings indicate the child's key social behaviors are problematic according to the norms on the scale, the child is subsequently observed for corroborating evidence. A teacher–consultant uses the CSIC to observe the child during recess activities on the playground for at least three days in order to determine his or her level of social behavior. These data are compared to group norms shown in Table 3. If the child's level of social behavior is below the normal range, he or she is so identified and the behavior is accepted as an intervention target.

To summarize, the diagnostic assessment process can involve up to four different steps. Initially, individual problematic children may be nominally referred for further assessment. Large-scale screening of *all* children within classrooms may be conducted using cost-efficient rank ordering (Greenwood *et al.*, 1977) or sociometrics (Asher *et al.*, 1976). Teachers' ratings on scales with established norms and empirically validated descriptive behavior items can be used to provide further and more precise evidence of social behavior deficit. Ratings may require that teachers compare the referred children with their peers on specific social strengths and deficits. Finally, observation coding of the children's behavior in the natural setting confirm and describe social behavior deficits in the subjects, both in terms of the magnitude of behavior and in reference to peer norm criteria. At each level of assessment, the data may indicate that a problem does not exist, precluding further assessment. Thus, in the final analysis, this procedure is cost effective, requiring more expensive observational measurement only for those children who have been identified as problematic in the earlier stages.

## Design

Behavioral assessment and intervention bear a close relationship to one another, one that is too often ignored (Mash & Terdal, 1974). In the past, decisions have

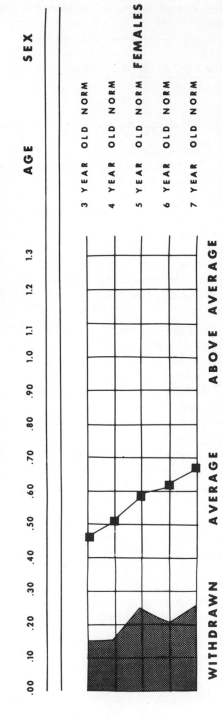

NORM TABLE FOR THE CHILDREN OBSERVED DURING 1975 (463 CHILDREN)

FREEPLAY INTERACTION RATE SCORE -- FEMALES

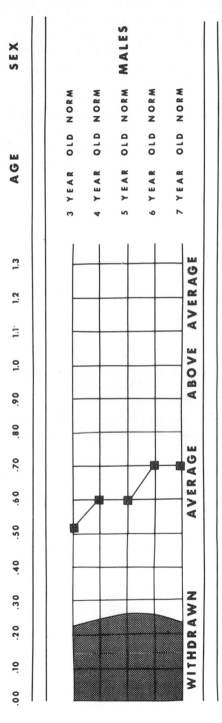

FIGURE 7

Normative data from the SAMPLE.

been made on the basis of a priori theoretical positions unrelated to assessment data. Assessment has been conducted in shotgun fashion in the hope that some measure may be sensitive to the actual treatment process. This use of assessment is likely to occur when the purpose of intervention is unclear and nonbehavioral. Functional assessment relates to treatment objectives in direct, meaningful ways.

Once the diagnostic phase has been completed, assessment must be concerned with (1) pinpointing the behaviors of interest, that is, the targets for change; (2) specifying the antecedent and consequent variables in the environment that may be controlling the targeted behaviors; and (3) selecting a particular intervention designed to lower excesses and increase competencies. This section will focus on assessment procedures that have been used to target behaviors and identify controlling stimulus conditions.

### Pinpointing

Precisely identifying or pinpointing the target behavior for intervention generally requires narrow-band, high-fidelity assessment measures (Cronbach, 1970). Traditional assessment measures used for this purpose involve content items varying in specificity. Behavior assessment generally operates at two distinct levels: (1) items identifying molar response classes, around which behavioral objectives or treatment behaviors can be created, and/or (2) specific pinpoints that are directly expressed as behavioral objectives, that is, those that are observable, clearly stated, and with both the context of the response and a criterion level attached. In the first instance, a response class is identified as problematic, but the specifics are left to the clinical judgment of the therapist. Thus, additional measures must be developed for monitoring these created pinpoints in intervention. Later, at postassessment, changes produced in the pinpoints may or may not show up as improvements on the response-class measure. In the second instance, the pinpoints and the targets of treatment are one and the same.

Current methods will now be examined in detail in order to evaluate their usefulness in pinpointing social behaviors.

SOCIOMETRIC MEASURES. Sociometric scores provide information about a child's (1) general level of social acceptance (roster-and-rating or positive nominations), (2) level of rejection (negative nominations), (3) degree of neglect (virtual absence of positive and negative nominations), and (4) friendships (reciprocal positive choices). The major shortcoming of sociometric measures in establishing pinpoints for intervention is their lack of behavioral specificity—they do not provide clear targets for behavior change. This is true even though a number of studies have found correlational relationships between popularity and specific responses (Gottman et al., 1975; Gottman 1977a; Ladd & Oden, 1979), and with few exceptions (Kelly, Furman, Phillips, Hathorn, & Wilson, 1979; Ladd, in press), these correlational and contrast group relationships of sociometrics to actual behavior have not been validated through experimental manipulations.

Interventions designed to increase sociometric scores by training children on specific correlated target behaviors must show that each of the low sociometric children had deficits in these *behaviors*, according to available norms, for example, and that training produced increases in these specific response *classes*, which, in turn, resulted in sociometric gains (Ladd, in press). Research is clearly needed in this area. Consequently, when determining intervention pinpoints, it appears more practical to use direct rating or observation methods in naturalistic or analogue settings to assess a child's ability to display these behaviors.

BEHAVIOR RATING SCALES AND CHECKLISTS. A multibehavior rating scale or checklist on which teachers or parents are asked to provide estimates of a child's social behavior has been used frequently as a diagnostic tool and less frequently for pinpointing social behavior targets for intervention (Achenbach, 1978; Spivack & Swift, 1973). Traditionally, rating scales have consisted of behavior descriptors not directly expressed as behavioral objectives. In fact, on many of these instruments single items may not be directly useful, as the items are averaged to form a scale score for use in the diagnostic process previously described. Thus, on the Walker Checklist (Walker, 1970), for example, the Distractability Scale may be normatively demonstrated to be problematic, with each item only suggestive of intervention pinpoints. Pinpointing in this case requires a further task analysis of behavior objectives targeted for specific intervention. In the PEERS (Hops *et al.*, Note 7) and the SAMPLE (Greenwood *et al.*, Note 6) teacher rating scales, each item has been demonstrated to be correlated with observational indexes of social behavior and can be interpreted singly. However, some items are in the form of general behavior response classes, and the specific pinpoint objectives must be created by the clinician.

Some data suggest that raters are more accurate in their ratings of more behavior-specific items (Bolstad & Johnson, 1977; Greenwood, Walker, & Hops, 1977; Jones & Cobb, Note 20). Unfortunately, it has also been noted that low reliabilities are more likely to occur with more specific items (Evans & Nelson, 1977), perhaps as a function of the fluctuation in judgment required to account for performances under changing stimulus conditions.

SELF-REPORT. Instruments that require children to report on how they view their feelings, behavior, and social relationships with peers may offer information to aid in the assessment and treatment of problems. For example, a child may show no specific skill deficits but may report discomfort or dissatisfaction with peer relationships. The target of the intervention, consequently, might be the child's own reported feelings rather than the social behavior.

Self-report indexes have been used more frequently with adults (Galassi & Galassi, 1976). As with other assessment instruments developed for children, they rely heavily on the adult literature, largely ignoring the unique developmental perspective (Achenbach, 1978). Two such instruments were developed to assess assertiveness in children: the 27-item Children's Assertiveness Behavior Scale (CABS) (Wood, Michelson, & Flynn, Note 21) and the Self-Report Assertiveness Test for Boys (SRAT-B) (Reardon, Hersen, Bellack, & Foley, Note 22).

The CABS is a group multiple-choice paper-and-pencil test, requiring responses to interpersonal situations along a passive–assertive–aggressive continuum. The 27 items represent five content areas, including conversation skills and responses to compliments, to complaints, to requests, and to empathy. Fourth-grade children provided feedback on the CABS and validated the situations as problem areas. Responses along the continuum were validated by independent raters and are illustrated in the following example (Wood & Michelson, Note 23, p. 7):

> You need *someone* to do something for you.
> You would usually:
>   a. Not ask for anything to be done.
>   b. Give a small hint that you need something done.
>   c. Say, "Would you please do something for me?" and then explain what you want.
>   d. Say, "I want you to do this for me."
>   e. Say, "You gotta do this for me."

Stability over a 6-week period and some evidence of internal consistency were demonstrated. Validation coefficients were significant, but they were low to moderate and highly variable against a teacher's rating scale and a behavioral analogue test measuring the same problem situations. The CABS was also found to be sensitive to the effects of an assertiveness training program (Michelson, Wood, & Flynn, Note 24). However, the weaknesses in the scale related to reliability, limited sampling, and external validity outweigh its being recommended at this time. Indications of its ability to predict actual behavior *in situ* is required.

The SRAT-B consists of 20 items eliciting both positive and negative assertive responses. Respondents can check as many of the five alternatives provided as they wish, in order to indicate their typical response in a real-life situation. No reliability data were provided. Moreover, moderate to high correlations between the scale scores and behavioral measures of assertiveness in role play situations was found only for older boys in the seventh and eighth grades (Reardon *et al.*, Note 22).

One wonders about the general use of group paper-and-pencil tests with children. Validation is predicated on children's being able to read, which may account for the low validity correlations obtained by Reardon *et al.* (Note 22) and Michelson *et al.* (Note 24) on young children. Further, as noted by Cox and Gunn (Note 25), such tests confound conceptual knowledge with performance, are subject to social desirability sets, and rest on the implication that a single response is synonymous with skill level. At best, the total score may be more useful as a screening instrument rather than as a precise indication of treatment focus.

BEHAVIORAL ANALOGUE SITUATIONS TEST. Several researchers have tried to duplicate the primary assessment procedures used in adult assertiveness training (Bornstein *et al.*, 1977). These involve measuring specific social responses in contrived settings designed to simulate actual interpersonal problem situations. Situations are presented to each subject verbally by a narrator present in the room or over an intercom from an adjoining room. A confederate in the room provides a verbal prompt at the end of the narration to initiate each situation. For example (Bornstein *et al.*, 1977, p. 186):

> NARRATOR: "Imagine you're standing in line for lunch. Jon comes over and cuts in front of you."
> PROMPT: "Let me cut in front of you."

The subject or client is then required to respond verbally to the prompt.

Analogue situational tests are potentially useful because (1) direct observation in the natural environment is not always possible, (2) laboratory settings can be controlled to test an individual's responsiveness to problem situations that are not available to external observers, (3) paper-and-pencil tests may not be appropriate, and (4) they provide a measure of objective performance.

In a more recent development, Edelson and Rose (Note 26) demonstrated how an assessment instrument can be empirically developed for a younger population (ages 8–12), based on the five-stage behavior-analytic model for assessing social competence developed by Goldfried and D'Zurilla (1969). Specific situations highly problematic for children were identified through interviews with 16 children who had kept weekly diaries for an 8-week period. Next, the list was summarized, condensed, and presented to a sample of 40 children, who were asked to provide responses in a role-play format. The responses were evaluated for social competence by expert judges, and ratings and criteria were established. A behavioral role-play test format was developed. The final test consisted of eight problem situations, four involving peer interaction at school and four with siblings and peers at home or in the neighborhood. Four additional items were created to measure generalization of training effects. The test is administered to an individual child by a tester. The final stage, still under development, requires the demonstration of reliability and validity indexes. Data are currently being collected on a sample of children who have been rated by their teachers and peers.

Cox and Gunn (Note 25) and Cox, Gunn, and Cox (Note 27) have developed a similar method for assessing social skills of elementary school children. They validated their film assessment procedure with a group of male students ($n = 16$) removed from the public schools for disruptive acting-out behavior and a contrast group of same-aged (10–14 years) males attending the public schools. Their groups did not differ on response classes that had been shown to discriminate between popular and unpopular children (Gottman et al., 1975) and on the basis of which others have developed treatment procedures (Kelly et al., 1979). However, the public school children provided more reasons for behavior and showed more appreciation in contrast to the problematic children, who were more argumentative and emphatic in their requests.

These studies demonstrate a preliminary step in the development of empirical bases for evaluating specific social competencies in children. As Cox and Gunn (Note 25) noted, further research is required. One major limitation of the analogue assessment is its complete reliance on verbal behavior, providing only a partial estimate of actual social behavior. More critical is the absence of external validation measures (i.e., direct observation *in situ*), which limits the current usefulness of such assessment. Studies with adult normal and psychiatric populations generally demonstrated little relationship between role play behavior and social behavior in natural settings (Bellack, Hersen, & Lamparski, 1979; Bellack, Hersen, & Turner, 1978, 1979). There is little reason to believe that these results do not hold for children as well.

DIRECT OBSERVATION IN THE NATURAL SETTING. Direct observation in the natural setting has been one of the most widely used assessment techniques for pinpointing social behaviors as targets for intervention (Hops, in press). The recording of social behaviors has occurred at the infant day care level (Meighan & Birr, Note 1), toddler preschool level (Mueller & Brenner, 1977), preschool level (Greenwood et al., Note 6; O'Connor, 1969), and elementary school level (Allen et al., 1976), and in both special (Strain & Timm, 1974) and regular classrooms (Hymel & Asher, Note 13). Observations have also occurred during instructional (Walker & Hops, 1973), free play (Greenwood et al., Note 17), and recess activities (Hops et al., 1979).

Pinpointing has generally followed one of two distinct strategies. A substantial number of investigators have obtained general measures of social behavior frequency, for example, rate of interaction per minute (Walker & Hops, 1973) or percentage of time spent in social behavior (Hops et al., 1979). Treatments were then designed to increase the level of these variables. This particular strategy has been criticized because of the absence of predictive or convergent validation indicating that these measures are, in fact, evidence of social disability (Gottman, 1977a). However, Greenwood et al. (Note 5) found that withdrawn children identified on the basis of such observation measures displayed low levels of component behaviors directly related to other measures of social disability. They noted that preschoolers with low interaction rates verbalized, initiated to others, responded to others' initiations to them, and were initiated to by others significantly less often than higher frequency interactors. Furthermore, these preschoolers spent more time observing peers, working alone on a task, and being alone and were less involved in tasks requiring peer participation and proximity to peers.

Global measures with demonstrated relations to specific deficits offer several advantages. They are easier to record, especially for relatively untrained practitioners with limited time for assessment. They also are extremely useful when accompanied by comprehensive treatment programs aimed at increasing a wide range of specific social deficits (e.g., PEERS for socially withdrawn children—Hops et al., Note 7; RECESS for socially aggressive children—Walker et al., Note 15).

A second strategy frequently employed is to specify and observe directly occurrences of precise behaviors. Examples have included smiling, sharing, positive physical contact, and compliments (Cooke & Apolloni, 1976); greeting by handwaving (Stokes, Baer, & Jackson, 1974); and initiating interactions, responding to others' initiations, and maintaining interactions (Walker et al., 1979). Moreover, each behavior can be precisely defined, and all have been shown to be modifiable. Yet, except in the case of extremely low-functioning developmentally delayed children, there has been little empirical evidence of a relationship between such specific behaviors and global social competence levels, even with precisely defined social situations (Gottman, 1977a; Hops, in press).

Research establishing the validity of component skills can be useful for targeting interventions. Kelly et al. (1979) trained retarded adolescents to provide information following direct questioning, to elicit information from others by questioning, and to extend social invitations to peers. These specific behaviors were selected for conversational skill training based on the previous work of Gottman et al. (1975), who established these skills as correlates of sociometric popularity. The subjects increased not only their frequencies of specific responses in the training sessions but also the percentage of time spent in social interaction on the playground with untrained peers.

Research must also be carried out to understand the effects that increasing specific skills will have on the general features of interaction. Walker *et al.* (1979) reinforced a group of socially withdrawn children for increasing initiating and then for increasing responding to others' initiations. Increases in the rates of either of these behaviors resulted in the suppression of total time spent in social responding. The decrease in social behavior was likely a function of the contingencies interfering with the subjects' natural interactive styles and regular peer partners.

Children's social behavior is extremely variable from day to day in contrast to academic-oriented behaviors in more structured settings. Free play behavior varies as a function of the weather, play materials (Quilitch & Risley, 1973), and the availability of specific peers (Hops, 1971). In an unpublished study of the social behavior of two preschoolers, lag 1, 2, and 3 correlations of daily rates of social interaction over a 3-month period were all found to be nonsignificant, averaging approximately .25. These data suggest that behavioral levels based on a single day's observation (Gottman, 1977b) are not likely to be a reliable or valid estimate of a child's general level of behavior over time. In our own programs, we recommend at least 3 days of data collection by interventionists within the same or similar stimulus conditions (e.g., recess) for pinpointing accurate baseline levels of social responding.

### Specifying Antecedent and Consequent Variables

As discussed previously in this chapter, an observational analysis of naturally occurring social exchange among peers shows great promise of yielding information on the controlling properties of social stimuli. In current practice, however, this new activity requires complex observational coding procedures. The observational assessment must be sequentially recorded, capturing who says or does what to whom in a string of events over time. Bakeman (1978) provides an excellent discussion of the types of observational data that his group has sequentially analyzed. In addition to the sequential requirement, the observational procedure must also include individual response codes or categories of behavior (e.g., initiate positive, greets, smiles at, play organizer).

Patterson (1974b, 1974c) has used sequential analyses to identify the specific behaviors emitted by family members, which, as antecedents or consequences, control the problematic behavior of socially aggressive children. For example, coercive behaviors have been shown to be powerful antecedents to like responding in the targeted child, but siblings in problem families produce significantly more coercive responses than those in nonproblem families (Patterson, 1976). The recent work of Strain and his colleagues in identifying specific initiations that reliably result in positive responses is an example of the methodology applied to peer interaction (Tremblay *et al.*, in press). In other studies, Strain's group has also demonstrated the functional effect of increasing peer initiations (antecedent) and its concomitant increase in peer responses (Strain, 1977).

The implications of this newly developing technology for selection of social behavior change targets and behavior change methods is aptly described by Patterson (Patterson & Whalen, Note 28): "In effect, we may have the bases for a new kind of precision intervention; this in contrast to the traditional shotgun approach of spraying contingencies willingly about the social system" (p. 16). This technology is extremely promising but is not widely available to many applied practitioners. Further research in the development of coding systems and methods for analyzing sequential interaction remains to be accomplished before Patterson's view of precision intervention can be widely implemented.

## *Intervention*

In contrast to traditional assessment strategies, with behavioral assessment, intervention may follow directly from the type of measure used in pinpointing target behaviors. For example, training in analogue settings will be applied to specific skill deficits determined in that setting (Bornstein *et al.*, 1977). Intervention, in this case, will involve a combination of instructions, behavioral rehearsal, and feedback, procedures likely to be most effective in a structured training setting. Specific responses can be practiced until proficiency is achieved. Such repeated practice in natural settings is inappropriate and may interfere with and suppress overall social responding (Walker *et al.*, 1979). During natural social situations, however, the teacher and/or parent can, at appropriate moments in the interactive process, prompt and positively reinforce target behaviors learned previously in tutoring sessions. Low sociometric acceptance scores may reflect a child's low stimulus value to the peer group (Evans & Nelson, 1977). Pairing the child with other events of high reinforcement value, such as candy (Kirby & Toler, 1970) or free time (Drabman, Spitalnik, & Spitalnik, 1974), or involving the child in group activities to demonstrate his or her competencies (Ballard *et al.*, 1977) may have the effect of increasing sociometric scores. Social withdrawal occurring across all settings may reflect general social skill deficiencies (Evans & Nelson, 1977) or more basic motor, intellectual, and language delays (Strain *et al.*, 1976). Consequently, interventions designed to increase social skills per se or specific behaviors that would facilitate the learning of social skills from peers (e.g., imitation; Peck *et al.*, 1975) must be specifically tailored to effect the measures used.

An intensive approach to assessment and treatment can be seen in the development of social skills training packages for remediating specific deficits/excesses and establishing social competencies in problematic children (Hops *et al.*, Note 7; Walker *et al.*, Note 15). These programs are advantageous because they include (1) comprehensive intervention procedures cutting across various skill deficits, (2) systematic and standardized implementation methodology described in procedural manuals, (3) assessment instruments for pinpointing and monitoring behavioral problems, and (4) implementation by briefly trained school personnel with primary-grade children.

The major shortcomings of such programs include (1) the lack of precise assessment procedures for targeting behavioral deficits and strengths, (2) not matching one-to-one specific intervention procedures with related deficits noted in assessment, and (3) the costliness of implementing the entire package, although only some of its components may be necessary for effective treatment.

## Treatment Evaluation

The reliance on an ongoing evaluative process for demonstrating the effectiveness of interventions (Mash & Terdal, 1974; Cone & Hawkins, 1977) reflects the empiricism that is the fundamental strength of the behavioral model (Biglan & Kass, 1977). Treatment evaluation has a twofold purpose: (1) the continued measurement of the behavioral pinpoints to determine whether the specific objectives or criterion levels of performance are being achieved and (2) the use of precise experimental designs to evaluate whether or not the changes can be causally attributed to the actual treatment procedures (Mash & Terdal, 1974, 1976).

This section will examine the purpose of continuous monitoring and of pretreatment, posttreatment, and follow-up monitoring, as well as the instruments that may be used to achieve these different objectives.

### *Continuous Monitoring*

Repeated assessment of behavior targeted for treatment provides the *process* data necessary for a precise evaluation of treatment effects for individuals. These data provide immediate feedback on how well intervention objectives are or are not being met. For example, in one study we established a token reinforcement procedure with a group backup to increase the positive social behavior of a first-grade female student (Hops, Guild, Fleischman, & Paine, Note 29). Initial effects were in the predicted direction, but continued monitoring over days revealed a concomitant increase in socially negative behavior (cf. Kirby & Toler, 1970). The child's attempts to interact were increasingly bossy and physically aggressive. Consequently, we introduced a response cost contingency to reduce this new aspect of the child's social behavior.

Continuous monitoring within a single-subject design is illustrated in Figure 8 (Hops *et al.*, 1979). The subject, a first-grade female, was well below her peers' level of social behavior (indicated by solid square boxes) at screening. The PEERS program procedures were implemented beginning with 3 days of social tutoring prior to recess and were followed by an individual social behavior contingency with a group backup reinforcer shared by the entire class, a contingency for increasing talk, a class pep talk prior to each session, special helpers selected daily, and a consultant who operated the procedures on the playground.

Daily observation demonstrated initial increases in the subject's social behavior following tutoring and a marked improvement with the introduction of the point system.[4] The data were used to monitor the effects of the contingency and to indicate when to begin fading each of the program's components. Significant drops

---

[4]The effect of the talk contingency is not reflected in these data.

and increased daily variation in social behavior were noted primarily with the removal of the consultant and group rewards. However, in comparison with the original baseline and screening levels, the subject maintained improvement above the normal range.

Although this is not a particularly powerful design (no reversals or multiple baseline), these procedures have been used in other research to demonstrate more clearly the causal relationship between the treatment procedures and social behavior improvements (Hops et al., 1979); this is a powerful method of assessing ongoing daily effects. Within this observation process, treatments can be continued or adjusted.

A second assessment criterion that can be used to evaluate the success of the intervention is the extent to which the child's social behavior approximates the normal level as defined by normative data. In the PEERS program (Hops et al., Note 7), normative data (see the shaded area in Figure 8) are used to set the criteria for effective intervention and maintenance once the fading procedures begin. Well aware that the effects of treatment are likely to dissipate over time with the withdrawal of the treatment components (Walker & Buckley, 1972), treatment continues until levels of social behavior are greater than one standard deviation above the mean of the age-appropriate normative group. After this level has been achieved for a predetermined number of consecutive days, the program's components are faded gradually, but with a concomitant decrease in the criterion level of social behavior (i.e., the criterion for reinforcement) dropping to the mean for the norm group. Our experience with PEERS has been that, with removal of the intervention procedures, the target child's behavior drops to near the mean of the grade-appropriate group. This appears satisfactory, since children are not expected to maintain at higher levels than their agemates.

Monitoring of intervention procedures can include assessment of the independent variable to demonstrate that the treatment was accurately implemented as intended. Strain and Timm (1974) and Strain (1977) demonstrated that both contingent teacher attention and peer confederate initiations, respectively, accounted for changes in targeted behaviors. In the majority of studies, we must accept the author's verbal report as validation that treatment was installed, thus often precluding accurate replication by others.

Monitoring of targeted behaviors in nontreatment settings or of nontreated target behaviors within the treatment setting can provide evidence of generalization and/or effects of generalization procedures. Cooke and Apolloni (1976) found that effective training in smiling among handicapped children produced concomitant increases in sharing and positive physical contact for some children. In addition, these increases in the trained responses were shown to generalize to the untrained setting. Similarly, increases in physical cooperative behavior followed contingent teacher attention for verbal cooperation (Slaby & Crowley, 1977). Generalization may also occur from trained to untrained subjects (Strain, Shores, & Kerr, 1976), likely as a function of social reciprocity (Cooke & Apolloni, 1976). Assessing cross-setting generalization should be a standard procedure within analogue training conditions, but this has seldom been carried out (Kelly et al., 1979; Ladd, in press).

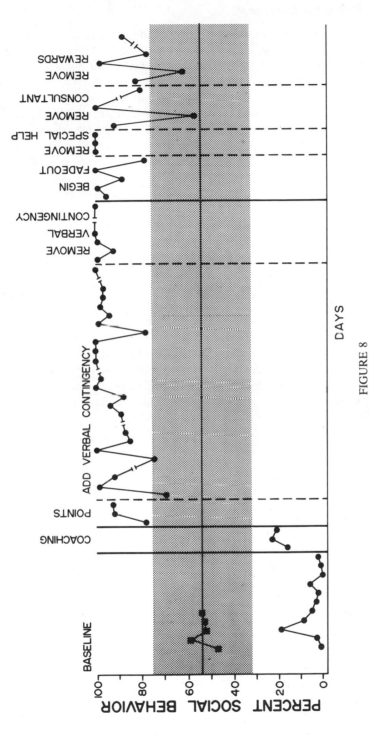

FIGURE 8

Illustration of continuous monitoring with a PEERS program intervention on a single subject.

*Pre–Post–Follow-Up Assessment*

Assessment following the removal of treatment can have several purposes. Within a single-subject reversal design (Baer, Wolf, & Risley, 1968), it can be used to establish the causal nature of the independent variables, for example, teacher attention (Allen *et al.*, 1964) and peer initiations (Strain *et al.*, 1977). Used within group designs, postassessment can establish the outcome, rather than the process, of the intervention. This is especially useful when "packages" developed within single-subject designs are being evaluated against the outcome of an untreated or alternatively packaged program (Hersen & Barlow, 1976; Walker *et al.*, in press).

Follow-up assessment indicates the power of the procedure to produce lasting gains over time. Long-term follow-up in schools generally occurs after the targeted children have changed classrooms, teachers, and peer groups. Consequently, changes in setting conditions must be accounted for in the follow-up assessment (Walker & Hops, 1976). Oden and Asher (1977) followed up their subjects in new classrooms one year after termination of treatment. They reanalyzed the peer ratings after standardizing the sociometric scores by classroom at each experimental phase (i.e., pretreatment, posttreatment, and follow-up). Controlling for stimulus changes with this procedure appeared to wash out some of the effects obtained earlier without standardization.

Street *et al.*, (Note 12) continued to observe a group of socially withdrawn children in new classrooms after treatment in an experimental classroom setting. In this case, each of the follow-up measures was obtained with peer groups other than those involved in treatment. Using a percentage score computed by dividing the subject's interaction rate by his or her respective peer group mean to control for setting changes, the data indicated that the children continued to improve up to 17 months later (see Figure 9).

# CONCLUSIONS

The recent proliferation of efforts to develop social skills training procedures and related assessment techniques follows a similar trend established with adults (Hersen & Bellack, 1977). As with so many attempts to develop interventions for problematic children, many of the social skills training procedures appear as inadequate imitations of those developed for adult populations. Little attention has been paid to such critical factors as normal developmental changes and their influence upon conceptual and behavioral responding at different age levels. What appears to be a deficit at one age turns out to be average social behavior at another. Ignoring developmental variables, the efforts often emphasize the remediation of social dysfunctioning rather than the teaching of those specific social competencies that are prerequisites for successful peer social interaction at varying developmental levels. When combined with the relatively brief history of social skills training and assessment, the results of these efforts still remain overshadowed by the general absence of either a consensual or empirical definition of social competence. This

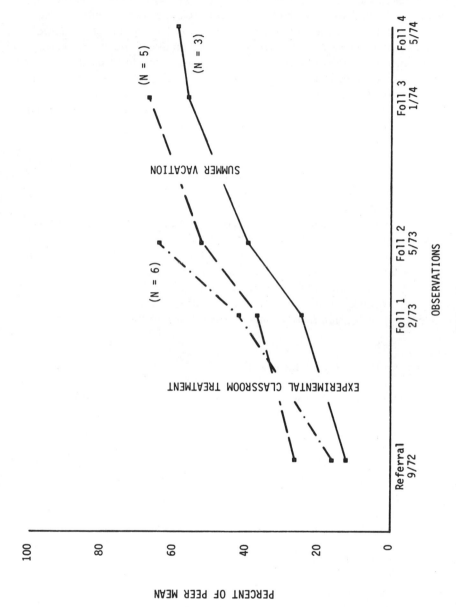

FIGURE 9

Follow-up data of withdrawn children treated in an experimental classroom setting.

is reflected in the heterogeneous array of treatment procedures evaluated by occasionally unrelated assessment techniques.

Our review of nonresearch settings concerned with the assessment of children's social behavior reveals discrete, noncontinuous systems wherein there is little assurance that each child will even be screened for social behavior problems. There is no absolute entry point for assessment. Screening in the sense of all children's coming under assessment even in schools is not commonly practiced. Rather, reliance on teacher or parent referral is the norm. Thus, it would be most effective to direct resources, procedures, and training toward teachers or other school personnel at this time (e.g., Greenwood *et al.*, Note 6; Hops *et al.*, Note 7).

We have argued that behavioral assessment of social skills in children can and must proceed purposefully and empirically. Within a multipurpose–multimethod framework, a number of assessment methods were described, ranging from simple nomination or ranking of adults to the direct observation of children's social behavior in the natural setting by highly trained professional observers. Each method was described as a research tool and reviewed for its practical utility with relatively untrained applied practitioners.

Although sequential analysis and packaged programs for applied personnel appear promising, it seems clear that few attempts have been made to select and/or develop assessment procedures purposefully and functionally. Many studies used broad-based variables as criteria for screening, pinpointing, and evaluation, but treatment is aimed at more precise behavioral pinpoints that have not been shown to be empirically related to the initial assessment criteria. Further, little evidence is presented to show that significant changes were produced in the targeted behavior.

## Future Research

Future research should focus on deriving functional definitions of social competence, empirically determining what behaviors are required for successful long-term social functioning. It is possible that situation- and age-specific behavioral taxonomies will have to be established. If so, the problem is enormous. We think, however, it is more likely that there are specific social responses that will be demonstrated to be functional across settings and time. Consequently, training these responses in one or two settings should produce greater generalization in others than will similar training in responses that are age- or setting-specific. The work in sequential analysis is a step toward a determination of such responses, those that produce positive reciprocal responses from peers. Similarly, it is likely that competencies developed at one age will continue to bear fruit at subsequent age levels, while others may be critical only for specific periods. Accordingly, training in those skills that continue to be important should occur as early as possible, perhaps within established preschool curriculums. However, each of these possibilities requires empirical demonstration rather than presumption. For example, analogue training will have to show that more precise training in highly controlled settings does generalize to the natural environment; otherwise, we have not improved much upon traditional office psychotherapy.

Only minor mention was made of the role of social validation measures in social skills training and assessment, because it has only been within the past three years that these procedures have been well understood by behaviorists and incorporated into their methodology. Few children's studies have used subjective reports of social agents in the field to select targets or alternatives. We know of no studies using indicators of consumer satisfaction, either from the children themselves or from other agents within the social environment. It is hoped that research on children's social skills will advance rapidly in this area.

We hope that our conclusions have not been overly pessimistic. We attempted only to show that the field is in its infancy and that much remains to be done. Beginnings are speckled with examples of exciting and promising developments.

## Acknowledgments

This chapter was prepared with assistance from NIH Biomedical Research Support Grant RR05612, Oregon Research Institute, and Program Project Grant, National Institute of Child Health and Human Development, No. 2 P01 HD 03144, University of Kansas. The authors wish to acknowledge the assistance of Susan Brewster and Deborah Millsap in the typing of this manuscript.

## Reference Notes

1. Meighan, M., & Birr, K. *The infant and its peers.* Unpublished manuscript, University of Kansas Medical Center, Kansas City, 1979.
2. Mueller, E., & Vandell, D. *Film 2: A methodology for the study of social interactions.* Boston: Boston University, Department of Psychology, Playgroup Project, 1976.
3. Greenwood, C. R., Walker, H. M., Todd, N. H., & Hops, H. *Description of withdrawn children's behavior in preschool settings* (Report No. 40). Eugene: University of Oregon, Center at Oregon for Research in the Behavioral Education of the Handicapped, 1978.
4. Singleton, L. C., Asher, S. R., & Alston, F. *Sociometric ratings and social interaction among third-grade children in an integrated school district.* Paper presented at the annual meeting of the American Educational Research Association, San Francisco, April 1976.
5. Greenwood, C. R., Walker, H. M., Todd, N. M., & Hops, H. *Preschool teachers' assessments of social interaction: Predictive success and normative data* (Report No. 26). Eugene: University of Oregon, Center at Oregon for Research in the Behavioral Education of the Handicapped, 1976.
6. Greenwood, C. R., Todd, N. M., Walker, H. M., & Hops, H. *Social assessment manual for preschool level (SAMPLE).* Eugene: University of Oregon, Center at Oregon for Research in the Behavioral Education of the Handicapped, 1978.
7. Hops, H., Fleischman, D. H., Guild, J., Paine, S., Street, H., Walker, H. M., & Greenwood, C. R. *Program for establishing effective relationships skills (PEERS): Consultant manual.* Eugene: University of Oregon, Center at Oregon for Research in the Behavioral Education of the Handicapped, 1978.
8. Alevizos, K., Labrecque, V. H., & Gregersen, G. F. *Effects of area size on play behaviors.* Salt Lake City: Salt Lake County Mental Health, Children's Behavior Therapy Unit, 1972.

9. White, J. A., Labrecque, V. H., & Gregersen, G. F. *The effect of spatial manipulation of group density on verbal behavior in retarded children.* Salt Lake City: Salt Lake County Mental Health, Children's Behavior Therapy Unit, 1973.

10. Todd, N. M. *The effects of verbal reporting and group reinforcement in increasing the interaction frequency of preschool socially withdrawn children.* Master's thesis, Department of Special Education, University of Oregon, Eugene, 1977.

11. Johnson, T. L., Goetz, E. M., Baer, D. M., & Green, D. R. *The effects of an experimental game on the classroom cooperative play of a preschool child.* Paper presented at the fifth annual Southern California Conference on Behavior Modification, Los Angeles, October 1973.

12. Street, A., Walker, H. M., Greenwood, C. R., Todd, N. M., & Hops, H. Normative peer interaction rate as a baseline for follow-up evaluation. In H. Hops (Chair), *Systematic analysis of social interaction: Assessments and interventions.* Symposium presented at the 84th annual meeting of the American Psychological Association, Washington, D.C., 1976. (ERIC Document Reproduction Service No. ED 131 937)

13. Hymel, S., & Asher, S. R. *Assessment and training of isolated children's social skills.* Paper presented at the biennial meeting of the Society for Research in Child Development, New Orleans, March 1977.

14. Greenwood, C. R., Walker, H. M., Todd, N. M., & Hops, H. *Cost effective prediction and screening variables for preschool social withdrawal* (Report No. 39). Eugene: University of Oregon, Center at Oregon for Research in the Behavioral Education of the Handicapped, July 1978.

15. Walker, H. M., Street, A., Garrett, B., Crossen, J., Hops, H., & Greenwood, C. R. *Reprogramming environmental contingencies for effective social skills (RECESS): Consultant manual.* Eugene: University of Oregon, Center at Oregon for Research in the Behavioral Education of the Handicapped, 1978.

16. Cohen, A. S. Personal communication, January 31, 1979.

17. Greenwood, C. R., Walker, H. M., Todd, N. M., & Hops, H. *Normative and descriptive analysis of preschool free play social interactions* (Report No. 29). Eugene: University of Oregon, Center at Oregon for Research in the Behavioral Education of the Handicapped, 1977.

18. Garrett, B., Hops, H., & Stevens, T. *Peer Interaction Recording System II (PIRS II).* Eugene: University of Oregon, Center at Oregon for Research in the Behavioral Education of the Handicapped, 1977.

19. Todd, N. M., Hudsen, D., & Greenwood, C. R. *Preschool Interaction Code.* Eugene: University of Oregon, Center at Oregon for Research in the Behavioral Education of the Handicapped, 1978.

20. Jones, R. R., & Cobb, J. A. *Validity of behavioral scores derived from teachers' ratings vs. naturalistic observations.* Paper presented at the meeting of the Western Psychological Association, Anaheim, Calif., April 1973.

21. Wood, R., Michelson, L., & Flynn, J. M. *Assessment of assertive behavior in elementary school children.* Paper presented at the annual meeting of the Association for the Advancement of Behavior Therapy, Chicago, November 1978.

22. Reardon, R. C., Hersen, M., Bellack, A. S., & Foley, J. M. *Measuring social skill in grade school boys.* Unpublished manuscript, University of Pittsburgh.

23. Wood, R., & Michelson, L. *Children's Assertive Behavior Scale.* Unpublished manuscript, Nova University, 1978.

24. Michelson, L., Wood, R., & Flynn, J. M. *Development and evaluation of an assertive training program for elementary school children.* Paper presented at the annual meeting of the Association for the Advancement of Behavior Therapy, Chicago, November 1978.

25. Cox, R. R., & Gunn, W. B. *Interpersonal skill development with the schools: The keep cool rules and other strategies.* Paper presented at the seventh annual symposium of the Houston Behavior Therapy Association, Houston, March 1977.

26. Edelson, J. L., & Rose, S. D. *A behavioral role play test for assessing children's social skills.* Paper presented at the 12th annual meeting of the Association for the Advancement of Behavior Therapy, Chicago, November 1978.

27. Cox, R. R., Gunn, W. B., & Cox, M. J. *A film assessment and comparison of the social skillfulness of behavior problem and non-problem children.* Paper presented at the meeting of the Association

for the Advancement of Behavior Therapy, New York, December 1976.
28. Patterson, G. R., & Whalen, K. *Determining the causal status of a controlling stimulus.* Eugene: Oregon Research Institute, 1975.
29. Hops, H., Guild, J. J., Fleischman, D. H., & Paine, S. *Preliminary evaluation of a programmed package for remediating socially withdrawn behavior in primary aged school children* (Report No. 36). Eugene: University of Oregon, Center at Oregon for Research in the Behavioral Education of the Handicapped, 1979.
30. Walker, H. M., Hops, H., Greenwood, C. R., & Todd, N. M. *Social interaction: Effects of symbolic modeling, individual and group reinforcement contingencies, and setting on the behavior of withdrawn children* (Report No. 15). Eugene: University of Oregon, Center at Oregon for Research in the Behavioral Education of the Handicapped, 1975.

# References

Achenbach, T. M. Psychopathology of childhood: Research problems and issues. *Journal of Consulting and Clinical Psychology*, 1978, *46*(4), 759–776.
Allen, G. J., Chinsky, J. M., Larson, S. W., Lockman, J. E., & Selinger, H. V. *Community psychology and the schools.* Hillsdale, N.J.: Lawrence Erlbaum, 1976.
Allen, K. E., Benning, P. M., & Drummond, T. W. Integration of normal and handicapped children in a behavior modification preschool: A case study. In G. Semb (Ed.), *Behavior analysis and education.* Lawrence: University of Kansas Press, 1972.
Allen, K. E., Hart, B., Buell, J. S., Harris, F. R., & Wolf, M. M. Effects of social reinforcement on isolate behavior of a nursery school child. *Child Development*, 1964, *35*, 511–518.
Anderson, S., & Messick, S. Social competency in young children. *Developmental Psychology*, 1974, *10*, 282–293.
Apolloni, T., & Cooke, T. P. Integrated programming at the infant, toddler, and preschool age levels. In M. Guralnick (Ed.), *Early intervention and the integration of handicapped and non-handicapped children.* Chicago: University Park Press, 1977.
Asher, S., Oden, S., & Gottman, J. Children's friendships in school settings. In L. Katz (Ed.), *Current topics in early childhood education* (Vol. I). Hillsdale, N.J.: Lawrence Erlbaum, 1976.
Asher, S. R., Singleton, L. C., Tinsley, B. R., & Hymel, S. The reliability of a rating scale sociometric method with preschool children. *Developmental Psychology*, 1979, *15*, 443–444.
Baer, D. M., & Wolf, M. M. The entry into natural communities of reinforcement. In R. Ulrich, T. Stachnik, & J. Mabry (Eds.), *Control of human behavior.* Glenview, Ill.: Scott Foresman, 1970.
Baer, D. M., Wolf, M. M., & Risley, T. R. Some current dimensions of applied behavior analysis. *Journal of Applied Behavior Analysis*, 1968, *1*, 91–97.
Bakeman, R. Untangling streams of behavior: Sequential analysis of observation data. In G. P. Sackett (Ed.), *Observing behavior: Data collection and analysis methods.* Baltimore: University Park Press, 1978.
Ballard, M., Corman, L., Gottlieb, J., & Kaufman, M. J. Improving the social status of mainstreamed retarded children. *Journal of Educational Psychology*, 1977, *69*, 605–611.
Barnes, K. E. Preschool play norms: A replication. *Developmental Psychology*, 1971, 5, 99–103.
Bellack, A. S., Hersen, M., & Lamparski, D. M. Role-play tests for assessing social skills: Are they valid? Are they useful? *Journal of Consulting and Clinical Psychology*, 1979, *47*, 335–342.
Bellack, A. S., Hersen, M., & Turner, S. M. Role-play tests for assessing social skills: Are they valid? *Behavior Therapy*, 1978, *9*, 448–461.
Bellack, A. S., Hersen, M., & Turner, S. M. The relationship of roleplaying and knowledge of appropriate behavior to assertion in the natural environment. *Journal of Consulting and Clinical Psychology*, 1979, *47*, 670–678.
Biglan, A., & Kass, D. J. The empirical nature of behavioral therapies. *Behaviorism*, 1977, *5*, 1–15.
Bolstad, O. D., & Johnson, S. M. The relationship between teacher's assessment of students and students' actual behavior in the classroom. *Child Development*, 1977, *48*, 570–578.

Bonney, M. E. Assessment of effort to aid socially isolated elementary school pupils. *Journal of Educational Research*, 1971, *64*, 359–364.

Bornstein, M. R., Bellack, A. S., & Hersen, M. Social skills training for unassertive children: A multiple baseline analysis. *Journal of Applied Behavior Analysis*, 1977, *10*, 183–195.

Broekhoff, J. Physique types and perceived physical characteristics of elementary school children with low and high social status. In J. Broekhoff (Ed.), *Physical education, sports, and the sciences*. Eugene, Ore.: Microform Publications, 1976.

Broekhoff, J. A search for relationships—Sociological and social–psychological considerations. *The Academy Papers*, 1977, *11*, 45–55.

Busk, P. L., Ford, R. C., & Schulman, J. L. Stability of sociometric responses in classrooms. *Journal of Genetic Psychology*, 1973, *123*, 69–84.

Campbell, D. E. Arguments for an expansion of behavior change concepts. In A. Rogers-Warren & S. T. Warren (Eds.), *Ecological perspectives in behavior analysis*. Baltimore: University Park Press, 1977.

Chittenden, G. F. An experimental study in measuring and modifying assertive behavior in young children. *Monographs of the Society for Research in Child Development*, 1942, *7*(1, Serial No. 31).

Cobb, J. A. Relationship of discrete classroom behaviors to fourth-grade academic achievement. *Journal of Educational Psychology*, 1972, *63*, 74–80.

Cohen, A. S., & Van Tassel, E. A comparison: Partial and complete paired comparisons in sociometric measurement of preschool groups. *Applied Psychological Measurement*, 1978, *2*, 31–40.

Combs, M. L., & Slaby, D. A. Social skills training with children. In B. Lahey & A. Kazdin (Eds.), *Advances in clinical child psychology* (Vol. I). New York: Plenum, 1977.

Cone, J. D., & Hawkins, R. P. *Behavioral assessment: New directions in clinical psychology*. New York: Brunner/Mazel, 1977.

Cooke, T. P., & Apolloni, T. Developing positive social–emotional behaviors: A study of training and generalization effects. *Journal of Applied Behavior Analysis*, 1976, *9*, 65–78.

Cowen, E. L., Dorr, D., Izzo, L. D., Madonia, A., & Trost, M. A. The primary mental health project: A new way to conceptualize and deliver school mental health service. *Psychology in the Schools*, 1971, *8*, 216–225.

Cowen, E. L., Pederson, A., Babigian, H., Izzo, L. D., & Trost, M. A. Longterm followup of early detected vulnerable children. *Journal of Consulting and Clinical Psychology*, 1973, *41*, 438–446.

Cronbach, L. J. *Essentials of psychological testing* (3rd ed.). New York: Harper & Row, 1970.

Drabman, R., Spitalnik, R., & Spitalnik, K. Sociometric and disruptive behavior as a function of four types of token reinforcement programs. *Journal of Applied Behavior Analysis*, 1974, *7*, 93–101.

Evans, I. M., & Nelson, R. O. Assessment of child behavior problems. In A. R. Ciminero, K. S. Calhoun, & H. E. Adams (Eds.), *Handbook of behavioral assessment*. New York: Wiley, 1977.

Evers, W. L., & Schwartz, J. C. Modifying social withdrawal in preschoolers: The effects of filmed modeling and teacher praise. *Journal of Abnormal Child Psychology*, 1973, *1*, 248–256.

Evers-Pasquale, W., & Sherman, M. The reward value of peers: A variable influencing the efficacy of filmed modeling in modifying social isolation in preschoolers. *Journal of Abnormal Child Psychology*, 1975, *3*(3), 179–189.

Fagot, B. I., & Patterson, G. R. An in vivo analysis of reinforcing contingencies for sex-role behaviors in the preschool child. *Developmental Psychology*, 1969, *5*, 563–568.

Furman, W. Promoting appropriate social behavior: A developmental perspective. In B. Lahey & A. Kazdin (Eds.), *Advances in clinical child psychology* (Vol. 3). New York: Plenum, 1980.

Furman, W., Rahe, D. F., & Hartup, W. W. Rehabilitation of socially-withdrawn preschool children. *Child Development*, 1979, *50*, 915–922.

Galassi, M. D., & Galassi, J. P. The effects of role playing variations on the assessment of assertive behavior. *Behavior Therapy*, 1976, *7*, 343–347.

Garmezy, M. Children at risk: The search for the antecedents of schizophrenia. Part I: Conceptual models and research methods. *Schizophrenia Bulletin*, 1973, *8* (Spring), 14–90.

Garvey, C. Some properties of social play. In J. S. Bruner, A. Jolly, & K. Sylva (Eds.), *Play—Its role in development and evolution*. New York: Basic Books, 1976.

Goldfried, M. R., & D'Zurilla, R. J. A behavioral analytic model for assessing competence. In C. D.

Spielberger (Ed.), *Current topics in clinical and community psychology* (Vol. I). New York: Academic Press, 1969.

Goodenough, F. L. Measuring behavior traits by means of repeated short samples. *Journal of Juvenile Research*, 1928, *12*, 230–235.

Gottlieb, J., Agard, J., Kaufman, M. J., & Semmel, M. I. Retarded children mainstreamed: Practices as they affect minority group children. In R. L. Jones (Ed.), *Mainstreaming the minority child*. Minneapolis: The Council for Exceptional Children, 1976.

Gottman, J. The effects of a modeling film on social isolation in preschool children: A methodological investigation. *Journal of Abnormal Child Psychology*, 1977, *5*, 69–78. (a)

Gottman, J. M. Toward a definition of social isolation in children. *Child Development*, 1977, *48*, 513–517. (b)

Gottman, J., Gonso, J., & Rasmussen, B. Social interaction, social competence, and friendship in children. *Child Development*, 1975, *46*, 709–718.

Gottman, J., Gonso, J., & Schuler, P. Teacher social skills in isolated children. *Journal of Abnormal Child Psychology*, 1976, *4*(2), 179–197.

Greenwood, C. R., Hops, H., & Walker, H. M. The durability of student behavior change: A comparative analysis at follow-up. *Behavior Therapy*, 1977, *8*, 631–638.

Greenwood, C. R., Hops, H., Walker, H. M., Guild, J. J., Stokes, J., Young, K. R., Keleman, K. S., & Willardson, M. A standard classroom behavior management program (PASS): Social validation and replication studies in Utah and Oregon. *Journal of Applied Behavior Analysis*, 1979, *12*, 235–253.

Greenwood, C. R., Walker, H. M., & Hops, H. Some issues in social interaction/withdrawal assessment. *Exceptional Children*, 1977, *43*, 490–499.

Greenwood, C. R., Walker, H. M., Todd, N. M., & Hops, H. Selecting a cost-effective screening device for the assessment of preschool social withdrawal. *Journal of Applied Behavior Analysis*, 1979, *12*, 639–652.

Guralnick, M. J. The value of integrating handicapped and nonhandicapped preschool children. *American Journal of Orthopsychiatry*, 1976, *42*, 236–245.

Hart, B. M., Reynolds, N. J., Baer, D. M., Brawley, E. R., & Harris, F. R. Effect of contingent and non-contingent social reinforcement on the cooperative play of a preschool child. *Journal of Applied Behavior Analysis*, 1968, *1*, 73–76.

Hartup, W. W. Peer interaction and social organization. In P. H. Mussen (Ed.), *Carmichael's manual of child psychology* (Vol. 2). New York: Wiley, 1970.

Hartup, W. W. Peer relations and the growth of social competence. In M. W. Kent & J. E. Rolf (Eds.), *Primary prevention of psychopathology* (Vol. 3): *Social competence in children*. Hanover, N.H.: University Press of New England, 1979.

Hartup, W. W., Glazer, J. A., & Charlesworth, R. Peer reinforcement and sociometric status. *Child Development*, 1967, *38*, 1017–1024.

Hersen, M., & Barlow, D. H. *Single-case experimental design: Strategies in studying behavior change*. New York: Pergamon, 1976.

Hersen, M., & Bellack, A. S. Assessment of social skills. In A. R. Ciminero, K. R. Calhoun, & H. E. Adams (Eds.), *Handbook of behavioral assessment*. New York: Wiley, 1977.

Hops, H. Covariation of social stimuli and interaction rates in the natural preschool environment (Doctoral dissertation, University of Oregon, 1971). *Dissertation Abstracts International*, 1971, *32*, 32109-B.

Hops, H. Social skills training for socially isolated children. In P. Karoly & J. Steffen (Eds.), *Intellectual and social deficiencies*. New York: Gardner Press, in press.

Hops, H., Walker, H. M., Fleischman, D. H., Nagoshi, J. T., Omura, R. T., Skindrud, K., & Taylor, J. CLASS: A standardized in-class program for acting-out children. II. Field test evaluations. *Journal of Educational Psychology*, 1978, *70*, 636–644.

Hops, H., Walker, H. M., & Greenwood, C. R. PEERS: A program for remediating social withdrawal in the school setting: Aspects of a research and development process. In L. A. Hamerlynck (Ed.), *The history and future of the developmentally disabled: Problematic and methodological issues*. New York: Brunner/Mazel, 1979.

Jakibchuk, Z., & Smeriglio, V. The influence of symbolic modeling on the social behavior of preschool children with low levels of social responsiveness. *Child Development*, 1976, *47*, 838–841.

Johnson, J. E. Relations of divergent thinking and intelligence of test scores with social and nonsocial make-believe play of preschool children. *Child Development*, 1976, *47*, 1200–1203.

Kazdin, A. E. Assessing the clinical or applied importance of behavior change through social validation. *Behavior Modification*, 1977, *1*, 427–452.

Keller, M. F., & Carlson, P. M. The use of symbolic modeling to promote social skills in preschool children with low levels of social responsiveness. *Child Development*, 1974, *45*, 912–919.

Kelly, J. A., Furman, W., Phillips, J., Hathorn, S., & Wilson, T. Teaching conversational skills to retarded adolescents. *Child Behavior Therapy*, 1979, *1*, 85–97.

Kent, M. W., & Rolf, J. E. (Eds.). *Primary prevention of psychopathology* (Vol. 3): *Social competence in children*. Hanover, N.H.: University Press of New England, 1979.

Kirby, F. D., & Toler, H. C. Modification of preschool isolate behavior: A case study. *Journal of Applied Behavior Analysis*, 1970, *3*, 309–314.

Kohn, M., & Rosman, B. L. Relationship of preschool social–emotional functioning to later intellectual achievement. *Developmental Psychology*, 1972, *6*, 445–452.

Ladd, G. W., Social skills and peer acceptance: Effects of a social learning method for training social skills. *Child Development*, in press.

Ladd, G. W., & Oden, S. L. The relationship between peer acceptance and children's ideas about helpfulness. *Child Development*, 1979, *50*, 402–408.

Lewis, M., & Rosenblum, L. A. *Friendship and peer relations*. New York: Wiley, 1975.

Mager, R. F. *Preparing instructional objectives*. Palo Alto, Calif.: Fearon Publishers, 1962.

Mash, E. J., & Terdal, L. G. Behavior-therapy assessment: Diagnosis, design and evaluation. *Psychological Reports*, 1974, *35*, 587–601.

Mash, E. J., & Terdal, L. G. (Eds.). *Behavior therapy assessment: Diagnosis, design and evaluation*. New York: Springer, 1976.

Mueller, E. The maintenance of verbal exchanges between young children. *Child Development*, 1972, *43*, 930–938.

Mueller, E., & Brenner, J. The origins of social skills and interaction among play group toddlers. *Child Development*, 1977, *48*, 854–861.

Mueller, E., & Vandell, D. Infant–infant interaction. In Osofsky, J. (Ed.), *Handbook of infant development*. New York: Wiley-Interscience, 1979.

O'Connor, M. The nursery school environment. *Developmental Psychology*, 1975, *11*(5), 556–561.

O'Connor, R. D. Modification of social withdrawal through symbolic modeling. *Journal of Applied Behavior Analysis*, 1969, *2*, 15–22.

O'Connor, R. D. The relative efficacy of modeling, shaping, and the combined procedures for the modification of social withdrawal. *Journal of Abnormal Psychology*, 1972, *79*(3), 327–334.

Oden, S., & Asher, S. R. Coaching children in social skills for friendship making. *Child Development*, 1977, *48*, 495–506.

Parten, M. B. Social participation among preschool children. *Journal of Abnormal and Social Psychology*, 1932, *27*, 243–269.

Patterson, G. R. Interventions for boys with conduct problems: Multiple settings, treatments, and criteria. *Journal of Consulting and Clinical Psychology*, 1974, *42*, 471–481. (a)

Patterson, G. R. Stimulus control in natural settings. In J. deWit & H. Hartup (Eds.), *Determinants and origins of aggressive behavior*. The Hague, Netherlands: Mouton Press, 1974. (b)

Patterson, G. R. A basis for identifying stimuli which control behaviors in natural settings. *Child Development*, 1974, *45*, 900–911. (c)

Patterson, G. R. The aggressive child: Victim and architect of a coercive system. In E. J. Mash, L. A. Hamerlynck, & L. C. Handy (Eds.), *Behavior modification and families*. New York: Brunner/Mazel, 1976.

Patterson, G. R. Mothers: The unacknowledged victims. *Monographs of the Society for Research in Child Development*, 1980, *45* (Serial No. 185).

Patterson, G. R. A performance theory for coercive family interaction. In R. Cairns, (Ed.), *The analysis of social interactions: Methods, issues, and illustrations*. New York: Wiley, 1979.

Patterson, G. R., & Reid, J. B. Reciprocity and coercion: Two facets of social systems. In C. Neuringer

& J. Michael (Eds.), *Behavior modification in clinical psychology*. New York: Appleton-Century-Crofts, 1970.

Patterson, G. R., Reid, J. B., Jones, R. R., & Conger, R. E. *A social learning approach to family intervention* (Vol. I): *Families with aggressive children*. Eugene, Ore.: Castalia Publishing Company, 1975.

Peck, C. A., Apolloni, T., Cooke, T. P., & Raver, S. A. Teaching retarded preschoolers to imitate the free-play behavior of non-retarded classmates: Trained and generalized effects. *Journal of Special Education*, 1975, *12*, 195–207.

Quilitch, H. R., & Risley, T. R. The effects of play materials on social play. *Journal of Applied Behavior Analysis*, 1973, *6*, 573–578.

Raph, J. B., Thomas, A., Chess, S., & Korn, S. J. The influence of nursery school on social interactions. *American Journal of Orthopsychiatry*, 1968, *38*, 144–152.

Reuter, J., & Yunik, G. Social interaction in nursery schools. *Developmental Psychology*, 1973, *9*(3), 319–325.

Risley, T. R. The ecology of applied behavior analysis. In A. Rogers-Warren & S. T. Warren (Eds.), *Ecological perspectives in behavior analysis*. Baltimore: University Park Press, 1977.

Roff, M., Sells, S. B., & Golden, M. M. *Social adjustment and personality development in children*. Minneapolis: The University of Minnesota, 1972.

Rolf, J. E., & Hasazi, J. E. Identification of preschool children at risk and some guidelines for primary intervention. In G. W. Albee & J. M. Joffe (Eds.), *Primary prevention of psychopathology* (Vol. I): *The issues*. Hanover, N.H.: University Press of New England, 1977.

Rubenstein, J., & Howes, C. The effects of peers on toddler interaction with mother and toys. *Child Development*, 1976, *47*, 597–605.

Rubin, K. H., Maioni, T. L., & Hornung, M. Free-play behaviors in middle and lower class preschoolers: Parten and Piaget revisited. *Child Development*, 1976, *47*, 414–419.

Sackett, G. P. Measurement in observational research. In G. P. Sackett (Ed.), *Observing behavior* (Vol. 2): *Data collection and analysis methods*. Baltimore: University Park Press, 1978.

Schulman, J. L., Ford, R. C., Busk, P., & Kaspar, J. C. Evaluation of a classroom program to alter friendship practices. *The Journal of Educational Psychology*, 1973, *67*, 99–102.

Slaby, R. G., & Crowley, C. G. Modification of cooperation and aggression through teacher attention to children's speech. *Journal of Experimental Child Psychology*, 1977, *23*, 442–458.

Spivack, G., & Shure, M. B. *Social adjustment of young children*. San Francisco: Jossey-Bass, 1974.

Spivack, G., & Swift, M. The classroom behavior of children: A critical review of teacher-administered rating scales. *The Journal of Special Education*, 1973, *1*, 55–89.

Stokes, T. F., Baer, D. M., & Jackson, R. L. Programming the generalization of a greeting response in four retarded children. *Journal of Applied Behavioral Analysis*, 1974, *7*, 599.

Strain, P. S., Cooke, T. P., & Apolloni, T. *Teaching exceptional children: Assessing and modifying social behavior*. New York: Academic Press, 1976.

Strain, P. S. An experimental analysis of peer social initiations on the behavior of withdrawn preschool children: Some training and generalization effects. *Journal of Abnormal Child Psychology*, 1977, *5*, 445–455.

Strain, P. S., & Shores, R. E. Social reciprocity: Review of research and educational implications. *Exceptional Children*, 1977, *43*, 526–531.

Strain, P. S., Shores, R. E., & Kerr, M. An experimental analysis of "spillover" effects on the social interactions of behaviorally handicapped preschool children. *Journal of Applied Behavior Analysis*, 1976, *9*, 31–40.

Strain, P. S., Shores, R. E., & Timm, M. A. Effects of peer social initiations on the behavior of a withdrawn child. *Journal of Applied Behavior Analysis*, 1977, *10*, 289–298.

Strain, P. S., & Timm, M. A. An experimental analysis of social interaction between a behaviorally disordered preschool child and her classroom peers. *Journal of Applied Behavior Analysis*, 1974, *7*(4), 583–590.

Suomi, S., & Harlow, H. F. Monkeys without play. In J. S. Bruner, A. Jolly, & K. Sylva (Eds.), *Play—Its role in development and evolution*. New York: Basic Books, 1976.

Tremblay, A., Strain, P. S., Hendrickson, J. M., & Shores, R. E. Social interactions of normally developing preschool children: Using normative data for subject and target behavior selection. *Behavior Modification,* in press.

Ullmann, C. A. Identification of maladjusted school children. *Public Health Monograph No. 7.* Washington, D.C.: Federal Security Agency, 1952.

Victor, J. B., & Halverson, C. F., Jr. Behavior problems in elementary school children: A follow-up study. *Journal of Abnormal Child Psychology,* 1976, *4,* 17–29.

Waldrop, M. F., Bell, R. Q., & Goering, J. D. Minor physical anomalies and inhibited behavior of elementary school girls. *Journal of Child Psychology and Psychiatry,* 1976, *17,* 113–122.

Waldrop, M. G., & Halverson, C. F. Intensive and extensive peer behavior: Longitudinal and cross-sectional analyses. *Child Development,* 1975, *46,* 19–26.

Walker, H. M. *The Walker Problem Behavior Identification Checklist: Test and manual.* Los Angeles: Western Psychological Services, 1970.

Walker, H. M., & Buckley, N. K. Programming generalization and maintenance of treatment effects across time and across settings. *Journal of Applied Behavior Analysis,* 1972, *5,* 209–224.

Walker, H. M., Greenwood, C. R., Hops, H., & Todd, N. Differential effects of reinforcing topographic components of free play social interaction: Analysis and systematic replication. *Behavior Modification,* 1979, *3,* 291–321.

Walker, H. M., & Hops, H. The use of group and individual reinforcement contingencies in the modification of social withdrawal. In L. A. Hamerlynck, L. C. Handy, & E. J. Mash (Eds.), *Behavior change: Methodology, concepts, and practice.* Champaign, Ill.: Research Press, 1973.

Walker, H. M., & Hops, H. Use of normative peer data as a standard for evaluating classroom treatment effects. *Journal of Applied Behavior Analysis,* 1976, *9,* 159–168.

Walker, H. M., Hops, H., & Greenwood, C. R. RECESS: Research and development of a behavior management package for remediating social aggression in the school setting. In P. S. Strain (Ed.), *The utilization of classroom peers as behavior change agents.* New York: Plenum Press, in press.

Weinrott, M. R., Corson, J. A., & Wilchesky, M. Teacher mediated treatment of social withdrawal. *Behavior Therapy,* 1979, *10,* 281–294.

Westbrook, A. Teachers' recognition of problem behavior and referrals of children to pupil personnel services. *The Journal of Education Research,* 1970, *63,* 391–394.

Zax, M., Cowen, E. L., Rappaport, J., Beach, D., & Laird, J. Follow-up study of children identified early as emotionally disturbed. *Journal of Consulting Psychology,* 1968, *32,* 369–373.

Zigler, E., & Trickett, P. K. IQ, social competence, and evaluation of early childhood intervention programs. *American Psychologist,* 1978, *33*(9), 789–798.

# DEVELOPMENTAL DISORDERS

# AUTISM

### Crighton Newsom
*Suffolk Child Development Center*
*and State University of New York at Stony Brook*

### Arnold Rincover
*University of North Carolina at Greensboro*

Autism may be the only childhood disorder with a history of behavioral assessment that antedates its history of cognitive assessment. Traditional, standardized intelligence testing was considered by most professionals to be unsuitable for autistic children until the late 1960s (Alpern, 1967), yet by 1962 Ferster had already concluded his classic studies involving the assessment of reinforcer preferences, persistence, speed of learning, stimulus control, conceptual performance, and drug effects (Ferster & DeMyer, 1961a, 1961b, 1962). Soon thereafter, automated and observational assessment procedures were applied routinely by the first behaviorally oriented clinicians who implemented and evaluated treatment programs for autistic children (Davison, 1964; Lovaas, Berberich, Perloff, & Schaeffer, 1966; Lovaas, Freitag, Gold, & Kassorla, 1965a, 1965b; Wetzel, Baker, Roney, & Martin, 1966; Wolf, Risley, & Mees, 1964).

This chapter selectively reviews contemporary assessment procedures. It is intended to serve more as a practical guide than as a critical review. Therefore, various aspects of "clinical lore" are included at several points, along with experimentally established techniques. The needs of the clinician/researcher have been the primary concern because most behavioral psychologists in this area wear both hats. We begin with a guide through the labyrinthine issues of definition and diagnosis, since "autism," after all this time, still exhibits a profound resistance to definition and remains as slippery a term as "hyperkinesis" or "learning disability." In this section we also discuss the unsolved problem of subclassification and the notion of autism as a unitary disease. The main purposes of assessment in placement, intervention, and research endeavors are described, with attention to decision-making activities in these areas. The remainder of the chapter reviews assessment methodologies, including both global, "total repertoire" procedures and some procedures for measuring fairly specific behaviors. The chapter concludes with a brief mention of some areas of assessment that stand in need of further development.

# MEANINGS OF AUTISM

The word *autism* serves as both a diagnostic label and a hypothetical construct (Rutter, 1978). That is, it is used as a classifying term for developmentally disabled children who exhibit certain behaviors and also as the name of an underlying, yet-to-be-discovered disease that accounts for those behaviors. However, in the absence of evidence that "autistic" children (classification) have "autism" (hypothetical disease), the behavioral clinician/researcher is well advised to discriminate between these usages. The following discussion is intended to establish just such a discrimination.

## Autism as a Label

As a summarizing word for a list of deviant behaviors, "autism" is potentially functional for diagnosticians, researchers, and administrators. However, its potential functionality has yet to be realized because different workers apply the word to different lists of behaviors. Not surprisingly, this lack of consensus creates considerable ambiguity and is one of the reasons for the current great concern over the elucidation of diagnostic issues. In spite of the amount of effort being spent on this question, there is still no objective, empirically derived basis for diagnostic decision making. The published diagnostic checklists designed to distinguish autism from other childhood disorders (British Working Party, in O'Gorman, 1967; Lotter, 1966; Polan & Spencer, 1959; Rimland, 1964) have in common only 35% of their items and, presumably as a result, correlate only moderately ($+.40$s to $+.60$s) in the hands of experienced clinicians applying them to the same children (DeMyer, Churchill, Pontius, & Gilkey, 1971). Rimland (1971) found that if a child were diagnosed as autistic by one professional, the probability that a second professional seeing the child would make the same diagnosis was less than .25. Researchers probably do little better. The well-established research centers in England and in the United States all go by rather different sets of criteria (Russo & Newsom, 1979; see Table 1). This "chaotic" (Rimland, 1971) state of affairs had an early onset, going all the way back to the introduction of the term by Kanner.

### Kanner's Syndrome

Kanner's (1943) original paper, "Autistic Disturbances of Affective Contact," presents 11 case histories, followed by a rambling discussion of observed and inferred characteristics that he believed distinguished these children from schizophrenic and retarded children. Because it is impossible to determine with certainty which characteristics Kanner meant to be extracted to form a set of diagnostic criteria (his later writings on the subject are of little help in this regard), we will list those that he seemed to emphasize as being especially important:

1. *Extreme autistic aloneness from birth that ignores or shuts out all exteroceptive stimuli*, as indicated by a failure to assume the normal anticipatory

TABLE 1
Diagnostic Criteria Used in Selected Research Centers

---

*Indiana University Clinical Research Center for Early Childhood Schizophrenia* (DeMyer, Churchill, Pontius, & Gilkey, 1971)
1. Serious emotional withdrawal before 3 years of age
2. Lack of speech for communication
3. Nonfunctional, repetitive use of objects
4. Failure to engage in role play alone or with peers

*UCLA Autism Project* (Lovaas, 1977)
1. Expressive and receptive language deficiencies
2. Apparent sensory deficit
3. Severe affect isolation
4. Self-stimulatory behavior
5. Absent or minimal social and self-help behaviors
6. Self-destructive behavior in some children

*UCLA Mental Retardation and Child Psychiatry Program* (Ornitz & Ritvo, 1976)
1. Disturbances of perception
2. Disturbances of development rate
3. Disturbances of relating
4. Disturbances of speech and language
5. Disturbances of motility

*Medical Research Council Development Psychology Unit, London* (Hermelin & O'Connor, 1970)
1. Abnormalities in auditory perception and speech
2. Abnormalities in motor control
3. Abnormalities in visual perception and imitation
4. Abnormalities in social relationships, mood, and play

---

    posture prior to being picked up in infancy, feeding problems, fear of loud noises and moving objects, unresponsiveness to other people's verbalizations, failure to look at others' faces, failure to play with other children, and failure to notice the comings and goings of the parents.

2. *Language abnormalities*, including mutism (which appears to be elective) in a minority of children and noncommunicative speech in the majority. The speaking children learn to name objects easily and repeat nursery rhymes, prayers, songs, and lists requiring an excellent rote memory but no comprehension. They also exhibit lack of spontaneous sentence formation and immediate or delayed echolalia, or exact repetitions of sentences heard at some previous time, resulting in the reversal of personal pronouns in requests (e.g., "Are you ready for your dessert?" is used to ask for dessert). There is extreme literalness in the use of prepositions (e.g., pictures are not hung "on" the wall but "near" the wall) and "affirmation by repetition" ("yes" is indicated by simply echoing the question).

3. *An anxiously obsessive desire for the maintenance of sameness* that nobody but the child may disrupt. Changes of daily routine, of furniture arrangement, of an arrangement of objects, or of the wording of requests, or the sight of anything broken or incomplete produce tantrums or despair. There

is a limitation in the variety of spontaneous activity, including rhythmic movements providing masturbatory orgastic gratification, and a preoccupation with objects that do not change their appearance or position except when manipulated by the child.

4. *Good cognitive potential*, as indicated by intelligent and serious-minded, yet "anxiously tense," facial expressions; excellent memory for previous events, poems, names, and complex patterns and sequences; and good performance on the Seguin Form Board.

5. *Essentially normal physical development*, with better fine motor than gross motor skills.

6. *Highly intelligent, obsessive, and cold parents*, as indicated by their advanced degrees, professional occupations, unhappy marriages, and detailed diaries and recollections of the child's early development.

Kanner's criteria, which have been held up as a model of "lucid description" and "clear, careful prose" (Schopler, 1978; Rutter, 1978), reflect the casual disregard for objectivity that was characteristic of psychiatry in that era. In light of current experimental knowledge, Kanner's criteria constitute a set of features that are loosely defined with unclear boundaries and seem to be ripe for misinterpretation and idiosyncratic application. It is therefore hardly surprising to find that the concept of autism has changed over the years to accommodate various investigators' perceptions as well as research needs and political interests. These pressures have produced multiple definitions of autism (Table 1) and have resulted in the broadening of the concept to include more children than Kanner originally intended (Kanner, 1958).

The *multiplicity* of definitions can probably be accounted for by the fact that each investigator sees a different group of children who resemble the children described by Kanner and, further, sees them with a unique perceptual set, determined by his or her professional background and interpretation of Kanner's descriptions. This result was inevitable, given Kanner's failure to provide reasonably objective criteria for the diagnosis.

The *broadening* of definitions appears to be the result of two very practical considerations. First, if autism were diagnosed only in strict accordance with Kanner's (1943) criteria, too few children would be available at any one laboratory at the same time for the basic medical and psychological investigations that require group designs. Rimland (1974) has calculated that the prevalence of Kanner's Syndrome children is about 1 in 20,000 live births, as compared with a prevalence rate for all autistic children of about 1 in 2500 (Lotter, 1967; Wing, Yeates, Brierley, & Gould, 1976). Second, parents and professionals lobbying for special treatment and educational programs need the weight of numbers to sway administrators and legislators. A clear example of how this need produces a broadening of the definition is provided by the elevation of "disturbances of developmental rates and sequences," not discussed by Kanner, to the status of a "cardinal symptom" by the Professional Advisory Board of the National Society for Autistic Children (NSAC), partly to take advantage of the new funding provided by the Developmental Disabilities Act (Schopler, 1978).

## Current Definitions

Because Kanner's criteria are dated and difficult to apply, and because the multiplicity of definitions impedes communication, most investigators would welcome a single definition of autism that reflects current knowledge and seems likely to be reliable. However, current developments suggest that the best that might be hoped for in the near future is the widespread adoption of one or the other of two key definitions as a replacement for the many now in use. One of these definitions has been provided by Rutter (1978) and is an attempt to update Kanner's criteria on the basis of current knowledge. The other is the NSAC Professional Advisory Board definition (1977, 1978), intended primarily for administrative and legislative uses. Both definitions have the imprimatur of the editors of the primary journal in the field (Schopler, 1978). The implication of this unusual move seems to be that either definition may be used in making the diagnosis.

Rutter's (1978) definition presents the following criteria for making the diagnosis in a child of 4 years or younger:

1. *Onset of symptoms before the age of 30 months.*
2. *Impaired social development that is below the child's tested intellectual level.* Specifically, there is a lack of attachment behavior and a relative failure of social bonding, as well as nondiscriminating use of eye contact.
3. *Delayed and deviant language development*, which includes failure to imitate, failure to engage in imaginative play, abnormal patterns of babbling, lack of comprehension, lack of gesture, immediate and delayed echolalia, I–You pronominal reversal, lack of conversational speech, and difficulty in talking about things outside the immediate situation.
4. *Insistence on sameness*, indicated by stereotyped play patterns, abnormal preoccupations with certain objects or activities, rigid routines, and resistance to changes in the environment.

Rutter's definition represents some gain in objectivity over Kanner's and organizes the salient behaviors of autistic children succinctly into four areas. It allows the concurrent diagnosis of autism, other medical conditions, and mental retardation. The inclusion of each item is supported by the citation of a number of research studies. This last characteristic makes the definition highly attractive, but it is not a guarantee of the validity of the points. The studies cited involved children diagnosed according to various criteria, so that the resulting "state of the art" presented by Rutter is based on a kind of "diagnostic averaging" across studies. Nevrtheless, Rutter's criteria do avoid giving undue weight to the preoccupations of any one research center and do capture the essential features of "autism" as the term is generally used.

The NSAC (1977, 1978) definition is the product of clinical observation and committee consensus rather than scholarly review. Its main points are the following:

1. *Onset of symptoms prior to 30 months of age.*
2. *Disturbances in the rate of appearance of physical, social, and language skills.*

3. *Abnormal responses to sensations.* Any one or a combination of sight, hearing, touch, pain, balance, smell, and taste are affected.
4. *Speech and language are absent or delayed*, while specific thinking capabilities may be present. Immature rhythms of speech, limited understanding of ideas, and the use of words without attaching the usual meaning to them are common.
5. *Abnormal ways of relating to people, objects, and events.* Typically, they do not respond appropriately to adults and other children. Objects and toys are not used as normally intended.

Each point is elaborated on with several examples of deviant behaviors drawn from clinical observation (NSAC, 1978), including those mentioned by Rutter (1978), but with additions. This definition goes on to list "associated features" that may be present in some cases, such as mental retardation; lability of mood; self-injurious behavior; stereotyped, repetitive behavior; and EEG abnormalities.

Given the existence of two "approved" definitions, the obvious question arises as to which should be used in making the diagnosis. In practice, it really does not matter which definition is used, since the two definitions overlap sufficiently to be virtually interchangeable for most clinical and research purposes. Rutter's criteria seem to best summarize current empirical knowledge. Further, there is the practical consideration that his criteria most resemble the criteria in the third edition of the *Diagnostic and Statistical Manual* of the American Psychiatric Association (DSM-III), a factor which should be kept in mind when a choice is made. The definitions are similar in the behavioral details used as examples in the complete texts and differ primarily in emphasis and in the theoretical biases determining their organization.

### Differential Diagnosis

Autistic children share many behaviors with children who are more appropriately located in other categories of childhood disorders, such as mental retardation, childhood schizophrenia, deafness, and aphasia. Appropriate differential diagnosis is based on historical information, psychological and audiological testing, and the overall "clinical impact" of the observed behaviors. The following considerations aid in making the decision.

"Mental retardation" is generally diagnosed in preference to autism when the deficits in motor, cognitive, social, and language functioning are at a fairly uniform level. In questionable cases, the degree of socialization becomes crucial: retarded children usually exhibit more appropriate social behaviors than autistic children.

In the psychiatric nomenclature of DSM-II, "autism" does not appear, with the result that autistic children are not diagnosed separately but receive the label of "childhood schizophrenia," often with the phrase "with autistic features" added. This practice changes with DSM-III, reflecting the increasingly common tendency to differentiate early-onset and late-onset childhood psychoses, with autistic children placed in the first category and schizophrenic children in the second. This distinction is the result of studies by Kolvin (1971), Makita (1966), and Vrono

(1974) showing a bipolar distribution in the ages of onset of childhood psychoses, with one peak in infancy and the other during or after pubescence, and the existence of important differences in the two groups of children. This research is the basis for the "under 30 months" criterion in current definitions of autism. Schizophrenic children also differ from older autistic children in being more sociable (sometimes excessively so) and less globally handicapped. Often, the major subjective impression is that of a "thought disorder" because of the nearly age-appropriate, but deviant, language behavior of schizophrenic children, which tends to be perseverative, grammatically immature, illogical, and often too idiosyncratic in content to be of any communicative value.

Variable responsiveness to sounds in young autistic children often suggests deafness, but the problem is usually attentional rather than sensory. Nonpsychotic deaf children usually distinguish themselves from autistic children by their use of communicative gesturing and their high degree of social relatedness. But the two conditions are not mutually exclusive; some autistic children are also deaf or have various degrees of measurable hearing loss that are not attributable to auditory attention deficits.

Aphasic children differ from autistic children primarily in their higher levels of intellectual and social development and their greater use of gesturing. They also tend to be less delayed motorically and less involved with self-stimulatory behaviors.

## A Behavioral Perspective on Diagnosis

The problem of diagnosis in autism involves larger issues than the search for a definition and its differential application. Certain professional and theoretical problems are important and far from resolution at the present time.

An argument can be made that diagnosis is the province of medicine, not psychology, and therefore psychologists should not concern themselves about diagnostic problems until an acceptable psychological diagnostic system is created. It is easy to sympathize with this argument in the abstract, but it overlooks the facts that, in reality, researchers often screen potential subjects to validate the medical diagnoses they have been given and some clinicians involved in assessment are expected to give diagnostic impressions. Intentional disregard of current developments in diagnosis would serve the interests of neither party. This view is based on the presupposition that, for behavioral psychologists, "autism" is used simply as a convenient label for those children who show the behaviors listed in Rutter's criteria or the NSAC criteria, without assuming that the label names an underlying disease. The deviant behaviors observed in autistic children may be closely related and attributable to a single physiological dysfunction or, on the other hand, may be relatively independent, resulting from multiple physiological and environmental variables. At present it is not at all clear that these deviant behaviors should be attributed to a "disturbance of affective contact" (Kanner, 1943), or to "faulty modulation of sensory input and motor output" (Ornitz, 1974). The use of the label need not imply acceptance of a one-to-one correspondence between the label and some yet-to-be-identified disease or abnormality but can, instead, be used simply as a summary term for classification purposes.

The foregoing observation points to a fundamental weakness of "autism" as a diagnosis. It serves only to classify. Unlike diagnoses in more technologically advanced areas of medicine, the autism diagnosis fails to indicate the etiology or the probable course of the disorder, does not narrow the range of potentially effective treatments, and does not specify the prognosis (Russo & Newsom, 1979).

The most serious weakness of the autism diagnosis, by whatever set of criteria it is made, is that it still leaves us with only one broad term with which to label a very heterogeneous population. It subsumes under the same label children who, for example, are profoundly retarded, mute, and totally preoccupied with self-stimulatory behavior and children whose IQs are in the normal range and have considerable communicative speech. Little progress in the identification of etiological factors or the prediction of likely outcomes to different treatments can be expected until we have a reliable system for subclassifying autistic children. This problem, of dividing autism into meaningful subtypes, is currently the most pressing and formidable task facing investigators concerned with classification, yet its surface has barely been scratched (DeMyer, Norton, & Barton, 1971; DeMyer, Barton, DeMyer, Norton, Allen, & Steele, 1973).

### The Problem of Subclassification

The meaningful subdivision of autistic children presents a formidable problem because it is unlikely that any single system of subclassification can be devised that will be generally useful for all purposes in all environments. Different, yet equally valid, systems will be required to meet the different needs for which subclassification is sought. For example, a neurophysiological researcher would probably subdivide autistic children in a different way than would an educational administrator. Each system could be valid and functional within the setting in which it is intended to be used, but neither could be expected to be valid or functional outside that setting.

A further source of difficulty in devising a subclassification system for a given purpose is our ignorance of which physiological, behavioral, and environmental dimensions would form the most useful basis for dividing the children. Some leads are available for those interested in subclassification for prognostic purposes. Several researchers have found that measured intelligence, language level, severity (a combination of IQ and degree of developmental milestone delay), and initial educational placement are highly correlated with outcome (DeMyer, et al., 1973; Lotter, 1974a, 1974b, 1978; Rutter, Greenfeld, & Lockyer, 1967). But these dimensions may be of limited usefulness to the contemporary prognostician, since they are derived from studies where the outcomes were probably affected by the rather primitive treatments available in the 1950s and 1960s (primarily custodial and pharmacological regimens, along with some early special education approaches).

At present, valid subclassification systems for the purposes of educational placement, basic medical research, behavioral treatment planning, and residential placement, to name a few, are conspicuously lacking. The reason for this state of affairs may be that too much effort is spent in trying to get more information out of traditional measures, such as medical histories, neurological examinations, and IQ tests, than they were ever meant to yield. Consideration of nontraditional variables might lead to useful systems with more meaningful subdivisions than are currently available. In educational settings, for example, classroom placements are often made on the basis of mastery of self-care skills, rate and intensity of disruptive and aggressive behaviors, level of language development, and chronological age. These dimensions are currently or potentially quantifiable and could enter into a subclassification system for educational placement purposes.

Another example occurs in the domain of behavioral treatment planning with children whose major presenting problem is self-injurious behavior (SIB). Here, subdivision is possible according to motivational considerations. Carr (1977) has suggested that SIB falls into two major classes: that which is extrinsically motivated (by positive social reinforcement or by negative reinforcement) and that which is intrinsically motivated (by self-stimulatory or organic factors). Each of these four motivational dimensions and their interactions carry unique implications for treatment (cf. Rincover & Koegel, 1977). This example is additionally instructive in relation to the fundamental and radical issue of the value of the autism diagnosis at all in treatment efforts. Carr's (1977) review demonstrates the irrelevance of psychiatric nosology to treatment efforts in the area of SIB, and its irrelevance to behavioral treatment considerations more generally in the field of autism has been previously argued (Lovaas & Newsom, 1976; Newsom, Carr, & Lovaas, 1979). For the present, it is sufficient to summarize by noting that subclassification efforts need not be constrained by medical models but could benefit from approaches based on known behavioral variables.

## Autism as a Construct

In addition to being an arbitrary label for a cluster of behavioral and developmental deviations, autism is often a reification of one or another of the published definitions into a hypothetical disease. The concept of autism-as-a-disease endures as a convenient fiction for journalists and for researchers engaged in the search for a biochemical or physiological substrate of the condition described in the definition. Implied in these efforts is the expectation of a "magic bullet" type of intervention, that is, a pharmacological or dietary treatment regimen that will have global curative effects. Or, if such a cure is not possible, there is still the expectation that a genetic or fetal "marker" will be identified that will serve as the basis for prenatal counseling, as in the case of Tay–Sachs disease, for example. The realization of either of these events would be a great breakthrough, but two considerations limit our anticipation of success in the immediate future.

First, it seems that some agreement on a meaningful way of subdividing autistic children for etiological research purposes is required. As has just been seen, "autism" includes a quite heterogeneous group of children, and none of the published definitions allows discriminations within this group. To paraphrase Bleuler, we are dealing with "the group of autisms," and it is possible that different sets of etiological variables will be necessary to account for the various possible subclassifications. Autism is known to be associated with maternal rubella (Chess, 1971, 1977), congential brain damage (DeMyer, 1976; Lotter, 1967; Rutter, Bartak, & Newman, 1971), and certain metabolic dysfunctions (Coleman, 1976). These underlying causes may be responsible for distinct subgroups, but their delineation remains to be accomplished. At present, the investigator concerned with physiological causes is faced with using one of the standard definitions and hoping to find a common factor that will account for all of the subgroups of autistic children or with limiting his or her sample to a subgroup selected according to a personal decision about which dimensions define a condition that will be vulnerable to systematic research.

Second, there is no evidence that autism is a disease in the sense that there is a one-to-one correspondence between one of the definitions and an underlying pathology. The characteristics listed in each definition represent clinical impressions regarding the essential features of autism, but they may not be the characteristics that will lead to knowledge about etiology. Some of the characteristics, such as social aloofness and insistence on sameness, may be very secondary to more basic deficiencies in language development, perception, or learning, for example. If so, investigations of the causes of retardation in language, perception, and learning in autistic children would be more productive of etiological knowledge than would investigations of autism as a unitary disease entity. Although there are occasional reports of biochemical and anatomical deviations in autistic children, such as impaired serotonin metabolism (Boullin, Coleman, O'Brien, & Rimland, 1971; Takahashi, Kanai, & Miyamoto, 1976; Yuwiler, Geller, & Ritvo, 1976), enlarged temporal lobe development (Hauser, DeLong, & Rosman, 1975), vestibular system dysfunction (Ornitz, 1978), and deviant hemispheric dominance (Blackstock, 1978), there is still no well-established abnormality known to be present in the majority of children diagnosed as autistic and specific to them. Thus autism is not reducible to an underlying physiological pathology at present, and it is incorrect to use the word as though it named a disease.

An alternative to attempts to identify "the" pathology underlying autism is the "divide-and-investigate" strategy preferred by behavioral investigators. Each of the behaviors traditionally associated with autism (and often shared with other diagnostic categories) may be studied separately, with due attention to possibly relevant physiological and behavioral variables. This approach has the weight of clinical utility behind it (Newsom et al., 1979) and may be more productive in uncovering etiological variables and suggesting treatment strategies than are the "whole-child" approaches common in traditional medical and psychological investigations. This position was most forcefully argued by Lovaas (1971) in his spontaneous remarks during the discussion of diagnostic issues at the Indiana Colloquium:

It seems we are trying to define autism here because of certain assumptions. The main assumption is that there is some kind of process going on in autism and that a whole set of behaviors follow or are related to this process. A further assumption is that if we change this process we will simultaneously change all sorts of behaviors. The self-stimulation will disappear, the language will come, the affect will come, and so on. I personally doubt that we have something of that kind called autism. . . . I see not one condition but a heterogeneity. Behaviors which we now call autistic, like self-stimulation, aloofness, interpersonal relationship distortions, other distortions in language, and so on, may be tied into rather separate types of environments or tied into separate types of treatment possibilities. One way to define autism is to try to work out the relationships that govern each one of these behaviors. The sum total of all these relationships will be your definition. (p. 110)

## PURPOSES AND SETTINGS

Behavioral assessment plays a part in decisions in the broad areas of placement, intervention, and research. The questions raised in each of these areas require familiarity with rather different assessment activities.

### Placement

Placement decisions are made intermittently throughout every autistic individual's life. The first formal assessment may take place as early as 2 or 3 years of age if the toddler's development is sufficiently abnormal to attract the attention of the parents or the pediatrician. The presenting complaints may include delays in reaching milestones, suspected deafness, social unresponsiveness, or feeding and sleeping problems. The major assessment question is whether the child should be diagnosed as retarded, autistic, or normal but slow in developing. Infant development scales, such as the Bayley Scales of Infant Development, the Merrill–Palmer Scale, or the Gesell Development Schedules, are often used to assess the degree of retardation, whereas physical and neurological examinations can determine whether medical or neurological problems exist. The diagnosing physician takes information from these sources into account, but also relies heavily on informal behavioral observations. The resulting diagnosis includes a large measure of clinical judgment and is often considered tentative at this early age. The autism diagnosis is usually made only when the child shows profound social unresponsiveness, as indicated by lack of eye contact, absence of a social smile, limpness or stiffness when held, use of another person's hand to get things, emotional flatness, or lack of comprehension and gesturing.

The primary placement question is usually whether the child should remain at home or be referred to a preschool program for developmentally disabled children. (Institutionalization is also a possibility, but more often than not it is immediately rejected by the parents at this stage unless severe medical problems are present.) The decision to recommend that the child stay at home or attend a preschool depends on several factors, which may be formulated as questions: (1) Does one of the parents have the time, energy, and personality (cf. Lovaas, Koegel, Simmons, & Long, 1973) to work successfully with the child at home? (2) What is the availability, quality, and cost of appropriate preschool programs? (3) Are there any good in-home training and support services available in the area? and (4) Are there additional problems in this family that may be important (e.g., marital problems, very low income, a large number of siblings, handicapped siblings)? Questions like these must be considered because the mere availability of a preschool program does not necessarily mean that placement there would be the best thing for the child or the family. Highly motivated parents who are relatively unencumbered by other problems can generally do more for their autistic child, if they are trained and supported, than can most preschool programs.

The autistic child who has not come to professional attention beforehand will almost certainly be referred for an evaluation within a few days or weeks after entering school. Social and language deficits will be glaringly apparent in the average kindergarten or first grade. After an evaluation of the child by the school psychologist or a psychologist in the community, which often includes administration of an intelligence test and informal classroom observations, the child's case comes before the committee on the handicapped of the local school district. The committee determines an appropriate school placement for the child, taking into account the diagnosis, level of intelligence, nature and severity of disruptive behavior, and available placement options.

In practice, the child is placed in a special education class within the district if one is available and if the child is independent in most self-care skills and has no serious disruptive behaviors; otherwise, he or she is referred to a school for retarded children or to a private school. The psychologist who assesses the child for the committee must be aware of the very low tolerance level of most public school teachers for self-care and self-control deficits. Special education teachers tend to be oriented by training and experience toward the problems of mildly retarded and learning-disabled children and often will not respond well to a child in need of individual attention in toileting or eating or who is aggressive or hyperactive. Rates and intensities of disruptive behavior that the professional who is familiar with autistic children would consider to be routine and relatively mild are often completely unacceptable to the public school teacher.

Within a school that specializes in the education of retarded and/or autistic children, some unusual dimensions often must be considered in making classroom placement recommendations (Koegel & Rincover, 1975; Rincover & Koegel, 1977). Variables such as age, sex, size, level of language usage, and "ability to work in a group" (i.e., low levels of disruptive behavior and manageability with intermittent, delayed, and often random social reinforcers), along with the available teachers' degrees of skill in controlling behavior, form the basis for most class placements. Traditional psychometric test data and psychiatric evaluations are functionally irrelevant in most placement decisions. The behavioral psychologist participating in such decisions currently must rely on informal observational knowledge of the children and teachers involved and his or her own clinical hunches to an uncomfortably large degree.

Concerns about institutional or residential placement become frequent in the adolescent years. These concerns are generally prompted by the parents' inability to continue managing the autistic adolescent in the home, because of a kind of cumulative fatigue with attending to his or her needs for so many years, to marital or financial problems, to their advancing ages, to restlessness with a constricted lifestyle, or to other factors. Sometimes the question of placement is raised by administrators at the aggressive adolescent's school, who may be reluctant to continue risking physical danger to teachers and peers as the child gets older and larger. When the request comes from the parents, the psychologist must be sensitive to the needs of the other family members and must try to match the adolescent's needs with the available institutional or residential options as well as possible. When the question of placement is raised by school personnel, the final decision may depend upon the psychologist's ability to assess and remediate the problem. Skill in designing, implementing, and evaluating behavior management procedures can often preclude, or at least delay, a decision to exclude an aggressive adolescent. In such cases, the psychologist's ability to devise an effective treatment and to monitor the problem behaviors with objective observational measures is essential in order to prevent incorrect decisions based on subjective impressions.

At the age of 21, the possibility of school placement ends and only three possible placements remain: institutional, residential, or sheltered workshop. Institutional placement is almost inevitable if the child is difficult to manage at home, because residential facilities (whether large facilities or small group homes) tend to reject aggressive persons and those who are deficient in basic self-care skills. Sheltered workshops for residential adults or for those still living at home are usually geared toward retarded persons, often expecting a relatively high degree of self-control and independence (i.e., zero aggressive and disruptive behaviors and the ability to work for long periods without close supervision). The probability of obtaining a residential or workshop placement for an autistic adolescent or adult can be enhanced by providing objective evidence of the attainment of such behaviors. Such evidence can take the form of data showing low weekly or monthly rates of disruptive behaviors, high mean durations of work periods between supervisory interactions, or similar measures. A knowledge of the expectations of available facilities is invaluable in this regard, along with coordination of efforts with a social worker.

## Intervention

Intervention efforts, whether described as education, rehabilitation, clinical treatment, language therapy, behavior management, or home living training, have in common the fundamental obligations of assessing entry behaviors in order to pinpoint excesses and deficits, selecting target behaviors, and subsequently tracking the behaviors selected for intervention. The first two needs are met through the use of interviews, standardized tests, checklists covering important domains of behavior, and pretreatment observation procedures, which range in degree of structure from highly informal (as in clinical observations and preplacement classrooms) to highly operationalized (as in baseline observations focused on a few specific behaviors). Assessment of the effects of intervention is conducted either continuously, through trial-by-trial or daily recording, or intermittently, through periodic testing or observational procedures.

Although the technology for meeting these obligations is fairly well developed, our experience in various applied settings suggests that the first two activities—assessment of entry behaviors and selection of targets for intervention—are the recipients of much more effort than is the latter activity—the subsequent tracking of target behaviors. The intake process in educational and rehabilitational settings and the diagnostic activities of clinics and institutions invariably generate considerable information from interviews, tests, checklists, and observations upon admission but usually fail to monitor the subsequent course of those behaviors that have been identified as being in need of intervention. This excessive emphasis on initial evaluation is probably attributable to the fact that interviewing, testing, and completing checklists are essentially one-shot efforts that require much less time and energy than devising counting, time-sampling, or work-sampling techniques; teaching staff, students, or teachers to use them (or setting aside the time to use them oneself); and analyzing and acting upon the resulting data. These problems are greatly reduced outside of institutions and schools. In university clinics and in the home, the responsible psychologist works with more motivated treatment agents (i.e., graduate students and parents) and with fewer children at one time. In such cases, the assessment techniques which will be reviewed later can often be brought to bear to their full advantage. But in community settings, with their large numbers of children and their assessment-naïve treatment agents, the task of tracking behavior change is much more difficult and requires more attention to considerations of efficiency and cost-effectiveness than has been evident thus far in the literature.

## Research

The demands made of behavioral assessment procedures in research endeavors are highly varied, limited only by the creativity of the investigator who asks questions about the behavior of autistic children. In comparative treatment studies and in studies concerned with identifying characteristics specific to autism, initial consideration is given to the degree to which the child's diagnosis of record is valid. Because those who conduct such studies intend to generalize beyond their samples to "all" autistic children, they usually screen the possible subjects through informal observation or checklists to make sure that those selected meet one of the published definitions of autism.

In studies concerned with the analysis and/or treatment of a characteristic behavior (e.g., immediate echolalia or self-stimulatory behavior), the investigator selects subjects on the basis of the presence of the behavior of interest. The children selected must exhibit the behavior in sufficient strength for meaningful analysis or treatment, and diagnosis is considered of secondary importance. What constitutes "sufficient" strength depends upon the behavior and the goals of the research. For example, a mild self-injurious response that occurs "only" one to five times a day might not be of interest to an investigator who wishes to assess a new technique for reducing self-injurious behavior, whereas the same behavior occurring at a rate of 60 times a minute would be of great interest.

Investigations of the causes of autistic behaviors ("basic" studies) often make use of measures of frequency, rate of responding (occurrences per unit of time), or percentage occurrence (occurrences per opportunities, or trials). Frequency and rate measures are common in studies of behavior that have the characteristics of free operants, such as self-injurious behavior, self-stimulatory behavior, and aggression. Percentage correct (or incorrect) measures are commonly found in studies of discrimination learning, attention, language, and other behaviors that lend themselves to discriminated-operant methods. Automated as well as observational techniques are used.

Investigations of treatment effects ("applied" studies) also involve measures of rate and percentage correct (or "appropriate") but may also involve the simple enumeration of behaviors acquired, as in studies of vocabulary expansion or multiple educational attainments. In prognostic and comparative treatment studies, socially relevant measures, such as living environment and school or work placement, are often used as outcome measures. One measure not used enough in applied research with autistic children is the subjective "social validation" (Wolf, 1978) measure, which reflects relevant others' evaluations of the behavior change reported. For example, if self-stimulatory behavior is reduced from 70% to 35% in a given study, it would be helpful to know how the parent, teacher, and other caretakers view that change—was it a highly valued change or only minimally beneficial?

## METHODS OF ASSESSMENT

The methodology for assessing autistic children includes the traditional inferential procedures (interviews and conventional intelligence tests) that are customary in clinical practice, as well as instruments such as checklists, educational tests, and direct-observation techniques that have become popular in recent years. The most commonly used of these "global" assessment procedures will be discussed in some detail here, primarily for the benefit of practicing clinicians and those researchers who are engaged in long-term treatment and follow-up studies. The second part of this section is concerned with recent developments in the assessment of certain relatively specific, characteristic behaviors that are often the subject of focused treatment efforts and experiments, namely, sensory functioning, echolalia, and classroom social and educational interactions.

## Global Assessment Procedures

Global, "whole-child" assessment procedures sample a broad spectrum of behaviors within a brief time span to gauge the child's deficiencies and strengths in various areas considered to be important in normal functioning. Global assessments are customarily conducted in every community setting whenever an autistic child is first admitted to the facility and when placement referrals are being made. In addition to these "coming in" and "going out" occasions, additional global assessments are undertaken periodically in special education settings at the request of a child's school district to justify continued placement, in some institutional and residential facilities on an annual basis to satisfy state legal requirements, and in long-term treatment and follow-up studies. Methods for the assessment of multiple behaviors include informal observations, intelligence testing, behavioral checklists, educational evaluations, and structured observation procedures.

### Informal Observations

Tentative information about an autistic child can be gained from informal observations during a screening interview, in a preplacement classroom, or in the home. The clinician will be alert to the dimensions tapped in the following questions:

1. How active is the child? In general, the lethargic child and the hyperactive child will require more intensive intervention mediated by stronger treatment agents than will the child showing a more normal activity level.

2. Is the child responsive to external stimuli or preoccupied with self-stimulatory behavior? Addressing the child by name, cuddling the child, and observing his or her responses to attempts to evoke imitative behaviors and to a few simple commands will provide a rough estimate of social accessibility and receptive language level.

3. How much speech does the child have? Does he or she seem completely mute, exhibit only self-stimulatory vocalizations, engage in "prelinguistic" babbling, use one- or two-word labels or mands, exhibit echolalia, produce functional phrases or sentences, or use language that is close to age level in structure but is socially inappropriate, repetitious, delusional, or incoherent? The results of these observations can form the basis for initial recommendations about the level and intensity of language training that will be required.

4. Is the child independent in feeding, dressing, and toileting? Where there are deficits, what degree of prompting is required?

5. How does the child react to demands, punishment, and frustration? The child who becomes unusually aggressive, tantrumous, or self-injurious will require special intervention efforts focused on the problem behavior.

6. What reinforcers are functional? Does the child respond to praise, caresses, or tickling, or will food reinforcers be necessary to motivate learning? Does he or she eat a variety of foods readily, only a few foods, or very little at all?

7. Is the child receiving a special diet or medication? What effects, if any, has it appeared to have? If the child has a history of epileptic seizures, what are

their type and rate of occurrence? Is he or she receiving an anticonvulsant drug? If so, how well does it control the seizures?

8. What unique features does this child present in the way of unusual strengths, problem behaviors, or medical problems? Although it is a truism that every child is unique, some autistic children are "more unique" than others, showing especially severe problems or unusual abilities that should be noted and promptly communicated to the treatment agents who will be spending the most time with them.

9. If the child is self-injurious, what is the topography, rate, and apparent motivation of the self-injurious behavior? A very useful set of guidelines for investigating the motivation of SIB has been presented by Carr (1977). His screening sequence lists key questions to consider and tentative conclusions to be drawn from the answers (see Table 2).

The parents are almost always present during screening procedures and should be questioned about the reinforcers, punishers, and management techniques they have tried. We have found it useful to have the mother fill out the Behavior Management Questionnaire shown in Figure 1 during or soon after the initial interview. The questionnaire was suggested by Clement and Richard's (1976) Children's Reinforcement Survey. It inquires about potential reinforcers (questions A and B), potential punishers (question C), and previously tried management techniques (questions D and E). The questionnaire is assumed to reflect the well-known

TABLE 2

A Screening Sequence to Determine the Motivation of Self-Injurious Behavior

---

*Step 1*
Screen for genetic abnormalities (e.g., Lesch–Nyhan and de Lange Syndromes), particularly if lip, finger, or tongue biting is present.
Screen for nongenetic abnormalities (e.g., otitis media), particularly if head banging is present.
If screening is positive, motivation may be organic.
If Step 1 is negative, proceed to Step 2.

*Step 2*
Does self-injurious behavior increase under one or more of the following circumstances:
  a. When the behavior is attended to?
  b. When reinforcers are withdrawn for behaviors other than self-injurious behavior?
  c. When the child is in the company of adults (rather than alone)?
If yes, motivation may be positive reinforcement.
Does self-injurious behaviors occur primarily when demands or other aversive stimuli are presented?
If yes, motivation may be negative reinforcement.
If Step 2 is negative, proceed to Step 3.

*Step 3*
Does self-injurious behavior occur primarily when there are no activities available and/or the environment is barren?
If yes, motivation may be self-stimulation.

---

*Note*. From "The Motivation of Self-Injurious Behavior: A Review of Some Hypotheses" by E. G. Carr, *Psychological Bulletin*, 1977, *84*, 800–816. Copyright 1977 by the American Psychological Association. Reprinted by permission.

A1. List below the 5 activities in which your child spends the most time when free to do whatever he/she wants. List them in the order of the amount of time devoted to them, from greatest to least. By activities, we mean such things as watching TV, being alone, playing with another family member, playing with a certain toy or object, sleeping, going shopping, going to a fastfood place, etc. If specific objects, toys, people, or locations are important in an activity, name them.

1.

2.

3.

4.

5.

A2. List below any activities which you think he or she would like to engage in more often than he/she does at present.

1.

2.

3.

B. List below your child's 5 best-liked foods and drinks. Include desserts, snacks, and other treats. List the items according to preference beginning with the most preferred. Include items which you may not allow your child to have very often, but which fall high on his or her list of preferences.

1.

2.

3.

4.

5.

FIGURE 1

C1. List your child's least-preferred activities. Consider such things as specific chores, certain parts of the daily routine, and other things he/she has to do occasionally but would avoid if given the chance.

1.

2.

3.

C2. List below any situations, activities, or objects which your child usually is fearful of.

1.

2.

3.

D. Are there any specific disciplinary methods you have found to be usually <u>effective</u> with certain recurring behavior problems? If so, please describe the problems and the specific things you do in each case to handle the problems successfully.

E. Are there any specific disciplinary methods you have found to be <u>ineffective</u> with certain recurring behavior problems? If so, please describe the problems and the things you have tried and found unsuccessful.

Behavior Management Questionnaire.

limitations of all verbal reports but has been found to be useful in narrowing down the range of variables to be explored in initial treatment efforts. In interviewing the parents, the clinician should also try to ascertain their ability to follow through on home treatment suggestions as indicated by, for example, their apparent acceptance of responsibility for training the child, their previous success in teaching the child a few behaviors (e.g., self-care skills and compliance with a few commands), and their apparent willingness to set limits and apply strong consequences (both positive and negative). Parents who may prove to be ineffectual tend to give some early warning by discussing pharmacological, dietary, neurological, and other "effortless" medical approaches at length and with conviction, by overemphasizing financial or work-related burdens, or by giving indications of severe depression, severe marital problems, or lack of concern for the child's welfare. However, clinical intuition in these matters should be held in abeyance until empirical validation occurs, since surprises sometimes occur.

### Intelligence Tests

An intelligence test generally contributes relatively little information to the assessment of autistic children because of the limited range of behaviors it samples, which have been selected on the basis of cognitive and developmental presuppositions and statistical utility. Many behavioral clinicians would dispense with them entirely, except that state laws and agency policies often require their use. Virtues can be made of this necessity. Stripped of its mentalistic connotations, an adequately standardized intelligence test still yields a quantitative measure of the degree to which an autistic child differs from a large control group of normal peers on certain tasks at a certain point. The IQ from a conventional test can be useful in at least two ways:

1. In the assessment of a nonretarded autistic child who is being considered for placement in a normal classroom, the IQ can serve in accordance with its conventional function as a rough predictor of scholastic aptitude.
2. In research concerned with long-term follow-up or comparative treatment outcome, intelligence test results are commonly obtained and reported.

In addition to providing an IQ and/or a "mental" age (MA), the administration of an intelligence test allows some useful informal observations to be made. The examiner should gain an impression of the child's general language level, fine motor skills, latency of responding ("impulsivity"), and breadth and span of attention. Additionally, the test administration constitutes a situation that is rich in adult demands and therefore provides some information about the child's characteristic responses to this important class of stimuli. It is essential to maintain the proper perspective in making such observations. Every test administration is only a brief, unreplicated observation of behavior on arbitrary tasks in an artificial situation. (The examiner is not "sinking shafts at critical points" and divining the hidden potentialities of the child in a manner analogous to petroleum exploration, as is sometimes assumed in psychometric theory.) The test results and the informal observations that are made must be interpreted to consumers cautiously, particularly in consideration of the undue credibility and faith accorded intelligence tests by many professionals, administrators, teachers, and parents.

The Stanford–Binet and the Wechsler scales can be used with autistic children and adolescents who use functional phrases and sentences. The obvious advantage of using one of these established scales whenever possible is their high degree of familiarity to other professionals. The proper use of these tests with autistic examinees entails the consideration of the following points. In using the Stanford–Binet, some examiners of functionally mute autistic children routinely substitute nonverbal alternate items for one of the verbal items at each age level. This nonstandard procedure generally produces artificially inflated IQs, which cannot be legitimately interpreted in the conventional way, and it is inadvisable, in spite of its helpfulness in making the scale apparently "fairer" to the child. In using the Stanford–Binet with children who fail to pass all of the items at the 2-year level, there is an alternative to simply reporting "no basal established." If the child passes at least one item at the 2-year level, a basal age of 1–6 years can be assigned and one month's credit given for each item passed at this year level (Sternlicht, 1965).

The Wechsler Intelligence Scale for Children—Revised (WISC-R) may have more construct validity than the Stanford–Binet with autistic children who function in the middle childhood to late-adolescent range, simply because its performance scale contributes to the full-scale IQ throughout its range, whereas the Stanford–Binet becomes increasingly loaded with abstract verbal items after the 3-year level. However, it should be remembered that the "performance" items on the WISC-R require considerable receptive language ability, with the possible exception of Block Design and Object Assembly (Maxwell, 1959), on which autistic children often achieve their highest scores (Rutter, 1966). Two cautions should be kept in mind when using the WISC-R with retarded autistic children: It does not provide IQs below 40, and it is not advisable to calculate a full-scale IQ unless the child obtains raw scores greater than zero on at least three verbal and three performance scale subtests (Wechsler, 1974). The Wechsler Preschool and Primary Scale of Intelligence (WPPSI) creates similar problems with its limited floor, but a full-scale IQ can be considered valid when only two verbal and two performance subtests yield raw scores greater than zero, according to Wechsler (1967). The WPPSI is a more difficult test than the Stanford–Binet for children in its age range (4 to 6½ years) (Sattler, 1974) and consequently is used much less often with young autistic children.

For autistic children who are functioning beyond infancy levels but who are mute, minimally verbal, or deaf, the Leiter International Performance Scale is a currently popular alternative to the Stanford–Binet and Wechsler scales. The main advantage of the Leiter is that it can be administered completely without verbal instructions. It does, however, require that the child be able to match to sample in an unusual task format, which occasionally makes it unusable with severely and profoundly retarded children.

In testing very young and very low-functioning children, a choice can be made between one of the developmental scales (e.g., Bayley Scales of Infant Development, Merrill–Palmer Scale of Mental Tests, Cattell Infant Intelligence Scale, Gesell Developmental Schedules) or Alpern and Kimberlin's (1970) Cattell–Binet Short Form. The Cattell–Binet has the widest range of applicability with retarded examinees, because it is a combination of the Cattell Scale and the Stanford–Binet, creating an IQ test having items extending down to the 2-months' age level. Its additional advantages include its brief administration time (less than 20 minutes) and its yield of MAs and IQs that are calculated in a similar way to those obtained from the Stanford–Binet. Its disadvantages include the high degree of judgment involved in scoring many of the infant items and the lack of reliability and validity data beyond those provided in the original article on a small sample of retarded autistic children.

In administering standardized tests to retarded autistic children, it is common practice to use food reinforcers, which are delivered noncontingently with praise for "good working" and "good sitting." The scale should be administered as efficiently and rapidly as possible, with periodic breaks for social "chatter." Still, it may be necessary to spread testing over two or three sessions, especially with disruptive or young children.

### Behavioral Checklists

Both *diagnostic* and *descriptive* checklists have been developed primarily for use with autistic children. As these labels imply, the essential difference in the two types of checklists lies in their intended uses. Diagnostic checklists are designed to differentiate autistic children from other severely deviant children, whereas descriptive checklists are designed to identify the presence and absence of behaviors deemed important in normal human functioning.

The most well-known diagnostic checklist is Rimland's Diagnostic Checklist for Behavior Disturbed Children. Form E-2 of this checklist (published as the appendix in Rimland, 1964) consists of 80 questions to be answered by the child's parents about development and behavior from birth through 5 years. The main goal of the checklist is to discriminate Kanner's Syndrome children from schizophrenic and other "autistic-type" children. Thus, the items cover the characteristics mentioned by Kanner, as well as various characteristics of schizophrenic children described by Despert, Bender, and other writers. A total "autism" score is derived by subtracting "nonautistic" points from "autistic" points, with + 20 being the conservative cutoff score for identifying Kanner's Syndrome children (Rimland, 1974). Rimland's checklist has been found to be useful in showing substantial, but less than perfect, agreement with diagnoses made by Kanner (Rimland, 1971) and with the results of a biochemical study of blood serotonin levels (Boullin *et al.*, 1971). An expanded version of the checklist (Form E-3) contains approximately 250 questions concerned with the child's behaviors, familial disorders, blood types, drugs taken during pregnancy, and the effects of various treatments (Rimland, 1974).

Other diagnostic checklists are designed to distinguish autistic children from retarded, schizophrenic, and brain-damaged children (British Working Party list, as revised by O'Gorman, 1967; Lotter, 1966; Polan & Spencer, 1959). None of these checklists has been established as sufficiently valid to be used as the sole means of diagnosis. They are best considered rough screening devices that can serve as adjuncts to clinical judgment (DeMyer, Churchill, Pontius, & Gilkey, 1971).

Kozloff's (1974) Behavior Evaluation Scale (BES) is a descriptive checklist that is also prescriptive, because it is accompanied by detailed instructions on its use in planning an educational program. (It could, therefore, be classified appropriately in the section on educational tests to follow. We discuss it here simply because its format is that of a checklist and because the procedures to follow are concerned with education in the narrow sense, that is, as an in-school activity.) The BES organizes approximately 90 behaviors into seven areas: learning readiness skills; looking, listening, and moving skills; motor imitation skills; verbal imitation skills; functional speech; chores and self-help skills; and problem behaviors. The behaviors in each area except the last are listed in an "easy-to-hard" sequence, prerequisite behaviors are listed, and the most important behaviors in each area are identified. Questions concerned with the frequency and the degree of prompting needed to evoke the behavior, as well as the child's reactions to attempts to teach the behavior, are included for most behaviors. The BES is most useful in helping parents and teachers of young and/or retarded autistic children to identify behavioral deficits and plan a remediation strategy. It has not been the subject of correlational or normative studies to date.

The Adaptive Behavior Scale (American Association on Mental Deficiency, 1975) is comprehensive in its sampling of behaviors and can be used with both children and adults. Although designed primarily for nonpsychotic retarded persons, its coverage of behaviors is sufficiently broad to encompass many of the psychotic behaviors of autistic individuals. It consists of two parts. The first is a comprehensive survey of behaviors in 10 socially desirable areas (e.g., independent functioning, language development, vocational activity, self-direction), whereas the second is concerned with maladaptive behaviors in 13 areas and with the use of medications. Many of the items in both parts are poorly operationalized and require inferential judgments. The scale yields profiles for each part in terms of percentile ranks based on the scores of institutional residents in 11 age categories from 3 to 69 years. Interrater reliability of the scale is good (.86) for the first part but poor (.57) for the second part. The scale appears to be useful in measuring changes with behavioral treatment and in assisting in placement decisions (American Association on Mental Deficiency, 1975).

The Vineland Social Maturity Scale (Doll, 1965) is another checklist that was originally devised for nonpsychotic retarded persons but that is extensively used with autistic children and adolescents. It consists of items sampling various self-help, motor, language, and social behaviors organized according to chronological age of their appearance in the normative sample. It provides a social age equivalent score, which can be used to calculate a "social quotient." Its disadvantages include the limited range of behaviors sampled, especially in the adolescent age range, and its lack of up-to-date normative data.

### Educational Tests

Three published instruments have been specifically designed to provide assessments of autistic children for classroom education purposes. Lacking adequate reliability, validity, and standardization data, they are useful primarily for individual program planning and for within-subject comparisons over time. They fill a long-standing need for educational tests for young and for low-functioning autistic children who are not appropriate candidates for conventional educational tests such as the Wide-Range Achievement Test or the Peabody Individual Achievement Test. These latter instruments are best reserved for mildly retarded and nonretarded autistic children.

The Psychoeducational Profile (PEP) (Schopler & Reichler, 1976) is intended for children 1 to 12 years of age who are functioning at a preschool level. It consists, first, of tasks similar to those found in infant development scales and IQ tests, which are organized into six developmental areas: imitation, perception, motor, eye–hand integration, cognitive–performance, and cognitive–verbal. In addition, there are a number of specified informal observations to be made in five "pathology" areas: affect, relating/cooperating/human interest, play and interest in materials, sensory modes, and language. The developmental scale yields a profile of raw scores, which is keyed to a hierarchy of chronological age norms obtained from a sample of normal children 1 to 7 years of age. The manual is comprehensive, providing detailed scoring criteria, recommendations for interpretation, and instructions for constructing the test materials.

The Evaluation and Prescription for Exceptional Children (EPEC) (Flaharty, 1976) is a compilation of a large number of items from the birth through 6th-year levels of various published developmental scales and IQ tests. The items are arranged by age level in each of 15 areas (e.g., fine motor, concepts, matching skills, expressive language, socialization and play). The EPEC yields a profile of age scores based on the locations of the items in their original published scales. Still in the process of development, the EPEC lacks standardized administration instructions; therefore, its use depends entirely on the examiner's familiarity with the published scales from which it is drawn.

The Autism Screening Instrument for Educational Planning (ASIEP) (Krug, Arick, & Almond, Note 1) is a package of five instruments that can be used in combination or separately. Its components include: (1) a 57-item diagnostic checklist; (2) a language sample; (3) a social interaction assessment procedure which utilizes direct-observation time sampling of several categories of behavior in a standard play setting; (4) an educational assessment procedure with tasks in the areas of in-seat behavior, receptive language, expressive language, body concept, and speech imitation; and (5) an assessment of "learning rate" based on a sequencing task. For each component, profiles of preliminary data from autistic and nonautistic severely retarded children are provided. The manual gives detailed directions for administration and scoring and comes with all materials necessary for using the scale. The ASIEP is most useful with young autistic children and with severely and profoundly retarded older autistic children.

## Structured Observational Procedures

These procedures involve direct observation and recording of multiple behaviors in controlled situations, often with standard social stimulus presentations. The studies selected for discussion here indicate some of the ways in which the assessment of multiple behaviors in autistic children have been conducted in various settings with direct-observation methods.

The Multiple-Response Recording (or "Extra-Experimental") procedure of Lovaas *et al.* (1965b, 1973) requires continuous recording of behaviors in five categories: self-stimulation, echolalic and bizarre speech, appropriate speech, social nonverbal behavior, and appropriate play. Each 35-minute session is divided into three conditions. During the "alone" condition, the child is observed while alone in a room containing a number of specified toys. During the "attending" condition, an unfamiliar adult is present and looks at the child but does not initiate interactions. During the "inviting" condition, the adult encourages the child to engage in play with the toys and in certain simple social and verbal interactions. The child's behaviors are recorded on a specially made button panel containing timers that accumulate the number of seconds each button is depressed. The panel is connected to an Esterline–Angus event recorder and a paper-tape punch, which allow determination of frequencies, durations, and response interactions. Observation sessions have been conducted over intervals ranging from one month to several years in order to measure behavior before, during, and after treatment and at follow-up (Lovaas *et al.*, 1973).

The main advantages of the procedure are (1) the high degree of validity it affords by recording behaviors simultaneously and continuously rather than intermittently and (2) the assessment of stimulus generalization of treatment gains, provided by the use of a novel room and an unfamiliar adult. The first advantage, validity, extracts a price. Reliability is attained only after extensive training when more than one or two behaviors are recorded simultaneously, primarily because observers must record onsets and durations of behaviors precisely.

One way to avoid prolonged observer training while still recording several behaviors simultaneously is to give up the moment-by-moment information afforded by continuous recording and to substitute a time-sampling schedule for recording. Newsom (Note 2) used the Multiple-Response Recording procedure to measure four to six self-stimulatory behaviors per subject with 2-second observation intervals separated by 8-second recording intervals. All behaviors observed within each brief "snapshot" observation interval were recorded with single depressions of their corresponding buttons during the subsequent recording interval. (Thus, a coded data sheet on which the behaviors were simply marked off could serve as an inexpensive way of using the same procedure.) Adequate reliability was obtained with naive observers who were simply given a list of behaviors and definitions to study and who then discussed the definitions with an experienced observer shortly before recording. The main disadvantages of this modification are its insensitivity to brief-duration behaviors, which limits the range of behaviors to which it can be applied with validity, and its inability to track shifts from one behavior to another, since these are lost between the 2-second observation intervals.

A second way of minimizing the time required to train observers is to sacrifice the recording of multiple behaviors simultaneously. Boer (1968) divided the behaviors of autistic children in a playroom into eight exhaustive and mutually exclusive categories. Although only one category could be scored in each observation interval, each interval was only a second in duration and followed immediately after the preceding interval. Intervals were signaled by the sound of a metronome, and recording consisted of depressing a key on a Stenograph. (Each depression automatically advances a paper tape, which permits discrimination of the intervals for data analysis.) Boer achieved high reliability figures after only three sessions of discussion and practice. This procedure retains the moment-to-moment detail of the Lovaas *et al.* procedure, but it does require that a priori decisions be made about which of several behaviors capable of simultaneous occurrence will be recorded when they do so occur.

The Baselines procedure of Graham, Kass, and Forness (Note 3) was developed to measure learning readiness behaviors in a preschool for autistic children. It closely resembles the Multiple-Response Recording procedure in its use of direct, continuous recording of multiple behaviors obtained with a button panel and an event recorder. The major differences are that the Baselines procedure records adult (teacher) as well as child behaviors and includes small-group as well as alone conditions. Twelve child behaviors are recorded in four categories: attention behaviors, verbal behaviors, appropriate task behaviors, and maladaptive behaviors. Two additional behaviors, specific to each child, are also recorded. Six teacher behaviors are recorded: attention to the child, attention to the other children, demands, redirections, prompts, and social and food reinforcer deliveries.

The child and teacher are observed in six daily sessions, which alternate between one-to-one and small-group instructional conditions. Within each 12-minute session, instructional task and type of reinforcer (social or food) are changed every 3 minutes. During one-to-one observations, an additional condition (teacher present but not attending) is included. The procedure is used to determine the child's reactions to different teaching methods, to obtain information on the stimuli likely to occasion disruptive behaviors, and to measure progress before, during, and after educational interventions (Graham, Kass, & Forness, Note 3). The disadvantages of the procedure are that it requires two observers for every session (each records ten behaviors) and its reliability remains to be adequately determined.

Strain and Cooke's (1976) Total Behavior Repertoire procedure puts the open observational technique common in ethology (Hutt & Hutt, 1970) to service in identifying the behaviors of autistic children in a free play setting. The technique is "open" in the sense that the observer is not constrained by preselected behavioral categories before making the observations. Narrative notes (e.g., "hits peer," "spins block") about a child are jotted down on a data sheet lined to represent 10-second intervals, which are signaled by a cassette tape. The behaviors identified in these "action–object" notes are subsequently sorted into categories that seem appropriate and relevant to the research questions. For example, in their study of two autistic children in a classroom during free play periods, Strain and Cooke (1976) collapsed the observed behaviors into nine categories, including self-stimulation, object manipulation, physical aggression, and bizarre verbalization.

A possible problem in using this procedure results when two or three brief-duration behaviors occur within a 10-second observation interval. One partial solution would simply be to shorten the observation interval. Another, more laborious solution would be to tape record observers' verbal notes and dispense with arbitrarily timed observation intervals (cf. Hutt & Hutt, 1970, pp. 48–51). Reliability could be assessed by comparing the reliability observer's narrative on a behavior-by-behavior basis with the main observer's narrative, scoring agreements when both observers described the same behaviors at the same times on the tapes. The main observer's changes from describing one behavior to describing another could define the (obviously variable) changes from one observation interval to another for the purpose of scoring agreements and disagreements. Presumably, a few seconds' latitude would have to be allowed at these change points to have reasonable expectation of obtaining adequate reliability figures. The use of this procedure would necessitate a prior decision as to whether the gain in validity is sufficient to warrant the amount of work it requires if numerous reliability checks are to be made.

### Recent Advances in the Assessment of Specific Behaviors

This section presents a sampling of recently developed techniques for the assessment of behaviors in certain delimited areas of functioning. These methods are merely representative of the behavioral technologies that are currently being applied in the study of various categories of autistic behaviors and do not constitute an exhaustive survey. They indicate the diversity and the limitations of current procedures in the areas selected: sensory functioning, echolalia, and educational and social interactions.

#### Sensory Functioning

The assessment of sensory functioning in autistic children presents serious difficulties because conventional clinical testing procedures require comprehension of verbal instructions by the child and reliable reporting of sensations. Such procedures are useless with autistic children whose linguistic behavior is nonexistent, minimal, or unreliable. What is needed are techniques that bypass the use of verbal instructions and, instead, provide nonverbal "instructions" in the form of stimulus shaping techniques (Sidman & Stoddard, 1966) similar to those used in the field of animal psychophysics (Stebbins, 1970). Until such procedures are developed and applied on a large scale, we will not know to what degree the widely held assumption of intact sensory functioning in autistic children is true. The feasibility of nonverbal sensory assessment procedures for autistic children is indicated by recent work in our laboratory.

Newsom and Simon (1977) used a stimulus-shaping procedure in measuring binocular visual acuity thresholds in nonverbal schizophrenic and autistic children. The first phase of the procedure taught the child to choose a card with three black, vertical stripes in preference to a card with three black, horizontal stripes from a distance of 20 feet (6.1 m), the conventional distance for the measurement of acuity. A room was arranged with tables and a blackboard (for display of the cards), as shown in Figure 2.

The vertical stripes on the "correct" card were always fully black, whereas the horizontal stripes on the "incorrect" card were faded in from white through darkening shades of gray to fully black in 16 steps. Once the vertical–horizontal discrimination was established, the stripes on each card were converted into Snellen E's by adding a black stripe to the top of the correct card and to the side of the incorrect card. In the test phase, the Snellen E's on each pair of cards decreased in size on each trial until the child began to make errors. At that point, all changes in the size of the E's, either to smaller or to larger E's, depended on whether the child passed or failed a criterion of five successive correct choices within eight trials. The test phase continued until the child's trial-by-trial record showed a regular oscillation between sizes only one step apart. The acuity ratio corresponding to the smallest size at which the child reliably discriminated the vertically oriented E was considered to be the distance acuity. Sample records of training and test performances are shown in Figure 3.

The Newsom–Simon (1977) procedure was found to be valid in comparison with the results of screening tests with the Illiterate E chart (which also requires discriminations of the orientation of Snellen E's) and was able to identify previously undiagnosed acuity impairments in nonverbal autistic children. Its main disadvantage is its reliance on an extradimensional shift in stimulus control during training, that is, from intensity to orientation. Some autistic children cannot make this shift (Koegel & Rincover, 1976; Newsom & Simon, 1977; Rincover, 1978a; Schreibman, 1975), which limits the applicability of the procedure.

FIGURE 2

Top view of the room arrangement for visual acuity testing. Each table was 1.5 × .74 m.

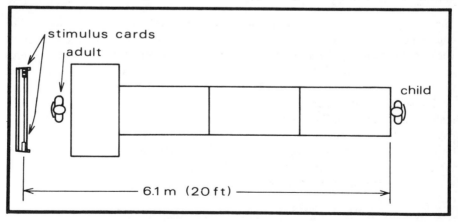

Measuring hearing in nonlinguistic autistic children presents the same difficulties as those involved in measuring vision. However, the technology for measuring hearing with operant procedures is much more advanced (e.g., Bricker, Bricker, & Larsen, 1968; Fulton, 1974; Fulton & Lloyd, 1969). Although these methods were developed for retarded and very young normal children, the many similarities that exist between those populations and autistic children render the methods usable with autistic children (Newsom & Williams, Note 4; described in Newsom *et al.*, 1979).

Other recent work in the area of sensory functioning has been concerned with measuring ear preferences in listening to different sounds and with the timing of motor responses in relation to auditory stimuli. Blackstock (1978) studied ear preference in listening to different types of auditory stimuli with a novel procedure he developed in the course of exploring hemispheric lateralization in autistic children. He constructed two boxes, each of which supported four small speakers on poles adjustable in height. Three of the speakers on each box were connected to the outputs of cassette recorders inside the boxes, which permitted the simultaneous presentation of six taped auditory stimuli. (Two control speakers were always silent.) The volume of each recorder was adjusted to a low level so that the child had to place one ear or the other against a speaker to hear a given selection. The experimenter recorded the child's choice of speakers, the use of each ear, and the duration of listening with a panel of 16 buttons connected to a pen recorder. A question that might be raised is whether the situation was overly complex (i.e., contained too many simultaneously available choices among stimuli) for valid conclusions to be drawn about preferences among the stimuli. Unfortunately, no indication of how many speakers were sampled by each child was given.

Condon (1975) has used detailed analyses of films of the motor behaviors of autistic children to study their relationship to auditory stimuli. In normal children and adults, bodily movements are closely synchronized with auditory stimuli. In autistic children, however, it appears that such movements occur both in synchrony with a sound and also after a delay of as much as a second. These findings result from analyses of sound films that involve the frame-by-frame coding of the auditory stimuli along with the movements of the head, eyes, mouth, shoulders, arms, and hands. Condon's (1975) procedure appears capable of providing important information about auditory functioning in autistic children, but its full utilization will depend on improvements in the realiability assessments that have been conducted thus far.

## Echolalia

Two types of echolalia—immediate and delayed—are found in autistic children. Immediate echolalia is the repetition of all or part of an utterance immediately after it is heard. Delayed echolalia is the repetition of all or part of an utterance several minutes, hours, or weeks after it is first heard. Echolalia is commonly assessed by tape recording the child's speech in a clinic setting during interviews or play

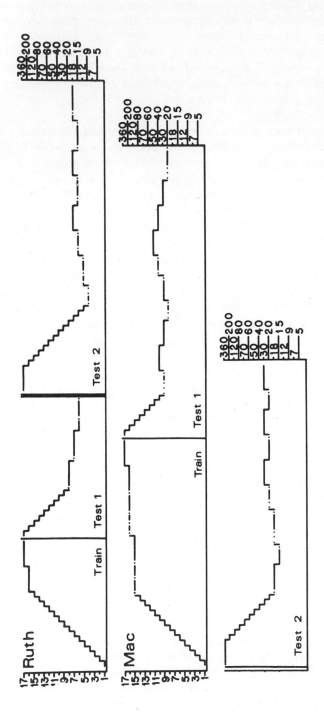

ACUITY RATIO (20/x)

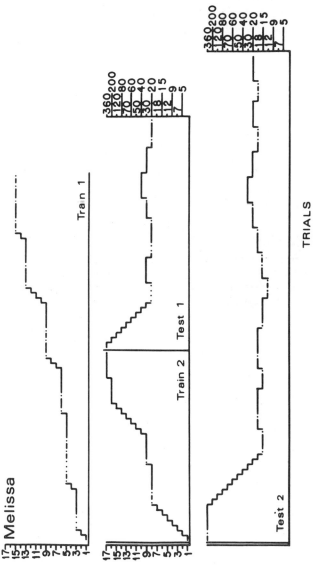

FIGURE 3

Performances during training and test phases of three nonverbal psychotic children. The left ordinate indicates fading steps during training phases; the right ordinate indicates the sizes of the test E's in terms of the denominators of their acuity ratios. The horizontal segments of each curve represent correct choices, and dots represent incorrect choices. Phases conducted within a session are separated by a single vertical line; phases conducted in different sessions are separated by double vertical lines. From "A Simultaneous Discrimination Procedure for the Measurement of Vision in Nonverbal Children" by C. D. Newsom and K. M. Simon, *Journal of Applied Behavior Analysis*, 1977, *10*, 633–644. Copyright 1977 by the Society for the Experimental Analysis of Behavior, Inc. Reprinted by permission.

interactions with an adult. Recently, other techniques have been reported that provide more information about echolalia than could be obtained from clinic speech samples.

Carr, Schreibman, and Lovaas (1975) constructed a list of 20 stimulus phrases for their study of immediate echolalia. There were two categories of phrases, "discriminative" and "neutral," with half of the phrases in each category calling for a verbal response and the other half designating a nonverbal response. The discriminative stimuli were defined as stimuli to which some appropriate response existed (e.g., "What's your name?" "Touch your head."). The neutral stimuli were nonsense phrases to which no appropriate responses existed (e.g., "Min dar snick," "Off plot"). Random presentations of these stimulus phrases to echolalic autistic children indicated a much greater probability of echolalia in response to the neutral phrases than to the discriminative phrases. The results of a second experiment in this study and a subsequent study (Schreibman & Carr, 1978) showed that neutral phrases need not be nonsense phrases to evoke echolalia; questions and commands currently beyond the child's level of comprehension (e.g., "What is baseball?" "Indicate the eraser.") have the same effect. This result suggests that an assessment device based on the Carr et al. (1975) and Schreibman and Carr (1978) procedure, but including test phrases that cover a greater range of comprehension levels, could be constructed for use in both basic and applied studies.

Delayed echolalia has not yet been the subject of experimental, manipulative studies, and, probably because it occurs infrequently, even correlational and structural studies based on tape recordings are rare. The assessment strategies currently being reported consist of taping the delayed echoer's verbalizations in novel settings. For example, Lovaas, Varni, Koegel, and Lorsch (1977) taped delayed echolalia in autistic children in a barren laboratory room and in a bathroom; Cantwell, Baker, and Rutter (1978) taped it in the children's homes; and Baltaxe and Simmons (1977) taped it in the bedroom after their subject had been put to bed for the night. Such procedures provide data for structural analyses similar to those that are common in psycholinguistic research but fail to contribute to a functional analysis of this behavior because no observation of the language input to the child is undertaken. In the absence of such observations, it is difficult to determine which of the child's utterances are instances of delayed echolalia and which are instances of creative, "propositional" speech (Baltaxe & Simmons, 1977).

Some preliminary data obtained by Rincover and Anderson constitute perhaps the first experimental analysis specifically addressing delayed echolalia and suggest that delayed echolalia has different determinants than immediate echolalia. Specifically, at least some delayed echolalia appears to be operant behavior maintained by its (auditory) sensory consequences. When children are prevented from hearing their own echoic responses, by earphones or masking sounds, echolalic behavior was dramatically reduced or eliminated, suggesting that the auditory consequences were in fact reinforcers for the echolalic behavior. Still, it is notable that some delayed echolalic responses remained—for example, "No," "Don't do that"—that seemed to have been related to punishment at one time. It was only the sing-song repetition of television commercials, songs, the alphabet, and the like, that was reduced with the "sensory extinction" procedure (Rincover, 1978; Rincover, Cook,

| | |
|---|---|
| Child:_____ | Teacher:_____ |
| Observer:_____ | Assistant(s):_____ |
| Date:_____ | Time: From_____ to_____ |

| | |
|---|---|
| Behavior | Behavior |
| Activity/Loc. | Activity/Loc. |
| Stimuli | Stimuli |
| Consequences | Consequences |
| | |
| Behavior | Behavior |
| Activity/Loc. | Activity/Loc. |
| Stimuli | Stimuli |
| Consequences | Consequences |
| | |
| Behavior | Behavior |
| Activity/Loc. | Activity/Loc. |
| Stimuli | Stimuli |
| Consequences | Consequences |

Additional observations

Possible treatments and priority

FIGURE 4

Informal Behavior Observation Form.

Peoples, & Packard, 1979). Consequently, as with self-injurious behavior (Carr, 1977), it is possible that there are subtypes of delayed echolalia, each having different motivational determinants (e.g., sensorily reinforced, punishment related).

## Classroom Interactions

As classroom programs for autistic children have multiplied in recent years, observational techniques for studying child and teacher behaviors and their interactions have appeared with increasing frequency. These techniques range from relatively informal methods for diagnosing management problems to relatively molecular analyses of teaching interactions.

In consulting with teachers about disruptive behaviors (e.g., aggression, tantrums), we have found the two forms shown in Figures 4 and 5 to be useful. The

Child: _____

Date: _____

| Time | Location | Activity | Behavior | Stimulus |
|------|----------|----------|----------|----------|
|      |          |          |          |          |
|      |          |          |          |          |
|      |          |          |          |          |
|      |          |          |          |          |
|      |          |          |          |          |
|      |          |          |          |          |
|      |          |          |          |          |
|      |          |          |          |          |
|      |          |          |          |          |
|      |          |          |          |          |
|      |          |          |          |          |
|      |          |          |          |          |
|      |          |          |          |          |
|      |          |          |          |          |
|      |          |          |          |          |
|      |          |          |          |          |

FIGURE 5

Daily Episode Log. (Time = time the behavior started; Location = table, play area, hallway, etc.; Activity = morning group, sign training, lunch, getting on bus, etc.; Behavior = hit (*name*), prolonged screaming, threw sandwich, etc.; Stimulus = any event or behavior of another person that immediately preceded the behavior, e.g., told to work, toy taken away, stranger walked in, (*name*) was crying.)

Informal Behavior Observation Form (Figure 4) is used by the psychologist simply to organize observations made when attempting to determine the causes of one or more frequent disruptive behaviors. Notations of the ongoing classroom activity, the problem behaviors, and their antecedents and consequences may be made during the course of an observation lasting half an hour to an hour or more. Space is included for noting any additional observations that seem relevant and for ranking possible treatment alternatives. In addition to providing a way in which to organize notes during informal observations, the form also helps to structure and focus consultations with the teacher and results in a permanent record for future reference.

The Daily Episode Log (Figure 5) is left in the classroom with the teacher to track relatively infrequent disruptive behaviors over the entire school day. It is generally used for several days in the earliest stages of consultation, before a more individualized data collection procedure has been decided upon. As the column headings suggest, information that aids in narrowing down the setting conditions for the problem behaviors is the primary concern. This emphasis serves two purposes: (1) it helps to sensitize teachers to the effects of their educational activities and their own behaviors in evoking some problem behaviors and (2) it helps to determine whether a problem behavior tends to occur in a certain place or during a certain activity rather than randomly throughout the day. If the behavior can be localized to some degree, then certain relatively simple stimulus manipulations may be considered or, at the very least, the most useful time to schedule personal observations to gather more information will be known. If the behavior appears to be randomly distributed across times, locations, and activities, then the focus of attention shifts to its consequences. In using this form with numerous teachers, we have found that the ''stimulus'' column occasionally yields repeated entries of the ''none apparent'' variety, despite the presence of a broad definition, with examples, at the bottom of the form and informal suggestions made during consultations. These entries are never taken at face value unless confirmed through personal observation. A column for ''consequences'' is not included in the form, because events belonging to this category are rarely recorded accurately or completely prior to special training.

The use of forms such as those just described to get an initial overview of problem behaviors is often followed by the implementation of formal observational procedures for more detailed analyses of selected behaviors and of the effects of treatment interventions. Several procedures for studying child–child and teacher–child interactions have been published recently.

Part of the Strain and Cooke (1976) study discussed previously was devoted to an analysis of child–child interactions in a free play situation. The experimenters divided the interactive behaviors of autistic children into two types: motor/gestural and vocal/verbal. Interactions of both types were coded in continuous 10-second intervals as having been emitted by a target subject or a peer, as being either positive (prosocial) or negative (rejecting or aggressive) in type, and as being either an initiated (''spontaneous'') behavior or a behavior in response to another child's behavior. This procedure allowed them to describe the frequencies of various types of social contacts that their target subjects had with their peers and to describe the probabilities of each target subjects' responses given the occurrence of certain peer-initiated behaviors.

In a subsequent study (Ragland, Kerr, & Strain, 1978), the procedure was used to measure the changes in positive and negative social behaviors of three autistic children when a normal peer attempted to engage each of them in play during succeeding phases of a multiple-baseline design. Play behaviors were also the focus of a study by Romanczyk, Diament, Goren, Trunell, and Harris (1975). They recorded 12 categories of behavior, including isolate play, social play, offer toy, and take toy, on a 20-second observe, 10-second record schedule and obtained respectable reliability coefficients with both two-observer and three-observer calculations.

A general coding system for recording teacher–child interactions during group instruction has been reported by Meyers and Craighead (1979). Their Teacher–Pupil Interaction Chronograph (TPIC) is an eight-by-ten matrix form, with eight categories of child behavior on one axis and ten categories of teacher behavior on the other. The child behaviors consist of seven categories of inappropriate behaviors (e.g., object noise, isolate play) and one category of appropriate behaviors (on-task and socially relevant behaviors). The teacher behaviors are divided into those occurring before pupil behaviors (i.e., positive and negative prompts and statements) and those occurring after pupil behaviors (e.g., positive verbal feedback, ignoring). An interaction is coded by marking the initials of the pupil(s) involved at the appropriate intersection in the matrix. In Meyers and Craighead's (1979) study, a single matrix was used to record interactions during each 20-second interval of a 6-minute observation period; observations were conducted four times daily. The interactions recorded on the TPIC matrices were subjected to an analysis which yielded four second-order categories of teacher behaviors: appropriate behavior appropriately applied, appropriate behavior inappropriately applied, inappropriate behavior, and neutral behavior. These categories were defined by examination of intersections of teacher and pupil behaviors prior to a functional analysis of their effects on pupil behaviors. (Potential users of the TPIC in an unmodified form should be alert to the inadvertent substitutions of "negative" for "positive" in the published definition of "positive prompt.")

Finally, Koegel, Russo, and Rincover (1977) developed a procedure for making fine-grain analyses of one-to-one teaching interactions. Observers recorded each of five teaching behaviors during a trial as correct, incorrect, or not present, according to the criteria listed in Table 3. The child's response was recorded as correct, incorrect, prompted, or an approximation of the target response. In addition to these trial-by-trial observations, a summary measure of the child's progress during the session was obtained by comparing the adequacy of responding during the last ten trials with that during the first ten trials. These procedures proved to be very sensitive to the effects of a training package on teacher performance and to permit the observation of changes in children's learning as a function of changes in teacher's performances.

## LOOKING AHEAD

The foregoing presentation shows that the assessment of autistic children is a multifaceted enterprise that requires the behavioral clinician/researcher in this field to be a generalist. Versatility is necessary because the field is still developing and there is no single set of procedures applicable to all situations. We conclude this chapter by briefly mentioning some of the areas most in need of further attention.

### Behavioral Subclassification

The problem of subclassification, discussed previously, needs creative solutions if any major progress in etiological research is to occur and if treatment planning

TABLE 3
Teacher Behaviors Recorded by Koegel, Russo, and Rincover (1977)

1. The teacher's instructions to the child should be:
   a. discriminable to the child;
   b. appropriate to the task;
   c. consistent over trials;
   d. uninterrupted;
   e. presented only when the child is attending.
2. Prompts must be effective in evoking correct responses.
3. Shaping: Each reinforced response should be at least as good as the preceding one.
4. Consequences should be:
   a. immediate;
   b. appropriate;
   c. unambiguous;
   d. consistent;
   e. effective.
5. Discrete trials: Each trial should have a distinct onset and offset and should be preceded and followed by an intertrial interval.

is to become more objective and less intuitive. Instead of waiting for medical breakthroughs to define a system based on physiological variables, behavioral investigators could attempt to construct systems based on levels of important behaviors, characteristic responses to important stimuli or consequences, rates or magnitudes of change observed under different treatment regimens, or combinations of these or other interactional variables.

## Assessment of Learning Ability

It would be very useful to have a standardized test that measured learning ability directly, through current performances, rather than inferentially, through current achievements, as conventional IQ tests do. What we are suggesting is a battery of learning tasks, each of which would be administered for a set number of trials under standard conditions, yielding a profile of scores or a single score that would have predictive validity with regard to progress in behavioral treatment. Ideally, the scale would be standardized on a large sample of autistic children of varying ages and levels of functioning, so that a given child could be described in reference to other autistic children.

The major stumbling block in devising such a scale would, of course, be the selection of tasks that would be sufficiently discriminating and that would contribute to meaningful final scores. It should be kept in mind that other researchers have found it difficult to assemble learning tasks that correlate more than moderately with IQ (Jensen, 1970, pp. 66–81), a different, but related, endeavor to that being proposed here. Although the job might turn out to be a little like Edison's testing hundreds of materials to find the best filament for his first light bulb, it seems to be a possible, if formidable, undertaking. One could begin by exploring batteries of simple successive and simultaneous discrimination tasks, matching-to-sample and oddity problems, short-term memory tasks, generalization problems, learning-set tasks, and other common paradigms from the basic learning laboratory. The success of the venture, however, might well hinge on the consideration of some apparently important, but unconventional, measures, such as "shapeability" (i.e., variety in reinforcement-induced behaviors), "reinforceability" (propensity to engage in food, sensory, or social consummatory behaviors), stimulus overselectivity, and imitative or observational-learning ability. Appropriate criterion measures might include number of words, signs, self-help skills, or vocational workshop skills learned in 6 months of behavioral training conducted at the rate of, say, 20 hours a week. The development of a convenient, useful scale would take a great deal of time, but the effort seems worthwhile in view of the failure of traditional cognitive and developmental scales to be either sufficiently discriminating or sufficiently predictive to make significant contributions to intervention planning.

## Prediction of Response to Treatment

A need also exists for the development of predictive procedures that are much more restricted in scope (and thus more easily attainable) than the hypothetical global scale just discussed. We are apparently within reach of procedures for predicting an autistic child's response to certain specified treatment interventions, such as time out, punishment, and sign language training. Solnick, Rincover, and Peterson (1977) have shown that the effectiveness of time out with autistic children depends on at least two factors—the presence versus the absence of self-stimulatory behavior during time out and whether or not the "time-in" environment is "enriched" (i.e., provides frequent, multiple reinforcers). Autistic children who engage in self-stimulatory behavior while in time out or who are provided with few reinforcers in their normal training settings can be expected to show increases in the disruptive behaviors upon which time out is made contingent. Further research could determine whether there is some critical rate of self-stimulatory behavior in the child and some critical density or variety of reinforcers in the environment that would predict whether time out will have punishing or reinforcing effects.

We have less information that might help to formulate predictions about response to pain-inflicting punishers, such as slaps or shock. At present, the only useful predictor seems to be the child's initial response to treatment. For example, in the use of shock with SIB, clinical experience suggests that unless the child shows marked suppression within five to ten applications of punishment (shock), it will not be effective (Lovaas & Newsom, 1976). It would be very useful to know, prior to treatment, whether the rate or topography of SIB is predictive of response to shock (or other punishers), but this may be an academic question since shock is only a last-resort treatment and the necessary research would be difficult, if not impossible, to conduct for ethical reasons.

Manual sign language training has become very popular in clinical and educational settings. Is there any way to predict an autistic child's response to sign training? Some leads are emerging from recent research. For example, Carr (1979) has marshalled the existing evidence to support the idea that mute children will probably not learn the auditory information provided in "simultaneous communication" training (i.e., both the word and the sign presented simultaneously), whereas echolalic children will. In other words, echolalic children may be expected to learn receptive and verbal labeling as well as signs when exposed to simultaneous communication training, but mute children may be expected to learn only receptive and expressive signs. Work in progress in Rincover's laboratory by Jeanne Devany is attempting to determine whether differential performances on visual and auditory discrimination tasks will predict subsequent performances in sign training and verbal language training. If so, then a valuable screening procedure for planning the most appropriate type of communication training will be available.

The foregoing points emphasize the underlying theme of this chapter, indeed, of this entire book. That is, there remains a continuing need for the development of assessment procedures that are functionally related to treatment rather than simply reflective of theories about the population of interest.

With regard to autistic children, the theories of intellectual, developmental, and personality processes that have inspired most conventional assessment instruments have been of scant utility in suggesting specific interventions and in predicting response to treatment. What is needed is essentially an atheoretical approach to assessment, in which assessment procedures are derived from functional analyses elucidating subject, stimulus, and motivational variables important in understanding and changing behavior. The strength of behavioral assessment is that it encourages a continuous interplay between measurement and treatment. The measurement of subject characteristics; of topographies, rates, and intensities of behaviors; of setting conditions and stimulus events; and of maintenance contingencies ideally should lead to suggestions about effective treatments. Reciprocally, the outcomes of treatment interventions should lead to modifications in the variables selected for assessment. Such an "interactional" approach to assessment can be expected to result in truly functional assessment.

## Reference Notes

1. Krug, D. A., Arick, J. R., & Almond, P. J. *Autism Screening Instrument for Educational Planning*. Portland, Ore.: Department of Special Education, Portland State University, 1978.
2. Newsom, C. D. *The role of sensory reinforcement in self-stimulatory behavior*. Unpublished doctoral dissertation, University of California at Los Angeles, 1974.
3. Graham, V., Kass, E. W., & Forness, S. R. *Development of a behavior baseline for educational intervention with atypical preschool children*. Paper presented at the meeting of the California Educational Research Association, San Diego, November 1971. (Available from S. R. Forness, Neuropsychiatric Institute, UCLA, 760 Westwood Plaza, Los Angeles, Calif. 90024.)
4. Newsom, C. D., & Williams, S. L. *Operant measurement of pure-tone thresholds in nonverbal autistic children*. Unpublished manuscript, Camarillo State Hospital, Children's Learning Laboratory, Camarillo, Calif., 1976.

# References

Alpern, G. D. Measurement of "untestable" autistic children. *Journal of Abnormal Psychology*, 1967, *72*, 478–486.

Alpern, G. D., & Kimberlin, C. C. Short intelligence test ranging from infancy levels through childhood levels for use with the retarded. *American Journal of Mental Deficiency*, 1970, *75*, 65–71.

American Association on Mental Deficiency. *Adaptive Behavior Scale* (1975 rev.). Washington, D.C.: Author, 1975.

Baltaxe, C. A. M., & Simmons, J. Q. Bedtime soliloquies and linguistic competence in autism. *Journal of Speech and Hearing Disorders*, 1977, *42*, 376–393.

Blackstock, E. G. Cerebral asymmetry and the development of early infantile autism. *Journal of Autism and Childhood Schizophrenia*, 1978, *8*, 339–353.

Boer, A. P. Application of a simple recording system to the analysis of free-play behavior in autistic children. *Journal of Applied Behavior Analysis*, 1968, *1*, 335–340.

Boullin, D., Coleman, M., O'Brien, R., & Rimland, B. Laboratory prediction of infantile autism based on 5-hydroxytryptamine efflux from blood platelets and their correlation with the Rimland E2 score. *Journal of Autism and Childhood Schizophrenia*, 1971, *1*, 63–71.

Bricker, D. D., Bricker, W. A., & Larsen, L. A. *Operant audiometry manual for difficult-to-test children*. Nashville: Kennedy Center for Research on Education and Human Development, 1968.

Cantwell, D., Baker, L., & Rutter, M. A comparative study of infantile autism and specific developmental receptive language disorder—IV. Analysis of syntax and language function. *Journal of Child Psychology and Psychiatry*, 1978, *19*, 351–362.

Carr, E. G. The motivation of self-injurious behavior: A review of some hypotheses. *Psychological Bulletin*, 1977, *84*, 800–816.

Carr, E. G. Teaching autistic children to use sign language: Some research issues. *Journal of Autism and Developmental Disorders*, 1979, *9*, 345–359.

Carr, E. G., Schreibman, L., & Lovaas, O. I. Control of echolalic speech in psychotic children. *Journal of Abnormal Child Psychology*, 1975, *3*, 331–351.

Chess, S. Autism in children with congenital rubella. *Journal of Autism and Childhood Schizophrenia*, 1971, *1*, 33–47.

Chess, S. Follow-up report on autism in congenital rubella. *Journal of Autism and Childhood Schizophrenia*, 1977, *7*, 69–81.

Clement, P. W., & Richard, R. C. Identifying reinforcers for children: A Children's Reinforcement Survey. In E. J. Mash & L. G. Terdal (Eds.), *Behavior therapy assessment: Diagnosis, design, and evaluation*. New York: Springer, 1976.

Coleman, M. (Ed.). *The autistic syndromes*. Amsterdam: Elsevier North-Holland, 1976.

Condon, W. S. Multiple response to sound in dysfunctional children. *Journal of Autism and Childhood Schizophrenia*, 1975, *5*, 37–56.

Davison, G. C. A social learning therapy programme with an autistic child. *Behaviour Research and Therapy*, 1964, *2*, 149–159.

DeMyer, M. K. Motor, perceptual–motor and intellectual disabilities of autistic children. In L. Wing (Ed.), *Early childhood autism: Clinical, educational and social aspects* (2nd ed.). London: Pergamon, 1976.

DeMyer, M. K., Barton, S., DeMyer, W. E., Norton, J. A., Allen, J., & Steele, R. Prognosis in autism: A follow-up study. *Journal of Autism and Childhood Schizophrenia*, 1973, *3*, 199–246.

DeMyer, M. K., Churchill, D., Pontius, W., and Gilkey, K. A comparison of five diagnostic systems for childhood schizophrenia and infantile autism. *Journal of Autism and Childhood Schizophrenia*, 1971, *1*, 175–189.

DeMyer, M. K., Norton, J. A., & Barton, S. Social and adaptive behaviors of autistic children as measured in a structured psychiatric interview. In D. W. Churchill, G. D. Alpern, & M. K. DeMyer (Eds.), *Infantile autism: Proceedings of the Indiana University Colloquium*. Springfield, Ill.: Charles C. Thomas, 1971.

Doll, E. A. *Vineland Social Maturity Scale: Manual of directions* (Rev. ed.). Minneapolis: American Guidance Service, 1965.

Ferster, C. B., & DeMyer, M. K. Increased performances of an autistic child with prochlorperizine administration. *Journal of the Experimental Analysis of Behavior*, 1961, *4*, 84. (a)

Ferster, C. B., & DeMyer, M. K. The development of performances in autistic children in an automatically controlled environment. *Journal of Chronic Diseases*, 1961, *13*, 312–245. (b)

Ferster, C. B., & DeMyer, M. K. A method for the experimental analysis of the behavior of autistic children. *American Journal of Orthopsychiatry*, 1962, *32*, 89–98.

Flaharty, R. EPEC: Evaluation and Prescription for Exceptional Children. In E. R. Ritvo (Ed.), *Autism: Diagnosis, current research and management*. New York: Spectrum, 1976.

Fulton, R. T. *Auditory stimulus–response control*. Baltimore: University Park Press, 1974.

Fulton, R. T., & Lloyd, L. L. *Audiometry for the retarded*. Baltimore: Williams & Wilkins, 1969.

Hauser, S. L., DeLong, G. R., & Rosman, N. P. Pneumographic findings in the infantile autism syndrome: A correlation with temporal lobe disease. *Brain*, 1975, *98*, 667–688.

Hermelin, B., & O'Connor, N. *Psychological experiments with autistic children*. New York: Pergamon, 1970.

Hutt, S. J., & Hutt, C. *Direct observation and measurement of behavior*. Springfield, Ill.: Charles C. Thomas, 1970.

Jensen, A. R. A theory of primary and secondary familial retardation. In N. R. Ellis (Ed.), *International review of research in mental retardation* (Vol. 4). New York: Academic Press, 1970.

Kanner, L. Autistic disturbances of affective contact. *Nervous Child*, 1943, *2*, 181–197.

Kanner, L. The specificity of early infantile autism. *Zeitschrift für Kinderpsychiatrie*, 1958, *25*, 108–113.

Koegel, R. L., & Rincover, A. Treatment of psychotic children in a classroom environment: I. Learning in a large group. In A. Graziano (Ed.), *Behavior therapy with children* (Vol. 2). Chicago: Aldine, 1975.

Koegel, R. L., & Rincover, A. Some detrimental effects of using extra stimuli to guide learning in normal and autistic children. *Journal of Abnormal Child Psychology*, 1976, *4*, 59–71.

Koegel, R. L., Russo, D. C., & Rincover, A. Assessing and training teachers in the generalized use of behavior modification with autistic children. *Journal of Applied Behavior Analysis*, 1977, *10*, 197–205.

Kolvin, I. Psychoses in childhood—A comparative study. In M. Rutter (Ed.), *Infantile autism: Concepts, characteristics, and treatment*. London: Churchill-Livingstone, 1971.

Kozloff, M. A. *Educating children with learning and behavior problems*. New York: Wiley, 1974.

Lotter, V. Epidemiology of autistic conditions in young children. I. Prevalence. *Social Psychiatry*, 1966, *1*, 124–137.

Lotter, V. Epidemiology of autistic conditions in young children. II. Some characteristics of the parents and children. *Social Psychiatry*, 1967, *1*, 163–173.

Lotter, V. Social adjustment and placement of autistic children in Middlesex: A follow-up study. *Journal of Autism and Childhood Schizophrenia*, 1974, *4*, 11–32. (a)

Lotter, V. Factors related to outcome in autistic children. *Journal of Autism and Childhood Schizophrenia*, 1974, *4*, 263–277. (b)

Lotter, V. Follow-up studies. In M. Rutter & E. Schopler (Eds.), *Autism: A reappraisal of concepts and treatment*. New York: Plenum, 1978.

Lovaas, O. I. General discussion. In D. W. Churchill, G. D. Alpern, & M. K. DeMyer (Eds.), *Infantile autism: Proceedings of the Indiana University Colloquium*. Springfield, Ill.: Charles C. Thomas, 1971.

Lovaas, O. I. *The autistic child: Language development through behavior modification*. New York: Irvington, 1977.

Lovaas, O. I., Berberich, J. P., Perloff, B. F., & Schaeffer, B. Acquisition of imitative speech by schizophrenic children. *Science*, 1966, *151*, 705–707.

Lovaas, O. I., Freitag, G., Gold, V. J., & Kassorla, I. C. Experimental studies in childhood schizophrenia: Analysis of self-destructive behavior. *Journal of Experimental Child Psychology*, 1965, *2*, 67–84. (a)

Lovaas, O. I., Freitag, G., Gold, V. J., & Kassorla, I. C. Recording apparatus and procedure for observation of behavior of children in free play settings. *Journal of Experimental Child Psychology*, 1965, *2*, 108–120. (b)

Lovaas, O. I., Koegel, R., Simmons, J. Q., & Long, J. S. Some generalization and follow-up measures on autistic children in behavior therapy. *Journal of Applied Behavior Analysis*, 1973, *6*, 131–166.

Lovaas, O. I., & Newsom, C. D. Behavior modification with psychotic children. In H. Leitenberg (Ed.), *Handbook of behavior modification and behavior therapy*. Englewood Cliffs, N.J.: Prentice-Hall, 1976.

Lovaas, O. I., Varni, J. W., Koegel, R. L., & Lorsch, N. Some observations on the nonextinguishability of children's speech. *Child Development*, 1977, *48*, 1121–1127.

Makita, K. The age of onset of childhood schizophrenia. *Folia Psychiatrica et Neurologica Japonica*, 1966, *20*, 111–121.

Maxwell, A. E. A factor analysis of the Wechsler Intelligence Scale for Children. *British Journal of Educational Psychology*, 1959, *29*, 237–241.

Meyers, A. W., & Craighead, W. E. Classroom treatment of psychotic children. *Behavior Modification*, 1979, *3*, 73–96.

National Society for Autistic Children. A short definition of autism. *NSAC Newsletter*, 1977, *9*, 6.

National Society for Autistic Children. Definition of the syndrome of autism. *Journal of Autism and Childhood Schizophrenia*, 1978, *8*, 162–167.

Newsom, C. D., Carr, E. G., & Lovaas, O. I. The experimental analysis and modification of autistic behavior. In R. S. Davidson (Ed.), *Modification of behavior pathology*. New York: Gardner Press, 1979.

Newsom, C. D., & Simon, K. M. A simultaneous discrimination procedure for the measurement of vision in nonverbal children. *Journal of Applied Behavior Analysis*, 1977, *10*, 633–644.

O'Gorman, G. *The nature of childhood autism*. London: Butterworths, 1967.

Ornitz, E. M. The modulation of sensory input and motor output in autistic children. *Journal of Autism and Childhood Schizophrenia*, 1974, *4*, 197–215.

Ornitz, E. M. Biological homogeneity or heterogeneity? In M. Rutter & E. Schopler (Eds.), *Autism: A reappraisal of concepts and treatment*. New York: Plenum, 1978.

Ornitz, E. M., & Ritvo, E. R. Medical assessment. In E. R. Ritvo (Ed.), *Autism: Diagnosis, current research and management*. New York: Spectrum, 1976.

Polan, C. C., & Spencer, B. L. Checklist of symptoms of autism in early life. *West Virginia Medical Journal*, 1959, *55*, 198–204.

Ragland, E. U., Kerr, M., & Strain, P. S. Behavior of withdrawn autistic children: Effects of peer social initiations. *Behavior Modification*, 1978, *2*, 565–578.

Rimland, B. *Infantile autism: The syndrome and its implications for a neural theory of behavior*. New York: Appleton-Century-Crofts, 1964.

Rimland, B. The differentiation of childhood psychoses: An analysis of checklists for 2218 psychotic children. *Journal of Autism and Childhood Schizophrenia*, 1971, *1*, 161–174.

Rimland, B. Infantile autism: Status and research. In A. Davids (Ed.), *Child personality and psychopathology* (Vol. 1). New York: Wiley, 1974.

Rincover, A. Variables influencing stimulus-fading and discriminative responding in psychotic children. *Journal of Abnormal Psychology*, 1978, 541–553. (a)

Rincover, A. Sensory extinction: A procedure for eliminating self-stimulatory behavior in autistic and retarded children. *Journal of Abnormal Child Psychology*, 1978, *6*, 299–310. (b)

Rincover, A., Cook, R., Peoples, A., & Packard, D. Using sensory extinction and sensory reinforcement principles for programming multiple adaptive behavior change. *Journal of Applied Behavior Analysis*, 1979, *12*, 221–233.

Rincover, A., & Koegel, R. L. Research on the education of autistic children: Current status and future directions. In B. B. Lahey & A. E. Kazdin (Eds.), *Advances in clinical child psychology* (Vol. 1). New York: Plenum, 1977. (a)

Rincover, A., & Koegel, R. L. Classroom treatment of autistic children: II. Individualized instruction in a group. *Journal of Abnormal Child Psychology*, 1977, *5*, 113–126. (b)

Ritvo, E. R. (Ed.). *Autism: Diagnosis, current research and management*. New York: Spectrum, 1976.

Romanczyk, R. G., Diament, C., Goren, E. R., Trunell, G., & Harris, S. L. Increasing isolate and social play in severely disturbed children: Intervention and postintervention effectiveness. *Journal of Autism and Childhood Schozphrenia*, 1975, *5*, 57–70.

Russo, D. C., & Newsom, C. D. Psychotic disorders of childhood. In J. R. Lackenmeyer & M. S. Gibbs (Eds.), *Psychology of the abnormal child*. New York: Gardner Press, 1979.

Rutter, M. Behavioral and cognitive characteristics of a series of psychotic children. In J. K. Wing (Ed.), *Childhood autism: Clinical, educational, and social aspects*. London: Pergamon, 1966.

Rutter, M. Concepts of autism: A review of research. *Journal of Child Psychology and Psychiatry*, 1968, *9*, 1–25.

Rutter, M. Diagnosis and definition of childhood autism. *Journal of Autism and Childhood Schizophrenia*, 1978, *8*, 139–161.

Rutter, M., Bartak, L., & Newman, S. Autism—A central disorder of cognition and language? In M. Rutter (Ed.), *Infantile autism: Concepts, characteristics and treatment*. London: Churchill-Livingstone, 1971.

Rutter, M., Greenfeld, D., & Lockyer, L. A five to fifteen year follow-up study of infantile psychosis. II. Social and behavioural outcome. *British Journal of Psychiatry*, 1967, *113*, 1183–1199.

Sattler, J. M. *Assessment of children's intelligence* (Rev. reprint). Philadelphia: W. B. Saunders, 1974.

Schopler, E. Discussion. *Journal of Autism and Childhood Schizophrenia*, 1978, *8*, 167–169.

Schopler, E., & Reichler, R. J. *Psychoeducational Profile*. Chapel Hill, N.C.: Child Development Products, 1976.

Schreibman, L. Effects of within-stimulus and extra-stimulus prompting on discrimination learning in autistic children. *Journal of Applied Behavior Analysis*, 1975, *8*, 91–112.

Schreibman, L., & Carr, E. G. Elimination of echolalic responding to questions through the training of a generalized verbal response. *Journal of Applied Behavior Analysis*, 1978, *11*, 453–463.

Sidman, M., & Stoddard, L. T. Programming perception and learning for retarded children. In N. R. Ellis (Ed.), *International review of research in mental retardation* (Vol. 2). New York: Academic Press, 1966.

Solnick, J., Rincover, A., & Peterson, C. Some determinants of the reinforcing and punishing effects of timeout. *Journal of Applied Behavior Analysis*, 1977, *10*, 415–424.

Stebbins, W. C. (Ed.). *Animal psychophysics*. New York: Appleton-Century-Crofts, 1970.

Sternlicht, M. A downward extension of the 1960 Revised Stanford–Binet with retardates. *Journal of Clinical Psychology*, 1965, *21*, 79.

Strain, P. S., & Cooke, T. P. An observational investigation of two elementary-age autistic children during free-play. *Psychology in the Schools*, 1976, *13*, 82–91.

Takahashi, S., Kanai, H., & Miyamoto, Y. Reassessment of elevated serotonin levels in blood platelets in early infantile autism. *Journal of Autism and Childhood Schizophrenia*, 1976, *6*, 317–326.

Vrono, M. Schizophrenia in childhood and adolescence. *International Journal of Mental Health*, 1974, *2*, 7–116.

Wechsler, D. *Manual for the Wechsler Preschool and Primary Scale of Intelligence*. New York: Psychological Corporation, 1967.

Wechsler, D. *Manual for the Wechsler Intelligence Scale for Children—Revised*. New York: Psychological Corporation, 1974.

Wetzel, R. J., Baker, J., Roney, M., & Martin, M. Outpatient treatment of autistic behavior. *Behaviour Research and Therapy*, 1966, *4*, 169–177.

Wing, L., Yeates, S. R., Brierley, L. M., & Gould, J. The prevalence of early childhood autism: A comparison of administrative and epidemiological studies. *Psychological Medicine*, 1976, *6*, 89–100.

Wolf, M. M. Social validity: The case for subjective measurement or how applied behavior analysis is finding its heart. *Journal of Applied Behavior Analysis*, 1978, *11*, 203–214.

Wolf, M. M., Risley, T., & Mees, H. Application of operant conditioning procedures to the behavior problems of an autistic child. *Behaviour Research and Therapy*, 1964, *1*, 305–312.

Yuwiler, A., Geller, E., & Ritvo, E. R. Neurobiochemical research. In E. R. Ritvo (Ed.), *Autism: Diagnosis, and current research and management*. New York: Spectrum, 1976.

# LEARNING DISABILITIES

### Russell A. Barkley
*The Medical College of Wisconsin and Milwaukee Children's Hospital*

The inability of children to perform adequately in areas of academic achievement despite seemingly adequate intellectual skills and educational opportunity has come to be recognized as a significant educational, social, and economic problem (Benton & Pearl, 1978). These children not only present problems in regard to the design of adequate educational programs, but also are likely to constitute a significant proportion of mental health problems. Many of these children go on to develop difficulties in conduct, self-esteem, anxiety, and depression after only a few years of frustration and failure in school. A substantial percentage drops out of school early, contributing in large measure to the population of juvenile delinquents in the country (Brown, 1978). The economic loss to society is immeasurable, not only in lost productivity for those who may become underemployed or unemployed but also in the expense of mental health and criminal facilities that must attend to the reactive conduct and emotional problems to which academic failure presumably leads.

Despite the significance of the problem, it remains one of the most confusing and disorganized areas in the literature of child psychology. The confusion in diagnostic terminology is but one example. Learning-disabled (LD) children are labeled with such terms as "minimal brain dysfunction" (Millichap, 1977), "brain-injured child" (Strauss & Lehtinen, 1947), "dyslexia" (Benton & Pearl, 1978), "dysphasia," "slow learner," and "underachiever." Some have argued that these disorders do not exist apart from mental subnormality or cultural deprivation (see Yule, Rutter, Berger, & Thompson, 1974, for a discussion). Others have stated that as many as 10% of school-age children may show learning disabilities of one form or another (Millichap, 1977). The confusion in labeling, also observed in efforts at definition and treatment, has promoted many fads (dietary changes, ocular motor training, etc.) to meet the increasing public demand that "something" be done now to meet the child's needs.

Taking these controversies into account, this chapter will suggest some practical guidelines for the behavioral assessment of learning disabilities. There will be no attempt to resolve the complex conceptual and methodological issues in this area or to present an exhaustive review of the literature. All of the disorders that could be broadly construed as learning disabilities will not be discussed here, such as severe language delay, blindness, deafness, cerebral palsy, and other developmental disabilities. Instead, attention will be given only to that group of children who, despite seemingly adequate language and intellectual development, as well as adequate exposure to educational opportunities, display deficits in one or more areas of academic achievement. More specifically, this chapter will focus on the assessment of selective deficits in reading, spelling, mathematics, and writing.

The behavioral approach to be taken here differs from most other approaches to LD children in that it greatly emphasizes the environmental antecedents and consequences of the child's academic performance problems. It does not eschew the importance of assessing cognitive or neuropsychological skills but views them as merely a starting, rather than an end, point in understanding the child's classroom achievement problems. The social context in which the performance difficulties occur, how they are consequated, and how the transaction among these variables transforms the child's classroom or academic behaviors are of equal importance in evaluating and treating the LD child.

# DEFINITION

The disorders referred to herein as specific learning disabilities do not in any sense imply that the child *cannot* learn academic material. Rather, they refer to children showing various *degrees* of difficulty in acquiring academic skills compared to normal children of similar age and intelligence. From a purely behavioral view, these children display deficiencies in age-appropriate responding to linguistic–numeric stimuli despite adequate exposure to the social contingencies generally provided to develop such responding. These deficiencies can be qualitative or quantitative and cannot be attributed to general mental retardation, severe psychiatric impairment, or problems in primary sensory modalities such as vision and hearing.

Although interest in the field of specific learning disabilities can be traced to the writings of Strauss and Lehtinen (1947) and Werner (1948), widespread professional attention did not begin until the learly 1960s (Cruickshank, 1967; Kephart, 1960; McCarthy & McCarthy, 1963). At this time, various schools of thought produced widely diverse definitions of, and causal explanations for, specific learning disabilities. These ranged from brain damage and dysfunction to visual–perceptual deficits, familial or genetic factors, and improper educational techniques. This controversy over definition and etiology has continued to the present and probably will exist for some time to come.

Nonetheless, those working in this area have come to accept the definition provided in U.S. Public Law 94-142 as at least a starting point for the allocation of educational resources to these children. This law states that LD children are as follows:

> Those children who have a disorder in one or more of the basic psychological processes involved in understanding or in using language, spoken or written, which disorder

may manifest itself in imperfect ability to listen, think, speak, read, write, spell, or do mathematical calculations. [*Federal Register*, 1977, Section 121a. 5(9)]

The definition attempts to exclude "children who have learning problems which are primarily the result of visual, hearing, or motor handicaps, or mental retardation, or emotional disturbance, or environmental, cultural, or economic disadvantage" [*Federal Register*, 1977, Section 121a. 5(9)].

To the behavioral scientist, this definition raises several issues that are worth brief mention. First, it does not clearly stipulate what is meant by a "disorder." That is, it fails to indicate how deficient a child must be in reading, spelling, writing, and so forth, before he or she can be called LD. Early efforts (*Federal Register*, 1976) defined the deficiency using a formula that took the child's IQ into consideration. This seems to have been abandoned for other criteria, such as two grade levels below that expected for age and intelligence, 50% below that grade level expected for age and intelligence, or two standard deviations below the mean for same-age children on academic achievement tests. Each of these criteria has its disadvantages. Second, the definition does not suggest a standard with which the deficit is compared, such as age, intelligence (verbal or nonverbal), or expected grade level. Third, the definition proposes that deficits may exist in cognitive skills that are quite difficult to assess, such as "thinking." And finally, it does not make clear just how one excludes educational or cultural deprivation or just what exactly is meant by these terms.

Despite these difficulties with the P.L. 94-142 definition, it is the one most frequently used to assign children to LD resources and therefore must be heeded by those who work in public school settings. The following are offered as tentative suggestions in working with LD children:

1. Where federal, state, or local definitions exist in law to define a child as LD, these will have to be consulted and followed.

2. Where none exists, the LD child can be considered one who falls at the 20th percentile or lower on well-standardized tests of reading, spelling, mathematics, or writing. Such a definition allows children between kindergarten and second grade to be considered LD (Rourke, 1976).

3. The child should have an IQ on a well-standardized intelligence test, such as the Wechsler Intelligence Scale for Children—Revised (WISC-R), that falls within the normal range for that test in either verbal or nonverbal abilities. Both types of abilities should be tested, as will become evident later.

4. The clinician should rule out primary sensory defects and should assess whether the child has had adequate exposure to and opportunity for formal schooling.

5. Finally, disorders such as psychosis, hyperactivity, depression, and anxiety should be ruled out as primary causes of the learning disorder. This does not mean that they may not coexist with the learning problems but that, in the clinician's view, they do not play a primary causal role in the genesis of the learning disability.

The definitions used here limit the disorder to school-age children (5 to 18 years, typically). Some would argue that this is arbitrary, since problems with reading or mathematics often persist into adulthood (see Trites & Fiedorowicz,

1976), and that some predictors of learning disorders may be apparent before 5 years of age (Trehub, 1977). However, the critical decisions as to the allocation of limited resources come when the child is of school age and necessarily decline once the child leaves the age of compulsory education.

Three exceptions to these guidelines should be noted. The first concerns the child who displays significant distress in academic settings because of deficits in achievement areas that may not be sufficient to warrant inclusion as an LD student under legal criteria. Although such children may not yet meet legal criteria, they will eventually as they continue to fall behind—hence services should be delivered now as an effort to prevent further backsliding or greater emotional distress. The second exception is the case of the child of above-average or superior intellectual skills who shows deficits in one or two academic areas. These deficits, however, may fall within the normal range. Despite these normal *levels* of performance in the relatively deficient areas, the child is not likely to perform adequately in class and is likely to find these subjects highly frustrating. As a few writers are beginning to stress (Guthrie, 1973; Rourke, 1976), it is the profile of *relative* deficits within a child's pattern of skills rather than his or her absolute level of deficiency that determines whether the child will manifest specific learning disabilities. The third exception is the child who may meet LD criteria yet reside within a community or school system in which most of the children are well below national norms on achievement tests, as in remote rural or poor inner-city areas. Community standards must therefore be considered when evaluating whether an LD child is really in need of special assistance.[1]

## GENERAL DESCRIPTION

Most research in the area of learning disabilities has compared children who are heterogeneous in terms of their achievement deficits with a group of normal children. Such studies seek to find whether the general population of LD children differs in any respect from normal children on measures other than those on which the groups were selected. Indeed, many studies have not even used measures of achievement to define their groups. Instead, they have used medical opinion, current placement of the child in some LD program, or the presence of "minimal brain dysfunction" as diagnosed by a neurologist or pediatrician. Not surprisingly, few reliable differences have emerged between LD and normal children (Rourke, 1978b).

---

[1]Although not the subject of this chapter, the opposite case is also likely to occur and to cause great consternation to those who would rigidly apply any definition of learning disability. More specifically, some children of average to slightly below-average skills find themselves attending schools in high-income school districts where most children perform above national norms in achievement skills. Such a child, though not formally learning disabled, is likely to experience great failure, anxiety, emotional difficulties, and related problems because of his or her substandard performance *in that setting*. Obviously, this child is in need of some special assistance under whatever program in the school best meets his or her needs.

Several studies have found LD children to have more neurologic "soft signs" (physical characteristics or responses that are not clear indications of brain damage but are abnormal for the child's age) than normal children (Dykman, Peters, & Ackerman, 1973; Eaves & Crichton, 1974–1975; Millman, 1970). Others have not found such differences (Black, 1973; Erickson, 1977; Myklebust, 1973; Rie, Rie, & Stewart, 1976).

Similar conclusions have been reached for visual–perceptual problems, attentional deficits, sequencing difficulties, motor clumsiness, and other possible deficiencies (see Benton & Pearl, 1978; Millichap, 1977; Rourke, 1976, 1978a, 1978b, for a more thorough review). Hence, no single characteristic reliably discriminates LD children. However, most of the children in these studies have been reading disabled, whereas others had problems in mathematics, spelling, or all three areas. It seems likely that any factors that might differentiate these subgroups would not be apparent when they are combined into one heterogeneous group of LD children. As Rourke (1978b) notes, this probably accounts for much of the heuristic infertility of the vast amount of research into the general population of LD children.

Estimates of the prevalence of LD children in the population must obviously be qualified by the lack of agreement in definition. The most widely accepted estimate appears to be 3–5% of the school-age population (Farnham-Diggory, 1978; Knights & Bakker, 1976; Ross, 1976). As with many childhood psychological disorders, boys are more likely to be LD than girls, with ratios ranging from 4:1 to 10:1 (Benton & Pearl, 1978; Ingram, Mason, & Blackburn, 1970). The reasons for greater male prevalence are not established.

Although school achievement would certainly be expected to vary with the socioeconomic level of the child's family, specific delays in reading, spelling, or mathematics are not found in greatest prevalence in the lowest socioeconomic groups. Rutter, Tizard, Yule, Graham, and Whitmore (1976) have shown that the majority of such children tend to come from the lower-middle or "manual" classes. Children with these disabilities are also more likely than normal children to have family members with histories of learning difficulties (Ingram et al., 1970; Rutter et al., 1976).

Studies of dyslexic children, in particular, have noted that they have a higher incidence of left-handedness, ambidexterity, psychiatric and conduct problems, allergies, and peer relationship problems than do normal children (see Benton & Pearl, 1978; Kinsbourne & Caplan, 1979; Knights & Bakker, 1976). However, this is also true of hyperactive children (see Chapter 3, this volume) and children with various acquired neurologic disorders (Rutter, 1978).

# SUBTYPES

As noted previously, many studies have compared children with various learning disabilities to normal children but with little success. This has led several investigators (Boder, 1973; Mattis, 1978; Rourke, 1976) to propose that only research that examines subgroups of learning disabilities is likely to yield reliable results. Early efforts appear to bear out this notion. Most of this research has been on reading disability, or dyslexia. Various factor-analytic studies of reading in normal and dyslexic children (Denckla, 1979; Mattis, 1978; Petrauskas & Rourke, 1979) suggest at least three, if not more, subtypes of reading/spelling disabilities. Little research has been conducted with arithmetic disabilities, but here, too, results have been promising in identifying some subtypes (Goodstein & Kahn, 1974; Rourke & Strang, 1978).

Certainly, this approach makes a great deal of sense, considering the complexity of academic skills and the numerous cognitive processes necessary for their adequate execution. Difficulties in any particular process will result in some deficiency in an achievement skill. The type of process affected determines the nature of the impairment in the achievement skill (Luria, 1973; Tarnopol & Tarnopol, 1977). For example, reading requires listening, attending, adequate vision and hearing, normal visual and auditory memory, satisfactory transmodal comparisons or processing of audiovisual stimuli, vocal and subvocal speech, and so forth. Deficits in any of these areas would lead to a certain type of reading problem, which might be quite different from that produced by deficits in a different prerequisite skill. Collapsing all children with reading problems into one group for comparison with normal readers would tend to obscure these differences, leading to inconsistent findings in research (Rourke, 1976). Thus, it no longer appears adequate simply to study children with general reading disability. One must go further in order to deduce the particularly deficient aspect of reading if research and clinical endeavors are to have much utility (Kinsbourne & Caplan, 1979).

## Disorders of Reading

Various efforts have been made to categorize reading disorders into more homogeneous groups. It is not the purpose of this chapter to review the merits of these classification schemes; for this, the reader is referred to Benton and Pearl (1978) for a more thorough review. Some of the more widely accepted schemes are listed in Table 1. These varying classifications seem to yield at least three subtypes of dyslexia.

### Disorders of Language Skills

This group constitutes by far the largest group of poor readers (approximately 60%). They typically show greater impairment of verbal or language skills on the Wechsler Intelligence Scale for Children (WISC or WISC-R) (Wechsler, 1949, 1974) compared to the nonverbal performance subtests (Mattis, French, & Rapin, 1975; Rourke, 1978b; Smith, 1970a, 1970b). According to Boder (1973), Rourke (1980), and others (Doehring, Hoshko, & Bryans, 1979; Mattis, 1978), they usually

## TABLE 1
Various Proposed Classification Schemes for Reading Disorders

*Boder (1973)*
1. Dysphonetic
2. Dyseidetic
3. Mixed dysphonetic–dyseidetic

*Mattis (1977)*
1. Language disorder
2. Articulatory and graphomotor incoordination
3. Visuospatial perceptual disorder

*Doehring, Hoshko, and Bryans (1979)*
1. Poor oral reading of letters, syllables, and words
2. Slow matching of spoken and written letters
3. Poor matching of spoken and written syllables and words

*Ingram, Mason, and Blackburn (1970)*
1. Audiophonic disorder
2. Visuospatial disorder

*Petrauskas and Rourke (1979)*
1. Language disorder
2. Sequential–analytic
3. Articulatory and graphomotor incoordination (poor expressive
   language and verbal conceptualizations)

show difficulties in matching the correct phoneme to its grapheme in both reading and spelling; that is, they have considerable problems in matching the sounds of words to their written representation. Boder (1973) suggests that they show frequent partial and gross mispronunciations in oral reading, often construed as poor phonetic or "word-attack" skills. They may guess wildly at words on the basis of the first one or two letters (i.e., saying "dinosaur" for "dangerous") and may make semantic substitutions for words, such as "quack" for "duck." Their spelling errors belie their reading problems, a truism for the other reading disorders as well (Boder, 1973; Rourke, 1980; Rutter, 1978). Efforts at spelling consist of wild or bizarre guesses at the word, with frequent letter omissions, substitutions, and repetitions. The pronunciation of the misspelling does not usually closely approximate its sound.

A history of delayed language development is common (Denckla, 1979; Ingram *et al.*, 1970; Mattis, 1978; Rutter, 1978). Many do poorly on tests involving language skills, especially auditory discrimination for word sounds and word-finding skills (dysnomia). Apparently good in visual memory for words, the children will often be able to say and spell correctly simple mono- and bisyllabic words that they frequently encounter, such as "go," "cat," and "boy." However, once they confront more complex words, their spelling and pronunciation contains many errors, as illustrated in Figure 1. They frequently do more poorly on tests of reading

| | | | |
|---|---|---|---|
| mokn | (MAKE) | aspln | (EXPLAIN) |
| him | (HIM) | ejj | (EDGE) |
| say | (SAY) | kien | (KITCHEN) |
| lat | (LIGHT) | | |
| must | (MUST) | | |
| Jes | (DRESS) | | |
| rech | (REACH) | | |
| ordr | (ORDER) | | |
| woch | (WATCH) | | |
| etr | (ENTER) | | |
| gon | (GROWN) | | |
| nach | (NATURE) | | |

FIGURE 1

Spelling errors characteristic of a dysphonetic reader.

and spelling than of arithmetic (Rourke, 1976, 1978b, 1980; Rourke & Finlayson, 1978), especially if the mathematical problems are not in verbal form.

Those children with language-based reading problems may have their greatest difficulty with phonetic–analytic skills. Hence, they are likely to be detected at a time when learning demands require a shift from sight-word reading to phonetic analysis (Boder, 1973). These dysphonetic readers/spellers may also have poor handwriting, though it may not be as poor as children with the other reading problems to be discussed.

### Disorders of Sequencing and Verbal Expression

This is the next most frequent type of reading disorder and accounts for approximately 10–20% of reading disabilities (Boder, 1973; Mattis, 1978). These children show poor articulation and handwriting skills. They seem to perform uniformly poorly on all achievement tests (mathematics, reading, and spelling), and there is little discrepancy between their WISC verbal and nonverbal performance scales (Mattis et al., 1975; Cohen & Netley, 1978). They are likely to perform poorest on the arithmetic, coding, information, and digit-span subtests, or what some call the ACID pattern (Bannatyne, 1968, 1971; Petrauskas & Rourke, 1979; Rugel, 1974a), on the WISC or WISC-R. Many seem to have poor recall of sentences whether read by them or to them.

This group probably corresponds to the group identified by Boder (1973) as a mixed dysphonetic–dyseidetic reading disability. They not only make the mistakes in reading and spelling noted on the first group described here but also are poor at whole-word or sight-word skills. They may misspell even the simplest of frequently encountered words. Some investigators (Mattis, 1978; Rourke, 1978a, 1980) believe that the disorder is in the sequential processing of verbal information, especially in memory. Poor at both phonics and sight-word reading, they are difficult to treat and may have the worst prognosis of the three disorders outlined (Boder, 1973; Rourke, 1980).

### Disorders of Visuospatial Skills

The least frequent of the reading disorders are those in which children do most poorly on tests of visuospatial construction or drawing and copying. Their nonverbal test scores are generally lower than their verbal scores on the WISC or WISC-R. In achievement skills, poorest performances are seen on mathematics tests, relative to reading and spelling (Ingram et al., 1970; Mattis et al., 1975; Petrauskas & Rourke, 1979; Rourke & Finlayson, 1978).

Boder (1973) and others (Mattis, 1978; Smith, Note 1, Note 2) believe that this group comprises approximately 5–10% of the poor readers. Characterized by good phonetic–analytic skills but poor sight-word reading, their oral reading is slow and laborious, even with frequently encountered words. Mispronunciations are less common than in the other groups, except for words whose written syllables do not suggest their sounds, such as "laugh" or "nature." Boder (1973) calls them dyseidetic readers, believing their deficit to be primarily one of poor visual memory for the total "gestalt" or written representation of words; hence their poor sight-word vocabulary.

The spelling errors of these children are marked by phonetic correctness despite their inaccuracy in the actual letters used for a word. That is, they spell the word like it sounds rather than as they recall seeing it (Boder, 1973; Rourke, 1978b), as illustrated in Figure 2. For instance, they are likely to spell "nature" as "nacher" and "reasonable" as "resinable." Unlike the children with the other reading disorders, these children do not make wild guesses at the spelling of words or in trying to pronounce them. Words that are not spelled like they sound will often be the most inaccurately spelled, such as "laf" for "laugh."

Mathematics is often their poorest area of achievement, with spelling being the second poorest and word pronunciation, as measured by the Wide-Range Achievement Test (WRAT), often being at, or only mildly below, grade level. Comprehension of reading is often normal, as is performance on most verbal tests. Performance on written mathematics, such as on the WRAT, is often poorer than auditory/verbal mathematics, as on the WISC-R or Peabody Individual Achievement Tests (Dunn & Markwardt, 1970). These readers are often the last to come to the attention of the professionals because their better phonetic–analytic skills assist them through the early years of reading.

Although other types of reading disorders probably exist to lesser degrees, these seem to be the most common. Yet, even these often do not present as quite so clearcut as the preceding descriptions may suggest. Often, they are mixed in

| | | | |
|---|---|---|---|
| *wotch* | (WATCH) | *am aaa ry* | (IMAGINARY) |
| *enter* | (ENTER) | *o k upie* | (OCCUPY) |
| *growen* | (GROWN) | *chariter* | (CHARACTER) |
| *natchur* | (NATURE) | *susiady* | (SOCIETY) |
| *explain* | (EXPLAIN) | *ofishle* | (OFFICIAL) |
| *edge* | (EDGE) | *re kan is* | (RECOGNIZE) |
| *kichen* | (KITCHEN) | | |
| *surprize* | (SURPRISE) | | |
| *resaut* | (RESULT) | | |
| *advice* | (ADVICE) | | |
| *pruchis* | (PURCHASE) | | |
| *breat* | (BRIEF) | | |
| *sucses* | (SUCCESS) | | |
| *resnable* | (REASONABLE) | | |

FIGURE 2

Spelling errors characteristic of a dyseidetic reader (poor visuospatial skills).

their deficits and error patterns. Nonetheless, these three types are likely to present frequently enough to make their delineation useful.

### Disorders of Arithmetic

Little research appears to have been conducted on children who perform poorly only on tests of mathematical skills (Kinsbourne & Caplan, 1979). Yet, children with specific deficits only in arithmetic undoubtedly exist. Because they have few, if any, problems with reading or spelling, they are less likely to come to professional attention until later in their education (Rourke & Strang, 1978). As noted previously, disorders of arithmetic, or *dyscalculia*, may and often do, co-exist with disorders of reading and/or spelling.

The research of Goodstein and Kahn (1974) and Rourke (1980) and his students (Petrauskas & Rourke, 1979; Rourke & Finlayson, 1978; Rourke & Strang, 1978) has examined the neuropsychological correlates of children who do poorly on mathematics. These children were compared to those who do more poorly on reading and spelling than on mathematics and those who do equally as poor in all three areas. These results suggest at least two types of mathematics disorders. Children who do most poorly on mathematics relative to much lesser deficits in reading and/or spelling are likely to show their greatest, and sometimes only, deficits in visuospatial skills, as on the performance subtests of the WISC. This suggests that adequate or normal development in visuospatial skills is a necessary, though not sufficient, condition for normal arithmetic development.

The second group of arithmetic disorders is that associated with poor language development, as seen in the first group of reading disorders. Children with such disorders do poorly on the verbal subtests of the WISC and have deficits in reading and spelling equal to, if not greater than, their deficits in mathematics. Little research is available to suggest what other correlates of these two mathematics disorders might exist relative to children who are normal in arithmetic development.

Kinsbourne (1977; Kinsbourne & Caplan, 1979) suggests two other problems that may lead to poor mathematics skills besides deficits in verbal and visuospatial skills. Some children may do poorly in mathematics because of poor ordering or sequencing of numbers in their appropriate positions. Recognizing the position of numbers within arrays is critical to the translation, meaning, and manipulation of numbers. These children may also be those noted in the second group of reading disorders who show problems in graphomotor, articulation, and sequencing skills. Another group of children with poor mathematics skills may be those who initially do well in mathematics but who, because of poor reading skills, begin to do less well as it comes to be taught more through reading-based methods. Kinsbourne (1977) notes that at the fourth grade or later, when mathematics is taught more by reading and verbal explanation, children poor in these skills may only then begin to show deficits in mathematics. Again, little research on arithmetic deficits exists to enable more critical evaluation of these notions.

### Disorders of Written Expression

Although little may be known of the disorders of arithmetic, even less is known about the specific disorders of written expression, or *dysgraphia*, yet they do exist. As with dyscalculia, dysgraphia can occur with, or independently of, disorders of reading. Drawing from the neuropsychological literature (Hecaen & Albert, 1978; Heilman & Valenstein, 1979), it would seem that disorders of written expression in children could be of at least three types, paralleling several of the reading disorders (Naidoo, 1972) and often co-existing with them.

The first disorder of handwriting seems to relate to deficits in language development, but especially to phonetic–analytic skills. As noted previously in the reading disorders, children with deficient phonics skills are likely to show delayed, wild, and often bizarre misspellings in their written expression. Obviously, such children are also likely to have a disorder of reading and possibly of mathematics. However, Naidoo (1972) has reported a group of children with adequate reading but poor spelling whose major deficit appeared to be in linguistic or phonics skills. Yet, compared to a group with both reading and spelling problems, the language deficits were less severe. This suggests that spelling may be a more complicated skill than reading, in which very mild deficits in language, especially phonetic–analytic skills, may have more apparent disruptions. This may explain why, in cases where reading and spelling are both poor, spelling is likely to be more severely impaired (Rutter, 1978).

The second type of dysgraphia is that seen in children with apparently poor visuospatial and constructive skills. Here, again, the spelling disorder is likely to occur with a reading problem. Yet, it is more often seen with disorders of arithmetic. In such children, arithmetic, especially written arithmetic, may be the severest deficit and spelling only somewhat less so, whereas reading may be near normal. As mentioned previously, these children are often adequate in phonics skills and make less bizarre or less wild spelling errors than dysphonetic spellers. Their errors, when they do occur, are likely to be phonetically accurate. Nonetheless, Naidoo (1972) reports a group of poor spellers who do not do poorly at reading but who show poor visuospatial deficits on neuropsychological measures. Again, the deficits are mild relative to children who are poor at both reading *and* spelling. This suggests that mild deficits in visuospatial and constructional skills are likely to affect spelling more than reading, although written arithmetic may also be deficient.

A third group of children who do poorly in written expression and who are probably much less frequently encountered than those already described are those who show deficits only in written expression, not in reading or mathematics skills. These are often children best thought of as *apraxic* (Heilman & Valenstein, 1979); that is, they show problems in the planning and execution of voluntary motor movements, but especially those involved in writing. Although they are normal in terms of oral expression, their ability to express their thoughts in writing is severely impaired. These children often show no problems on intellectual tests, except those that require handwriting, such as the coding subtests on the WISC, on which they will do singularly poorly. This child is likely to come to the attention of professionals late in his or her elementary or middle school years, since written expression receives ever greater emphasis in class assignments, tests, and homework. Time pressures particularly seem to exacerbate their written expression problems.

## Issues Related to Learning Disability Subtypes

This necessarily brief descriptive review raises several issues important to the understanding, assessment, and treatment of children with these problems. These issues are as follows:

1. It is no longer acceptable in research or clinical practice to consider children with learning disabilities as a single homogeneous group of children who differ from other children in any consistent respect.

2. Neither is it acceptable to view specific disorders of reading, spelling, mathematics, or written expression as homogeneous subtypes of learning disorders. As has been seen, even children specifically deficient in reading will vary as to the nature of their skills and deficits as well as to the quality of their errors. Rourke (1980) has repeatedly indicated that a level of performance definition of these learning disorders is outdated and without merit in treatment planning. Instead, the profile of the child's cognitive, intellectual, and academic skills and deficits must be studied. It is this *profile of relative deficits* for a child that will offer hypotheses as to the specific nature of the child's academic learning problem(s).

3. In addition to this profile analysis, the clinician must pay close attention to the nature and quality of the child's errors in the performance (Kinsbourne, 1977; Kinsbourne & Caplan, 1979). Simply knowing the child's score on a reading

test does not permit one to know how the child did poorly on the test and what erroneous behavioral strategies he or she is using to accomplish the test. The interested reader is referred to Luria (1973) for a thorough discussion of this more idiopathic approach to assessment.

4. Despite their initial etiologies, the learning disabilities described here do not appear to result from simply a critical deficit level in any one skill. That is, a deficient score on a particular test does not necessarily argue, one way or the other, that a child will have a learning disability. Instead, it appears to be the degree of deficit relative to the child's other skill levels that determines the presence and nature of the learning disability (Applebee, 1971; Guthrie, 1973; Luria, 1973; Mattis *et al.*, 1975; Rourke, 1980). As a result, children of above-average skills may show a severe deficit in visuospatial skills relative to their language skills, although the actual level of their visuospatial skills falls within the normal range. It is the severity of the discrepancy in these skill levels, not their absolute levels, that seems to create learning disabilities in academic achievement (Cohen & Netley, 1978; Smith, 1970a, 1970b). Even so, on achievement tests, their scores may range from average to superior, suggesting, at first glance, the absence of a disability. This is erroneous, however, as the child is likely to be struggling to barely achieve normal grade levels in one or two areas. He or she may also show the characteristic errors of more impaired learners who are actually below grade level in these areas and may begin to display the reactive emotional problems seen in the more deficient learner. Applebee (1971) and Guthrie (1973) suggest that a relative disequilibrium in the development of cognitive skills necessary for the performance of highly complex achievement skills results in disorders of reading. One would expect that a similar principle operates in determining disorders of mathematics, spelling, or written expression.

5. In this regard, at least four general areas of cognitive development appear to be important to adequate achievement skills, and these must develop with relative equilibrium among themselves (i.e., with an absence of sharp discrepancies or delays in any one area). Not only do factor-analytic studies of intellectual and achievement tests reveal these factors (see Bannatyne, 1968, 1971; Rugel, 1974a, 1974b), but various neuropsychological studies (see Hecaen & Albert, 1978; Heilman & Valenstein, 1979; Luria, 1973) support their neuroanatomic localization in children and adults. These skills appear to be (1) linguistic–conceptual skills; (2) visuospatial–constructive skills; (3) sequential–analytic skills; and (4) motor planning, execution, and regulation skills. Where these develop seriously out of synchrony from each other, regardless of the cause or the possible "normalcy" of the discrepant area(s), problems with achievement skills are likely to occur.


# RELATED BEHAVIORAL AND SOCIAL CHARACTERISTICS

Several behavioral and social problems are found to occur more often in LD than in normal children. Primary among these seem to be conduct problems (Douglas

& Peters, 1979; Kinsbourne & Caplan, 1979; Rutter, 1978). Aggression, hyper-activity, social withdrawal, anxiety, school phobias, depression, and low self-esteem may also be seen in greater frequency in children with learning disabilities (Balow & Bloomquist, 1965; Boder, 1973; Peter & Spreen, 1979; Rutter et al., 1976). Poor peer relationships also characterize some of these children (Bryan, 1974, 1976; Greca & Mesibov, Note 3).

Although these behavior problems may occur simultaneously with learning disabilities, they may also develop in response to extended failure in the classroom. Many of these children begin school as highly motivated students who eventually lose interest in academic material after several years' experience of classroom failure. Over time, the child feels less certain of his or her academic abilities and may often become significantly anxious or depressed by the end of elementary school. When emotional problems come to the forefront of the child's difficulties, they are often mistakenly viewed as the cause, rather than the result, of academic failure (Kinsbourne & Caplan, 1979). Such emotional or social problems may be so apparent that they draw the clinician's attention away from more subtle learning problems that may cause or contribute significantly to the former problems. Certainly, where a formerly well-behaved child has developed emotional or conduct problems, especially surrounding school activities, evaluation for possible learning problems would seem to be imperative. The reader is referred to those chapters dealing with the aforementioned conduct and emotional problems for their assessment and treatment.

Cunningham and Barkley (1978) have demonstrated how academic failure can come to create classroom behavior problems, seeming inattentiveness, off-task behavior, aggression, and social withdrawal in children. As seen in Figure 3, a variety of conditions may predispose a child to poor classroom achievement, one of which may be specific learning disabilities. Once classroom failure becomes chronic, it may lead to a variety of undesirable behaviors. These can, in turn, serve to further increase academic failure as well as alienation of the child from his or her peers. The response of the social environment to these behaviors further determines their expression. Various treatment approaches may produce varying degrees of change in the child's behavior problems and classroom failure, depending on their focus of intervention in this process. In any event, Figure 3 simply shows how initially specific learning deficits affect a child's classroom behavior and social conduct, perhaps resulting in the development of social maladjustment where none formerly existed (Douglas & Peters, 1979).

As discussed in Chapter 3 of this volume, a child's behavior obviously occurs in a social context that not only is changing but is being changed by the reaction of the social context (parents, teachers, peers, etc.) to the child's initial difficulties. This bidirectional, reciprocal nature of social interactions (see Bell & Harper, 1977) suggests that initial problems on achievement tasks have some impact on those individuals who interact with the child around that task. This individual can be the teacher during a classroom assignment in the deficient skill or a parent who must struggle to keep the child's attention directed toward homework with which he or she is having little success. The reactions of these individuals to the child's task

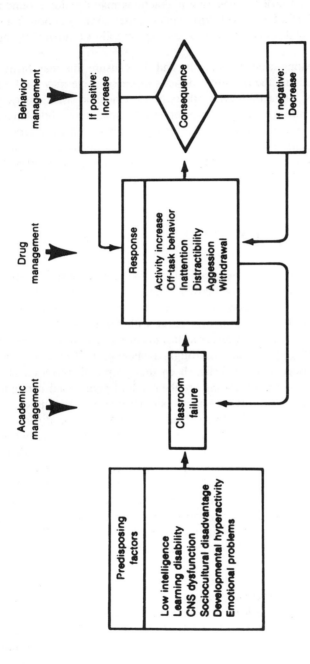

FIGURE 3

Diagram of factors leading to academic failure, the behavioral responses to that failure, and the possible avenues of intervention. From "The Role of Academic Failure in Hyperactive Behavior" by C. Cunningham and R. Barkley, *Journal of Learning Disabilities*, 1978, *11*, 15–21. Reprinted by permission of *Journal of Learning Disabilities* printed by The Professional Press, Inc.

performance not only greatly affect his or her persistence on and attitude toward the task but deleteriously influence the child's reactions and attitudes toward that particular adult. Hence, a series of negative interactions may develop around performance on the deficient achievement skill. This requires some attention from the clinician, over and above that given toward assessing the child's academic strengths and deficits.

In addition to creating academic deficits and the censure this may bring the child from peers and adults, the cognitive deficits discussed here may well affect the child's direct social interactions with others in nonacademic situations (Mash, Note 4). That is, the child with a reading disorder attributable to subtle language difficulties might be expected to use poorer language skills in general interactions with others, leading them to respond differently to him as opposed to a child of normal language skills. I am not aware of any researchers who have examined this issue, though clearly it should receive some emphasis in future studies.

# ETIOLOGY

As with many other childhood psychological disorders, the causes of specific learning disabilities are not precisely known. Many single- and multiple-factor theories of etiology exist. It is outside the purview of this chapter to review them in great detail. Almost all of these theories deal with disorders of reading and spelling, where the vast majority of research has occurred. The reader is referred to Benton and Pearl (1978) for a more thorough consideration of these theories.

One of the most popular theories has been that proposed by Orton (1925, 1937)—that specific disabilities of reading are the result of poor visual perception. After reviewing the research support for this and similar theories, Vellutino (1978) concludes that such problems are unlikely causes of most reading disorders. A subgroup of reading problems, however, might possibly be caused by visual processing problems. Vellutino (1978) and others (Denckla, 1979) believe that the research supports the more likely etiology of linguistic deficiencies as causes of most dyslexia in children. Yet, as Doehring (1978) cautions, this approach erroneously assumes that dyslexia is a unitary, homogeneous disorder. Although disorders of reading may be most frequently caused by language disorders (as yet not fully specified), difficulties in visuospatial and sequential–analytic skills may also underlie other types of dyslexia of lesser frequency (Bannatyne, 1968; Petrauskas & Rourke, 1979; Rugel, 1974a).

A second, and perhaps not unrelated, direction of research on etiology has been on the role of familial–genetic factors. For some time, it has been known that 30–60% of poor readers have at least one or more family members who are also poor readers (Boder, 1973; Ingram et al., 1970; Rutter et al., 1976). Although this may intimate genetic factors at work in some reading problems, the role of family environments that are not conducive to developing reading skills cannot be ruled out. Hallgren (1950) reported a high concordance rate for dyslexia among identical versus fraternal twins, suggesting a genetic etiology, but the research suffered numerous methodological flaws that lead one to question its results (Owen, 1978). Finucci, Guthrie, Childs, Abbey, and Childs (1976) present data showing that 45% of the first-degree relatives of dyslexic children were also disabled readers. They conclude that reading disorders are probably genetically heterogeneous in etiology. A careful review of the genetic literature by Owen (1978) indicates that a multifactorial genetic predisposition is involved in some types of learning disabilities, the expression of which is modulated by environmental experiences and resources. McClearn (1978) further states that this situation is unlikely to become any more discernible until genetic studies are conducted on more homogeneous subgroups of dyslexics.

Other theorists (Ross, 1976) have proposed that disorders of attention underlie most learning disabilities. Black (1974) and Harris (1976) have reviewed the studies in this area and find little support for this hypothesis.

Satz, Taylor, Friel, and Fletcher (1978) have suggested that developmental dyslexia is attributable to a lag in the development of linguistic skills mediated by the left cerebral hemisphere. Data from the extensive follow-up studies by Satz are reported as generally supporting this notion. Kinsbourne (1977; Kinsbourne & Caplan, 1979) similarly hypothesizes a developmental immaturity in the efficiency of higher cortical processes subserving reading as the cause of reading and other learning disorders. The research of Rourke (1978b) also points to immaturity or dysfunction of various neuropsychological processes as causative in learning disabilities. Although promising, much more research at the neuroanatomic and neurophysiologic levels is required before these theories can be more thoroughly tested.

One clearly demonstrated etiology of childhood learning disabilities is acquired focal neurologic insults, such as that produced by stroke, head trauma, tumor, and other neurologic diseases. Large insults to the brain typically produce widespread and relatively severe cognitive and behavioral deficits. However, highly focal lesions in relatively circumscribed regions of the brain often produce learning disorders similar to those seen in the more developmental–idiopathic forms of learning disabilities. A distinction between acquired versus developmental–idiopathic causes of learning disabilities is often helpful from the standpoint of litigation or in providing a greater understanding of the disability. Treatment approaches, however, are often the same despite the etiology.

At present, speculations as to possible environmental or social causes of specific learning disabilities have not mustered much support and are apparently not taken very seriously by experienced investigators in this field (see Benton & Pearl, 1978; Denckla, 1979; Rourke, 1976, 1978b). An obstacle for such theories is explaining how children can manifest highly specific delays in only one or two areas of achievement on the basis of environmental disadvantage or neglectful teaching methods.

# PROGNOSIS

Research on the outcome of children with specific learning disabilities has focused almost exclusively on children with reading disabilities. At this point, however, there is no reason to assume that children with deficits in mathematics or written expression would have a substantially different outcome. A few early and less methodologically rigorous studies appear to have found favorable outcomes for reading disabled children when they reached adulthood as determined by measures of occupational success (Balow & Bloomquist, 1965; Rawson, 1968; Robinson & Smith, 1962). However, more recent studies (Boder, 1973; Satz et al., 1978; Silver & Hagin, 1964, 1966; Trites & Fiedorowicz, 1976) indicate that deficits in reading persist beyond two or more years and often into adulthood, with the child tending to fall further behind his peers in reading level over time (Trites & Fiedorowicz, 1976). Peter and Spreen (1979) have shown that social problems are also likely to persist in these children into adolescence, with those children having lower IQs and those being female having the poorest outcome. There appear to be few, if any, studies that have examined the outcome of children receiving different types of intervention versus no intervention for their learning disabilities.

# EARLY PREDICTORS

A few investigators have begun to examine whether characteristics exist in the preschool years that predict later reading disorders in children. Predictors of other learning disabilities have received little or no scrutiny. The work of Satz et al. (1978) and Rourke (1978a) suggests that children who show poor finger graphesthesia, finger localization, and verbal recitation–discrimination skills are at high risk for developing later disorders of reading. *Finger graphesthesia* is an inability to recognize letters or numbers written on the child's fingertips while he or she is blindfolded. *Finger localization* refers to the ability to detect which finger has been touched by the examiner while one's eyes are closed. These tests are of interest from a neuropsychological standpoint since both are quite sensitive to impairment of the posterior parietal regions of the brain, especially in the left cerebral hemisphere. This location of the brain is known to subserve a critical function in reading in most individuals (Hecaen & Albert, 1978).

A third predictor of reading failure is suggested by Boder (1973), Denckla (1979), and others (Rutter, 1978) to be mild delays in language development. Although not severe enough to suggest aphasia or serious impairments in language in early childhood, language delays of more than a few months may forebode difficulties with reading at school age. Future research needs to be done in this area before efforts at early intervention and prevention can begin.

# GENERAL ASSESSMENT CONSIDERATIONS

The preceding review has indicated that specific learning disabilities do not constitute a homogeneous group of children. Instead, they are more appropriately viewed as a collection of more homogeneous subtypes of reading, spelling, mathematics, and written expression disorders. Nonetheless, it appears that a set of at least four cognitive or neuropsychological skills interact during development and participate in the highly complex activities involved in academic achievement. The relatively unequal development of these skills seems to result in specific learning disabilities. The severity of the discrepancy or the number of these four processes that are relatively delayed in development seem to determine the type(s) and severity of the disorder in achievement skills.

This review also suggests, however, that these initial cognitive–developmental deficits will have some influence on, and will be influenced by, the social context in which they occur and the types of task demands to which the child is exposed. Over time, the transaction between these specific learning disorders and the child's social environment will inevitably alter the nature, extent, and secondary reactions to those disorders. Older LD children may therefore present with more widespread and severe disorders of both learning and adaptive socioemotional behavior relative to a younger child having essentially the same specific learning disability.

The prognosis of specific learning disabilities in terms of recovery to normal levels has not been shown to occur, though more research on outcome is obviously required. The etiology of these disabilities is no doubt multiple. Neuropsychological lags or immaturities in the development of prerequisite skills, familial–genetic factors, and, in some cases, demonstrable acquired neurologic lesions receive the greatest support from the meager research in this area. Certainly, adequate environmental explanations of specific learning disabilities remain to be proposed.

The foregoing review, albeit brief, clearly shows at least four levels of assessment of LD children:

1. *Developmental–cognitive processes.* It seems imperative that the child's pattern of skills in verbal–linguistic, visuospatial–constructional, sequential–analytic, and response planning, implementing, and regulating processes all require some assessment. In addition, assessment of reading, spelling, mathematics, and written expression is required. Analysis of the profile of performances (and not simply their absolute levels) is required, as well as of the qualitative errors made on the measures of achievement.

2. *Community task demands.* Besides determining the profile of cognitive abilities of the child, one must determine the nature of the demands being placed on the child by his school teacher or the community at large. The severity of the learning problem and the urgency for intervention can be judged only relative to the particular levels of productivity and performance accuracy being asked of the child, to the achievement areas designated, and to the situational circumstances.

3. *Social context and interactions.* One must examine the effects of the LD child's cognitive deficits and academic failure on significant others in his or her social settings (parents, teachers, peers, etc.), particularly on their responses to the child.

4. *Transactional effects over time.* Once levels 1 through 3 have been addressed, some determination can be made as to how they have interacted

over time to culminate in the child's current array of cognitive, behavioral, emotional, and social difficulties. In addition, some consideration should be given to how they might continue to interact over time to produce possible future difficulties. Assessment at this level probably requires more clinical expertise and subjective impressions than objective data, as these are likely to be difficult to obtain. Nonetheless, the child's past, present, and future problems are likely to be the result of the transaction among the other three levels over some extended period; hence, some appreciation for the transaction must be gained. A narrow focus on just a single level, such as only on the psychometric profile of the child's cognitive abilities or only on the social interactions or learning history variables of the child, is likely to be of limited value in planning intervention approaches.

## THE NEED FOR A BEHAVIORAL– NEUROPSYCHOLOGICAL APPROACH

It is obvious that a strictly behavioral approach to learning disabilities has not been advanced in this chapter. Such an approach, which focuses primarily on functional relationships between antecedent events and consequent responses in the child's present and past learning, cannot adequately account for the nature of these disorders. Clearly, organismic variables must be considered, especially those pertaining to the anatomy and function of the central nervous system in general and to the cerebral hemispheres in particular. The best approach to their assessment appears to be one that focuses on both the neuropsychological and the behavioral aspects of the disorder.

The utility of this combined approach has been discussed elsewhere (Goldstein, 1979). It need only be said here that such an approach would truly emphasize each component of the *S-O-R-K-C* framework in which current behavioral views are couched (see Chapter 1, this volume). Neuropsychological data provide a necessary understanding of those organismic independent variables affecting the brain, of which behavioral responses are certainly a function. Additionally, they serve, perhaps, to pinpoint more accurately the target behaviors that should become the focus of behavioral interventions.

A closer consideration reveals that these two approaches to studying behavior are not as divergent as one might assume. Behaviorism stresses the environmental stimulus and consequent events that surround a given behavior in order to reveal the variables of which that behavior is a function. Neuropsychology focuses on altered states of the central nervous system as independent variables affecting that behavior. Both are legitimate sciences subject to rigorous methodological requirements. Only their independent variables and sources of data seem somewhat different. Neuropsychologists frequently use psychometric data, whereas behaviorists seek more naturalistic measures. Changes in behavior can result from focal neurologic events, such as a stroke, but these events are clearly affected and altered to some extent by the situational variables and response consequences surrounding their occurrence. Thus, a combined approach is necessary for a complete understanding of the behavior of the neurologically compromised individual.

With regard to learning disorders in children, it has grown increasingly obvious that neuropsychological theories offer highly promising ways of conceptualizing these disorders (Denckla, 1979; Kinsbourne & Caplan, 1979; Rourke, 1980). The great similarity of learning disorders to acquired neurologic disorders of both adults and children (Benton, 1978), the findings of impaired performance by LD children on neuropsychological tests shown to be highly sensitive to brain impairment (Rourke, 1978b), and the association of learning disabilities with familial–hereditary and physical factors (Rutter, 1978) point in the unmistakable direction that neurologic processes of one form or another probably play a role in the etiology of learning disorders. Yet, as noted previously, these cognitive or neuropsychological deficits do not occur in a vacuum; they are molded and shaped by environmental events, culminating in the cognitive, social, and emotional difficulties that are the objects of assessment. Thus, deciding whether the behavior in question is either "organic" or "learned" is academic, since both factors are obviously at work in the child with specific learning disabilities. The question is the degree of influence exerted by both sources of variation, and the answer comes only from a careful assessment of both domains.

### Goals of Behavioral–Neuropsychological Assessment

The major goals of behavioral–neuropsychological assessment are indicated in the following questions:

1. What is the nature and extent of deficits in those cognitive skills that are important to academic achievement? What is the nature of the errors in performance?

2. Can the origin be determined? Although most learning disorders are of a developmental–idiopathic sort, a few will be the result of demonstrable neurologic insults. Of these, most will be static in nature. That is, they occurred at some time in the child's past but are not operating at present. Birth complications, head trauma, strokes, or other acute events in the child's past are examples of static insults, which usually leave specific marks on the child's neuropsychological functions. These are of lesser concern to the clinician than those rarer, but more medically significant, progressive neurologic diseases, such as infections, encephalitis, tumor growth, metabolic-storage diseases, and degenerations of brain tissue. Such events are often fatal or of high morbidity and will often present initially as changes in, or loss of, cognitive skills. Failure by the clinician to recognize the early signs of such rare disorders as they appear in learning might well contribute to increased morbidity. Probably the best indicator of the presence of a progressive disease is regression in already acquired skills. Where language, sensory, or motor skills show behavioral evidence of deterioration, progressive illnesses should be suspected and the child referred immediately for neurologic evaluation.

3. With what particular tasks in the classroom are the cognitive deficits interfering (i.e., mathematics, reading, spelling, etc.)?

4. What is the nature and extent of primary or secondary emotional behaviors that may occur with, or be a reaction to, the learning disability?

5. How is the learning disability and its concomitant behavioral–emotional disorders affecting the child's interactions with and reactions from parents, teachers, and peers? In what setting are these interactional problems more likely to occur?

6. How will the factors at these various levels of analysis interact over time to improve or exacerbate the child's well-being?

7. How can the child's remaining cognitive "strengths" be used in habilitating or coping with the existing problems?

8. What resources exist within the family, school, and community that can be used to assist in item 7?

The manner in which these and other goals of the assessment process can best be addressed is the subject of the remainder of this chapter.

# ASSESSMENT OF LEARNING DISABILITIES

The general methods of evaluating learning disabilities are (1) interviews with parents, teacher(s), and child; (2) psychometric assessment of developmental–cognitive skills; (3) direct observations of the child's classroom academic performance; and (4) direct assessment of the social interactions of the child with his or her parents and teacher(s) in problematic settings.

## Interviews

### Parental Interview

In the parental interview, as in any initial clinical interview, it is necessary to obtain demographic data, information on the current concerns of the family with respect to the child, the history of these concerns, and what the parents have already attempted to do to address them, if anything. Initial concerns are likely to be expressed in such terms as "Billy doesn't seem to read very well" or "Johnny isn't doing as well as he should in school." Where necessary, parents should be queried on the specific academic tasks with which their child has trouble.

It is important to question whether the parents work with the child on homework in the deficient areas. If so, then they should be asked how they teach, direct, or supervise the homework; what the child's reactions are; how they will manage these reactions if they are negative; what the general outcome of the homework interactions is; and how often the problem interactions are likely to occur (see the chapter on hyperactivity for a more thorough discussion of the important mechanisms involved in negative parent–child interactions). Finally, parents should be asked how they generally feel about the outcome of these interactions and where they are likely to lead in the future if intervention is not undertaken. For cases where concomitant problems such as hyperactivity, social skills deficits, self-control problems, depression, and other behavioral disorders are noted, the reader is directed to the appropriate chapters in this volume.

Information on the pregnancy, delivery, and developmental and medical histories should, of course, be obtained. The possible occurrence of seizures in the past or present should also receive brief attention.

The parents should then be questioned about the child's academic history, including when school was first begun, how the child has progressed in each grade, what problems began to develop in each grade and how they were handled, whether and what school evaluations have already occurred, and what plans school personnel have already made for the immediate and future education of the child. It is also important to ask for the parents' opinion on academic achievement and its value to the child (How important is his or her education?), as well as their opinion on the school itself.

The interview should then progress to a consideration of parent and family variables. The parents' educational level, the existence of learning problems in the parents and in other family members, and parental psychiatric, marital, financial, or emotional problems should be determined. Also deserving attention are the progress of the child's siblings in school; whether interactional problems exist among the children, particularly over academic competitiveness; and how the parents manage these interaction problems when they occur.

The impression of the parents should be obtained as to what has caused or contributed to the child's learning disability, what they feel is the likely outcome for the child, and what they expect from the school staff or the examiner in terms of the outcome of any interventions. Questioning such as this may reveal certain erroneous beliefs and expectations that will have to be discussed during the feedback discussion on the results of the evaluation or during the first treatment session.

Finally, some assessment of possible reinforcers to use with the child should be made. With some reflection, parents can often generate ideas as to what activities, privileges, and tangible reinforcers can be used with the child to increase motivation to perform in the classroom.

### Teacher Interview

Prior to or following the parental interview, it is imperative that the examiner discuss with the teacher his or her impressions of the child's learning problems, how they are currently being dealt with, and what the reactions of other classmates are toward this child. Following the evaluation, it is essential that a conference be scheduled with the parents and relevant school staff in order to review the results and their implications for the design of intervention programs for the child. At this time, information should be obtained from the teacher on possible reinforcers available in the classroom, to assist in designing these programs. Often, those clean-up and clerical chores considered menial by the teacher may prove to be quite reinforcing to the child and can therefore be employed in behavioral programs in class.

### Child Interview

During the initial assessment, some time should be devoted to questioning the child as to what subjects he or she has greatest difficulty with, how the child views the causes of this difficulty, and how he or she would like to be helped in school. The child's impression of his or her teachers and parents, the manner in which they work with him or her on problematic skills (and their willingness to do so), and the child's impression of himself or herself in school are also areas deserving attention. Certainly, the assessment of possible reinforcing events or activities is needed for the later designing of intervention programs.

## Psychometric Assessment

In the assessment process, opinions are likely to differ most on the issue of what tests and measures should be employed with the LD child. Each school of thought on the causes and remediation of these disorders has its own favored test batteries, some of which take as long as 6–8 hours to administer over 2 or 3 days (Rourke, 1976). Certainly, testing cannot be dispensed with altogether, as some would suggest (Coles, 1978), for many legal definitions of these disorders rely heavily on test data, if only in the measurement of general intelligence. It is not within the scope of this chapter to evaluate all possible tests that have been or could be used with these children. General areas of cognitive development requiring assessment have already been mentioned, and tests should be selected on the basis of how well they assess these areas. Whatever tests are selected, they should have acceptable standardization data (see *APA Standards for Tests*, 1974), adequate "floors" and "ceilings" for the various ages of interest here (ages 5–18 years), and some data supporting their predictive and concurrent validity (Guion, 1965).

### Tests of Intelligence

Several tests of intelligence exist that have been used with LD children. The most common are the Stanford–Binet Intelligence Scale (1973), the Wechsler Intelligence Scale for Children (1949) and its revised version (Wechsler, 1974), the McCarthy Scale of Children's Abilities (McCarthy, 1972), and the Slosson Intelligence Test (Slosson, 1963). The two most useful among these are the Wechsler Intelligence Scale for Children—Revised (WISC-R) and the McCarthy Scale of Children's Abilities. Both tests are quite psychometrically sophisticated and are the best standardized instruments of children's intelligence (see Sattler, 1974, for an overview of the issues surrounding the use of these and other widely used intellectual tests). The older WISC (Wechsler, 1949) is to be avoided in evaluating children because of its considerably older normative data and reports that it tends to overestimate IQ by an average of 7 to 10 points, and as much as 30 points in some cases, relative to the WISC-R (Barkley & Murphy, 1978).

Of greatest importance to this discussion is that both the WISC-R and McCarthy tests yield data on most or all of the cognitive–developmental skills subserving the acquisition of more complex achievement skills. Using Bannatyne's (1968, 1971) and Rugel's (1974a, 1974b) approach to factor sorting on the WISC-R yields scores for verbal–linguistic skills, visuospatial–construction skills, and sequential–analytic skills. At the very least, the verbal and performance scale IQs on this test should be examined for possible hypotheses as to the cognitive deficits contributing to the learning disability. It has been shown that children, especially older children, who show discrepancies greater than 10–15 points on the WISC are likely to have different performance profiles and deficits on the Wide-Range Achievement Test (WRAT), depending on which scale IQ is higher or lower (Rourke & Telegdy, 1971; Rourke, Young, & Flewelling, 1971). Although the significance that should be attributed to this verbal-performance discrepancy is in doubt (Black, 1974; Coles, 1978; Rourke, Dietrich, & Young, 1973), large discrepancies can often generate hypotheses on the possible nature of the type of learning disability experienced by the child when coupled with results of the achievement tests.

One subtest pattern that appears to occur with unusual frequency in children with reading disorders is the ACID pattern. This refers to especially low performances by a child on the arithmetic, coding, information, and digit-span subtests of the WISC-R. Ackerman, Peters, and Dykman (1971) believe that these subtests evaluate the sequential analysis of symbolic information, suggesting that problems in this "skill" underlie the learning disability. Rourke (1978a) provides evidence for its relatively consistent appearance in the test profiles of LD children but is unable to explain adequately its significance to the disorders. At present, the utility of this pattern for prescribing particular interventions has yet to be demonstrated (Coles, 1978).

Like the WISC-R, the McCarthy scales yield not only a general IQ score but various subscale scores for different cognitive–perceptual–motor skills. Scaled scores for memory, motor, perceptual organization, verbal, and numerical reasoning abilities are provided, which can serve to generate hypotheses about the nature of the child's learning disability that are worthy of closer scrutiny.

Both tests show relatively high correlations with measures of reading, spelling, and mathematics, depending on the subscales examined and the nature of the achievement tests. The McCarthy test is more appropriate for children aged 5–8 years (or younger), whereas the WISC-R should not be used with children younger than 6½–7 years because of relatively insensitive "floors" and "ceilings" on the subtests. I prefer the WISC-R for children older than 8 years because of the wealth of data it yields, the greater amount of research that has been conducted with it, and its higher upper age limits (16 years and 11 months) compared to the McCarthy test. This permits more consistent test–retest data to be collected during the repeated evaluations likely to occur over the academic career of the child.

TABLE 2
Achievement Tests Commonly Used with Learning-Disabled Children

| Test | Publisher |
| --- | --- |
| Classroom Reading Inventory | William C. Brown |
| Doren Diagnostic Reading Test | American Guidance Services |
| Durrell Analysis of Reading Difficulty | Jovanovich |
| Follett Individual Reading Test | Follett |
| Gates–McKillop Reading Diagnostic Tests | Teachers College Press |
| Gilmore Oral Reading Test | Harcourt Brace Jovanovich |
| Gray Oral Reading Test | Bobbs-Merrill |
| Kay Math Diagnostic Arithmetic Test | American Guidance Services |
| Peabody Individual Achievement Test | American Guidance Services |
| Sequential Tests of Educational Progress | Educational Testing Services |
| Spache Diagnostic Reading Scales | California Test Bureau |
| Wide-Range Achievement Test | Guidance Associates |
| Woodcock Reading Mastery Tests | American Guidance Services |

## Achievement Tests

The most commonly used achievement tests are listed in Table 2. I am most comfortable using the Peabody Individual Achievement Tests (PIAT), the WRAT, and the Gray Oral Reading Test (Gray, 1967). Since both the PIAT and the WRAT contain reading recognition (word pronunciation) subtests that are highly similar, only one of the two should be given for cost efficiency of testing.

It is recommended that all three tests be given because they assess somewhat different types of academic achievement, with comparisons among them likely to generate valuable hypotheses as to target problems and planning for intervention. The PIAT yields both age- and grade-level equivalents and percentiles for children at any grade level from kindergarten through grade 12. Subtests assess mathematics, reading recognition (single-word pronunciation), reading comprehension (from silent reading of sentences), spelling (recognition), and general information (factual knowledge). Except for those on reading recognition and general information, the subtests provide multiple-choice answers. Hence, verbal explanation of the answer is not required, nor is a written response—the child just points to the answer.

The WRAT (Jastak, Bijou, & Jastak, 1978) also evaluates children across all grade levels. It yields scores (grade levels or percentiles) in arithmetic, spelling, and reading recognition. As noted previously, this last subtest is not given if the full PIAT is administered. Because the mathematics and spelling subtests require timed written responses, the results can be compared with the mathematics and spelling scores of the PIAT, which are untimed and involve no writing. Thus, children doing substantially more poorly on the WRAT subtests as compared to these PIAT subtests would appear to have greater difficulties with written expression than with skill knowledge. Furthermore, the written spelling sample from the WRAT is essential in suggesting possible subtypes of reading problems.

Neither the PIAT nor the WRAT assesses reading beyond a single-word level.

Hence, some test of oral reading, such as the Gray Oral Reading Test, is imperative since it assesses oral reading of paragraphs as well as comprehension. To illustrate, a child with a visuospatial, or dyseidetic (Boder, 1973), type of reading problem is likely to perform at near-normal levels on the PIAT reading subtests (both recognition and comprehension), because the child has near-normal phonetic–analytic (word-attack) skills. However, where more protracted reading is involved, especially under timed circumstances, as on the Gray test, problems in reading will emerge. These are likely to be word-by-word, slow, and laborious reading problems, as well as multiple partial mispronunciations. The Gray test permits some breakdown into types of oral reading errors, which is critical to understanding the nature of the reading problem. The types of errors are: requires aid, gross and partial mispronunciations, omissions, insertions, substitutions, repetitions, and inversions. Scores on paragraph comprehension are also yielded by this test.

### Tests of Tactile Perception

As noted previously, two tests of tactile sensory perception have shown consistent reliability in predicting reading problems in children. These are the finger localization and fingertip symbol writing tests from the Halstead–Reitan Neuropsychological Test Battery (see Reitan & Davison, 1974). I am likely to use these tests more often with children 8 years of age or younger, since the direct assessment of reading at this age may reveal only minor problems. In such cases, where significant deficits (greater than 1.5 $SD$ from normal) are seen on the two tests, I am likely to bring this child to the attention of the school as being at high risk for later reading failure. In evaluating children 9 years of age or older, these tests are of limited utility, since many, though not all, reading deficits are fairly apparent by this age.

### Other Clinical Measures

Besides the preceding measures, the child's handwriting should be assessed further by having the child write his or her name as many times as possible in 1 or 2 minutes, as well as writing sentences to dictation. The latter test is given by selecting one sentence above and one below the child's failure level on the WRAT spelling test and dictating each to the child. Both of these nonstandardized tests assess handwriting skill, as well as providing another sample of written spelling ability.

In addition to standardized tests, the examiner should not hesitate to use more nonstandardized tests or to use tests in nonstandardized ways to pursue hypotheses as to the nature of the child's problems. If an apraxia is suspected as a problem in written expression, then simply asking the child to *demonstrate* the use of commonly encountered items in the absence of the item can be helpful in revealing such problems.

Various neuropsychological tests and tests of mental skills exist that have been used with LD children. Rourke (1976) advocates the use of the Halstead–Reitan

Neuropsychological Test Battery (Reitan & Davison, 1974) in evaluating learning disabilities. The Luria Neuropsychological Test Battery (Golden, Hammeke, & Purisch, 1978) is also being standardized for use with children. Although these and other tests may be helpful where questions of neurologic impairment, recovery of skills following impairment, or degree of deficits in cases of litigation are raised, they are not likely to be cost effective in assessment and treatment planning with most LD children. Not only are they extremely time consuming to administer, but they tend to overlap considerably with intellectual tests, such as the WISC-R or the McCarthy, in most of the skills they assess. Furthermore, they are not likely to yield information that is any more useful to treatment planning than the recommended tests of intelligence and achievement already discussed (see Feuerstein, Ward, & LeBaron, 1979, and Baron, 1978, for further discussion on using these tests with children).

## General Testing Considerations

The examiner is interested not only in the child's scores on the aforementioned tests but also in the quality of his or her performance and the nature of the errors made. In addition, note should be taken of the child's awareness of and reaction to errors, general demeanor during testing, and sustained performance or concentration to the tasks as they increase in level of difficulty. LD children are more likely than normal children to express aversion to the task, ask for greater feedback on their performances, and give up more readily as difficult item levels are achieved. These should serve to raise hypotheses for further assessment during direct classroom observation.

In agreeing with Rourke (1976), I believe that the examiner should make every effort to motivate the child to perform at his or her best possible level. Hence, great amounts of encouragement, praise (not contingent on correctness of performance), and generally positive feedback are provided. The goal of testing is not so much to achieve a representative sample of in-class performance but to see exactly what the child can do when motivation is heightened. It is assumed that this approach yields information about cognitive deficits less confounded by motivational deficiencies than is to be found in the classroom observations to be made later.

It can be useful to vary the presentation of test items from the manner in which they were standardized once the standardized version has been given and the score obtained. For instance, periodically, a child with a dysphonetic form of poor reading is likely to achieve a score on reading comprehension that is as poor as, if not poorer than, the low score on reading recognition on the PIAT. Is the child's understanding of word meanings as poor as his or her word pronunciation skills in this case? This question cannot be answered from the test scores because the child's poor silent reading may preclude the correct identification and hence the meaning of a word. When in doubt about this, I return to the PIAT at the end of testing and repeat the reading comprehension subtest. However, at this point, I read the sentences to the child and have the child point to the picture that best describes what was read. In most cases, the child's comprehension score will improve dramatically, suggesting that the problem was one of word pronunciation, not comprehension or meaning. In the few cases where the score fails to improve, a problem in sentence comprehension has been demonstrated in addition to the problem in word pronunciation.

In summary, the purpose of testing is to raise hypotheses about academic performance problems in the LD child rather than to provide definitive conclusions about the problem. Only when the test data, testing observations of behavior, and analysis of error patterns are combined with interview and classroom observation data can one have any sense of confidence in pinpointing the nature of the child's problems and how best to approach their habilitation or retraining.

## Direct Behavioral Observations

Where time and resources permit, it is essential that observations be made of the child's actual classroom performance, interactions with the teacher and peers in the classroom, and interactions with the parent who is most likely to supervise his or her homework accomplishment. Where such observations are not possible, greater attention should be paid to these areas, and to others described subsequently, during the parent and teacher interviews.

### Classroom Observations

Of the three aforementioned areas of observation, this area is most important. The examiner should plan to visit the school classroom and observe the child during structured group and individual academic performance (small group reading, individual desk work, attention to teacher lectures, etc.).

At this point, there may be some question as to what types of behavior are most important for observation and recording and, of course, for later treatment planning. At first glance, it might seem meaningful to assess classroom behaviors related to sitting still, paying attention, and not disrupting others, since these are prerequisites to satisfactory task accomplishment. If such assessment is desired, then those behavioral coding systems described in Chapter 3 of this volume would be of some assistance in evaluating on-task behaviors. Recent research (see Ayllon & Rosenbaum, 1977; Cunningham & Barkley, 1978), however, suggests that behavioral programs designed to increase on-task behaviors do not necessarily result in increases in classroom productivity or in accuracy in the academic work assigned to the child.

In agreeing with Ayllon and Rosenbaum (1977), I believe that more appropriate targets for assessment and treatment are academic productivity (amount of work accomplished) and accuracy (number of problems completed correctly). Several studies (Ayllon, Layman, & Kandel, 1975; Ayllon & Roberts, 1974; Cunningham & Barkley, 1978) suggest that when the consequences surrounding the occurrence of these behaviors are manipulated, drastic improvements in their frequency can occur. In addition, decreases in off-task and disruptive behavior are likely to be seen without any direct intervention for these behaviors. Thus, when making class-room observations, it is important to record the child's rate of productivity and accuracy in the deficient subject areas. These rates can be expressed as absolute numbers or as percentages of problems assigned by the teacher.

The examiner should also ask the teacher to have available during the school visit samples of the child's previous classwork, as well as any significant obser-vations he or she may have made on the child. Although it is desirable to have the teacher collect records of the child's academic accuracy and productivity over several days, it may not be feasible given the large number of other responsibilities the teacher may have.

If possible, and without violating the confidentiality of other students, the examiner should ask to see the classwork of one or two average students in the class for comparison with the samples for the LD child. Such comparison serves to address the issue of community standards and task expectations raised previously in this chapter. In addition, the child's level of academic accuracy and productivity relative to his peers can be assessed.

Some attention should also be given to the antecedent and consequent events surrounding the child's poor academic performance in the class. How does the teacher provide corrective feedback to the child? What do other children say or do to the child during class performance? Is the child likely to seek out help for difficult problems, and if so, how? How much time is provided the child for doing classwork? These stimulus and consequent parameters are likely to help explain the interaction between the child's deficits and the reactions of people in the classroom environment to those deficits, which help account for the present state of the child's problems.

Although more than one classroom visit would seem desirable, it may not prove feasible from a cost-efficient standpoint. Therefore, such a visit should be critically considered as to its incremental utility in decision making, based on what data have already been collected. In any case, the examiner should query the teacher on what resources are available to the child in that class, in the school, and in the school district.

## Parent–Child Interactions

Although likely to be inconvenient or inefficient from a cost standpoint, obser-vations of the parent–child interactions surrounding homework accomplishment may prove helpful where convenient. If not convenient, the parent should be encouraged to keep a diary of these interactions when they are problematic, as a source of both baseline data and data on treatment outcome. Observational systems for capturing parent–child interactions were discussed in Chapter 3 of this volume and are likely to be helpful if used in these circumstances as well.

If home observations are impossible, clinic analogue observations may be arranged should one-way viewing facilities be available. If so, it will be useful to ask the parent to bring the child's most recent homework assignment to the clinic for use in these observations on the day of evaluation; otherwise, material for academic tasks can be provided by the examiner. In either case, the parent and child should be placed in a room with writing supplies and observed as they interact in working on the academic problems. Although normative data on such interactions are not available, this does not preclude the observations' suggesting possible problem areas in the interactions. The parent should be queried afterward as to how representative the analogue observations were of home interactions during homework accomplishment.

## COST EFFICIENCY OF ASSESSMENT

One important issue not often considered by clinicians is the cost efficiency of their methods of assessment. Thus, one is likely to see decisions about LD children being based upon assessment procedures that range from brief, 15-minute office physical examinations to 10-hour test batteries of broad-spectrum neuropsychological tests. Between these inefficient extremes lies an approach in which the clinician evaluates the time and expense involved in a particular assessment procedure in relation to the utility of the information likely to be derived from the test or measure.

The goal of assessment is not to evaluate as many cognitive processes or behaviors as possible but only those that are relevant to the particular learning disability involved. On the other hand, the goal clearly involves more than simply saying whether or not a child is LD. There is no simple and general rule that solves this dilemma. What should be common to all cases, however, is a critical appraisal as to which methods are essential to addressing the issues raised by a case and which are gratuitous. The range of time required for making initial treatment decisions will likely fall between 3 and 5 hours. These decisions can then be modified and refined during the ongoing process of assessment that occurs with any particular mode of intervention.

## CASE ILLUSTRATION

Space limitations do not permit illustration of the variety of learning disabilities that one is likely to encounter in clinical practice. The following case, however, is likely to illustrate the approach recommended in this chapter for LD children.

Cory is a right-handed Caucasian boy, 9 years and 10 months old, who was referred by a neurologist for evaluation of a possible learning disability. He is in a third-grade class, having repeated the first grade because of difficulties in academic performance. Developmental history was significant for a long labor (about 30 hours) during his birth and a difficult forceps delivery. Walking and speech milestones were only slightly late—14 and 24 months, respectively, at time of onset. The boy received speech therapy for 6 months at age 3½ years. At the time of referral, he was described as unhappy and as showing a developing disinterest in academic work. Other than his shyness and apparent depression, he was not considered to be a serious conduct problem at home or at school. His parents did note, however, that they had had significant problems in getting their boy to do his homework in the evening. Records kept by the family describing this time at home indicated that the parents had spent as long as 2–3 hours trying to get this boy to complete 20–30 minutes of homework. At the end of this time, Cory was said to be generally withdrawn and depressed, while his parents were quite angry at the amount of time they had to spend supervising his performance. A review of family history indicated that both parents had siblings who had had significant learning problems in school as children.

Table 3 lists the tests that Cory was given and their respective scores and percentiles. As this table shows, Cory was of normal intelligence, but he had relatively greater problems on the verbal subtests of the WISC-R, especially the subtest of general information. Relative to his scores on the other performance subtests, his score on the coding subtest appears somewhat low. Many of the verbal items on the WISC-R had to be repeated to Cory, because he frequently appeared not to remember them. Analysis of the achievement test scores indicates greatest difficulty in word pronunciation (reading recognition) and in written spelling. Comparing the two spelling subtests, it is apparent that Cory recognizes more correctly

TABLE 3
Test Results for a 9-Year-Old Learning-Disabled Boy

| WISC-R | | PIAT | | |
|---|---|---|---|---|
| Full-scale IQ | = 96 | Subtest | Grade | %ᵃ |
| Verbal IQ | = 86 | Arithmetic | 3.4 | 23 |
| Performance IQ | = 109 | Reading recognition | 1.8 | 3 |
| Subtest | Scaled score | Reading comprehension | 2.7 | 10 |
| General Information | 4 | Spelling | 3.2 | 16 |
| Similarities | 10 | General information | 2.2 | 11 |
| Arithmetic | 7 | | | |
| Vocabulary | 9 | WRAT | | |
| Comprehension | 9 | | | |
| Digit span | 10 | Subtest | Grade | %ᵃ |
| Picture completion | 9 | Arithmetic | 3.1 | 13 |
| Picture arrangement | 16 | Spelling | 1.9 | 1 |
| Block design | 11 | | | |
| Object assembly | 14 | | | |
| Coding | 7 | | | |

ᵃIndicates percentile for age level.

spelled words than he is able to write from memory. He also appears to have somewhat greater difficulty with written versus oral arithmetic. Performance on the Gray Oral Reading Test was at a 1.0 grade level and was characterized by numerous gross and partial mispronunciations and substitutions of incorrect words for those in the paragraphs. Wild guessing at words was common. Of 15 words in one paragraph at the second-grade level, Cory pronounced only 3 correctly on this first attempt at sounding them out.

A sample of Cory's handwriting and spelling is shown in Figure 4. It can be seen that this boy's spelling errors are not phonetically correct if one attempts to pronounce them. This was also evident on the WRAT written spelling test.

These test results suggest that Cory has a reading disability characterized by dysphonetic reading and spelling errors. The history of mild developmental language delay and the lower verbal IQ (as compared to performance IQ) are consistent with this hypothesis. Oral reading is marked by significant gross mispronunciations. A mild problem with written expression exists, which is largely attributable to the dysphonetic spelling errors.

Besides these cognitive problems, home and classroom reports and classroom observations reveal problems with depression and social withdrawal, as well as protracted negative interactions with the parents and teachers regarding homework and individual desk work in class, respectively. Records kept on classroom productivity and accuracy indicate that less than 40% of the assignments in reading workbooks and spelling tests were accomplished and that less than half of these

FIGURE 4
Spelling errors made during dictation by a 9-year-old learning-disabled boy.

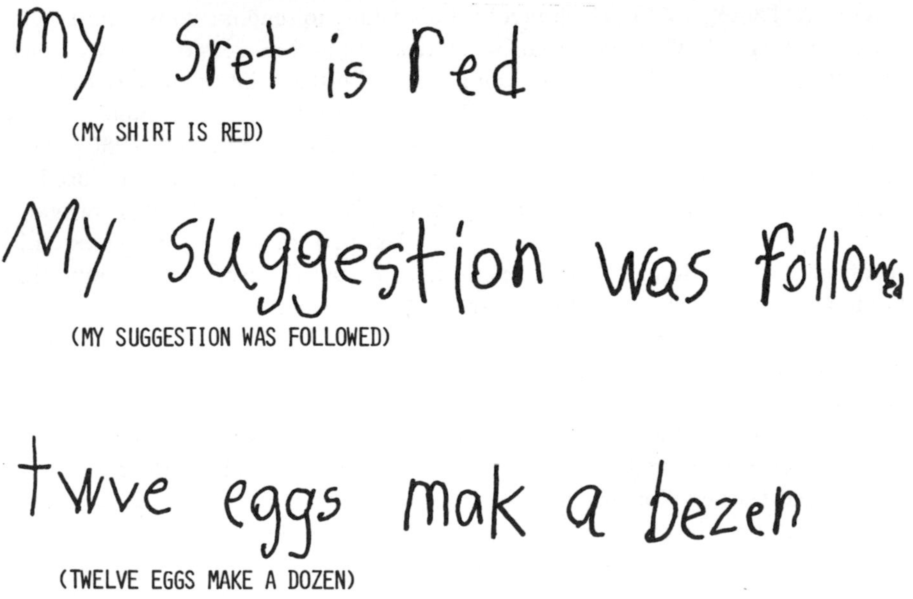

my Sret is red
(MY SHIRT IS RED)

My suggestion was follows
(MY SUGGESTION WAS FOLLOWED)

twve eggs mak a bezen
(TWELVE EGGS MAKE A DOZEN)

responses were accurate (20% of the assignments). Performance on written mathematics assignments were only somewhat better, with an average of 60–70% of the problems being attempted and 40–50% of those attempted being accurate.

Treatment recommendations for this boy were as follows:

1. Cory was placed in a learning disabilities resource program at school, where he attends regular third-grade classes but goes to a resource tutor for reading and spelling instruction.

2. The resource tutor was requested to stress whole-word-attack skills (sight-word recognition) in initially working with the dysphonetic reading problems (Boder, 1973). Flash cards were used to train the boy in using his better visual memory for the "gestalt" of words and their complete sounds instead of phonetic word analysis skills.

3. As sight-word vocabulary improved, the tutor was asked to begin to train Cory in phonetic reading skills (Boder, 1973) as direct habilitation of his poor word-attack skills.

4. The parents received four sessions of behavior management training designed to lessen their directiveness during homework interactions, to have them rely on positive attention and privileges as ways of motivating better homework performance, and to have them provide positive and negative consequences contingent on the boy's productivity and accuracy in completing his homework within 30 minutes. A timer was set for 15 minutes, during which half of the homework had to be completed. The timer was then reset for a second 15 minutes, at which point all homework was to be completed.

5. Reductions were also made by school staff in the level of difficulty in reading and spelling assignments in class and homework.

6. Cory was placed on a home-based token system (see Barkley, Hastings, Tousel, & Tousel, 1976), which involved his taking to school a daily report card, shown in Figure 5. Cory was rated by his teachers in five areas of behavior each day. When he returned home, the ratings were translated into points as follows: 1 rating = +25 points; 2 rating = +10 points; 3 rating = −10 points; and 4 rating = −25 points. Losing the card at school resulted in a fine of −250 points, and missing a teacher's rating was −50 points. Points were then to be used to purchase extra privileges at home. This system is advantageous in that it (1) provides daily feedback to the parents on the child's class performance, (2) provides daily feedback to the child on his or her performance, and (3) uses highly reinforcing home activities to motivate better classroom performance.

7. During a school conference, the teacher was instructed in methods of in-class behavior management designed to increase accuracy and productivity on academic assignments (Ayllon & Rosenbaum, 1977).

Within one month after treatment began, there were noticeable improvements in Cory's classroom productivity and accuracy, as well as in his interactions with parents and teachers. The parents also reported their boy to be happier, less withdrawn, and more involved with his siblings and peers. Psychometric testing was to be repeated during a six-month follow-up.

| SCHOOL PERFORMANCE CARD for (student's name) | | | | | |
|---|---|---|---|---|---|
| WEEK                          DAY····· | MON | TUES | WED | THURS | FRI |
| TEACHER'S INITIALS | | | | | |
| ATTENTIVE in CLASS | | | | | |
| COMPLETED IN-CLASS WORK | | | | | |
| COMPLETED HOMEWORK | | | | | |
| PARTICIPATED IN CLASS | | | | | |
| RELATED WELL TO TEACHER | | | | | |
| RELATED WELL TO STUDENTS | | | | | |

1 = ALWAYS          2 = MOST of           3 = SOME of           4 = HARDLY EVER
                                    the TIME              the TIME
                (Please list homework on other side)

FIGURE 5
Daily school evaluation card.

# TREATMENT CONSIDERATIONS

It is not within the purview of this chapter to thoroughly review treatment approaches for learning disabilities. Reviews and more detailed suggestions can be found elsewhere (Boder, 1973; Johnson, 1978; Kinsbourne & Caplan, 1979; Rourke, 1976). Treatment approaches stressing dietary changes, oculomotor training, balance training, and reinforcement for on-task behaviors alone are not felt to be useful (Ayllon & Rosenbaum, 1977; Cunningham & Barkley, 1978; Kinsbourne & Caplan, 1979; Millichap, 1977). However, little research currently exists to suggest which of the remaining therapies are of any long-term benefit to the child. In general, the following treatment steps seem to be desirable, at least on an intuitive basis:

1. *Providing information.* This step involves educating the parents and teachers about the nature of the child's learning problems and the possibility that they may persist as handicapping conditions throughout his or her academic career. At this point, the best approach to take seems to be one of training parents and children to cope with the disability rather than hoping for an outright cure. If, as most investigators believe, the disorder has a neurologic basis, then this will set limits on habilitation. As is the case for the neuropsychologically impaired person, however, habilitation includes both retraining through use of the child's cognitive

strengths and a frontal assault on the deficient areas themselves (Rourke, 1976). This attitude of coping rather than curing appears to be essential for realistic planning.

2. *Cognitive retraining.* As noted previously, this step involves special educational tutoring incorporating the relative strengths seen in the child's test performances. For instance, the dysphonetic reader is trained to use visual memorization of word gestalts and their complete sounds, whereas the poor reader with intact phonetic analysis is further trained in this skill to compensate for poor sight-word recognition (Boder, 1973; Rourke, 1976). At present, however, such approaches have not been empirically tested to determine their efficacy.

3. *Cognitive habilitation.* Once the child strengthens his or her skill using step 2, then a direct attack on the deficient area can begin. For example, phonetic analysis is emphasized at this stage for the dysphonetic reader, whereas sight-word recognition is stressed for the dyseidetic or poor visuospatial reader. Again, this step in treatment is intuitive and awaits empirical testing and support.

4. *Decreasing standards for success.* This step can be accomplished by lowering the expectations of the adults in authority as to what performances by the child are deserving of reinforcement. Rather than relying on age-appropriate levels of performance, reinforcement is instead made contingent on performance at the developmental level indicated by the achievement tests. Thus, the child works at his or her own level rather than at that expected for the child's age group. This can also be accomplished by removing the child from a regular class and placing him or her in a self-contained learning disabilities class where peer competition is diminished and additional teacher assistance can be provided. This should only be considered, however, for the severely disabled child.

5. *Increasing motivation.* This step is accomplished by providing the child with more frequent positive feedback and reinforcement for increased accuracy and productivity on class assignments and homework. This should also serve to compensate for the prior experiences of academic failure and to increase interest in the deficient area.

6. *Modifying adult–child interactions.* Using programs similar to those outlined in Chapter 3 of this volume, the training of parents and teachers should focus on reducing commands, punishment, and negative interactions while increasing encouragement and positive attention. This step is specifically directed toward school work performance both at home with the parents and in class with the teacher. Both parents and teachers are encouraged to place appropriate formal time limits on task accomplishment, to provide frequent feedback to the child on his or her accuracy in solving problems, and to utilize rewards and privileges immediately on task completion (see Houten, Hill, & Parsons, 1975; Stromer, 1975).

7. *Assessing responsiveness to treatment.* The direct behavioral measures of classroom accuracy and productivity, homework accomplishment, and parent–child interactions can be obtained daily, as necessary, as ways of monitoring treatment outcome. Changes in the behavioral educational programs can then be made where indicated.

8. *Providing periodic reevaluation.* At least once per year, or earlier when

necessary, the child should be reevaluated on the psychometric tests and behavioral measures to assess response to treatment, developmental gains, and residual learning and behavior problems. Based upon the results, ongoing interventions are modified or booster sessions provided to the parents, teacher, or child as needed. As the child enters high school, the results can be used for vocational/occupational counseling and training to capitalize on the child's strongest skills and to prepare him or her for entry in the job market or for college, should it prove appropriate.

# SUMMARY

At this time, specific learning disabilities in academic performance must be viewed as a heterogeneous group of differing disorders of reading, writing, spelling, and mathematics. Some homogeneous subgroups are being identified on the basis of difficulties in linguistic, visuospatial, or sequential–analytic skills or in planning and execution of responses to linguistic–numeric stimuli. Disequilibrium in the development of these skills seems to account for the emergence of problems related to accomplishing complex academic achievement skills. These developmental–cognitive deficits are modified by the antecedent and consequent events surrounding their occurrence, which may lead to further declines in performance as well as to reactive conduct problems over time.

A combined behavioral–neuropsychological approach to LD children stresses four levels of assessment: developmental–cognitive, community standards and task expectations, social interactions, and transactions among the first three levels over time. Specific assessment methods include interviewing, psychometric assessment, and direct behavioral observations of both academic performance and social interactions surrounding the performance. Repeated assessment permits a greater understanding of the transaction between cognitive deficits and environmental influences. Suggested treatment approaches emphasize coping with these developmental academic handicapping conditions through (1) educating adults as to the problem and its nature, (2) cognitive retraining, (3) cognitive habilitation, (4) reduced performance standards, (5) increased reinforcement and positive feedback, (6) alteration of adult–child interactions, (7) monitoring treatment, and (8) periodic reevaluation and treatment.

## Acknowledgment

Sincere appreciation is expressed to Eric Mash and Thomas Hammeke for their review of an earlier version of this chapter.

## Reference Notes

1. Smith, M. M. *Patterns of intellectual functioning in E. H. children.* Unpublished doctoral dissertation, Claremont College, Claremont, Calif., 1970.

2. Smith, M. M. *Patterns of intellectual functioning in educationally handicapped children*. Proceedings of the Fourth Annual Conference on the Educationally Handicapped, University of Redlands, Redlands, Calif., 1970.
3. Greca, A. M., & Mesibov, G. B. *Social intervention with learning disabled children*. Paper presented at the meeting of the American Psychological Association, New York, September 1979.
4. Mash, E. Personal communication, October 19, 1979.

# References

Ackerman, P., Peters, J. E., & Dykman, R. A. Children with specific learning disabilities: WISC profiles. *Journal of Learning Disabilities*, 1971, *4*, 150–166.

Ayllon, T., Layman, D., & Kandel, H. J. A behavioral–educational alternative to drug control of hyperactive children. *Journal of Applied Behavior Analysis*, 1975, *8*, 137–146.

Ayllon, T., & Roberts, M. D. Eliminating discipline problems by strengthening academic performance. *Journal of Applied Behavior Analysis*, 1974, *7*, 71–76.

Ayllon, T., & Rosenbaum, M. S. The behavioral treatment of disruption and hyperactivity in school settings. In B. Lahey & A. Kazdin (Eds.), *Advances in clinical child psychology* (Vol. 1). New York: Plenum, 1977.

*APA standards for educational and psychological tests*. Washington, D.C.: American Psychological Association, 1974.

Applebee, A. N. Research in reading retardation: Two critical problems. *Journal of Child Psychology and Psychiatry*, 1971, *12*, 91–113.

Balow, B., & Bloomquist, M. Young adults ten to fifteen years after severe reading disability. *Elementary School Journal*, 1965, *66*, 44–48.

Bannatyne, A. Diagnosing learning disabilities and writing remedial prescriptions. *Journal of Learning Disabilities*, 1968, *1*, 28–35.

Bannatyne, A. *Language, reading and learning disabilities*. Springfield, Ill.: Charles C. Thomas, 1971.

Barkley, R. A., Hastings, J. E., Tousel, R. E., & Tousel, S. E. Evaluation of a token system for juvenile delinquents in a residential setting. *Journal of Behavior Therapy and Experimental Psychiatry*, 1976, *7*, 227–230.

Barkley, R. A., & Murphy, J. V. Pseudodeterioration of intelligence in children. *Annals of Neurology*, 1978, *4*, 388.

Bell, R. Q., & Harper, L. V. *Child effects on adults*. New York: Wiley, 1977.

Benton, A. Some conclusions about dyslexia. In A. Benton & D. Pearl (Eds.), *Dyslexia: An appraisal of current knowledge*. New York: Oxford University Press, 1978.

Benton, A., & Pearl, D. (Eds.). *Dyslexia: An appraisal of current knowledge*. New York: Oxford University Press, 1978.

Black, F. W. Neurological dysfunction and reading disorders. *Journal of Learning Disabilities*, 1973, *6*, 313–316.

Black, F. W. WISC verbal–performance discrepancies as indicators of neurological dysfunction in pediatric patients. *Journal of Clinical Psychology*, 1974, *30*, 165–167.

Boder, E. Developmental dyslexia: A diagnostic approach based on three atypical reading–spelling patterns. *Developmental Medicine and Child Neurology*, 1973, *15*, 63–687.

Brown, B. S. Foreword. In A. Benton & D. Pearl (Eds.), *Dyslexia: An appraisal of current knowledge*. New York: Oxford University Press, 1978.

Bryan, T. Peer popularity of learning disabled children. *Journal of Learning Disabilities*, 1974, *7*, 621–626.

Bryan, T. Peer popularity of learning disabled children: A replication. *Journal of Learning Disabilities*, 1976, *9*, 49–53.

Cohen, R. L., & Netley, C. Cognitive deficits, learning disabilities, and WISC verbal–performance consistency. *Developmental Psychology*, 1978, *14*, 624–634.

Coles, G. S. The learning disabilities test battery: Empirical and social issues. *Harvard Educational*

*Review*, 1978, *48*, 313–340.

Cruickshank, W. M. *The brain-injured child in home, school, and community*. Syracuse, N.Y.: Syracuse University Press, 1967.

Cunningham, C. E., & Barkley, R. A. The role of academic failure in hyperactive behavior. *Journal of Learning Disabilities*, 1978, *11*, 15–21.

Denckla, M. B. Childhood learning disabilities. In K. M. Heilman & E. Valenstein (Eds.), *Clinical neuropsychology*. New York: Oxford University Press, 1979.

Doehring, D. G. The tangled web of behavioral research on developmental dyslexia. In A. Benton & D. Pearl (Eds.), *Dyslexia: An appraisal of current knowledge*. New York: Oxford University Press, 1978.

Doehring, D. G., Hoshko, I. M., & Bryans, B. N. Statistical classification of children with reading problems. *Journal of Clinical Neuropsychology*, 1979, *1*, 5–16.

Douglas, V. I., & Peters, K. G. Toward a clearer definition of the attentional deficit of hyperactive children. In G. A. Hale & M. Lewis (Eds.), *Attention and the development of cognitive skills*. New York: Plenum, 1979.

Dunn, L. M., & Markwardt, F. C. *Peabody individual achievement test*. Minneapolis: American Guidance Service, 1970.

Dykman, R. A., Peters, J. E., & Ackerman, P. T. Experimental approaches to the study of minimal brain dysfunction: A follow-up study. *Annals of the New York Academy of Science*, 1973, *205*, 93–108.

Eaves, L. C., & Crichton, J. U. A five year follow-up of children with minimal brain dysfunction. *Academic Therapy*, 1974–1975, *10*, 173–180.

Erickson, M. T. Reading disability in relation to performance on neurological tests for minimal brain dysfunction. *Developmental Medicine and Child Neurology*, 1977, *19*, 768–775.

Farnham-Diggory, S. *Learning disabilities*. Cambridge, Mass.: Harvard University Press, 1978.

*Federal Register, 41* (252), December 30, 1976, pp. 56966–56998.

*Federal Register, 42* (163). August 23. 1977.

Feuerstein, M., Ward, M. M., & LeBaron, S. W. M. Neuropsychological and neurophysiological assessment of children with learning and behavior problems: A critical appraisal. In B. Lahey & A. Kazdin (Eds.), *Advances in clinical child psychology* (Vol. 2). New York: Plenum, 1979.

Finucci, J. M., Guthrie, J. T., Childs, A. L., Abbey, H., & Childs, B. The genetics of specific reading disability. *Annals of Human Genetics*, 1976, *40*, 1–23.

Golden, C. J., Hammeke, T. A., & Purisch, A. D. Diagnostic validity of a standardized neuropsychological battery derived from Luria's neuropsychological tests. *Journal of Consulting and Clinical Psychology*, 1978, *46*, 1258–1265.

Goldstein, G. Methodological and theoretical issues in neuropsychological assessment. *Journal of Behavioral Assessment*, 1979, 1, 23–41.

Goodstein, H. A., & Kahn, H. Pattern of achievement among children with learning difficulties. *Exceptional Children*, 1974, *41*, 47–49.

Gray, W. S. *Gray oral reading test*. New York: Bobbs-Merrill, 1967.

Guion, R. M. *Personnel testing*. New York: McGraw-Hill, 1965.

Guthrie, J. T. Models of reading and reading disability. *Journal of Educational Psychology*, 1973, *65*, 9–18.

Hallgren, B. Specific dyslexia ("congenital word blindness"): A clinical and genetic study. *Acta Psychiatrica et Neurologica Scandinavica*, 1950, Supplement 65.

Harris, L. A. Attention and learning disordered children: A review of theory and remediation. *Journal of Learning Disabilities*, 1976, *9*, 47–57.

Hecaen, H., & Albert, M. L. *Human neuropsychology*. New York: Wiley, 1978.

Heilman, K. M., & Valenstein, E. (Eds.). *Clinical neuropsychology*. New York: Oxford University Press, 1979.

Houton, R., Hill, S., & Parsons, M. An analysis of a performance feedback system: The effects of timing and feedback, public posting, and praise upon academic performance and peer interaction. *Journal of Applied Behavior Analysis*, 1975, *8*, 449–457.

Ingram, T. T. S., Mason, A. W., & Blackburn, I. A retrospective study of 82 children with reading disability. *Developmental Medicine and Child Neurology*, 1970, *12*, 271–281.

Jastak, J. F., Bijou, S. W., & Jastak, S. *Wide range achievement test*. Wilmington, Del.: Jastak Associates, 1978.

Johnson, D. J. Remedial approaches to dyslexia. In A. Benton & D. Pearl (Eds.), *Dyslexia: An appraisal of current knowledge*. New York: Oxford University Press, 1978.

Kephart, N. C. *The slow learner in the classroom*. Columbus, Ohio: Charles E. Merrill, 1960.

Kinsbourne, M. Selective disorders in learning to read, write, and calculate. In J. G. Millichap (Ed.), *Learning disabilities and related disorders*. Chicago: Year Book Medical Publishers, 1977.

Kinsbourne, M., & Caplan, P. J. *Children's learning and attention problems*. Boston: Little, Brown, 1979.

Knights, R. M., & Bakker, D. J. (Eds.). *The neuropsychology of learning disorders*. Baltimore: University Park Press, 1976.

Luria, A. R. *Higher cortical functions in man*. New York: Basic Books, 1973.

Mattis, S. Dyslexia syndromes: A working hypothesis that works. In A. Benton & D. Pearl (Eds.), *Dyslexia: An appraisal of current knowledge*. New York: Oxford University Press, 1978.

Mattis, S., French, J. H., & Rapin, I. Dyslexia in children and young adults: Three independent neuropsychological syndromes. *Developmental Medicine and Child Neurology*, 1975, *17*, 150–163.

McCarthy, D. *McCarthy scales of children's abilities*. New York: The Psychological Corporation, 1972.

McCarthy, J. J., & McCarthy, J. F. *Learning disabilities*. Boston: Allyn & Bacon, 1963.

McClearn, G. E. Review of "Dyslexia—Genetic Aspects." In A. Benton & D. Pearl (Eds.), *Dyslexia: An appraisal of current knowledge*. New York: Oxford University Press, 1978.

Millichap, J. G. (Ed.). *Learning disabilities and related disorders*. Chicago: Year Book Medical Publishers, 1977.

Millman, H. L. Minimal brain dysfunction in children—Evaluation and treatment. *Journal of Learning Disabilities*, 1970, *3*, 89–99.

Myklebust, H. F. Identification and diagnosis of children with learning disabilities: An interdisciplinary study of criteria. *Seminars in Psychiatry*, 1973, *5*, 55–77.

Naidoo, S. *Specific dyslexia*. New York: Wiley, 1972.

Owen, F. W. Dyslexia—Genetic aspects. In A. Benton & D. Pearl (Eds.), *Dyslexia: An appraisal of current knowledge*. New York: Oxford University Press, 1978.

Orton, S. T. "Word-blindness" in school children. *Archives of Neurology and Psychiatry*, 1925, *14*, 581–615.

Orton, S. T. *Reading, writing and speech problems in children*. New York: Norton, 1937.

Peter, B. M., & Spreen, O. Behavior rating and personal adjustment scales of neurologically and learning handicapped children during adolescence and early adulthood: Results of a follow-up study. *Journal of Clinical Neuropsychology*, 1979, *1*, 75–92.

Petrauskas, R. J., & Rourke, B. P. Identification of subtypes of retarded readers: A neuropsychological, multivariate approach. *Journal of Clinical Neuropsychology*, 1979, *1*, 17–37.

Rawson, M. *Developmental language disability: Adult accomplishment of dyslexic boys*. Baltimore: Johns Hopkins University Press, 1968.

Reitan, R. M., & Davison, L. A. *Clinical neuropsychology: Current status and applications*. New York: Wiley, 1974.

Rie, H. E., Rie, E. D., & Stewart, S. Effects of methylphenidate on underachieving children. *Journal of Consulting and Clinical Psychology*, 1976, *44*, 250–260.

Robinson, H. M., & Smith, H. K. Reading clinic—Ten years after. *The Elementary School Journal*, 1962, *63*, 22–27.

Ross, A. O. *Psychological aspects of learning disabilities and reading disorders*. New York: McGraw-Hill, 1976.

Rourke, B. P. Issues in the neuropsychological assessment of children with learning disabilities. *Canadian Psychological Review*, 1976, *17*, 89–102.

Rourke, P. B. Neuropsychological research in reading retardation: A review. In A. Benton & D. Pearl (Eds.), *Dyslexia: An appraisal of current knowledge*. New York: Oxford University Press, 1978. (a)

Rourke, B. P. Reading, spelling, and arithmetic disabilities: A neuropsychological perspective. In H.

R. Myklebust (Ed.), *Progress in learning disabilities* (Vol. 4). New York: Grune & Stratton, 1978. (b)

Rourke, B. P. Neuropsychological assessment of children with learning disabilities. In S. Filskov & T. Boll (Ed.), *Handbook of clinical neuropsychology*. New York: Wiley, 1980.

Rourke, B. P., Dietrich, D. M., & Young, G. C. Significance of WISC verbal–performance discrepancies for younger children with learning disabilities. *Perceptual and Motor Skills*, 1973, *36*, 275–282.

Rourke, B. P., & Finlayson, M. A. J. Neuropsychological significance of variations in patterns of academic performance: Verbal and visual–spatial abilities. *Journal of Abnormal Child Psychology*, 1978, *6*, 121–133.

Rourke, B. P., & Strang, J. D. Neuropsychological significance of variations in patterns of academic performance: Motor, psychomotor, and tactual–perceptual abilities. *Journal of Pediatric Psychology*, 1978, *3*, 62–66.

Rourke, B. P., & Telegdy, G. A. Lateralizing significance of WISC verbal–performance discrepancies for older children with learning disabilities. *Perceptual and Motor Skills*, 1971, *33*, 875–883.

Rourke, B. P., Young, G. C., & Flewelling, R. W. The relationships between WISC verbal–performance discrepancies and selected verbal, auditory–perceptual, visual–perceptual, and problem-solving abilities in children with learning disabilities. *Journal of Clinical Psychology*, 1971, *27*, 475–479.

Rugel, R. P. WISC subtest scores of disabled readers: A review with respect to Bannatyne's recategorization. *Journal of Learning Disabilities*, 1974, *7*, 57–64. (a)

Rugel, R. P. The factor structure of the WISC in two populations of disabled readers. *Journal of Learning Disabilities*, 1974, *7*, 57–61. (b)

Rutter, M. Prevalence and types of dyslexia. In A. Benton & D. Pearl (Eds.), *Dyslexia: An appraisal of current knowledge*. New York: Oxford University Press, 1978.

Rutter, M., Tizard, J., Yule, W., Graham, P., & Whitmore, K. Research report: Isle of Wight Studies. *Psychological Medicine*, 1976, *6*, 313–332.

Sattler, J. M. *Assessment of children's intelligence*. Philadelphia: W. B. Saunders, 1974.

Satz, P., Taylor, H. G., Friel, J., & Fletcher, J. Some developmental and predictive precursors of reading disabilities: A six year follow-up. In A. Benton & D. Pearl (Eds.), *Dyslexia: An appraisal of current knowledge*. New York: Oxford University Press, 1978.

Silver, A. A., & Hagin, R. A. Specific reading disability: Follow-up studies. *American Journal of Orthopsychiatry*, 1964, *35*, 95–102.

Silver, A. A., & Hagin, R. A. Maturation of perceptual functions in children with specific reading disability. *The Reading Teacher*, 1966, 253–259.

Slosson, R. L. *Slosson intelligence test for children and adults*. New York: Slosson Educational Publications, 1963.

*Stanford–Binet Intelligence Scale*. Boston: Houghton Mifflin Co., 1973.

Strauss, A., & Lehtinen, L. S. *Psychopathology and education of the brain-injured child*. New York: Grune & Stratton, 1947.

Stromer, R. Modifying letter and number reversals in elementary school children. *Journal of Applied Behavior Analysis*, 1975, *8*, 211.

Tarnopol, L., & Tarnopol, M. *Brain function and reading disabilities*. Baltimore: University Park Press, 1977.

Trehub, S. E. Infant antecedents: A search for the precursors of learning disabilities. In M. E. Blaw, I. Rapin, & M. Kinsbourne (Eds.), *Topics in child neurology*. New York: Spectrum, 1977.

Trites, R., & Fiedorowicz, C. Follow-up study of children with specific (or primary) reading disability. In R. Knights & D. Bakker (Eds.), *The neuropsychology of learning disorders*. Baltimore: University Park Press, 1976.

Vellutino, F. R. Toward an understanding of dyslexia: Psychological factors in specific reading disability. In A. Benton & D. Pearl (Eds.), *Dyslexia: An appraisal of current knowledge*. New York: Oxford University Press, 1978.

Wechsler, D. *Manual for the Wechsler Intelligence Scale for Children*. New York: The Psychological Corporation, 1949.

Wechsler, D. *Manual for the Wechsler Intelligence Scale for Children—Revised*. New York: The Psychological Corporation, 1974.

Werner, H. *Comparative psychology of mental development*. New York: Science Editions, 1948.

Yule, W., Rutter, M., Berger, M., & Thompson, J. Over- and under-achievement in reading: Distribution in the general population. *British Journal of Educational Psychology*, 1974, *44*, 1–12.

# PSYCHOSEXUAL AND GENDER PROBLEMS

## George A. Rekers

*Kansas State University*
*and Logos Research Institute, Inc.*

Early detection and psychological treatment of psychosexual problems must be based upon a multimethod behavioral assessment of the individual in several major living environments in addition to standardized psychodiagnostic procedures administered in the clinic setting. Initially, one of the clinician's tasks is to differentiate normal adjustment phases in psychosexual development from psychological disturbances that require specific intervention. This task is complicated by the wide range of normal developmental adjustments that individuals must make pertaining to their physical sex status, sex-role learning, and rate of sexual maturation across the years before and during puberty. Parents, and sometimes children themselves, will ask the practicing clinician about masculine role behaviors, feminine role behaviors, boy–girl relations, sexual behaviors, the psychological impact of sexual maturation, and sexual identity issues. The clinician's knowledge of normal psychosexual development provides a context for differentiating normal needs for sex education and guidance in gender development from specific adjustment problems.

In the course of normal psychosexual development, children will typically perform a wide variety of sex-role behaviors as they learn to make the fine discriminations between masculine and feminine social roles. Young boys will occasionally explore behaviors that society traditionally has assigned to girls and women, such as putting on a dress, using lipstick and mascara, and playacting the roles of bearing and nursing infants. Similarly, young girls sometimes assume a masculine role, such as playing "daddy" while playing house, or adopt a cluster of masculine behaviors to the exclusion of feminine behaviors, which leads to the social labeling of "tomboy." This type of episodic and flexible exploration of sex-typed behaviors is typical of many boys and girls and represents a component of the normal sex-role socialization process (Maccoby, 1966; Maccoby & Jacklin, 1974; Mischel, 1970; Mussen, 1969).

In rare cases, however, the child deviates from the normal pattern of trying out the opposite sex-role behaviors and develops a persistent, compulsive, and rigidly stereotyped pattern. At one extreme is the excessive hypermasculinity of boys who are interpersonally violent, destructive, uncontrolled, and belligerent and who lack gentle and socially sensitive behaviors (Harrington, 1970). Behavioral intervention is required for these exaggeratedly "super masculine" boys who have adopted a caricature of the masculine social role. The opposite extreme is observed in boys who reject their male role to the extent of insisting that they are girls or that they want to grow up to be mothers and to bear children. Such a boy frequently dresses in girls' clothes; avoids boys' clothing; plays predominantly with girls; tries on cosmetics, wigs, and other feminine attire; and displays stereotypically feminine arm movements, gait, and body gestures. Such hyperfemininity in boys goes beyond normal curiosity-induced exploration of feminine stereotypic behavior to constitute a serious clinical problem. Although there has been a dearth of research on female childhood gender disorders, it is theoretically possible to identify the parallel conditions of hyperfemininity and hypermasculinity in girls.

## ETHICAL AND LEGAL CONSIDERATIONS

Although the potentially destructive components of traditional sex-role stereotyping are receiving a contemporary social challenge, the scientific literature does provide a framework for differentiating normal gender development from problems in psychosexual adjustment. Changes in conceptualizations of sex roles by social psychologists, although being idealistic, may ignore the scientific findings suggesting that nontraditional sex roles may be associated with serious and chronic problems in psychological adjustment. It is consistent with accepted professional ethics and widely held community standards for a psychologist to provide assessment and treatment interventions for children who exhibit deviant and maladaptive behavior, including psychosexual and gender disturbances.

There is no more appropriate reference group to make the social value judgment regarding clinical intervention for a child than the parent or guardian in cooperative consultation with licensed professionals who are, in turn, sensitive to the broader social codes and moral expectations of the community (see Principle 3, *Ethical Standards of Psychologists*, American Psychological Association, 1977). All helping professions have the same ethical obligation to offer children a foundation for happy and productive lives. In this regard, it is not logical to distinguish behavioral intervention from other forms of intervention for children (such as educational intervention, dental intervention, and medical intervention)—such a distinction would imply that psychological assessment and treatment should follow different ethical standards than other intervention approaches (Rosen, Rekers, & Bentler, 1978).

The early identification and prevention of sexual maladjustment is preferable to waiting until adulthood when intervention is time consuming and difficult, as is the case with transvestism and homosexuality, or nearly impossible, as in the case of adult transsexualism (Qualls, 1978; Rekers, 1972, 1978a, in press-b; Rekers, Bentler, Rosen, & Lovaas, 1977; Rekers & Mead, 1980; Rekers & Milner, 1981; Rekers, Rosen, Lovaas, & Bentler, 1978; Zuger, 1978). Compulsive cross-dressing behavior requires intervention to prevent adult transvestic sexual disturbances. For the cross-gender-identified child in particular, there is the additional need for treatment because the child is at high risk for adult transsexualism, which is a condition with an extremely poor prognosis even with psychological treatment, typically accompanied by severe depressive episodes, suicide ideation, actual suicide attempt, and/or genital self-mutilation (Rekers, 1977b; Zuger, 1978). Many clinicians previously thought that radical surgical and hormonal sex reassignment procedures were the only treatment of choice for adult transsexuals, but a longitudinal follow-up of operated and unoperated transsexuals found significant improvement in the adjustment of the group of unoperated patients and no significant change in the adjustment scores of the operated transsexuals (Meyer & Reter, 1979). Consequently, the historically leading center for transsexual surgery at the Johns Hopkins University Hospital for two decades decided in 1979 to terminate its surgical treatment approach to transsexuals (Note 1).

Now that a treatment approach based on social learning principles has been isolated which holds great promise for helping children with gender and psychosexual problems (e.g., Bates, Skilbeck, Smith, & Bentler, 1975; Rekers, 1972, 1977a, 1978b; Rekers & Mead, 1979a) it would be unethical not to use the behavioral assessment procedures that have been developed to identify and treat gender and sexual behavior disorders in children.

### Proper Legal Consent

Even though there is no legal requirement to obtain a minor's consent (Martin, 1975), some critics question the initiation of intervention by helping professionals at the request of the parent without a special attempt to obtain the child's informed consent. Ferguson (1978) has outlined four distinct childhood developmental age groups that should be considered to have different and separate criteria for obtaining informed consent. Members of the "gay" community have insisted that children should not be deterred from a course toward a homosexual lifestyle. These critics imply that a boy's exclusive preference for play with feminine objects and with girls should be honored and that any assessment or treatment intervention for this unusual sex-typed behavior is a direct violation of the child's right to consent to treatment. The fallacy of this position is that a minor child does not have the capacity to grant proper consent (Rekers, 1978a, in press-a).

Martin (1975) has discussed at length the three conceptually distinct, and yet equally necessary, conditions for morally and legally proper consent from an individual: information, competence, and voluntariness. Although children may meet the voluntariness criterion, they are not capable of providing fully informed or competent consent for all kinds of social interventions because of their relative lack of social decision-making power resulting from their restricted mental capabilities and legal status. It is therefore the consensus of the legal and judicial systems that consent decisions must be left to the responsible surrogate for the child—the parent or legal guardian.

Rosen *et al.* (1978) have argued that though it may be desirable for a behavior therapist to work in consonance with the child's expressed wishes, the clinician need not require the child's consent to behavior change interventions if the deviance of that child requires direct action to alleviate the present state of misery and discomfort and/or to prevent future maladjustment and unhappiness. Although the rights of children need to be protected against any possible malicious intrusions into their inalienable dignity and freedom as individuals, therapists must be equally conscientious in their professional attempts to ensure that children simultaneously retain their right to be given new and possibly very beneficial forms of behavioral assessment and treatment.

It is appropriate for the parent to request behavioral assessment and potential treatment for a child with atypical sex-typed behaviors because such children are quite typically in a chronic state of isolation and misery. Principle 6 of the *Ethical Standards of Psychologists* (American Psychological Association, 1977) states that psychologists must do nothing to cause harm to clients, whether passively or actively. In the case of a gender-disturbed child, the psychologist's responsibility is to do a careful behavioral assessment either to confirm or to disconfirm the parents' concerns over potential deviance in their child, with the goal of alleviating the child's present and potential future maladjustment.

A related ethical issue concerns the psychological implications of even attempting to obtain "informed" consent, even if it were legally possible for a child to grant consent at that level. If clinicians attempted to satisfy the normal definition of obtaining *informed* consent from a child before they conducted a behavioral assessment for a gender problem, they would face the serious problem of the gross undesirability of informing the referred boy that he is being evaluated to determine whether or not he is at high risk for transsexualism or transvestism or homosexuality. Because the self sex-labeling process is crucial in psychosexual development, the very process of satisfying the requirement of informed consent from the child might adversely affect the child's psychological adjustment. Even the most careful phrasing would yield an anxiety-producing encounter and would constitute a risk for the boy's psychosexual adjustment. Therefore, the process of obtaining proper informed consent in the case of evaluating a gender disturbance would create an overwhelming risk of social injury and psychological harm to the child, which would in itself possibly override any intended therapeutic benefit of the assessment.

We must conclude that though deception (misinformation given) should be avoided, concealment (information withheld) would be the most therapeutic approach with such a child. Ethically and legally, the parent or guardian must grant the consent for assessment for the child in order to protect his or her rights, freedom, and human dignity.

## Social and Professional Ethics

Once it is understood that no North American court would expect a minor child to grant full proper consent for behavioral assessment and treatment intervention, the next question is who should be permitted to determine the assessment and treatment goals? Who should define the appropriate range of child behavior? Health caretakers? Parents? Legislators? The courts? Concerned professionals? A select group of social advocates?

The parents of an individual child may have one set of personal values, clinical professionals may hold another set of values, gay activist groups may advocate a vastly different set of values, extremist feminist groups may espouse another position, and the gender-disturbed child may possess yet another set of values. If the parent requests professional assistance from a psychologist, whose set of values should be followed?

The American Psychological Association's *Ethical Standards of Psychologists* make it clear that the set of values certainly should not be that of the psychologist alone or of the minority extremist group. Principle 3 of the *Ethical Standards* states that the psychologist must show serious regard for the social codes and moral expectations of the community in which service is provided. The psychologist must take into account data from a variety of sources in order to make the most responsible ethical decision.

The complaint of the parent regarding the child's behavior must be taken seriously because the parent is the legal agent responsible for the child's care. The psychologist makes a judgment as to whether the parent has the best wishes of the child in mind. The psychologist should be familiar with the current literature regarding the presenting problem as it becomes focused after a thorough behavioral assessment of the individual child. The broader social values of the larger community may also come into play in the final decision.

The psychologist must make the distinction between appropriate sex-typing and arbitrary sex-role stereotypes. Within the domain of arbitrary sex-role stereotypes, the psychologist must make a distinction between benign and harmful arbitrary stereotypes. Although the psychologist should provide leadership for advancing the social codes by breaking down harmful arbitrary sex-role stereotypes, he or she must, at the same time, help a deviant child make a number of distinctions between men and women that are appropriate (Rekers *et al.,* 1978).

In childhood, for example, most girls learn to imitate a maternal role, which includes fantasies or playacting about growing up, having marital sexual relations with a man, being pregnant, delivering babies, breast-feeding infants, and caring for them. It is important for the boy to learn that he will not grow up with the biological possibility of having sexual intercourse with a man, of getting pregnant, of delivering a baby, and of breast-feeding the infant. Although the boy should be encouraged to be nurturant, sensitive, and caring for infants, an important part of the socialization process involves the boy's learning that his culture has a legitimate right to expect that he will not wear dresses or marry a man.

There is no evidence to indicate that a parent would be requesting an unethical or illegal act by a psychologist by requesting that the psychologist assist in helping to prevent a deviant psychosexual outcome in his or her own child. The normalization of sex-typed behaviors is a legitimate goal for behavioral assessment and treatment.

# SEVEN PSYCHOSEXUAL DIMENSIONS FOR ASSESSMENT

Rather than assigning children to global and inarticulated diagnostic categories of sexual deviancy, it is more helpful to assess a particular child across several major psychosexual dimensions (Rosen & Rekers, 1980), outlined in Table 1.

TABLE 1
Dimensions for Psychosexual Assessment

| Level of assessment | Dimension | Major categories |
|---|---|---|
| Sexual status | Physical | Male, female, or intersexed; Tanner's stages for prepubertal, pubertal, or postpubertal development |
| | Social assignment | Male, female, or intersexed; child, adolescent, or adult (boy, girl, man, woman) |
| Intrapersonal behavior | Sexual identity self-labeling behavior | Normal, undifferentiated, cross-gender, or conflicted |
| | Sex-role self-labeling behavior | Heterosexual, bisexual, homosexual, transsexual, transvestite, "queen," "fag," "drag queen," "gay," etc. |
| | Sexual arousal behavior | Human object choice (Kinsey scale rating); animal object choice; magnitude and frequency; fantasies |
| Interpersonal behavior | Gender sex-role behavior | Masculine, feminine, undifferentiated, androgynous |
| | Genital sex-role behavior | Human partner (Kinsey scale rating); animal partner; inanimate object; intrusive versus receptive roles; group versus individual partner; etc. |

## Sexual Status Dimensions

### *Physical Sex Status*

The physical dimension consists of the five variables of sex: genetic constitution, gonads, external sex organ anatomy, internal accessory genital structures, and sex endocrinology. The three major categories of physical sex status for the individual refer to the interrelationship of these five variables, yielding "male," "female," or "intersexed (hermaphroditic)," where the term *intersexed* denotes a condition of incongruity among the variables or incomplete physical differentiation. Assessment of physical sexual status is further refined by physician ratings of the stage of prepubertal, pubertal, or postpubertal development on the Tanner Scale (Marshall & Tanner, 1969, 1970; Tanner, 1955).

### *Social Sex of Assignment*

The social sex of assignment is the sex into which the child is reared and is usually established at birth by the attending physician. In normal individuals, the adults rearing the child accept the physician's decision, resulting in congruence between the dimensions of physical sex status and social sex of assignment. Intersexed individuals are assigned to male or female, while parents are told that the physical sexual differentiation process is incomplete and requires medical intervention to finish the development.

## Intrapersonal Behavioral Dimensions

In assessing the individual, there are three psychological dimensions pertaining primarily to intrapersonal processes.

### *Sexual Identity Self-Labeling Behavior*

The term *sexual identity* (which parallels the psychoanalytic concept of "core gender identity") refers to the possible types of self-labeling as male or female at the covert and overt verbal response levels. *Normal sexual identity* is the state in which a person's self-label as male or female is strong and matches one's physical sex status. *Ambiguous* or *undifferentiated sexual identity* designates either (1) the developmental period of infancy or (2) the abnormal condition in later life in which a firm and consistent verbal self-assignment as male or female is lacking. A *cross-gender identity* is the strong belief that one is a member of the opposite physical sex; the transsexual individual has the normal physical anatomy of one sex while identifying strongly with the opposite sex. A *conflicted sexual identity* would be the state in which strong feelings of masculine and feminine identity co-exist or alternate in a personality.

### Sex-Role Self-Labeling Behavior

Another aspect of self-labeling behavior refers to personal assignment by the individual of the label "homosexual" or "heterosexual" or similar label (e.g., "queer," "drag queen"), which categorizes the individual's own expectations for his or her gender and genital sex-role behaviors. Some investigators refer to these sex-role labeling behaviors as "orientation," which may or may not match one's actual interpersonal behaviors or arousal patterns.

### Sexual Arousal Behavior

The individual's development of sex-object arousal patterns for exclusively opposite-sex persons, for exclusively same-sex persons, for animals or inanimate objects, or for some combination of these possibilities constitutes the intrapersonal arousal dimension for assessment. The descriptive terms "heterosexual," "homosexual," and "bisexual" should not be used to describe the sexual arousal pattern of the person until (1) the person attains adulthood, (2) hermaphroditism is ruled out, and (3) transsexualism is ruled out. Early in development, it is most convenient to assess the specific stimulus objects for arousal and the magnitude and frequency of such arousal rather than using general descriptive terms.

## Interpersonal Behavioral Dimensions

With regard to interpersonal dimensions for analysis, there are two general, but interrelated, types of sex-role behavior to assess.

### Gender Sex-Role Behavior

The term *gender sex-role*, or, more simply, *gender role*, describes the psychological dimensions of masculine and feminine behavior and personality characteristics (as measured by test behavior or self-report inventory behavior). Recent psychological research does not conceptualize masculinity–femininity as a unidimensional, bipolar phenomenon. Two separate continua are now measured—namely, the degree of masculinity, which can range from low to high, and separately, the degree of femininity, from low to high. A person measuring low in frequency or range on masculine behavior *and* low on feminine behavior is called "undifferentiated" in sex-role. A person scoring high on masculine behavior and low on feminine behavior is designated "masculine," and a person high on femininity and low on masculinity is called "feminine." A person who is high on both masculinity *and* femininity is considered "androgynous" (Bem, 1974, 1975).

Masculine and feminine sex-role behaviors are (1) purely biologically defined (e.g., feminine = breast-feeding behavior; masculine = impregnating a female by sexual intercourse); (2) socially defined, based on physical sex differences (e.g., feminine = modesty behavior associated with upper torso; masculine = hunting or athletic involvement based on strength differences); (3) legitimate, but arbitrary, social assignments with no direct biological basis (e.g., feminine = wearing lipstick; masculine = wearing neckties); or (4) harmful arbitrary social stereotypes (e.g., feminine = nurse; masculine = doctor). This aspect of sex-role behavior may or may not parallel sex-labeling behavior in a given individual. As a consequence, gender sex-role behavior in an individual should be assessed separately from sex-role labeling behaviors.

### Genital Sex-Role Behavior

One subcategory of sex-role behavior is genital behavior, which is distinguished from nongenital, or gender, sex-role behavior. At the interpersonal level, genital sex-role behavior may or may not parallel the sexual arousal behavior at the intrapersonal level. As a consequence, actual genital sex-role behavior should be assessed separately from an individual's sexual arousal patterns of behavior.

The Kinsey scale would rate genital sex-role behavior on a continuum from exclusive activity with female partners to exclusive activity with male partners, with five patterns of "bisexual" behavior scored between. Some overt sexual behavior cannot be rated on the Kinsey scale because it is oriented toward animals or inanimate objects (e.g., with fetishisms).

## INCONGRUITIES ACROSS THE PSYCHOSEXUAL DIMENSIONS

An incongruity across any two of the several dimensions for assessment can create psychological conflict and associated maladjustment problems (Rosen & Rekers, 1980). Although in the past investigators were engrossed with the problem of cross-gender identity in children (e.g., Green, 1974, who uses the term *sexual identity conflict*), more detailed assessment data have differentiated two basic problems: sex-role behavior disturbance and cross-gender identification in physically normal prepubescent boys who display feminine sex-typed behavior (Rosen, Rekers, & Friar, 1977; Bentler, Rekers, & Rosen, 1979).

### Sex-Role Behavior Disturbance

A sex-role behavior disturbance may be present in a boy who is as young as 4 or 5 years and who has normal male physical sex status (as measured by current biomedical testing procedures outlined by Rekers, Crandall, Rosen, & Bentler, 1979). Typically, the sex assignment has been male, although cases have been reported where child-rearing agents may give incongruent or ambiguous messages to the young child regarding his physical sex status. With regard to intrapersonal dimensions, self-labeling behavior is typically male in identity, although self-labeling of role may range from male gender role to "fag," "queer," or "drag queen" to female gender role, or it may vacillate over time across settings. Sexual arousal behavior may be absent, unreported, or varied, including sexual arousal to feminine clothing and/or to male and female sexual fantasies.

The distinguishing features of this disorder, however, exist at the level of interpersonal dimensions, where any of several behaviors are observed over a long period. At the gender sex-role level, the boy has a behavioral history of (1) actual or improvised cross-dressing in feminine clothing; (2) actual use or playacting use of female cosmetic articles; (3) use of feminine-appearing mannerisms, behavioral gestures, or gait; (4) aversion toward or avoidance of peer activities with other boys, or preoccupation with feminine sex-typed activities and games; (5) the use of high, feminine-like voice inflection and/or predominantly feminine speech content; and (6) taking a feminine role in play. At the genital sex-role level, the boy may or may not have a documented history of deviant sexual behavior or masturbation patterns associated with feminine clothing or articles.

The detection of sex-role behavior disturbance in a girl is a much more complex task (Rekers & Mead, 1979a, 1980; Rekers & Milner, 1979) because of the relatively greater social acceptance of "masculine" behaviors in girls, including the wearing of "masculine" clothing, as contrasted with the social concern in our society over boys wearing dresses, for example. Because the transient phase of taking on the "tomboy" role appears to be part of adaptive behavioral development in many girls, the chronicity of deviant sex-role behavior patterns and the general psychological adjustment of the girl are important variables that must be taken into account before considering any of the following gender sex-role behaviors as potentially problematic in girls: (1) rigid insistence on wearing masculine sex-typed clothing, coupled with chronic rejection of dresses, skirts, cosmetic articles, and feminine jewelry; (2) use of masculine-appearing behavioral gestures, postures, and gait, to the exclusion of feminine mannerisms; (3) avoidance of female peer activities and preoccupation with playing exclusively with boys, often with the expressed desire to be considered "one of the boys"; (4) use of an artificially induced low voice inflection and/or predominantly masculine topics in speech content; and (5) the request to be called by a boy's name or nickname. At the level of genital sex-role behavior, some girls with sex-role behavior disturbance have a history of deviant sexual behavior or masturbation patterns associated with masculine clothing items.

## Cross-Gender Identification

This disorder is potentially more serious than sex-role behavior disturbance and involves cross-sexual identity self-labeling behaviors, including requests to change one's sex. Assessment would indicate this diagnosis in boys if either of the following behavior patterns is manifested alone or in combination with any of the sex-role behavior disturbances (gender or genital) discussed previously: (1) self-labeling as a female as evidenced by a stated desire to be a girl or a woman (cross-sex identity) or by excessive female role taking, often including fantasies of bearing children and of breast-feeding infants; or (2) a request by the boy to have his penis removed or other sex-reassignment medical procedures performed, potentially indicative of a deviant self-labeling as female identity or role and/or of a deviant sexual arousal pattern (Greenson, 1966; Rekers, 1972, 1977a, 1977b; Stoller, 1964, 1965, 1968a).

Similarly for girls, cross-gender identification is indicated if either of the following two behaviors occur alone or in combination with any of the sex-role behavior deviance (gender or genital) discussed previously: (1) an 18-month or longer history of having verbalized the desire to be a boy or a man or taking predominantly male roles in play, possibly including fantasies of having a penis; or (2) a repeated request for male hormones, breast removal, or other sex-reassignment medical procedures.

## Genital Sex-Role Behavior Disorders

Children from early childhood to late adolescence may indicate the beginnings of a chronic "sexual deviation" if they exhibit excessive public masturbation (Bitter-Lebert, 1956; Gilbert, 1916; Levine & Bell, 1956; Rudolf, 1954; Stirt, 1940), masturbation with ropes or objects (Coe, 1974; Edmondson, 1972; Resnik, 1972; Shankel & Carr, 1956; Stearns, 1953), sexual assault behaviors (e.g., Atcheson & Williams, 1954; Roberts, McBee, & Bettis, 1969; Shoor, Speed, & Bartlett, 1966; Vanden Bergh & Kelly, 1964), object fetishes (e.g., Salfield, 1957), extreme anxiety over the process of puberty (Brown, 1972; Grover, 1973; Hamelstein, 1974), delinquency or truancy involving sexual acting-out (Craft, 1966; Deisher, 1970; Deisher, Eisner, & Sulzbacher, 1969; Gandy & Deisher, 1970; Ginsburg, 1967; Hackett, 1971; Hartmann, 1973; Mohr & Turner, 1967; Nadler, 1968; Pittman, 1971; Raven, 1963; Reiss, 1963; Roberts, Abrams, & Finch, 1973; Russell, 1971), excessive homosexual behavior, or other sexual adjustment difficulties, or a history of sexual abuse (Bender & Blau, 1937; Brunold, 1964; Katzman, 1972; Langsley, Schwartz, & Fairbairn, 1968; Mangus, 1932; Schultz, 1972, 1973; Weiss, Rogers, Darwin, & Dutton, 1955). One or more of these behavior patterns would indicate the need for a thorough assessment to determine whether psychotherapeutic intervention is necessary.

## Psychosexual Problems Secondary to Medical Conditions

Some children or adolescents have emotional reactions to physical abnormalities or diseases of the genital system. Other nongenital-related diseases may have a psychological impact on sex-role and sexual identity adjustment. For example, chronic illnesses that restrict the physical movement or activities of boys may interfere with their sex-role development in terms of their perception of a lack in "masculine" image. Such illnesses may therefore interfere with the normal progression of self-labeling processes as male or female and may thereby generate secondary difficulties in sexual identity formation (Rekers & Milner, 1978).

# INCIDENCE OF PSYCHOSEXUAL PROBLEMS

Four general types of childhood sex-role behavior disturbance may be distinguished: (1) excessive feminine behavior in boys, (2) pathological hypermasculinity in boys, (3) pathological hyperfemininity in girls, and (4) excessive masculine behavior in girls. Similarly, four general types of self sex-labeling behavior problems can be distinguished: (1) female self-labeling in boys, (2) distorted hypermasculine self-labeling in boys, (3) pathological hyperfeminine self-labeling in girls, and (4) masculine self-labeling in girls. In addition, a number of genital sex-role behavior disorders have been enumerated in children. Of these many potential types of psychosexual disturbances in children, the systematic research deals almost exclusively with the cases of deficit masculine development in boys, involving a sex-role gender behavior disturbance, a cross-gender identity disturbance, or homosexual behavior development. This state of the literature is, in part, a function of the finding that problems of sexual dysphoria and deviation occur more frequently in males than in females (Green & Money, 1969; Kinsey, Pomeroy, & Martin, 1948; Money & Ehrhardt, 1972; Stoller, 1968b) and of the relatively greater concern by American parents over feminine sex-role behavior in their sons.

The feminine sex-typed behaviors (whether they be gender- or genital-related) that are used as the initial screening criteria for assessment of boys can exist in many contexts. Theoretically speaking, it is probable that the prognosis and treatment of sex-role behavior disturbance, cross-gender identity disturbance, and homosexual behavior are not the same (Rekers, Bentler, Rosen, & Lovaas, 1977), but research on this question has not yet been conducted. The developmental histories of all these types of deviant boys parallel the retrospective reports of adult male transsexuals, transvestites, and some homosexuals. The feminine behaviors used as the initial screening criteria may therefore exist in a variety of different developmental or situational contexts. Unfortunately, there are no published experimental studies that report on the base rate for feminine sex-role behaviors in the general population of boys that would be potentially predictive of normal versus deviant adult adjustment. Nor are there adequate longitudinal data to indicate what percentage of feminine boys spontaneously outgrow a "phase" of deviant sex-role development, what percentage grow up to be adult transsexuals, what percentage develop as transvestites, and what percentage become adult male homosexuals.

Although there are no base-rate data on the occurrence of these various types of sex-role disturbance, investigators have relied on their clinical experience to make various estimates that sex-role behavior disturbance occurs in one out of 25,000 to 80,000 children and that cross-gender identity disturbance occurs in one out of 100,000 to 200,000 children (Rekers, Bentler, Rosen, & Lovaas, 1977; Rekers et al., 1978). These conservative estimates do suggest that such disturbances are rare phenomena and that the full-time private practitioner might see a true case of childhood gender identity disturbance only once in every 2 years on the average.

It is fortunate that these conditions are relatively infrequent in the general population, but on the other hand, it may be that professionals detect less than 15% of these cases because of the embarrassment of parents in confronting the problems directly or the secretiveness of children in their cross-dressing or deviant sexual behaviors, enabling them to elude normal observation and detection.

# PROBABLE ETIOLOGY

Unfortunately, no reliable scientific data exist on the differential etiology of these conditions, although plausible developmental theories have been postulated (e.g., Bradley, Steiner, Zucker, Doering, Sullivan, Finegan, & Richardson, 1978). Social learning variables have been considered to be the main source for sex-role deviance and sexual identity disturbances (e.g., Meyer-Bahlburg, 1977), although biological abnormalities may theoretically be a potential contributing factor (e.g., Hutt, 1978). An excellent review of the available data in the context of a theory of sexual identity development has been offered by Bentler (1976). Although there is little published information about the causes of the development of deviations in sex-role adjustment, established findings provide the basis for understanding the theoretical context for potential causes. There is also a substantial body of evidence suggesting the developmental outcome for such children.

Theoretically, psychosexual development and the differentiation of sexual identity in individuals can be best conceptualized as a complex sequential interaction among biological, psychological, and social variables. Money and Ehrhardt (1972) have comprehensively reviewed research on the components of sexual identity development. Developmental events that result in a person's adult sexual identity begin with the individual's chromosomal status at the fertilization of the egg. It is useful to conceptualize the sequence of psychosexual development as a series of pathways in a relay race.

The earliest programming for sexual dimorphism is initially carried in this relay race by the sex chromosome (either an X or a Y) supplied by the male parent and paired with the X chromosome from the mother. Then, either the XX or the XY chromosomal combination takes a turn in this relay race by passing the program on to the undifferentiated gonad, to determine its outcome as a testis or ovary. Next, the gonad becomes differentiated as male or female and subsequently passes the program on to the sex hormonal secretions of its own cells. Research has found that in the total absence of fetal gonadal hormones, the fetus will always develop the female reproductive anatomy. The testis passes the program on to the testicular hormones that it secretes, which are, in turn, essential for the differentiation of male reproductive structures, for the shape of the external genitals, and for the patterns of organization in the brain that can influence future behavioral temperament. [This is a theoretical inference by Money and Ehrhardt (1972), who localize the hormonal action as "in the hypothalamic pathways that will subsequently influence certain aspects of sexual behavior" (p. 2).]

At birth, the child is socially identified as a boy or a girl based on external anatomy, which immediately results in the major differences in day-to-day practices of child rearing for boys and girls (see Rekers & Milner, 1979). Money and Ehrhardt (1972) theorize that the central nervous system passes on the program accounting for behavioral tendencies that are culturally classified as predominantly boyish or girlish.

Taking into account all the available research, it appears that the major part of sexual identity and sex-role development receives its program in this relay race by way of the consequent social sex assignment by leading to the different day-to-day practices of child rearing received by boys and girls. Although sex self-labeling behaviors in a child are developed in early childhood, the onset of hormonal changes in puberty eventually will confirm psychologically the sense of sexual identity or will provide a source of emotional conflict for persons who have incongruent sex self-labeling.

Money, Hampson, and Hampson (1955) studied test pairs of hermaphroditic individuals who had been matched chromosomally and gonadally and who were otherwise physically the same, with the exception that one member of each pair had been raised as a boy and the other as a girl. These studies suggested that socialization aspects of child rearing are the strongest potential variables in the formation of a sexual identity in a child, even though it was not possible to specify precise child-rearing variables and the cause-and-effect relationship among them. However, the available literature on sex-role development (see Maccoby & Jacklin, 1974; Money & Ehrhardt, 1972) suggests that the most significant of the child-rearing components are (1) identification with and role-modeling of the parent-figure and peers of the same sex, (2) development of complementary role behaviors toward members of the opposite sex, and (3) the child's recognition of and identification with his or her sexual anatomy and its reproductive function.

In this relay race of psychosexual differentiation, abnormalities along any of these pathways may lead to clinical problems in the individual's ultimate psychosexual adjustment. On the one hand, abnormalities may occur in any of the five physical variables of sex, which may place the individual at risk for problems in sexual identity development. On the other hand, sexual identity problems occur in some individuals without any detectable or measurable abnormality in any of the five physical variables of sex (Green, 1974, 1976; Rekers et al., 1979). In these cases, the postnatal social environment of child rearing is primarily implicated in the etiology of psychosexual disturbance. Nevertheless, we must entertain the possibility that some degree of prenatally determined disposition may make certain children easily vulnerable to disorders of sexual identity differentiation, even though we may not be able to detect such variables with our current methods of biomedical testing.

In sex-role behavior disturbance and cross-sex gender identity disturbance, overt sexual behaviors are not differential diagnostic criteria. However, as the child with a gender identity problem moves into adolescence, heterosocial dating deficits can serve to reinforce the development of transsexualism and may contribute to the problem of arousal to same-sex partners. Deviance in sex-role behavior patterns predisposes the child away from heterosexual development and toward homosexual or other sexual behavior problems. Peers are highly likely to label the feminine boy as homosexual ("queer" or "fag"), and some boys may make sexual advances toward the gender-identity-disturbed child because of his behavioral presentation in the peer group. Such social events have an impact upon the intrapersonal self-labeling behaviors of the child and also upon the overt sex-role behavioral development of the individual. With such limited social alternatives, a child is at high risk for the development of homosexual arousal. On the other hand, the boy with a sex-role behavior disturbance may move his compulsion to the privacy of his bedroom, where masturbation becomes paired with cross-dressing, often resulting in a fixated form of atypical, but heterosexual, fantasy.

Some individual children may become directly involved in deviant genital sex-role behavior patterns at an early age quite independent of other deviant gender behavior patterns. These children may also be at high risk for abnormal sexual development (Rekers & Milner, 1978).

Although etiological variables in deviant sex-role development are not yet fully understood (Bentler, 1976; Money, 1970a, 1970b; Money & Ehrhardt, 1972; Rosen, 1969; Zuger, 1970a, 1970b), the available prospective longitudinal data do indicate that effeminate behavior in boys is fairly predictive of male homosexuality (Bakwin, 1968; Green, 1974, 1979; Lebovitz, 1972; Zuger, 1966, 1970a, 1978; Zuger & Taylor, 1969; Money & Russo, Note 2) and is retrospectively reported by adult male homosexuals (Bieber, Dain, Dince, Drellich, Grand, Gundlach, Kremer, Rifkin, Wilber, & Bieber, 1962; Evans, 1969; Holemon & Winokur, 1965; Whitam, 1977), adult male transvestites (Prince & Bentler, 1972), and adult male transsexuals (Benjamin, 1966; Bentler, 1976; Bentler & Prince, 1970; Green & Money, 1969). The majority of adult transsexuals and transvestites report retrospectively that their cross-sex behavior began in early childhood (Green, 1974; Money & Primrose, 1968; Prince & Bentler, 1972; Walinder, 1967; Zuger, 1966). Zuger's (1978) long-term prospective follow-up of a small sample of untreated gender-disturbed boys found 63% to be homosexual, 6% transvestite, 6% transsexual, and 12% heterosexual; 25% attempted suicide, and 6% committed suicide. The various prospective studies of gender-disturbed boys predict a deviant sexual outcome in from 40% to 75% of cases. All available evidence, therefore, indicates that childhood sex-role deviations are strongly predictive of homosexual orientation disturbance, transsexualism, or transvestism in adulthood (Bender & Paster, 1941; Green, 1974, 1979; Green & Money, 1961, 1969; Pauly, 1969; Qualls, 1978; Rekers, 1977b, in press-b; Stoller, 1967, 1968a, 1968b, 1970–1971). Based on all the available literature, the best scientific prediction must be that a sex-role-disturbed boy will be at high risk for transsexualism, transvestism, or homosexuality as opposed to normal heterosexual development.

## COMMON ASSESSMENT PURPOSES

Child psychiatrists and clinical psychologists see referrals from family members, school personnel, pediatricians, family practitioners, and social agency personnel who express concern over an individual child's stereotypically extreme sex-role behaviors, cross-sex self-labeling statements, or deviant sexual behavior patterns.

## Clinical Reasons for Assessment

Because the clinical rationale for intervening in the case of a suspected gender disturbance has been discussed at length by a number of clinicians (Bates, Skilbeck, Smith, & Bentler, 1975; Braun & Rekers, 1981; Green, 1974; Qualls, 1978; Rekers, 1977a, 1977b, 1978a, 1981b; Rekers, Bentler, Rosen, & Lovaas, 1977; Rekers & Lovaas, 1974; Rekers et al., 1978; Rosen et al., 1978; Stoller, 1968a, 1970–1971), only the major points will be summarized here.

### Detection of Psychosocial Maladjustment

The most adaptive psychological state appears to be that in which the essential (biologically mandated and socially defined) distinctions between male and female roles are mastered by the child, with sex-role flexibility beyond those basic distinctions. The gender-disturbed child is rigid in a strong inhibition for same-sex-typed activities and is compulsive in cross-sex behaviors (Green, 1974; Green & Money, 1961, 1969; Rekers, Lovaas, & Low, 1974; Stoller, 1968a, 1970–1971) as contrasted to the behavioral flexibility that is systematically observed in normal boys and girls (Bates & Bentler, 1973; Rekers & Yates, 1976). There is conflict and confusion in identity because of the dissonance between rigidly held self-labels and the reality demands of everyday society. The child suffers unhappiness and is, for example, typically scapegoated with cruel and insulting labels such as "sissy," "fag," "queer," and "girly" (Green, 1974; Green, Newman, & Stoller, 1972; Rekers & Lovaas, 1974; Rekers, Willis, Yates, Rosen, & Low, 1977; Stoller, 1970–1971).

The assessment task should be to ask the question of whether or not the child's unhappiness, obsessive–compulsive trends, isolation and withdrawal, negativistic behavior, detachment, inability to form close interpersonal peer relationships, and low self-esteem are products of a primary sex-role disturbance.

### Identifying Children at High Risk for Adulthood Sexual Deviance and Secondary Problems

Detection of a childhood sex-role disturbance not only would allow potential prevention of adulthood sexual problems (Green, 1979; Rekers, 1977b, in press-b; Stoller, 1968a) but also prevention of the secondary problems associated with adult gender dysphoria, such as severe depression, suicidal ideation, suicide attempt, self-mutilation in the form of autocastration or autopenectomy, and extremely rigid and compulsive sex-role maladjustment (Qualls, 1978; Rekers, 1977b; Rekers, Bentler, Rosen, & Lovaas, 1977; Rosen et al., 1978), and potential prevention of untreated venereal disease, which occurs at significantly higher rates in adult sexual deviants (Meyer & Rekers, in press).

## Answering Parental Questions

Parents typically seek to prevent sexual deviance in their child and to improve the child's social and psychological adjustment. There is no empirical evidence that the values of society have changed so radically that 'parents, if given a choice, would consider it desirable to foster homosexuality, transsexualism, or transvestism in their own child. It is an appropriate therapeutic goal to reduce the maladaptive sex-role rigidity in the sex-role-disturbed child in order to increase the life options of the individual (Gray, 1971; Thoresen & Mahoney, 1974, p. 5). It is reasonable for parents to promote adaptive sex-role development and satisfaction with one's physical sex status in their child. For example, promoting nurturance toward babies in both boys and girls is desirable, but behavioral intervention is necessary for the boy who chronically playacts the roles of bearing and breast-feeding infants while cross-dressing as a "mother."

## Common Assessment Questions

*Is the child's psychosexual behavior deviant?* Do the child's atypical sex-role behaviors (their duration, their clustering, their frequency) constitute merely a "passing phase" of development, or do they represent a current psychological adjustment problem with potentially debilitating adulthood prognosis (see Stoller, 1967)? It is essential to interpret sex-role behaviors in their cultural and temporal contexts (Rosen *et al.*, 1977). For example, it is not unusual for girls in 1979 Californian culture to wear jeans to school that were designed for males with a zipper in the front. However, it may be indicative of a sex-role problem if the same girl is unable to wear a dress to Sunday school where all the other girls wear dresses. Sex-role rigidity is best assessed across a number of situational contexts. Conceptualizing deviance both clinically and statistically, the assessment task involves a survey of the available body of empirical data on sex-role development (e.g., Bates & Bentler, 1973; Bates, Bentler, & Thompson, 1973; Maccoby & Jacklin, 1974; Rekers, Amaro-Plotkin, & Low, 1977; Rekers & Rudy, 1978; Rekers & Yates, 1976), assessments of the child with available psychometric and behavioral measures, and judgments regarding the presence and magnitude of sex-role deviance in the child.

*What is the meaning of the deviant psychosexual behavior to the child?* Unfortunately, many applied behavior analysts have ignored the meaning (i.e., the total situational context) of behavior in their definition of target responses for treatment (Rekers, 1977a). For example, although nurturant behavior in a boy is normally desirable, when that behavior is accompanied by verbalizations of female sex self-labeling, it is undesirable. In the latter case, the boy unfortunately sex-types nurturance as a *female* quality, and the assessment may therefore determine for an individual boy that his inability to perform nurturant behaviors in the context of covert male sex self-labeling is a problem.

*What is the prognosis?* Is this child simply demonstrating sex-role flexibility, or does the behavior pattern represent an excessive and compulsive pattern which would place him at high risk for a sexual problem in adulthood? In assessment, the psychologist can compare the data obtained from an individual child with the data reported in the literature in order to formulate the most accurate estimate of the child's outcome in the absence of treatment intervention.

*What are the treatment goals?* Even though contemporary American society may encourage sex-role rigidity, Rosen *et al.* (1978) have argued that the socialization of the child into some sex-role flexibility is in the best interest of both the child and society. For this reason, the treatment goal would be to expand the behavioral repertoire of the child in order to increase his or her future choices among a larger number of alternative behaviors. To establish appropriate sex-typed behaviors, it is often necessary to reduce substantially the cross-sex behaviors that serve as competing responses to appropriate responding (Rekers, 1977a). The treatment goals would be (1) to teach the disturbed child to discriminate the small number of behaviors that are appropriately sex-typed masculine and feminine, (2) to decrease the child's compulsive cross-sex behavior, and (3) to encourage sex-role flexibility in the areas that go beyond the few essential distinctions between masculine and feminine roles (Rekers, 1977b, 1978a).

*What are the concurrent potential risks and benefits of treatment for this child?* Rekers *et al.* (1978) provided a detailed review of the potential risks versus the potential benefits of treating a gender-disturbed child. In general, the more extreme the child's sex-role behavior disturbance, the greater the potential benefits as compared to the potential risks.

Clinical psychologists must recognize the arbitrary nature of some sex-role distinctions in the child's culture which impose unnecessary limitations on an individual's optimal personal development. However, the presence of crippling sex-role stereotypes does not lead to the conclusion that there are no legitimate distinctions between masculine and feminine roles that the child must master. But even for arbitrarily sex-role-stereotyped behaviors, the assessment process involves the determination of the psychological significance of specific sex-role behaviors for the individual child.

For example, it is normally appropriate for parents to encourage their male children to be flexible enough to wear aprons to wash dishes, even though those behaviors have a mild feminine valence that is arbitrarily culturally defined. However, there are gender-disturbed boys who fantasize that they are women when they wear aprons to wash dishes. Part of the assessment task is to make this conceptual distinction when evaluating the individual. One goal in treatment for a gender-disturbed boy, for example, would be to assist him to become comfortable with male self-labeling behaviors while washing dishes. Normally, therefore, it would be undesirable to allow boys to avoid dish washing by their insistence that the task is exclusively for girls. In the case of a gender-identity-disturbed boy, however, it may be placing the child at risk to allow him continually to wear aprons (which symbolize dresses for him) and to wash dishes (which may symbolize taking on the "mother" role).

*What is the social reaction to the child's deviance?* Sex-role behavior deviance often leads to severe and chronic social rejection by the peer group. One typical example was a boy who was called Karl, who, unfortunately, was labeled "sissy," "queer," and "fag" by his peer group (Rekers et al., 1974). This boy referred to himself by these same names. During the course of behavioral treatment, the boy's behavior was changed, and he expressed pleasant surprise that he no longer behaved as a "queer" (particularly since he had believed that his previous condition was a chronically internalized personality disposition). However, after the child's social behaviors had changed through treatment, his peer group at school continued to reject him on the basis of his acquired social reputation as "queer." This was an important issue in behavioral assessment before and after treatment. As a result of the continued peer rejection, the child was transferred to a different school at which he could establish a new social reputation based on his new behavioral repertoire. The important assessment question is whether the reaction that the child receives from the peer group and/or family members is a direct function of his current sex-role behavior or a reflection of past deviance, which resulted in a continued deviant definition for the child.

*Is the child physically normal?* Some children referred for sex-role behavior disturbance or cross-gender identification may be previously undetected cases of pseudohermaphroditism or true hermaphroditism. Many parents inquire as to whether the child's behavior is caused by "hormones" or "genes." Theoretically, the prenatal variables of chromosomal status, fetal gonadal development, fetal hormonal development, maternal hormones, brain dimorphism, and the development of genital dimorphism cannot be overlooked as potential etiological variables that could make certain children easily vulnerable to disorders of sexual identity differentiation.

As a consequence, Rekers et al. (1979) have given a pediatric evaluation of gender-disturbed boys that consists of a medical history, a complete physical examination (including examination of the external genitalia), a chromosome analysis (including 2 cells karyotyped and 15 counted), and sex chromatin studies for buccal smear and hair root sheath cells. Baseline endocrinological studies were considered unnecessary unless abnormalities were detected in the physical examination. These investigators found all 12 of the gender-disturbed boys to be normal genetically and physically, with the exception of one boy with one undescended testicle. No evidence was found for maternal hormone treatment during pregnancy, nor were there any histories of hormonal imbalance in the mothers.


# SETTINGS AND SOURCES FOR ASSESSMENT


Research data suggest that childhood sex-role behavior deviance is characterized by stimulus specificity and by response specificity of sex-typed masculine and feminine play behaviors. Sex-typed play was found to vary as a function of the social stimulus situation and of the type of play response required (Rekers, 1975). The occurrence of cross-sex behaviors does not represent a simple function of a generalized response disposition (Rekers, 1977a). Certain environmental events may become discriminative for specific sex-typed play behaviors in a certain child, and reinforcement may be delivered in some situations but not in others. This is one possible theoretical explanation for the finding of stimulus specificity of sex-role behavior deviance in boys. Similarly, different sex-typed behaviors may elicit different response consequences from the same person, thereby accounting (theoretically) for the finding of response specificity of sex-typed behaviors.

Furthermore, numerous studies have found behavioral treatment effects for sex-typed behaviors to be stimulus-specific and response-specific (Rekers, 1977a). Therapeutic interventions in the clinic setting have not readily generalized to the home or school setting. Similarly, the effects of intervention in the home setting do not always automatically generalize to the school setting.

These findings complicate the assessment procedure for identifying cross-sex-role problems in children. Rekers (1975) specifically reported that the sex-typed behaviors of cross-gender-identified children will differ in the presence of the mother, the father, a male examiner, or a female examiner. Only sex-typed play in an "alone" condition (by observation behind a one-way mirror) was reliably correlated with the clinical diagnosis of childhood cross-gender identification.

Therefore, the child's ratio of masculine to feminine sex-typed behaviors should be assessed in all the child's major *in vivo* living environments, including the home and school classroom settings. The multisetting analysis also benefits from a multimethod approach in which direct behavioral observations (using time-sampling) are made over time, in addition to collecting data from validated parent-report inventories and from multiple informants (including mother and father separately, peers, siblings, teachers, and relatives) in order to assess the situational occurrence of deviant sex-role behaviors. It is helpful to obtain a developmental baseline by careful interviewing of the parents with regard to the frequencies of behaviors at different times in the child's development.

Rosen et al. (1977) have presented a detailed review of the sources relevant to the assessment process. They discuss the situational and temporal contexts of identity statements, cross-dressing behavior, deviant sex-role play behavior, diagnostically significant parent–child relationship behaviors, parental reaction to cross-sex-role behavior, physical appearance of the child, presence of other psychological deviance, and the interrelationship among these various factors.


# ASSESSMENT METHODS


The most reliable diagnosis of a childhood psychosexual problem requires the use of several different assessment techniques in combination in order to contribute data from many sources across several major living environments of the child. Prior to the behavioral assessment, referral information is typically obtained from pediatricians, school psychologists, teachers, or others who may have referred the child for an initial evaluation. When data collection from the significant adults in the child's daily life would not pose the risk of adversely labeling the child, clinical reports should be obtained from these individuals prior to or concurrent with a complete behavioral assessment of the individual. If the child has not been referred by a physician, a complete physical examination and medical history should await the outcome of the behavioral assessment unless the child has an urgent and un-tended medical need. Once a psychosexual problem has been documented by a complete behavioral assessment, the child should be referred to a pediatrician for a physical examination (Rekers *et al.*, 1979).

In general, the clinician should keep in mind that as children become older, they become aware of the socially defined sex-roles and discriminate sex-typed behaviors in their own and other's behavior to a greater degree as a function of learning. Children under 6 years of age may readily display deviant sex-role be-haviors, whereas older children may deliberately inhibit deviant sex-role behaviors in the clinic setting. Particularly where the child is aware of the reason for the referral to the clinician, he or she may rarely admit to cross-sex self-labeling or deviant patterns of sex-typing. Because of the artificiality introduced by the be-havioral recording procedures in the clinic for older children, it becomes increas-ingly necessary to obtain multiple types of assessment from numerous sources for older children. Some behaviors may have more diagnostic significance in the context of evaluating a self-conscious older child. For example, it appears that cross-gender-identified boys are unable to adequately discriminate their feminine-appearing ges-tures and mannerisms, yielding a higher correlation between the observations of such mannerisms in the clinic and reports of their occurrence in the home and school settings. On the other hand, the delicate situation specificity of sex-typed *play* behaviors make it necessary to record those responses across a number of *in vivo* settings.

## Analysis in the Clinic

In the clinic setting, it is useful to obtain not only direct behavioral recordings of sex-role behavior but also interview data from the child and parents, test responses on conventional psychological instruments, and more global clinical ratings.

### Measurement of Sex-Typed Play Behaviors

Clinicians cannot directly use most of the existing methods for assessing sex-typed play in children that have been devised by developmental psychologists (see Mac-coby & Jacklin, 1974) because of the critical limitations on the kinds of conclusions that could be drawn from the data obtained from an individual child. For example, many observational techniques in the child development literature involve only the child's initial choice of a toy or pictorial representation of a toy rather than con-tinuous play over a period of time (e.g., Brown, 1956; Sutton-Smith, Rosenberg, & Morgan, 1963). Many other measures of sex-typed behavior require that an adult examiner be present for the administration of the experimental procedure (e.g., Rabban, 1950), which poses a stimulus-specific condition that limits generalizations as to the critical variables controlling the individual child's sex-typed play. When such techniques are used clinically to detect sex-role behavior disturbance, those methods yield uninterpretable data in light of the finding that sex-typed play of gender-disturbed boys is a direct function of the presence of male versus female experimenters (Rekers, 1975; Rekers & Lovaas, 1971). Furthermore, another large number of conventional measures of sex-typing lose predictive power in the process of clinical interpretation of the data that requires a considerable theoretical inference from the responses of the child (such as in the use of projective tests).

BEHAVIORAL ASSESSMENT PROCEDURE. For these reasons, Rekers (1972) developed a behavioral assessment measure of play that (1) consisted of toy stimuli related to significant differences in sex-typed play behavior of normal boys and girls; (2) provided clinically meaningful data when readministered as a repeated dependent measure over time; (3) did not require the presence of a male or female examiner, thus eliminating a potential source of variance; and (4) was appropriate for administration to children ranging from ages 3 to 8 years.

This specific procedure consisted of unobtrusive recording (from behind a one-way mirror) of the individual child's continuous play with masculine and feminine toys. Because of its diagnostic usefulness, this procedure will be described in enough detail for the clinician to replicate this measure in a standard clinic setting where a one-way mirror is available. Two child-sized tables were placed in a playroom. On one end of the first table were placed girls' cosmetic articles and apparel—a wig; a pair of small, high-heeled shoes; a child-sized dress; a play cosmetic set with lipstick and manicure items; and a set of jewelry consisting of bracelets, necklaces, rings, and earrings. On the other end of this dress-up table was placed boys' apparel, consisting of a plastic football helmet, a sea captain's hat, an army helmet, an army fatigue shirt, an army belt with hatchet holder and canteen holder (all available in army surplus stores), and a battery-operated play electric razor. The second table had feminine toys on one end, including a baby doll in a 3-foot crib with sliding side, a baby bottle, baby powder, and a Barbie doll with two sets of clothes. Masculine toys on the other end of this table consisted of two dart guns with darts, a small target, a rubber knife, plastic handcuffs, and a set of 42 cowboys and Indians (each approximately 2 inches tall).

In the normative validation study using these stimuli, Rekers and Yates (1976) recorded children's continuous play (from behind a one-way mirror) in four sessions totaling 20 minutes. This procedure could be adapted in the clinic setting by having the observers use two stopwatches—one to record cumulative seconds of masculine play and the other to record cumulative seconds of contact with the feminine toys. The child is told that he or she can play with any of the toys on the dress-up table for two of the 5-minute sessions and with any of the toys on the other table for the other two 5-minute sessions. (The examiner gives instructions that alternate from the first table to the second table to the first table again, and then to the second table for a final session.)

In the validation study of the play behavior of 60 normal boys, 60 normal girls, and 15 gender-disturbed boys, no significant age effects or age–sex interactions were obtained. An analysis of variance found a highly significant sex effect

($p < .001$), indicating that the measures of masculine and feminine play discriminated between the sex-typed play preferences of normal males and females. The mean percentages of feminine play were 19% for normal boys, 76% for normal girls, and 72% for gender-disturbed boys. The highest feminine play score found among the normal boys was 56%. These results provide base-rate data on children aged 3 years and zero months to 8 years and 11 months.

It is necessary to formulate an assessment-decision rule that maximizes the probability of accurate diagnosis of gender disturbance in boys. The clinician could require that the boy obtain a score that exceeded the mean of the gender-disturbed boy group (72%) before making the diagnosis of a sex-role behavior disturbance. False positives using this decision rule should be extremely rare. With the same decision rule, however, these data indicate that the proportion of false negatives would be approximately 33%. This would not constitute a serious clinical assessment problem so long as the clinician used more than one data source for finalizing a diagnosis (Rosen et al., 1977).

This procedure is a reliable measure of sex-typed play behaviors in an "alone" condition, which has been validated for clinical use across an age range of 6 years in early childhood. It is necessary to assess the child during solitary play in this way in contrast to play in the presence of various observers in the playroom in light of the findings of the intrasubject replication study of cross-gender-identified boys reported by Rekers (1975). This study investigated various potential discriminative stimuli for feminine and masculine play with the sex-typed toys in this play procedure. An ABA reversal design demonstrated that certain stimulus conditions (such as the presence of the mother or the father or of a male or a female stranger) were discriminative for reliable intrasubject changes in sex-typed play. Although all the children played predominantly feminine while alone in the playroom, no single environmental stimulus was consistently discriminative for masculine play across the boys, although one stimulus condition was found for each boy under which he played predominantly masculine. For this reason, it is essential to administer this procedure and make the observations from behind a one-way mirror, because only the "alone" play condition (the child was informed that he would be observed) was reliably correlated with the clinical diagnosis of cross-gender identification.

It has been useful to repeat this play procedure at various stages in treatment as a replicated baseline condition in order to trace the treatment effects over time in "alone," mother-present, father-present, and stranger-present conditions (e.g., Rekers & Lovaas, 1974; Rekers, Yates, Willis, Rosen, & Taubman, 1976). This procedure was not designed to obtain independent measures of masculine play versus feminine play, because it is the ratio of masculine to feminine play that is the assessment datum of clinical significance. If the child plays for the majority of the play session, feminine play (in this calculation) tends to be a direct inverse function of masculine play.

Because this method is a forced-choice technique with only two play options, the data do not address the empirical issue of whether or not masculinity–femininity is best understood theoretically as a unidimensional, bipolar function. Clinically speaking, it would not be particularly useful to record the amount of masculine play in the presence of exclusively masculine toys or the presence of feminine play in the presence of exclusively feminine toys. The assessment of sex-role rigidity versus sex-role flexibility requires a measure of choice behavior over a period of time.

For example, different children may engage in feminine play for 10 minutes out of the total 20-minute play period. The first child may also play another 10 minutes with the masculine toys, which would be interpreted as the kind of sex-role flexibility that is often found in normal samples. The second child, however, might have displayed absolutely no play with the masculine toys, which, if replicated over many sessions, would indicate sex-role behavioral inflexibility. If feminine play alone were scored, these children would appear identical, but if feminine play were interpreted as a function of total play, the distinctions between the play behavior patterns of these two children would be readily apparent.

Some preliminary studies indicate that the procedure of training a child to *self-monitor* sex-typed play results in therapeutic behavior change to more appropriate sex-typed play patterns when used either alone or with "self-reinforcement" procedures (Rekers & Varni, 1977a, 1977b; Rekers & Mead, 1979a) in gender-disturbed boys and girls in clinic and school settings.

### Measures of Sex-Typed Mannerisms and Body Gestures

Although body gestures and behavioral mannerisms have been recognized as important characteristics reflecting sex-role, past experimental investigations of these behaviors have focused largely on the sex differences between adults and late adolescent males and females in characteristics of body position and movement (Birdwhistell, 1970; Jenni, 1976; Jenni & Jenni, 1976). It has been only very recently that developmental investigations of childhood body gestures have been conducted, even though Michael and Willis (1968) found that the first year of school was formative in the development of a child's repertoire of gestures.

Eight expressive "feminine" gestures and behavioral mannerisms have been operationally defined and systematically observed in gender-disturbed boys by Rekers (1977a). These behaviors, which have been characterized as "effeminate" by the peers, families, and clinicians describing these gender-disturbed boys, were investigated in two studies of normal boys and girls to ascertain whether the behaviors do, in fact, appear more frequently in normal girls than in normal boys.

Rekers, Amaro-Plotkin, and Low (1977) recorded these behaviors while 48 normal boys and girls in two age groups (4–5 years and 11–12 years) individually performed a standardized play task. Rekers and Rudy (1978) added a ninth body gesture and replicated these procedures while 180 boys and girls in three age groups (4–5 years, 7–8 years, and 10–11 years) were observed performing the same task. The following behaviors were found to occur significantly more frequently in girls than in boys:

1. Limp wrist—operationally defined as flexing the wrist toward the palmar surface of the forearm or upper arm while the elbow is either flexed or extended

2. Arm flutters—the rapid succession of up-and-down movements of the forearm and/or upper arm while the wrist remains relaxed
3. Flexed elbow—walking or standing with the arm(s) held such that the angle between the forearm and the upper arm is between zero and 135 degrees (approximately)
4. Hand clasp—touching the hands together in front of the body
5. Palming—touching the palm(s) to the back, front, or sides of the head above the ear level

There was an interaction between sex and age for the "hands-on-hips-with-fingers-forward" gesture, which was defined as resting the palm(s) on the waist or hips with fingers pointed forward; this gesture appeared significantly more frequently in 10- to 11-year-old boys than in younger boys and in the girls of all age groups. No other age differences were found, and sex of experimenter did not produce any significant group differences.

While clarifying behavioral differences in sex-role development, these normative base-rate data also provide a clinically useful standard for assessing children with cross-gender behavioral disturbances. Table 2 provides the group means and standard deviations for the five feminine gestures and the single masculine gesture identified by Rekers and Rudy (1978). As can be seen, the base rate for performance

TABLE 2

Group Means and Standard Deviations for Five Feminine Gestures and One Masculine Gesture

| Gesture | 4- to 5-year-olds | | 7- to 8-year-olds | | 10- to 11-year-olds | |
|---|---|---|---|---|---|---|
| | Boy | Girl | Boy | Girl | Boy | Girl |
| *Feminine* | | | | | | |
| Hand clasp | | | | | | |
| Mean | 2.47 | 4.13 | 1.80 | 4.97 | 4.17 | 4.40 |
| SD | 3.28 | 6.07 | 2.84 | 4.35 | 7.6 | 4.8 |
| Limp wrist | | | | | | |
| Mean | 0.77 | 2.53 | 1.50 | 1.87 | 0.47 | 2.60 |
| SD | 1.30 | 3.54 | 2.07 | 2.66 | 0.92 | 3.68 |
| Arm flutters | | | | | | |
| Mean | 0.13 | 0.57 | 0.07 | 0.56 | 0.06 | 0.20 |
| SD | 0.57 | 1.20 | 0.35 | 0.95 | 0.25 | 0.54 |
| Palming | | | | | | |
| Mean | 1.50 | 3.00 | 0.50 | 1.87 | 1.23 | 2.40 |
| SD | 2.68 | 3.89 | 1.02 | 4.42 | 2.09 | 3.78 |
| Flexed elbow | | | | | | |
| Mean | 13.00 | 15.06 | 13.03 | 19.63 | 14.90 | 19.36 |
| SD | 10.76 | 12.14 | 9.36 | 14.90 | 11.17 | 9.52 |
| *Masculine* | | | | | | |
| Hands on hips, fingers forward | | | | | | |
| Mean | 1.40 | 0.93 | 2.43 | 2.80 | 8.30 | 2.90 |
| SD | 3.14 | 2.03 | 3.94 | 4.92 | 10.39 | 7.43 |

for all of these gestures is generally low, occurring in from zero to 12% of the 100 6-second intervals for which the behaviors were scored. Even a moderate frequency rate for these behaviors would mark a girl, or especially a boy, as being different and would possibly provoke the peer ridicule that is typically suffered by children with deviant sex-role behaviors. If a boy between the ages of 4 and 11 years displayed a frequency of hand clasp, limp wrist, flutters, palming, or flexed elbow above the second standard deviation for normal boys, a clinician could hypothesize that the client's pattern of gestures was atypical, thereby warranting further assessment to determine the possibility of a gender disturbance. Rekers, Sanders, and Strauss (1981) have reported base rates of these same gestures in adolescent boys and girls through age 17 years.

It should be noted that some of the behavioral mannerisms displayed by gender-disturbed boys are caricatures of femininity and are different from those behaviors that are displayed both by normal boys and by normal girls. In any case, an unusually high frequency rate of any of these behaviors demonstrated to be "feminine" in this study would constitute one diagnostic sign for a serious problem of social adjustment, if not gender disturbance (Bates et al., 1973; Rekers et al., 1974; Rekers & Rudy, 1978; Stoller, 1970–1971).

Rekers (1977a) has not found the kind of discriminative stimulus control over sex-typed mannerisms and behavioral gestures that operates over sex-typed play behaviors in gender-disturbed boys. Although sex-typed play behavior is a function of definable stimulus conditions with gender-disturbed subjects (Rekers, 1975), feminine mannerisms and gestures are apparently quite stable in gender-disturbed boys, even under heavy peer criticism and the child's desire to change (Rekers, 1977a). Rekers, Willis, Yates, Rosen, and Low (1977) demonstrated that a gender-disturbed boy was not able to discriminate his sex-typed gestures adequately, which may account for these children's inability to inhibit these behaviors even under social criticism. For this reason, the clinician could easily record the occurrence of these sex-typed behavior mannerisms in a play session, which would serve as one useful assessment tool for discriminating the gender-disturbed boy from the normal child.

It is also clinically useful to assess the book-carrying behavior of the child or adolescent because the observation takes only a few minutes and large sex differences have been reported in children, adolescents, and adults (Hanaway & Burghardt, 1976; Jenni & Jenni, 1976; Rekers & Mead, 1979b). Normal males typically carry books to their side in one hand. In clear contrast, females generally carry books against their bodies with one or both arms. These sex differences have been reported to be consistent both within individuals and across cultures, and they occur regardless of the grip strength of the individual, the size of the load to be carried, or the book weight (Jenni, 1976; Spottswood & Burghardt, 1976).

### Measures of Athletic Game Skills

Rekers (Note 3) developed a specific set of assessment and training procedures to shape athletic behaviors in gender-disturbed boys. Because of the situational differences in the game skills required by the environments of different boys at different ages, it was not found to be useful to establish normative ranges of skills for children at different ages. The individualized procedure employed was to obtain information from the school, parents, and others in the boy's major living environments in order to ascertain the particular skills that would be useful for social success in the child's physical education period at school and in neighborhood peer groups.

For example, some gender-disturbed boys have notable deficits in throwing a football, socking a school playground ball, playing kickball, tossing baskets, or throwing a softball. After observation of the child's peers, an estimate is established for the average skill for the child's peer group in terms of distance in throwing a football, distance in socking a playground ball, distance and accuracy in kicking a kickball, percentage of baskets made from the free-throw line, and accuracy and distance in throwing a softball (if those are skills commonly employed by that particular child's peer group). Then a number of baseline trials are run in a testing procedure to ascertain the mean performance of the gender-disturbed boy for each of these skills. The boy's ability is then compared to those in his own peer group in order to isolate areas of skill deficit.

Once areas are targeted for remediation, a simple behavior-shaping procedure involving reinforcement of successive approximations to the desired criterion can be instituted for one play skill at a time, replicating the treatment effect across behaviors in a multiple-baseline design (Rekers *et al.*, 1974; Rekers, Willis, Yates, Rosen, & Low, 1977).

### Interview with the Child

It is essential to interview or observe the child alone as well as conjointly with the mother and the father, if possible, in order to observe mother–child behaviors, father–child behaviors, and parental responses to the child's sex-typed behaviors. It is useful to ask the child to provide the clinician with the first names of his friends at school and in the home neighborhood. The ratio of male to female names of playmates is often indicative of the peer preferences and/or social acceptance of the child. The child should describe friendship patterns, relationships with peers, favorite activities and games, and any difficulties he or she may verbalize spontaneously. It is useful to the eventual treatment process to obtain a reinforcement survey for the child by asking him or her to name favorite people, places, and things in order of the amount of time spent with each. The interviewer can also ask the child to name people, places, and things with which he or she would like to spend more time. In some cases, it is appropriate to assess by interview the child's knowledge of the physical differences between the sexes and his or her level of knowledge regarding reproductive anatomy and sexual behavior.

Whereas the younger child may be observed primarily in a play setting, children 7 and 8 years and older may be able to verbalize their sex self-labeling and to describe their family relationships and peer relationships in some detail.

In some cases, it is helpful to tape record the interview and to spend the first

20 minutes of the interview in a baseline condition in which the examiner limits his or her verbal interaction to short, nonleading, direct answers to the child's questions. If the examiner refrains from initiating any conversation but attends positively to all the child's speech irrespective of content or voice inflection, it is then possible to later score those 20 minutes of verbal behavior for a sex-typed verbal content and voice inflection. Each verbal phrase can be rated from the tape by assigning it to one of three mutually exclusive content categories: (1) *neutral speech*, consisting of references to non-sex-typed objects (e.g., telephone), to persons in which the gender is left unspecified (e.g., a swimmer), and to non-sex-typed activities (e.g., watching television); (2) *masculine speech*, consisting of words denoting masculine sex-typed objects (e.g., man's suit), masculine persons (e.g., fireman), and masculine sex-typed activities (e.g., camping with the Boy Scouts); and (3) *feminine speech*, consisting of words denoting feminine sex-typed objects (e.g., girls' toys), feminine persons (e.g., sister), and feminine sex-typed activities (e.g., putting on a dress). In addition, feminine voice inflection can be coded as the boy's verbal pronunciation of any word with a voice pitch markedly higher than his normal range of voice inflection (Rekers et al., 1974). This behavioral coding of the verbal behavior can be interpreted in terms of the ratio of feminine to masculine content by calculating the percentage of masculine content and feminine content with regard to the total number of seconds of verbal behavior (total = feminine + masculine + neutral).

### Interview with the Parents

The interview situation provides the opportunity to evaluate the severity of the potential sex-role disturbance by weighing the qualitative and quantitative aspects of sex-typed behaviors recorded in the other behavioral assessment methods. By comparing interviews with medical records, it is possible to determine whether the parents appropriately accepted the sex of assignment congruent with the child's physical sex status; nonacceptance of or ambivalence toward the child's sex is of diagnostic significance. A developmental history is important because the age of onset of the cross-sex-typed behavior is of interpretative importance. Gender identification begins to develop normally at the age of 1½–2 years and is typically established by age 5 or 6 years. In cases in which a deviant sex-typed *behavior* did not occur historically with any significant frequency until age 8 or later, it is relatively less likely that a true cross-gender *identity* is present. This would suggest that a more appropriate diagnosis might be some level of sex-role behavior disturbance.

The Rekers Behavior Checklist for Childhood Gender Problems (Rekers, 1972) can be followed for a structured interview in which (1) father–mother relationships and father–child and mother–child relationships are historically examined; (2) retrospective information is derived from the parents on the behavior rate frequencies of a large number of feminine, masculine, and neutral sex-typed behaviors; and (3) a report is obtained from the parents on their own reinforcement for each behavior in terms of several categories of possible positive, negative, or neutral contingencies. It is also helpful to have the parent list the child's overall behavioral assets, excesses, and deficits and to observe how many behaviors of psychosexual significance are included in each category.

Informally, it is helpful to ascertain the parental attitude toward sex-typed behaviors. Some parents report that effeminate behavior in a boy is amusing. Others tend to perceive the problem as innate (e.g., "The boy was always like that."). Other parents may have wittingly or unwittingly reinforced cross-sex-typed behaviors, which may be revealed by such comments as, "The second child should have been a girl."

### Conventional Psychological Tests

The child's responses to selected clinical psychological tests are useful in the assessment process in supplementing the referral information, developmental history data, interviews, and *in vivo* behavioral observations in the clinic and natural environmental settings.

A standardized intelligence test should be administered either in its full form or in an acceptable short form, to screen for deficits in intellectual functioning that could potentially interfere with the normal sex-role learning processes of childhood.

Human figure drawings can provide assessment data indicative of a sex-role behavior disturbance because the majority of normal children tend to draw a person of their own sex (Jolles, 1952), whereas the drawing of a female figure by boys has been somewhat predictive of childhood gender disturbance (Green, Fuller, & Rutley, 1972). Skilbeck, Bates, and Bentler (1975) reported that in response to a "draw a person" instruction, gender-problem boys, as contrasted to school-problem boys, were more likely (1) to draw a female figure, (2) to draw figures with enhanced body proportion, (3) to draw more articles of clothing on the figures, and (4) to draw their female figure larger than their male figure. Although these studies lend some construct–validational evidence for the Draw-a-Person Test, the variability of scores within the gender-problem and school-problem groups limits the usefulness of this assessment procedure because individual results of this test alone cannot be interpreted confidently. For this reason, this test should not be interpreted independently from data from objective parent-report inventories regarding childhood behavior and play preferences and from behavioral recordings of sex-typed play.

It has been recommended by Rosen *et al.* (1977) that a standard administration of the Schneidman Make-a-Picture Story Test can be used in which sex self-labeling can be inferred from the ratio of the total number of male to female figures in the stories generated by the child and from the sex of the main character. The use of this test for this purpose is still in the process of validation, and it is recognized that the interpretation of sex self-labeling from these data is still theoretical in basis.

To obtain a quantitative measure of the child's reported feelings toward each member of the family, the Family Relations Test (Bene & Anthony, 1957) can be administered by the standard procedure. Rosen *et al.* (1977) recommend interpretation of the correlation between the gender of each family member and the child's incoming and outgoing feelings for them. Theoretically, the test results can also be analyzed for typical defense mechanisms employed by the child and thereby yield a measure of overall degree of emotional disturbance. A lack of involvement with the father coupled with a high degree of involvement and dependence upon the mother in the individual child's score is theoretically interpreted as substantiating a diagnosis of a cross-gender identity problem as distinguished from a simple sex-role behavior disturbance (Rosen et al., 1977; Rosen & Teague, 1974).

Although the Brown IT-Scale for Children has been recommended for the assessment of sex-role disturbances in children (Green, Fuller, & Rutley, 1972), Rosen et al. (1977) have employed the measure on a series of 47 cases referred for gender disturbance and have found that the results of the IT-Scale do not correlate with final outcome diagnosis except for children under 6 years, primarily because the purpose of the test is very transparent to a child referred for evaluation for a gender-related problem.

### Measures of Sexual Arousal

The two types of measures of sexual arousal that have been used for assessing deviant patterns in adolescent children have been (1) various verbal reports or written recordings by the patient of the occurrence of sexual fantasies, urges for deviant behavior, and actual perception of sexual arousal in the clinic or natural environments of the adolescent and (2) direct measurement of penile circumference changes to sexual stimuli recorded by plethysmography.

Several investigators have obtained reports on the frequency of homosexual fantasy in adolescents before and after aversion therapy (Callahan & Leitenberg, 1973; Canton-Dutari, 1974; Davison, Brierly, & Smith, 1971; Larson, 1970). Bentler (1968) and Huff (1970) similarly obtained verbal reports on frequency of homosexual fantasy before and after treatment and upon follow-up of adolescents who were treated with nonaversive behavioral techniques. Barlow, Reynolds, and Agras (1973) instructed a 17-year-old transsexual boy to make daily records in a notebook of homosexual and heterosexual urges and fantasies. Similarly, a 17-year-old boy with deviant sexual fantasies (of physically binding and injuring women and about being injured while dressing as a woman) was taught by Mees (1966) to keep detailed records of fantasies on an inpatient hospital basis for a 25-week baseline period prior to behavioral treatment. MacCulloch, Williams, and Birtles (1971) assessed a 12-year-old boy who had a compulsion to undress and expose his erect penis to older women. These investigators used a modified Sexual Orientation Measure questionnaire, which yielded a score for sexual fantasy for "older women" and "girls my age" prior to treatment, during treatment, and after treatment; with this measure, the investigators calculated a percentage ratio of the boy's sexual fantasy for older versus younger females. Callahan and Leitenberg (1973) assessed a 15-year-old boy with a 4-year history of exposure by having the boy record daily urges to expose himself during a baseline period, during treatment, and in follow-up assessment. Lowenstein (1973) similarly instructed a 17-year-old boy to use a running diary to record a baseline of drive to expose himself, daily setting events, and experiences of sexual stimulation. The boy was instructed to record his thoughts of exposure and to rate the strength of the need to expose on a 1–10 scale.

A more direct behavioral measure of sexual arousal is plethysmography to measure penile circumference changes by mechanical strain gauge (Barlow, Becker, Leitenberg, & Agras, 1970). Prior to aversion therapy, penile volume responses have been measured as responses to pictures of male nudes and pictures of female nudes or pictures of heterosexual relationships (Callahan & Leitenberg, 1973, who translated the penile volume measure into percentage of full erection; McConaghy, 1969, 1970, 1975; McConaghy & Barr, 1973). Barlow, Agras, Abel, Blanchard, and Young (1975) recorded penile circumference changes in their studies to evaluate the separate effects of feedback and reinforcement to increase heterosexual arousal in two 15-year-old boys. Barlow *et al.* (1973) similarly recorded daily measures of penile circumference changes as a response to male nude slides and to female nude slides (calculated as percentage of full erection) in the 17-year-old transsexual boy whom they treated. Callahan and Leitenberg (1973) recorded erection to slides during exhibition exposure fantasy in a 15-year-old boy who was treated with aversive conditioning; by this method of assessment, the investigators were able to demonstrate that the effects of the behavioral treatment indicated that the boy's erectile response to slides of nude females under instructions to fantasize intercourse was 83% of maximum, whereas instructions to think of exposure resulted in only 14% erection after the treatment was completed.

### Measures of Genital Sex-Role Behavior

The two types of assessment of overt sexual behavior have been (1) verbal reports or written records by the patient of sexual fantasies during masturbation and (2) verbal reports or daily diary recordings of interpersonal sexual behavior, although validity studies on these measures have not been reported by investigators using them in clinical case studies.

Larson (1970) and Bentler (1968) reported on adolescent boys' ratio of homosexual to heterosexual masturbatory fantasies before and after treatment for homosexuality. Bentler (1968) similarly reported on pretreatment and posttreatment reports of heterosexual fantasy during masturbation in three boys, aged 11, 13, and 16 years, whom he treated for transvestism. Bond and Evans (1967) obtained periodic verbal reports from two adolescent boys (one 16 years of age, and the other 17 years) whom they treated for underwear fetishism. Similarly, Mees (1966) taught the 17-year-old boy whom he treated on an inpatient basis for sadistic and fetishistic fantasies to record on a daily basis for 25 weeks his imagery regarding deviant and normal fantasies during masturbation. MacCulloch, Williams, and Birtles (1971) obtained verbal reports on masturbatory fantasies before and after treatment of a 12-year-old boy with a compulsion for exposure. Callahan and Leitenberg (1973) also obtained patient report data on fantasies during masturbation for a 15-year-old exhibitionist.

A similar type of daily recording or periodic verbal reports have been obtained from adolescents with sexual deviations with regard to their genital sex-role behavior in their natural environment. Several investigators have obtained reports on heterosocial interaction and dating; heterosexual behaviors, including intercourse, as contrasted to frequency of homosexual behaviors in adolescents (Bentler, 1968; Callahan & Leitenberg, 1973; Gold & Neufeld, 1965; Herman, Barlow, & Agras, 1974; Huff, 1970; Larson, 1970; MacCulloch, Birtles, & Feldman, 1971; MacCulloch & Feldman, 1967); social dating behavior versus transvestic behavior (Bentler, 1968); dating behavior after behavioral treatment for transsexualism (Barlow et al., 1973); fetishistic sexual behavior before and after treatment (Strzyewsky & Zierhoffer, 1967); patterns of sexual behavior based on daily records of the 17-year-old boy with sadistic fantasies (Mees, 1966); appropriate dating behavior versus exhibitionistic behavior in teenage boys (Callahan & Leitenberg, 1973; Lowenstein, 1973); promiscuous sexual behavior in a retarded adolescent girl (Anant, 1968); and appropriate heterosocial and heterosexual dating behavior in older adolescents with avoidance of dating behavior (e.g., Melnick, 1973).

## Clinical Ratings on Sexual Identity and Gender Sex-Role Behavior

Once data have been obtained on all seven psychosexual dimensions for assessment, it becomes necessary to organize the clinical data systematically for the individually assessed child. Bates, Skilbeck, Smith, and Bentler (1974) argue that clinical impressions of children with abnormal sex-role behaviors have a unique value that is lost in more objective descriptions. They have reported on their analyses of extensive clinical ratings on a series of 29 boys, aged 5 to 13 years, referred for potential gender disturbance. They developed an extensive clinical rating form of 88 items, covering gender-appropriate behaviors, gender-inappropriate behaviors, family interaction patterns, physical characteristics of the child, traumatic history, preferences, and interpersonal characteristics of the child. To minimize individual bias, pooled scores of two or three clinicians familiar with the case were used to consolidate clinical impressions in a uniform way. Then the clinical ratings were subjected to a principal components analysis, and scores based on the principal components were computed for each individual child.

Their data suggested that clinical screening judgments regarding the presence or absence of gender disturbance are positively associated with differential ratings of specific effeminate behaviors. The boys who were clinically judged to have a significant sex-role disturbance received high ratings on a cluster of effeminate behaviors to a greater degree in early childhood than in middle childhood. A number of investigators have reported that peer and family pressures on effeminate boys (Rosen et al., 1977; Zuger, 1970b) and the situation specificity of cross-sex-typed behaviors (demonstrated by Rekers, 1975) can lead to an overt conformity in sex-role behavior at later ages, although the effeminate preferences may reappear in later life. For this reason, the observed reduction in overt effeminacy from early to middle childhood is not likely to represent a meaningful change in gender identification. Because higher rates of uninhibited cross-sex-role behavior are more likely in earlier childhood, the clinician should carefully compare the reports of earlier behavioral history with the present behavioral assessment data for the diagnosis of an individual child.

In the study by Bates *et al.* (1974), boys who were clinically judged not to have a significant gender disturbance were found to be rated as coming from relatively normal family environments and as being more popular in their peer groups as compared to the gender-disordered boys. In addition, those boys judged to have gender disturbance received clinical ratings of observable passivity, harm avoidance, and associated parental overprotectiveness. The data also suggested that boys referred for effeminacy tend to show a lack of normal response to social situations, regardless of the level or degree of gender disturbance. The referred boys were rated as being uniformly unable to deal successfully in interpersonal situations. Of the referrals, 20 were judged to be less happy than most children, and only 1 was judged to be more happy; 15 were rated as less independent than normal, and only 4 as more independent; and 18 were rated as psychologically immature, and only 3 as more mature. Within the group of boys clinically judged to have a gender disturbance, the general findings were that the mothers were not accepting of masculinity, and the families were characterized by overprotectiveness and punishment of noisy, aggressive behavior.

In a study by Bentler, Rekers, and Rosen (1979), 38 children (aged 4 to 12 years) who were referred for potential gender disturbances were given three independent clinical psychological assessments using two numbered clinical rating scales: one for sex-role behavior disturbance and another for sex-role identity disturbance. Three independent clinical ratings of sex-role behavior were based on psychodynamic assessment procedures, behavioral assessment, and psychometric instruments, respectively, using this five-point scale: (1) extreme sex-role behavior disturbance, (2) marked sex-role behavior disturbance, (3) moderate sex-role behavior disturbance, (4) mild sex-role behavior disturbance, and (5) no sex-role behavior disturbance. The ratings derived from behavioral and psychodynamic procedures were intercorrelated ($r = +.692$). Alpha (.654) and theta (.692) coefficients for the mean sex-role behavior disturbance rating demonstrated internal consistency.

Two of the clinical psychologists in this same study made ratings on a five-point scale of sex-role identity disturbance: (1) profound cross-sex-role identification, (2) moderate cross-sex-role identification, (3) sex-role identity confusion, (4) moderate sex-role identity confusion, and (5) normal sex-role identification. These two independent clinical ratings of sex-role identity disturbance, which were derived from a psychodynamic evaluation and a behavioral assessment, yielded moderate interrater agreement ($r = +.593$). The mean rating of sex-role identity provided a high degree of internal consistency (alpha = theta = .813). The pooled mean ratings for sex-role behavior disturbance and for sex-role identity disturbance were positively correlated ($r = +.708$). An overall diagnosis for each subject, which was derived by combining the behavior and identity mean ratings, yielded a high internal consistency coefficient, demonstrating reliable discrimination among the children in terms of the measurement dimensions of sex-role behavior and sex-role identity.

## Analysis in the Home

Because of the situational specificity of sex-typed behavior (Rekers, 1972, 1975, 1977a), it is essential to obtain assessment data in the natural living environments of the child, including the home. Assessment of the child's sex-typed behavior is most directly accomplished by systematic behavioral recordings in the home environment by parents and external observers. A supplemental, but less direct, procedure would be to use the two validated parent-report inventories available.

### Direct Observational Recordings

Parents can be taught to use time-sampling procedures to record reliably the frequency of excessive public masturbation (Ferguson & Rekers, 1979; Wagner, 1968) and the frequency of such sex-typed behaviors as play with girls, play with boys, play with dolls, taking female roles in play, taking male roles in play, and feminine gestures (Rekers & Lovaas, 1974; Rekers et al., 1974; Rekers, Willis, Yates, Rosen, & Low, 1977). External observers can be sent to the home to obtain simultaneous recordings to check for observer reliability. If the parent is instructed to make time-sampled recordings at specific times twice or three times daily, an adequate baseline frequency of these behaviors can be obtained over a 3-week period. Some of the more complex sex-typed behaviors, such as masculine content versus feminine content in speech, feminine voice inflection, and specific subtypes of sex-typed behavior mannerisms or body gestures, are more difficult for parents to record reliably in the home setting and are better recorded by trained external observers who make visits to the home (e.g., Rekers et al., 1974; Rekers, Willis, Yates, Rosen, & Low, 1977).

### Parent-Report Inventories

Two parent-report instruments have been developed and validated which are quick and useful measures of gender disturbance in boys: the Child Game Participation Questionnaire (based on the research on normal and gender-disturbed boys reported in Bates & Bentler, 1973) and the Child Behavior and Attitude Questionnaire (based on the research on normal and gender-disturbed samples reported in Bates et al., 1973). The questionnaire items and scoring procedures are available in the publications cited; the clinical diagnoses regarding sex-role behavior disturbance made primarily on the basis of data from those inventories alone have been found to be somewhat correlated with more clinical ratings based on more extensive behavioral assessment ($r = +.250$) and assessments based on a comprehensive psychodynamic evaluation of children ($r = +.233$) as reported by Bentler et al. (1979).

### Self-Monitoring

For adolescents, various self-recording procedures have been used for the problems of homosexuality, transvestism, transsexualism, fetishism, exhibitionism, and promiscuous sexual behavior (see review by Rekers, 1978b).

## Analysis in the School

Without identifying the child as having been referred for a potential gender problem, it is useful to obtain school records, school psychological testing, and counselor reports. If the school has already referred the child for potential gender disturbance, there is no risk of adversely labeling the child by sending behavioral observers to the school setting to train the teacher to make simple time-sampled recordings of behaviors such as cross-dressing, effeminate voice inflection, feminine content in speech versus masculine content in speech, and feminine mannerisms and gestures. External observers can be sent to the school classroom to pose as student teachers and to make ratings on an individual child. If there is concern regarding adversely labeling a child as potentially gender-disturbed for the teacher who may be unaware of the potential difficulty, it is often possible to obtain permission from the principal of the school to send the observer to pose as a student teacher in the class and to make ratings on three children, only one of which is the target child for clinical evaluation, without the teacher knowing which one is genuinely being observed. Reliable observational data from teachers and external observers have been obtained in the school setting (e.g., Rekers *et al.*, 1974; Rekers & Varni, 1977b).

## Integration of Assessment for Diagnostic Formulation

Until more longitudinal developmental research data are available, the diagnosis of the various childhood psychosexual problems must be based upon a weighing of the assessment data collected on the individual child as compared to the data available on the limited prospective studies on untreated child cases followed longitudinally, the data obtained retrospectively from adult cases, and the developmental theories. Parental reports alone would be considered insufficient data to lead to a positive diagnosis and must be supplemented with behavioral assessment data obtained in the clinic and by direct observation in the child's major living environments. It is important to consider the ratio of masculine to feminine sex-typed behavior, the number of different cross-sex behaviors, the chronicity of the behavior patterns, the situational contexts in which the deviant behaviors occur, the child's own verbal statements regarding his or her behavior, the reaction of the peer group and parents to the child's deviant behavior, and the general psychological adjustment of the child.

It is helpful to summarize the assessment data for an individual child in terms of the outline of the seven psychosexual dimensions. In this way, overt sex-typed behavior patterns can be compared with sex self-labeling behaviors, for example. It is relatively less likely that a true cross-gender identity is present in cases where compulsive cross-sex behavior has not occurred at any significant frequency until age 9 or 10 years. It is more common for the cross-gender syndrome to be evidenced at a much younger age, usually before 6 years.

## ILLUSTRATIVE CASE MATERIAL

Several detailed intrasubject case studies of gender-disturbed children have been published elsewhere in the recent literature. These cases are simply cited here, since the reader can obtain the journal articles for more specific review. Rekers and Lovaas (1971, 1974, 1979) describe the behavioral assessment of cross-gender-identified boys who were evaluated in the clinic and home settings using primarily direct behavioral observation of sex-typed play behavior and body gestures. Rekers, Lovaas, and Low (1974) present the assessment of an 8-year-old boy with cross-gender identification who was evaluated in the clinic, home, and school settings with direct observational measures of sex-typed speech content, voice inflection, play patterns, body gestures and mannerisms, athletic skill behavior, and overall psychological adjustment.

Rekers *et al.* (1976) present the assessment of a 5-year-old cross-gender-identified boy that was accomplished primarily by using methods in the clinic and assessing carefully a variety of stimulus setting events for the cross-gender behavior in the clinic setting. Rekers and Varni (1977a) report a 6-year-old cross-gender-identified boy who was evaluated primarily in the clinic setting but also in the home environment. Rekers, Willis, Yates, Rosen, and Low (1977) report the most comprehensive assessment of a sex-role behavior disturbed 8-year-old boy in the home and clinic settings, with detailed procedures on the recording of behavioral mannerisms in particular. Rekers and Varni (1977b) report the behavioral observations of a 4-year-old boy with gender identity confusion in the clinic and preschool settings and illustrate the therapeutic goal of using self-regulation strategies to enhance more androgynous play behavior rather than stereotyped cross-sex behavior patterns. Rekers and Mead (1979a) similarly report the behavioral observations made of an 8-year-old gender-identity-disturbed girl in clinical and home settings, before and after a self-monitoring treatment intervention.

Rekers and Milner (1978) provide five diagnostic case examples illustrating the variety of different disorders that can be detected in assessment. Rekers (1978b) surveyed case studies and intrasubject research studies on the behavioral assessment and treatment of a variety of child and adolescent psychosexual disorders.

## ASSESSMENT–TREATMENT IMPLICATIONS

The formulation of specific treatment intervention goals for an individual child must await the outcome of the comprehensive behavioral assessment. Rekers (1977a, 1978b) has reviewed the behavioral treatment strategies that have been reported in the literature, with particular emphasis upon those strategies that have been evaluated by the use of intrasubject replication designs. If a child has a cross-sex self-labeling problem in conjunction with a deviant pattern of sex-role behavior, the treatment objectives would include decreasing the cross-sex behavior and increasing the child's repertoire of appropriate sex-role behaviors. On the other hand, if there is little presumptive evidence of a cross-sex identity problem although a number of deviant sex-role behavior patterns are present, it may be more helpful to the child to increase the repertoire of appropriate sex-role behaviors to increase sex-role flexibility and perhaps to decrease only one or two discrete behaviors such as cross-dressing, which may be eliciting social ostracism or which may place the child at high risk for sexual adjustment difficulties in the future.

In the same way, deviant sexual behaviors need to be interpreted in their situational context. Patterns of simple masturbation may not warrant treatment intervention, but if the behavior occurs excessively in public so as to disrupt school classroom activities for peers and teachers, it would be important to train the child to inhibit the behavior in public settings (Ferguson & Rekers, 1979; Rekers, in press-c).

For a discussion of specific treatment strategies as they evolve from the findings of behavioral assessment of childhood gender problems, the reader is referred to a growing literature (Bates *et al.*, 1974; Rekers, 1977a, 1978b, 1981a). After treatment has been carried out, identical outcome measures should be used to evaluate the effects of treatment across the seven dimensions of psychosexual adjustment. In a follow-up assessment study that is in progress, Rekers is recontacting all children previously referred for psychosexual and gender disturbances to readminister a comprehensive battery of clinical psychological and behavioral assessment measures. These measures are being administered in a different clinic setting and by clinicians other than those who initially dealt with the child, in order to provide some independence of the posttreatment follow-up evaluation.

## Acknowledgments

The author's original research presented in this chapter was supported by a National Science Foundation graduate fellowship at the University of California at Los Angeles, a postdoctoral fellowship grant at Harvard University from the Foundations' Fund for Research in Psychiatry, and U.S. Public Health Service research grants MH21803, MH28240, and MH29945, the latter at the Logos Research Institute, Inc. Appreciation is expressed to Dr. Judy A. Sanders, who assisted in the technical preparation of the manuscript.

## Reference Notes

1. No surgery for transsexuals. *Time*, August 27, 1979, p. 73.
2. Money, J., & Russo, A. *Establishment of homosexual gender identity/role: Longitudinal follow-up of discordant gender identity/role in childhood.* Paper presented at the meeting of the American Psychological Association, Toronto, Ontario, Canada, August 28–September 1, 1978.
3. Rekers, G. A. *Shaping athletic behaviors in children.* Training manual, University of California at Los Angeles, 1973.

# References

American Psychological Association. *Ethical standards of psychologists* (Rev. ed.). Washington, D.C.: Author, 1977.

Anant, S. S. Verbal aversion therapy with a promiscuous girl: Case report. *Psychological Reports*, 1968, *22*, 795–796.

Atcheson, J. D., & Williams, D. C. A study of juvenile sex offenders. *American Journal of Psychiatry*, 1954, *111*, 336–370.

Bakwin, H. Deviant gender-role behavior in children: Relation to homosexuality. *Pediatrics*, 1968, *41*, 620–629.

Barlow, D. H., Agras, W. S., Abel, G. G., Blanchard, E. B., & Young, L. D. Biofeedback and reinforcement to increase heterosexual arousal in homosexuals. *Behaviour Research and Therapy*, 1975, *13*, 45–50.

Barlow, D. H., Becker, R., Leitenberg, H., & Agras, W. S. A mechanical strain gauge for recording penile circumference change. *Journal of Applied Behavior Analysis*, 1970, *3*, 73–76.

Barlow, D. H., Reynolds, E. J., & Agras, W. S. Gender identity change in a transsexual. *Archives of General Psychiatry*, 1973, *28*, 569–576.

Bates, J. E., & Bentler, P. M. Play activities of normal and effeminate boys. *Developmental Psychology*, 1973, *9*, 20–27.

Bates, J. E., Bentler, P. M., & Thompson, S. Measurement of deviant gender development in boys. *Child Development*, 1973, *44*, 591–598.

Bates, J. E., Skilbeck, W. M., Smith, K. V. R., & Bentler, P. M. Gender role abnormalities in boys: An analysis of clinical ratings. *Journal of Abnormal Child Psychology*, 1974, *2*, 1–16.

Bates, J. E., Skilbeck, W. M., Smith, K. V. R., & Bentler, P. M. Intervention with families of gender-disturbed boys. *American Journal of Orthopsychiatry*, 1975, *45*, 150–157.

Bem, S. L. The measurement of psychological androgyny. *Journal of Consulting and Clinical Psychology*, 1974, *42*, 155–162.

Bem, S. L. Sex role adaptability: One consequence of psychological androgyny. *Journal of Personality and Social Psychology*, 1975, *31*, 634–643.

Bender, L., & Blau, A. The reaction of children to sexual relations with adults. *American Journal of Orthopsychiatry*, 1937, *7*, 500–518.

Bender, L., & Paster, S. Homosexual trends in children. *American Journal of Orthopsychiatry*, 1941, *11*, 730–743.

Bene, E., & Anthony, J. *Manual for the Family Relations Test*. London: National Foundation for Educational Research, 1957.

Benjamin, H. *The transsexual phenomenon*. New York: The Julian Press, 1966.

Bentler, P. M. Heterosexual behavior assessment—1. Males. *Behaviour Research and Therapy*, 1968, *6*, 21–25.

Bentler, P. M. A typology of transsexualism: Gender identity theory and data. *Archives of Sexual Behavior*, 1976, *5*, 567–584.

Bentler, P. M., & Prince, C. Psychiatric symptomatology in transvestites. *Journal of Clinical Psychology*, 1970, *26*, 434–435.

Bentler, P. M., Rekers, G. A., & Rosen, A. C. Congruence of childhood sex-role identity and behaviour disturbances. *Child: Care, Health and Development*, 1979, *5*, 267–284.

Bieber, I., Dain, H. J., Dince, P. R., Drellich, M. G., Grand, H. G., Gundlach, R. H., Kremer, M. W., Rifkin, A. H., Wilber, C. B., & Bieber, T. B. *Homosexuality: A psychoanalytic study*. New York: Basic Books, 1962.

Birdwhistell, R. L. *Kinesics and context*. Philadelphia: University of Pennsylvania Press, 1970.

Bitter-Lebert, I. [A case of excessive masturbation]. *Praxis der Kinderpsychologie und Kinderpsychiatrie*, 1956, *6*(2/3), 44–48.

Bond, I., & Evans, D. Avoidance therapy: Its uses in two cases of underwear fetishism. *Canadian Medical Association Journal*, 1967, *96*, 1160–1162.

Bradley, S. J., Steiner, B., Zucker, K., Doering, R. W., Sullivan, J., Finegan, J. K., & Richardson,

M. Gender identity problems of children and adolescents. *Canadian Psychiatric Association Journal*, 1978, *23*, 175–183.

Braun, M., & Rekers, G.A. *The Christian in an age of sexual eclipse*. Wheaton, Ill.: Tyndale House Publishers, 1981.

Brown, D. G. Sex-role preference in young children. *Psychological Monographs: General and Applied*, 1956, *70* (14, Whole No. 421), 1–19.

Brown, F. Sexual problems of the adolescent girl. *Pediatric Clinics of North America*, 1972, *19*, 759–764.

Brunold, H. Observations after sexual traumata suffered in childhood. *Excerpta Criminologica (Netherlands)*, 1964, *4*(1), 5–8.

Callahan, E. J., & Leitenberg, H. Aversion therapy for sexual deviation: Contingent shock and covert sensitization. *Journal of Abnormal Psychology*, 1973, *81*, 60–73.

Canton-Dutari, A. Combined intervention for controlling unwanted homosexual behavior. *Archives of Sexual Behavior*, 1974, *3*, 367–371.

Coe, J. I. Sexual asphyxias. *Life-Threatening Behavior*, 1974, *4*, 171–175.

Craft, M. Boy prostitutes and their fate. *British Journal of Psychiatry*, 1966, *112*, 1111–1114.

Davison, K., Brierley, H., & Smith, C. A male monozygotic twinship discordant for homosexuality. *British Journal of Psychiatry*, 1971, *118*, 675–682.

Deisher, R. W. The young male prostitute. *Pediatrics*, 1970, *45*, 153–154.

Deisher, R. W., Eisner, V., & Sulzbacher, S. I. The young male prostitute. *Pediatrics*, 1969, *43*, 936–941.

Edmondson, J. S. A case of sexual asphyxia without fatal termination. *British Journal of Psychiatry*, 1972, *121*, 437–438.

Evans, R. B. Childhood parental relationships of homosexual men. *Journal of Consulting and Clinical Psychology*, 1969, *33*, 129–135.

Ferguson, L. N., & Rekers, G. A. Non-aversive intervention for public childhood masturbation. *The Journal of Sex Research*, 1979, *15*, 213–223.

Ferguson, L. R. The competence and freedom of children to make choices regarding participation in research: A statement. *Journal of Social Issues*, 1978, *34*, 114–121.

Gandy, P., & Deisher, R. Young male prostitutes: The physician's role in social rehabilitation. *Journal of the American Medical Association*, 1970, *212*, 1661–1666.

Gilbert, J. A. An unusual case of masturbation. *American Journal of Urology and Sexology*, 1916, *12*, 82–87.

Ginsburg, K. N. The "meat-rack": A study of the male homosexual prostitute. *American Journal of Psychotherapy*, 1967, *21*, 170–185.

Gold, S., & Neufeld, I. L. A learning approach to the treatment of homosexuality. *Behaviour Research and Therapy*, 1965, *2*, 201–204.

Gray, S. W. Ethical issues in research in early childhood education. *Children*, 1971, *18*, 83–89.

Green, R. *Sexual identity conflict in children and adults*. New York: Basic Books, 1974.

Green, R. One hundred ten feminine and masculine boys: Behavioral contrasts and demographic similarities. *Archives of Sexual Behavior*, 1976, *5*, 425–446.

Green, R. Childhood cross-gender behavior and subsequent sexual preference. *American Journal of Psychiatry*, 1979, *136*, 106–108.

Green, R., Fuller, M., & Rutley, B. IT-scale for children and Draw-A-Person Test: 30 feminine vs. 25 masculine boys. *Journal of Personality Assessment*, 1972, *36*, 349–352.

Green, R., & Money, J. Effeminacy in prepubertal boys: Summary of eleven cases and recommendations for case management. *Pediatrics*, 1961, *27*, 286–291.

Green, R., & Money, J. (Eds.). *Transsexualism and sex reassignment*. Baltimore: Johns Hopkins University Press, 1969.

Green, R., Newman, L. E., & Stoller, R. J. Treatment of boyhood "transsexualism"—An interim report of four years' experience. *Archives of General Psychiatry*, 1972, *26*, 213–217.

Greenson, R. R. A transvestite boy and a hypothesis. *International Journal of Psychoanalysis*, 1966, *47*, 396–403.

Grover, J. W. Problems of emerging sexuality and their management. *Rhode Island Medical Journal*, 1973, *56*, 274–279; 298.

Hackett, T. P. The psychotherapy of exhibitionists in a court clinic setting. *Seminars in Psychiatry*, 1971, *3*, 297–306.

Hamelstein, H. Youth and *their* sexual problems. *Journal of Clinical Child Psychology*, 1974, *3*(3), 31–33.

Hanaway, T. P., & Burghardt, G. M. The development of sexually dimorphic book-carrying behavior. *Bulletin of the Psychonomic Society*, 1976, *7*, 267–270.

Harrington, C. C. *Errors in sex-role behavior in teenage boys*. New York: Teachers College Press, 1970.

Hartmann, L. Some uses of dirty words by children. *Journal of the American Academy of Child Psychiatry*, 1973, *12*, 108–122.

Herman, S. H., Barlow, D. H., & Agras, W. S. An experimental analysis of classical conditioning as a method of increasing heterosexual arousal in homosexuals. *Behavior Therapy*, 1974, *5*, 33–47.

Holemon, E. R., & Winokur, G. Effeminate homosexuality: A disease of childhood. *American Journal of Orthopsychiatry*, 1965, *35*, 48–56.

Huff, F. W. The desensitization of a homosexual. *Behaviour Research and Therapy*, 1970, *8*, 99–102.

Hutt, C. Biological bases of psychological sex differences. *American Journal of Diseases in Childhood*, 1978, *132*, 170–177.

Jenni, D. A., & Jenni, M. A. Carrying behavior in humans: Analysis of sex differences. *Science*, 1976, *194*, 859–860.

Jenni, M. A. Sex differences in carrying behavior. *Perceptual and Motor Skills*, 1976, *43*, 323–330.

Jolles, I. A study of the validity of some hypotheses for the qualitative interpretation of the H-T-P for children of elementary school age. *Journal of Clinical Psychology*, 1952, *8*, 113–118.

Katzman, M. Early sexual trauma. *Sexual Behavior*, 1972, *2*(2), 13–17.

Kinsey, A. C., Pomeroy, W. B., & Martin, C. E. *Sexual behavior in the human male*. Philadelphia: W. B. Saunders, 1948.

Langsley, D. G., Schwartz, M. N., & Fairbairn, R. H. Father–son incest. *Comprehensive Psychiatry*, 1968, *9*, 218–226.

Larson, D. E. An adaptation of the Feldman and MacCulloch approach to treatment of homosexuality by the application of anticipatory avoidance learning. *Behaviour Research and Therapy*, 1970, *8*, 209–210.

Lebovitz, P. S. Feminine behavior in boys: Aspects of its outcome. *American Journal of Psychiatry*, 1972, *128*, 1283–1289.

Levine, M. I., & Bell, A. I. Psychological aspects of pediatric practice. II. Masturbation. *Pediatrics*, 1956, *18*, 803–808.

Lowenstein, L. F. A case of exhibitionism treated by counter-conditioning. *Adolescence*, 1973, *8*, 213–218.

Maccoby, E. E. (Ed.). *The development of sex differences*. Stanford, Calif.: Stanford University Press, 1966.

Maccoby, E. E., & Jacklin, C. N. *The psychology of sex differences*. Stanford, Calif.: Stanford University Press, 1974.

MacCulloch, M. J., Birtles, C. J., & Feldman, M. P. Anticipatory avoidance learning for the treatment of homosexuality: Recent developments and an automatic aversion therapy system. *Behavior Therapy*, 1971, *2*, 151–169.

MacCulloch, M. J., & Feldman, M. P. Aversion therapy in management of 43 homosexuals. *British Medical Journal*, 1967, *2*, 594–597.

MacCulloch, M. J., Williams, C., & Birtles, C. J. The successful application of aversion therapy to an adolescent exhibitionist. *Journal of Behavior Therapy and Experimental Psychiatry*, 1971, *2*, 61–66.

Mangus, A. R. Sex crimes against children. In K. M. Bournen (Ed.), *Sexual deviation research*. Sacramento: Assembly of the State of California, March 1932.

Marshall, W., & Tanner, J. Variations in the pattern of pubertal changes in girls. *Archives of Disease in Childhood*, 1969, *44*, 291–303.

Marshall, W., & Tanner, J. Variations in the pattern of pubertal changes in boys. *Archives of Disease in Childhood*, 1970, *45*, 13–23.

Martin, R. *Legal challenges to behavior modification*. Champaign, Ill.: Research Press, 1975.

McConaghy, N. Subjective and penile plethysmograph responses following aversion–relief and apomorphine aversion therapy for homosexual impulses. *British Journal of Psychiatry*, 1969, *115*, 723–730.

McConaghy, N. Penile response conditioning and its relationship to aversion therapy in homosexuals. *Behavior Therapy*, 1970, *1*, 213–221.

McConaghy, N. Aversive and positive conditioning treatments of homosexuality. *Behaviour Research and Therapy*, 1975, *13*, 309–319.

McConaghy, N., & Barr, R. F. Classical, avoidance and backward conditioning treatments of homosexuality. *British Journal of Psychiatry*, 1973, *122*, 151–162.

Mees, H. L. Sadistic fantasies modified by aversive conditioning and substitution: A case study. *Behaviour Research and Therapy*, 1966, *4*, 317–320.

Melnick, J. A comparison of replication techniques in the modification of minimal dating behavior. *Journal of Abnormal Psychology*, 1973, *81*, 51–59.

Meyer, J. K., & Reter, D. J. Sex reassignment: Follow-up. *Archives of General Psychiatry*, 1979, *36*, 1010–1015.

Meyer, S. A., & Rekers, G. A. Venereal disease. In W. A. Elwell (Ed.), *Tyndale encylcopedia of Christian knowledge*. Wheaton, Ill.: Tyndale House Publishers, in press.

Meyer-Bahlburg, H. F. L. Sex hormones and male homosexuality in comparative perspective. *Archives of Sexual Behavior*, 1977, *6*, 297–325.

Michael, G., & Willis, F. N., Jr. The development of gestures as a function of social class, educational level, and sex. *Psychological Record*, 1968, *18*, 515–519.

Mischel, W. Sex-typing and socialization. In P. H. Mussen (Ed.), *Carmichael's manual of child psychology* (3rd ed., Vol. 2). New York: Wiley, 1970.

Mohr, J. W., & Turner, R. E. Sexual deviations. Part III: Exhibitionism. *Applied Therapeutics*, 1967, *9*, 263–265.

Money, J. Critique of Dr. Zuger's manuscript. *Psychosomatic Medicine*, 1970, *32*, 463–465. (a)

Money, J. Sexual dimorphism and homosexual gender identity. *Psychological Bulletin*, 1970, *74*, 425–440. (b)

Money, J., & Ehrhardt, A. A. *Man and woman, boy and girl: The differentiation and dimorphism of gender identity from conception to maturity*. Baltimore: Johns Hopkins University Press, 1972.

Money, J., Hampson, J. G., & Hampson, J. L. An examination of some basic sexual concepts: Evidence of human hermaphroditism. *Bulletin of the Johns Hopkins Hospital*, 1955, *97*, 301–319.

Money, J., & Primrose, C. Sexual dimorphism and dissociation in the psychology of male transsexuals. *Journal of Nervous and Mental Disease*, 1968, *147*, 472–486.

Mussen, P. H. Early sex-role development. In D. A. Goslin (Ed.), *Handbook of socialization theory and research*. Chicago: Rand McNally, 1969.

Nadler, R. P. Approach to psychodynamics of obscene telephone calls. *New York State Journal of Medicine*, 1968, *68*, 521–526.

Pauly, I. Adult manifestations of male transsexualism. In R. Green & J. Money (Eds.), *Transsexualism and sex reassignment*. Baltimore: Johns Hopkins University Press, 1969.

Pittman, D. J. The male house of prostitution. *Trans-Action*, 1971, *8*(5, 6), 21–27.

Prince, C. V., & Bentler, P. M. A survey of 504 cases of transvestism. *Psychological Reports*, 1972, *31*, 903–917.

Qualls, C. B. The prevention of sexual disorders: An overview. In C. B. Qualls, J. P. Wincze, & D. H. Barlow (Eds.), *The prevention of sexual disorders: Issues and approaches*. New York: Plenum, 1978.

Rabban, M. Sex-role identification in young children in two diverse social groups. *Genetic Psychology Monographs*, 1950, *42*, 81–158.

Raven, S. Boys will be boys: The male prostitute in London. In H. M. Ruitenbeek (Ed.), *Problem of homosexuality in modern society*. New York: E. P. Dutton, 1963.

Reiss, A. J. Social integration of queers and peers. In H. M. Ruitenbeek (Ed.), *Problem of homosexuality in modern society*. New York: E. P. Dutton, 1963.

Rekers, G. A. Pathological sex-role development in boys: Behavioral treatment and assessment (Doctoral dissertation, University of California, Los Angeles, 1972). *Dissertation Abstracts International*, 1972, *33*, 3321B. (University Microfilms No. 72-33, 978)

Rekers, G. A. Stimulus control over sex-typed play in cross-gender identified boys. *Journal of Experimental Child Psychology*, 1975, *20*, 136–148.

Rekers, G. A. Assessment and treatment of childhood gender problems. In B. B. Lahey & A. E. Kazdin (Eds.), *Advances in clinical child psychology* (Vol. 1). New York: Plenum, 1977. (a)

Rekers, G. A. Atypical gender development and psychosocial adjustment. *Journal of Applied Behavior Analysis*, 1977, *10*, 559–571. (b)

Rekers, G. A. A priori values and research on homosexuality. *American Psychologist*, 1978, *33*, 510–512. (a)

Rekers, G. A. Sexual problems: Behavior modification. In B. B. Wolman (Ed.), *Handbook of treatment of mental disorders in childhood and adolescence*. Englewood Cliffs, N.J.: Prentice-Hall, 1978. (b)

Rekers, G. A. Sex-role behavior change: Intrasubject studies of boyhood gender disturbance. *Journal of Psychology*, 1979, *103*, 255–269.

Rekers, G. A. Childhood identity disorders. *Medical Aspects of Human Sexuality*, 1981, *15*, in press. (a)

Rekers, G.A. *Your child's future: Homosexuality or family fulfilment?* Chicago: Moody Press, 1981, in press. (b)

Rekers, G. A. Gay liberation. In W. A. Elwell (Ed.), *Tyndale encyclopedia of Christian knowledge*. Wheaton, Ill.: Tyndale House Publishers, in press. (a)

Rekers, G. A. Homosexuality. In W. A. Elwell (Ed.), *Tyndale encyclopedia of Christian knowledge*. Wheaton, Ill.: Tyndale House Publishers, in press. (b)

Rekers, G. A. Masturbation. In W. A. Elwell (Ed.), *Tyndale encyclopedia of Christian knowledge*. Wheaton, Ill.: Tyndale House Publishers, in press. (c)

Rekers, G. A., Amaro-Plotkin, H., & Low, B. P. Sex-typed mannerisms in normal boys and girls as a function of sex and age. *Child Development*, 1977, *48*, 275–278.

Rekers, G. A., Bentler, P. M., Rosen, A. C., & Lovaas, O. I. Child gender disturbances: A clinical rationale for intervention. *Psychotherapy: Theory, Research and Practice*, 1977, *14*, 2–11.

Rekers, G. A., Crandall, B. F., Rosen, A. C., & Bentler, P. M. Genetic and physical studies of male children with psychological gender disturbances. *Psychological Medicine*, 1979, *9*, 373–375.

Rekers, G. A., & Lovaas, O. I. Experimental analysis of cross-sex behavior in male children. *Research Relating to Children*, 1971, *28*, 68. (Abstract)

Rekers, G. A., & Lovaas, O. I. Behavioral treatment of deviant sex-role behaviors in a male child. *Journal of Applied Behavior Analysis*, 1974, *7*, 173–190.

Rekers, G. A., Lovaas, O. I., & Low, B. P. The behavioral treatment of a "transsexual" preadolescent boy. *Journal of Abnormal Child Psychology*, 1974, *2*, 99–116.

Rekers, G. A., & Mead, S. Early intervention for female sexual identity disturbance: Self-monitoring of play behavior. *Journal of Abnormal Child Psychology*, 1979, *7*, 405–423. (a)

Rekers, G. A., & Mead, S. Human sex differences in carrying behaviors: A replication and extension. *Perceptual and Motor Skills*, 1979, *48*, 625–626. (b)

Rekers, G. A., & Mead, S. Female sex-role deviance: Early identification and developmental intervention. *Journal of Clinical Child Psychology*, 1980, *8*, 199–203.

Rekers, G. A., & Milner, G. C., III. Sexual identity disorders in childhood and adolescence. *Journal of the Florida Medical Association*, 1978, *65*, 962–964.

Rekers, G. A., & Milner, G. C., III. How to diagnose and manage childhood sexual disorders. *Behavioral Medicine*, 1979, *6*(4), 18–21.

Rekers, G. A., & Milner, G. C., III. Early detection of sexual identity disorders. *Medical Aspects of Human Sexuality*, 1981, *15*, in press.

Rekers, G. A., Rosen, A. C., Lovaas, O. I., & Bentler, P. M. Sex-role stereotypy and professional intervention for childhood gender disturbances. *Professional Psychology*, 1978, *9*, 127–136.

Rekers, G. A., & Rudy, J. P. Differentiation of childhood body gestures. *Perceptual and Motor Skills*, 1978, *46*, 839–845.

Rekers, G. A., Sanders, J. A., & Strauss, C. C. Developmental differentiation of adolescent body gestures. *Journal of Genetic Psychology*, 1981, *138*(1), 123–131.

Rekers, G. A., & Varni, J. W. Self-monitoring and self-reinforcement processes in a pre-transsexual boy. *Behaviour Research and Therapy*, 1977, *15*, 177–180. (a)

Rekers, G. A., & Varni, J. W. Self-regulation of gender-role behaviors: A case study. *Journal of Behavior Therapy and Experimental Psychiatry*, 1977, *8*, 427–432. (b)

Rekers, G. A., Willis, T. J., Yates, C. E., Rosen, A. C., & Low, B. P. Assessment of childhood gender behavior change. *Journal of Child Psychology and Psychiatry*, 1977, *18*, 53–65.

Rekers, G. A., & Yates, C. E. Sex-typed play in feminoid boys vs. normal boys and girls. *Journal of Abnormal Child Psychology*, 1976, *4*, 1–8.

Rekers, G. A., Yates, C. E., Willis, T. J., Rosen, A. C., & Taubman, M. Childhood gender identity change: Operant control over sex-typed play and mannerisms. *Journal of Behavior Therapy and Experimental Psychiatry*, 1976, *7*, 51–57.

Resnik, H. L. P. Erotized repetitive hangings: A form of self-destructive behavior. *American Journal of Psychotherapy*, 1972, *26*, 4–21.

Roberts, R. E., Abrams, L., & Finch, J. R. Delinquent sex behavior among adolescents. *Medical Aspects of Human Sexuality*, 1973, *7*(1), 162–175.

Roberts, R. E., McBee, G. W., & Bettis, M. C. Youthful sex offenders: An epidemiologic comparison of types. *Journal of Sex Research*, 1969, *5*, 29–40.

Rosen, A. C. The intersex: Gender identity, genetics, and mental health. In S. Plog & R. Edgerton (Eds.), *Changing perspectives in mental illness*. New York: Holt, 1969.

Rosen, A. C., & Rekers, G. A. Toward a taxonomic framework for variables of sex and gender. *Genetic Psychology Monographs*, 1980, *102*, 191–218.

Rosen, A. C., Rekers, G. A., & Bentler, P. M. Ethical issues in the treatment of children. *Journal of Social Issues*, 1978, *34*, 122–136.

Rosen, A. C., Rekers, G. A., & Friar, L. R. Theoretical and diagnostic issues in child gender disturbances. *The Journal of Sex Research*, 1977, *13*(2), 89–103.

Rosen, A. C., & Teague, J. Case studies in development of masculinity and femininity in male children. *Psychological Reports*, 1974, *34*, 971–983.

Rudolf, G. de M. An experiment in the treatment of masturbation in oligophrenia. *American Journal of Mental Deficiency*, 1954, *58*, 644–649.

Russell, D. H. On the psychopathology of boy prostitutes. *International Journal of Offender Therapy*, 1971, *15*(1), 49–52.

Salfield, D. J. [Juvenile fetishism]. *Zeitschrift für Kinderpsychiatrie*, 1957, *24*(6), 183–188.

Schultz, L. G. Psychotherapeutic and legal approaches to the sexually victimized child. *International Journal of Child Psychotherapy*, 1972, *1*(4), 115–128.

Schultz, L. G. The child sex victim: Social, psychological and legal perspectives. *Child Welfare*, 1973, *52*, 147–157.

Shankel, L. W., & Carr, A. C. Transvestism and hanging episodes in a male adolescent. *Psychiatric Quarterly*, 1956, *30*, 478–493.

Shoor, M., Speed, M. H., & Bartlett, C. Syndrome of the adolescent child molester. *American Journal of Psychiatry*, 1966, *122*, 783–789.

Skilbeck, W. M., Bates, J. E., & Bentler, P. M. Human figure drawings of gender-problem and school-problem boys. *Journal of Abnormal Child Psychology*, 1975, *3*, 191–199.

Spottswood, P. J., & Burghardt, G. M. The effects of sex, book weight, and grip strength on book-carrying styles. *Bulletin of the Psychonomic Society*, 1976, *8*, 150–152.

Stearns, A. W. Cases of probable suicide in young persons without obvious motivation. *Journal of the Maine Medical Association*, 1953, *44*(1), 16–23.

Stirt, S. S. Overt mass masturbation in the classroom. *American Journal of Orthopsychiatry*, 1940, *10*, 801–804.

Stoller, R. J. A contribution to the study of gender identity. *International Journal of Psychoanalysis*,

1964, *45*, 220–226.

Stoller, R. J. Passing in the continuum of gender identity. In J. Marmer (Ed.), *Sexual inversion: The multiple roots of homosexuality*. New York: Basic Books, 1965.

Stoller, R. J. "It's only a phase." *Journal of the American Medical Association*, 1967, *201*, 98–99.

Stoller, R. J. Male childhood transsexualism. *Journal of the American Academy of Child Psychiatry*, 1968, *7*, 193–209. (a)

Stoller, R. J. *Sex and gender: The development of masculinity and femininity*. New York: Science House, 1968. (b)

Stoller, R. J. Psychotherapy of extremely feminine boys. *International Journal of Psychiatry*, 1970–1971, *9*, 278–280.

Strzyewsky, J., & Zierhoffer, M. Aversion therapy in a case of fetishism with transvestic component. *The Journal of Sex Research*, 1967, *3*, 163–167.

Sutton-Smith, B., Rosenberg, B. G., & Morgan, E. R. Development of sex differences in play choices during preadolescence. *Child Development*, 1963, *34*, 119–126.

Tanner, J. M. *Growth at adolescence*. Oxford: Blackwell Scientific Publications, 1955. (2nd ed., 1962.)

Thoresen, C. E., & Mahoney, M. J. *Behavioral self-control*. New York: Holt, 1974.

Vanden Bergh, R. L., & Kelly, J. F. Vampirism: A review with new observations. *Archives of General Psychiatry*, 1964, *11*, 543–547.

Wagner, M. K. A case of public masturbation treated by operant conditioning. *Journal of Child Psychology and Psychiatry*, 1968, *9*, 61–65.

Walinder, J. *Transsexualism: A study of forty-three cases*. Goteborg: Scandinavian University Books, 1967.

Weiss, J., Rogers, E., Darwin, M. R., & Dutton, C. E. A study of girl sex victims. *Psychiatric Quarterly*, 1955, *29*, 1–27.

Whitam, F. L. Childhood indicators of male homosexuality. *Archives of Sexual Behavior*, 1977, *6*, 89–96.

Zuger, B. Effeminate behavior present in boys from early childhood: I. The clinical syndrome and follow-up studies. *Journal of Pediatrics*, 1966, *69*, 1098–1107.

Zuger, B. Gender role determination: A critical review of the evidence from hermaphroditism. *Psychosomatic Medicine*, 1970, *32*, 449–467. (a)

Zuger, B. The role of familial factors in persistent effeminate behavior in boys. *American Journal of Psychiatry*, 1970, *126*, 1167–1170. (b)

Zuger, B. Effeminate behavior present in boys from childhood: Ten additional years of follow-up. *Comprehensive Psychiatry*, 1978, *19*, 363–369.

Zuger, B., & Taylor, P. Effeminate behavior present in boys from early childhood. II. Comparison with similar symptoms in non-effeminate boys. *Pediatrics*, 1969, *44*, 375–380.

# HEALTH-RELATED DISORDERS

# CHRONIC ILLNESS: ASTHMA AND JUVENILE DIABETES

**Barbara G. Melamed**     **Suzanne Bennett Johnson**
*University of Florida*             *University of Florida*

## RATIONALE FOR A BEHAVIORAL APPROACH TO PSYCHOSOMATIC DISORDERS

It is widely recognized that the interaction of multiple, complex factors (physical, constitutional, environmental, and social) contributes to the development and maintenance of most physical disorders (Kimball, 1970; Lipton, Sternschneider, & Richmond, 1966). The emotional state of the patient is now recognized as playing an important role in the precipitation of many illnesses (Davison & Neale, 1974). Regardless of the specific etiology or bodily dysfunction, there is evidence that learning or conditioning mechanisms can be significant contributing or exacerbating factors in a variety of disorders.

Childhood disorders of both organic and nonorganic origin, such as enuresis (see Chapter 16), seizures (see Chapter 14), and asthma, have been successfully treated with behavioral techniques. The efficacy of a particular treatment strategy does not necessarily provide information about the etiology of a given disorder. However, research has demonstrated that autonomic responses themselves can be affected and modified by both respondent and operant conditioning (Blanchard & Young, 1974; Miller, 1969). Recent clinical evidence indicates that autonomic responses such as heart rate (Bleeker & Engle, 1973), blood pressure (Elder, Ruiz, Deabler, & Dillenkoffer, 1973) and pulmonary resistance (Kotses, Glaus, Crawford, Edwards, & Scherr, 1976) can be subject to voluntary control through operant conditioning mechanisms. This opens the field to the use of biofeedback procedures in directly helping the patient control overreactive systems, such as those often associated with psychosomatic disturbances.

In addition, behavioral approaches have been useful in modifying dysfunc-

529

tional behavior patterns that may have developed while the medical problem was in existence. For instance, severe dependency upon tracheostomy cannula (Wright, Nunnery, Eichel, & Scott, 1969) or nebulizers (Sirota & Mahoney, 1974) has been alleviated. Wright (1977) argued for consideration of all behavioral concomitants of physical illness as possible targets of psychological treatment. This would provide the rationale for considering the secondary gain associated with increased parental attention or the patient's avoidance of responsibilities as possibly maintaining the illness-related behavior. The personality of the individual may predispose him or her to adopt certain coping behaviors. It is also possible that the illness may lead an individual to develop personality styles in reaction to the sickness, such as overdependency.

In analyzing the impact of a chronic disease on a child, the behavioral assessment task follows that of any careful functional analysis. Most studies fail to identify which conditions existed prior to the disease and which are associated with the course of illness. Therefore, a multifaceted approach looking at the pre-illness history as well as the current family environment is needed in the assessment of child health problems. Some of the factors needing evaluation include understanding the nature of the chronic disease, the age and emotional adjustment of the child at the onset of the disease, and parental attitudes and behaviors regarding the illness. One must then evaluate what current threats the illness presents for the basic emotional adjustment of the child and the family. The need for the child to learn new coping strategies in regulating medical and behavioral aspects of the disease involves assessing the abilities and motivations of all the family members. It is part of the responsibility of the assessor to investigate what special facilities and programs might be appropriate.

Asthma and juvenile diabetes will be used as illustrations of behavioral assessment of chronic illness. Studies of psychosomatic disorders in children often stress the co-existence of psychopathology in the child and/or family with chronic illness. Such broad generalizations grow out of false assumptions and methodological errors in the clinical and research literature. These will be briefly reviewed in an attempt to impress the evaluator with the importance of an individual functional analysis.

# METHODOLOGICAL CONSIDERATIONS

The misconception most often promulgated by the literature is that a chronic medical ailment is by itself an overriding factor determining the psychological development of the child. This misconception has led to characterizing as a homogeneous sample children who are heterogeneous in terms of life experiences. This step has led to futile searches for the personality types that go with a particular diagnosis. The associated emphasis on discovering parental deviations that may influence the process of illness has led the researcher astray. Thus, divergent findings and erroneous conclusions based on questionnaires and interviews with families or sick children are not surprising.

There is also a bias in the types of children who come to the attention of mental health professionals and who make up the bulk of the research populations. These children have often failed to benefit from the drug regimen. The families may have been unable to carry out the behavioral management of the illness. The child's illness may serve a role in maintaining some cohesiveness in a disturbed family. The child may be reinforced for the symptoms of the illness by providing for the avoidance of family conflict (Minuchin, Baker, Rosman, Liebman, Milman, & Todd, 1975). The lack of a representative sampling of the entire population of children with a specific illness limits generalizations that can be made from existing studies and overemphasizes psychopathology.

Appropriate control groups are often lacking. The theories that stress the interaction between psychopathology in the family and in the child with chronic illness often fail to differentiate the chronically ill child and his or her family from control groups of physically handicapped children. The use of so-called normal comparison groups does not adequately control for the effect of the illness on the child or the sampling bias in studying children and families seen by doctors and other health-related specialists.

In fact, several studies (Tavormina, Kastner, Slater, & Watt, 1976) have failed to find differences between psychological test responses given by chronically ill children and those of a normalization sample. Teacher and parent ratings of psychopathology did not discriminate asthmatic children from normal children in a sample of all children on the Isle of Wight (Graham, Rutter, Yule, & Pless, 1967). Werry (1979) pointed out that several studies (Purcell & his colleagues, 1961, 1962, 1975) found that parents of asthmatic children described their children as having more problems than normal children. However, studies exist that demonstrate similarities between asthmatic children and children with other chronic illnesses, such as heart disorder and diabetes (Cernelc, Hafner, Kos, & Cenlec, 1977; Graham *et al.*, 1967; Neuhaus, 1958). These disturbances may therefore be the result of a general adaptation to illness. The correlational nature of most of the studies makes it impossible to separate out the relationship between emotional illness antecedent to or concomitant with the physiological disturbance.

# STATEMENT OF THE PROBLEM

Asthma, long recognized as an illness with psychological concomitants, has generated many studies that provide a convergence of factors that allow us to predict the interaction between individual personality variables and the course of the illness. Many rigorous controls have been considered. Subclassification of asthmatics on both somatic predisposition and personality coping style has proven useful for predicting those individuals at high risk for psychopathology. These subtypings have also led to prediction of the behavioral treatment approaches most likely to reduce symptomatology. Therefore, a detailed functional analysis can be developed in light of the availability of a systematic battery of assessment tools and predictions from the research literature.

In contrast, the study of juvenile diabetes, a chronic illness involving radical medical intervention and strict control of dietary regimens, has often neglected psychological factors. It is only recently that emotional disturbances other than "self-concept" have been explored. Wright (1977) provided examples of behavioral problems caused indirectly from this physical illness. Adolescent diabetics often engage in a passive form of self-destructive behavior that contrasts with the more active self-destruction of some illnesses such as hemophilia. Diabetic youngsters may refuse to collect their urine samples or may not administer their insulin, allowing the disease to slip out of control. Our work at the University of Florida is an attempt to extend the use of a behavioral assessment to defining the problem, predicting the risk of brittle out-of-control diabetes, and planning treatment. Suggestions are made regarding the need for a more empirical approach to the assessment of psychological correlates of this disorder.

# ASTHMA

## Definition of the Problem

Asthma is a disorder of the respiratory system. It is estimated that 2–4% of the population has asthma. Asthma most often has its onset between ages 3 and 8 years. In 1964 asthma accounted for 6.5 million days of school absence, or 25% of school days lost for all chronic diseases combined. This disruption alone suggests that the disease is going to involve major social–psychological factors no matter what its etiology (Bronheim, 1978).

A functional analysis of the disorder involves understanding the physiological, behavioral, and subjective concomitants. The wheezing, characteristically observed, results from an episodic narrowing of bronchioles in the lung with resulting difficulty in breathing, particularly expiration. Its severest form, status asthmaticus, threatens life and calls for immediate medical emergency procedures. The child with asthma has often suffered periods of repeated respiratory infections or chronic allergic rhinitis. Therefore, the warning signals often precipitate anticipatory anxiety in both the patient and the family. A useful behavioral assessment must consider the physiological state of the patient and the behavior that precedes and follows this reaction in order to predict the most appropriate course of action. The etiology of the disorder may differ in patients showing the same symptom patterns. Although some children have a high somatic predisposition, suggesting hereditary factors, others have severe physiological reactions with little history of allergic reaction. From the physiological point of view there is an overreaction of the parasympathetic nervous system. Some evidence (Criep, 1976) suggests that asthmatics have a deficient adenylate cyclase class system. This receptor enzyme responds to stimulation of the sympathetic nervous system inefficiently in counteracting the constriction caused by parasympathetic stimulation and triggers an attack. Among the stimulants are cold, infection, allergies, and emotions. In view of the fact that sympathomimetic drugs (e.g., epinephrine) often fail to be effective or produce undesirable side effects, a behavioral functional analysis would be useful in identifying emotional factors that are important in different attacks. By determining the functional relationships among the problem behaviors the patients emit, their emotional attitude, and the events in the environment, the therapist is in a better position to alter the conditions and to produce a desirable change in behavior.

## Selecting a Target Behavior

The first task in any functional analysis is to define what behaviors need to be modified. This involves an analysis of behaviors that occur too frequently (behavioral excesses), behaviors that are absent or that occur too infrequently (behavioral deficits), inappropriate or defective stimulus control, and the child's assets in dealing with the problem behaviors.

The behavioral excesses associated with asthma include episodes of wheezing, repeated emergency room visits, and frequent hospitalizations. Children who suffer chronic, perennial asthma often have deficits in their social skills because of absences from school, which limit the opportunities for normal peer relationships. This situation often leads to a sense of alienation. Classroom behaviors that appear disruptive may result from the child's inability to catch up with missed schoolwork. Parents often report that their children make excessive dependency demands and exhibit a variety of other immature behaviors. Other deficits involve the child's inability to cope with the anxiety of illness. The literature reveals that many asthmatics tend to overrespond to their symptoms of an impending attack. Both extremes are maladaptive in terms of ensuring appropriate medical intervention.

The inappropriate stimulus control arises from the fact that a variety of stressors elicit changes in physical structures leading to excessive bronchial constriction rather than other more adaptive coping mechanisms. In fact, the symptoms of the stress reaction themselves become triggers for anxiety (i.e., fear of attack); thus a vicious cycle is set in motion.

In assessing the child's strengths, the ability to understand the illness and to carry out the management program are of primary importance. The child must exhibit flexibility in adapting to his or her limitations and in finding substitute sources of gratification where restrictions on physical activity or diet are involved for successful coping. The support of the family and the physician is also a necessary part of the evaluation prior to the selection of any treatment plan.

## Methods of Collecting Information

The need to select behaviors that can be readily modified involves a clear operational definition of the primary symptoms.

The goal is to restore normal breathing patterns. A child with the most severe case of status asthmaticus could go into respiratory failure, as medication often does not reverse the symptoms. Therefore, it is necessary to define the breathing difficulties in the earliest stages. The wheezing that characteristically defines an asthmatic episode is a difficult response to define and measure accurately. The length of a wheezing episode would require an operational definition of onset and offset. This would be difficult to detect from patient self-report because concern with the wheezing has been indicated to vary with personality types (Dirks, Jones, & Kinsman, 1977; Dirks, Kinsman, Jones, & Fross, 1978; Dirks, Kleiger, & Evans, 1978). Asthmatics who are high on the panic–fear (P-F) dimension would tend to overreact to their symptoms, whereas others would tend to minimize or deny their symptoms until severe asthma existed. Thus, self-monitoring of episodes would involve experiential factors that would make it less than reliable. The duration of wheezing has been employed successfully in treatment programs where others in the environment have been the observers (Neisworth & Moore, 1972). However, in an outpatient setting, or even in residential treatment, the continuous monitoring of frequency or duration of wheezing would be a cumbersome task. Time-sampling techniques might, by the nature of their timing, fail to reflect the course of the disorder as it varies with the time of day or emotional precipitants. Therefore, it is necessary to obtain both more reliable and more practical measures to reflect asthma severity.

### Physiological Measures

Since wheezing is a reflection of respiratory action, a direct measure of pulmonary function is justified.

There are several measures of pulmonary functioning and airway obstruction that are practical to use. Selection of a measure involves a trade-off between accuracy and practicality. Regardless of the precipitating factor, physical alterations accompanying asthma produce increases in the resistance of the airways to air flow. Thus, regardless of whether the narrowing of the bronchial lumen occurs with muscle spasm, edema, bronchial mucosa, or hypersecretion, the measures of air flow reflect pulmonary functioning.

Early assessment techniques such as esophageal balloon or whole-body plethysmography are impractical in that these techniques require the use of elaborate equipment and skilled technicians (DuBois, Botelho, & Comroe, 1956). In addition, the amount of disruption they impose on the child make them impossible for use in identifying triggering events.

The most frequent alternatives involve relatively insensitive measures of ventilatory flow and volume (Stein, 1962). The measures reported as Peak Expiratory Flow Rate (PEFR) and Forced Expiratory Volume (FEV) (one second) involve effort on the part of the patient, thus introducing variability due to motivation factors. Both of these measures require an apparatus (flow meter) into which the patient exhales with as much force as possible following an inspiration of maximum capacity. The PEFR is the rate of air outflow at the peak of the expiration curve, whereas the FEV is the volume of air expired during the first second. These measures are often expressed as a percentage of that predicted from values based on normal population parameters. This has the advantage of data normalization, thus providing a general indication of severity. The difficulties with these measures involve (1) their effort-dependent nature (Alexander, Miklich, Hershkoff, 1972); (2) excessive exertion on repeated trials, which may be harmful to the patient (Danker, Miklich, Pratt, & Creer, 1975); and (3) extensive cooperation on the part of the patient.

A promising innovation uses a Forced Oscillation Technique (FOT), which yields the total respiratory resistance (TRR) (DuBois, Brody, Lewis, & Burgess, 1956). This technique has been automated (Levenson, 1974). The technique involves treating the airways as analogous to an electrical circuit with properties of current (air flow), voltage (pressure), and resistance. By imposing a low-frequency pulsation below the resonant frequency at a known pressure and determining air flow produced by that pressure, the resistance of the total respiratory system can be computed. The significant correlations between forced oscillation measures of resistance and whole-body plethysmography during both baseline ($r = +.81$) and bronchodilator trials ($r = +.93$) argue for its validity. It also has the advantage of not being effort-dependent, and it does not require maximum exertion or patient cooperation. The earliest stages of pulmonary dysfunction can be detected. In addition, the measure is amenable to immediate analysis and can be used in a feedback situation.

### Self-Report Measures

Several measures of subjective symptomatology have been developed. Because it has been shown that a person's subjective reaction to his or her symptoms is often translated into behavior that affects the course of the illness, it is useful to assess the reactions that patients have to their asthma. Kinsman, O'Banion, Resnikoff, Luparello, and Spector (1973) developed the Asthma Symptom Checklist to describe five symptom categories: panic–fear, irritability, fatigue, hyperventilation–hypocapnia, and airway obstruction.

The P-F dimension, which reflects the patient's feeling scared, panicky, worried, and frightened, has been found to relate to the length of hospitalization and the type of medical regimen. Thus, it reflects the medical intractibility of some patients. In an attempt to look at this personality trait in more general coping-style terms, the Minnesota Multiphasic Personality Inventory (MMPI) Panic–Fear Scale was derived empirically from the Asthma Symptom Checklist's P-F symptom category (Dirks, Kinsman, Jones, & Fross, 1978). The 15 items on the MMPI, which include statements about being more easily hurt than others and about frequently worrying, were validated by Dirks, Kleiger, and Evans (1978). They demonstrated that the measure was valid in predicting patients' reactions to illness across a broad range of chronic illnesses. The degree to which differences in high or low panic scores predict coping styles makes it particularly useful in evaluating asthmatic patients. The patients who score high on this scale demonstrate ineffective helplessness and dependency, whereas extreme low-scale scorers show rigid counter-dependence and denial. It would appear that either extreme rating on the scale indicates a need for intervention, since the medical aspects of treatment, including requests for medication, length of hospital stay, and frequency of admissions, are related to the patient's subjective style of reacting. Whether or not there will be a change in coping style if the patient receives therapy in how to deal more effectively with his or her illness remains to be tested.

In dealing with asthmatic children, it has been useful to subclassify them with regard to the influence of psychological factors as triggering events relative to the physical factors that predispose one to asthma. A scale to index emotional precipitants (Purcell & Weiss, 1970) serves the function of identifying triggering events. It can be particularly useful in the early planning of systematic desensitization and results in a rank-ordering of situations that seem to precede asthmatic episodes. Kagan and Weiss (1976) used this scale in a semistructured interview with outpatient families. They found that there were a significantly greater number of emotional precipitants in children scoring low on the Asthmatic Potential Scale (Block, Jennings, Harvey, & Simpson, 1964) when compared with high scorers, even though the two groups were matched on severity of asthma, as defined by the use of corticosteroid drugs. That these differences were reflected in children not seriously ill enough to require hospitalization makes the scale particularly useful in a test battery designed to evaluate the child in the earliest stages of this chronic illness.

A self-report of anxiety on a rating scale such as the Fear Thermometer (Lang, Melamed, & Hart, 1970) would be a useful measure of anxiety during and between attacks and might also identify emotional precipitants.

Attitude questionnaires are useful in helping to evaluate how realistically patients view their problems. Some children may feel highly stigmatized by the illness and may be unable to accept it. Their degree of denial may be so pervasive that they are unable to report reliably whether or not they are wheezing. Other children may develop ambivalence toward physicians and reduce their receptiveness to medical advice and prescriptions. Still others may despair, and with loss of hope, the motivation to help themselves may diminish.

Attitudes have been shown to change with the child's age and experience with the illness. The Children's Respiratory Illness Opinion Survey (Matus, Kinsman, & Jones, 1978) is a 46-statement questionnaire that measures seven attitude dimensions related to chronic respiratory illness and hospitalization in a residential treatment program. The seven dimensions are: minimization of severity, passive observance, bravado, expectation of staff rejection, moralistic authoritarianism, stigma, and external control. Matus et al. (1978) tested 72 children, aged 7–15 years, who were admitted to an extended care program at the National Jewish Hospital and Research Center. The distribution of items suggested that stable attitude structures in regard to chronic asthma and medical personnel were already present during childhood. They compared the children's responses with those of adolescent and adult asthmatics on a scale with 29 communal items. These results suggested that magical beliefs become less apparent in the older group and are replaced by greater bitterness. The older group associates action and involvement with perceptions of exacerbation, and the younger group associates helplessness and passivity with this perception. The issue of whether attitude patterns are related to success in self-management still needs to be addressed. It is a potentially useful tool in tailoring programs to unique individual coping styles.

## Medical or Somatic Indexes

Research has been able to identify subclassifications that make it possible to pinpoint which families are at risk for psychological disturbances associated with illness, so that therapeutic efforts may be appropriately directed.

The development of the Asthmatic Potential Scale (APS) (Block *et al.*, 1964) allowed for greater distinctions to be made between individuals with more psychopathology involvement and those where drug regimens are likely to relieve symptoms. The genetic component of asthma is suggested by a high frequency of family history of atopic disease (Kempe, Silver, & O'Brien, 1974). Therefore, the first factor of the APS includes factors from family history of allergy. Other "objective factors" included in this scale relate to specific somatic factors, including (1) highest blood eosinophil percentage during any episode, (2) skin test reactivity, (3) the total number of allergies, and (4) ease of diagnosability of specific allergies.

The studies in which high- and low-APS groups are compared with each other and with a matched contrast group of children suffering from congenital heart disease yielded clear differences in emotional maturity among individuals within the subtypes of asthma. The outpatient asthmatic group as a whole differed from the physical disability group in projective measures and parental ratings of maladjustment. However, important distinctions were discovered when the subgrouping was made. The high-APS asthmatic children were more similar to the disabled group. Despite a careful matching for severity of asthma, emotional factors were more prominent in the low-APS children. The parents described these children as more demanding and petulant. The mothers were found in psychiatric interviews and in Q-sort responses to be more fearful, pessimistic, anxious, and rejecting. They were more intolerant of frustration and described ambivalent relationships with their own parents. The data suggested that since the severity of asthma had been equated and blind raters used, psychopathology was not reactive to the illness. That children low in somatic predisposition had more psychological problems implies that psychological intervention would be an important adjunct with these children. The usefulness of this subtyping has been illustrated by different patterns of parent–child interaction and different responsivity to behavioral interventions, as described in the section on functional analysis.

A widely used medical indication of severity involves the recording of medication regimens. Those children kept on daily corticosteroids are usually considered more intractable asthmatics. In attempting to assess psychological severity, it might be useful to obtain an indication of the individuals' dependence upon nebulizers. A permanent product measure of the number of empty inhalant dispensers would be useful to obtain.

## Behavioral Data

Behavioral concomitants of impaired pulmonary functioning are often more practical to obtain in most settings. They often are useful in reflecting the changes in severity attributable to environmental or therapeutic manipulations. Such data as the number of attacks per week, the duration of wheezing episodes, the number of emergency visits, and the number of hospital admissions are usually valid sources of information. There is a dearth of good research into the behavior of the patient during the actual attack. The available observational scales of children's anxiety (Melamed & Siegel, 1975) might be adapted to measuring the anxiety-related behaviors of asthmatic children during an attack.

## A Functional Analysis of Behavior

In evaluating the role of environmental factors, it is sometimes possible to rearrange what happens before or after the target behavior. Several studies have attempted to identify causal relationships in the onset and maintenance of asthmatic symptoms by controlled presentation of precipitating events or by rearrangement of consequences. These attempts have ranged from presenting emotional stressors, such as frightening images, to the extreme of actually separating the child from his or her family. The studies of biofeedback procedures also give information as to the use of operant procedures to directly alter the visceral responses. The role of other operant factors, such as parental attention or withdrawal of reinforcers, sheds light on the maintenance of the symptoms. Cognitive factors, such as internal–external control, related to personality variables have also been shown to affect the course of the illness.

### Emotional Precipitants

In a retrospective clinical review of 406 acute asthmatic attacks in more than 50 patients with bronchial asthma (Knapp & Nemetz, 1960), data indicated that during the attack the patient was absorbed in the physical illness. In terms of prodromal features, the emotions of anger or anxiety were often prominent. Following an attack, individuals reported depressive attitudes, including a sense of sadness, helplessness, and hopelessness.

Several research studies have demonstrated a functional relationship between emotional precipitants and the induction of an asthmatic episode (Alexander, 1972; Clarke, 1970; Hahn, 1966; Straker & Tamerin, 1974; Tal & Miklich, 1976). Use has been made of hypnosis, emotive imagery, and/or placing the subject in a stressful situation in order to examine psychophysiological indicants of asthma.

Clarke (1970) found that hypnotically induced anger and fear reduced the forced expiration volume (one second) in three cases of clinical asthma. In a more sophisticated study, Tal and Miklich (1976) also found evidence for anger and fear as emotions inducing asthmatic symptoms. They found that in children with perennial asthma severe enough to require frequent residential treatment, imaginary reinstigation of affect could directly influence the pulmonary functioning of the patient. Of the children instructed to revisualize the most frightening and most angry experience in their life, 38% had a significant reduction in airway flow and showed an increased heart rate. This was particularly true for the anger scenes. This finding is interesting in that in children given assertiveness training for dealing with anger (Hock, Rodgers, Reddi, & Kennard, 1978) pulmonary functioning tended to worsen and the number of asthmatic attacks after treatment increased. It was only when assertiveness training was combined with relaxation training that there was a significant reduction of attacks and improvement in pulmonary functioning. The stress aroused by the assertive skills training itself may have interfered with the potential benefits.

Other stressors have also been found to precipitate asthma symptoms. Mathé and Knapp (1971) compared the reactions of asthmatics and nonasthmatics in a relaxation condition (music, travelog), an active stress condition (timed mental arithmetic), and a passive stress condition (watching a film depicting burn accidents and autopsies). Using the most sensitive measure of airway conductance (full-body plethsysmograph), they found that stress caused a decrease in pulmonary functioning in asthmatics but not in nonasthmatics. The lowered airway conductance scores were observed in asthmatics during the stress condition but not during the relaxation condition. Hahn (1966) had also demonstrated, relative to normal persons, a decrease in respiratory rate and higher heart-rate responses in asthmatics exposed to criticism or unsolvable problems. Thus, it is not only the nature of the stressor but also the physiological vulnerability of the subject that must be considered in making predictions. A study in which asthmatics observed films of other children in the midst of an attack caused empathic wheezing in the asthmatic viewer but had no effect on nonasthmatic viewers (Levenson, 1979; Straker & Tamerin, 1974).

## Biofeedback and Relaxation

Given that pulmonary functioning can be affected by emotional stimuli, it is interesting to view the therapy outcome literature in which biofeedback procedures have been employed in an attempt to regulate specific systems, such as airway resistance or muscle tension, in an attempt to short-circuit an attack. It is important to examine the differential effectiveness of these nonpharmacological approaches in terms of subclassifications based on asthma potential scores or emotional precipitant indexes. It would be predicted that children with less corticosteroid-dependent asthma would be more reactive to behavioral intervention. This, in fact, has often been the case.

The procedures in these biofeedback studies often involve making reward contingent upon improvement; thus, motivational effects on the pulmonary effectiveness measures are maximized. Davis, Saunders, Creer, and Chai (1973) found that biofeedback of electromyograms (EMG), as an adjunct to Jacobsen's relaxation procedures, improved nonsevere asthmatics in terms of increasing their peak respiratory flow, in comparison to severe asthmatics (those receiving steroid drugs). Unfortunately, there was a lack of generalization. The improvement of PEFR did not hold up the week following treatment. The motivational incentives must be considered, because they might have been strong enough to produce temporary change but not maintenance of a new habit.

In a similar fashion, it was found by Kahn (1977) that a different subclassification of asthmatics helped predict responsiveness to biofeedback. Children were classified as reactors and nonreactors to a saline vapor inhalation test. Children showing bronchial constriction (as defined by a fall in FEV greater than 15%) to vapors described as containing allergen were labeled "reactors." Those showing no tendency to respond to this type of test were labeled "nonreactors." The feedback apparatus displayed increasing numbers related to decrease of airway resistance. Therapy consisted of 50-minute sessions for 5–8 weeks. Children were also praised for progressive decreases in airway resistance. An attempt to improve generalization consisted of giving them the opportunity to use their skill in a situation in which bronchial constriction was induced by suggestion or inhalation of a bronchoconstrictor. Feedback was provided as to how successful they were. We view this attempt as a counterconditioning process in which the child substitutes bronchodilation in situations known to precipitate bronchial constriction. The control-group children were not given any such training. Data were collected over one year on the number of attacks, total length of attacks, number of emergency room visits, number of hospital admissions, amount of medication taken, and severity of asthma. The combined experimental treatment helped to reduce the frequency, duration, and severity of asthmatic attack in both reactors and nonreactors. Reactors in the control group receiving supportive therapy also showed significant improvement. The factor of attention being paid to the group alone seemed sufficiently anxiety-reducing to explain the results. Thus, one questions the need of elaborate biofeedback procedures with nonsevere asthmatics who are easily influenced by cognitive factors.

Given the great difficulty in reliably assessing PEFR because of the motivation of the patient, EMG biofeedback might prove more expedient in severe asthmatics. In fact, Kotses *et al.* (1976) demonstrated a relationship between frontalis EMG and peak expiratory flow in asthmatic children. In this study, the use of a group receiving noncontingent feedback provided some support that the biofeedback training was indeed facilitating change beyond the possible placebo effect of being hooked up to the apparatus. The children receiving contingent EMG feedback showed greater increase in PEFR from pretraining when the effects were measured inconspicuously throughout the day. Thus, support for the generalization of effects was obtained because training and test sessions were several days apart.

In a subsequent study (Kotses, Glaus, Bricel, Edwards, & Crawford, 1978), the investigators replicated their findings with a measure of PEFR immediately prior to and after each frontalis EMG training session, thereby providing direct support for the relationship between frontalis relaxation and concident PEFR changes in asthmatic children. In both of these studies, there were no systematic effects of medication, with equal numbers of severe and nonsevere asthmatics being assigned to each group.

If the improvement of asthmatics with biofeedback training is attributable to a reduction of arousal, it would be likely that other anxiety-reducing procedures, such as systematic desensitization (SD), would also be useful in promoting more change than medical treatment alone. This would be particularly true when a low somatic predisposition for asthma existed. The children studied by Miklich, Renne, Creer, Alexander, Chai, Davis, Hoffman, and Danker-Brown (1977) were moderate-to-severe perennial asthmatics, responsive to emotional arousal, and thereby likely to improve following change in a stressful environment. In this study, EMG frontalis feedback was used to assist relaxation training of some patients. Long-term follow-up of patients was reported for many variables, including medication regimens. Although support for improved FEV and for reduced medication was obtained at posttreatment and at 6-month follow-up for subjects receiving systematic desensitization, we conclude that the data have little clinical utility because all the patients remained chronically ill, moderately severe asthmatics. Thus, the multi-faceted nature of asthma suggests other regulating factors in addition to emotional precipitants or autonomic variables.

## *Parental Contributing Factors*

Psychodynamic theories have hypothesized that asthmatics have an excessive, un-resolved dependency upon the mother. The threat of separation could bring on an attack. The wheezing and dyspenia were viewed as the child's suppressed cry for his or her mother. Crying is a way to reestablish the dependent bond, and asthma may develop when the crying and the longing it represents are not tolerable to the mother (French, 1950; Saul & Lyons, 1951; Weiss, 1950).

Unfortunately, there has been little in the research literature to support causal relationships. A study by Neuhaus (1958) generated more support for the idea that the problems of the asthmatic are reactive to the illness rather than caused by parental conflicts. Neuhaus compared 84 asthmatic children and their siblings with 84 cardiac patients and their siblings and a matched group of healthy normal persons. The data, primarily projective test responses, showed that the asthmatic children, although rated as more neurotic and dependent than normal children, did not differ from their siblings or the children with cardiac disease and their siblings.

An interaction between somatic predisposition (APS) and family conflicts was reported in a series of outpatient studies (Block et al., 1964) in which structured interviews of parent–child interactions were obtained in addition to psychiatric ratings. It was found that mothers in the low-APS group were more competitive with their child, were disappointed in the child's performance, and tended to ignore the child's difficult behavior. The mothers were rated as more rejecting of the child and had more frustrating interactions. In contrast, the children who were high on the APS had more compatible interactions. Their mothers gave them more autonomy and were more responsive to them and less intrusive.

These findings suggested that relationships between the parents, as judged in a psychiatric interview and corroborated in a structured conflict interview, were more satisfactory in parents of high-APS children. There was more friction in the parental interaction of low-APS children, with the wife excluding the husband from the mother–child relationship. She was more depreciating of her husband.

Purcell, Muser, Miklich, and Dietiker (1969) replicated many of these findings in children and parents who were separated because of the child's institutionalization in a residential treatment center. In studying children whose symptoms diminished dramatically with separation (rapid remitters), the differences between families of low-APS and high-APS children were replicated. The investigators found more psychopathology in children and more negative child-rearing attitudes in parents of low-APS rapid remitters.

In a clever design to unconfound family and environmental allergens as precipitating factors (Purcell, Brady, Chai, Muser, Molk, Gordon, & Means, 1969), children were studied on a daily basis during periods in which they lived with their families and during an experimental period in which they had no contact with their families but were cared for in their own homes by a substitute parent. Two subgroups were established, using parents' rankings on the scale of emotional precipitants to isolate those children for whom emotional indicants were probable from those whose asthma was more likely to be precipitated by allergies, weather, or overexertion. As predicted, for children high in emotional precipitants, there was improvement in expiratory peak flow rates, amount of medication required, daily history of asthma, and daily clinical examination for wheezing during the period of family separation, followed by an increase in symptoms upon the family's return home. Little change was found in the group low on emotional precipitants.

Although much theorizing has been done regarding family system relationships as a factor maintaining the illness (Minuchin et al., 1975), little substantive research has resulted. The family system model is based on a triad of factors: (1) family organization that encourages somaticization, (2) involvement of the children in parental conflict, and (3) physiological vulnerability. This is a general model for psychosomatic illness in children and has not been empirically tested with asthmatic families. In a study that attempted to assess communication patterns of parents of asthmatic children in a conflict situation (Wikran, Faleide, & Blakar, 1978), there was no difference found in conflict resolution patterns when such parents were compared with parents of children with chronic heart disease. Unfortunately, the selection of an analogue task (maze solution) and the absence of the child in the situation minimize the interpretation of these data as relevant to the theory. Also, there was no attempt to subclassify parents as to whether subgroups of high or low somatic predisposition existed.

Although the role of the parent in eliciting emotional arousal that might trigger an attack is not clearly understood, there is evidence that the frequency of asthmatic episodes can be reduced if parental attention is withdrawn contingent upon wheezing (Neisworth & Moore, 1972). Thus, in planning an operant treatment program where parental attention is going to be used, it might be useful to subtype the asthmatic children regarding APS scores and indexes of emotional precipitants. The data strongly predict greater effectiveness of this manipulation in families where low APS scores and high emotional precipitants are obtained.

## Consequent Factors

Several therapy studies demonstrate effective control over symptoms associated with asthma by merely rearranging parental attention or reducing the avoidance of unpleasant activities associated with playing "sick." This suggests that the increased attention the patient receives from others in the environment may have the paradoxical effect of maintaining the symptoms even in the absence of serious physiological disturbance.

Miklich (1973) successfully decreased the number of attacks in an asthmatic child when reinforcement was given for increasing periods without attacks. Creer (1970) demonstrated that the residential treatment setting could provide too much support for continued illness. He used time out from positive reinforcement to decrease both the frequency and the duration of hospitalization. In essence, this procedure made continued hospitalization less desirable than return to the real world. While hospitalized, the resident was placed in a room by himself and denied visits from other patients. Only school work was permitted to be in his possession. A reversal procedure clearly demonstrated the importance of social consequences in maintaining the frequency and duration of hospitalization.

Classroom behavior of a child frequently absent because of illness may reflect inattentiveness and hyperactivity that results from being overwhelmed by peer interactions or from the inability to catch up on missed work. This may result in a vicious cycle of the child's desiring to stay home because of the unpleasant classroom encounters. Creer and Yoches (1971) found that behavioral disruptions in the classroom could be easily controlled if rewards were given to appropriate task-relevant behavior.

### Personality Factors

It has already been mentioned that cognitive factors such as hypnosis, attention placebo, and suggestibility can alter the occurrence of wheezing even in the absence of bronchial constriction. The importance of attitude in inducing asthma has been emphasized by Purcell (1975). He felt that it was the emotional state that occurred immediately antecedent to an asthmatic attack rather than the personality or conflict in the parent or child that was the critical variable. Even in steroid-dependent children, it was found that negative mood was more frequently associated with attacks than with asthma-free periods (Weiss, 1966).

More recent data on asthmatic adolescents and adults provide further support that the individual's attitude about his or her symptoms does effect the course of the illness. The research on the P-F dimension (Dahlem, Kinsman, & Horton, 1977) finds a strong relationship between individuals' coping styles and their adherence to medication regimens, their requests for medication, and the length of hospitalization. Asthmatics at the extreme end of the P-F scale show medication-requesting behavior that is independent of objective measures of airway obstruction. High-P-F patients requested more medication regardless of the level of pulmonary function. Moderate scorers showed a progressive increase in the percentage of days in which they requested medication as pulmonary function was impaired. The low-P-F patients very rarely asked for medication.

The checklist P-F scale seems to serve as a signal to anxiety, whereas the MMPI P-F scale is thought to reflect an underlying coping strategy that had more to do with characteristic ego resources of the individual. High scores on this personality scale relate to length of hospitalization and intensity of prescribed oral corticosteroids (Dirks, Jones, & Kinsman, 1977; Dirks, Kinsman, Jones, Spector, Davidson, & Evans, 1977). These patients describe themselves as generally fearful, highly emotional individuals who have their feelings hurt more easily than others and as feeling helpless and inclined to give up easily in the face of difficulty. Patients low on the MMPI P-F dimension describe themselves as experiencing little discomfort or anxiety and as being unusually calm, stable, and self-controlled. Both of these styles may be maladaptive in ensuring the prompt appropriate treatment of their illness. For example, physicians are influenced by patients' self-reports about symptom anxiety in recommending medication regimens. Kinsman, Dahlem, Spector, and Staudenmayer (1977) found that physicians rated as being highly sensitive to the patients' whole well-being prescribed less intensive steroid regimens for low-P-F patients, whereas physicians with less sensitivity weighted objective indexes of pulmonary functioning more highly. This fact has important implications for the influence of persons' coping styles on the course of illness. If patients minimized or denied their stress, they would fail to monitor symptoms early enough to receive medication in order to short-circuit serious attack. In fact, these patients are more often rehospitalized than those who exaggerate their symptoms and receive more medications.

These data have implications for differential treatment of patients depending on their coping style. Low-P-F patients need to be reinforced for adhering to medication regimens and attending to their symptoms of distress. Those therapies that focus on alleviating anxiety may be better applied to patients high in P-F. Some anxiety is adaptive in self-monitoring of symptoms, whereas too much may lead to overmedication. Physicians must be cautioned not to be overly influenced by the patients' complaints but to judge severity in conjunction with objective evidence of airway obstruction. Although research with young children in terms of P-F characteristics has not yet been done, the Respiratory Illness Opinion Survey (Matus *et al.*, 1978) does indicate that these coping styles are set early in life. Therefore, preventive efforts at improving the ability of the patient to self-monitor his or her symptoms might reduce the tendency to develop maladaptive habits.

### Selecting a Treatment Program

From the functional analysis, it is clear that asthma is not an all-or-none response. For some patients, it is primarily somatic arousal precipitated by allergic factors, whereas for others, it is more strongly influenced by situational factors such as emotional attitude and reinforcing consequences. Still others lack certain coping skills to use in regulating their own treatment program. In developing an individualized treatment program, the therapist is wise to analyze the patient's profile of responses and decide whether the symptoms are associated primarily with physiological arousal, behavior deficits (such as poor peer relationships), or excess secondary gain.

Lang (1977) suggests that a three-system profile might provide a rationale for which therapy approach to emphasize first. Relaxation or biofeedback training might be initiated if the patient suffers physiological excesses. Systematic desensitization would be beneficial if emotional precipitants can be clearly identified. Assertiveness training should be part of a program where anger or shyness is associated with wheezing episodes. The cognitive self-control strategies would be the treatment of choice for individuals whose self-statements reflect a tendency to minimize or exaggerate symptoms. The sick-role behaviors that are maintained by secondary gain can best be altered by changing incentives via operant approaches. Certainly, combined approaches can be evaluated in terms of how they change these patterns of responding. The research literature does provide some evidence that behavioral programs would be most effective with children who have low somatic predispositions to asthma and where family conflict is more evident. Early intervention with these patients and families can prevent many of the problems typically faced when treating the chronically ill child. By teaching young children to be more independent in dealing with their drug regimens, they may develop a less pessimistic attitude about their limitations resulting from illness. The parents' awareness of the importance of maintaining good school attendance may lessen the likelihood that peer relationship problems will develop. Parental attention should be focused on age-appropriate success and not on dependency demands.

## Evaluation of Program

The three-system evaluation-of-illness profile also provides a means of evaluating treatment progress. If one focuses on reinforcing independent, assertive skills in patients, it is important to observe the concomitant change in self-attitude. There is no guarantee that change in one system will automatically promote change in the other systems. More may yet be learned about predicting those asthmatic youngsters who are at risk for developing psychological problems secondary to asthma by studying the interactions and lack of concordance between systems while applying different programs. The assessment task thus generates more research upon which to base future treatments. Therefore, systematic use of dependent variables to monitor a change within individual patients and across different patients should be encouraged.

# JUVENILE DIABETES

## Definition of the Problem

Juvenile, or insulin-dependent, diabetes is the result of insufficient insulin production by the pancreas. It is the most common endocrine disorder of childhood, affecting approximately 150,000 people. Only about 5% of all persons with diabetes have the juvenile form of this disorder. Most people have the "adult type," which often can be controlled through diet or weight reduction. In contrast, youngsters with juvenile diabetes are entirely dependent upon daily injections of insulin for their survival.

Glucose or sugar is used by the body for energy. Insulin is responsible for the transport of glucose from the blood stream to the muscle and fat cells. Without insulin, the body literally starves, despite high levels of available glucose. The body reacts by breaking down muscle and fat as it normally does in the starvation state. However, the free fatty acids or ketones produced cannot be metabolized without insulin. The high levels of glucose and ketones in the blood result in osmolar diuresis and excretion of large amounts of ketones and glucose by the kidneys. Excessive water loss will ultimately have central nervous system effects (Rosenbloom, 1978).

Classic symptoms of diabetes onset include excessive thirst and urination, fatigue, weakness, and weight loss despite ingestion of large quantities of food. Without medical attention, the child will lapse into a coma. Prior to the discovery of insulin in 1922, youngsters with this disorder had only a few years in which to live. Today, they have a reasonable life expectancy, although a variety of serious complications affecting neural, visual, and kidney functioning is associated with this disorder. Most of these complications occur quite some time after diabetes onset but necessarily demand further readjustment to the real or possible functional losses they create. Because the disease is hereditary, questions concerning marriage and childbearing also arise.

Controlling insulin-dependent diabetes requires a relatively complicated treatment regimen. Injections are given one or two times a day, urine is tested two to four times a day, and dietary restrictions are imposed. The youngster must eat frequently but must avoid concentrated sugar. The amount of insulin required varies, depending upon diet, exercise, physical health, and emotional state. Consequently, taking the same dose of insulin daily will not necessarily control the child's diabetes. If the youngster takes too much insulin or does not eat often enough, he or she may have a hypoglycemic or "insulin" reaction resulting from abnormally low blood sugar. Such reactions involve irritability, confusion, shakiness, and, ultimately, unconsciousness. In other words, the child must adjust his or her insulin dose to prevent both hyperglycemic (excessive blood sugar) and hypoglycemic (abnormally low blood sugar) effects.

## Selecting a Target Behavior

Some youngsters have a "brittle" form of juvenile diabetes, resulting in frequent episodes of hyperglycemia, ketoacidosis and hospitalization. This instability is of particular concern because it is associated with poor school performance (Koski, 1969), psychological difficulties (Koski, 1969; Loughlin & Mosenthal, 1944; Simonds, 1976–1977; Stersky, 1963; Swift, Seidman, & Stein, 1967), and an increased incidence of physical complications (e.g., loss of vision, kidney failure—Cahill, Etzwiler, & Freinkel, 1976). Several investigators report that problems in managing diabetes are particularly common among adolescents (Fallstrom,

1974; Koski & Kumento, 1975). Because emotional factors are often implicated, a psychologist or psychiatrist is frequently asked to evaluate the child or adolescent who is repeatedly in poor diabetes control. A careful assessment should target and define those behaviors or situations that contribute most to the youngster's diabetes instability. At least four areas should be assessed: (1) knowledge of diabetes management, (2) compliance to treatment regimen, (3) the youngster's emotional state, and (4) family and environmental influences.

### Knowledge of Diabetes Management

Adequate diabetes management often involves a relatively sophisticated understanding of diabetes. The youngster or his or her parents must know how to test for urine glucose and ketones and to interpret test results appropriately in order to adjust the insulin dosage. The insulin must be drawn up accurately and injected skillfully. The youngster must learn to eat often but must generally avoid certain foods (e.g., candy, soda pop). He or she must learn to attend to internal cues in order to act on early signs of hypoglycemic or hyperglycemic reactions. The youngster and/or his or her parents must understand the potential effects of exercise, diet, stress, illness, and so forth on diabetes stability. Poor understanding in any of these areas could result in too much or too little insulin being administered and in poor dietary habits, including infrequent eating or excessive ingestion of sweets.

Data reported in several studies suggest that understanding of diabetes increases as the child grows older. Between the ages of 12 and 15 years, understanding is sufficient for the youngster to manage his or her own diabetes (Etzwiler, 1962; Garner, Thompson, & Partridge, 1969; Partridge, Garner, Thompson, & Cherry, 1972). Nevertheless, teenagers frequently have misconceptions about this disorder (Frankel, 1975; Kaufman & Hersher, 1971). Parents do not always have sufficient knowledge of diabetes to assist their youngsters (Collier & Etzwiler, 1971; Etzwiler & Sines, 1962), and medication errors are common even among adult diabetics (Watkins, Roberts, Williams, Martin, & Coyle, 1967).

### Compliance to Treatment Regimen

Adequate knowledge and understanding of diabetes is a necessary prerequisite for good diabetes management. Adequate knowledge, however, does not ensure adequate compliance to treatment regimen. Etzwiler and Robb (1972), for example, used programmed education to improve knowledge of diabetes among a group of youngsters and their parents. This increased knowledge did not improve these youngsters' diabetes stability. In other words, a youngster may understand how to care for his or her diabetes but not behave in accordance with this understanding. A child may "know" how to do urine tests but may never do them. He or she may "know" when and what to eat but will eat irregularly and inappropriately. Consequently, the psychologist or psychiatrist must target both the behaviors related to an understanding of diabetes and the behaviors related to compliance to prescribed treatment procedures.

*Emotional State*

That emotional factors may influence diabetes stability has long been recognized. In the 17th century, Thomas Willis wrote that he believed that the disorder was the result of "prolonged sorrow." In the 1930s, Menninger described changes in his patients' diabetes stability that seemed to be correlated with changes in mental state (Treuting, 1962). As mentioned previously, a number of investigators have reported poorer adjustment among youngsters with poorly controlled diabetes (Koski, 1969; Loughlin & Mosenthal, 1944; Simonds, 1976–1977; Stersky, 1963; Swift *et al.*, 1967). In these studies, however, psychological difficulties could have been the result of diabetes instability rather than its cause.

Better evidence for the direct effect of psychic stress on the levels of blood glucose and free fatty acids (ketones) is provided in a series of laboratory studies employing adolescent and adult diabetics as subjects. In normal individuals, stress results in the production of pituitary hormones and catecholamines. These hormones and catecholamines lead to decreased insulin production and increased free fatty acids in the blood. Under prolonged stress, blood glucose may also increase, ensuring an adequate energy supply for body tissues (which can employ either glucose or fats for fuel) and the central nervous system (which uses only glucose). When the stress ends, there is a temporary rise in insulin, a decline in the stress hormones, and a subsequent return to normal levels of blood glucose and free fatty acids. Because the youngster with diabetes has insufficient insulin, his or her system is unable to counteract the effects of the stress hormones. Exogenous administration of insulin is helpful but still leaves the patient with an insensitive system unable to fluctuate in response to momentary needs (Efendic, Cerasi, & Luft, 1974).

Hinkle, Conger, and Wolf (1950) and Hinkle and Wolf (1952) studied the effect of a stress interview on adult and adolescent diabetics and normal persons in a fasting state. The patients with diabetes had taken no insulin prior to the interview. Blood and urine glucose and ketones, as well as the amount of urine excreted, were monitored. The physiological effects of the stress interview were compared to nonstressful periods prior to and after the stress interview. Stress was associated with an increase in blood ketones and urine output both for the patients with diabetes and for the normal persons. However, patients with elevated ketones prior to the stress interview showed a particularly exaggerated increase in free fatty acids. Blood and urine glucose levels did not appear to be particularly reliable indications of the patient's clinical state.

Other stress-induction laboratory studies of diabetics have been conducted by Baker, Barcai, Kaye, and Hague (1969); Vandenbergh, Sussman, and Titus (1966); and Vandenbergh, Sussman, and Vaughn (1967). As a group, these studies strongly suggest that stress can affect diabetes stability. A rise in free fatty acids and urine volume in response to stress is consistently reported for both normal persons and persons with diabetes. Blood and urine glucose levels, however, appear to be much more variable and may not be the best measure of the patient's diabetes stability. Unfortunately, results of urine glucose tests are used by most patients to determine their daily insulin requirement.

Although these studies support the possible impact of stress on diabetes, they tell us little about the effects of emotional states within the natural environment.

A careful assessment will necessarily involve some attempt to delineate possible emotional reactions and coping styles that may be affecting the youngster's diabetes stability.

It is also possible that emotional states or coping styles may be a target for further assessment and intervention even when the youngster's diabetes is well controlled. Many studies have assessed the personality characteristics of children and adolescents with diabetes. Most report that these youngsters function within normal limits on a variety of standardized tests measuring self-concept, aggression, frustration threshold, personal adjustment, introversion–extroversion, psychopathology, and intelligence (Delbridge, 1975; Galatzer, Frish, & Laron, 1977; Koski, 1969; Kubany, Danowski, & Moses, 1956; Steinhauser, Borner, & Koepp, 1977; Tavormina, Kastner, Slater, & Watt, 1976). Tavormina et al. (1976) reported greater alienation and Delbridge (1975) reported poorer social adjustment compared to the standardization sample. These findings, however, seem to be the exception rather than the rule.

Other investigators have compared the responses of youngsters with diabetes with those of nondiabetic controls matched on variables such as age, sex, and social class. Most report no major differences in the psychiatric status of patients with diabetes compared to matched controls, although differences on one or two specific measures may emerge (Cernelc et al., 1977; Olatawura, 1972; Sayed & Leaverton, 1974; Stersky, 1963; Sullivan, 1978; Laron, Karp, & Frankel, Note 1). Swift et al. (1967) found greater psychological disturbance among youngsters with diabetes. However, the psychologist and psychiatrist who assessed these children were aware of the youngsters' diabetic or nondiabetic status, possibly biasing their results. Fallstrom (1974) also reported poorer adjustment among patients with diabetes, although this study has been criticized on methodological grounds (McCraw & Tuma, 1977).

More often than not, youngsters with diabetes seem to respond "normally" to psychological tests and assessment procedures. However, some investigators do report significant psychological disturbance among these youngsters. Peer or social problems and feelings of alienation seem to be the most frequently reported difficulties (Delbridge, 1975; Fallstrom, 1974; Sayed & Leaverton, 1974; Tavormina et al. 1976; Laron et al., Note 1). It seems reasonable to conclude that some children with diabetes have psychological problems. Although most youngsters seem to cope reasonably well, an individual child may worry excessively about becoming sick or may feel "different" from other youngsters. An adolescent may have real concerns about acceptance by his or her peers, employers, and possible marriage partners. The older child may be unsure of his or her ability to cope with physical complications that may result from diabetes. Certainly, these are all affective and cognitive concerns that are appropriate targets for assessment and treatment.

## Family and Environmental Influences

Environmental factors may also affect the youngster's diabetes stability and/or emotional state. In particular, the family may exert a powerful influence on the child. Several studies report greater family disturbance among children in poor diabetes control compared to those with highly stable diabetes (Delbridge, 1975; Koski, 1969; Koski & Kumento, 1977). In one study, changes from good or fair to poor control were associated with a high incidence of family disruption (Koski & Kumento, 1975). Simonds (1977) found an unusually low rate of divorce in families of well-controlled youngsters as compared to unstable diabetic or nondiabetic comparison groups. Most clinicians point to particular pathological family patterns as important influences on the child's diabetes stability. Parents of children in poor control are described as overanxious, overindulgent, overcontrolling, resentful, rejecting, or disinterested (Bruch, 1949; Katz, 1957; Khurana & White, 1970; Kravitz, Isenberg, Shore, & Barnett, 1971; Starr, 1955). However, there is little empirical support for these clinical impressions.

More objective data assessing the interrelationship of family patterns and the youngster's diabetes stability have been provided by Minuchin and Baker and their colleagues. In their model, a "psychosomatic family" is one that seeks to avoid conflict. However, conflict necessarily occurs, and family members become emotionally and physiologically aroused. This situation is described as the "turn on" phase. In this particular type of family, the "turn off" phase (or return to normal levels of physiological responding) is handicapped by the family's attempts to avoid conflict, with a consequent lack of conflict resolution (Baker, Minuchin, Milman, Liebman, & Todd, 1975; Minuchin et al., 1975; Minuchin, Rosman, & Baker, 1978). These authors have tested this model by monitoring physiological responding during a stressful family interview. The stress led to an increase in arousal and free fatty acid production in the youngsters studied that did not "turn off" once the interview was terminated (Baker et al., 1975; Minuchin et al., 1978). Further, children with unstable diabetes from psychosomatic families seem to improve in response to family therapy, although no appropriate control group comparisons have been conducted (Minuchin et al., 1975).

This work is commendable as an initial attempt to study objectively the effect of family patterns on diabetes stability. Nevertheless, the number of subjects studied is small, and it is unclear how often pathological family patterns play a causal role in children's diabetes instability. Perhaps some youngsters are particularly stress-sensitive, and any stress, including "normal" family conflict, could result in diabetes instability. In any event, it seems reasonable to assume that family patterns or other environmental stressors could affect a particular child's diabetes stability. Similarly, the family may be seriously affected by the child's diabetes. Parents may argue over how to manage the child's illness. Siblings may feel jealous of the extra attention that may be paid to a child with diabetes. The illness may be a strain on the family's financial resources. Although the impact of diabetes on the family has not been adequately studied, it remains an important target for assessment.

## Methods of Collecting Information

In conducting an assessment, the psychologist or psychiatrist may employ several methods for collecting information. An initial interview with the youngster and his or her parents is essential. However, important information can also be obtained through the use of self-report instruments, self-recording, behavioral observations, physiological measures, and the collection of permanent products.

### Self-Report Instruments

The usual method for assessing a youngster's or parent's knowledge of diabetes is a paper-and-pencil test such as those developed by Etzwiler (1962) and Collier and Etzwiler (1971). These instruments generally ask very specific questions about diabetes (e.g., What causes diabetes? When should you routinely test your urine?). Little reliability or standardization data are available. At the University of Florida, we have developed a test of the youngster's or parent's ability to solve problems in managing diabetes. Sample items are provided in Table 1. We have found that scores on our test of problem solving correlate only moderately ($r = +.5$ to $+.7$) with scores on a test of general information, suggesting that the two tests are measuring different, but related, knowledge. Tests of problem-solving skills may

TABLE 1

Test of Diabetes Knowledge: Problem Solving (Sample Items)

1. You are at a school football game and begin to feel dizzy, shaky, and faint. You should:
   a. Leave the game right away and go straight home.
   b. Buy a coke and a hot dog and eat them.
   c. Lie down, until you feel better.
   d. I don't know.
2. You are trying out for the swimming team and practice is in midafternoon. Your urine tests are usually negative before lunch and in midafternoon. You should:
   a. Decrease your insulin the days you practice.
   b. Eat a particularly big lunch that day.
   c. Increase your insulin to give you more energy that day.
   d. I don't know.
3. You have a big test coming up next period in your hardest subject. You are worried about it, because you feel unprepared. Thirty minutes before the test is to begin you begin to feel weak, shaky, and sweaty, and your heart begins to beat fast. You should:
   a. Go to the school nurse so you won't have to take the test.
   b. Eat something.
   c. Take extra regular insulin so you'll be ready for the test.
   d. I don't know.
4. You take 30 units of NPH insulin each morning. One day your urine at 10:00 a.m. has 5% sugar and "large" acetone. In this situation you should:
   a. Eat less today.
   b. Eat more to counteract the ketones.
   c. Drink extra fluids and check your urine again in an hour or two.
   d. I don't know.
5. You have the flu, with a high fever, and you don't feel like eating. You check your urine and it is 8% and large. You should:
   a. Hold your morning insulin because you're not eating as much.
   b. Add regular insulin to your usual morning dose and call your doctor.
   c. Do nothing different because everybody gets the flu.
   d. I don't know.

be important for assessing the youngster's or parent's ability to make appropriate insulin dose or diet changes depending upon daily fluctuations in the child's health, exercise, emotional state, and so forth. Knowing the "facts" about diabetes does not ensure that the youngster knows how to regulate his or her diabetes under variable conditions.

Standardized psychological tests or behavioral checklists can be used as self-report measures of the youngster's general psychological well-being. The examiner can assess, for example, whether the youngster is more or less anxious, aggressive, or withdrawn than other youngsters his or her age. A thorough discussion of available psychological tests and behavioral checklists is beyond the scope of this chapter. The interested reader is referred to recent reviews by O'Leary and Johnson (1979) on the assessment of psychopathology in children and by Johnson and Melamed (1979) on the assessment of children's anxiety states and fears (see Chapter 6).

Several self-report instruments designed to assess family patterns and environments are also available. The Family Functioning Index was developed by Pless and Satterwhite (1973) to study the characteristics of families with chronically ill children. The authors report good interrater and test–retest reliability and some data supporting the instrument's validity (Pless, Roghmann, & Haggerty, 1972; Satterwhite, Zweig, Ikes, & Pless, 1976). Moos (1973, 1976) has developed the Family Environment Inventory, which is composed of 90 true–false items falling into ten subscales (e.g., cohesiveness, expressiveness, conflict). Adequate internal consistency and test–retest reliability have been reported. Both of these instruments should be considered experimental, and they have not been used extensively with youngsters who have diabetes.

The number and extent of life stress events have also been assessed using self-report instruments for both children (Coddington, 1972) and adults (Holmes & Rahe, 1967). Using these measures, life stress has been related to number of sickness episodes in children (Bedell, Giordani, Amour, Tavormina, & Boll, 1977) and adults (Grant, Kyle, Teichman, & Mendels, 1974). These instruments have been used to study groups of individuals rather than the single case. Consequently, the clinician assessing a particular youngster and his or her family should be aware of their limitations.

In general, self-report instruments are open to a number of criticisms. They are easily affected by demand characteristics, the care with which the respondent chooses to answer the questions, and his or her desire to "look good" (or "look bad"). Nevertheless, they serve as one possible data source, albeit an imperfect one. As has been seen in the asthma literature, self-report instruments assessing patients' attitudes toward their illness and subjective symptoms occurring during asthma attacks can serve as important predictors of treatment outcome (e.g., Kinsman et al., 1977; Staudenmayer, Kinsman, & Jones, 1978).

Perhaps questionnaires focusing on a specific illness (e.g., asthma) are more helpful than instruments asking more general questions about overall family functioning or psychological health. To address this issue, we have developed and are currently testing the Diabetes Opinion Survey. This is a self-report instrument designed to assess youngsters' attitudes toward diabetes. Similar in concept to the

Respiratory Illness Opinion Survey, this instrument attempts to assess attitudes specifically related to diabetes, such as psychological stigma (i.e., feeling different from others), feelings toward medical staff, subjective awareness of diabetes symptomatology, optimism concerning the future, and denial of realities about diabetes. A second form has been developed for parents, with which we are attempting to assess parental overprotectiveness toward the child, the impact of diabetes on the family, the parent's optimism or pessimism about the child's future, and the child's manipulative use of his or her illness.

### Self-Recording

Self-recording is probably one of the most convenient ways to collect data as to a youngster's daily functioning. Usually, the youngster is asked to keep records of urine glucose levels and time, type, and dose of insulin administered. For some youngsters, extensive information is needed as to their dietary and exercise habits as well (see Chapter 13, this volume). At the University of Florida, we ask these youngsters to complete the Diabetes Daily Record for 1-week to 2-week intervals (see Figure 1). On each day, the child or parent is to record (1) each administration of insulin, including information as to time administered, type of insulin, and dose level; (2) each urine test, including time of test, levels of glucose, and amount of ketones; (3) any food or drink ingested, including time of day eating or drinking occurred and type of food or fluid taken; and (4) type and duration of any physical activity, including time of day it occurred. The Diabetes Daily Record can be used as a measure of the youngster's "usual" behavior. Both parents and child are told *not* to change the way in which they typically behave (e.g., if they never test the youngster's urine, no urine test data are recorded). The record also can be used as an intervention procedure to encourage adequate compliance to treatment regimen.

Self-recording can also be used to measure a youngster's daily fluctuations between hypoglycemic and hyperglycemic states. Fowler, Budzynski, and Vandenbergh (1976) had a 20-year-old woman record her subjective state on a nine-point scale from severe hypoglycemia to severe hyperglycemia. Each point on this Self-Rated Diabetic Scale was defined by a specific set of symptoms in order to enhance consistent use of the scale (see Table 2). Each day, the young woman recorded her subjective state prior to testing her urine. The authors report a substantial correlation between the woman's subjective diabetes symptomatology and the amount of daily insulin self-administered ($r = +.77; p < .01$).

These same authors also had this woman record her emotional state on a five-point scale from very tense to very calm. She did this at the same time she used the Self-Rated Diabetic Scale. This procedure was an attempt to assess this young woman's emotional state as well as daily fluctuation in her diabetes symptomatology. In this particular case study, the correlation between the two was moderate and statistically significant ($r = +.49; p < .05$).

Although the self-recording methods developed by Fowler et al. (1976) could probably be used with adolescents, a simpler version of this procedure would be necessary for younger children. We are currently experimenting with a modified version of Fowler et al.'s Self-Rated Diabetic Scale for children. We are also

Name: _____

Date: _____

*Insulin injection(s)*

| Time | AM<br>PM | AM<br>PM | AM<br>PM |
|---|---|---|---|
| Units/type | R<br>NPH<br>Lente | R<br>NPH<br>Lente | R<br>NPH<br>Lente |

*Urine testing*

| Time | AM<br>PM | AM<br>PM | AM<br>PM | AM<br>PM |
|---|---|---|---|---|
| Sugar | <2% 2–6% >6% | <2% 2–6% >6% | <2% 2–6% >6% | <2% 2–6% >6% |
| Acetone | neg sml mod lrg | neg sml mod lrg | neg sml mod lrg | neg sml mod lrg |

*Diet*

| Time | AM  PM | AM  PM | AM  PM | AM  PM | AM  PM | AM  PM |
|---|---|---|---|---|---|---|
| Food and/or drink | | | | | | |

*Exercise*

| Time | AM  PM | AM  PM | AM  PM | AM  PM | AM  PM |
|---|---|---|---|---|---|
| Activity | | | | | |
| Duration (how long activity lasts) | | | | | |

FIGURE 1
Diabetes Daily Record.

TABLE 2
Self-Rated Diabetic Scale

| Rating | Description |
| --- | --- |
| −4 | Severe hypoglycemia<br>Unconscious<br>Convulsions<br>Little or no recall of events<br>Hospitalization |
| −3 | Moderate hypoglycemia<br>Some lapse in memory<br>Insulin reaction requiring large amounts of glucose, etc.<br>Strange behavior, that is, acting drunk<br>Nervousness, anxiety, and/or apprehension<br>Confusion, difficulty in thinking<br>Difficulty in focusing eyes<br>Poor coordination<br>Speech difficulties |
| −2 | Mild hypoglycemia<br>Hunger<br>Sweating<br>Cold, shivering<br>Tachycardia<br>Able to recall all events<br>Shaking<br>Drowsy<br>Weak |
| −1 | Feel drop in blood sugar, but no insulin reaction<br>Tired<br>Hunger<br>Mild weakness |
| 0 | Feel fine: no signs of hypoglycemia or hyperglycemia |
| +1 | Mild symptoms of hyperglycemia and/or acetone<br>Weakness<br>Thirsty<br>Easily fatigued during mild exercise, for example, walking |
| +2 | Moderate symptoms<br>Increasing nausea<br>Weakness<br>Starting to become dehydrated<br>Headache |
| +3 | Serious symptoms<br>Extreme weakness<br>Dehydrated<br>Dizziness |

*(continued)*

TABLE 2 *(continued)*

| Rating | Description |
|---|---|
| | Blurred vision |
| | Drowsy, tired |
| | Difficulty in concentrating |
| | Severe nausea and/or vomiting |
| | Kussmaul breathing |
| | Aches (muscular, joint) |
| | Difficulty in extending arms, legs, fingers |
| +4 | Ketoacidosis requiring hospitalization |

*Note.* From "Effects of an EMG Biofeedback Relaxation Program on the Control of Diabetes: A Case Study" by J. Fowler, T. Budzynski, and R. Vandenbergh, *Biofeedback and Self-Regulation*, 1976, *1*, 105–112. Copyright 1976 by Plenum Publishing Corporation. Reprinted by permission.

assessing the utility of the state anxiety portion of Spielberger's State–Trait Anxiety Inventory for Children (1973) as a means of collecting daily measures of anxiety in preadolescent youngsters.

If the psychologist or psychiatrist suspects that a particular environmental event is triggering a youngster's instability, he or she may ask the child to record the frequency of these events daily. A good example of this approach is provided in an early study reported by Hinkle and Wolf (1949). A 15-year-old school girl with frequent episodes of hospitalized ketoacidosis was asked to keep a diary of significant events, feelings, and levels of urine glucose and acetone. These records indicated a striking correlation between conflict with her mother and increased levels of acetone in her urine (see Figure 2). In a second case study, the same authors suspected that the diabetes instability in an adolescent girl was associated with scholastic examinations (Hinkle & Wolf, 1952). When the youngster self-recorded daily levels of urine acetone and noted when examinations occurred, a clear relationship between the two was found.

It is important to note that the use of self-recording among youngsters with diabetes has not been well researched. Although such procedures have been used in one or two published studies, we know nothing of their reliability, validity, or reactivity. Although we have presented examples of various self-recording procedures, caution must be exercised when interpreting any information obtained in this manner. The adequacy of these procedures as measurement techniques has not been established.

### Behavioral Observations

Observational data may be collected in either analogue settings or in the natural environment.

In assessing a youngster's ability to conduct urine tests and to administer insulin, it is important to have the child demonstrate the necessary steps and procedures. Watkins *et al.* (1967) asked adult diabetics to measure the insulin they were currently using. Measurement errors occurred in 28% of the patients studied. Consequently, it seems prudent to assess through observation whether a child or parent is accurately measuring and administering the correct amount of insulin. Self-report data may not be sufficient. We have observed over 150 youngsters with diabetes testing their own urine and preparing to self-inject insulin. The observer watches the child and scores each step in the procedure as pass (P) or fail (F). The score sheet for observing self-injection is provided in Figure 3.

We have obtained excellent interrater reliability with this procedure (87–93% agreement). We have also found that more than 50% of the youngsters studied made "serious" errors when urine testing and that more than 24% made such errors when preparing to self-inject. A "serious" error was defined as a failure on specified items that should result in incorrect readings on the urine test or incorrect administration of insulin on the self-injection test.

In an effort to assess the role of the family in cases of unstable diabetes, Baker and Minuchin and their co-workers have used observational procedures in an analogue setting (Baker *et al.*, 1975; Minuchin *et al.*, 1978). The family is given a "task," such as planning a menu for the evening dinner. The interaction is videotaped and then rated for overprotectiveness, enmeshment, rigidity, and lack of conflict resolution. These concepts are apparently operationalized within their scoring system. However, published reports describing this procedure do not provide adequate detail as to the coding system employed, nor do they present sufficient reliability data. Certainly this is a critical, but difficult, area for assessment. Baker and Minuchin and their co-workers should be commended for their pioneering efforts. Nevertheless, additional research must be done if we are to develop reliable and valid measures of family interactions.

A recent study provides an excellent example of the use of observational procedures in a natural setting. Lowe and Lutzer (1979) monitored three behaviors in a 9-year-old girl that the investigators considered important to her diabetes management. These included (1) urine testing, (2) eating, and (3) foot care. This child's mother recorded observations daily on all three behaviors. Occasionally, an older sister independently observed the same behaviors to check for reliability. The experimenter also made unannounced visits to corroborate the child's and mother's reports.

Despite an extensive literature on observational assessment procedures, only recently have these techniques been applied to the study of youngsters with diabetes and their families. It is hoped that future assessment efforts in this area will rely more heavily on this particular information collection method.

### Physiological Measures

Physiological measures are particularly important because diabetes stability or instability is defined by such indexes. Unfortunately, no one physiological measure can be used to assess the youngster's diabetes control. For example, blood glucose

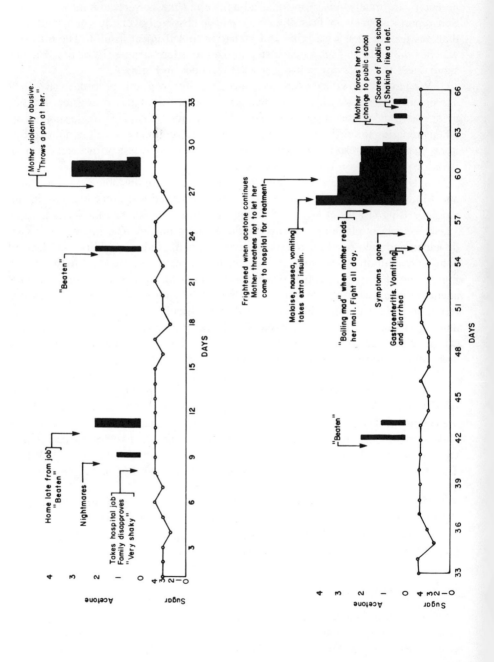

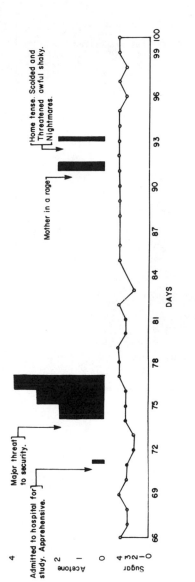

FIGURE 2

Detailed correlation of urinary findings with events, attitudes, and emotions in a 15-year-old girl reported by Hinkle and Wolf (1949). From "Experimental Study of Life Situations, Emotions, and the Occurrence of Acidosis in a Juvenile Diabetic" by L. Hinkle and S. Wolf, *American Journal of Medical Sciences*, 1949, *217*, 130–135. Copyright 1949 by Lea & Febiger. Reprinted by permission.

Examiner: Ask the child how much insulin the doctor has prescribed for
him or her.

*1.    States prescribed amount. _____
                                 (write in response)
         (Score after checking dose in medical record.)        P         F

Examiner: Tell the youngster you would like him or her to
demonstrate how to self-inject.

*2.    Chooses correct insulin bottle.                          P         F

3.    Mixes insulin appropriately (rolls, does not shake).      P         F

4.    Cleans top of insulin bottle with alcohol pad.           P         F

5.    Pulls plunger back so that syringe fills with air and the
top of the plunger is within $\pm$ 5 unit marks of the previously
stated amount of insulin (see #1).                      P         F

6.    Takes top off needle properly.                           P         F

7.    Inserts needle into rubber top of insulin bottle.         P         F

8.    Injects air into the bottle, but not into the insulin.     P         F

9.    Turns bottle upside down with syringe in place.           P         F

10.    Pulls back insulin.                                   P         F

11.    Looks for air bubbles. (Inquire about what youngster
is doing.)                                        P         F

12.    Flicks syringe with finger or uses some other method to remove
air bubbles. (Inquire: "What are you doing that for?")   P         F

Examiner: Reach for syringe and say, "Can I see that?"
Examine closely for next two items.

*13.    No air bubbles are visible.                           P         F

*14.    Amount of insulin in syringe is at the unit mark previously
stated by the youngster after syringe is removed from bottle.  P         F

FIGURE 3

15. Needle cover is placed back on.                                              P        F

    Examiner: Ask the child, "Point to where you injected
              the last time."

16. Points to abdomen, thigh, buttock, or arm.                                  P        F

    Examiner: "If you were going to give a shot now, point to
              where you would do it."

*17. Indicates a different injection site.                                       P        F

    Examiner: "Show me what you would do next, as if you were
              giving a shot there."

18. Cleans area with alcohol.                                                    P        F

19. Makes skin taut or pinches skin up.                                          P        F

    Examiner: "Instead of pushing the needle into your skin,
              pretend this is you (indicate foam pad) and
              show me how you would give the shot.

20. Inserts needle vertically (not less than 45° angle).                         P        F

21. Inserts needle completely.                                                   P        F

^22. Pushes plunger down all the way.                                            P        F

23. Wipes injection site with alcohol.                                          P        F

24. Breaks needle and destroys syringe.                                         P        F

25. Throws away syringe in the proper receptacle.                               P        F

26. Spontaneously records insulin dose on the record sheet.                     P        F

    Examiner: If recording is not done spontaneously, prompt
              with "What should you do next?" Then try, "What's
              the last thing you should do?" or "If you were at
              home, what's one more thing you should do?"
              When two (2) prompts fail, ask "What about writing
              it all down?" This usually produces the desired
              response, but is scored F (fail).

27. Recording is done in response to prompting.                                 P        F

Score sheet for skills demonstration: self-injection (P = pass; F = fail; asterisked items are important items where failures may result in administration of improper insulin dose).

concentration is a direct measure of sugar levels in the blood. However, since it is taken at a single time, it may not reflect the patient's "usual" or "average" blood glucose concentration. Similarly, a measure of 24-hour urinary excretion of glucose is dependent on the patient's willingness to collect complete specimens and is influenced by exercise, food ingested, and the child's health on the day the urine is collected. Consequently, diabetes control has been difficult to define (Malone, Hellrung, Malphus, Rosenbloom, Girgic, & Weber, 1976). Different physicians use different criteria. Simply pointing to "normal" blood glucose levels as the index of control is not sufficient; current treatment techniques simply do not permit blood glucose regulation in a normal fashion (Bruck & MacGillivray, 1974; Rosenbloom & Giordano, 1977; Service, Molnar, Rosevear, Ackerman, Gatewood, & Taylor, 1970).

This issue is further complicated by the fact that the youngster uses his or her urine glucose and acetone levels (acetone is a type of ketone) as a basis for changing the frequency and dose of insulin administered. As noted previously, urine glucose is not always a reliable measure of the patient's diabetic state (Hinkle et al., 1950; Hinkle & Wolf, 1949, 1952; Vandenbergh et al., 1966, 1967). In addition, ingesting aspirin and ascorbic acid (a common additive to man-made foods and drinks) can produce inaccurate readings of urine glucose levels when testing with the usual procedures (e.g., Clinitest Tablets, Diastix, Clinistix, or Tes-Tape strips—Travis, 1978). Other more reliable measures such as hemoglobin $A_{1c}$ are available but require blood samples and expensive laboratory equipment (Tze, Thompson, & Leichter, 1978). Consequently, they cannot be conveniently used on a daily basis in the youngster's home environment. Perhaps levels of urine acetone and urine volume would be better measures of a youngster's diabetic state than levels of urine glucose (Hinkle & Wolf, 1949, 1952; Vandenbergh et al., 1966). Certainly, this is a critical area in need of further research.

Although physiological measures have been used primarily as indexes of diabetes stability, they can also be used to assess a youngster's response to a particular stress. Baker et al. (1969), for example, suspected that a preadolescent girl's repeated episodes of ketoacidosis were related to emotional arousal. Using a repeated blood-sampling procedure, they compared the physiological effects of a stressful interview with those of a nonstressful discussion. Increases in blood glucose, ketones, and free fatty acids occurred when the youngster was stressed.

A similar procedure was used by Baker et al. (1975) to monitor a youngster's physiological responsiveness to a stressful family interview. Increases in free fatty acids were reported. This procedure requires frequent blood sampling and close monitoring of the participants. In the Baker et al. (1975) study, a small needle was inserted into the youngster's peripheral vein with a stopcock arrangement, which permitted frequent, but relatively "unobtrusive," blood sampling. It is clear that this procedure must be used only in a highly controlled setting with adequate medical attention to the youngster's physical condition. It is possible that some individuals are particularly responsive physiologically to emotional and stressful events. This procedure offers a method of assessing a youngster's reactivity to one or more specific stresses. Nevertheless, it should be used with appropriate caution.

*Permanent Products*

Many times, a particular behavior results in a "product" that can be measured. Counting these products is one way in which to help confirm the occurrence of a specific behavior. Lowe and Lutzer (1979), for example, asked a youngster to test her urine four times daily. Each time she was to save half of the urine specimen collected. The experimenter then arbitrarily tested some of these specimens to corroborate the child's test data. This child was also asked to wash her feet carefully once a day and to use a clean washcloth on each occasion. She was given seven washcloths for the week. The experimenter simply counted the number of dirty washcloths in the laundry on unannounced home visits as a means of confirming the mother's reports of the child's compliance to this procedure.

There are a number of other permanent products that are useful in studying youngster's with diabetes. Many syringes are disposable and could be counted. Discarded cotton swabs dipped in alcohol and used to clean the skin prior to injection could be counted. The amount of insulin left in its container could be measured. All of these permanent products are useful indicators of insulin administration. In addition to saving urine samples as Lowe and Lutzer did (1979), the number of unused Clinitest tablets or the number of used Tes-Tape or Clinistix strips could be counted as measures of urine testing frequency. Dietary behavior is more difficult to monitor. Discarded food wrappers could be collected as a means of assessing the number and type of snacks eaten. Weight gain or loss might serve as an indicator of compliance or noncompliance to a prescribed diet. Exercise could be assessed by noting wear on a youngster's sports shoes, the number of miles on a bike's speedometer, or the amount of exercise shorts, shirts, and socks thrown into the laundry hamper.

Of course, permanent products are not necessarily valid indications that a particular behavior occurred. A youngster could draw up insulin, throw it down the sink, and then discard the syringe along with a piece of cotton dipped in alcohol to make it look like he or she had actually self-injected insulin. Although this is not extremely common, it does occur. In such cases, the psychiatrist or psychologist must conduct a functional analysis of both the noncompliance behavior (e.g., not injecting insulin) and the youngster's elaborate efforts to "cover up."

## A Functional Analysis of Behavior

Using information obtained through various data collection procedures, the psychologist or psychiatrist conducts a functional analysis of the target behavior(s). In an *S-O-R* model, stimulus or eliciting events may be discriminative cues for the behavior to occur. Organismic characteristics of the child may be influential in maintaining the behavior. Response or consequence variables may be important as well.

In some youngsters, a psychic stressor is a common antecedent event to poor diabetes control. In case studies provided by Hinkle and Wolf (1949, 1952), increases in urine acetone seemed to be "set-off" by mother–child conflicts for one youngster and by scholastic examinations for another. The work of Baker and Minuchin described previously also assumes that unresolved family conflicts are important eliciting events in diabetes instability. Other potentially influential antecedent events include peer or sibling pressure to eat highly concentrated sugars or to "forget" taking insulin. Such events are described anecdotally but have not been well researched.

Specific characteristics of the child may also serve to maintain targeted behavioral deficits or excesses. For example, noncompliance to treatment regimen could be a function of insufficient knowledge about diabetes. Lowe and Lutzer (1979) were careful to assess their 9-year-old subject's urine testing skills and dietary knowledge prior to implementing a program to increase the frequency of this child's self-administered urine tests and her compliance to dietary restrictions. A number of skill deficits were noted and subsequently corrected. Other children may be overanxious or may show heightened physiological sensitivity. Baker and Minuchin's work suggested that some youngsters show high arousal in response to stress that does not "turn-off" once the stress is terminated. Research cited previously from the asthma literature indicates that the patient's level of anxiety may be an important predictor of treatment outcome. Poor social or coping skills may prevent a youngster from appropriately handling pressures from peers or the normal stresses of everyday life.

The responses of significant others in the child's life will also be critical. If the parent attends to the child more when he or she is sick than well, sickness behavior may be inadvertently rewarded and actually increase. Similarly, youngsters with diabetes are frequently permitted to leave the classroom whenever they feel ill. The child may begin to miss more and more school and to fall farther behind academically. The child's academic deficits may further increase school-avoidant sickness behavior. Parents who overprotect their youngsters by carrying out all aspects of their child's therapy (e.g., urine tests, insulin administration) may be encouraging poorer compliance to treatment regimen when the child is on his or her own in an unsupervised situation. Certainly, a chronic illness like diabetes is cause for concern. Sickness episodes can have serious consequences. It is difficult for a parent to always know how much concern is necessary and how much may be inadvertently rewarding inappropriate child behaviors.

Of course, not all parents show overconcern or overprotectiveness. Some are on the opposite end of the continuum, neglecting their child and his or her particular needs. These unhappy youngsters may find special comfort in a hospital setting where they are cared for and attended to by pleasant, concerned staff. It is not surprising that such children show high rates of hospital readmission.

Only very recently have behaviorally oriented psychologists begun to employ their skills with youngsters who have diabetes and their families. Consequently, there are few data as to common antecedent or consequent events or organismic variables that are specific to problems of children with diabetes. Research is clearly needed. In the meantime, it seems wise to continue to rely on principles that have proved useful with other problems of childhood.

## Selecting a Treatment Program

Once the psychologist or psychiatrist has completed a thorough assessment, a treatment program must be selected and implemented. One or more behaviors may be targeted for change. The therapist may choose to focus on events presumed to elicit child problems (e.g., family arguments) or on specific characteristics of the child (e.g., deficits in diabetes knowledge, poor skills to cope with stress). The therapist might also choose to work with significant others in the child's world if he or she suspects their responses may be maintaining some of the child's problem behavior. In many cases, more than one area will be targeted for change. However, those aspects of the child or the environment selected for therapeutic intervention will necessarily depend on the viability of such change efforts.

Hinkle and Wolf (1952), for example, described a youngster who showed high levels of urine acetone during periods of academic examinations. In this case, it seems unreasonable to remove the eliciting event (scholastic examinations) because this is a normal stress of daily life. Instead, the authors chose to focus on the attitudes toward school performance of this youngster's parents. When her parents put less emphasis on extremely high levels of academic achievement, this youngster reportedly improved. Good results using family therapy have also been described by Minuchin et al. (1975), although appropriate control groups were not employed.

Not all parents are amenable to treatment programs whether their behavior is eliciting the child's problem behavior or reinforcing it. In such cases, it may be particularly important to focus on the youngster. Presumably, children as young as 7 years can be taught coping and many diabetes self-management skills, although this area has not been carefully researched. In one of the few studies focusing on improving coping skills, Fowler et al. (1976) trained a young woman in EMG biofeedback and muscle relaxation. The patient reported decreased emotionality and more stable diabetes in response to training. Her daily insulin dose was substantially reduced.

Lowe and Lutzer (1979) used both a written prompt to elicit compliance behavior in their young subject and a reward system to reinforce it. For one of the targeted behaviors, the introduction of the prompt was associated with high rates of compliant behavior. For two other behaviors, the prompt was not particularly effective, and back-up rewards were introduced with good success.

There are numerous treatment programs one could devise depending upon the specific problems and strengths of an individual child and his or her family. We have made no attempt to be comprehensive in this regard. Instead, we have chosen to highlight a few studies that describe various intervention strategies. Despite extensive discussion in the literature of the problems youngsters with diabetes encounter, well-controlled treatment research with this population is almost nonexistent.

Before leaving the subject of treatment planning, it seems important to reiterate the point that assessment does not stop when an intervention program is selected and implemented. Ongoing assessment is critical to the evaluation of any treatment program. It provides the necessary data on which the therapist bases his or her decisions concerning treatment program changes and treatment termination.

## SUMMARY

Although asthma and juvenile diabetes are among the most common chronic illnesses of childhood, behavioral assessment or treatment procedures have not been extensively applied to these problems. Most studies have focused on one or more personality traits of youngsters with asthma or diabetes in comparison to nonasthmatic or nondiabetic persons. Consequently, there is little available data as to the best assessment methods or intervention procedures to use with children who have these chronic disorders.

In view of this inadequate data base, we have attempted to provide a number of suggestions regarding selecting and defining target behaviors, methods of data collection, conducting a functional analysis, and selecting a treatment program. Where possible, we have provided examples from the literature. At times, however, we have been forced to rely on our own experiences in working with these populations. We would like to encourage the reader to use this discussion as a guide to or as "pilot data" for further research efforts in this area. Well-trained behavioral psychologists and psychiatrists can make important contributions to the study of these particular childhood health problems. Research is critically needed.

### Acknowledgments

The authors wish to acknowledge Janet Silverstein, MD, Arlan Rosenbloom, MD, William Riley, MD, R. Timothy Pollak, PhD, Brenda Gilbert, MSW, Rebecca Spillar, MA, and Martha McCallum, RN, who are the integral members of our research team studying psychosocial aspects of juvenile diabetes. The support of the National Institute of Dental Research through Grant No. DE05305-01 is gratefully acknowledged.

### Reference Note

1. Laron, Z., Karp, M., & Frankel, J. J. *A study of the rehabilitation of juvenile and adolescent diabetics in the central region of Israel.* Final report, Pediatric, Metabolic, and Endocrine Service, Beilinson Hospital Medical Center, Petach-Tiqva, Israel, 1972.

### References

Alexander, A. B., Miklich, D. R., & Hershkoff, H. The immediate effects of systematic relaxation training on peak expiratory flow rates in asthmatic children. *Psychosomatic Medicine*, 1972, *34*, 388–394.

Baker, L., Barcai, A., Kaye, R., & Hague, N. Beta adrenergic blockade and juvenile diabetes: Acute studies and long-term therapeutic trial. *Journal of Pediatrics*, 1969, *75*(1), 19–29.

Baker, L., Minuchin, S., Milman, L., Leibman, R., & Todd, T. Psychosomatic aspects of juvenile diabetes mellitus: A progress report. In Z. Laron (Ed.), *Modern problems in pediatrics* (Vol. 12): *Diabetes in juveniles: Medical and rehabilitation aspects*. New York: Karger, 1975.

Bedell, J., Giordani, B., Amour, J., Tavormina, J., & Boll, T. Life stress and the psychological and medical adjustment of chronically ill children. *Journal of Psychosomatic Research*, 1977, *21*, 237–242.

Blanchard, E. B., & Young, L. D. Clinical applications of biofeedback. *Archives of General Psychiatry*, 1974, *30*, 573–389.

Bleeker, E. R., & Engle, B. T. Learned control of cardiac rate and cardiac conduction in Wolff–Parkinson–White syndrome. *Seminars in Psychiatry*, 1973, *5*, 465–479.

Block, J., Jennings, P. H., Harvey, E., & Simpson, E. Interaction between allergic potential and psychopathology in childhood. *Psychosomatic Medicine*, 1964, *26*, 307–320.

Bronheim, S. P. Pulmonary disorders: Asthma and cystic fibrosis. In P. R. Magrab, (Ed.), *Psychological management of pediatric problems* (Vol. 1). Baltimore: University Park Press, 1978.

Bruch, M. Physiological and psychological interrelationships in diabetes in children. *Psychosomatic Medicine*, 1949, *11*, 200–210.

Bruck, E., & MacGillivray, M. Posthypoglycemic hyperglycemia in diabetic children. *Journal of Pediatrics*, 1974, *84*, 672–680.

Cahill, G., Etzwiler, D., & Freinkel, N. "Control" and diabetes. *New England Journal of Medicine*, 1976, *294*, 1004.

Cernelc, D., Hafner, G., Kos, S., & Cenlec, P. Comparative study of social and psychological analyses in asthmatic, rheumatic and diabetic children. *Allergie und Immunologie*, 1977, *23*, 214–220.

Clarke, P. S. Effects of emotion and cough on airways obstruction in asthma. *Medical Journal of Australia*, 1970, *1*, 535.

Coddington, R. The significance of life events as etiologic factors in the diseases of children. II. A Study of a normal population. *Journal of Psychosomatic Research*, 1972, *16*, 205–213.

Collier, B., & Etzwiler, D. Comparative study of diabetes knowledge among juvenile diabetics and their parents. *Diabetes*, 1971, *20*(1), 51–57.

Creer, T. The use of a time-out from positive reinforcement procedure with asthmatic children. *Journal of Psychosomatic Research*, 1970, *14*, 117–120.

Creer, T. L., & Yoches, C. The modification of an inappropriate behavioral pattern in asthmatic children. *Journal of Chronic Disease*, 1971, *24*, 507–513.

Criep, L. Pharmacologic modulation of antigen antibody release of chemical mediators. In L. Criep (Ed.), *Allergy and clinical immunology*. New York: Grune & Stratton, 1976.

Dahlem, N. W., Kinsman, R. A., & Horton, D. J. Requests for as-needed (PRN) medications by asthmatic patients: Relationships to prescribed oral corticosteroid regimens and length of hospitalization. *Journal of Allergy and Clinical Immunology*, 1977, *60*(5), 295–300.

Danker, P. S., Miklich, D. R., Pratt, C., & Creer, T. L. An unsuccessful attempt to instrumentally condition peak expiratory flow rates in asthmatic children. *Journal of Psychosomatic Research*, 1975, *19*, 209–213.

Davis, M. H., Saunders, D. R., Creer, T. L., Chai, H. Relaxation training facilitated by biofeedback apparatus as a supplemental treatment in bronchial asthma. *Journal of Psychosomatic Research*, 1973, *17*, 121–128.

Davison, D. G., & Neale, J. M. *Abnormal psychology: An experimental clinical approach*. New York: Wiley, 1974.

Delbridge, L. Educational and psychological factors in the management of diabetes in childhood. *Medical Journal of Australia*, 1975, *2*, 737–739.

Dirks, J. F., Jones, N. F., & Kinsman, R. A. Panic–fear: A personality dimension related to intractability in asthma. *Psychosomatic Medicine*, 1977, *39*, 120–126.

Dirks, J. F., Kinsman, R. A., Jones, N. F., & Fross, K. H. New developments in panic–fear research in asthma: Validity and stability of the MMPI panic–fear scale. *British Journal of Medical Psychology*, 1978, *51*, 119–126.

Dirks, J. F., Kinsman, R. A., Jones, N. F., Spector, S. L., Davidson, P. T., & Evans, N. W. Panic–fear:

A personality dimension related to length of hospitalization in respiratory illness. *Journal of Asthma Research*, 1977, *14*, 61–71.

Dirks, J. F., Kleiger, J. H., & Evans, N. W. ASC panic–fear and length of hospitalization in asthma. *Journal of Asthma Research*, 1978, *15*(2), 95–97.

DuBois, A. B., Botelho, S. Y., & Comroe, J. H. A new method for measuring airway resistance in man using a body plethysmograph: Values in normal subjects and in patients with respiratory disease. *Journal of Clinical Investigation*, 1956, *35*, 327–335.

DuBois, A. B., Brody, A. W., Lewis, D. H., & Burgess, B. F. Oscillation mechanics of lungs and chest in man. *Journal of Applied Physiology*, 1956, *28*, 113–116.

Efendic, S., Cerasi, E., & Luft, R. Trauma: Hormonal factors with special reference to diabetes mellitus. *Acta Anaesthesiologica Scandinavica (Supplement)*, 1974, *55*, 107–119.

Elder, S. T., Ruiz, Z. R., Deabler, H. L., & Dillenkoffer, R. L. Instrumental conditioning of diastolic blood pressure in essential hypertensive patients. *Journal of Applied Behavior Analysis*, 1973, *6*, 377–382.

Etzwiler, D. What the juvenile diabetic knows about his disease. *Pediatrics*, 1962, *29*, 135–141.

Etzwiler, D., & Robb, J. Evaluation of programmed education among juvenile diabetics and their families. *Diabetes*, 1972, *21*, 967–971.

Etzwiler, D., & Sines, L. Juvenile diabetes and its management: Family, social and academic implications. *Journal of the American Medical Association*, 1962, *181*(4), 94–98.

Fallstrom, K. On the personality structure in diabetic school children. *Acta Paediatrica Scandinavica (Supplement)*, 1974, *251*, 5–71.

Fowler, J., Budzynski, T., & Vandenbergh, R. Effects of an EMG biofeedback relaxation program on the control of diabetes: A case study. *Biofeedback and Self-Regulation*, 1976, *1*(1), 105–112.

Frankel, A. Juvenile diabetes—The look from within. In Z. Laron (Ed.), *Modern problems in pediatrics* (Vol. 12): *Diabetes in juveniles: Medical and rehabilitation aspects*. New York: Karger, 1975.

French, T. M. Emotional conflict and allergy. *International Archives of Allergy and Applied Immunology*, 1950, *1*, 28–40.

Galatzer, A., Frish, M., & Laron, Z. Changes in self-concept and feelings towards diabetic adolescents. In Z. Laron (Ed.), *Pediatric and adolescent endocrinology* (Vol. 3): *Psychological aspects of balance of diabetes in juveniles*. New York: Karger, 1977.

Garner, A., Thompson, C., & Partridge, J. Who knows best? *Diabetes Bulletin*, 1969, *45*, 3–4.

Graham, P., Rutter, M., Yule, W., & Pless, I. Childhood asthma: A psychosomatic disorder? Some epidemiological considerations. *British Journal of Preventive and Social Medicine*, 1967, *21*, 78–85.

Grant, I., Kyle, G., Teichman, A., & Mendels, J. Recent life events and diabetes in adults. *Psychosomatic Medicine*, 1974, *36*(2), 121–128.

Hahn, W. W. Autonomic responses of asthmatic children. *Psychosomatic Medicine*, 1966, *28*, 323–332.

Hinkle, L. E., Conger, C., & Wolf, S. Studies on diabetes mellitus: Relation of stressful life situations to the concentration of ketone bodies in the blood of diabetic and nondiabetic humans. *Journal of Clinical Investigation*, 1950, *29*, 754–769.

Hinkle, L. E., & Wolf, S. Experimental study of life situations, emotions, and the occurrence of acidosis in a juvenile diabetic. *American Journal of Medical Sciences*, 1949, *217*, 130–135.

Hinkle, L. E., & Wolf, S. Importance of life stress in the course and management of diabetes mellitus. *Journal of the American Medical Association*, 1952, *148*, 513–520.

Hock, R. A., Rodgers, C. H., Reddi, C., & Kennard, D. W. Asthmatic children: An evaluation of physiological change. *Psychosomatic Medicine*, 1978, *40*, 210–215.

Holmes, T., & Rahe, R. The social readjustment rating scale. *Journal of Psychosomatic Research*, 1967, *11*, 213–218.

Johnson, S. B., & Melamed, B. G. The assessment and treatment of children's fears. In B. Lahey & A. Kazdin (Eds.), *Advances in clinical child psychology* (Vol. 2). New York: Plenum, 1979.

Kagan, S. G., & Weiss, J. H. Allergic potential and emotional precipitants of asthma in children. *Journal of Psychosomatic Research*, 1976, *20*, 135–139.

Kahn, A. U. Effectiveness of biofeedback and counter-conditioning in the treatment of bronchial asthma. *Journal of Psychomatic Research*, 1977, *21*, 97–104.

Katz, P. Behavior problems in juvenile diabetes. *Canadian Medical Association Journal*, 1957, *76*, 738–743.

Kaufman, R. V., & Hersher, B. Body image changes in teen-age diabetics. *Pediatrics*, 1971, *48*(1), 123–128.

Kempe, C., Silver, H., & O'Brien, D. *Current pediatric diagnosis and treatment* (3rd ed.). Los Altos, Calif.: Lange Medical Publications, 1974.

Khurana, R., & White, P. Attitudes of the diabetic child and his parents toward his illness. *Postgraduate Medicine*, 1970, *48*(2), 72–77.

Kimball, C. P. Conceptual developments in psychosomatic medicine: 1939–1969. *Annals of Internal Medicine*, 1970, *73*, 307–316.

Kinsman, R. A., Dahlem, N. W., Spector, S., & Staudenmayer, H. Observations on subjective symptomatology, coping behavior, and medical decisions in asthma. *Psychosomatic Medicine*, 1977, *39*, 102–119.

Kinsman, R. A., O'Banion, K., Resnikoff, P., Luparello, T. J., & Spector, S. L. Subjective symptoms of acute asthma within a heterogeneous sample of asthmatics. *Journal of Allergy and Clinical Immunology*, 1973, *52*, 284.

Knapp, P. H., & Nemetz, S. J. Acute bronchial asthma. I. Concomitant depression and excitement, and varied antecedent patterns in 406 attacks. *Psychosomatic Medicine*, 1960, *22*, 42–55.

Koski, M. L. The coping processes in childhood diabetes. *Acta Paediatrica Scandinavica (Supplement)*, 1969, *198*, 7–56.

Koski, M., & Kumento, A. Adolescent development and behavior: A psychosomatic follow-up study of childhood diabetes. In Z. Laron (Ed.), *Modern problems in pediatrics* (Vol. 12): *Diabetes in juveniles: Medical and rehabilitation aspects*. New York: Karger, 1975.

Koski, M., & Kumento, A. The interrelationship between diabetic control and family life. In Z. Laron (Ed.), *Pediatric and adolescent endocrinology* (Vol. 3): *Psychological aspects of balance of diabetes in juveniles*. New York: Karger, 1977.

Kotses, H., Glaus, K. D., Bricel, S. K., Edwards, J. E., & Crawford, P. L. Operant muscular relaxation and peak expiratory flow rate in asthmatic children. *Journal of Psychosomatic Research*, 1978, *22*, 17–23.

Kotses, H., Glaus, K. D., Crawford, P. L., Edwards, J. E., & Scherr, M. S. Operant reduction of frontalis EMG activity in the treatment of asthmatic children. *Journal of Psychosomatic Research*, 1976, *20*, 453–459.

Kravitz, A., Isenberg, P., Shore, M., & Barnett, D. Emotional factors in diabetes mellitus. In A. Marble (Ed.), *Joslin's diabetes*. Philadelphia: Lea & Febiger, 1971.

Kubany, A., Danowski, T., & Moses, C. The personality and intelligence of diabetics. *Diabetes*, 1956, *5*, 462–467.

Lang, P. J. Physiological assessment of anxiety and fear. In J. D. Cone & R. P. Hawkins (Eds.), *Behavioral assessment: New directions in clinical psychology*. New York: Brunner/Mazel, 1977.

Lang, P. J., Melamed, B. G., & Hart, J. A. A psychophysiological analysis for fear modification using an automated desensitization procedure. *Journal of Abnormal Psychology*, 1970, *76*, 220–234.

Levenson, R. W. Automated system for direct measurement and feedback of total respiratory resistance by the forced oscillation technique. *Psychophysiology*, 1974, *11*, 86–90.

Levenson, R. W. Effects of thematically relevant and general stressors on specificity of responding in asthmatic and nonasthmatic subjects. *Psychosomatic Medicine*, 1979, *41*, 28–39.

Lipton, E. L., Sternschneider, A., & Richmond, J. B. Psychophysiological disorders in children. In L. W. Hoffman & M. L. Hoffman (Eds.), *Review of child development research* (Vol. 2). New York: Russell Sage Foundation, 1966.

Loughlin, W., & Mosenthal, H. Study of the personalities of children with diabetes. *American Journal of Diseases of Children*, 1944, *68*, 13–15.

Lowe, K., & Lutzer, J. Increasing compliance to a medical regimen with a juvenile diabetic. *Behavior Therapy*, 1979, *10*(1), 57–64.

Malone, J., Hellrung, J., Malphus, E., Rosenbloom, A., Girgic, A., & Weber, F. Good diabetic control—A study in mass delusion. *Journal of Pediatrics*, 1976, *88*(6), 943–947.

Mathé, A., & Knapp, P. H. Emotional and adrenal reactions to stress in bronchial asthma. *Psychosomatic*

*Medicine*, 1971, *33*, 323–340.

Matus, I., Kinsman, R. A., & Jones, N. F. Pediatric patient attitudes toward chronic asthma and hospitalization. *Journal of Chronic Diseases*, 1978, *31*, 611–618.

McCraw, R. K., & Tuma, J. M. Rorschach content categories of juvenile diabetics. *Psychological Reports*, 1977, *40*, 818.

Melamed, B. G., & Siegel, L. J. Reduction of anxiety in children facing hospitalization and surgery by the use of filmed models. *Journal of Consulting and Clinical Psychology*, 1975, *43*, 511–521.

Miklich, D. R. Operant conditioning procedures with systematic desensitization in a hyperkinetic asthmatic boy. *Journal of Behavior Therapy and Experimental Psychiatry*, 1973, *4*, 177–182.

Miklich, D. R., Renne, C. M., Creer, T. L., Alexander, A. B., Chai, H., Davis, M. H., Hoffman, A., & Danker-Brown, P. The clinical utility of behavior therapy as an adjunctive treatment for asthma. *Journal of Allergy and Clinical Immunology*, 1977, *60*, 285–294.

Miller, N. E. Learning of visceral and glandular responses. *Science*, 1969, *163*, 434–445.

Minuchin, S., Baker, L., Rosman, B., Liebman, R., Milman, L., & Todd, T. A conceptual model of psychosomatic illness in children. *Archives of General Psychiatry*, 1975, *32*, 1031–1038.

Minuchin, S., Rosman, B., & Baker, L. *Psychosomatic families*. Cambridge, Mass.: Harvard University Press, 1978.

Moos, R. *The Family Environment Inventory*. Palo Alto, Calif.: Social Ecology Laboratory, Department of Psychiatry, Stanford University, 1973.

Moos, R. Typology of family social environments. *Journal of Family Process*, 1976, *15*(4), 357–371.

Neisworth, J. T., & Moore, F. Operant treatment of asthmatic responding with the parent as therapist. *Behavior Therapy*, 1972, *3*, 95–99.

Neuhaus, E. C. A personality study of asthmatic and cardiac children. *Psychosomatic Medicine*, 1958, *20*, 181–186.

Olatawura, M. The psychiatric complications of diabetes in children. *African Journal of Medical Sciences*, 1972, *2*(3), 231–240.

O'Leary, K. D., & Johnson, S. B. The assessment of psychopathology in children. In H. Quay & J. Werry (Eds.), *Psychopathological disorders of childhood* (2nd ed.). New York: Wiley, 1979.

Partridge, J. W., Garner, A. M., Thompson, C. W., & Cherry, T. Attitudes of adolescents toward their diabetes. *American Journal of Diseases of Children*, 1972, *124*, 226–229.

Pless, I., & Roghmann, K., & Haggerty, R. Chronic illness, family functioning, and psychological adjustment: A model for the allocation of preventive mental health services. *International Journal of Epidemiology*, 1972, *1*, 271–277.

Pless, I., & Satterwhite, B. A measure of family functioning and its application. *Social Science and Medicine*, 1973, *7*, 613; 621.

Purcell, K. Childhood asthma, the role of family relationships, personality, and emotions. In R. Davids (Ed.), *Child personality and psychopathology: Current topics* (Vol. 2). New York: Wiley, 1975.

Purcell, K., Bernstein, L., & Bukantz, S. A preliminary comparison of rapidly remitting and persistently "steroid-dependent" asthmatic children. *Psychosomatic Medicine*, 1961, *23*, 305–310.

Purcell, K., Brady, K., Chai, H., Muser, J., Molk, L., Gordon, N., & Means, J. The effect on asthma in children of experimental separation from the family. *Psychosomatic Medicine*, 1969, *31*, 144–164.

Purcell, K., Muser, J., Miklich, D., & Dietiker, K. E. A comparison of psychologic findings in variously defined asthmatic subgroups. *Journal of Psychosomatic Research*, 1969, *13*, 67.

Purcell, K., Turnbull, J., & Bernstein, L. Distinctions between subgroups of asthmatic children: Psychological test and behavior rating comparisons. *Journal of Psychosomatic Research*, 1962, *6*, 283–291.

Purcell, K., & Weiss, J. Asthma. In C. Costello (Ed.), *Symptoms of psychopathology*. New York: Wiley, 1970.

Rosenbloom, A. The adolescent and young adult with diabetes mellitus. In I. Shenker (Ed.), *Topics in adolescent medicine*. New York: Stratton Intercontinental Medical Book Corporation, 1978.

Rosenbloom, A., & Giordano, B. Chronic overtreatment with insulin in children and adolescents. *American Journal of Diseases of Children*, 1977, *131*, 881–885.

Satterwhite, B., Zweig, S., Ikes, H., and Pless, I. The family functioning index—Five year test–retest reliability and implications for use. *Journal of Comparative Family Studies*, 1976, *7*, 111–116.

Saul, L. J., & Lyons, J. W. The psychodynamics of respiration. In H. A. Abramson (Ed.), *Somatic and psychiatric treatment of asthma*. Baltimore: Williams & Wilkins, 1951.

Sayed, A. J., & Leaverton, D. R. Kinetic-family-drawings of children with diabetes. *Child Psychiatry and Human Development*, 1974, *5*(1), 40–50.

Service, F., Molnar, G., Rosevear, J., Ackerman, E., Gatewood, L., & Taylor, W. Mean amplitude of glycemic excursions: A measure of diabetic stability. *Diabetes*, 1970, *19*, 644–655.

Simonds, J. Psychiatric status of diabetic youth in good and non-control. *International Journal of Psychiatry in Medicine*, 1976–1977, *7*(2), 133–151.

Simonds, J. F. Psychiatric status of diabetic youth matched with a control group. *Diabetes*, 1977, *26*(10), 921–925.

Sirota, A. D., & Mahoney, M. J. Relaxing on cue: The self-regulation of asthma. *Journal of Behavior Therapy and Experimental Psychiatry*, 1974, *5*, 65–66.

Spielberger, C. *Manual for the State–Trait Inventory for Children*. Palo Alto, Calif.: Consulting Psychologists Press, 1973.

Starr, P. Psychosomatic considerations of diabetes in childhood. *Journal of Nervous and Mental Disease*, 1955, *121*(6), 493–504.

Staudenmayer, H., Kinsman, R., & Jones, N. Attitudes toward respiratory illness and hospitalization in asthma. *Journal of Nervous and Mental Disease*, 1978, *166*(9), 624–634.

Stein, M. Etiology and mechanisms in the development of asthma. In J. H. Nodine & J. H. Moyer (Eds.), *The first Hahnemann Symposium on Psychosomatic Medicine*. Philadelphia: Lea & Febiger, 1962.

Steinhauser, H., Borner, S., & Koepp, P. The personality of juvenile diabetics. In Z. Laron (Ed.), *Pediatric and adolescent endocrinology* (Vol. 3): *Psychological aspects of balance of diabetes in juveniles*. Basel: Karger, 1977.

Stersky, G. Family background and state of mental health in a group of diabetic school children. *Acta Paediatrica*, 1963, *52*, 377–390.

Straker, N., & Tamerin, J. Aggression and childhood asthma: A study in a natural setting. *Journal of Psychosomatic Research*, 1974, *18*, 131–135.

Sullivan, B. J. Self-esteem and depression in adolescent diabetic girls. *Diabetes Care*, 1978, *1*(1), 18–22.

Swift, C. R., Seidman, F., & Stein, H. Adjustment problems in juvenile diabetes. *Psychosomatic Medicine*, 1967, *29*(6), 555–571.

Tal, A., & Miklich, D. R. Emotionally induced decreases in pulmonary flow rates in asthmatic children. *Psychosomatic Medicine*, 1976, *38*, 190–199.

Tavormina, J. B., Kastner, L. S., Slater, P. M., & Watt, S. L. Chronically ill children: A psychologically and emotionally deviant population? *Journal of Abnormal Child Psychology*, 1976, *4*, 99–110.

Travis, L. *An instructional aid on juvenile diabetes mellitus*. Austin, Tex.: American Diabetes Association, 1978.

Treuting, T. F. The role of emotional factors in the etiology and course of diabetes mellitus: A review of the recent literature. *American Journal of Medical Science*, 1962, *244*, 93–109.

Tze, W. J., Thompson, K. H., & Leichter, J. Hemoglobin Alc—An indicator of diabetes control. *Journal of Pediatrics*, 1978, *93*, 13–16.

Vandenbergh, R., Sussman, K., & Titus, C. Effects of hypnotically induced acute emotional stress on carbohydrate and lipid metabolism in patients with diabetes mellitus. *Psychosomatic Medicine*, 1966, *28*, 382–390.

Vandenbergh, R. L., Sussman, K. E., and Vaughn, G. D. Effects of combined physical–anticipatory stress on carbohydrate–lipid metabolism in patients with diabetes mellitus. *Psychosomatics*, 1967, *8*(1), 16–19.

Watkins, J., Roberts, D., Williams, T., Martin, D., & Coyle, V. Observations of medication errors made by diabetic patients in the home. *Diabetes*, 1967, *16*, 882–885.

Weiss, E. Psychosomatic aspects of certain allergic disorders. *International Archives of Allergy*, 1950, *1*, 4–28.

Weiss, J. Mood states associated with asthma in children. *Journal of Psychosomatic Research*, 1966,

*10*, 267–373.

Werry, J. Psychosomatic disorders, psychogenic symptoms and hospitalization. In H. Quay & J. Werry (Eds.), *Psychopathological disorders of childhood* (2nd ed.). New York: Wiley, 1979.

Wikran, R., Faleide, A., & Blakar, R. M. Communication in the family of the asthmatic child. *Acta Psychiatrica Scandinavica*, 1978, *57*, 11–26.

Wright, L. Conceptualizing and defining psychosomatic disorders. *American Psychologist*, 1977, *32*, 625–628.

Wright, L., Nunnery, A., Eichel, B., & Scott, R. Behavioral tactics for reinstating natural breathing in infants with tracheostomy. *Pediatrics Research*, 1969, *3*, 275–278.

CHAPTER 13

# CHILDHOOD OBESITY

John P. Foreyt

*Baylor College of Medicine and The Methodist Hospital*

G. Ken Goodrick

*University of Houston*

Assessment of childhood obesity seems a simple enough task. Weigh the child and compare the result to a table of normal body weights for the child's age and height. Treatment is even more straightforward. Determine how many pounds need to be lost to reach goal weight and instruct the parents and the child (if old enough) to eat a low-calorie diet. Stress cutting out snacks and junk food and encourage the child to watch less television and to get more exercise. Would that it were that easy.

Unfortunately, many investigators and practitioners have thought the task was that simple, and as a result, very little has been done other than weighing, comparing, and treating with diet. Assessment of the *causes* of the obese state, for example, are almost always assumed rather than measured. Consequently, treatment may be inappropriate and chances of failure almost certain.

The purpose of this chapter is to examine in detail the assessment of childhood obesity. It is divided into the following sections:

1. Assessment of obesity
2. Assessment of dietary input and activity output
3. Assessment of degree and types of external environmental control
4. Assessment for maintenance
5. Recommended assessment plan

The same assumptions underlie each section: (1) obesity is an excess of body fat resulting from an imbalance between caloric input and expenditure; (2) this imbalance is attributable to overeating and/or underactivity and is subject to some degree of external control; and (3) manipulations of the external controlling factors can result in changes in caloric input and expenditure and thus result in changes in percentage of body fat. Sometimes obesity is attributable to other factors. These cases are rare and are not discussed in this chapter. To rule them out, however, the child should always be evaluated by a physician.

The topic of each section is discussed and evaluated in terms of the relevance of the data obtained for successful treatment and the feasibility for use in typical intervention programs. We are, unfortunately, limited in our discussion of each

573

topic because even the most effective treatment procedures to date result in only small reductions in percentage of body fat, and these reductions have not lasted for clinically significant periods.

# ASSESSMENT OF OBESITY

## Operational Definition

*Obesity* is an excess of body fat. The word *excess* implies comparative judgments involving both the effect of body fat on the present and future health status of the child and its effect on social psychological functioning.

Regarding health, for example, childhood relative weight at ages 9–13 years has no relationship to adult levels of blood sugar, cholesterol, beta-lipoprotein, blood pressure, or cardiovascular renal disease (Weil, 1977). However, there is a significant relationship between childhood relative weight and hypertensive vascular disease. Children who are less than average weight or more than 20% above average weight are more susceptible than children at or slightly above average weight (Weil, 1977).

Childhood obesity is a predictor of adult obesity. According to one study, 80% of children who were obese at ages 10–13 years were still overweight at ages 26–35 years (Abraham & Nordsieck, 1960). Thus, the health risks of obese adults, including cerebrovascular accidents and maturity-onset diabetes mellitus (Mann, 1974), accrue in many obese children.

Percentage of body fat is an indicator of the relationship between dietary input and activity output. It is one index of relative health risk due to sedentary lifestyle. Although there is little research on the effects of insufficient exercise on children, the long-term effects of inactivity on the health of adults is well documented (Leon & Blackburn, 1977). Thus, a judgment of "excess" for the assessment of obesity must take into account both body fat and inactivity in terms of the health risks created by the static (fat) and dynamic (inactivity) features of obesity.

Body fat with a high caloric-input/output ratio can also be defined as "excess" when the social psychological functioning of the child is adversely affected. Obese children are generally less popular with peers, are discriminated against by adults, have poorer self-concepts, and show more personality disturbance than children of normal weight (Coates & Thoresen, 1978). The high input/output ratio may lead to characterizations that the child is lazy, self-indulgent, or gluttonous. Cosmetic considerations may also have a strong effect on the child independent of health risks.

*Excess of body fat* is most easily defined as a departure from some population norm and can then be assessed using arbitrary cut-off points (e.g., Cheek, 1968). The specific points at which health risks become indicated have not been clearly established through prospective studies; however, the 97th percentile for skinfold (Tanner & Whitehouse, 1975) and either 10% (Lauer, Connor, Leaverton, Reiter, & Clarke, 1975) or 20% (Weil, 1977) over ideal body weight at different ages and heights have been suggested.

TABLE 1
Obesity Standards for Caucasian Americans

| Age (years) | Skinfold measurements[a] | |
|---|---|---|
| | Males | Females |
| 5 | 12 | 14 |
| 6 | 12 | 15 |
| 7 | 13 | 16 |
| 8 | 14 | 17 |
| 9 | 15 | 18 |
| 10 | 16 | 20 |
| 11 | 17 | 21 |
| 12 | 18 | 22 |
| 13 | 18 | 23 |
| 14 | 17 | 23 |
| 15 | 16 | 24 |
| 16 | 15 | 25 |
| 17 | 14 | 26 |
| 18 | 15 | 27 |

*Note.* Adapted from Seltzer and Mayer (1965). Copyright 1965 by McGraw-Hill, Inc. Used with permission of Drs. Seltzer and Mayer and the publisher, McGraw-Hill, Inc. Figures represent the logarithmic means of the frequency distributions plus one standard deviation.

[a]Minimum triceps skinfold thickness in millimeters indicating obesity.

Defining excess body fat psychosocially or cosmetically is a subjective judgment of child, parents, and therapists. Operationally, it can be defined in several ways, including scores on psychological tests or structured interviews standardized across a pediatric population. It is likely that most children referred for psychosocial or cosmetic reasons also are at risk for present or future health problems.

## Assessment of Body Fat

*Body fat* is the quantity of triglyceride and other fats contained in the body. It forms the major component of adipose tissue. The density of fat is about .90 (90% as dense as water), whereas the lean body mass (everything except fat) has a density of about 1.10 (Bray, 1976). When a child is totally immersed in water, the amount of water displaced equals the child's volume; weight divided by volume equals density. From this, an approximation of percentage fat can be made. This technique requires elaborate equipment and the acceptance of assumptions regarding the constancy of lean body mass, which is also difficult to measure (Weil, 1977). Most behavior therapists will need to use simpler, indirect measures.

Skinfold measurement is the most common indirect technique for approximating percentage body fat. However, utilization of this technique has not been standardized for children, and reliability and validity of the measurement for obese individuals are questionable. The most commonly used standards for children are shown in Table 1. These measurements are for Caucasian children, ages 5–18 years. The table includes skinfold thicknesses greater than one standard deviation above the mean on a log normal scale; these thicknesses are intended to represent the lower limits of obesity. Operationally, 16% of the population is defined as obese.

Variability in skinfold measurements is common. Greater degrees of obesity, for example, can cause increased measurement error. One way to decrease this problem is to identify the site more clearly by marking the skin (Bray, 1976; Johnson & Stalonas, 1977). Several investigators (e.g., Franzini & Grimes, 1976; Grimes & Franzini, 1977; Weil, 1977) believe that skinfold measurement is the method of choice for assessing body fat because the most common alternate techniques, such as height/weight tables, are less related to the concept of obesity as excess body fat. Others (e.g., Bray, 1976; Johnson & Stalonas, 1977) disagree, because of the difficulty in achieving adequate reliability and validity.

Standardized skinfold techniques for children need to be developed and related to percentage body fat. At present, standards for triceps and subscapular skinfold measurements have been published (Tanner & Whitehouse, 1975):

> The triceps should be measured half-way down the left arm, which should hang relaxed at the subject's side. The tips of the acromial process and the olecranon are palpated, and a point halfway between marked on the skin. The skinfold is picked up over the posterior surface of the triceps muscle on a vertical axis of the limb, and the caliper jaws are applied at the marked level. Care should be taken to locate the site right on the back of the arm. . . . The subscapular skinfold is picked up just below the angle of the left scapula with the fold either in a vertical line or slightly inclined, in the natural cleavage line of the skin. (pp. 142–143)

For children aged 6–17 years, the triceps measurement can be compared to the norms shown in Figures 1 and 2. It is hoped that an easy, reliable measure for skinfold approximation of child body fat will be developed, along with norms and definitions of health-risk ranges.

Weight is another commonly used indirect assessment technique for approximating excess body fat. A child's weight at any given time is dependent on age, sex, height, body build, and composition (percentage fat). *Relative weight* has been defined as a percentage of the median weight for age, sex, and height (Lauer *et al.*, 1975; Wheeler & Hess, 1976). Figures 3 and 4 show mean weight norms for the United States for age, sex, and height. Unfortunately, relative weight does not take body build into account; a normal large-frame child may have a relative weight indicating obesity. Under 7 years of age, use of relative weight tends to result in an underestimation of fatness; at adolescence, such use may result in an overestimation (Weil, 1977).

Edwards (1978) has proposed a *weight index*, defined as the difference between actual weight/height ratio and normed weight/height ratio for the appropriate age and sex. There are at least two disadvantages to this approach. First, body build is not taken into account, and second, norms do not exist for weight/height ratios. Although weight and height are positively correlated at a given age, the relationship is far from perfect, and comparisons based on weight/height ratios would introduce variance unrelated to obesity.

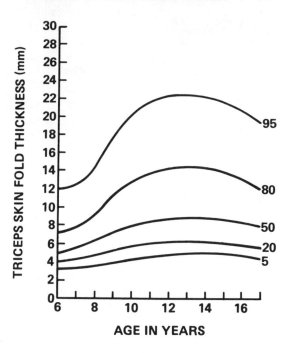

FIGURE 1

Triceps skinfold percentiles for boys. Adapted from "Coronary Heart Disease Risk Factors in School Children: The Muscatine Study" by R. M. Lauer, W. E. Connor, P. E. Leaverton, M. A. Reiter, and W. R. Clarke, *The Journal of Pediatrics*, 1975, *86*, 697–706. Used with permission of Dr. Lauer and the publisher, The C. V. Mosby Company.

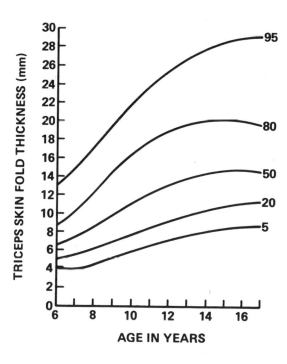

FIGURE 2

Triceps skinfold percentiles for girls. Adapted from "Coronary Heart Disease Risk Factors in School Children: The Muscatine Study" by R. M. Lauer, W. E. Connor, P. E. Leaverton, M. A. Reiter, and W. R. Clarke, *The Journal of Pediatrics*, 1975, *86*, 697–706. Used with permission of Dr. Lauer and the publisher, The C. V. Mosby Company.

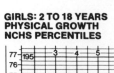

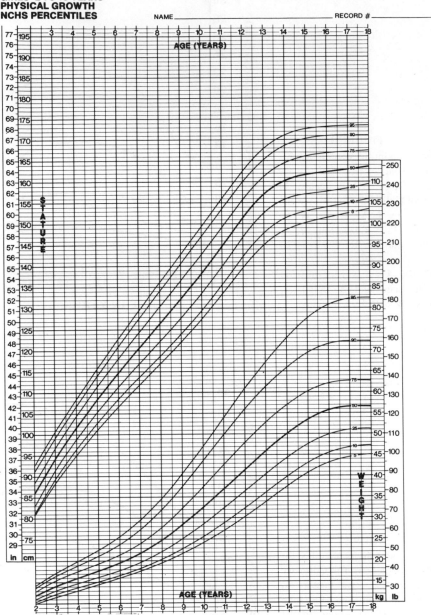

FIGURE 3

Height and weight norms for girls. To find goal weight, find stature percentile rank from
upper set of curves. Goal weight is weight for the same percentile ranking and age from the
lower set of curves. Adapted from National Center for Health Statistics: NCHS Growth
Charts, 1976. Monthly Vital Statistics Reports. Vol. 25, No. 3, Suppl. (HRA) 76-1120.
Health Resources Administration, Rockville, Md., June 1976. Data from the National Center
for Health Statistics. Copyright 1976 by Ross Laboratories. Used with permission of Ross
Laboratories.

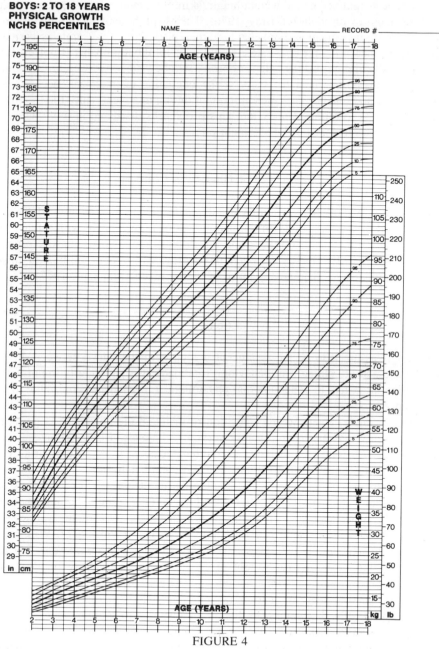

BOYS: 2 TO 18 YEARS
PHYSICAL GROWTH
NCHS PERCENTILES

NAME_____ RECORD #_____

FIGURE 4

Height and weight norms for boys. To find goal weight, find stature percentile rank from
upper set of curves. Goal weight is weight for the same percentile ranking and age from the
lower set of curves. Adapted from National Center for Health Statistics: NCHS Growth
Charts, 1976. Monthly Vital Statistics Reports. Vol. 25, No. 3, Suppl. (HRA) 76-1120.
Health Resources Administration, Rockville, Md., June 1976. Data from the National Center
for Health Statistics. Copyright 1976 by Ross Laboratories. Used with permission of Ross
Laboratories.

Other weight/height and weight/height/skinfold methods for assessing obesity have been used with adults (cf. Bray, 1976). The use of these methods with children awaits further investigation. For behavioral therapists, a totally accurate assessment method for measuring the obese state would be helpful but probably is not critical. Virtually all children seeking help for obesity will be visibly overweight. Although visual diagnosis may be satisfactory at the beginning of treatment, accurate assessment of body fat becomes most important during treatment, since the treatment goal should be lowering of body fat. This problem is discussed in more detail in the section on recommended assessment plan.

## Prevalence of Obesity in Children

The prevalence of obesity in children also depends upon what operational definition is used and the cut-off points on the parameters of measurement within that definition. One estimate is that at least one-fourth of all children are obese (Brownell & Stunkard, 1978). Obesity is much more prevalent among children of lower socioeconomic status than among those of higher levels (Stunkard, 1977).

## Etiology

Obesity is assumed to be the residue of a long-term imbalance between dietary intake and activity output. For behavioral treatment, it is particularly important to determine the extent to which internal physiological mechanisms contribute to the imbalance.

For example, a genetic predisposition to maintain the imbalance is possible. Using adoptive- versus natural-parent survey techniques, Biron, Mongeau, and Bertrand (1977) found that heredity accounted for about 9.5% of the variance in weight and about 6.6% of the variance in the weight/height ratio. They point out, however, that weight indexes in children do not accurately reflect excess fat tissue. Using similar techniques, Hartz, Giefer, and Rimm (1977) found heritability to be about 11%, whereas family environment accounted for 39% of the variance in obesity. About 45% of adult obesity begins in infancy (Weil, 1977; Wilkinson, Parkin, Pearlson, Phillips, & Sykes, 1977). Of children who are obese at 5 years, only 35% will be of normal weight at 15 years. The variability in onset and remission argues against a strong heritability characteristic.

It has been thought that excess fat in infancy leads to an abnormally large number of fat cells. The child may then be predisposed to eat more at a later time in order to satisfy these cells. Doubt has been expressed about this hypothesis because of the imperfect relationship between infant, childhood, and adult obesity (Coates & Thoresen, 1978). Jeffery, Wing, and Stunkard (1978) for example, found that adults with early-onset obesity and those with late-onset obesity had equivalent weight losses in a reduction program. Jung, Gurr, Robinson, and James (1978), using biopsy techniques on subcutaneous and intraabdominal sites in adults, found no relationship between fat-cell number and childhood-onset obesity. They felt that earlier findings of hypercellularity were artifacts of research based solely on subcutaneous samples.

## ASSESSMENT OF DIETARY INPUT AND ACTIVITY OUTPUT

In the behavioral treatment of childhood obesity, it is assumed that physiological dysfunction has been eliminated as a major cause and that the excess fat is the residue of a history of imbalance between diet and exercise, that is, that obesity is the result of behavioral surfeits and deficits. The first problem of assessment is to evaluate the nature of the imbalance so that appropriate behaviors can be targeted for change.

### Assessment of Dietary Input

Griffiths and Payne (1976) assessed caloric intake in children by actually analyzing in a ballistic bomb calorimeter, duplicate portions of everything each child ate for a week. This method is clearly not feasible in normal clinical practice.

The most frequently used technique is a food diary, which children or parents fill out daily. An example of a diary is pictured in Figure 5. It illustrates one day's intake of a tenth-grade student in Houston. Aragona, Cassady, and Drabman (1975) used a daily food diary and then graphed the reported caloric intake using a calorie-counter guide. Coates (1977) has developed The Eating Analysis and Treatment Schedule (EATS), and Wheeler and Hess (1976), a Food Intake Record. There have been few attempts to validate these measures with children. If some of these measures are validated, then calculation of calories from them is simply a matter of looking up the caloric values for the foods in nutrition tables (U.S. Department of Agriculture, 1975).

### Assessment of Activity Output

To assess all activity of a child over a baseline and treatment period would be a monumental task. Using complex oxygen-consumption and heart-rate monitors, Griffiths and Payne (1976) measured integrated pulse rate, based on the relationship between oxygen consumption and actual pulse rate. Jordan and Levitz (1975) developed a daily activity record, which categorized activity into five levels depending upon caloric expenditure. Aragona et al. (1975) had mothers put a check mark on an exercise chart when their children did about 30 minutes of exercise per day. Stunkard (Note 1) suggested the use of trained observers in watching children and recording six levels of activity. Caloric expenditure could be estimated by oxygen consumption rates at each of these levels.

Daily activity records kept by children, parents, or observers are difficult to

**Food Record**

Name ___Debbie K._____ Day _Thursday_ Date _10/12_

Write **ONE** food on each line.

| Time | Place | Amount | Food - How Prepared | Do Not Write Here | |
|------|-------|--------|---------------------|-------------------|---|
| 8:10a | School cafeteria | 1 | apple fried pie | | |
| 1:00p | School cafeteria | 1 | bean burrito | | |
| | | 1 pack | Dorritos 1-1/2 oz. | | |
| | | 12 oz | Dr. Pepper | | |
| 4:00p | den | 2 scoops | cherry vanilla ice cream | | |
| | | 1 can | Coke | | |
| 8:15p | in car | 1 can | Welch's grape soda | | |
| 10:00p | breakfast room | 2 | hamburgers | | |
| | | 2 T | mustard | | |
| | | 2 T | catsup | | |
| | | 30 | French fries | | |
| | | 1 can | Dr. Pepper | | |
| | | | | | |
| | | | | | |
| | | | | | |
| | | | | | |
| | | | | | |

FIGURE 5

Example of a food diary of a tenth-grade student in Houston.

validate and are subject to much variability because of inaccuracy in estimating the level of activity and the imperfect relationship between this level and caloric expenditure.

Daily activity has relatively little effect on caloric expenditure unless it is somewhat strenuous. Some exercises, if performed at durations and intensities that will have a significant caloric and health impact on the child, will produce a change in aerobic capacity. A clinically significant measure of childhood activity would be the child's aerobic fitness level (Cooper, 1977). Measuring activity based on aerobic fitness level has the advantage of simplifying behavioral assessment, since only these activities would need to be monitored and aerobic fitness is a relatively easy-to-assess measure of activity level. It also has a direct relationship to the health status of the child.

## Assessment of Input/Output Imbalance

Carrera (1967) found that only 4% of obese children were hyperphagic (overeaters). Most were characterized by below-normal activity levels. Several studies (e.g., Hampton, Huenemann, Shapiro, & Mitchell, 1967; Huenemann, 1972, 1974; Johnson, Burke, & Mayer, 1956) reported that obese children eat no more than their normal-weight peers. In light of this growing amount of data suggesting that obese children eat no more than their lean peers but are less active, it is interesting that behavioral treatment programs still almost always stress reducing caloric input rather than increasing caloric output.

Assessment of exercise level and aerobic fitness is important in treatment of obesity for several reasons. From an evolutionary perspective, *Homo sapiens* was designed to expend a far greater caloric output than is typical in today's society. Primitive tribes who survived by hunting and foraging had few problems with obesity. Even as recently as the 1930s, children expended two to four times as many calories in activity as do today's children (Griffiths & Payne, 1976). The culprits seem to be television and the general trend toward more sedentary lifestyles and occupations.

Other evidence also points to the need to focus on activity in the assessment of childhood obesity. Rats restricted in exercise become twice as heavy as rats who exercise *ad libitum* (Bray, 1976). This can be explained in the following way. It would probably be adaptive for animals to eat slightly more than their normal daily basal and activity needs dictated so that there is a small reserve of stored energy for combating illness or for coping with unexpected dangers. The set point for satiety would then be at a level inappropriate for sedentary existence. Even in a normal state, a surplus of calories is stored in the short term for the energy used in food-seeking behavior. If this surplus accumulates as fat because of inactivity, the set point for satiety may remain at a level that will supply a surplus of calories, since the presence of the fat will not produce a feedback signal to the hunger-controlling center of the brain.

A few treatment programs for obese children have included an exercise component. For example, Christakis, Sajeckie, Hillman, Miller, Blumenthal, and Archer (1966) found an 11% drop in percentage overweight for a group receiving daily exercise and nutrition information. Moody, Wilmore, Girandola, and Royce (1972) reported a significant reduction in body fat without much weight change in a group of females who received daily exercise, and Jokl (1969) found dramatic weight losses in children using endurance exercises. Although the amount of weight lost in treatment programs may not have a significant effect on health status, aerobic exercise does yield psychosocial and health benefits and should be given more prominence in the behavioral assessment and treatment of obesity.

To assess hyperphagia or excessive caloric input, Figure 6 can be used to estimate a desired allowance for calories based on a goal weight. Hypoactivity can be assessed using aerobic indexes. Since many obese children's caloric imbalance is due to hypoactivity, the aerobic criterion alone may suffice to describe the condition needing behavior change. However, caloric comparisons can be made between input and output using approximations in Figure 6 when hyperphagia is expected. If hypoactivity is reported, the approximated caloric expenditure beyond basal level would be best calculated as 50% or less of basal calories. Norms need to be developed for caloric requirements over a range of aerobic fitness levels.

Once input and output caloric expenditures have been assessed on the basis of eating and exercise behaviors, the controlling variables for these behaviors must be determined. These variables then need to be manipulated, and long-term compliance assured.

# ASSESSMENT OF DEGREE AND TYPES OF EXTERNAL ENVIRONMENTAL CONTROL

Figure 7 illustrates the relationships among some of the controlling factors in the eating and exercise behavior of a child. The "eating mediation" box shows the relationships among available food, situational–parental–social conditions, physiological feedback, and resultant caloric intake. The "exercise mediation" box shows the relationship with respect to exercise output. Arrows with heads on both ends indicate interactive processes. This figure is shown in order to point out that the parent–child–society system is complex and that intervention at one point may have effects throughout the system that should be assessed in terms of their impact on obesity.

## Assessment of Control of Eating

If the input–output imbalance indicates that the child is consuming too many calories, it will be necessary to discover what is controlling this excessive eating. Even though evidence points away from overeating as a major cause of childhood

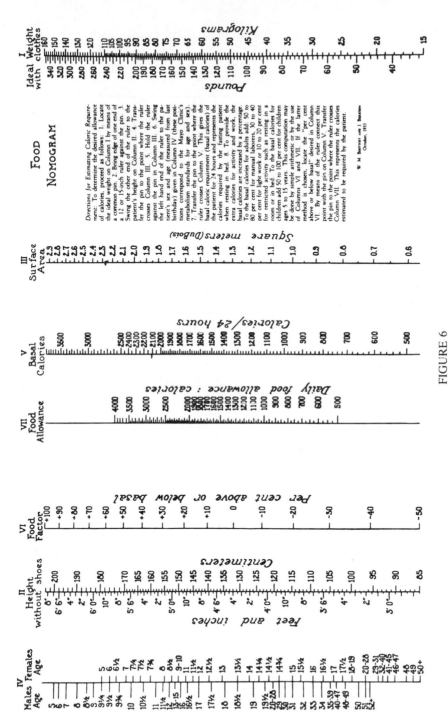

FIGURE 6

Nomogram for calculating basal calories and recommended caloric input for a goal weight. Reprinted by permission.

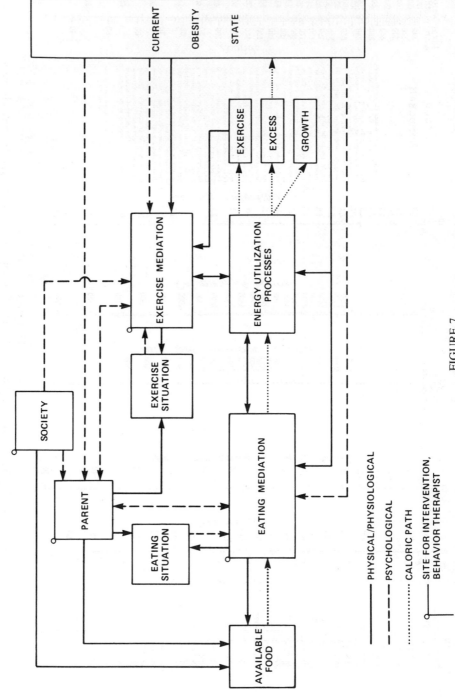

FIGURE 7

Systems model of childhood obesity.

obesity, almost all behavioral research has been aimed at eating behaviors. Interestingly, few studies have actually demonstrated a relationship between changes in eating behavior and weight changes (cf. Brownell and Stunkard, 1978).

The following controlling factors should be considered as *possibilities* in each individual case of child obesity. It will be necessary to monitor changes in the controlling factors over time and to relate them to weight loss before selecting which factors to target for a continued intervention program. Such an individually tailored program is necessary, since each child may have a unique set of controlling factors (Coates & Thoresen, 1980). If a multimethod therapeutic approach is used, it will be difficult to determine which factors were prepotent in controlling the change in eating behavior leading to weight loss.

To assess the factors controlling eating, it is helpful to use trained nonparticipant observers in the natural eating environment, such as at school and at home. Accurate behavioral assessment of this type cannot be adequately performed through clinical interviews. Validity of parental reports of child diet history has not been established. Baseline observation should extend for 2 weeks to ensure the assessment of reliable patterns.

The first task of the observers is to establish that dietary input is excessive, based on previous calculations of recommended input (as already discussed), and then to look for controlling factors, which can be categorized roughly as (1) situational control, (2) skills deficits, and (3) cognitive control. In an initial assessment interview, some of these factors may be easily identified, so that observational techniques can be somewhat directed. Table 2 summarizes typical areas for assessment.

## Situational Control

Two factors contribute in a major way to the amount of food eaten: first, the availability and type of food, and second, the cues that prompt eating behavior independently of biological need. Availability and type of food for younger children are under parental control. For older children, however, overeating is frequently a function of environmental situations, as it frequently is with adults (Stunkard & Kaplan, 1977). Observation of the sources of food will provide information needed to plan control strategies, which generally involve making food more difficult to obtain and prepare and avoiding places where overeating occurs.

There is no strong evidence that obese persons are more subject to eating cues than are normal persons (Coates, 1977; Mahoney, 1975a, 1975b). However, assessment of the degree of hunger reported by children trained to focus on physical cues of hunger would be helpful in reducing unnecessary eating in routine situations. The Eating Analysis and Treatment Schedule (Coates & Thoresen, 1980) and the Food Intake Record (Wheeler & Hess, 1976) can be used for situational assessment.

The parents are also an important component of the eating situation. They exert control far beyond merely providing the food. Areas of parental permissiveness and eating consequation that have an effect on the child's eating include catering to the child's food preferences, allowing free meals and snacks, using food as a

TABLE 2
Factors That May Control Eating Behavior

| Factor | How assessed | Research examples |
|---|---|---|
| *Situational control* | | |
| Food availability | EATS[a] | Coates (1977) |
| Food cues | EATS/FIR[b] | Wheeler and Hess (1976) |
| Eating locations | | |
| School | | |
| Restaurants | | |
| Parental factors | | |
| Reinforcement | Diary | Aragona, Cassady, and Drabman (1975) |
| Permissiveness | | Owen, Kram, Garry, Lowe, and Lubin |
| Caters to food preference | | (1974) |
| Food used as reward | | |
| Allows snacking | | |
| Withholds food as punishment | | |
| Degree of control | FIR | Wheeler and Hess (1976) |
| Attention during eating | | |
| versus at other times | | |
| Peer modeling | | |
| *Skills deficits* | | |
| Eating style | Observation | Drabman, Hammer, and Jarvie (1977) |
| Bite rate | | Epstein, Parker, McCoy, and McGee |
| Sip rate | | (1976) |
| Chew rate | | |
| Food energy-density preferences | | Hunt, Cash, and Newland (1975) |
| Nutritional skills | | |
| Caloric knowledge | | |
| Erroneous beliefs | | Coates (1977) |
| *Cognitive control* | | |
| Food thoughts | | Mahoney and Mahoney (1976) |
| Self-statement regarding predicted be- | | Bandura (1977) |
| haviors (self-efficacy) | | |
| Perceived consequences of staying fat | | Court, Johns, and Wilson (1977) |
| or losing weight | | |

[a]The Eating Analysis and Treatment Schedule.
[b]Food Intake Record.

reward, and withholding food when the child misbehaves (Owen, Kram, Garry, Lowe, & Lubin, 1974). Other areas to look for include increased attention or affection during meals (food as love) or urgings to clean one's plate (the "wasting-food-is-a-sin" or "children-in-far-off-lands-are-starving" ploys). The degree of parental control over the child's eating behavior is an important area to assess before intervention.

### Skills Deficits

Depending upon the degree of control asserted by the parents, assessment of nutritional skills should be made of both parents and child. Caloric knowledge of foods and of low-calorie substitutions can be assessed by written test. In addition to parents' and children's knowing what to eat, much recent research has focused on *how* to eat. Evidence of an "obese eating style" is equivocal for adults (Mahoney, 1975a, 1975b). Drabman, Hammer, and Jarvie (1977) found that obese children take more bites and chew less than normal children. Epstein, Parker, McCoy, and McGee (1976) reported no difference in bite rate between obese and normal 7-year-olds. Even if differences do exist, a causal relationship between eating rate and obesity cannot be inferred.

There are several good reasons, however, for assessing eating style. One is that a slower rate may allow for physiological satiety signals to occur sooner and thereby limit the amount eaten. A slower rate may also influence the number of "second helpings" or may provide more cognitive satisfaction with less food (Coates, 1977). Another possibility is that an eating style may be characterized by a tendency to eat foods that have a *high energy density* (defined as calories per volume). High-energy-dense foods leave the stomach faster than low-energy-dense foods, with feelings of hunger returning sooner (Hunt, Cash, & Newland, 1975). Obese children, for example, drink more milk and eat less bread than their normal peers (Epstein *et al.*, 1976).

We want to emphasize again that there is little experimental evidence suggesting that any of the preceding skills deficits necessarily leads to obesity. Cause–effect relationships must be determined on a case-by-case basis by introducing changes in skills behaviors, assessing compliance with the changes, and measuring body fat and weight reduction. Ideally, each area would be changed while the others remain constant, using an ABAB reversal design. The efficacy of any procedure will be assessed by the subjective evaluations of parents, child, and therapist.

### Cognitive Control

Self-statements can have an effect on obesity-control behaviors (Mahoney & Mahoney, 1976). For example, some individuals may frequently have the feeling that they cannot succeed in losing weight because they have never been able to lose more than a few pounds. Simple repetition of a counterthought, such as "Things will be different this time with behavior modification—it works," may have a positive effect on behavior change. This technique is limited in use to older children who are better able to communicate their thoughts about obesity and who are usually more highly motivated. Assessment of negative self-defeating thoughts is usually done in a clinical interview.

Other cognitive factors that may affect therapeutic outcome are the perceived consequences of staying fat or of losing weight (Court, Johns, & Wilson, 1977), attitude toward treatment, and perceived efficacy of the procedures (Wheeler & Hess, 1976; Kingsley & Shapiro, 1977). All of these may be measured by questionnaires and discussion. Table 2 lists areas for cognitive restructuring that can be probed during initial clinical visits. Assessment of the effectiveness of the cognitive restructuring in changing behavior can only be done by subjective report of the individual.

TABLE 3
Factors That May Control Exercise Behavior

*Situational control*
Exercise facility availability
Exercise facility safety
School program availability
Parental reinforcement, attention for exercise
Parental degree of control
Peer modeling
Sports personality modeling
Self-monitoring
*Skills deficits*
How to exercise
Equipment
Learning to judge body's feedback (pain)
Caloric knowledge
Aerobic knowledge
*Cognitive control*
Exercise thoughts
Self-efficacy

## Assessment of Control of Exercise

Although a few treatment programs for childhood obesity have included exercise, minimal weight loss occurs and children stop exercising when the formal structured programs terminate (Coates & Thoresen, 1978). Some studies suggest that minimal exercise, such as walking up the stairs rather than riding an elevator or parking in the far corner of a shopping center lot, increases caloric expenditure. However, for any appreciable effect on body fat, aerobic exercise is required. Since there is essentially no research on the controlling factors of exercise in obese children, we suggest that aerobics be selected as the goal behavior. Anything less has little beneficial effect on health and can only have a slight impact on reduction in body fat. Also, the performance and residue of aerobics are easier to assess, since only a brief exercise period of about 30 minutes a day is required, obviating the need to follow the child all day, observing a range of behaviors. The results of the exercise can be assessed using the aerobic point system developed by Cooper (1977).

Even though research on controlling factors in childhood exercise has not really begun, therapists can explore the following areas (summarized in Table 3) for possible influence in much the same way as with eating behavior.

## Situational Control

Jogging is one of the easiest and most convenient aerobic exercises. Lack of proper facilities, that is, a safe outside area where jogging is socially acceptable, is a situational factor working against the development of exercise behavior. Just as eating may be under stimulus control, so may be jogging. Stimuli to increase exercise might include hanging posters depicting runners, setting aside regular times for activity, arranging equipment the night before for convenient use, placing a graph on the refrigerator door showing exercise completed, and parents' reinforcing exercise behavior.

Assessment of any of these techniques in changing behavior may come from parental report. However, the therapist could structure such a program at the child's school, where monitoring by teachers and coaches might be possible. School systems should routinely assess all children's percentage body fat and aerobic fitness level as they now assess vision, audition, and teeth.

## Skills Deficits

Unless the therapist is an experienced runner or an expert in aerobic conditioning, a coach or similar instructor should be consulted to help assess skills deficits. There are many mistakes that beginning aerobics exercisers can make, such as beginning too fast, jogging incorrectly, or not warming up or cooling down properly. Improving such skills should have a positive effect on exercise progress and maintenance.

## Cognitive Control

Any number of negative self-statements, such as "Exercise is work and therefore punishing," may tend to inhibit such behavior. Counterthoughts such as "Millions of people are now jogging and enjoying it—it can be fun and rewarding" may be helpful to the person. Self-statements can be probed in clinical interviews.

# ASSESSMENT FOR MAINTENANCE

In the previous section, assessment was for the purpose of finding factors that controlled eating and exercise behaviors, so that a treatment program could be designed to alter those factors and bring about behavior change. If the new positive behaviors were maintained indefinitely, dramatic changes in health, weight, and body fat would occur. Unfortunately, maintenance of prescribed behaviors seems to be difficult to establish during treatment programs. In truth, few data on actual performance of prescribed behavioral changes exist for either during or after treatment. Research detailing the process of recidivism is also lacking. Some factors have been hypothesized to have a bearing on long-term maintenance. Assessment of the presence of these factors near the end of formal treatment may help in augmenting the intervention strategies at that point, assuming that performance of prescribed changes has not already stopped.

Wheeler and Hess (1976) point out that factors associated with relative program success need to be separated into those related to success of treatment (as discussed in the preceding section) and those related to continuation of the prescribed behaviors. Continuation in treatment may be a function of the perceived difficulty in carrying out the regimen as assessed by the individual and the therapist (Court, Johns, & Wilson, 1977). Perceived efficacy of the program may also be assessed during treatment apart from objective measures such as weight loss. Unrealistic expectations for success may have relevancy in these perceptions, as well as in perceptions of self-efficacy (Bandura, 1977) or in the self-perceived ability to succeed using the recommended treatment program. These perceptions should be assessed and discussed whenever contact with the individual occurs.

Although studies have not assessed performance of prescribed behaviors up to the point of recidivism, data from weight-loss programs suggest that a return to old behavior patterns usually occurs after the individual leaves the close scrutiny of the therapist. Thus, periodic checks on performance may be indicated over the course of 1 or 2 years.

Factors applicable to drop-out during clinical contact also apply to maintenance. Techniques for improving maintenance may include family support, use of peer models, and the structuring of a supportive environment (response cost and reinforcement) (Coates & Thoresen, 1980; Stunkard & Mahoney, 1976). Degree of family support can be assessed through family group discussion with the therapist, although a nonparticipant observer at home meals might provide more valid information. This would also be the method of choice for assessing use of peer models and contingency programs.

Cognitive factors related to recidivism in addictive behaviors have been studied by Marlatt and Gordon (1980). Likelihood of relapse can be a function of erroneous beliefs or self-statements related to perceived failure or lack of self-efficacy. Role playing near the end of clinical treatment could assess the beliefs and feelings associated with projected relapse; cognitive restructuring would then be directed toward correcting these thoughts. Some factors that may affect maintenance are summarized in Table 4.

## RECOMMENDED ASSESSMENT PLAN

An example of an assessment plan for behavioral treatment of childhood obesity is shown in Figure 8. It is based on a treatment program that is individually tailored to each child in terms of the relative emphases given to diet and exercise and of the idiosyncratic nature of the controlling factors for eating and activity. The data collected include those directly related to health status (body fat and aerobic fitness) and the traditional weight measure.

TABLE 4

Factors That May Affect Maintenance of a Behavior
Therapy Regimen for Obese Children

---

Perceived self-efficacy of child and parent
Degree of success at end of intensive treatment period
Attitude toward dietary and exercise regimens
Perceived difficulty and expense of techniques
Perceived efficacy of techniques
Unrealistic expectations
Family, school, social support
Relapse prevention skills

---

At the initial clinical visit, the child's goal weight can be approximated from Figures 3 or 4. The weights in these figures take into account age and height but not body type. The goal weight is taken to be the median weight for children of the same age, sex, and height. Percentage overweight for age, sex, and height percentile is then calculated as (initial weight/goal weight) × 100. Note that goal weight is a function of age and will be different each time percentage overweight is calculated. Since there are no normed conversion tables that approximate percentage body fat from children's skinfold, the skinfold thickness itself is used. The triceps skinfold percentile ranking can be obtained from Figures 1 or 2. Table 2 shows the cut-off points for obesity (one standard deviation above the mean). Both triceps and subscapular measurements should be recorded.

During the 2-week baseline period, an accurate account of all foods eaten is kept in a food diary, together with a record of any aerobic activities. Also helpful is a record of sedentary behaviors such as television viewing. Most children will be unable to take an aerobics fitness test until they have been in an activity program for at least 6 weeks. Directions for giving an aerobics fitness test can be found in Cooper (1977). Calories from the food diary can be approximated using published tables of caloric content of foods (U.S. Department of Agriculture, 1975).

Also during baseline, observers should look at situational controlling factors for eating and exercise, some of which are listed in Tables 2 and 3. Six home visits during mealtime will help assess control of eating. Ideally, observations at school lunches and weekend meals away from home could be done; however, parental reports are more feasible. The therapist should also assess beliefs and attitudes about eating and exercise during baseline visits.

After the baseline period, average daily caloric intake can be computed from the food diary. Assuming that weight and activity levels remain stable during this period, daily caloric output will equal caloric input. From Figure 6, an approximation of basal caloric expenditure can be determined. The difference between the daily caloric output and the basal figure gives an approximation of the caloric expenditure due to activity. For hypoactive children, this figure will be about 50% of basal, whereas for active children it will be closer to 100% of basal. Norms of activity levels in terms of caloric expenditure still need to be developed for children.

Based on dietary intake/activity output levels, and using the major postulated

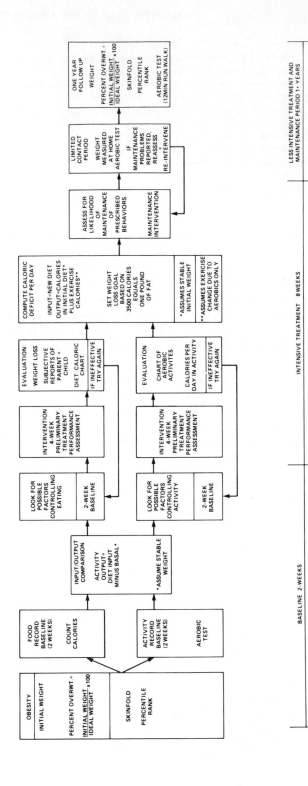

FIGURE 8

Assessment plan for the behavioral treatment of childhood obesity.

TABLE 5
Energy Expenditure for Selected Aerobic Activities

| Activity | kcal/min kg |
|---|---|
| *Bicycling* | |
| 5 mph | .06 |
| 10 mph | .11 |
| *Jogging* | |
| 11 min, 30 sec per mile | .135 |
| 9 min per mile | .193 |
| 8 min per mile | .208 |
| *Swimming, crawl* | .130 |
| *Tennis* | .109 |
| *Walking, normal pace* | .080 |

*Note.* Adapted from Katch and McArdle (1977).

controlling factors for eating and exercise, a preliminary treatment program can be implemented. The critical assessment during the month of implementation is the process evaluation of performance of the prescribed intervention methodologies. Ideally, observers might make spot checks in addition to the record keeping by parents and child. Because skinfold and aerobic fitness will not show much change in the short term, evaluation of preliminary treatment should use weight change as a criterion for success in eating and exercise changes. The ultimate treatment program will be based on the judgments of parents, child, and therapist of what seems to work best.

Once a preliminary treatment package has been designed, dietary and exercise assessment is needed to develop realistic goals. Caloric input can be determined from the average daily diet under the preliminary treatment plan, assuming a stable level of input over the past 2 weeks. Also, the record of aerobic exercise over the past 2 weeks will show average daily caloric expenditure over and above the baseline level.

Table 5 shows calorie expenditure for typical aerobic exercises. The average daily caloric deficit is calculated as the input diet calories minus the calories in the baseline diet minus the calories for aerobic exercise. If other nonaerobic activity is also increased, the projections will be that much more conservative. Note that caloric deficit can be achieved if the diet remains unchanged or even if it is increased, provided there is a sufficient amount of exercise.

The average daily caloric deficit is then divided into 3500 calories per pound of fat to determine how many days per one pound of weight loss. For example, if the daily deficit is 350 calories, the weight loss goal should be set at one pound every ten days.

TABLE 6

Aerobic Fitness Classification for Children—12-Minute Run

| Fitness category | Males, 8–19 yr | Females, 8–12 yr | Females, 13–19 yr |
|---|---|---|---|
| I Very poor | < 1.25[a] | < .83 | < 1.00 |
| II Poor | 1.26–1.37 | .84–.96 | 1.00–1.18 |
| III Fair | 1.38–1.56 | .97–1.12 | 1.19–1.29 |
| IV Good | 1.57–1.72 | 1.13–1.25 | 1.30–1.43 |
| V Excellent | 1.73–1.86 | 1.26–1.38 | 1.44–1.51 |
| VI Superior | > 1.87 | > 1.39 | > 1.52 |

*Note*. Adapted from *The Aerobics Way* by K. H. Cooper. Copyright 1977 by K. H. Cooper. Used with permission of Dr. Cooper and the publisher, M. Evans and Company, Inc. Also adapted from the Governor's Commission on Physical Fitness (1974).

[a]Distance in miles.

Before beginning the phase of treatment in which parents and child are on their own, assessment for maintenance is necessary. Areas for assessment are listed in Table 4. Assessment can then follow recommended procedures common to all behavior-change therapies. Parents and child are encouraged to continue to keep records of weight, exercise, and results of·periodic aerobic fitness tests. Fitness norms are shown in Table 6.

At 1-year posttreatment follow-up, changes in percentage overweight, percentile for skinfold, and improvement in aerobic capacity can be assessed. Changes in percentage overweight will take into account height and age change, since these changes are based on median weights for percentile height and age (Figures 3 and 4). Percentile change in skinfold also takes age into account, as calculated from Figures 1 and 2.

## CONCLUSION

The assessment of childhood obesity is a particularly intriguing problem because of the complex variables involved and the difficulty of singling out the most important ones. To date, much of the research has assumed overeating to be the major cause. Underactivity has received little systematic investigation by behavior therapists. This chapter stresses the interdependence of the two and the need to assess accurately the entire behavioral repertoire of the child. The poor treatment data seen in the literature may partially be a function of poor assessment. As researchers gain in their understanding of the causes of the obese state through better assessment, treatment results should begin to improve.

## Acknowledgment

This research is supported by Grant No. HL17269 from the National Heart, Lung, and Blood Institute, National Institutes of Health, Bethesda, Md. Dr. Goodrick is a research fellow in behavioral medicine at the University of Houston, supported by National Heart, Lung, and Blood Vessel Institute Grant No. 1 T32 HL07258-01A1.

## Reference Note

1. Stunkard, A. J. Personal communication, June 5, 1978.

## References

Abraham, S., & Nordsieck, M. Relationship of excess weight in children and adults. *Public Health Reports*, 1960, *75*, 263–273.

Aragona, J., Cassady, J., & Drabman, R. S. Treating overweight children through parental training and contingency contracting. *Journal of Applied Behavior Analysis*, 1975, *8*, 269–278.

Bandura, A. Self-efficacy: Toward a unifying theory of behavior change. *Psychological Review*, 1977, *84*, 191–215.

Biron, P., Mongeau, J., & Bertrand, D. Familial resemblance of body weight and weight/height in 374 homes with adopted children. *The Journal of Pediatrics*, 1977, *91*, 555–558.

Bray, G. A. *The obese patient*. Philadelphia: W. B. Saunders, 1976.

Brownell, K. D., & Stunkard, A. J. Behavioral treatment of obesity in children. *American Journal of Diseases of Children*, 1978, *132*, 403–412.

Carrera, F. Obesity in adolescence. *Psychosomatics*, 1967, *8*, 342–349.

Cheek, D. B. *Human growth*. Philadelphia: Lea & Febiger, 1968.

Christakis, G., Sajeckie, G., Hillman, R. W., Miller, E., Blumenthal, S., & Archer, M. Effect of a combined nutrition education–physical fitness program on weight status of obese high school boys. *Federation Proceedings*, 1966, *25*, 15–19.

Coates, T. J. Theory, research and practice in treating obesity: Are they really all the same? *Addictive Behaviors*, 1977, *2*, 95–103.

Coates, T. J., & Thoresen, C. E. Treating obesity in children and adolescents: A review. *American Journal of Public Health*, 1978, *68*, 143–151.

Coates, T. J., & Thoresen, C. E. Treating obesity in children and adolescents: Is there any hope? In J. M. Ferguson & C. B. Taylor (Eds.), *Advances in behavioral medicine*. Englewood Cliffs, N.J.: Spectrum, 1980.

Cooper, K. H. *The aerobics way*. New York: M. Evans, 1977.

Court, J. M., Johns, N., & Wilson, M. Obese children and their families: A study of a discussion group. *Australian Paediatric Journal*, 1977, *13*, 170–175.

Drabman, R. S., Hammer, D., & Jarvie, G. J. Eating styles of obese and nonobese black and white children in a naturalistic setting. *Addictive Behaviors*, 1977, *2*, 83–86.

Edwards, K. A. An index for addressing weight change in children: Weight/height ratios. *Journal of Applied Behavior Analysis*, 1978, *11*, 421–429.

Epstein, L. H., Parker, L., McCoy, J. F., & McGee, G. Descriptive analysis of eating regulation in obese and nonobese children. *Journal of Applied Behavior Analysis*, 1976, *9*, 407–415.

Franzini, L. R., & Grimes, W. B. Skinfold measures as the criterion of change in weight control studies. *Behavior Therapy*, 1976, *7*, 256–260.

Governor's Commission on Physical Fitness. *The Texas physical fitness–motor ability test*. Austin, Tex.: State of Texas, 1974.

Griffiths, M., & Payne, P. R. Energy expenditure in small children of obese and nonobese patients. *Nature*, 1976, *260*, 698–700.

Grimes, W. B., & Franzini, L. R. Skinfold measurement techniques for estimating percentage body fat. *Journal of Behavior Therapy and Experimental Psychiatry*, 1977, *8*, 65–69.

Hampton, M. C., Huenemann, R. L., Shapiro, L. R., & Mitchell, B. W. Caloric and nutrient intakes of teenagers. *Journal of the American Dietetic Association*, 1967, *50*, 385–396.

Hartz, A., Giefer, E., & Rimm, A. A. Relative importance of the effect of family environment and heredity on obesity. *Annals of Human Genetics*, 1977, *41*, 185–193.

Huenemann, R. L. Food habits of obese and nonobese adolescents. *Postgraduate Medicine*, 1972, *51*, 99–105.

Huenemann, R. L. Environmental factors associated with preschool obesity. *Journal of the American Dietetic Association*, 1974, *64*, 488–491.

Hunt, J. N., Cash, R., & Newland, P. Energy density of food, gastric emptying, and obesity. *Lancet*, 1975, *2*, 905–906.

Jeffery, R. W., Wing, R. R., & Stunkard, A. J. Behavioral treatment of obesity: The state of the art 1976. *Behavior Therapy*, 1978, *9*, 189–199.

Johnson, M. L., Burke, B. S., & Mayer, J. Relative importance of inactivity and overeating in the energy balance of obese high school girls. *American Journal of Clinical Nutrition*, 1956, *4*, 37–44.

Johnson, W. G., & Stalonas, P. Measuring skinfold thickness—A cautionary note. *Addictive Behaviors*, 1977, *2*, 105–107.

Jokl, E. *Exercise, nutrition, and body composition*. Springfield, Ill.: Charles C. Thomas, 1969.

Jordan, H. A., & Levitz, L. S. Behavior modification in the treatment of childhood obesity. In M. Winick (Ed.), *Childhood obesity*. New York: Wiley, 1975.

Jung, R. T., Gurr, M. I., Robinson, M. P., & James, W. P. Does adipocyte hypercellularity in obesity exist? *British Medical Journal*, 1978, *2*(6133), 319–321.

Katch, F. I., & McArdle, W. D. *Nutrition, weight control, and exercise*. Boston: Houghton Mifflin, 1977.

Kingsley, R. B., & Shapiro, J. A comparison of three behavioral programs for the control of obesity in children. *Behavior Therapy*, 1977, *8*, 30–36.

Lauer, R. M., Connor, W. E., Leaverton, P. E., Reiter, M. A., & Clarke, W. R. Coronary heart disease risk factors in school children: The Muscatine study. *The Journal of Pediatrics*, 1975, *86*, 697–706.

Leon, A. S., & Blackburn, H. The relationship of physical activity to coronary heart disease and life expectancy. *Annals of the New York Academy of Science*, 1977, *301*, 561–578.

Mahoney, K., & Mahoney, M. J. Cognitive factors in weight reduction. In J. D. Krumboltz & C. E. Thoresen (Eds.), *Counseling methods*. New York: Holt, Rinehart & Winston, 1976.

Mahoney, M. J. Fat fiction. *Behavior Therapy*, 1975, *6*, 416–418. (a)

Mahoney, M. J. The obese eating style: Bites, beliefs and behavior modification. *Addictive Behaviors*, 1975, *1*, 47–53. (b)

Mann, G. V. The influence of obesity on health. *New England Journal of Medicine*, 1974, *291*, 178–185; 226–232.

Marlatt, G. A., & Gordon, J. R. Determinants of relapse: Implications for the maintenance of behavior change. In P. O. Davidson & S. M. Davidson (Eds.), *Behavioral medicine: Changing health lifestyles*. New York: Brunner/Mazel, 1980.

Moody, D. L., Wilmore, J. H., Girandola, R. N., & Royce, J. P. The effects of a jogging program on the body composition of normal and obese high school girls. *Medicine and Science in Sports*, 1972, *4*, 210–213.

Owen, G. M., Kram, K. M., Garry, P. J., Lowe, J. E., & Lubin, A. H. A study of nutritional status of preschool children in the United States, 1968–1970. *Pediatrics*, 1974, *53* (Supplement, Pt. 2), 597–625.

Seltzer, C. C., & Mayer, J. A simple criterion of obesity. *Postgraduate Medicine*, 1965, *38*(2), A101–107.

Stunkard, A. J. Obesity and the social environment: Current status, future prospects. *Annals of the New York Academy of Science*, 1977, *300*, 298–320.

Stunkard, A. J., & Kaplan, D. Eating in public places: A review of reports of the direct observation of eating behavior. *International Journal of Obesity*, 1977, *1*, 89–101.

Stunkard, A. J., & Mahoney, M. J. Behavioral treatment of the eating disorders. In H. Leitenberg (Ed.), *Handbook of behavior modification and behavior therapy*. Englewood Cliffs, N.J.: Prentice-Hall, 1976.

Tanner, J. M., & Whitehouse, R. H. Revised standards for triceps and subscapular skinfolds in British children. *Archives of Diseases in Childhood*, 1975, *50*, 142–145.

U.S. Department of Agriculture. *Nutritive value of American foods in common units. Agriculture handbook #456*. Washington, D.C.: U.S. Government Printing Office, 1975.

Weil, W. B. Current controversies in childhood obesity. *The Journal of Pediatrics*, 1977, *91*, 175–187.

Wheeler, M. E., & Hess, K. W. Treatment of juvenile obesity by successive approximation control of eating. *Journal of Behavior Therapy and Experimental Psychiatry*, 1976, *7*, 235–241.

Wilkinson, P. W., Parkin, J. M., Pearlson, J., Phillips, P. R., & Sykes, P. Obesity in childhood: A community study in Newcastle upon Tyne. *Lancet*, 1977, *1*, 350–352.

# SEIZURE DISORDERS

**Barbara A. Balaschak**

*Children's Hospital Medical Center of Boston*

**David I. Mostofsky**

*Boston University and Children's Hospital Medical Center of Boston*

Seizure disorders present distinctly different problems of assessment for psychologists. Various conditions, such as central nervous system infections, metabolic disturbances, toxic agents, and expanding brain lesions, may be causative factors in the development of a seizure disorder. The organicity that contributes to the pathophysiology of seizures and the alternatives among the various anticonvulsant medications appropriate for the separate conditions among the epilepsies are reasonably understood and constitute a voluminous literature in neurology and neurophysiology (Magnus & DeHaas, 1974). This literature, however, provides little guidance to an appreciation of the difficulties that children with epilepsy face in their natural environment, that is, the social and psychological consequences of their seizures to themselves and others.

The assessment provided by traditional pediatric neurological examinations includes a basic neurological examination and medical history, along with blood chemistry, cranial nerve studies, and various types of radiological examinations, including computerized axial tomography (CAT) scans, history, and so forth. This standard medical assessment, though still the primary and most essential manner in which childhood seizure disorders must be assessed, does not provide a complete picture of the child's functioning in daily life. The neurological assessment often leaves uncompleted the task of determining the behavioral problems of the child. These problems may include (1) seizures that are not fully controlled by anticonvulsants, (2) the reactions of the child and his or her family to the seizures, and (3) the effect of the disorder on the child's social, emotional, and academic experiences. Each of these is an area in which behavioral assessment can be of value in providing direction for specific behavioral interventions or for more traditional psychotherapy involvement by mental health professionals normally available in hospital settings and in the child's larger community.

# DEFINITION

*Epilepsy* is a symptom complex characterized as follows:

1. It consists of recurrent paroxysmal aberrations of brain function.
2. The seizures are usually brief, from a few seconds to several minutes, depending on the type of seizure, and are self-limited.
3. The seizures may be of diverse etiologies.
4. The seizures are secondary to recurrent abnormal electrical discharges from neuronal aggregates in the brain.
5. The source of the paroxysmal disorder resides within the brain itself.

Seizures are characterized by alterations in or loss of consciousness (Khoshbin, Note 1). In addition to changes in the state of consciousness, a seizure may also result in changes in the child's motor activity or sensory phenomena (Holvey, 1972). With some forms of seizure, the attacks are often accompanied by a convulsion in which the child suddenly falls and undergoes violent, involuntary tonic and clonic contractions of the arms and legs. A more complete description of the most frequently occurring types of seizures will be presented later.

# ETIOLOGY

Convulsive disorders may be attributable to or associated with a variety of cerebral disorders. Convulsions are among the most frequently observed neurologic disorders in children. The most common form of seizure in children is the febrile convulsion, which occurs in association with fever and acute systemic infections in approximately 2–3% of all children. Recurrent convulsive seizures that are not associated with fever or systemic infection occur in .5% of children (Farmer, 1964).

Epilepsy has traditionally been divided into two broad etiological categories: symptomatic and idiopathic. The term *symptomatic epilepsy* is given to seizure disorders with an identifiable cause, such as encephalitis, tumor, trauma, or known metabolic disease. In these conditions, seizures are considered to be a symptom of another disease. The term *idiopathic epilepsy* means that the seizure disorder seems to arise spontaneously in the absence of other diseases of the nervous system (Pincus & Tucker, 1978). In approximately half of the children with convulsive disorders, careful study fails to reveal evidence of a specific cerebral lesion or of an extracerebral cause for the attacks. Farmer (1964) believes it is likely that in these individuals there is a biochemical defect that results in periodic seizure activity. Although the etiology is not known, the electrophysiologic cerebral activity that accompanies these seizures is well established.

# INCIDENCE

Despite its centuries-old existence in the literature of illness and disease, epilepsy continues to be a major medical problem for millions of people, particularly children. Although exact epidemiological data are not available, the estimate lies somewhere between 1–2% of the American population. The census figures of 1976 place the annual health care cost for this disorder at two billion dollars. Clearly, epilepsy is a major national health problem.

Though epilepsy can occur at any age, 76.7% of those who develop epilepsy have their first seizure before 20 years of age (Epilepsy Foundation of America, 1975). There are some data that indicate that the onset of epilepsy in persons under age 20 is most frequent in the first two years of life and during adolescence (Bridge, 1949; Debakan, 1959). The Epilepsy Foundtaion of American (EFA) (1975) estimates that there will be more than 537,000 new cases of epilepsy diagnosed in the age group 0–19 years in the years 1970–1980. This is based on the 2% prevalence rate. Statistical studies differ regarding the incidence of epilepsy, although the popular view is that the incidence in males is slightly higher than in females. Millon (1969) reported that the incidence was about equal for the two sexes. As of 1975, the officials of the EFA had not attempted to draw conclusions about age and sex prevelance. More extensive data on the incidence of various types of epilepsy can be found in the EFA's *Basic Statistics on the Epilepsies* (1975).

# TYPES OF TREATMENTS AVAILABLE

## Pharmacological Management

The primary method of treatment for epilepsy is anticonvulsant drug therapy. With efficient therapy, adequate control can be achieved in some 70–80% of patients. Side effects of drug therapy, however, are not uncommon, and a number of patients' epilepsies remain resistant to any drug or combination of drugs available at present (Sutherland, Tait, & Eadie, 1974).

The rate of metabolizing anticonvulsants varies considerably from person to person but usually is slow enough for plasma and brain concentrations of the drug to remain relatively constant if the drug is taken once or twice daily. When anticonvulsant treatment is begun, or anticonvulsant doses are changed, it usually requires several days for plasma and brain levels of the drug to reach a steady state. The main factors governing tissue levels of an anticonvulsant are the dosage in which the drug is given and the liver's rate of metabolizing the drug. At present, the mechanism of action of the anticonvulsant drugs is poorly understood and no general theory of anticonvulsant action is possible.

An anticonvulsant drug is usually introduced in a small dosage, with gradual increments generally made not more often than once a week until control is achieved, until therapeutic blood levels are reached as determined by gas liquid chromatography, or until toxic effects appear. If the seizures are controlled, the therapy is continued for a period of at least 2 years. If they are partially controlled, the first drug is taken to its limit of tolerance and the next safest effective preparation is added in gradually increasing doses. If the first drug had no therapeutic effect, or if toxic effects appeared, the second safest effective anticonvulsant is added and the first one is gradually withdrawn. This is continued until an effective drug combination is found. Maintenance therapy should be continued in full dosage in order to maintain the control of epilepsy for at least 2 years, with occasional monitoring of plasma anticonvulsant levels (Sutherland et al., 1974).

A wide variety of anticonvulsant medications is now available for the treatment of seizures. Some of the more common ones used in treating grand mal include phenytoin (Dilantin), phenobarbitone, primidone (Mysoline), carbamazepine (Tegretol), and methoin (Mesantoin). For petit mal, some of the more familiar ones include ethosuximide (Zarontin), methsuximide (Celontin), troxidone (Tridione), and acetazoleamide (Diamox). One of the most recent additions to the U.S. market is sodium valproate (Depakane), which is used primarily for myoclonic seizures.

Such medications are used singly or in combination, depending on the individual patient's seizure type(s). The dosage is gradually built up until seizure control is achieved, toxic side effects occur, or plasma levels indicate therapeutic level has been achieved. If full control is not achieved, the next safest drug thought to be effective is gradually added. Also, one drug may be added while the previous one is gradually withdrawn. Achieving an adequate anticonvulsant regimen may take a few weeks or many months or may never occur. In addition, a patient who has been maintained successfully on a particular regimen for some time may experience an increase in seizures, which requires concomitant medication changes.

The emphasis is on dispensing the smallest dosage of the most effective, least harmful anticonvulsants. These medications carry with them a wide variety of side effects ranging from benign to serious, including rashes, gum hyperplasia, hirsutism (excess hair), ataxia, vertigo, anemia, lethargy, and neuropsychiatric symptoms. Because of this variety of side effects, seizure patients have their blood levels monitored on a regular basis. Some require blood levels to be determined as frequently as once a month, whereas others may require checking only once or twice a year (Sutherland et al., 1974).

## Ketogenic Diet

A ketogenic diet, which includes a ratio of three to four parts fat to one part carbohydrate plus protein, sometimes benefits children with minor motor seizures (especially those between the ages of 2 and 5 years). Livingston (1972) reports that the ketogenic diet controlled seizures in 50% of 426 patients with minor motor seizures and brought about improvement in another 27%. Four-fifths of these children had experienced no benefit from previous drug therapy. This diet is also occasionally prescribed for major motor, psychomotor, or intractable petit mal attacks. It is not a regimen of choice in these conditions. Many children on this diet become lethargic from it. It is usually not continued for more than 1 or 2 years at most, because it may impair growth and also predisposes to hypoglycemia and other toxic side effects (Solomon & Plum, 1976).

## Surgical Procedures

It is generally agreed that surgery is indicated for demonstrable structural epileptogenic lesions such as neoplasms, arteriovenous malformations, or cysts lying in accessible areas of the cerebral hemisphere. There is less agreement as to the guidelines for surgery when the anatomic lesions cannot be demonstrated, even when the seizures are intractable (Solomon & Plum, 1976).

A hemispherectomy can sometimes be beneficial in controlling seizures in children with cerebral palsy. It is worth considering in children with intractable epilepsy associated with hemiplegia but with good function in the remainder of the brain. Other patients for whom surgery is sometimes considered are those who have temporal lobe seizures with no apparent structural abnormality. Sometimes in older patients, a small benign tumor, undetectable until the operation, may be present. For these patients, a temporal lobectomy may be considered. However, the risks and complications of this surgery often outweigh the predicted benefits. This is particularly true when the focus is in the hemisphere responsible for language (Sutherland et al., 1974).

A new surgical approach that has received much publicity in recent years involves the implantation of electrodes in the brain. Cooper and his associates have reported on their initial findings in the use of chronic cerebellar stimulation for both cerebral palsy patients (Cooper, Riklan, Amin, Waltz, & Cullinan, 1976). In the latter study, Cooper reported on 15 patients with intractable epilepsy treated by means of cerebral stimulation. Six had mainly psychomotor seizures, six had grand mal, and three had myoclonic seizures. Cooper and his colleagues reported that in 10 of these 15 patients chronic cerebellar stimulation was followed by modification or inhibition of the clinical seizure pattern. All ten reported being more alert, attentive, and capable of improved study or work activities. In two patients, uncontrolled interictal rage reaction was suppressed.

Caution must be used to guard against overoptimism in the use of cerebellar stimulation. The exact mechanism presumably operating to diminish seizures is not understood. In addition, only a very small number of patients have been accepted by Cooper for continued study of this technique. The long-term risks and effects are, of course, unknown at this time. Of special interest are some recent personal communications indicating that some cases presumed to be improved as a result of cerebellar stimulation were found to have nonfunctioning stimulators.

# CONTROLLABILITY

It is a common misconception that all epileptics are "controlled" by medication. Unfortunately, despite developments of new drugs and other advances in pharmacological management of various types of seizures there are still many epileptics whose seizures are not fully controlled (Table 1). According to Rodin (1972), approximately 85% of those with epilepsy can achieve enough seizure control to lead essentially normal lives. The *control* of a seizure disorder is a very individual problem. No two seizure patients are the same—even if they have the same types of seizures—because many factors, some known and some unknown, affect the degree of controllability that an individual patient experiences. The Epilepsy Foundation of America (1975) has summarized seven sets of data on seizure control for all ages of patients using proper medications across all types of seizures. The data describing percentage of "complete control" range from 48% to 70%; for partial control, they range from 14% to 37%; and for "no control," they range from 12% to 20%.

With children who were otherwise intellectually and emotionally normal and who complied with anticonvulsant drugs and/or diet therapy, a complete cessation of seizures was found in 70% of the sample, a significant reduction in 14%, and no change in 16% (Bratanov & Kerekovski, 1970). On a less enthusiastic note, a similar study of 801 children by Fukuyama, Arima, Nagahata, and Okada (1963) reported 90–100% seizure control in 53% of the children, 19–87% control in 36% of the children, and less than 18% control (i.e., no significant effect) in 12% of the children.

Regardless of differing definitions of adequate seizure control, it seems clear from these statistics that even if one uses a conservative percentage (12%) to estimate the uncontrolled epileptics of all ages in the United States, this represents a large number of people, approximately 480,000. Of this number, it is likely that the majority are below the age of 20 years.

# INTERNATIONAL CLASSIFICATION OF EPILEPTIC SEIZURES

The ability to record cortical activity noninvasively was a major landmark in epileptology. Electroencephalography (EEG), part science and part art, is a fundamental and necessary element in ascertaining a condition of epilepsy. A standardized classification of seizure disorders was proposed by a committee of the International League Against Epilepsy (ILAE), which met in 1964 to develop a standardized and uniform system based on clinical and encephalographic factors. Gastaut presented the classification scheme in 1965 and later reviewed and revised it into its present form (Gastaut, 1970), as shown in Table 2.

This taxonomic system adequately complements the anatomical and neurophysiological considerations for which is was designed. The classification scheme does not, however, reflect behavioral aspects of the disorders, such as controllability, limitations on cognitive and/or interpersonal functioning, severity, and responsivity to either medication or other methods of intervention such as biofeedback, behavioral therapy, and psychiatric intervention. The committee itself has been

TABLE 1
Pinpointing the Type of Seizure

| Epileptic type | EEG type | Onset | Etiology | Treatment |
|---|---|---|---|---|
| *Partial seizures* | | | | |
| With elementary symptomatology: | | | | |
| Focal seizures (motor, sensory, or autonomic) | Usually unilateral spike and/or slow wave discharge | Depends on area | Organic | Carbamazepine or phenytoin |
| With complex symptomatology: | | | | |
| Complex–partial seizures | Anterior temporal discharge | Young adults | Organic | Carbamazepine, primidone |
| Partial seizures with secondary generalization: | | | | |
| Tonic–clonic seizures beginning locally | Focal discharge | Increases with age | Organic | Carbamazepine or phenytoin |
| *Generalized seizures—bilaterally symmetrical* | | | | |
| Infantile spasms | Hypsarrhythmia | First year | Organic | ACTH, phenobarbital, diazepam, clonazepam |
| Atonic and akinetic seizures | Slow spike and wave (petit mal variant) | 1–5 years | Organic | Diazepam or clonazepam |
| Simple absence (petit mal) | 3/sec spikes and waves | About 5 years | Idiopathic | Ethosuximide |
| Complex absences (including autonomic manifestations) | Nonspecific or paroxysmal discharges | Between 2–20 years | Usually idiopathic | Phenobarbital and ethosuximide, clonazepam |
| Myoclonic jerks | Mixed spike and slow wave | 5–20 years | Idiopathic | Phenobarbital or phenytoin or clonazepam |
| Tonic–clonic seizures (grand mal) | Interseizure record normal or sharp and paroxysmal | Before 20 years | Frequently idiopathic | Phenytoin, carbamazepine, primidone |
| *Unilateral seizures* | | | | |
| Tonic–clonic seizures of infancy | Focal discharges, usually spike wave complexes | Usually first year | Idiopathic or organic | Correct metabolic disturbance and/or phenobarbital |

TABLE 2

International Classification of Epileptic Seizures

---

I.  Partial seizures (seizures beginning locally)
    A. Partial seizures with elementary symptomatology (generally without impairment of consciousness)
        1. With motor symptoms (includes Jacksonian seizures)
        2. With special sensory or somatosensory symptoms
        3. With autonomic symptoms
        4. Compound forms
    B. Partial seizures with complex symptomatology (generally with impairment of consciousness)
       (temporal lobe or psychomotor seizures)
        1. With impairment of consciousness only
        2. With cognitive symptomatology
        3. With affective symptomatology
        4. With "psychosensory" symptomatology
        5. With "psychomotor" symptomatology (automatisms)
        6. Compound forms
    C. Partial seizures secondarily generalized
II. Generalized seizures (bilaterally symmetrical and without local onset)
        1. Absences (petit mal)
        2. Bilateral massive epileptic myoclonus
        3. Infantile spasms
        4. Clonic seizures
        5. Tonic seizures
        6. Tonic–clonic seizures (grand mal)
        7. Atonic seizures
        8. Akinetic seizures
III. Unilateral seizures (or predominantly)
IV. Unclassified epileptic seizures (due to incomplete data)

---

*Note.* From "Clinical and Electroencephalographical Classification of Epileptic Seizures" by H. Gastaut, *Epilepsia*, 1970, *11*, 102–113. Copyright 1970 by Elsevier Publishing Co. Reprinted by permission.

aware of these problems and is continuing in its efforts to revise the classification system.

Research into the basic electrochemical mechanisms of epilepsy and development of effective diagnostic and treatment techniques are continuing. These techniques include new medications, new surgical methods, and new nondrug methods. The latter category underscores the need for an aggressive involvement of behavioral medicine in neurology. It includes biofeedback as well as other behavior modification techniques, such as relaxation training, systematic desensitization, cognitive strategies, and management of environmental contingencies.

Because assessment procedures are anchored either to theoretical accounts of psychological dynamics presumed to govern seizure activity or to treatment tactics designed to introduce an avenue for controllability, we shall first consider the larger body of behavior-related theories surrounding the epilepsies and then return to the specific considerations of assessment itself.

# PSYCHOLOGICAL THEORIES OF EPILEPSY

Historically, epilepsy has moved from being viewed as a superstitious or demonic event to being viewed primarily as a neurophysiological event with electrical and possibly chemical mechanisms. Between these two ends of the continuum are the psychological theories about epilepsy. These theories vary according to the degree of emphasis placed on psychological components, ranging from the psychoanalytic interpretations of seizures and epilepsy as arising from basic unresolved emotional conflicts to the more widely accepted view concerning emotional and even environmental precipitants. None of the psychological theories to be described provides a comprehensive view of the epilepsies or directions for effective behavioral treatment. However, they all suggest a number of nonmedical, social–emotional factors that seem to be important in a comprehensive assessment program. Included in this section are some examples of psychoanalytic formulations, a more recent reformulation of epilepsy as a psychosomatic/behavioral problem, and a learning-theory-oriented formulation of the epilepsy problem that represents the most current and acceptable position. Each theoretical system implies the need for appropriate measurement of dependent variables critical to an adequate description of the nonorganic variables that exert control over the course of the disorder.

## Psychoanalytic Formulations

In their psychoanalytic explanations of the psychosomatic approach, Alexander and Flagg (1965) discuss epilepsy along with narcolepsy. They indicate that the role of emotional conflict in narcolepsy, catalepsy, and epilepsy has long been recognized. More specifically, they cite Epstein and Ervin (1956), who concluded that the psychomotor seizures of two patients receiving intensive psychotherapy were highly organized discharges of dynamic conflictual material. They viewed the seizure as a motivated behavior, in that it dispelled mounting psychological tension of nonreported thought. Bandler, Kaufman, Dykens, Schleifer, Shapiro, and Arico (1958) attribute seizures to sexual, rather than aggressive, psychodynamic conflict. Sexual fantasies and unconscious, inhibited rage were hypothesized by Alexander and Flagg (1965) as causes of petit mal and grand mal seizures in an 18-year-old female. Reportedly, her seizures decreased when her rage was reduced over 4 years of psychotherapy.

The cases of three epileptic boys treated analytically were reported by Gottschalk (1953), who noted that psychological factors play a role in the elaboration or exacerbation of epileptic phenomena. For these cases, Gottschalk presents information about events occurring at the onset of the patient's seizures, Rorschach interpretations, and a psychodynamic formulation of each patient's personality disorder. In all three cases, he analyzed some components of inhibition of anger or rage along with fixation at a dependent stage.

In a study of 120 children with "limbic epilepsy" (or temporal lobe seizures), Glaser (1967) reports that projective tests such as the Rorschach showed evidence of difficulty with control of violent hostile and aggressive impulses. The cases of temporal lobe seizure present a special challenge both diagnostically and theoretically because the seizure often involves behavioral automatisms, visceral disturbances, and personality and thought disorders. Symptoms of temporal lobe epilepsy (TLE) are sometimes misdiagnosed as psychiatric problems. On the other hand, the frequency of psychiatric problems in adults with TLE is higher than for other types of seizure disorders.

"Assessment" in this context follows traditional psychodiagnostics and clinical interviews as they might be undertaken for mental health objectives. The ability to obtain such information reliably in a child population is not clear. The emphasis, however, is upon unconscious and unresolved conflicts and dynamisms. Their documentation would allow the conduct of appropriately structured psychotherapy relevant to the manifestation of the seizures.

## Emotional Precipitants

Lennox and Markham (1953) disagree vehemently with "some Freudians who insist that a devastating convulsion is the person's unconscious attempt to retreat to the comfortable cavern of the uterus" (p. 1690). They correctly emphasize that emotional problems may accentuate, but do not initiate, epilepsy; if emotions initiate the illness, it is not epilepsy by hysteria. Fremont-Smith (1934) reported that 31 out of 42 patients showed a direct relationship between emotion and one or more major convulsions. In addition to strong emotion, pain, cold, and the onset of acute infections were other physiologic mechanisms noted by Fremont-Smith as seizure precipitants. He suggests that such factors stimulate the sympathetic nervous system, which by some as yet undetermined mechanism, precipitates a seizure in a person whose brain is predisposed to seizures. Some researchers feel that seizures are more frequent and severe during periods when emotional factors are operating (Bridge, 1949). Fear, frustration, tension, and anxiety are the emotional situations that Livingston (1954) regards as the most common emotional precipitants of seizures in epileptic children. Case studies to support the importance of examining the role of emotional factors in epileptics are presented by Caveness (1955) and Jensen (1947). Gottschalk (1953) speculated that the blocking of any nonspecific drive or strong emotion from gratification or expression by either an internal autonomous inhibiting factor or an external agent could lead to seizures. This was felt to be the case especially in children who have a lower seizure threshold and less mature, more primitive impulses and emotions than other children.

The notion that psychological stress can trigger seizures is supported by an experiment by Barker and Barker (1950). They utilized psychological stress to elicit EEG seizure discharges from known epileptics. These stress factors consisted of "insight" and "awareness" information that the patient found difficult to accept. Greenson (1944) described an epileptic patient who had his first seizure during the analytic hour when he began discussing certain dreams. The dreams were later interpreted to be a part of a complex of disruptively stressful and therefore seizure-triggering dreams. Supporting this viewpoint, Barker and Barker (1950) concluded:

> At one time or another, either suddenness, conflictual reaction, or intensity of response seemed to be the outstanding factor in the situations characterized by convulsive reaction. The convulsive reactions to sudden stimulation seemed to represent reactions to stress when no other response could be organized. (p. 110)

According to their view, psychotherapy proves useful because it teaches patients how to organize their reactions. The seizures then become replaced either by more minor seizure forms or by disruptive reactions such as belching, yawning, sighing, complaints of pain and distress, or temper tantrums. The value of psychotherapy can presumably also be shown by the EEG records for several subjects described by Gottschalk (1953).

Most recently, Williams (Note 2) reported the results of psychotherapy carried out with 37 diagnosed (and poorly controlled) epileptics. Where IQ and emotional stability were normal, marked reduction or elimination of the seizure problem was reported for most patients presenting with a neurogenic etiology.

Recent research in the area of emotional precipitants has emphasized an experimental design to evoke various emotional responses in seizure patients and to observe their effect on the EEG (Small, Stevens, & Milstein, 1964; Stevens, 1959). Overall, the research literature on emotional precipitants of seizures is sparse, although there are many articles about the general psychological effects of epilepsy (Hermann, 1977).

In medical practice, too little time is spent by medical and staff persons in determining the existence of emotional precipitants or in devising a plan for the patient to deal effectively with them in the hope of reducing his or her seizure rate. Sometimes, even if a patient reports what he or she believes to be a reliable emotional precipitant, the physician may view this as superstitious thinking or an hysterical tendency on the part of the patient. More often than not, reported emotional and conditioned environmental precipitants to seizures are not thought to be serious diagnostic data and are not utilized in the medical treatment of the patient.

Psychiatric studies of epilepsy largely assume a biological predisposition augmented by psychological factors that contribute to the development and continuance of the epileptic disorder. Heredity is seen as an important factor, considering the evidence that an average of one parent and at least one-half of the relatives of all epileptics show dysrhythmia, although not all of them suffer from seizures (Greenson, 1944). This evidence would seem to indicate that other factors, such as psychological ones, may be operating. This has been recognized particularly with children (Gottschalk, 1953):

> Neuropsychiatrically, their seizure threshold was lower than that of other children. Psychologically they had a predisposition to paroxysmal, explosive and sensory activity. Their impulses were more punative, less mature than those of other children of comparable age. Consequently, perhaps psychologic conflicts were more overwhelming. (p. 23)

## Psychosomatic Theory Applied to Epilepsy

Mostofsky (1972) noted that the professional community and the general public are adjusted to the notion that asthma, ulcers, eczema, and other "real," organically obvious conditions are directly related to psychological dynamisms. However, these same people have been rigid in their preconceptions that the psychosomatic illness model cannot be extended to describe pathologies of the central nervous system. Despite recent dramatic advances in the application of behavioral techniques to the modification of heart rate and other autonomic nervous system functions, the possibility of comparable clinical effects for treating seizures behaviorally is still met with considerable resistance. This is especially strange considering the wealth of documented and anecdotal evidence pointing to anxiety states, environmental traumas, and a variety of psychogenic factors as precipitants and triggers for petit mal and grand mal episodes.

Neurologists have long recognized the psychosomatic consequences of epilepsy and even the contribution of psychodynamics in aggravating the "neurological" problem. The literature is careful to distinguish "genuine" epilepsy from the hysterical illnesses clinically resembling epileptic convulsions. It is surprising that little effort has been exerted in understanding such factors with a view toward their elimination or reduction or in formulating psychotherapeutic programs that would seek to function as "anticonvulsant agents." Little effort has been dedicated to incorporating psychiatric or behavior modification protocols into dealing with the seizure problem itself, although traditional psychotherapy (limited to dealing with the social, emotional, and personality problems of the epileptic patient) is increasingly a recommended adjunct to neurological practice.

## Learning Approaches

One of the earliest suggestions that seizures may be conditioned responses to emotional stimuli was made by Cannon (1933) in discussing the papers presented by Lennox and Fremont-Smith at the 1932 meeting of the Boston Society of Psychiatry and Neurology. Cannon (1933) noted that:

> An emotional response can be conditioned just as in dogs the salivary flow can be conditioned, by association with any stimulus. The situation is similar when a person has had an emotional experience and a convulsive attack; anything that brings back the original circumstances may also bring back the attack, because these circumstances make the conditioned stimulus. (p. 236)

As an extension, some, if not all, seizure activity can also be conceived of as having operant properties (no matter what its etiology). That is, once the seizure occurs, it is reinforced in both direct and indirect ways, thus increasing the probability of its recurrence. Such reinforcement may also serve to increase the intensity or duration of a seizure—a possibility that is alluded to by Freedman and Kaplan (1967) in discussing patients who "malinger seizures" for their own benefit. To be sure, any analogy to classical or instrumental conditioning is decidedly imperfect.

One may speculate on the many possible reinforcers (both immediate and long term) that may be thought of as being contingent upon seizure activity. They may include such things as immediate attention, physical proximity to and contact from others, expressions of concern, regular medical appointments, medication, precautionary planning by parents, and other forms of "special" treatment. The rationale for such reinforcement of physiological responses in a child was proposed by Miller (1969) in his classic paper on the learning of visceral and glandular responses. This is not to suggest that seizures may not also have negative, even injurious, consequences such as fear, loss of control, embarrassment, and possible physical, and even brain, injury. However, it is hypothesized that for some children with seizures, the rewarding aspects of the seizure activity far outweigh the punishing ones. Indeed, for some children, the social attention they receive because of their seizures may be greater than the attention they receive for any other single activity. Therefore, one may postulate that the seizures of these people are strengthened and/or maintained by environmental and social contingencies such that medication alone cannot adequately eliminate them. A data bank does not currently exist that would rigorously confirm these hypotheses. The individuality of the person is preserved in the seizure patient, and only the fragmentary reports of the separate case studies that have appeared in the literature can be offered in support of these premises (Balaschak, 1978).

It appears that for some epileptics intense emotions (Freedman & Kaplan, 1967) or specific stimuli (Forster, 1977) may be precipitants for seizure activity. The seizure activity may both remove the child from an emotionally arousing situation (i.e., a negative reinforcement) and net for him, on a fairly reliable schedule, a variety of other rewards such as those mentioned previously, in this chapter. If one construes the seizure activity in this manner, the treatment may focus on (1) changing the person's manner of dealing with these emotionally charged situations, thus presumably lessening the probability of their precipitating a seizure (this can be tried through traditional psychotherapy, systematic desensitization, or relaxation training, procedures that have been successfully used with older patients Parrino, 1971; Williams et al., 1978; Meyer, Bock, Johnson, & Woodward, Note 3; Mostofsky & Vick, Note 4; Muthen, Note 5); or (2) modifying the rewards that are contingent upon the behavior and thereby lessening the probability of the seizure's recurrence.

It is our contention that some portion of the seizure activity otherwise satisfactorily controlled by chemotherapy can be considered an operant that is reinforced and maintained by a variety of positive and negative reinforcers. For example, that epilepsy has historically been a frightening and misunderstood medical problem has probably heightened parents' responsiveness to seizure activity. Similarly, well-meaning attention and concern by the parents, designed to ensure the child's physical safety during a seizure and to reassure the frightened child afterward, may unintentionally reinforce such behaviors. Continued intermittent reinforcement may then make the behavior difficult to extinguish.

# ASSESSMENT

The issue of assessment as it relates to the epilepsies embraces at least three domains of data relevant to patient characteristics and a separate set of considerations that must be assessed relating to the intended behavioral-service-providing system. These elements are summarized in Table 3.

Such a broad and encompassing perspective of assessment needs is necessary to appreciating the concern for admitting discussions of both theories on epilepsy and treatment alternatives for this condition. A broad-based assessment of the epileptic patient has been a seriously neglected ingredient in epilepsy research, and the development of appropriate instruments will depend on an appreciation of related literature and thought. The delineation of variables in Table 3, however incomplete, will provide some guidance on (1) the limitations of any proposed treatment plan (or more important, may allow for a rational selection among behavior treatment alternatives, (2) potential targets for focused intervention, and (3) sensitization to sources of interaction and interference.

## Physiological Domain

Although most epileptic children are routinely assessed physiologically, fewer are assessed with reference to cognitive, social, or emotional problems. Still fewer are assessed in terms of the interaction of their seizure disorder with factors in their daily life environments. The physiological assessment category includes the taking of pertinent medical history information, the general neurological workup, and an EEG. No seizure patient should be lacking any aspect of these basic physiological examinations.

The conventional "assessment" data that may be sufficient for the neurologist are largely inadequate for the psychologist, counselor, or teacher whose concerns do not relate to drug selection or surgical consultation. The standard procedure in the initial assessment of a child suspected to have seizures begins with a general neurological examination, the gathering of a complete medical history (usually from the child's mother), and an EEG. The neurologist relies heavily on the parent's clinical descriptions of the possible seizures, along with confirming evidence on the EEG. This is especially so because the EEG does not always confirm nor disconfirm the presence of seizures. The neurologist's goals are to determine the presence or absence of a seizure disorder, to specify its type, and to institute appropriate drug treatment in an attempt to eliminate completely or to reduce greatly the further occurrence of seizures.

The adult patient has the advantage of being more actively involved in the diagnostic process as well as in coordinating with his or her physician concerning the effects of medications. The child patient is at a great disadvantage in both of these processes. The degree to which the child is actively involved in the interview process with the physician depends on a variety of factors, the first of which is the particular neurologist's style of relating to the child patient. In addition, variables

TABLE 3
Assessment Checklist

| Patient characteristics |
| --- |

*Physiological domain*
EEG profile
Serum/hormonal levels
Anatomical structures
Multiple handicaps
Genetic history

*Psychological domain*
IQ
Cognitive development
Emotional/affective stability
Social/family status
Phobias, anxieties, addictions

*Environmental domain*
School/vocational performance
Leisure activities
Rewards, punishers, motivators
Compliance and life style
Coping skills

| Behavioral clinic qualifications |
| --- |

Personnel—number of therapists, psychodiagnosticians, field observers
Facilities—hospitalization capability; biofeedback equipment; technicians
Location—geographic accessibility; nonthreatening setting
Team cooperation—neurologist; psychologist; social worker
Economics (patient costs)—research funds; third-party payment; patient payment
Program support—secretarial; data analysis; bioengineering
Consultations—psychiatry; medical diagnostics; teacher

such as the patient's age, level of intelligence, language skills, and emotional state may all play a role in deciding whether and to what degree he or she may become an active participant in the diagnostic process.

In our experience, even when the patient is a teenager of at least average intelligence, the diagnostic interview too often is limited to the parent. This is partly justified because the youngster may not be fully cognizant of his or her seizure-related symptoms or may be amnesic for the episodes. However, we cannot help but believe that often when the child or teenage patient is present during such discussions, he or she may inadvertently be made to feel like an object of just so many medical symptoms. Because of the issue of short- and long-term compliance with the drug regimen that every epileptic patient faces, we feel that the patient's initial involvement in the diagnostic process is of great importance.

## Psychological Domain

Some or all aspects of assessment listed in this second domain are carried out with many child epileptics. Questions about a child's general cognitive functioning are usually examined by means of standard, individually administered intelligence tests. Other tests that address specific skills such as perceptual–motor tasks, language functioning, and auditory or visual memory are also administered to epileptic children as they would be to any other child. No special scoring systems for epileptics exist for any of these tests. One may well presume that an epileptic child may manifest some deficit, especially on timed tasks such as those on the performance half of the Wechsler Intelligence Scale for Children, because of medication effects. However, one can also argue that although the child's score may be diminished because of medication, it is an accurate representation of the child's functioning level. It is incumbent upon the diagnostician to recognize and report the interplay of the epileptic child's medication or actual seizures with his or her fine motor coordination and speed, his or her rate of processing auditorially presented material, and any other cognitive skills.

Questions about the general emotional status of an epileptic child are usually addressed where there are specific symptoms in evidence. Signs of depression, mood swings, inability to form adequate peer relationships, somatic complaints with no clear organic basis, and self-precipitated seizures are the types of indications that often result in the referral of an epileptic child for further psychological assessment. Some of these issues may be pursued by the primary physician, but most often a referral is made to some mental health professional.

A typical diagnostic intake interview is the primary method of assessment. Though there appear to be some moves toward family interviews, it is still likely the practice of most therapists to interview the child's parents and to have a separate diagnostic session with the child. The treatment of emotional problems of an epileptic varies with the preference of the therapist and is not linked to the epilepsy itself. The prevalence of emotional problems in epileptics versus the nonepileptic population is a much-debated topic, with studies on each side of the argument. A recent review (Hermann, 1977) addresses these issues. Many researchers point to temporal lobe epileptics as being especially subject to emotional problems (Glaser, 1967). Whatever one's opinion about the prevalence of emotional problems in epileptics, there are no specialized assessment or treatment techniques for this population. Perhaps even the standard diagnostic interview is too infrequently employed.

It is our opinion that even if a child does not display overt psychiatric symptoms, there is some value in having the child and his or her parents interviewed by a mental health professional for preventive reasons. Often potential problems can be averted by early intervention. For example, a child who does not understand what a seizure is may build up unnecessary anxieties from lack of an adequate explanation. The child may have felt uncomfortable asking his or her parents or physician certain questions about the seizure disorder. For example, in our experience, it is not uncommon for a child to believe that he or she caused the seizure disorder by doing something disobedient. Some children associate the seizure with death but are afraid to ask about the possibility. Such issues should be explored with the child and his or her parents in a sensitive manner before they precipitate an emotional symptom.

It is also important for the therapist to provide the parents with a balanced view of the need for supervising or protecting the child. The child will require guidance on accepting the disorder and the limitations it is likely to impose. As with many other chronic disorders, such early preventative interventions can be important contributions to the effective management of the disorder and to the patient's general quality of life.

## Specific Assessment Materials

Data from the environmental domain will usually be derived from histories and interviews as previously recommended. To ensure that pertinent areas of inquiry are not overlooked, we have developed three paper-and-pencil inventories.

The Seizure Disorder Survey Schedule (SDSS) is designed to provide a standardized data profile on the patient and his or her problem(s). The various sections of the inventory allow for entry of sociofamilial information; detailed descriptions of the observable features of the clinicl seizure; possible seizure precipitants; relevant medical, surgical, and drug histories; other behavioral complaints (phobias, bed wetting, etc.); subjective impressions; and psychometric results. Sample items are given in Figure 1.

The Pre-Behavioral-Treatment Questionnaire, particularly valuable for young children, is designed to elicit the level of the patient's understanding about his or her disorder and the potential reinforcement value that the disorder may offer (Figure 2). This questionnaire can be used with a child as young as 5 years old.

The Weekly Chart was designed to facilitate the recording of seizure occurrences, and often patients or monitors enter (on the blank reverse side) additional data concerning duration or severity or the particular social–psychological situation that attended the occasion of the seizure. A sample weekly chart, completed for a fictitious patient, is always supplied as a guide to the novice user (Figure 3). It should be noted that although neurologists will often request the patient or parent ''to keep a record,'' such a log is usually impressionistic, and the few forms for record keeping that several pharmaceutical companies provide as a service do not allow for an easy and accurate description of the relevant phenomena.

The SDSS and Pre-Behavioral-Treatment Questionnaire provide a framework of questions that encompass primarily issues in the psychological domain of assessment as well as many of those in the physiological realm. The SDSS is usually administered to the parents of the child. If the patient is an adolescent or young adult, he or she would answer many of the questions without the involvement of parents.

The SDSS and the Pre-Behavioral-Treatment Questionnaire (Balaschak, 1978) also attempt to explore the more minute details of the patient's seizures as they

-1-

Date_____

Age of Onset

Name:_____DOB_____Age_____ of Puberty_____

Address:_____    Referring Physician:_____

_____    Neurologist:_____

_____    Completed by:_____

Phone: _____    Information Supplied by:

Hospital Number:_____    _____

Type(s) of Seizure:_____    School/Business Address:_____

_____    _____

Age of First Onset:_____    _____

Brief Description of Seizures:    _____

_____    Phone_____

_____    Contact Person:_____

1.  Number of seizures on increase    Yes ( )      No ( )

2.  Number of seizures on decrease    Yes ( )      No ( )          Same ( )

3.  Number of seizures per day    (small)_____ (severe)_____

4.  Number of seizures per week    (small)_____ (severe)_____

5.  Usual time between seizures    _____

6.  Seizures occur during day only    Yes ( )      No ( )

7.  Seizures occur during night only    Yes ( )      No ( )      Either ( )

8.  Seizures occur during sleep    Yes ( )      No ( )    Only  ( )

9.  Prodromal symptoms(irritability,    Yes ( )      No ( )
              mood....)

FIGURE 1
Seizure Disorder Survey Schedule.

-2-

Seizure onset

10. Aura                                Yes ( )          No ( )

    If yes .... Duration               _____

    Aura signs                         _____
    (sensory, autonomic, covert)

11. Known seizures, stimuli, or events(including thoughts) which precede or trigger
    seizures:

    _____

12. Seizure sensory precipitated        Yes ( )          No ( )

    If yes..Startle onset(high intensity)   Yes ( )          No ( )

          Unexpected only (any intensity)   Yes ( )          No ( )

          Specific pattern or passage       Yes ( )          No ( )

Seizure

13. Seizure activity can be prevented    Yes ( )          No ( )

    If yes.. Known conditions

    _____

14. Seizure activity can be aborted after onset   Yes ( )          No ( )

    If yes.. Known conditions

    _____

15. Known conditions when seizure never occurs    Yes ( )          No ( )

    _____

16. Stare before muscular contractions   Yes ( )          No ( )

17. Absence before muscular contractions  Yes ( )          No ( )

18. Atonic, akinetic reaction            Yes ( )          No ( )

19. Cry or scream                        Yes ( )          No ( )

20. Tonic muscular stiffening            Yes ( )          No ( )

                              Arm    Right ( )        Left ( )

                              Leg    Right ( )        Left ( )

                            Other    _____

FIGURE 1
*(continued)*

-3-

21. Body stiffens in arched position on floor    Yes ( )      No ( )

22. Arms flexed    Yes ( )      No ( )

       Right ( )    Left ( )      Both ( )

23. Arms extended    Yes ( )      No ( )

       Right ( )    Left ( )      Both ( )

24. Proceeds from clonic to tonic    Yes ( )      No ( )

25. Clonic jerks    Yes ( )      No ( )

26. Bladder empties    Yes ( )      No ( )

    a. During seizure

    b. During post convulsive stupor

27. Sphincter control loss    Yes ( )      No ( )

    a. During seizure

    b. During post convulsive stupor

28. Duration of seizure (not including stupor)    _____

29. Sweating    Yes ( )      No ( )

30. Pupils contract and dilate    Yes ( )      No ( )

31 Profuse salivation    Yes ( )      No ( )

32 Cyanosis    Yes ( )      No ( )

33. Duration of stupor after seizures and before awakening.

                               _____

34. Confused or disoriented upon awakening    Yes ( )      No ( )

35. Sleep following seizures    Yes ( )      No ( )

    If yes.. Duration of sleep (range)    _____

36. Symptoms upon awakening    Yes ( )      No ( )

    Autonomic complaints

    Headache

    Sore muscles

    Other

FIGURE 1
*(continued)*

-4-

Covert events (e.g. funny thoughts, images)

_____

37. Complete amnesia                          Yes ( )          No ( )

    If partial, describe nature of recollection

_____

Neurological History

38. Institutionalization or hospitalization for seizure or related disorder

    Date        Age           Institution        Length of Stay     Reason

    _____      _____    _____  _____ _____

    _____      _____    _____  _____ _____

39. Neurological Examinations and findings

    General Neurological Exam    _____

    Pneumogram                   _____

    Arteriogram                  _____

    Skull                        _____
                                 A
    Scan          Echo           B          CAT          Radioisotope

    Serum (GLC)                  _____

    Average Evoked Response      _____

        Auditory                    Visual              Somatosensory

_____

40. Presumed etiology

_____

41. Clinical Impression (diagnostic category for seizure disorder)

        Date                          Impression

    _____         _____

    _____         _____

42. Neurosurgery                              Yes ( )          No ( )

_____

FIGURE 1
*(continued)*

-5-

Related History

43. Family Constellation                          Yes ( )          No ( )

| Names | Age | Relation | Seizure Disorder(Y/N) |
|-------|-----|----------|------------------------|
| _____ | _____ | _____ | _____ |
| _____ | _____ | _____ | _____ |
| _____ | _____ | _____ | _____ |
| _____ | _____ | _____ | _____ |

44. Other handicaps or dysfunctions

    Sensory (blind, deaf...)_____

    Motor (coordination, ability)_____

    Language _____

    IQ (score and test if known)_____

    Personality (inc. tests, if known)_____

    Sexual _____

45. Full term Delivery                     Yes ( )          No ( )

46. Caesarean Delivery                     Yes ( )          No ( )

47. Nutrition (inc. diabetic mother)      Yes ( )          No ( )

| | Date | Findings or Action Taken | Person Seen |
|--|------|--------------------------|-------------|
| 48. Developmental Evaluation Clinic | _____ | _____ | _____ |
| 49. Psychiatry Clinic | _____ | _____ | _____ |
| 50. Social Service Clinic | _____ | _____ | _____ |

DRUG HISTORY (INCLUDING TRANQUILIZERS)

| Date | Age | Drug | Dosage | Treatment Duration | Effect |
|------|-----|------|--------|--------------------|--------|
| _____ | _____ | _____ | _____ | _____ | _____ |
| _____ | _____ | _____ | _____ | _____ | _____ |
| _____ | _____ | _____ | _____ | _____ | _____ |
| _____ | _____ | _____ | _____ | _____ | _____ |

FIGURE 1
*(continued)*

-6-

Present Drug Therapy

| Date | Age | Drug | Treatment Duration | Effect |
|------|-----|------|-------------------|--------|
| _____ | _____ | _____ | _____ | _____ |
| _____ | _____ | _____ | _____ | _____ |
| _____ | _____ | _____ | _____ | _____ |
| _____ | _____ | _____ | _____ | _____ |

EEG REPORTS

NAME_____DATE_____SERVICE_____

EEG NUMBER_____AGE_____(Dr.)_____

BACKGROUND ACTIVITY(alpha rate & voltage)_____

_____

FAST ACTIVITY_____

SLOWING_____

ASYMMETRIES & LOCALIZING SIGNS_____

_____

HYPERVENTILATION(how long deep breathing was done, how well, what it produced)

_____

PHOTIC STIMULATION_____

EEG IMPRESSION_____

_____

_____

Psycho-social Impression

1.  Does the patient have other symtpoms not related to seizure disorder(e.g., phobias,

    enuresis, tics, negativism, controllingness?_____

    _____

2.  What is the patient's understanding of his/her seizure disorder?_____

    _____

FIGURE 1
*(continued)*

-7-

3. What are the patient's own techniques for preventing, interrupting or diminishing a seizure?_____

_____

4. Would you describe the patient as being:

<u>Circle One</u>

| | | |
|---|---|---|
| anxious | - | relaxed |
| dependent | - | independent |
| hostile | - | pleasure |
| immature | - | mature |
| manipulative | - | not manipulative |
| craves attention | - | does not crave attention |
| cannot tolerate stress | - | tolerate stress well |
| cannot make friends | - | makes friends on his own |

5. Are there any obvious connections between environmental or emotional factors and seizure onset? If so, describe:_____

_____

_____

BEHAVIORAL TREATMENT PROGRAM

1. Withdrawal of Positive Reinforcement(e.g. ignoring behavior)

2. Time Out from Reinforcement (e.g. "time out room"; interruption of activity)

3. Avoidance (e.g. relief from unpleasant medication schedule)

4. Suppression by punishment (e.g. shock; criticism)

5. Relaxation, autogenic

FIGURE 1
(continued)

-8-

6. Habituation; coverant extinction

7. Token Reward for desired behavior (e.g. praise; privileges)

8. Covert Reward/Extinction

9. Systematic Desensitization and Hypnosis

10. Biofeedback

11. Self-Control; overcorrection

12. Dynamic/Traditional Psychotherapy

NOTES

_____

_____

_____

_____

FIGURE 1
*(continued)*

```
                          -1-              Name:_____

                                           Date:_____

                                           Age:_____
```

1.  Why do you come here to the hospital?

2.  What is the name of your problem?(For subsequent questions, use the patient's own term for seizures, tics, or other symptoms. If he has no particular term use the word which you fell best describes his problem).

3.  In your own words tell me what a (seizure,tic, etc.) is.

4.  How long have you had (seizure, tics, etc.)? How old were you when they first started?

5.  Do you remember the very first (seizure, tic, etc.) you ever had?

6.  How often do you have (seizures, tics, etc.)? How many do you usually have in a week?

7. Can you tell when you are going to have a(seizure, tic, etc)?(If yes) How?

8.  Are there certain times or situations when you <u>almost always</u> have a (seizure, tic, etc.)? Describe them.

9.  Are there certain times or situations when you <u>almost never</u> have a (seizure, tic, etc.)? Describe them.

10.  Tell me all about your symptom. What happens and what does it feel like?

FIGURE 2
Patient's Pre-Behavioral-Treatment Questionnaire.

-2-

11. Have you or anyone else ever prevented one of your (seizures, tics, etc.) from happening? (If yes) How?

12. Have you or anyone else stopped one of your (seizures, tics, etc.) once it had started? (If yes) How?

13. What else helps you prevent or stop your (seizure, tic, etc)?

14. (a) Do you take medicine?

    (b) What kind of medicine do you take, how much, and how often?

    (c) How does it make you feel to have to take medicine?

    (d) What do you think that the medicine does for you?

15. (a) What do your family members (parents, husband, wife, etc.) do when you have a (seizure, tic, etc.)?

    (b) How does that make you feel?

16. (a) What do other people do when you have a (seizure, tic, etc)? Your friends? Your teachers (or co-workers)?

    (b) Tell me how that makes you feel.

17. (a) What is the worst thing about having your symptoms?

    (b) Are you aware of when your symptom is occurring?

    (c) Do you ever feel embarrassed by your symptom?

    (d) Do other people notice your symptom?

FIGURE 2
*(continued)*

-3-

    (e) How has your symptom affected or changed your life?

18. What is the best thing about having (seizures, tics, etc.)

19. (a) If you could choose, would you like to have more (seizures, tics, etc.) or less or just the same number you have now?

    (b) How many (seizures, tics, etc.) would you like to have every week?

    (c) When, where and with whom would you prefer to have them?

20. What methods have you tried to reduce your symptom?

21. Is there anything else that you would like to tell me about your symptom?

--------------------------------------------------------------------------------

NOTES:

FIGURE 2
*(continued)*

relate to his or her daily life. For example, what events or emotions seem to precipitate a seizure, or in what ways is the child able to avoid or abort a seizure? What is the child's attitude about taking medication?

The information obtained from the SDSS and the questionnaire has been useful in designing behavioral treatments for seizure reduction. It is our contention that more emphasis needs to be placed on this third domain—that is, the assessment of the chain of behavioral events that occur before, during, and after a seizure. Furthermore, the patient's seizures should be looked at not only in terms of rate of occurrence but also in terms of time of occurrence, pattern throughout a day or week or longer time span, duration, and intensity. Of perhaps equal importance to behavioral therapists are the relationships of the seizure to secondary gain, avoidance of responsibilities, disruption of peer interactions, interference with cognitive tasks, and so forth. It is the social–psychological disruption aspect of their disorder and not so much the seizures themselves that adult patients report as their main problems (EFA, 1979). Unfortunately, these problems are seldom addressed unless the patient exhibits severe psychiatric symptoms or refers himself or herself. It can be presumed that because epilepsy still carries a large stigma, both children and adults with this disorder will have many additional social–psychological and vocational issues to deal with that are not experienced by people with other disorders, such as obesity or asthma. It is therefore ironic that some type of standard assessment techniques specifically addressing issues common to many epileptics have not been developed.

Furthermore, there has been little research into the patient's subjective feelings about the seizures themselves with regard to what might precipitate a seizure or what the patient may view as a self-control procedure to avoid or interrupt a seizure. The general lack of credence given to the patient's view of his or her own seizure has resulted in a concomitant lack of serious development of behavioral assessment techniques and treatment methods to enable epileptics to try to control their own seizures. The potential clinical application of behavioral control methods deserves more serious consideration, not only in view of the large numbers of epileptics whose seizure disorders are refractory to current anticonvulsants but also in view of the side effects that are inherent in all anticonvulsants and for which a hoped-for reduction is a commonly stated goal of the "controlled" epileptic as well.

## The Role of Assessment

In most general terms, assessment can be seen as an activity that is important for meeting four distinct objectives: (1) determining the patency of the functioning system, that is, the relative strengths and deficiencies of selected performance or capabilities (learning; ability to exercise self-control); (2) predicting the course of behavioral development (will learning or emotional difficulties be encountered if no intervention is undertaken?); (3) providing a rationale for selecting the appropriate interventions (therapy vs. biofeedback); and (4) establishing a baseline against which subsequent developments can be reliably measured. In the neurological

HOME

Name CHRIS EGAN          Dates 3/30/80 to 4/5/80

| | Hour | Sun. 3/30 | Mon. 3/31 | Tues. 4/1 | Wed. 4/2 | Thurs. 4/3 | No school Fri. 4/4 | Sat. 4/5 | Totals |
|---|---|---|---|---|---|---|---|---|---|
| AM | 6 | Asleep | Asleep | Asleep | Asleep | Asleep | Asleep | Asleep | |
| | 7 | | 0 | 0 | 0 | 0 | | | |
| | 8 | | | — | — | 1 at 8:15 in car – brief | 0 | | 1 |
| | 9 | 0 | At | A+ | A+ | A+ | 0 | 0 * | |
| | 10 | 0 | school | school | school | school | 0 | 0 | |
| | 11 | 0 | | | | | 0 | 0 | |
| Noon | 12 | 0 | | | | | 1 falling seizure while playing outside | 0 | 1 |
| PM | 1 | 0 | | | | | 0 | 0 | |
| | 2 | 1 seiz. at 2:15 (2 min.) | | | | | 0 | 0 | 3 |
| | 3 | 0 | 0 | 0 | 2 at 2:40 in car – brief | 1 – fell off chair – doing homework | 0 | 0 | 1 |
| | 4 | 0 | 0 | 0 | 0 | 0 | 0 | 0 | |
| | 5 | 0 | 0 | 0 | 1 brief petit mal just before dinner | 0 | 0 | 1 at 5:10 fell 1 at 5:30 brief | 3 |
| | 6 | 2 at 6:30 brief | 0 | 0 | 0 | 0 | 0 | 0 | 2 |
| | 7 | 0 | 0 | 0 | 0 | 0 | 0 | 0 | |
| | 8 | 0 | 0 | 0 | 0 | 0 | 0 | 0 | |
| | 9 | In bed | In bed | In bed | In bed | Did to 2 at 9:30 not want go to bed fell down In bed | 0 | 0 | 2 |
| | 10 | | | | | | In bed | 0 | |
| | 11 | | | | | | | In bed | |

Totals:     3          0          0          3          4          1          2          13

\* Forgot to give morning medication.

FIGURE 3

3/30    1  2 min. seizure while playing alone. Loud noise — door slam. Included staring and hand and arm movements

          2  brief ones during dinner — arguing with sister — about 30 sec. each seizure

4/1    Very good day — in good mood about field trip at school today

4/2    2 brief seizures while in car on the way home. Seemed upset, but would not say why

          1 just before dinner

4/3    BAD DAY! In grouchy mood at breakfast

          1 in car (10 sec. or so) just before school

          1 after school, at home doing homework — Fell out of chair — not hurt. Did not complete math homework.

          2 around 9:30 — argued about going to bed. Fell once in bedroom

4/4    School holiday

          1 falling seizure while outside playing alone. Came in to tell me about it, then stayed in to watch TV

4/5    1 at 5:10 · fell in living room — bumped head slightly on coffee table

          1 at 5:30 — brief

      *  Forgot to give morning medication

TOTAL 13

Sample Weekly Chart.

setting, the various medical determinations and the development of a patient history are relevant to each of these objectives. The neurological and general physical status of the person provides information about the severity of disability and its implications for fostering normal behavior (objectives 1 and 2), suggests the judicious selection among the many anticonvulsants appropriate for the specific profile of the presenting disorder (objective 3), and simultaneously enables an evaluation of the course of treatment (objective 4).

The *behavioral* assessment objectives parallel those of the medical assessment. However, although the classes of objectives are very much the same, the specific concerns are substantially different. The evaluation of behavioral patency goes well beyond specific skills, abilities, and aptitudes and is necessarily concerned with the abilities for coping, life-style, personal and interpersonal growth, and optimum navigation in both friendly and hostile environments (objective 1). The predictive objective in the case of seizure disorders is focused on determining whether any behavioral intervention (given the current state of the arts and technologies in applied behavior science) should be tried and, if so, which of the many possible techniques might most likely be effective with a particular patient's characteristics (seizure type, aura, etc.). The last objective is to establish a referent for evaluating the selected behavioral intervention(s). This is especially critical in seizure disorders. The inherent variability in severity and frequency of seizure episodes is notorious—ranging from several seconds of interruptions of consciousness once a month to weekly and daily convulsions, sometimes accompanied by physical and/or psychological trauma—and anecdotal or retrospective reconstructions of the patient's status, whether by the patient himself or herself or by another, are simply unreliable.

The structure provided by both the SDSS and the Pre-Behavioral-Treatment Questionnaire for the patient have been valuable in acquiring diagnostic information that might not have been obtained in a more standard type of diagnostic interview. For example, the SDSS contains questions regarding the bladder and sphincter control, as well as one concerning other symptoms such as enuresis and phobias. Answers to these questions supplied by the parents of an epileptic child have been helpful in determining that parents had been overestimating the number of seizures the child was experiencing because they had incorrectly presumed that the child's long-standing bed wetting was seizure-related. In one such case, an 11½-year-old boy with petit mal and photosensitive seizures was found to have nocturnal enuresis, instead of nocturnal seizures, resulting in bladder loss. A behavioral program was instituted with his parents as the main therapeutic agents. Within 10 weeks of a contingency reward program, he was free of nocturnal enuresis. The mother's description of this boy's photosensitive seizures and the manner in which he tended to look up at the sun or at any bright light source and blink led to the design of a behavioral program to interrupt this youngster's habit. A time-out procedure was designed for use by the child's parents and teacher. The procedure called for the adult to require the child to close his eyes and keep his hands at his sides for one minute. This was effective in reducing the seizures caused by blinking at a light source from a baseline rate of 3.5 incidents per day to .8 incidents per day.

In the case of a 19-year-old woman with TLE, her mother's replies to questions on the SDSS seemed to indicate that in times of emotional stress, with support from her boyfriend or other friends, her daughter seemed to "hold herself together" and not have as many seizures. The daughter reported a similar feeling about her seizure pattern when responding to the Pre-Behavioral-Treatment Questionnaire. It was also determined from these interviews that seizure-precipitating factors included accidents, illness (especially if accompanied by fever), arguments with her alcoholic father, and lack of sleep. This patient was urged to interrupt any impending seizure by remaining calm and relaxed and by thinking about her boyfriend and her previously demonstrated emotional strength, which seemed related to lower seizure rates. This patient's seizure rate went from 42 (during a 10-week baseline) to zero (during a 10-week treatment period) with no change in medications. She had two seizures during the next 10 weeks of no treatment. These two seizures occurred during a week in which she had a sore throat and intermittent fevers. It is likely that the patient was continuing her self-control methods even into the follow-up weeks.

These are but two examples of the ways in which the SDSS and the Pre-Behavioral-Treatment Questionnaire are of value diagnostically and in designing behaviorally oriented programs aimed at seizure reduction. In addition, the SDSS in particular has been therapeutic in helping parents express various feelings such as frustration, fear, guilt, and anger about their child's seizure disorder.

### Other Standard Psychological Assessment Techniques

With the possible exception of the use of occasional IQ tests such as the Wechsler Intelligence Scale for Children and the Stanford-Binet, there are no standard psychological assessment instruments specifically in use with epileptic children. Even these IQ tests should not be administered routinely just because a youngster has been diagnosed as having a seizure disorder. Previous studies indicate that intelligence levels among epileptics are distributed similarly as among the nonepileptic population. Therefore, standardized intelligence tests are usually administered only where there is some question of learning problems, retardation, or organic brain damage. Similarly, a psychiatric evaluation including projective tests should not be fixed as a standard part of an assessment of an epileptic child. The type of seizure disorder that, in our experience, is most likely to prompt a neurologist's request for a psychiatric evaluation is TLE. This order is its relationship to personality dysfunction is the topic of much research and will not be reviewed here. Recently, Dodrill (1978) has attempted to standardize a battery of neuropsychological tests specifically designed for assessment with adult epileptics. Perhaps this effort may stimulate the development of a standardized and clinically practical battery of tests for child epileptics as well, although no such battery is currently available. In addition, the types of questions on standardized projective tests do not directly address some of the specific concerns of epileptics, nor do such test results obviously imply preferred strategies for intervention and management.

# BEHAVIORAL ASSESSMENT

## Procedure for Seizure Patients

When a child is referred for behavioral treatment of his or her seizures, our standard procedure is to speak with the referring person and to review the child's medical chart. The initial session consists of an interview of approximately one hour with the parent(s) using the SDSS as the primary structure. During this session, the parents are also asked about potential reinforcers for the child, often guided by a structured reinforcement inventory form. Finally, the parent (usually the mother) is given specific instructions on how to take a 10-week baseline count of the child's seizures (recording them on the Weekly Charts). The directions emphasize the necessity of noting the frequency and time of occurrence of the seizures. Where a child has more than one type of seizure, the parent is asked to note the types. Where possible, the mother is encouraged to note other aspects of the seizures, such as duration or severity. In particular, the parent is instructed to note the child's activity and/or emotional state before, during, and after the seizure. In brief, she is told to note any behavioral or stimulus events occurring in close proximity to the seizure in the hope that one or more specific precipitants might be found that might be amenable to behavioral intervention. However, even in cases where no precipitant emerges, the child can still be involved in some types of behavioral treatments.

Following this interview with the parents, the child is interviewed utilizing the Pre-Behavioral-Treatment Questionnaire as the main format. He or she is also asked about potential types of rewards. These answers are later compared to those of the parents. Those rewards that are mentioned by both parent and child are usually the ones utilized later if a contingency reward program is used. The child is also informed about the baseline recording by his mother and is encouraged to tell her if he knows he has had a seizure that she did not see. The child is also encouraged to try to notice any other behavioral aspects of his or her seizures that may be helpful in designing a treatment program.

The child and his or her mother return in 10 weeks. This length of time is seen as a minimum requirement to control for any cyclical patterns and to ensure that a fair sample of activities in the natural environment can be assessed in relations to the seizure problem. The therapist reviews the baseline charts and discusses any new findings (e.g., daily or weekly time pattern related to frequency, additional suspected precipitants). The average weekly seizure rate for the 10-week baseline is calculated. The popular "first strategy" for a behavioral therapy program is to set a 10% reduction in this mean seizure rate as a goal for the child to meet during the first week of behavioral treatment. If the child meets the goal, he or she receives a reward at the end of that week. In some cases, the behavioral therapist can offer suggestions on how to meet the goal from the information provided in the initial session as well as from the baseline data. For example, where evenings of less than usual amounts of sleep occur, followed by a morning of increased seizure activity, the child and parent are reminded of the probable importance of sufficient sleep. Where heightened emotions (whether positive or negative) appear to be related to even a small percentage of seizures, the patient is made aware of this possible interaction and encouraged to try to cope effectively with such situations.

The variety of behavioral treatment programs available for seizure problems have been reviewed elsewhere (Mostofsky & Balaschak, 1977). The assemblage of techniques and procedures can be conveniently grouped into three broad categories: (1) reward management (which is characterized by the major emphasis being placed on reward and punishment consequences of seizure and preseizure behaviors), (2) self-control (where the therapist and patient explore the role and often the redirection of motivation, expectancies, and other cognitive variables, either in the theoretical framework or behavior therapy or in traditional psychotherapy), and (3) psychophysiological procedures. This third category is defined by (1) the habituation/desensitization protocols used with patients for whom specific sensory stimuli precipitate seizures and where the treatment objective is to alter the critical trigger threshold and (2) the cortical EEG biofeedback protocols, where patients are trained to generate brain waves that lead to a diminution of slow-wave and spike activity with an increase in arousal frequencies, with treatment outcomes of reduced incidences of frank clinical seizures.

The data derived from the assessment of both the patient and the family will provide directions for the therapist in arriving at a judicious selection of the appropriate treatment program. Critical in deciding upon a treatment strategy (or more likely, the elimination from consideration of clearly unworkable tactics) will be considerations of age, of intellectual and emotional functioning, and an appreciation of the patient's denial, compliance, hostility, and so forth with respect to his or her disorder together with the behaviors and range of reinforcers that may be responsible for maintaining the behavioral repertoire. Achieving success will mean the real promise of reduced medications to accompany the reduction in the seizure problem.

## Conclusion

As a general rule, there has not been sufficient research into the application of behavioral procedures to seizure disorders to allow us to suggest which procedures are optimal for which types of patients. However, given our clinical experience over the past 6 years, as well as our clinical research with 24 refractory seizure cases (Balaschak, 1978), we feel that the procedures are safe, are commonly beneficial, and do not present a risk of increased seizure rates. Indeed, a few cases have shown fairly dramatic reductions in seizure rate. Although we are not yet able to specify the important variables to be considered, we do urge that more psychologists consider the importance of developing reliable assessment procedures and the use of behavioral techniques. Our instruments and procedures are offered as a starting point in that process.

## Reference Notes

1. Khoshbin, S. *Epileptic seizures: An introduction.* Unpublished manuscript, Children's Hospital Medical Center of Boston, Department of Neurology, 1976.
2. Williams, D. T. *The impact of psychiatric intervention on patients with uncontrolled seizures.* Paper presented at the International Symposium on Psychological Treatments of Epilepsia, Trondheim, Norway, May 1979.
3. Meyer, R. G., Bock, P., Johnson, R., & Woodward, D. *A biofeedback approach to epileptic seizure control.* Unpublished manuscript, University of Louisville, Psychology Clinic, Louisville, Ky., 1973.
4. Mostofsky, D. I., & Vick, S. H. *The therapeutic value of muscle relaxation in seizure control: A case study.* Unpublished manuscript, Boston University, 1973.
5. Muthen, J. *Psychological treatment of epileptic seizures.* Thesis, Institute for Applied Psychology, Uppsala University, Sweden, 1978.

## References

Alexander, F., & Flagg, W. The psychosomatic approach. In B. B. Wolman (Ed.), *Handbook of clinical psychology.* New York: McGraw-Hill, 1965.

Balaschak, B. A. *Behavior modification techniques with refractory epileptics.* Doctoral dissertation, Miami University, Oxford, Ohio, 1978. (University Microfilms No. 79-03168)

Bandler, B., Kaufman, E. I., Dykens, J. W., Schleifer, M. Shapiro, L. N., & Arico, J. F. The role of sexuality in epilepsy: Hypothesis, analysis of two cases. *Psychosomatic Medicine*, 1958, *20*, 227–234.

Barker, W., & Barker, S. Experimental production of human convulsive brain potentials of stress-induced effects upon neural integrative function: Dynamics of the convulsive reaction to stress. *Life Stress and Bodily Disease: Proceedings of the Association of Research in Nervous and Mental Diseases*, 1950, *24*, 90–113.

Bratanov, B., & Kerekovski, I. Experience in the treatment of some forms of epilepsy in children (Bulgarian). *Pediatria*, 1970, *9*, 376–386.

Bridge, E. M. *Epilepsy and convulsive disorders in children.* New York: McGraw-Hill, 1949.

Cannon, W. B. Discussion: Boston Society of Psychiatry and Neurology. *Archives of Neurology*, 1933, *30*, 232–236.

Caveness, W. E. Emotional and psychological factors in epilepsy (general clinical and neurological considerations). *American Journal of Psychiatry*, 1955, *112*, 190–193.

Cooper, I. S., Amin, I., Riklan, M., Waltz, J. M., & Poon, T. P. Chronic cerebellar stimulation in epilepsy. *Archives of Neurology*, 1976, *33*, 559–570.

Cooper, I. S., Riklan, M., Amin, I., Waltz, J. M., & Cullinan, T. Chronic cerebellar stimulation in cerebral palsy. *Neurology*, 1976, *26*(8), 774–753.

Debakan, A. *Neurology of infancy.* Baltimore: Williams & Wilkins, 1959.

Dodrill, C. B. A neurophysiological battery for epilepsy. *Epilepsies*, 1978, *19*, 611–623.

Epilepsy Foundation of America. *Basic statistics on the epilepsies.* Philadelphia: F. A. Davis, 1975.

Epilepsy Foundation of America. *Survey, 1979.* Washington, D.C.: Author, 1979.

Epstein, A., & Ervin, F. Psychodynamic significance of seizure content in psychomotor epilepsy. *Psychosomatic Medicine*, 1956, *18*, 43–55.

Farmer, T. W. *Pediatric neurology.* New York: Harper & Row, 1964.

Forster, F. M. *Reflex epilepsy: Behavioral therapy and conditional reflexes.* Springfield, Ill.: Charles C. Thomas, 1977.

Freedman, A. M., & Kaplan, H. I. (Eds.). *Comprehensive textbook of psychiatry.* Baltimore: Williams & Wilkins, 1967.

Fremont-Smith, F. The influence of emotion in precipitating convulsions (a preliminary report). *American Journal of Psychiatry*, 1934, *13*(4), 717–719.

Fukuyama, Y., Arima, M., Nagahata, M., & Okada, R. Medical treatment of the epilepsies in childhood: A long term survey of 801 patients. *Epilepsia*, 1963, *4*, 207–224.

Gastaut, H. Clinical and electroencephalographical classification of epileptic seizures. *Epilepsia*, 1970, *11*, 102–113.

Glaser, G. H. Limbic epilepsy in childhood. *Journal of Nervous and Mental Disease*, 1967, *144*, 391–397.

Gottschalk, L. A. Effects of intensive psychotherapy on epileptic children: Report on three children with idiopathic epilepsy. *American Medical Association Archives of Neurology and Psychiatry*, 1953, *70*, 461–384.

Greenson, R. R. On genuine epilepsy. *Psychoanalytic Quarterly*, 1944, *13*, 139–159.

Hermann, B. P. Psychological effects of epilepsy: A review. Abstracted in the Journal Supplement Abstract Service *Catalog of Selected Documents in Psychology*, MS 1430, 1977, 1(i), 16.

Holvey, D. N. (Ed.). *Merck manual of diagnosis and therapy*. Rahway, N.J.: Merck, Sharp & Dohme Research Laboratories, 1972.

Jensen, R. A. The importance of the emotional factor in the convulsive disorders of children (a preliminary report). *American Journal of Psychiatry*, 1947, *104*, 126–131.

Lennox, W. G., & Markham, C. H. *The sociopsychological treatment of epilepsy. The Journal of the American Medical Association*, 1953, *152*, 1690–1694.

Livingston, S. *Comprehensive management of epilepsy in infancy, childhood, and adolescence*. Springfield, Ill.: Charles C. Thomas, 1972.

Livingston, S. *The diagnosis and treatment of convulsive disorders in children*. Springfield, Ill.: Charles C. Thomas, 1954.

Lovaas, I. Letter to editor. *Psychology Today*, November 1970, *4*, 4.

Magnus, O., & DeHaas, A. M. L. The epilepsies. In P. J. Vinken & G. W. Bruyn (Eds.), *Handbook of clinical neurology* (Vol. 15). New York: Elsevier, 1974.

Miller, N. Learning of visceral and glandular responses. *Science*, 1969, *163*, 433–445.

Millon, T. *Modern psychopathology: A biosocial approach to maladaptive learning and functioning*. Philadelphia: W. B. Saunders, 1969.

Mostofsky, D. I. Behavior modification and the psychosomatic aspects of epilepsy. In D. Upper & D. S. Goodenough (Eds.), *Behavior modification with the individual patient*. Nutley, N.J.: Roche Laboratories, 1972.

Mostofsky, D. I., & Balaschak, B. A. Psychobiological control of seizures. *Psychological Bulletin*, 1977, *84*, 4, 723–250.

Parrino, J. J. Reduction of seizures by desensitization. *Journal of Behavior Therapy and Experimental Psychiatry*, 1971, *2*, 215–218.

Pincus, J. H., & Tucker, G. J. *Behavioral neurology* (2nd ed.). New York: Oxford University Press, 1978.

Rodin, E. A. Medical and social prognosis in epilepsy. *Epilepsia*, 1972, *13*, 121–131.

Small, J. G., Stevens, J. R., & Milstein, V. Electro-clinical correlates of emotional activation of the electroencephalogram. *Journal of Nervous and Mental Disease*, 1964, *138*, 146–155.

Solomon, G. E., & Plum, F. *Clinical management of seizures*. Philadelphia: W. B. Saunders, 1976.

Stevens, J. R. Emotional activation of the electroencephalogram in patients with convulsive disorders. *Journal of Nervous and Mental Disease*, 1959, *128*, 339–351.

Sutherland, J. M., Tait, H., & Eadie, M. J. *The epilepsies: Modern diagnosis and treatment*. Edinburgh and London: Churchill-Livingston, 1974.

Williams, D. T., Spiegel, H. I., & Mostofsky, D. I. Neurogenic and hysterical seizures in children and adolescents: Differential diagnostic and therapeutic considerations. *American Journal of Psychiatry*, 1978, *135*, 82–86.

# SLEEP DISTURBANCE IN CHILDREN AND ADOLESCENTS

**Thomas J. Coates**
*The Johns Hopkins University School of Medicine*

**Carl E. Thoresen**
*Stanford University*

> Once in every four-and-twenty hours, the gay and the gloomy, the witty and the dull, the clamorous and the silent, the busy and the idle, are all overpowered by the gentle tyrant, and all lie down in the equality of sleep.
>
> SAMUEL JOHNSON

Equality, however, extends only to those who can experience sleep easily.

> How many thousand of my poorest subjects
> Are at this hour asleep! O Sleep, O Gentle Sleep,
> Nature's soft nurse, how have I frighted thee,
> That thou no more wilt weigh my eyelids down
> And steep my senses in forgetfulness?
>
> (HENRY IV, III, i, 4–31)

Disturbances in sleep are nondiscriminatory, affecting not only adults but also the youngest of children, sometimes with merciless intensity. What to do about these disturbances may presume an understanding of what causes them, which, in turn, may assume the foundation of basic knowledge about sleep. Sleep is common among humans, and sleep disorders are not uncommon. Despite these shared experiences, we know relatively little about sleep, less about sleep disorders in adults, and frightfully little about assessing and treating sleep disorders in children and adolescents.

This lack of information regarding assessment and treatment (especially using behavioral science perspectives and tools) makes it all the more urgent that more persons become involved in this area. In this chapter we have attempted to wed existing knowledge with a perspective on sleep and sleep disorders in young persons that might suggest important assessment questions leading eventually to more useful clinical strategies and research programs.

## THE PROCESS VIEW OF SLEEP

The "process view" of sleep suggests that an adequate account of sleep phenomena can be derived only when sleep is viewed as one part of a person's 24-hour sleep–wake cycle (Dement & Mitler, 1976). The biological clock found in all organisms accounts for variations in man in hormone secretion, body temperature, cardiac output, venous pressure, urine secretion, and enzyme synthesis over a 24-hour period. Factors in the environment (e.g., light and dark) termed *Zeitgebers* apparently pace these biological rhythms but do not act as their immediate cause, much as a discriminative stimulus ($S^D$) cues, but does not cause, behavior. Circadian rhythms seem to be inherent in the structural nature of organisms (cf. Aschoff, 1965).

The process view has two important implications for assessing and treating sleep disorders:

1. Sleep and disorders associated with sleep can be understood best as they are related to and studied within the context of these circadian cycles.
2. Because rapid-eye-movement (REM) sleep, non-rapid-eye-movement (NREM) sleep, and wakefulness are linked and interdependent components of overall cycles, assessment and treatment of sleep disorders require that *daytime* as well as *nighttime* variables be considered. Behaviors, thoughts, moods, environments, and biological functions need to be studied and may need to be modified.

In light of these implications, the term *sleep disorder* may be misleading, implying problems only with sleep. We prefer to call this class of problems *behaviors and complaints associated with sleep*. The disorders are associated with, or occur during, sleep, but their cause and treatment may be linked to waking states as well.

## NORMAL SLEEP: A BACKGROUND PERSPECTIVE

"Normal" sleep is divided into two relatively different states: *REM sleep* and *NREM sleep*. NREM sleep is composed of sleep Stages 1, 2, 3, and 4. These are distinguished from one another primarily by electroencephalogram (EEG) patterns and the subject's responsiveness to the external environment.

Figure 1 presents EEG, electrooculogram (EOG), and electromyogram (EMG) tracings from laboratory and home recordings typical of each sleep stage. Wakefulness prior to sleep onset is characterized by alpha in the EEG (8–12 cps) and by random eye movements. As a person enters sleep, Stage 1 appears first and is characterized by slow, rolling eye movements and low-amplitude, mixed-frequency (3–7 cps) EEG activity. Stage 1 sleep is sometimes viewed as a transition from

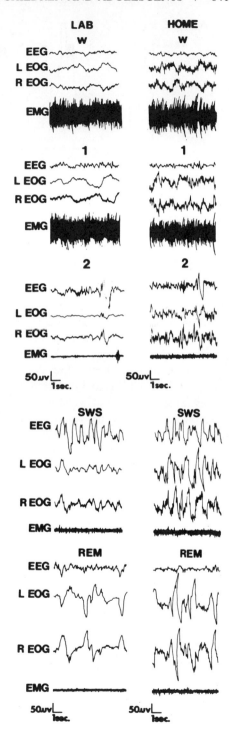

FIGURE 1

States and stages of sleep recorded at home and in the lab for a normal 30-year-old male sleeper. From "Telephone Transmission of Polysomnographic Data from Subjects' Homes by Telephone" by M. R. Rosekind, T. J. Coates, and C. E. Thoresen, *Journal of Nervous and Mental Disease*, 1978, *166*, 438–441. Copyright 1978 by the Williams & Wilkins Co. Reprinted by permission.

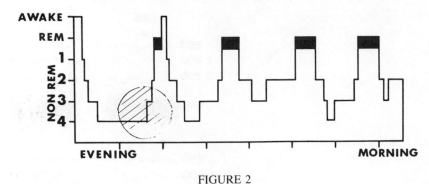

FIGURE 2

Progression of sleep throughout the night for an idealized child. Notice that REM periods (shaded areas) become longer and that Stages 3 and 4 sleep decrease as the night progresses. The shaded area in the circle represents the time during which the disorders of arousal (enuresis, somnambulism, *pavor nocturnus*) tend to occur.

wakefulness to sleep; mental and physiological activity is still quite pronounced (Johnson, 1975). Stage 2 sleep is characterized by sleep spindles (13–16 cps lasting .5 to 2 seconds) and K-complexes (sharp rise and fall in the brain wave pattern). Delta waves (.5 to 2 cps; 75 $\mu$V in amplitude) characterize Stages 3 and 4 (slow-wave or delta) sleep. These slow and high-amplitude brain waves signal that brain activity is reduced. Stage 3 is scored when 20% to 50% of the EEG contains delta waves. Stage 4 is scored when more than 50% of the EEG contains delta waves. Physiological activity and responsiveness to the external environment diminish as the person progresses from NREM Stage 1 to Stage 4 sleep.

REM sleep is characterized by fast, sawtoothed waves in the EEG; rapid, strong eye movements in the EOG; and absence of muscle tension in the EMG.

Figure 2 presents a histogram showing the progression of sleep through the night for an idealized 10- to 12-year-old child. He or she lies awake for a brief period; sleep onset occurs rapidly. Slow-wave (Stages 3–4) sleep predominates in the early part of the night. After 60–90 minutes, the child experiences a brief period of Stage 2 sleep, followed immediately by the first REM period of the night. The cycle is repeated through the night. Periods of slow-wave sleep become shorter and shorter toward morning, whereas REM sleep beings to predominate as morning approaches.

Sleep changes markedly with age. Sleep in the newborn infant can be classified into only three sleep states: *active REM, quiet sleep* (the precursor to NREM sleep), and *indeterminate sleep* (Anders, Emde, & Parmelee, 1971). At birth, REM sleep occupies 40–50% of total sleep time, quiet sleep occupies 35–45%, and indeterminate sleep occupies 10–15%. By 3 months of age, quiet sleep EEG patterns can begin to be classified into NREM Stages 1, 2, 3, and 4 (Metcalf, 1972). REM decreases to about 30% in the latter 6 months of the first year (Petre-Quadens, 1966). On the average, neonates spend 17 of 24 hours sleeping at birth, and 14 or 15 hours at the 15th week. After this, total sleep time declines gradually (Parmelee, 1974; Parmelee, Schultz, & Disbrow, 1961).

Table 1 presents some common sleep variables that change with maturation. REM sleep decreases and number of awakenings increase throughout childhood. Considerable variability is found among subjects on some variables (e.g., time in bed, total sleep time). Time in bed and total sleep time decrease at the beginning of the school years (6–9 years) and again in adolescence, with no decrease in sleep efficiency (minutes of sleep divided by minutes in bed). Of special interest is the dramatic decrease in total sleep time during adolescence. Anders, Carskadon, Dement, and Harvey (1978) surveyed 218 children from 10 to 13 years. They found that sleep on nonschool nights tended to remain constant between these ages, whereas sleep on school nights decreased significantly in 12- and 13-year-olds. They suggested that extreme sleepiness found in older adolescents may be related to cumulative sleep deprivation imposed by social and other demands. Clearly, more studies of the natural history of sleep and sleepiness among children and adolescents need to be completed.

It should be noted that the data presented in Table 1 are from *small samples* of subjects recorded for only two nights in one laboratory. They may not represent sleep under other conditions, as normal sleepers have complained about sleeping more poorly in the lab than at home (Frankel, Coursey, Buchbinder, & Snyder, 1976), and sleep recorded in the home may be different from sleep recorded in the lab (Coates, Rosekind, Strossen, Thoresen, & Kirmil-Gray, 1979). Additional studies of the sleep of normal children are needed to establish a normative base.[1]

### Behaviors and Complaints Associated with Sleep

Table 2 lists specific complaints associated with sleep observed commonly in infants, young children, and adolescents. Figure 2 illustrates where some of these behaviors and complaints occur during sleep.

Bixler, Kales, Scharf, Kales, and Leo (1976) provided data on the incidence of these behaviors and complaints in general practice. A total of 4358 physicians nationwide were surveyed and asked to report the percentage of patients presenting these specific problems. Pediatricians and child psychiatrists, respectively, reported the following percentages: insomnia, 5.3% and 19.4%; hypersomnia, 1.3% and 5.2%; narcolepsy, .2% and .2%; enuresis, 7.5% and 10.8%; somnambulism, 1.5% and 1.4%; nightmares, 7.8% and 18.3%; and night terrors, 2.4% and 5.5%.

Teeth grinding, sleep talking, and head banging can occur during any state or stage of sleep during any part of the night. Night terrors, nocturnal enuresis, and sleepwalking are termed *disorders of arousal* because they appear to be as-

---

[1]Some data on the sleep of normal children are being collected at Western Psychiatric Institute and Clinic at the University of Pittsburgh by David Kupfer, MD, and Patricia Coble, RN. Mary Carskadon and William Dement, MD, PhD, at Stanford University Sleep Disorders Clinic are also studying normal children longitudinally (cf. Carskadon *et al.*, 1978; Carskadon, Harvey, & Dement, 1977).

TABLE 1

Average Values on Common Sleep Variables for Males in Various Age Groupings

| Variable | 3–5 years (n = 10) | 6–9 years (n = 12) | 10–12 years (n = 13) | 13–15 years (n = 10) | 16–19 years (n = 13) |
|---|---|---|---|---|---|
| Total time in bed[a] | 633.4 (41.1) | 589.8 (20.1)[b] | 585 (24.3) | 510.6 (15.7)[c] | 475.2 (25.5)[c] |
| Total sleep time[a] | 610.6 (36.6) | 572.9 (20.3)[b] | 557.5 (23.9) | 488.8 (11.9)[c] | 448.6 (31.1)[c] |
| Sleep efficiency | .96 (.03) | .97 (.02) | .95 (.02) | .96 (.02) | .94 (.03) |
| Number of awakenings | 1.25 (1.11) | .67 (.86) | 1.58 (1.15)[d] | 3.2 (2.66) | 2.81 (1.80) |
| Percentage of time in REM sleep | 30.3 (3.6) | 27.3 (3.5) | 26.4 (1.9) | 26.7 (3.1) | 22 (3.3)[b] |
| Number of REM periods | 6.7 (.75) | 5.5 (.64)[b] | 5.1 (.96) | 4.7 (.47) | 4 (.75)[d] |

Note. Adapted from findings for males in each age group reported in Williams, Karacan, and Hursch (1974).

[a]Times are given in minutes.

[b]Indicates significant difference from immediately younger age group (p < .01 level).

[c]Indicates significant difference from immediately younger age group (p < .001 level).

[d]Indicates significant difference from immediately younger age group (p < .05 level).

TABLE 2
Behaviors and Complaints Associated with Sleep Observed in Children and Adolescents

| Behavior or complaint | Description |
|---|---|
| Insomnia | A complaint of daytime fatigue attributed to poor sleep at night; poor sleep can be marked by difficulty in falling asleep, difficulty in staying asleep, short total sleep time, or combinations of these difficulties. |
| Hypersomnia (excessive daytime sleepiness) | Excessive sleepiness during the day or excessively long sleep at night with difficulty in awakening. |
| Narcolepsy | Recurrent daytime episodes of irresistible drowsiness and sleep. May be associated with the "narcoleptic tetrad": <br>• Cataplexy—sudden loss of muscle tone, with person falling to the ground while maintaining consciousness <br>• Sleep paralysis—sudden awareness while falling asleep or during sleep that one cannot move or talk <br>• Hypnogogic hallucinations—vivid visual or auditory imagery occurring at sleep onset |
| Sleep apnea | An apnea is defined as cessation of airflow at the nostrils and mouth lasting at least 10 seconds. Sleep apnea is diagnosed if at least 30 apneic episodes are observed in REM and NREM sleep during 7 hours of nocturnal sleep. |
| Nocturnal bruxism | Repetitive teeth grinding or jaw clenching during sleep. |
| Somniloquy (sleep talking) | Spontaneous talk during NREM or REM sleep. |
| Nightmares | Arousal and fright characterized by elaborate dream content usually during REM sleep. |
| *Jactatio capitus nocturna* (head banging) | Rhythmical rocking movements of the head or body before or during sleep. Believed to be voluntary, even though the person does not remember them in the morning. Can occur during REM and slow-wave sleep. |
| *Pavor nocturnus* (night terrors) | Person sits up in bed and screams, appears to be staring at an imaginary object, breathes heavily, perspires; immediate dream recall is fragmentary, and there is amnesia for the event in the morning. Usually experiences tachycardia and rapid heart rates during the episodes, usually during NREM sleep. |
| Nocturnal enuresis (bed wetting) | Bed wetting at night: primary—person has |

*(continued)*

TABLE 2 *(continued)*

| Behavior or complaint | Description |
| --- | --- |
| | never developed bladder control; secondary—bladder control gained but lost; usually associated in children with arousal from Stage 3/4 to the first REM period; sleep stage change is often associated with increased body movements, heart rate, erection in males, and bed wetting. |
| Somnambulism (sleepwalking) | A body movement followed by the person sitting up in bed, with the eyes open and glassy, staring straight ahead; the person may get up and manipulate objects; person is generally uncommunicative. |

sociated with atypical arousal patterns in slow-wave sleep. Episodes of night terrors, sleepwalking, or enuresis begin in Stage 4 sleep with a burst of rhythmic delta waves, followed by a body movement and a transition to Stage 1 or Stage 2 sleep (Broughton, 1968). The episode follows. Night terrors and nightmares are distinguished in terms of several factors (cf. Table 3). Night terrors are a phenomenon of NREM sleep, whereas nightmares are associated with dreaming activity in REM sleep.

*Insomnia* is a common descriptive term used to refer to perceived or actual impairment in sleep that can include difficulty in falling to sleep, difficulty in maintaining sleep, or premature awakening. The complaint of insomnia in adolescents and adults is usually associated with complaints of daytime fatigue, irritability, or depression. Younger persons may experience disrupted sleep at night without complaining of impairment in daytime function.[2]

*Hypersomnia* refers to a general complaint of excessive daytime sleepiness, whereas *narcolepsy* and *sleep apnea* refer to specific syndromes that can impair sleep at night and cause excessive sleepiness during the day (Zarcone, 1977). Most disorders generally come to the attention of physicians because of the inconvenience and worry they cause parents. The "sleepy" child, however, is seldom bothersome and often is not even viewed as having a disorder. Consequently, in spite of the potential deleterious effects of excessive sleepiness, the child may not receive treatment, and professionals have given little attention to the problem.

---

[2]The relationship of chronic fatigue and stress has not yet been systematically studied with sleep complaints. Jenkins (1978) reports that the single most common correlate of chronic stress in adults (e.g., "Type A" behavior pattern) is the complaint of insomnia. Thomas (1976) also found stress-related problems highly associated with complaints about sleep (e.g., onset and reawakenings among medical students). It is not known at present if chronic stress in children and adolescents is similarly related.

TABLE 3
Factors Distinguishing Nightmares and Night Terrors

| Factor | Night terrors | Nightmares |
|--------|---------------|------------|
| EEG | Associated with transition from Stage 3 or 4 to Stage 2, usually in the first third of the night. | Associated with a REM period in any part of the night. |
| Mental content | Vague: overwhelming feeling of anxiety. Person is confused and disoriented when awakened. | Elaborate, vivid. Person can recall dream vividly when awakened. |
| Movement | Thrashing | Little or no movement |
| Physiology | Rapid increase in pulse and respiration rate, intense autonomic activity (e.g., sweating). | Gradual increase in pulse (typical of REM sleep) but no major change in autonomic activity. |

*Note.* Adapted from Keith (1975).

# ASSESSMENT AND ACTION: INTEGRATING MEDICAL AND BEHAVIORAL APPROACHES

Behaviors and complaints associated with sleep are complex phenomena potentially related to a variety of biological, psychological, and environmental conditions. These three classes of variables should be considered in designing treatment or research programs for the individual case or in selecting homogeneous groups for research or group treatment. Figure 3 presents an algorithm for a comprehensive assessment of possible medical and behavioral factors responsible for initiating or maintaining behaviors and complaints associated with sleep.

## Medical Examination

Once the child or his or her parents, teachers, or siblings complain, a medical examination is indicated. Many of the behaviors and complaints listed in Table 3 can be associated with kidney, liver, or thyroid disorders or anemia, brain tumors, epilepsy, or hyperglycemia. Any condition associated with pain or other discomfort at night should also be investigated. Similarly, nutritional disorders, as well as low-grade poisonings, allergies, asthma, and bronchial distress, can influence sleep and sleepiness (Williams, Karacan, & Hursch, 1974). Guilleminault and Dement (1977) suggested that a "normal" physical examination is usually sufficient. If physical illness is not obvious, it seems reasonable that the sleep complaint is primary, and assessment and treatment should continue on this assumption.

During the medical examination, it is important to inquire about the possibility

Complaint of sleep disturbance by child, parents, teachers, etc.

Medical examination

- Physical history and medical examination to assess if disturbance is secondary to physical disorder

  If illness is not obvious, assume that sleep disturbance is primary complaint and continue assessment and treatment.

- Interview with parents and child to assess if disturbance may be secondary to neurological dysfunction.

  If neurological dysfunction is obvious or suspected (by interview, diaries, and tape recordings), refer person to competent sleep specialist for further diagnosis and appropriate treatment.

Assessment of drug use

- To determine if complaint is a result of the use of hypnotics or stimulants (including alcohol).

  If excessive hypnotics and/or stimulants are used, consult physician about considering gradual withdrawal regimen.

All-night sleep recording

- May be needed in selected cases to provide more definitive diagnosis.
- Essential in research to document nature and extent of disturbed sleep.
- May be helpful in clinical practice to document nature of sleep disturbance.

Behavior analysis

- Use variety of assessment methods to determine cognitive, behavioral, and environmental patterns potentially related to sleep disturbance.

  Structured interviews with child.

  Structured interviews with significant others (parents, teachers, siblings).

  Self-report.

  Direct observation by parents, nurses, or observers.

  Time-lapse photography.

  Audiotape recordings.

FIGURE 3

Steps in assessing behaviors and complaints associated with sleep. Adapted from Coates and Thoresen (1980).

of narcolepsy and sleep apnea if the complaint involves excessive daytime sleepiness and/or poor sleep at night.

### Narcolepsy

The narcolepsy syndrome involves excessive daytime sleepiness, sleep episodes, and cataplexy, with or without sleep paralysis, frightening hypnogogic hallucinations, and disturbed nocturnal sleep (Guilleminault & Dement, 1977). Children with narcolepsy may also present a history of sleeping excessively at night. Bruhova and Roth (1972) estimated prevalence in the general population at 2 per 1000, whereas Dement, Carskadon, and Ley (1973) estimated prevalence at 5 times this rate. Other estimates suggest that there are from 40,000 to 80,000 persons with narcolepsy in the United States (Zarcone, 1975). The prevalence of narcolepsy in children is not known because the question has never been asked.

Narcolepsy is frequently first observed in adolescence. Yoss and Daly (1975) reported that of 241 narcolepsy patients, 22 showed symptoms before age 10, whereas more than 80 others showed symptoms before age 20. Kessler, Guilleminault, and Dement (1974) reported that the mean age of onset in 50 patients was 19.4 years, with 60% of the sample reporting onset before age 20. Narcolepsy also seems to be family-related. Kessler et al. (1974) reported that 52% of their samples showed positive family history. Krabbe and Magnussen (1942) found that 54 cases out of 300 clustered into 19 families, with two to eight afflicted members per family.

In preliminary diagnosis of narcolepsy, the child or significant others can be questioned in two areas: "Does he or she experience *sudden* and *irresistible* urges to sleep during the day?" "Does he or she have peculiar attacks of muscular weakness brought on by strong emotions such as laughter, anger, or fright?" Further questions about hallucinations and sleep paralysis may be asked. If facilities are available, daytime and nighttime sleep recordings may help with accurate diagnosis. Narcoleptic patients show REM periods at sleep onset (Rechtschaffen, Wolpert, Dement, Mitchell, & Fisher, 1963; Dement, Zarcone, Guilleminault, Carskadon, Hoddes et al., 1973). If the syndrome is suspected, the client can be referred to a competent specialist for definitive diagnosis and medical management.[3]

The usual treatment involves drugs such as stimulants and REM suppressants. Because of the syndrome's probable neurological determination, it may not be possible to dispense with drug therapy altogether. It may be feasible, however, to combine drug and behavior therapy to provide better management at lower drug levels. It would seem useful to use a behavior analysis to identify situations leading to sleepiness, cataplexy and perhaps drug overuse and then to teach the person procedures for managing narcoleptic symptoms without overreliance on medications.

---

[3]See Coates and Thoresen (1977) and Hauri (1977) for a listing of sleep disorders clinics in the United States. The Association of Sleep Disorders Centers (Stanford University Sleep Disorders Clinic, Stanford University, Stanford, Calif. 94305) also maintains a listing of accredited clinics.

### Sleep Apnea

An *apnea* is defined as a cessation of airflow at the nostrils and mouth lasting at least 10 seconds. Sleep apnea is diagnosed if at least 30 episodes are observed during 7 hours of nocturnal sleep. The prevalence of sleep apnea is also unknown, but it has been related to sudden infant death syndrome (Guilleminault *et al.*, 1975) and has also been documented in young children. Guilleminault, Eldridge, Simmons, and Dement (1976) reported symptoms present in 8 children: snoring (8 of 8), nocturnal enuresis (7 of 8), decreased school performance (5 of 8), morning headaches (5 of 8), emotional problems (4 of 8), hyperactivity (3 of 8), refusal to go to bed (3 of 8), underweight (5 of 8), overweight (2 of 8), and hypertension (5 of 8).

The child of his or her significant others can be questioned about the occurrence of heavy snoring at night. In particular, *sleep apnea is characterized by lapses in breathing followed by a snoring gasp for air*. If significant others are uncertain, 1- or 2-hour observations, combined with audiotape recordings while the child is sleeping, can be used to diagnose the disorder (Guilleminault & Dement, 1977). All-night sleep recordings with nasal thermistors to detect airflow and strain gauges to detect diaphragm movement are definitive. If the disorder is suspected, the person can be referred to a specialist competent to carry out the necessary treatments, such as tonsillectomy, adenoidectomy, or tracheotomy (Guilleminault, Tilikan, & Dement, 1976).

### Assessment of Drug History and Drug Use

Complaints of disturbed sleep and daytime sleepiness can be secondary to chronic or occasional use of stimulants, tranquilizers, or a variety of drugs that alter sleep. Careful questioning should be pursued in order to document all prescription and over-the-counter medication, alcoholic beverages, and drugs and foods potentially stimulating or tranquilizing to the person. The *Physicians' Desk Reference* (PDR), which is published annually, describes potential side-effects of any prescription drugs distributed legally in the United States. (Note, however, that the PDR is not a vigorous or critical source of scientific data or analysis of drugs.)

Drug-dependent insomnia, common among adults in the United States, refers to insomnia maintained by the chronic use of hypnotics or tranquilizers. Ironically, most sleep medications make sleep worse rather than better (Kales & Kales, 1974), since persons habituate rapidly, requiring larger doses to maintain sleep of any kind. At the same time, the person becomes dependent on the medication, so that sleep without the drug is worse than when the person began to use the medication to obtain relief (Coates & Thoresen, 1978).

The natural history of hypnotic drug use has not been documented systematically, but some preliminary data suggest that many persons might begin use in adolescence (Kales, 1971). Abelson *et al.* (1977) surveyed a random probability sample; 2.9% of the 12- to 17-year-olds reported using a sedative or tranquilizer during the past month, whereas 6.9% reported drug use during the past year. Price, Coates, Thoresen, and Grinstead (1978) surveyed 629 12th-grade students; 12% reported frequent sleep problems, and another 37.6% reported occasional sleep disturbance three or fewer times per week. In the sample, 20% of the chronic poor sleepers and 5% of the occasional poor sleepers had begun to use medications at least occasionally. Kirmil-Gray, Coates, Thoresen, and Rosekind (1978) reported that adolescents used caffeinated remedies (cola, aspirin, cocoa), high-sugared foods (cocoa, ice cream), and prescription and over-the-counter medications in attempting to relieve sleep problems.

Finally, some medications prescribed for other problems may affect sleep. Antihistamines, for example, can cause drowsiness during the day and perhaps the perception that sleep at night is poor. Cold remedies (e.g., codeine) can suppress REM. The person may then experience "REM rebound," an increase in REM accompanied by vivid dreams and nightmares later in the night or when drug use is terminated.

## The All-Night Sleep Recording

The all-night sleep recording is a continuous polysomnographic recording of the EEG, the EOG, and the EMG. Other physiological functions can also be monitored, depending upon specific research or treatment objectives. These include the electrocardiogram (ECG), respiration using nasal and mouth thermistors, diaphragm movement using strain gauges, movement of the lower extremities using EMG leads on the legs, frontalis or massetcr EMG, and blood pressure.

At least three functions must be monitored so that sleep states and stages can be discriminated (Rechtschaffen & Kales, 1968).[4] The EEG is recorded from the two central positions (C3 and C4) and sometimes from the two occipital positions (O1 and O2), according to the 10–20 Jaspar International System. The EOG is recorded from the outer canthi of the eyes, and the EMG is recorded from the digastric chin muscles. Two reference electrodes (A1 and A2) are placed on the ear lobes or mastoids. Once electrodes are in place, the subject retires to a relatively quiet bedroom. The electrode leads are gathered into a ponytail behind the subject's head and plugged into a headboard that leads to a polygraph. A technician remains on duty throughout the night to monitor the equipment and attend to subject needs. While the subject tries to sleep, a continuous record of the person's EEG, eye movements, and muscle tension is printed out on a polygraph is an adjoining room.

Table 4 lists some common measures derived from the all-night sleep recording. Each of these can be used in several ways, depending upon the purposes of the assessment. First, values can be compared to norms to determine if the person deviates in significant ways from values obtained in normative studies. A child

---

[4]Rechtschaffen and Kales (1968) is the standard reference for scoring states and stages of sleep in adults. Anders, Emde, and Parmelee (1971) have developed a similar standardized guide for scoring sleep stages in infants.

TABLE 4

Common Measures Obtained from All-Night Sleep Recordings

| Recording | Measure |
| --- | --- |
| Total sleep time | Total time person is asleep while in bed. |
| Time in bed | Time from when the subject is settled in bed and the light is turned out until the polygraph is turned off in the morning so that the subject may arise. |
| Sleep efficiency | Total sleep time divided by time in bed. |
| Minutes spent in each sleep stage | Total minutes spent in NREM Stages 1, 2, 3, 4 or in REM. |
| Percentage in each sleep stage | Number of minutes in each stage divided by total sleep time. |
| Latency to sleep onset | The time from lights out until the appearance of the first sleep stage. |
| Number of awakenings | Number of times subject reaches full wakefulness. |
| Wake time after sleep onset | Amount of time subject is awake after sleep onset. |

showing relatively little deep or REM sleep, for example, would be considered quite atypical. Second, many of these variables relate to quality of sleep, and specific types of problems could lead to different treatment programs. Difficulty in falling to sleep might be treated differently than a problem in maintaining sleep. Third, the recording can be used to pinpoint sleep disturbance phenomena. We noted previously, for example, the importance of discriminating between nightmares and night terrors. Nightmares might respond to a procedure such as systematic desensitization, whereas night terrors might require nocturnal biofeedback or response interruption methods.

As might be expected, all-night sleep recordings can alter sleep. "First night" effects are common: sleep on the first, and sometimes the second, night in the laboratory is more disrupted than sleep on subsequent nights in that setting (Agnew, Webb, & Williams, 1966; Karacan, Anch, Thornby, Okawa, & Williams, 1975). Scharf, Kales, and Bixler (1975) also found that persons returning to the lab for a second series of consecutive recordings after sleeping at home for one week needed one night to readapt to the laboratory. Persons who were accustomed to sleeping with a bed partner showed more Stage 4 and less REM sleep than when they slept alone in the laboratory (Monroe, 1969). Good sleepers have reported that sleep in the lab is generally worse than at home (Frankel et al., 1976). Infants also need to adapt when brought to the laboratory so that their sleep can be monitored. REM sleep can be decreased (Bernstein, Emde, & Campos, 1973) and rhythms of active and quiet sleep disrupted until a period of adaptation has been completed (Sostek, Anders, & Sostek, 1975).

Procedures have been developed to move the "sleep laboratory" to persons' homes so that more naturalistic and perhaps generalizable estimates of persons' sleep can be obtained. Rosekind, Coates, and Thoresen (1978), for example, developed a system for transmitting all-night EEG data from subjects' homes by telephone. A transmission unit, housed in a suitcase and powered by four 6-volt batteries, amplifies and transmits eight separate channels of biological signal over a single telephone line. The signal is received at the central laboratory where the record can be written out on a polygraph or stored on magnetic tape. A technician remains on duty to monitor the recording. The transmission unit is also equipped with a microphone for two-way voice communication between the subject at home and the technician in the laboratory.

To use this system, the technician goes to the subject's home in the evening and attaches the full electrode array needed to complete the all-night sleep recording. The individual electrodes are plugged into a master headboard, which interfaces with the transmitter via a polarized plug. The technician can depart at any time. When ready to retire, the subject goes to bed, inserts the plug, informs the lab technician that the lights are being turned out, and sleeps (or stays awake) in accustomed surroundings.

Other home-based systems involve the use of multichannel FM tape recorders left in the home overnight. The technician returns in the morning, retrieves the tape, and takes it to the laboratory where it is written out or analyzed on-line by a computer (Ellis, Randall, Johns, & Dudley, 1976). Wilkinson and Mullaney (1976) adapted the Medilog, a four-channel cassette recorder, to record the EEG, EMG, and EOG. Frost and Delucchi (1975) described an easy method for applying electrodes. A snug cap, which fits over the head, contained prefilled electrolyte-saturated rubber electrodes fitted and positioned precisely for the subject. No technician was required at bedtime. When ready to retire, the subject placed the cap on his head, plugged himself into the FM recorder, and retired. Home-based sleep recordings could supplement laboratory studies in important ways. It is commonly reported from laboratory studies, for example, that noise will not disrupt sleep, especially if the noise is constant (Ruckebusch, 1977). Globus, Friedman, and Cohen (1973), however, found that in home recordings, the sleep of people living for 6 years in the Los Angeles area was still disturbed by jet noise.

Coates et al. (1979) compared the sleep of eight insomniacs who had received self-management training when their sleep was recorded at home and when it was recorded in a laboratory. Significant differences were found between mean values on four parameters (minutes of Stage 3 sleep, percentage of Stage 2 sleep, percentage of Stage 3 sleep, number of REM periods). Variances on two parameters (total sleep time, latency to sleep onset) were greater in the laboratory than at home. These data indicated that recordings in different locations may yield different values on some variables for groups of persons and for some individuals within those groups.

EXEMPLARY APPLICATION:
TREATING THE COMPLAINTS OF INSOMNIA IN ADOLESCENTS

Kirmil-Gray et al. (1978) reported three case studies of treatments for the complaint of insomnia in young persons. Subjects were three adolescents (male, aged 16; females, aged 16 and 17). All complained of difficulty in initiating and maintaining sleep and of fatigue and depression during the day.

Laboratory baseline sleep recordings were quite essential in designing treatment programs for these persons. The male did not show short or abnormal sleep. He was referred to a counseling institute so that his complaints and problems could be pinpointed directly and programs appropriate to his needs could be developed and implemented. Focusing on sleep in the absence of the sleep recording may have led to unproductive counseling and client frustration.

The 17-year-old female (Client 1) showed difficulty in falling asleep and an unusual number of awakenings during the night, while the 16-year-old female (Client 2) showed difficulty in falling asleep. Because difficulty in falling asleep is treated easily using relaxation (Killen & Coates, 1979), Client 1 was given eight sessions of progressive muscle relaxation training. Sleep-maintenance insomnia has been much more resistant to treatment (Coates & Thoresen, 1980; Thoresen, Coates, Zarcone, Kirmil-Gray, & Rosekind, 1980) and may be related to excessive mental activity at night due to unresolved daytime worries and anxieties (Coates & Thoresen, 1979). For that reason, Client 2 was given 16 sessions that combined relaxation with training and guided practice in problem solving. Sleep recordings immediately following treatment (laboratory only) and at follow-up (laboratory and home) confirmed the maintained and generalized efficacy of these treatment programs (cf. Table 5).

## The Importance and Inherent Limitation of Sleep Recordings

Modern sleep research is built on the all-night EEG. The sleep recording has enabled researchers and clinicians to advance knowledge and treatment of behaviors and complaints associated with sleep. Narcolepsy and sleep apnea, discussed earlier, represent two areas in which understanding was facilitated by the sleep recording. As a second example, identifying nightmares associated with REM sleep and night terrors (along with enuresis and somnambulism as associated with NREM sleep) may lead to different treatments for each.

SELF-REPORT. Studies of behavioral treatments for sleep disorders have relied primarily on self-reported sleep to document outcomes (Coates & Thoresen, 1980; Thoresen et al., 1980). Studies of the correspondence between reported and recorded sleep have been conducted only with adults, but they might shed some light on issues for assessing sleep in young persons.

Self-reports have been disparaged and all-night sleep recordings have been exalted as an "objective" measure of sleep (Carskadon, Dement, Mitler, Guilleminault, Zarcone, & Spiegel, 1976; Dement, 1972; Weiss, McPartland, & Kupfer, 1973). Individuals vary in the degree to which reported and recorded sleep agree. In studying a sample of 122 drug-free adult insomniacs, Carskadon et al. (1976) reported that there were 21 persons whose estimates of total sleep time were within 15 minutes of recorded sleep time, but 42 subjects underestimated total sleep time

## TABLE 5

All-Night Sleep Recording Data for Two Adolescent Subjects Treated for the Complaint of Insomnia

| All-night sleep recordings | Phase (number of consecutive recordings) | | | | Norms[a] |
|---|---|---|---|---|---|
| | Baseline (2) (lab) | Treatment (2) (lab) | Follow-up (3) (lab) | Follow-up (3) (home) | |
| **Client 1** | | | | | |
| Total sleep time[b] | 427.0 | 410.5 | 361.5 | 373.0 | 454.80 ± 27.56 |
| Latency to sleep onset[b] | 12.5 | 5.0 | 3.3 | 1.0 | 18.45 ± 8.60 |
| Minutes awake after sleep onset | 50.5 | 22.5 | 6.0 | 7.0 | 5.85 ± 1.19 |
| Number of awakenings | 14.5 | 10.5 | 3.7 | 5.5 | 1.70 ± 1.14 |
| Number of Stage 1 arousals | 10.5 | 9.5 | 5.0 | 5.0 | 5.70 ± 2.21 |
| Percentage Stage 1 | 4.1 | 2.9 | 2.4 | 2.0 | 3.74 ± 1.59 |
| Percentage Stage 2 | 54.2 | 54.5 | 49.2 | 55.3 | 49.43 ± 4.51 |
| Percentage Stage 3 | 3.8 | 4.7 | 13.3 | 10.6 | 5.65 ± 2.65 |
| Percentage Stage 4 | 21.1 | 22.5 | 19.8 | 21.3 | 17.78 ± 3.17 |
| Percentage REM | 14.1 | 11.3 | 14.0 | 9.4 | 22.12 ± 3.55 |
| **Client 2** | | | | | |
| Total sleep time[b] | 464.0 | 435.0 | 494.2 | 430.3 | 480.4 ± 34.6 |
| Latency to sleep onset[b] | 80.0 | 6.5 | 9.0 | 4.7 | 15.5 ± 6.7 |
| Minutes awake after sleep onset | 10.0 | 6.5 | 3.7 | 2.8 | 5.75 ± 4.99 |
| Number of awakenings | 3.0 | 3.0 | 4.1 | 4.5 | 1.9 ± 1.9 |
| Number of Stage 1 arousals | 28.0 | 19.0 | 15.0 | 15.0 | 5.5 ± 2.4 |
| Percentage Stage 1 | 8.9 | 5.1 | 3.8 | 4.4 | 3.0 ± 1.3 |
| Percentage Stage 2 | 54.4 | 41.5 | 46.1 | 53.7 | 48.7 ± 6.2 |
| Percentage Stage 3 | 3.9 | 7.0 | 13.7 | 11.5 | 5.2 ± 1.4 |
| Percentage Stage 4 | 8.5 | 26.5 | 15.9 | 12.2 | 16.5 ± 3.3 |
| Percentage REM | 21.7 | 16.3 | 18.1 | 15.7 | 25.6 ± 3.8 |

*Note.* Adapted from Kirmil-Gray, Coates, Thoresen, and Rosekind (1978).

[a] From Williams, Karacan, and Hursch (1974).

[b] Time expressed in minutes.

by more than 60 minutes. A total of 54 subjects estimated sleep latency within 15 minutes of the recorded value, whereas the discrepancy was greater than 15 minutes in 45 subjects and greater than 1 hour in 15 other subjects.[5] Roth, Lutz, Kramer, and Tietz (1977) reported that 81% of their normal sleepers estimated sleep latency within 10 minutes of recorded values, whereas only 25% of the persons complaining of insomnia were able to do so. A total of 70% of the normal sleepers were within 15 minutes of recorded sleep time, whereas only 25% of the persons complaining of insomnia agreed that closely. Clearly, the degree to which self-reports reflect electrophysiological activity as documented in all-night sleep recordings varies from sample to sample and from normal sleepers to persons complaining of sleep disorders. Finally, there is considerable interindividual variability in agreement between reported and recorded sleep.

Agreement and accuracy must be distinguished in considering the utility of an assessment device. Agreement refers to the degree to which independent assessments correlate, and accuracy refers to the correlation between an assessment and a criterion measure. The all-night EEG provides only one method of assessing sleep and the quality of sleep. Because it appeared promising quite early, because it was correlated with early advances in sleep research, and because it can provide a continuous measure over time without apparently disturbing the arousal level of the subject, it is understandable that the EEG has become regarded as *the* criterion of sleep (Kamiya, 1961).

The all-night EEG, however, provides only one method of assessing sleep and provides no information about the perceived quality of sleep. Self-reports serve two functions: they can be used to obtain information about events that potentially can be verified by other methods, and they can provide data about the subject's experience (Hersen & Bellack, 1976). From this perspective, it seems essential that all-night sleep recordings be used in combination with self-report (and other measures) to study which electrophysiological variables might lead to the complaint in the first place as well as to document which variables are correlated with perceived improvements in sleep and reductions of the complaint of a sleep disorder.

The all-night sleep recording is an invaluable tool in diagnosing, documenting, and treating behaviors and complaints. The need to supplement it with other measures is crucial, especially in clinical studies. The need for convergent validity should always be recognized.

## Measuring Sleep in Other Ways

All-night sleep recordings are time consuming, expensive, and difficult to use in or out of the laboratory. In many cases, the amount of data yielded by one recording

---

[5]Persons complaining of insomnia but showing "normal sleep" on the all-night sleep recording have been labeled "pseudo-insomniacs" (Dement, 1972). In a case series analysis of persons complaining of insomnia in the Dartmouth Sleep Laboratory, Hauri (1976) reported that 51 of 141 persons (36%) slept well in the lab despite complaints at home. Of these 51 who slept well, 32, or 62%, reported sleeping *poorly* in the lab.

may be more than is needed for obtaining adequate information for assessment and treatment. Videotapes, audiotapes, activity monitors, and direct observation might provide feasible, reliable, and less expensive data that are adequate for many assessment purposes.

## Videotape and Time-Lapse Photography

Anders and Sostek (1976) developed a time-lapse video recording system for observing sleep of infants. A Sony camera with zoom lens, placed on a tripod 4 feet above the infant, was focused on the face and upper trunk. A clock in the crib displayed real time, while a microphone recorded crying and verbalizations. The time-lapse system recorded 1.5 frames per second, resulting in a 24:1 reduction of real time. Thus, 24 hours of behavior could be collapsed into one hour of half-inch tape.

Observers later reviewed the tape to record five behavioral states: fussy–crying, alertness, drowsiness, active-REM sleep, quiet-NREM sleep. Correlations between video and polygraphically recorded sleep–wake state durations were robust for infants at 2 and 8 weeks of age. When used in the home, it might also be possible to monitor environmental events (e.g., mother–child interactions) potentially related to disturbance of sleep–wake patterns.

Hobson, Spagna, and Malenka (1978) photographed six poor and six good adult sleepers at 15-minute intervals through the night. Poor sleepers showed a significant number of body movements through the night, and poor and good sleepers showed no overlap on the "consolidation index" (the relative amount of time immobile in the night). Again, the technique could lend itself easily to a functional analysis. Both videotape and time-lapse still photography are inexpensive and apparently reliable and could be used in settings outside of the laboratory.

EXEMPLARY CASE: ROCKING AND HEAD BANGING

Linscheid, Copeland, Jacobstein, and Smith (Note 1) reported two case studies (a 4-year-old female and a 13-year-old male) documenting a treatment for *jactatio capitus nocturna*. Both subjects, hospitalized at night but allowed to go home and to school during the day, were observed continuously at night via closed-circuit television. Observers watched the monitor and recorded the occurrences of rocking (the 4-year-old) and of head banging (the 13-year-old).

The baseline data documented the occurrence and topography of the target behaviors. The use of video monitors made it possible to apply the overcorrection treatment strategy. When the 4-year-old began to rock, the observer entered the room and led her through some "exercises": rolling her on her stomach and having her lie completely still for 15 seconds, repeated 15 times. When the male client banged his head, he was required to turn from his stomach to his back, to stretch out, and to hold perfectly still for 15 seconds, to be repeated 15 times. Unfortunately, both subjects were discharged at the end of three nights of treatment. Parents, instructed to continue treatment and to monitor results, reported cessation of both problems.

It would seem feasible, in both cases, to use time-lapse video systems and home-based assessment and treatment.

## Audiotapes

Guilleminault and Dement (1977), in discussing their case series analysis of patients presenting with daytime sleepiness, mentioned that audiotape recordings can be used to document the gasping–snoring sounds of sleep apnea. Timers to turn recorders on or off or multiple or long-playing recorders to collect more extensive samples might be useful in discriminating persons suspected of apnea and for making decisions regarding referral to sleep specialists.

## Monitoring Nighttime Activity

Activity monitors have been attached to the bed and to the person. In one very early application, Giddings (1934) monitored the effects of milk and of a heavy meal on children's movement during sleep by means of a mechanical event recorder attached to the mattress. Predictably, milk led to more periods of quiet activity, whereas the heavy meal led to increased restlessness during sleep.

The study of movements during sleep may help in understanding the complaint of insomnia, especially when the complaint fails to be verified using standard EEG criteria. Phillips, Spiegel, Clayton, and Dement (1975) reported that alpha bursts combined with body movements discriminated persons complaining of insomnia from normal sleepers. Takahashi, Guilleminault, and Dement (1974) studied four "pseudo-insomniacs." One subject showed an abnormal number of body movements, and two others showed movements associated with arousals. The fourth showed no abnormalities. Thus, the study of movements could be of some importance in documenting and treating certain cases of poor sleep.

Continuous 24-hour measurements of activity appear feasible and highly reliable in discriminating sleep from wakefulness in adults (Foster, Kupfer, Weiss et al., 1972; Kupfer, Detre, Foster et al., 1972). Kripke, Messin, Mullaney, and Wyborney (1977) described a transducer excited by omnidirectional movements of a small, weighted level. The transducer was mounted on the wrist and connected to a Medilog recorder worn on the belt. When compared to all-night sleep recordings, the transducer method was highly reliable for estimating total sleep period ($r = +.95$), total minutes of sleep ($r = +.98$), and minutes of wake time within sleep ($r = +.85$).

Observations by significant others might prove feasible for some age groups. Weiss, McPartland, and Kupfer (1973) presented data showing that nurses provided highly inaccurate data about patients' sleep when compared to all-night sleep recordings. On the other hand, Parmelee, Schultz, and Distrow (1961) trained mothers to record sleeping and waking intervals of their newborn infants. Aserinsky and Kleitman (1955) combined mechanical and human recorders to study movement cycles in the newborn. It may be that accurate records can be obtained with sufficient training of observers.

# BEHAVIORAL ANALYSIS OF BEHAVIORS AND COMPLAINTS ASSOCIATED WITH SLEEP

The process view of sleep suggests that sleep disorders are associated with disturbances in specific circadian cycles, anomalies in the sleep–wake cycle, or disassociations between sleep–wake and circadian cycles. Behavior analysis is designed to illuminate the environmental, social-psychological, behavioral, or physiological factors associated with disturbed circadian cycles or dissociations between sleep–wake and circadian cycles. From the analysis, interventions can be developed and tested empirically until the therapist and client are satisfied with the outcomes. The functional approach proceeds by (1) describing explicitly the specific behavior or complaint, (2) examining a variety of physical, environmental, and psychological antecedents and consequences to determine possible causes of the behavior pattern or complaint, and (3) designing a treatment program to modify these causes and thus improve sleep. Emphasis is placed on assessing those variables that can be modified to produce changes in the behavior or the complaint.

Table 6 presents a variety of environmental, behavioral, and cognitive factors that can be related to good and poor sleep. The list is illustrative and not meant to be exhaustive. The clinician–researcher needs to be alert continually to the multitude of idiosyncratic factors that can influence sleep.

Young children and adolescents are most likely to present with complaints of sleeplessness or excessive sleepiness. Research has focused on identifying traits of caretakers correlated with sleep problems in infants and young children. Moore and Ucho (1957) studied 160 infants; about 70% slept from midnight to 5 a.m. by 3 months, and 83% did so by 6 months. Ten percent were not sleeping through the night at their first birthday. About 50% of those who had started sleeping through the night had subsequent spells of night waking of more than 4 weeks' duration. From interviews, these night-wakening episodes were correlated with high levels of "maternal anxiety," reflected by inconsistent handling and little playing time. Bernal (1973) found parents very responsive to infant waking. Feeding, handling, or taking the child into the parents' bed were common responses to awakening. Similarly, Hirschberg (1957) reported that parental anger and concern seemed to compound sleeping disturbances after 6 months of age. Roberts and Schoellkopf (1951) reported common sleep problems among 783 2½-year-olds: resistance to nap (2%), resistance to going to bed (12%), night terrors and nightmares (8.6%), and getting into parents' bed (4.6%).

Poor sleep among older children and adolescents has been attributed to "emotional disturbances." In a study of 627 high school students, Price et al. (1978) reported that poor sleepers reported significantly more negative mood states (e.g., depression, tension) and also described themselves more negatively than good sleepers. Marks and Monroe (1976) completed a study of 831 emotionally disturbed adolescents, of whom 53 were poor sleepers. Poor sleepers showed more anxiety, tension, depression, sensitivity, and somatic concerns than good sleepers

TABLE 6

Some Factors to Assess in Treating Behaviors and Complaints Associated with Sleep

| Factor | Description |
| --- | --- |
| Pre-bedtime (evening) activities | Evening activities (e.g., family arguments, exciting television program) can promote physical and mental arousal, making sleep onset difficult. |
| Responses to problems | Social reinforcement (intended or unintended) in response to problem or expression of problem. |
| Circadian rhythm | Shifts in sleep schedule will produce sleep disturbance. |
| | Failure to maintain regular sleep–wake schedule can result in disturbed sleep. |
| | Child's sleep–wake cycle may be out of phase with demands of external environment. |
| | Child may have an irregular or atypical circadian rhythm. |
| Daytime activities and environment | Child under chronic stress; stress can also contribute to physical or mental fatigue that is not related to poor sleep. |
| | Daytime environment that is noisy, crowded, light, hot, or humid. |
| | Excessive exercise or lack of exercise may promote feelings of fatigue or sleepiness. |
| Diet | Specific foods (e.g., caffeine, heavy meals), eaten prior to bedtime, may improve or diminish sleep quality. |
| | Weight loss may shorten sleep time, whereas weight gain may increase sleep time. |
| | Specific foods or food allergies may promote sleepiness or fatigue. |
| Mental activity, thoughts, and emotions | Persistent thinking about problems; excessive "worries" may be a characteristic response of the child. Includes recurring thoughts about being unable to sleep well and beliefs about ability to do what is necessary to fall to sleep. |
| | Phobias about loss of consciousness, fear of nightmares (intermittent and/or recurring). |
| Sleep environment | Sleep environment may be excessively noisy, light, hot, humid, or crowded. |
| | Stimuli in the immediate sleep environment (bedroom) may evoke activities or thoughts incompatible with sleep. |
| | Activities conducted in bedroom may be incompatible or may interfere with good sleep. |

*Note.* Adapted from Coates and Thoresen (1980).

(see also Monroe & Marks, 1977a). The poor sleepers also scored significantly higher on the *Hs, D, Hy,* and *Si,* and lower on the *Ma* scale of the Minnesota Multiphasic Personality Inventory (MMPI) than good sleepers (Monroe & Marks, 1977b). Similarly, individual case reports have identified stress and anxiety as central to complaints of insomnia (e.g., Weil & Goldfried, 1973), sleepwalking (Meyer, 1975), and nightmares (Handler, 1972).

Although these studies are informative in pointing out areas related to the complaint of poor sleep, they give few data upon which to build practical change strategies. Needed is a variety of methods for assessing functional relationships between the environment; person's behaviors, thoughts, and mood; and their sleep at night. We will present five possible alternatives:

1. The structured interview
2. Sleep and activity diaries
3. Automatic monitoring devices
4. Video recordings
5. Daytime activity monitors

## Structured Interviews

The structured interview is a relatively inexpensive and efficient method for obtaining information about the problem behavior and potentially related environmental events, behaviors, thoughts, and moods. General principles of behavioral interviewing, discussed by several authors (Cautela & Upper, 1975; Linehan, 1977; Morganstern, 1976; Stuart & Stuart, 1976), are relevant to analysis and treatment of behaviors and complaints associated with sleep. In the case of behaviors and complaints associated with sleep, it is essential to interview the client (in this case, the child) and also significant others (e.g., parents, teachers, siblings) who can provide insight into the nature of the problem and factors associated with it.

The structured interview serves two functions: to gather information about the problem and to develop hypotheses about factors responsible for initiating and maintaining the problem. As the interview (and also therapy) progresses, the two functions interact in a cyclical process. As information is gathered, hypotheses are developed and tested through the gathering of additional information.

The first task in the interview involves obtaining from the client and significant others a clear and complete statement of the nature of the problem, including its frequency, intensity, and duration. Especially important is determining from everyone why the complaint should be considered a problem. Myths about sleep are rampant, and persons entertain quite rigid notions about normal and abnormal sleep patterns. The range of sleep experienced by humans is quite wide (Williams *et al.*, 1974). When advertising for participants in our studies, we invariably receive several calls from persons who have atypical sleeping patterns. Our first question always is: "Does this bother you or anyone else?" If the answer is "No," then the person does not have a sleeping problem, no matter how unusual the sleeping pattern may seem to be. In working with children and adolescents, it is quite important to discriminate between atypical sleep patterns, those that cause the person harm or discomfort, and those that are of concern to a significant other. If the complaint is only of concern to a significant other, then the major problem may have nothing to do with sleep but rather may be related to some other feature of the interaction between the child or adolescent and the significant others in the environment.

Following the steps outlined in Figure 3, evaluation of physical condiions and drug use comes next. Judicious and probing questions can reveal obvious signs of a physical disorder. Complete and careful evaluation, however, is accomplished best through a medical–behavioral scientist team in which each person can contribute skills and expertise to problems that frequently bridge disciplines.

The behavior analysis is designed to assess history, external environment, and associated behaviors, events, and thoughts in turn.

## History

Assessment of the duration of the problem and events associated with the beginning of the problem can often provide clues about events initiating, and also currently maintaining, the disorder. Family history of similar or related complaints can also be important in determining if sleep disorders are experienced or modeled by family members.

## Environment

Several features of the environment should be assessed. Degree of crowding, noise, heat, and type of bed are important physical characteristics related to good and poor sleep. Equally important is the meaning the environment has for the person. We routinely ask questions regarding whether the person likes and feels comfortable in the neighborhood and in the bedroom and the emotional associations evoked by the neighborhood and bedroom environments. The physical arrangement and complete range of activities performed in the bedroom should also be assessed, as some of these may be incompatible with sleep. One client, for example, kept her desk in her bedroom. Because she was reentering the job market, her desk was cluttered with job listings and resumés. Every time she entered the bedroom, she was cued by the desk to reflect on her unemployed status. Similarly, if the bedroom is used for emotional altercations or punishment, it may come to evoke negative feelings that can interfere with sleep.

The home all-night sleep recording system is advantageous in that it enables us to observe other relevant features of the home environment. With minimal training, technicians can observe such things as noise, light, heat, and the number of appliances (e.g., radio, television, stereo) in the bedroom. In our experience, technicians have also been able to identify medications and family interactions likely to produce poor sleep. Often subjects have not been able or have not been willing to report these same features to us directly.

### Sleep Routine and Schedule

The process view places sleep in the context of inherent circadian rhythms. Sleep and wakefulness are favored at alternating phases of the cycle. Persons who sleep poorly can fall into some habits that may contribute to or exacerbate the sleep problem. It is tempting, for example, to sleep any time the urge is present in the belief that there is no other way to make up lost sleep. Poor sleepers may sleep late in the mornings if they can or may retire early, whenever possible, to obtain extra needed sleep. In general, extending sleep, reducing sleep, or shifting habitual sleep time reduces sleep efficiency and degrades daytime performance (Taub & Berger, 1976).

These practices can result in greater feelings of fatigue because persons are attempting to sleep at times not favored by their circadian cycle. It is also possible to shift the circadian cycle so that it is out of phase with the external environment. Persons who sleep poorly at night may gradually extend morning arising times. This delays bedtime and sleep onset the following night, which, in turn, extends arising time the next morning. Atypical schedules can be tolerated if the person does not have to meet external environmental demands, but the person will experience a sleep problem if he or she has to conform to routines established by others.

Finally, atypical rhythms resulting in periodic sleep disturbance have been documented.

EXEMPLARY CASE: 24.9-HOUR CIRCADIAN RHYTHM

Miles, Raynal, and Wilson (1977) reported a case of a blind man with a 24.9-hour circadian cycle. The individual functioned well for 2–3 weeks, but his circadian cycle would gradually get out of phase with his sleep–wake cycle. He would begin experiencing difficulty in falling asleep at night and in remaining alert during the day. Heavy use of medications allowed him to sleep and to maintain a somewhat normal schedule until his circadian cycle came back into phase with his imposed sleep–wake cycle. Attempts to re-entrain the cycle were unsuccessful.

### Behavioral Antecedents to Sleep Problems

Areas of exploration can include: (1) activities in the evening prior to bedtime, (2) diet, and (3) mental activity, thoughts, and emotions. Although it might be useful to focus first on factors occurring close in time to bedtime, it may also be important to explore the person's daytime activities and environment. A person who is under stress all day long or who is restricted to an environment that is unpleasant (noisy, hot, humid) may experience fatigue in the absence of poor sleep or may experience poor sleep at night because of the intimate linkage of daytime and nighttime thoughts, behaviors, environments, and physical reactions.

## *Thoughts and Beliefs*

Persons who experience sleep disorders often report a sense of powerlessness and lack of ability to control or produce good sleep. Combined with these can be persistent concern about sleep and the ability to perform adequately during the day because of poor sleep. It is also possible that children experience terror or fear of the bedroom or of sleep because they fear loss of consciousness or the experience of nightmares or night terrors.

These habit patterns can be explored in a variety of ways in the structured interview. Persons can be asked, in a straightforward way, about their internal experiences. They can also be asked to imagine themselves in bed and to free associate on the thoughts and images they experience. If these procedures fail, *in vivo* assessments might be necessary. It might be very enlightening and essential to conduct some assessment sessions in the home. As an alternative, we have issued miniature dictaphones to clients and have asked them to record their thoughts and feelings during the day, at night prior to retiring, and during the night when they awaken. These provide a rich source of assessment information and also can be used as outcome measures. The tapes can be transcribed and coded to assess changes in thoughts and feelings as the person progresses through a therapy strategy.

## *Reactions of Significant Others*

Reinforcement patterns could be maintaining the problem behavior. A straightforward assessment of events surrounding the experience of the sleep problem may be sufficient to yield data about important consequences.

### EXEMPLARY CASE: INSOMNIA

Yen, McIntire, and Berkowitz (1972) reported the case of a 17-year-old male who had difficulty sleeping for 2 years. The behavior analysis, conducted during interviews supplemented with self-monitoring records, revealed that the subject would lie awake worrying unless he was able to enter his mother's room before bedtime and talk about his worries. The behavior analysis suggested that the mother's attention was sustaining these behaviors. The mother and son agreed to the following strategy. Conversations about worries were shifted to a time earlier in the evening. If the son did enter his mother's bedroom prior to retiring, the following evening's conversation time was cancelled. Within 3 weeks, the strategy was reportedly highly successful in eliminating the son's poor sleep and his disturbing his mother.

## Sleep and Activity Diaries

Coates and Thoresen (1977) developed a sleep diary (Figure 4) and an analysis form (Figure 5) that asks clients to record events, thoughts, and moods regardless of their presumed relationship to sleep. With slight modifications, these forms could also be used by parents to monitor their children's sleep behavior. Because

Name _Patrick Thomas_ Date _July 21_

1. Bedtime __10:30__ Sleep time _12:00 p.m._

2. It took me __90__ minutes to fall asleep last night.

3. I awakened __2__ times last night.
   Indicate *times* and *how long* it took to fall back asleep each time:
   
   __2:30__ ___40___ minutes
   __3:45__ ___10___ minutes
   _____ _____ minutes

4. I woke up for the last time at __7:00__ and slept a total of __6¹/₁₀__ hours.

5. Rate your level of physical arousal when you went to bed.

   | Extremely<br>calm/relaxed | | | | | | Extremely<br>tense/aroused | |
   
   1  2  3  4  5  6  ⑦  8

6. Write down what you were thinking about as you were in bed:
   _Bills and finances, trip to Los Angeles next week, children; disagreement with boss last week, whether or not I was going to get a good night's sleep_

7. Write down your activities from dinner time to bedtime:
   _Washed dinner dishes Conversed with wife Fixed lamp cord. about work Skimmed Time magazine Watched 10:00 news_

8. Write down your activities once you got into bed:
   _Talked with wife Read New Yorker article about trip on education Talked about bills_

FIGURE 4

Sample sleep diary. From *How To Sleep Better: A Drug-Free Program for Overcoming Insomnia* by T. J. Coates and C. E. Thoresen. Copyright 1977 by Prentice-Hall, Inc. Reprinted by permission.

| Name _Jim Stone_ | |
|---|---|
| Dates: From _March 29_ to _May 17_ | |
| *Good Nights* | *Bad Nights* |

| | Good Nights | Bad Nights |
|---|---|---|
| **Daily Sleep Diary** Number of nights | 8 | 4 |
| **Physical arousal** | 4.5 | 5.0 |
| **Thoughts upon retiring** | _Daytime accom- plishments_ _Vacation plans_ | _Tomorrow's schedule_ _Problem situation_ |
| **Activities from dinner to bedtime** | _Television_ _Novel reading_ _Playing with children_ | _Television_ _Playing with children_ _Read novel_ |
| **Bedtime activities** | _Talk to spouse about pleasant events_ _Stay in bed once there_ | _Talk to spouse about finances, kid's problems_ _Get up several times to do things I forgot to do_ |
| **Brainstorm** | | _"Beat myself mentally Take long naps Really warm bedroom Make a phone call Think about un- friendly exchange with co-workers_ |
| **Other factors** | _Transition between work and bed_ _Physical exercise during day_ | _Noises outside_ _Tense, uptight day_ |

FIGURE 5

Sample self-analysis worksheet for discovering variables related to good and poor sleep. From *How To Sleep Better: A Drug-Free Program for Overcoming Insomnia* by T. J. Coates and C. E. Thoresen. Copyright 1977 by Prentice-Hall, Inc. Reprinted by permission.

children and parents may be unaware of, or may deny, factors related to good or poor sleep, the sleep diary requests subjects to record *all* events before retiring in the evening. Upon arising in the morning, data regarding sleep can be completed. After diaries have been collected for several weeks, they can be sorted into piles representing good, mixed, or poor sleep nights. Therapists and clients can then sort through each pile to look for factors common to good and poor sleep.

Figure 5, for example, shows bedtime activities possibly related to good and poor sleep. On nights when the person experienced good sleep, the person talked to his spouse about pleasant events and stayed in bed once he was there. By contrast, on nights when poor sleep was experienced, they discussed a range of serious matters, and he got up and down several times before retiring.

Not all events related to good and poor sleep may be recorded on the sleep diary. For that reason, Coates and Thoresen (1977) suggested brainstorming, in which subjects were encouraged to list factors (as many as possible) that might hypothetically be related to poor sleep. Brainstorming without censoring is essential, as subjects typically can find exceptions to any factor seemingly related to good and poor sleep.

From the data that are collected, strategies for change can be generated.

EXEMPLARY CASE: PROCRASTINATION AND INSOMNIA

Coates and Thoresen (1979) reported the case of a 58-year-old woman who had complained of insomnia for 30 years. She responded well to progressive relaxation but experienced poor sleep on at least two nights each week. When the sleep diaries were sorted, a common factor discriminated nights of good sleep from nights of poor sleep. Days following nights with poor sleep often involved teaching, whereas days following nights with good sleep often did not. Further interviewing revealed that evenings preceding classes were marked by extensive lecture preparation, often until late in the evening. The client would work late and then attempt to go to bed and to sleep. The solution was straightforward. Time had to be set aside during the day to complete preparations so that it was not delayed until the last part of the day.

Adolescents have had no difficulty in using these sleep diaries (Kirmil-Gray *et al.*, 1978), and simpler forms might be kept by younger children. In both cases, it might be possible to supplement them with diaries kept by parents or siblings.

Three issues merit attention in assessing behaviors and complaints associated with sleep using interviews and sleep diaries. First, it is essential that significant others be interviewed along with the client. Behaviors and complaints associated with sleep involve actions performed by the child when he or she may not be awake and able to process information adequately. Nocturnal myoclonus and sleep apnea, for example, may be discernible only to bed partners and persons listening to the child's sleep, whereas teachers may be able to comment on daytime behaviors associated with these disorders.

Second, information obtained from self-reports may or may not reflect the data that would be obtained from other physiological (e.g., all-night sleep recordings) or behavioral (e.g., videotape recordings) sources. Insomnia and daytime sleepiness are complaints that may not be related to one another or to poor sleep as measured in all-night sleep recordings. Persons complaining of insomnia *perceive* a relationship between daytime problems and nocturnal sleep disturbance. However, daytime sleepiness cannot always be attributed to disturbances in nighttime sleep. Dement (1972) has commented on the problem of "pseudo-insomnia." There are persons whose sleep appears normal by EEG standards but who complain of poor sleep. Pollak, McGregor, and Weitzmann (1975) put normal-sleeper volunteers on a reversed sleep–wake cycle: They slept at times when they would normally be awake and were given usual clinical doses of flurazepam (Dalmane ®) to ensure that they would sleep at times called for in the protocol. Despite their sleeping well according to usual EEG criteria, they still experienced severe sleepiness when awake.

Subjects receiving behavioral treatments for complaints of insomnia have reported improvement in nighttime sleep and daytime sleepiness without significant change being found in EEG variables derived from all-night sleep recordings (e.g., Hauri, 1978). What is happening to modify perceptions of sleep and sleepiness in the absence of changes in the EEG remains a mysterious, but seemingly important, phenomenon to explore. It reinforces the notion that sleep and sleepiness may or may not be related in specific cases and that adequate assessment of behaviors or complaints associated with sleep requires careful analyses of *waking and sleeping* behaviors and environments.

Third, when treating a case using only self-report, it is possible to show success but to misattribute the reason for success.

### Exemplary Case: Nightmares

Clement (1970) described a therapy program for sleepwalking in a 7-year-old boy. Sleepwalking was attributed to the need to escape "a big black bug," which was reportedly the content of the boy's nightmares. The first treatment strategy, involving identification of feelings and expressions of hostility, was ineffective. The second strategy eliminated sleepwalking immediately and results were sustained at follow-up. The treatment was simple: every time the boy began sleepwalking, his mother took him to the bathroom and washed his face and neck completely with cold water until there was no doubt that he was fully awake. Clement (1970) attributed the success of the procedure to breaking stimulus associations between the dream and sleepwalking.

In this case, the treatment may have worked for reasons other than those cited, because sleepwalking is most commonly associated with arousals from Stage 4 sleep (Broughton, 1968). NREM dreams do occur (Brown & Cartwright, 1978; Cartwright, 1977), and it has been suggested that increases in incidence of all kinds of behaviors and complaints associated with sleep in children and adolescents may be associated with stress (Anders & Guilleminault, 1976). Without benefit of more extensive documentation, however, these attributions must remain quite speculative. When proceeding without benefit of multiple assessments, the clinician or researcher needs to realize that though a sleep disorder may be the primary complaint, the person may not be experiencing a sleep disorder at all. Client perceptions regarding causation may or may not be accurate. When subjects report improvement, treatment may have influenced sleep or some daytime correlates such as sleepiness or anxiety, or it may have influenced only the perception that each has been changed.

## Automatic Monitoring Devices

Korner, Thomson, and Glick (1974) devised a neonatal monitoring system to discriminate large, medium, and small movements and to screen out movements induced by caretakers so as to provide counts unconfounded by the infant's crying. A foam rubber mattress provided signal input to an analog recorder, six movement counters, and an integrator which accumulated activity counts over 5-minute epochs. A unidirectional microphone connected to a voice-activated switch provided a signal to yield measures of crying and noncrying activity. The signal also started a clock which accumulated crying time. A switchmat in front of the crib provided a signal to a clock which recorded the cumulative time in which a caretaker tended to the child.

Sander, Stechler, Julia, and Burns (1970) used a similar system to study relationships between environments and establishment of sleep–wake cycles in infants. Predictably, infants in a nursery established regular rhythm and day–night differentiation much more quickly than infants at home. In a second study, Sander, Julia, Stechler, and Burns (1972) reported that infants having a single caretaker in the nursery showed accelerated rates of day–night differentation compared to infants with multiple caretakers.

These mechanical recording strategies could be used by themselves or in combination with video monitoring to assess antecedents and consequences of a wide range of sleeping problems among infants and young children. If persons could adapt to their presence, they might even be useful in discriminating factors associated with sleep disturbance among older children and adolescents.

## Videotape Combined with Sleep Recordings

Nocturnal polygraphic recordings in combination with videotape recordings have been invaluable in documenting the occurrences of night terrors, somnambulism, and enuresis in the transition between Stage 4 and Stage 2 sleep. The combination of videotape and sleep recordings might also be essential for a definitive diagnosis of nightmares or night terrors or for documenting relationships between other abnormal nocturnal behaviors and specific states or stages of sleep.

### EXEMPLARY CASES: FAMILY PROBLEMS AND EPILEPSY

Guilleminault, Korobkin, Anders, and Dement (1977) used a combined sleep-recording and videotape procedure to diagnose the probable cause of two cases of abnormal nocturnal behaviors. An 8-year-old child was referred for night terrors and uncontrollable sobbing, supposedly Stage 4 phenomena. However, observations revealed that both occurred during wakefulness. Discussions with parents and subsequent family therapy resulted in a cessation of the problem.

A 6-year-old child presented a case of nocturnal head banging which occurred for 100 minutes during one night of sleep recording. Typical epileptic temporal spikes, activated during REM sleep, preceded each head-banging episode.

## Monitoring Circadian Rhythms

Kokkoris, Weitzmann, Pollak, Spielman, Czeisler, and Bradlow (1978) described a device for recording rectal body temperature from ambulatory subjects at frequent intervals over an extended period. The instrument consists of a solid-state memory, internal clock, four AA batteries carried in the pocket, and the thermistor probe worn comfortably in the rectum. Though still in the trial stages, these devices may prove useful in studying and treating various sleep disorders in children.

EXEMPLARY CASE: FREE-RUNNING RHYTHM
Kokkoris *et al.* (1979) reported using this instrument for 3½ months with a 34-year-old male. In addition to the temperature monitors, the subject also recorded lights-out, sleep, meals, physical activities, and special events. The plot of temperatures revealed a 24.8-hour cycle, and sleep periods always coincided with drops in the cycle.

Activity monitors might be adaptable for similar purposes and also to study relationships between level and timing of daytime activity in relation to past or future nighttime sleep. McPartland and associates (1976a, 1976b), for example, presented preliminary data on relationships between depression, sleep, and daytime activity using normals and controls. Schulman, Stevens, Suran, Kupst, and Naughton (1978) reported using activity monitors in a biofeedback mode in order to decrease activity in an 11-year-old hyperactive boy and to increase activity in a 10-year-old hyperactive boy. It might be feasible to use similar strategies to study and treat relationships between activity and sleep in children and adolescents.

In summary, these alternative assessment strategies represent what has been reported and not what could be done. Assessment of behaviors and complaints associated with sleep is a young and emerging field. Clinicians and researchers need to give their imagination freedom in devising ingenious and novel ways in which to measure variables related to sleep.

# SLEEPINESS: WHAT IS IT?

Sleepiness is one of those ubiquitous phenomena (not unlike fear or stress) experienced by everyone, easily labeled and expressed when experienced, but operationalized and studied only with great difficulty. Zarcone (1977) summarized the state of the art in understanding hypersomnia quite succinctly:

> Chronic idiopathic hypersomnia is characterized by prolonged amounts of normally staged sleep in individuals who complain of sleeping too much and of feeling too sleepy in the daytime. The problem with the definition of this syndrome is that we do not know how much sleep is normal, nor how many times most people get sleepy. (p. 295)

Ironically, the complaint of sleepiness is one of the indicators that persons use to seek help for a "sleep disorder."

Dement, Carskadon, and Richardson (1978) noted that, in spite of its clinical importance, the empirical study of sleepiness has lagged considerably. The Stanford Sleepiness Scale, one of the early measures developed to study sleepiness, is a Likert-type self-rating scale, with seven dimensions ranging from "fully awake" to "sleep onset soon" (Hoddes, Zarcone, Smythe, Phillips, & Dement, 1973). The scale is useful clinically but possibly deficient by itself for scientific studies because of subjects' tendencies to rate idiosyncratically or to adjust the scale over a period of time.

Performance testing is a conventional alternative (cf. Webb, 1977). These tests typically require persons to perform some task that requires continual attention (e.g., Wilkinson Vigilance Task) or use of complex cognitive functions (e.g., Wilkinson Addition Task). The use of these tests to measure sleepiness is based on the view that deprivation of sleep interferes with both simple and complex cognitive function. However, these tests are insensitive to all but the most extreme sleep deprivation (Johnson, 1975). They have proven insensitive in discriminating relatively minor sleep deprivation, the problem experienced by a majority of persons complaining of poor sleep. Moreover, when persons are deprived of some sleep over a long period, they adapt and are able to perform as well on these performance tests as they did during baseline.

Anders, Carskadon, Dement, and Harvey (1978) described a Sleep Habits Questionnaire (SHQ) designed to measure nighttime sleep and daytime sleepiness among adolescents. Twelve items were selected to form an index of sleepiness, including latency to sleep onset, daytime naps, sleeping through alarms, sleep "attacks" during school, snoring, daytime energy levels, and impaired daytime functioning. The majority of children scored zero, while 2.4% of the children scored above 6 (range = 0 to 22). They suggested that the instrument might have promise in screening children with sleep problems who are failing in school for no apparent reason.

The Multiple Sleep Latency Test (Dement et al., 1978; Richardson, Carskadon, Flagg et al., 1978) was designed to provide a laboratory-based procedure, sensitive to varying degrees of sleep deprivation, for measuring the effects of lack of sleep. The test is based on the operationalization that sleepiness represents an increased tendency to fall asleep. Electrodes are attacked to record the EEG, the EOG, and the EMG. Persons are placed in bed and told to lie there or to fall asleep. They remain in bed at various times during the day until they experience unambiguous Stage 1 sleep (390 seconds of 3–7 cps brainwave activity combined with slow, rolling eye movements). The test is terminated after 20 minutes if the person fails to fall asleep. Preliminary studies show that the test discriminates persons with narcolepsy and sleep apnea from persons with no sleep complaint. Dramatic reduction in sleepiness has been found after tracheotomy for sleep apnea (Dement et al., 1978). Total sleep loss results in marked increases in "sleepiness" in young children (Carskadon, Harvey, & Dement, 1977), and there appear to be increases in sleepiness with physical maturation in adolescents (Carskadon, Harvey, Dement, & Anders, 1977).

The Multiple Sleep Latency Test is not without problems. Motivation and demand, for example, could influence outcomes. Falling asleep may be a skill that persons need to learn regardless of their state of sleepiness. A person complaining of insomnia may be experiencing sleepiness but could be unable to fall sleep because of inability to control extraneous and unwanted mental activity. At the opposite side, a person may not experience sleepiness but could fall asleep because of developed cognitive control skills.

Nonetheless, these techniques undoubtedly represent preliminary, but important, attempts to conceptualize and operationalize a very important dimension of behaviors and complaints associated with sleep.

Sleepiness is central to the complaint of poor sleep, and reductions in sleepiness should be an important outcome for interventions. Moreover, sleepiness and sleep may be quite independent. The relationship between the two cannot be studied adequately unless sleepiness can be measured reliably and satisfactorily. Conceptual and methodological work is needed so that this elusive, but important, phenomenon and experience might be studied.

# SUMMARY

We have presented several potentially useful methods for assessing the sleep experience in young persons. Many of these methods have not been used with children but might be adapted for such use. The novelty of these procedures, however, should not be allowed to obscure their obvious shortcomings. They provide only glimpses of sleep phenomena, and the assessment program presented remains mostly speculative.

Except for the current interest in the behavioral treatment of insomnia (primarily sleep onset problems), sleep and behaviors and complaints associated with sleep have received little attention from psychologists and other persons interested in behavioral approaches to clinical problems. Two consequences emerge. First, the treatment of sleep and sleep disorders is reported without acknowledging (and perhaps without awareness of) important assessment issues and basic physiology underlying phenomena observed (Coates & Thoresen, 1980). Second, the psychological understanding of these phenomena remains markedly underdeveloped.

The consequences of such lack of attention can be harmful. On the one hand, treatment success can be attributed to reasons that are inconsistent with what is known about specific sleep phenomena. On the other hand, we may remain enamored for too long with existing methods, failing to develop new perspectives and views inspired by psychological approaches. Sleep, behaviors and complaints associated with sleep, and sleepiness are complex. Adequate models and treatments require attention to physiology, behavior, environment, and experience. Somehow these must be better integrated in studying and treating these phenomena.

Finally, the need for treatment is real and pressing (cf. Cooper, 1977). Treatment recommendations involve using drugs (e.g., imipramine, diazepam) or remain generally vague and limited (Anders & Guilleminault, 1976).[6] The challenge of integrating improved assessment with better treatment is clear and impelling.

## Acknowledgments

Preparation of this chapter was supported in part by Grant No. MH27551 from the Clinical Research Branch of the National Institute of Mental Health, by the Spencer Foundation, by the Luke Hancock Foundation, and by the Boys Town Center for Youth Development at Stanford. The views expressed do not necessarily reflect those of the agencies.

## Reference Note

1. Linscheid, T. R., Copeland, A. P., Jacobstein, D. M., & Smith, J. L. *Overcorrection treatment for nighttime self-injurious behavior in two normal children.* Unpublished manuscript, Georgetown University School of Medicine, Washington, D.C., 1977.

## References

Abelson, H. I., Fishburne, P. M., & Cisin, I. *National survey on drug abuse.* Rockville, Md.: National Institute on Drug Abuse, 1977.

Agnew, H. W., Jr., Webb, W. B., & Williams, R. L. The first night effect. An EEG study of sleep. *Psychophysiology*, 1966, 2, 263–266.

Anders, T. F., Carskadon, M. A., Dement, W. C., & Harvey, K. Sleep habits of children and the identification of pathologically sleepy children. *Child Psychiatry and Human Development*, 1978, 9, 56–62.

Anders, T., Emde, R., & Parmelee, A. (Eds.). *A manual of standardized terminology, techniques, and criteria for scoring states of sleep and wakefulness in newborn infants.* Los Angeles: UCLA Brain Information Service, National Institute of Neurological Diseases and Stroke, 1971.

Anders, T. F., & Guilleminault, C. The pathophysiology of sleep disorders in pediatrics. *Advances in Pediatrics*, 1976, 22, 137–174.

---

[6]Kripke, Simons, Garfinkel, and Hammond (1979) reported in a prospective epidemiological study that questionnaire reports of short and long sleep durations and of sleeping pill use are major mortality risk predictors. Cause-and-effect relations, of course, cannot be established, but these data do suggest that use of hypnotic medications could carry serious risk and that the benefits of correcting curtailed sleep could be quite large.

Anders, T., & Sostek, A. M: The use of time lapse video recording of sleep–wake behavior in human infants. *Psychophysiology*, 1976, *13*, 155–158.

Aschoff, J. Circadian rhythms in man. *Science*, 1965, *148*, 1427–1432.

Aserinsky, E., & Kleitman, N. A motility cycle in sleeping infants as manifested by ocular and gross bodily activity. *Journal of Applied Physiology*, 1955, *8*, 11–18.

Bernal, J. F. Night waking in infants during the first 14 months. *Developmental Medicine and Child Neurology*, 1973, *15*, 760–769.

Bernstein, P., Emde, R., & Campos, J. REM sleep in four-month-old infants under home and laboratory conditions. *Psychosomatic Medicine*, 1973, *35*, 322–329.

Bixler, E. O., Kales, J. D., Scharf, M. B., Kales, A., & Leo, L. A. Incidence of sleep disorders in medical practice: A physician survey. *Sleep Research*, 1976, *5*, 62. (Abstract)

Broughton, R. J. Sleep disorders: Disorders of arousal? *Science*, 1968, *159*, 1070–1078.

Brown, J. N., & Cartwright, R. D. Locating NREM dreaming through instrumental responses. *Psychophysiology*, 1978, *15*, 35–39.

Bruhova, S., & Roth, B. Heredo-familial aspects of narcolepsy and hypersomnia. *Archives Suisses de Neurologie, de Neurochirurgie, et, de Psychiatrie*, 1972, *110*, 45–54.

Carskadon, M. A., Dement, W. C., Mitler, M. M., Guilleminault, C., Zarcone, V. P., & Spiegel, R. Self-reports versus sleep laboratory findings in 122 drug-free subjects with complaints of chronic insomnia. *American Journal of Psychiatry*, 1976, *133*, 1382–1388.

Carskadon, M. A., Harvey, K., & Dement, W. C. Sleep tendency in children. *Sleep Research*, 1977, *6*, 91. (Abstract)

Carskadon, M. A., Harvey, R., Dement, W. C., & Anders, T. F. Acute partial sleep deprivation in children. *Sleep Research*, 1977, *6*, 92. (Abstract)

Carskadon, M. A., Harvey, K., Dement, W. C., Guilleminault, C., Simmons, F. B., & Anders, T. F. Respiration during sleep in children. *Western Journal of Medicine*, 1978, *128*, 477–481.

Cartwright, R. D. *Nightlife: Explorations in dreaming*. Englewood Cliffs, N.J.: Prentice-Hall, 1977.

Cautela, J. R., & Upper, D. The process of individual behavior therapy. In M. Hersen, R. M. Eisler, & P. M. Miller, (Eds.), *Progress in behavior modification* (Vol. 1). New York: Academic Press, 1975.

Clement, P. W. Elimination of sleepwalking in a seven-year-old boy. *Journal of Consulting and Clinical Psychology*, 1970, *34*, 22–26.

Coates, T. J., Rosekind, M. R., & Thoresen, C. E. All night sleep recordings in clients' homes by telephone. *Journal of Behavior Therapy and Experimental Psychiatry*, 1978, *9*, 157–162.

Coates, T. J., Rosekind, M. R., Strossen, R. J., Thoresen, C. E., & Kirmil-Gray, K. Sleep recordings in the laboratory and the home: A comparative analysis. *Psychophysiology*, 1979, *16*, 339–346.

Coates, T. J., & Thoresen, C. E. *How to sleep better: A drug-free program for overcoming insomnia*. Englewood Cliffs, N.J.: Prentice-Hall, 1977.

Coates, T. J., & Thoresen, C. E. What to prescribe instead of sleep pills. *Journal of the American Medical Association*, 1978, *240*, 2311–2312.

Coates, T. J., & Thoresen, C. E. Treating arousals during sleep using behavioral self-management. *Journal of Consulting and Clinical Psychology*, 1979, *47*, 603–605.

Coates, T. J., & Thoresen, C. E. Treating sleep disorders. In S. Turner, H. C. Adams, & K. Calhoun (Eds.), *Handbook of clinical behavior therapy*. New York: Wiley, 1980.

Cooper, J. R. *Sedative–hypnotic drugs: Risks and benefits*. Rockville, Md.: National Institute of Drug Abuse, 1977.

Dement, W. C. *Some must watch whild some must sleep*. Stanford, Calif.: Stanford Alumni Association, 1972.

Dement, W. C., Carskadon, M., & Ley, R. The prevalence of REM narcolepsy. *Sleep Research*, 1973, *2*, 147. (Abstract)

Dement, W. C., Carskadon, M. A., & Richardson, G. Excessive daytime sleepiness in the sleep apnea syndrome. In C. Guilleminault & W. C. Dement (Eds.), *Sleep apnea syndromes*. New York: Alan Liss, 1978.

Dement, W. C., & Mitler, M. M. An overview of sleep research: Past, present, and future. In D,

Hamburg & K. Brodie (Eds.), *American handbook of psychiatry* (Vol. 6). New York: Basic Books, 1976.

Dement, W., Zarcone, V., Guilleminault, C., Carskadon, M., Hoddes, E., *et al.* Daytime sleep recordings in narcoleptics and hypersomniacs. *Sleep Research*, 1973, *2*, 147. (Abstract)

Ellis, W., Randall, N. J., Johns, M. W., & Dudley, H. A. F. A transportable sleep recording system. *Biomedical Engineering*, 1976, *11*, 246–248.

Foster, F. G., Kupfer, D. J., Weiss, G., *et al.* Mobility recordings and cycle research in neuropsychiatry. *Interdisciplinary Journal of Cycle Research*, 1972, *3*, 60–72.

Frankel, B. L., Coursey, R. D., Buchbinder, R., & Snyder, F. Recorded and reported sleep in chronic primary insomnia. *Archives of General Psychiatry*, 1976, *33*, 615–623.

Frost, J. D., & Delucchi, M. R. Electrophysiological home-recorded sleep study in insomnia. In N. Burch & W. L. Altshuler (Eds.), *Behavior and brain electrical activity*. New York: Plenum, 1975.

Giddings, G. Child's sleep: Effect of certain foods and beverages on sleep motility. *American Journal of Public Health*, 1934, *24*, 609–614.

Globus, G., Friedman, J., & Cohen, H. Effect of aircraft noise on sleep as recorded in the home. *Sleep Research*, 1973, *2*, 116. (Abstract)

Guilleminault, C., & Dement, W. C. 235 cases of excessive daytime sleepiness. *Journal of the Neurological Sciences*, 1977, *31*, 13–27.

Guilleminault, C., Eldridge, F. L., Simmons, F. B., & Dement, W. C. Sleep apnea in eight children. *Pediatrics*, 1976, *58*, 23–30.

Guilleminault, C., Korobkin, R., Anders, T. A., & Dement, W. C. Nocturnal disturbances in children: NREM dyssomnia or other? *Sleep Research*, 1977, *6*, 169. (Abstract)

Guilleminault, C., Persita, R., Sonquet, M., & Dement, W. C. Apneas during sleep in infants: Possible relationship with sudden infant death syndrome. *Science*, 1975, *190*, 677–679.

Guilleminault, C., Tilikan, A. G., & Dement, W. D. Sleep and respiration in children with sleep apnea syndrome. *Electroencephalography and Clinical Neurophysiology*, 1976. *41*, 367–378.

Handler, L. The use of a relationship and implosive therapy in ameliorating nightmares. *Psychotherapy: Theory, Research and Practice*, 1972, *9*, 54–56.

Hauri, P. A case series analysis of 141 consecutive insomniacs evaluated at the Dartmouth Sleep Lab. *Sleep Research*, 1976, *5*, 173. (Abstract)

Hauri, P. *The sleep disorders.* Kalamazo, Mich.: Upjohn, 1977.

Hauri, P. Biofeedback techniques in the treatment of chronic insomnia. In R. L. Williams & I. Karacan (Eds.), *Sleep disorders: Diagnosis and treatment*. New York: Wiley, 1978.

Hersen, M., & Bellack, A. S. (Eds.). *Behavioral assessment: A practical handbook*. New York: Pergamon, 1976.

Hirschberg, J. Parental anxieties accompanying sleep disturbance in young children. *Bulletin of the Menninger Clinic*, 1957, *21*, 129–138.

Hobson, J. A., Spagna, T., & Malenka, R. Ethology of sleep studied with time-lapse photography: Postural immobility and sleep-cycle phase in humans. *Science*, 1978, *201*, 1251–1253.

Hoddes, E., Zarcone, V. P., Smythe, H., Phillips, R., & Dement, W. C. Quantification of sleepiness: A new approach. *Psychophysiology*, 1973, *10*, 431–436.

Jenkins, C. D. A comparative review of the interview and questionnaire methods in the assessment of the coronary-prone behavior pattern. In T. M. Dembroski, S. M. Weiss, J. C. Shields, S. G. Haynes, & M. Feinheib (Eds.), *Coronary-prone behavior*. New York: Springer, 1978.

Johnson, L. C. The effect of total, partial, and stage sleep deprivation on EEG patterns and performance. In N. Burch & W. L. Altshuler (Eds.), *Behavior and brain electrical activity*. New York: Plenum, 1975.

Kales, A. Hypnotic drug abuse: Clinical and experimental aspects. *Medical Counterpoint*, 1971, *3*, 13.

Kales, A., & Kales, J. D. Sleep disorders: Recent findings in the diagnosis and treatment of disturbed sleep. *New England Journal of Medicine*, 1974, *299*, 487–497.

Kamiya, J. Behavioral, subjective, and physiological aspects of drowsiness and sleep. In D. W. Fiske & S. R. Maddi (Eds.), *Functions of varied experience*. Homewood, Ill.: Dorsey Press, 1961.

Karacan, I., Anch, M., Thornby, J. I., Okawa, M., & Williams, R. L. Longitudinal sleep patterns during pubertal growth: Four-year follow-up. *Pediatric Research*, 1975, *9*, 842–846.

Keith, P. R. Night terrors: A review of the psychology, neurophysiology, and therapy. *Journal of Child Psychiatry*, 1975, *14*, 477–489.

Kessler, S., Guilleminault, C., & Dement, W. C. A family study of 50 REM narcoleptics. *Acta Neurologica Scandanavica*, 1974, *50*, 503–512.

Killen, J., & Coates, T. J. The complaint of insomnia: What is it and how do we treat it? *Clinical Behavior Therapy Reviews*, 1979, *1*(4), 1–15.

Kirmil-Gray, K., Coates, T. J., Thoresen, C. E., & Rosekind, M. R. Treating insomnia in adolescents. *Sleep Research*, 1978, *7*, 237. (Abstract)

Kokkoris, C. P., Weitzmann, E., Pollak, C., Spielman, A. J., Czeisler, C. A., & Bradlow, H. Long-term ambulatory temperature monitoring in a subject with a hypernychthermeral sleep–wake cycle disturbance. *Sleep*, 1978, *1*, 177–190.

Korner, A., Thomson, E., & Glick, J. A system for monitoring crying and non-crying, large, medium, and small neonatal movements. *Child Development*, 1974, *45*, 946–952.

Krabbe, F., & Magnussen, G. On narcolepsy: I: Familial narcolepsy. *Acta Psychiatrica et Neurologica*, 1942, *17*, 149–173.

Kripke, D. F., Messin, S., Mullaney, D. J., & Wyborney, V. G. Wrist actigraph measures sleep. *Sleep Research*, 1977, *6*, 210. (Abstract)

Kripke, D. F., Simons, R. N., Garfinkel, L., & Hammond, E. C. Short and long sleep and sleeping pills. *Archives of General Psychiatry*, 1979, *36*, 103–116.

Kupfer, D. F., Detre, T. P., Foster, F. G., *et al*. The application of Delgado's telemetric mobility recorder for human sleep studies. *Behavioral Biology*, 1972, *7*, 858–590.

Linehan, M. M. Issues in behavioral interviewing. In J. D. Cone & R. P. Hawkins (Eds.), *Behavioral assessment: New directions in clinical psychology*. New York: Brunner/Mazel, 1977.

Marks, P. A., & Monroe, L. J. Correlates of adolescent poor sleepers. *Journal of Abnormal Psychology*, 1976, *85*, 243–246.

McPartland, R. J., Foster, F. G., Reisler, K. L., *et al*. Application of the LSI motor activity monitor. Part II: Patient studies. *Sleep Research*, 1976, *5*, 206. (Abstract) (a)

McPartland, R. J., Matthews, G., Reisler, K. L., *et al*. Application of the LSI motor activity monitor. Part I: Normative study. *Sleep Research*, 1976, *5*, 205. (Abstract) (b)

Metcalf, D. EEG sleep spindle autogenesis in normal children. In W. L. Smith (Ed.), *Drugs, development and cerebral function*. Springfield, Ill.: Charles C. Thomas, 1972.

Meyer, R. G. A behavioral treatment of sleepwalking associated with test anxiety. *Journal of Behavior Therapy and Experimental Psychiatry*, 1975, *6*, 167–168.

Miles, L. E. M., Raynal, D. M., & Wilson, M. A. Blind man living in normal society has circadian rhythms of 24.9 hours. *Science*, 1977, *198*, 421–423.

Monroe, L. J. Transient changes in EEG sleep patterns of married good sleepers: The effects of altering sleeping arrangement. *Psychophysiology*, 1969, *6*, 330–337.

Monroe, L. J., & Marks, P. A. Psychotherapists' descriptions of emotionally disturbed adolescent poor and good sleepers. *Journal of Clinical Psychology*, 1977, *33*, 263–269. (a)

Monroe, L. J., & Marks, P. A. MMPI differences between adolescent poor and good sleepers. *Journal of Consulting and Clinical Psychology*, 1977, *45*, 151–152. (b)

Moore, T., & Ucho, L. Night waking in early infancy. Part 1. *Archives of Diseases of Childhood*, 1957, *32*, 333–342.

Morganstern, K. P. Behavioral interviewing: The initial stages of assessment. In M. Hersen & A. S. Bellack (Eds.), *Behavioral assessment: A practical handbook*. New York: Pergamon, 1976.

Parmelee, A. The ontogeny of sleep patterns and associated periodicities in infants. In F. Falhner, N. Kretchmer, & E. Rossi (Eds.), *Modern problems in pediatrics*. New York: Karger, 1974.

Parmelee, A. H., Schultz, H. R., & Distrow, M. A. Sleep patterns of the newborn. *Journal of Pediatrics*, 1961, *58*, 241–250.

Petre-Quadens, A. On the different phases of sleep in the newborn with special reference to the activated phase or phase-d. *Journal of Neurological Sciences*, 1966, *3*, 151.

Phillips, R. L., Spiegel, R., Clayton, D., & Dement, W. C. A study of short arousals in insomniacs and normals. *Sleep Research*, 1975, *4*, 231. (Abstract)

Pollak, C., McGregor, P., & Weitzmann, E. D. The effects of flurazepam on daytime sleep after acute sleep–wake cycle reversal. *Sleep Research,* 1975, *4,* 112. (Abstract)

Price, V. A., Coates, T. J., Thoresen, C. E., & Grinstead, O. The prevalence and correlates of poor sleep among adolescents. *American Journal of Diseases of Children,* 1978, *132,* 583–586.

Rechtschaffen, A., & Kales, A. (Eds.). *A manual of standardized terminology, techniques, and scoring system for sleep stages of human subjects.* Washington, D.C.: Public Health Service, U.S. Government Printing Office, 1968.

Rechtschaffen, A., Wolpert, E., Dement, W. C., Mitchell, S., & Fisher, C. Nocturnal sleep of narcoleptics. *Electroencephalography and Clinical Neurophysiology,* 1963, *15,* 599–609.

Richardson, G. S., Carskadon, M. A., Flagg, W., van den Hoed, J., *et al.* Excessive daytime sleepiness in man: Multiple sleep latency measurement in narcoleptic and control subjects. *Electroencephalography and Clinical Neurophysiology,* 1978, *45,* 621–627.

Roberts, K. E., & Schoellkopf, J. A. Eating, sleeping, and elimination practice in a group of two-and-a-half-year-old children. *American Journal of Diseases of Children,* 1951, *82,* 121–152.

Rosekind, M. R., Coates, T. J., & Thoresen, C. E. Telephone transmission of polysomnographic data from subjects' homes. *Journal of Nervous and Mental Disease,* 1978, *166,* 438–441.

Roth, T., Lutz, T., Kramer, M., & Tietz, E. The relationship between objective and subjective evaluations of sleep in insomniacs. *Sleep Research,* 1977, *6,* 178. (Abstract)

Ruckebusch, Y. Sleep and environment. In W. P. Koella & P. Levin (Eds.), *Sleep, 1976.* Basel: Karger, 1977.

Sander, L., Julia, H., Stechler, G., & Burns, P. Continuous 24-hour interactional monitoring in infants reared in two caretaking environments. *Psychosomatic Medicine,* 1972, *34,* 270–282.

Sander, L., Stechler, G., Julia, H., & Burns, P. Early mother–infant interaction and 24-hour patterns of activity and sleep. *Journal of the American Academy of Child Psychiatry,* 1970, *9,* 103–123.

Scharf, M. B., Kales, A., & Bixler, E. O. Readaptation to the sleep laboratory in insomniac subjects. *Psychophysiology,* 1975, *12,* 412–415.

Schulman, J. L., Stevens, T. M., Suran, B. G., Kupst, M. J., & Naughton, M. J. Modification of activity level through biofeedback and operant conditioning. *Journal of Applied Behavior Analysis,* 1978, *11,* 145–152.

Sostek, A. M., Anders, T. F., & Sostek, A. J. Diurnal variability in sleep and waking states as a function of age and stress in human infants. *Sleep Research,* 1975, *4,* 133. (Abstract)

Stuart, R. B., & Stuart, F. Prestructuring behavior therapy through precounseling assessment. In E. J. Mash & L. G. Terdal (Eds.), *Behavior-therapy assessment: Diagnosis, design, and evaluation.* New York: Springer, 1976.

Takahashi, S., Guilleminault, C., & Dement W. A study of body movements in pseudo-incomniacs. *Sleep Research,* 1974, *3,* 146. (Abstract)

Taub, J. M., & Berger, R. J. Altered sleep duration and sleep period time displacements: Effects on performance in habitual long sleepers. *Physiology and Behavior,* 1976, *16,* 177–184.

Taub, J. M., & Hawkins, D. R. Nocturnal sleep schedules, performance, mood and diurnal rhythms. *Sleep Research,* 1977, *6,* 115. (Abstract)

Thomas, C. B. Precursors of premature diseases and death: The predictive potential of habits and family attitudes. *Annals of Internal Medicine,* 1976, *85,* 613–658.

Thoresen, C. E., Coates, T. J., Zarcone, V. P., Kirmil-Gray, K. R., & Rosekind, M. R. Treating the complaint of insomnia: Self-management perspectives. In J. M. Ferguson & C. B. Taylor (Eds.), *A comprehensive handbook of behavioral medicine.* New York: Spectrum, 1980.

Webb, W. B. Sleep and performance. In W. P. Koella & P. Levin (Eds.), *Sleep, 1976.* Basel: Karger, 1977.

Weil, G., & Goldfried, M. Treatment of insomnia in an eleven-year-old child through self-relaxation. *Behavior Therapy,* 1973, *4,* 282–294.

Weiss, B. L., McPartland, R. J., & Kupfer, D. J. Once more: The inaccuracy of non-EEG estimations of sleep. *American Journal of Psychiatry,* 1973, *130,* 1282–1285.

Wilkinson, R. T., & Mullaney, D. Electroencephalogram recording of sleep in the home. *Postgraduate Medical Journal,* 1976, *52,* 92–96.

Williams, R. L., Karacan, I., & Hursch, C. J. *Electroencephalography (EEG) of human sleep: Clinical applications*. New York: Wiley, 1974.

Yen, S., McIntire, R. W., & Berkowitz, S. Extinction of inappropriate sleeping behavior: Multiple assessment. *Psychological Reports*, 1972, *30*, 375–378.

Yoss, R., & Daly, D. Criteria for the diagnosis of the narcoleptic syndrome. *Proceedings of the Staff Meetings of the Mayo Clinic*, 1957, *32*, 320–328.

Zarcone, V. P. Narcolepsy. *New England Journal of Medicine*, 1975, *288*, 1156–1166.

Zarcone, V. P. Diagnosis and treatment of excessive daytime sleepiness. In H. I. Klawans (Ed.), *Clinical neuropharmacology*. New York: Raven Press, 1977.

CHAPTER 16

# ELIMINATION PROBLEMS: ENURESIS AND ENCOPRESIS

**Daniel M. Doleys**          **Mark S. Schwartz**

*The University of Alabama in Birmingham*          *Mayo Clinic*

**Anthony R. Ciminero**

*Veterans Administration Medical Center, Miami*

There are many problems involving the process of elimination. Lund (1963) noted some 90 different types of urinary incontinence alone. This chapter, however, will focus on the more common elimination disorders and on those that the behavioral psychologist is most likely to be called upon to treat. These include diurnal and nocturnal enuresis and encopresis. The philosophical approach and assessment procedures outlined can be generalized to other problems of elimination.

Perhaps more so with problems of elimination than with other behavioral disorders, anatomical and physiological integrity of the client or patient must be given full consideration. This is not to imply that if some biological mechanism is not functioning properly that behavior therapy can be of no use, but it is to imply that basic knowledge of these mechanisms, how they function, and their status, is important in designing an effective treatment program and one that is in line with the capabilities of the child. For example, complete daytime and nighttime continence may not be a reasonable goal for a multiply handicapped child, and standardized treatment regimens may have to be modified to meet his or her special needs. For these reasons, an adequate evaluation of problems of elimination also involves a multidisciplinary approach wherein the role of the behavioral psychologist may be to integrate the information into a meaningful treatment protocol. Although this chapter will focus upon behavioral assessment procedures, it will also try to show how these data tie in with data obtained from medicine, nutrition, and other disciplines.

# GENERAL PHILOSOPHY AND STRATEGY

Philosophically, problems of elimination will be examined from a functional analysis perspective. In each case, it is necessary to determine the situation(s) $(S)$ in which the behavior occurs, the relevant characteristics of the child $(O)$, an exact description of the problem or response to be treated $(R)$, and the consequences $(C)$ that are produced by the behavior and that influence its strength and frequency. This general $S$-$O$-$R$-$C$ model is similar to that described by Goldfried and Sprafkin (1974).

There are three goals in the assessment of problems of elimination: (1) to obtain an adequate description of the problem behavior, the client, and potential contributing factors; (2) to yield data that will meaningfully guide the selection or development of a treatment procedure; and (3) to establish guidelines relating to the implementation of the treatment (e.g., degree of supervision necessary). This third goal is frequently ignored or not sufficiently attended to. Often, the way in which we introduce a procedure, how we interact with the client and his or her family, how we instruct the parents to respond to their child, and how we respond to the parents are critical to ensuring compliance. Some children and parents have to be handled more "delicately," monitored more closely, and given more specific instructions than others.

To accomplish these three goals, the assessment of problems of elimination is conducted in four steps: (1) medical screening, (2) clinical interview, (3) baseline recording of the problem behavior, and (4) ongoing evaluation. The initial pretreatment assessment process may involve several visits and can take 2–4 weeks or longer. The time, however, is well spent, because it often yields a more efficient and effective treatment. Ongoing evaluation during treatment is vital to determining the impact of the intervention and to identifying necessary treatment modification.

Enuresis and encopresis are complex behavioral problems. Appropriate toileting is the terminal behavior in a complex chain of events and should be viewed as such. If approached too simplistically, subtle features of these problems may be undiscovered and contribute to prolonged treatment or relapse. One does not treat enuresis or encopresis but, rather, individual children, many of whom happen to respond positively to a given procedure. Therefore, assessment must focus on the individual child and his or her special circumstances and not only the problem behavior.

# ENURESIS

## Definition

*Functional nocturnal enuresis* can be defined as persistent wetting of the bed in the absence of neurologic or urologic pathology (Doleys, 1977, 1978). The minimum age at which a child can be considered enuretic varies from 3 to 5 years,

TABLE 1
Classification System for Enuresis

| Category | Percentage dry | Description |
|---|---|---|
| 1 | 100% dry | Never wet |
| 2 | "100%" dry | 1–2 wets per year |
| 3 | 98–99% dry | 1–2 wets per 4 months or 3–6 wets per year |
| 4 | 90–97% dry | Less than 1 wet per week or 1–3 wets per month |
| 5 | 50–87% dry | 1 wet per week to less than 4 wets per week or 4–15 wets per month |
| 6 | 13–47% dry | 4–6 wets per week or 16–26 wets per month |
| 7 | 3–10% dry | 27–29 wets per month or 1–3 dries per month |
| 8 | 1–2% dry | 1–2 dries per 4 months |
| 9 | 0% dry | 0–2 dries per year |
| 0 | Variable | Intermittent and unpredictable periods of wetting |

depending upon the researcher. Similarly, the frequency of bed wetting required to define enuresis has ranged from 1 to 21 wets per month (Forsythe & Redmond, 1974; Hallgren, 1965; Oppel, Harper, & Rider, 1968a; Groenhart, Note 1). Enuresis is more common in males than in females (about 2:1) up to age 11, after which the ratio is approximately equal (deJonge, 1973).

Incidence figures vary, but most report 15–20% of 5-year-olds, 5% of 10-year-olds, and about 2% of 12- to 14-year-olds to be enuretic (Lovibond & Coote, 1970; Oppel, Harper, & Rider, 1968b). The percentage of children expected to become dry in a given year without systematic professional treatment also varies and is a function of age. deJonge (1973) estimated the average to be 13.5% for ages 7.5–12 years. Forsythe and Redmond (1974), in a study of 1129 children, noted remission rates of 14–16% from ages 5 to 19 years. Approximately 80% of younger enuretic children and about 50% of 12- to 14-year-old enuretics will have never been continent for 6 months or more and will fall in the category of primary or continuous enuretics. The remainder of enuretics will have been consistently dry but then began wetting (i.e., secondary, acquired, or onset enuresis—deJonge, 1973).

Given the variety of criteria used to define bed wetting, Table 1 is presented as a proposed guide to classification. This scheme will allow for a more exact description of enuresis and may help in providing a more precise analysis of treatment outcome in studies involving large numbers of children.

## Physiology of Micturition

Basic knowledge of the physiology of micturition and the developmental steps related to daytime and nighttime continence will be useful in assessing the problem, designing a treatment, and communicating the rationale for treatment. Yeates (1973) noted five steps in the functioning of the mature bladder: (1) bladder filling by flow of urine into the bladder from the kidneys via the ureters, (2) desire to void initiated by stretching and relaxing of the detrusor muscle surrounding the bladder, (3) inhibition of voiding by maintaining pressure on the sphincter muscles and perineal pressure, (4) onset of voiding following bladder fullness as a result of rhythmical contractions of the bladder, and (5) sustained bladder contractions and sphincter relaxation until bladder is empty. A more detailed description can be found in Yeates (1973) and Muellner (1951).

Muellner (1960a, 1960b) identified four developmental stages encountered in the acquisition of mature bladder functioning: (1) demonstrated awareness of bladder fullness (1–2 years of age), (2) ability to retain urine voluntarily (about 3 years of age), (3) capacity to start and stop the flow of urine in midstream (4.5 years), and (4) ability to initiate and terminate the flow of urine at any degree of bladder fullness (about 5 years of age). It should be self-evident that these skills are not prerequisites to achieving urinary control and that the ages listed are mean estimates. In the older incontinent child, the absence of one or more of these skills may be a contributing factor to the enuresis or indicative of a developmental delay.

## Etiology

The intention of this section is to acquaint the reader with the various hypothesized etiologies of enuresis. Each will be examined briefly. A more thorough discussion can be found in Kolvin, MacKeith, and Meadows (1973) and Perlmutter (1976). Because enuresis is not a disease, no single etiological factor appears to be sufficient to account for all cases. Many of the factors may be independent, but they are not necessarily mutually exclusive.

### Functional Bladder Capacity

*Functional bladder capacity* (FBC) refers to the volume of urine retained before voiding occurs and is not a measure of the structural size of the bladder. Several studies have shown enuretics to have smaller FBCs than nonenuretics (Esperanca & Gerrard, 1969; Starfield, 1967; Zaleski, Gerrard, & Shokeir, 1973). It has been suggested that this reduced FBC is a result of inadequate cortical inhibition over afferent bladder stimuli, which may be part of a developmental delay. It has also been suggested (Esperanca & Gerrard, 1969) that a low FBC may be indicative of an allergenic reaction wherein the bladder is maintained in spasm, preventing it from accommodating larger volumes of urine. Several studies have documented the effectiveness of bladder-stretching or retention-control exercises for increasing FBC (Harris & Purohit, 1977; Starfield & Mellits, 1968; Zaleski *et al.*, 1973). Some authors (Kimmel & Kimmel, 1970; Paschalis, Kimmel, & Kimmel, 1972) have proposed such exercises as a viable treatment for nocturnal enuresis. Recent data by Harris and Purohit (1977) and Doleys, Ciminero, Tollison, Williams, and Wells (1977) cast serious doubt on the utility of such bladder-stretching or retention-control exercises as the sole treatment procedure for enuresis.

In examining the question of the relationship of FBC to enuresis, Rutter (1973) notes that there is considerable overlap in the FBCs of nocturnal enuretics and nonenuretics of the same age (Starfield, 1967; Starfield & Mellits, 1968; Esperanca & Gerrard, 1969), eliminating it as a sufficient explanation. In addition, an 8-year-old enuretic may have a larger bladder capacity than a 4-year-old nonenuretic. Rutter (1973) suggests that a small FBC could reflect a compensatory response. That is, the bladder remains small since it has not been stretched by dilation at nighttime.

## *Sleep*

Parents and professionals alike have indicted "deep sleep" as a causative factor in enuresis. Many parents of enuretic children will readily volunteer testimonials on the difficulty they have in awakening their children. Several researchers have also described enuresis as an arousal disorder (Finley, 1971; Perlmutter, 1976; Ritvo, Ornitz, Gottlieb, Poussaint, Maron, Ditman, & Blinn, 1969).

When discussing this issue, it is important to differentiate between depth of sleep and arousability. Depth of sleep is determined by electroencephalographic (EEG) patterns as being Stage 1, 2, 3, 4, or REM (rapid eye movement), which is associated with dreaming (Kales & Kales, 1974). Arousability is a behavioral measure of how easily the child can be awakened from sleep. These two measures of sleep are not necessarily associated with one another (Graham, 1973).

The research in the sleep area has been revealing, though the data are inconsistent and the conclusions tentative (Graham, 1973; Salmon, Taylor, & Lee, 1973; see Chapter 15). In general, it appears as though wetting occurs in all of the four stages of sleep, but typically not in REM. Kales, Kales, Jacobson, Humphrey, and Soldatos (1977) suggest that the stage of sleep in which the enuretic episodes occur is proportional to the amount of time spent in that stage. Younger children tend to spend proportionally more time in deeper stages (3 and 4) than older children, which coincides with Finley's (1971) observations that as age increases, wetting tends to occur more frequently in the lighter stages of sleep. This may, in part, account for children "outgrowing" their enuresis, since bladder distention cues insufficient to arouse the child from Stage 4 sleep may be sufficient to arouse him or her from Stage 2 or 3. In reviewing 62 all-night EEG records of seven males, Ritvo et al. (1969) divided enuretic episodes into three classes: awake enuresis, nonarousal enuresis, and arousal enuresis. No "arousal signals" from bladder distention were recorded for the nonarousal cases, whereas they were noted in the arousal group but did not result in the child's awakening. These data seem to be compatible with Di Perri and Meduri's (1972) observation that enuretic children are generally less responsive to interoceptive stimulation, such as a distended, rapidly contracting bladder.

With regard to arousability, studies by Bostack (1958), Boyd (1960), Braithwaithe (1956), and Kaffman and Elizur (1977) provide conflicting data as to whether enuretics are more difficult to awaken than nonenuretics. Variations in methodology, however, make comparisons across studies difficult. Similarly, studies of the relationship of intensity of urine alarms to acquisition of nighttime continence (Young & Morgan, 1973; Finley & Wansley, 1977) have produced equivocal outcomes. Again, different methodologies and intensity ranges were used. Finley and Wansley (1977), however, did note the treatment of "slow responders" to be facilitated by using a louder alarm, whereas the acquisition rate of faster responders was not differentially affected.

In summary, the relationship between enuresis, sleep arousal, and depth of sleep is not yet clear. Some enuretic children may indeed have an arousal problem and would benefit from the use of a louder stimulus and nighttime conditioning using a urine alarm, but to date we have no statistics as to what percentage of the total population of enuretics this might be. Practical considerations, such as parental cooperation, might preclude the use of louder alarms with all children, and assessment can be helpful in determining where such an alarm may or may not be needed.

## Psychological Factors

The psychodynamic and psychoanalytical models propose that diurnal and nocturnal enuresis are a result of some underlying conflict, anxiety, or emotional stress (Pierce, 1975; Sperling, 1965). There is some evidence that enuretic children display a higher incidence of behavioral disturbances than other children (Rutter, Yule, & Graham, 1973; Shaffer, 1973). This relationship is stronger for girls than for boys. Such problems, however, may not have any etiological significance and could be a result of the enuresis (Werry, 1967). Posttreatment measures have not revealed the appearance of any new "symptoms" following the remediation of enuresis (Baker, 1969; Dische, 1971; Werry & Cohrssen, 1965). Such symptom substitution would be predicted from an analytic model.

Stress such as mother–child separation in a critical period of development (2–4 years of age) may result in the onset of enuresis or incomplete toilet training. Douglas (1973) and Shaffer (1973) have described some data that suggest that such events may interfere with the acquisition or development of normal inhibitory controls. Nevertheless, it is important to remember that events that may be judged to be significant in the onset of enuresis are often not present or influential in later years.

## Genetics

As always, it is difficult to interpret the role of genetics. The views as to the importance of genetics vary according to the writer's bias toward family history and concordance rates as data. Generally, it has been noted that concordance rates for enuresis are twice as high for monozygotic as for dyzygotic twins. Regarding familial history, where both parents were enuretics, 77% of children were enuretic, as opposed to 44% when one parent was, and 15% if neither were enuretic. There are obviously many alternative explanations and speculations regarding these data. A more thorough discussion of these and other issues related to genetic factors and enuresis can be found in Faray (1935), Cohen (1975), and Bakwin (1973).

## Learning–Behavioral Model

This approach emphasizes the learned nature of functional enuresis and attributes it to habit deficiency, inadequate learning experiences, and inappropriate reinforcement contingencies (Atthowe, 1973; Lovibond & Coote, 1970; Yeates, 1973; Young, 1965). Enuresis has been approached from several different paradigms within learning theory. Mowrer and Mowrer (1938) proposed a classical conditioning model as the foundation for treatment. Lovibond and Coote (1970) preferred to view control of micturition as an instrumental response acquired through the process of avoidance conditioning. Turner, Young, and Rachman (1970) described acquisition of continence via the urine alarm in terms of a punishment or passive avoidance paradigm, while Azrin, Sneed, and Foxx (1973, 1974) focused on the operant, social–motivational aspects involved in the acquisition of urinary control.

Briefly, the learning–behavioral approach attempts to rearrange environmental circumstances so that appropriate control responses can be acquired. This model, unlike others, attends closely to the presence and acquisition of prerequisite skills such as undressing, particularly in work with handicapped children (Foxx & Azrin, 1973; Edwards, Note 2). In the general case, bladder fullness is interpreted as a stimulus event that, in the continent child, has acquired discriminative properties, cuing nighttime awakening and/or proper toileting. For the child with enuresis, bladder stimuli have not acquired these properties or other contingencies (e.g., avoidance or fear in the case of the toilet phobic) exert a stronger influence over responding.

## Assessment

### Medical Screening

All children presenting with enuresis should undergo a medical examination. Many, if not all, will have done so in the recent past, and the results of these evaluations should be requested. Most enuretics will not have any urological or neurological pathology. This, of course, is less true when treatment involves multiply handicapped or developmentally disabled children, where knowledge of the pathology will guide the establishing of realistic goals and procedures. With this population, consultation with a physical therapist or physical medicine specialist may also be needed to determine posturing on the commode, need for special equipment (Edwards, Note 2), and the degree to which the child is ambulatory. Ability to detect bladder fullness may be inhibited in some cases and special signaling devices may be needed for the noncommunicative child (Edwards, Note 2).

Extensive urological examinations are generally not needed at the outset (Perlmutter, 1976; Campbell, 1970). A urinalysis and urine culture to rule out renal pathology and infection should be standard. Infections are much more common among females than among males but occur in only about 5–10% of girls (Jones, Gerrard, Shokeir, & Houston, 1972; Stansfeld, 1973). The presence of significant bacteria, recurrent urinary tract infection, diurnal patterns (Arnold & Ginsburg,

1975; Smith, 1967), and repeated failure of systematic supervised treatment are indicative of a need for more comprehensive urological evaluations. Residual urine in the bladder after voiding, a poor stream (small, irregular), daytime disturbances in mictruition such as dribbling, dysuria (painful urination), urgency, significan polyuria (frequent urination), and daytime incontinence should result in a more extensive medical evaluation. In general, it has been noted that enuretics void more frequently during the day than nonenuretics (Esperanca & Gerrard, 1969; Starfield, 1972). In one study enuretics aged 4–14 were noted to void 12–14 times per 24 hours as contrasted with nonenuretics, who voided 4–6 times over the same period (Esperanca & Gerrard, 1969).

Urological examinations typically undertaken, when indicated, include an excretory urogram (intravenous pyelogram, or IVP), voiding cystourethrogram, and cystoscopy. An IVP is typically performed where there is a question of obstruction, structural damage, or inappropriate functioning of the genetourinary system. Briefly, the IVP involves injection of a chemical containing iodine. This chemical is excreted rapidly by the kidney into the urine, which makes the kidneys, ureters, and bladder opaque to X rays taken serially over about a half-hour period. The procedure is somewhat uncomfortable and in rare occasions produces side effects such as nausea, vomiting, itching, hives, and respiratory discomfort. This examination will help rule out obstructions, blockages, tumors, stones, and congenital abnormalities. Residual urine following voiding can also be detected.

The voiding cystourethrogram is the visualization of the urethra and bladder during retrograde insertion of a contract material through a catheter. This procedure, often referred to as "cystometry," can provide precise information regarding the functioning of the bladder, the point at which contractions begin to appear, the strength of the contractions, and when voiding is initiated (Wear, 1974).

Cystoscopy involves the insertion into the bladder via the urethra of a telescopic-like instrument, which magnifies and illuminates the bladder. This procedure is most frequently carried out only when there is strong indication of organic disease.

### Clinical Interview

The clinical interview is divided into five areas: (1) history and description of problem, (2) family and medical history, (3) other problems, (4) home and family environment, and (5) previous treatment. The interview can be conducted with the child and/or the parent. If the child is embarrassed or very young, his or her presence during the entire interview may be distracting and unnecessary. It is important, however, for the therapist to have some contact with the child. At some point during the initial assessment, the parent and child should be observed together in order to determine the degree of control that the parent is able to exercise over the child's behavior.

The child and parent should be set at ease early. Children and sometimes parents can get very anxious and embarrassed when discussing the problem. It is important to listen to both the child and the parent during the interview and to establish rapport. This rapport will be helpful in developing and maintaining parental cooperation and can result in the therapist becoming a positive reinforcer for the child. Talking *with* and not *at* the child is recommended. The interview should be somewhat structured, but the therapist should be flexible and willing to let the parent or child "ramble" some. Many times, parents have become very frustrated with the ineffectiveness of earlier treatments and need or would like a chance to discuss these experiences. The general tone of the interview should be a reassuring and confident one. The child should be informed that the problem is rather common and one that others in his or her school probably share.

It is important to impress upon the parent and the child that everyone will be working toward the resolution of the problem, rather than allowing the child to feel that this is "his or her problem" and that success or failure of treatment is solely his or her responsibility.

HISTORY OF ENURESIS. Information regarding the history of the enuresis should include data relating to the onset and severity of the wetting. Medical factors (e.g., infection) and stress factors (divorce, moving, etc.) are often related to the onset of enuresis after continence has been obtained. Continuation of these circumstances could influence the efficacy of treatment and should be investigated. If a child has never achieved total continence, greater attention should be given to assessing the basic prerequisite skills (Azrin & Foxx, 1974; Foxx & Azrin, 1973), such as dressing, finding the bathroom at night and so forth. If the parents describe brief periods of continence, it is important to determine whether these were a result of parental nighttime awakening of the child, unusual circumstances in the home, or fluid restriction. Continence obtained under these situations is artificial and may be misleading in that it could erroneously be interpreted as indicating skills that the child does not have.

Inquiries should be made as to the parents' perceptions of the child's ability to retain urine after he or she has indicated the urge to void, the daily frequency of voiding, and the presence of pain. Some children display an urgency syndrome, characterized by a sudden and intense urge to void and an inability to retain. The presence of high-rate voiding during the day (polyuria) and painful urination (dysuria) may indicate abnormalities in the structure or functioning of the genitourinary system. Some children will not display enuretic behavior when they stay away from home or have company. This information is suggestive of the presence of appropriate inhibitory controls in specific situations.

FAMILIAL HISTORY. Another area of questioning focuses on the family history and background. Information should be obtained about other enuretic siblings and any history of enuresis, diabetes, or urinary tract infections on either the paternal or maternal side of the family. Parents who themselves have been enuretic or who have had other enuretic children may be overly demanding or complacent based upon their own experiences.

Competence and mental status of the parents are important in determining the type and amount of supervision that will be needed and the ability of the parents to understand and interpret directions, organize schedules, tolerate the frustrations of treatment, and maintain compliance throughout. The clinical interview should be sufficient to evaluate parental competence. Where questions arise, they should be followed up prior to the onset of treatment.

Interest in the child, parenting skills, and attitudes should be considered in the interview. Attitudes specifically toward bed wetting can be assessed using the Morgan and Young (1975) tolerance scale of 20 items. Scores indicative of intolerance obtained on this scale have been found to be associated with early withdrawal from treatment utilizing the urine-alarm procedure. If identified early, closer supervision, more support, and the use of techniques that require minimal parental time and involvement can be employed to enhance the likelihood of success.

Recent, expected, or ongoing life changes (e.g. moves, trips, pregnancies, hospitalizations, starting or changing of school, change in parental marriage status, and death of close relatives) are all important in assessing contributing factors to the enuresis and the development of a treatment protocol. Although recent or expected changes do not necessarily preclude treatment, they can alter the type and time of the treatment. The parents frequently will not mention what might be considered important events unless specifically asked. Treatment is sometimes best deferred pending other anticipated changes that might be occurring in the child's or family's life.

OTHER PROBLEMS. The third area of assessment involves gathering general information regarding the presence of additional problems with the child. In planning treatment for enuresis, it is useful to know about the child's general health, level of intellectual functioning, emotional stability, behavioral problems, and general motor and social development. Standard assessment techniques such as the Minnesota Child Development Inventory for children up to 6½ years (Ireton & Thwing, 1972), the Personality Inventory for Children (ages 6–16—Wirt, Loeba, Klinedinst, & Seat, 1977), and the Children's Behavior Checklist (Achenbach, 1978) can be used. Children with emotional problems can still be treated for enuresis but may require closer supervision and additional treatment for preexisting problems. There are also data indicating a differential rate of relapse between children who are described as emotionally disturbed and enuretic children who are not (Sacks & DeLeon, 1978). Children who are functioning in the lower-than-average range of intelligence may also require closer attention.

The use of parent questionnaires and brief observations of parent–child interactions can yield an estimate of the child's compliance. Certain treatment procedures, such as dry-bed training (DBT—Azrin, Sneed, & Foxx, 1973), require a considerable amount of child–parent interaction and may be contraindicated where the child appears to be very noncompliant. There may also be situations where noncompliance should be treated prior to the enuresis. In one report, this approach was effective in reducing the enuresis (Nordquist, 1971).

HOME ENVIRONMENT. Knowledge of the physical environment (home, institution, boarding house, etc.) in which the child is living needs to be obtained. For example: Does the child sleep alone or share a room, and if the latter, with whom? Do any siblings wet? What is the location of the parent or other care giver to the child? What is the proximity of the bathroom? Are there night-lights? What is the temperature in the home at night? What does the child prefer to wear to bed?

It is more common and probably preferable for the enuretic child to remain in his or her own room during treatment, but temporary arrangements are sometimes necessary as might be the case in an institutional setting or where bedrooms are shared with other children. Enuretic siblings should probably be separated from the treated child, especially if the urine alarm is being used, so they do not become desensitized to it. Nonenuretic siblings sleeping in the same room during the urine-alarm treatment can usually learn to sleep through the alarm or return to sleep quickly after they have been awakened.

The major consideration is to make treatment as unobtrusive and nonaversive as possible for other family members and for the child. If the separation cannot be achieved practically, then other treatment approaches should be considered. Ideally, the toilet should be near the child's bedroom regardless of the treatment approach used, especially for younger children or when household temperatures are cool. The sleeping–bedroom area temperature should be kept comfortable enough for the child to get out of bed. If the bathroom is not close, serious consideration should be given to a portable toilet or to moving the child. At least one parent should sleep nearby to help the younger, less competent child or the child who is having trouble in awakening and who may require shaping and praise.

PREVIOUS TREATMENTS. Parents have usually attempted other treatment, including support, fluid restriction, punishment, nighttime awakening, positive reinforcement for dryness, self-monitoring, medication for enuresis or urinary tract infection, counseling, urine alarm, dry-bed training, psychotherapy, retention-control training, hypnosis, sleep interval training, dietary modification, urological instrumentation, and surgery. Details on supervised and unsupervised treatment attempts, how systematically they were carried out, the outcome of these attempts, problems incurred, attitudes of the parents toward treatment of the enuresis, and knowledge and expectations of the parent and the child should be evaluated. Often, parents will have implemented any one or more of the preceding treatment techniques but will have done so in a very unsystematic or unsupervised fashion. Nevertheless, they will often report, "I have used the urine alarm before without success." Upon careful questioning, however, one frequently discovers that it was used intermittently and for brief periods, that treatment was interrupted, or that the apparatus malfunctioned or was insensitive. The prior use of unsystematic and inappropriate reinforcement and punishment in an attempt to modify the enuresis is common. Suggestions involving the use of reinforcement and tokens will frequently elicit comments that this has been tried and failed. It behooves the clinician to obtain full and complete details of any unsystematic or systematic treatment attempts so as to prevent the parents from not accepting or from criticizing the proposed treatment on the basis of unsuccessful early attempts.

The use of imipramine (Tofranil), a tricyclic antidepressant, is quite common among enuretic children treated by physicians. Assessment of the effects of medication should include knowing when the medication was administered, the dose level, the age of the child, and the degree and duration of any side effects experienced. The child's and parents' attitudes toward treatment may be affected to prior failures, especially if their hopes were unrealistically high. Without necessarily criticizing the use of medication, the therapist should be aware of the data on the efficacy of the medication and report this to the parents. Discussion of the speculated mechanism of action will help parents to be more confident in the therapist's skill and will enhance their willingness to cooperate. Some families have already had unsuccessful and unpleasant experiences with the urine-alarm approach. Equipment malfunctions, use with too young a child, the child's fear of the alarm, inadequate supervision or instructions, insufficient treatment duration, inadequate explanation of relapse, and/or inadequate fluid regulation contribute to treatment failures. Motivation to reinitiate treatment will often be low.

Some treatments such as fluid restrictions, nighttime awakening, reprimands, and punishment often seem logical to parents and are sometimes recommended by professionals. If any such treatments are ongoing, the parents should be encouraged to stop but should not be chastised for having tried. It is more helpful if the parents and the child feel that the therapist is attempting to improve upon what they have been trying to do.

### Assessment of Enuretic Behavior

The assessment of enuretic behavior involves data gathering relevant to the child's (1) nighttime (nocturnal) patterns, (2) daytime (diurnal) patterns, and (3) bladder capacity. This information is obtained during a 1- to 3-week baseline period. The procedure for recording these data should be written out in clear, simple language; reviewed with the parent and child; and sent home with them. Recording sheets should be prepared in advance so that the parents do not have to construct their own. Telephone contact or an office visit should occur during the early part of the baseline to ensure that directions are being followed.

This data collection period can fulfill several functions. First, it provides a baseline against which to evaluate the effects of treatment. Second, it yields information that can be useful in the selection of a treatment technique. Third, it provides a check on the parents' motivation via their willingness to keep records. Fourth, it assesses parental ability to follow directions. And fifth, it may itself become the treatment, since some children become dry during self-monitoring. The baseline period allows for this trend to be observed and may thus eliminate the need to use a complicated procedure. It is important that during baseline, fluid restrictions be removed and the child not wear protective clothing such as diapers. Rather, the child should sleep in underwear, pajamas, or nude.

NOCTURNAL PATTERNS. An accurate record of the *frequency* of nocturnal wets can be obtained by bed checks made about 2 hours after the child is asleep, in the middle of the night, and in early morning. This helps determine the approximate time of wetting and if the child is a multiple wetter. Reduction in the frequency of multiple wets and delay of wetting until later in the night, during treatment, are positive signs and may precede a noticeable decrease in the number of wet nights per week (Schwartz, Colligan, & O'Connell, 1972).

If wetting is intermittent, knowledge of this *pattern* may help to identify contributing variables such as fluid intake, stress, fatigue, and illness. For example, intermittent periods of wetting followed by continence have been associated with recurrent urinary tract infection, especially in girls (Gerrard & Zaleski, 1974). The parents can also obtain an estimate of the size of the wet spots by measuring across the widest part or by judging it to be size of a half dollar, saucer, dinner plate, meat platter, or larger. A reduction in the size of the wet spot may precede a decrease in wetting frequency, although this particular measure is not used with great regularity.

In terms of *sleep behavior*, parents should be instructed to note any somnabulism, nightmares, restlessness, partial awakening, bruxism, and so forth. Some children become partially awake prior to, or immediately after, wetting, which may indicate sensitivity to bladder distention–contractions or wetness of the bed. This appears to be more true of older (9–14 years) children, who seem to sleep during lighter stages of sleep.

As a measure of arousability, parents can be asked to place an alarm clock or urine alarm near the child's bed and to activate it 1–2 hours after the child is asleep. The amount of time (up to 5 minutes) it takes the child to awaken and whether or not physical prompts after 5 minutes are needed give a global estimate of arousability (Boyd, 1960). This information can influence the decision as to whether or not to use a urine alarm and, if so, as to what kind (i.e., loudness) of urine alarm should be used. Arousal conditioning (Browning, 1967) may be necessary in some cases. It has frequently been assumed, although not experimentally demonstrated, that wet beds are "naturally" aversive and will arouse the child (Peterson, 1971).

DIURNAL PATTERNS. Information relating to diurnal patterns should be obtained whether or not there is a history of daytime incontinence. Starfield (1972) and Esperanca and Gerrard (1969) have noted that many enuretic children void more frequently than nonenuretics. deJonge (1973) stated that about 15% of nocturnal enuretics will exhibit excessive diurnal frequency. Periodic diurnal wetting and excessive frequency may be indicative of stress incontinence (Shingleton & Davis, 1977), bladder infection (most often in females), urgency syndrome (de-Jonge, 1973) small bladder capacity, or an organic lesion. The child should be questioned about whether he or she senses the urge to void or has fears of the bathroom. Some children find public bathrooms very aversive because of the lack of privacy, the smell, or filthy conditions. Parents should be encouraged to check the child after each voiding episode to ensure that there is no daytime dribbling. Dribbling can occur in response to incomplete bladder evacuation or inadequate sphincter control.

Assessment of the frequency, duration, and location of diurnal wetting should be made. If the wetting is frequent (e.g., one or more times a day), additional medical and/or psychosocial–behavioral evaluation is indicated. Practical and individual professional considerations will influence whether one treats the diurnal problem first or later.

FUNCTIONAL BLADDER CAPACITY. Zaleski *et al.* (1973) found the bladder capacity of a group of enuretic children to be significantly lower than that of nonenuretics. Inadequate retention ability, infection, and neurogenic bladder have been associated with small functional bladder capacities.

There are two measures of bladder capacity: average bladder capacity (ABC) and maximum bladder capacity (MBC). The ABC is obtained by having the parents or child measure as many voiding episodes as possible for 3–7 days. This is accomplished by providing a data sheet and a plastic beaker or special container fitting on the commode, graded in milliliters or ounces, into which the child can void. The average amount voided over the collection period is considered the ABC. Collecting measures outside the home is difficult. Therefore, parents are encouraged to obtain as many measures as possible in the evenings and on the weekends.

The MBC can be derived in two ways. First, the largest recorded voiding while collecting data for the ABC can be considered the MBC. This is the easiest method and perhaps the most valid (Zaleski et al., 1973). The second procedure is called the "water load" test. The child is given water, tea, juice, soda, or other beverage (except milk) at the rate of 30 milliliters per kilogram (1 ounce per 2.2 pounds) up to 17 ounces and is asked to drink it as rapidly as is comfortable. He or she is then asked to announce when the urge to void is felt and to refrain from voiding until it is very uncomfortable. The retention interval and the amount voided are measured. The child is again asked to indicate when he or she feels the next urge to void (which will usually be within an hour or so) and to retain as before. The retention time and magnitude of the second voiding are also recorded. The larger of these two voiding episodes is considered the MBC. This water load procedure can be carried out at the home or in the office (Harris & Purohit, 1977). Parents must be cautioned to be supportive and not punitive during data collection. For the "shy" child, this procedure can be embarrassing, and avoidance behavior should be expected.

There are other measures of bladder functioning that have been proposed as being prerequisite to the acquisition of continence (Muellner, 1960a, 1960b) and that can be obtained during baseline. At 4–5 years of age, children should be able to start and stop the flow of urine in midstream without pain and to void in the absence of any significant urge to void. Parents should be asked to observe these responses and to indicate whether or not the child experienced any difficulty or pain in accomplishing them. Retention training and sphincter control exercises may be useful if these behaviors are not present, although the relationship between these behaviors and enuresis has not yet been experimentally validated.

To date, there appears to be no single set of guidelines by which to determine how to treat the child who is enuretic during the day and at night. One general rule of thumb is to intervene where the likelihood of success seems to be the greatest but not for both daytime and nighttime incontinence at the same time. Availability of a caregiver, history of continence, severity of the problem, and treatment techniques being considered enter into the decision. In most instances, treatment of nocturnal enuresis is the most practical because the parents are available and the inappropriate behavior can be detected and consequated as soon as it occurs. However, where no toilet training appears to have been achieved, it may be more judicious to begin with daytime training, especially with a developmentally disabled child. With the child who shows some degree of control but who has not obtained total continence, one can start with either problem.

### *Ongoing Evaluation*

After treatment has been initiated, weekly contacts should be maintained. If possible, office visits should occur on a regular basis. Periodic contact by telephone or mail may be used as an alternative if the initial consultation(s) are comprehensive and office visits are not practical. During these contacts, the data collected should be reviewed and discussed. The specific type of data collected will vary as a function of the treatment program utilized. Wet night, time of each wet, and time of each self-awake are preferred for nocturnal enuresis.

There is a plethora of management problems that can arise during treatment and that require the therapist's attention. These include noncompliance, fear of the alarm, resistance to treatment, parental disagreement about the utility of treatment, financial considerations, diminished motivation, malfunctioning equipment, and family disruption. Although many of these can be anticipated, some cannot. Information regarding problems may not always be volunteered.

It is helpful to maintain a frequency graph of the child's progress. Under the pressure of other demands, charting of data is sometimes ignored. Ongoing charting (1) provides a ready source of feedback to the child, (2) provides a model of appropriate behavior for the parent, and (3) focuses the therapist's attention upon behavioral trends in treatment. If the child is being maintained on any medication, continuing consultation with the primary physician is also advisable.

# ENCOPRESIS

## Definition

*Functional encopresis* has been defined as "the passage of fecal material of any amount of consistency into the clothing or other generally unacceptable areas in the absence of any organic pathology beyond the age of 3 years" (Doleys, 1979a, p. 186). This condition has also been referred to as "fecal incontinence" and "psychogenic megacolon" when soiling occurs in response to excessive retention and an enlarged colon is noted. There is considerable disagreement about the age at which a child can be considered encopretic. It is sometimes difficult to discriminate between an encopretic child and one who has not been toilet trained. Knowledge of the child's general developmental rate, prior attempts at toilet training, and the presence of bladder control influence which descriptive label applies. However, the assessment and treatment procedures are often very similar.

There is a variety of subclassifications for functional encopresis. Encopresis is generally divided into primary (continuous) and secondary (discontinuous) cases.

TABLE 2

Classification System for Encopresis

| Degree of constipation | Degree of incontinence |
| --- | --- |
| Straining, hard stools (by history or examination), or bowel movements every 2 days or less. | Soiling infrequent (less than weekly) and amounts small. |
| Palpable fecal mass throughout abdomen; fecal masses visible on X ray; bowel movements every 3–5 days. | Occasional large accidents (less than weekly). |
| Large stools; fecal mass visible throughout colon on X ray; bowel movements every 7–14 days. | Light to moderate soiling frequently (one or more times per week) or one large accident per week, and/or absence of sensation prior to accidents. |
| Abdominal detention from several fecal impactions; diffuse, enlarged colon by X ray; bowel movements every 14–21 days. | Soiling daily or almost daily. |

Note. Adapted from Levine and Bakow, Pediatrics, 1976, 58, p. 90.

The latter term is applied to those patients who have demonstrated independent bowel control for at least 6 months. Encopretic children are further subdivided into retentive and nonretentive types (Gavanski, 1971; Walker, 1978) and those who display an exaggerated fear of defecation (toilet phobia—Doleys, 1978), refusal to defecate (pot refusal syndrome—Berg & Jones, 1964), smearing of feces (copraphagia), and stress incontinence (Berg & Jones, 1964). A majority of encopretics display some degree of constipation or retention (Fitzgerald, 1975; Levine, 1975).

A somewhat more qualitative system of classifying encopretics has been illustrated by Levine and Bakow (1976) in describing their study sample. Table 2 shows a version of the schema, which allows for a description of the severity and degree of constipation and incontinence to be made. Such a system is not only more descriptive but also more adequately suited for summarizing and evaluating treatment outcome.

Estimates of the incidence of functional encopresis vary from 1.5% to 7.5% of children. Levine (1975) and Yates (1970) cite 3%. Bellman (1966) noted that 8.1% of 3-year-olds still soil their pants, 2.8% of 4-year-olds, and 2.2% of 5-year-olds. Newson and Newson (1968) reported an incidence of 2.3% for males of 7–8 years and of .7% for females of the same age. At the 10- to 12-year range, these figures drop to 1.2% and .3% for males and females, respectively (Rutter, Tizard, & Whitmore, 1970). It also appears that children who are late in the acquisition of bowel control show delays in other areas (Stein & Susser, 1967).

A recent study of 102 encopretics (Levine, 1975) showed 87 to be 4–13 years of age. Of the total, 85% were males and nearly 50% were incontinent during day and night. Most indicated that they could not detect the urge to defecate. Complaints of abdominal pain, poor appetite, and lethargy were common. Fecal impactions were discovered in 75%, and 40% were classified as continuous encopretics. Familial, marital, and behavioral pathology are not major contributing factors, but they do co-exist with encopresis in more instances than with enuresis (Hersov, 1977; Wolters, 1974a, 1974b).

The general assessment philosophy and strategy outlined for enuresis applies to encopresis. Nevertheless, in spite of some of the apparent similarities in these two problems of elimination, there are also differences that make the assessment and treatment of encopresis somewhat unique (Doleys, 1978). For example, loss of sensation regarding the need to evacuate and painful elimination due to retention are more frequently observed in encopresis. Excessive retention is a more common problem in encopresis and may result in bladder dysfunctioning. Furthermore, parents tend to be less tolerant of encopresis than of enuresis, particularly nocturnal enuresis.

## Physiology

The physiological mechanism involved in fecal continence and defecation has been outlined in a number of sources. Gaston (1948) provides one of the more detailed and experimentally based descriptions. Briefly, however, Anthony (1963) notes the process to be reflexive in nature, initiated by stimulation of receptors in the rectal mucosa. Defecation typically occurs in response to distention of the rectum produced by mass peristalsis of fecal material out of the colon. Filling and distention of the rectum results in (1) increased colonic peristalsis, (2) reflexive relaxation of internal anal sphincters, and (3) desire to defecate. Voluntary contraction of thoracic and abdominal muscles and relaxation of the external anal sphincters bring about defecation. If defecation is voluntarily inhibited by maintenance of pressure on the external anal sphincter in the absence of thoracic and abdominal muscular contraction, rectal receptors adapt to existing pressure and the urge to defecate is suppressed. Subsequent urges may not occur until 24 hours later or when mass peristalsis begins again. During retention, moisture from the fecal mass can be absorbed, producing a hard stool and more painful defecation.

From this description, it is easy to understand how children can come to retain fecal mass for extended periods. Second, normal defecation is an active, not a passive, process. Muscle contractions and external anal sphincter relaxation must be coordinated. And third, excessive parental pressure during toileting can interfere with this process, making defecation more difficult.

## Etiology

Theories about etiology can be separated into three major classes: psychodynamic (psychoanalytic), medical–constitutional, and learning–behavioral.

### *Psychodynamic*

The psychodynamically oriented theorists and clinicians tend to view encopresis as they do enuresis—as a symptom of some unconscious conflict. Lack of parental love, guilt value of feces, separation anxiety, fear of loss of the feces, pregnancy wishes, aggression against a hostile world, response to familial dysfunction, and traumatic separation from the mother between the oral and anal stages of psychosexual development involvement have been postulated as sources of the underlying conflict (Lehman, 1944; Pierce, 1975; Silber, 1969). The "power struggle" that often develops during toileting has been given a good deal of attention (Anthony, 1957; Hilburn, 1968). Several writers have spoken specifically about mother–child relationships during toilet training (cf. Hersov, 1977). Although the use of inappropriate (i.e., coercive) training methods may contribute to the development of encopresis, it does not seem likely that it is a result of an unconscious conflict. Such a theoretical approach has been most nonproductive when applied clinically. Furthermore, it is of little use in working with the developmentally disabled child.

## Medical–Constitutional

The medical approach to the etiology of encopresis seems to encompass a neurodevelopmental model. From this perspective, lack of neurological integrity, inappropriate functioning of the physiologic mechanisms, and anatomical malfunctions are examined. Consideration is also given to diet and constitutional factors (Davidson, 1958). The medical approach cannot be discarded, because many cases of encopresis have an organic component. However, the presence of organic pathology should not imply that behavioral procedures are of no use (Epstein & McCoy, 1977). Similarly, appropriate toileting does not always follow correction of anatomical anomalies. Neurological pathology is common among the moderately and severely developmentally disabled child, yet toileting skills can be acquired. Medical personnel are sometimes insensitive to the impact of environmental contingencies and the presence of prerequisite skills, and behavioral psychologists are occasionally too candid about the functional nature of encopresis.

## Learning–Behavioral

From a learning–behavioral (conditioning) perspective, inadequate or inappropriate learning experiences are major factors in the development and maintenance of encopresis. In the case of the primary encopretic, the learning model would speculate on the presence of prerequisite skills (i.e., undressing) and on whether or not reinforcement sufficient to strengthen the proper toileting behavior has been applied. It would also be assumed that the cues emanating from rectal distention and internal anal sphincter relaxation have not become discriminative cues for temporary retention and bowel movements in the commode.

Secondary encopresis, on the other hand, is often accounted for in terms of avoidance conditioning principles, where pain or fear-arousing events can be associated with the onset of encopresis, or of inadvertent shaping, where untimely reinforcement (parental attention following soiling) can be identified. A functional analysis is used to isolate these faulty environmental contingencies. Rearranging such contingencies is a major focus in therapy. An important consideration in the application of a conditioning model is the understanding that one set of circumstances can operate to promote the development of encopresis but that a separate set of circumstances could be maintaining it. For this reason, a precise analysis of current conditions is often seen as more critical to treatment than a comprehensive understanding of the patient's early history.

## Assessment

### *Medical Evaluation*

The medical evaluation is a critical aspect in the assessment procedure for the encopretic. A majority of encopretics will have some degree of constipation. This problem, particularly if present early in life, is frequently associated with congenital hypothyroidism, anorectal anomalies (Hendren, 1978; Leape & Ramenofsky, 1978), and Hirschsprung's disease (Ravitch, 1958). Hirschsprung's disease (aganglionic megacolon) is characterized by nerve fiber innervation inadequate for the detection or production of normal peristaltic movement (Silber, 1969). Each of these disorders must be ruled out. A medical history, rectal examination, barium enema, or biopsy may be required. Vaughan, McKay, and Nelson (1975) have delineated several criteria for differentiating Hirschsprung's disease from functional constipation.

Other factors that might contribute to constipation include (1) a constitutional predisposition; (2) dietary intake; (3) difficulty in passing large, hard stools because of failure to provide proper leverage; (4) presence of pain and voluntary resistance; and (5) presence of fecal impactions (Davidson, 1958).

Other needed information includes whether or not megacolon is evidenced and to what degree. If soiling episodes are frequent, are they a result of an irritable bowel syndrome or a malabsorption disorder? In the first case, incontinence may occur up to 10 times per day and the stools often contain mucus. What laxatives or stool softeners will be required, if any? Some children with megacolon will not feel the urge to defecate and bowel movements will have to be induced. It is important to keep the colon sufficiently cleared so that it will have an opportunity to recover its original shape. Medical consultation is required regarding what purgatives should be used, how much, and for how long.

### *Clinical Interview*

The clinical interview serves the same functions as outlined for enuresis and is conducted in much the same manner. Basically, the interview should (1) help to differentiate among the various types of encopresis, (2) help to determine related environmental contingencies and circumstances, and (3) provide data relevant to the emotional and behavioral competencies of the parents (caregivers) and the child. At first contact, the clinician might develop a strong notion as to the nature of the encopresis and the contingencies operating to maintain it. It is nonetheless important to follow through with a comprehensive evaluation and to avoid the obvious pitfalls identified by Wright (1978) when he indicated that we tend to find what we look for.

DISTINGUISHING PRIMARY VERSUS SECONDARY ENCOPRESIS. First, it is important to differentiate between the primary and the secondary encopretic. Treatment can vary for the two subtypes. The secondary encopretic has the necessary basic toileting skills, but these may not be present for the primary encopretic. The latter is most likely to be the case with handicapped or developmentally disabled children. Here, consideration must be given to such basic skills as whether or not the child is capable of removing his or her clothes and of reaching to clean himself or herself. Children can be so disabled as to be unable to reach behind themselves, and thus they need to be taught to reach between their legs.

The focus of assessment and intervention for the secondary encopretic often emphasizes the discovery of stimulus conditions that accompany soiling behavior and the consequences, immediate or delayed, that follow. It is important to remember that elimination problems can be functionally autonomous. That is, the conditions associated with the onset of incontinence may no longer be influential, and a new set of circumstances may serve to maintain the behavior. For example, a child may have several accidents during an illness but may continue to be encopretic after the illness because of the attention received for the soiling. Primary encopresis tends to be more indicative of underlying organic pathology and genetic disorders than does secondary encopresis.

DISTINGUISHING BETWEEN RETENTIVE AND NONRETENTIVE TYPES. Second, it is important to differentiate between retentive and nonretentive types. Parents will often remark about the low frequency of accidents or bowel movements. Retention may be voluntary or involuntary, resulting from other factors, such as diet or stress, which can lead to chronic constipation. Enlarged colon (megacolon) and subsequent loss of sensation to defecate are frequent by-products of constipation. A majority of encopretics fall into this category (Levine, 1975; Walker, 1978). If constipation begins in the first year of life or shortly after weaning, is persistent, and resists standard medical treatment with stool softeners and laxatives, congenital hypothyroidism, anorectal anomalies (Hendren, 1978; Leape & Ramenofsky, 1978), and Hirschsprung's disease (Ravitch, 1958) must be ruled out.

If accidents are frequent, if the child appears unaware of the sensation to defecate, and if there is a history of retention, then overflow incontinence must be considered. This condition is marked by the passage of small amounts of stool, often thin and ribbon-like or diarrhea-like in appearance and frequently very odorous. Davidson (1958) claims that this soiling pattern so mimics common diarrhea that he refers to it as "paradoxical diarrhea." In fact, overflow incontinence is created by excessive retention. With continuous retention, feces accumulate in the upper regions of the colon and form an impaction. Additional softer fecal masses may be forced around this impaction and ejected, giving the appearance of diarrhea. If treated as diarrhea (with constipating agents, increased bulk in the diet, etc.), the underlying condition will most certainly be exacerbated. Inquiry into the appearance of the stool passed during an accident and careful record keeping can help determine the need for close medical examination relating to the presence of an impaction.

Severe retention with or without overflow incontinence will also reduce the child's appetite and should be inquired about. Many children will have a nutritionally deficient diet because of their decreased appetite, lethargy, and increased pickiness. Further problems can ensue if the child is taking mineral oil or other agents that deplete the body's needed vitamins and minerals. Therefore, a 7-day intake log should be obtained and analyzed by a nutritionist.

Cases of excessive retention and impaction often develop into megacolon, loss of sensation to defecate, and minimal muscular control and may require frequent artificial evacuation (e.g., enemas). It should be remembered that normal muscle tonus, control, and toileting behavior are not likely to return by removing the impaction. Toileting skills and proper muscular control may have to be retrained. It can take months for the muscle tonus to return to normal. Normal eating patterns may also have to be shaped. Some children will experience abdominal pain following eating and develop a conditioned avoidance response either to eating in general or to certain foods. Fear of defecating because of prior pain experienced in the passing of large stools should be looked for and incorporated into the treatment plan. A history of the use of purgatives and enemas should be sought in detail. Some parents are indiscriminate and harsh in their use of these procedures. Careful questioning concerning the efficacy of such procedures, their frequency of use, and the child's response may uncover potentially problematic parents.

DETERMINING WHEN THE ACCIDENTS OCCUR. A fourth major type of encopresis is differentiated on the basis of when the accidents occur. Most encopretics soil during the day, though Levine (1975) noted that half of his population also soiled at night. However, the child who is encopretic only at night is rare. In these cases, the encopresis is most frequently organic in nature.

OTHER INFORMATION. Other information to be gained from the clinical interview regarding the child's general behavior, the family's adjustment, and the home physical environment is the same as discussed previously for enuresis. Although the incidence of other behavioral problems and pathology is not as high with encopretics as is commonly thought, it is more frequent than with enuretics and should be pursued in the initial assessment.

### Behavioral Records

Parents who report their children's encopresis as a major problem often express a deep sense of urgency about beginning treatment. They frequently have been to many other professionals, mostly medical. It is important to put them at ease and to explain the need to obtain pretreatment baseline records. The therapist should not initiate treatment without an adequate description of the problem. Although an interview with the parents and the child can be very revealing, it is not a substitute for collecting baseline data, particularly for cases with extended histories of treatment failure. As mentioned previously, baseline periods can help to assess parental motivation and ability to follow instructions and to collect data. Each is an integral part of successful treatment. Levine and Bakow (1976), for example, found a significant positive relationship between parental compliance and remission of soiling during treatment.

Data and instruction sheets should be blocked out in hours of the day and days of the week. The parents or caregivers should record the time of each accident. This can be accurately estimated by checking the child's pants every 1–2 hours. Attempts to defecate, bowel movements in the commode, and when these occurred should be noted. Parents should be instructed to try to confirm the occurrence of bowel movements rather than to rely upon the child's reports. When accidents to occur, the child's response to them (e.g., hides his or her pants, ignores it, cleans clothes immediately) should also be noted. An estimate of the magnitude of each accident (e.g., a stain, small pellet-like deposits, full bowel movement) and of the consistency of the stool is needed.

Information on the timing of accidents can be used to guide when to take the child to the bathroom. Although having a bowel movement in the morning may be the most desirable, it may not be a realistic goal at the beginning of treatment. Initially, the focus should be on maximizing the likelihood of the child's having a bowel movement while sitting on the commode, so that this response can be reinforced and strengthened.

Many children will attempt to hide or discard their soiled underwear. Some identifying mark should be put on each of the encopretic's pairs of underwear to ensure the accuracy of records. Underwear can then be kept separately and given to the child one pair at a time as he or she turns in a soiled or clean pair. It is best to terminate any major discipline procedures for accidents during baseline. Weekly contacts by telephone or in the office will help to maintain compliance.

The caregiver should be certain to observe the child's attempts to defecate. Some children will sit very passively on the commode, without exerting the proper or necessary muscular pressure. These children have not learned to exert such pressure, are fearful of defecating, or are voluntarily retaining. Such observations can also confirm the presence of a "toilet phobia" (Ashkenazi, 1975; Doleys & Arnold, 1975), where the child is fearful of sitting on the commode or being near the commode. Anthony (1957) described a number of cases where children have developed unusual concerns and feas. Gavanski (1971) described a "pot refusal" syndrome brought about by coersive toilet training procedures, which resulted in the child's refusing to sit on a commode.

Complete records should be kept of laxatives, stool softeners, and other medication taken during baseline; of when they were taken, and of the dose level. Often, especially in the case of chronic constipation, such regimens will have to be continued into therapy and gradually faded out. As mentioned previously, a dietary intake record should be obtained where there is serious question of the nutritional status of the child because of low intake or extended use of mineral oil and the like. In cases where diarrhea is common, a nutritional evaluation would be indicated, because such children may have absorption or other medically related disorders. Many parents may require brief nutritional counseling on what foods facilitate bowel movements, softer stools, and so forth. This can be done early in order to remove eating habits as a contributing factor to encopresis, particularly the retentive type.

Children can be questioned as to whether they sense the urge to defecate and where it is felt. They should be asked to demonstrate how they "push" when they try to go to the bathroom. In discussing these issues with the child, it is best to discover beforehand his or her terms for bowel movement and commode and to use these terms during the discussion.

## Prior Treatment

Information regarding previous treatment attempts can be invaluable to achieving an understanding of how the parents and others have perceived the problem and which procedures should be avoided because of documented failure. The use of harsh punishment is not uncommon, but it is not frequently freely volunteered. Such parents could be potential child abusers. Indeed, it appears in England that the second most frequently cited problem resulting in child abuse relates to toileting and toileting accidents (Turner, Note 3). When several procedures have been applied over a relatively brief period and the parents are discouraged, they often present the problem as a "challenge" to the therapist in a "Here, see what you can do about it" fashion without accepting their own role in therapy. Close supervision, encouragement, and support will inevitably be required.

Children who have been exposed to punitive measures, may have become very stressed over toileting. This, of course, is incompatible with the coordination of muscular tensing and sphincter relaxation required for bowel movements to occur. Excessive retention can result from harsh discipline procedures. These children will require a program of positive reinforcement and perhaps desensitization or relaxation training. This is not to imply that negative consequences cannot be used but that they need to be explained carefully and balanced with positive reinforcement for appropriate behavior. Furthermore, the situation will require close monitoring so that the use of mild punishment in the treatment of encopresis is not interpreted as condoning the application of punishment for any maladaptive behavior displayed by the child. Doleys (1978, 1979a) has summarized much of the work in this area and notes the utility of programs that combine positive reinforcement with mild punishment.

The effect of some laxatives and stool softeners will be diminished over time. Larger doses will be required to produce the same results. In children with extended histories of taking purgatives, medical consultation regarding the types administered, the amount to administer, and their efficacy should be sought.

## Ongoing Evaluation

The following criteria should be used in evaluating treatment outcome: (1) frequency of appropriate toileting, (2) percentage of toileting that is self-initiated, (3) frequency of accidents, (4) degree of assistance or prompts required, (5) situation generality of toileting skills, and (6) the need for laxatives, stool softeners, or other medications. Each of these criteria is related to assessment and should be examined during baseline. Reporting the frequency of accidents is necessary but not sufficient. The goal of treatment should be independent, regular toileting. The frequency of accidents for a retentive encopretic may be reduced to zero, but if purgatives and prompts are required to induce proper toileting, it would seem that treatment is incomplete and that a relapse is most probable. As with enuresis, there can be degrees of success. Periodic accidents (one every 3–4 weeks) are to be expected during the first 6 months posttreatment, while habit patterns continue to be strengthened. The parents or caregivers should be instructed to exercise considerable caution in responding to accidents that may occur during an illness, so as not to inadvertently reinforce encopretic behavior. Encopretics and enuretics should be followed for 18–24 months posttreatment.

# MULTIPLY DISORDERED CHILDREN

Some children will display both enuresis and encopresis. The assessment procedures are as outlined. In addition, bladder dysfunctioning due to excessive retention must be ruled out. This is best accomplished through medical consultation. If retention is a confounding factor, it should be treated first. Except for this situation, there are few other guidelines to use in selecting which problem to treat initially. It is suggested that the problems not be treated simultaneously. Simultaneous treatment could create undue stress for the child and the parents. The best strategy is to treat the problem that appears most modifiable. This is determined by considering the history and severity of the two problems and the availability of proper supervision for treatment.

# HOSPITALIZATION

Some children may be candidates for brief hospitalization for assessment and initiation of treatment.

## A CASE SUMMARY

In a recent case of secondary, nonretentive encopresis, evaluation and treatment began on an outpatient basis. The child was a 9-year-old male with a history of school and home problems. The mother was divorced but was contemplating remarriage to a much younger man who was quite immature and irresponsible. She worked full time. In spite of apparent interest in her son, the mother semed involved in her own problems. The initial attempt at treatment of the encopresis was only moderately successful and contact was gradually lost as the mother noted increasing difficulty in getting time from work to keep appointments. About 18 months after the onset of treatment, the child was referred for treatment again. His pattern of soiling had not changed. The mother, however, was giving him enemas nightly, contrary to the initial program guidelines, and was not employing any type of systematic reinforcement procedures.

Because of the multiplicity of problems the child was experiencing, he was hospitalized and a behavioral program for encopresis was begun. The treatment program involved self-monitoring and reinforcement, with continued staff feedback and support. Time outside the ward was gradually increased. After about 8 weeks, he was discharged to the home and attended a hospital-affiliated school. Six months posthospitalization, the child continued to be free from accidents and displayed self-initiated toileting. According to the child's report and available information from the mother, he is engaging in appropriate toileting behavior at home.

The purpose of describing this case is twofold. First, it illustrates how hospitalization may be used to bring about proper toileting skills when the natural environment cannot be sufficiently structured to do so. The major emphasis is then on generalization of these skills. Second, this case shows how parents may abuse certain aspects of a treatment program when not carefully supervised. Although frequent telephone contacts or office visits may be cumbersome, they are ultimately in the best interest of everyone involved and will help to ensure compliance. It should be emphasized that most encopretics can be treated as outpatients. Hospitalization should be used only as a last resort.

## INTRODUCTION OF TREATMENT

There are various treatment procedures applicable to enuresis and encopresis, all of which have been adequately described elsewhere (Doleys, 1977, 1978, 1979a, 1979b, in press-a; in press-b; Perlmutter, 1976; Walker, 1978). The importance of how the treatment program is introduced, however, is frequently not attended to. It is discussed briefly here because this is the event that marks the transition from initial assessment and baseline to treatment and the onset of ongoing evaluation.

After collecting behavioral data, arranging for past medical records, attending one or more interviews, and having tried other procedures and professionals, parents (caregivers) are inclined to hope for some reasonable explanation for the child's behavior. To suggest only that the problem behavior has arisen out of inadequate learning experiences provides parents with little information and may enhance already present guilt feelings. The therapist should attempt to integrate the medical, social interview, and behavioral data into a parsimonious and understandable description of the problem. How these data relate logically to the selection of a treatment approach should also be outlined. A detailed description of the program, data relating to its efficacy, and the therapist's, parents', and child's role in treatment should be described. It is better to be forthright and honest than to try to create unreasonable expectations for treatment success. The cooperative nature of treatment should be emphasized, so that the child or parent does not feel "under the gun." Expectations can be very tenuous and may change as treatment progresses. However, maintenance of motivation and compliance to the treatment protocol will help ensure success or the ability to determine the reason for treatment failure if it occurs.

When possible, treatment procedures should be demonstrated in the office or in the therapeutic setting. To simply distribute a urine alarm, for example, is, in our view, inappropriate. Instruction manuals and demonstrations (Dische, 1971; cf. Doleys, 1977) are invaluable. The fear a child or parent may have for the urine alarm can be overcome if the device is introduced in a relaxed, nonprescriptive fashion. Furthermore, urine alarms should be selected on the basis of recommended safety requirements (Kolvin et al., 1973), which can be described to the parents as evidence of the existence of quality control and continued concern over the safety of the child.

The relatively high relapse rates noted for enuretics and for some programs for encopresis make retreatment highly probable. It is prudent behavior for the therapist to discuss this point at the onset of treatment. Retreatment following relapse is often successful and should be considered part of the treatment protocol. In addition, if parents and the child are aware of this eventuality, they are not as likely to overreact to episodic accidents during follow-up.


# CONSULTATION

A little-discussed area in the treatment of problems of elimination is consultation that is provided to agencies and individuals. Institutions for the developmentally disabled, community-based residential facilities, hospital wards, and residential facilities for adjudicated children and adolescents are but a few of the types of agencies that require consultation, assessment, and treatment in problems of elimination. All of the assessment considerations described previously are important. However, it must be recognized that assessment and treatment of such problems often are of relatively low priority in many of the facilities, and excessive demands for precise data collection may result in nothing being accomplished. A compromise between the ideal and the realistic goal may be required (Bellack & Franks, 1975; Hersen & Bellack, 1978).

More often than not, there will be insufficient staff and funding to carry out the needed programs. The consultant must assess what the most realistic goal for a given situation is. In some instances, dry-bed training (Azrin, Sneed, & Foxx, 1974) or the urine alarm (Jehu, Morgan, Turner, & Jones, 1977) can be used. In other cases, procedures that are less demanding in terms of time, less expensive, and less complex (e.g., regular awakening, use of an alarm clock, or restricted fluids) will be required. If the facility is operating under a token reinforcement program, tokens for dry nights could be suggested. However, the consultant must be aware of other potential problems when using tokens, such as fading the tokens, adjustment of economy, and impact on nonwetting children (c.f. Kazdin, 1977). Staggered nighttime awakening, self-monitoring, and retention training during the day may be viable alternatives. Sometimes simply rearranging the environment, that is, moving the wetters closer to the bathroom, can be helpful. Reinforcement of staff compliance and staff motivation are critical factors that should not be taken for granted.

Recently, Doleys visited a residential program for adjudicated adolescents to consult regarding three enuretics. In one case, the client was a moderately retarded, aggressive female who was under medication to reduce her physically aggressive behavior. The enuresis had worsened as the medication was introduced and increased. The facility was equipped with a community bathroom, and each resident had his or her own room, which was occasionally locked at night. This client was one of 20–30 who were housed along a corridor that was presumably monitored by a staff member during the night. No one was supposed to leave his or her room without permission, which may have to be gained by calling out to the staff. The client was reportedly difficult to awaken at night and frequently unmanageable.

The second case was an adolescent male, functioning in the mild range of retardation and living under similar circumstances. It was noted that Tofranil had been tried with little success and that his enuresis would improve and then worsen during weekend stays away from the institution. During a brief interview, it became evident that he was under the impression that he could not leave the room at all during the night, even to go to the bathroom. In addition, it was clear that he was concerned about calling out for permission because of ridicule and harassment from peers.

The third case was a moderate to mildly retarded female living in a remodeled dorm with more convenient and clean bathrooms. The staff station was in clear view of the client's room. Staff were awakening her every 2 hours, guiding her to the bathroom, and requesting that she void. She was described as relatively easy to awaken and generally compliant.

In each case, the recommendations varied, noting that total continence during the night might be an unreasonable goal. General suggestions included holding regular staff meetings to enable everyone to be familiar with the problem and treatment, maintenance of daily records, use of a portable toilet that could be kept in the resident's room, and positioning of the staff so as to be more accessible to the client during the night. There is a temptation to consider Tofranil in these situations, but drug interactions, maintenance of treatment away from the institution, withdrawal, and side-effects contraindicate its use.

Uninformed staff do not always appreciate the various factors that influence continence but see it solely as a problem of patient motivation. A brief discussion of the various contributing factors can enhance staff awareness and compliance to recommendations.

Consultation that is provided to individual professionals and paraprofessionals presents a somewhat different set of concerns. Many times, information is sought regarding the most effective treatment approach to a specific problem. To answer this question is to deny the importance of the role of assessment as described in this chapter. The effectiveness of various procedures can be described in statistical terms only. We encourage the conducting of workshops as a vehicle by which to acquaint groups of professionals and paraprofessionals with the basic elements of assessment and the problems of elimination. Follow-up consultation can then be provided regarding individual cases.

## Acknowledgment

Preparation of this chapter was supported in part by Project 910, U.S. Maternal and Child Health, HSMSA, Department of Health, Education and Welfare, as awarded to the Center for Developmental and Learning Disorders, The University of Alabama in Birmingham.

## Reference Notes

1. Groenhart, P. *Enuresis nocturna.* Thesis, Ultrecht, 1943.
2. Edwards, G. *Toilet training for the multiply handicapped.* Unpublished manuscript, Center for Developmental and Learning Disorders, Birmingham, Ala., 1979.
3. Turner, R. K. Personal communication, September 1979.

## References

Achenbach, T. The Child Behavior Profile: I. Boys aged 6–11. *Journal of Consulting and Clinical Psychology,* 1978, *46,* 478–488.

Anthony, C. P. *Textbook of anatomy and physiology* (6th ed.). St. Louis: C. V. Mosby, 1963.

Anthony, E. J. An experimental approach to the psychopathology of childhood encopresis. *British Journal of Medical Psychology,* 1957, *30,* 146–175.

Arnold, S. J., & Ginsburg, A. Understanding and managing enuresis in children. *Postgraduate Medicine,* 1975, *58*(6), 73–81.

Ashkenazi, Z. The treatment of encopresis using a discriminative stimulus and positive reinforcement. *Journal of Behavior Therapy and Experimental Psychiatry,* 1975, *6,* 155–157.

Atthowe, J. M. Nocturnal enuresis and behavior therapy: A functional analysis. In R. B. Rubin, J. Henderson, H. Fensterheim, & L. P. Ullmann (Eds.), *Advances in behavior therapy* (Vol. 4). New York: Academic Press, 1973.

Azrin, N. H., & Foxx, R. M. *Toilet training in less than a day.* New York; Simon & Schuster, 1974.

Azrin, N. H., Sneed, T. J., & Foxx, R. M. Dry bed: A rapid method of eliminating bedwetting (enuresis) of the retarded. *Behaviour Research and Therapy,* 1973, *11,* 427–434.

Azrin, N. H., Sneed, T. J., & Foxx, R. M. Dry-bed training: Rapid elimination of childhood enuresis. *Behaviour Research and Therapy,* 1974, *12,* 147–156.

Baker, B. L. Symptom treatment and symptom substitution in enuresis. *Journal of Abnormal Psychology,* 1969, *74,* 42–49.

Bakwin, H. The genetics of enuresis. *Clinics in Developmental Medicine,* 1973, *48/49,* 73–77.

Bellack, A. S., & Franks, C. M. Behavioral consultation in the community mental health center. *Behavior Therapy*, 1975, *6*, 388–391.

Bellman, M. Studies on encopresis. *Acta Paediatrica Scandinavica* (Supplement No. 70), 1966.

Berg, I., & Jones, K. V. Functional fecal incontinence in children. *Archives of Disease in Childhood*, 1964, *39*, 465–472.

Boyd, M. M. The depth of sleep in enuretic school children and in non-enuretic controls. *Journal of Psychosomatic Research*, 1960, *4*, 274–281.

Bostack, J. Exterior gestation, primitive sleep, enuresis and asthma: A study in aetiology. *Medical Journal of Australia*, 1958, *149*, 185–192.

Braithwaite, J. V. Some problems associated with enuresis. *Proceedings of the Royal Society of Medicine*, 1956, *49*, 33–39.

Browning, R. M. Operantly strengthening UCR (awakening) as a prerequisite to treatment of persistent enuresis. *Behaviour Research and Therapy*, 1967, *5*, 371–372.

Campbell, M. F. Neuromuscular uropathy. In M. F. Campbell & T. H. Harrison (Eds.), *Urology* (Vol. 2). Philadelphia: W. B. Saunders, 1970.

Ciminero, A. R., & Doleys, D. M. Childhood enuresis: Considerations in assessment. *Journal of Pediatric Psychology*, 1976, *4*, 17–20.

Cohen, M. W. Enuresis. In S. B. Friedman (Ed.), *Pediatric clinics of North America*. Philadelphia: W. B. Saunders, 1975.

Davidson, M. Constipation and fecal incontinence. In H. Bakwin (Ed.), *Pediatric clinics of North America*. Philadelphia: W. B. Saunders, 1958.

Davidson, M. D., Kugler, M. M., & Bauer, C. H. Diagnosis and management in children with severe and protracted constipation and obstipation. *Journal of Pediatrics*, 1963, *62*, 261–266.

deJonge, G. A. Epidemilogy of enuresis: A survey of the literature. In I. Kolvin, R. C. MacKeith, & S. R. Meadow (Eds.), *Bladder control and enuresis*. Philadelphia: J. B. Lippincott, 1973.

Di Perri, R., & Meduri, M. L'enuresi notturna: Ulteriori elementi in tema di diagnostica strumentali. *Acta Neurologica*, 1972, *27*, 22–27.

Dische, S. Management of enuresis. *British Medical Journal*, 1971, *2*, 33–36.

Doleys, D. M. Behavioral treatments for nocturnal enuresis in children: A review of the recent literature. *Psychological Bulletin*, 1977, *84*, 30–54.

Doleys, D. M. Assessment and treatment of enuresis and encopresis in children. In M. Hersen, R. Eisler, & P. Miller (Eds.), *Progress in behavior modification* (Vol. 6). New York: Academic Press, 1978, 85–123.

Doleys, D. M. Assessment and treatment of childhood encopresis. In A. J. Finch & P. C. Kendall (Eds.), *Treatment and research in child psychopathology*. New York: Spectrum, 1979. (a)

Doleys, D. M. Assessment and treatment of childhood enuresis. In A. J. Finch & P. C. Kendall (Eds.), *Treatment and research in child psychopathology*. New York: Spectrum, 1979. (b)

Doleys, D. M. Enuresis. In J. Ferguson & C. B. Taylor (Eds.), *Advances in behavioral medicine*. New York: Spectrum, in press. (a)

Doleys, D. M. Encopresis. In J. Ferguson & C. B. Taylor (Eds.), *Advances in behavioral medicine*. New York: Spectrum, in press. (b)

Doleys, D. M., & Arnold, S. Treatment of childhood encopresis: Full cleanliness training. *Mental Retardation*, 1975, *13*, 14–16.

Doleys, D. M., Ciminero, A. R., Tollison, J. W., Williams, C. L., & Wells, K. C. Dry-bed training and retention control training: A comparison. *Behavior Therapy*, 1977, *8*, 541–548.

Douglas, J. W. B. Early disturbing events and later enuresis. In I. Kolvin, R. C. MacKeith, & S. R. Meadows (Eds.), *Bladder control and enuresis*. Philadelphia: J. B. Lippincott, 1973.

Epstein, L. H., & McCoy, J. F. Bladder and bowel control in Hirschsprung's disease. *Journal of Behavior Therapy and Experimental Psychiatry*, 1977, *8*, 197–99.

Esperanca, M., & Gerrard, J. W. A comparison of the effect of imipramine and dietary restriction on bladder capacity. *Canadian Medical Association Journal*, 1969, *101*, 721.

Faray, L. G. Enuresis: A genetic study. *American Journal of Diseases of Childhood*, 1935, *49*, 557–578.

Finley, W. W. An EEG study of the sleep of enuretics at three age levels. *Clinical Electroencephal-

*ography*, 1971, *2*, 35–39.

Finley, W. W., & Wansley, R. A. Auditory intensity as a variable in the conditioning treatment of enuresis nocturna. *Behaviour Research and Therapy*, 1977, *15*, 181–185.

Fitzgerald, J. F. Encopresis, soiling, constipation: What's to be done? *Pediatrics*, 1975, *56*, 348–349.

Forsythe, W. I., & Redmond, A. Enuresis and spontaneous cure rate: Study of 1129 enuretics. *Archives of Diseases in Childhood*, 1974, *49*, 259–263.

Foxx, R. M., & Azrin, N. H. *Toilet training the retarded*. Champaign, Ill.: Research Press, 1973.

Gaston, E. A. The physiology of fecal continence. *Surgery, Gynecology, and Obstetrics*, 1948, *87*, 280–290.

Gavanski, M. Treatment of non-retentive secondary encopresis with imipramine and psychotherapy. *Canadian Medical Association Journal*, 1971, *104*, 227–231.

Gerrard, J. W., & Zaleski, A. Nocturnal enuresis. *Pakistan Medical Review*, 1969, November, 77–82.

Gerrard, J. W., & Zaleski, A. Functional bladder capacities in children with enuresis and recurrent urinary infections. In L. D. Dickey (Ed.), *Clinical ecology*. Springfield, Ill.: Charles C. Thomas, 1974.

Goldfried, M. R., & Sprafkin, J. N. *Behavioral personality assessment*. Morristown, N.J.: General Learning Press, 1974.

Graham, P. Depth of sleep and enuresis: A critical review. In I. Kolvin, R. C. MacKeith, & S. R. Meadow (Eds.), *Bladder control and enuresis*. Philadelphia: J. B. Lippincott, 1973.

Hallgren, B. Enuresis: I. A study with reference to the morbidity risk and symptomatology. *Acta Psychiatrica et Neurologica Scandinavica*, 1965, *31*, 379–403.

Harris, L. S., & Purohit, A. P. Bladder training and enuresis: A controlled trial. *Behaviour Research and Therapy*, 1977, *15*, 485–490.

Hendren, W. H. Constipation caused by anterior location of the anus and its surgical correction. *Journal of Pediatric Surgery*, 1978, *13*, 505–512.

Hersen, M., & Bellack, A. S. Staff training and consultation. In M. Hersen & A. S. Bellack (Eds.), *Behavior therapy in the psychiatric setting*. Baltimore: Williams & Wilkins, 1978.

Hersov, L. Fecal soiling. In M. Rutter & L. Hersov (Eds.), *Child psychiatry: Modern approaches*. Philadelphia: Blackwell Scientific Publications, 1977.

Hilburn, W. B. Encopresis in childhood. *Journal of Kentucky Medical Association*, 1968, *66*, 978.

Ireton, H. R., & Thwing, E. J. *Minnesota Child Development Inventory*. Minneapolis: Interpretive Scoring Systems, 1972.

Jehu, D., Morgan, T., Turner, R., & Jones. A. A controlled trial of the treatment of nocturnal enuresis in residential homes for children. *Behaviour Research and Therapy*, 1977, *15*, 1–16.

Jones, B., Gerrard, J. W., Shokeir, M. K., & Houston, C. S. Recurrent urinary infections in girls: Relation to enuresis. *Canadian Medical Association Journal*, 1972, *106*, 127–130.

Kaffman, M., & Elizur, E. Infants who became enuretic: A longitudinal study of 161 kibbutz children. *Child Development Monographs*, 1977, No. 42.

Kales, A., & Kales, J. D. Sleep disorders. *New England Journal of Medicine*, 1974, *290*, 487–499.

Kales, A., Kales, J. D., Jacobson, A., Humbrey, F. J., & Soldatos, C. R. Effects of imipramine on enuretic frequency and sleep stages. *Pediatrics*, 1977, *60*, 431–436.

Kazdin, A. E. *The token economy*. New York: Plenum, 1977.

Kimmel, H. D., & Kimmel, E. C. An instrumental conditioning method for the treatment of enuresis. *Journal of Behavior Therapy and Experimental Psychiatry*, 1970, *1*, 121–123.

Kolvin, I., MacKeith, R. S., & Meadow, S. R. (Eds.). *Bladder control and enuresis*. Philadelphia: J. B. Lippincott, 1973.

Kolvin, I., Tounch, J., Currah, J., Garside, R. F., Norlan, J., & Shaw, W. B. Enuresis: A descriptive analysis and a controlled trial. *Developmental Medicine and Child Neurology*, 1972, *14*, 715–720.

Leape, L. L., & Ramenofsky, M. L. Anterior ectopic anus: A common cause of constipation in children. *Journal of Pediatric Surgery*, 1978, *13*, 627–630.

Lehman, E. Psychogenic incontinence of feces (encopresis) in children. *American Journal of Diseases of Childhood*, 1944, *68*, 190–198.

Levine, M. D. Children with encopresis: A descriptive analysis. *Pediatrics*, 1975, *56*, 412–416.

Levine, M. D., & Bakow, H. Children with encopresis: A study of treatment outcome. *Pediatrics*, 1976, *58*, 845–852.

Lovibond, S. H., & Coote, M. A. Enuresis. In C: G. Costello (Ed.), *Symptoms of psychopathology*. New York: Wiley, 1970.

Lund, C. J. Types of urinary incontinence. In C. J. Lund (Ed.), *Clinical obstetrics and gynecology*. New York: Harper & Row, 1963.

MacKeith, R., Meadow, R., & Turner, R. K. How children become dry. *Clinics in Developmental Medicine*, 1973, *48/49*, 3–21.

Morgan, R. T. T., & Young, G. C. Parental attitudes and the conditioning treatment of childhood enuresis. *Behaviour Research and Therapy*, 1975, *13*, 197–199.

Mowrer, O. H., & Mowrer, W. M. Enuresis: A method for its study and treatment. *American Journal of Orthopsychiatry*, 1938, *8*, 436–459.

Muellner, S. R. The physiology of micturition. *Journal of Urology*, 1951, *65*, 805–814.

Muellner, S. R. Development of urinary control in children: A new concept in cause, prevention and treatment of primary enuresis. *Journal of Urology*, 1960, *84*, 714–716. (a)

Muellner, S. R. Development of urinary control in children. *Journal of the American Medical Association*, 1960, *172*, 1256–1261. (b)

Newson, J., & Newson, E. *Four-year-old in the urban community*. London: Allen & Unwin, 1968.

Nordquist, V. M. The modification of a child's enuresis: Some response–response relationships. *Journal of Applied Behavior Analysis*, 1971, *5*, 241–247.

Oppel, W. C., Harper, P. A., & Rider, R. V. The age of obtaining bladder control. *Pediatrics*, 1968, *42*, 614–626. (a)

Oppel, W. C., Harper, P. A., & Rider, R. V. Social, psychological, and neurological factors associated with nocturnal enuresis. *Pediatrics*, 1968, *42*, 627–641. (b)

Paschalis, A. P., Kimmel, H. D., & Kimmel, E. Further study of diurnal instrumental conditioning in the treatment of enuresis nocturna. *Journal of Behavior Therapy and Experimental Psychiatry*, 1972, *3*, 253–256.

Perlmutter, A. D. Enuresis. In Kelalis (Ed.), *Clinical pediatric urology*. Philadelphia: W. B. Saunders, 1976.

Peterson, R. A. The natural development of nocturnal bladder control. *Developmental Medical Child Neurology*, 1971, *13*, 730–734.

Pierce, C. M. Enuresis and encopresis. In A. M. Friedman, H. I. Kaplan, & B. J. Sadock (Eds.), *Comprehensive textbook of psychiatry II*. Baltimore: Williams & Wilkins, 1975.

Ravitch, M. M. Pseudo Hirschsprung's disease. *Annals of Surgery*, 1958, *148*, 781–795.

Ritvo, E. R., Ornitz, E. M., Gottlieb, F., Poussaint, A. F., Maron, B. J., Ditman, K. S., & Blinn, K. A. Arousal and non-arousal of enuretic events. *American Journal of Psychiatry*, 1969, *126*, 77–84.

Rutter, M. Indications for research: III. In I. Kolvin, R C. MacKeith, & S. R. Meadow (Eds.), *Bladder control and enuresis*. Philadelphia: J. B. Lippincott, 1973.

Rutter, M., Tizard, J., & Whitmore, K. (Eds.). *Education, health and behavior*. London: Longman, 1970.

Rutter, M., Yule, W., & Graham, P. Enuresis and behavioral deviance: Some epidemiological considerations. In I. Kolvin, R. C. MacKeith, & S. R. Meadow (Eds.), *Bladder control and enuresis*. Philadelphia: J. B. Lippincott, 1973.

Sacks, S., & DeLeon, G. Training the disturbed enuretic. *Behaviour Research and Therapy*, 1978, *16*, 296–299.

Salmon, M. A., Taylor, C. D., & Lee, D. On the EEG in enuresis. In I. Kolvin, R. C. MacKeith, & S. R. Meadow (Eds.), *Bladder control and enuresis*. Philadelphia: J B. Lippincott, 1973.

Schwartz, M. S., Colligan, R. C., & O'Connell, E. J. Behavior modification of nocturnal enuresis: A treatment and research program at the Mayo Clinic. *Professional Psychology*, 1972, Spring, 169–171.

Shaffer, D. The association between enuresis and emotional disorder: A review of the literature. In I. Kolvin, R. C. MacKeith, & S. R. Meadow (Eds.), *Bladder control and enuresis*. Philadelphia:

J. B. Lippincott, 1973.

Shaffer, D. Enuresis. In M. Rutter & L. Hersov (Eds.), *Child psychiatry: Modern approaches*. Philadelphia: Blackwell Scientific Publications, 1977.

Shingleton, H. M., & Davis, R. O. Stress incontinence in perspective. *Journal of Continuing Education in Obstetrics and Gynecology*, 1977, *48*, 15–26.

Silber, D. L. Encopresis: Discussion of etiology and management. *Clinical Pediatrics*, 1969, *8*, 225–231.

Smith, E. D. Diagnosis and management of the child with wetting. *Australian Pediatric Journal*, 1967, *3*, 193–205.

Sperling, M. Dynamic considerations and treatment of enuresis. *Journal of American Academy of Child Psychiatry*, 1965, *4*, 19–31.

Stansfeld, J. M. Enuresis and urinary tract infection. In I. Kolvin, R. C. MacKeith, & S. R. Meadow (Eds.), *Bladder control and enuresis*. Philadelphia: J. B. Lippincott, 1973.

Starfield, B. Functional bladder capacity in enuretic and non-enuretic children. *Journal of Pediatrics*, 1967, *70*, 777–782.

Starfield, B. Enuresis: Its pathogenesis and management. *Clinical Pediatrics*, 1972, *11*, 343–350.

Starfield, B., & Mellits, E. D. Increase in functional bladder capacity and improvements in enuresis. *Journal of Pediatrics*, 1968, *72*, 483–487.

Stein, Z. A., & Susser, M. The social dimensions of a symptom: A social–medical study of enuresis. *Social Science and Medicine*, 1967, *1*, 183–201.

Turner, R. K., Young, G. C., & Rachman, S. Treatment of nocturnal enuresis by conditioning techniques. *Behaviour Research and Therapy*, 1970, *8*, 367–381.

Vaughan, V. C., McKay, R. J., & Nelson, W. E. *Textbook of pediatrics* (10th ed.). Philadelphia: W. B. Saunders, 1975.

Walker, C. E. Toilet training, enuresis, encopresis. In P. R. Magrad (Ed.), *Psychological management of pediatric problems* (Vol. 1). Baltimore: University Park Press, 1978.

Wear, J. B. Cystometry. *Urologic clinics of North America*, 1974, *1*, 45–80.

Werry, J. S., Enuresis: A psychosomatic entity? *Canadian Medical Association Journal*, 1967, *97*, 319–327.

Werry, J. S., & Cohrssen, J. Enuresis: An etiologic and therapeutic study. *Journal of Pediatrics*, 1965, *67*, 423–431.

Wirt, R. D., Loebar, D., Klinedinst, J. K., & Seat, P. *Personality Inventory for Children*. Los Angeles: Western Psychological Services, 1977.

Wolters, S. Encopresis. *Psychotherapy and Psychosomatics*, 1971, *19*, 266–287.

Wolters, W. H. G. *Kinderin mit encopresia, een psychosomatische benadering*. Utrecht: Elinhivyk, BV, 1974. (a)

Wolters, W. H. G. A comparative study of behavioral aspects in encopretic children. *Psychotherapy and Psychosomatics*, 1974, *24*, 86–97. (b)

Wright, L. Psychogenic encopresis. *Ross Timesaver: Feelings and Their Medical Significance*, 1978, *20*, 11–16.

Wright, L., & Walker, C. E. A simple behavioral treatment program for psychogenic encopresis. *Behaviour Research and Therapy*, 1978, *16*, 209–242.

Yates, A. J. *Behavior therapy*. New York: Wiley, 1970.

Yeates, W. K. Bladder function in normal micturition. In I. Kolvin, R. C. MacKeith, & S. R. Meadow (Eds.), *Bladder control and enuresis*. Philadelphia: J. B. Lippincott, 1973.

Young, G. C. The aetiology of enuresis in terms of learning theory. *The Medical Officer*, 1965, *113*, 19–22.

Young, G. C. The problem of enuresis. *British Journal of Hospital Medicine*, 1969, *2*, 628–632.

Young, G. C., & Morgan, R. T. T. Conditioning treatment of enuresis: Auditory intensity. *Behaviour Research and Therapy*, 1973, *11*, 411–416.

Zaleski, A., Gerrard, J. W., & Shokeir, M. H. K. Nocturnal enuresis: The importance of a small bladder capacity. In I. Kolvin, R. C. MacKeith, & S. R. Meadow (Eds.), *Bladder control and enuresis*. Philadelphia: J. B. Lippincott, 1973.

# AUTHOR INDEX

Italicized page numbers indicate names in tables and figures.

# SUBJECT INDEX

Italicized page numbers indicate material in tables and figures.